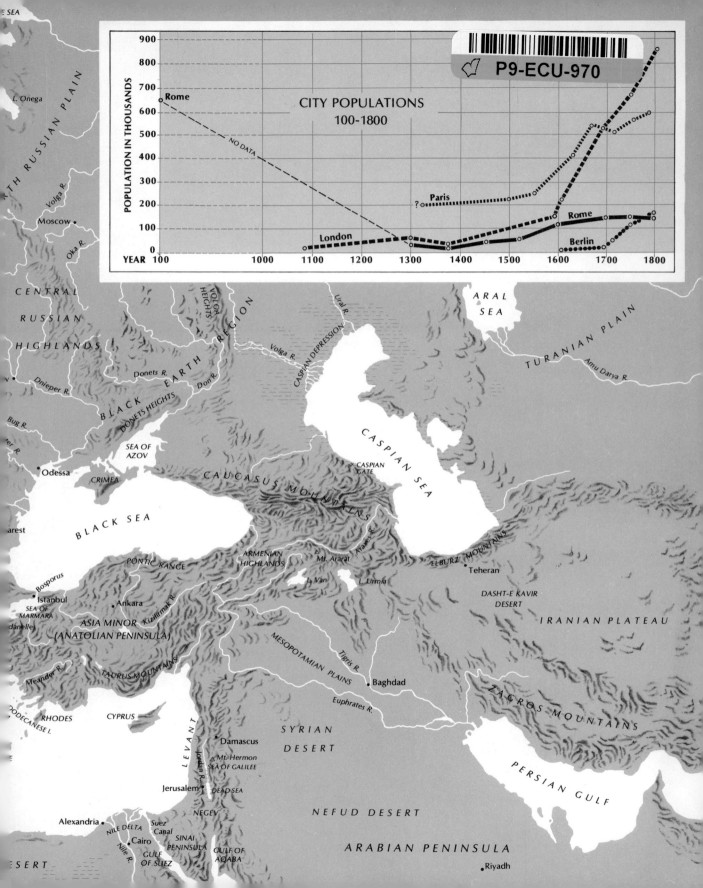

P9-ECU-970

CITY POPULATIONS
100-1800

POPULATION IN THOUSANDS

Rome

NO DATA

Paris
?

London

Rome

Berlin

YEAR 100 | 1000 | 1100 | 1200 | 1300 | 1400 | 1500 | 1600 | 1700 | 1800

THE WESTERN EXPERIENCE

SECOND EDITION

MORTIMER CHAMBERS / *University of California at Los Angeles*

RAYMOND GREW / *University of Michigan*

DAVID HERLIHY / *Harvard University*

THEODORE K. RABB / *Princeton University*

ISSER WOLOCH / *Columbia University*

ART ESSAYS BY H. W. JANSON / *New York University*

ADVISORY EDITOR / EUGENE RICE *Columbia University*
CONSULTANT / ALVIN BERNSTEIN *Cornell University*

THE WESTERN EXPERIENCE

SECOND EDITION

ALFRED A. KNOPF NEW YORK

THIS IS A BORZOI BOOK
PUBLISHED BY ALFRED A. KNOPF, INC.

Second Edition
987654321
Copyright © 1974, 1979 by Alfred A. Knopf, Inc.

Library of Congress Cataloging in Publication Data

Main entry under title:
The Western experience
    Includes index.
    1. Civilization—History. 2. Civilization,
Occidental—History. I. Chambers, Mortimer.
CB59.W38 1978   909   78-12117

ISBN: 0-394-32135-9

Book Design by Dana Kasarsky

Cover illustration: Detail from *The Harvesters*, a painting by Pieter Brueghel, the Elder. The Metropolitan Museum of Art, Rogers Fund, 1919.

Map consultant: D. W. Meinig
Maps were executed by Jean Tremblay.

Manufactured in the United States of America

Men and women use their knowledge of the past in legitimately different and sometimes contradictory ways. Two ways especially have satisfied the needs of civilized peoples: the way of the artist and the way of the historian.

The artist, like the scientist and the philosopher, raids his cultural inheritance in order to make something new and personal. Untroubled by anachronism, he repossesses and reshapes only those ideas and images that serve his own work, that nourish his own sensibility, values, and obsessions. The past speaks to the artist, the scientist, and the philosopher in the present tense.

Historians are past-minded. They want to preserve in archives and libraries as complete a record of the past as possible and to transmit the sum of historical sources and knowledge intact to their successors. Sensitive to context and nuance, their professional concern is to avoid anachronism, that is, to understand the past as it really was, in its own terms rather than in present-day terms. They try not to manipulate or distort it but to make it live again in its uniqueness.

The relation of past to present is paradoxical because human beings are both myth makers and truth seekers. As individuals we must be free to use the past as we wish—to plunder it unhistorically, to misunderstand it creatively. This liberty is our guarantee of innovation, our assurance that the past will continue to be used in the interests of the future. As historians, however, our obligation and responsibility are different. We have the duty to correct misconceptions about the past, even fruitful ones, and to expose the myths created by misunderstanding or malice.

The reason for this is not simply that truth is superior to falsehood—as niggling accuracy is to high-minded nonsense—although this is the best reason. We guide our most ordinary thought and action by past experience. The authenticity of what we think and do depends on the accuracy with which our memories reproduce that experience. In the same way the authenticity of our collective lives and the quality of our culture rest on the extent and truthfulness of our memory of history. If our historical memory is defective, it serves the present badly and impoverishes the future.

Sound historical knowledge is useful to us because it makes past experience accessible for our instruction and delight, because it guards us from temporal provincialism and ethnocentrism, and because it helps us understand ourselves better.

Our collective memory is a museum of the mind. Museums preserve the material artifacts of past generations; histories are records of alternatives. Human beings have located the highest good by turns in wisdom, virtue, pleasure, utility, and power, to give a far from exhaustive list. They have worshiped one god, two gods, three gods, many gods, and they have invented a bewildering variety of magical, metaphysical, religious, and scientific hypotheses to

PAST & PRESENT

explain the human condition and the end and purpose of human life. They have considered desirable or necessary alternative kinds of rule—by one, by the wellborn few, by the rich, by priests, by a majority of all; alternative modes of production—craft, capitalist, and socialist; alternative patterns of social stratification—by birth or occupation, education or income; alternative systems of dominance and subjection—slavery, serfdom, or the free exchange of labor for wages. As skeptics of every age have pointed out, nothing is so characteristic of human life as its diversity.

So great is the diversity of mankind and so heterogeneous the possible lessons of the past that we cannot plausibly expect historical precedent to solve our personal or public difficulties in any direct or simple way. If we could the conduct of our affairs would have improved long ago. On the other hand it is precisely the wealth of alternatives preserved in our memory of things said and done that enables us to experiment and suggests the possibility and directions of change. Where there are no alternatives, there can be no choice.

The study of history is a liberating discipline because it offers us, choosing in the present, an ever broadening spectrum of alternatives. This is important. Most people—the exceptions are geniuses, rare in any age—find only what they have been sensitized to see. Transmitting knowledge of past problems and solutions performs the absolutely critical function of alerting each successive generation to a maximum number of possibilities. A clean slate is a wholly unsatisfactory foundation for a better world, and those who wish to free themselves from the past enslave themselves to the present.

The heresies of present-mindedness are temporal provincialism and ethnocentrism. Temporal provincialism is a vulgar conviction that current ways of doing things are normative. It confers a timeless validity on transient contemporary taste. Unlike the present-mindedness of artists, philosophers, and scientists, which manipulates knowledge of the past in the interest of innovation, it is blinkered by ignorance. Ethnocentrism is a cultural bias, the notion (in our own case) that Western civilization is the proper yardstick for judging all others. Knowledge of other cultures and of our own remoter past points up the relativity of the present, induces a healthy skepticism about current arrangements and achievements, and exposes the status quo to continuous critical reappraisal.

Socializing the young, defining the roles of men and women, and preparing for death are permanent human problems. It is narrowing to imagine that our ways of meeting them are the only ones or the best. Knowledge of other ways allows us to reexamine our own with something of the dispassion of foreigners. The hero of one of Voltaire's novels is a Huron Indian traveling in eighteenth-century France. His innocent astonishment at the peculiar customs of the French forced Voltaire's readers to look at themselves with heightened awareness. Not the least benefit of historical study is to make Voltairian Hurons of us all.

History is useful to us in short because it helps us understand ourselves better. By comparing our present behavior and institutions with those of earlier ages and other peoples, we learn more of their real character. Listening to Indian music sharpens our ear to what is distinctive in Western music. A study of feudalism, a system of government in which the exercise of public powers like taxation and the administration of justice rests on the ownership of private property, clarifies the very different nature of the modern sovereign state. Only a comparative investigation of how painters in various periods and cultures have met the problems of representing a three-dimensional world on a two-dimensional surface will turn up the fact that true geometrical perspective is to be found only in Western art between its discovery in Florence in the early fifteenth-century and its abandonment in the first decade of our own. Such a study will show that Western perspective was not the end of a long historical progression, a perfection toward which painters in other times and places worked with greater or lesser success, but rather a stylistic peculiarity of a particular culture during a well-defined period of its history—an alternative open to twentieth-century artists but deliberately rejected by most of them. The same comparative method, by isolating causal variables absent in the ancient Mediterranean world and East Asia but present in late medieval and early modern Europe, offers the best hope of explaining why perspective was unique to Western civilization for roughly five hundred years.

Constantly changing criteria of relevance determine what successive generations will select from the past to illuminate the present. Historians share with everyone else the mental structures of their time and place. However free they may be of temporal provincialism, however discriminatingly past-minded, they ask questions suggested by the preoccupations of their own day. This does not mean that every man is his own historian or that historical knowledge lacks a solid foundation but rather that every new question gets a new answer. Historical writing is always in flux because historians ask their sources questions newly shaped by changing social and cultural needs.

The questions many historians have been asking for the past twenty years or so have created a distinctive kind of historical writing. Contemporary historians commonly call it "social history." The name is not new; and the impulse behind it goes back a long way too. In antiquity and from the Renaissance until far into the nineteenth century, almost everybody took it for granted that the proper subject of history was past politics, diplomacy, and war. Only gradually were perma- nently successful efforts made to broaden the subject matter of history to include law, religion, constitutional and economic change, and intellectual and cultural developments. The field of social history and its name emerged at the same time.

But what social history *was* remained vague. It could mean the study of ideas about society. Some narrowed the meaning of "social" to "working class," and social history became the history of labor movements. For others its subject matter was daily life: daily life in ancient Rome, or in Renaissance Florence, or old New York—studies of dress, diet, pots, and pans, salted with anecdote and picturesque detail of manners. Or it was just plain history with the politics left out.

Today historians have a broader notion of social history. They think that the proper object of study is society in all its manifestations. They do not define social history by what it excludes. It can include anything. It certainly includes politics and war. Its defining characteristics are rather ones of emphasis, method, and point of view.

Its sources are anything that records the pulse of human life: pots, coins, paintings, fiscal records, novels and plays, diplomatic correspondence and private letters, account books, publishers' lists, political and theological tracts, and government reports. It tends to be analytical rather than narrative and to emphasize long views. It borrows from the social sciences (as they borrow from it)—terms and ideas such as "growth" and "modernization," categories of stratification, types of family structure —and makes sophisticated use of the techniques and theories of statisticians, demographers, and psychologists. Today's historians are sensitive to the fact that most historical writing has been about the tiny minority of the powerful and rich (they, after all, have left behind the fullest and most accessible records of their activities). The new social history is as mindful of popular culture as it is of the culture of the elite, as interested in the family as in the state, in patronage as in diplomacy, in plague and famine as in political theory. It tries to recover as much as it can of the living experience of ordinary people, to look at a society from the bottom up as well as from the top down.

Another characteristic of today's history is quantification. Counting is important because it helps us test hypotheses and verify generalizations. Even the best historical writing is peppered with words like "typical," "representative," and "widespread." These are implicitly quantitative generalizations. What even a simple quantitative technique enables us to do is to reveal the merits or defects of such impressionistic generalizations by giving them a statistical base. There are problems with quantification, of course, the main one being that before the seventeenth century quantifiable data are scarce; indeed, only from the nineteenth century on can we easily gather samples large enough to make quantitative analysis effective. It is well to remember too that although quantification can often settle what the facts are, it does not often tell us what they mean. Historians must still interpret the results of calculation. Baldly put, though, the message is this: If you wish to generalize about a group or class, it is better to count than to guess; and if you can't count, admit you are guessing (mind you, some guesses are more educated than others).

Equally characteristic of today's history is the way it measures historical time. Since it is typically a study of social and cultural processes, more often a history of structures than a history of events (without abandoning narrative where it is necessary or appropriate), a history of problems rather than of presidencies or reigns, it emphasizes the long haul, moving at the slower tempo of long-term trends in production and consumption, the expansion and contraction of population, or the displacement of one class by another at the levers of political and economic command. Its periodization therefore tends to be different from the familiar one dictated by traditional political and military history. At one level of abstraction, indeed, human history divides plausibly into three periods only: the 100,000 years of prehistory from the emergence of *homo sapiens* to the appearance of the first civilizations in the ancient Near East, when a planned increase in agricultural productivity freed creative energies from the need to supply daily food; the very brief, very recent period initiated by the modern technological and economic revolution at the end of the eighteenth century; and in between virtually the whole of human history, properly speaking, from Sumer and Egypt to the industrial and French revolutions, the many centuries during which the texture of ordinary people's experience remained extraordinarily stable and the rate and character of change extraordinarily slow—slow, that is, by the hectic standards of the modern period.

A minor consequence of living in a rapidly changing society and world is that each generation exaggerates the novelty of what it does. Historians are no exception. The best current work, which seems to us so fresh, its explanations so satisfactory, its subject matter so relevant to our present needs and tastes, its periodization so reflective of what is really important in the Western experience, will no doubt seem to our successors as partial as much of the history written by earlier generations seems to us. In the meantime, though, history speaks directly to us now from the pages that follow.

Eugene Rice

CONTENTS

ART ESSAYS

MAPS

ONE

THE FIRST CIVILIZATIONS

The subject of this book is the Western experience. By Western experience we mean the history of European civilization and its remoter origins in earlier civilizations located in Mesopotamia and around the Mediterranean.

Man began to abandon a nomadic existence and live in settled agricultural communities only about 10,000 years ago. The earliest farming villages so far identified appeared in the hills of Asia Minor. Some 5,000 years later, settlements grew up along the banks of the Tigris, Euphrates, Nile, and Indus. The richer lands irrigated by these rivers supported many more people than could the highlands and did not require the effort of the whole population to guarantee a stable supply of food. This margin of freedom and leisure made possible a diversity of occupations, specialization of skills, and experiments in building, thought, law, government, and military organization. Permanence, complexity, and sophisticated social organization transformed the agricultural village into something we can recognize as urban, the form of habitation crucial for the development of civilization.

Expansion caused these early societies to develop still more complicated forms of political and social control. Powerful kingdoms and great empires, dotted with sizable cities, arose in Asia Minor and in Egypt. For a time, the Persian Empire united the entire Near East under its Great King. The achievement of literacy and a proliferation of written records, long-distance trade, the invention of increasingly ingenious tools, utensils, vehicles, and weapons, the development of monumental architecture and representative art, advances in medicine, astronomy, and mathematics document the change from primitive to civilized conditions.

The most distinctive contribution of the ancient Near East to the unity of the Western experience was religious: the monotheism of the Old Testament. Other kingdoms conquered territory (and lost it); Israel permanently conquered people's imaginations.

I. WESTERN CIVILIZATION

Naming this book *The Western Experience* and then defining "Western experience" as the history of European civilization and its remoter origins may seem at first glance easy to justify. On examination, though, the adjective "Western" turns out to be far from clear, while the noun "civilization" is even harder to define. And both words conceal value judgments that we need to make explicit.

WHAT IS THE WEST?

Columbus sailed west in order to reach the East. This reminds us not only that the earth is a sphere, but also that the notions of west and east are relative. Because the Greeks gave the names east and west to the points on the horizon where the sun rises and sets and then correctly located the Persian Empire and India to their east, the Greeks were the first "Westerners." The historian Herodotus, chronicling the great war between the Greeks and the Persians, described it as a struggle between Europe and Asia. Since Greece is in Europe and Persia in Asia, Europe became the West and Asia the East. We still speak conventionally of the Near East because it is east of Europe and nearer to Europe than China and Japan, which we name, equally conventionally, the Far East. Such usage is ethnocentric: Europeans, that is, imagined themselves at the center of the world and placed other peoples and countries in relation to themselves. (This is why historians today prefer the terms East Asia for China and Japan, South Asia for India, and West Asia for Turkey.) Our situation as Americans is even more complicated. We are North Americans, not Europeans. In the strained sense that New York is west of London we remain "Westerners." California, though, is more plausibly described as east of China than west of it. So if we imagine California as our point of reference and if we imagine (which is more difficult) that as Californians we are free of the conventions of our European past and language, we could with equal justice think of the Chinese as Westerners and think of ourselves as Orientals.

Other usages, common today, may cause misunderstanding. Western Europeans distinguish themselves from Eastern Europeans, a distinction that has acquired a special ideological coloration since the Second World War, giving to the struggle of East and West a different meaning from that of Herodotus. The revolutionary economic and social changes associated with industrialization and modernization, most marked in Europe and North America, have given to "Western" the added connotations of developed or advanced, with the paradoxical result that for purposes of economic analysis Japan is today sometimes called a "Western" nation.

We need not, for all this, abandon the traditional usage which has made synonyms of European, or indeed European-American, and Western. Having banished the grosser forms of ethnocentrism and recognized the relative character of our terminology, we rightly continue to describe our historical experience as Western for the simple reason that American civilization is an offshoot of European civilization. To be sure, American Indians, black Americans, and Chinese-Americans have non-European roots as well. It is also true that since the seventeenth century all the peoples of the Americas have developed distinctive cultural traits that in some measure distinguish them from Europeans. But the fact remains that before the seventeenth century the ancestors of many of us were Europeans and that nineteenth- and twentieth-century Europeans are the ancestors of many more of us. In order to learn who we are and where we came from we must regularly retrace the course of European history and its antecedents. Europeans must naturally do the same. But they have no real need to call their historical experience Western. They more accurately call it simply European. "Western" and "Western Civilization" appear much less often on European title pages than they do on American. Americans, on the other hand, need the adjective "Western" in order to express the truth that they share with Europeans a common past and a common civilization.

CIVILIZATION

If by "Western" we mean European or European-American, what do we mean by "civilization" when we say that our subject of study is European civilization? The difficulty is the greater when the word we are trying to define is as varied in usage and as rich in meaning as the word "civilization" is.

A useful beginning is to ask what civilization

is not. We distinguish civilization from barbarism, for example, from an existence that is akin to that of beasts, wild, cruel, and inhuman, or, less pejoratively, one that is uncultivated, rude, rough, ignorant, and illiterate. Conversely, characteristics of civilization are obedience to law, an ordered life in a community, the cultivation of letters and the arts, and refinement of manners and behavior.

But here too there are traps. The words "barbarous" and "barbarian" go back to the Greek, and they meant originally no more than "foreigner," "non-Hellenic." For the Romans, as for the Chinese, barbarians were people who lived outside their empire. In the Middle Ages, heathen and infidels, everyone living beyond the limits of Christendom, were barbarians. Renaissance Italians revived classical usage and called non-Italians barbarians. But even in antiquity the ironies built into the word were beginning to surface. Ovid, in exile, lamented that he, a poet and Roman citizen, was a barbarian to his rude neighbors. And by the sixteenth century it was commonly recognized that the inhabitants of every nation considered those of other nations barbarians, that a barbarian is a person who does not talk as we talk, dress as we dress, eat as we eat. Thus, while "barbarism" continues to suggest by contrast important characteristics of civilization, the possibility always lurks that in our complacent superiority we call someone a barbarian only because he is different from us.

A more interesting contrast is that between civilization and the condition of the savage. In European art and literature, the savage is pictured as a wild man, naked and hairy, or clothed in moss and ivy (he is ignorant of the arts of spinning and weaving). Like animals he is fierce, undomesticated, untamed, and ungoverned. He lives in the state of nature. The seventeenth-century English philosopher Thomas Hobbes described what the savage lacked: he had no industry or agriculture, no navigation or trade, no commodious building, no mechanical devices to move heavy objects, no knowledge of geography, no conception of time, "no Arts, no Letters, no Society, and which is worst of all, continual fear and danger of violent death."

But again the root meaning of the word makes the essential point. "Savage" comes from the late Latin word *silvaticus*, "wooded." The savage inhabits forest and grasslands and lives by hunting and by gathering uncultivated fruits, nuts, and roots. The civilized person is precisely the reverse. He lives in a town or city. Because his environment is urban, he is himself urbane. The word "civilized" is a derivative of *civis* (citizen) and *civitas* (city or city-state, translation of the Greek *polis*). In the same cluster of words and ideas is "civility," from the Latin *civitas*, which translates the Greek *politera*, a community of citizens, a polity, as in the phrases "politic government" or the government of a commonwealth or civil society." The root of "civilization," a word first popularized by intellectuals in eighteenth-century France, is the same.

We commonly make another contrast and distinguish civilized from primitive peoples and societies. The English "primitive" comes from the Latin *primitivus*, which means "first," "original," "earliest of its kind." Its connotations can be flattering or pejorative, for it suggests, on the one hand, an original purity untouched by later corruption, as in the phrase "the primitive Church," so often used by ecclesiastical reformers to criticize contemporary abuses; again, on the other hand, it suggests that the earliest times were far less advanced than the civilized present. The contrast runs like a red thread through all of Western thought, separating optimists from pessimists. Optimists imagined the first age as one of gold and put the first humans in a Garden of Eden; pessimists imagined an initial age of iron and pictured the first inhabitants of the planet as centaurs, hippocamps, or mermaids, half human, half bestial. Optimists thought that men and women in the state of nature were healthy, free, honest, and happy, as free and happy, wrote the poet Dryden in the seventeenth century,

> as Nature first made man,
> 'Ere the base Laws of Servitude began,
> When wild in woods the Noble Savage ran.

For pessimists like Hobbes, the life of man in the state of nature was "solitary, poor, nasty, brutish, and short." Modern scholars have summed up the contrast in the phrases "hard primitivism" (life was worst at the beginning and has gradually become better) and "soft primitivism" (things were best in the beginning and have become progressively worse).

What remains useful in the distinction between "primitive" and "civilized" is the notion of evolution and development inherent in it. Peoples and cultures in early stages of development are primitive; peoples and cultures in later stages, those with more complex and sophisticated institutional and intellectual structures, with a more elaborate social stratification and varied economic life, are, by comparison, more advanced or civilized. Civilization, then, is a particular stage in the development of a human community or culture.

CULTURE AND CIVILIZATION

The author of a recent study of the meanings of the word "culture" has managed to assemble 164 definitions. Anthropologists use the word most broadly. They mean by it the whole way of life of a particular community or group, its language, traditions, customs, and institutions, its ideas, beliefs, and values, and their embodiment in material instruments and artifacts. The influential American anthropologist Ruth Benedict defined it briefly this way: "A culture . . . is a more or less consistent pattern of thought and action." It follows that man is as much a culture-producing animal as he is a tool-making animal. Wherever he has lived in a group, however remotely or crudely, the whole of the group's burial practices and types of settlement, means of livelihood, artistic motifs, rituals, and social bonds defines his culture. It also follows that there are primitive, prehistoric cultures. Indeed, in this context the very notion of an "uncultured" human being is a contradiction.

Every civilization then is a culture in the anthropological sense. But not every culture is a civilization. What distinguishes a culture that is also a civilization from a primitive culture that is not civilized?

The least controversial and most important criterion is literacy. Primitive, prehistoric cultures are illiterate. Civilization and history begin with writing.

A second criterion is the existence of cities. From antiquity on, as we have seen, the contrast between the isolated, undomesticated life of woods and savannah, of a life supported by hunting and food gathering, and the ordered, communal life of urban populations fed by farmers clustered in settled agricultural villages has been understood to distinguish the savage, barbarian, and primitive from the civilized. Under the name of the "urban revolution" the contrast has been used to describe the origin of civilization and to underline this important characteristic. Civilization exists when men and women begin to live together in cities and when, supported by the surplus of grains made possible by a developed agriculture, some of them are free for the first time to turn their energy to technological innovation, commerce, and the arts—in sum, to begin to supply those necessities and amenities that Hobbes found wanting in the state of nature.

The third criterion by which we distinguish civilized from primitive conditions rests on a meaning of "culture" narrower than the all-

This painting of a horse (ca. 15,000 B.C.), taken from a cave at Lascaux in southwestern France, displays the remarkable naturalistic style typical of primitive cave art. Most of these paintings are located deep within caves, where prehistoric man did not live; some were painted directly over earlier pictures. (Photo: Douglas Mazonowicz for Thames and Hudson Ltd.)

embracing definition of the anthropologists. Primitive people worshiped the gods, made tools, painted pictures in the dark recesses of their caves, participated in ritual dances, hunted with skill and daring, endured puberty initiations, and modified their behavior to conform to a variety of political and social rules. Civilized people have done, and do, the same. But civilized people also produce and appreciate high culture, the traits of which are more difficult to define than literacy or urbanism but are recognizable precisely in those characteristics commonly thought to be the opposite of savagery or barbarism: refinement of manners, humane behavior, respect for reason, and love of art.

The root meaning of "culture" (Latin: *cultura*) is cultivation of the soil (thus *agriculture*). Cicero, Roman politician and man of letters, extended it to mean training and cultivation of the mind. Philosophy, he said, is cultivation of the mind (*cultura animi*). By a further extension, we define high culture as marked intellectual development and notable achievement in the arts and sciences. Civilized men and women are reflective and self-conscious. They possess a sense of values, discrimination of taste, and a critical spirit. They honor poets and painters, philosophers and scholars. They create and appreciate literature. They seek to understand nature rationally. They control in some measure their instinctual drives. The marks of high culture are subtlety and profundity of thought and the creation of works of art charged with aesthetic emotion. A society so marked is civilized. Whether primitives in actual fact live in a state of nature is debatable; what is certain is that civilization is not natural, but itself a work of art.

A survey of the Western experience is, therefore, the study both of a culture in the anthropological meaning of the word and of a civilization, of popular culture and high culture. Its scope is correspondingly large, for its overriding themes touch now on historical geography and demography or marriage and the family, now on the Pythagorean theorem or the image of man in Renaissance art; explore shifting patterns of freedom and bondage, tradition and innovation, expansion and decline, as well as the teachings of prophets or the structures of metaphysicians and architects; range from the small and apparently banal to the infinitely great and, in time, from the beginning of humanity to the anxious present.

II. EARLY MAN

The earth may be about 4 to 6 billion years old. For more than half that time it lacked life entirely. Then for millions of years only lower forms of life existed—vegetation, insects, and fish. Much later, about 20 million years ago, the first manlike creatures appeared, but the process of man's evolution was long and slow; the human species did not assume its present form until about 30,000 years ago. For most of his time on earth man has had to struggle for some kind of control over his environment, to escape bad weather and predatory animals and, above all, to get enough to eat. By far the longest phase of human history has been that devoted to hunting and gathering; only fairly recently has man become a food producer. With that development, settled, complex, and rich civilizations could now come into being.

MAN THE FOOD GATHERER

Changes in climate had a profound effect on early man. When the glaciers moved over the face of Europe and Asia he, with the animals, was driven south before them to return north only after the glaciers had receded. For many thousands of years, early man roamed about in small bands, hunting and gathering, following the movements of the animals on which he preyed, ever restless, always in search of food. He found shelter in caves, and his mastery of fire together with a limited ability to fashion crude stone tools was the extent of his technical achievements.

We know nothing of the internal organizations of these early societies, yet we glimpse man's creative nature at work in the cave paintings, which survive to the present day. These paintings, normally of wild animals, are sometimes taken to be symbolic attempts to gain power over man's quarry. They may, of course, be simply artistic interpretations of essential reality for early man, the wandering hunter.

MAN THE FOOD PRODUCER

Man's transition from hunting and gathering his food to producing it from the soil marked a crucial turning point in his development as a social and eventually as a civilized animal. The discovery of agriculture did not herald the evolution of some higher human species, since hunting often requires greater skill, cunning, and knowledge than growing grain. What farming did was to introduce new attitudes and therefore the potential for radically new forms of behavior. Hunting requires quick, instinctive action; a successful harvest demands long-term planning. The art of farming caused people to settle in fixed locations where they raised their crops and domesticated their animals; they thus created new stability that gave their existence identity and continuity. For security in the new habitat more sophisticated defenses became necessary; the ditches and stockades that these agriculturalists devised as protection from wild beasts and human enemies were the original precursors of the city's limits and its walls. Finally, farming is a much surer way of producing a food surplus than hunting, and this surplus meant that a larger population could be supported. Increased numbers allowed the development of new skills and occupations, freeing those not needed for agricultural production to engage in pottery making, weaving, metalwork, and trade.

Experts believe that this revolutionary change to agriculture first occurred about 10,000 B.C. among the hills of what is now southern Turkey and northern Iraq, when the last glaciers retreated (see Map 1.1). In these hills man learned to grow wheat and barley, perhaps from the chance observation that discarded grains sprouted new shoots in the ground. Villages began to appear in the area soon after 8000. The oldest known communities are Jericho and Jarmo, while the largest known food-producing village of early times is Çatal Hüyük (*sha-tal hoo-yook*). It lies in what is now Turkey, covers thirty-two acres, and contains twelve successive levels of building thought to range in date from 6500 to 5650. Çatal Hüyük is also the oldest known village with buildings constructed for exclusively religious purposes,

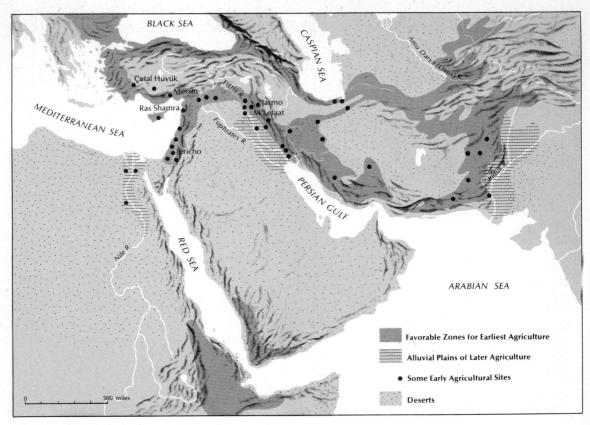

MAP 1.1: THE EARLIEST CIVILIZATIONS

and its archaeological remains preserve an unusually clear record of some early religious practices. As we might expect, these early agriculturalists were mostly concerned with breeding and fertility; the ruins of Çatal Hüyük contained female statuettes, idols of unmistakable earth-mother types, with enormous buttocks and breasts, whose fertile bodies, it was hoped, would make the soil productive. Evidence exists also of the technical advances and new economic practices that accompanied this settled, agricultural existence. The art of weaving was being practiced in Anatolia by about 6000, and about the same time people began to travel in crude rafts and in carts with wheels (this latter being, oddly enough, an invention never made by either the Aztecs or the Mayas).

Craftsmen were now learning to fashion pots on the surface of a turning wheel, so that they could make in minutes what had previously taken days, and the pot, the raft, and the wheel combined to provide the vessels and the means to transport grain and imperishables. A rudimentary trading economy thus emerged.

By such steps, then, primitive agrarian communities with communal gods, domesticated animals, simple technologies and economies, and elementary regulation of social behavior came into existence. We must bear in mind, however, how painfully slow was the transition from nomadic hunter to food-producing villager. The change from a hunting economy to one of controlled food production, crop growing, and animal husbandry is the greatest event of prehistory, yet civilization still lay far in the future.

III. THE FIRST CIVILIZATIONS IN MESOPOTAMIA

The development of civilization coincides with the emergence of cities, just as the demise of a civilization follows on their disappearance. There was no dramatic moment in history when civilizations suddenly arose. Some 5000 years elapsed between the earliest farming villages in Asia Minor and northern Mesopotamia and the first urban civilizations along the great river valleys. Why the change occurred is not entirely clear.

EARLY URBAN SOCIETIES

Urbanization complicates human existence. It brings greater numbers of people together, requiring more sophisticated rules to regulate their associations and therefore more complex political organization. The formalizing of relationships among citizens is often expressed in detailed law codes that not only tell the historian how the rulers controlled their populations but also reveal interesting facts about the life style of these early societies. Cities, being larger than villages, are stronger, with the resources to dominate the hinterland and even to enslave its population. Social controls maintaining a system of slavery will, of course, be rigid and repressive, while the institution of slavery itself allows the enslavers to engage in more varied occupations and in greater specialization by freeing them from the more mundane requirements of existence. In antiquity, it often heralds the appearance of a leisure class that has the time to develop such intellectual skills as mathematics, surveying, and astronomy (a subject often closely associated with religion).

SUMER

Mesopotamia is a rich alluvial plain created by deposits from the Tigris and Euphrates rivers. The first cities appeared in the territory known as Sumer, at the southern end of this long valley. Early settlers apparently came from the neighboring highlands, attracted by rich soil and plentiful game. To take advantage of the fertile land as well as to channel and control the periodic floods, they had to construct a complex system of canals for irrigation.

By about 3000 Sumer contained a dozen or more city-states, each independent of the others, worshiping its own patron deity, and ruled by its own king. Jealousy among them led to almost constant fighting for power and land, but no single community was able to dominate the others permanently. Ur, the largest of these cities, covering about 150 acres, had a population of about 25,000 people—perhaps 200,000 if we add those living in the suburbs and hinterland. The citizens of each city were divided into three classes—nobles and priests, commoners, and slaves—the first evidence of any division of citizens into a political and social order. The king was not considered divine; he held power only so long as he could command support from the more important priests and nobles.

At the center of a Sumerian city there usually stood a ziggurat—a terraced tower built of baked brick and culminating in a temple for a god, probably the patron deity of the city. A ziggurat might be a stupendous structure: the wall surrounding one of them was some thirty-six feet thick. The Old Testament contains many traces of Sumerian civilization and it seems likely that the Tower of Babel was ultimately modeled on the memory of a ziggurat.

The Sumerians' great contribution to civilization was their development of the art of writing. The most important intellectual tool ever discovered, writing enables man to keep records, codify laws, and transmit knowledge.

Through it man can build civilization in confidence that its achievements will not be lost and he can take advantage of the experience of his predecessors. He can, in short, think and act historically. Although some earlier attempts at writing occurred elsewhere, the Sumerians developed it in an efficient form. Their writing was originally pictographic; each sign was a simplified picture of the article that the scribe had in mind. In time scribes reduced the complexity of the system by simplifying individual pictures and by combining several pictures into one. In this process of abstraction the meaning of a given sign might change. For example, a crude picture of a star was simplified into four wedge-shaped marks and given the meaning "god" or "heaven".[1] This is the kind of symbolic transformation that occurs in the evolution of any script. Sumerian texts were written on clay tablets by pressing the end of a reed or bone stylus into the wet clay; modern scholars call the resulting wedge-shaped marks "cuneiform" (Latin *cuneus*, "wedge"), a name used for all varieties of this kind of script.

Among the clay tablets found in Sumer is the first record that historians have of a developed mythology. Here we witness man beginning to speculate about causes, trying to explain divine action, and perhaps attempting to control the supernatural by considering the purposes and desires of the gods.

The Sumerians believed that their gods had established the standards by which man must live. One of their main deities, Enlil, was primarily a storm god who lived in heaven. Normally kind and fatherly, Enlil made the rich soil of Mesopotamia fertile, and he was even credited with designing the plow. At times, however, when Enlil had to carry out harsh decrees of the other gods, he became terrify-

ing. This alternation reflects the uncertainty bred by the threat of floods that always hovered over Sumer. When the rivers overflowed and destroyed the crops, the gods had suddenly ceased to be favorable, and Sumerians rationalized this by assuming that they had somehow offended the gods' strict codes.

Some Sumerian myths passed into the traditions of other peoples. For example, one tale about the Sumerian hero Gilgamesh anticipates a scene in Homer's *Odyssey*, Book 11. In each case the hero stands at the entrance to the underworld and talks with the spirit of a departed comrade. Neither the Sumerian nor the Greek poem attempts to make the world of the dead attractive; the concept of fulfillment after death was foreign to both cultures.

Other Sumerian myths foreshadow the biblical accounts of Creation, of eating from the tree of knowledge in the garden of Paradise, and of the Flood. Yet it is important to recognize the differences between Sumerian myths and their parallels in the Bible. The Hebrew Scriptures place more emphasis on divine initiative and on the central place of man. In both Sumerian and biblical accounts man is fashioned of clay and then given the breath of life. Sumerian myths explained that man was created because the gods required slaves to relieve themselves of certain burdens; but the Bible shows a more humane kind of relationship between God and man. Thus although the authors of the Bible borrowed from traditional Near Eastern themes, they transformed them within the system of Hebraic monotheism. Both these ancient sources demonstrate how man has focused on certain symbols and parables in his efforts to interpret his place on earth and his relationship to the gods.

---

[1] The method of Sumerian writing is described by S. N. Kramer, *The Sumerians*, pp. 302 ff.

Sumerian cuneiform tablet, "The Creation of Man." (Photo: The University of Pennsylvania)

THE BABYLONIAN KINGDOM

Wars among the cities weakened Sumer and prepared the way for its conquest about 2340 by the Akkadians, a Semitic people from the north. The Sumerians regained control some two centuries later; but then invasions by other peoples weakened their leadership and brought about a slow revolution in the political structure of Mesopotamia. Finally, a supreme power emerged—the kingdom of Babylonia, centered on the city of Babylon, north of Sumer. The Babylonians were Semites, and their language, Akkadian, became the official language of the kingdom. Sumerian, a non-Semitic language, passed out of use.[2]

The leading ruler of Babylonia was Hammurabi (1792?–1750?). His most famous legacy is a cuneiform inscription, now in the Louvre in Paris, recording a long series of legal judgments published under his name. The Code of Hammurabi regulated nearly every aspect of Babylonian private life and shows how strongly centralized within the kingdom was the authority of Babylon and its ruler. It laid stress on retribution and fair dealing, but at the same time revealed a highly stratified society and a conception of justice that was avowedly non-egalitarian: "If a man has destroyed the eye of an aristocrat, they shall destroy his eye. . . . If he has destroyed the eye of a commoner or broken the bone of a commoner, he shall pay one mina of silver." Hammurabi used to be called the first lawgiver, but discoveries in Sumer have revealed that there were several earlier collections of legal decrees.

Hammurabi's subjects recognized the importance of commercial records, and their knowledge of mathematics was remarkably advanced. Yet this achievement rested on foundations laid by the Sumerians, who had already discovered many rules of mathematics. Among the mathematical tools the Babylonians used were multiplication tables, lists of squares and cubes, exponents, and tables for computing interest. They also devised methods of solving quadratic equations and produced textbooks with practical problems for use in schools.

Babylonian mathematics used positional notation with the number 60 as the base (in our conventional mathematics 10 is the base). Many features of this sexagesimal system (*sexaginta*, Latin for 60) have endured until today: the circle has 360 degrees, the hour has 60 minutes, and the year has 12 months. Babylonians also knew the Pythagorean theorem about the right triangle over a thousand years before Pythagoras stated it. They also developed complex systems of astronomy and astrology. Many tablets contain observations of heavenly omens, and one tablet notes Venus as the planet that disappears and reappears behind the sun.

THE FIRST INDO-EUROPEANS

Babylonia was weakened and overthrown about 1600 by invaders who spoke an Indo-European dialect and were therefore linguistically separate from the Semites of Babylonia and from the Sumerians. The Indo-European people came from the area around the lower Volga River and the southern Urals. Between 5000 and 4000 they began a slow dispersion across Europe and parts of Asia. Some of them ultimately migrated southward through Afghanistan into the Indian subcontinent.

Another group of Indo-European peoples moved westward into Italy, Greece, central Europe, and Asia Minor. Those who entered Asia Minor shattered the kingdom of Babylonia and established new kingdoms in its place. Among this group of peoples the Hittites are especially prominent; but before we consider

---

[2] The Babylonian and Assyrian dialects are closely related. The term "Akkadian" is now used to refer to Assyrio-Babylonian; Akkadian was a Semitic language.

the Hittites we must turn to another spectacular river civilization.

IV. EGYPTIAN SOCIETY

No other ancient people can match the Egyptians for the longevity of their civilization, and one is tempted to think that nothing ever changed along the Nile. This is far from true. There were wars of conquest, periods of disruption, and religious battles. In variety of experience and creative scope Egypt has in fact a strong claim to being the richest of all Near Eastern civilizations.

THE ROLE OF THE NILE

The basic element in Egyptian history and culture is the Nile River. It rises from the lakes of central Africa as the White Nile and from the mountains of Ethiopia as the Blue Nile; these two branches join at Khartoum to form the Nile River, which flows some 4,000 miles northward to the delta, where at last it empties into the Mediterranean Sea. Less than two inches of rain a year falls in the delta; rain is altogether unknown in much of Egypt. Most of the land is therefore uninhabitable. These geographic facts determined much of the character of the country. The people living along the Nile could be controlled with comparative ease by a central government, and the inhospitable desert that locks the river within its valley protected Egypt from invasion.

One miracle stood between the Egyptians and starvation. The Nile swells each summer as the snow melts on the mountains; it overflows its banks, reviving the land with fresh water and depositing a thick layer of alluvial soil for cultivation. The Egyptians would then plant their grain and often reap two harvests before winter. This yearly flood gave them a natural beginning for their year, and their 365-day calendar is the direct forerunner of the calendar now used throughout the Western world. In case the Nile failed to rise to its usual height, they developed an elaborate storage system for grain. Normally, Egypt could support more than its own population; Greeks, Romans, and others drew large portions of their food supply from the wheat grown in Egypt.

THE LIST OF KINGS

The basic source for Egyptian history is a list of the kings compiled by an Egyptian priest named Manetho, who wrote his history nearly 3,000 years after the reign of the first kings. Manetho wrote in Greek in about 280 B.C., after Alexander's conquest, for the Macedonians who ruled Egypt. He divided the kings into thirty dynasties (later chroniclers added a thirty-first). Modern scholars accept these divisions and have grouped the dynasties in this manner:

Archaic Period (Dynasties 1–2)	3100–2700
Old Kingdom (Dynasties 3–6)	2700–2200
Intermediate Period (Dynasties 7–10)	2200–2050
Middle Kingdom (Dynasties 11–12)	2050–1800
Intermediate Period (Dynasties 13–17)	1800–1570
New Kingdom (Dynasties 18–20)	1570–1085
Postempire (Dynasties 21–31)	1085– 332

The first Egyptians appear to have used a Hamitic language that was probably native to Africa. A later group of Semitic immigrants fused with the Hamites, but their precise background is unclear. Early Egypt was divided into two kingdoms, one in Upper Egypt (the Nile valley) and one in Lower Egypt (the delta). This distinction may reflect two different groups of people among the ancient Egyptians.

THE OLD KINGDOM

Menes (also known as Narmer), who lived about 3000, unified Upper and Lower Egypt and established a capital at Memphis. By the

The Pyramids of Giza. (Photo: Elliott Erwitt, Magnum)

time of the Old Kingdom, the land had been consolidated under the strong central power of the king, who enjoyed a supremacy that we can hardly imagine today. The king (he was not called "pharaoh" until the New Kingdom) was the owner of all Egypt and supposedly a god as well. As such he stood above the priests and was considered the only direct contact with the other gods. Under the king was a hierarchy of officials, ranging from governors of provinces down through local mayors and tax collectors. Artisans, peasants, and slaves nourished the whole system.

The Old Kingdom reached its zenith in the Fourth Dynasty. Wealth and prosperity in-creased greatly. The rulers waged successful wars with Libya and the Sudan. Overseas trade with Byblos, on the coast of Palestine, produced cedar for houses, furniture, and sailing craft, and copper mines were operated in the Sinai Peninsula. The appropriate symbols of this period of greatness are the three immense pyramids built at Giza between 2600 and 2500, staggering feats of engineering that still dwarf any other monuments to individual men from any age. Building such a pyramid may well have been the chief activity of the king during his rule. These were built by Khufu (called Cheops by the Greeks), Khafre, and Menkure.

The priests, an important body within the ruling class, were a social force working to modify the king's supremacy. Yielding to the demands of the priests of Re, a sun-god, kings

The ceremonial palette of King Narmer is a symbolic representation of the unification of Upper and Lower Egypt. This side of the palette shows the king, wearing the white crown of Upper Egypt, smashing the head of an enemy. The god Horus, in the form of a falcon, holds a rope attached to a captive of Lower Egypt, a region symbolized by six papyrus plants.

began to call themselves sons of Re, adding his name as a suffix to their own: Khafre, Neuserre, and so on. Re was also worshiped in temples that were sometimes larger than the pyramids of later kings.

Beginning with the Fifth Dynasty (about 2500) there are signs that the nobles were also forcing some decentralization of power. Titles such as "governor" and "sealbearer" were assumed by dozens of officials. This could be due to increased administrative work, but it also shows that authority was being placed in more hands.

EGYPTIAN CULTURE

By the end of the Old Kingdom, a recognizably Egyptian culture had emerged. The great amount of documentation, both artistic and literary, presents a full picture of life and thought in this civilization.

Religion

The king and the gods closely associated with him stood at the pinnacle of Egyptian religion. Numerous other gods occupied lesser positions in the pantheon. These others appeared in a

On this side of the palette King Narmer has completed his conquest of Lower Egypt and wears the red crown of that kingdom. He is reviewing the bodies of decapitated victims. The exotic beasts with necks intertwined may symbolize the unity of the two Egypts. (Photo: Hirmer Fotoarchiv München)

variety of forms, often as animals, and in origin were probably deities of the villages up and down the Nile. Patron deities presided over many aspects of Egyptian civilization.

Unlike some other peoples, the Egyptians believed in a pleasant life after death. The general conception of the hereafter had men performing their usual tasks but with more success. The king, already a god, would become a greater god; viziers, priests, and administrators would hold more responsible positions. For everyone there would be pleasures such as boating and duck hunting.

Death was not considered a welcome event, but the Egyptians lessened the dread, and they made careful preparations for the physical needs of the afterlife. To preserve their bodies after death they perfected the art of embalming; the mummies have survived and can be seen in our museums. Statues sat in the tombs of kings as receptacles for their spirits in case their bodies should be destroyed.

The wish to provide housing for the dead led to the most renowned monuments of Egypt, the pyramids. The earliest tombs were much smaller than the massive pyramids already mentioned. They were low structures with flat tops called mastabas, built of brick and decorated with brick paneling; most scholars see in this method of building an influence from Mesopotamia, where brick rather than stone was used.

Maat

The Egyptians recognized an abstract ethical quality called *maat*, which Egyptologists translate roughly as "right order" or "just state of things." It combines the concepts of order, justice, and truth. *Maat* existed if everything was in the order that the gods ordained. The idea of *maat* shows a new way of reflecting on morality. Sumerian religion, for example, does not seem to have had any purely ethical ideas

of right order. When a society can give a name to the abstract idea of true order without having to attach it to a god, a new and subtler kind of thinking is evident. *Maat* moreover had implications for both ruler and ruled. Right order would help to hold Egyptian society together. Thus *maat* illustrates another frequent use of religion in many civilizations —as a carefully crafted tool of politics in addition to a method of expressing the feelings of a people toward divine powers.

Art and Writing

Much of the surviving art of Egypt comes from the interior of tombs and is closely associated with Egyptian religion. Artists tried to represent scenes and pastimes familiar to the deceased: a king is shown defeating his enemies or in the company of his family; workers are shown building boats or tending fields. On the whole, the art is optimistic. Both inside and outside the tombs there were serene and imposing statues of the kings, often several identical ones located together, as if to emphasize by repetition the monumental strength of the rulers.

Egyptians developed a form of writing known as hieroglyphics ("sacred carvings"). The indispensable key to the Egyptian past was the Rosetta stone, discovered when Napoleon occupied part of Egypt at the end of the eighteenth century. This stone, now in the British Museum, contains a partly preserved hieroglyphic text along with translations in the cursive Egyptian script that evolved from hieroglyphics and also in Greek, a known language that offered a way of penetrating the other two. The decisive stage in decipherment came with the work of J. F. Champollion in 1822.

Like the cuneiform script of Mesopotamia, hieroglyphics began as pictorial signs. It is likely that the Sumerians influenced the Egyptians in the early stages, around 3000; but the pictures that the Egyptians developed were mostly original. Hieroglyphics sometimes use merely a picture of the object represented; for example, a small oval represents "mouth." But at some point the scribes decided to use the pictograms as phonetic signs; thus *ra* continued to mean "mouth" but was also used for the sound *r*. Fully developed hieroglyphics are therefore a combination of pictograms and phonetic signs.

The Egyptians learned to make writing material from the papyrus plants that grow in abundance along the Nile. From papyrus comes our word "paper." The reeds of the plant were placed crosswise in layers, then soaked, pressed, and dried to produce sheets and rolls. Because of the dry climate, thousands of papyri have survived in excellent condition; most of these come from the later period when the Romans administered Egypt.

Literature

The rich variety of Egyptian literature illustrates the creativity of the early Egyptians and the liveliness of their culture. Their works often dealt, as did their art, with mythology and the afterlife, and their hymns to various deities, poems celebrating the king's victory over death, and stories about the gods reflect the serene Egyptian confidence in the beneficence of the gods. Various texts, collectively known as the *Book of the Dead*, provide charms and other methods of assuring a successful transition to the other world.

Success in this world appears as the central concern of another literary genre, appropriately known as "instructions" or "instructions in wisdom." These books, in which a wise man gives advice about how to get ahead in the world, reveal much about Egyptian social attitudes, especially the supreme position of the king; they counsel discretion and loyalty: "If you are a man of note sitting in the council of your lord, fix your heart upon what is good.

Be silent—this is better than flowers. Speak only if you can unravel the difficulty . . . to speak is harder than any other work. . . . Bend your back to him that is over you, your superior in the king's administration. So will your house endure with its substance, and your pay be duly awarded. To resist him that is set in authority is evil."[3]

We also have scraps of Egyptian love poetry: "It is pleasant to go to the pond in order to bathe in your presence, that I may let you see my beauty in my tunic of finest royal linen, when it is wet." And there are meditations, songs, ghost stories, and fables of all kinds. In fact, not until the Greeks did the ancient world possess a literature with the diversity and charm of that of Egypt.

Mathematics and Medicine

The Egyptians were the forerunners of the Greeks in applied science too. The need for careful planting in the silt deposits of the Nile forced them to master the art of surveying, for an unusually rich overflow might wipe out the boundaries between plots of land, and when this happened the land had to be remeasured. As to ordinary reckoning, the Egyptians developed a rather elementary system of multiplication and division.

Medicine in Egypt depended largely on driving out demons from the body. The Egyptians believed that a separate god ruled over each organ and limb, and treatment consisted largely in finding the right chant to appease the appropriate deity and then delivering it in the right tone of voice. Sometimes the sorcerer simply threatened the demon by promising to invoke the aid of the gods if it did not depart at once.

---

[3] Adolf Erman, *The Ancient Egyptians: A Sourcebook of Their Writings* (1966), pp. 61–62 (language slightly modified).

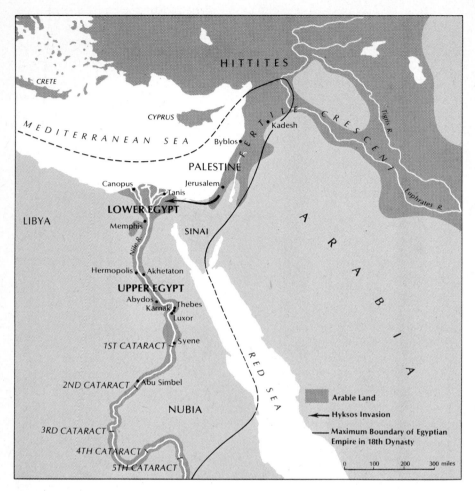

MAP 1.2: ANCIENT EGYPT

Medicine was not entirely based on magic. One papyrus, a treatise on surgery, displays a more empirical approach to illness. It discusses some forty-eight medical problems, classified according to the various parts of the body. Whenever possible the author gives a diagnosis and suggests a treatment. A verdict is often given in one of three forms—"An ailment that I will treat," "An ailment with which I will contend," or "An ailment not to be treated"—probably according to whether the prognosis was favorable, uncertain, or unfavorable. This text is a witness to the birth of a kind of inquiry that transcends haphazard folk medicine. The maturing and broadening of knowledge independent of magic characterizes the civilizing process throughout history.

THE MIDDLE KINGDOM

Political division and rivalry lie close beneath the surface in any state. The Old Kingdom dissolved into an intermediate period of anarchy that ended in the victory of a faction from the city of Thebes. This faction reunited Egypt and supplied kings during the Middle Kingdom.

A sign of Theban supremacy was the prominence of the god Amen, whose principal seat of worship was Thebes. He was merged with Re as Amen-Re and became the Egyptian national god. In his honor, rulers of the Middle Kingdom began the construction of the stupendous temple at Karnak, the largest ever erected to an ancient god. Rulers of the Twelfth Dynasty also took Amen into their names: four of them were named Amenemhet, an indication of the new respect paid to this god.

Rulers of the Middle Kingdom expanded Egyptian influence toward Palestine and Asia and also southward up the Nile (see Map 1.2). Sources tell of one military expedition into Palestine, but apparently the Egyptians did not dominate any part of this region through direct military occupation. Their influence was, rather, economic and cultural. It was different with the territory southward up the Nile, where the Egyptians pushed their frontier beyond the First Cataract and penetrated the area south of the Second Cataract.

THE INVASION OF THE HYKSOS

The prosperity and success of the Middle Kingdom declined in the late Twelfth and early Thirteenth Dynasties. The invasion by the so-called Hyksos, about 1720, ended the Middle Kingdom and led to the second intermediate period. Archaeologists are still not certain who these invaders were, but they were probably a Semitic group from Syria and Palestine.

The Hyksos controlled mainly the region of the delta. At about the time of their invasion, other tribes were overrunning Babylonia, and the activities of the Hyksos appear to have been part of a general disturbance in the Fertile Crescent that lasted from about 1750 to 1550. The Hyksos' invasion was a shock to Egyptian civilization, but it had some positive effects. The conquerors brought in the horse-drawn chariot as a vehicle in war and established the use of bronze rather than copper for weapons. They also stimulated the Egyptians to regroup and counterattack. By about 1570 Egyptian warriors from Thebes had driven the Hyksos from the delta and back into Asia Minor. The period following the expulsion is called the New Kingdom or the Egyptian Empire.

THE NEW KINGDOM

During the Eighteenth Dynasty the rulers from Thebes, now called "pharaohs," established the power of the central government over the nobles and organized Egypt into a military state. They enlarged their domain by encroaching on Asia Minor, where they encountered another large kingdom, that of the Hittites. These two kingdoms, the Egyptian and the Hittite, were the most powerful ones known down to their time, and also the last great kingdoms of the Bronze Age, that period from about 2000 to 1100, when military supremacy rested on weapons fashioned of bronze.

Thutmose III (1490?–1436?) was Egypt's most dynamic military statesman. He made seventeen expeditions into Asia Minor and established his reign as far as the Euphrates River. His successors, exploiting these conquests, grew rich on the tribute paid by subject peoples. Many captives, such as the Israelites, became slaves, and with this new economic force the Egyptians were able to expand their trade, build temples, and work the mines in the Sinai Peninsula.

AKHNATON'S RELIGIOUS REFORM

After the conquests of Thutmose, a dramatic conflict of religions took place in the New Kingdom—a battle of gods that had its roots in a battle between the pharaoh and certain priests and nobles. It was but one event during the centuries of the New Kingdom, but its humanistic interest carries special fascination. Early in

his reign King Amenhotep IV (1369?–1353?) began to oppose Amen-Re, for centuries the traditional god of Thebes, and sponsored the worship of the aton, the physical disk, or circle, of the sun. Supported by his wife, the exquisite Nefertiti, the pharaoh appears to have been trying to overcome the influence of priests and bureaucrats in Thebes. To advertise the new faith among his people, he changed his own name to Akhnaton, which may be translated as "He who serves Aton," and sent workers around Egypt to chisel off the name of Amen-Re from monuments. He moved his capital from Thebes to a completely new city called Akhetaton, "the horizon of Aton" (a village called Tell el Amarna today), where he built a temple to Aton and lived rather like a pope serving his god. He composed a soaring hymn in praise of Aton, hailing him as the creator of the world—another account of creation that stands beside those of the Sumerians and the Israelites.

There is evidence that Akhnaton fought the worship of other gods, and some historians have gone so far as to call him the first monotheist. Such a conception is anachronistic and overlooks the real conditions of the worship of Aton. The royal family alone worshiped the god; the Egyptian people were expected to worship the pharaoh himself. Artistic scenes show priests and nobles in attitudes of reverence, but they are addressing their prayers to the pharaoh, not directly to Aton.

During the reign of Akhnaton even artistic traditions, unchanged for hundreds of years, did not escape reform. Most portraits of Egyptian kings show them as handsome, massive creatures, but Akhnaton appears as a slender, aesthetic-looking man, with thin legs and a pot

Amenhotep IV-Akhnaton and his wife Nefertiti, accompanied by one of their daughters, make offerings to Aton, the disk of the sun. (Photo: The Metropolitan Museum of Art)

belly. This strain of realism could not have arisen without the king's approval.

Akhnaton fostered his new religion with passionate commitment, but in his zeal he neglected the kingdom. Princes took advantage of his inattention and, abandoning their loyalty to him, seized their independence. First in Syria and then in Palestine, Egyptian control was shaken loose. The Asiatic holdings fell away.

In the struggle between ideas, political authority is often ineffective. The more conservative priests, and probably most Egyptians, continued to worship Amen-Re, and the upheaval in religious and cultural life that Akhnaton had instigated came to an end with his death. The next pharaoh changed his name from Tutankhaton to Tutankhamen, thus indicating that Amen-Re, the older chief deity, was again in favor. The royal court moved back to Thebes, and the Theban priests of Amen-Re enjoyed their victory. The city named for Aton, Akhetaton, was first abandoned, then destroyed, and Akhnaton's name was savagely effaced from monuments and king lists. Indeed, he was now known as "the criminal of Akhetaton." The young king Tutankhamen, the heir of this quarrel, reigned for only seven years and was buried with dazzling splendor. The discovery of his tomb in 1922, intact with all its treasures, has remained one of the most impressive finds in the history of Egyptology.

The New Kingdom emerged from its weakness in the Eighteenth Dynasty under the pharaoh Haremhab, who reestablished a strong central government and destroyed the final vestiges of the religious reform. The first pharaohs of the Nineteenth Dynasty continued the rebuilding. Seti captured portions of Syria and restored Egyptian power in Palestine. Ramses II had difficulty in maintaining Egyptian holdings. He fought a great battle at Kadesh with the Hittites in 1286, but conflict continued for years until the two kingdoms signed a peace treaty about 1280. The temporary peace that Ramses achieved allowed him to spend time and money on building projects. He renamed the city of Tanis in the delta for himself; and, according to tradition, he exacted forced labor from the Israelites in Egypt. At Karnak he completed an enormous hall of columns sacred to Amen-Re, who had now fully regained his old position. Even more impressive are the monuments that Ramses II built to himself. In front of the temple at Luxor, built by his predecessors, he constructed an entrance court, guarded by six colossal statues of himself. His supreme achievement as a builder is the temple that he had carved out of the rocky cliffs along the Nile at Abu Simbel. The building of the Aswan Dam by the modern Egyptians would have drowned the temple and its statues beneath the waters of an artificial lake; but an international group of engineers preserved Ramses' desire to be remembered for all time by cutting the outer monuments free and raising them above the level of the water.

A VIEW OF EGYPTIAN SOCIETY

In antiquity, communication over navigable waterways in ships was greatly superior to overland transportation in animal-drawn carts. The Nile therefore imposed a natural administrative unity on Egypt. Bureaucratic and military control came far more easily to Egypt's rulers than to those of other ancient nations because the people of Egypt dwelt clustered along the river. As a result, Egypt remained united for most of 3000 years. The kings secured their power through cooperation with ministers and advisers, especially with the class of priests, while a complex bureaucracy carried out the routine work of government. The ultimate economic basis for the regime was the peasants, whose lives changed little from one generation to another.

Slavery existed in Egypt, although the economic difference between free man and slave was not always clear since both classes worked the fields and labored on the pyramids. Yet Egypt was not seriously threatened by the enormous stresses that have troubled some other slave-owning societies, where mass rebellion was a permanent possibility.

The Egyptians solved religious questions with easy pragmatism and a fertile spirit of invention. They discovered gods everywhere—in the Nile, in the sun, in the pharaoh himself. Life, like the Nile, flowed predictably, making severe demands but bringing the material for prosperity and a well-earned reward.

v. THE HITTITES

The first powerful society located outside the fertile river valleys that cradled civilization was that of the Hittites. They were an Indo-European people (that is to say, they spoke a language belonging to the great Indo-European group) who formed a major kingdom in Asia Minor. In the Hittite civilization, Indo-Europeans first blended their culture with that of the Near East on a significant scale.

RISE OF THE HITTITE KINGDOM

The Hittites had probably begun infiltrating Asia Minor before 2000. By about 1650 they had established a unified kingdom in northwest Turkey and had brought some neighboring tribes under their rule. Their capital was ancient Hattushash (Bogazköy in modern Turkey). Excavations here have disclosed about 10,000 cuneiform tablets, the decipherment of which has made it possible to write at least an outline of Hittite history.

The greatest early warrior of this nation, Mursilis, led armies south as far as Babylon, which he sacked about 1595, thus destroying the kingdom once ruled by Hammurabi. Between 1400 and 1200 the Hittite Kingdom reached its zenith, as it became the most formidable state in the Near East. The reign of its most renowned king, Suppiluliumas (about 1380–1340), coincided with that of Akhnaton in Egypt and the Hittite took advantage of the pharaoh's preoccupation with religious reform to tear away from Egypt the region of northern Syria. Under Ramses II, Egypt's unsuccessful attempt to regain the territory resulted in the signing of a treaty of nonaggression between the two nations about 1280. This modern-sounding document indicates a growth in the techniques of diplomacy among ancient states.[4]

One innovation of the Hittites was their system of government. In the civilizations of Mesopotamia and Egypt kings held their power through dynastic succession; in Egypt they were considered divine. The Hittites, however, elected their kings in an assembly composed of members of the army, a pattern later adopted by other states such as Macedonia and Rome. The king also acted as general, chief judge, and high priest; in the latter role he served the many Hittite gods, most of whom were deities that the Hittites had adopted when they entered Asia Minor. Their practice of adoption also extended to law codes, which they published in the tradition of older societies.

CLOSE OF THE BRONZE AGE

An important legacy of the Hittites was the use of iron. One of the commonest minerals on earth, iron had been known for many hundreds of years, but one of the tribes conquered by the Hittites had discovered a means of producing it in large quantities. Had the Hittites exploited it to make weapons, they might have managed to preserve their supremacy for a while longer than they actually did.

Between 1250 and 1200 new waves of invaders from the north and east poured into Asia

Minor, breaking up the Hittite Kingdom. These peoples had learned the secret of working iron but they, unlike their more civilized Hittite contemporaries, promptly applied their knowledge to weaponry. As a result, they overcame the older and higher civilizations that still relied on bronze weapons. After about 1100 the Bronze Age came to an end, replaced by an Age of Iron.

The introduction of iron had profound social and political consequences for the development of civilization. Iron, more readily available than bronze, is not only harder but, most important for this discussion, was cheaper as well. As a result, more people came to own weapons, and Iron Age states grew militarily more formidable. As more of the population obtained weapons, there followed a partial shrinking of the distance between some socioeconomic groups in the society. Those who now served the state in the field began to claim some role in determining its policies, and the ruling elites had to open their ranks to the newcomers in order to maintain control over the masses.

The closing of the Bronze Age in the decades before and after 1200 marks a major turning point in the history of Near Eastern civilizations. Not only the Hittites but nearly every society in this part of the world experienced an upheaval at this time. The disturbances threatened, and in some places ended, various forms of political domination. But one society, more notable for its ideas than for its conquests, now began to emerge.

VI. PALESTINE

The Hittites and their older neighbors shaped civilization in the ancient Near East, but the direct continuity of their influence stopped many centuries ago. The Israelites, however, provide a sharp contrast, for modern Jews feel

---

[4] Both versions of this document are translated in James B. Pritchard (ed.), *Ancient Near Eastern Texts Relating to the Old Testament* (1955), pp. 199–203.

an intimate kinship with their ancient ancestors.[5] The modern state of Israel considers itself a child of the Israelite Kingdom of antiquity, and three of the great religions of the world—Judaism, Christianity, and Islam—descend from the Israelites' belief in a single, all-powerful god.

CANAANITES AND PHOENICIANS

Israelites did not create the first civilization in the region of Palestine. A group of Semitic tribes, the Canaanites, originally inhabited the area and established flourishing urban civilizations about the time of the Egyptian Old Kingdom. Among their cities were Jericho and Jerusalem. By about 1200 the Canaanites lost control of most of their domain and were forced into Phoenicia, a narrow region along the Mediterranean Sea.

The Canaanites in Phoenicia drew part of their culture from the Mesopotamian and Egyptian states nearby, but they were also innovators. They developed a simplified alphabet with only about thirty characters that was later adopted by the Greeks and became the ancestor of Western alphabets.

The Phoenicians conducted intensive trade on land and sea with other Mediterranean peoples and established colonies or trading posts with a commercial dynamism unique in the ancient Near East. Their most famous colony was Carthage, on the Mediterranean coast of Africa, a powerful city that controlled parts of North Africa and Spain. Among their articles of trade was a reddish dye that the ancients called

purple. Cloth dyed in this color was considered a luxury, and purple clothing became a mark of royalty or eminence.

Trade and the dissemination of the alphabet helped to spread the culture of the Phoenicians. They were also the first people to treat the art of war as a profession; they became mercenaries in the Persian navy because of their sailing ability. Lacking the manpower to achieve a great kingdom, they used their resources to influence other states. They and other Canaanite peoples had developed a high urban civilization by the time the Israelites began their invasion of the Palestinian coast.

THE OLD TESTAMENT AS A HISTORICAL SOURCE

The Old Testament provides a continuous record of how the Israelites viewed their own past. But before the historian can use the legends and chronicles of the Scriptures as a source, he must settle his attitude toward their credibility. Scholars in the nineteenth century questioned whether the Old Testament contained unchallengeable, revealed truth. Archaeology in recent years has often confirmed the Bible, at least in questions of geography and topography, but literal accuracy is not, after all, the central issue. Legends can provide historical information, just as law codes and king lists do, and the twentieth century has a subtler appreciation of how to recover the history of a society from religious traditions.

The unique cultural contribution of the various writers in the Old Testament was to make creative use of familiar material, some of it descending from other Near Eastern peoples and some of it native to the Israelites themselves. These writers also demythologized much Canaanite literature. For example, the word *yam* meant "god of the sea" in prebiblical legends, but the Israelite chroniclers made this a nonmythical concept, "the sea." As they elimi-

---

[5] The term "Hebrew" should be restricted to the language and writings of this general group of people. They called themselves "Israel" or "sons of Israel." We shall hold to this usage: the term *hapiru* is found in Egyptian sources and probably means "caravaneer." It is the ancestor of the term "Hebrew," but it is not an ethnic designation. The word "Judean," from which "Jew" is derived, arose when Israel survived only in the southern kingdom called Judah.

nated such deities, they concentrated on a single god and on man's relationship to him. This great theme, varied in countless ways, fuses the Old Testament into a story about one god and the history of his chosen people. The Bible deals with real people and real times; it combines ethics, poetry, and history into the most influential book in the Western tradition.

The Old Testament was formed over many hundreds of years, starting perhaps in the twelfth century B.C. It probably assumed its present shape between A.D. 70 and 135. The long process of revision has left some interesting traces, such as parallel accounts of the same event. Chapters 1 and 2 of the Book of Genesis contain a classic example, for they offer two different views of the Creation, accounts that passed through oral tradition and were not reconciled when the text received its final polishing.

THE EARLY ISRAELITES

There is no good reason to doubt the tradition that one of the founders of the Israelite nation was Abraham, who led his clan away from the Sumerian city of Ur between 1800 and 1700 and followed a wandering course toward Egypt. Jacob, the grandson of Abraham, is said to have organized the growing nomadic people into twelve tribes under the jurisdiction of his twelve sons. Israel was therefore politically a tribal society, unlike the urban society of Sumer and the unified monarchy of Egypt. Their primitive tribal organization made the Israelites disciplined, loyal, and fit for the stern challenges they would face in founding their nation.

Some of the Israelite tribes settled in Canaan; the remainder migrated to Egypt, where they were subjects under various pharaohs. Then, probably under Ramses II or his successor, Merneptah, they left Egypt, led by a man with the Egyptian name of Moses. He crossed the Sinai Peninsula with them at some time before 1200, during the period of general unrest in the Near East.

Moses organized the tribes of Israel and some neighboring Canaanites into a confederation bound by a covenant to the god he named YHWH, which we write as Yahweh or Jehovah, and placed all the people in Jehovah's service. He proclaimed the new covenant between God and man on Mount Sinai, in the pitiless wastes of the desert. According to the Book of Exodus, he received his instructions directly from Jehovah. These instructions, a document of the greatest historical interest, include the Ten Commandments, in which Jehovah issues the terse order, "Thou shalt have no other gods before me." A god who insisted on being worshiped alone was rare in the ancient world, where families of deities were the rule. The Old Testament states that the Israelites did at times worship other gods and that they did not easily accept Jehovah as their only god.

Moses also laid down a complex code of laws, only part of which has survived. It is clearly analogous to the earlier Mesopotamian and Hittite codes, but it differs from them in one basic aspect: it is a series of laws prescribing ethically right conduct. The historical reality of Moses and the fact that his laws are connected with the experience of a people have given the faith of Israel an immediacy to which Sumerian or Egyptian religion could hardly pretend.

THE ISRAELITE MONARCHY

By a series of attacks on Canaanite cities and covenants made with other tribes, the Israelites established themselves in Palestine. About 1200, if not a little earlier, they invaded Canaanite territory—a fertile, hilly refuge overlooking the Mediterranean. Biblical stories say that Joshua, the successor of Moses, led the tribe of Israel across the Jordan River and took the Canaanite city of Jericho by siege.

Traditionally, each of the twelve Israelite tribes had been ruled by a judge, but the settlement of Canaan demanded a more efficient system; the result was the formation of a strong central government under a monarchy. Saul became king about 1020. His successor, David (1010?–960?), conquered Jerusalem and made it his capital. The entire nation now took the name Israel. During his reign David extended the kingdom to its farthest boundaries.

Solomon, David's son and successor (960?–920?), was famed for his skillful administration and wisdom; he passed into Muslim literature as the clever and powerful Suleiman. He is the purported author of some books of the Bible—Proverbs, Ecclesiastes, and the Song of Solomon—but it is clear that these works were composed considerably later.

Solomon ruled in a period when other Near Eastern powers were weak. He maintained peace by increasing the size of the standing army and equipping it with chariots; he also made a series of alliances with neighboring rulers who often sent him princesses in marriage as a token of good faith. These princesses, in a harem, provided political links to other important tribes. Thus a harem was actually a political device and was often used as such in the Near East.

Like all great kings of the period, Solomon was a builder. He left behind him the physical memorial that symbolized the faith of Israel through the centuries—the Temple in Jerusalem. But the temple could not compare in size with his magnificent palace and citadel. The tradition that the stables housed 12,000 horses gives some indication of its scale.

Solomon's autocratic rule and his extravagance caused resentment among his people, who were heavily taxed to pay for his palace and army. After his death his son was unable to control the kingdom, and it split into two parts. The northern half, based on the ancient town of Shechem, retained the name of Israel; the southern half was now called Judah and had its capital in Jerusalem. This division denied Israel the chance for further political expansion and in fact led to the long period of tragedy that the people were now to suffer.

Weakened by internal quarrels, the northern kingdom of Israel was conquered in 722 by the Assyrians, who dispersed all its leaders into Assyrian territories. This scattered people became known in biblical lore as the ten lost tribes of Israel.

Judah was now the only Israelite kingdom, and from this point on the remaining Israelites are known as Jews. *Yehudim* was the name for those who settled around Jerusalem and from the Greek version of this name, Ioudaioi, was derived the English word "Jews." Judah fell in 586 to the Chaldean, or New Babylonian, Kingdom. The captives were deported to Babylon—the so-called Babylonian captivity—but later in the same century were allowed to trickle back to Palestine. There were occasional revivals of an independent Jewish kingdom at other times, but in general the Jews became pawns of the various forces that ruled Palestine: Persians, Macedonians, Romans, Arabs, Turks. Only in our own day has a revived Jewish state taken its place among sovereign nations.

THE STRENGTHENING OF JUDAISM

The time of troubles witnessed a further solidifying of the Jewish faith. In the history of the Near East the Israelite kingdom lacked the power and expanse of other kingdoms, but in the history of man's thought the Jewish tradition has exerted an influence impossible to overstate.

The Jewish religion, like any institution tied to the fortunes of a people, changed and grew during more than a thousand years. One of the strongest forces that shaped it came from a few resolute social critics whose passionate conviction was sometimes close to fanaticism. These were the prophets—men of the people, tradesmen, preachers—who emerged in all periods of Israel's history. The most authoritative was Moses, and all successors looked back to him for guidance. They spoke one general message: Israel was becoming corrupt and only a rigid moral reform could save her. Worship of Jehovah had sometimes been blended with that of the gods, or Baalim, of the Canaanites. Luxury, promiscuity, and extravagance were weakening the discipline of Israelite society, a society built not only on belief but also on definite customs and behavior. But even as they denounced the prevalent wickedness, the prophets—men like Amos, Micah, Hosea, Jeremiah, Ezekiel, and the two Isaiahs—promised that God would forgive Israel if the people repented. God would prove his love to Israel by providing a redeeming king, or Messiah. The famous Dead Sea Scrolls, ranging in date from the second century B.C. through the first century A.D. (see Chapter 5), often speak of the awaited Messiah. To Jews he is still unborn or unknown; to Christians he has already appeared in the person of Jesus, who they believe is the son of God.

Another event that strengthened Judaism was the organization of the sacred writings. Ezra, whose work dates to about 445 B.C., is the prototype of a new kind of spiritual leader—the scribe and scholar. He collected and published the first five books of the Old Testament (the Pentateuch); later scholars collected the books of the prophets. The Temple in Jerusalem, destroyed during the Babylonian invasion, was rebuilt during the 500s and, in the absence of a free Jewish state, assumed even greater importance as the nucleus of the faith. It fell once more, in A.D. 70, this time to the Romans who destroyed it. But part of the western wall of the outer court survived, and at this site, the "Wailing Wall," the Jews were permitted to weep and pray.

THE JEWISH LEGACY

The Jews are the only society originating in the ancient Near East whose traditions have remained vital in modern times. For reasons that no one can fully explain, adversity has never broken the Jewish spirit, and over many centuries the Jews have persisted as a society even without an independent state. Their faith provided the most persuasive answer to the problem that also troubled their neighbors—the nature of the relationship between man and God. There was only one God; he was a jealous, vindictive God and, unlike the gods of the pagans, he was an exclusive and intolerant one. He judged severely, but was also prepared to forgive those who sincerely regretted wrong behavior. He created the world and stood outside the world; he had no association with the world of nature and never appeared as an animal or in any other form. Above all, he was a god for everyone, not just for nobles, priests, and kings. This simple but lofty conception of the divine, formed over the course of seven or eight centuries, drew its decisive impetus from the revelation granted to Moses, whose message was reinforced by the later prophets. To the Jews, history moves to and from three points—creation, revelation, and redemption. Moses stood at the central point, and only obedience to the laws that he transmitted can guarantee man's progress from revelation to final redemption.

Moses and the other prophets were not kings and could not force Jews to observe the law. The fact that ordinary men could influence the ethical behavior of a nation solely through their moral convictions anchored Judaism forever among the people. The Jewish religion is the experience of a people and the Bible is their

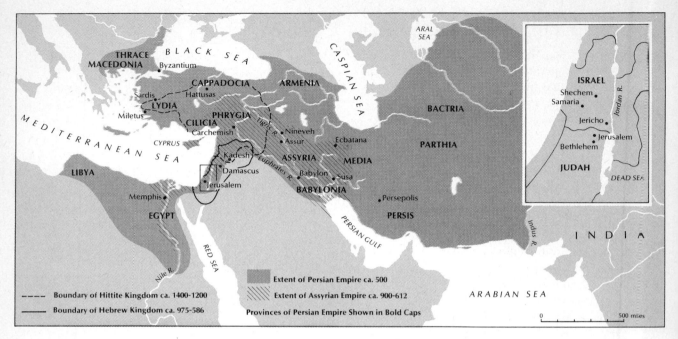

MAP 1.3: FOUR ANCIENT STATES

record. Christianity, the religion of medieval and modern Europe, is a daughter of Judaism and has drawn upon the morality and ethics of the older faith. No matter how deep the wounds of persecution or how widely Jews were scattered in later times, nothing destroyed their loyalty to their traditions. They stand alone as the most influential culture of the ancient Near East.

VII. THE NEAR EASTERN EMPIRES

A series of general disruptions about 1200 left no state dominant for the next few centuries until the Assyrians began their conquests. They became the first people to accomplish a political unification of the entire Near East and thus formed the first true empire in history (see Map 1.3). The Persians, the next great im-

perialists of this region, built on foundations laid by the Assyrians, and ruled with an administrative skill that only the Roman Empire would surpass in ancient times. They also developed a widely accepted religion, Zoroastrianism, some of whose doctrines persisted long after the Persian Empire had been destroyed.

THE ASSYRIAN STATE

The Assyrians were descended from Semitic nomads who had entered northern Mesopotamia about 2500 and founded the city of Ashur, named after their chief god. From this name comes the designation "Assyrian" for the people. Their language was a Semitic dialect closely resembling that of the Babylonians, and they wrote in the cuneiform script that had originated in Sumer and had been adopted by others.

About 900 the Assyrians began their most important period of conquest and expansion. They became masters of the upper reaches of Mesopotamia, and their territory included Babylonia to the south, the cities of Palestine to the west, and Egypt. By the late seventh century their empire embraced most of the Near East.

If any one concept could characterize Assyrian society it would be militarism. The army was especially dominant and efficient, and the Assyrians greatly extended the use of iron weapons. In administering their empire the Assyrians faced a greater challenge than any earlier state, for they had to absorb large kingdoms such as Egypt and Babylonia. They ruled with a degree of control unknown in any of the earlier conglomerates. In order to reflect the marked difference it is best to call the Assyrian domain the first empire and to designate those of earlier states as enlarged kingdoms.

The Assyrian kings exacted heavy payments of tribute as the price of leaving the conquered territories in peace. Some peoples, such as the inhabitants of Judah, escaped further burdens, but other, less independent people had to accept a vizier, or governor, serving the king. In

Assyrian reliefs usually show kings with long curled beards and lofty headdresses receiving prisoners or slaughtering enemies, scenes closely related to historical events. In this relief the Israelite king Jehu prostrates himself before the Assyrians, to whom he paid tribute money in exchange for peace. (Photo: British Museum)

some cases the imperial government deported subject peoples who might prove troublesome—for example, the inhabitants of Israel who were dispersed within the Assyrian Empire. Assyrian armies stationed in the provinces were a further guarantee of stability.

Language became another means of unifying the empire, for the Semitic language known as Aramaic was ultimately spoken everywhere in lands dominated by Assyria and became the common tongue of the Near East. In Palestine it was spoken by the Jews, including Jesus.

Among the brighter products of this harsh imperialism was Assyrian art. Much of the wealth extracted from the empire was spent on artistic glorifications of the king and his conquests. This art survives most notably in reliefs cut on the palace walls at Nineveh, the capital, and elsewhere.

The last important Assyrian king, Ashurbanipal (668–627?) created a library of cuneiform texts, which have been translated in modern times. The largest single group of these texts concerns omens, divination, or observations of the stars, for Assyrian kings relied heavily on omens to guide their policy. Some scholars believe that this practice gave influence to the aristocratic priests of the state, whose interpretations of divine signs could sway the monarch's decisions.

It is hardly surprising that subject kingdoms within the Assyrian Empire watched for any chance to rebel. Finally, in 612, a combination of forces, led by Babylonians, captured Nineveh, and the Assyrians lost control of their empire.

THE CHALDEANS AND THE MEDES

The Assyrian Empire gave way to two successor states: the Chaldean, or Neo-Babylonian, Kingdom and the Kingdom of the Medes. Seen in historical perspective, these mark the transi-

tion between the two great empires of the Assyrians and the Persians.

The Chaldeans, the dominant tribe within the new kingdom based on Babylon, were the most learned astronomers of antiquity. They kept a minute record of eclipses, charted a plan of the heavens, and, most impressive of all, calculated the length of the year mathematically and not by mere observation. Their accomplishments in astronomy were passed on to the Greeks and Romans and influenced all medieval and modern astronomy.

Babylon, the capital of the Chaldean Kingdom, became notorious as a center of luxury and wealth. Nebuchadnezzar (604–562), the most famous king of the Chaldean dynasty, built numerous lavish temples to the gods and also constructed the terraced roof garden known as the Hanging Gardens, which was considered one of the seven wonders of the ancient world. In the Book of Daniel it is written that Nebuchadnezzar made an immense golden image that all his subjects were ordered to worship. According to the same book, Daniel interpreted for Belshazzar, a later king, a message written on a wall by a mysterious hand. The message, *mene, mene, tekel, upharsin,* meant that the Chaldean Kingdom would soon fall to the control of the Medes and the Persians.

Media, the territory of the Indo-European Medes, was located east of Mesopotamia and became a coherent kingdom about 650. Among its subjects was another Indo-European group, the Persians. The Kingdom of Media retained much of its prestige even after the Persians actually conquered it. Probably because Media was an older state than Persia, it was referred to first in official documents in which both states were named. The Greeks used "Medes" as the single term embracing both Medes and Persians, and called their crucial war with the Persians the Medic War.

THE PERSIAN EMPIRE

It was the careful planning of Persia's resolute King Cyrus (559–530) that laid the basis for the Persian Empire. The Persians first extended their dominion by conquering the Medes, to their north, about 550. A few years later they expanded into western Asia Minor and confronted the recently formed kingdom of Lydia, whose ruler, Croesus, was famous as the richest man in the world, a reputation that may have derived partly from the fact that coins were invented in Lydia.[6]

Croesus, realizing that he would need allies against Persia, turned to the cities of Greece for help. Thus he involved European states for the first time in the affairs of the kingdoms of Asia Minor. Sparta agreed to join Croesus in war against Persia, but Athens refused. Croesus also asked advice from the renowned oracle at Delphi, a shrine sacred to Apollo where the god supposedly spoke in prophecy through the mouth of a young girl. The shrewd Delphic priests gave Croesus a deliberately ambiguous reply: "If Croesus crosses the Halys River [the frontier between Lydia and Persia], he will destroy a mighty empire."

Croesus lost his ambitious campaign. It was the Lydian Kingdom that fell, and Cyrus took the capital city of Sardis. This conquest brought the Persian Empire westward as far as the Aegean Sea, which separates Asia Minor from Greece. Now the stage was set for a direct clash between the vast empire of the Near East and the new culture of the Greeks, but this clash was not to come for another two generations.

To secure the southern flank of his growing empire, Cyrus led his forces against the Chaldeans and captured Babylon. Evidently, the inhabitants welcomed him, for they offered little resistance. Their judgment was sound; Cyrus treated the city with moderation, not sacking it as an Assyrian conqueror might have done. His wisdom is evident in his treatment of the Jews, whom he allowed to return to Jerusalem and rebuild their holy temple.

He did not live to make the third great conquest that enlarged the Persian Empire. His successor, Cambyses (529–522), conquered Egypt in 525, and the rich valley of the Nile remained under Persian rule until Alexander the Great captured it in 332 B.C. No Egyptian ruled independently over this ancient land again until A.D. 1952, when the government of Naguib and Nasser was established.

The most skillful administrator of the huge Persian Empire was Darius (521–486). He divided it into some twenty provinces, each ruled by a satrap ("protector of the realm"). The system worked successfully for the Persians because they had enough spies and civil servants to enable the king to keep close watch on his subordinates. The king was regarded as the supreme glory of the state, but the satraps had a high degree of independence; they dispensed justice, designed foreign policy, and were in charge of finance. Each one was responsible for an assigned amount of revenue from his province.

The Greek historian Herodotus mentions with admiration the Persian system of roads begun by Cyrus and perfected by Darius. A great highway ran across the empire from the capital at Susa to Sardis in Lydia, a distance of more than 1,000 miles. The first long highway built anywhere, this road bound together the gigantic empire of the Persians.

---

[6] Ancient coins were lumps of precious metal stamped by the ruler to guarantee their weight and therefore their value. As coinage gradually replaced trade by bartering, it transformed methods of trade and crucially influenced Western civilization. Without acknowledged systems of trading in precious metal, the commerce of later antiquity and of the modern world would have been inconceivable.

Darius also built a lavish capital at the new city of Persepolis. The efficiency of his reign can be seen in his coinage, for he made creative use of this Lydian invention by issuing a famous series of gold coins called darics. He also installed a standard system of weights and measures for the empire.

ZOROASTRIANISM

The predominant influence on Persian religion was the prophet Zarathustra—more familiarly, Zoroaster, the Greek form of his name—who probably lived soon after 600 B.C. Zoroastrianism was a dualistic religion, unlike the monotheistic creed of the Jews. The prophet taught that the world had been created by a god of light and truth who was engaged in a struggle with a god of evil and darkness. After some thousands of years, good would prevail and the day of judgment arrive. Those who had clung to the principles of the god of light would then be admitted to Paradise; the rest would suffer in the realm of endless darkness.

The teachings of Zoroaster survived through the centuries, long after the demise of the Persian Empire, and exerted a strong influence on other faiths. During the Roman Empire, this religion survived in the worship of Mithras, a Persian deity who rivaled Jesus in popularity. The dualism of the Persian religion is reflected in Manicheanism, a religious belief of late antiquity, and in the Albigensianism of southern France during the twelfth century.

Zoroaster lived at the same time as the Israelite prophets and the earliest Greek philosophers. Gautama, the Buddha, who founded the great Eastern religion of Buddhism, was active about 500 B.C.; and in distant China the philosopher Confucius was a precise contemporary of the Buddha. We shall not, in this book, study the thought of India and China, but it seems highly significant that men throughout the world felt, at about the same time, the need to restate their religious and moral creeds.

From the time of the earliest agricultural settlements some degree of civilization appears as man began to fashion communities with specialized social structures and some degree of wealth and luxury. In Sumer, the oldest civilized region in the Mesopotamian plain, city-states took the place of villages, and the closer intellectual contact among people in an urbanized society must have stimulated the pictographic writing invented in Sumer and later simplified into cuneiform. About the same time the Egyptians began to write in hieroglyphics, learned the science of surveying, and devised the technique of creating monumental architecture. Other societies developed in the Near East, some of them controlling large sections of neighboring lands. The Persian Empire, the youngest and largest of these states, succeeded in unifying the entire Near East.

These early civilizations had different ways of looking at the two problems that will always concern man most deeply: his relationship to others of his own kind and his relationship to those forces that he considers divine. The Near Eastern peoples made basic discoveries regarding these problems, and without their explorations of human experience, our own culture would not have become what it is. In particular, the ethical monotheism of Israel is the root of the three main Western religions: Judaism, Christianity, and Islam. The God of Israel became that of the Western world.

But we are also close in spirit to the civilizations of Greece and Rome. In literature and thought they drew on the legacy of the ancient Near East, but they added a deep measure of individualism and a passion for logical thought. Our politics and institutions also descend from Greco-Roman society. We shall therefore turn to the Mediterranean world and trace the rise of the highly urbanized cultures of Greece and Rome.

RECOMMENDED READING

Sources

*Erman, Adolf. *The Ancient Egyptians: A Sourcebook of Their Writings.* 1966.

Lichtheim, Miriam. *Ancient Egyptian Literature: A Book of Readings.* Vol. 1: *The Old and Middle Kingdom.* 1973.

Pritchard, James B. (ed.). *Ancient Near Eastern Texts Relating to the Old Testament.* 1955. A collection of translations from cuneiform and hieroglyphic texts, with brief commentaries, by the most eminent scholars in the field.

Studies

*Albright, William Foxwell. *The Biblical Period from Abraham to Ezra.* 1963. A brief history of the Israelites.

———. *From the Stone Age to Christianity.* 1957. A survey of modern historical knowledge for this long period.

*Frankfort, Henri. *The Art and Architecture of the Ancient Orient.* 1971.

*———. *The Birth of Civilization in the Near East.*
1951. A comparison of Mesopotamian and Egyptian history in early stages.

*Gardiner, Sir Alan. *Egypt of the Pharaohs.* 1966. Essentially a political narrative by one of the masters of Egyptology.

*Gurney, O. R. *The Hittites.* 1961.

Kramer, Samuel Noah. *The Sumerians: Their History, Culture and Character.* 1963. The fullest presentation of Sumerian civilization by a leading authority.

*Mellaart, James. *The Earliest Civilizations of the Near East.* 1966.

*Olmstead, A. T. *History of the Persian Empire.* 1948.

*Oppenheim, A. Leo. *Ancient Mesopotamia: Portrait of a Dead Civilization.* 1968. A cultural study of Assyrio-Babylonian society.

Piggott, Stuart (ed.). *The Dawn of Civilization.* 1961. A far-flung anthropological survey.

*Wilson, John A. *The Culture of Ancient Egypt.* 1956. A subtle treatment of Egyptian cultural history; excellent for the history of ideas.

*Available in paperback.

TWO

THE FOUNDATIONS
OF GREEK CIVILIZATION

With the Greeks we stand at the threshold of European civilization. These curious, contentious people were the first to attempt to explain the physical world exclusively in natural terms. For religious faith they substituted canons that approximate the assumptions of modern scientific thought. They believed that the visible world concealed a rational order and that human reason, unaided, could discover the causes of natural phenomena. They applied this secular viewpoint to the mysteries of the human condition, and tried to define ethical, political, and aesthetic values by reference not to the will of the gods, but to human needs and aspirations. In the process they created tragic and lyric poetry, philosophy, government by consent, and democracy. The importance of these achievements for the Western experience can hardly be overestimated. To the extent that Europeans and their descendants living outside Europe share a common cultural tradition, they owe it in significant part to the unifying influence of Greek philosophy. Carried throughout their empire by the Romans, assimilated and restated by Jewish and Christian theologians, the perennial philosophy of the Greeks has nourished Western thought in every century from late antiquity to the present day.

These intellectual discoveries did not spring full-blown from the foreheads of the classical Greeks, as Athena did from that of Zeus. They emerged gradually from the unique history of the ancient Hellenes. The Greek enlightenment can only be understood when viewed against the background of that singular, historical experience.

I. EARLY GREECE

Our knowledge of the origins of Greek civilization comes mainly from archaeological excavations. They reveal that a culture based on many small cities developed in Greece during the Bronze Age. For centuries it was clearly inferior to the more advanced culture on the island of Crete, where an attractive civilization flourished, one notable for its wealth and elegance. Crete influenced early Greece in art and religion, but in time the Greek city of Mycenae became the leading center in the Aegean area. Mycenaean civilization in turn survived until the general upheavals that occurred around 1200. This era of troubles in the eastern Mediterranean and the Near East greatly weakened early Greek civilization; but much of its cultural legacy passed on to the Greek city-states that revived after 800.

THE AEGEAN WORLD

The earliest inhabitants of Greece were not Greeks; they did not speak the Greek language, nor can they yet be identified with any known ethnic group. True Greek civilization began about 2000, when a group of Indo-Europeans migrated from the northern Balkans, seeking a warmer climate and better access to the sea. They imposed their language upon, and probably intermarried with, the earlier inhabitants. Slowly, a new culture evolved, influenced in its early centuries by the more highly developed civilization of Crete, which lies just south of the Aegean. The history of Greece must, then, begin with Crete, the island that served as a link between the ancient Near Eastern kingdoms and the mainland of Greece.

Minoan Civilization

The first inhabitants of Crete probably came from western Asia Minor well before 3000. In time, as the islanders mastered the sea, Crete became a thriving maritime power. Trade with the older civilizations of Egypt and Asia introduced new ideas and new skills. These, combined with the creative energy of the Cretans, produced a distinctive civilization.

We owe our knowledge of Cretan civilization to the work of the English archaeologist Sir Arthur Evans. In 1900 Evans began to excavate Knossos, the leading city of ancient Crete. There he uncovered a magnificent structure that he called the Palace of Minos, so naming it from the legendary king of Crete (hence the civilization of Crete is often called Minoan). Evans also established the usually accepted chronology for the history of Crete: Early Minoan (2600–2200), Middle Minoan (2200–1500), and Late Minoan (1500–1200).[1] He based his chronology on the residue of pottery found at Knossos, for different styles of pottery provide an accurate record of the successive stages of civilization at a site.

The Palace of Minos was built over several centuries from about 2000 onward. It was an extensive structure, with an impressive grand staircase and many wings, additions, and storage chambers. In designing some of its architectural features the Minoans displayed remarkable technical ability. The palace had a plumbing system with water running through fitted clay pipes, and the palace windows were covered with a form of glazed windowpane.

It was in the grace and beauty of their art that the Minoans achieved their greatest distinction. Minoan art bears witness to a civilization that valued elegance and style. The walls of the palace were decorated with frescoes showing jeweled ladies in elaborate gowns and graceful young men bearing cups and vases; paintings of gardens, birds, and animals express the Minoans' delight in nature. Minoan pottery, far more colorful than that of any previous Western culture, often depicts marine themes: plants from the sea, flying fish, and lively renderings of the octopus. The gaiety and freedom of these designs are almost unique to Minoan artists.

The peaceful nature of Minoan civilization is suggested by the absence of fortifications at Knossos and at palaces excavated at other sites in Crete. Knossos was clearly the wealthiest of the Cretan cities and, judging from the size of its palace, was the center of a complex administration. Surviving records indicate that the king was served by an efficient bureaucracy. He probably acted as priest in religious ceremonies, for there is no evidence of a powerful priesthood such as the Egyptians had. Nor were there any temples on Crete; the people worshiped at shrines, either in their homes or outdoors. Among the deities worshiped—and perhaps the chief one—was a bare-breasted goddess, probably a goddess of nature.

Much of the wealth of Crete came from trade. The Greek historian Thucydides wrote that Minos was the first man to have a sea empire. But any Cretan dominion overseas was not an empire in the modern sense, for Crete lacked the manpower to control it directly. At most, her dominion consisted of a group of

---

[1] The system of Cretan chronology was established by Evans in his *The Palace of Minos* (1921–1936). Some scholars have attacked Evans' scheme. The most important difference is that they date the Linear B tablets to about 1200 rather than about 1400 (Evans). See, for example, L. R. Palmer, *Mycenaeans and Minoans* (1965).

Sea creatures were often used in the designs of Minoan pottery, and the octopus on this vase is an excellent example of the free-flowing style of Minoan artists. (Photo: Hirmer Fotoarchiv München)

trading posts distributing the products of Crete.

Minoan civilization reached its height between 1550 and 1400, when Crete enjoyed her greatest influence in the Aegean world. Minoan pottery was widely distributed, and there are several sites in the Aegean area named Minoa. Early mainland Greek art, architecture, and religion reveal Minoan influence. At least two Greek goddesses, Athena and Artemis, are believed to have been adopted from Crete.

Striking evidence of the Minoan-Greek interchange comes from Cretan writing on tablets that Evans and others discovered at Knossos.

Most of the tablets fall into two classes, Linear A and Linear B. (Evans called them "linear" because the symbols are outlines rather than the detailed drawing found in hieroglyphics.) Both linear scripts are syllabic: each symbol represents a sound, such as *ko*, rather than a letter of an alphabet. Linear A, the older script, has not yet been deciphered; but in 1952 a British linguist and architect, Michael Ventris, showed that Linear B could be reconciled with an archaic form of classical Greek. The tablets he deciphered are inventories, rosters, and records of all kinds, listing foot stools, helmets, horses, vessels, seeds, and the like.

That these tablets were written in a form of Greek is highly significant, for it shows that Greeks were in Knossos during the period between 1450 and 1400, when the currently accepted chronology dates the Linear B tablets. While the Greeks were there, they learned to use the Cretan script in writing their own language. Another important clue suggests that there were Greeks on Crete. At this time the pottery made at Knossos changed in style; the painting became more regular and formalized. This change is probably due to Greek influence. There is evidence that they also introduced larger swords and the use of the horse both as a mount and with chariots. These changes at Knossos suggest that Greeks dominated the city not long before 1400, conceivably through outright military seizure.

About 1400 disaster engulfed Knossos and other Cretan cities. The palaces were burned or destroyed. There is continuing debate about what caused this destruction. A series of earthquakes or a huge volcanic eruption may have been responsible for it, but the most plausible explanation is that Greeks from the mainland raided the island. If so, they must have been led by forces from Mycenae, which by this time had become the most powerful Greek city.

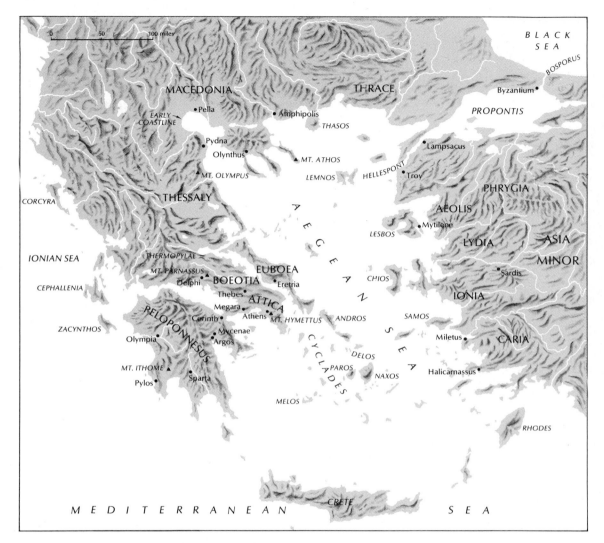

MAP 2.1: EARLY AND CLASSICAL GREECE

Mycenaean Civilization

As it does in all civilizations, geography played a part in the formation of Greek society. Mountain ranges divide Greece into many small valleys. The resulting pattern of settlement, so different from that of Egypt, encouraged the Greeks to develop independent political communities without the direction—or oppression—of a central ruler. The broken coastline, in-dented with countless small harbors, invited the people to become sailors, traders, and warriors at sea (see Map 2.1). By 1600 enterprises by sea had transformed a number of the independent Greek communities into wealthy, fortified states. Chief among them was Mycenae; therefore the years from 1600 to 1100 are often called the Mycenaean Age.

Two sets of graves found in the soil at

Mycenae have given us a fascinating glimpse of early Greek culture. The graves in each were enclosed within a circular wall. The older set, tentatively dated between 1700 and 1600, was outside the walls that surround the citadel of Mycenae. Interred there were wealthy Greeks, perhaps from a royal family or clan. Alongside the bodies, the surviving relatives had deposited various offerings, for example, a golden rattle in a child's grave. The second set of graves, inside the citadel walls, far surpassed the older ones in wealth. These graves, dated between 1600 and 1500, were discovered in 1876 by one of the founders of Greek archaeology, Heinrich Schliemann, and are still among the wonders of archaeology. They include such stunning luxuries as three masks of gold foil that were pressed on the faces of the dead and a complete burial suit of gold foil wrapped around a child as well as swords, knives, daggers, and hundreds of gold ornaments. Bulls' heads in the graves indicate the influence of Crete on artifacts made in Greece.

The graves tell us little about the political or social history of Mycenae, but they do demonstrate her growing wealth in the sixteenth century. We know that the city's king was also its chief religious officer as well as commander of the army. Elaborate fortifications at Mycenae and other early Greek cities indicate that Greece was a more warlike society than Crete.

Linear B tablets have been found at Mycenae, Thebes, and Pylos. The Pylos tablets can be dated soon after 1200 from the evidence of pottery fragments found with them. These tablets, like those at Knossos, are inventories and rosters, more evidence of the bureaucratic tidiness which was characteristic of the early Greeks.

Between 1400 and 1200, Mycenae reached the height of her prosperity. This period saw the creation of the most splendid monuments in all Bronze Age Greece. Between 1350 and 1300 the walls around the citadel were built in their present form; the mighty Gate of the Lionesses (or Lion Gate) was erected as an entrance to the city, and the most imposing of the Mycenaean tombs came into use. These are the beehive, or *tholos*, tombs, large vaults with walled entranceways. The grandest and best preserved is the Treasury of Atreus, named for the legendary father of Agamemnon. The high vaulted ceiling is still intact, and the effect made by the somber cavern is breathtaking.

Each city of the Mycenaean period was probably independent under its own king. The only time these cities appear to have united in league was during the war against Troy, a prosperous city in Asia Minor near the Dardanelles. The origin of the Trojans is not yet clear, but some of their pottery suggests a close relationship to the Greeks. Apparently the Trojans were rich and offered a tempting prospect to pirates and looters. This was probably the real cause of the Trojan War, but ultimately Greeks explained the origins of the war by the romantic story in Homer's *Iliad* about the seduction by a Trojan of Helen, the wife of the king of Sparta. The excavation of Troy, begun by Schliemann at Hissarlik in Turkey, has disclosed several layers of building. One layer, called Troy VII A, was destroyed by an enemy about 1250. This evidence suggests that Homer's account of a successful Greek expedition against Troy contains some historical truth.

The war against Troy was the last feat of the Mycenaean Age. About 1300 or a little later, various marauders began to attack Greek ships

Mycenaean gold funeral mask. (Photo: Hirmer Fotoarchiv München)

and even mainland Greece. The identity of these warriors is still uncertain. Historians usually call them sea-peoples, and their homes were probably somewhere in Asia Minor. Whoever they were, they made trading by sea so dangerous that the export of Mycenaean pottery virtually ended. The raids by sea were temporarily destructive. But much more significant was a series of attacks by land, lasting roughly from 1200 to 1100. Near 1100, Mycenae itself was overrun and destroyed.

It is still not wholly clear who these land invaders were. Recent excavations have uncovered remains of a wall built across the isthmus that leads to the Peloponnesus—evidently an attempt to stop invasions by land. We can at least say that among the invaders were the Dorian Greeks. Historians can trace them through the presence of their dialect, Doric Greek, in Corinth, Argos, and other cities. They settled above all in Sparta, which became the most important Dorian city in Greek history.

The period from 1100 to 800 is known as the Dark Age of Greece. Throughout the area there are signs of a sharp cultural decline. Some sites, formerly inhabited, were now abandoned. Pottery was much less elegant; burials were made without expensive ornaments; and the construction of massive buildings came to a halt. Even the art of writing in Linear B vanished. The palace-centered bureaucracies no longer existed, but of the political machinery that replaced them we know almost nothing.

Still, the cultural decline was not quite a cultural break. Farming, weaving, and other technological skills survived; pottery, though it was for a while much less gracious, revived and developed the so-called Geometric style. Nor was the Greek language submerged. Many Greeks found safety for their families by settling in other areas.

In a larger sense, the shattering of the mon-archic pattern in the Mycenaean Age can be viewed as a liberating and constructive event. We cannot show that the kings and dynasties in Greece were dependent on or were imitating kings in the ancient Near East, but the two systems of monarchy resembled each other. If the Mycenaean kings had survived, mainland Greece might have developed as Anatolia did, with strong monarchies and priests who interpreted and refined religious thought in ways that would justify the divine right of kings. Self-government within Greek states might not have emerged for centuries if it appeared at all. But the invasions of the twelfth century, in which the Dorians at least played a part, ended forever the domination of the palace-centered kings.

II. THE GREEK RENAISSANCE

The so-called Dark Ages following the destruction of the Mycenaean world were far darker, for the modern historian, than the Christian Dark Ages of Europe. Much archaeological evidence survives, but there is little to help us reconstruct the social and political paths that led to the city-state or *polis*. After 800 Greek culture displays a richness and creativity never before seen. A new spirit of optimism and adventure awakened the Greeks from the comparative lethargy of the Dark Age. One phrase, imprecise but still effective, has been used to designate the period from about 800 to 600: the Greek Renaissance.

COLONIZATION

During the Dark Age, for all its lack of dramatic activity, the population of Greece must have increased. This growth had unfortunate consequences. In antiquity, as also today,

Greece was relatively poor in agricultural resources, and by about 750 the population threatened to outgrow the local capacity to feed it. The problem of limited resources grew more and more acute: the struggle for survival caused social and economic conflict as people turned on each other. They solved this problem through foreign colonization. In effect, the mainland Greeks of the eighth and seventh centuries, instead of importing foodstuffs, exported their excess population. They colonized vigorously from about 750 to 600 and by the end of this period had spread over an enormous area, stretching from the northern, western, and southern shores of the Black Sea through Western Asia Minor and Greece proper, including the Aegean islands, to much of Sicily and southern Italy, then continuing west along both shores of the Mediterranean to Cyrene in Libya, to Marseilles, and to Spanish coastal sites. Wherever they went, the Greeks settled on the edge of the sea, never in the hinterland. Among their colonies are some of the great ports of modern Europe: Byzantium (today Istanbul), Naples, and Syracuse.

This overseas expansion led to a revival of trade. The colonies supplied needed raw materials to the mainland Greeks, who in turn furnished them with manufactured goods. The Greeks proved to be enterprising traders; by about 500 they dominated commerce in the Mediterranean. Trade brought prosperity to many of the Greek cities and, even more important, the intangible benefits of contact with other peoples and other ideas.

One of these intangible—and incalculable— benefits was the alphabet. By about 750 the

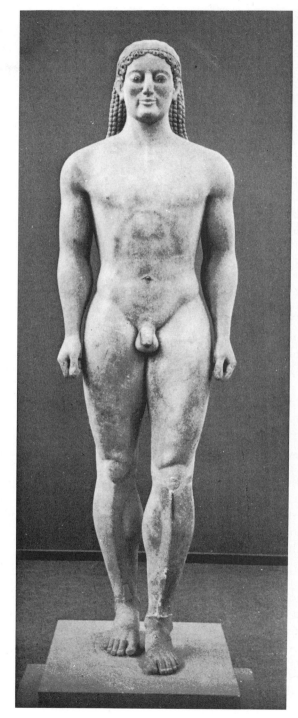

The kouros is characteristic of the rigid, formalized style of early Greek sculpture and clearly suggests the influences of Egypt and the Near East. (Photo: Boudot-LaMotte)

Greeks began to trade with the Phoenicians, who were using a Semitic script called the alphabet (from the first two characters, *aleph*, which seems to mean "ox," and *beth*, "house"). The Greeks adapted this script to their own language. To historians the advent of Greek writing marks the end of the prehistoric period in Greece.

Two versions of the alphabet developed. A Western version made its way to Cumae, a Greek town in Italy, and then to the Etruscans. They in turn passed it on to the Romans, who developed it into the alphabet that is now prevalent throughout the Western world and is being used more and more in such recently literate regions as Africa. Much later, many letters of the alphabet were used in an Eastern version, the Cyrillic form, the script for Russian and other Slavic languages. Thus large regions of the world use one or another derivative of the Phoenician alphabet in the form that the Greeks gave it.[2]

POLIS AND POLITICS IN ARCHAIC GREECE

The economic crisis to which colonization was a reaction had its roots in the nature of aristocratic society and in the ways in which that society developed during the Dark Ages. Though no evidence for its development has survived, we know that it underwent a transition that subjected even the most powerful individuals to formal rules of organization and authority. This transition cannot have been either simple or natural, for the existence of constitutional government, which we today take so much for granted, is really, like much else in our society, quite anomalous. A student of

history cannot help but be struck by the extreme improbability of this kind of system ever emerging anywhere or managing to endure once it has emerged. There is much truth in Adlai Stevenson's observation that "the natural government of man is servitude. Tyranny is the normal pattern of human government." How frustrating it is, therefore, that the light of history should fail us at that very moment when Western man first undertook the experiment in constitutional government that would distinguish him from his Eastern predecessors and produce such profound repercussions for his descendants.

One major step in the progress toward constitutional government must have been the elimination of kingship, but it was a step that, curiously, went unnoticed even in the legends and traditions of the Greeks. The silence suggests that there was no great stimulus to record the feat. Despite the colorful Agamemnons and Odysseuses of Homer's epics, the monarchs of the Dark Ages must have been petty chieftains whose disappearance from the scene was neither dramatic nor memorable. In their place emerged councils and offices that previously must have provided advice to the monarch but now assumed and more or less defined the responsibilities of government. The breadth of this new governing oligarchy should not be overestimated, for its members undoubtedly came from a narrow and socially closed landed aristocracy. The political divisions of the archaic Greek city-state, or polis—to use the word the Greeks themselves used—consisted of competing tribal and family groups, each containing members from every socioeconomic level of society, and led by wealthy landowning magnates who were the ruling aristocrats. In the political system of the archaic age, various aristocratic clan leaders allied their families with other friendly clan leaders against an opposition similarly constituted, and politics consisted of

---

[2] The best study of the Greek alphabet is L. H. Jeffery's *The Local Scripts of Archaic Greece* (1961). She reviews the evidence for dating the adaptation of the alphabet to about 750.

the alignments and realignments of such groups. One way of controlling the members of a clan was to manipulate their common religion. For the various tribes had their own cults, controlled by the aristocratic clan leaders who were part-time head priests as well, since the Greeks lacked the full-time priestly class of many of their Near Eastern contemporaries. This whole political and religious structure would have to be destroyed before the democratic polis of the classical period could exist and be governed by its sovereign and autonomous popular assembly.

GOVERNMENT AND ECONOMIC LIFE

The polis (plural "poleis") usually consisted of a city built around a citadel known as an *acropolis,* or "high city," and the surrounding area of farms. In size the poleis varied from a few hundred citizens to tens of thousands. Statistics are notoriously scarce and unreliable for the ancient world, but the best estimates put the citizen population of Athens, the most populous city-state, at about 30,000 during the fifth century. Citizenship, however, was restricted to free, native-born, adult males. The total population of Athens and her outlying villages (that is, the region known as Attica) was presumably over 200,000, a figure which would include all men, women, children, and slaves.

We saw how, at the beginning of the Archaic Age, these poleis were governed by narrow, landowning aristocracies. The aristocrats would have governed through assemblies which, in origin, were probably the cities' armies. They, naturally, would have had the right to vote on declarations of war and treaties of peace. But in time their legislative powers expanded, and they became electoral bodies as well, choosing their own magistrates from among the competing aristocratic candidates. As population increased and as methods of warfare changed, more of the poorer classes of

citizens gained admission to the army and so to the legislative and electoral bodies of the state. As political power expanded into the lower levels of Greek society, the ruling aristocracy could only neglect the interests of the citizenry at the risk of losing its monopoly of political power. Indeed, legal codes defining citizens' rights were published in the course of the seventh and sixth centuries, dramatic evidence of the shift in political power.

This whole process was, eventually, hastened by the effects of colonization. At first, the mainland Greeks had resorted to colonizing in order to stave off the social upheaval attendant on overpopulation. But one of the early effects of their vigorous colonizing was the growth of trade. Profits came either directly through the trading itself, or indirectly through some of the economic side effects that frequently accompany trade, such as an increased demand for small handicrafts and vessels in which the exported products can be transported. At any rate, new markets encouraged new entrepreneurs or, at least, gave old entrepreneurs new avenues for investment and capital accumulation. Most often, wealth gathered from commerce was at once invested in land, because throughout antiquity land was regarded not only as the safest investment, as compared, say, with the hazards of putting one's wealth out to sea, but also as the most prestigious, unsullied, as it was, by barter or the effort to buy cheap and sell dear. In antiquity, as in modernity, wealth bought power, and colonization would, in the long run, have political as well as social and economic effects.

Not all poleis conducted their economic affairs in the same way, but there were enough similar features to give us a general picture of conditions in the city-states. The basic element in economic life was agriculture, but in most places the soil of Greece is thin and rocky, not conducive to raising grain or pasturing cattle.

Therefore at times the farmer was threatened with a limited food supply.

It was the task of political reformers to discover new ways for Greeks to feed themselves. One such way was increased trade, which revolutionized agriculture in many poleis by putting it on a commercial basis. More effort could be devoted to the growth of olive trees and grapevines, both better suited than grain to the rocky soil and rough terrain of Greece. There was a ready market for olive oil and wine abroad, and these were easily transportable commodities. In return, the Greeks could import more grain than they were able to grow locally.

Trading was mainly a venture of small, independent businessmen rather than organized corporations. For a long period Corinth was the leader in trade, but by the fifth century Athens had become dominant and had taken over from Corinth the trade with Sicily and other Greek cities to the west.

Trade stimulated industry at home, particularly the manufacture of pottery. In general, industry was operated on a limited scale, almost like a household craft. A worker might have two or three slaves helping him in his trade as a potter, shoemaker, or stonecutter. A few larger workshops are known. One shield maker employed 120 slaves, and the father of the orator Demosthenes owned about 30 slaves and was considered fairly wealthy. The most skilled workers were makers of jewelry and fine pottery. Ordinary pots had little decoration and were simply containers for goods, but luxury pots, exquisitely painted, were objects for trade.

The development of an economy based on money seems to have been rather slow. Greece did not begin to use coins until nearly 600, and even then the smallest unit of coinage was usually a drachma, one day's pay for workers on the Athenian Parthenon; therefore the Greeks must have continued to use barter as their medium of exchange for some time after coinage was adopted from Lydia.

Taxation was haphazard in the poleis, for Greeks had little grasp of the mechanics of public finance. There was no permanent military treasury in the poleis until the 300s. In some ways this is surprising, since the cities were so often at war. Infantry soldiers were expected to arm themselves, but they did receive pay, and for this the state had to find money. When large amounts were needed for projects such as public buildings and maintenance of ships, the expenses were assigned to citizens judged capable of bearing the cost. This was only one of many services to the state that were imposed on the rich; others included paying for the training of the choruses in Greek dramas and seeing to the upkeep of gymnasiums for athletic contests.

MILITARY REFORM AND THE RISE OF TYRANNY

At the beginning of the seventh century a virtual revolution in military tactics, connected with the changes we have been describing, helped to promote political revolution. Before this time war seems to have been fought exclusively by the aristocracy and consisted of such hand-to-hand combats between warrior nobles as Homer describes in the *Iliad*. But soon after 700, the art of the period depicts soldiers fighting in tight, well-disciplined formations. They were heavily armed and their task was to charge the enemy's line and break it. Such warfare required large numbers of men, because success often depended on the weight of the attacking line.

The social and political bases of these two styles of warfare are entirely different. The earlier style depends on a warrior aristocracy, the latter on a broader society, since it involved a greater number of trained soldiers, accustomed to fighting together as an efficient machine instead of displaying their individual prowess. The new soldiers were called hoplites, and when we see them more clearly during the fifth century they are solidly middle-class types. The arms of a Greek soldier were provided not by the state but by himself, so that the hoplites came from the income group that could afford hoplite armor.

Not surprisingly, the change to hoplite tactics, which incorporated a new class into the military arrangements of the state, inspired those in the ranks to demand a share of power in government. Equality in the field led, inevitably, to a demand for equality in the forum, and the aristocracy could no longer defend its monopoly of power on the ground that it, as a class, also bore exclusive responsibility for the state's defense.

In the generation after the introduction of this change, a series of revolutions shook the Greek mainland and installed tyrants[3] in many of the poleis. The accounts we possess of the establishment of the individual tyrannies support the view that the new tyrants both relied on hoplite support and climbed to power after making reputations as commanders in war. Moreover, the revolutions played a part in creating the democratic systems of government that appeared in the next century. As the tyrants took power away from their aristocratic predecessors and set up new institutions to guard against a resurgence of aristocratic power, they transformed the shape of Greek politics for all time to come, for they set themselves to weaken the old tribal loyalties and to redirect those loyalties toward the state.

---

[3] The Greek word *tyrannos* means an autocrat who ruled without a strict legal foundation, not necessarily a bloodthirsty villain. Oedipus, in Sophocles' play *Oedipus Tyrannos,* was the ruler (almost "dictator") of Thebes.

LIFE IN THE POLIS

Greek city-states allowed their inhabitants more social mobility than did any Near Eastern kingdom. They lacked the rigid divisions between citizens that form true social classes. Although some rich landed families had more influence than other citizens, and in that sense formed an aristocracy, there was no hereditary nobility. Moreover, the new wealth brought into prominence many men outside the ranks of the well-born. It was legally possible for any citizen to make a reputation and eventually hold some kind of public office.

The society of the polis did, indeed, have a substratum of slavery. The slaves—mostly prisoners of war—were considered property. Some had to perform harsh, dangerous work, such as toiling in the silver mines of Attica, where they were little more than beasts of burden. But for most slaves life was less arduous. Generally, they worked in the household, in industry, or on farms, or became tutors, bankers, hotel keepers, cooks, and porters. Slaves who worked on buildings of the Athenian Acropolis received the same pay as free citizens. Though they were legally bound to turn their earnings over to their masters, they were probably allowed to keep some money. A slave who saved enough might obtain his master's permission to buy his freedom.

Home life in the polis, even for the wealthy, was far less luxurious than that of an Egyptian noble or a lord within a palace in Crete. All dwellings were modest, and sanitation barely existed. Fish, grain, and bread were staples of the diet; meat was usually reserved for festival days. The Greeks used olive oil extensively—as fat in cooking, as fuel for lamps, and even as a kind of soap. Breakfast, if taken at all, was a lump of bread dipped in olive oil.

With few luxuries available, the Greeks could subsist on small incomes. A skilled worker on public buildings earned a drachma a day in the fifth century, and it has been estimated that 180 drachmas a year could support a married couple. It is clear that a Greek did not have to work unduly hard to make a living and that he had abundant free time. Even the farmer, given the seasonal nature of Greek farming, had several months of leisure a year.

This leisure time the Greek spent mostly in public places. All life—religious, cultural, economic, and social—was centered in the town. The austerity of a Greek's home was balanced by the splendor of his public buildings. Civic life was in fact an immediate extension of the Greek's personal life, and this is what gave the polis its distinctive character.

SPARTA

Sparta, the leader of the Dorian states in the Peloponnesus, achieved greatness by imposing on herself a rigid political system that made every citizen the unflinching servant of the state. At the cost of artistic and literary development, she conquered nearby territory and set the military standard for all other Greeks.

Sparta's militarism was the outgrowth of a problem common to all the Greek poleis: overpopulation. Instead of sending out colonies to relieve this pressure, Sparta, around 720, conquered a neighboring people, the Messenians, and divided their land among the Spartan warriors. The subject peoples outnumbered the Spartans by about seven or eight to one, and every able-bodied Spartan was needed in the army to maintain control over them. As a result Spartan landowners spent their lives in constant military training, while the subjected Messenians worked the land for them.

In the seventh century the Messenians rebelled. The revolt failed, and Sparta reacted by making her army even more invincible and revising her constitution to establish a stricter

system. This constitution, attributed to a legendary lawgiver named Lycurgus, dates from about 600. As finally evolved, the constitution established a government in which oligarchy, or the rule of a small number, was tempered with a measure of democracy. Sparta always retained two kings, a survival from prehistoric times. The ruling circle also included five ephors (overseers), elected annually by the citizens. Any Spartan could become a candidate for this office. The ephors acted as an executive body and also had great influence over Sparta's foreign policy. They initiated legislation, summoned the assembly and council, and wielded both police and judicial powers. The council of elders, the gerousía, consisted of the two kings and twenty-eight other men, who were chosen for life. The assembly, the legislative body, comprised every male over thirty who could demonstrate that he was the child of full-fledged Spartan citizens. The assembly's powers were limited; the council brought before it the proposals for action, and the people voted yes or no. As a further safeguard against too much popular control, the leaders could dismiss the assembly if in their opinion it made the wrong decision. Thus the limited democracy of Sparta yielded to her ultimate faith in oligarchy.

In foreign affairs Sparta had tried to dominate other Peloponnesian states by outright conquest. When this policy failed, she sought strength through alliance rather than warfare. An interstate system arose, probably about 530, which Greeks called "The Spartans and their allies"; modern historians call it the Peloponnesian League. Sparta led but did not control the league, although if she refused to call the states to meet, no action could be taken. The league is one of the earliest examples of alliance in the Greek world and is a rare instance of the Greeks transcending the normal exclusiveness of city-state politics.

The Spartan male dedicated most of his life to military service. Training started in boyhood. The Spartan warriors lived and ate together, and their military discipline approached sadism. As tests of their manhood, young men were required to go without food and shelter and received severe floggings, which sometimes proved fatal. Boys were taught to steal, and the crime lay in being caught. Spartan girls were also given rigorous training so that they would bear healthy children.

Sparta was cut off from the other Greek poleis by two mountain ranges, and this geographic isolation was reinforced by the state. The need for manpower at home made it difficult for Spartans to engage in international trade (we know of only one Spartan colony, the modern city of Taranto in Italy). Trade with others was further discouraged by the adoption of an intrinsically worthless iron currency. Perhaps because of this isolation and the rigors of military life, the Spartan's laconic way of speaking (so named from the plain of Laconia around Sparta) came to denote extreme terseness.

The isolation also cut her people off from new ideas that might have sparked creativity. The Spartans did not cultivate philosophic debate or historical writing. Though they did make fine pottery, at least until 525, the martial spirit of the society did not provide the right atmosphere for the general development of the arts.

Whatever we think of the principles of the Spartan regime, it was successful in preserving itself. The Spartan people, having to dominate a much larger population of potential enemies, chose to embrace rigid militarism. Yet the citizens were sovereign over the question of war or peace, and when they chose war, they were voting to put themselves in the field. To other Greeks, Sparta became a symbol of tenacity and strength. Plato approved of Spartan virility and lack of democratic follies; Aristotle and later philosophers praised Sparta for her mixed constitution, in which the kings represented the element of monarchy, the gerousía that of oligarchy, and the assembly that of democracy.

ATHENS

The city of Athens expanded her domain early in history until she controlled the whole plain of Attica, but she did not reduce the inhabitants of the other villages to a condition of servitude; thus she was free of the terrible problem that the Spartans created for themselves in having to restrain large numbers of angry subjects. Athens was a large polis with widespread trading interests, and her political currents were stronger and more turbulent. These are among the conditions that caused Athens to experiment again and again with her constitution; her political history is the most varied of all the city-states of Greece.

At one time Athens had a king as other poleis did. He was advised by a council of senior men, known as the Areopagus. When the monarchy ended about 683, the king was replaced by three (later nine) archons, or administrators. At first the archons probably had to come from established families—the people whom we may loosely call the aristocracy. They were elected annually by the assembly of adult male citizens. After completing their year's term of office, the archons became permanent members of the Areopagus. Thus each year the Areopagus acquired nine new members with experience in high office, and eventually it numbered about three hundred men. Since it was composed of senior men with permanent membership, the Areopagus was probably more influential than the board of archons in determining public policy.

Our first information about a major reform in Athens is dated about 621 when Draco, an otherwise unknown statesman, published or codified the law on homicide. That the law on homicide was now published for all to know was an important step forward for Athens. Draco's laws were later considered severe (such is the meaning of "Draconian"); but they did establish a better judicial procedure than simply relying on the opinion of tribal elders. Among his other legal reforms Draco apparently made a distinction between voluntary and involuntary homicide, which in itself was significant. Early societies often looked on any kind of homicide as defiling the community in the eyes of the gods.

About 600, when Sparta was revising its state in the reform associated with Lycurgus, Athens was also dealing with a political crisis. The differing methods used by these states to solve their problems present an interesting contrast within the world of the poleis. Athens faced a serious agricultural crisis as her increasing population found it ever more difficult to feed itself from the available land. During lean years some farmers began to obtain additional food by pledging away a portion of the next year's crop. As they assigned more and more of their crops, they finally began to use the land itself as collateral. Some dispossessed peasants became tenant farmers, working the land for a portion of the crop (probably one-sixth). If they defaulted on this rent, their creditors had the right to enslave them.

The resentment of the bankrupt peasants might have exploded into violent revolution had not the Athenians managed to solve the problem peacefully. They gave powers of arbitration to Solon, one of the archons, in 594.[4] Aware that there was little hope that the poor farmers could ever repay their debts, Solon adopted a course of radical simplicity: he canceled all agricultural debts. At one stroke the enslaved men were free. As for the land, it probably remained in the hands of its new owners. The important thing was that Solon had prevented civil war, at least for the time being.

Solon also undertook constitutional reforms. He divided all Athenian citizens into four classes based on their income from the land rather than on family background. Members of the three higher classes could hold public office. Those in the lowest class, common laborers, could hold no office, but as members of the assembly they could vote in elections. This system for choosing officials indicates the importance of owning land in early Athens, for it apparently excluded all who did not own productive land, even traders and artisans. The significance of the new system was that it ended privileges based on birth. If men from newer families could work their way up economically, no one could deny them a post of leadership merely because of family background.

Solon also seems to have created a court of appeal, called the Heliaea, somehow drawn from the people at large, but our sources tell us little of how it worked. Over the years other reforms became associated with him. Aristotle says, for example, that he created a second council of 400 citizens alongside the older Areopagus, but many modern historians reject this council as inauthentic. The best information about his work comes from surviving quotations from his poetry, and these show that he considered himself a moderate: "I gave the people just enough privilege, neither taking away nor adding anything." His chief contribution was recognizing the needs of the

---

[4] That Solon was archon in 594 is fairly certain, and most scholars follow ancient tradition in dating his reforms to the same year. We accept this date for the sake of convenience. In all probability the assumed synchronism between his archonship and his reforms was an inference drawn in antiquity, and there is some reason to think that the reforms actually took place in the 570s: see C. Hignett, *A History of the Athenian Constitution* (1952), p. 316.

The single most inspired architectural achievement of the Classical Age is the Athenian Acropolis, which dominated the surrounding city and could be seen from the marketplace below. Construc- tion began in the sixth century, but the largest and most magnificent of its temples, the marble Par- thenon dedicated to Athena, was built during the Age of Pericles. (Photo: Alison Frantz)

whole state; for the first time someone considered the common people as a group with justified grievances and took bold steps to solve them. We hear of no such arbitration in any ancient Near Eastern kingdom.

Solon's humane legislation did not end the agricultural crisis. Freeing the peasants from servitude was not the same as guaranteeing them enough to eat; hungry tenant farmers had become hungry free citizens, and the discontent remained. Pisistratus, an Athenian military leader supported by the poorer farmers from the hill country, saw his opportunity in this turmoil. In 561 he appeared in the city, displaying wounds that he had allegedly received from his enemies. His supporters demanded that the assembly give him a bodyguard. With the help of these club-bearers, as they were called, he seized the Acropolis and began to rule as a tyrant. Though he was driven from the city twice, he returned in 546 to seize authority decisively, and he ruled Athens from that year until his death in 528.

Pisistratus fits well the pattern of the Greek tyrant sketched earlier. Solon's failure to institute a distribution of land meant that Attica still suffered from her agricultural difficulties. Since Pisistratus had drawn some of his support from disgruntled farmers and workers, he now rewarded them with land grants from the confiscated estates of the wealthy landowning aristocrats who had opposed him. Responding to the changed conditions of the times, he sought to ameliorate the plight of the poor by further encouraging trade and industry. Under his aegis Athens became an important commercial center.

In order to turn men's loyalties away from their clan leaders and toward the new, larger unit he was attempting to create, Pisistratus initiated a splendid program of public works. He built a temple to Athena, the patron goddess of Athens, and in another part of the city he began a temple to Zeus, largest of all Greek temples, not completed until about A.D. 120, when Athens was under the Roman Empire. He also established a yearly festival in Athens honoring the god Dionysus, and by encouraging dramatic contests at these festivals he opened the way for the development of Athenian tragedy in the next century.

The tyranny of Pisistratus, like many tyrannies that have come after his, conferred many material benefits. Moreover, Pisistratus ruled by masking despotic realities in constitutional forms. For example, the archons were still elected by the assembly, though the candidates were almost certainly selected by the tyrant himself and would have had far less freedom of initiative than in a free society. The façade did at least mean that Athenians grew accustomed to having some role in the choice of their magistrates, and this maintenance of democratic form made them receptive to real democracy when it finally came into existence at the end of the sixth century.

For some years after Pisistratus' death in 528, his son Hippias ruled securely; but a conspiracy eventually frightened him into using terror as a means to keep peace. Some Athenians were forced into exile, among them Cleisthenes, the leader of a noted family. While in exile, Cleisthenes and his supporters managed to enlist the help of the Spartans in a plan to drive the new tyrant from Athens. In 510 a Spartan army invaded Athens and exiled Hippias. Cleisthenes returned to his native city, determined to make himself the dominant Athenian politician.

Having observed how Pisistratus overcame all rivals by making the poor his supporters, Cleisthenes decided to use the same strategy. In 508 he proposed a scheme whereby the masses would participate more directly in running the state. Although Cleisthenes himself probably did not use the term, the Greeks eventually called this system *demokratia*, the rule of the demos or the entire body of citizens.

Cleisthenes' aim in founding democracy was probably to secure his own supremacy and that of his associates rather than to further any special political theory. The basic reform was the creation of a Council of 500 (members). This council planned business for the public assembly and gradually surpassed the old Areopagus in political power. But Cleisthenes' *demokratia* did have its limits. Members of the lowest property-class, the *thetes*, were ineligible to serve on the council; and they probably numbered about half the adult male citizens. All other male citizens above thirty could serve for one year, and the council was chosen afresh every year. In later times—or perhaps from the beginning—the members were chosen by drawing lots; this eliminated the influence of any special groups who might try to dominate the council. No man could serve more than twice: in this way political experience was shared by a great many citizens of the middle class and above, even if this led to government by amateurs rather than professionals.

The enforced rotation of service in the council was Cleisthenes' master stroke. There was a fair chance that every eligible Athenian would be chosen to serve on it once during his lifetime. With such a personal stake in democracy citizens would not conspire with those who wanted to abolish the system. The success of Cleisthenes' plan is evident from the remarkable tenacity of Athenian democracy, which endured for several centuries in its Cleisthenic form.

The Council of 500 had wide powers. It prepared business for the assembly, administered domestic and foreign policies, and controlled finance. The assembly included all adult males. They could debate motions and suggest amendments, but they could not initiate legislation; that was the duty of the council.

Cleisthenes also directed a radical revision of the Athenian social structure. He was evidently trying to break up the possible influence of regional groups. For political purposes he divided all Athenians into ten tribes. The determining factor was the particular village, or deme, that a man lived in at the time of the reform. These villages, well over one hundred in number, were grouped into thirty sets, called trittyes (the word means "thirds"). Three trittyes were grouped together to form a tribe, the thirty trittyes thus forming ten tribes in all. A tribe included men dwelling in trittyes that were geographically separated from each other; thus no tribe came from a single region of Attica. This complex scheme assured that no local interests would dominate the opinions of a tribe. The Council of 500 included fifty men from each tribe, chosen from candidates selected by the individual demes.

Cleisthenes left the magistracies untouched. There were still nine archons, as before, and after their year in office they became permanent members of the Areopagus. The qualifications for office remained as they had been under Solon: only the upper two property-classes could be archons. We are not well informed about the judicial system at this time, but it seems that the archons conducted their own trials. Two ancient features of judicial procedure continued. The Areopagus judged cases of homicide; and at times the people, or a section somehow formed into the Heliaea, acted as a court of appeal (this, as we saw, may have been a reform of Solon). It must be stressed that all adult male citizens, whether landowners or not, could vote in the assembly; and it was the assembly of citizens that passed legislation, elected magistrates, and voted for or against war.

After the passing of his reforms, Cleisthenes is heard of no more in our sources; but the Athenians continued to develop his system, es-

The interesting procedure of ostracism was instituted in Athens about the time of Cleisthenes. Once a year the Athenians voted for the man they considered most dangerous to the state by inscribing his name on ostraka, *or scraps of pottery, such as those shown here. The one on the right bears the name of Themistocles. Six thousand votes in all had to be cast, and the "winner" went at once into exile for ten years. Themistocles was ostracized after the Persian Wars, when his influence had waned.* (Photo: American School of Classical Studies at Athens)

pecially through the use of drawing lots for office. In 487, for example, they began choosing their nine archons, from a preselected group of candidates, by this method. Later, in the fifth and fourth centuries, many other officials were so chosen, such as public auditors and managers of public land and mines. The officers chosen by lot, even the archons, surely lost some of their former prestige; but the political theory underlying allotment was that there were many men equally honest and capable of holding office in a democracy. Again, allotment eliminated much of the quarrelsome rivalry over office. Also in 487 we hear for

the first time of a man expelled from Athens for ten years by the colorful process of ostracism (Aristotle assigns this reform to Cleisthenes himself, but this remains controversial). In 457, by another extension of democracy, the third highest property-class was made eligible for the archonships.

Thus more and more citizens shared in running the state. By stages that we cannot trace precisely, the judicial system also came into the hands of the people. Trials were held (though never for homicide)[5] before juries numbering 200, 500, or more citizens—chosen by lot; and here even the lower class could serve. Aristotle observed that "when the people gain control of the juries they are masters of the state." It is clear that the great majority of Athenians supported this constitution. This is shown by the abysmal failure of revolutions led by oligarchs. Intellectuals, such as Plato, deplored the power of the untaught masses, but the attachment of the people to their *demokratia* prevailed over all.

Cleisthenes' constitution endured with slight modifications well into the third century A.D.,

---

[5] The Areopagus retained jurisdiction over homicide.

long after Athens had lost political independence. Thus the system lasted for more than 700 years; it was easily the most stable one in the ancient world, and no other democratic constitution has ever had such a long life.

III. THE ORIGINS OF THE GREEK ENLIGHTENMENT

There has come down to us, even through the Dark Ages, a large sample of the old Mycenaean mythology. It survives in Homer's two great epic poems, the *Iliad* and the *Odyssey*, and in the fragments of myth presented in later Greek literature. The total does not tell us a great deal about the gods of the Greeks. We often know their lineages and a fair amount about sexual alliances, especially with mortals, since later on, Greek nobles traced their own lineage back to these gods, but there is less information about their specialties and their formal relations with each other. Rather Greek mythology is full of exciting adventure stories and violent tales of murder, incest, rape, patricide, matricide, and fratricide. In what sense, then, can we properly speak of Greek mythology forming the basis for a true religion?

RELIGION AND MYTHOLOGY

Historically, there are two distinct sorts of mythology. One, transmitted by priests, is usually quite decorous, dedicated above all to explaining why the world is the way it is. This mythology has been carefully worked over, and kept up to date, by full-time, professional priests. The other kind, popular mythology, consists of adventure stories about gods, demigods, and heroes. In some societies, such as Egypt and Polynesia, both varieties of mythology coexist. The Greeks, however, lacking professional priests, had little priestly mythology, with the result that there were relatively few mythological explanations of natural phenomena, while those that did exist were quite primitive. For example, there is next to nothing in Greek mythology about the origin of man, about the reason for and the origin of death, about why the gods no longer live near man; there is nothing that explains the fall of man and the reason for evil. Even in the famous tale of Pandora's box, the Greek word *kakia*, usually translated "evil," really means disease, as is perfectly clear from the context. In any case, the tale certainly does not mean to deal with man's capacity for evil. Man receives Pandora's box as a consequence of Prometheus' stealing fire; so we have here only a limited attempt to explain minor aspects of the human condition. Any respectable priestly mythology does far more.

We have seen that, toward the year 700, the Greeks were emerging from their Dark Age. Colonization and contact with other civilizations in the Mediterranean made them more sophisticated. They had reached the point where philosophy comes into existence—that is, when people are no longer satisfied with supernatural explanations for the nature of things. It is hard to say just why the Greeks gradually became skeptical about the truth of their myths. But the beginning of philosophical inquiry among the Greeks was a turning point in man's view of the world and of himself: it implied that there was a logical order in the world and that man had the ability to discover it.

At the same time the Greeks were in a unique historical situation. For reasons that we also do not know, they had never developed a priestly hierarchy that might have made new myths for them. There were indeed priests in Greece, but they mainly presided over shrines to local gods and were not built into the ruling system; the Athenians built the

Parthenon for Athena as a civic project, not because some priests ordered them to do it. The task of interpreting the world was left to secular intellectuals, natural philosophers, and poets. How they accomplished it requires explanation.

THE MILESIAN SCHOOL[6]

It is appropriate that the first natural philosophers should have been citizens of Miletus, an Ionian Greek city on the west coast of Asia Minor. They lived during the sixth century when their city had already existed for some hundreds of years. During their lifetime Miletus was a city of tremendous fertility; ancient tradition claims that she was responsible for founding no less than ninety colonies, half of which have been confirmed by the archaeological evidence. She was extraordinarily wealthy, functioning as a trading center for materials and manufactured goods brought to the coast from inner Anatolia. These she exported, along with a variety of her own manufactured goods, to the Black Sea in the north, to Mesopotamia in the east, to Egypt in the south, and to the Greek colonies of southern Italy in the west. When the moment came to abandon mythological and theological modes of thought, the change was facilitated, as we have seen, by the fact that neither here nor in any other Greek state was freedom of thought inhibited by the demands of a religious, theocratic form of society such as existed in the neighboring oriental countries.

Miletus' geographical position also helps explain why philosophy was born here. The city stood on the eastern frontier of the Greek-speaking peoples and had direct contact with

the ideas and achievements of the Near East. Indeed, most of these Ionian Greeks were ruled by Lydia from about 610 to 560, a span covering almost the entire lifetime of Thales. They must, therefore, have had the opportunity of getting to know at first hand the achievements of their neighbors to the east and south.

In Egypt and Babylonia, for all the high level of their civilization, the demands of religion prevented free expression and weighed heavily on every branch of life; religion was used in the interests of a monarch who embodied divinity, and of a priesthood that surrounded the king and ensured that its own authority was not diminished by any intrusion of independent thought. Yet these great empires contributed indispensable technical knowledge to the Greeks. Thales of Miletus is said to have predicted an eclipse. If he did so, he must have known Babylonian astronomy, and the Greeks' debt to Babylonian and Egyptian mathematics is one that they themselves freely acknowledged. Herodotus believed that geometry was invented in Egypt and brought from there to Greece, and that it was from the Babylonians that the Greeks learned to divide the day into twelve parts as well as to use instruments for marking the times of the day and the chief turning points of the year, such as the solstice and equinox.

All this knowledge, and much else, the Greeks acquired from contacts with their Near Eastern neighbors. It was not, therefore, science that the Greeks invented, but philosophy, for they lifted scientific inquiries onto a different plane. The Greeks—for reasons that still elude us—were the first people to evince any interest in knowledge for its own sake rather than because it served some practical purpose. The implications of this new attitude were truly revolutionary. The Egyptians were interested in geometry because they required it to survey the land and make their complicated system of

---

[6] In my treatment of this subject I have partly followed the excellent discussion of W. K. C. Guthrie in his *History of Greek Philosophy* (1962, 1965).

taxation function properly. In Egypt, geometry and mathematics were therefore handmaidens of land measurement and, eventually, of pyramid building. In Babylonia, religious considerations strongly affected the conduct of practical life. Since their religion was a stellar one, Babylonian astronomy was a practical study which explained to educated men the behavior of the stellar gods. The observations derived from it were impressively accurate but always served the established religion. Only the Greeks asked the question "why," and this interest in causes led, almost immediately, to a demand for generalization.

An ancient Egyptian might observe that fire hardens his bricks, warms his house, turns sand to glass, tempers steel, and boils his water. He is happy to observe and enjoy the results. The ancient Greek, on the other hand, asks why the same thing, fire, does all those different things. Such a question means that the Greek will seek out the nature of fire, in general, and attempt to discover its properties. This is the essence of the new step taken by the Greeks: their demand for generalization lifts, say, triangles and rectangles from the concrete plane to the abstract as they inquire now about the nature of triangularity and rectangularity. This concern with form and essence was eventually to impress itself on every aspect of intellectual activity, so that even Greek art would be concerned, not only with the nature of individual men, but with the ideal of humanity.

THE RATIONALIZATION OF MYTH

Greek philosophy, for all its originality, was born into a certain intellectual climate. Both early Greek and Near Eastern theories about the world included the idea of unity. In the beginning, for both thought-worlds, the universe was a great formless mass. The initial act of making the world was achieved by a process of separation and division, as in the familiar biblical myth that tells how "God divided the light from the darkness, and divided the waters which were under the firmament from the waters which were above the firmament," and so on. For an example of a similar Greek myth of underlying unity in the world we may turn to the poet Hesiod, who, in his *Theogony*, tells the primitive story of how Uranus and Gaia (Heaven and Earth), conceived as anthropomorphic figures, lay locked in an embrace until Kronos (Time) forced them apart.

Both Near Eastern and Greek mythology seem to imagine water as the first principle of all things. The Old Testament portrays the earth itself rising out of the primordial waters, and the Babylonian cosmology of the Enuma Elish, dating from about 1500, presents a similar picture of the primacy of water. As for the Greeks, in Homer's *Iliad* (Book 16, lines 241 and 246) Oceanus is the parent of the gods, though for Hesiod he is the son of Uranus and Gaia.

In their attempt to understand the nature of the universe, Greek philosophers of Miletus asked such questions as: Can the apparently disordered world be reduced to simple principles? What is the world made of? How does change occur? Why do things spring up, grow, decline, and die? Thales is the first thinker whose answer to these questions is preserved for us. He sought to discover a substance that persisted through change, an element that survived all transformations. Thales found this element, as his predecessors in the Near East had done, in water. For Thales, everything was but water in one or another form.

Greek thinkers loved not only thought but argument as well, and any philosophical statement was likely to provoke a reply. Another Milesian, Anaximander (611?–547?), held that the origin of all things was an infinite body of matter, which he called the "boundless." A whirling motion within the boundless divided its substance into the hot, which rose to form the heavens, and the cold, which sank and took form as the earth and the air surrounding it. A further division into wet and dry created the oceans and the land. This theory pointed toward a later classification of matter into the four elements: earth, air, fire, and water.

One of the most influential theories of the nature of the world was proposed by Pythagoras of Samos. He approached the question through the study of numbers and was thus the first to abandon water and all other kinds of matter and to deal with reality in abstract terms. He discovered the harmonic intervals within the musical scale and formulated the Pythagorean theorem about the sum of the sides of a right triangle, which is familiar to all students of geometry. He went on to conclude that the basic principle of the universe was number: within all things there is a harmonious or numerically balanced arrangement of parts. Pythagoras, in a sense, anticipated the mathematical relationships that modern physicists have established. He was also the first to call the universe the Cosmos (in Greek, "order").

The basic social organization of Greece was the independent city-state. These states existed in the hundreds and were not united by any central leadership or control. The civilization within these states surpassed anything in the Near Eastern kingdoms in diversity and richness of thought. Here political forms changed more rapidly than they did in Egypt or Mesopotamia. Aristocratic families gave way to tyrants as the dominant political element. The tyrants in turn awakened and represented the wish of the people themselves to manage their own affairs. Democracy, in varying degrees, became a common form of government. This was an extraordinary, and probably unpredictable, departure from the monarchies of the Near East and of Mycenaean Greece.

The establishment of self-government in Greek states reflects the willingness of Greek citizens to trust themselves in politics. Kings no longer held power through inheritance, and the people gave orders to themselves through elected officers. The Greeks believed that their own intelligence was capable of governing. This daring innovation, democracy, arose at about the same time as philosophic speculation. The universe was explained through conjectures derived from reason rather than through traditional, received myths. These political and intellectual discoveries had barely been made when the Greek states had to face their supreme challenge—an attack from the Persian Empire, the state that had unified the political heritage of the Near East.

RECOMMENDED READING

Sources

*Herodotus. *The Persian Wars*. Aubrey de Sélin-court (tr.). 1954.

*Homer. *The Iliad*. Richmond Lattimore (tr.). 1951. The best of many translations.

*———. *The Odyssey*. Richmond Lattimore (tr.). 1968.

Studies

*Andrewes, A. *The Greek Tyrants*. 1966.

*———. *The Greeks*. 1973.

*Burn, A. R. *The Lyric Age of Greece*. 1960.

Bury, J. B., and Russell Meiggs. *A History of Greece*. 4th ed. 1975. The best one-volume history of Greece.

*Chadwick, John. *The Decipherment of Linear B*. 1970. The best brief study of the Cretan scripts.

*Finley, M. I. *Early Greece: The Bronze and Archaic Ages*. 1970.

Guthrie, W. K. C. *A History of Greek Philosophy*. Vols. I–IV, 1975. Brilliant, sensitive, and elegant.

Hignett, C. *A History of the Athenian Constitution*. 1952. An important revisionist study, critical of ancient sources.

Hopper, R. J. *The Early Greeks*. 1976. Highly readable survey of ancient Greece from its origins to the beginning of the Classical period. Has a full, up-to-date bibliography.

*Hutchinson, R. W. *Prehistoric Crete*. 1962.

Lesky, Albin. *A History of Greek Literature*. 1966. Superb history with trenchant discussions.

Mylonas, George. *Mycenae and the Mycenaean Age*. 1966. Now the fullest report on Mycenaean archaeology.

*Nilsson, Martin P. *The Mycenaean Origin of Greek Mythology*. 1972.

*Page, Denys L. *History and the Homeric Iliad*. 1959.

*Pendlebury, J. D. S. *The Archaeology of Crete*. 1965. Still unreplaced as a survey.

*Vermeule, Emily. *Greece in the Bronze Age*. 1972. An exact and comprehensive treatment; the best work available.

---

*Available in paperback.

THREE

CLASSICAL AND
HELLENISTIC GREECE

At the beginning of the fifth century the mighty Persian Empire under Darius and Xerxes twice tried to conquer the small city-states of mainland Greece. Against all likelihood, in a series of military encounters that culminated in the famous battles at Plataea and Mycale in 479, a heavily outnumbered Greek hoplite army smashed the Persian invaders and drove them from Europe. The poleis of Greece, especially Sparta and Athens, had performed the miracle of routing the Persians. As the Persians withdrew from the Aegean, the crucial question became, Who should lead the Greeks? For the rest of the fifth century the inability of the Greeks to unite inspired a struggle for leadership that in 431 led to war. Almost all the poleis were drawn in eventually, forced to take sides as Sparta and Athens fought for hegemony. The war raged till 404, leaving the participants weak and demoralized. Thus it prepared the way for the conquest of Greece in the next century by the Macedonian king Philip II and his son Alexander the Great. These two monarchs then went on to conquer Egypt, Persia, and Asia Minor.

In the fifth and fourth centuries, the intellectual and artistic achievements of the Greeks reached their apex. Despite tumultuous political conditions—perhaps in some measure because of them—a sudden burst of creative energy occurred, concentrated in time and space to a degree that was then unprecedented and, some would argue, has never been duplicated. In these years lived the tragedians Aeschylus, Sophocles, and Euripides, and the comic poet Aristophanes; the philosophers Parmenides, Protagoras, Socrates, Plato, and Aristotle; the historians Herodotus and Thucydides; the sculptors Phidias, Polyclitus, and Praxiteles.

After the Macedonians had destroyed the autonomy of the polis, Greek culture took a decisive turning. During the last decades of the fourth century the Greeks, having lost the world of the independent polis, found the new, wider world of Alexander's empire. There followed a fascinating series of intellectual developments, including Stoicism and Epicureanism, that were to affect dramatically the future intellectual experience of the West.

I. THE CHALLENGE OF PERSIA

The Greeks had enjoyed many contacts with the Near East, but shortly after 500 they had to face the most enormous of ancient empires in the field. An observer from Crete or Egypt, asked to predict the result of a war between the wealthy Persian dominion and the disunited city-states of Greece, would have considered a Greek victory impossible. Yet the amazing victory was won—and in all Greek history there is no more significant event. If Persia had converted Greece into another satrapy of her empire, no one can say how different Western culture might have been.

INVASIONS OF GREECE

Among the territories controlled by King Darius of Persia were the Greek cities on the western coast of Asia Minor. These Greeks rebelled against Persian control in 499—a prelude to the Persian Wars. This event is called the Ionian Revolt, after Ionia, the central portion of the shoreline. Athens supported the revolt, and for a time it was successful, until it finally collapsed in 493.

Darius had no wish to leave the matter there. He now proposed to invade Greece herself, and one of the prime victims was to be Athens, the city that had dared to help the rebels. Darius probably also planned to conquer much or all of Greece; had he succeeded, he would have been the first ruler in history whose empire joined Asia and Europe. In pursuit of this aim, Darius sent a fleet across the Aegean Sea in 490 and confidently awaited news of the fall of Athens.

The Persians landed at Marathon, a village near Athens (see Map 3.1), where they were opposed by the Athenians under the command of Miltiades, a member of a prominent Athenian family. The Greek force was perhaps 10,000 men and the Persian, 20,000. The Greeks trapped most of the Persians in the center of their wing formation. Those who escaped ran down to their ships and sailed against Athens. The Athenians marched back to the city in time to prevent its betrayal by a pro-Persian group, and the Persians had no choice but to return to Asia. Herodotus reports that the Athenians lost only 192 men and the Persians, 6,400.

Stung by this defeat, Darius began at once to prepare a second invasion but he did not live to attempt it. The next king, Xerxes (486–465), took up the task. He devoted four full years to preparing a huge force that would attack by land and sea. This time there would be no mistake.

Fortunately for Greece, there came to power in 480 the shrewdest creative strategist in her history, Themistocles. A few years earlier he had persuaded the Athenians to build a navy of a hundred triremes, the classical Greek warship, and since then more had been added. In this navy Themistocles saw the chance for Athenian survival. About the same time other Greek poleis began to fear annihilation from a Persian invasion—nothing less than the threat of foreign conquest could force the independent city-states to stand together. Early in 480 some thirty states formed an alliance; Sparta, Athens, and Corinth were its most powerful members. Sparta's tradition of discipline in war and her clear military superiority caused the other allies to entrust to her the command on both land and sea.

A few months later Xerxes began his march toward Greece. Historians estimate the strength of his force at about 60,000 men and 600 ships.[1] Whatever its exact size, this was the most grandiose invasion of Europe by sea until the Allied invasions of Sicily and Italy in 1943. The Persian infantry crossed into Europe on a pontoon bridge built across the Hellespont and soon arrived in Greece proper.

The Greeks decided to make a stand at Thermopylae, a narrow defile that a few men could hold against a much larger force. About 5,000 men from various states, including 300 Spartans under King Leonidas, blocked the pass against a horde of Persians. When one Spartan was warned that the massive barrage of Persian arrows would conceal the sun in the sky, he replied with laconic wit, "Excellent news: if the Persians darken the sun, we shall be able to fight in the shade." A traitorous Greek led a Persian force through the hills to the rear of the Greeks, who were thus made to fight on two fronts. This transformed the battle into a Persian victory. The Greeks were killed nearly to the last man, and King Leonidas of Sparta fell along with his countrymen.

---

[1] Herodotus, our source for the Persian Wars, was given fantastic reports and reckoned the total Persian force at more than 5 million men. The figure here is only an estimate.

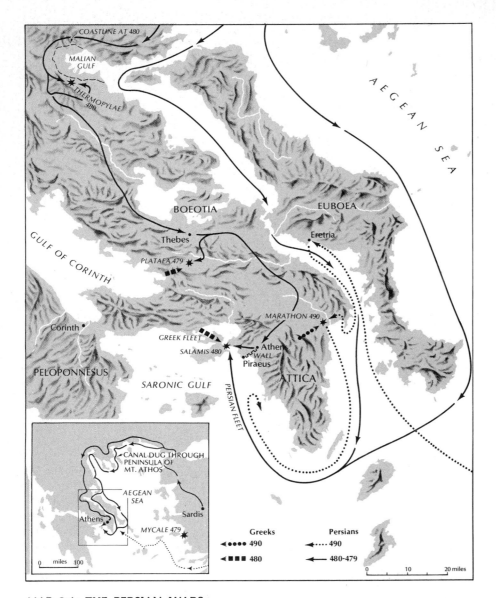

MAP 3.1: THE PERSIAN WARS

Map labels:
COASTLINE AT 480
MALIAN GULF
THERMOPYLAE 480
AEGEAN SEA
BOEOTIA
EUBOEA
GULF OF CORINTH
Thebes
Eretria
PLATAEA 479
Corinth
MARATHON 490
GREEK FLEET
SALAMIS 480
Athens
WALL
Piraeus
PELOPONNESUS
ATTICA
SARONIC GULF
PERSIAN FLEET

Inset map labels:
CANAL DUG THROUGH PENINSULA OF MT. ATHOS
AEGEAN SEA
Athens
Sardis
MYCALE 479
miles 100

Legend:
Greeks
● ● ● ● 490
■ ■ ■ 480
Persians
← · · · · 490
← 480-479

0   10   20 miles

GREEK VICTORY

Southern Greece now lay open to the slowly advancing Persian armada. The Persian army had won the costly victory at Thermopylae, and the navy, though seriously damaged by a storm, had come south and waited off the coast of Attica. The people abandoned Athens ahead of the Persian army, which marched across Attica and burned the city. In the nearly desperate situation, Themistocles devised an ingenious stratagem. He sent a slave to the Persian king with a false message: Themistocles wished him well and advised him to strike at once in order to prevent the demoralized Greeks from escaping; if he attacked quickly, he might win the decisive battle practically without a blow. Themistocles then persuaded the council of Greek commanders to follow his strategy.

The Persians were taken in by the ruse and sent their navy into the narrows between Athens and the island of Salamis. This put the Persian ships at a disadvantage. The Greek fleet, some 380 ships, rammed the Persians, thus shearing off and fouling their oars. At this point heavily armed Greek soldiers boarded the enemy's ships and fought as if on land. The Persian navy broke and retreated. On all sides the Greek victory was decisive. Wrecks and remnants of the Persian ships drifted along the coast of Attica. Xerxes sailed back toward the Dardanelles with his shattered navy. A Persian king had gazed upon Europe for the last time.

Salamis is one of the most important battles in history. Yet the Persian Wars were not over, for a Persian army remained in Greece. The reckoning with this force came in 479, at the village of Plataea. The Spartan regent, Pausanias, directed the battle. Once more the Greek army utterly defeated the Persians; out of perhaps 50,000 Persians, only a few thousand survived the day.

From this point on the tide of Greek victory and liberation could not be stopped. The Greeks won a further battle at Mycale on the shore of Asia Minor in 479. The Ionian Greeks proclaimed their freedom and thus completed the work of throwing off Persian control that they had begun twenty years earlier. The final reckoning with Persia did not come until Alexander the Great finally dissolved the empire. For the present, the Greek poleis had thrust back their most formidable enemy.

II. THE SUPREMACY OF ATHENS

After the Persian Wars Athens was dominant in the Greek world for the next half-century. She headed a confederation of Greek states that gradually became an Athenian empire. With political leadership came commercial dominance; her trading activities spread throughout the Aegean and eastern Mediterranean. At home her democratic institutions were further strengthened as the citizens gained a full voice in all governmental affairs.

THE ATHENIAN EMPIRE

The Greek victories over the Persians in 480 and 479 secured mainland Greece from further attacks, but the presence of Persian troops in Asia Minor continued to pose a threat. Sparta, reverting to her traditional policy of isolation, withdrew from further campaigning. Other members of the Greek alliance continued to make war against Persian holdings in Asia Minor and soon decided to form a permanent union for this purpose. Meeting on the island of Delos in the winter of 478–477, they formed a new alliance, the Delian League, under Athenian leadership. Each city-state was to have one vote in determining policy, and all agreed to make regular contributions of either money or manned ships for campaigns against Persia. Athens was assigned the command of the fleet.

The campaigns were successful. The Greeks liberated the cities in Asia Minor still held by the Persians and drove the Persian navy from the Aegean. Warfare between Greeks and Persians ended by about 450. During the intervening years Athens had initially acted with restraint in exercising her leadership over the

A detail from the Parthenon frieze (completed in 432 B.C.) showing horsemen in the festal procession organized every four years to honor Athena, titulary goddess of the city-state of Athens. (Photo: Alinari-Scala)

other members of the league. Gradually, however, she began to extend her political influence, forcing some cities into the league against their will and refusing to allow others to withdraw.

On occasion she intervened in the local politics of the member states, usually supporting the democratic faction. Athenian dominance was tacitly acknowledged in 454 when the league's treasury was transferred from Delos to Athens. Henceforth, cash contributions to the league were actually tribute payments to Athens: the alliance of equals had become an Athenian empire.

THE AGE OF PERICLES

Athens entered her greatest period under the leadership of Pericles (490?–429), a brilliant statesman from an aristocratic family. From 450 to the time of his death Pericles dominated the competitive world of Athenian politics. He held the post of general year after year, but this alone does not account for his political supremacy. The historian Thucydides reports that Pericles was respected for his financial honesty; moreover, through his personality and oratory he "controlled the masses rather than letting them control him."

Pericles was determined to make Athens preeminent in Greece. To ensure her military strength he extended the system of alliances. He used her expanded fleet to make Athens the supreme commercial power in the Aegean. He undertook a great building program to beautify the city; the Parthenon is his legacy.

Athens grew prosperous. Her trade network extended into the Black Sea and throughout the eastern Mediterranean. Tribute continued to flow in from her allies in the Delian League and newly discovered silver deposits in Attica added to her income. Even the poorest citizens shared in the increased prosperity since many were hired for Pericles' building program. The fleet also provided jobs, both in building and in manning the ships.

The basis of Athenian military power became, more and more, the navy. This fact gave more importance to poorer citizens, who

The most significant stylistic change in Greek sculpture of the fifth century is illustrated in this bronze statue of Zeus. The figure has a special dynamism; strength, resolve, and action are implicit in its form, a striking contrast to the earlier kouros. (Photo: Hirmer Fotoarchiv München)

rowed in the fleet—just as, long before, the spread of iron weapons had made the armed warrior more of a political force. The constitution of Cleisthenes was still in force. The assembly of all male citizens voted only on business brought before it by the council of 500, in which poorer citizens did not serve. As we have seen, the judicial system in the fifth century operated largely through juries numbering 200, 500, or even more citizens. There was no detailed body of civil or criminal law: juries had wide powers of interpretation, and there was normally no appeal from their decisions. Pericles instituted pay for jury duty in order to provide enough jurors to man the

This vase painting depicts a warrior's departure and is a fine example of the Red Figure style, which reversed the earlier Black Figure work; here the background is painted black and the figures are left in the natural orange. (Photo: Hirmer Fotoarchiv München)

expanding system of courts. This judicial system was viewed by critics as too democratic, but it expressed the opinion of most Athenians —that the intelligence and dedication of the average citizen were reliable political controls.

III. THE PELOPONNESIAN WAR

The Age of Pericles closed with a ruinous war between Athens and Sparta and their respective allies that spelled disaster for the poleis. When it finally came to an end after almost thirty years, Athens was defeated.

THE WAR YEARS

Sparta and other independent city-states had long viewed the growth of the Athenian Empire with suspicion (see Map 3.2). When Athens began to intervene in matters involving the states allied with Sparta in the Peloponnesian League, these allies became convinced that war was the only solution. Corinth, which felt her position jeopardized by the Athenian actions, finally persuaded the reluctant Spartans to lead the Peloponnesian League into war.

The war opposed two kinds of political states. Sparta controlled no empire and relied on internal resources to maintain herself. Athens, the center of an empire, relied on her imperial system to provide grain for her people and tribute to pay for her navy. Sparta had the strongest army in Greece and Athens the strongest navy.

Fighting began in 431 but was inconclusive for several years. Sparta sought to break Athenian morale by invading Attica annually; her troops inflicted some damage and then departed in time for the Peloponnesian harvest. But the Athenians merely withdrew behind fortifications until the Spartans retreated. Pericles, still the leader of Athens, refused to allow the Athenian infantry to challenge Sparta on the field; instead, he launched sea-borne raids against various points in the Peloponnesus. These raids left Sparta untouched and her infantry undefeated. Far more damaging than any offensive policy of Sparta was a serious plague that afflicted Athens in 430 and intermittently thereafter. The plague took many lives within the crowded and unsanitary city. Pericles was one of the victims.

In 425 both Athens and Sparta achieved certain successes, but the losses that both sides suffered in the next few years made all parties ready to end, or at least suspend, the war. A peace treaty was signed in 421 (the Peace of Nicias, named for the Athenian general who led the negotiations). At this point the poleis could have turned their backs on war, for both Athens and Sparta had shown their courage and neither one had gained any dominant position.

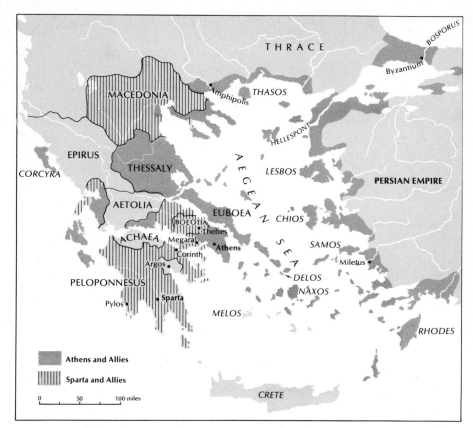

MAP 3.2: GREECE 431 B.C.

After 421 a few years of suspicious peace did in fact follow, but the issues that had caused the war had not been settled.

In 415 an occasion for renewed war arose. The people of Segesta, a polis in Sicily, appealed to Athens for help against another city on that island. The issue of war in Sicily was the subject of a crucial debate in Athens. The eloquence of Alcibiades, a talented young political leader of enormous ambition and—as it later turned out—few scruples, persuaded the Athenian assembly to raise a large fleet and sail to Sicily.

The original plan of aiding Segesta had to be deferred when Syracuse, the largest Sicilian city, entered the war against the Athenians. The Athenians laid siege to Syracuse. Thucydides, who chronicled the war, makes it clear that a resolute attack might well have succeeded, but the Athenians failed to strike when they had a clear advantage. One event that blunted the Athenian attack was the loss of Alcibiades, one of the leaders of the expedition. He was recalled to Athens to stand trial on charges of violating the state's religion. Fearing that his political enemies would be able to secure his conviction, he defected to Sparta.

The Athenians finally lost a critical naval battle at Syracuse in 413 and had to retreat toward the interior of the island. During this desperate march the Syracusans and their allies cut the Athenians off and decimated them as they tried to cross a river. Those who survived this calamity surrendered; as Thucydides grimly says, "few out of many returned home."

The disaster in Sicily caused many defections

This bronze statuette of a Spartan soldier illustrates the helmet and draped garment worn during the time of the Peloponnesian War. (Photo: Wadsworth Atheneum, Hartford)

among the members of the Delian League. The war dragged on inconclusively for eight more years; Sparta sought decisive help by enlisting the aid of Persia, promising her control over the cities in Asia Minor that had freed themselves during the Persian Wars. In 405 a Spartan admiral captured the Athenian fleet on the shore of the Hellespont. Athens, no longer able to assure her food supply through the straits, had to surrender. She renounced control over her empire and, as a guarantee for the future and a symbol of humiliation, had to demolish the defensive walls that reached from the city down to the coast of Attica. Sparta pronounced this event in April 404 as "the liberation of Greece."

Athens had lost her empire, most of her navy, and much of her trade; and she never recovered her former power. Though democracy was able to survive in Athens for long years afterward, the quality of political leadership had declined after the death of Pericles.

Some ambitious leaders were demagogic, able to sway the assembly at will. On a number of occasions when the war appeared to be at an end, they could command support for rash ventures that ended in disaster, such as Alcibiades' expedition to Syracuse. Moreover, the war produced a number of atrocities by various parties. A striking example is the Athenian treatment of the island of Melos. When the Melians refused to renounce their neutrality and give their support to Athens, the Athenians massacred the male population and took the women and children as slaves.

One of the effects of the war was a spirit of pessimism and disillusionment among Athenian intellectuals. To many of them it appeared that uncontrolled democracy had led to social decline and military disaster. They compared the discipline and single-mindedness of Sparta, the victor in the war, with the frequent chaos of Athenian democracy. Such ideas run through the work of Plato and other philosophers, who asked what had gone wrong with democracy and what system should replace it. Political philosophy was founded in the aftermath of the Peloponnesian War, and virtually every conceivable problem in this field was discovered and debated by Greeks in the fourth century.

IV. CLASSICAL GREEK CULTURE

Historians usually call the period from about 500 to 323 the Classical Age of Greece. Athens was preeminent culturally in this period. Her citizens attended extraordinarily subtle dramas, meant to emphasize the complexities of the human condition; they heard brilliant philosophical debates between Socrates and his opponents, the Sophists. Athens housed philosophical schools, and moral issues found their way into historical writing.

THE IDEA OF MAN IN GREEK DRAMA

We saw earlier how Milesian philosophers tried to explain the physical world through scientific theories that were partly derived from mythological tradition. In Athens, playwrights turned to the problem of value and presented a more sophisticated view of man than current mythology provided. They did this by drawing on familiar legends, reinterpreting them so as to ask radical questions about morality and the justice that supposedly derives from the gods.

Greek tragedy debated the timeless questions that would later be the province of philosophers and theologians: What is man's relationship to the gods? What is justice? And if the gods are just, why do they make man suffer? Dramatic performances began in Athens, probably in the sixth century at festivals honoring the god Dionysus. In the fifth century they were presented before audiences of several thousand; they were practically an education in ethics for citizens. Prizes were awarded for the best dramas, and the winning plays combine, in amazing fashion, dramatic effectiveness with subtle moral dilemmas. The stature of the tragic characters gave additional force to these dramas: they deal with heroic, strong-willed men and women like Oedipus and Antigone, powerful personalities caught in fearful dilemmas. These unique dramas are still performed, filmed, and used as the matter for operas and ballets, over two thousand years after their creation.

Playwrights commonly presented dramas in sets of three, but only one such trilogy has survived, the tragedy of Orestes, son of Agamemnon (the *Oresteia*), by Aeschylus (525?–456). The central theme is the nature of justice, which Aeschylus explores in a tale of multiple murders and vengeance. Even before the trilogy opens, the problem has been exposed: the Greek king Agamemnon sails against Troy in accordance with his oath, but on the way his fleet is becalmed. If the fleet is to continue, he must sacrifice his daughter to the gods (this episode recalls another archetypal myth, in which the god of Israel commands Abraham to sacrifice his son Isaac). Agamemnon must decide which is the more just action, to kill his daughter and thus fulfill his oath, or to spare her and thus break his promise to attack Troy.

He follows the gods' orders, but on his return to Greece his wife, Clytemnestra, avenges the girl's death by murdering Agamemnon and assuming the throne with her lover. The chain of vengeance continues as Orestes, Agamemnon's son, kills Clytemnestra and the lover in turn. But now he too must expiate his (partly justified) crime. Orestes is pursued by the Furies, hostile demons who nearly drive him

mad. Finally, in Athens, he is tried for homicide by the court of the Areopagus, with the goddess Athena presiding. When the jury's vote is tied, Athena herself acquits Orestes by casting her vote in his favor. Thus he has been forgiven in the sight of the gods. For the Athenian audience, the final scene reveals that their system of justice, divinely inspired by Athena, has supplanted the old tribal custom of personal vengeance.

The resonance of Greek drama is most evident in *Oedipus the King* by Sophocles (496?–406), perhaps the most nearly perfect specimen of Greek tragedy that survives. Freud drew on it in his theory of the Oedipus complex, which describes a child's desire for his parent of the opposite sex and rejection of the parent of the same sex. The play is about Oedipus, King of Thebes, who had unknowingly committed the terrible crimes of killing his father and marrying his mother. As the play opens, a religious curse has brought a plague on the people. Oedipus orders a search to eliminate the offender who has polluted the city, but the search narrows with terrifying logic to Oedipus himself. His crimes of patricide and incest, though unintentional, have disturbed the order of the universe, and he must atone for them. When the truth emerges, Oedipus' wife-mother hangs herself. Oedipus, in a frenzy of remorse, plunges her brooches into his eyes and begins a life of wandering as a blind outcast.

The plays of Euripides (480?–406?) are characterized by greater realism than those of Aeschylus and Sophocles. Euripides is interested in how the inner workings of man's mind and emotions shape his destiny. Thus the passions of the characters rather than the workings of fate determine the course of events in his plays. Euripides' characters are intense, often neurotic, and even fanatical.

Euripides' most familiar play is *Medea*. Jason, the husband of Medea, has deserted her for a princess of Corinth. To revenge herself, Medea kills the Corinthian girl and then her own children. She is a woman of strong, often conflicting, emotions. She weeps over her children but, despite a momentary weakening of her resolve, fulfills her plan to kill them. Vicious and at times depraved, Medea is nonetheless heroic and terrifying in her determination.

THE SOPHISTS: CONVENTION AND NATURE

Euripides' plays seem to many to tend toward a kind of irreligion. There was, however, a group of thinkers at this time who openly avowed agnosticism. Their conclusions may be summed up in the words of Protagoras, earliest and greatest of the sophists; he claimed that "man is the measure" of whether anything exists and that the existence of the gods is an undemonstrable assumption.

When their faith in the gods grew uncertain, the Greeks turned to "nature," as Europeans would centuries later. The most fundamental characteristic of the fifth-century intellectual revolution is the distinction between man-made custom (*nomos*), on the one hand, and the law of nature (*physis*), on the other. For Protagoras and his followers, what was man-made was arbitrary and inferior; what was natural was immutable and proper. Accordingly, Protagoras could argue that the accepted canons of good behavior, including some restraint of the selfish appetites and impulses, and the time-honored practice of acting with consideration for others, were not essential parts of human nature. Such things belonged to *nomos*, not *physis*.

Athena leaning on her spear. (Photo: Acropolis Museum, Athens)

Moral relativism flourished now in the Greek world for many reasons, but most of all because the Greeks' contacts with other peoples were increasing through travel, foundation of colonies, and war. These widening horizons made it evident that customs and standards previously accepted as absolute, decreed by the gods for all people, were in fact local and relative. European explorations of Africa and the Americas in the sixteenth century and resultant knowledge of the customs of the inhabitants produced an analogous crisis of values among Europeans then. The Greeks learned that habits wicked and disgusting in their eyes, such as marriage between brother and sister, might seem to the Egyptian normal and even enjoined by religion. The great Greek historian and father of history, Herodotus, whose work has many sixteenth-century analogues, is typical of the fifth century in the enthusiasm with which he describes the customs of Scythians, Persians, Lydians, and others, pointing out their divergence from Greek usage. If all men, Herodotus says, were asked to name the best laws and customs, each would certainly choose his own. The playwright Euripides noted that incest was practiced among non-Greek peoples and that no law forbade it, and shocked his audience by having one of his characters say, with reference to incest, that absolutely no behavior is shameful if it does not seem so to those who practice it.

In the end, the sophistic movement attacked all established ideas and institutions, and its scepticism worked to undermine the bases on which the polis rested. Earlier political thought on the polis had drawn a close connection between the laws and morality, believing that the state had an obligation not only to prevent and punish wrongdoing, but also to make its citizens virtuous. Gradual acceptance of the relativity of values undermined acceptance of the state's moral purpose. The proper relationship between the laws and morality became one of the burning issues of the day. Some of the early and more traditional of the sophists, such as Protagoras, seem to have retained a thoroughly orthodox view of the state's moral function; but later sophists argued that the state must assume a morally neutral position. Antiphon, for example, admitted that some few laws were necessary for life. Thus law might reasonably be introduced as a pragmatic measure to prevent some kinds of wrongdoing; it must not, however, try to serve as a positive moral agent.

The great war between Sparta and Athens relaxed further the connection between law and morality. Participants in a given war may begin by arguing its morality, but the nature of war undermines moral values and creates circumstances where moral considerations appear simply inappropriate. There is no more explicit illustration of this new climate of opinion than the famous Mytilene debate, as preserved for us by the second Greek historian, Thucydides, in his account of the war itself. Mytilene, a subject city of Athens, rebelled during the course of the war. The Athenians crushed the rebellion, and the debate concerns the fate of the city: what punishment to mete out to its citizens. One Athenian leader, Cleon, argues for executing the entire male population and enslaving all women and children in order to make Mytilene an object lesson for any other allies who might be contemplating rebellion. Arguing against Cleon, Diodotus recommends much milder treatment, on the grounds that Cleon's punishment would ensure that the next subject ally to revolt would fight to the finish against the Athenians, knowing the dreadful fate awaiting it. Throughout the debate morality is beside the point. As one speaker aptly puts it: "We are not in a court of justice, but in a political assembly. The question at issue is not justice, but how to make the people of Mytilene useful to the Athenians."

A final, extremist fringe of the sophistic movement appeared at the very end of the war.

Characteristic of it was Critias, a right-wing revolutionary who advocated a theory of government based, not on divine sanction or even on consent, but on fraud. He conceived of religion as a device through which the deception that was the task of government and the laws might be carried out more efficiently. Law, according to this view, should be neither conducive to morality nor morally neutral, but a means of tricking people into acting in ways contrary to their natures; that is, they must be made to act against the dictates of *physis*, and so, immorally. Plato in his great work of political theory, *The Republic*, makes a certain Thrasymachus the spokesman for a variation on this theme. Thrasymachus defines justice as "what is in the interests of the stronger," thus anticipating Karl Marx's statement that political power is merely the organized power of one class to oppress another. Like Marx, Thrasymachus sees conventional morality as a by-product of the process of oppression and exploitation.

HISTORICAL WRITING

The spirit of inquiry and analysis led the sophists to examine man's condition. Another way of doing this is to write history—to analyze the past and compare it with the present. Herodotus (484?–425?) is rightly called the "Father of History," for he was the first to write an analysis of political events, in his case the Greek war with Persia. In his investigation he grasped the essential fact that large historical events are often the result of a meeting between two differing cultures. He therefore sought to learn the history of the Persian Empire and the reasons for its pressure on Europe.

Herodotus traveled throughout the Greek world and the Near East to gather the data for his *History*. He was a curious and open-minded traveler; he judged each society on its own terms rather than according to Greek standards of behavior. Though he often displays a shrewd scepticism, Herodotus did not always try to separate truth from legend. He sometimes reports two versions of one event, leaving it to the reader to make his own assessment. He partly disarms critics by saying "my duty is to report what is told me, but not to believe it all." He attributed the Greek victory in the Persian Wars to the inevitable triumph of a free society over a despotic one. The most impressive dimension of his work is his demonstration that all the cultures of the ancient world were interconnected: Greece and Persia were both parts of the whole.

Thucydides (455?–399?), the successor of Herodotus, participated in the Peloponnesian War and wrote its history; in fact he did not live to finish his work, which breaks off within 411, seven years before the end of the war. Thucydides perfectly represents the relentlessly analytical thought of the late fifth century. The speeches and debates that he reproduces reflect sophistic techniques of argument, and the speakers are usually contemptuous of any moral principles. Arguments based on justice and mercy, if brought up at all, are ruthlessly swept aside by whichever person or force has the upper hand. It is by no means clear that Thucydides himself had no use for compassion, but he presents the whole war as a coldly realistic pursuit of power.

In his view, the Athenian state was well led under Pericles because this statesman controlled the masses. His successors in power flattered the people for the sake of political advantage and allowed the masses to influence decisions, with tragic consequences for Athens. Thucydides' literary art is superb, particularly when he describes a scene of horror. No reader can avoid a chill over the clinical description of the plague that attacked Athens or the shattering defeat of the Athenian force in Sicily. Modern historians can sometimes convict him of error, but he remains the undisputed standard for ancient historians and has few if any superiors in any age.

COMEDY

To extract the comic from a situation was the aim of Aristophanes (448?–385?). His plays give the reader a graphic picture of everyday life in classical Athens because they satirize real people and events, ridicule the war, the political leaders, and the intellectuals (both the sophists and Socrates), and deride the inadequacies of democracy. Typically, Aristophanes' comedies present solutions to real problems, and his heroes appear as dropouts from society who escape in fantasy what his contemporaries cannot escape in real life. His characters will make peace with the world armed with nothing but a wine skin, or they will found a city in the sky, a society whose institutions satisfy the needs that earthly cities are failing to satisfy. At the same time, the Aristophanic hero is something more sinister than a mere dropout. He often embodies, to an exaggerated degree, the qualities of his society as it perceives itself: he is the typical Athenian, except in two conspicuous respects. First, he pursues openly and unscrupulously what his contemporaries pursue disingenuously, covering their real aims by professing ideals they no longer believe. Second, he succeeds where his real contemporaries fail. He deals with trickery by being trickier, he fights lawlessness with greater lawlessness, and he combats others' lack of restraint with unbridled license. In *The Birds*, the main character, Pithetaerus, escapes the earthly imperial city to found an even more repressive empire in the sky, one which tyrannizes not just over men, but over the gods as well. His behavior accords perfectly with Thrasymachus' sophistic morality, which took it as axiomatic that the pursuit of self-interest, in its **narrowest** form, was natural and right, and that such conduct achieved its most perfect and uninhibited expression in the person of the tyrant.

SOCRATES, PLATO, AND ARISTOTLE

The main critic of the sophists was Socrates (469–399). He transformed philosophy into an inquiry about the moral responsibility of man. His basic question was not, What is the world made of? but, What is right action and how can I know it is right? He was concerned with the loss of ethical values during the Peloponnesian War. His mission, as he saw it, was to persuade young men of Athens to examine their lives in the pursuit of moral truth, for "the unexamined life is not worth living." His technique was to question his pupils—even many who were not his pupils—refuting, correcting, and guiding them by his "Socratic" method to the right answers. He held that no man is wise who cannot give a logical account of his actions; this belief led to the statement that "knowledge is virtue," one of several Socratic theses that seem paradoxical, for even ignorant men may have virtues. But such paradoxes were intended to make people think critically in order to discover the truth.

Socrates' doctrines and his insistent questioning annoyed many Athenians. He also had political critics, for he had been the tutor of several Athenians who had opposed democracy during the last years of the Peloponnesian War (Alcibiades had been one of his hearers). In 399 he was brought to trial on the charges of "worshiping strange gods and corrupting the youth"—a way of hinting that Socrates had connections with enemies of the democratic state. In a fever of misguided patriotism, an Athenian jury condemned him to death. He accepted his fate and drank the famous cup of poison with simple courage.

Our knowledge of Socrates' thought comes mainly from the writings of his most famous pupil, Plato (428–347), for Socrates wrote nothing. Plato continued Socrates' investigation of moral conduct. He has left a massive series of philosophical books, mainly in the form of dialogues in which Socrates is the main speaker. But Plato went far beyond the homely paradoxes of Socrates and sought truth through a complex system that is still endlessly discussed and probed by critics.

Plato made his greatest impact on the future of philosophy with his theory of knowledge. Some sophists, as we have seen, practically denied that it was possible to know anything: in the absence of objective knowledge, the only recourse was to make your way through the world by coolly exploiting any situation at hand. Socrates rebelled against this view, but his answer to the question, How can I know what is right?, was simply that one must listen to one's conscience.

Plato believed that we must go beyond the evidence of our senses to find ultimate reality. We see objects as real, but in fact they are only poor reflections of ideal models, or "forms," which are eternal, perfect originals of any given object or notion.[2] What we see as justice, for example, is only an approximation of the true form of justice. Only through long training in philosophy can we learn how to perceive and understand these forms, which exist somewhere outside our world. This view of reality is the foundation of the philosophical movement known as Idealism.

Plato presents this thesis in several dialogues, of which the most read is *The Republic*. Like other Athenian intellectuals, Plato was an op-

ponent of democracy, and his repudiation of this system was strengthened when a jury of 500 was persuaded to condemn Socrates to death, even though the master had served the state as a soldier and had committed no crime. Disillusioned by the excesses of democracy, Plato sought to design a more stable form of government, one in which "everyone will do his proper task." The state would be guided by statesmen trained in philosophy to perceive the Forms. A second class, warriors, would defend the state; a third, artisans, would produce the needed material goods. Plato sums up his conception of the proper rulers in the epigram, "the state will be ruled well when kings become philosophers and philosophers become kings."

Like other visions of utopia, Plato's *Republic* had little effect on actual constitutions, but it seems to touch nearly every problem of philosophy, from statesmanship to perception, linguistics, and psychology. Through this rich book run many threads, but one above all: the question, What is justice? As we have seen, this had been worked over in the legendary material of Greek drama and in some of the debates in the history of Thucydides. The pupil of Socrates, who had seen his teacher condemned in a brutal distortion of justice, could hardly be indifferent to this question.

Plato, in turn, had an equally famous pupil, Aristotle (384–322), who was for a time the teacher of Alexander the Great of Macedonia. His investigations, in which he was assisted by his pupils in Athens, extended to all fields of learning known to the ancients: logic, metaphysics, astronomy, biology, physics, politics, and poetry among them. His contributions to each of these subjects were not to be surpassed for many centuries; not until the fourteenth century did anyone seriously question Aristotle's theory of motion (see Chapter 12).

Aristotle departed from Plato's theory of

---

[2] This theory of Plato's is often called the theory of Ideas; but the Greek word *idea* means something that can be seen—thus the *idea* of anything is its pattern or form.

ideal forms that cannot be perceived by the senses. He believed that every object has both form and matter, which are inseparable and can be studied only in that object. When we generalize about a group or class of objects, we are not referring to some ideal form but merely making a statement about what the particular objects in that group have in common. Form shapes matter; thus the form of "man" in the human embryo makes the child and, eventually, the man. For Aristotle each object had a purpose as part of a grand design of the universe. "Nature does nothing by accident," he said. The task of the philosopher is to study individual objects to discover their purpose; then, from the conclusions he draws, he may ultimately be able to perceive the grand design.

Aristotle made that task his life's work. He and his pupils devoted themselves to collecting and systematizing knowledge in all fields. For his *Politics* he studied the governments of over 150 contemporary states, comparing the merits of each. In the work he distinguishes three different types of constitution: monarchy, aristocracy, and moderate democracy. But he warns that monarchy can turn into tyranny; aristocracy into oligarchy; and moderate democracy into radical democracy, or anarchy. Of the three pure forms, Aristotle expresses a preference for moderate democracy. The chief end of government, in his view, is the good life, for both the individual and the community as a whole. This is an extension of the view expressed in his *Ethics* that happiness is the greatest good of the individual. To achieve it man must seek moderation, a mean between extremes of excessive pleasure and ascetic denial. This is in accord with the Greek principle of harmony and balance.

Aristotle was the last of the great Greek philosophers. The techniques of logical argument perfected in the polis had given birth to philosophy, but by the time of Aristotle's death

in 322, the self-contained polis had been absorbed into a larger world of empire. Greek philosophy thereafter became narrower in focus, concentrating on practical rules for ethical conduct.

v. THE RISE OF MACEDONIA

The Peloponnesian War seriously undermined the Greek system of city-states. During the next few decades, the city-states continued to quarrel among themselves. This further weakened their defenses and left them prey to the advance of the emerging kingdom of Macedonia. The intervention of Macedonia may therefore be viewed as a disastrous consequence of a number of errors made by the poleis. Yet at the same time the Macedonian conquest of Greece opened a new period in the history of the ancient world, an outward movement of Greek civilization into the ancient Near Eastern and newer Mediterranean kingdoms.

THE ERA OF HEGEMONIES

The beginning of the fourth century is usually called the "era of hegemonies," because first one polis and then another held the hegemony, or leadership, over a group of allies. Sparta, the winner in the Peloponnesian War, was the first state to establish hegemony, but Spartan traditions of isolation within the Peloponnesus did not fit her to govern as the successor to Athens. She established a docile government of oligarchs in Athens, but within a few months popular opposition swept this group away; and soon Athens revived her naval league, though with fewer members than it had had in the fifth century.

The polis of Thebes became an important power, siding now with Athens, now with Sparta, in a series of never-ending quarrels.

The quarrels themselves and their causes are too complicated to follow in detail, and no clear trend emerges except one of constant intrigue and war. During one of the struggles in these decades, the brilliant Theban general Epaminondas won a victory over Sparta in 371, exploding the belief, held with almost religious faith, that the Spartan infantry was invincible. Sparta continued to decline, partly through a shortage of manpower; Aristotle informs us that her armies in the field were now fewer than 1,000 in size, rather than the 4,000 or 5,000 who went into battle during the wars of the fifth century.

The period of the hegemonies practically brought to a close the era of self-governing poleis. Constant struggles and internal weaknesses had made the system vulnerable. It was replaced by a reversion to monarchy, as the kingdom of Macedonia spread its influence over the Greek mainland.

The head of Alexander the Great in heroic profile; the obverse of a silver coin issued by Lysimachus, one of Alexander's bodyguards, who after his master's death became king of Thrace. (Photo: Courtesy, Museum of Fine Arts, Boston)

THE MONARCHS OF MACEDONIA

Macedonia (or Macedon) was an ancient, somewhat backward kingdom in northern Greece. Its emergence as a Hellenic power was due to a resourceful king, Philip II (359–336), whose career has been unjustly overshadowed by the deeds of his son, Alexander the Great. With shrewd political skill Philip developed his kingdom, built up a powerful army, and planned a program of conquest.

Using both aggression and diplomacy, Philip added poleis and large territories to his kingdom and extended his control into central Greece. The great Athenian orator Demosthenes, in a series of fiery speeches ("Philippics"), called on his countrymen to recognize the danger and fight for Greek liberty. But by the time the Athenians responded, it was too late to halt the Macedonian advance. Philip won a decisive battle against Athens and several other poleis at Chaeronea in 338. All the city-states of southern Greece, except isolated Sparta, now lay at his disposal. He could have devastated many of them, including Athens, but his shrewd sense of tactics warned him not to do so. Therefore, he gathered the more important poleis, again excepting Sparta, into an obedient alliance called the League of Corinth. The league automatically recognized Philip as its leader and agreed to follow him in his next project, an invasion of Persia. But before he could open his Persian War, Philip was murdered in 336 by one of his officers.

The powerful empire built by Philip now passed to his son, Alexander III (336–323), and never has a young warrior prince made more productive use of his opportunities. During his brief reign Alexander created the largest empire the ancient world had known, and, more

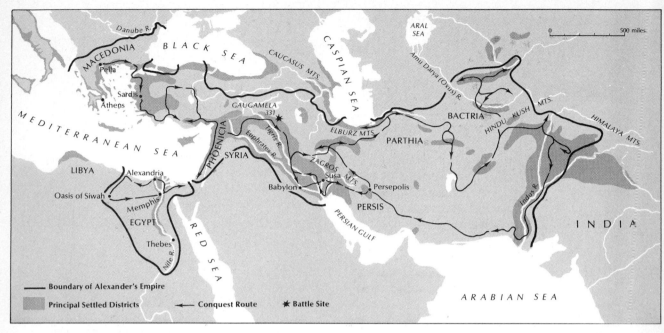

MAP 3.3: ALEXANDER'S EMPIRE 336–323 B.C.

than any other man, he was responsible for the diffusion of Greek culture.

After he consolidated his rule in his Greek territory, Alexander began the invasion of the Persian Empire. The Persia that he attacked was a much weaker state than the one that conquered Croesus and Babylon or the one that Xerxes led against the Greeks in 480. Intrigue and disloyalty had weakened the administration of the empire. Moreover, the king, Darius III, had to rely on Greek mercenary soldiers as the disciplined element in the infantry, for native troops were mainly untrained serfs. These facts must be taken into account to understand Alexander's success, but in no way do they diminish his reputation as one of the supreme generals in history. His campaigns show physical courage, strategic cleverness, and superb leadership.

Alexander swept the Persians away from the coast of Asia Minor and in 332 drove them out of Egypt, a land they had held for two centuries. The Egyptians welcomed him as a liberator and recognized him as their pharaoh. In the next season Alexander fought Darius III at Gaugamela. A complete victory there opened the way for him to capture the rich cities of Susa and Persepolis.

From 331 onward Alexander met little opposition in Persia. Darius III was murdered by disloyal officers in 330, and Alexander assumed the title of King of Persia. The expedition had now achieved its professed aim; yet Alexander continued to make war. During the next few years he campaigned as far east as India, where he crossed the Indus River (see Map 3.3). Finally in 326 he began his march back. At Babylon, where he was preparing an Arabian expedition, he caught a fever, and within a few days he died, not yet thirty-three.

VI. THE HELLENISTIC AGE

One of Alexander's modern admirers has said that he lifted the civilized world from one groove and set it in another. He conquered the Persian Empire and opened its enormous territory to Greek culture, which was transmitted through the dozens of garrisons and towns that he and his successors founded. The mere presence of Greeks inevitably exposed the East to the influence of their ways. Many features of Eastern life were changed over the decade of conquests. The process is called Hellenization, and the period from the death of Alexander in 323 to that of Cleopatra in Egypt two centuries later is known as the Hellenistic Age.

DISSOLUTION OF ALEXANDER'S EMPIRE

After Alexander's death his generals struggled for control of his empire. By about 275, after years of warfare and diplomatic intrigue, the empire had been carved into three large kingdoms ruled by the descendants of three of these generals: Macedonia under the Antigonids; Egypt under the Ptolemies; and western Asia under the Seleucids. A fourth kingdom was formed somewhat later around the city of Pergamum in western Asia Minor. The division of the empire did not end the strife. The subsequent history of these kingdoms is one of continual warfare until they were eventually absorbed by the Roman Republic.

The king of Macedonia controlled northern Greece. The poleis in the south continued to retain their autonomy. To protect their independence from the monarchy they formed defensive leagues, the most influential of which were the Aetolian League in western Greece and the Achaean League on the northern coast of the Peloponnesus.

The Greek rulers of Egypt and the Seleucid kingdom transformed themselves into Eastern monarchs in the style of their Egyptian and Persian predecessors. The inhabitants of these areas had long worshiped their rulers as divine or semidivine beings, and the Hellenistic kings exploited this tendency to identify man and god. Such propaganda lent authority and stability to their rule; they presented themselves to their subjects as saviors and enjoyed the worship offered to benefactors in the ancient world. The glorified position of the king may have given meaning to life for some subjects who found security in honoring such a father figure.

Hellenistic kings ruled through strong armies and large bureaucracies; their systems of taxation were efficient, to say the least. Certain products were royal monopolies and could be traded only at official prices. Greeks usually held the chief public offices in the army and bureaucracy. The kings did allow some democratic institutions to function in the Near Eastern cities. But the autonomy of these cities was limited to local affairs; they had no independent foreign policy within the monarchic framework.

ECONOMIC LIFE

One of the sharpest contrasts between the classical and Hellenistic worlds is in the scale of their economic operations. In classical Greece farmers worked small plots of land, and industry and commerce were ventures of small entrepreneurs. In the Hellenistic states of Egypt and the Seleucid kingdom vast estates predominated. Industry and trade operated on a larger scale than ever before in the ancient world, requiring the services of bankers and other financial agents.

The Hellenistic world prospered under Greek rule. Enterprising Greeks emigrating from their homeland to make their fortunes brought new vigor to the economies of Egypt and the

Near East. They introduced new crops and new techniques in agriculture to make production more efficient. In Egypt, for example, they encouraged the cultivation of grapes for wine and improved and extended the irrigation system. They also devoted more acreage to pasturing animals, which provided leather and cloth for the people and horses for the cavalry.

The growth of industry and trade was even more remarkable. The Hellenistic kings encouraged these efforts by establishing a sound money system, building roads and canals, and clearing the seas of pirates. Traders ventured eastward to India and, in the west, beyond the Mediterranean to the Atlantic coasts of Africa and Europe.

The resulting prosperity, however, was unevenly distributed. Kings and members of the upper classes (usually Greek) amassed great fortunes, but little of this wealth filtered down to the peasants and laborers. This great disparity between rich and poor led to increasing social conflict. Moreover, mainland Greece did not share in the new prosperity. Athens became little more than a university town after the center of trade had shifted from Greece to cities on the eastern Mediterranean coast. And the departure of the more venturesome Greeks for the Near East and Egypt depleted the Greek cities of the leadership that might have reversed the economic decline.

HELLENISTIC CITIES

Hellenistic civilization, like Greek civilization, was predominantly urban. Though the greater part of the vast lands of the kingdoms was devoted to agricultural pursuits, it was in the numerous Greek cities founded by Alexander and his successors that the culture of the Near East was transformed into the civilization that we call Hellenistic. Most of these new cities were in western Asia, in the Seleucid kingdom. With the brilliant exception of Alexandria, the Ptolemies founded few cities in Egypt, for a docile, rustic civilization was easier to control than citizens of a politically active urban society.

The Hellenistic cities were centers of government, trade, and culture. They were extremely large by ancient standards. Some had ten times as many inhabitants as the average polis in Greece; Alexandria, the largest of them, had at least a half-million inhabitants.

Besides their political institutions the Greeks brought from their homeland many of the amenities of polis life: temples, theaters, gymnasiums, and other public buildings. Natives in the upper classes copied Greek ways and sent their children to Greek schools. Moreover, a version of their language, koiné ("common") Greek, based mainly on the Attic dialect, became an international tongue. Now, for the first time, an individual could travel to any city in the known civilized world and make himself understood.

This traveling and intermingling account for the cosmopolitanism of the Hellenistic cities. None was more cosmopolitan than Alexandria, the greatest of the Hellenistic cities. The city attracted scholars from all over the Greek world, for there the Ptolemies had built a museum and the greatest library of ancient times. Though Athens still retained its leadership in philosophy, Alexandria became the cultural center of the Hellenistic Age. Scholars at Alexandria specialized in literary, historical, and scientific research.

The specialization of scholars was characteristic of the growing professionalism of the age. Whereas the citizen of fifth-century Athens could in turn be a farmer, a politician, a soldier, and even an actor (all the performers in the great dramas were amateurs), now these roles were filled by professionals. The army consisted of professional soldiers. Though the private citizen could cast a vote in the city's as-

The theater at Epidaurus, built in the 200s B.C., is testimony to the importance the Greeks placed upon drama. The theater was designed to seat more than 12,000 people. (Photo: Alison Frantz)

sembly, the professional bureaucrats ran the government. Professional theatrical groups replaced the amateurs.

Increased professionalism, by narrowing the focus of a citizen's life, engendered a growing individualism. Once a participant in all activities of the polis, the citizen was now a spectator, except in his own professional field. Moreover, the Greek inhabitants of the Near Eastern cities were uprooted; they had no ancestral ties to the community. Therefore they began to withdraw from community life to the privacy of their families or to private clubs. They abandoned public religious ceremonies for private cults.

LITERATURE, ART, AND SCIENCE

The Hellenistic Age was not a particularly fertile period in literature. Poets were concerned chiefly with style. Many of them achieved a certain technical perfection in their lyrics, but the works had little emotional depth. One of the few to rise above mere technical proficiency was Theocritus, a third-century poet who wrote charming lyrics about nature. His influence is evident in Vergil's *Bucolics* (or *Eclogues*) and, in a later period, in some of the work of Spenser and Milton.

The most significant literary achievements of the Hellenistic Age came from scholarship, a sign of the growing professionalism of the period. The literary capital of the Greek world was no longer Athens but Alexandria. By about 200 the library there probably housed a half-million papyrus rolls, the ancient form of the book. Scholars in Alexandria worked to preserve the literature of earlier times. Their outstanding achievement was the standardization of the text of Homer. By comparing the many versions that had been handed down over the centuries, they were able to establish the text on which modern versions of Homer are based.

Hellenistic kings subsidized art and architecture. As a result the architecture of the age tends to emphasize size and grandeur, as compared with the simplicity and human scale of classical architecture. An example is the Altar of Zeus from Pergamum (now in Berlin). A great stairway leading to the altar is flanked by a frieze 400 feet long. The figures on the frieze are typical of Hellenistic sculpture. They are carved in a high relief, with a realism that makes them seem to burst out of the background. The almost extravagant emotionalism of the work is only one of the characteristics that distinguishes Hellenistic sculpture from that of the classical period. Instead of idealized figures artists now showed genuine individuality in faces and bodies (see Plate 5). They often portrayed physical imperfection or even frank ugliness. Their attempts to portray strong emotion in their subjects sometimes led merely to exaggeration.

The most remarkable example of the cross-fertilization of cultures in the Hellenistic Age was in the field of science. The Greeks had long speculated about the nature of the universe, and the Near East had an even longer scientific tradition, particularly in the fields of astronomy and mathematics, as we have seen. After Alexander's conquests joined the two cultures, other conditions favored scientific advance: the increased professionalism of the age, the use of Greek as an international language, and the research facilities established in Alexandria. The result was an age of scientific achievement that was not surpassed until the seventeenth century.

In mathematics Euclid (about 300) compiled a textbook of geometry that is still used in American colleges. The most gifted mathematician of Hellenistic times was Archimedes, who calculated the value of *pi* (the ratio between the circumference and the diameter of a circle), developed a system for expressing large numbers, and discovered the ratio between the volumes of a cylinder and a sphere. Archimedes was also interested in physics and applied physics. He demonstrated that a floating body will sink only so far, until it displaces its own weight in a liquid. He is said to have lifted a loaded ship with a mechanical device (perhaps a lever), boasting, "Give me a place to stand and I will move the earth."

About 250 Aristarchus, an astronomer and mathematician, advanced a heliocentric theory of the movement of the planets. The theory that the earth revolves around the sun was not new, but Aristarchus refined it. He stated that the earth revolves on its own axis; the sun, as the center of the universe, remains immobile; and the planets circle the sun in orbit. This theory was not generally accepted by Hellenistic astronomers; it remained for Copernicus in the sixteenth century to prove the soundness of Aristarchus' system.

One of the most important contributions of Hellenistic scientists was the development of more precise measurements. Hipparchus (about 150), the greatest Hellenistic astronomer, calculated the length of the average lunar month to within one second of the accepted figure. Eratosthenes (275?–194?) computed the circumference of the earth to be about 28,000 miles, only 4,000 miles more than the actual figure. Other scientists worked out the division of time into hours, minutes, and seconds and of circles into degrees, minutes, and seconds.

PHILOSOPHY AND RELIGION

The change in life style from the security of the polis to the sophistication, variety, and loneliness of a large cosmopolitan world produced corresponding changes in Greek philosophy. Plato and Aristotle had been philosophers of the polis in the sense that they were concerned with man's role in the intimate world of the city-state. But now the state was a large kingdom headed by a remote ruler. Individual men and women could hardly influence its policies and yet were caught up in wars and other changes of fortune. In such conditions, philosophies were needed that offered the possibility of survival in this world. The two most important schools of Hellenistic philosophy, Stoicism and Epicureanism, were addressed to an individualistic age in which men sought guidance in their personal lives and were unconcerned about the nature of the political framework.

Zeno (335–263), who founded Stoicism, taught that a single divine reason, or plan, governs the universe, and that to find happiness man must act in harmony with this plan. He should be patient in adversity, for it is a necessary part of the divine plan and he can do nothing to change it. By cultivating a sense of duty and self-discipline, man can learn to accept his fate; he will then become immune to earthly anxieties and will achieve inner freedom and tranquillity. The Stoics did not advocate withdrawal from the world. They believed that all men, as rational beings, are brothers. Therefore, men should be tolerant. Moreover, to ensure justice for all, the rational man should consider it his duty to engage in public affairs.

The Stoics were advancing ideas that were to have a profound influence on later Western history: universal brotherhood, the virtue of tolerance, and compassion for the less fortunate members of the human race. The concept of the brotherhood of man was the product of a cosmopolitan society; in the Greek city-states non-Greeks had been called "barbarians." Furthermore, most earlier Greeks had accepted the institution of slavery, but the Stoics believed that the practice of exploiting others corrupted the master (the slave himself could endure his bondage by achieving inner freedom). Stoicism became the most influential philosophy among educated men of the Hellenistic Age and achieved great influence among the Romans.

Like the Stoics, Epicurus (341–270) believed that men should strive for tranquillity, but he differed with them on the means of attaining it. Addressing himself to the anxieties of his contemporaries—fear of the gods and fear of death—and their general sense of purposelessness, he said that the gods were indifferent to man, thus not intimidating. As for death, "good and bad exist only by being perceived, and death deprives us of perception; . . . while we are, death is not, and when death is, we are not." Men should therefore concern themselves only with leading pleasurable lives. To Epicurus pleasure was not self-indulgence but, rather, the avoidance of physical and mental pain. Since political and emotional involvement can cause pain, the wise man withdraws from the world to study philosophy and enjoy the companionship of a few friends.

The search for meaning in life existed at all

levels of Hellenistic society, but nowhere so much as among the great masses of the poor. The answers of philosophy were addressed to an intellectual elite—the gentleman-scholar, as it were, meditating in his study. But the poor lacked the education, leisure, and detachment for such a pursuit. They sought spiritual and emotional sustenance for their daily encounters with the harshness of Hellenistic life.

For many the mystery religions of the Near East filled this need. The influence of the old Greek civic religion had declined along with the polis and by now had almost disappeared. Thus Greek religion was never firmly transplanted in the East. Rather, the religious influence gradually moved in the opposite direction until finally Eastern religions dominated the West.

There were numerous mystery cults that had some features in common as a result of the frequent intermingling of cultures in the cosmopolitan Near East. They centered on the worship of a savior whose death and resurrection would redeem the sins of mankind; their rituals were elaborate, often wildly emotional; and they nourished hope by promising an afterlife that would compensate for the rigors of this one. Among the more important mystery cults was the worship of Isis and Osiris, deities from Egypt.

The Eastern god who was to achieve the greatest acceptance in the West was Jehovah, the god of the Israelites and then of the Jews and Christians. Much in the development of Christianity was Israelite in origin, but some of its practices emerged from other Near Eastern religions. Baptism, the confession of sins, sacrificial meals, and a general growth of mysticism all were part of the spiritual heritage of the Hellenistic Age. We might indeed say that Christianity became the most widespread and successful of all the mystery religions.

The Greeks of the Classical Age established standards of beauty and wisdom that have inspired people ever since. Greek civilization at its height explored and analyzed nearly every aspect of man and his potential. Even when the world of the poleis was shattering, philosophers reaffirmed that man has reason and that he can therefore devise a more just society.

The long Peloponnesian War between Athens and Sparta caused the decline of the poleis and opened the way for the domination of Greece by Philip II of Macedonia. His son Alexander was responsible for a dramatic expansion of Greek culture; with his conquering armies he brought Greek civilization into Asia Minor, Syria, and India.

A fusion of cultures took place as different societies were drawn into the orbit of Greek language and thought. A new Hellenistic civilization emerged as the polis gave way to the "cosmopolis." The Greeks themselves underwent some changes. They transplanted many institutions of their poleis to the Near East, but the ties within the community that had char-

acterized the society of the polis were weakened. The cultural interchange in the Hellenistic world was to have a profound influence on religion in the West. Christianity started as a small cult in the Near East. The man who brought its message to the Greeks, and then to the Romans, was Paul of Tarsus, a Hellenized Jew from Asia Minor.

But the Greeks could not maintain permanent control over the Hellenized world. Another state was to succeed even beyond the achievements of Alexander. Not Greece but Rome became the uniting force that passed the legacy of the classical world to medieval and then to modern Europe.

RECOMMENDED READING

Sources

Aristotle. *Athenian Constitution.* H. Rackham (tr.). 1935.

*Arrian. *Life of Alexander the Great.* Aubrey de Sélincourt (tr.). 1958.

The Complete Greek Tragedies. David Grene and Richmond Lattimore (eds.). 1959. The best collection of translations.

*Thucydides. *The Peloponnesian War.* Rex Warner (tr.). 1954.

Studies

*Andrewes, A. *The Greeks.* 1973. Has a full, up-to-date bibliography.

Bell, H. I. *Egypt from Alexander the Great to the Arab Conquest.* 1948.

Burn, A. R. *Persia and the Greeks.* 1962.

Cary, Max. *A History of the Greek World, from 323 to 146 B.C.* 1951. Contains well-organized chapters on Hellenistic culture.

*Ehrenberg, Victor. *From Solon to Socrates.* 1968.

*Forrest, W. G. *A History of Sparta, 950–192 B.C.* 1968.

Green, P. *Alexander of Macedon.* 1975.

Jones, A. H. M. *Athenian Democracy.* 1960.

Kagan, Donald. *The Great Dialogue: A History of Greek Political Thought.* 1965.

*Kitto, H. D. F. *Greek Tragedy: A Literary Study.* 1969.

*Lloyd-Jones, Hugh (ed.). *The Greek World.* 1965. Essays by several experts on all phases of Greek culture.

Meiggs, Russell. *The Athenian Empire.* 1972.

*Ross, W. D. *Aristotle.* 1956.

Rostovtzeff, M. *The Social and Economic History of the Hellenistic World.* 1941. The final work of the leading ancient historian of his time.

*Taylor, A. E. *Plato, the Man and His Work.* 1966.

*———. *Socrates: The Man and His Thought.* 1959.

*Zimmern, Alfred. *The Greek Commonwealth.* 1931. An ever-fresh and perceptive study of life in a Greek polis.

*Available in paperback.

FOUR

THE ROMAN REPUBLIC

The history of the Roman Republic is the record, first, of a remarkably successful imperialistic venture. In origin a small agricultural village on the Tiber River, Rome grew until she was able to unite the Italian Peninsula under her rule, a unification of Italy not duplicated until the nineteenth century. With the resources of the whole of Italy at her disposal, Rome subdued the western Mediterranean countries—Sicily, Sardinia, Corsica, Spain, northern Africa, and southern France—and then went on to dominate the lands of the eastern Mediterranean as well. Her Empire eventually stretched from Scotland in the north to the Sahara in the south, from the Rock of Gibraltar in the west to Armenia in the east. It was not only an extraordinary feat of conquest, but also a fascinating exercise in internationalism. Ironically, the vehicle for this internationalism was extreme nationalism, the desire of a people to impose its will and its name on all others.

Second, the history of Republican Rome is the story of a remarkable revolution. This revolution killed whatever elements of political freedom existed in the Republic and established a powerful autocracy. Yet despite its violence it did not weaken Rome as an imperial power. On the contrary, it made her a more efficient administrator of her foreign dominions.

1. THE UNIFICATION OF ITALY

No central power unified Italy in earliest times. Etruscans, Greeks, and various Italic tribes lacked the ability to establish a powerful kingdom. About 625 the Etruscans ruled over the city of Rome. When their domination ended, the Romans feared their return and sought allies among neighboring tribes. Rome now began a course of expansion and, in a long series of wars, managed to unite and control the Italian Peninsula.

GEOGRAPHY OF ITALY

Italy is not, like Greece, divided into many small valleys. The main geographic feature is the Apennine range, which runs diagonally across Italy in the north and then turns southward to bisect the peninsula. The central portion of this peninsula has plenty of water and good soil, benefits that most Greeks would have

envied, but the extreme south is poor and sun-baked. North of the Apennines is the valley of the Po River, fertile and desirable, irrigated by rivers that drain the Apennines and the Alps, even farther north. Its rich land was for centuries the home of Celtic peoples known collectively as Gauls. The hills of Italy are gentle enough for pasturing, unlike those of Greece; and wood, scarce in Greece, was plentiful.

THE ORIGINS OF ROME

The legends about the founding of Rome by Aeneas or by Romulus and Remus are myths, so we must depend on evidence gathered by archaeologists to describe early Roman history. Scraps of pottery suggest that the site of Rome was inhabited as early as 1400; certainly between 900 and 600 there was a series of cemeteries on the famous seven hills that bound Rome.

The ancients believed that Rome was founded

in 753 (slight variations from this date occur in the sources). In any case, there must have been considerable inhabitation in the area around Rome by that time. About 625 the marshes below the seven hills were drained and a central marketplace, the Forum, was built. At about this time the Etruscans united the Latin-speaking tribes in the hills around Rome and ruled the city under an Etruscan monarch.

The origins of the Etruscans are obscure. They appeared in Italy soon after 800, in the region north of the Tiber River known as Etruria (modern Tuscany). They may have been a native people who were reinforced by immigrants from Asia Minor. Their language, which was not an Italic dialect, is still undeciphered even though thousands of short Etruscan inscriptions exist.

During their period of rule the Etruscans left their stamp on the future Roman civilization. They were a relatively sophisticated culture—urbane, literate, and technologically advanced—and they developed a flourishing international trade, which brought them into contact with the culture of the Greeks and Phoenicians. Part of the Etruscan legacy is seen in the monumental architecture of Roman temples and tombs. They provide the best evidence that historians have about these early people. On the coffins are reliefs or statues that show a lively and individual art, adapted mainly from Greek models. The Etruscans also introduced to Rome the worship of a triad of gods (Juno, Minerva, Jupiter) and the custom of examining the innards of animals to foretell the future.

The Greeks, beginning about 750, had established about fifty poleis on the southern and western shores of Italy and on the island of Sicily. The Romans called the area of southern Italy Magna Graecia ("Great Greece") and thus gave us the name "Greeks" for the people who called themselves Hellenes. Greek culture from the colonies influenced the Etruscans and,

This sarcophagus is from a late sixth-century Etruscan tomb. The reclining couple on the lid reflects the synthesis of Grecian art and the individualized style of the Etruscans. (Photo: Alinari-Art Reference Bureau)

in turn, the Romans. For example, from the village of Cumae, the oldest Greek colony in Italy, the Etruscans learned the Western version of the Greek alphabet and passed it on to Rome. These Greek colonies survived until the third century, when they were brought under the control of the Roman Republic.

About 500 (the Romans reckoned the date as 509) Etruscan sovereignty over Rome ended. The legends invented to account for this revolution need not be taken seriously, but somehow Rome freed herself of her last king and established her republican form of government. Afterward the Etruscans gradually declined as a power until they were finally absorbed by the Roman Republic in the fourth century.

THE EARLY CONSTITUTION

Much of the political history of the Republic revolves around the constitution, which was never a written document but rather a set of carefully observed procedures and customs. Romans had a deep reverence for precedent, and so for law, as is made abundantly clear by the fact that the Latin for "revolution" is *res novae*: literally, "new things."

Structurally, the Roman system, like both the Athenian and the Spartan systems, had three major components, which tended to offset and balance each other. These were the elected magistrates, including and in particular the consuls who were executives and represented the regal element; the Senate, an aristocratic advisory body of elder statesmen and clan leaders; and the popular assemblies, which theoretically embodied the democratic elements in the state.

The consuls were elected annually by the

A sixth-century Etruscan chariot, done in bronze sheathing over a wood frame. (Photo: Metropolitan Museum of Art, Rogers Fund, 1903)

Assembly of the Centuries, which comprised the entire army and in which a man's voting power was proportionate to his wealth. This arrangement illustrates the conservative nature of the Roman mind, as does the law that, in cases where the two executives disagreed, the consul advocating no action should prevail. Consuls (and lower-ranking officers called praetors) possessed imperium, which gave them the power to command troops and to govern the foreign province to which they were assigned after their year of office.

Control of both foreign and domestic policy belonged to the Senate. It was originally an advisory body (the word *senatus* means "council of elders"), but it came to be the guiding element in the Roman constitution. Its members (usually about three hundred) were ex-consuls and other magistrates; membership was for life. Its solid conservatism acted to restrain hotheaded politicians, and more than once it provided the moral leadership that brought the state to victory in war. Rome lacked defined political parties, and this large body naturally divided itself into smaller units, rivals in the struggle to hold power and to determine policy. The real nucleus of power was the *gens*, or clan; this was a group of related families—for example, all those whose second name was Cornelius or Aemilius (this was the "gentile" name). The great clans and their subdivisions contrived to maintain such firm control over high office that by about 100 B.C. it was rare for any man to attain the consulship who did not have ancestors who had already held the office. Such an outsider (for example, the orator Cicero) was referred to as a "new man" (*novus homo*). Throughout all Italian history, even down to the present, the family unit has remained the focus of social and political life.

In addition to the Assembly of the Centuries there was an Assembly of Tribes, which also included all citizens but not arranged hierarchically as in the Centuriate Assembly. The Tribal

Assembly consisted of 35 voting units, or tribes, and the criterion for membership in a specific tribe was place of birth or residence. Between them these two citizen assemblies passed laws, elected magistrates, and served as criminal and civil courts. Yet for most of the Republic's history both bodies, in all their capacities, required that their members give their votes openly, making them vulnerable to the crudest forms of economic intimidation should they fail to vote as their wealthy patrons instructed.

THE STRUGGLE OF THE ORDERS

Rome followed the traditional Greek pattern of substituting an oligarchy for a patriarchal or hereditary kingship. The next centuries saw a struggle in which a small hereditary upper class, the patricians, battled against the political demands of the much larger class of common people, or plebeians. This struggle, however, unlike that in Greece, did not issue in dictatorship, at least not for the time being. The Roman tradition instead records a series of constitutional compromises, which we call the Struggle of the Orders. For the most part these compromises did not lead to establishment of many new organs of government but rather admission to the old institutions of wealthy men from the inferior plebeian order, and thus creation of a new patrician-plebeian governing oligarchy.

Like the founding fathers of our own country, the prominent plebeian families who led the Struggle of the Orders succeeded in stopping their revolution at the most advantageous point. Not only did the new combined oligarchy of patricians and plebeians retain power, but it was able to use the progress of the revolution to hold power more securely. The plebeians' spokesmen, called the college of the People's tribunes, consisted of ten annually elected members, each having the power to veto (through *intercessio*) any and all public business: elections, legislative enactments, legal proceedings, even meetings of the Senate. A tribune could thereby halt the process of government indefinitely. A similar right of veto in medieval Poland made it almost impossible for government to be carried on at all. In Rome it should have meant that government could be carried on only by consent of the People's tribunes. Yet, as the Roman historian Livy tells us, the tribunes were, in fact, instruments of senatorial policy, for they were usually tied to some strong senatorial faction and under an obligation to do its bidding. Since the veto of a single tribune could paralyze the activities of his colleagues, the tribunician college and the Tribal Assembly over which it presided were rendered harmless, provided that the senatorial factions commanded the loyalty of at least one member of the board. The paralyzing power of the tribunes had the potential for great disruption. But in effect that power now meant simply that the Senate could disrupt any activity of the plebeian assembly that it found uncongenial. As a result, political debate was rendered ineffective on all but the senatorial level. This clever and subtle transformation of a theoretical revolution could only work if all concerned agreed to allow it to work. In the centuries of external danger, of conflict with competing foreign states in Italy, Africa, and the Greek East, all were so agreed.

Before the revolution, as the Romans surely knew regardless of what they claimed in their public traditions, the management of the state in practice rested in the hands of the Senate in virtue of its *auctoritas*, a word that means "authority" but carries with it also the mystique of leadership. The second-century Greek historian Polybius called the Roman constitution a perfect blend of regal, aristocratic, and democratic elements. His error was analogous to that committed by Montesquieu in regard to the English mixed constitution of the eighteenth century: the poor exercised their votes not in their class interests, but in the interests of the various aristocrats to whose houses they and their families had a traditional attachment. They were, as the Latin put it, *clientes* of these aristocratic patrons, giving them their votes, generation after generation. Political power in Rome during the third and much of the second centuries remained the preserve of the ruling classes; the lower classes made no demands that threatened this system. Nor were they likely to do so as long as Rome was still fighting for her very existence.

EARLY EXPANSION OF ROME

While the Romans were developing their form of government, they were also expanding their holdings on the Italian Peninsula. Except for the Greek city-states in the south and the Etruscan power in the north, most of the peninsula was occupied by tribes with little organization. The Romans first conquered the tribes in the nearby plain of Latium and then advanced into other territories. Roman historians of these early wars of conquest saw them through a haze of legend, but their narratives convince us that the battles were long and severe.

The period of conquest was punctuated by one major disaster. About 390 a large force of Gauls left their stronghold in the Po valley and captured part of Rome herself. They exacted a ransom as the price of their withdrawal. Rome then renewed her policy of expansion, showing the resilience that made her, in the words of the historian Edward Gibbon, "sometimes vanquished in battle, always victorious in war." Shortly after 300 Rome dominated the Italian Peninsula as far south as the Greek city-states of Magna Graecia.

A series of quarrels led to a war between Rome and these city-states. At this point Roman history emerges into clear light, with secure dates and no legendary decorations. The Greek city of Tarentum summoned Pyrrhus, a prince from the half-Greek region of Epirus (modern Albania), to direct the campaign against Rome. Pyrrhus fought two successful battles in 280, but at a heavy cost in casualties to his own men (whence comes the phrase "a Pyrrhic victory").

Pyrrhus sent an envoy to invite the Romans to surrender; the aged censor Appius Claudius declared in the Senate that Rome would never negotiate with an enemy so long as he was on Roman soil. His statement epitomized the Roman spirit. Pyrrhus might have achieved more than he did if he had stuck to his war, but he became diverted to military adventures in Sicily, and in 275 he abandoned Italy, leaving the Romans to pursue their conquests. By 265 Rome controlled the entire Italian Peninsula, but she had not yet mastered the Po valley (see Map 4.1).

THE ROMAN FEDERATION

Rome organized the conquered communities by establishing several different degrees of privilege and responsibility among them. Residents of a few favored communities were granted the most highly prized status, full Roman citizenship. This meant that they were on the same legal footing as the Romans; they enjoyed the protection of Roman law and could hold office in Rome. Members of some other communities became citizens *sine suffragio* (without the vote); such citizens had the right of intermarriage with Romans and had to supply troops to the Roman army on demand. At a lower level of privilege were the *socii* ("allies"). They received Rome's protection from other peoples and were also liable for troops. None of these groups, once joined to

MAP 4.1: ITALY 265 B.C.

Rome in whatever status, could follow independent foreign policies, but progress upward within the ranks of citizenship was possible. This system of confederation enabled the Romans to solve an administrative problem that had frustrated the Greek poleis: how to control a large territory without having to demolish or transform the conqueror's own institutions.

II. THE AGE OF IMPERIALISM

After unifying peninsular Italy, Rome—by which we now mean not only the city of Rome but the peoples of Italy allied with that city in the system—began to intervene in the quarrels of other states. Within a little more than a century, from 264 to 133, Rome became the supreme Mediterranean power. This imperialism influenced nearly everything in Roman life from government and society to literature and art.

THE PUNIC WARS

Three wars with Carthage established the foundations of Roman imperialism. The city of Carthage in North Africa had been founded by the Phoenicians about 700, but within the next century she became independent of Phoenicia and began to establish her own Mediterranean empire. By the time Rome had unified the Italian Peninsula, the Carthaginian Empire included cities in northern Africa, parts of Spain, the islands of Corsica and Sardinia, and much of Sicily.

The confrontation with Rome began in 264 as a minor conflict over the presence of Carthaginian troops in the Sicilian city of Messana, which lay outside the Carthaginian territory there. Messana had invited the troops into the city as protection against other enemies but then decided to replace them with a Roman force. When Carthage refused to tolerate Roman interference, war broke out between Carthage and Rome. The war soon became a contest for control of the island of Sicily itself and it was the first of the three Punic Wars, so named from the Latin word *Poeni*, or Phoenicians, who had founded Carthage. Roman tenacity finally won this war in 241, but with heavy casualties. Carthage abandoned Sicily entirely, and large parts of the island passed to Rome. In 238 the Romans seized the Carthaginian islands of Corsica and Sardinia. These islands, together with Sicily, became the first Roman provinces.

The second Punic War (219–202) was the most critical. The conflict arose in Spain, where Rome protested to Carthage about her treatment of the town of Saguntum, which was friendly to Rome but located well within the agreed Carthaginian sphere of influence in Spain. The Romans had only weak grounds for protest. During negotiations Hannibal, the brilliant Carthaginian general, seized Saguntum, and this action made war inevitable. He welcomed a chance for war against the power that had humiliated his nation, and he decided to carry the war to the enemy. During the autumn of 218 he led his army from Spain across the Alps and down into Italy. Once there he hoped to arouse the Gallic tribes in the Po valley and break up the alliances of the various peoples with Rome; then he planned to go on to conquer Rome itself. This two-fold strategy failed. Hannibal won a brilliant victory against the Romans at Cannae in 216, but he could not arouse the allies to revolt. At least half of them chose to remain loyal to Rome. Without revolts Hannibal's manpower was insufficient to defeat the Romans. The war dragged on for more than a decade, and gradually it became clear that the Carthaginians lacked the strength to make Rome surrender.

In 203 Hannibal returned to Carthage to defend it against a Roman invasion under the command of Publius Cornelius Scipio, but Carthage was defeated in the following year at Zama in North Africa. In honor of the victory Scipio received the name "Africanus," and proudly added it to his traditional Roman name. Besides paying Rome a huge indemnity, Carthage had to give up all her territory except that immediately around the city in Africa, and she was forbidden to raise an army without Roman permission.

The third and final Punic War was a squalid affair, lasting from 149 to 146. An anti-Carthaginian group in Rome, led by the elder Cato, succeeded in provoking this war and making it a campaign of punishment against Carthage, which had broken the peace terms by raising an army against a nearby aggressor. Another Scipio, Aemilianus, captured and destroyed Carthage in 146. The territory became the Roman province of Africa. In the aftermath of the victories over Carthage, Rome went on to conquer almost all of Spain in a series of wars lasting until 133.

ROME'S EASTERN WARS

In the 220s the Romans began to intervene along the shore of Illyria (modern Yugoslavia), when piracy and disturbed political conditions threatened their trade and commerce in this region. Philip V, who became ruler of Macedonia in 221, was alarmed by this extension of Roman interest. During the second Punic War he thought he saw his chance to remove the Roman presence; he formed an alliance with Hannibal after the battle of Cannae. To frustrate this combination, the Romans sent a force toward Greece. Thus by drawing the Romans across the Adriatic into Greek lands, Philip unwittingly opened the gate through which, over several centuries, Roman troops and administrators poured as far east as Armenia. This is one of the milestones in European history.

The war against Philip (214–205) was the first of four wars between Rome and Macedonia. In the earlier years of these wars the Romans tried to avoid entangling commitments in the Greek world. For example, in 197 they won a decisive victory over Philip in the second Macedonian War, but a year later they withdrew from Greece. In doing this they were not acting in a spirit of innocent devotion to liberty, for they expected the Greeks to remain loyal and obedient subject allies and to respect Roman leadership.

Warfare in Asia Minor

Almost at once the Romans had to plunge back into Greek affairs. Antiochus III, the Macedonian king of the Syrian Empire, invaded Greece in 192 at the request of the Aetolian League, one of the groups of city-states that were created as a counterbalance to Macedonian monarchy. The Aetolians had been allies of Rome in the Macedonian Wars against Philip, but now betrayed her because they had not been allowed to expand their holdings as much as they had wanted after the recent defeats of Macedonia. The Romans had no choice but to drive Antiochus out of Greece. It is true that no single Hellenistic power could challenge Roman hegemony; all the same, a coalition of the Aetolians, Philip, and Antiochus might try to contend with her on equal terms.

In 191 the Romans defeated Antiochus at Thermopylae and decided to pursue him into Asia Minor—another important step in the Roman conquest of the Mediterranean world, as Roman legions first left Europe for warfare in Asia. Scipio Africanus, the man who had defeated Hannibal, and his brother Lucius won a crushing victory over Antiochus at the town of Magnesia in 190. Antiochus was not actually disarmed, but he was forced to pay huge reparations and was excluded from western Asia Minor.

Annexation of Greece and Asia Minor

Rome now found it impossible to withdraw from Greek affairs. A further quarrel with Macedonia—the third Macedonian War—ended with a Roman victory at the village of Pydna in 168. The Romans divided Macedonia into four separate districts, but even this severe policy did not produce a calm situation. Further disturbances provoked the Romans into invading again and thus opening the fourth war

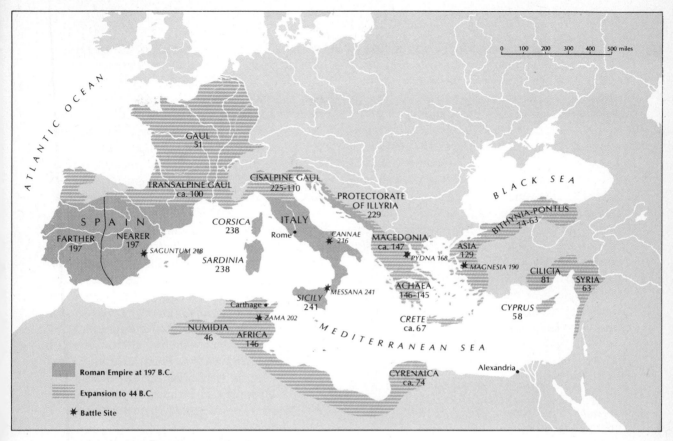

MAP 4.2: THE ROMAN EMPIRE 197–44 B.C.

in 149. By this time the Senate realized that outright annexation was the only way to secure its interests. Therefore, in 147 or 146, Macedonia was officially made a province—Rome's first acquisition of territory in the Hellenistic world. In 146 she added most of southern Greece to this province, which was placed under the authority of the governor of Macedonia (in 27 B.C. this newer region became the separate province of Achaea). Thus the Romans brought to an end the independent political life of mainland Greece, and from this time on their dominance in the Mediterranean could not be denied or reversed.

In 133, the last king of Pergamum died without leaving a successor and willed his kingdom to Rome. In doing so he was aiding destiny, for Rome's influence in the East practically assured that the kingdom of Pergamum could not long survive without Roman protection. Four years later Rome created the province of Asia, based on the territory of Pergamum (see Map 4.2). Because this province possessed great wealth, the office of governor of Asia became highly desirable for ambitious men pursuing careers in politics.

THE NATURE OF ROMAN IMPERIALISM

What distinctive strength made Rome so successful in her rise to imperial power? Early in the city's history, events had forced her to seek defensive alliances. After the expulsion of the Tarquins, Rome had to unite militarily with her Latin neighbors against the possibility of the Etruscans' return. What is more, internecine struggles among city-states in the area must have come to an abrupt halt when the invading Gauls swept down to devastate Italy in 390. After their withdrawal, they still presented a threat that encouraged the peoples of Italy to band together for protection, and the resultant alliances would eventually lead to unification under Rome's aegis.

The psychological result of such conditions stands out more clearly by contrast with the experience of the early Greek city-states. During the Dark Ages the polis matured unperturbed by any outside power. Not until the beginning of the fifth century B.C. did outside dangers threaten the city-states of mainland Greece, causing them to unite temporarily in face of superior forces. The Greeks therefore developed an attitude to the state, based on that early historical experience, that greatly valued local autonomy and political independence. In the Italian Peninsula, on the other hand, there was far less security, and independence would have seemed a secondary consideration to city-states driven, from the earliest stages of their political development, to unite for a common defense. Success remained the only true test of whether any particular policy was good or not. Romans therefore had few inhibitions impeding the development of a highly effective and utterly ruthless policy of foreign domination. Scipio Aemilianus, for example, forced the people of Numantia, in Spain, to surrender in 133 by reducing them to cannibalism, and cut off the hands of four hundred young men in a neighboring city who had advocated aiding their Spanish brethren. The Senate at home deemed his achievements worthy of a triumph, the highest military honor the Romans could bestow on a successful commander.

This stone relief shows one aspect of daily life in Rome: tradespeople at a market stall selling fruits, vegetables, and game. (Photo: Gabinetto Fotografico Nazionale)

Rome's first great accomplishment on her way to complete imperial dominion was the unification of the Italian Peninsula. Military necessity required common efforts at defense, and the allies that eventually concluded treaties with Rome, always more or less to her advantage, simply agreed to furnish the Romans with troops, such as they could muster and the Romans thought sufficient. Moreover, unlike their Athenian imperial counterparts, the Romans studiously remained aloof from any involvement in the internal affairs of their subject allies, who surrendered only their autonomy in foreign affairs in return for Roman protection and what the Romans called their friendship (Latin *amicitia*). This, a crucial word in Roman politics, external and internal, means a more binding obligation than the English translation suggests.

Through such friendships, Rome expanded over the years beyond the shores of Italy to the rest of the Mediterranean world, constructing an ever-lengthening skein of defensive alliances. The Romans did not, however, simply place themselves at the mercy of some friend's good offices. The safest way to assure that today's friends would not become tomorrow's betrayers was to humble any competing foreign power that might rival Rome's hegemony.

The demands of national security, as the Romans conceived it, lay behind their conquest of the Mediterranean. The expansion of Carthage northward through Sicily and later through the Spanish Peninsula in the direction of Italy caused that state's eventual destruction. Then the growth of Illyrian, Macedonian, and finally Asiatic powers across the Adriatic Sea attracted the attention of Roman senators and ended in the spread of Roman rule to those areas, together with loss of their autonomy. When each of these nations began to look as though it might constitute a threat to the latest perimeter of Rome's circle of friends, it had to be dealt with and itself become the newest segment of the outer ring.

Provincial Administration

The Latin word *provincia* means any duty assigned to a magistrate, and the Romans extended it to include the governing of the various regions that they had acquired through their conquests. They found governors for the earliest provinces simply by raising the number of praetors from two to four; the two new ones governed over Sicily and the combined province of Corsica and Sardinia. The same expedient was used in Spain. There were two Spanish provinces, Nearer and Farther Spain, and to provide governors for them two more praetors were created. Because of the distance from Spain to Italy and the importance of the Spanish provinces, these praetors were given a higher rank of imperium than the governors of Sicily and Corsica-Sardinia: they were called proconsuls (*pro consule*, "in place of a consul"), a title that the Romans used when they wanted to have an officer wield the powers of a consul even though he was not strictly one of the consuls for the year. Similar officials were used in other provinces.

Governors of provinces were appointed by the Senate. They ruled the provinces with absolute power, though they could not violate Roman law or act illegally against Roman citizens. Some provinces were well ruled, but others were notorious for their corrupt governors. From the Roman view the system was efficient: rebellions were not common, and troops stationed in the provinces did not resort to massacres to maintain control.

The provinces furnished the financial support for the Roman Republic. Some had to pay tribute in tithes of various kinds, usually food, while others were assigned a fixed sum. In order to obtain these taxes the state devised a convenient, but corruptible, system of tax collection. Companies of tax collectors bid for contracts to collect the taxes of certain provinces, especially Asia. They paid the state a fixed sum in advance and then tried to make their profit by collecting taxes in excess of what they had paid. The natives of the provinces were nearly helpless against the raids of the *publicani*, as tax collectors were called. Their only protection was the governor of the province, who was supposed to see that the *publicani* did not collect more than a reasonable amount. Unfortunately, however, sometimes the collectors could use their funds as bribes to persuade the governor to overlook their rapacity.[1]

Religion

Religion in Rome consisted largely in forms of worship that guaranteed obedience to established customs. This was true in both private and public worship. The father acted as the priest within the household and led the family in its worship of household gods—for example, Janus, the god of the doorway; Vesta, the spirit of the hearth; and other household spirits called Lares and Penates. The main concept underlying Roman religion was that some objects possessed divine power, or *numen*, which probably means "the power to influence things." For example, a boundary or terminal stone marking the edge of a family's property was sacred and had numen, perhaps because it supposedly had the power to deter intruders.

Nearly all Roman mythology was an adaptation of Greek legend, and Roman gods were often Greek deities with Roman names: the Greek father-god Zeus became Iuppiter, or Jupiter; Zeus's wife Hera became Juno; Athena became Minerva; Heracles became Hercules; and so on. These gods were the ones officially worshiped in public, though they might also be worshiped within the family along with the household deities. Perhaps because Greek myths often show gods behaving spitefully or immorally, the Romans also created other deities to personify certain uplifting ideas, such as Virtus (manly conduct), Pax (peace), Fides (loyalty), and Pudor (modesty).

The Romans showed their usual concern for order by creating several groups of priests, thus excluding the ordinary man from any connection with public worship. That does not mean that Romans took religion lightly; rather, they feared what might happen if the gods were not pleased with the sacrifices. Eventually their rites hardened into patterns whose original meaning was sometimes forgotten, but so long as the priests did not deviate from routine, the Romans assumed that the gods were satisfied and would not interfere in their enterprises.

Literature

As their conquests brought the Romans into contact with other civilizations, their cultural horizons widened immeasurably. The Greek literature that the Romans brought back with them from the East exerted a strong influence.

The real founder of literature written in the Latin language—the Roman Chaucer, as he has been called—was Quintus Ennius (239–169). His writings now survive only through quotations in other works. He was not a Roman (almost none of the more famous Latin authors were from Rome) but an Italian who lived near Tarentum. His most important original work was his *Annales*, a patriotic historical poem. Ennius was the first poet to translate into Latin the Greek tragedies, which were to influence the still immature Latin literature.

The influence of Greek comedy can be seen in the plays of Plautus (250?–184?) and Terence (190?–159?). Their works were based on the New Comedy of Menander and his contemporaries, for the Romans did not

---

[1] Cicero, a firm supporter of the *publicani*, called them "the flower of the Roman equestrians, the ornament of the state, and the foundation of the Republic."

approve of the Old Comedy of Aristophanes, which savagely lampooned active politicians. Plautus filled his comedies with stock situations such as mistaken identities, frustrated romances, and the like. One of his plays about mistaken identities, the *Menaechmi*, was used by Shakespeare as the model for his *Comedy of Errors*. Terence wrote comedy in a more refined and delicate style than did Plautus. His influence on later ages was strong, for he became the model for the comedy of manners of Molière and Sheridan.

One of the most dynamic poets of the Republic was Lucretius (94–55), whose masterpiece, *De rerum natura* (*On the Nature of the Universe*), reveals just how much Greek thought influenced Latin literature. His model was the Hellenistic philosopher Epicurus. Lucretius wanted to use his poetry to spread Epicurus' doctrine of tranquillity and withdrawal from the world. Although it did gain some converts, Epicureanism was less congenial to the Romans than were the more austere beliefs of Stoicism, which preached devotion to duty.

Catullus (84?–54?) wrote poetry of a more personal nature. It suggests the subjectivity and emotional qualities of the work of the Hellenistic poets in Alexandria. Many of Catullus' poems are addressed to his mistress, Clodia (whom he calls Lesbia), a flagrantly promiscuous woman. Their affair burned fiercely, as some poems show, but finally turned to disillusion and hate. Catullus also experimented with miniature epic poems in the Alexandrian fashion, and he was capable of a solemn grief, as he demonstrates in a sorrowful poem that he composed at his brother's grave in Asia Minor. In all his works Catullus displays his feelings with a frankness that was rare in a society where external dignity and self-discipline were considered the main social virtues.

The Greek Polybius (200?–120?), though not a Latin writer, deserves a place here as a historian of the Roman Republic. Along with several other prominent Greeks Polybius was deported to Rome as a hostage in the 160s; there he met many Roman statesmen and became an expert in Roman history. He wrote a general history of the Greco-Roman world from the first Punic War down to his own times, largely to demonstrate the inevitable domination of the Mediterranean by the Romans. He is the only surviving source for some of the wars of Greece and Rome.

Polybius believed that much of Rome's success in government was due to her well-designed constitution, an example of the commendable mixed form of state that would probably preserve Rome despite the difficulties of maintaining any constitution. Polybius traveled widely and insisted on the need to visit sites in order to grasp the importance of geography to history. His work is therefore professional and methodical, though often pedantic. He is both the most important Hellenistic historian and the most reliable guide to earlier Roman history.

Marcus Tullius Cicero (106–43) was the most versatile Latin writer of his time. His polished prose style became the model for clarity and elegance. At the same time his orations, essays, and letters are among the best sources for the political history of the later Republic. Cicero's philosophical treatises do not follow the doctrines of any particular philosophic school; he was equally interested in Stoicism, the thought of Plato, and several other methods, and he chose whatever seemed persuasive from Greek models for his own theories. In *On the Republic*, for example, he accepted the Platonic view that wise leaders ought to govern the state, but disregarded the more technical points in Plato's philosophical system.

Cicero's political speeches are a continuous record of his career and his frustrated ambitions. He was the first of his family to attain the consulship and therefore ranked as a "new man." He enjoyed his political success and sought a place for himself among the upper classes, believing that they should guide the state along established constitutional lines. Unfortunately, most members of the governing class in the later Republic were willing to be tempted away from their normal allegiance to the constitution and selfishly followed their own personal advantage. Cicero never became a magnetic leader around whom others gathered. His letters are a frank and often painful record of the compromises that he was forced to make in the treacherous world of Roman politics.

III. THE ROMAN REVOLUTION

By 133 the Roman state was rich, proud, and powerful, but its expansion had created power blocs or pressure groups whose authority might threaten the senatorial government. New wealth had given rise to a class of influential men who owned large estates, and this wealth threatened to unbalance the traditional economy. The need for armies to control the provinces offered an opportunity for generals to use their loyal troops against the state itself. Individuals and groups began to intrigue for their own power. Under these strains the senatorial government began to give way, and from 133 to 31 Rome went through a violent but surprisingly slow revolution. This upheaval destroyed the Republic and cleared a path for the Roman Empire.

THE CHANGING WORLD OF ITALY

The breakdown of the Roman Republic has been called Hannibal's legacy, and there is some truth in the epigram. A century of successful warfare saw Carthage destroyed and Rome became the ruler of the Greek-speaking Hellen-

ANCIENT AND MODERN MORTALITY COMPARED

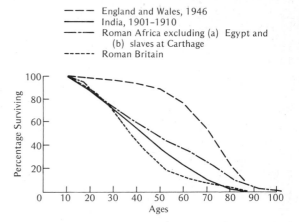

The graph shows the percentages of males alive at the age of 10 who remain alive at successive ages up to the age of 100 (alleged). (From Born, A. R., "Hic breve vivitur," Past and Present, 4, 1953)

istic world; but the ravages of years of fighting up and down Italy, and long periods of military service at home and abroad, had impoverished the Italian peasantry, bringing great numbers of them to ruin. After the second Punic War, pacification of the new province of Spain meant more long terms of service abroad and therefore more time away from the farm. Ironically, Rome's great successes in the East made matters worse, for the booty brought back by some of the Roman legionaries and their generals was to have a catastrophic effect on economic and social conditions in the peninsula. Disruption of the socioeconomic structure of Italy eventually created turmoil in the Forum, which ended only when the institutions of the Republic gave way to an imperial autocracy.

The flood of new wealth from the East, the result of war-profiteering, was, of course, unevenly distributed. Wealthy citizens into whose hands came booty and the spoils of war had not only the capital, but a market in which to invest it. Land was plentiful and cheap.

The less fortunate, who lacked the cash to maintain their farms, lost either possession or ownership of them, often unwillingly. The enormous increase of the slave population on Italian soil, prisoners of war from the East who came into the peninsula by the tens of thousands, decreased demand for the poor farmer's labor and depressed wages when he did manage to find work. Often the displaced farmers had little choice but to join the ranks of the permanently unemployed.

New conditions of farming also made it difficult for the small farmer to survive. The market in one important product, wine, was now expanding. This crop demands a heavy outlay for pressing machinery and periodic replacement of stocks. Even the cheapest wines cannot be put on the market at once; thus wine growing requires capital that can be invested for some years. It is not an occupation for a poor man, unless he is backed by a cooperative movement or a political party. The wealthy had both the opportunity and a market. Posidonius, who was born about 135, wrote from personal knowledge that Gauls were prepared to trade a slave for a jar of wine and that the slave was likely to become a unit in the production of many more jars. Archaeological evidence is even more convincing. Ancient inhabitants of hill forts in Provence and Languedoc strewed their area with so many broken wine jars that the fragments impede cultivation even today.

STRAINS ON THE CONSTITUTION

For some years before 133 the small farmers displaced by large landowners had added to the economic problems of the state, and the decline in their fortunes threatened to impede the recruitment of soldiers into the Roman army. Rome had nothing like a modern war treasury, and only men who had enough money to arm themselves could be drafted into the legions.

Without sufficient recruits, the gains of imperialism might be lost.

About 136 a revolt among the slaves in the province of Sicily dramatically emphasized the need for a strong army. The revolt directly threatened a part of the Roman food supply since grain was imported from Sicily. Thus in the late 130s two crises faced Rome: a decline in military manpower and the possibility of a serious grain shortage.

Tiberius and Gaius Gracchus

Two ambitious young Roman aristocrats, Tiberius and Gaius Gracchus, moved to solve these problems. Tiberius, the older brother, became tribune for 133 and proposed a land bill to the Tribal Assembly that would allow the state to assign parcels of public land, reclaimed from the wealthy, to dispossessed farmers, with the double aim of increasing both the supply of potential recruits for the army and his own political support. The bill was opposed by another tribune, who tried to veto it on behalf of vested interests. Tiberius persuaded the people to remove this tribune, and the bill was passed.

The distribution of land was in progress when Tiberius decided to run for reelection. This was a breach of custom, for tribunes held office for only one year. Some of his opponents feared that he might seize permanent leadership of the propertyless as a demagogue. A group of senators, late in 133, took the law into their own hands, raised a gang of thugs, and hunted Tiberius down. He was clubbed to death in a riot. His death gave grim warning of a new intensity in the political struggle. Above all, the taboo against assassination had been violated and this first step, once taken, became easier to repeat. Despite Tiberius' death, the distribution of land continued, and his enemies even took credit for the success of the project.

Gaius Gracchus became tribune ten years

later, in 123. He authored several measures with a common theme, mainly limiting the prerogatives of the Senate. One of the most important concerned the extortion court, which investigated cases of alleged extortion by provincial governors and tax collectors. The jurors, all senators, were usually not severe in judging governors, who were fellow members of the Senate. Gaius had a bill passed that assigned the seats on this jury to members of the equestrian class (*equites:* the common translation "knights" is misleading). Equestrians were wealthy nonsenatorials: tax collectors, builders of roads, entrepreneurs of all kinds, and owners of land. One might hesitantly call them a middle class because they stood between the working masses and the Senate.

All tax collectors were equestrians, and when Gaius Gracchus placed them on the jury of the extortion court, they gained the power to protect members of their group who might be denounced and brought to trial. Provincial governors now feared unfavorable decisions handed down by equestrian jurors. Gaius' arrangements were later revised, but he was the first to make the extortion court the subject of a bitter political quarrel. Since money and politics were as deeply entwined in Rome as they are in America, Gaius' concessions to these wealthy nonsenatorials may not have been entirely disinterested, especially in a society where favors always created obligations.

To further his brother's program of relocating farmers on the land, Gaius also sponsored the founding of several colonies. The choice of one of them—near the site of the hated Carthage, which only about twenty years earlier had been destroyed in the third Punic War—exposed him to criticism and seriously weakened his standing with the masses. He also proposed that Roman citizenship be offered to large numbers of people in rural districts who were not yet Roman citizens. They had been asking for this status to protect themselves against having their land confiscated for distribution to those whom the Romans were resettling. But the voters of Rome, warned by Gaius' opponents that they would be sharing their privileges with outsiders, refused to extend their citizenship.

Like his brother, Gaius Gracchus came to a violent end. After he left office his enemies asserted that he was planning a revolution. The Senate then instructed one of the consuls for the year 121 to "see to it that the state suffered no harm," thus inviting the consul to use force to suppress the younger Gracchus. When the consul raised an armed force to hunt him down, Gaius, at his own instructions, was killed by one of his slaves.

The Gracchi had tried to adapt Roman procedure to new social and economic realities. When he began to lose support, Gaius turned to new political groups—Italians who lacked Roman citizenship and equestrians who now stood against senators through their control of the extortion court. Above all, the Gracchi had unleashed a force whose working could not easily be controlled when they invited the Tribal Assembly to take a more activist role. It is true that the people had long possessed the right to legislate in the Tribal Assembly, but they had not always had the will; nor had ambitious tribunes always dared to use this weapon. The Gracchi greatly increased the activity of the assembly. From this moment began the slow but sure Roman revolution.

Marius and the Roman Army

The Gracchi could not protect themselves from the violence of the Senate because they had no army. But as Roman imperialism brought the state into further wars, powerful generals appeared who did have the support of their armies. And they used their military power to fulfill their political aims. The first such general was Gaius Marius (157?–86), a "new man" from the country near Rome. He is important because he changed, radically and forever, the composition of the Roman army and the nature of its loyalties.

With the support of a powerful family, the Metelli, Marius made his way upward in politics until he reached the consulship in 107. At this time Rome was involved in war with the African king Jugurtha; the historian Sallust has left us a narrative of this conflict. As soon as Marius became consul he persuaded the Tribal Assembly to hand over to him the conduct of the war. In doing so the assembly was encroaching upon the power of the Senate, which customarily appointed military commanders and designated their *provincia*, or sphere of activity.

When Marius ended the war in 105, his victory seemed to many people proof that the Senate was no longer the bulwark of the state as it had been in the Punic Wars. His prestige grew even more after he drove back an attempted invasion of Italy by some Germanic tribes from the north.

In order to raise large numbers of men for these German wars, Marius abolished the old requirement that a soldier must own at least a modest amount of property, and he also accepted volunteers instead of just drafting men for service. As a result, the army came to be composed largely of poor men who served their commander, received booty from him, relied on him as their main patron, and expected him to obtain a grant of land for them when they were discharged. Thus Marius became involved with the problem of displaced farmers that the Gracchi had addressed. He may not have foreseen the political results of his action, but he converted the army into an instrument for ambitious commanders down through the Republic and indeed throughout the history of the Roman Empire.

The War with the Italians

In the 90s the dispute over citizenship for the allies of Rome came to a head. The attitude of the Senate convinced these people that only military rebellion would gain them the right of citizenship, which brought with it the privileges of voting and holding office. In 91 some Italian tribes proclaimed themselves independent and opened a guerrilla war that lasted until 88. In the end the Romans negotiated with the Italians and allowed them to acquire citizenship. But the fact that it required a war to obtain this concession shows that both the upper classes—the senators and equestrians—and the common people as well were still jealous of their privileges.[2]

Senatorial Reaction Under Sulla

The Italian War helped make the reputation of another powerful general, Lucius Cornelius Sulla. In the 80s civil war broke out in Rome between various factions of senators. One group rallied behind Sulla and his legions, seeing him the best vehicle for their own ambitions. Sulla's supporters finally prevailed when he landed in Italy after a campaign in Greece; his troops marched with him against Rome herself, which was held by his enemies. It is doubtful they would have done so a generation earlier. Such was the legacy of agrarian discontent and the military reforms of Marius. Late in 82 he entered the city as her conqueror. He killed hundreds of his opponents and had himself named dictator, suspending the customary six-month time limit for that office.

Sulla reshaped the state on apparently conservative principles. Two forces, he thought, menaced the rigid control of the Senate: the tribunes of the people, who made the Tribal

---

[2] Historians have compared the Italian War to the war between the American states, 1861–1865. Each war finally decided whether the nation was to split apart or remain united.

Assembly more conscious of its power, and the strong generals who used the loyalty of their armies to gain political leverage. To deal with the first of these threats, Sulla passed a law forbidding tribunes to offer legislation without prior approval from the Senate, a clear historical rebuke to Tiberius Gracchus. Another law prevented tribunes from ever holding another office, a stratagem that was designed to make the office of tribune unattractive to young men with political ambitions.

Sulla handled the army commanders by restricting their service as governor of a province to a period of one year. This scheme neatly assured that no commander would remain on the scene long enough to become a familiar hero to his troops and possibly the leader of a new march on Rome. It would appear that there were to be no Sullas after Sulla.

Among Sulla's other reforms the most important was his restructuring of the jury system. He canceled the legislation of Gaius Gracchus, who had put juries in the hands of equestrians, and restricted seats on the juries to senators. There were now seven permanent courts dealing with various offenses. To provide enough jurors for them, and perhaps to reward some of his loyal followers, Sulla raised the membership of the Senate to about 600.

Sulla completed this far-reaching legislation, which remained largely in force until the end of the Republic, and then in 79 resigned the dictatorship, a rare act in any supreme ruler. To his enemies he was ruthless, but he was also a clever political strategist. He had bolstered the power of his Senate, but events soon exposed its real weakness, as it proved unable to manage generals who commanded Roman armies. More and more, such generals manipulated their forces so as to dominate the civilian government.

The Rise of Pompey

The new military potentate after Sulla was Pompey. He had his first opportunity to gain a reputation in 77, when he was sent to Spain with instructions to end a revolt there. After completing this task and while his army was still intact, he helped to suppress a rebellion of slaves in Italy led by the famous Thracian slave Spartacus. This campaign was already in the hands of another ambitious Roman, Marcus Licinius Crassus, the richest man of his time. No sooner was the slave revolt crushed in 71 than the joint commanders, Pompey and Crassus, marched their armies to the gates of Rome and demanded both consulships for the year 70. Pompey was legally unqualified for this office, for he was only thirty-six and had never held any previous magistracy. The Senate, however, had not the will to resist the two men, and they were elected consuls.

During their consulship Pompey and Crassus canceled several other of Sulla's arrangements. They restored to the tribunes their right to propose legislation, and they mixed senators and equestrians in the always controversial juries. At the end of their year in office both consuls retired without demanding any further appointment. This action, at first surprising, was really consistent with Pompey's ambitions. He wanted a position of the first rank in the state, but he disliked committing himself to open revolution. A modern historian has said of him that he would not play false and yet would wrongly win.

Pompey was given an extraordinary command in 67 to deal with pirates operating in the Mediterranean who were interfering with the grain supply for Rome. In a swift campaign he cleared the seas of pirates. The following year he received an even more important command in the East, where Rome by now

A first-century B.C. *wall painting from the cubiculum of the Villa at Boscoreale, a town in southern Italy.* (Photo: Metropolitan Museum of Art, Rogers Fund, 1903)

had several territories. The province of Cilicia had been organized as early as 102, and that of Bithynia in 74, when the king of that region willed his country to Rome (in the same way the king of Cyrene had done in 96). Pompey was now assigned the provinces of Bithynia and Cilicia, where the current governor was involved in a war with Mithridates, a powerful local king. Cynical political considerations played a part in getting Pompey this large new command. The previous governor, Lucullus, had tried to protect the helpless provincials from the tax collectors and had drastically lowered the amount the equestrian tax collectors could collect. Therefore the equestrian class, representing their own financial interests, demanded the governor's removal and his replacement by Pompey.

Pompey successfully fought the difficult war in Asia Minor and established a secure base for Roman interests there. He annexed the province of Syria in 64–63; he enlarged Cilicia; and he extended Bithynia so that it included part of the kingdom of Pontus. Around these provinces he created a system of client kings, rulers of smaller states whose loyalty to Rome was assured by the familiar device of *amicitia*. For some time this group of kingdoms, to the east of the province of Asia, offered an effective solution to threats on the eastern front.

Cicero and Catiline

During Pompey's absence overseas Cicero became a potent statesman in Rome. His superb oratorical style and his administrative skill won him each successive political office at the earliest possible legal age. He was genuinely dedicated to compromise and political negotiation and thought that such procedures would establish a rule of the two upper classes, senatorial and equestrian. This potential system he often called *concordia ordinum*—harmony within the ranks. But other, less scrupulous men believed that while orators debated, the sword might decide the issue.

One such renegade was a fiery patrician of undoubted courage, Lucius Sergius Catilina, usually called Catiline. He had gone heavily into debt through extravagance, and in 63 he formed a conspiracy to murder the consuls, seize the state, and pass laws to abolish debts. Cicero, one of the consuls that year, easily frustrated the plot.[3] He hoped that this success would enable him to form a circle of eminent men, including the powerful Pompey, who would be dedicated to traditional, lawful government. Past problems and future events would prove his hope vain.

The First Triumvirate

When Pompey returned to Rome from his Eastern victories, he found some influential members in the Senate resentful of his prestige. Many feared that he might use his huge army to become a second Sulla but might not step aside as Sulla had finally done. Pompey actually had two aims. He wanted the Senate to ratify the arrangements he had made in Asia Minor and to bestow a grant of land on his men. But his enemies in the Senate combined to frustrate both these wishes.

The returning governor of Spain, Gaius Julius Caesar (100–44), also had enemies within the Senate. Caesar's political expenses had placed him heavily in debt to the wealthy Crassus, who had served as consul with Pompey in 70. To solve his financial problems, Caesar hoped to win the consulship for 59 and then obtain another provincial command, which would provide enough income to pay off his debts. A small faction in the Senate looked on Caesar as a brash upstart. First they refused him the honor of a triumphal parade through Rome on his return from Spain. Then they tried to block his plans to secure a major provincial command after his consulship of 59.

---

[3] Cicero tells his version of the suppression of the conspiracy in his four orations *In Catilinam (Against Catiline);* see also Sallust's *War with Catiline.*

Faced with this obvious affront to his dignity, Caesar made a political bargain with Pompey and Crassus, who was also at odds with some powerful senators over a financial matter. The three formed a coalition known to modern historians as the First Triumvirate, and their united influence at the polls elected Caesar as one of the consuls for 59.

Caesar's Consulship and the Gallic War

Pompey's aims were met after Caesar himself introduced a bill in the Tribal Assembly that would provide allotments of land for his army; a tribune then offered another bill ratifying Pompey's arrangements in the East. Both bills were passed by the Tribal Assembly, which supported the triumvirate against such opposition as the Senate could put forth. Crassus' financial quarrel was also settled to his satisfaction. Lastly, Caesar, looking to his own future command, arranged to have a bill passed that gave him the command over Cisalpine Gaul (the Po valley) and the coast of Illyria (Albania and Yugoslavia) for a guaranteed period of five years beginning on March 1, 59. About this time the governor of Transalpine Gaul (Provence, in the south of France) died, and Caesar also acquired this province within his command.

Caesar actively sought opportunities to extend Roman rule outside the borders of the province. He intervened in the politics of the Gallic tribes and opened a series of campaigns that finally brought the whole area of modern France and Belgium under Roman rule, implanting there the Latin language and Roman culture. Caesar narrates his actions and justifies his motives in his *Commentaries on the Gallic War*. To this day the book remains a superb textbook in political-military decision making.

The Gallic War lasted from 58 to 50. Caesar's two partners in the triumvirate, Pompey and Crassus, were always suspicious of each other, but they did maintain fairly good rela-

tions and even held a second consulship together in 55. At Caesar's wish, they had his command in Gaul renewed for another five years, so that it would not expire until March 1, 49.[4] Through the Tribal Assembly Pompey and Crassus also took on commands for themselves. Crassus became proconsul of Syria and fought against the Parthian kingdom on the Syrian frontier, where he was killed in 53. Pompey was given command over the two provinces of Spain, which he governed through assistants (legates), preferring to remain near Rome and thus at the center of power.

The Break Between Caesar and the Senate

Caesar's enemies in the Senate feared that he might use his victories in Gaul to make himself more powerful in Rome. His preeminence and opportunism made such a fear reasonable. As protection against Caesar these senators began to draw Pompey into their camp. Some of them had quarreled with him in the past, but they were willing to gamble that he could be dispensed with when the time was ripe. "Divide and conquer" was a Roman maxim that did not apply to foreign affairs only.

Caesar planned to return to Rome in 49 after his command in Gaul ended. He would seek the consulship in 48 and then would probably accept another command such as the one Crassus had had in the East. Neither Caesar nor any other Roman politician was thinking of staging a revolution. Yet Caesar would not shrink from revolution if his personal position was at stake.

As 49 opened, the Senate met in a state of near hysteria. Caesar's enemies were seeking some way to strip him of his command in Gaul even before it expired. Some cooler heads proposed that both Caesar and Pompey should end the tension by resigning their commands at the

---

[4] The exact date on which Caesar's command was to expire is still a controversial question. March 1, 49 seems to accord best with the ancient evidence.

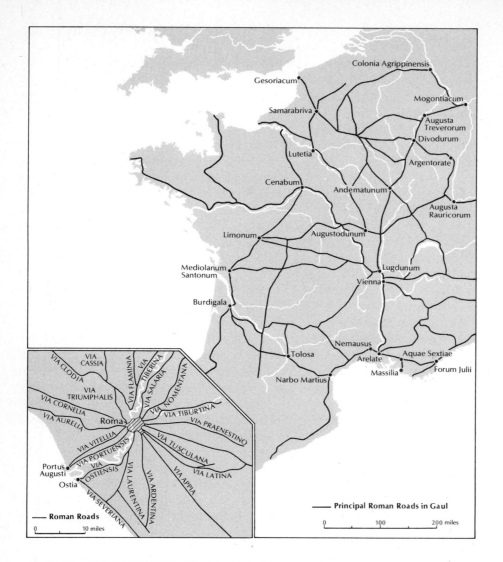

MAP 4.3: THE NETWORK OF ROMAN ROADS (A) FROM THE CITY AND (B) IN GAUL

(From Chevallier, Raymond, "Roman Roads," University of California Press, 1976)

same time. Caesar would have agreed to this, but the small band of implacable senators forced through a motion ordering him to lay down his command, even though he was then taking no action beyond remaining in his province of Cisalpine Gaul. The Senate passed a decree establishing martial law and ordering Pompey to command the armies of the state against Caesar. Finally, they threatened the lives of any tribunes who tried to oppose these extreme measures, thus handing Caesar a superb subject for propaganda: he could claim that he was defending the prerogatives of the tribunes, the common people of Rome, and the men in his army.

Caesar's Invasion of Italy

While some hot-blooded senators were driving Rome nearer to civil war, Caesar was stationed in his province just across the Rubicon River, a tiny stream that divided Italy from Cisalpine Gaul. Learning that his enemies were challenging him to war, he decided that he had no course but to fight for his dignity and, as he could now claim, for the rights of the people and their sacred tribunes. On about January 11, 49, he invaded his own country at the head of Roman legions.

Caesar's own men supported him loyally, and as he moved southward through Italy more and more people joined his cause. Pompey and his followers retreated to Greece; Caesar pursued them and won a decisive battle at the town of Pharsalus in Thessaly. Pompey tried to find refuge in Egypt, but as he stepped on shore he was murdered by renegades who realized that Caesar had been victorious. Caesar himself reached Egypt, where he met the shrewd Macedonian queen, Cleopatra. No one has ever been certain whether he actually fathered a son by her, but he did spend several months with her in Alexandria. He then returned to battle and after other victories in Africa and Spain he returned to Rome in 46.

Caesar's Rule

Caesar assumed the position of dictator and consul. On the model of Sulla he extended his dictatorship beyond the legal six-month limit; then, in 44, he had himself named dictator for life. All restraints on his power that Roman tradition might have imposed were swept aside. He had complete authority to pass laws, declare war, and appoint men to office.

As dictator, Caesar passed a series of rapid reforms in many areas of Roman life. To reward his followers with public office he raised the number of praetors and quaestors. Along with this expansion went a dramatic increase in the size of the Senate; he raised the membership to about 900. Many of Caesar's veteran officers became members of this body, assuring Caesar a rubber stamp for anything he wanted. Loyalty and discreet service in the Senate might bring important provincial commands, and we may be sure that few senators dared to challenge the dictator's wishes. From this time onward the Senate rapidly lost its former authority as the bulwark of the state. Caesar also divided all Italy into municipal areas, probably for the sake of greater administrative efficiency; he gave each town control over the surrounding countryside.

Caesar settled many of his soldiers in colonies throughout the Roman provinces, especially Spain, Transalpine Gaul, and northern Africa. He also extended Roman citizenship into some of the provinces. His most lasting reform, however, was one by which we still regulate our lives—the establishment of a calendar based on the old Egyptian reckoning of 365 days, with one day added every fourth year (this was done simply by observing February 24 twice; the modern February 29 was unknown to the Romans). This Julian calendar lasted until 1582; it was then revised by Pope Gregory XIII to our present Gregorian calendar.

The Death of Caesar

The full effect of Caesar's plans was not to be realized, for on March 15, 44, after four years of supremacy, he fell to the daggers of conspirators led by two of his lieutenants, Marcus Brutus and Gaius Cassius. His autocracy had been a grave affront to the upper class; they still wanted the chance to win political leadership rather than be appointed by a high and mighty ruler. Because they were being denied these traditional rights of Roman aristocrats, they turned against Caesar and committed the

The Roman aqueduct at Segovia in Spain (first century A.D.*), nearly 100 feet at its highest point, impressively combines strength, elegance, and utility. It still carries the city's water supply.* (Photo: Editorial Photocolor Archives)

most famous political assassination of ancient times.

Caesar's career was controversial and baffling, even to his contemporaries. He was pitiless toward Gauls and Germans, and he enriched himself by selling prisoners of war as slaves. In Rome he showed too little desire to revive Republican forms once he became dictator, and for this he paid with his life. On the other hand, he often forgave his enemies: in the civil war he dismissed opposing generals whom he had captured, and they lived to fight him another day. Such actions may have rested on cool calculation of their value as propaganda, but they may also show genuine gallantry. No one can question Caesar's fiery leadership. His troops followed him into Italy with enthusiasm and fought with amazing discipline.

Caesar left no memoirs of his later years, and it is difficult to know what he would have done to the Roman system if he had lived to carry out all his plans. He evidently thought that the old institutions of the Senate and the assemblies had lost their political potency. "The Republic," he is said to have remarked, "is only a name without body or face, and Sulla did not know the ABCs of politics in resigning his dictatorship." The political weakness of the late Republic largely confirms this harsh evaluation. In the end, the experienced politicians whom Caesar needed in his administration were not prepared to accept his verdict; but history was shortly to prove him right and them wrong.

There has been much modern discussion about one possible aim of Caesar—to return Rome to monarchy and make himself a semi-divine ruler. The historians who support this view point to his acquaintance with Hellenistic monarchies (Cleopatra's, in Egypt, survived his death) and argue that he would have imposed some such system in Rome; Caesar is shown wearing a diadem on some coins, and a monarchy would indeed have been the final logical step beyond his perpetual dictatorship. On balance, the evidence does not seem strong enough to prove that he had such a plan, at least at the moment of his death. Later rulers of Rome did install a cult of the Emperor and were converted into gods after they died—and Caesar's adopted son did much to further this kind of propaganda by calling Caesar the "divine Julius" almost at once.

IV. THE FOUNDING OF THE ROMAN EMPIRE

After Caesar's death there remained some in Rome who hoped for a return to the old system of competitive elections and government by ancient tradition. However, this was not to be; the slide toward dictatorship could not be stopped, and the result was the founding of an enduring autocracy by Caesar's adopted son.

THE VICTORY OF AUGUSTUS

For several decades the structure of the Republic had been dissolving as generals, beginning with Marius, used their armies as private instruments of power. The emperor Augustus was the last and most successful of these generals. Almost the entire military force of the state became his private army, making him even more potent than Caesar.

The Second Triumvirate

Brutus, Cassius, and the other liberators imagined that republican government could be restored with Caesar out of the way. Yet partisans of Caesar commanded armies throughout the Roman world. The removal of their leader still left them in charge, and they were not men who would meekly surrender their powers to the Senate. One such man was Marcus Antonius, or Mark Antony, a follower of Caesar and consul for the year 44. He managed to maintain his position, for the liberators had not had the foresight to remove him as well. Antony tried to seize for himself the provincial command in Cisalpine Gaul, even though the Senate had already assigned it to another governor for the year 43. When Antony tried to take over this province and drive out its duly appointed commander, the Senate turned on him with the now senior statesman Cicero leading the attack.

Among the commanders whom the Senate put in action against Antony was a young man of nineteen—Caesar's grandnephew and adopted son. His name, originally Gaius Octavius, became Gaius Julius Caesar Octavianus upon his adoption; modern historians call him Octavian, but he called himself Caesar. He used his name skillfully to win a following among Caesar's former soldiers, but he also played the part of

Gaius Octavius, granted the title "Augustus" by the Senate, is portrayed as ruler in this idealized statue. (Photo: Vatican Museum)

they marched on Rome. The Senate had to acknowledge their leadership, and a tribune proposed a law that turned the state over to their control for a period of five years; their official duties were "to provide order for the state"—a charge broad enough to provide a legal basis for nearly any action they might wish to take. In due course their power was renewed for another five years.

Brutus and Cassius, seeing that they did not have popular support, went to the East and managed to gain control of the provinces of Syria and Macedonia. But within a year the triumvirs eliminated these enemies at the Battle of Philippi in northern Greece. To reward their troops with land, the rulers had already marked out the territory of no fewer than eighteen prosperous towns in Italy. The rule of the Second Triumvirate was thus made secure by the seizure and redistribution of property. Further security was provided by a series of "trials" against those who had the bad luck to be on the losing side. Now, as in the time of Sulla, autocrats brushed aside the traditional guarantees of Roman law as they coldly purged their enemies. One of those killed without trial was Cicero.

Tension and suspicion now began to grow between the two major partners, Antony and Octavian (Lepidus had been forced into retirement when he tried to take control of ·Sicily away from Octavian). Antony did his own cause grave harm by remaining in the East for long periods, fighting the Parthian kingdom,· which had taken certain Roman territories after the death of Crassus in 53. The basic cause of enmity between Antony and Octavian was the lust for supreme power. The publicly announced issue, which Octavian skillfully exploited as propaganda, was Antony's romance with Cleopatra. The relationship had distinct political overtones. Cleopatra had the resources to support Antony's Parthian War; in return she wanted to extend the boundaries of

a discreet young supporter of the Senate in its battle against Antony. Cicero, one of the chief supporters of the old constitution, wrote of Octavian after their first meeting, "The young man is completely dedicated to me."

Octavian and Antony realized that the Senate was committed to the destruction of the Caesarian faction upon whom both depended for their political support. Therefore, in 43, they joined with a lesser commander, Lepidus, and formed a political partnership known as the Second Triumvirate. With their armies

her kingdom northward along the coast of Palestine.

The final break between the two men came in 32. By this time Octavian had secured control of all the western provinces and felt strong enough to challenge Antony in the field. Octavian and his supporters denounced Antony for having granted to Cleopatra and her children (he was the father of two of her sons) certain eastern territories belonging to Rome. Octavian raised a large force from Italy and the western provinces; his allies included many people who had been encouraged to fear an eastern domination of Rome. Some 300 opponents of Octavian out of a Senate now swollen to about 1,000 fled to the East to join Antony's side. Octavian's forces won the only battle, fought in 31 at Actium, a promontory on the western coast of Greece. Cleopatra withdrew to Egypt and Antony followed her, his army surrendering to Octavian's.

The next year Octavian unhurriedly advanced on Alexandria for the reckoning with Antony and Cleopatra. Antony took his own life, and Cleopatra was left to confront Octavian. She scorned to decorate a triumphal parade in Rome as his captive and killed herself—according to one famous account, by pressing a poisonous asp to her breast. With her ended the last Macedonian kingdom and, therefore, the Hellenistic Age.

The Rule of Augustus

When Octavian returned to Rome in 29 from his conquest of Egypt, his supremacy was beyond challenge. He was the leader of a huge army commanded by loyal generals, and for several years he had been consul with a dedicated political following. The issue now was whether he would solve the problem that had defeated Caesar: how to rule without seeming to be an autocrat. He achieved this by restoring the appearance—but no more—of Republi-

can government. Candidates ran for office, but only when he designated them; a willing Senate executed only the policies that he favored. Republican structures remained intact, but they were staffed by loyal adherents. He also avoided any offensive displays of authority. At no time did he announce that he was converting the Republic into an empire. Therefore historians can find no official beginning for the Roman Empire; the best date is probably 27 B.C., for in that year Octavian laid the foundations of his system.

In 27 Octavian assumed control of an enormous provincial command, including Farther Spain, Gaul (the regions newly conquered by Caesar, not the old province of Transalpine Gaul), and Syria. Most of the legions were concentrated in these provinces; thus Octavian was the legal commander of an unrivaled military force. He ruled his provinces through assistants, or legates, as Pompey had ruled his Spanish command. Egypt was handled in a special manner; it was treated as a private possession of Octavian and governed by an equestrian appointee who merely directed the governmental machinery that the Ptolemies had set up.

Along with this command the Senate conferred on Octavian the name Augustus, meaning "blessed" or "fortunate." This title brought with it no powers, but its semidivine overtones were useful to Augustus in establishing his eminence. In 23 he received two additional powers from the Senate. His imperium (the word means power of command) was extended to cover not only his former provinces but the whole Roman world. He also obtained the authority of a tribune (*tribunicia potestas*). As a patrician (by his adoption into Caesar's family), Augustus could not actually be a tribune. Yet his having the power of a tribune suggested that Augustus was the patron and defender of the common people of Rome.

Augustus' control really rested on his *auc-*

This superb onyx cameo (carved about A.D. 1) commemorates a Triumph accorded Tiberius for victories over the Germans. Tiberius steps down from his chariot (top left) into the presence of The Emperor Augustus and of a personification of Rome; below, warriors with trophies and prisoners. (Photo: Alinari-Art Reference Bureau)

toritas—that indefinable quality of authority that makes it unnecessary for the ruler to murder his critics. Augustus' rule was absolute, and all candidates who were elected to office had received his approval. No tribunes inflamed the assembly, though they were still elected; and few proconsuls showed indiscretion. He was usually called the *princeps*, an old Republican title denoting the senior ex-consul in the Senate, who had the right to speak first in the carefully controlled senatorial debates. Modern writers ofter refer to the system of Augustus as the Principate.

The long reign of Augustus from 27 B.C. to

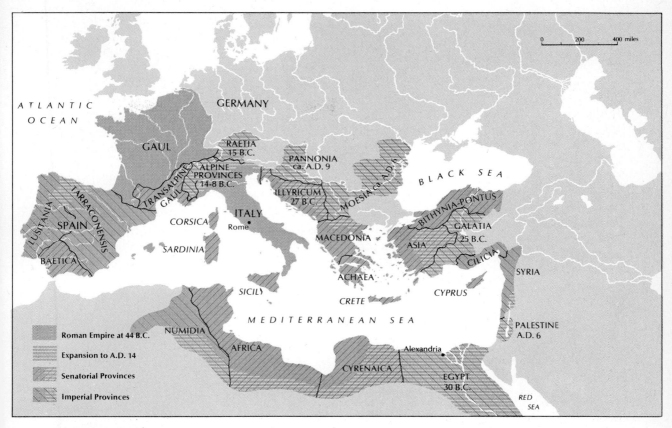

MAP 4.4: THE ROMAN EMPIRE A.D. 14

A.D. 14 established many abiding features of the autocracy. He provided a cash payment from the public treasury to soldiers who had served for twenty years, thus securing the loyalty of the legions to the state, not to their generals. He also gave security to the Empire by extending and solidifying the northern frontier (see Map 4.4). The provinces north of Italy now reached as far as the Rhine and Danube rivers.

Augustus also created a force of soldiers known as the Praetorian Guard, which was stationed in Rome. This group of some 9,000 men was recruited from Italians (no provincials, even if citizens, could serve in it under Augustus) and received higher pay than the soldiers in legions. The guard served as the city's police force and as Augustus' personal bodyguard, but after a few decades it came to play a crucial, and violent, role in the designation of new emperors.

Augustus assumed the office of Pontifex Maximus, or high priest, and made attempts to revive the old Roman religion, probably as a device promoting political stability. He also grasped the possibilities of ruler-cult. First he assigned Julius Caesar a place among the Roman gods and built a Temple to the Deified Julius. He also called himself "Divi Filius," or son of the divine one, though he was only the adopted son of Caesar. This verbal trick invited people to imagine that Augustus, though not strictly divine, might some day become so. Vergil and Horace, who were practically court poets, discreetly referred to Augustus as a future deity. He also sponsored the building of temples to "Rome and Augustus"—a further suggestion, though not an offensive demand, that the Emperor should be worshiped. It became customary to make an offering to the Genius (protecting spirit) of the Emperor. In the eastern parts of the Empire the line between man and deity had long been blurred, and the institution of ruler-cult developed more quickly in such regions.

Part of the religious revival was the rebuilding of scores of temples; but temples were by no means the only Augustan buildings; a famous saying tells us that "he found Rome made of brick and left it made of marble." The prosperity of the later years of Augustus' rule reflects the general peace that he brought to the Roman world. Freed of the expense of wars, Rome enjoyed a confidence that expressed itself in cultural creativity, which will be discussed in the next chapter.

Augustus died in A.D. 14. Through his careful control of the army and magistrates, he had given Rome three decades of healing after the civil wars. Rome did not relapse into civil war after Augustus' death. The Empire he designed and guided in its formative years lasted for two centuries in much the same condition as it had been at his death. For centuries more it survived as the Byzantine Empire in the East, and it was the ancestor of the Holy Roman Empire in the West.

The development of Rome from a village south of the Tiber River into an imperial state follows a course marked by political discipline. No Greek city-state showed such perseverance once a policy was determined. Why did Rome become the empire builder? One answer is the large reserves of manpower that enabled the Romans to overcome Carthage. Another answer, perhaps more abstract, is the rigorous character of the Roman people. In daily life the word of the father was law. In the state the power of the Senate to direct public affairs was unquestioned for many decades. This authoritarian view of life was reinforced by Roman religion, a group of cults with only one fixed doctrine: conservative obedience to established customs.

As Rome extended her power a wealthy aristocracy, composed of both patricians and plebeians, absorbed the small holdings of peasants. The brothers Gracchus tried to restore displaced farmers to their lands, but another use was finally made of this manpower when poor men were admitted to the Roman legions.

Generals became warlords and troops became their followers. The prizes of supremacy became more valuable. Julius Caesar played for absolute control and won the contest. It is far from certain that he set out to destroy the Roman constitution, but in the civil war between him and the conservatives that was the result. Another period of intrigues led to the more discreet supremacy of Augustus who designed the permanent structure of the Roman Empire. He led Rome through a transformation that most Romans found acceptable.

An empire, once established, will face various challenges. The Roman Empire was to be threatened by enemies outside its borders and by rebellions and conspiracies within them. Not all these challenges were equally effective, but over several centuries the Empire was transformed, and at its close it dissolved into the states of the Early Middle Ages.

RECOMMENDED READING

Sources

*Caesar. *War Commentaries*. Rex Warner (tr.). 1960.
Livy. *History of Rome*. B. O. Foster and others (trs.). 14 vols. 1919–1959.
Polybius. *The Histories*. E. Shuckburgh (tr.). 2 vols. 1962.
*Sallust. *Jugurthine War* and *Conspiracy of Catiline*. S. A. Handford (tr.). 1963.

Studies

Badian, E. *Foreign Clientelae, 264–70 B.C.* 1958.
*———. *Roman Imperialism in the Late Republic*. 1967. Together, the two books provide a comprehensive and brilliant analysis of Roman imperialism.
Bloch, Raymond. *The Origins of Rome*. 1960. A concise statement of Etruscan and early Roman history.
Boak, Arthur E., and William G. Sinnigen. *A History of Rome to A.D. 565*. 1965. A reliable American textbook for consultation.

Brunt, P. A. *Italian Manpower 225 B.C.–A.D. 14.* 1971.
Gelzer, Matthias. *Caesar: Politician and Statesman.* 1968.
Mommsen, Theodor. *A History of Rome*. Originally 3 vols., 1854–1856; many modern editions. The classic history of the Republic, still a gripping narrative.
Richardson, Emeline. *The Etruscans: Their Art and Civilization*. 1964.
*Rose, H. J. *A Handbook of Latin Literature*. 1954. The best brief history of the subject.
*———. *Religion in Greece and Rome*. 1959.
*Scullard, H. H. *From the Gracchi to Nero*. 1971. The best textbook for this period; good references.
*Syme, Ronald. *The Roman Revolution*. 1960. Brilliant analysis of the founding of the Empire by Augustus.
*Taylor, Lily Ross. *Party Politics in the Age of Caesar*. 1949.
Toynbee, Arnold. *Hannibal's Legacy*. 2 vols. 1965.

*Available in paperback.

FIVE

THE EMPIRE
AND CHRISTIANITY

The history of the Roman Empire is one of both transformation and remarkable continuity. The system of government devised by Augustus and maintained by his successors gave the Empire two centuries of solid prosperity. The provinces were peaceful and soon began to rival Rome in economic strength. Wars on the frontiers did strain the imperial resources at times, but there was no enemy strong enough to threaten Roman domination of Europe.

At the beginning of the third century the Empire entered a period of crisis. Control of the army became the key to power, and emperors and would-be emperors followed one another in rapid succession. When order finally returned during the fourth century, the old Roman Empire was no more. In the East the Byzantine Empire was formed; in the West the Empire steadily declined, finally ceasing to be governed by Roman emperors altogether in 476.

The passing of the Roman Empire marked the end of the ancient world. The undoing of a marvelous civilization has long held a special fascination for historians, perhaps because it reminds them of the impermanence that threatens all human institutions and every civilization. Many factors weakened the Empire—the inadequacies of the slave system, the plight of the poor, the dearth of effective leaders, the desires of subject peoples for autonomy, the insufficiency of classical values to command allegiance and sustain morale among the Empire's inhabitants. There is no single, simple explanation for Rome's decline, but there is still much to be learned in the contemplation of this transformation.

Even as antiquity was passing, ancient peoples were laying the basis for a new form of civilization. Here the most important innovation was the gradual formation and slow spread of a new set of religious beliefs. This was Christianity, which was destined to inform the life and culture of the Western heirs of the Roman Empire.

The ancient world declined, but the memory of its achievements never entirely faded. Rather, the magnificence and grace of antiquity's monuments, the range and subtlety of its thought, the elegance and interest of its literature—all this remained to fascinate and inspire future generations. So also the social ideals that the Empire embodied—unity among nations, peace throughout the world, the rule of reason, law, and justice in human affairs—retained their appeal to Rome's heirs and successors. The political regime of the Roman emperors ended in the West in 476. But the intellectual and artistic accomplishments and social ideals of the ancient world have survived to form a living, stimulating, challenging part of Western cultural tradition.

I. THE EMPIRE AT ITS HEIGHT

For two centuries after the death of Augustus his solution to the problem of ruling a Mediterranean empire proved workable. Except for one outburst of violence in 69, emperor succeeded emperor in peaceful continuity. But the true nature of the imperial constitution, which Augustus had partially concealed, became clearer. The will of the emperors counted for much more than the resolutions of the Senate, and the traditional popular assemblies seem to have lost all function in the legislative process. Still, peace was preserved, and this Pax Romana allowed both the economy and culture to flourish. The Empire enjoyed its most prosperous, most creative age.

THE SUCCESSORS OF AUGUSTUS

After the death of Augustus his stepson, Tiberius, whom he had adopted, became leader of the state. In recognizing Tiberius the Senate confirmed the principle of dynastic succession and established the fact that an empire, not a republic, now existed. The dynastic line established by Augustus, called the Julio-Claudian dynasty, reigned until A.D. 68.

Much can be said against the rule of the Julio-Claudians. Tiberius was morbid, suspicious, and vengeful. His successor, Gaius, or Caligula, suffered from insanity. Claudius was gullible and manipulated by his wives and freedmen. Nero, the last of the Julio-Claudians, was one of the worst emperors in Roman history. His tyranny led to a rebellion in Gaul. When the revolt spread to Rome, he saw he was doomed and killed himself.

Yet these emperors did maintain, and even increased, the Augustan heritage. Claudius, for example, conquered Britain, thus completing the work begun by Caesar's brief invasions of Britain in 55 and 54 B.C. Moreover, within the peaceful Empire, the provincial administration that Augustus had established continued to function effectively.

The process of centralization of power continued. Tiberius stripped the assemblies of the right to elect magistrates and gave this responsibility to the Senate. This reform was little more than a recognition of the true state of affairs, for the assemblies were by now only a formality. From this time onward it was but a short step to allowing the emperor to appoint magistrates directly; the Senate merely made the formal gesture of conferring their imperium. Claudius withdrew more affairs of state from the Senate and turned them over to his trusted assistants. These were usually Greeks who had been freed from slavery and given high positions because of their astuteness.

Another factor that weakened Senatorial power was the frequent interference by the Praetorian Guard. The Guard first intervened in politics when it forced the Senate to recognize Claudius as Emperor. It also played a decisive role in the selection of Nero in 54; his mother bribed the Guard for its support, and the Senate had no choice but to acclaim him as Emperor. This repeated invasion of civil authority by the Praetorian Guard was another step on the road toward militarization; within a little more than a century the emperors were to become totally dependent on being able to buy the good will of the soldiery.

The military played a significant role in the struggle over the succession after Nero's death in 68. Troops in various quarters of the Empire backed their own candidates for emperor. The year 69 is often called "the year of the four emperors" because at one time four men claimed to be emperor. Vespasian finally stabilized the situation and emerged as sole ruler late in 69. He founded the Flavian dynasty, which lasted through the reigns of his two sons.

Vespasian was an efficient administrator. He

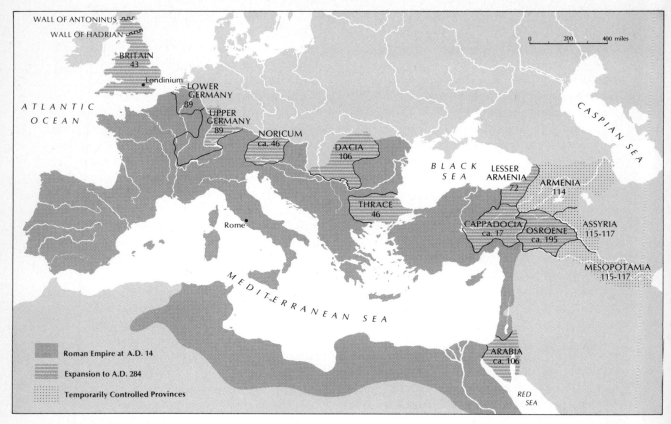

MAP 5.1: THE ROMAN EMPIRE A.D. **14–284**

provided a strong central government for Rome that further augmented the powers of the emperor. The old republican institutions, the Senate and the assemblies, no longer retained any power. The emperor appointed the consuls and other officers.

THE FIVE GOOD EMPERORS

The Flavian dynasty ended in violence in 96, when a group of senators instigated the murder of the Emperor Domitian, Vespasian's despotic son. Domitian had no son, so the Senate picked the best man available, Nerva, and designated him as emperor. For almost a century thereafter the problem of succession was solved.

An emperor would choose a qualified successor and adopt him as his son, thus assuring a peaceful transfer of power. The system functioned so well, and the men chosen were so capable, that historians have called Nerva and the next four rulers the "five good emperors."

Nerva was little more than an elderly presiding officer without much real power. After less than two years he was succeeded by his adopted son, Trajan, who had been chosen because of his high military reputation. Trajan was later viewed as a model emperor; he ruled with an unusual blend of fairness and freedom, even issuing warnings not to hunt down Christians or listen to anonymous accusations. He was followed by Hadrian, who claimed that

Trajan had adopted him. Hadrian was strong enough to take and maintain control, and he saw to the succession of the next two emperors, Antoninus Pius and Marcus Aurelius. Antoninus' rule was peaceful, but Marcus was forced to fight repeated wars on the Eastern and Danubian frontiers.

The Empire continued to expand during this period. Trajan led successful campaigns against the tribes north of the Danube River. The result of these wars was the creation of the province of Dacia in the large plain that is today the heart of Rumania. Trajan also declared war against the kingdom of Parthia in 113, when the local monarch set up a government in violation of a compromise made with Nero. During the campaign Trajan led his troops down the valley to the head of the Persian Gulf, forming the provinces of Mesopotamia and Assyria. By 116 the Roman Empire reached its furthest extension to the east (see Map 5.1). But Trajan could not hold these areas in the midst of revolts, and while he was retreating he fell ill and died in 117. Hadrian, who succeeded him, decided to cut Rome's losses by withdrawing from the extreme eastern positions that Trajan had taken.

The assumption of power by the emperor became even more evident during the reign of Hadrian. He issued laws directly from the throne, without working them through the Senate; these were called *constitutiones* ("decisions"). He was advised by an informal council, the *amici* ("friends") of the emperor.

These emperors undertook a vast building program. Trajan erected many structures throughout the Empire and added an impressive column to the Roman Forum, on which are carved a series of scenes recording episodes in the wars against the trans-Danubian tribes. Hadrian undertook various building projects in the provinces. Most famous is the wall he built across Britain from Newcastle to Carlisle,

A detail from the column commemorating Marcus Aurelius' victories shows the beheading of defeated soldiers. (Photo: Anderson-Giraudon)

to mark the boundary between the Roman province of Britain and the areas controlled by Celtic tribes to the north.

The Empire enjoyed its last years of prosperity under the reign of Marcus Aurelius. But in his final years the gathering storm broke in all its fury. Marcus had to fight invasions by tribes on the Danube River and in the East. One campaign was especially disastrous, for the army returning from Asia Minor in the 160s brought with it a devastating plague that spread through much of Europe. This plague must have been one cause of the weakening of Rome, but the nearly total lack of records prevents our knowing how many died.

Marcus wanted to advance the position of his

worthless son, Commodus, and this caused him to give up the principle of adoption in choosing the next ruler. He passed the imperium to Commodus, whose extravagance and cruelty were reminiscent of Nero and Domitian. Commodus was murdered in 192.

At the beginning of the third century the Empire was nearly destroyed during a period of prolonged crisis. The difficulties were both political and social, and partly transformed the elegant civilization that had endured for almost two centuries after the reign of Augustus.

ROMAN IMPERIAL CIVILIZATION

No ancient empire except Rome ever controlled so much of the civilized world or exploited its successes so well. The Romans studied and imitated Greek drama, literature, philosophy, and art. They adapted much of the architecture, religion, and science of Greece and the Near East. The civilization of the Empire was therefore the final repository of the culture of the ancient world.

Economy

In the late Republic and the first two centuries of the Empire, economic life in Italy and the provinces reached a level of prosperity that would not again be equaled for the next thousand years. The results of Roman censuses, which have partially survived, indicate that Italy at the death of Augustus (including Cisalpine Gaul but excluding the islands) contained probably 7.5 million inhabitants. (In about 1500, the earliest date at which we can make a comparable estimate, the same area contained about 10 million people.)

A distinctive feature of settlement throughout the Empire was the importance of cities. In the western provinces, these were for the most part tiny; to judge from the area enclosed by the Roman walls, most towns contained only a few thousand residents. And yet they characteristically possessed temples, markets, arenas, courthouses, and other public buildings; they display, in other words, an authentic urban character. In the East, cities were much larger. Alexandria in Egypt contained probably 400,000 inhabitants; Ephesus in Asia Minor, 200,000; Antioch in Syria, 150,000. The existence of these numerous and occasionally large urban centers is testimony to the vitality of industries, markets, and trade within the imperial economy that supported them.

Largest of all the imperial cities, and a true wonder of the ancient world, was Rome. Estimates of its size range from 450,000 to 1 million inhabitants. Not until the eighteenth century would other European cities, London and Paris, again contain like concentrations of humanity. The masses of Rome's inhabitants lived in high-rise tenements, called "islands" (*insulae*), the like of which would also not be seen again until the eighteenth and nineteenth centuries. The maintenance under crowded conditions of acceptable standards of public hygiene, the supply of enormous quantities of pure water and food, challenged but did not defeat Roman skills in civil engineering and in administration. Rome's central position, both geographically and economically, made the city a metropolis comparable to New York or London today. No other city in the ancient world drew the variety of travelers that came to Rome, and the city's harbor, Ostia, was crowded with goods from the various provinces of the Empire and from such distant lands as China (see Map 5.2). Many writers have portrayed the city as an immense parasite, feeding on the tribute and products of the Empire. This seems unfair. It is true that Rome could not feed herself from the produce of Italy alone, but the city provided economic leadership for the Empire in banking and trade.

In spite of the importance of manufacture

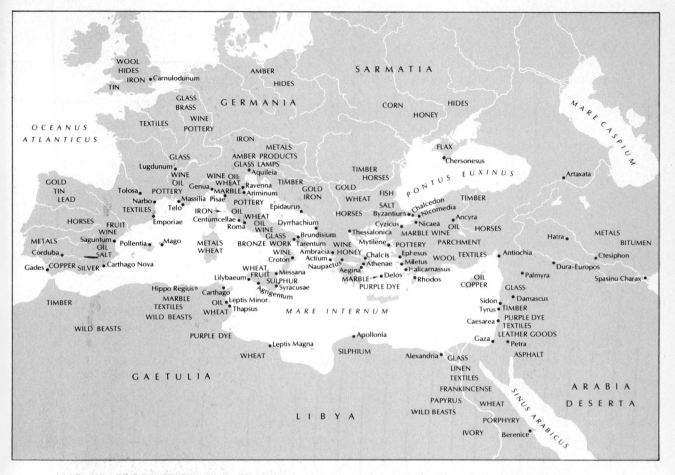

MAP 5.2: PRODUCTION AND TRADE IN THE ROMAN EMPIRE IN THE 2ND CENTURY A.D.

(From Hayden, *Atlas of the Classical World*, London: Nelson & Sons, Ltd., 1959, p. 1.51)

and trade, agriculture remained the basic support of the economy; it supplied, according to rough estimates, upward of 75 percent of the total product of the Empire. One important change in Italian agriculture in the last century of the Republic had been the triumph of the great slave-run estates, called latifundia, at the expense of small farms and holdings. At the same time, the managers of these vast planta-tions favored extensive forms of agriculture— the cultivation of vines, olives, and fruit; and the raising of large numbers of cattle, sheep, and goats. Only enough grain was cultivated to feed the *familia*, the resident staff of workers, most of them slaves. On some latifundia, particularly in the south of Italy, cattle were counted in the hundreds and sheep and goats in the tens of thousands. The great estates also supplied the cities with building stone, lumber, and firewood; huge quantities of wood were required, for example, to keep the Roman baths at comfortable temperatures. The widespread abandonment of cereal cultivation left the Italian cities, and Rome especially, critically dependent on imported wheat, which came mainly from Egypt. In the view of some historians, extensive deforestation and overgrazing led inevitably to erosion of the land and the loss of fertile topsoil, and were principal factors in the economic decline of Roman Italy. Even ancient peoples had the power to injure their environments.

Large estates were growing in the provinces as well, but they did not dominate the agricultural economy as in Italy. Moreover, the "Roman peace" favored the development of these once backward areas to the point where they threatened Italy's economic leadership. Provinces such as Spain and Gaul, and those along the Danube River, possessed superior natural resources. The wine market, for example, passed into the hands of Spanish cultivators within the second century, for Spanish wine was better than Italian and was cheaper to produce because of lower labor costs. In some forms of industry, too, the provinces began to outrun Italian production. One of the main Italian industries was pottery, especially the Arretine ware made at Arretium (modern Arezzo). But by about A.D. 50 Gallic pottery (Samian ware) had replaced Italian pottery even in Italy and had also taken over the market in the provinces and military camps. Thus Rome's success in establishing a commercial network created markets for products of the provinces and eventually contributed to her own economic decline.

Slavery

As in most other ancient states, slaves were widely used in the Roman economy, but no earlier society had organized the institution of slavery to such a degree or used slaves in such large numbers. During the late Republic, the number of available slaves increased dramatically, as Rome overran Greece, Asia Minor, Spain, and Gaul. Julius Caesar reports in his *Gallic War* that he once sold 53,000 Gauls into slavery in a single day.[1] One owner of a large estate, who died in A.D. 8, mentioned in his will that he owned no fewer than 4116 slaves. Of the 7.5 million inhabitants of Italy at the death of Augustus, an estimated 3 million were slaves. It is easy to appreciate how the prospect of a slave uprising terrified the free classes. Slaves were probably not so numerous in other parts of the Empire, but everywhere they comprised a substantial segment of the laboring population.

Many slaves were employed on the latifundia; they were especially suitable as workers in extensive types of agriculture, which required effort but not much skill or commitment. Indeed, the mounting flood of cheap slaves seems to have been decisive in the expansion of the great plantations during the last century of the Roman Republic. Rural slaves were known in legal terminology as the "talking stock," to distinguish them from the "dumb stock," or farm animals. In most places they lived in modest quarters and were properly fed, more or less. On the other hand, in Sicily they were often turned loose without shelter to feed off the land. Usually, they labored in gangs under the supervision of a steward or *vilicus*, himself a slave; stewards were, however, usually allowed to marry, in order to assure their loyalty and diligence.

Slaves were better treated in the cities, where they were employed in almost every occupation. They served as artisans, hair dressers, hotel keepers, secretaries, bankers, and, of course, personal servants. Slaves from the East, Greeks in particular, commonly tutored the children of the free classes. Slaves supplied much of the entertainment in ancient society.

---

[1] These Gauls had violated their pledge to surrender and tried to ambush Roman troops; this partially explains Caesar's ferocious response.

Girls and boys who could sing, dance, or recite were highly valued; there was also active traffic in beautiful young slaves of both sexes, for unwholesome purposes. Gladiators were slaves, and reputedly fought harder because of it. If they prevailed over an opponent, they might win their freedom; if they lost, they forfeited nothing more than a miserable existence. Many urban slaves were highly regarded by their masters, who often expressed their affection and gratitude with the gift of freedom. Moreover, slaves were usually allowed to accumulate some property of their own (occasionally including even other slaves); often, their wealth enabled them to buy manumission. As a freedman, the emancipated slave retained ties of dependence to his former owner, but the master's rights were now narrowly prescribed. Along with slaves, freedmen were everywhere found in ancient cities.

Judged as an economic system, ancient slavery offered certain substantial advantages. It permitted a rational utilization of labor in relation to land and capital—an optimum combination of what economists call the "factors of production." The owner of a great estate or an urban shop could maintain his staff of workers at optimum size by purchasing new hands when he needed them or by selling superfluous workers. As long as the market in adult slaves remained favorable, he did not have to pay the costs of supporting unproductive children. Nor was he required to maintain aging slaves. The elder Cato (234–149 B.C.), who enjoyed a durable reputation for wisdom among the Romans, advised estate owners to sell at once worn-out plow animals, diseased sheep, broken tools, aged and feeble slaves, "and other useless things."

But in the long run, the slave system of antiquity also revealed certain serious weaknesses. We shall examine what they were when we consider the reasons for the decline of Rome.

Social Conditions

The upper class in Rome lived on a far higher scale, and was more widely separated from the common people, than the rich of Greece. The wealthy had running water tapped into their homes, slaves to tend them hand and foot, and elegant country villas for recreation. These villas approached economic self-sufficiency, for slaves manufactured articles of light industry on the farms.

A modern aspect of Roman cities was the existence of suburbs and resorts. Capri was, as it is now, a resort, and Ostia served as both a harbor and a seaside resort. Pompeii was a commercial town, but its neighbor Herculaneum was a residential suburb. Both towns, buried by the eruption of Vesuvius in 79, provide examples of the airy Roman house, built around an atrium, a central open court, and decorated with graceful wall paintings.

Eating was a species of amusement for the wealthy. Even the most athletic glutton could be more than satisfied at a dinner that began in the late afternoon and lasted until after midnight. Romans always ate in a reclining position without using knives and forks; servants washed their hands and kept up the flow of wine mixed with water. The Romans' devotion to food is symbolized in their offensive invention, the special room for vomiting, a device that enabled the gourmand to prolong and renew his pleasure.

The workers of Rome lived in housing that was acceptable by ancient standards, though flimsy and inflammable. Their apartments had no running water, but a system of aqueducts gave easy access to water. Rome always took pride in her enormous, cheap public baths.

There were corporations in Rome for every kind of worker—fishermen, engineers, cobblers, carpenters, silk workers, and so on. These city laborers had working conditions that were beyond the dreams of a Near Eastern peasant.

POPULATION OF THE ROMAN EMPIRE

These estimates of Roman populations were formulated by the German historian K. J. Beloch in 1886. More recent studies would set the totals perhaps as high as 80 million, but Beloch's estimates still have not been superseded.

COUNTRY	AREA IN KM²	NUMBER OF INHAB-ITANTS	NUMBER OF INHAB-ITANTS PER KM²
EUROPE			
Italy	250,000	6,000,000	24
Sicily	26,000	600,000	23
Sardinia	33,000	500,000	15
Spain	590,000	6,000,000	10
Narbonese Gaul	100,000	1,500,000	15
Gaul	535,000	3,400,000	6.3
Danubian Provinces	430,000	2,000,000	4.7
Greece	267,000	3,000,000	11.2
Total	2,231,000	23,000,000	9.7
ASIA			
Asia	135,000	6,000,000	44
Asia Minor (except Asia)	412,000	7,000,000	17
Syria	109,000	6,000,000	55
Cyprus	9,500	500,000	52
Total	665,500	19,500,000	34
AFRICA			
Egypt	28,000	5,000,000	179
Cyrenaica	15,000	500,000	33
Africa	400,000	6,000,000	15
Total	443,000	11,500,000	26
ROMAN EMPIRE	3,339,500	54,000,000	16

Source: Salmon, P., *Population et Depopulation*, pp. 22–24.

They worked only about six or seven hours a day, and the Roman year contained about 160 holidays. To these were added from time to time special days of celebration. Thus a worker could expect a day of holiday for each day of work.

The major amusements during days of leisure were public games, especially chariot races in one of the arenas such as the great Circus Maximus. These races brought honor and wealth to the skilled charioteers. Besides races the Romans enjoyed watching contests between

Atrium house, Pompeii. (Photo: Anderson-Giraudon)

gladiators and between men and animals. The Colosseum, whose ruins still stand, was the most grandiose Roman arena.

It is a measure of Rome's prosperity that the city was able to support roughly half its population at public expense, through free allotments of food. These were the poor, who lived in slums and were able to find little or no work. In the later, less prosperous years the cost of maintaining 50 percent of the city's population was to strain the Empire's economy.

Social mobility became easier within the Empire. Some Greeks who had been freed from slavery enjoyed enviable careers as secretaries to emperors or as businessmen, and they were able to join the wealthier class. The need for troops opened new opportunities for provincials. Italian manpower alone was not enough to patrol Rome's extended frontiers, so the use of native troops for such service became more common. Men from the provinces entered the Roman legions, especially during the second century and later; they finally made their way into the Praetorian Guard, once recruited from Italians and considered an elite corps. Even the Senate began to include men born in the provinces, often not even Italian in descent. In time the Empire became less "Roman," for Rome was no longer the only center of activity. In both manpower and economic strength the primacy of Italy was of the past. This movement away from Rome as the all-important city led to the transfer of political control from Rome to Byzantium in the fourth and fifth centuries.

Law

An ever-developing, complex system of law and procedure was one of the chief cultural contributions of Rome. Naturally, Roman law developed under the Republic, but its growth under the Empire suggests that we treat it here. The earliest codified Roman law was the Laws of the Twelve Tables, published about 450 B.C. As the state developed, the Romans recognized that the Laws of the Twelve Tables were no longer adequate to their needs, and the law of Rome began a long process of modification. Normally, a case was heard before a judge, or *iudex*, who was a private citizen of high standing. The judges were drawn from the Senate and later from equestrians as well.

The judges often relied on the advice of other private citizens who were reputed to understand the law. These men were called jurists (*iurisprudentes, iurisconsulti*), and their opinions and advice constantly influenced and reshaped the law. Another influence on the law came from magistrates, especially praetors, who had the right to issue edicts in which they explained how they would interpret the law during their year in office. These edicts acquired the authority of tradition and were, in effect, a means of shaping the law.

The Romans distinguished their own citizens from members of their dominion who did not possess strict Roman citizenship. The citizens were subject to the *ius civile*, or law applying to citizens; the rest were allowed, in various ways, to maintain many of their own customs, and these customs gradually came to form the *ius gentium*, or law of other nations in general. These two kinds of law were assigned, logically enough, to two magistrates for administration, the *praetor urbanus* ("urban praetor") and the *praetor peregrinus* ("traveling praetor").

During the earlier Empire the process of modifying the law continued, with a new influence appearing—the intervention of emperors. Their orders and provisions were now also incorporated into the body of law. Jurists continued to play an important part in this process. Sabinus, Gaius, and Papinian are among the most important jurists of the first three centuries. The Emperor Hadrian seems to have recognized the need for a consistent revision of the many edicts laid down by praetors over the decades, and Salvius, one of his jurists, made such a revision. This codification pointed the way toward the final revisions of Roman law in the fifth and sixth centuries. The Emperor Justinian presided over the most important of these revisions.

The Romans' respect for their law expresses the remarkable discipline and cohesiveness that one sees throughout their society. In war they were often brutal, but then so were many others in all periods of history. Rome's achievement in designing and preserving a rich system of laws governing the behavior of citizens toward one another has served as a model for the law of Western Europe generally (an exception is the English-speaking group of states, which derive their law from the common law of England). The enormous codifications of the late Empire overshadow any other law codes within ancient societies.

Engineering and Architecture

The Romans showed their greatest competence in the fields of engineering and construction. The most enduring monument to Roman civilization is the impressive network of roads found everywhere from Britain to Africa. Originally designed as highways for the rapid movement of legions, these roads became trade routes in more peaceful times. The great highways, with their offshoots, eliminated all barriers to travel; even the mountains and deserts yielded to these everlasting ribbons of flagstone.

From the earliest times they built aqueducts that converged toward the cities with fresh water from the mountains; Rome also had an imposing system of sewers, which were constantly flushed by water from the aqueducts.

The Romans placed more emphasis on personal cleanliness than any other civilization down to modern times. One of the largest buildings in Rome was the Baths of Caracalla built in the third century, and the English city of Bath is named for the facilities that the Romans built there. Like the gymnasiums in Greek poleis, the Roman baths served as social centers.

In architecture the Romans adapted Greek techniques to Roman taste. Their temples, like those of the Greeks, were supported by columns, primarily in the Corinthian style. They had larger interiors because the Romans congregated indoors to perform their sacrifices, while the Greeks performed theirs in front of the temple and reserved the interior as a room for the deity. Roman builders solved the problem of how to create these larger spaces with two devices: the arch and concrete. The Romans were the first to grasp the possibilities of using arches and vaults on a large scale, and this gave their buildings a vastness that the Greeks could not achieve. Arches were prominent in the design of public buildings, sewers, and aqueducts, and the freestanding triumphal arch was an imposing commemoration of various imperial victories. They also invented concrete and it became their principal building material. It has clear advantages over stone and marble: it is inexpensive, its components are readily available, and it can be laid by relatively unskilled labor, which the Romans had in abundance. It can also be shaped into forms impossible in marble, and it is lighter in weight and can easily be supported in vaulted buildings.

The Forum at Rome was expanded at various times with the addition of libraries, colonnades of shops, and many temples. Its original function was as a town market but it became a meeting place for various assemblies from the second century B.C. on. Monumental columns and arches, rostra for speakers, and other decorations adorned it. Provincial towns also built forums, bathhouses, temples, and public halls. They often added an arch, an aqueduct, or a

The Forum, originally Rome's central market, became in the period of the late Republic and Empire the political, administrative, and religious center of the city. Its ruins, shown here in a recent photograph, have over the centuries reminded visitors of the Roman achievement. (Photo: Editorial Photocolor Archives)

theater to express their civic pride and their desire to resemble Rome even in a modest way.

Sculpture and architecture were blended in the triumphal arches, which were often embellished with reliefs depicting the historical event that the arch was meant to celebrate. Roman sculpture was based on Greek models of the Hellenistic Age, when realism came to be valued as highly as the perpetuation of ideal types. In the later Empire, sculpture tended to be more stylized, although realism was never wholly abandoned.

Our knowledge of Roman painting is derived mainly from the wall paintings at Pompeii and Herculaneum. Many of these were done by Greeks and comprise our most important samples of Greek wall painting (almost none have survived from classical Greece). Later, Italian artists began to do more of the decorations

Since homes were lighted only through the doorways, these paintings were intended to relieve the confining feeling of the bare walls. Landscapes were one of the favorite subjects (see Plate 6). Along with the wall paintings there were many mosaic compositions, also a legacy from Greek art. A famous one at Pompeii shows several street musicians at their work and is signed by a Greek artist.

Poets

The leisure provided by Rome's prosperity created a receptive audience for poets, especially among the educated class. The most famous Latin poet, Vergil (70–19 B.C.) borrowed from Greek models, as Roman poets often did. His early poems, the *Bucolics* and *Georgics*, are polished hymns of praise to the Italian landscape, which reflect the style of Theocritus and Hesiod; but the gentle, human spirit of Vergil himself is always present.

The best qualities of Vergil appear when he treats civilized emotions—mercy, compassion, and sadness; then his work is touched with a graceful melancholy. These qualities are demonstrated in his Roman epic, the *Aeneid*, which borrows and transforms material from Homer. In this work Vergil narrates the wanderings of Aeneas, the Trojan who was the legendary founder of Rome. His aim was to sing the glory of Rome and its salvation by Augustus. No one after Vergil tried to write a patriotic Roman epic. Even in antiquity it was recognized that he used the epic tradition in a way that no other Latin writer could challenge.

A contemporary of Vergil was Horace, whose brief *Odes*, *Epodes*, and *Sermones* (or *Satires*) examine love, amusement, annoyance, contentment—in short, the feelings of everyday life. Now and then Horace makes an attempt at serious patriotic verse, but these poems are self-conscious and moralizing and do not speak with the real Horatian voice of gentle, amusing irony.

The subject of love continued to inspire Roman poets. The most polished poet of love was Ovid (43 B.C.–A.D. 17?). His most famous work is *Ars Amatoria* (*The Art of Love*), a witty discourse on how to find and keep mistresses and lovers. The late medieval romances, including many studies of courtly love, are based largely on Ovid. His most complex poem is *Metamorphoses*, a series of fifteen mythological tales about transformations of various kinds. In two famous episodes, for example, Hercules turns into a bull and Julius Caesar into a star. Ovid is a representative of the Roman Empire: elegant, highly civilized, and accomplished. He does not have the elemental power of Homer; rather, he is a poet of wit, rhetoric, and learning.

Juvenal, a more pungent satirist than Horace, wrote shortly after A.D. 100. He took as his motto "indignation inspires my poetry" (*facit indignatio versum*). His poems denounce the excesses of pride and elegance in Roman society. His language is colorful, often bitter and obscene. One of his richest and wisest satires concerns the vanity of human wishes. After reviewing the foolishness of man, Juvenal gives his advice in a famous epigram: one should pray for "a sound mind in a sound body" (*mens sana in corpore sano*).

Historians

The histories of Rome written during the Republic were usually the work of men directly involved in politics. Under the Empire this changed, for political contest itself had almost come to an end. It was therefore time for someone to look back on the Republic and write a final history of its politics and imperialism. Livy (59 B.C.–A.D. 17) undertook this task during the reign of Augustus, when the decisive political transformation occurred.

Livy narrated Roman history from its legendary beginnings until 9 B.C. Because he usually drew on the work of earlier historians, he was

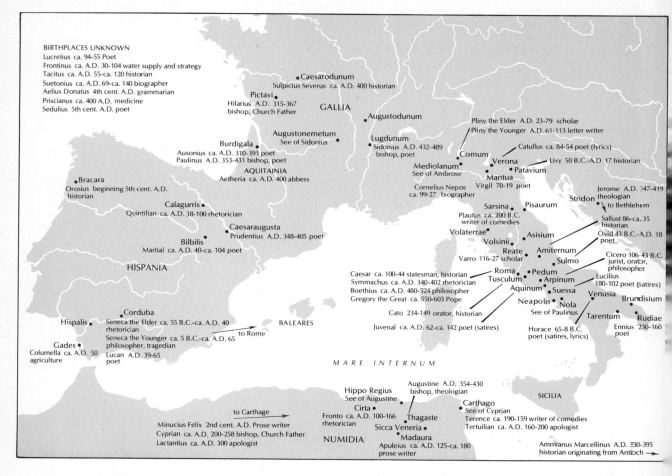

BIRTHPLACES UNKNOWN
Lucretius ca. 94-55 Poet
Frontinus ca. A.D. 30-104 water supply and strategy
Tacitus ca. A.D. 55-ca. 120 historian
Suetonius ca. A.D. 69-ca. 140 biographer
Aelius Donatus 4th cent. A.D. grammarian
Priscianus ca. 400 A.D. medicine
Sedulius 5th cent. A.D. poet

• Caesarodunum
Sulpicius Severus ca. A.D. 400 historian

Pictavi •
Hilarius A.D. 315-367   GALLIA
bishop, Church Father

• Augustodunum

Pliny the Elder A.D. 23-79 scholar
/ Pliny the Younger A.D. 61-113 letter writer

Augustonemetum •
See of Sidonius

Lugdunum
• Sidonius A.D. 432-489
bishop, poet

Burdigala •
Ausonius ca. A.D. 310-393 poet
Paulinus A.D. 353-431 bishop, poet

AQUITAINIA
Aetheria ca. A.D. 400 abbess

• Comum   Catullus ca. 84-54 poet (lyrics)
Verona •   — Livy 50 B.C.-A.D. 17 historian
Mediolanum •   • Patavium
See of Ambrose   Mantua
• Bracara   Cornelius Nepos   Virgil 70-19 poet
Orosius beginning 5th cent. A.D.   ca. 99-27 biographer
historian   Jerome A.D. 347-419
Sarsina •   Pisaurum   Stridon • theologian
Calagurris •   \ to Bethlehem
Quintilian ca. A.D. 38-100 rhetorician   Plautus ca. 200 B.C.   • Sallust 86-ca. 35
writer of comedies   Asisium   historian
Caesaraugusta   Volaterrae•   Ovid 43 B.C.-A.D. 18
• Prudentius A.D. 348-405 poet   Volsinii •   • poet
Bilbilis •   Reate   Amiternum   Cicero 106-43 B.C.
Martial ca. A.D. 40-ca. 104 poet   Varro 116-27 scholar   • Sulmo   jurist, orator,
HISPANIA   Roma • • Pedum   philosopher
Caesar ca. 100-44 statesman, historian   Tusculum • • Arpinum   Lucilius
Symmachus ca. A.D. 340-402 rhetorician   Aquinum •   180-102 poet (satires)
Boethius ca. A.D. 480-524 philosopher   • Suessa   Venusia
Gregory the Great ca. 550-603 Pope   Neapolis •   • Nola   • Brundisium
• Corduba   Cato 234-149 orator, historian   See of Paulinus   Tarentum •   • Rudiae
Hispalis •   Seneca the Elder ca. 55 B.C.-ca. A.D. 40   BALEARES   Horace 65-8 B.C.   Ennius 230-160
rhetorician   → to Rome   poet (satires, lyrics)   poet
Gades •   Seneca the Younger ca. 5 B.C.-ca. A.D. 65   Juvenal ca. A.D. 62-ca. 142 poet (satires)
Columella ca. A.D. 50   philosopher, tragedian
agriculture   Lucan A.D. 39-65
poet   MARE INTERNUM

Augustine A.D. 354-430
bishop, theologian   SICILIA

Hippo Regius •   Carthago
See of Augustine   Cirta •   • See of Cyprian
Fronto ca. A.D. 100-166   Thagaste •   Terence ca. 190-159 writer of comedies
rhetorician   Sicca Veneria •   Tertullian ca. A.D. 160-200 apologist
to Carthage →   • Madaura
Minucius Felix 2nd cent. A.D. Prose writer   Apuleius ca. A.D. 125-ca. 180   Ammianus Marcellinus A.D. 330-395
Cyprian ca. A.D. 200-258 bishop, Church Father   prose writer   historian originating from Antioch →
Lactantius ca. A.D. 300 apologist   NUMIDIA

MAP 5.3: THE MOST IMPORTANT WRITERS WHO USED THE LATIN LANGUAGE 300 B.C.–A.D. 600

(From Hayden, *Atlas of the Classical World*, London: Nelson & Sons, Ltd., 1959, p. 1.73)

sometimes unable to escape the influence of the myths that had clouded the history of the early Republic.[2] He was well aware of this problem

and complained about the poor sources available to him. Livy is at his best when he uses a good source such as Polybius.

Livy's *Roman History* is a kind of prose epic, filled with patriotism and admiration for the great men who had led Rome when the Republic was conquering the Mediterranean. Just as Vergil became the last Roman epic poet, so Livy was the last writer in Latin to attempt a full history of Rome. His work was ac-

[2] Livy's usual sources were "annalists," writers of year-by-year histories, often with a strong pro-Roman bias.

cepted as authoritative until soon after 1800. Modern criticism has shown how untrustworthy are the legends that Livy accepted for the earliest period of Rome, but there is no denying the rhetorical skill with which he presented his monument to the Roman Republic.

The best Roman historian, and the one who is most like Thucydides in accuracy and seriousness, is Cornelius Tacitus (55?–120?). One early booklet by Tacitus is the *Germania*, a description of the customs of the Germanic tribes and practically the only portrait of the society that was ultimately to rule over large areas of northern Europe.[3] In it Tacitus carefully describes the tribal organization, the weaponry, and the assemblies of the Germans.

The first major work of Tacitus is the *Histories*, in which he treats Roman history from 69, the year of the four emperors, through the death of Domitian in 96. His chief interest was the analysis of characters during revolution. Deeply influenced by satire, the dominant literary form of his age, Tacitus loved to fashion stinging epigrams aimed at members of the governing class, and he treated nearly all his main characters as selfish or corrupt. His disillusioned attitude was partly caused by his being an outsider, probably from southern Gaul; he saw Roman society through the cool eyes of a provincial who became a senator.

His other major work is the *Annals*, which covers the reign of the Julio-Claudian emperors from Tiberius through Nero (14–68). Tacitus looked back at the early Empire from a vantage point in a happier period, and he saw there little but despotism. By this time his style had reached its perfection. His irony found inviting targets in the Julio-Claudian dynasty, and his epigrams are masterpieces of terse brilliance.

---

[3] The *Germania* is especially valuable because of the absence of other records concerning the early Germans, but it was probably based on literary sources rather than on Tacitus' personal observation.

II. CHANGES IN ANCIENT SOCIETY

By the end of the second century the Augustan compromise, which had effectively maintained peace and prosperity, was breaking down. There followed a century of instability that almost proved fatal to the Empire. This instability was most dramatically visible in the near-collapse of the government. Rulers held the throne only at the pleasure of their armies, and invasions ripped open the frontiers of the Empire. But on other levels, too, it is clear that the society built on classical models was going through a deep transformation.

THE PERIOD OF CRISIS

Rome's two centuries of prosperity ended with the death of the Emperor Commodus in 192. In the following years the political balance shifted to the military. Leaders of the Praetorian Guard and the army began to murder emperors almost at will and to replace them with new rulers, who in turn were murdered one after another. During the third century dozens of emperors claimed the throne, but many of these men were really no more than political gamblers or warlords who for a short time purchased the loyalty of soldiers within the army.

More and more, the emperors assumed dictatorial powers and governed through court favorites, bypassing the Senate. They also removed the Senate's remaining traditional powers, such as commanding legions and governing provinces, and conferred them on equestrians. This weakening of the Senate, which on the whole had supplied a fairly responsible group of public servants, indicates the radical change that was taking place in the political structure.

The economy of the Empire nearly collapsed during this period. Defense costs had risen as raiders plundered the holdings of the Empire on several frontiers. (The historical effect of these invasions will be discussed in the next chapter.) Moreover, the emperors had been supplying the inhabitants of Rome with free food and public games—a fairly effective means of political domination, but a heavy drain on the economy. Adding to these financial problems was a shortage of silver, on which the imperial currency was based. The emperors resorted to depreciating the currency, but this forced people to hoard what silver they had and actually drove more of the metal out of circulation.[4] The result was a disastrous inflation. In fact, experts conclude that during the third century prices in Egypt soared to between fourteen and twenty times their earlier level.

A further problem faced by the government was the increasing reluctance of people to hold civic office. No Roman office paid a salary, so only men of independent means could seek political careers. The problem was not new; in the second century the Romans had begun a system of "liturgies," that is, services performed for the state under official orders. Finally, the government was forced to compel people to take office, a step that pointed to the practice, which was to become common in the fourth century, of binding men to their occupations.

It would be confusing to narrate the careers of the emperors who tried to hold the state together through its period of crisis. Many of them were men of little leadership. On the other hand, some of them must have been among the most able rulers in the history of Rome, for otherwise the Empire would have totally disintegrated. It is also difficult to analyze the exact causes for the crisis. Was it a failure of leadership at the highest level? Did the plague that attacked the Empire under

Marcus Aurelius so weaken the army that peoples outside the Empire could at last invade the wealthy domains of Rome? However historians balance the causes, they must also consider what was now happening to ancient society.

THE DILEMMAS OF SLAVERY

Rome declined because its economy could no longer support the huge military expenditures, needed to defend the frontiers against the ever-threatening invaders. Why was the economy not equal to the task? One principal reason was this: the slave system, in spite of the short-term efficiencies we have already discussed, revealed in the long term certain fatal flaws. In particular it could not satisfactorily resolve two problems that every economy must face: the creation of incentives, to assure that the primary producers will labor hard and well; and the recruitment of new workers, to replace the aging and the dead.

Especially in the countryside, the principal incentive that bent slaves to their tasks was coercion, or the dread of punishment. For this reason, they were best employed in work that required little skill, diligence, or effort. (Urban slaves, able to acquire property and enjoy some prospect of eventual freedom, were better off.) The association of slavery with physical labor drained work of its dignity and discouraged even freedmen from engaging in "servile" tasks. The low prestige accorded labor also dampened interest in technological innovation. The great minds of the classical world, so powerful in the speculative arts, were rarely concerned with practical matters, with easing human efforts, with making life less onerous for chattel. Finally, in the belief of most historians, demoralized slaves were poor producers of children, even when they were allowed to marry. Why pass misery down the generations? The

---

[4] For example, Caracalla (211–217) tried to stabilize the currency by introducing a large new coin, but this soon became nothing but copper dipped in silver.

Roman estates counted among their gangs of bondsmen some offspring of slaves, but these *vernae*, as they were called, evidently constituted only a minute part of the corps of workers.

Slaves were recruited primarily from two sources: wars of conquest, which resulted in the enslavement of defeated armies and sometimes entire communities; and piracy. But under Augustus and his successors, the tempo of conquests gradually waned, and they ceased altogether from the time of Hadrian. And the government itself struggled long and successfully to suppress piracy and other violations of the Roman peace.

Slaves were the machines of the ancient economy, the basic capital equipment that supported society and the state. Declining numbers of slaves inevitably meant reduced outputs. What would happen if, in our own society, we faced continuously declining numbers of engines or relentlessly shrinking sources of power? To this critical situation, ancient society could not respond by quickly developing labor-saving devices; here, its splendid culture, its grand intellectual traditions, could offer no aid. Society could respond only by providing to the unfree new incentives for working well, new reasons for wanting and rearing children.

One example of this response was the spreading practice of "housing" the slave in the countryside, that is, of providing him with a house, farm, and wife; with her and with their eventual children, he might work the land and enjoy at least part of its produce. The farm he worked and improved was analogous to the wealth acquired by urban slaves. It belonged to his master, but he gained a moral right to its use and to pass it on to his children after him. The numbers of these "housed slaves" multiplied in late antiquity, even as the gangs of landless slaves diminished. This change was clearly in the long-term interest of society, but there were

penalties too. From the housed slave, now truly a peasant, the landlord and the state could expropriate in rent and taxes only a limited portion of his output. The effort to provide incentives to the lowest order of society diminished the surplus that might meet the needs of the elites and the state itself. Paradoxically, the move to a fairer social system weakened the fiscal resources of the beleaguered Empire.

The trend to freedom was manifest in cities too, where it had begun probably sooner than in rural areas. Highly skilled slaves expected to receive for their services both property and, eventually, freedom. By the time of the Emperor Diocletian, who sought to impose maximum limits on urban salaries, most of the artisans in the imperial cities must have been free.

THE PLIGHT OF THE POOR

Within the free population, contrasts between rich and poor were extreme, and social tensions and violent social uprisings further disturbed the stability of the Empire. In Italy, the spread of the great estates in the last century of the Republic had driven many small cultivators off the land. Many drifted to the Roman metropolis, where bread and circuses, provided free by the government, purchased their docility. In many provinces, too, rural depopulation and the abandonment of cultivated fields had become a major problem in the centuries after Augustus. It has been estimated that one-third of the lands of North Africa passed from cultivation under Augustus' successors. The reasons for the spread of these empty tracts were several: fiscal oppression in the provinces; the taint associated with servile labor; the lure of cities; and presumably low birth rates among the poorest rural classes.

Faced with shrinking numbers of cultivators and taxpayers, the Roman government sought desperately to reclaim and resettle the abandoned fields. Marcus Aurelius initiated a policy of settling outsiders on deserted lands within the Empire, even in regions as far removed from the frontier as the Po valley. Emperors or their officials also sought to attract free Roman cultivators back to the countryside. The free cultivator settled on another's land is technically called a *colonus*, and the institutions affecting his tenure are referred to as the *colonate*.

Roman policy toward the *coloni* and other free cultivators was ambivalent and shifting. Their status was determined both by imperial legislation and by customary or vulgar law, which must be reconstructed from inscriptions and other records showing private practices. In the customary or vulgar law known from North African sources, the *colonus* held the land under favorable terms. He was charged with a light and fixed rent, which he paid to the landlord or *dominus*. He could sell the land he improved or pass it on to his heirs, and he could depart from it at will. This favorable regimen was doubtless characteristic of other provinces too. The imperial legislation, on the other hand, most of which dates from the fourth century, gives a much different picture: the *colonus* was bound to the soil as were his children after him, and he was subject to the personal jurisdiction of his lord. As envisioned by the emperors, he was already a serf.

This flagrant inconsistency in our sources seems to reflect a basic dilemma in Roman social policy. The long-term interests of society and government dictated that resettlement within family-owned farms should be encouraged. On the other hand, the hard-pressed government could not overlook any source of revenue. Even while favoring resettlement, it frequently resorted to outrageous fiscal practices. It ruthlessly requisitioned food; it forced settlers to pay the taxes of their absent neighbors; it subjugated them to the authority of the great lords, who could be held responsible for collecting from them services and taxes. By the fourth and fifth centuries, under conditions of devastating fiscal oppression, some peasants preferred to flee the Empire rather than face ruin at home.

The plight of the harassed cultivator at times ignited violent social upheavals. In Gaul and northern Spain, for example, peasants known as the *Bacaudae* rose in revolt against tax collectors and judges in the third century and were suppressed, but rebelled again with even greater violence in the fifth century, even as the western provinces were succumbing to the invaders. A Russian classical historian of great insight, M. I. Rostovtzeff, maintained that the turmoil of the third century thinly disguised a class war. The peasant masses, notably those settled in the Illyrian provinces, rejected the traditional leadership of Rome. Because they filled the frontier legions, they were able to raise up their lowly-born commanders to imperial dignity. Several prominent rulers of the third century—Aurelian, who rebuilt the walls of Rome (270–275), and Diocletian—were Illyrians of rural or at least humble origins. Rostovtzeff has been faulted for seeing in the "revolution" of the third century too close an analogy with the downfall of Tsarist Russia in 1917. Was the Roman Empire, like the Russian, engulfed by an uprising of the lower classes? The model is assuredly too simple. But it can hardly be denied that social and class tensions and a violent rejection in the provinces of Roman leadership were powerful forces, working to undermine the Empire.

THE PROBLEM OF THE NATIONS

It is often difficult to distinguish social uprisings from ethnic or national movements, or social grievances from protests against cultural oppression. Rome had been surprisingly successful in extending and long maintaining her rule over so many nations (*gentes*) and cultures. Her success rested on two strategies. Incorporation within the Empire and loyalty to it guaranteed to the nations peace and protection, with justice. And the national elites were allowed wide local autonomy and a gradually extending participation in the affairs of the universal Empire. Local leaders were thus effectively coopted into the imperial system. But these social ideals, and Greco-Roman culture itself, had little direct appeal to the broad masses of the Empire. In the East, outside the great cities where Hellenistic culture prevailed, the largely Semitic peoples retained their own languages, cultures, and surely, too, resentments. In the Christian Book of Revelations, which views the world from a Semitic perspective, Rome, "that great city that bears rule over the rulers of the earth," is viciously depicted as a scarlet whore, committing fornication with kings, corrupting peoples, persecuting the just. There is no mistaking this raging hatred of the Roman name.

In western North Africa, Berber cultural nationalism seems to have inflamed from the fourth century onward the protracted war of the *circumcelliones;* the word means literally "those who prowl around storehouses," perhaps in the sense of rural guerrillas. The revolts of the *Bacaudae* in Gaul and Spain may have reflected the ethnic dissatisfactions of Celts as well as the social protest of peasants. Other examples could be given of the restlessness of nations under Roman rule.

Rome could never have built and preserved her vast Empire by material force alone. She had to hold out to the classes and nations of the Empire splendid social and cultural ideals that would hold their allegiance when arms could not. The failure of the Roman system was therefore not exclusively military, eco-nomic, or political. It was spiritual too; Rome fell when classes and nations rejected the values with which she had sought to woo them.

CULTURAL DISINTEGRATION

The Greco-Roman tradition, which was the spiritual cement of ancient society and of the Empire, succeeded for two centuries and more in maintaining among the nations morale, loyalty, and peace. Essentially, the promise of classical civilization under the Empire was universal peace. Amid peaceful conditions, individuals could pursue personal fulfillment as the classical poets and moralists had defined it. The tradition of Greco-Roman thought identified fulfillment with the cultivation and perfection of every human faculty or power—physical or athletic, literary, intellectual, artistic, or aesthetic. The wise man must of course seek his destiny in this life; the hereafter held out no certain hopes. He must live his life according to nature, which was, in the opinion of most ancient philosophers, the best leader, the *optima dux*. In responding to human needs, nature was both sufficient and benevolent. Even death, for all its mysteries, presented no terrors to the wise. Nature treats us well and fairly throughout our life. Will she change character and be mean to us in the end?

In spite of its manifest appeal, the cultural system of classical antiquity had some crucial weaknesses. It spoke preeminently to the privileged and the gifted, the elites of ancient society. Even as they failed to develop a technology which might have eased the labors of slaves and the poor, so also the intellectual leaders of the age could point out little meaning in the lives of the unfree, the unhealthy, the disadvantaged, those without property, those without talents.

Moreover, during the last centuries of the Empire, pagan thinkers were clearly losing the capacity to examine, elaborate, and develop their own ideals. They could no longer guide or inspire. After the Augustan age Roman civilization produced fewer original thinkers. A certain morose resignation pervades their writings. The earth was in decline, and history was approaching its term; everything worth accomplishing had been done, every limit had been reached. Already in the final decades of the Republican epoch, the Epicurean philosopher Lucretius, in his great poem *On the Nature of the Universe*, proclaimed that the earth "can scarce grow anything, for all our toil." "All," he continues, "is gradually decaying, nearing the end, worn out by the long span of years."

According to this oft-reiterated theme, there were no new worlds to conquer, no beckoning and challenging frontiers, no new destinies to be pursued. Christian authors fully shared this opinion, that life on earth offered nothing, challenged no one. In a remarkable passage, Tertullian, the first major Christian writer to use the Latin language, describes the state of the world in about 200:

> Everything has been visited, everything known, everything exploited. Now pleasant estates obliterate the famous wilderness areas of the past. Plowed fields have replaced the forests; domesticated animals have dispersed wild life. Beaches are plowed, mountains smoothed and swamps drained. There are as many cities as, in former years, there were houses. Islands do not frighten [settlers], nor cliffs deter. Everywhere there are buildings, everywhere people, everywhere communities, everywhere life.[5]

In averring that the earth was excessively burdened with people and their works, Tertul-

lian shows an acute lack of perception. Even as he wrote, the emperors were settling foreigners on deserted fields and recruiting them for their depleted armies. But his attitude alone concerns us here. Weighed down by the sense that every earthly limit had been reached, both pagans and Christians were psychologically ill-equipped to propose and to lead major social reforms. The pagans, who could see no destiny for mankind beyond the present life, were particularly muted and ineffectual. There is little wonder that they abandoned the rostra of society to the new group of vocal Christians. For Christians triumphantly affirmed that a further and unfulfilled destiny did indeed await mankind, but that man could only achieve it in life after death.

III. CHRISTIANITY

The triumph of Christianity within the Roman Empire represents one of the most remarkable cultural revolutions in history. The victory of the new religion is the more extraordinary, since the values it preached were opposed to those of classical thought. The great pagan philosophers had for the most part taught that the good life must be sought in the present world. *Carpe diem:* "seize the day"; there is no surety about tomorrow, no hope at all in an imagined life beyond death. To Christians, on the other hand, this visible world was a place of exile, a vale of tears through which we must pass, as we hurry toward our true homeland in heaven. Life was a pilgrimage in a foreign, hostile, hated land.

Cultural systems, if they are to survive, must discover and proclaim meaning and purpose in the varied events of life, the joyous and the sorrowful. Classical values, as we have mentioned, were failing to reach important sectors of ancient society: the slaves, the disadvantaged,

---

[5] Tertulliani Opera monastica, *Corpus Christianorum,* Series Latina, II (1954), p. 827, tr. D. Herlihy.

the subjugated, the losers. There is little wonder that the inhabitants of the Empire sought reason for their existence in new cultural and religious movements.

THE MYSTERY RELIGIONS

Part of this spreading religious ferment was the growing popularity of the so-called mystery religions, "salvationist eschatologies." They were eschatologies because they claimed to explain the "last things" (Greek, *eskhata*), the ultimate purposes of human life. They were salvationist because they offered to their adherents personal salvation, life after death. Their common formula for salvation was the association of the believer, through a mystical rite, with a hero who had conquered death. Thus, the cult of Mithras, which enjoyed particular popularity within the Roman army, required that the believer bathe in the blood of a slaughtered ox. Other heroes, conquerors of death, were Orpheus, Adonis, and Osiris.

Jesus was such a hero; he too claimed the faith of his followers because he had risen from the dead: he too (or only he, as Christians believed) had conquered death. But the cult of Jesus also differed from the other mystery religions. Salvation for the Christian required ritual, mysteries, sacraments; but it required too an upright, moral life. The Christian religion was from its origins a complex mixture of ritual and ethics, sacraments and commandments. Then, too, the redeeming Jesus was a historical person, who had come upon earth "in the fullness of time," as Christian texts affirmed. All other cultic heroes were mythical figures, who may never have walked the earth. Finally, the cult of Jesus drew decisive benefits from its close associations with the richest and most powerful religious tradition of the ancient world: Judaism.

THE JEWS IN THE ROMAN EMPIRE

The Jewish people had been subjects of the Persian Empire until the Greek and Macedonian invasion of the East swept away Persian rule. In the Hellenistic Age they were governed mainly by the Seleucid kings of Syria. During the Syrian rule one event inspired them to a strong reaffirmation of their faith. This was the ill-advised decision of Antiochus IV, the king of Syria, to impose the worship of Greek gods on the Jews. He installed a statue of Olympian Zeus in the sacred temple in Jerusalem and prohibited several Jewish religious practices.

A rebellion of the Jews, led by Judas Maccabaeus, forced the Seleucids to concede religious freedom in Jerusalem. The temple was cleansed and rededicated in 165 B.C., an event commemorated by the Jewish feast of Hanukkah. Eventually, the Jews, led by the family of Judas, gained independence from Syria and established their own kingdom; but in 63 B.C. the Roman general Pompey dissolved this kingdom and the Jews fell under the control of Rome. For some time Judea, now a small region in the south of Palestine, was ruled by client-kings, leaders who pledged loyalty to Rome; one of them was the notorious Herod the Great (40–4 B.C.). Herod was a harsh dictator, hated by the Jews, but he did maintain order. After his death Rome was forced to take a more direct role in administering Judea: This was done through a series of civil servants, usually called procurators.

Constant quarrels between the Roman officers and the Jews reached a climax in A.D. 66 when Jerusalem burst into rebellion. This great Jewish War, as the Romans called it, lasted until 70; the Romans then entered Jerusalem and demolished the temple, except for one outer wall, known as the Wailing Wall, at which the Jews were allowed to pray once a year. The Romans did not at first try to suppress the Jewish faith itself, but this step was finally taken after another Jewish rebellion (132–134). Nonetheless, Judaism retained its coherence and strength, and it assured its people that God would one day send them their redeemer.

The Sects

The plight of the Jews under Roman rule raised religious tensions among them; numerous sects appeared, each advancing its own interpretation of the common Jewish traditions. Among them were the Sadducees, who advocated strict adherence to Jewish law, but rejected belief in an afterlife, in angels, and even (if their enemies can be believed) in a personal, redeeming God. The more liberal Pharisees believed in a life after death and in angels; they accepted gentile converts, and were willing to make some modifications of Jewish law to allow some accommodation with Greco-Roman culture. They were popular preachers in the synagogue. The New Testament, in accusing them of hypocrisy —"whitened sepulchers" they are called—has permanently and unfairly sullied their name.

The Jewish sect that in recent years has attracted the most concentrated attention is the Essenes. The Essenes formed an ascetic community that sought isolation from the world. In 1947, several rolls of leather and papyrus were found in Qumran, a village near the Dead Sea in Jordan. These Dead Sea Scrolls, which are still being found in the region, have given historians an extraordinary view of the beliefs and practices of this pious Jewish sect in the decades immediately preceding the appearance of Jesus.

The most important scrolls are hymns and guides to moral living. The writings mention a Teacher of Righteousness who had died before the scrolls were written and they also predict that three more leaders will save the Jews:

a prophet, a Messiah of Aaron, and a Messiah of Israel. Until the day of salvation, the members of the community must observe the laws included in a document called the Manual of Discipline.

The relations of the Essenes to Jesus and the Christians remain obscure. The New Testament mentions them not at all. Essene beliefs seem to have been strongly touched by Persian (Zoroastrian) influences. A Wicked Priest, serving the powers of darkness, contends with the Teacher of Righteousness, the champion of the forces of light. This pronounced religious dualism is not a dominant theme, although occasionally present, in early Christian texts. On the other hand, the asceticism of the Qumran community and its withdrawal from worldly entanglements anticipate the style of life of the first Christians. And the very existence of the Essenes shows the intensity of religious expectations within Judaism on the eve of Jesus' career.

ORIGINS OF CHRISTIANITY

The historical investigation of Jesus[6] and his message, the "search for the historical Jesus" in the phrase of a modern theologian, presents formidable difficulties. Jesus wrote nothing at all. We can view him only through the writings of others—his immediate followers and early converts such as St. Paul, who formed the first Christian communities. Jesus himself invited his followers to reflect upon the meaning of his life: "What do men say of the Son of Man? Who do they think he is?" (Matthew 16:13). We can study what some men thought

---

[6] "Jesus" was his name: after his death he was called *ho Christos*, "the anointed one" or the Messiah, by his followers. Thus the familiar names "Christ" and "Jesus Christ," though universally used, are not historically correct; and "Jesus, called the Christ" is cumbersome.

of Jesus; but we cannot penetrate the abiding mystery of the man.

The first Christians recorded nothing of their memories and impressions of Jesus until probably two decades after his death, perhaps because they expected his imminent return in triumph and glory. The oldest parts of the New Testament are the Pauline Epistles, and Paul himself never knew Jesus personally. The youngest books of the New Testament—the Gospel according to St. John and the Book of Revelations—date probably from the last decade of the first century. Even within the books of the New Testament, the authors' interpretations of Jesus and his message are selective.

As his followers eventually recalled his career, Jesus was born of a virgin named Mary, married to a man named Joseph, "in the days of King Herod," at a date that modern scholarship would set at 7 B.C. At about the age of thirty, he was publicly baptized by an ascetic preacher called John, and he entered upon a public life of teaching. In the Sermon on the Mount, the best summary of his ethical principles, he affirmed that the blessings of God went to the poor, the meek, the pure, those who make peace, those who seek justice. He taught that true prayer and piety were movements of the spirit, not public gestures designed to win society's acclaim. But he also engaged in ritual practices ("sacraments" in later terminology), which implied that his followers formed an organized community or cult. At his last supper with his apostles, he urged them to continue in his memory the ritual consumption of consecrated bread and wine, which he identified with his own body. He called himself the Son of Man, the Son of God, and a king, but affirmed that his kingdom was not of this world. And he promised eternal life to those who accepted him. According to our texts, he worked miracles to show the truth of his mission. Christian sources further say that he was accused by the Jewish high priests of blasphemy. He was then crucified by order of the Roman governor Pontius Pilate (probably about A.D. 30). His followers were convinced that after three days in the tomb he rose again, and later ascended bodily into heaven. But he would, in their belief, come again, to save his followers and establish his kingdom.

PAUL AND HIS MISSION

After he departed from them, the followers of Jesus initially formed only one of many sects within the larger body of Judaism. They called themselves Christians, followers of the new Messiah. They seem to have had no clear notion of the persons—Jews only or gentiles too?—to whom he had directed his message; nor did they know what and where the kingdom was he had promised them. The man who clarified these crucial issues, reformed Christianity into a distinct and autonomous religion, and infused it with burning missionary fervor was a Jew from Tarsus, Saul, or in the name he chiefly used after his conversion, Paul.

Paul is by far the best known of all the early Christian teachers; the Acts of the Apostles is largely concerned with his career, and we have his own epistles. He enjoyed the privileges of Roman citizenship, knew Greek, and was evidently a learned man. As a pious Jew, he initially considered the followers of Christ blasphemous, and even aided in their early persecution. He held the cloaks of some irate Jews who stoned to death a man named Stephen, now regarded as the first martyr of the Christian Church. Then, as he journeyed to Damascus to organize still further persecutions, he was visited on the road by an apparition of the risen Jesus, who asked him to explain his hatred (A.D. ca. 38). Paul then accepted Christianity. He began to preach in Damascus, and from there he traversed the Roman world, organizing

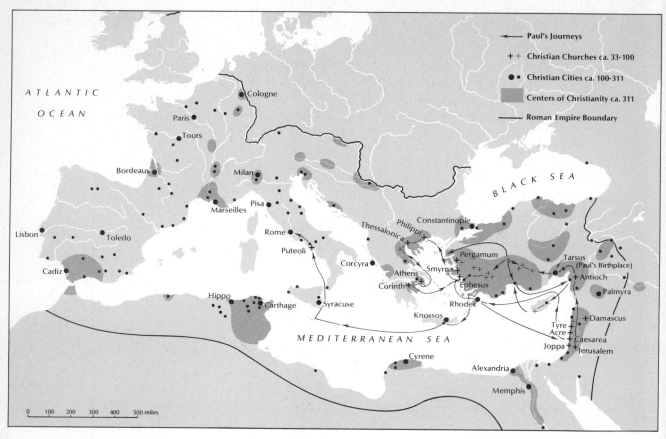

MAP 5.4: THE SPREAD OF CHRISTIANITY

Christian communities and advising and encouraging their members through letters (see Map 5.4). He began the mission of preaching to the gentiles, which would eventually spread Christianity across the Empire.

In his writings Paul elaborated several points of doctrine that have endured throughout the history of Christianity. He developed, in other words, the first coherent Christian theology. He rejected the conservative policy of some early Christians who would have restricted the preaching of the new faith to Jews alone. All peoples ought to worship the true God and hear the message of his only Son. "Is he the God of the Jews only? Is he not also of the Gentiles? Yes, of the Gentiles also" (Romans 3:29). To facilitate their conversion, Paul did not require Christian gentiles to be circumcised or to follow the Mosaic law.

Paul also began the theological exploration of the notion of grace—the special power by which God redeems sinners. The core of the Christian revelation was initially (insofar as we can judge at all) not so much an idea at all as an emotion, a hope, that there was life beyond life. In elaborating a coherent view of the nature of man and the providence of God, Paul and later Christian teachers were deeply indebted to the

Jewish tradition, of which they felt themselves the direct heirs and successors. To ancient Israel, they owed their concept of one God and their notions of creation, the fall of Adam and Eve, and the early history of mankind. They also accepted the view that God the creator had not abandoned his creation. Implicit in Old Testament history is the assumption of a return by God to his creation, to achieve, through the instrumentality of the Jewish people, a special providence for mankind. God comes back to his creation in order, as it were, to recreate, to undo the damage caused by Adam's disobedience.

To Paul, this idea of a return by God to a humanity enslaved by sin explained at least partially the mystery of Jesus' mission. Through one man (Adam) sin had entered the world, and with sin, death. The offense of one man had condemned all persons of every generation. But also through one man (Jesus), through his willing sacrifice, grace once more abounded, and many would be saved. By nature, Adam was founder and head of the human race. By grace, Jesus was its second founder, its restorer and redeemer.

In the new Christian perspective shaped by Paul, the universe was organized on two principles: an order of nature, established by original creation but faulted by sin; and an order of grace, founded in God's willingness to save mankind in spite of Adam's fall and brought to fulfillment with the coming of Jesus. The reconciliation of these two powers of nature and of grace and the determination of their purposes and their limits have remained over the centuries central problems of Christian theology.

THE CHURCH IN THE ROMAN EMPIRE

The death of St. John about A.D. 100 brings to an end the so-called apostolic age, the period of origins of the Christian Church.

From then until the reign of the Emperor Constantine, the Church remained an illegal, sometimes persecuted sect within the Empire. But it still succeeded in increasing its numbers and in developing remarkably both its theology and its government. Its numbers, to be sure, continued to form a small minority within the Empire, probably never exceeding 10 percent of the population. By about 300, the Christian message had penetrated nearly everywhere in the Roman world. At the council of Arles in southern France, held in 314, three bishops from distant Britain made an appearance. But the chief centers of Christian belief remained the regions of the Middle East; among them, Asia Minor (modern Turkey) held a special prominence.

The reasons for the Christian advance were many. The Roman peace facilitated communications and the exchange of ideas. Christians moved easily from community to community within the Jewish Diaspora, and they found a convenient forum for their preaching in the synagogues. By claiming for their own the sacred writings of the Jews (the Christian Old Testament), they appropriated a rich and impressive collection of religious law and literature. They also pointed to a historic founder, who was represented as the central figure in a total explanation of human history. Like the Jews, they made no compromises with paganism—either with pagan polytheism or pagan morality. Above all, they claimed to have an explanation for suffering and misfortune—evils, to be sure, in the pagan view, but benefits, in God's gracious governance, for those who must bear them. The meek, they promised, in a future life and another world, would inherit the earth.

Understandably, the teachings of the new religion initially appealed to slaves and the poor. A pagan, writing about 177–180, referred sarcastically to this superstition of wool carders,

This fresco of Adam and Eve is from an underground catacomb in Rome where early Christians met for refuge during the persecutions. (Photo: The Granger Collection)

shoemakers, and launderers. But even as he wrote, Christianity was making inroads among the intellectuals, who found the teachings of the pagans stale and unconvincing.

PERSECUTIONS

Toward the many religious sects of the Empire, the Roman government adopted, on the whole, a policy of toleration. It asked only that veneration be shown on official occasions to the "genius" (spirit) of Rome, to the traditional gods, and to the persons of deceased and deified emperors. This civic religion asked for little more than a public declaration of loyalty and patriotism, but the Christians, as the Jews before them, refused to make even this small compromise with polytheism. As a result, they earned the hatred and contempt of numerous pagans, who viewed them as enemies of the human race. In 64, the Emperor Nero perpetrated the first official persecution of the Christians in Rome. He falsely accused them of setting fire to parts of the city. The opprobrium in which Christians were held made them convenient scapegoats.

Sporadic persecutions, the severity of which is difficult to judge, and long periods of peace marked the history of the Church into the third century. Then only, amid general social crisis, did the government attempt a systematic suppression of the Christians. Decius in 250–251, Valerian in 257–260, and above all Diocletian in 303–313, sought to extirpate the Christian name; their concern with this menace to the state was a tribute to its now established strength. The persecutions probably cost few lives, but they did create a list of venerated Christian martyrs. The cult of saints, thereafter an integral part of Christian piety, began originally as a cult of martyrs. And the death of these few but visible members inspired the Christian community with constancy and pride and impressed even pagan observers. Tertullian was right in his judgment that the blood of martyrs was the seed of the Church.

THE CONVERSION OF CONSTANTINE

The conversion of the Emperor Constantine to Christianity in 312 marked a revolution in the Church and in its relations with the Roman Empire. The circumstances attending this dramatic event are obscure. In the traditional pious story, first appearing in 318–320, Constantine had a dream on the evening before he was to fight a rival emperor for supremacy over Italy, at the Milvian bridge near Rome. He was instructed in the dream to decorate the shields of his soldiers with the monogram of Christ: "in this sign you shall conquer." Constantine won the battle and recognized the divine power in the name of Christ.

Constantine's conversion was a political as well as a psychological event. Many of his subjects were now Christians, and the Christian Church had shown itself strong enough to survive persecution. In modern terminology, Constantine was trying to bring the opposition into the government. As emperor of what was still a pagan state, he continued to use pagan titles and symbols on his coinage; his personal life was hardly one of strict morality; and he delayed baptism until the year of his death, 337. He seems to have accepted the cult of Christ as one among many sources of divine help. Only gradually did he recognize its claim to be the one true faith.

In 313, at a conference held at Milan with a pagan coemperor named Licinius, Constantine extended complete freedom of worship to the Christians and ordered the return of their confiscated goods. This misnamed "Edict of Milan" (the official document was issued some months later and not at Milan) ended the age of persecutions. Other favors followed: churches could own property and enjoyed exemptions from certain taxes; bishops were allowed to judge the legal disputes of the members of their congregations, and their decisions were binding. Christianity did not become the official or established religion of the Empire until Theodosius the Great outlawed heresy (381) and closed the pagan temples (391). But the Church had already acquired a privileged juridical status which it would retain, in many Western lands, until the eighteenth and nineteenth centuries.

DOGMA AND GOVERNMENT

The Christians within the Roman Empire did not hasten to elaborate a systematic theology, or to develop a systematic government of the Church. Hope in a life after death, not learning or law, was the authentic spirit of the movement. Still, the early Christians inherited from their Jewish origins a strong sense of community. They viewed themselves as the new Israel, members of a holy nation, a chosen people, facing an unbelieving, hostile world. This sense of unity and separateness provided the foundation for a constitution for the Church and for taking fixed dogmatic positions in regard to fundamental beliefs. Usually, the Christian community did not bother to define these matters of dogma or of discipline until the outbreak of disputes threatened its internal unity and peace. The losers in these disputes, if they did not amend their beliefs, were regarded as heretics. The rise and resolution of these controversies forced the orthodox to refine their beliefs. The history of dogmatic and constitutional development in the early Church is related to the history of heresies.

An early dispute was with the Gnostics, beginning even before the year 100 and long persisting. Gnosticism in fact antedates the origins of Christianity, and was more an independent religion than a Christian heresy. The essence of its beliefs was that the mastery of special knowledge (*gnosis*) assured salvation. The Gnostics proceeded to elaborate complicated myths, which constituted the gnosis needed for salvation. They further attempted to incorporate the history of Jesus on earth into their mythological systems. To them, Jesus was not a real, material being; he only appeared to have arrived on earth. Against this, orthodox fathers such as Ignatius of Antioch in the early second century reaffirmed the historical reality of Christ; his sacrifice was an act of history and not an allegorical symbol. Through this stance, the Church retained its appeal to the poor and uneducated, who were unable to comprehend the complicated myths of the gnosis, but readily appreciated that a living person, a historical savior, had come to help them.

A heresy that touched on the character of the Christian revelation was that of Marcion, bishop of the town of Sinope in Asia Minor, who taught about the middle of the second century. A gifted organizer and controversialist, he attracted followers from Mesopotamia to Africa. On dualist principles, he condemned the God of the Old Testament as the god of darkness, and the Testament itself as a record of abominations. Even among the books of the New Testament, he accepted as binding only the Gospel according to Luke and the Epistles of St. Paul. In response to this rejection of a substantial part of the Scriptures, the orthodox Church defined its canon of sacred writings, virtually the modern Bible, as the basic source of Christian teaching.

Issues of ecclesiastical government were raised by another bishop from Asia Minor, Montanus (about 150–200). He maintained that certain living believers were prophets, who were continuously receiving direct inspiration from the Holy Spirit. Women were prominent among the prophets, and the belief eventually won the allegiance of the great North African writer Tertullian. The movement raised the question: Who should rule the Christian congregations—prophets, who might expect continuing new revelations, or priests, who could only interpret a past and closed deposit of faith?

The likelihood of conflict between priests and prophets was present from earliest Christian times but had not previously been resolved. The government of the early Christian community had rested with several officers. A board of elders (*presbuteroi*, from which we get the word "priests") presided over the community. In early times, a bishop (*episcopos* or "overseer") appears among them; sometimes he seems to have been president of the elders, sometimes an official with independent authority. Separate from the elders was a body of deacons; seven served the church of Jerusalem, according to the Acts of the Apostles. The deacons were responsible for collecting donations, distributing charities, and managing the material affairs of the community. It is interesting to note that women too enjoyed considerable prominence, which they subsequently lost, in the administration of these early churches; they formed recognized orders of widows and virgins, and served as deaconesses. But the continued presence of prophets (many of them also women) within the congregation was a source of uncertainty and disturbance. If the prophet spoke with the voice of the Holy Spirit, who could question his or her utterances?

Faced with the claims of the Montanists, who seem to have instigated orgies of prophecy, the orthodox Church denied the need for new revelations. The deposit of faith, all the truths needed for salvation, had been completed upon the death of the evangelist St. John, the last inspired author. At the same time, the Church confirmed the authority of the bishops as sole guardians and interpreters of the body of revelation.

By the third century the Church had acquired those characteristics which it was to preserve through the Middle Ages and beyond: faith in a historical redeemer, a canon of sacred books, and a hierarchical organization based on bishops.

DONATISTS AND ARIANS

The conversion of Constantine and the peace of the Church within the Empire did not bring theological peace. On the contrary, theological controversy mounted in intensity.

In 303, in proclaiming the last persecution of the Christians, Diocletian had ordered priests to surrender their sacred books. Those "traitors" (*traditores*, literally those who "delivered" the Scriptures) earned the lasting hatred of the more steadfast Christians. At the end of the persecution in 313, a party of zealous Christians in North Africa, led by a bishop named Donatus, declared that the traitors, even if repentant, had forever lost membership in the Church; all the sacraments they had ever administered—all baptisms, marriages, ordinations, and the like—were worthless. Since the traitors were many, acceptance of the Donatist program would have brought chaos and revolution to the African church. Moderate Christians won the support of Constantine, who tried to suppress the Donatists by force.

The result was violent schism, which mounted on occasion to civil war. Refusing to accept the rule of traitors, the Donatists established their own bishops and hierarchy. To explain this zeal, modern historians have argued that the movement was in fact an expression of Berber nationalism or an uprising of the oppressed peasantry against the exploitation of the cities. In any case, the schism was still not healed when North Africa was overrun by the barbarian Vandals in 429 and 430.

In response to the Donatists, the orthodox Church determined that the sacraments conferred grace on the recipients *ex opere operato*, "from the work having been worked," automatically, as it were. The spiritual state of the officiating priests did not matter. This remained the accepted position until the issue was raised again in the theological controversies accompanying the Protestant Reformation.

Arius was a priest of Alexandria in Egypt. At some time between 318 and 323 he began to teach that Jesus was not coequal with the Father in the Trinity, but was begotten by him in time: "there was a time when he [Jesus] was not." Arius, in sum, wished to emphasize the monotheistic as opposed to the trinitarian aspects of Christian theology. His teachings raised a furor in Egypt and soon beyond its borders. To restore peace among the theologians, Constantine summoned the first "ecumenical" council (that is, representing the entire inhabited world) of the Christian Church, which met at Nicea in Asia Minor in May 325. With Constantine in attendance, the council condemned Arius, and in the Nicene Creed—the first authoritative declaration of the principal tenets of the Christian faith—it declared that Jesus was coeternal with the Father, and of one substance with him. The pronouncement hardly placated the Arians, and in the years following Nicea they spread their teachings widely in the Empire and even among the Goths settled beyond its borders.

The dispute over the nature of the Trinity inspired further speculations—and new heresies—about the nature of Jesus' humanity. Not until the Council of Chalcedon (held in 451 and regarded as the fourth ecumenical council) was the theology of Jesus clearly defined. He was one person with two natures joined in union. He was both true man and true God. As man, he was authentically the son of Mary, and hence a fitting representative of the human race; as God, he was coequal with the Father and had reigned with him and would reign with him eternally. This definition has since remained the belief of orthodox Christians.

The theological turmoil of the fourth and fifth centuries indicates that Christian thinkers were applying the subtleties of classical philosophy to the deepest mysteries of their faith. Christianity and classical culture had come into intimate, even explosive, contact and on the highest philosophical levels.

THE CHURCH AND CLASSICAL CULTURE

Christian writers had consistently pretended to disparage the learning and literature of the classical world, which were filled, in their estimation, with indecencies, lies, and absurdities. "What has Athens to do with Jerusalem?" demanded Tertullian. But Christians remained indebted to pagan intellectual traditions. They had no choice. The schools of antiquity were all pagan, as were the basic grammars and texts, the authoritative models of argument and style. Moreover, Christianity was a religion based on a book, and the theologians who interpreted the sacred page had to master the arts of exegesis (interpretation), of which the pagans were the accomplished masters. Finally, to defend the faith against pagan detractors, Christian apologists had to master the art of rhetoric; they had to use the arsenal of pagan learning. As St. Augustine urged, Christians were allowed, like the ancient Israelites, to carry off the treasures of the Egyptians (that is, the learning of the pagans) in order to place them at the service of the one true God. This Christian accommodation with pagan learning had decisive repercussions. Nearly all the texts of the great pagan authors have reached us in copies made by Christians. They preserved them because they believed they would be useful in Christian education and theology. Paradoxically, these outspoken enemies of pagan values were instrumental in the survival of a rich cultural heritage, which they claimed to hate.

THE FATHERS OF THE CHURCH

The authoritative writers of the early Christian Church are traditionally called fathers, and the great age of patristic (*pater*, "father") learning is the fourth and early fifth centuries. Their works, in both Latin and Greek, give a kind of late, autumnal splendor to the great literary traditions of both the ancient languages.

Among the Latin fathers, the three great figures of the fourth century are Ambrose, who served as bishop of Milan from 374 until 397; Jerome (340?–420), chiefly known for his translation of the New and Old Testaments from Greek and Hebrew into Latin, in the so-called Vulgate version; and Augustine of Hippo (354–430), greatest of the fathers and perhaps the most influential of Christian theologians.

AUGUSTINE

Augustine was born amid fairly modest circumstances at Tagaste in northern Africa of a Christian mother and a pagan father. (Most of the fathers were of high aristocratic origins.) He studied at Carthage, Rome, and Milan and acquired some reputation as a teacher of rhetoric. In early manhood he had been attracted by the teachings of the Manichees—dualists who were impressed by the power of evil, and saw the world in terms of conflict between the principles of darkness and of light. But under the influence of Ambrose, he converted to Christianity (387), the religion of his childhood. He accepted election as bishop of Hippo in his native northern Africa (395), and spent the last years of his long life writing, preaching, and administering his see. He died even as the Vandals were besieging the city.

Augustine's influence is partially based on his enormous literary output. He had something to say about almost every question of Christian theology. He profoundly influenced, for example, Christian teachings on sexual morality and marriage. His principles were rigorous. Like his pagan contemporaries, he believed that the world was already filled with people. "The coming of Christ," he wrote, "is not served by the begetting of children." "There is not the need of procreation that there once was." He therefore urged all Christians to a life of celibacy, even though this would mean their own declining numbers: "marriage is not expedient, except for those who do not have self-control."

All sexual activity was, of course, banned

for the unmarried. Even within marriage, husband and wife could unite sexually only for procreation. Even so, the pleasure they took in the act, representing a triumph of passion over reason, was at least a small, venial sin. His moral teachings were too rigorous for most pagans, and yet there was one point of agreement between them. Both Augustine and the pagans saw little purpose in further procreation. The human race had already reached the limits of the world.

In theological matters, Augustine was passionately interested in the operations of grace —the special power by which God brought sinful man and faulted creation back to their original destinies. He sought to discern the work of grace in his own life, and the result was his *Confessions*, an intensely personal autobiography and a celebration of the providence that had guided him. This masterpiece of introspective analysis represents a type of literature virtually unknown in the classical tradition.

In questions of dogma, Augustine distinguished between God the creator (the author of nature) and God the redeemer (the source of grace), and insisted that these two operations not be confused. God as creator, or the nature he has created, gives man certain powers, but those powers, injured by the original fall, are insufficient for him to earn his salvation. When an Irish monk named Pelagius declared that people might gain salvation through good works, Augustine sprang into the lists against him. In numerous treatises, he accused Pelagius of magnifying the role of God the creator at the expense of God the redeemer. If people by their unsupported, natural acts might merit salvation, then the cross of Christ was foolish and unneeded. Only through a special power (grace), which Jesus' sacrifice had earned, could man hope to be saved. Moreover, God had known and decided from eternity to whom he would make this gift of grace;

hence, even before we are born, we are all predestined either to heaven or hell.

Augustine did not limit his meditations on grace to the living community of believers. He further believed that the whole course of human history was touched by its power. In his greatest work, the *City of God*, he set forth to show that there was order in history, conferred by a history beyond history, in the sense that behind the manifold events of the human past there was evident the hand of God, directing man through his grace along the ways of his providence. Into this immense panorama, Augustine brought the sacred history of the Jewish Testament, the secular history of his own times, and the Christian expectation of a future resurrection. This total picture of human history and human destiny resembles an epic poem of unrivaled grandeur.

At the same time, Augustine envisioned that the grace and love of God united the chosen in a form of community or city, which was set against the community of those joined by the love of earthly things. The city of God was as yet invisible, and the elect who were its members should recognize that this present earth was not their homeland. The earthly city, identified with the Empire, was not totally evil; it kept the peace, which the elect also enjoyed. Still, it is remarkable how coldly Augustine viewed the wondrous accomplishments of Rome. At all events, to Christians of his own troubled age and to those of later ages, he held out the beckoning vision of a heavenly city, a celestial Jerusalem, where at last they would be home.

IV. THE LATE ROMAN EMPIRE

History is always in transition, and the turning points chosen by historians to mark the beginning and the end of an era are matters of in-

WOMEN'S MARRIAGE AGES AND MEN'S ENLISTMENT AGES COMPARED

AGE OF ROMAN WOMEN AT DATE OF MARRIAGE.

Age	Number of Women	Age	Number of Women	Age	Number of Women
7	1	17	1	28	1
10	3	18	4	30	1
12	7	19	2	31	1
13	6	20	6	32	1
14	6	21	2	56	1
15	8	24	1		
16	5	25	2		59

AGE OF THE SOLDIERS OF THE ROMAN GARRISON ON ENTERING THE ARMY.

Age	Number of Soldiers	Age	Number of Soldiers	Age	Number of Soldiers
15	2	24	8	33	1
16	15	25	12	38	1
17	28	26	7	43	1
18	72	27	9	45	1
19	59	28	1	47	2
20	91	29	2	52	1
21	31	30	3		
22	29	31	2		400
23	18	32	4		

(Source: MacDonnell, "On the Expectation of Life in Ancient Rome," *Biometrika*, 9, 1913)

tellectual convenience; we cannot look back at history without dividing it in some way. Among the more important historical landmarks in the period so far covered by this book, we might mention the unification of the Near East by the rulers of Persia and the expansion of Greek culture into the East as a result of Alexander's conquests. No less a turning point in history was the dissolution of the Roman Empire in the West and its replacement by the young states of medieval Europe.

RESTORATION AND REFORM

The severe political crisis of the third century finally ended in 284 when Diocletian, a high army officer, gained power. He was from the peasantry of Illyria (modern Yugoslavia) and was a strong, ruthless, and heroic man. In order to strengthen the administration, he ruled through an elaborate bureaucracy. His system was authoritarian, almost oriental in its despotism.

Recognizing that the Empire was too large and too unstable to be directed any longer by one man, Diocletian reorganized it into smaller units that could be ruled by a single official. He enlisted three other men to share his rule with him, forming the Tetrarchy (rule of four). Diocletian gave himself and one of the other three the title "Augustus," the other two took the title "Caesar." The two Caesars, who were younger men, were expected to become Augusti in their turn. There was no precise division of the Empire into four parts; each ruler was placed where it seemed most appropriate.

In order to solve the financial crisis and guarantee income for the Empire, Diocletian devised a new system of taxation under which every plot of land was assessed a certain amount, based on productivity and available labor, to be paid to the emperor's agents. There were also taxes on trades and professions so that the burden would not fall solely on landowners. Local officials (*curiales*) were made personally responsible for the required tax and had to pay it themselves if they could not collect it from others. Diocletian also strengthened the secret service unit that was responsible for seeing that taxes were collected. Further, he tried to hold back inflation with a famous Edict on Prices, which fixed a maximum price for nearly all goods. But natural economic forces evidently led to further inflation, and he had to let the edict lapse after a few years.

Diocletian retired in 305 and forced the re-

THE
IMAGE
OF
MAN
IN ANCIENT AND MEDIEVAL ART

Man, however else we choose to define him, is the one creature on this earth capable of asking, "Who am I?" Not only is he capable of asking this question, but he has been asking it so persistently that he seems to be "the animal with the built-in identity crisis."

The question can be asked in a thousand ways, and the responses to it have been equally varied. Modern man tends to define himself, to resolve his doubts about the meaning of life, in terms of his relationships to other people. Until recently, however, man defined himself by relating to unseen forces, immeasurably more powerful than he, whose presence he sensed in the world of nature and to whose will he felt he must submit. We do not know when in the dawn of human history man first attained the degree of self-awareness that made him inquire into his own identity. It seems likely that this stage of man's evolution coincided with the emergence of language and the making of images. Language enabled man to name things and thereby to gain a degree of control over them. For that reason, the name of god remains a carefully guarded secret in some religions; even if known, it may be invoked only on solemn occasions, and profaning it is a grave offense. On the other hand, according to the Bible, Adam named the animals in the Garden of Eden and in doing so became their master. Images, too, confer a kind of power over the things they represent. This is their everlasting fascination, attested by the snapshots in our wallets as much as by the biblical prohibition against "graven images" of the Lord.

By giving names or making images, then, man defined himself in relation to that which was named or represented. Representation implies the idea of substitution; the image is a stand-in for its model. But if the model is known only through a substitute, as was true for images of spirits or deities, then the substitute tends to assume the reality of the original; it becomes an idol, the dwelling place of the god. Early man believed that by providing a dwelling place for the god he compelled the disembodied spirit to inhabit it; and since the dwelling place, the image, was under man's control, the spirit within it was too; that is, it was ready to be coaxed, bargained with, or propitiated by sacrifice and prayer.

If this need to gain control over the uncontrollable was a primary impulse in the development of art, it is not surprising that for many thousands of years the image of man played only a minor role. There are numerous images of man in the art of the Old and New Stone ages, but they are incidental rather than dominant in relation to those of animals, which usually strike us as far more organic and keenly observed. The human form in these images is subject to radical abbreviation, distortion, or transformation, often merging with animal features. Clearly, prehistoric man did not yet claim a privileged status for himself with respect to his fellow creatures; he resolved his identity crisis by relating his own existence to the rest of nature through an intricate system of magic kinship expressed in the concepts of totem and taboo.

In the course of the fourth millennium B.C. several interdependent developments occurred in Egypt and the Middle East that gave man a radically different view of himself: the growth of cities and of a more highly organized society divided into distinct classes, the invention of writing, and the emergence of a new concept of divinity. Totem and taboo gradually gave way to the belief in gods that had human shape, although many of them retained animal heads or wings to differentiate them from ordinary mortals; and man learned how to see himself in relation to these gods rather than to rocks, plants, or animals. It was his claim to a special relationship with the gods that differentiated man from all other creatures and gave him a unique, privileged status. The words of the Old Testament, "And the Lord said, Let us make man in our image and likeness," have their counterpart in the mythology of many peoples in the ancient world.

It now became the artist's task to make gods in the image and likeness of man. Faced with this challenge, the artist evolved a stable concept of human perfection, an ideal image of man; and the same ideal served him when he had to portray individual men, for only those were so honored who could claim kinship with the divine. In Egypt, where the ruler himself had the status of a god, this included members of his family and court, such as Ankh-haf (see Plate 1). The bust is a majestic likeness; over and above all its personal traits, it reflects a well-defined ideal of human perfection in the broad shoulders, the emphasis on smooth, rounded shapes, the proportional relationship of head, neck, and body. Yet this ideal physical image, however impressive, gives no hint of animation or action.

The very opposite may be said of Abikhil, Ankh-haf's Mesopotamian contemporary (see Plate 2). His physical presence is unimpressive, but he radiates a quality of spiritual communication with the deity that is lacking in Egyptian art. Although motionless, the figure acts, through the energetically clasped hands, the smile, the huge eyes. The image of Abikhil's god, had it been preserved, would show the same qualities in still more emphatic form; he would be communicating with his worshipers. These contrasting conceptions of man's relationship to the divine—the Egyptian emphasis on physical beauty, the Mesopotamian emphasis on communication—became the basis for the image of man in Greece, which in turn bequeathed it to Rome, to the Middle Ages, and to the Renaissance. The Greeks, after borrowing first from the Mesopotamians (see Plate 3), then the Egyptians, arrived at a balanced synthesis that was to remain a model for Western civilization until modern times (see Plate 4). Cicero defined the classical image of man for all posterity when he spoke of man as a "mortal god"; that is, a being who, though mortal, shares not only the physical beauty of the gods but their power to act and communicate. Even the portrait heads of Hellenistic Greece and the Roman Empire, however much they may reflect the troubled uncertainties of the individual psyche, still reveal a kinship with the physical nobility of the gods (see Plate 5).

The early images of Christ and the saints followed this classical tradition (see Plate 10); they could be distinguished from their pagan models only by such external attributes as haloes. Christ in his human incarnation was assumed to have looked like any other man. When the Christian emperors, claiming to rule by divine grace, wanted this special relationship to God conveyed in visual terms, the Mesopotamian tradition of man's spiritual likeness to the divine reasserted itself and the classical balance of body and spirit was lost; the figures became rigid and attenuated, their structure concealed behind heavy ceremonial garments, and expression was centered in the head, with its huge staring eyes (see Plates 7 and 11). The image of Christ, too, evolved from that of a man among men to that of the awesome ruler of the universe (see Plate 8). Not until the twelfth and thirteenth centuries did the humanity of Christ return to Western art and, in its train, the humanity of those to whom he had brought redemption, be they participants in the drama of the lamentation (see Plate 14) or simple peasants working their fields (see Plate 15). The image of man that evolved during the later Middle Ages conveys man's openness to emotional experience, his vulnerability and humility—qualities never stressed before. Yet it was the soil from which grew the Renaissance, the rebirth of the classical concept of man as a "mortal god."

These two figures in Plates 1 and 2, about the same date and similar in material, show how differently the oldest historic civilizations conceived the image of man. In ancient Egypt, the sculptor's most important task was to carve tomb statues of the Pharaoh—the divine ruler—and of the members of his court who could claim a share of his divinity through their relationship to him. Such statues were not meant for the eyes of ordinary mortals, but were permanent substitutes for the mummified body, so that the soul might always have an abode to come back to. The bust of Ankh-haf is a fully individual portrait —it fits no other soul but his— yet we could not possibly call it a speaking likeness. No hint of action—physical or psychological— disturbs the calm of its powerful shapes. The bust is a work designed for eternity, waiting to be animated by the recurrent visits of the spirit.

The statue of Abikhil, by contrast, is a portrait in name only, through its inscription, which also tells us that the figure was a present for the goddess Ishtar. Its purpose was to serve as a substitute for Abikhil in the act of communicating with the deity, and this act it conveys with extraordinary concentration. The hands are firmly locked in the Sumerian gesture of worship; a smile—denoting aliveness rather than a specific emotional state— makes the corners of the mouth curl upward. But the chief instruments of communication are the huge, luminous eyes, inlaid with shell and lapis lazuli and outlined in black, with their fixed wide-open stare. These clearly were the essential aspects for both sculptor and patron. Individuality is established by the written name, not by the facial features, which here simply repeat the racial type. Nor, unlike the Egyptian sculptor, does the artist show any interest in the subtleties of man's anatomy; in Ankh-haf the sculptor shows the firm presence of the skull beneath the flesh, but in Abikhil the artist makes no differentiation except in the fleecy waves of the beard. Yet the figure speaks, while Ankh-haf is forever mute.

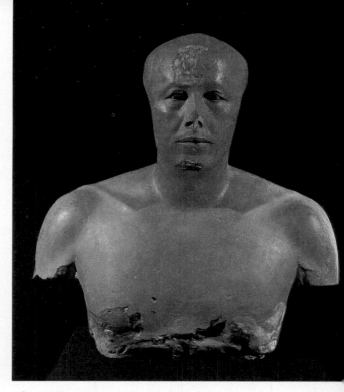

Plate 1. *Egypt,* BUST OF PRINCE ANKH-HAF
ca. 2600 B.C., *painted limestone, lifesize*
Museum of Fine Arts, Boston

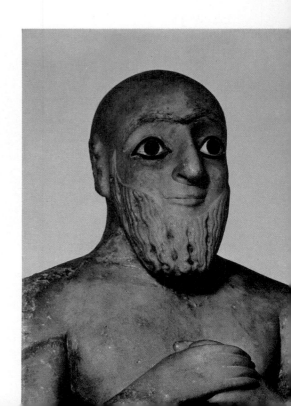

Plate 2. *Mesopotamia,* ABIKHIL
SUPERINTENDENT OF THE ISHTAR TEMPLE AT MARI
ca. 2750 B.C., *alabaster, height of portion shown about 10"*
Louvre Museum, Paris

Plate 3.
Greece, THE BLINDING OF POLYPHEMUS
ca. 675–650 B.C., *Proto-Attic amphora,*
height of portion shown about 16″
Museum, Eleusis

Greek artists built on the work of their predecessors in Egypt and Mesopotamia, but they profoundly transformed this heritage in keeping with the dynamic, man-centered world view that is the hallmark of Greek civilization. The gods now became human, not only in shape but in their relations with men; they no longer dominated life on earth or in the hereafter, and eventually were rationalized as the glorified memories of heroes. Such a hero was Odysseus, whose greatest exploit, the blinding of the one-eyed giant Polyphemus, is depicted on the neck of the two-handled storage jar (amphora) in Plate 3. The huge vessel, 56 inches tall, once held the body of a child. Its decoration, however, is not concerned with afterlife; instead, it celebrates man's victory over the forces of darkness. It takes three men to thrust the spear into the giant's eye, and their action is portrayed with great directness and expressive force. The heads, with their large noses and oversized eyes, still recall the art of the ancient Near East (compare Plate 2), but the muscular bodies and agitated movements bespeak the Greek painter's emphasis on doing rather than being.

Odysseus and his companions do not yet show the ideal of physical beauty we have come to expect of Greek art. That ideal made its appearance only two hundred years later in what we call the classic period of Greece—classic because its achievements set a standard of perfection which Western civilization has acknowledged ever since. We can see it in the graceful outlines, the harmonious proportions, and the balanced, self-contained pose of the lyre-playing maiden in Plate 4. She is painted on the body of a slender oil jug (lekythos), a funerary offering found in the grave of a girl. The instrument is Apollo's, and Mount Helicon is his abode; perhaps, then, the Muse was meant to commemorate the musical gifts of the deceased. Painted pottery, despite its narrow range of means—outline drawing, flat color, and a severely limited choice of pigments—was highly prized by the Greeks. Its finest masters, such as the Achilles Painter, were great artists of such individuality that we can recognize their personal styles even if we do not know their names. By careful observation of nature, they learned how to draw the human form in such a way that the outlines alone convey its roundness and weight.

Plate 4.
The Achilles Painter, MUSE ON MOUNT HELICON
ca. 445 B.C., *white-ground lekythos,*
height of portion shown about 6"
Private Collection, Lugano

Individual portraiture became an important concern of Greek artists only after the classic ideal of physical beauty had been established, and even the most striking portraits reflect a residue of this ideal. The ideal serves as a kind of matrix within which the sitter's unique features are embedded and lends him a heroic air although, as in Plate 5, his personality may be quite unheroic. The somewhat flabby features, the plaintive mouth, the unhappy eyes under furrowed brows, reveal a man beset by doubts and anxieties strangely akin to our own. Such men had surely existed earlier in the Greek world as they exist today, but only now, near the end of Greek independence, could the artist grasp such psychological complexity. This intensely private view of the sitter immediately captures our sympathy.

Landscape made its appearance in Greek art even later than portraiture. How indeed could a civilization that viewed man as the measure of all things be expected to celebrate the unbounded immensity of nature? Yet at some point—perhaps only after they had become part of the Roman world—the Greeks added this achievement to their many others. It matters little whether the artist who painted the impressive series of *Odysseus Landscapes* (of which Plate 6 shows one section) on the walls of a house in ancient Rome was a Greek or a Roman. What he shows us, framed by pilasters as if seen through a window, is the sun-drenched shore of the Mediterranean with masses of rock abruptly rising from deep blue waters that stretch to the very limits of our vision. A fine haze marks the meeting of sea and sky at the line of the horizon. In this timeless world, the human drama of the foreground is merely a passing episode; Odysseus, the great hero whose blinding of Polyphemus had been so impressively celebrated on the Proto-Attic amphora, no longer dominates the scene. His adventures have receded from the center of consciousness. Here, they are no more than an excuse for the landscape painter's art.

Plate 5. Greece, PORTRAIT HEAD *(from Delos)*
ca. 80 B.C., *bronze, lifesize*
National Archeological Museum, Athens

Plate 6. Rome, ODYSSEUS LANDSCAPE
late 1st century B.C., *wall painting*
Museo Profano, Vatican

Plate 7. Byzantine
THE EMPEROR JUSTINIAN AND ATTENDANTS *(detail)*
ca. 547, mosaic
San Vitale, Ravenna

The classical ideal of beauty had begun to decay from the third century on when the Roman world entered an ever deepening social and political crisis. A new ideal emerged only after Christianity became the official religion of what remained of the Roman Empire and artists had learned how to give visible form to the truths of the new faith. How remote this image of man is from the classical tradition can be seen in the portrait of Justinian and his entourage in Plate 7: the human body—flattened, attenuated, motionless, rigidly frontal—disappears behind a screen of ceremonial garments; it is these garments that signal rank, dignity, and station in life, which now are far more important than the individual's physical appearance. All the faces tend to look alike, sharing a dominant feature: the huge staring eyes, which recall those of the superintendent of the Ishtar Temple (compare Plate 2) and are meant to convey the same intense relationship to the deity.

This style, called Byzantine (after Byzantium, the old Greek name of the capital of Justinian's empire), was created by painters rather than by

Plate 8. Byzantine
CHRIST IN MAJESTY
ca. 1148, mosaic
Cathedral, Cefalù

sculptors. Free-standing statuary soon disappeared altogether, not to be revived until the Italian Renaissance. Among all the techniques of painting, mosaic was the one best adapted to the new ideal of beauty. Greeks and Romans had used colored marble cubes in floor mosaics; the Byzantines used cubes of tinted glass and glass backed with gold leaf to cover the walls and vaults of their churches with images of dazzling brilliance and luminosity. What ancient artists must have regarded as the limitations of the medium—its patternlike flatness and lack of delicate tonal gradation —now became its chief virtues: if mosaic could not create an illusion of reality such as the landscape in Plate 6, it was superbly suited to project an illusion of celestial space. The huge image of Christ in Plate 8 that fills the half-dome behind the altar in the Cathedral of Cefalù in Sicily is a truly awesome figure whose intense gaze endows the concept of the all-present God with overpowering reality.

Plate 9. Irish
ST. MARK AND THE SYMBOLS OF
THE FOUR EVANGELISTS
(from a Gospel Book)
8th century, miniature
Stiftsbibliothek, St. Gall

Plate 10. Carolingian
ST. MATTHEW
(from the Gospel Book of Charlemagne)
ca. 810, miniature
Kunsthistorisches Museum, Vienna

Far removed as it was from that of the Greeks and Romans, Byzantine art remained true to the classical past in that its central concern continued to be the human form. The Celtic and Germanic peoples of northwestern Europe shared an artistic heritage of a radically different sort: theirs was an art of ornament, mingling abstract linear rhythms, geometric patterns, and animal motifs. In accepting Christianity, they also accepted the Mediterranean tradition of the image of man, but their first impulse was to assimilate it as much as possible to their own sense of design. The strange result may be seen in the St. Mark in Plate 9: the figure shows no feeling for the organic continuity of the human body. It resembles an intricate knot that seems far more closely related to the ornamental panels surrounding it than to the classical model from which the image is ultimately derived.

The model must have been a picture in another Gospel manuscript, produced in one of the ancient centers of the Mediterranean world from which the missionaries set out to convert the heathen of the North. Christianity was a scriptural religion, hence the book containing the Word of God became a precious object, the copying and embellishment of the sacred text a pious act. The portraits of the evangelists in the earliest Gospel books were patterned on those of Greek and Roman artists. We can infer this from such miniatures as the St. Matthew in Plate 10, which was painted less than a century after the St. Mark but with a wholly new understanding of the classical tradition. Except for the large halo, the visible symbol of his sanctity, this evangelist is easily recognizable as a descendant of the *Muse on Mount Helicon* (compare Plate 4), even though separated from her by no less than 1,250 years. How could this picture have been done in northern Europe around the year 800? We know nothing about the artist, but his work is striking evidence of the Carolingian Renaissance, the classical revival in politics, art, and literature radiating from the court of Charlemagne, the first medieval ruler to assume the mantle of the Roman emperors of old. His empire did not survive long, but he revived the classical tradition that continued to inspire medieval civilization.

Plate 11. Medieval, RELIQUARY OF SAINTE-FOY
9th—10th century, gold, enamel, and gems,
height of portion shown about 9"
Abbey Church, Conques

If the connection linking the Carolingian St. Matthew and the Greek Muse (Plates 10 and 4) is readily apparent, it takes a sharp eye indeed to perceive any relationship between the head of Sainte-Foy in Plate 11 and the portrait in Plate 5. Yet such a link exists, for the face of the saint was originally the portrait of a late Roman ruler reworked and adapted to its present purpose in the wake of the Carolingian Renaissance. The large eyes and impersonal features betray a closer kinship to the Justinian mosaic (compare Plate 7) than to the Greek head; still, it is a product of pagan antiquity, and we are surprised to see it surviving in a Christian context.

How was this possible? Free-standing sculpture had disappeared with the victory of Christianity, and ancient statues had been destroyed by the thousands as pagan idols. The Middle Ages knew only applied sculpture, that is, sculpture which was an integral part of the architecture of churches and palaces or of their furnishings. The one apparent exception are reliquaries, but even these obey the rule: as sculptured containers of holy relics, they too had a service function which saved them from the evil odor of idolatry.

Let us turn once more to the two evangelists in Plates 9 and 10. What might be the outcome if two styles as different as these could somehow be merged? This is what happened in the years after the Carolingian Renaissance; and the new style, called Romanesque, emerged everywhere in Western Europe toward the end of the eleventh century. The *Annunciation* miniature in Plate 12 is a powerful example, combining the Celtic-Germanic sense of linear pattern with the Mediterranean figurative tradition. Unlike the St. Matthew, this miniature has no depth; all forms remain on the surface. Yet the picture plane is not simply flat, it is a field of force. The urgency of the angel's message, conveyed through his glance and gestures, is matched by the response of the Virgin Mary, awestruck and submissive at once. The contrast of active and passive could hardly be expressed with greater eloquence.

Plate 12. Romanesque, THE ANNUNCIATION *(from the* St. Albans Psalter)
ca. 1120, miniature
St. Godehard, Hildesheim

Plate 13. *Gothic*
CHARLEMAGNE BUILDING A CHURCH
ca. 1220, stained glass
Chartres Cathedral

Plate 14. *Giotto*
LAMENTATION
1305—1306, wall painting
Scrovegni Chapel, Padua

The great Gothic cathedrals which rose in France between 1150 and 1250 reflect a religious fervor among all strata of the population such as the Middles Ages had not known before. This newly felt devotion profoundly transformed the image of man as seen in the sculpture and painting of the time: the harsh expressiveness of the Roman-esque yields to a gentler, more realistic art stressing the human aspect of Christ and the saints. This is true even of stained glass, a pictorial technique that does not lend itself to realism. Plate 13 shows a small part of one of the windows at Chartres Cathedral, devoted to the deeds of Charlemagne (who wears a halo, having become a saint). The unknown artist does not present him as an awesome figure; the workmen busily erecting the church on the right are the same size as the emperor and attract our attention as much as he does. There is an attempt, by means of curving, hooklike lines, to endow the drapery folds with a measure of three-dimensionality, but such realistic impulses are severely limited by the nature of stained-glass

images (black outline drawings on pieces of brilliantly tinted glass).

It was in Italy, less than a century later, that Gothic realism was to bear its most important fruits. Compared to our sample of stained glass, Giotto's *Lamentation* over the dead Christ in Plate 14 looks like a direct revival of ancient painting (compare Plate 10) with its full-bodied, weighty figures seen against a background of landscape and blue sky. Giotto had surely studied the remains of ancient Roman murals, yet the way

he approaches his subject—as an emotion-filled human drama rather than as solemn ritual—derives from the Gothic north. To his contemporaries, Giotto's pictures seemed as real as nature itself: not only did the figures have all the solid, tangible qualities of statues, they were animated by feelings that made the beholder see himself as a participant of the scene. Giotto thus became the fountainhead of a great new tradition which was to transform all of European painting within the next hundred years.

Plate 15.
Ambrogio Lorenzetti, GOOD GOVERNMENT *(detail)*
1338—1340, wall painting
Palazzo Pubblico, Siena

If Giotto's *Lamentation* impresses us with its simple and direct humanity, the setting of the figures is severely limited—a stage barely deep enough to hold them and a minimum of props. The exploration of spatial depth was left to younger Italian painters such as Ambrogio Lorenzetti. In his view of country life in Plate 15, the setting is no longer a backdrop, but an environment within which men move as they do in the *Odysseus Landscape* (compare Plate 6). Cottages, fields, and orchards, peasants harvesting, threshing, and driving their heavily burdened donkeys—

every detail of this scene will seem familiar to the traveler who knows the countryside between Florence and Siena.

In the fourteenth century, such travelers included a number of painters from north of the Alps who went south while some of the Italian masters went north to the art centers of Paris or Prague. As a consequence of these exchanges, there developed toward 1400 the International Gothic style, so called because it prevailed all over Europe with only minor local variations. It was the last phase of medieval art, soon to give way

to the revolutionary developments of the following century. And the dawn of a new era announced itself in at least one respect: most medieval art was supported by the patronage of institutions, but the International Gothic was to a large extent sustained by the taste of individual collectors such as the duke who commissioned the *Très riches heures.* This is a book of hours, a personal prayerbook, but one designed as a magnificent showpiece rather than for actual use. Our miniature in Plate 16 belongs to the calendar that forms part of a book of hours. Clearly, the Limbourg Brothers must have known landscapes such as Lorenzetti's; how else could they have caught the seasonal features of country life—the flowering trees in the walled garden, the fishermen on the river—with such fidelity? But the seasonal activity of the foreground, a tender betrothal scene, relates directly to their patron. It probably shows the betrothal of the duke's granddaughter, and the participants are portraits, even though differentiated mainly by their extravagantly lavish costumes. In a history of fashion, the International Gothic must figure as the earliest Age of Elegance.

tirement of Maximian, the other Augustus. The two Caesars of the Tetrarchy then became Augusti in turn, but they were unable to maintain stable rule. They did appoint two new Caesars in an effort to continue the system of the Tetrarchy, but the arrangement soon broke down. Years of complex intrigue and civil war followed, as several leaders fought for the throne. Constantine, the son of Constantius, one of the current Augusti, began to call himself Augustus in 306 when his father died. We need not follow the course of the battles fought by the several rivals for the throne. Finally, in 324, Constantine overcame the opposition and gained recognition as sole emperor of Rome. Thus forty years after the accession of Diocletian the Empire was once again guided by a single mind.

CONSTANTINE AND THE BUREAUCRACY

Constantine expanded the bureaucracy established by Diocletian. By the end of his reign in 337 the pattern was set that remained throughout the fourth and later centuries. The whole state was cast into a rigid structure, almost one massive corporation, in which individual initiative was brutally discouraged.

For the sake of administrative efficiency the provinces were divided into more manageable units, numbering about 120. In no case did the governor of a province command the troops, as had been the custom earlier; instead, the troops were commanded by *duces* (leaders, or dukes). This separated the governors from any force that they might have used in order to revolt. The provinces were grouped into 14 (later 12) units called dioceses, each of them administered by a *vicarius* ("vicar"). The dioceses were in turn grouped into 4 larger structures called prefectures.

The old Roman Senate was now powerless and became only the town council of Rome, but the title "senator" continued to be used to

The Emperor Constantine tried to increase his glory by commissioning colossal portraits of himself, such as the one shown here. (Photo: Hirmer Fotoarchiv München)

denote civil servants close to the emperor. Further bureaucratic posts were established just below this new senatorial order. Far lower in the bureaucratic hierarchy were the local city councils, whose members, the *curiales*, served under compulsion. These councils were the foundation of the whole administrative structure.

Economic life suffered. Members of all trades and professions were grouped into *corpora*, or corporations, and to change profession was difficult. To make certain that the various services would be performed, the state made professions hereditary. We have seen that the state bound the tenant farmers, or coloni, to the soil. A small class of independent farmers clung to their existence, but the general trend was toward converting agricultural workers into near slaves.

Many features of absolute monarchy are common to the reigns of Diocletian and Constantine. Taxation was oppressive, and no manner of complaints from the people made the least difference. There was a deep gulf between the monarch's court and the common people. Even within the court the emperor stood apart from the rest, surrounded by oriental ceremony. Fourth-century rulers wore expensive cloaks dyed in purple, and courtiers had to kiss a corner of their robes when approaching the throne. Diadems, the custom of kneeling before the emperor, and other marks of royalty became traditional and have remained so in European monarchies.

Constantine, it is true, was never worshiped as a god. Rather, he chose to exploit his new position as patron of the Christian faith to claim for himself a sacred aura. Even when still unbaptized, he consorted with the bishops at Nicea as their equal, or rather as their mentor. He appropriated the title of sacred for his person, his family, his officials, his army, and his palaces. He was the first ruler to discern and exploit that divinity which hedges, but does not quite infuse, the Christian king.

The reforms of Diocletian and Constantine won two additional centuries of survival for the Western Empire (to 476). Even more lasting were the benefits conferred on the Eastern Empire. Constantine established as its capital the new city of Constantinople, founded on the site of the Greek colony of Byzantium. This city stood as a living monument to his name for more than 1000 years, until taken by the Ottoman Turks in 1453. The reforms of these two emperors, in sum, helped the Eastern Empire to become one of the most long-lived states in human history.

THE COURSE OF THE LATER EMPIRE

After the death of Constantine in 337, the chief administrative problem of the Empire for more than a century was whether one man could be strong enough to rule as sole monarch. For most of the time this proved impossible, and some kind of shared rule on the pattern established by Diocletian became regular. On the death of Theodosius, in 395, the Empire was divided into an Eastern and a Western half, with the dividing line just east of Italy. This was only formal recognition of a state of affairs that had existed for decades.

PROBLEMS OF THE WESTERN EMPIRE

The rigid society that developed during the last centuries of the Western Empire did not, and perhaps could not, allow people to move freely from one class to another. The coloni were bound to the soil chiefly because foreign conquest could no longer provide a regular flow of slaves who might replace them in agriculture. As the central government weakened, the estates, usually called villas, became more independent, and the coloni became more dependent on the owners for protection. Thus the villas developed into the political unit to which the coloni felt allegiance. Many villas were completely self-sufficient units resembling the later manors of the Middle Ages, with hunting lands and workshops that supplied the goods needed by the local population. The villas therefore became the main economic and political units of the Western empire.

CAUSES FOR THE DECLINE

The formal end of the Western Empire is traditionally dated at 476, when a Germanic warlord deposed the man who is called the last emperor, Romulus Augustulus.[7] Modern readers inevitably think of this event in the terminology imposed by the historical masterpiece of Edward Gibbon: that is, as the "decline and fall" of the Empire. But, of course, no political structure as large as the Roman Empire really falls like a tree in a forest without further influence or legacy. The survival of the Christian religion through the medium of classical languages alone is sufficient proof that the Empire and its heritage did not vanish without a trace.

Yet even though historians take care to speak of the transformation of the Empire rather than of its disappearance, there is no doubt that the Empire in the West did pass away while the Byzantine Empire in the East survived for nearly another thousand years. The problem is to explain why the regions of Italy, Spain, and Gaul could not maintain themselves under a continuous government and why at the same time no dissolution threatened the Eastern regions of the Empire. In other words, the causes for Rome's decline that the historian identifies must operate only in the Western half of the Empire.

Many explanations have been given. Gibbon, for example, assigned the cause to the destructive work of "barbarism and religion." But to say that Rome declined because of invasions by Germans, Franks, and Goths only pushes the inquiry back one step: Why were these tribes at last able to defeat an Empire that had ruled the civilized world through disciplined armies for centuries? And why did not the Eastern part of the Empire decline along with the Western?

Some historians have said that the mixing

of peoples within the Empire, a process that certainly did take place during the centuries, produced an inferior population that lacked the virility to withstand the invasions of the third and fourth centuries. This racial theory is, however, highly unscientific and would appeal to few historians today. After all, the Greeks, Germans, and Slavs who mixed with the Romans were not physically inferior to them and could have fought effectively enough in the armies. A more plausible supplement to this theory is the view that the emperors unintentionally paved the way for the fall of Rome by exterminating possible political rivals in the upper class; thus they weakened this class and prevented it from contributing leadership to the state. It is true that the Senate of the later Empire became feebler and less able to resist the dictatorial rule of emperors, a condition caused largely by the arbitrary execution of senators at the hands of emperors. Recently, an older theory of lead poisoning among the aristocracy has been revived. The wealthier Romans adopted Greek methods of cooking with lead utensils and drank water that was funneled through lead pipes. The theory postulates that the diluted lead made the wealthy classes progressively sterile; thus they failed to reproduce potential leaders.

Some scholars have advanced an economic argument, saying that the Empire was bound to decline because it never really emerged from a domestic economy to an industrial one. But this theory is hardly convincing, for some societies—admittedly much less complex than the Empire—have existed for many centuries with no more than a domestic economy. If there had been no convulsions and strains in the Empire, the production of goods and food could have continued more or less unchanged. Soil exhaustion and fluctuating cycles of rainfall and drought have also been proposed in

---

[7] Romulus himself was not the legal emperor but only the son of a usurper; the recognized Western emperor, Nepos, lived until 480. But within the sixth century, 476 became recognized as the date for the fall.

order to explain Rome's economic depression, but there is little exact knowledge about the cycles of crops and weather conditions that would indubitably account for the fall of the Empire.

Other scholars have suggested that the weakness of the Western Empire was due to a shortage of manpower. This explanation does seem fairly sound; the Eastern cities appear to have been more populous than the Western ones, and they had more strength and resilience. The numerical inferiority of the West became even more serious when the villas began to operate as self-sufficient units and the population no longer manned an army that was directed by a central authority. It was much easier for outsiders to invade the Empire when they met haphazard resistance from local forces. The relocation of the capital to Constantinople moved the administrative center even farther from the Western provinces; probably this accelerated the dissolution of the regions of Italy and Gaul.

But the shortage of manpower was not the only factor in the weakening of the Western Empire. Its physical geography doomed it to be more vulnerable to invasion than the Eastern Empire. Warlike tribes streamed along the Danube valley and through the terrain of Central Europe into the Western provinces, a less hazardous route than the journey south through the difficult mountains of the Balkans, Greece, and Asia Minor into the Eastern Empire.

Other conditions made the Western Empire less able to resist destructive invasions. In the late second and third centuries the emperors had deliberately increased the prestige of the army and depressed the Senate and the civil service. The creature that they fashioned soon began to rule them, for the armies and their leaders made and unmade emperors at will. The only way to preserve civilian control over the military machine would have been to entrust more responsibility to the Senate and maintain strong civil servants. But the emperors simply continued along the path of absolute coercion. This repression stifled initiative and made the lower classes apathetic and resentful. Nearly the whole economic strength of the state was now devoted to paying and equipping the army, and the system of tax collecting probably left little to the citizen for expanding or repairing his possessions. These conditions gave citizens only slight motivation to defend their oppressive government; domination by invading tribes may have seemed not much worse than being in the grip of the Roman state.

One must also look at the great number of holidays and forms of amusement within the city of Rome: To what degree did laziness and luxury contribute to the fall of the Empire? It seems clear that the masses in the city, scarcely required to work and pampered with free amusements, gradually lost their feelings of responsibility. In 69, as Tacitus reports, the crowd cheered with pleasure as rival troops fought in the streets for the throne. When the masses no longer had to exert more than minimal effort to survive, they abandoned the discipline and civic cooperation that had created the Empire. Public office was shunned, non-Italians supplied the troops, and appeals to the people to show traditional Roman firmness in danger found little response. The high price that Rome finally paid for her luxury was the destruction of the state.

Finally, historians must consider the great upheaval in the sphere of ideas and faith. We cannot express this view in the language of science or statistics, but Christianity must have weakened the defenses of the Empire. In the Roman scheme the emperors, governors, and administrators stood far above the people, and the objective in life was to attain a higher position. Roman religion offered little spiritual compensation for a low rank in the world. The Judeo-Christian faith, as we have seen, offered something better: the message that all persons are potentially equal in the eyes of God and may hope for a better afterlife through salvation. Were the increasing numbers of Christians really prepared to fight for the preservation of the old system? This spiritual rejection, as we might call it, worked along with the mighty pressures of invasion to cause the "fall" of Rome—an event that the modern world sees as a possible model of its own fate. The fall, a challenge and a warning to all who read history, is the recognized end of the ancient world and the beginning of a long period in which new nations would use the legacy of antiquity in their own development.

The constitutional order established by Augustus gave to the Roman Empire two centuries of peace. The economy attained a material prosperity that would not again be reached, at least in the West, for 1000 years. Populous cities dotted the Empire; Rome herself, with upwards of 500,000 people, was a wonder of the world. Gifted writers—Vergil, Tacitus, and others—made this a resplendent age for Latin letters.

And yet the imperial colossus concealed certain fatal flaws, which became manifest in the rampant chaos of the third century. The slave economy demanded a constant supply of human chattel, which it rapidly consumed. The end of aggressive wars and the suppression of piracy cut off this critical recruitment of slaves. And the values preached by pagan philosophy, urging the pursuit of the good life here and now, had little to offer to the enslaved, the exploited, the subjugated.

Ancient society responded to these pressures with new ways of organizing and rewarding labor and with new cultural attitudes. In agriculture, the small farm, run by housed slaves or free tenants called coloni, *slowly replaced the large slave-run estate. In towns, the victory of free labor over slavery seems to have been even more rapid and decisive. But in committing a larger and fairer share of the social product to its humblest classes, ancient society deprived itself of the disposable resources it needed to meet the menace of invading peoples beyond the imperial frontiers.*

Values, too, were changing. The peoples of the Empire, disillusioned with or unconvinced by the official paganism, sought new visions of the cosmos, new reasons for living. Mystery religions, holding out the promise of eternal life, gained unprecedented popularity. But Christianity eventually won out over all its rivals; with the conversion of Constantine, it became the favored, and not long after the established, religion of the late Empire.

Witness to profound changes in every sector of her life, Rome could not maintain the continuity of her rule in all her provinces, across this tumultuous age. But in economy and culture, the late Empire had already laid the foundations upon which would rise the new states of the Middle Ages.

RECOMMENDED READING

Sources

Ayer, Joseph Cullen. *A Source Book for Ancient Church History.* 1913.

Suetonius. *Lives of the Caesars.* Robert Graves (tr.). 1972.

Tacitus. *Complete Works.* A. J. Church and W. J. Brodribb (trs.). 1942.

Studies

Alföldi, A. *The Conversion of Constantine and Pagan Rome.* 1948.

*Chambers, Mortimer (ed.). *The Fall of Rome—Can It Be Explained?* 1970. A collection of modern attempts to explain the decline of Rome.

*Cochrane, Charles Norris. *Christianity and Classical Culture.* 1957. A highly sympathetic study of interaction between the two cultures.

Daniélou, Jean, and Henri Marrou. *The First Six Hundred Years.* Vol. 1 of *The Christian Centuries,* L. J. Rogier and others (eds.). 1964. Now the most comprehensive history of the Catholic Church.

Driver, G. R. *The Judaean Scrolls: The Problem and a Solution.* 1946.

Gibbon, Edward. *The History of the Decline and Fall of the Roman Empire* (originally 1776–1788; best edition by J. B. Bury, 7 vols., 1896–1900).

———. *Autobiography* (sometimes called *Memoirs of My Life and Writings;* good edition by J. B. Bury 1907). A delightful memoir of the eighteenth-century mind; explains Gibbon's choice of a theme.

Jones, A. H. M. *The Later Roman Empire, 284–602.* 1964.

MacMullen, Ramsay. *Enemies of the Roman Order.* 1966. On the internal causes of Rome's decline.

*Nock, Arthur Darby. *Conversion.* 1961. The transition from paganism to Christianity; the best book of its kind.

Rostovtzeff, M. *The Social and Economic History of the Roman Empire.* 1957. Explains the decline of Rome as caused by a conflict between classes.

Syme, Ronald. *Tacitus.* 1958. Not only a study of the historian, but a microscopic analysis of the politics of the Empire.

Vogt, Joseph. *The Decline of Rome: The Metamorphosis of Ancient Civilization.* 1969.

---

*Available in paperback.

SIX

THE MAKING
OF WESTERN EUROPE

Three new civilizations fell heir to the classical tradition after the fall of Rome. A distinctive system of religious belief marked each of them—Roman, or Catholic, Christianity in Western Europe; Eastern, or Orthodox, Christianity in Asia Minor, the Balkan Peninsula, and Russia; and Islam in the Middle East and North Africa. These new civilizations differed from their common parent in two fundamental ways. The new societies were predominantly peasant; they were based upon willing, if not exactly free, labor. Although slavery remained important, it no longer provided a principal support to their economic systems. The new cultures were dominated by the Christian and Muslim visions of an afterlife and the hope of personal salvation, while scholars in both East and West sought to combine these religious views with the cultural heritage of Greece and Rome.

These "higher religions," as they are sometimes called, offered to even the humblest members of society a sense of individual dignity and destiny. Unlike the slaves of antiquity who lived and died with little sustaining hope, the peasants believed that their lives and labors, however hard and cruel, were not meaningless. They learned from Christianity and Islam that God had created them and that, if they did God's will on earth, they would ultimately attain eternal life.

Many other changes accompanied the change in religion. A vast movement of peoples took place. Celts, Germans, and Slavs in the north and east, Arabs in the south, and other barbarians shifted or enlarged the areas of their former settlements; their migrations permanently affected the composition of the populations in Europe and the Middle East. In spite of these migrations and the violence that accompanied them, Western and Eastern peoples slowly rebuilt their economies.

Technological innovations aided the peasants to carry on intensive agriculture in areas, principally in northern Europe, that had not been efficiently cultivated before. These medieval societies also developed new economic and social institutions, such as the large estate or manor, based in Europe on semifree or serf labor. Upon these institutions they raised new political structures. Western and Eastern peoples also combined elements from both the barbarian and classical inheritances to form their distinctive cultures.

This chapter examines the emergence of Western Europe—one of the three successor civilizations to arise in the Early Middle Ages upon the twin supports of peasant labor and a confident expectation of life after death.

1. THE NEW COMMUNITY OF PEOPLES

The civilization that took root in the west and north of Europe after the decline of the Roman Empire was unmistakably the direct ancestor of the modern Western world. Traditionally, historians have called the millennium between the fall of the empire and approximately 1500 the Middle Ages of European history. Today, almost all historians further divide the European Middle Ages into three distinct periods:

Early Middle Ages	500–1000
Central Middle Ages	1000–1350
Late Middle Ages	1350–1500

The Early Middle Ages witnessed the emergence from the shambles of the Roman Empire of the first, recognizably Western civilization.

Early medieval Europe was founded upon a new community of peoples, which embraced both the former subjects of the empire and "barbarians" beyond its borders. The Romans called these peoples barbarians because of their unintelligible languages and their strange customs. They had been settled for centuries beyond the frontiers of the Roman Empire and had played only minor roles in the cultural life of the ancient world.

BARBARIAN INVASIONS

On the island fringes of northern Europe were Celtic tribes, Gaels in Ireland and Picts in Scotland, who had escaped the Roman domination to which their cousins, the Britons and the Gauls, had fallen subject. More numerous and more formidable than the Celts were the Germans, who were settled in a great territorial arc that stretched from Scandinavia to the Black Sea and rimmed the Roman frontier on the Rhine and Danube rivers. The Germans had benefited from strong Mediterranean influences and were culturally the most advanced of the barbarian peoples. From about 350 through the preaching of a missionary called Ulfilas, Christianity spread among the Germans north of the Danube, but in its Arian form (see p. 153). The adherence of many Germanic tribes—Goths, Vandals, and Lombards—to Arianism later obstructed their assimilation with the largely orthodox Romans. Beyond this Germanic cordon lived the still pagan Slavic tribes, probably the most numerous of the barbarians.

The Germanic tribes had for centuries challenged the Roman frontiers. Their primitive and poorly productive economies forced them to search constantly for new lands to plunder or settle. Understandably, the Germans were attracted by the wealth and splendor of the Roman world. Even while resisting their armies, the Romans had admitted barbarians into the empire. Initially, the barbarians came as slaves or prisoners of war, then as free peasants to settle on deserted lands of the empire, and finally as mercenary soldiers and officers.

This barbarian penetration into the Roman Empire acquired a new urgency and a new violence in the fourth century. Pressed by nomadic hordes from central Asia, the Germanic tribes that lived beyond the frontier moved to find more protected homes; and the Roman Empire, weakened by internal troubles, could no longer mount an effective guard over its borders.

The nomads who sowed tumult in the barbarian world were the Huns, a people probably of Mongolian or Tatar origin. For reasons still not fully understood, but perhaps in reaction to weather changes and the desiccation of their pastures, they swept out of their Asiatic homeland and terrorized Western Europe. In 375 the Huns subjugated the Ostrogoths, who were settled in what is now the Ukraine, and routed the Visigoths on the Dniester River. Their great chief Attila (433?–453), the "scourge of God" according to Christian writers, established his horde on the plain of the middle Danube, and from there led them on raids into both Gaul and Italy in search of plunder and tribute. With Attila's death in 453, the Hunnic Empire disintegrated, but the Huns had already given impetus to the great movement of peoples which better than any other event marks the beginning of the Middle Ages.

The Visigoths, first of the Germanic tribes to be dislodged by the Hunnic conquests, in 376 petitioned Emperor Valens, the ruler of the Eastern Roman Empire, to settle within its borders. They were admitted, but the hungry barbarians soon rebelled at the high prices which Roman officials demanded for food. To put down the uprising, Valens led an expedition against them but rashly disdained to await reinforcements from the West. The Visigothic cavalry scattered the ranks of the Roman legions at Adrianople in 378. This battle marked the end of the Romans' military advantage over the barbarians and showed the superiority of the mounted warrior (the prototype of the medieval knight) over the foot soldier. The Visigoths settled for a while in the Balkan Peninsula, then continued on a westward movement. They sacked Rome in 410 and crossed the Alps into Gaul where they established the first autonomous kingdom on Roman soil in 418. At its height in the mid-fifth century the kingdom of the Visigoths extended from Gibraltar to the Loire River. The Franks conquered the kingdom in Gaul in the sixth century; the Saracens, the surviving kingdom in Spain in the eighth century.

Another tribe pushed by the Hunnic conquests were the Vandals. They broke across the Rhine River into Gaul in 406 and embarked upon a career of conquest that within three years took them over the Pyrenees into Spain and south to the shores of the Mediterranean Sea. The Vandals crossed to North Africa where they established a permanent kingdom in 429. They were the only barbarians to become a power on the Mediterranean Sea, and from their base in North Africa they subjected Rome to fourteen days of ferocious plundering in 455 and harried western waters until destroyed by the Byzantines in the next century.

Not long after the Vandals crossed the Rhine River, the Burgundians followed them into Gaul, probably in 411. These Germans established an independent kingdom in the valleys of the upper Rhone and Saône rivers in 443 and preserved their independence until the Franks conquered them. The region they settled retained thereafter the name of Burgundy.

The ease with which these Germans invaded the Roman frontiers and sacked Rome indicates that the authority of the empire had almost vanished by the middle of the fifth century. Emperor Valentinian III was the last Roman to exercise any real power in the West. After his death in 455 a series of shadow emperors followed. They were raised to the throne, deposed, or murdered by German officials in the palace, who were the effective rulers. One of those barbarians, Odoacer, deposed the last emperor in 476. Although no more than a palace mutiny, this coup marks the final passage of power from Roman to German hands.

Odoacer remained in control until overthrown by Theodoric, who was the leader of the Ostrogoths. After the disintegration of the Hunnic Empire the Ostrogoths penetrated the Roman frontiers in the East and besieged Constantinople in 487. As a diversionary tactic the Eastern Emperor Zeno persuaded Theodoric to invade Italy, which he did in 489. Odoacer resisted tenaciously, but after years of struggle Theodoric tricked, ambushed, and murdered him, and established his own Ostrogothic kingdom in Italy in 493. A shrewd ruler, he gave Italy more than thirty years of peace.

In the third and fourth centuries the Germanic tribes living just beyond the Roman frontier in the Rhine valley coalesced into two large federations, the Alemanni in the upper valley and the Franks in the lower valley. The Alemanni pushed beyond the Rhine into the middle of Gaul and founded a kingdom in 420. The Franks slowly penetrated into northern Gaul, moving across the valley of the Seine up to the Loire River. By the fifth century they had separated into two peoples: the Salian or "salty" Franks, who successfully established their area of settlement from the shores of the British Channel to the Loire valley (excluding only Brittany); and the Ripuarian or "river bank" Franks, whose history is wrapped in obscurity, but who seem to have remained settled between the Rhine and Meuse rivers. The first-mentioned king of the Salians, a figure who stands

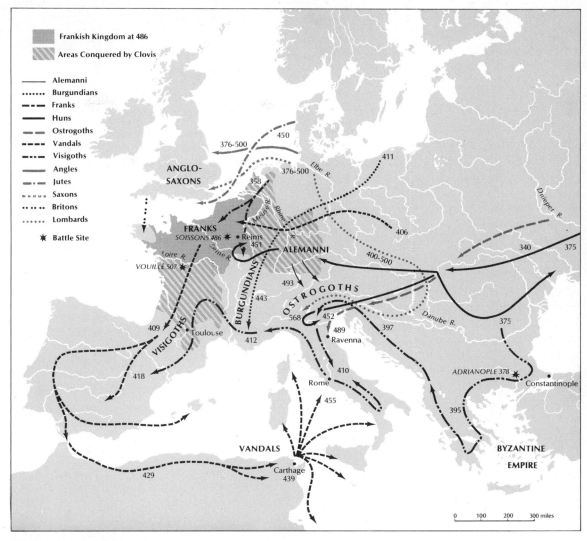

MAP 6.1: BARBARIAN INVASIONS 4TH–6TH CENTURIES

on the dark margin between legend and history, was called Merovech, and he gave his name to the first dynasty of Frankish kings, the Merovingians. The true founder of the kingdom of the Franks, however, was his putative grandson Clovis (481–511).[1]

At the time of Clovis's accession the various

Germanic tribes were contending for supremacy over each other and the native Gallo-Romans. Clovis's great accomplishment was the political unification of nearly the whole of Gaul. Already king of the Salians he had himself elected king of the Ripuarians and thus ruled a united Frankish people. He then conquered the Gallo-Romans at Soissons, the Alemanni, and the Visigoths at Vouillé (see Map 6.1). His sons added both Burgundy and Provence to the kingdom, nearly completing the conquest of Gaul.

---

[1] His name is really a cognate of Louis; thus, by this historical oddity, all the Louis's in the long line of French kings are misnumbered.

No less important for unification was Clovis's conversion, probably about 496, to Roman, rather than Arian, Christianity. This step won him the sympathy and support of the orthodox Gallo-Romans, facilitated his conquests, spared his kingdom the religious divisions between ruler and ruled which debilitated the regimes of the Visigoths and Vandals, and made possible the peaceful assimilation of the diverse peoples he ruled. As the first barbarians to accept Roman Christianity, the Franks became the "eldest daughter" of the Western Church and soon its acknowledged sword and champion.

The Germanic invasions of Britain differed from the barbarian conquests on the Continent. The Germans—Angles, Saxons, and Jutes—never constituted a single community; many chiefs led these barbarian bands. The Germans did not settle and assimilate with the native Britons, as they did in most other Roman provinces; they either exterminated the Britons or pushed them westward into Cornwall and Wales. While seeking safer homes some Britons crossed the Channel to settle in the Roman province of Armorica, which therefore came to be called Brittany. For a few decades in the early sixth century the Britons rallied against the Germanic incursions under a king whom later sources call Arthur, but they could not permanently resist the inundation of their home. After 550 the Germans rapidly consolidated their conquests and imposed their language on the region. So sharp is the linguistic break that modern English, apart from place names, shows little trace of the speech of the original inhabitants.

The Slavic tribes to the east of the Germanic cordon embarked on their own extensive migrations. In the fifth and sixth centuries some Slavic tribes pushed their settlements as far west as the Elbe River and as far north as the Baltic Sea; they are the ancestors of the modern West Slavs, the Poles, Czechs, and Slovaks. During the same years other Slavic tribes penetrated into the Balkan Peninsula and Greece; their descendants are the modern South Slavs, the Serbs, Croats, Bulgarians, and Macedonians. Still other tribes moved east beyond the Dnieper River and north into the forest regions of Russia; they are the ancestors of the modern East Slavs, the Great Russians, Ukrainians, and Byelo-, or White, Russians.

No other Indo-European peoples came to occupy so extensive a geographic area as the Slavs, although distance inevitably weakened their ethnic and cultural unity. The West Slavs were influenced primarily by Germanic and Latin culture, and the East Slavs and most of the South Slavs by the civilization of the Eastern or Byzantine Empire.

BARBARIANS IN THE ROMAN EMPIRE

The most numerous of the barbarian invaders of the Roman Empire in the West and the most important for the future history of Western Europe were the Germans. Most of this section, therefore, is devoted to Germanic institutions and culture, but there are some allusions to the institutions and culture of the other barbarian peoples.

Historians have estimated, although on flimsy evidence, that the Germans who settled within the Roman Empire constituted no more than 5 percent of the total population. The Germanic tribes apparently claimed one-third of the land or its revenues for themselves; this was the share traditionally allotted to an army quartered in a Roman province under an established practice known as "hospitality." How the tribes redivided the land among their members is not known. The kings and great warriors seem to have retained a greater part of the land. Most of the humble freemen seem to have settled as cultivators, obligated to pay rents and perform services to the owners of the land; but, unlike the *coloni* in the Late Roman Empire,

MAP 6.2: FORESTED AREAS OF WESTERN EUROPE IN THE EARLY MIDDLE AGES

these freemen retained their liberty of movement.

The Germans did not exterminate the Roman curial and senatorial classes or establish an exclusively Germanic aristocracy; rather, they gradually intermarried and made use of the inhabitants' skills. The Germans, great or humble, rich or poor, thus adopted lives that made them

Geographers estimate that not less than three-quarters of the surface area of Western Europe remained heavily forested in the Early Middle Ages. Human settlements in the small clearances sometimes achieved a high density of inhabitants but remained separated from one another by vast reaches of wilderness.

The Anglo-Saxon buckle belonged to an East Anglian king who died in 654. It is made of gold and niello, a black metallic substance that lends itself to incision of a design; the cuts are then filled in to produce the ornamental effect. The interlaced beasts in the ornamentation illustrate the Animal style of barbarian art. This buckle is one of forty-one solid gold items recovered from the ship burial at Sutton Hoo, England, and shows the great value given to gold jewelry by the barbarian kings. (Photo: British Museum)

almost indistinguishable from their Roman counterparts. This favored assimilation.

Historians no longer speak confidently, as they once did, of specifically Germanic or barbarian contributions to medieval and Western civilizations. Even before their invasions many Germans, particularly those settled near the frontiers of the empire, had achieved a cultural level that nearly resembled that of the Romans; moreover, the great majority of the Roman subjects did not share the sophisticated culture of the Roman aristocracy. The Germans were certainly more civilized and the Romans more barbarous than was once believed. Some historians today speak of the formation during the Late Roman Empire of a vulgar culture, that is, one that reflected the lives of the majority of the people rather than the aristocracy; it did not respect political boundaries and joined barbarians and Romans in one cultural community.

The Germans reinforced certain pronounced characteristics of the late Roman and early medieval civilizations. The destruction wrought by the invasions and the barbarians' apparent aversion to urban settlement accelerated and confirmed the decline of cities and the appearance of the small peasant village and rural estates. This was a critical change, for the cities had dominated the economy and culture of the classical Mediterranean world.

German Institutions

Writing, though not unknown, was little utilized in Germanic societies, and this explains several salient peculiarities of their institutions. Without written records how were legal obligations created and proved, juridical disputes settled, and governmental policies set and maintained? To record the creation of contractual obligations, the Germans (and the medieval world after them) relied heavily on symbolic gestures publicly performed. In conveying property, for example, the former owner would hand a twig or a clod of earth to its recipient; witnesses would note the act and later testify to its occurrence. But depending on the testimony of witnesses was a very precarious method for solving juridical disputes. Therefore, the Germans determined truth or falsehood, guilt or innocence, by investigating the characters of the litigants or appealing to magic. In a practice known as compurgation twelve good men who typically knew nothing at all about the facts at issue would swear to the honest reputation and presumed innocence of the accused. Or the accused would undergo an ordeal, such as running barefoot over hot irons or immersing his hand in a cauldron of boiling water; if his feet or hand showed no severe burns, he was declared innocent. Sometimes two contenders in a litigation would simply duel before the court on the assumption that God would not allow the innocent to be vanquished. To set and maintain policies, the Germans relied on old and respected men of the community to recall and state the ancient customs. This explains one of the most distinctive features of tribal government: the use of large councils or assemblies. The barbarian chief never made decisions alone; he always acted in an assembly or council of freemen who could help him recall the customs and aid him in making his judgments.

These barbarian practices influenced the development of several institutions of medieval law and government. The use of juries in trials, a common practice in Europe in the Middle Ages, was based on the assumption that the entire community, represented by sworn men, and not by the judge alone, should determine when a law was broken. The medieval king, like his barbarian predecessor, was also expected to make his major decisions with the advice of the great men of the realm, assembled in councils or parliaments. The connection between the later juries and parliaments and these

barbarian traditions is admittedly distant, but certainly exists.

The German chief had an ambiguous position in relation to the tribe and its members. Before their invasions the barbarians did not usually have kings; only the invasions, which required a continuing military command, made kings usual within Germanic society. The king was thus primarily a military leader and chief priest. He could not change the old customs, legislate, or demand obedience from his free subjects. His power rested less on the accepted prerogative and law and more on the naked violence he could threaten or apply.

The uncertain powers of the chief left to the family or kinship group the responsibility for avenging injuries done to its members. Custom eventually sought to regulate this violent practice by defining in monetary terms how much compensation could be demanded for a man's life (his *Wergeld*), arm, eye, or nose; but the responsibility and initiative in punishing or avenging a crime remained the family's and not the chief's.

Because the family was frequently unable to protect its members, Germanic societies were prolific in forming associations of self-help. The Roman historian Tacitus wrote a description of such an association, which he called a *comitatus* ("following").[2] Young warriors would join the retinue of an established chief, follow him to battle, and fight under his leadership in return for his protection, a share of his booty, and a reflection of his glory. The social and moral tie between chief and follower much resembles the ethical relationship between lord and vassal in the later feudal system. Another association of self-help was the guild. Unlike the *comitatus* this was an association of equals, and in its early appearances had no relation to

---

[2] *Agricola and the Germania*, Hugh Mattingly (tr.), 1971, chaps. 13–14. Among the Eastern Slavs the comparable institution was the *druzhina*.

economic life. The guild brothers offered gifts to the gods, feasted and drank together, and aided one another against common dangers. Like the *comitatus* the guild was to have a long and important "afterlife" in medieval social history.

German Culture

Since the Germans made little use of writing, their literature was preserved by oral transmission. Poetry, more easily memorized than prose, was the favored form of literary expression. The earliest surviving examples of Germanic poetry were not written down until the ninth century, but they still provide an authentic reflection of barbarian culture. Military values saturated barbarian literature because society looked primarily to its warriors for security. In the Anglo-Saxon epic *Beowulf* the King of the Danes, Hrothgar, was powerless against the terrible monster Grendel; and his plight illustrates the weakness of barbarian kingship and government. Hrothgar had to appeal for help to the hero Beowulf with whom the community's one hope of security rested. There is little wonder that the barbarians (and medieval society after them) looked upon warriors and their virtues with awe and admiration. Understandably, an analysis of heroism is the chief theme and interest of their literature.

Religion was marked by an abiding sense of pessimism. The Germans saw nature as a cruel and hostile force controlled by two sets of gods. Minor deities and spirits, both good and bad, dwelt in groves, streams, fields, and seas and directly affected men. Through incantations, spells, or charms men tried to influence the actions of these spirits. These magical practices (foreign to the paganism of the ancient world) strongly influenced popular religion and mixed with it a large element of superstition, which would persist for the entire length of the Middle Ages and for a long time thereafter. The high gods lived in the sky and took a

remote interest in the affairs of men. Chief among them was Woden or Odin, god of magic and victory, whom Tacitus equates with the Roman Mercury. Woden, his wife Friia or Frig, Thor the thunderer, Ti or Tyr the god of war—all give their names to days of the week in all Germanic languages, including English. According to late Scandinavian myth, warriors who died in battle joined the following of Odin in a great banquet hall, Valhalla. War, in other words, was a holy, redemptive exercise. But the entire company of gods and heroes was doomed to destruction by fire during a cosmic twilight when the ravaged earth would sink entirely into the sea. It is not known whether the early Germans shared this elaborate myth. They certainly shared in the exaltation of heroes and in a deep pessimism about mankind's ultimate fate.

The fundamental circumstances of Germanic life also influenced artistic forms. Because they changed their homes so frequently, the Germans developed no monumental art—no temples, palaces, or large statues—before they were settled within the empire. Their loveliest form of artistic expression was jewelry—buckles, brooches, necklaces, and crowns—made from precious metals. Many of these pieces show the Animal style, which embodied the forms of animals in the design of the jewelry. This style seems to have originated in the steppe region of Eastern Europe and Asia and then to have spread westward among both Slavs and Germans. The Animal style exerted a wide influence upon early medieval art; even the lettering and illuminations in the manuscripts of that epoch reflect some of its motifs (see Plate 9).

The period after the barbarian invasions witnessed a near triumph of vulgar, nonliterate culture over the literate, urban culture of the Roman aristocracy. The barbarians were not alone responsible for this vulgarization of the West. Undoubtedly, the great, unlettered masses of the Roman Empire shared many of the barbarian attitudes and practices; but the invasions did lend this vulgar culture a new strength and visibility. These popular attitudes and practices tell us more than does the literature of the learned about how for many centuries most Western Europeans were actually to live and view the world.

II. THE NEW ECONOMY

The great achievement of the Early Middle Ages was the emergence of the single-family farm as the basic unit of agricultural production. Europe became and long remained a peasant society. Several factors contributed to the formation of the medieval peasantry. The declining supply of slaves seems to have persuaded many villa owners to settle their slaves on family farms rather than to work them in gangs. The changes in warfare, specifically the new supremacy of the mounted warrior, made fighting an expensive, hence exclusive, profession and forced many freemen into the ranks of full-time cultivators. And a series of technological innovations in agriculture aided the peasant in supporting himself, his family, and the new society.

AGRICULTURE

The most favored agricultural region of Europe in terms of fertility and climate is the great alluvial plain that stretches from southeast England and France to the Urals. The men of the ancient world had not been able to farm it efficiently. The light plow of the ancient world only scratched the earth, though it was suitable enough for the thin soil and dry climate in the Mediterranean areas. Cultivation there required that the surface be pulverized to retain moisture, but not cut deeply. On the northern plain, however, the earth had to be cut and turned to form the furrows needed to carry away excess water from the abundant rains. Thus a heavier plow was necessary, one that was more complex and powerful. An obscure passage in Pliny suggests that the Germans had such a plow as early as the first century after Christ; but most historians date its diffusion, simultaneously among the Germans and the Slavs, only from the sixth century.

The light plow, which continued to be used in Mediterranean lands during the Middle Ages, was dragged by two oxen. The heavy plow, used on the plain of northern Europe, required the use of teams of as many as eight oxen. The Romans had harnessed the horse with almost incredible inefficiency. He was bound to his load by pliant straps around his throat and belly that rewarded his best efforts by strangling him. Moreover, he was hitched to his load so high on his withers that he could not throw his full weight against the harness. Northern Europeans did not develop a collar and harness that made efficient use of the horse as a draft animal until the ninth century. At about the same time the tandem harness, which permitted teams of horses to be hitched one behind the other, and the horseshoe, which gave the animal better traction and protected his sensitive hoofs, came into common use in Europe. By virtue of all these devices the Early Middle Ages, in the words of one historian, "discovered horse-power."[3]

Northern Europeans also developed a new method of crop rotation: the three-field system, first documented in 763. This routine of cultivation was based on a triennial cycle. The field was planted in winter wheat, then in a spring crop—oats, barley, peas, or beans—then permitted to lie fallow for a year. The older two-field system, which continued to be used in Mediterranean lands, was based on the yearly alternation of winter wheat and fallow. Spring

---

[3] Lynn White, Jr., *Medieval Technology and Social Change*, 1966, pp. 57–69.

tatis : qui fingis laborem in precepto.
Captabunt in animam iusti : + san
guinem innocentem condempnabunt.

The Luttrell Psalter, produced in England about 1340, is particularly known for its scenes of rural life. This fragment from the psalter illustrates the act of plowing. The heavy plow used on the plain of northern Europe included three indispensable parts: a colter or knife to cut the soil, a share or wedge to widen the breech and the clods, and a moldboard to lift the earth and turn the furrow. (Photo: British Museum)

crops were difficult to grow in the south because rain was scarce in the spring and summer months, but they were easy to cultivate in the north because there was an abundant year-round rainfall.

The three-field system kept a larger portion (two-thirds) of the soil under crops. It raised the productive efficiency of the peasant's labor by an even higher degree; the fallow, although it returned no crop, still had to be worked, and with a smaller fallow (one-third rather than one-half the land) the peasant had more time

for productive labors. The spring crop restored fertility to the soil, provided a more varied diet for the people, and lessened the risk of total failure because two crops were planted in one year. Since the spring crop was often intended for fodder, it also helped support a larger number of animals. The animals in turn provided manure for more abundant crops. The intensified exchange between animals and land, fertilizer and fodder, thus assured a higher level of abundance. For the first time the agricultural resources of the northern plain were used with some measure of efficiency, and the three-field system remained the most common pattern of cultivation in northern Europe until the agricultural revolution of the eighteenth and nineteenth centuries.

These technological innovations did not transform agriculture overnight. Their use spread through Europe at a glacial pace, and not without resistance; but it remains accurate to say that these technological innovations profoundly affected the character of the new Western civilization. They allowed the regions of northern Europe to support a denser population and established a tradition of technical innovation that has remained alive and unbroken to the present.

The Manor

Europeans developed a new form of agricultural organization: the manor, or large estate. Its origins are obscure. Documents from the Continent do not mention the manor with any clarity or frequency until the middle of the eighth century; it does not fully appear in English sources until the eleventh century. Many historians believe that the manor emerged directly out of the Roman villa and that the *coloni* of the Late Roman Empire were already serfs because they were legally bound to the soil. However, certain contrasts distinguish the manor from the villa. Although bound to the soil, the Roman *coloni* were not obligated, as far as sources inform us, to the labor requirements that were imposed on the medieval serfs. The lord of the villa was primarily dependent upon slaves or hired labor to work his lands, whereas the lord of the manor relied upon his serfs. It seems, then, that the manor was not truly an inheritance from the late empire but acquired its characteristic organization during the opening centuries of the Middle Ages.

Manorial organizations never extended over the whole of Europe and perhaps never included even a majority of the peasants. The manor

This figure is a simplified reconstruction of a medieval village under the "open field" system of cultivation. Each peasant household owns a strip of land in each of nine large, cultivated fields. The holdings of each family (its hide or mansus) *are designated by the letter a, b, c, etc. The strips are "open," that is no fence or barrier encloses them. The village, and not the individual owners, determines the rotation which each cultivator must follow. Here, the large fields are cultivated according to a three-course rotation— winter crop, spring crop, and fallow. The owners of the separate strips also have the right to graze a set number of animals in the common meadow and woods. If the village formed part of a manor, the lord's demesne would probably also consist of open strips distributed across the large fields.*

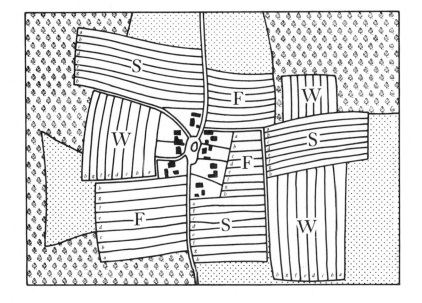

W = Winter crop
S = Spring crop
F = Fallow
Dwellings = ■
Commons:

Meadow =

Woods =

was characteristic of southeast England, northern France, western Germany, and certain areas of the south, such as the Rhone and Po valleys. These were regions of fertile soil where cereals in particular could be cultivated intensively. In its idealized form the manor may be defined as a tightly disciplined community of peasants organized under the authority of a lord. The manor should be thought of as a fundamental unit of economic, political, and social organization.

The lands of most manors were divided into two roughly equal parts: the small farms (called hides in England and *mansi* on the Continent) that belonged to the peasants, and the large demesne that the peasants worked for the lord. All manors possessed extensive meadows, forests, and wastelands where the lord hunted and the peasant grazed his animals or collected firewood. Forests and wastelands were usually part of the lord's demesne; but the peasants too would often have their own commons, a collectively owned meadow in which each resident had the right to graze a fixed number of animals. Many manors also had workshops that produced garments, tools, and other products needed by the community. Self-sufficiency, in other words, remained an ideal in manorial organization, although it could never be completely realized.

The lord was the chief police officer and judge. He or his steward ran the court, which was an important source of revenues. The lord held the rights to operate the bakery, brewery, mill, and winepress on the manor and to sell the peasants salt or iron. He was also the chief military officer, recruiting soldiers from among the free peasants and leading them to war. For many peasants the manorial lord was the only government they ever directly confronted.

Most of the peasants inhabiting the manor were serfs; they, and their children after them, could not leave the land without the lord's permission. Men were usually obligated to work three days a week upon the lord's demesne and

to fulfill additional services at other times of the year, particularly at harvest. Women were required to spend some time in the workshops producing cloth and clothing. The serfs paid, usually in kind, a yearly rental on their land and sometimes a small head tax to the lord. They also honored him with yearly gifts, such as eggs in the spring or a capon in the fall. When a serf died and his farm passed to a son, the family usually paid an inheritance tax, either the best animal or piece of furniture, to the lord. If a serf wished to marry someone outside the manor, he had to seek, and usually purchase, the lord's permission. Besides the serfs most manors had a smaller number of free peasants. They had to pay a yearly rent for land they held but were not subject to the labor obligation or (usually) to the head tax.

Although serfs lived harsh lives, their condition was still superior to that of the Roman *coloni*. Serfs had a moral right to their land, and the lord who took it away from them committed, in the opinion of the age, a grievous sin; therefore, they and their children could profit from the improvements they made on the land. Moreover, the serfs' obligations were traditional and fixed and could not be raised.

This highly disciplined community was well adapted to the age. The manor offered protection to its members and promoted group cooperation. Few peasants could afford, as individuals, the expensive heavy plow and the large team of animals required to pull it. In working collectively for the lord, the peasants learned to work collectively for one another. From what historians can reconstruct, the great manors supported the best and most progressive technological innovations in agriculture; thus, they served as a kind of school for the peasantry.

COMMERCE AND INDUSTRY

The economy of early medieval Europe became and long remained overwhelmingly agricultural. Commerce and industry, on the other hand, faded in significance. The Romans had relied heavily on commerce to meet their essential needs. Within the Western provinces, they had organized industries producing cloth, metal, and pottery to serve distant markets. By the seventh century, such export industries had all but disappeared from the West. The once vigorous commerce on the waters of the Mediterranean Sea, joining East and West, similarly suffered a sharp decline.

What had happened? The Germanic migrations certainly obstructed production and peaceful exchange. "Where are the riches of the great men of the world?" a Gallo-Roman, Prosper of Aquitaine, exclaimed in the fifth century. "Nothing in the countryside, nothing in the towns, retains its former state." Some historians also claim that the Islamic invasions of the seventh century (see p. 219) turned the Mediterranean Sea from a peaceful highway into a battlefield, ended trade upon its waters, and in consequence undermined commerce within Europe. But the most fundamental reasons for the decline in ancient commerce seem to have been social and cultural. The ancient cities, which lived by industry and trade, lost size and vitality in the West. The class of prosperous Roman landlords, who had been great consumers of imported luxuries, similarly disappeared. The new peasant society differed in tastes and living standards from the Romans; its leaders preferred pillage over production. Finally, the West was a poor society in the seventh century. Agriculture, the essential basis of its wealth, was not yet productive enough to support many merchants, artisans, and cities. In this perspective declining trade was only a further symptom of the profound economic crisis of ancient civilization.

The West in the Early Middle Ages was poor but not stagnant. The new peasant society would support advances, both agricultural and industrial, which would surpass the highest material achievements of the ancient world.

III. THE LEADERSHIP OF THE CHURCH

The Church exercised an unrivaled leadership in the Early Middle Ages. In an age of turbulence this institution retained the Roman tradition of effective social organization and social action. It also kept alive the classical tradition of literacy, rhetoric, and logic amid the upsurge of a nonliterate culture. One of history's great paradoxes is that the Church, so hostile to many values of the classical tradition, was more effective than any other institution in preserving those very values from total extinction in a barbarous age.

ORIGINS OF THE PAPACY

The papacy is the oldest living institution in the Western world; it is the only institution that can trace its history back without interruption to the age of the Caesars. According to the traditional Catholic (and medieval) view Jesus himself endowed the apostle Peter with supreme responsibility for his church.

> And I say unto thee, thou art Peter and upon this rock I will build my church, and the gates of hell shall not prevail against it.
> [*Matthew 16:18*]

In the Aramaic language that Jesus spoke, as well as in Greek and Latin, "Peter" and "rock" are the same words, implying that the Church was to be founded upon Peter. Medieval tradition further held that Peter became the first bishop of Rome and was martyred there.

Modern historians can neither confirm nor refute this traditional interpretation with certainty because the evidence is sparse and often ambiguous. Records show that the pronouncements of the Roman bishops were often accepted by the bishops of other churches with extraordinary reverence. The earliest nonscriptural text showing the influence of the Roman bishops is a letter that Clement, fourth in the traditional list of popes, wrote to the Corinthians in 95. Clement clearly considered it his duty to counsel them. In the second century Ignatius, bishop of Lyons, taught that beliefs accepted by the Roman bishops as orthodox should be considered orthodox by the entire Church. But in the third century Cyprian, bishop of Carthage, maintained that all bishops were equal in responsibility and authority; there could be within the Church no "bishop of bishops."

Whatever the validity of these arguments, it is hardly surprising that the church at Rome should have acquired preeminence. Rome was, after all, the city of the Caesars, the capital of the world, and the center of Latin culture; men were accustomed to seeking guidance from Rome. The Christian community there dated from apostolic times, and it had no Western rival in age, size, wealth, and talent. Furthermore, the Roman bishops, although not distinguished speculative theologians, had an uncanny ability to recognize and support dogmatic positions which the Church was ultimately to accept as orthodox. In contrast some bishops in other cities supported positions that later became heresies. These bishops could not rival the Roman bishops' reputation as defenders of orthodox belief.

Growth of Papal Primacy

The idea of a Roman primacy gained support and was expressed with clarity in the fourth and fifth centuries. The emperors, anxious to use the Church as an adjunct to their own imperial administration, favored the concentration of religious authority in Roman hands. The Council of Sardica (modern Sofia) in 343 affirmed the right of the Roman bishop to hear appeals from bishops deposed by provincial councils. Damasus (366–384) was the first pope to base his authority on the text of Matthew and the first to attach the term "apostolic" permanently to the Roman bishopric, or see. The most effective promoter of the conception of Roman primacy was Pope Leo I (440–461). In numerous letters

Leo I the Great was the first pope to give clear and forceful expression to the Petrine theory of papal supremacy. This late portrait shows how subsequent centuries imagined his appearance. (Photo: New York Public Library/Picture Collection)

and sermons Leo identified the person of the living pope with the person of Peter and with his divine commission to rule the Church. At the Council of Chalcedon in 451 the bishops received the declaration of the papal legates with the words "Peter speaks through Leo."

These claims for Roman primacy, however, went largely unsupported by any administrative apparatus; there was no machinery for taking appeals to Rome. Furthermore, the popes rarely intervened in the affairs of local churches outside Italy. The Western churches chose their own bishops, managed their own affairs, and had little occasion to invite intervention. Although the popes were not exercising an autocracy over the Church, their prestige in the Western world was unrivaled.

Gregory the Great

In the absence of effective secular authority, the popes had to assume responsibility for the security of Italy and the defense of the Church. They negotiated with a whole sequence of invaders—Huns, Vandals, Ostrogoths, and Lombards—and repeatedly sought help from the distant and distracted Eastern emperors. The pope who best exemplifies the problems and accomplishments of the early medieval papacy is Gregory I (590–604).

Gregory was both a writer of great influence and a man of action. His career illustrates the survival of Roman governmental skill in the service of the Church. As a layman he had been a prefect of Rome, its highest official. Then he became a priest and served as papal emissary to Constantinople and as deacon of the Church, managing its estates and supporting its charitable services. When Gregory became pope, the Lombards were plundering the Roman countryside and threatening Rome with destruction and starvation. Under these difficult conditions he maintained the productive capacity of the Church's estates, kept food coming to Rome, ransomed captives, aided widows and orphans, and organized the defense of the city. Gregory finally negotiated a truce with the Lombards in 598, although they continued to pose a threat to the security of Rome for more than a century.

Gregory was no less solicitous for the welfare of the entire Church. During his pontificate Gregory gave new momentum to missionary efforts and achieved some momentous successes. He sent a monk named Augustine and thirty companions to bring Christianity to England. The missionaries encountered strong opposition from the Anglo-Saxons, but ultimately converted them to Christianity. The new converts developed a strong veneration for St. Peter and a firm loyalty to Rome; some, including many kings, became pilgrims who visited Rome, and others became missionaries who carried the message to other barbarians. The Spanish Visigoths were also converted from Arian to Roman Christianity. By establishing a tradition of active involvement in the affairs of the world, to which most of his medieval successors would faithfully adhere, Gregory widened enormously, the influence of the Roman see.

MONASTICISM

Even more effective than the papacy in shaping medieval civilization was monasticism. The ascetic ideal of fleeing the world in order to devote oneself to worship is common to many religions and could almost be considered the natural fulfillment of religious aspiration.

Christian monasticism began in Egypt in the third century where St. Anthony entered the desert to live a solitary life of rigorous asceticism. But severe practical difficulties limited the spread of this solitary monasticism. The lone hermit could not easily find food or participate in the common liturgical prayer required of all Christians; moreover, the harsh, solitary life often brought on all sorts of psychological disturbances. To meet these practical needs and spiritual dangers, Pachomius, another "desert father," grouped his followers into a community and drew up for them the first monastic rule. He enjoined upon his monks the practice of chastity, poverty, and obedience to a spiritual abbot (from the Semitic *abba*, "father"). Pachomius's cenobitic (literally, "living in common") monasticism was readily received in other lands.

The Benedictine Rule

By the fifth century cenobitic monasticism had gained a powerful appeal in the West; but it was practiced in a bewildering variety of forms because all the great fathers of the Church—Augustine, Jerome, and Ambrose—gave advice in their writings to monks and ascetics. The monastic idea evoked a particularly fervent response among the Irish. Entire clans and tribes adopted the monastic life, with the chief assuming the title and functions of abbot. In the sixth and seventh centuries Irish monks gave their land and their people a preeminence in Western piety and letters. Roaming the Continent, the monks founded monasteries, preached to the heathen, reformed the Church, and corrected kings. Their work kept alive learning and intellectual life amid the chaos of the age.

The monk who brought uniformity and order into the movement, the great legislator of Western monasticism, was St. Benedict (480?–543?) from Nursia, in Italy. His rule is the only surviving literary work from his own hand, and much obscurity surrounds its origin and composition.[4]

As a young student at Rome Benedict was appalled by the vice he encountered there and fled into the wilderness. His growing reputation for sanctity soon attracted numerous disciples. He organized them into cenobitic communities, initially at Subiaco. When a jealous priest drove him from Subiaco, Benedict founded a new community at Monte Cassino in 529. Near the end of his life he drew up his famous rule for this community.

The Benedictine rule was an abstract constitution meant to be generally applicable to many individual communities. It was the product of a conscious reflection upon the purposes and needs of monastic life. Monasteries were thus the one social group of early medieval Europe to possess a written, carefully constructed constitution. The monastic constitution is another example of the survival of Roman governmental genius in the service of the Church. The rule endowed the abbot with full authority (sovereignty, really) over the community; he was to be elected for life and could not be replaced. To assure that the monastery was a disciplined and stable community the rule instructed a monk not to wander from house to house or refuse obedience. The abbot was to consult regularly the elder brothers and, in important matters, to consider even the opinions of the youngest members, on the scriptural ground that God frequently makes known his will to children.

The Benedictine rule also included references to all the principal problems, practical and spiritual, of monastic life; but Benedict made the regulations simple and elastic. In order to test a monk's suitability for the monastic life, for example, he was to take his vows only after a trial period of one year. In setting the daily schedule of the monk he was to say prayers at regular intervals throughout the day (the liturgical hours) rather than as private acts of asceticism. One of the most famous regulations enjoined upon the monks some manual labor, lending to it a dignity which both the Romans and the barbarians had denied. "Idleness," said the regulation, "is the enemy of the soul."

The Role of the Monk

The monks exerted an extraordinary influence on every level of medieval civilization. They were the most successful agriculturists of the age, first as farmers in their own right and then gradually as managers of ever larger estates; thus, they set an example of good farming practices from which laymen could benefit. The weak governments relied heavily on monastic farms to supply food for their administrations and armies and often appropriated part of the

---

[4] Historians still discuss the relationship of the Benedictine rule to an apparently older, longer, and cruder monastic code known as the *Regula magistri*. The best opinion now seems to be that Benedict made wide use of this older code but still impressed his own personality and genius upon the rule which bears his name. For a discussion of the controversy see David Knowles, "The *Regula Magistri* and the Rule of St. Benedict," *Great Historical Enterprises: Problems in Monastic History*, 1963, pp. 135–196.

monks' income from estates to finance their own needs. Monks were almost the only people who were literate and learned. The Benedictine rule assumed that the monk could read; and the monasteries, although not expressly obliged to do so, maintained both libraries and schools for the training of young monks and, sometimes, lay children. The monks also organized *scriptoria*, or writing offices, in which manuscripts that were needed for liturgy or education were copied. The great bulk of the surviving Latin literary works of both pagan and Christian antiquity were preserved in copies made in monasteries. Sometimes monks decorated, or illuminated, the manuscript pages; manuscript illuminations are among the loveliest art forms that have come from the age. Because they maintained the schools and libraries, the monks were virtually the only intellectuals in society. Rulers recruited their counselors and officials from the monasteries; and nearly all the administrative records which have survived were written by monastic scribes. Finally, the monks, as holy men, were thought to assure God's blessings for the world, and this helped support the morale of the troubled peoples of the Early Middle Ages.

Why were monks so important in medieval society? One reason is that the communal organization enabled the monks to cope more effectively with the problems of a turbulent age. They could divide essential tasks among their members, assigning some monks to work the earth, others to arrange for the defense of the community, and still others to read and study. The community was also, in a real sense, immortal and could maintain continuity of effort over generations.

A second reason is that the ascetic temperament equipped monks to be powerful instruments of both economic and cultural change. Early medieval society was desperately poor. Like every poor society its hope for a better future rested on an ability to save and invest

some part of the current, meager production. Grain uneaten, cattle not slaughtered, meant more abundant harvests and larger herds the next year; whether the motivation which saved the grain or cattle was religious or economic hardly matters. Monks were the great savers and investors of the age, and this partially explains their own considerable economic success.[5] Asceticism seems also peculiarly suited to an age of transition. The ascetic by his life calls into question the accepted attitudes of his age. The monks rejected both the classical and barbarian systems of value and helped uproot or weaken such attitudes as the classical aversion to physical labor and the barbarian love of violence. They thus prepared the way for the elaboration of the new values and the new culture of the Middle Ages.

IV. THE NEW POLITICAL STRUCTURES

Early medieval men sought to create new political structures and stable cultures by combining barbarian institutions and classical survivals. In the eighth and ninth centuries the Franks actually succeeded in building out of Germanic and Roman elements an empire. The empire failed to survive internal difficulties and renewed invasions in the late ninth century, but it left a lasting mark on Western culture. In the ninth and tenth centuries various Anglo-Saxon kings established a hegemony over England, but invasions in the late tenth century destroyed their efforts to achieve a lasting political entity.

---

[5] Some historians have discerned a similar link between religious asceticism and economic investment in the growth of capitalism in the sixteenth and seventeenth centuries. Specifically, they have argued that the ascetic attitudes of the Calvinists, especially the Puritans, aided their success in business. For this viewpoint see R. H. Tawney, *Religion and the Rise of Capitalism*, 1926.

THE FRANKISH KINGDOM

Clovis had established a strong Frankish kingdom in Gaul; but his Merovingian successors, known traditionally as the "do-nothing kings," showed the weaknesses of barbarian monarchy. Unable to conceive of the kingdom as anything but a private estate, they divided and redivided their lands among their heirs. They showed no sense of political responsibility and relied primarily upon violence to define their powers. The history of their reigns is largely a dismal story of intrigue and destructive feuds.

Yet amid the wars and rivalries the character of Frankish society was changing; the decisive shift was in the technique of making war. The introduction of the stirrup, probably in the early eighth century, gave a final advantage to the mounted warrior over the foot soldier (he could now strike a hard blow without falling from his horse) and confirmed the superiority, which had been evident for several centuries, of the cavalry over the infantry. Since horses were expensive, war became a preeminently aristocratic occupation. A new functional and social division appeared in Frankish society. In the past most freemen had been both peasants and warriors. Now those freemen who could not afford horses and arms—they were a majority of the population—became full-time peasants and soon serfs; those freemen who could afford the new implements of battle became full-time fighters. They constituted the new military aristocracy.

Because of the negligence of the Merovingian kings, their chief household official, known as the mayor of the palace, gradually took over the real powers of government. The mayor's functions were to manage the palaces and supervise the royal lands; he was also able to distribute the lands largely as he saw fit. Using

Spanish manuscript illumination of daily life in the monastery. (Photo: The Pierpont Morgan Library)

this privilege, some of the mayors began to supply the aristocracy with the estates they needed to maintain the expensive animals and arms in return for their service. The mayors thus built a following among the new military aristocracy that supported them in their acquisitions of further territory and power. One mayor, Pepin of Heristal, who already administered the eastern lands of the kingdom, gained control over the western lands in 687, unifying nearly all of the kingdom under him.

Pepin's son and successor, Charles Martel, cultivated the support of the warrior aristocracy. With their military assistance and the help he gave Christian missionaries, Charles began to extend Christianity and Frankish domination (the two were virtually indistinguishable) over the Germanic tribes settled beyond the Rhine River.

Charles's son, Pepin the Short, courted the allegiance of the other aristocracy of Frankish society, the great churchmen, by making a lasting alliance with the pope. The continuing support of the military aristocracy and the new sympathy of the ecclesiastical aristocracy enabled Pepin to effect a major constitutional change. In 751 an assembly of Frankish notables declared that the last Merovingian king was not truly a king, and they recognized Pepin as their legitimate sovereign. The pope confirmed the wisdom and justice of the act. In return for this expression of support Pepin confirmed papal possession of the Patrimony of St. Peter and defeated the Lombards, who had been harassing the papal lands in Italy. Later popes would repeatedly point to this Donation of Pepin as establishing the Papal States.

Roman tradition affirmed that the king exercised sovereign power; by exposing the character of Frankish kingship to strong Christian and Roman influences, Pepin strengthened and transformed it. He bequeathed to his successors a monarchy founded on the support of great warriors and priests and dignified by association with the Christian and Roman past.

Charlemagne

Pepin's son, Charles the Great, or Charlemagne (768–814), followed the policies of his predecessors; but, pursuing them with unprecedented energy, he achieved unprecedented success. His biographer, the court scholar Einhard, says that he was a large man, "seven times the length of his own foot," and that he delighted in physical exercise, particularly hunting, riding, bathing, and swimming. His taste for food and women seems to have been no less exuberant. Perhaps more remarkable in this man whose very life was war were his intellectual curiosity and alertness. He was probably illiterate; at least, Einhard says that he kept tablets by his bed to practice forming letters at night though with "ill success." But Einhard also says that he spoke and understood Latin, comprehended Greek, and enjoyed the company of learned men. The vast empire Charlemagne built was in large measure a personal accomplishment, a tribute to his bounding physical energy and open intelligence.

Charlemagne's success as king depended on his success as a military leader. On every frontier he waged long wars. His chief concern was to spread Christianity and thus subservience to Frankish authority among still pagan peoples. If permanent conquest and conversion were not possible, the expeditions would still weaken neighboring enemies and prevent them from striking into the Frankish domains. At the pope's request he campaigned four times in Italy against the Lombards and against factions at Rome opposed to the pope. He suppressed the independent Bavarians and overcame the Saxons after thirty-three years of fighting, bringing these peoples fully and finally into the community of Western peoples. These victorious wars added new territories to his empire (see Map 6.3). Charlemagne also organized punitive expeditions against the Danes, Slavs, and Avars beyond his eastern borders and against the Saracens beyond the Pyrenees.

On Charlemagne's fourth visit to Italy in 800, when he was praying before St. Peter's altar on Christmas night, Pope Leo III crowned him emperor of the Romans. The coronation of 800 added nothing to his possessions, but still retains great symbolic importance. It confirmed the alliance of the papacy and the Frankish monarchy, defined the political axis of subsequent Western history, and gave it its pronounced north-south orientation. It was a public declaration of the independence of the West, a final rejection of even a theoretical submission to the Eastern Empire. The coronation of 800 marks the birth of Europe, for it proclaimed the complete political and cultural autonomy of the Western community of peoples.

Government

The coronation gave Charlemagne no new powers; but it added much to his dignity, and a grandiose imperial ideology developed around his person. The cult of the emperor played a vital role in preserving the unity of the empire because the government did not have the material force to hold it together. Charlemagne was presented to the people as the new David (the ideal king of the Old Testament), the new Augustus (the greatest of the pagan emperors), and the new Constantine (the champion of the Church). By presenting the emperor as a figure of such sanctity and brilliance, the government hoped that rebellion against him would be unthinkable. Ideas might thus accomplish what armies could not do alone.

The emperor was, of course, the head of the government; and he was aided by several officials. The head of the palace clergy, and the chief ecclesiastic of the realm, was the chaplain, who advised the emperor and the entire court in matters of conscience. The chaplain also supervised the chancery, or secretariat, where the official documents were written. The chief lay official was the count of the palace, who supervised the administration, judged cases that the

This twelfth-century silver reliquary from Aachen represents Charlemagne as emperor, saint, and protector of the Church. After his death, through all the subsequent medieval centuries, Charlemagne was remembered and viewed as the ideal Christian emperor. (Photo: E.P.A./Scala)

emperor did not personally handle, and acted as regent during the emperor's frequent absences. The chamberlain took care of the royal bedroom and the treasury, the seneschal kept the palace provisioned with food and staffed with servants, the butler supplied the beer and wine, and the constable cared for the horses. These officials and others whom the emperor invited made up the court that advised him.

At the local level the fundamental administrative unit was the county, which in many parts of the empire resembled in its extent the Roman provinces or *civitates*. The count was the administrator, judge, and military leader of the county. The county was further divided into small judicial units under a *vicarius*, who heard minor cases.

Charlemagne's great administrative problem was to maintain an effective supervision and control over the local officials. He used three devices to resolve this problem. Charlemagne himself traveled widely to ascertain how the land was being administered and to hear appeals from the decisions of the counts. He appointed special traveling inspectors, called *missi dominici*, to inspect a particular county every year.

MAP 6.3: FRANKISH EMPIRE UNDER CHARLEMAGNE

The dates indicate the years that the regions were added to the empire. Marches were the frontier provinces (except Brittany, which was a maritime province) especially organized for the military defense of the empire. Magdeburg was the episcopal see that took the leadership in the conversion of the Danes and Slavs to Christianity. Aix-la-Chapelle was the capital of the empire. The tributary peoples were those beyond the frontiers of the empire over whom the emperor exercised a loose authority. They owed allegiance to him but were never integrated administratively into the empire.

They scrutinized the behavior of both the lay and ecclesiastical officials, heard complaints, published imperial directives, and reported their findings to the emperor. They were in fact surrogate emperors who made the emperor's power felt everywhere in his vast domain. Charlemagne further required that the great men of his realm, both laymen and ecclesiastics, attend a general assembly almost every year. There they reported on conditions in their local areas, advised the emperor on important matters, and heard his directives. Many of the imperial directives have survived. They are called capitularies because they are divided into chapters (*capitula*), and they are among the most important sources illuminating Carolingian government and society.

Decline of the Empire

Charlemagne passed on to his single surviving son, Louis the Pious, a united and apparently strong empire at his death. His successors in the ninth century proved unable to maintain that unity. Louis, a weak and indecisive man, soon lost control over his own family; and his sons rebelled against him. After his death the three surviving sons partitioned the empire at the Treaty of Verdun in 843 and established their own kingdoms (see Map 6.4).

As the family of Carolingian rulers divided amid civil wars and partitions, the loyalty of the military aristocracy also waned. The new rulers conquered no new lands; so they had no new offices or properties to buy the loyalties of the aristocracy. The office of count, appointive under Charlemagne, became hereditary under his successors. The Carolingian rulers no longer summoned the great men of the realm to the yearly assemblies and no longer dispatched the *missi dominici* on their circuits. The institutional and moral bonds tying their central governments to the peripheral territories were thus broken or abandoned.

NEW BARBARIAN INVASIONS

Charlemagne's military successes had kept the borders of his empire relatively secure against invaders; but under his weak successors the invasions were renewed, and they added critically to the centrifugal forces tearing at the empire. From the south Saracens established in North Africa invaded Sicily and southern Italy in 827, attacked the valley of the Rhone in 842, and raided Rome in 846. They held a pirate

fortress at Fraxinetum (Freinet) on the French Riviera, threatening Western ships and even harassing travel over the Alpine passes between Italy and France for over a century. From the East a new nomadic people, the Magyars, established themselves by about 895 in the valley of the Danube; and from this base for the next fifty years they struck repeatedly into France, Germany, and Italy.

The most wide-ranging and destructive of the new invasions were those mounted by the Northmen, or Vikings, who were the Germanic

Norwegian burial mounds have yielded to archaeologists three specimens of Viking ships, although it is nearly impossible to know how closely these ceremonial barges correspond with the ships in daily use. The largest of these barges, found at Gokstad, is shown here. It is only 76 feet long, 17.5 feet wide, and 6.5 feet deep. It was propelled by 16 pairs of oars. This seems like a small ship to challenge the North Atlantic. (Photo: Universiteteis Oldsaksamling, Oslo)

MAP 6.4: PARTITION OF THE FRANKISH EMPIRE

The division of the Frankish Empire at Verdun was only one of several partitions in the ninth century, but historians have traditionally considered that the date 843 marks the beginnings of the separate national histories of France, Germany, and Italy. The kingdom of Lothar I was soon divided into Lorraine, Burgundy, and Italy.

tribes settled in Scandinavia. Their movements may be considered the last phase of the Germanic invasions begun in the fourth century. Several facts explain their invasions. The tribes could not support a large population in the harsh northern climate; through commercial contacts and mercenary service they were familiar with the attractive wealth of the neighboring areas. The tribes were constantly at war with one another because there was no stable kingdom; a defeated chief, rather than accept a demeaning vassalage under his conqueror, often preferred to seek out new land overseas for his tribe. The Vikings were skilled and versatile seamen; their ships enabled them to master both the rivers of the Continent and the open ocean. Explorations took them as far as a western territory they called Vinland, which was undoubtedly part of the North American continent. Iceland, settled as a result of these

TO GREENLAND AND
NORTH AMERICA

ICELAND

874

FAEROES
800

SHETLANDS
700

VIKINGS

Novgorod
820

ATLANTIC OCEAN

Dublin
839

DANELAW

866-878

841-884

Hamburg

Kiev
882

Dnieper R.

Volga R.

WESSEX

Rouen   Aix-la-Chapelle
Seine R.   Paris
NORMANDY   *Rhine R.*
896-911   • Tours
Loire R.

895

843-882

Bordeaux

917

899

900

MAGYARS

895

866,907,941

BLACK SEA

Santiago

Marseilles   Nice
Fraxinetum

Danube R.

Constantinople

Barcelona   *CORSICA*   Rome
846

Lisbon
844

859-861

BALEARICS   *SARDINIA*

Monte
Cassino

Valencia

Seville
844

842

SICILY
827

840-896

SARACENS

MEDITERRANEAN SEA

0   100   200   300 miles

MAP 6.5: BARBARIAN INVASIONS 8TH–10TH CENTURIES

explorations, became the great center of medieval Scandinavian culture.

In England and on the Continent the Vikings appeared first as merchants and pirates, then as conquerors and colonists. Vikings, chiefly Danes, began raiding England in 787; then in 866 a Danish army landed in eastern England and established a permanent settlement. The Vikings followed the same pattern on the Continent. They attacked cities along the western coast of Europe, penetrated into the Mediterranean Sea, and invaded the valley of the Rhone.

They sailed over the Russian river system to reach the Black Sea and raided Constantinople (see Map 6.5). This initial period of piratical forays was followed by the establishment of permanent settlements. In 911 the Viking Rollo secured from King Charles the Simple the territory near the mouth of the Seine River, which henceforth was known as Normandy.

This new wave of invasions was not as disruptive as the great movements of peoples in the fourth and fifth centuries, but they were for Western Europe a new dark age. Amid the violence, however, the work of Christianizing the barbarians continued and helped to abate the invasions. Missionaries in the tenth century successfully converted the Magyars, Poles, and Vikings. With their acceptance of Christianity and simultaneous establishment of a stable kingdom, the Magyars, alone among the many nomadic tribes of Europe, succeeded in preserving their linguistic and ethnic identity until the present; they are the modern Hungarians. From about the year 1000 these barbarians no longer represented a foreign and heathen threat to Christian Europe; rather, they had become full partners in the association of Western peoples.

ANGLO-SAXON ENGLAND

England was divided among more than a score of petty dynasties and kingdoms as a direct result of the Germanic invasions in the fourth through sixth centuries. These many petty dynasties became fused into a single kingdom, but the climax of this trend toward political unity was not reached until after the Norman Conquest in 1066.

England achieved religious unity before political unity. Augustine and his fellow missionaries dispatched by Pope Gregory arrived in Kent in 597; but other Christian missionaries, the Franks and particularly the Irish, were already evangelizing the island. Irish, or Celtic,

Christianity differed from Roman Christianity.[6] Not until 663 or 664 did the Council of Whitby finally determine that the English Church should follow Roman rather than Celtic practices. Later in the century Theodore of Tarsus, a monk from the Middle East who served as archbishop of Canterbury, completed this work of ecclesiastical unification. He reformed monastic education, held numerous councils, made the authority of Canterbury felt throughout the land, and helped give England one of the most vigorous and learned churches of the age.

Political unity came more slowly. The numerous petty dynasties coalesced into seven fairly stable kingdoms, traditionally known as the heptarchy: Northumbria, Mercia, East Anglia, Essex, Sussex, Kent, and Wessex (see Map 6.6). The first kings to exert a stable hegemony over England were the rulers of Northumbria in the seventh and eighth centuries. This was the golden age of Northumbrian culture; the monastery at Wearmouth-Jarrow then counted among its members Bede the Venerable, the greatest scholar of his day. By the late eighth century the hegemony over England passed to the rulers of Mercia. King Offa, a contemporary of Charlemagne, was known even to the pope as King of Britain. Mercian leadership was, however, short-lived; and after Offa's death the honor passed to Egbert of Wessex and his successors.

Alfred the Great
To the kings of Wessex fell the task of defending England against the Danes. The greatest of these kings was Alfred (871–899). After experiencing military defeats by the Danes in the early years of his reign, Alfred reorganized

---

[6] Irish Christians calculated the date of Easter in a different fashion, applied the tonsure (the cut of hair symbolizing clerical status) in their own distinct way, and had a different concept of the role and powers of the bishop.

the defense of the kingdom. He reformed the militia to keep a larger and more mobile army in the field and built fortresses to defend the land and ships to defend the coast. His reforms proved successful. In 886 the Danes agreed to accept Christianity and settle in the Danelaw, a region north and east in England. Alfred was the first king effectively to rule over the entire English people. He also renewed intellectual activity. Alfred gathered a group of scholars and began a program of translating into Anglo-Saxon the works of several historians and theologians. During his reign an official record of events in England, the *Anglo-Saxon Chronicle*, was begun, which is an indispensable source for early English history.

The English resurgence initiated under Alfred continued under his successors for almost a century. However, by 991 King Ethelred was unable to overcome the renewed Danish advances and agreed to pay tribute to the Danes. The tax he imposed to meet the tribute was called the Danegeld. Its payment was a mark of weakness, but the Danegeld was still a national tax and shows the solid and continuing unity achieved by the kingdom. In 1013 the Danish King Swein invaded and conquered England, which became a province in a great northern empire. His son Canute ruled both Denmark and England; but at his death in 1035 the empire disintegrated and Edward, a descendant of Alfred, became the king of England. The work of building a unified community and effective monarchy in England was left to the Norman conquerors to complete after 1066.

v. LETTERS AND LEARNING

The great movement of peoples in the fourth and fifth centuries nearly extinguished in the West the urban, literate, aristocratic culture of the ancient world. Early medieval Europe almost lapsed into complete barbarism in the sense

MAP 6.6: ANGLO-SAXON ENGLAND

that the nonliterate, nonurban, vernacular culture of the barbarian peoples and the unlettered masses of the Roman Empire all but triumphed. But the tradition of classical learning did not entirely succumb. It survived in a peculiar context and for a peculiar purpose: to serve the Christian Church and to promote the interests of the Christian religion.

THE CHURCH AND CLASSICAL LEARNING

Because Christianity rebelled against classical values, it is understandable that many prominent Christian writers condemned classical literature as foolishness and an incitement to sin. Yet almost from the beginning Christianity had to make some accommodation to secular learning. Christianity was a religion founded on a book, the Bible. God had spoken to his people through the written word, and Christian theologians had to have the skill to read and interpret the sacred texts. The only way they could obtain this skill was to study at secular schools because the Church had no schools of its own. The leaders of the Christian community, therefore, had to study under the same teachers, read the same authors, and master the same techniques of philosophical argument and rhetorical expression as their pagan neighbors.

Christian scholars preserved a tradition of literacy in the fifth and sixth centuries, but their output accurately reflects the difficult conditions of their times and the biases of their own mental outlook. An important part of their literary effort was devoted to the preparation of textbooks that would preserve a modicum of ancient learning and the ability to read the ancient authors. One of the most influential of these textbooks was the *Introductions to Divine and Human Readings* by the Italian official, finally monk, Cassiodorus (490?–585?). In it he listed the religious and secular books that he felt a monk should copy and read. This book is about as appealing to modern readers as a library catalog, but it was carefully studied and helped to determine the holdings of medieval libraries. A contemporary Italian scholar, Boethius, translated into Latin some of Aristotle's treatises on logic. Through this work early medieval men acquired their limited, but significant, familiarity with Aristotelian logic. Boethius was even more famed for his *Consolation of Philosophy*, a meditation on death. It helped to preserve the dignity of learning by showing the role that reason and philosophy played in solving human problems. Less elegant than the *Consolation*, but equally popular, was the *Etymologies* by Isidore, bishop of Seville, which was a vast encyclopedia of ancient learning, covering in twenty books sub-

jects from theology to furniture. It provided a rich source of classical lore and learning for medieval writers.

Besides providing the medieval world with textbooks, translations, and compendia of classical learning, scholars also helped through original works to shape the character and interest of the age. Many of them were monks who believed that the highest human calling was the contemplation of the boundless wonders of God. Chief among these wonders was the Bible itself; and a primary concern of the scholars was exegesis, or comment and interpretation, of the sacred text. In this field the most important writer after St. Augustine was Pope Gregory. In his *Moralia in Job,* a commentary on the Book of Job, Gregory made extravagant use of allegory in explaining the biblical text and set the style for biblical exegesis in the medieval world. Another wonder of God was the lives of the saints and the miracles he wrought through them. In this field, too, Pope Gregory educated tastes, notably through his *Dialogues,* a record of the lives and miracles of the holy men of Italy. Since history was viewed as a vast panorama illustrating and proclaiming God's miraculous providence, it too evoked great interest among scholars. One of the most influential accounts was the *History of the Franks* by Gregory, bishop of Tours. Beginning with Creation (to show the entire range of God's providential concern with human affairs), Gregory recounted the history of the human race up to 591.

The modern reader is often surprised by the endless parade of miracles and slightly stunned by the apparent gullibility of the scholars who reported them, but he must view the miracles as did the authors who recorded them. For these men the miraculous interventions of God leading men to salvation gave purpose to human life and order to an otherwise chaotic world. In a universe shaped by the operations of grace, the miraculous was the natural and the expected.

Scholarship on the Continent sank to its lowest level in the seventh and early eighth centuries. The most important centers of scholarship were Ireland in the seventh and England in the early eighth century. Scholars there enjoyed the relative shelter of an insular home. They had the zeal of new converts and a strong monastic system that supported the schools. They had never shared deeply in pagan classical culture and could study it without fear of contaminating their Christianity. Since they did not speak a vernacular language derived from Latin, they could learn a correct Latin in schools without being confused by related vernacular forms.

The finest English scholar was undoubtedly Bede the Venerable (673?–735), whose *Ecclesiastical History of the English People,* an account of the conversion of the English and the growth of their Church, established his fame even until today. His high sense of scholarship is evident in the careful way he collected and used documents and interviewed witnesses. Bede, of course, accepted miracles, and the story of salvation is the principal theme to his history. But his views on the ultimate purpose of history did not lead him to do violence to his sources. He is a man whom any age would recognize as a scholar.

THE CAROLINGIAN RENAISSANCE

The Frankish rulers—Pepin, Charlemagne, and their successors—sought energetically to promote learning within their domains; and historians call the results of their efforts the Carolingian Renaissance. These rulers were interested in learning for several reasons. In the sixth and seventh centuries, when the Continent was divided among many barbarian kingdoms, different styles of writing, known as

national hands (Visigothic, Merovingian, Lombard, Beneventan, and so forth), had developed, and numerous variant readings had slipped into such basic texts as the Bible and the Benedictine rule. The Latin grammar used by scholars had also absorbed many regional peculiarities. Literate men in one part of Europe thus had great difficulty recognizing or reading a text written in another. The widespread decline in education had left few persons who could read at all. The paucity of literate men and the illegibility and diversity of texts undermined the cultural unity of Europe and deprived governments from employing learned men in their administrations. Furthermore, poorly educated priests could not properly perform the liturgy, upon which God's blessings on the community were thought to depend; and variations in religious rituals were also growing. Both situations weakened the unity of the Church as well as the state.

Pepin and Charlemagne attempted to develop a standardized curriculum, based on the same versions of the same texts and written in the same form of handwriting. They invited to court scholars from all over Europe for this purpose. To increase the supply of locally trained scholars both Pepin and Charlemagne ordered all bishops and monasteries to establish schools to educate boys; however, only the monasteries apparently had the resources to follow this order to any significant degree. Charlemagne himself set the example by founding a palace school for the sons of his own courtiers, but the school seems to have had little permanent impact upon the intellectual life of the age.

One great achievement of this educational revival was a reform in handwriting. About the year 800, monks at the monasteries of Corbie and Tours devised a new type of formal, literary writing, a "book-hand," based on small letters and now called the Carolingian minuscule.

The ninth-century manuscript illumination from the first Bible of Charles the Bald displays the Carolingian miniscule, which is the model for the small letters used today in what printers call Roman type. (Photo: Bibliothéque Nationale)

Previously, the book-hands used for important texts had been based on various styles of capital letters only. Small letters appeared only in informal, cursive scripts. But a book page written entirely in capitals is difficult to read rapidly; the eye is not aided in distinguishing letters by protrusions above and below the line. The Carolingian minuscule, the first book-hand based on small letters, made rapid reading easier. In addition, more letters could be written on a page with this new script; thus, more books were produced at less expense. Use of this graceful new script eventually spread across Europe.

Another achievement of this educational revival was the development of a common scholarly language. Carolingian scholars perfected and standardized a distinctive language known as Medieval Latin, which largely retained the grammatical rules of classical Latin but was more flexible and open in its vocabulary, freely coining new words to express the new realities of the age. Medieval Latin was also clearly different from the vulgar, or Romance, Latin spoken by the people. The establishment of Medieval Latin as a distinct language of learning thus freed the Romance vernaculars to develop on their own. The earliest surviving text in Old French dates from 842.

The Latin created by the Carolingian scholars enabled travelers, administrators, and scholars to make themselves understood from one part of Europe to another; and it continued to serve this function until the modern era. Even when it disappeared as an international language, it helped to promote European unity. All the modern vernacular tongues of Europe developed under the strong influence of this scholars' Latin. One of the reasons it is possible to translate quickly and accurately from one European language to another is that their learned vocabularies are in large measure based upon common Latin models.

A further achievement of the educational revival was the standardization of important texts. Pepin "decorated all the churches of the Gauls with the songs of the Roman church"; that is, he sought to standardize the liturgy on the basis of Roman practice. Charlemagne continued this policy of standardization. He had the English scholar Alcuin of York, who served as a sort of minister of cultural affairs from about 782 until 794, prepare a new edition of Jerome's Vulgate translation of the Bible. This edition became the common biblical text for the entire Western Church. Charlemagne procured from Monte Cassino a copy of the Benedictine rule and had it copied and distributed, so that monks everywhere would follow a standard code. He also initiated standardization into the school curriculum, based on the seven liberal arts. Alcuin divided the curriculum into the trivium, or verbal arts—grammar, rhetoric, and logic—and the quadrivium, or mathematical arts—arithmetic, astronomy, geometry, and music.

Carolingian scholars wrote lengthy educational tracts and huge quantities of didactic poetry, but little of their work can be considered notable for original thought or rhetorical grace. This is understandable. Most of the scholars were grammarians and educators, engaged in producing teachers' manuals, textbooks, and school exercises; they went back to the Latin classics to find models of correct grammar, usage, and vocabulary but not for aesthetic satisfaction or philosophical insights. Their work was nonetheless of the greatest importance for the intellectual growth of Europe. The revived mastery of correct Latin equipped scholars of later generations to return to the classical heritage and to recover from it philosophic and aesthetic values. The Carolingian Renaissance made possible all subsequent renaissances in the history of Western thought. The establishment of Latin as a universal language permitted easy communications within Europe and made possible that vigorous and creative dialogue across linguistic frontiers upon which the growth of Western scholarship has since depended.

Europe, in the sense of an association of Western peoples preserving their individual cultural identities and yet sharing certain fundamental attitudes and values, did not exist in the ancient world. This association was formed during the Early Middle Ages. After the politically and culturally disruptive barbarian invasions ended Roman rule in the West, medieval men sought to create a new stability out of the chaos. Charlemagne's conquests unified a new community of peoples and a wide area of Western Europe. Although his empire was not permanent, it left to every region included in it common institutions and a lasting memory of former unity. The missionary successes extended the religious and moral unity of the West even beyond the frontiers of his empire.

Early medieval society was desperately poor. Trade declined; commercial contact with the East was broken; cities shrank in size. Yet some remarkable achievements mitigated this misfortune. The labor of the settled peasant-family replaced that of the gang slave as the basis of agricultural production. Technological innovations made possible the efficient exploitation of the fertile plain of northern Europe. The three-field system of cultivation and the new manorial organization gradually produced a surplus of food.

By about the year 1000 the population began expanding for the first time since perhaps the second century after Christ. A distinctive Western culture was taking shape, based on the customs and practices of the barbarians and the unlettered masses of the former Roman Empire, the teachings of Christianity, and the heritage of classical learning, which the Church largely preserved. The Early Middle Ages left no brilliant cultural monuments, but it did lay the foundations upon which the achievements of all subsequent periods of Western history have rested.

RECOMMENDED READING

Sources

*Einhard. *The Life of Charlemagne.* 1962.

*Herlihy, David (ed.). *Medieval Culture and Society.* 1968.

*Hillgarth, J. N. (ed.). *The Conversion of Western Europe: 350–750.* 1969.

Studies

*Boussard, Jacques. *The Civilization of Charlemagne.* 1968.

Cambridge Economic History of Europe. 1941–. Four volumes to date comprise the standard reference for all economic questions. A revised edition of the first volume on medieval agrarian life was published in 1966.

Cambridge Medieval History. 1911–1936. These eight volumes are partially outdated, but still indispensable.

*Dawson, Christopher. *The Making of Europe.* 1956. Discusses the origins of European cultural unity.

Duby, Georges. *The Early Growth of the European Economy: Warriors and Peasants from the Seventh to the Twelfth Century.* Howard B. Clarke (tr.). 1974. The early medieval economy viewed in terms of "gift and pillage."

*Fichtenau, Heinrich. *The Carolingian Empire.* P. Munz (tr.). 1963. An unsympathetic treatment of Charlemagne and his policies.

Folz, Robert. *The Coronation of Charlemagne, 25 December 800.* J. E. Anderson (tr.). 1974. A thoughtful analysis.

*Laistner, Max. *Thought and Letters in Western Europe: A.D. 500 to 900.* 1955. Basic guide to writers of the period.

*Leclercq, Jean. *The Love of Learning and the Desire for God.* Catherine Misrah (tr.). 1961. Monastic culture of the Middle Ages interpreted by a modern Benedictine.

Musset, Lucien. *The Germanic Invasions: The Making of Europe, A.D. 400–600.* Edward and Columba James (trs.). 1975. Excellent recent survey.

Stenton, Frank. *Anglo-Saxon England.* 1971. Basic introductory text.

*Wallace-Hadrill, J. M. *The Barbarian West.* 1962. Brief and readable essays.

*Wolff, Philippe. *The Cultural Awakening.* Anne Carter (tr.). 1969. The Carolingian period and beyond, viewed by a prominent French scholar.

---

* Available in paperback.

SEVEN

THE EARLY MEDIEVAL EAST

The Early Middle Ages was a period of profound social and spiritual change in the East as well as the West. In both regions a new peasant economy replaced the slave systems that had principally supported ancient civilizations. Unlike classical beliefs, the triumphant new religions of Christianity and Islam taught their followers that human destiny or salvation lay in a life beyond death, to which even the poorest and the humblest could aspire.

The three most prominent civilizations of the East—Byzantine, Kievan, and Islamic— were nonetheless very different from barbarian-dominated Western Europe. The Roman Empire did not fall in the East, and Roman governmental institutions lived on in the Byzantine Empire. The Hellenistic cultural heritage, based on the Greek language, also survived in the East and gave to Byzantine civilization a distinctive character. Although Islam developed from a semibarbarous people, its expansion brought the new religion into areas—Egypt, Palestine, Syria, Persia—that had ancient and rich traditions of literate culture. Islamic civilization was deeply affected by the Hellenistic, Semitic, and Persian cultures that flourished in those areas it overran.

A further, decisive contrast between the East and the West was the survival of cities and an authentic urban life in both the Byzantine and Islamic worlds. Even the Principality of Kiev, founded by a new people—the East Slavs—rapidly developed cities and an urban culture. The presence of cities in the East helped maintain the vigor of commercial exchange, sophisticated governmental institutions, and high levels of learning. All these accomplishments gave the Eastern civilizations a marked superiority over contemporary Western societies in the Early Middle Ages.

After the eleventh century, however, new incursions of barbarians as well as internal changes undermined or transformed these Eastern civilizations. But all of them left cultural heritages that have profoundly influenced Eastern societies until the present day; all of them, likewise, played a role in stimulating the Western revival after the year 1000.

1. THE BYZANTINE EMPIRE

The name "Byzantine" is, strictly speaking, a historical misnomer. The men of the Eastern Empire recognized no break in continuity between their own civilization and that of classical Rome. Throughout their history they called themselves Romans, even after Rome had slipped from their power and they had adopted Greek as their official language. The men of the Eastern Empire acknowledged what modern Western historians sometimes forget: the Roman Empire did not fall in the East until 1453. Historians differ in their periodizations of Byzantine history, but the following one probably enjoys the widest acceptance.

Early Byzantine Period	324–632
Middle Byzantine Period	632–1071
Late Byzantine Period	1071–1453

EARLY BYZANTINE PERIOD

Emperor Constantine transferred the capital of the Roman Empire from the West to the East in 324. This act marks the beginning of Byzantine history. The emperor's motives were primarily military. Many powerful enemies—Persians beyond the Euphrates River, Germans beyond the Danube River, and Germanic pirates in the Black Sea—were menacing the Eastern provinces, the wealthiest and most populous in the empire.

Constantine chose as his new capital the site of the ancient Greek colony of Byzantium. The colony had been founded about 660 B.C. on a narrow peninsula that juts into the Sea of Marmara like a hand extended from Europe toward Asia. The official name of the rebuilt city was New Rome; however, it soon came to be called the City of Constantine, or Constantinople, after its founder.

The location of this capital influenced the character of Byzantium and the course of its history. The city stood at the intersection of two of the most traveled routes: the overland highway from the Balkans to Asia Minor and the maritime route between the Black and Mediterranean seas. Inevitably, the city came to serve as the commercial and cultural link among many peoples and cultures.

Constantinople at once acquired the aura of a Christian city, the capital of the Christian empire. No ancient monuments or old families were present to remind men of the past glories of pagan Rome. Because of his close association with the emperor, the bishop of New Rome was accorded the high status of patriarch. In the entire Church only the bishop of Rome ranked above him.

The successors of Constantine had no intention of abandoning the territories or the powers of the old Roman Empire in either the West or the East. Memories of the old empire dominated their policies; and they struggled continu-ously, if futilely, to restore the empire to its former size, power, and glory. The emperor whose actions best illustrate the ideals and policies of these early rulers was Justinian (527–565).

Justinian the Great

Historians have much information, or at least allegations, about Justinian, his family, and his household from the court historian Procopius. While the emperor lived, Procopius praised him in two histories: *On the Wars* recounts Justinian's victorious campaigns, and *On Buildings* describes his architectural achievements. But after Justinian's death, Procopius also wrote one of the most vicious efforts at character assassination in history. The *Secret History* paints Justinian, Empress Theodora, and several high officials of the court as monsters of public and private vice. Historians still have not satisfactorily reconciled the contradictory portraits left to us by the two-tongued Procopius.

Justinian seems to have been a vacillating man; but his will was stiffened by his ambitious wife Theodora and made effective by capable men in his service. Born about 500, the daughter of the keeper of the bears in the circus, Theodora became a famous actress and a celebrated courtesan before she was twenty. She traveled through the cities of the empire, earning her way, according to Procopius, by skillful prostitution. In her early twenties she returned to Constantinople, mended her morals but lost none of her charm, and married Justinian. She was, in sum, an outsider, with no roots in the social establishment of the capital and no inclinations to respect its conventions. In this she resembles other active rulers of history—Catherine the Great, the German empress of Russia; Napoleon; Eva Perón in twentieth-century Argentina; and many others.

Theodora's influence on her husband was decisive from the start. In 532, for reasons not entirely known, the popular factions of Con-

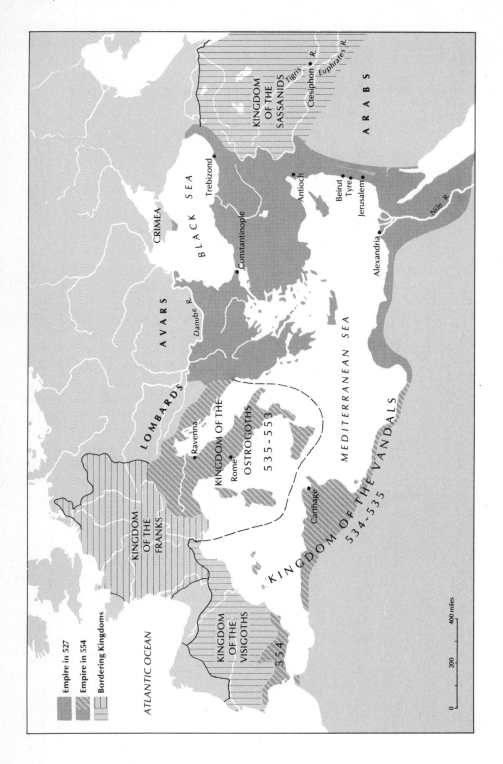

Empire in 527

Empire in 554

Bordering Kingdoms

ATLANTIC OCEAN

KINGDOM OF THE VISIGOTHS

554

KINGDOM OF THE FRANKS

LOMBARDS

AVARS

CRIMEA

BLACK SEA

Trebizond

Constantinople

Danube R.

Ravenna

Rome

KINGDOM OF THE OSTROGOTHS

535-553

Carthage

KINGDOM OF THE VANDALS

534-535

MEDITERRANEAN SEA

KINGDOM OF THE SASSANIDS

Ctesiphon

Tigris R.

Euphrates R.

ARABS

Antioch

Beirut

Tyre

Jerusalem

Alexandria

Nile R.

0   200   400 miles

MAP 7.1: BYZANTINE EMPIRE UNDER JUSTINIAN

stantinople rose in rebellion. Justinian panicked, and decided to flee. But in a moving speech, as recorded by Procopius, Theodora urged her husband to choose death rather than exile. Justinian remained and crushed the uprising. The suppression of this rebellion freed Justinian to pursue the three principal goals of his reign: the restoration of the Western provinces to the empire, the reformation of laws and institutions, and the promotion of physical splendor through an ambitious program of public works.

To restore imperial rule over the lost Western provinces, Justinian directed his armies against the kingdoms of the Vandals, Ostrogoths, and Visigoths and sought at the same time to maintain a precarious peace with the menacing Persians beyond his eastern frontier. By 554 his troops had destroyed the Vandal kingdom in North Africa and established Byzantine rule there, had triumphed, at least for awhile, over the Ostrogoth kingdom in Italy, and had forced the Visigoths in Spain to cede the southern tip of the peninsula (see Map 7.1). Justinian sought to reconcile the Eastern and Western branches of the Church, which were bitterly divided over a theological question concerning the nature of Christ.[1] He had the pope abducted by force from Rome and taken to Constantinople, where he bullied him into accepting an unwelcome compromise. His coercive tactics did not bring union and peace to the Church and were bitterly resented by all the conflicting parties.

One of the chief glories of the Roman Empire, its legal system, was extremely disordered by the early sixth century. Imperial edicts had been added to edicts over the centuries, but they had been placed in no systematic order. Lawyers could not readily ascertain which laws were relevant to which cases or which law should be followed in instances of conflict. Moreover, the great classical jurists had produced extensive legal comments, which rivaled in importance the laws themselves. But these opinions were preserved in no organized way, and lawyers could not easily consult this important body of commentary.

In 528 Justinian appointed a commission to prepare a systematic codification of Roman law. The result was the *Corpus Iuris Civilis* ("Body of Civil Law"). It consisted of four compilations: the *Codex Justinianus*, an arrangement of the imperial edicts according to topics in an easily consulted order; the *Digest*, or *Pandects*, a summary of legal opinions; the *Institutes*, a textbook to introduce students to the reformed legal system; and the *Novellae*, a collection of new imperial edicts issued after 534.

It would be hard to exaggerate the importance of the *Corpus Iuris Civilis*. It has remained for all subsequent generations the largest and richest source of information concerning the legal institutions and thought of Roman antiquity. Paradoxically, it ultimately exerted a more profound influence upon the juridical development of the Western peoples than upon the Byzantines or their heirs. The modern legal systems of most Western countries except the British Commonwealth and the United States (excluding Louisiana) are based on Roman law as represented by the *Corpus*. These two countries live under a legal system known as Common Law. Although Common Law is not a direct descendant of the *Corpus*, it has been strongly influenced by Roman legal concepts.

The destruction caused by the rebellion in Constantinople gave Justinian the chance to initiate an extensive rebuilding of the capital. His

---

[1] The Monophysite theory holds that Christ has one nature, partly divine and partly human; he was not, in other words, true man. Condemned as heretical at the Council of Chalcedon in 451, the belief remained strong in the East. The Dyophysitic theory holds that Christ has two natures, one human and one divine; he was both true God and true man.

desire was to make Byzantium reflect the physical splendor of Rome. The most spectacular of his many new churches, palaces, and public works was the great church of Hagia Sophia, or Holy Wisdom.

Justinian was remarkably successful in all his ambitious policies until the last years of his reign. Beginning in 542, a terrible plague—not again equaled in virulence until the Black Death (1348)—repeatedly struck the imperial lands. By then he had to wage a two-front war against the Persians to the east and the resurgent Ostrogoths on the western frontier. Justinian simply did not have the military power to fight on both fronts. At his death the Byzantine troops were everywhere on the defensive.

Modern historians have tended to view Justinian's policies as unrealistic, excessively ambitious, and ultimately disastrous. Memories of ancient Roman greatness blinded him to the inadequacy of his own resources. Yet Hagia Sophia and the *Corpus Iuris Civilis* assure him a permanent and brilliant reputation in both the East and the West.

In the years following Justinian's death new invaders overwhelmed the frontiers and wrested from his successors most of the emperor's territorial acquisitions. The Lombards' invasion of Italy in 568 undid many of Justinian's conquests there; his successors were able to retain control only over Ravenna, Rome, Naples, and the extreme south of the peninsula. They also held on to Carthage and Sicily. These emperors were not able to recover the Western provinces of the old Roman Empire; therefore, the Byzantine Empire could no longer aspire to the status of a universal state. She had to find her way as an Eastern, and exclusively Hellenic, empire.

MIDDLE BYZANTINE PERIOD

The reign of Emperor Heraclius (610–641) was pivotal in giving Byzantine policy and civilization their new Eastern orientation. His reign began amid repeated military disasters. The aggressive Persians took Antioch, Jerusalem, and Alexandria. With the aid of treasures donated by the churches, Heraclius reorganized and strengthened the army and then boldly took the offensive against the Persians in 622. His success was astonishing. In campaigns waged over six years Heraclius fought his way to the Persian capital of Ctesiphon. The Persians agreed to a humiliating peace. Then a new menace arose. After the death of Muhammad in 632 his Muslim followers embarked upon a tidal wave of conquests, overrunning most of the empire in scarcely more than ten years.

At the same time that Heraclius was defending the empire against invaders, he was also reforming its administration. One of his predecessors had begun to give land to the soldiers to work for themselves in exchange for military service. The military units and the provinces where they were settled were called themes. Heraclius and his successors extended this system to the navy and the entire empire. The soldier or sailor settled upon his own farm and fighting in his provincial army or navy proved to be far more effective both as a worker and a warrior than the slave, conscript, and mercenary upon whom the empire had earlier and chiefly relied.

A century elapsed before the Byzantines were able to take the offensive against the Muslims. Emperor Leo III (717–741) beat back a Muslim attack on Constantinople in 717 and 718 and then began a reconquest of Asia Minor.

In 726 Leo forbade the veneration of images within the churches of the empire. Historians still do not agree about his motives. His iconoclastic (image-breaking) policy may have been a legal pretext for seizing the land of the monasteries, which fully condoned image worship, because he needed additional lands to support his army; or it may have been an attempt to make Christianity more appealing to the Muslims whom he was seeking to conquer, by emulating the Islamic condemnation of image worship. Whatever the reasons, his iconoclastic policy had a disastrous effect on relations with the West; it antagonized the popes and was a major factor in their decision to seek out a Frankish champion. The veneration of images was restored in the Byzantine Empire between 784 and 813 and permanently after 843. But the iconoclastic policy helped to widen the cleavage between the Western and Eastern churches.

The military revival reached its height under the great warrior emperors of the ninth through eleventh centuries. They pushed the Muslims back into Syria and waged successful wars in southern Italy, the Balkan Peninsula, and the Caucasus. Their principal military accomplishment was in the Balkan Peninsula, where they defeated the Bulgars, a nomadic people who had set themselves over a Slavic population in the lands south of the Danube River. The Bulgars had abandoned their nomadic ways, adopted the language and culture of the Slavs, and established a kingdom during the ninth century. The modern Bulgarians, who are entirely Slavic in language and culture, retain only the name of the original nomadic conquerors.

BYZANTINE CIVILIZATION

Political philosophers of the Hellenistic world, chiefly Epicureans and Stoics, had maintained that all men were one in nature and subject to a single natural law; therefore, all men should be included in a single state. The Byzantines adopted these assumptions and gave them new meanings. As there was one God, one true faith, and one universal Church, so there should be only one empire to rule all Christian peoples, to protect and aid the Church, and to advance the faith among nonbelievers. The empire was thus given the sacred, quasi-messianic function

of aiding the salvation of the human race. The Byzantines believed that if the empire served this function, then God would never permit its destruction. This idea (the French would call it an *idée force*, an idea exerting power, comparable to ideas of nationalism or patriotism in the modern world) helped preserve unity among the many diverse nationalities that comprised the empire. It gave to the Byzantine peoples the spirit they needed to resist for centuries a nearly continuous onslaught of invaders.

The Byzantines also believed that the emperor was a holy figure because he was head of a state with a sacred function. Of course, a Christian emperor could not claim divinity; but the emperor lived surrounded by ceremony that imparted an aura of sanctity to his person, and the term "sacred" was liberally applied to his person, palace, and office. The word "sacred" was used as much as we use the word "public," a usage that illuminates the character of Byzantine civilization.

Modern historians have traditionally used the term "caesaropapism" to describe the emperor's position in the Church. This term suggests that the emperor was both caesar and pope, the true head of both Church and state. Recently, objections have been raised against the use of this term because the emperor's powers over the Church were restricted. He could not repeal the Nicene Creed or personally flout laws of Christian morality. He was not a priest and therefore could not say mass or administer the sacraments.

Yet the emperor exercised an impressive authority over ecclesiastical affairs. He supervised the discipline of the Church, set the qualifications for ordinations, created bishoprics and changed their boundaries, investigated the monasteries and reformed them when needed, and appointed patriarchs and at times forced their resignation. Even dogma was not beyond his influence. The emperor summoned councils, supervised their proceedings, and enforced their decisions. Some emperors believed they had the right to settle dogmatic disputes through edicts.

Because the emperor was responsible for the peace and welfare of the Church, the clergy was largely limited in its functions to the work of mediation, the performance of the sacred liturgy, and the administration of the sacraments. Even in matters closely touching ecclesiastical interests the clergy characteristically deferred to the wishes of the emperor.

The Church

The Eastern Church developed and functioned under close secular supervision. In the West, on the other hand, the vacuum of public authority following the collapse of the Roman Empire gave to the clergy a position of leadership in secular affairs. These contrasting experiences in the Early Middle Ages deeply affected the character and spirit of the two major branches of Christianity. The differences between the two Churches are worth reviewing because they help to make more understandable other contrasts in the history and cultural development of the Eastern and Western peoples.

Both the Eastern Church and the Western Church considered themselves catholic (that is, universal) and orthodox (that is, holding true beliefs); the terms "Roman Catholic" or "Greek Orthodox" used to identify the Churches today are exclusively modern usages. The two Churches maintained nearly identical beliefs. Perhaps the principal, or at least the most famous, disagreement was, and still is, the *filioque* dispute, which concerns the relationship among members of the Trinity: the Father, Son, and Holy Spirit. The Eastern Church held, and still holds, that the Holy Spirit proceeds only from the Father; whereas the Western Church maintained that the Holy Spirit proceeds from the Father and the Son. The Eastern Church did not share the Western belief in purgatory, an intermediate state between heaven and hell

where some souls are cleansed of minor faults before entering heaven. Both Churches, however, prayed for the dead to ensure that the departed souls would get into heaven.[2] In discipline, too, the differences in fasting, penitence, and morality were minor. The Eastern Church permitted, as the Western Church did not, divorce for reasons of adultery and the ordination of married men to the priesthood, although bishops had to be celibate.

The difference between the two Churches in liturgy were many but not momentous. The most significant difference was that the Eastern Church tolerated the use of vernacular languages—Greek, Coptic, Ethiopian, Syriac, Armenian, Georgian, Slavonic, and others—in the liturgy. Liturgical usage added great dignity to these Eastern languages and stimulated their development. The Russians, for example, possessed a rich vernacular literature in writing within a century after their conversion to Christianity. Western vernacular literature was much slower in developing. On the other hand, the toleration of many vernacular languages weakened the unity of the Eastern Church. An Eastern cleric who needed to know only his vernacular language for liturgical purposes could not easily communicate with clerics from other regions, whereas a Western cleric who had to learn Latin could make himself understood anywhere in the West. Because of language differences Eastern churches tended to develop in isolation from one another; they could not learn easily from their neighbors. Moreover, the toleration of many vernacular languages made difficult the revival of classical learning. A Western cleric in learning Latin also acquired, whether he

---

[2] The present disagreements concerning papal infallibility, the Immaculate Conception, and the Assumption of the Virgin Mary (dogmas all recently defined by the Roman Catholic Church) did not disturb relations in the Middle Ages.

wanted it or not, the ability to read the great Latin classics. An Eastern cleric who did not have to learn Greek never acquired the ability to read the great Greek classics. Eastern cultures were thus deprived of one avenue of enrichment.

The Western Church and the Eastern Church also differed in their organization and relations with secular authority. In the Early Middle Ages the Western Church began to separate itself from secular authority and develop a centralized government under the papacy. By the late twelfth century the pope had become the absolute ruler of the Western Church, which he governed with the aid of an elaborate bureaucracy and a sophisticated system of canon law common to the whole Western Church. The Eastern Church, however, remained thoroughly decentralized. It developed into a loose confederation of independent national churches that relied upon secular authority to defend their temporal interests.

The close ties between Church and state in the East conferred advantages on both. The Church devoted itself to its essential functions of liturgical service and the administration of the sacraments; the state made full use of the great wealth and spiritual power of the Church. This was a critical advantage for rulers and peoples struggling to survive on the eastern frontier of Europe, where all resources had to be enlisted in the battle for existence. The East was largely spared, and could have ill afforded, the prolonged disputes between Church and state which marked Western history.

Yet the disputes between Church and state in the West, while often damaging and unseemly, served as a powerful stimulus to intellectual and constitutional changes. The disputes led to fruitful and original analyses of the nature of society and of authority and favored the emergence of balanced constitutions, in which neither the king nor the Church exercised a monopoly of power. In the East the submissiveness and withdrawal of the churches from temporal concerns favored a tradition of autocracy, which lived on among the heirs of Byzantium.

BYZANTINE SOCIETY

The outstanding feature of Byzantine civilization, compared with contemporary Western civilization, was the continuing vitality of urban life. The empire included such great urban centers as Alexandria, Antioch, Beirut, Constantinople, Trebizond, and Tyre; the loss of all of these except Trebizond and Constantinople after the Muslim conquests of the seventh century still left the empire with two of the greatest cities of the age. Constantinople had paved and illuminated streets and many splendid churches and palaces. Urban society was marked by a wide division between rich and poor. The rich lived among magnificent surroundings in huge palaces; the poor in sprawling slums. Crimes committed in broad daylight were commonplace. The cities seem to have faced most of the social problems with which our own great cities are painfully familiar.

Rural society consisted largely of peasants whose status changed greatly over the centuries. An agrarian law, dating probably from the early eighth century, mentions slaves; but clearly the society it describes consisted of free peasants. The most striking feature revealed in the law is the highly developed village government. The peasants owning property assembled together, made decisions concerning the use of uncultivated or common lands, assumed (or were required to assume) collective responsibility for the payment of taxes, and elected judges and other officials to supervise the village government. Serfdom is not mentioned in the law; it probably began in the tenth century.

The Byzantine Empire was wealthy compared with other political entities of the age. One great source of wealth came from the commerce that passed through the ports and gates of Constantinople. Russians and other Slavs from the north carried amber, fur, honey, slaves, wax, and wheat; Armenians and Syrians from the east brought clothing, fruit, glass, steel, and spices; merchants from the west contributed arms, iron, slaves, and wood. The vigorous commerce attracted large colonies of foreign merchants who maintained their own churches, mosques, residences, storage houses, and even baths in Constantinople. The commercial importance of Byzantium is revealed in the prestige of its gold coin, the bezant. Its weight and purity were kept constant from the reign of Constantine to the late eleventh century; no other major system of coinage can match its record of stability.

Another source of wealth came from the numerous active guilds. There were at least twenty-one professional and craft guilds in the tenth century; most of these were involved with making luxury products, especially silk cloth. Byzantine craftsmen were also famed for goldwork, cups, ivories, jewelry, and reliquaries. These items were shipped to all parts of the known world. The government closely supervised merchants and artisans, regulating prices and the movement of goods. It also maintained state monopolies, particularly over silk products. The best silk, rich purple cloths, could not be exported. The strict regulations enabled the government to profit from this active commerce and were not injurious to it, at least not before the eleventh century.

The empire had a strong central government. The emperor, like his predecessors in the old Roman Empire, enjoyed absolute authority to make or unmake laws at will. He governed with the aid of an elaborate civil service. A master of offices served as a prime minister, a quaestor of the sacred palace presided over the courts and ran the chancery, a count of sacred largesses supervised the treasury, a count of private properties ran the imperial estates,

and a provost of the sacred bedroom administered the household affairs. Military affairs were entirely separated from civil administration and entrusted to masters of the soldiers directly responsible to the emperor. All these offices functioned with the aid of a large professional bureaucracy. These great offices were decentralized and simplified when Heraclius reformed the government in the seventh century; then civil and military administrations were combined on the local level under the general who governed the themes. All justice was considered to flow from the emperor, and he or his chief officials could hear appeals from any local court in the empire.

There were great contrasts between the Byzantine government and contemporary Western governments. Even after Heraclius reformed the government, it continued to be served by a well-organized local administration and an elaborate, professional bureaucracy. Western kingdoms, on the other hand, functioned with a rudimentary administration and without a professional civil service. The Byzantine government supported such refinements as an effective fiscal system, a state post, and even a secret police, ominously called the *agentes in rebus* ("those doing things"). Western governments had none of these. At a time when Western governments operated almost without a monetary budget the Byzantine government collected large revenues from the 10 percent tariff it imposed upon trade and from the profit it received from the state monopolies. The government also enjoyed the services of trained diplomats, who were celebrated by contemporary observers for their ability to keep enemies divided and their liberal use of bribes, tributes, and subsidies.

The bureaucracy was largely staffed by literate and trained laymen. Eunuchs were preferred for important positions in the government because it was believed that they would not be tempted by sexual intrigue and would have no wife or children to compete with the emperor for their loyalties. Reliance upon eunuchs in palace administration had an interesting social effect. They performed managerial functions which in the West were assumed by queens and women of the court. The services of eunuchs thus restricted the private and public influence of women and led to their progressive seclusion within the inner reaches of the household. This was a gradual tendency, but unmistakable in direction, and set a model for the heirs of the Byzantine Empire.

Culture

Byzantine wealth supported a tradition of learning which benefited not only the clergy but also many laymen. There were three institutions of higher learning: a palace school trained civil servants in language, law, and rhetoric; a patriarchal school instructed priests in rhetoric and theology; and monastic schools taught young monks the mystical writings of the past. The poor people were dependent on the guilds for what education they received.

Scholars used the Greek language almost exclusively after the sixth century. They composed large numbers of school manuals, histories, saints' lives, biblical commentaries, and encyclopedias of ancient science and lore. Their greatest accomplishment, however, was the preservation of classical Greek literature. With the exception of some few works preserved on papyri, virtually all the Western world possesses of classical Greek authors has come down through Byzantine copies, most of which date from the tenth to the twelfth centuries.

The first flowering of artistic achievement occurred in the sixth century, when Justinian literally rebuilt Constantinople. Among his many buildings is Hagia Sophia, designed by Isidore of Miletus and Anthemius of Tralles. Work was begun in 532 and completed in 537. As Procopius described it, its great dome seemed to float in the air, as if suspended by a chain from heaven. Hagia Sophia is one of the acknowledged architectural masterpieces of the world. Hagia Sophia, like other Byzantine churches, was decorated with brilliant mosaics, but most of these were destroyed by the iconoclasts in the eighth and ninth centuries. Because of the iconoclastic movement the richest examples of the early mosaics are not to be found in Constantinople and Asia Minor, but rather in areas that were no longer under Byzantine rule in those centuries. San Vitale and Sant' Apollinare in Ravenna, Italy, are particularly noted for early Byzantine mosaics.

With the final rejection of iconoclasm in the middle of the ninth century there was a resurgence of artistic endeavor. Byzantine craftsmen designed and decorated many churches throughout the empire. Their work is found in such places as Messina and Palermo in Sicily and Venice in Italy. Artists were summoned to such distant places as Kiev in Russia to aid in the design, construction, and decoration of churches.

The mosaics make vividly concrete the Byzantine concepts of empire, emperor, and church. The emperor is always presented as the august figure which Byzantine ideology made of him (see Plate 7). Christ is never shown as suffering; he is, in other words, always God and never man (see Plate 8). The reason for this seems to have been the close association which the figure of Christ bore to the living emperor. To show Christ as suffering would suggest that the emperor too might be a weak and vulnerable man. The mosaics have no sense of movement, admission of human frailty, or recognition of the reality of change. Operating within this picture of the world, the artists nevertheless portrayed their solemn figures with a rich variety of forms and garments and illumined them with a splendid array of colors. Byzantine mosaics may be static, but they are neither drab nor monotonous.

The greatest monument of the Byzantine Empire is the church of Hagia Sophia (Holy Wisdom) in Istanbul, which was begun in 532, during the reign of Emperor Justinian. The four minarets were added when the church became a mosque after the Turkish conquest. (Photo: G. E. Kidder Smith)

DECLINE OF THE EMPIRE

The military power of the empire in its middle period was largely based upon the system of themes that created an army and navy of free peasant-warriors. But from the early tenth century these free peasant-warriors, apparently to escape mounting fiscal and military burdens, began to abandon their farms to more powerful neighbors. In the eleventh century many of them became serfs. The disintegration of the theme system reduced the military manpower and contributed to the growth of a rural aristocracy of landlords, which in turn weakened the strength of the central government.

The weak emperors of the late eleventh century sought to purchase the loyalty of the rural aristocracy by distributing imperial estates to them. During the same time, the aristocracy was gaining control over the ecclesiastical lands. The Church had been granting to them entire monasteries as *charistikaria* (literally, "charitable donations") to administer in the best interest of the monks and the Church. But in fact these concessions represented virtually gifts of monastic properties.

Socially, Byzantium was being transformed from a disciplined society of peasant-warriors under a strong central government to a feudal society with a dependent peasantry, a strong local landlord, and a weak central government. The transition was costly in a military sense; the emperors had to seek outside help to compensate for the shrinking contingents they could marshal and command from among their own subjects. Control of the sea was essential to the security of Constantinople. To assure sufficient naval strength the emperors sought the support of the growing naval power of Venice. In 998 and 1082 they gave generous trading concessions to the Venetians, which were major steps in the growth of Italian (and Western) naval strength in the waters of the eastern Mediterranean. The problem of land defense was even more pressing. The eastern frontiers were being threatened by a new people, the Seljuk Turks, who had recently emerged from the steppes.

The Seljuks

The Byzantines gave the name "Turk" to a number of nomadic tribes who lived in the region east and north of the Caspian Sea (modern Soviet Republic of Turkestan). They had long posed a threat to the settled Islamic and Christian populations. In the eleventh century members of one of the nomadic tribes, the Seljuks, penetrated beyond the eastern borders of the empire into Asia Minor. Emperor Romanus Diogenes tried to expel them but succeeded only in provoking open war. The Seljuks shattered the largely mercenary army of the Byzantines and took Romanus himself captive at Manzikert in 1071.

The disaster at Manzikert broke down the eastern defenses of the Byzantine Empire and opened Asia Minor to the Seljuks. One Turkish chieftain, Suleiman, established himself and his warriors at Nicaea, only a few miles from Constantinople. He founded what eventually became the most powerful Turkish principality in Asia Minor: the Sultanate of Rum. The virtual loss of Asia Minor forced the Byzantine emperor to appeal to the West for help. This was the immediate prologue to the First Crusade and also the end of the Byzantine Empire as a great power in the East.

Schism with the West

The second disaster of the eleventh century was the formal schism between the Eastern and Western branches of the Church. The schism was provoked not by major dogmatic differences but by rivalry, disputes, and snobbery. For years the popes at Rome and the patriarchs at Constantinople had been rivals in converting the East Slavs and had been bitterly disputing the ecclesiastical jurisdiction over southern Italy and Illyria (modern Yugoslavia). Furthermore, the Byzantines resented the papal claim to primacy within the Church. Rome by this time appeared to them as a provincial town without an empire and subject territory, whereas Constantinople was the seat of wealth and power; it was, therefore, the more appropriate capital for the Church.[3]

Perhaps even more fundamentally the rupture of relations reflected the breakdown in communications between the East and West, which had begun when Justinian failed in the sixth century to reconcile the two branches of the Church within the old Roman Empire. After his reign the two halves of the Roman Empire ceased entirely to speak or understand a common language; misunderstandings came easily and were overcome with difficulty. Commercial and diplomatic contacts between the East and West also became sporadic.

Personalities played a major role in the actual schism of 1054. A dedicated but rigid reformer, Cardinal Humbert of Silva Candida, led a papal delegation to Constantinople. Failing to secure satisfactory concessions from Patriarch Michael Cerularius, the papal legates deposited a bull of excommunication on the high altar of Hagia Sophia and left the city in

---

[3] In the tenth century the Byzantines told Liutprand, bishop of Cremona, that they, and not the residents of Rome, were the true Romans and that Rome was a town inhabited exclusively by "vile slaves, fishermen, confectioners, poulterers, bastards, plebians, underlings."

anger. Cerularius, a haughty and ambitious prelate who welcomed a break with the Western Church and had labored to provoke it, publicly declared to the other Eastern patriarchs that the supporters of the pope were steeped in heresy and had taken themselves out of the true Church since the sixth century.

The schism of 1054 destroyed the hope for a united Christian Church, although only later centuries showed the full extent of the damage. Even today, more than nine hundred years after the event, men of Western and Eastern traditions are trying to overcome the rift. Only in 1965 did the pope and the Greek patriarch formally remove the excommunication of 1054.

THE WESTERN DEBT TO BYZANTINE CIVILIZATION

The East Slavs were the true, direct heirs of Byzantine civilization; but the Western peoples also accumulated a large debt to this civilization. Byzantine scholars preserved the classical Greek literature. This permitted Western scholars to establish direct contact with the most original thinkers of the ancient world. Neither the Western classical renaissance nor modern European culture would have been the same without their contribution.

The very existence of the Byzantine Empire, guarding the approaches to Europe, gave the Western peoples a measure of immunity from the destructive incursions of Arabs, Persians, Turks, and others. The sophisticated Byzantine economy and government served as a kind of school of civilized practices from which less advanced peoples could learn new techniques. The greatest contribution Byzantine civilization made to the West was that, through its own achievements, it showed the uncouth Western peoples the possibilities and rewards of civilized life.

II. THE PRINCIPALITY OF KIEV

During the Early Middle Ages a new people, the East Slavs, set about building a civilization that was based primarily on the values of Eastern Christianity. Three modern Slavic peoples —the Russians, Ukrainians, and White (Byelo-) Russians—trace their ancestry directly to these East Slavs, and all regard the foundation of the first East Slavic state as the beginnings of their own national histories. For this reason, it is inappropriate to speak, as is often done, of the first Russian state, as the Russians are not its exclusive heirs. In referring to these East Slavs we shall rather use a contemporary term, the "Rus," a name of obscure origins, which first referred to a dominant tribe or group and then came to signify the entire people.

THE FOUNDATIONS OF KIEV RUS

The East Slavs greatly expanded their area of settlement between the sixth and ninth centuries. Some East Slavic tribes pushed to the east as far as the Volga River. There they encountered on the lower course of the river a Turkish-speaking people called the Khazars. The Khazars (or at least their upper classes) practiced Judaism; their obscure history has its own special fascination. Other Slavic tribes moved to the north nearly to the Baltic Sea. Two of their most important settlements were Kiev on the Dnieper River and Novgorod on Lake Ilmen, within easy access of the Baltic Sea.

About 830 Vikings from Scandinavia, embarking upon a vigorous wave of expansion in all directions, penetrated into the lands of the East Slavs in quest of booty and profit. They also established trade routes that ran from the Baltic Sea over the rivers of Eastern Europe to the Black Sea and thence to Constantinople, thus linking Scandinavia with Byzantium. The invasions brought the Vikings and East Slavs into close contact. Out of this encounter emerged the first East Slavic state.

The most detailed and important source for the birth of the Rus state is the *Primary Chronicle*. Many hands contributed to this work; and it was not written down in its present form until 1117 or 1118, some 250 years after the events it describes. According to the *Primary Chronicle* the Varangians, as the East Slavs called the Vikings, ruled Novgorod until the Slavic population rebelled against them and drove them back beyond the sea. Soon, however, the people of Novgorod fell to fighting among themselves. Unable to overcome their discord, they invited the Varangians to rule them once again. In response a prince named Rurik, his two brothers, and "all the Rus" came to govern Novgorod in 862. "On account of these Varangians," the *Primary Chronicle* explains, "the district of Novgorod became known as Russian land."

Historians have long argued vigorously and even bitterly over the dating and terminology used in this account. The date of 862 is certainly wrong, and the meaning of "Rus" is obscure. Byzantine sources mention a Rus attack on Constantinople in 860, and there are earlier references to a mysterious people by that name settled in what is now the Ukraine.

The *Primary Chronicle* goes on to say that Rurik soon left Novgorod and that his follower Oleg assumed authority in Novgorod and then Kiev. Oleg (873?–913) is thus considered the true founder of the Rus state because he united under his rule the two chief cities of Kiev and Novgorod. In 907 he led a fleet, allegedly containing two thousand ships, on a raid against Constantinople. The Byzantine emperor granted both tribute and trading concessions in order to purchase peace with the Rus. Oleg's successors completed the unification of the East Slavic tribes. This brought under their rule an area that stretched from the Baltic to the Black seas and from the Danube to the Volga rivers. They also made war against the nomadic peoples of the steppes and strengthened commercial, diplomatic, and cultural ties with the Byzantine Empire. In 989 the ruler, Vladimir, converted to Christianity (the Eastern Church) and imposed baptism on his subjects. These people, the most numerous of all the Slavs, were thus brought within the Eastern cultural world.

Yaroslav the Wise

The Principality of Kiev reached its height of power under Vladimir's son Yaroslav (1015–1054), who might well be termed the Slavic Justinian. Like Justinian, Yaroslav was a successful warrior, administrator, and builder. He defeated the Pechenegs, a nomadic people who roamed the grasslands south and east of Kiev and hampered contact with the Black Sea, and extended his territory to the north at the expense of the Finns (see Map 7.2). He won self-government for the Rus Church from the patriarch of Constantinople in 1037. The head of the Church was called the metropolitan. Kiev became the ecclesiastical as well as the political capital of the East Slavs. During his reign Yaroslav had prepared the first written codification of East Slavic law, the *Russkaia Pravda*. He built many churches and brought in skilled Byzantine artisans to decorate them. His masterpiece was the cathedral at Kiev. The *Primary Chronicle* says that Yaroslav loved books "and read them continually day and night," and that he wrote many books himself. He tried to promote learning in his principality and assembled many scribes to translate religious books from Greek into Slavic.

The Principality of Kiev maintained closer ties with Western Europe than any other Russian state for centuries. Russia is mentioned in the eleventh-century French epic, the *Song of Roland*. The family of Yaroslav had marriage

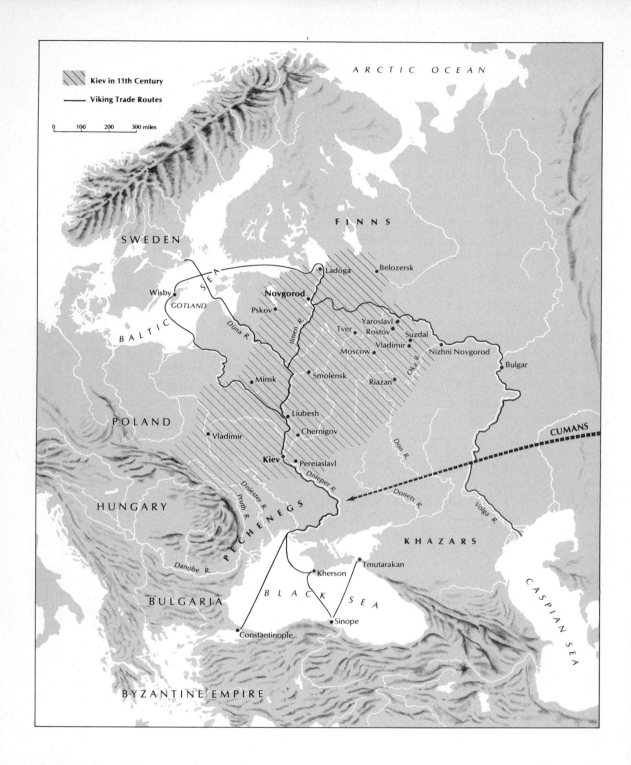

MAP 7.2: PRINCIPALITY OF KIEV

connections with the ruling dynasties of Byzantium, England, France, Germany, Norway, Poland, and Hungary. Yaroslav's own daughter Anna married King Henry I of France. Charters with her signature survive, carefully inscribed with Cyrillic letters; she seems to have been the only lay person in the French court who could write. Kiev was also a refuge for Western princes; Edwin and Edward, sons of the English king Edmund Ironside, fled there during Canute's reign in England.

KIEVAN CIVILIZATION

Kievan economy was both vigorous and balanced. Agriculture was productive on the fertile steppes. The *Primary Chronicle* describes peasants plowing with horses at a time when the less efficient oxen were the more common draft animals in the West. Trade was conducted with the Scandinavians, the steppe peoples, the Muslims at Baghdad, and especially the Byzantines. Every year a great fleet of boats assembled at Kiev and floated down the Dnieper River to the Black Sea and across to Constantinople. The princes themselves led these expeditions. Amber, fur, honey, slaves, and wheat were exchanged for silks, spices, and other luxuries of the East. In recent years Russian archaeologists excavating at Novgorod have uncovered numerous commercial documents written on birch bark that illuminate this lively trade. These documents indicate that the Rus merchants were not as sophisticated in their business practices as the Byzantines, but they establish the variety and quality of the products the Rus offered for trade.

Most of the population was free peasants, but there were slaves and some enserfed peasants. Although its foundations were agricultural, Kievan society had an important urban life. Within the many towns a wealthy aristocracy of princes, warriors, and great merchants rubbed shoulders with artisans, workers, and large numbers of destitute persons. The princes had to concern themselves with such social problems as the oppression of the poor, usury, and enslavement for debt.

Kiev in the eleventh century was one of the great cities of the age. The German chronicler Adam of Bremen considered Kiev a rival in size to Constantinople; Metropolitan Hilarion described it as "glittering with grandeur"; another German chronicler, Thietmar of Merseburg, said it had four hundred churches, eight marketplaces, and unnumbered inhabitants. In 1124 a fire allegedly destroyed six hundred churches. Kiev must have included twenty to thirty thousand people, which would be above the size of any contemporary Western city.

The head of the Kievan government was the prince, who selected nobles, called boyars, to aid him in governing. The boyars formed the prince's *druzhina* ("friendship").[4] In all important matters the prince consulted his boyars for advice. The towns had large citizen assemblies, called *veches*, that the prince also consulted for advice. The government was thus based on a balance of monarchial, aristocratic, and popular elements. The prince, unlike the Byzantine emperor, was not the fountain of justice. Most cases were settled in popular courts from which there was no organized system of appeal. Kievan justice was closer to the Germanic system than to the Byzantine system. The limitations upon princely autocracy imposed by the boyars and the *veches* make the Kievan period distinctive in Russian constitutional history.

The central event in Kievan cultural development was the acceptance of Eastern Christianity in 989. The arrival of some Byzantine clergy in Kiev changed the character of its culture. They established a formal educational system primarily to train a clergy; but their

---

[4] The *druzhina* was the equivalent of the Germanic *comitatus* (see Chapter 6).

Prince Yaroslav built St. Sophia Cathedral at Kiev in 1038, modeling it after Hagia Sophia at Constantinople. It is famous for its outstanding mosaics and frescoes. The present domes were built in the seventeenth century in Ukranian baroque style. In 1934 it was declared a state museum. (Photo: Novosti from Sovfoto)

schools, were open to the sons of ruling families, and a number of women, too, were educated in convents. Monks, as the first scholars in Kiev, used a modification of the Greek alphabet that missionaries had devised years before to convert the Slavs. They employed this alphabet in the translations of parts of the Bible and other ecclesiastical writings. These works constituted the dominant body of contemporary

literature, and their religious themes served as models for the native writers.

The literary masterpiece of the age is the *Primary Chronicle.* Its principal theme is the conversion of the Rus to Christianity and their battles against the pagan peoples who surrounded them. This work gave to the East Slavs a sense of national identity within a Christian scheme of history. Although the account is of questionable accuracy in its earliest passages, it remains a classic of medieval literature. Few Western chronicles of comparable age can equal it in the wealth of information and liveliness of narration. The monks, of whom Metropolitan Hilarion was perhaps the most gifted, also produced many sermons, doctrinal and devotional tracts, and histories of saints' lives. These histories and the *Primary Chronicle* provide the best picture of the society and culture of medieval Rus. The poetry of medieval Rus is represented by the short heroic epic the *Song of Igor's Campaign.*[5] The poem records an unsuccessful campaign that the Rus princes conducted against the pagan Polovtsi in 1185 and depicts with considerable feeling the tragic but necessary costs of battle against the steppe peoples.

Christianity also had an immense influence on architectural and artistic development. After the conversion the East Slavs built many churches based on Byzantine models. The familiar onion domes of the Russian churches, for example, were a late effort to imitate in wood the domes on ecclesiastical architecture at Constantinople. The East Slavs loved magnificence and splendor in their churches and liturgical

---

[5] The original manuscript was discovered about 1790 by Count Aleksey Musin-Pushkin but was destroyed during the Napoleonic invasion in 1812, when Moscow was burned. Those who accept its authenticity usually date its composition to 1187. The *Song* is available in a fine English translation by the distinguished novelist Vladimir Nabokov.

services. They learned the art of painting from the Byzantines and decorated their churches with icons (from the Greek, *eikón*, meaning "image"). The icon is a representation in painting or enamel of some sacred personage, such as Christ, a saint, or an angel.

Christianity imparted to the East Slavs a sense of world history and of their own place in it. They came to view their country as Holy Rus, the defender of the true faith, facing and fighting a sea of pagan barbarians. Even though many accomplishments of the Kievan era were not maintained in the succeeding periods of East Slavic history, the Russians, Ukrainians, and Byelo-Russians themselves did not lapse into barbarism.

DECLINE OF THE PRINCIPALITY

Both internal and external troubles destroyed the peace of the land after Yaroslav's death. To select his successor Yaroslav introduced an extraordinarily complex procedure known as the rota system. The entire land was considered to be the property of the ruling family, and the towns were ranked in order of their importance and allotted to the princes according to their position within the family. When the senior prince of Kiev died, each of the junior princes transferred his rule to the next greater town; brothers were given preference over sons. This cumbersome system of succession led to a constant movement of princes, to frequent bickerings, and often to civil wars. The political history after the reign of Yaroslav becomes an involved and dismal story of unending princely quarrels.

These struggles left the people unable to resist the renewed menace of the steppe nomads. In 1061 the Cumans began harassing the frontier, and they eventually cut off Kiev from contact with the Black Sea. This sundering of the trade route to Constantinople was a disaster for commerce and culture because it deprived Kiev of contact with the Byzantine Empire and the Western world.

Pressure from the nomads pushed the area of East Slavic settlement to the north and west, where extensive forests offered protection from their forays. This dispersal prepared the way for the eventual differentiation of the East Slavs into three culturally distinct peoples. The Rus of the north—soon Russians—were forced into a kind of isolation, removed and remote from the major centers of civilization. A new city, Moscow (not mentioned in the sources until 1147), assumed the arduous task of forming a united Russian state. In 1169 the soldiers of a northern prince, Andrew Bogoliubsky of Suzdal, sacked Kiev. With the ruin of Kiev, perpetrated by the steppe nomads and by the Rus themselves, the first major chapter of East Slavic history closes.

III. ISLAM

Sometime about 610 in the Arabian town of Mecca, a merchant's son named Muhammad began to preach to the people, summoning them to repentance and reform. Gradually, he brought his teachings together to form a new system of religious belief that he called Islam. The explosive impact of his preaching must be reckoned as one of the most extraordinary events of world history. Within a century after Muhammad's death his followers had conquered and partially converted territories larger than the old Roman Empire. Even today Islam remains the faith of more than 513 million people, about an eighth of the world's population.

THE ARABS

The Arabian Peninsula, the homeland of the Arabs, profoundly influenced their culture and history. Its vast interior and northern regions are dominated by steppes, wastelands, and some of the hottest and driest deserts of the world. The Arabs, however, had adapted to this harsh environment. They supported themselves by raising sheep and camels. These animals provided nearly all their necessities: meat, milk, wool and skins for clothes and tents, and fuel from dried camel dung. The Arabs were extremely proud of their family, race, language, skill, and way of life. The harsh environment and fierce pride made them spirited, tenacious, and formidable warriors.

The Arabian Peninsula was in a state of intense political and social ferment on the eve of Muhammad's appearance. The stronger political powers—the Persians, Byzantines, and Abyssinians across the Red Sea—tried repeatedly to subdue the Arabs, but they could not dominate them in their desert home. Religious ferment was no less pronounced. Several prophets, preaching new religious beliefs, had appeared in Arabia before Muhammad; and this indicates a growing dissatisfaction among the Arabs with their traditional paganism that gave no promise of an afterlife and offered no image of human destiny and the role of the Arabs in it. Both Christianity and Judaism had won numerous converts, but neither one was able to gain the adherence of the larger part of the people. The Arabs awaited a man who by the force of his vision could fuse these contending ideas—pagan, Christian, and Jewish—into a single, commanding, and authentic Arabian religion.

MUHAMMAD

Historians have little information that is certain about the founder of Islam. Muhammad was born at Mecca about 570 or 571. His father died before his birth, and his mother when he was six. After being raised by his uncle, Muhammad worked as a camel driver in mercantile caravans. He may have been illiterate and may have had no direct knowledge of the Jewish and Christian scriptures; but he did acquire a wide, if sometimes inaccurate, knowledge of the history and teaching of those two religions. About the age of twenty-five Muhammad married the widow of a rich merchant; thus freed from economic concerns, he gave himself to religious meditations in the desert outside Mecca.

In 610 the voice of the angel Gabriel spoke to Muhammad, and he continued to receive revelations in increasing frequency and length for the remainder of his life. After that event Muhammad began to preach publicly about personal moral reform, but only his wife and a small group of relatives initially accepted his teachings. The Meccans feared him because his strictures against paganism seemed to threaten the position of Mecca as a center of pilgrimages. Mecca possessed a renowned shrine containing the Kaaba, a sacred black stone that was the object of pagan worship. Rejected in his native city, Muhammad accepted an invitation to come to Yathrib, a trading town 270 miles to the north, which he later renamed Medina.

Muhammad's flight from Mecca to Yathrib is called the Hegira and occurred in 622; it later became the year 1 of the Islamic calendar. The Hegira was a turning point in Muhammad's career for two reasons: he became the political leader and governor of an important town, which gave him a base for the military expansion of the Islamic community; and his responsibilities as head of an independent town affected the character of his religious message. More and more it was concerned with public law, administration, and the practical problems of government.

Muhammad was more successful at Yathrib than he had been at Mecca in making converts. He told them that God ordered them to convert or conquer their neighbors; through enthusiastic proselytizing and war the community of believers grew rapidly. With this support Muhammad marched against the Meccans, defeating

them at Badr in 624 and taking Mecca in 630. By his death in 632, Muhammad had given his religion a firm foundation on Arabian soil.

In this fourteenth-century Persian painting Muhammad sets in place the sacred black stone known as the Kaaba. Veneration of the Kaaba had been an important rite under Arabic paganism, and Muhammad enjoined his followers to continue the practice. This is a further illustration of his skill in synthesizing many older beliefs and rites into the new religion of Islam. (Photo: University of Edinburgh Library)

THE RELIGION OF ISLAM

Instructed by the angel Gabriel, Muhammad passed on to his followers the words or prophecies of Allah (from *al ilāh*, "the God"). The collection of prophecies is known as the Koran; and Allah, in Islamic theology, is its true author. The Koran was written down in its present, official version from 651 to 652. The Koran often impresses the non-Muslim reader as chaotic and repetitious, but to the sympathetic reader it imparts a powerful mood, one of uncompromising monotheism, of repeated and impassioned emphasis upon the unity, power, and presence of Allah. The mood is sustained by constant reiterations of set formulas praising Allah, his power, knowledge, mercy, justice, and concern for his people.

The chief obligation which Muhammad im-

posed upon his followers was submission (the literal meaning of "Islam") to the will of Allah. Those who submit are Muslims. ("Muhammadan," which suggests that Muhammad claimed divinity, is an inappropriate usage.) Muhammad was little concerned with the subtleties of theology; he was interested in defining for Muslims the ethical and legal requirements for an upright life. Unlike Christianity, Islam retained this practical emphasis; jurisprudence, even more than speculative theology, remained the great intellectual interest of scholarship. Also in contrast to Christianity, Islam did not recognize a separate clergy and church, for there was no need for specialized intermediaries between Allah and his people. Allah was the direct ruler of the faithful on earth; he legislated for them in the Koran and administered through Muhammad, the Prophet, and his successors, the caliphs. Church and state were not separate entities, at least in theory. There was only the single, sacred community of Allah.

Expansion of Islam

The message of Islam exerted a powerful appeal to the Arabs. Compared with Christianity and Judaism, Islam was a starkly simple belief, easily explained and easily grasped. It was an effective fusion of religious ideas from Christianity, Judaism, paganism, and perhaps Zoroastrianism. Judaism influenced the legal code regulating diet and behavior. Judaism and Christianity provided the notion of prophecy (Muhammad considered himself the last of a line of prophets that began with Abraham and included Christ). Christianity gave the concepts of Last Judgment, personal salvation, heaven and hell, charity to the poor and weak, and a universal religion. Christianity or perhaps Zoroastrianism suggested the figures of Satan and evil demons. Paganism contributed the veneration of the Kaaba at Mecca and the requirement of pilgrimage to the sacred city. Islam was the fulfillment of religious ideas already familiar to the Arabs. Perhaps most important, Islam appealed strongly to the intense racial and cultural pride of the Arabs. The Koran was written in their native language, Arabic, and only in Arabic could Allah be addressed. Islam was the final revelation, bringing to completion the message that God had partially conveyed through the Hebrew prophets and Christ. The Arabs, a semibarbarous people who had hitherto played a negligible role in history, were given an important mission in life: to carry to the world the ultimate saving message. Even as Muhammad supplanted Christ as the supreme prophet, so the Arabs replaced the Jews as God's chosen people, with a sacred right to his holy places, including Jerusalem.

It is remarkable that these ideas retain power even in the contemporary world. The present conflict in the Middle East between Israelis and Arabs, among Jews, Muslims, and Christians, is not primarily a reflection of modern political and economic rivalries. Rather, it is grounded in ancient theologies and long-ingrained cultural pride; it is history's anguished legacy.

Allah instructed his followers to convert or conquer nonbelievers. Several factors aided the extraordinary expansion of Islam in the first century of its existence. Islam fused the once contending Arab clans and tribes into a unified and dedicated force. The Arabs, long familiar with camels, were masters of desert warfare. Their enemies, relying on horses, could not challenge them on desert terrain. Using the desert much as English imperialists later used the sea, the Arabs moved armies and supplies with impunity across vast arid stretches, struck the enemy at places and times of their own choosing, and retreated to the safety of the desert when the odds turned against them. Moreover, the Arabs' immediate neighbors, the Byzantines and Persians, were mutually exhausted by their recurrent wars. Both empires included large Semitic populations that were linguistically and culturally related to the Arabs and, therefore, could comprehend the message of Islam. The Arabs were able to make and hold their conquests through a unique combination of fanaticism and toleration. They were inspired to battle by the Prophet's promise of vast rewards to those who died in the Holy War against the nonbelievers and by the very real prospect of considerable booty if victory accompanied their efforts. The Prophet, however, also enjoined a policy of partial toleration toward the Christians and Jews, the "people of the Book." They were permitted to live under their own laws, but they paid a special tax for the privilege and were prohibited from serving in the government or military. Finally, because the Arabs did not have the numbers and the skills to govern all the territories they conquered, they opened the ranks of government to men from the newly conquered and converted peoples. This added stability to Islamic rule.

The period of most rapid expansion of Islam followed Muhammad's death in 632 and coincided with the rule of the first four caliphs. Arabian forces seized the Byzantine provinces of Palestine and Syria, overran Persia, and conquered Egypt. By 661 Islam was firmly established as a world power. Islamic conquests continued under the Omayyad caliphs, the first line of hereditary rulers. The Omayyads moved the capital from Mecca to Damascus. Under their rule the Muslims conquered North Africa and overran the Kingdom of the Visigoths. After crossing the Pyrenees into the Kingdom of the Franks, Muslim raiders were finally defeated by Charles Martel at Tours in 732. This battle, one hundred years after Muhammad's death, marked the extent of the western advance and stabilized the frontier of Islam for the next several centuries (see Map 7.3).

As the territory under Islamic control grew to enormous size, powerful movements threatened and finally shattered Islamic unity. Jealousies and frictions disturbed the relations among the various peoples who had accepted Islam, and religious divisions also appeared. Islam had been an open and fluid religion at the death of Muhammad, but scholars and teachers gradually elaborated a theology which a majority of the believers accepted as orthodox. The scholars based the new orthodoxy not only upon the Koran but also upon the Sunnas, or traditions, which were writings that purported to describe how the first companions of Muhammad or Muhammad himself dealt with various problems. Some Muslims, however, rejected the new orthodoxy of the Sunnites, as

they came to be called. Those who opposed the Sunnites were called the Shiites, or schismatics.

This earliest schism was more a political than a religious protest. The Shiites maintained that only the descendants of Muhammad's son-in-law, Ali, who was the fourth caliph, could lawfully rule the Islamic community; therefore, they rejected the Omayyads (and later the Abbasids) as usurpers. Shiism soon became a cloak for all sorts of antagonisms, protests, and revolts. It struck deep roots among the mixed populations, reflecting the dissatisfactions of non-Arabs with Arab preponderance and channeling the antagonism between the poorer classes and their masters.

The growing social and religious dissensions finally broke the Omayyad caliphate. A descendant of Muhammad's uncle Abbas revolted against the Omayyads, captured Damascus, and ruthlessly massacred the caliph's family in 750. Only one member escaped, Abdurrahman. He fled to Spain, where he set up an independent caliphate at Cordoba in 755. Other split-offs soon followed: Morocco in 788, Tunisia in 800, eastern Persia in 820, and Egypt in 868. All became virtually independent under their local dynasties. The new Abbasid caliph moved the capital from Damascus to a new city, Baghdad. The community of Islam was never again to be united.

ISLAMIC CIVILIZATION

Medieval Islamic civilization reached its peak of prosperity, refinement, and learning in the ninth and tenth centuries. The name of Caliph Harun al-Rashid is known throughout the world by virtue of the tales of the *Arabian Nights*. These exotic stories, put into their present form in the fourteenth century, convey a glamorous and idealized, but not a false, picture of the luxurious life at Baghdad during its most splendid age. Harun's son Al-Mamun

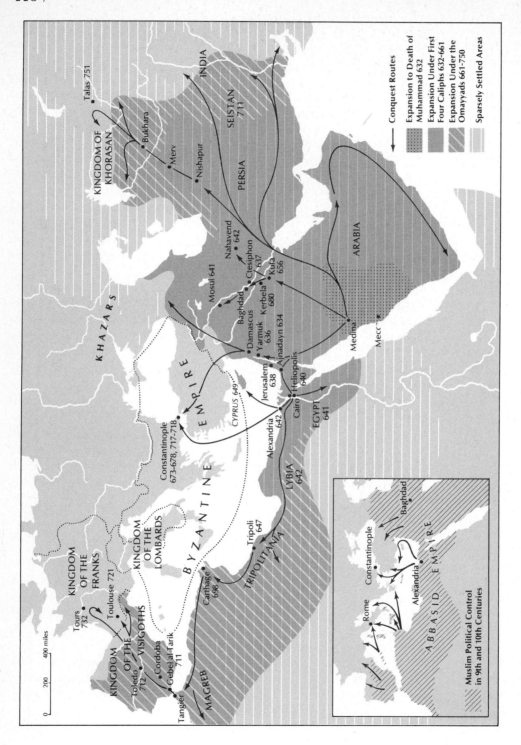

Talas 751

KINGDOM OF
KHORASAN

Bukhara

Merv

Nishapur

INDIA

SEISTAN
711

PERSIA

ARABIA

Nahavend
642

Ctesiphon
637

Kufa
656

Mosul 641

Baghdad

Kerbela
680

Damascus

Yarmuk
636

Ajnadayn 634

Jerusalem
638

Heliopolis
640

Medina

Mecc

KHAZARS

B Y Z A N T I N E   E M P I R E

CYPRUS 649

Alexandria
642

Cairo

EGYPT
641

Constantinople
673-678, 717-718

KINGDOM
OF THE
FRANKS

Toulouse 721

Tours
732

KINGDOM
OF THE
LOMBARDS

Carthage
698

Tripoli
647

TRIPOLITANIA

LYBIA
642

KINGDOM
OF THE
VISIGOTHS

Toledo
712

Cordoba

Gebel al-Tarik
711

Tangier

MAGREB

400 miles

200

0

Conquest Routes

Expansion to Death of
Muhammad 632

Expansion Under First
Four Caliphs 632-661

Expansion Under the
Omayyads 661-750

Sparsely Settled Areas

Baghdad

A B B A S I D   E M P I R E

Rome

Constantinople

Alexandria

Muslim Political Control
in 9th and 10th Centuries

MAP 7.3: EXPANSION OF ISLAM

reigned even more splendidly than his father. He was also a patron of learning. Al-Mamun founded an observatory for the study of the heavens and established a "House of Wisdom" (sometimes referred to as the first Islamic institute of higher education), where translations could be made and a library collected for the use of scholars.

Spain was also a center of medieval Islamic civilization. The brilliance of Islamic-Spanish civilization is best reflected in three great architectural monuments: the mosque (now a cathedral) at Cordoba, the Alhambra Palace at Granada, and the Alcazar at Seville. Jewish communities in Spain contributed to the high quality of intellectual life. It was in Spain that Western Christians came into intimate contact with Islamic learning and drew from it the greatest benefits.

· The expansion of Islam brought within the Muslim world a great variety of economic systems. The Bedouins in the Arabian Peninsula, the Berbers in North Africa, and the Turkish peoples on the Eurasian steppes continued to follow an essentially pastoral economy. The majority of the population in Egypt, Persia, Sicily, and Spain lived from settled agriculture. The inhabitants of cities, particularly those found along the caravan routes which tied the Middle East to India and central Asia, depended on commerce.

Islamic religion contributed to the economic life of these many peoples and regions by facilitating communication and commercial exchange. The imposition of a universal language, Arabic, enabled travelers and merchants to make themselves understood from Spain to India. The obligation of pilgrimage to Mecca assured that travel would be frequent. Moreover, Muhammad had been a merchant, and the earliest centers of his religion, Medina and Mecca, were important caravan cities; therefore, Islamic law was favorable to commercial transactions, and Islamic society held the merchant in high esteem. Merchants not only con-

The Book of the 1001 Nights, *first redacted in Arabic at Baghdad in the ninth century, made use of much Persian and Indian materials and remains a world classic of imaginative story telling. This bizarre representation of a monster, taken from a late-medieval Urdu (Hindustani) edition of the work, illustrates both its romantic content and lasting appeal.* (Photo: The Granger Collection)

tinued the caravan trade, but also developed an important maritime commerce in the Mediterranean Sea, the Red Sea, and the Indian Ocean. Their ships provided until the sixteenth century the chief commercial link between India and the West.

Commercial exchange stimulated agriculture. Cultivators in Sicily and Spain learned of, and

adopted, new plants from Asia, such as rice, and new techniques of cultivation, such as the irrigation of fields. Muslims from Persia to Spain practiced an agriculture remarkably advanced for the age. Commercial exchange also stimulated urban artisans to improve the quality of their products. The steel of Damascus, the leather of Cordoba, and the fine cotton, linen, and silk of many Eastern towns were desired and imitated in the West. These same products were shipped to India and Indonesia, where they were traded for spices and other products.

The practice of a common religion assured that there would be similarities in Islamic societies everywhere in the world. Religious law allowed the male Muslim to have as many as four legal wives and an unlimited number of concubines. In fact, because the number of men and women are approximately equal in all populations, polygamy remained an ideal more than a social reality; only the very rich had an opportunity to practice it. More important than polygamy in determining the position of women were the relative ease of divorce and the life of seclusion imposed upon all women after puberty. Religious laws permitted the husband to dismiss his wife almost at will and prohibited a woman from revealing her face except to her husband. These laws were not enforced everywhere with equal rigor; they primarily weighed upon women of the upper classes. Moreover, within the cities, at least in certain periods, women enjoyed relative freedom. Variety, in other words, rather than uniformity, was the more prominent characteristic of medieval Islamic society.

That society was also distinguished by a vigorous urban life, concentrated in the cities of Baghdad, Cairo, Cordoba, and Damascus. According to travelers' reports, Damascus had

The Alhambra Palace in Granada. (Photo: G. E. Kidder Smith, New York)

113,000 homes and 70 libraries. Baghdad surpassed all cities with the number of palaces, libraries, and public baths. In all the major cities products from almost all parts of the known world could be purchased at the markets, or bazaars. The streets teemed with slaves, servants, artisans, merchants, administrators, and beggars. The aura of the Islamic cities was preeminently cosmopolitan.

Muhammad died before making provision for the government of Islam, and his immediate followers elected Abu Bakr as his successor, or caliph. Because Islam recognized no distinction between church and state, the caliph was the supreme religious and civil head of the Muslim world. But he was not free to change the laws at will since Allah had already provided all the laws his people needed; therefore, he was primarily a military chief and a judge. The government tended to retain the administrative institutions of the preceding rulers in territories that were overrun. Among the Muslims the chief administrator on the local level was the kadi. He was primarily a judge, and his importance reflects the concern of the faithful to live according to the dictates of the Koranic law.

The Islamic conquests brought the Arabs into intimate contact with older and more accomplished civilizations than their own, particularly the intellectual achievements of Hellenism, which they were eager to preserve. During the eighth and ninth centuries scholars translated into Arabic many Greek authors: Aristotle, Euclid, Archimedes, Hippocrates, and Galen. These works, most of which were translated from the Syriac rather than directly from the Greek, provided the foundations for Islamic learning.

Scholars were especially interested in astronomy, astrology, mathematics, medicine, and optics; and in these areas their writings exerted a great influence on the Western world. Al-Razi (known as Rhazes in the West) of Baghdad wrote some 140 medical treatises, including an admirable description of smallpox. Mathematicians took the numbers from the Hindus, but made the critical addition of the zero, which is itself an Arabic word. Italian merchants became familiar with the Arabic numbers shortly before the year 1200 and carried them back to the West. Mathematicians also developed algebra. Astronomers and astrologers invented an improved astrolabe (which measures the angular declination of heavenly bodies above the horizon) and were able to correct the astronomical tables of antiquity.

Scholars also wrote philosophical and theological treatises. The most important Islamic philosopher was the Spaniard ibn-Rushd, or Averroës (1126?–1198), who wrote commentaries on Aristotle and exerted a profound influence on Christian as well as Islamic philosophy in the subsequent Middle Ages. Islamic philosophical speculations aided intellectual life in the West in two ways: Western philosophers gained a much broader familiarity with the scientific and philosophical heritage of classical Greece through translations made from the Arabic, chiefly in Spain; and Islamic philosophers explored issues central to religious philosophy much earlier than Christian thinkers. What is the relation between faith and reason, between an all-powerful, all-encompassing God and the freedom, dignity, and individuality of the human person? In posing these problems and in suggesting answers, the Muslims stimulated and enriched thought in the West.

DECLINE OF ISLAM

The earliest indication of decline was the growing military debility of the various Islamic states in the face of new invasions in the middle eleventh century. In the West, Christian armies embarked on the reconquest of the Iberian Peninsula, and Christian fleets broke the Islamic domination of the western Mediterranean islands. The Christian offensive blends imper-

ceptibly with the First Crusade, which wrested Jerusalem from Islamic control in 1099. In the East, Turkish nomads infiltrated the Abbasid caliphate in considerable numbers, and the Seljuks seized Baghdad in 1055. Turkish rulers gained supremacy in all the Eastern Islamic states over the next few centuries.

The economic basis was also changing. Commerce had been vigorous and was the chief economic resource. By the thirteenth century, however, maritime and commercial supremacy on the Mediterranean Sea passed to the Italians and other Westerners. Arabian coins largely disappeared from circulation in the West, documenting a headlong retreat from commerce. Simultaneously, the Islamic states were no longer supporting their warriors by salaries but by grants of land, which weakened central authority. The growing importance of an aristocracy of rural warriors seems to have brought a new rigidity into society.

Caution, to be sure, must be utilized in speaking of the decline of medieval Islam. Islamic civilization continued to support some great cultural centers and to inspire some great individuals; but after the eleventh century Islamic civilization lost those qualities of openness, flexibility, and intellectual daring which had so distinguished it in the ninth and tenth centuries.

THE WESTERN DEBT TO ISLAMIC CIVILIZATION

Almost every aspect of medieval Western life was influenced by Islamic civilization. Western farmers imitated the techniques of irrigation developed by the Muslims and learned to grow many new plants, such as rice, citrus fruits, and peaches. Western merchants adopted the system of numbers and probably some forms of business partnerships. Western scientists, philosophers, and theologians were influenced by Islamic scholars.

However, what Western civilization took

from Islamic civilization did not decisively change the course of Western cultural development. The more remarkable aspect is really how little these two medieval civilizations affected one another in their fundamental cultural attitudes, apart from specific techniques and institutions. The Islamic historian Sir Hamilton Gibb remarked that a civilization will resist foreign borrowings which threaten the character of its aesthetics, philosophy, or religious thought and will "absorb elements from other cultures only within a limited range and in forms adapted to its own temperament and psychological structure."[6] The medieval West was not much influenced by, and in fact poorly understood, the fundamental theology or the spirit of Islam. But it still enlisted many Islamic accomplishments in the service of its own civilization.

---

[6] "The Influence of Islamic Culture on Medieval Europe," in Sylvia L. Thrupp (ed.), *Change in Medieval Society*, 1964, p. 167.

 *The East preserved the urban culture of antiquity better than the West, and this largely explains the evident superiority of the East in the Early Middle Ages. Even in classical times the Eastern provinces of the Roman Empire had been more populous and more urbanized than the Western ones, and the Islamic conquests did not disturb the continuity and vitality of urban life. The Principality of Kiev, although the creation of a people only recently emerged from barbarism, still benefited from its close proximity to the ancient Mediterranean centers of civilization.*

These Eastern communities performed inestimable services for Western civilization. The Byzantine Empire and the Principality of Kiev helped shield the West from destructive invasions coming out of Asia. Byzantium and Islam offered the West enlarged access to the classical Greek heritage. They further passed on numerous techniques and skills and were for the backward West models of high accomplishment. From about the year 1000 the West embarked on a great age of growth. That it could work in relative security, that it could take full advantage of the heritage of antiquity, and that it could learn from gifted neighbors were in no small measure due to the presence and the power of these Eastern civilizations.

RECOMMENDED READING

Sources

Cross, Samuel Hazard (ed.). *Russian Primary Chronicle: Laurentian Text.* O. P. Sherbowitz-Wetzor (tr.). 1968.

*Ibn, Khaldun. *The Muqaddimah: An Introduction to World History.* Franz Rosenthal (tr.). 1969.

The Meaning of the Glorious Koran. M. Marmaduke Pickthall (tr.). 1948.

Procopius. *Secret History.* Richard Atwater (tr.). 1961. Full of scandal, sure to hold reader's attention.

*Vernadsky, George (ed.). *Medieval Russian Laws.* 1969.

Studies

*Baynes, Norman H., and Moss, Henry (eds.). *Byzantium: An Introduction to East Roman Civilization.* 1948. Elegant essays written by the founders of modern Byzantine studies.

*Geanakoplos, Deno J. *Byzantine East and Latin West: Two Worlds of Christendom in the Middle Ages and Renaissance.* 1966.

*Gibb, Hamilton A. *Mohammedanism: An Historical Survey.* 1962. Reflections of a distinguished scholar, now deceased.

Grekov, B. D. *Kiev Rus.* Dennis Ogden (ed.). 1959. From the viewpoint of a modern Soviet historian.

Hodgson, Marshall G. *The Venture of Islam: Conscience and History in a World Civilization.* 1974. A lengthy examination of the traditional beliefs and values of Islam.

*Lewis, Bernard. *The Arabs in History.* 1966. Short, graceful, and thoughtful.

Ostrogorski, George. *History of the Byzantine State.* Joan Hussey (tr.). 1969. The basic reference for all matters of political history.

*Runciman, Steven. *Byzantine Civilization.* 1933. An essay, many times reprinted, by a prominent English scholar.

*Vasiliev, A. A. *History of the Byzantine Empire: 324–1453.* 1953–1959. Stronger on cultural matters than Ostrogorski, by a great Russian scholar.

*Vernadsky, George. *A History of Russia.* 1946–1963. In five parts and six volumes, the most comprehensive, if still controversial, history of early Russia by a single historian in any language.

*Von Grunebaum, Gustave E. (ed.). *Medieval Islam: A Study in Cultural Orientation.* 1966. By one of the late, great figures in Islamic studies.

_____

* Available in paperback.

EIGHT

TWO CENTURIES OF
CREATIVITY

The present historical view of the Middle Ages recognizes the year 1000 as a watershed between two contrasting periods. Before 1000, Western civilization changed slowly, nearly imperceptibly. Europe's population was small, and the economy remained overwhelmingly agricultural in character. Trade was sporadic, and the few cities which survived the repeated invasions played only a minor role in economic life. Governments tended to be weak and unstable. In art and literature, there were few works produced which we would today regard as masterpieces.

After 1000, change came rapidly on virtually every level. Population, stagnant or declining since the last years of the Roman Empire, increased. People cleared and settled new lands and extended Europe's land frontiers in every direction. Commerce grew; and the resulting expansion of wealth restored vitality to urban life, moribund in the West since the decline of Rome. Rulers reorganized their governments in an effort to adapt the institutions of feudalism to a more stable political environment. Western philosophers embarked on a penetrating and even audacious examination of Christian theology, and the Church itself was subject to a major reform. Artists were once again productive, primarily in service to the Church.

Only recently have historians come to appreciate the dimensions of these changes, and this appreciation has led many of them to make a radical reassessment of the contribution of the Middle Ages to Western development. From the time of the Italian Renaissance, humanists and other scholars had dismissed the period as barbarous, and the prejudice against the Middle Ages remained strong in scholarly circles until the twentieth century. Today, however, many historians actually speak of a medieval renaissance. They have, in fact, gone so far as to propose a new periodization of Western history which dispenses with the old division between the medieval and modern periods. For these historians the eleventh and twelfth centuries, more than the Italian Renaissance or the Reformation, created the civilization that they label "traditional Europe." This civilization lasted until the revolutionary upheavals of the eighteenth and nineteenth centuries, the beginning of the authentically modern world. Not all historians would want to discount, as this view does, the impact of the Renaissance and the Reformation; but nearly all agree that the eleventh and twelfth centuries gave new impetus and new directions to the course of Western history.

1. THE ECONOMIC AND SOCIAL CHANGES

From the year 1000, European society showed many signs of growth, in its human numbers and in its geographic area of settlement. More-over, these greater numbers of people were earning their living in novel ways; in particular, there occurred a revival of trade and a rebirth of urban life. Simultaneously, Europeans were creating new forms of social and political organization and of cultural expression.

THE BEGINNINGS OF EXPANSION

Europe's population in the Early Middle Ages, to about the year 1000, was small in absolute numbers and was not distributed evenly across the countryside. Rather, the people tended to cluster into crowded communities—"population islands" they are sometimes called—separated from one another by vast stretches of wilderness. Within these islands there is much evidence of acute population pressures, even though there was little or no absolute growth. Peasant farms (the *mansi*), each intended for the support of a single family, often contained several by the ninth century. Average family size tended to be small—fewer than five persons per family, for example, on the estates of the monastery of Saint-Germain-des-Prés near Paris in the early ninth century. Men greatly outnumbered women; there were 130 men for every 100 women on these same estates. Perhaps female infanticide was practiced; perhaps women died sooner than men because of the hard agricultural labors they were expected to perform. Historians can only say with certainty that women did not survive well in the early medieval countryside.

Why did the population not spread out from these impacted settlements and clear new farms in the extensive surrounding wilderness? Many factors obstructed such an exodus: the trammels of serfdom; the safety provided by close settlement in a period of invasions; the bonds of kinship; a traditional fear of the wilderness. Other factors too, still undiscerned by historians, undoubtedly played a role.

This pattern of settlement changes from about the year 1000. Peasants pour out of their older centers of settlement to newly opened frontiers, both within Europe and beyond its former borders. What had happened? Perhaps improving conditions of climate encouraged the colonization of new lands. By the middle and late tenth century, the incursions of Vikings, Hun-garians, and Saracens were waning, and the new security made the wilderness less intimidating. Beginning in the late tenth century many lords and princes began to encourage the settlement of the wilderness areas they controlled; others assumed leadership in the expansion of the external frontier. They offered land to new settlers under favorable terms and assured them protection in the work of colonization. Their interest in increased rents perhaps indicates that the warrior aristocracy of Europe could no longer live, as it had in the past, predominantly from royal gifts and pillage taken in the frequent wars. The Church too, Europe's largest landlord, by the late tenth century actively sought to increase its own revenues from the land in the interest of supporting a celibate and reformed clergy (see p. 253). These changes further imply that Europeans, or at least their lay and ecclesiastical leaders, were developing a new self-consciousness. They were able to analyze their situation, evaluate their needs, and act rationally in order to obtain them.

The opening of new lands encouraged reproduction. Children became an asset to families engaged in the hard work of clearing land. Women survived better than before. More land in cultivation meant more food. For the first time since the fall of the Western Roman Empire, Europe's population gives evidence of sustained and substantial growth.

Frontiers

In England, France, and Germany, the peasants leveled forests and drained marshes; in England and the Low Countries they won land from the sea by building dikes and polders. Other pioneers, chiefly German peasants and knights looking for new lands to settle, pushed eastward beyond the former borders of the Frankish Empire (see Map 6.1) into territories which were thinly inhabited by Slavs, Prussians, Letts, and Lithuanians. Some Germans settled just beyond the Elbe River and established the Prin-

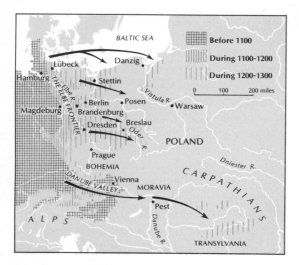

MAP 8.1: GERMAN MIGRATION EASTWARD

cipality of Brandenburg. Other Germans advanced along the shores of the Baltic Sea at the same time that Swedes began to move across Finland. The Russian prince of Novgorod, Alexander Nevsky, defeated the Swedes on the Neva River close to the Baltic Sea in 1240, and repulsed the Germans at Lake Peipus in 1242. Although these defeats halted further advances in northeastern Europe, the Germans and Swedes controlled the shores of the Baltic Sea. The Germans had by then pushed through the middle Danube valley and founded another principality: Austria. By the mid-thirteenth century the *Drang nach Osten* ("drive to the east") had clearly spent its strength, but it had tripled the area of German settlement over what it had been in Carolingian times (see Map 8.1).

Settlers also moved into the Iberian Peninsula. In the mid-eleventh century the Christian kings, whose kingdoms were confined to the extreme north of the peninsula, began an offensive against the Muslims, who ruled most of Iberia. These kings actively recruited Christian settlers for the territories they reconquered and gave them land under favorable terms. The Christian domina-

tion of the peninsula was confirmed in 1212 at Las Navas de Tolosa, when an allied Christian army defeated an invading Muslim army from North Africa. Only the Principality of Granada in the south remained under Muslim rule; the Iberian frontier remained almost unchanged for the next 280 years. The reconquest and resettlement of the Iberian Peninsula, known as the *Reconquista*, are the dominant themes of medieval Iberian history.

In Italy, too, pioneers pushed the Christian frontier to the south. In the early eleventh century knights from Normandy began fighting in southern Italy against Muslims, Byzantines, and local lords who had long been disputing dominion there. By 1124 they finally drove the Muslims and Byzantines from southern Italy and Sicily and united the two regions into the Kingdom of Naples and Sicily.

European power swept over the sea as well as the land. The leaders were the maritime cities of Pisa and Genoa. In 1015 and 1016 fleets from Pisa and Genoa freed Sardinia from Islamic rule; and between 1113 and 1115 an allied Christian army, carried by a Pisan fleet, drove the Muslims from the Balearic Islands.

SOCIAL CHANGES

In many regions of Europe the expansion in settlement shifted the balance between the free and unfree classes. To attract settlers onto previously uncultivated lands, lords had to offer generous terms, frequently guaranteed in a written charter. Many landlords established on their properties free or new villages. The peasant who settled in a free village usually paid only a small, fixed rent for the lands he cleared and was not required to labor for the landlord. He could leave the village at will, selling his lands and the house he had built at their market value. A runaway serf who resided in a free village for one year and one day without being claimed by his owner was thenceforth free. The settlers in the free villages were usually given the right to run their own courts and, for all but the gravest offenses, to judge their peers according to their own customs.

The social conditions of the serfs also improved; a number of factors contributed to this. Emancipation was considered a religiously meritorious act, and the period was one of marked religious enthusiasm. The increase in population eliminated the need for landlords to keep the entire labor force tied to the soil. Moreover, since the new frontiers attracted the serfs, only better terms, not brute force, could hold the laborers on the lord's land. Revived trade enabled some serfs to sell their produce at market; they could thus earn money with which to buy their freedom. Finally, serfdom bound landlords as well as serfs. Enterprising lords who wished to raise their rents or even change routines of cultivation were blocked by the custom making servile obligations fixed and immutable. To reorganize their estates, to free their lands, to free themselves, the landlords had also to free their serfs.

By the early thirteenth century serfdom had almost disappeared in France, Spain, Italy, and western Germany, although some vestiges of it were to remain until the eighteenth century. In England serfdom also declined until the thirteenth century; but the growing cities of the Continent created a large, profitable market for cereals, and English landlords were eager to produce for it. Rather than leasing out their estates, they continued to cultivate them directly. To find the necessary laborers, English lords maintained, or reimposed, conditions of serfdom over their peasants. But this Indian summer of English serfdom did not last much beyond the fourteenth century.

The changes in agriculture altered the character of noble life. Most landlords now rented their lands to peasants to cultivate; they were no longer direct cultivators but rent collectors. Since this new function did not require the constant supervision of their lands, the lords were free to live away from home for extended periods, perhaps traveling as pilgrims or crusaders to distant lands or mingling with their peers at the courts of great nobles. The new agricultural system, and the physical freedom it allowed the lords, permitted the growth of a courtly society, which in turn brought with it a rich lay culture.

Life continued to be very hard, of course, for the peasants of Western Europe, but there were some improvements. To judge from skeletons found in medieval churchyards and from other slight evidence, the incidence of violent death declined, and life expectancy was growing; by the thirteenth century, the average newborn might expect to live as long as forty years. Evidence of female infanticide declines, but rural conditions continued to be taxing for women. In the typical peasant village, men continued to outnumber, and presumably to outlive, women.

Although most peasants no longer lived in packed settlements, they still saw a good deal of their fellows. Markets and market days became a characteristic feature of rural life in Europe. Peasants slowly grew accustomed to selling or exchanging their surplus produce, purchasing their needs, borrowing money, or simply sharing information with their neighbors at the markets. The influence of markets further stimulated the growth of cottage industries, especially in the vicinity of towns. Within their homes, after their agricultural tasks were accomplished, the peasants and their families spun yarn, wove cloth, cured leather, made wood products, and produced other commodities which they could exchange at the urban markets.

The rural Church acquired new importance, and it is to this period that the rural parishes of Europe (and the Christianization of the countryside) must be dated. Churches were built at an extraordinary pace. A contemporary remarked that churches came to cover the landscape like a blanket of snow. The parish priest was usually of peasant origins and was often assisted by a young cleric or clerics in training for the priesthood (there were no seminaries). Because the priest was frequently the only member of the community who could read, he aided the peasants in their contacts with merchants, tax collectors, and other representatives of the literate culture of the city. Sundays and feast days brought the people together for divine services and for boisterous celebrations too. Church councils repeatedly condemned dancing and singing in the churchyard, especially since the songs on such occasions tended to be indecent, but the denunciations had scant effect. Many of these boisterous customs continued to mark rural life in the West until the twentieth century.

COMMERCE

The European economy remained predominantly agricultural, although new forms of economic endeavor were emerging. Trade, which had dwindled to scant importance in the Carolingian Age, became more vigorous. Most of the trade was local between rural areas or between city and countryside, but there was a dramatic rebirth of trade with regions beyond the European frontiers. Three trading zones developed; they were based upon the Mediterranean Sea in the south, the Baltic Sea in the north, and the overland routes that linked the two seas (see Map 8.2).

The leaders of this commercial revolution were Venice, Pisa, and Genoa. In the tenth and eleventh centuries the Venetians received from the Byzantine emperors charters that gave them complete freedom of Byzantine waters. In the twelfth century, Pisans and Genoese negotiated formal treaties with Islamic rulers which allowed them to establish commercial colonies in the Middle East and North Africa.

Marseilles and Barcelona soon began to participate in the profitable Eastern trade.

In this Mediterranean exchange, the East shipped condiments, medicines, perfumes, dyes, paper, ivories, porcelain, pearls and precious stones, rare metals such as mercury—all of which were known in the West under the generic name of "spices." It also sent a variety of fine linens and cottons (damask, muslin, organdy) as well as brocades and other silks. Western North Africa supplied animal skins, leather, cheese, ivory, and gold. Europe shipped wood, iron, and products made from them (including entire ships), grain, wine, and other agricultural commodities. By 1200 manufactured goods, especially woolen cloth woven in Flanders and finished in Italy, began to play an increasingly important role in the Mediterranean exchange. This cloth gave European merchants a product valued in the Eastern markets; with it they were able not only to pay for Eastern imports but to generate a flow of precious metals into Europe.

Trade in northern Europe among the lands bordering the Baltic Sea linked the great ports of London, Bruges, Bergen, Cologne, Lübeck, and Novgorod with the many smaller maritime towns. The eastern Baltic regions sold grain, lumber and forest products, amber, and furs. Scandinavia supplied wood and fish. England provided raw wool and cereals. Flanders was the great industrial area of the north, taking food and raw material for its excellent cloth.

The northern and Mediterranean trading zones were joined by numerous overland routes. After 1100 the most active exchange between north and south was concentrated at six great fairs, held at various times of the year in the province of Champagne in France. Merchants could find at least one fair open no matter what time of year they came. They were guaranteed personal security at the fairs, low tariffs, and quick and fair justice. For two

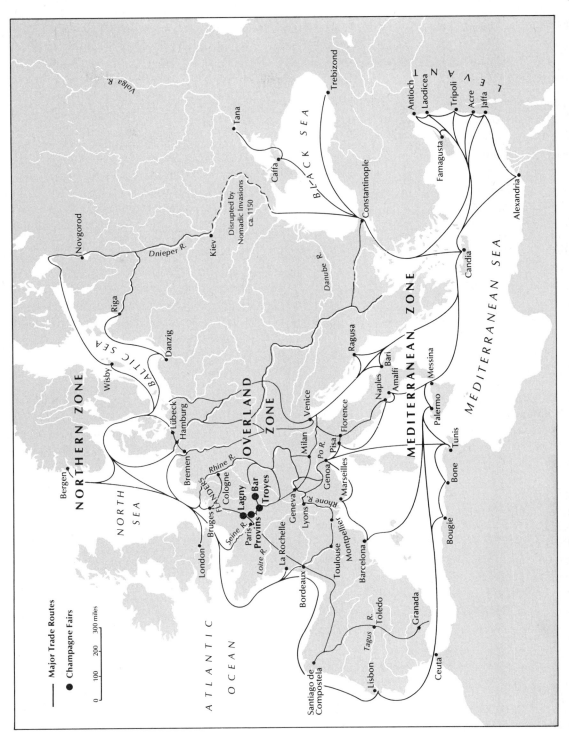

MAP 8.2: MEDIEVAL TRADE ROUTES

centuries the fairs remained the greatest markets in Europe.

THE REBIRTH OF URBAN LIFE

Although the towns in Western Europe were increasing in size and social complexity, their growth was very slow even in this age of economic expansion. Before 1200 probably no town in Western Europe included more than 30,000 inhabitants. These small towns, however, were assuming new functions.

In the Early Middle Ages the towns had been chiefly administrative centers, serving as the residence of bishops—or, much more rarely, of counts—and as fortified enclosures to which the surrounding rural population fled when under attack. (The original sense of the English word "borough" and of the German *burg* is fortress.) As the revival of trade made many of them centers of local or international exchange, permanent colonies of merchants grew up around the older fortresses. These merchant quarters were sometimes called a *foris burgus*, or faubourg ("outside the fortress"), or a *vicus* ("street" or "neighborhood"; preserved in such names as Brunswick and Greenwich). Many European towns, especially in the north, still show these two phases of their early history in their central fortress and surrounding settlements (see Map 8.3).[1] Some towns in the twelfth century added to their administrative and commercial services a third function: they became centers of large-scale industrial produc-

tion, especially of woolen cloth. However, the great industrial town of the Middle Ages is more characteristic of the thirteenth century.

While growing in size, town populations, or at least their richest merchants, began demanding a greater measure of liberty from the bishop or lords who ruled them. They resented the lord's cumbersome, expensive, and undiscerning justice (he probably knew little about commercial needs); they feared his powers to tax and to demand military service. The instrument by which the medieval townsmen sought to govern themselves was the commune, a permanent association created by the oath of its members and under the authority of several elected officials. Communes first appear late in the eleventh century in northern Italy and Flanders, the two most heavily urbanized areas of Europe. Through force, persuasion, or purchase, many communes acquired from their lords charters that recognized their right to judge and tax themselves. Others gained similar rights by simple usurpation.

Urban society also began to show considerable complexity. At the top of the social scale was a small aristocracy; historians now usually call its members the patricians. In Italy this aristocracy included many nobles and great landlords from the countryside, who lived for part or all of the year in the towns. In Flanders nobles and great landlords tended to keep to their rural estates, whence they viewed with disdain and fear the growing wealth of the towns. The powerful urban families in the north came chiefly from common origins, and most of them founded their fortunes upon commerce or the management of urban property. Social and cultural contrasts between town and countryside, then, were much sharper in the north than in Italy.

Below the patricians were the small merchants and shopkeepers, who were at first unspecialized in their economic interests. Most towns in the twelfth century still had only a

---

[1] In Italy, for example, it is rare to find a physical contrast between a central fortress and surrounding faubourgs, but population growth is amply documented by the successive circles of walls built to protect the urban settlement. By comparing the oldest, or Roman, circle of walls with those constructed in the thirteenth century, historians have concluded that some Italian towns must have expanded from five or six thousand inhabitants in about 1100 to some thirty thousand or more by about 1300.

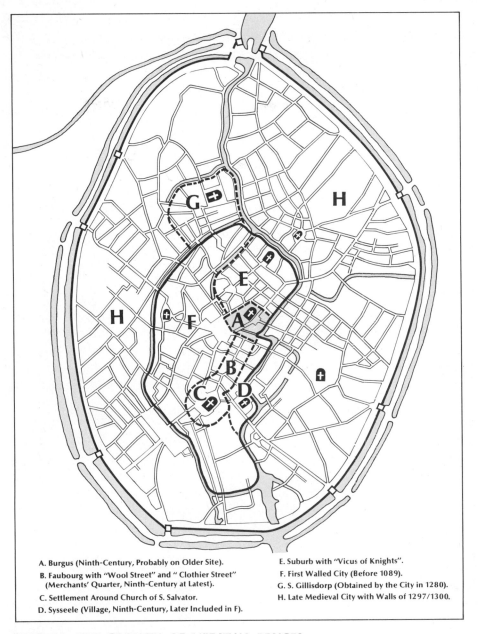

A. Burgus (Ninth-Century, Probably on Older Site).

B. Faubourg with "Wool Street" and "Clothier Street" (Merchants' Quarter, Ninth-Century at Latest).

C. Settlement Around Church of S. Salvator.

D. Sysseele (Village, Ninth-Century, Later Included in F).

E. Suburb with "Vicus of Knights".

F. First Walled City (Before 1089).

G. S. Gillisdorp (Obtained by the City in 1280).

H. Late Medieval City with Walls of 1297/1300.

MAP 8.3: THE GROWTH OF MEDIEVAL BRUGES

Bruges presents a fine example of the topographical dualism of many commercial towns of northern Europe. The town grew from two centers: the central fortress (A) and the merchant's settlement (B), gradually absorbing surrounding parishes and villages. The size of the late medieval walls conveys an accurate impression of the dimensions of medieval urban growth. (Grosser historischer Weltatlas, II: Mittelalter, Munich, 1970, p. 129)

primeres telles choses prouffitablees selon le langaige du prie pour
instruire tous les assistens. Donc cestes choses ainsi traictees du
regime de maison en passent soubz selance auances choses parti
culieres dignes de narracion. Nous faisons fin de ce second liure
ou quel nous auons baille art du regime domestique selon nre
science par laide de celui dont toute science et bonte vient.

Yci fine le second liure du regime des princes ou quel est traicte
du gouuernement de maison. Et comance le tiers liure le quel traicte
du regime de cite et comunisme. Tout le premier chapitre declaire
que la comunite de cite est anciennement principale et est constituee
pour cause de bien.

single guild, or association of merchants. Soon after 1200, however, the guilds multiplied, showing an ever greater diversification in the commercial enterprises of the mercantile classes. At the same time the small merchants and shop-keepers were disputing, often with violence and soon with some success, the political domination of the patricians. Before the coming of industries the cities did not support a large class of artisans and workers. But here, too, the city presents a dynamic picture, and the commercial growth in the twelfth century was laying the basis for industrial expansion in the thirteenth. Perhaps the most distinctive feature of urban society, even in the twelfth century, was the fluid divisions separating the classes. Vertical social mobility was easier in the city than in any other part of the medieval world, the only possible exception being the Church. The patrician class was always admitting new members, chiefly recent immigrants from the countryside whom the buoyant economy of the city had carried to wealth and power. The towns of the Middle Ages were much more efficient than rural society in recognizing, utilizing, and rewarding talent.

The dynamic towns of the Middle Ages, like the cities of the ancient world, shaped culture more than size alone might indicate. Urban commercial life required skill in calculations and a high level of literacy. The towns provided adept administrators who soon figured prominently in the governments of both Church and state. The urban milieu fostered new cultural attitudes, an approach to life based on exact observations and reasoned decisions. Medieval townsmen were by no means indifferent to religion or the afterlife, but they wanted the Church to respond more directly to the moral and religious problems characteristic of the city, in terms comprehensible to them. From the eleventh and twelfth centuries the medieval towns exerted a profound influence on the developing culture of the Middle Ages; moreover, that influence was growing.

II. FEUDALISM AND THE SEARCH FOR POLITICAL ORDER

Growth in population, expansion in trade, and changes in society in the eleventh and twelfth centuries were in part made possible by, and in part helped produce, a higher degree of security and political order than Europe had possessed in the chaotic tenth century. The European communities sought to achieve this renewed stability through a set of institutions that constituted what is traditionally called the feudal system. Although in different ways, the governments of England, France, the Holy Roman Empire, and other European states may all be called feudal.

FEUDAL INSTITUTIONS

"Feudalism," "feudal systems," *la féodalité* must be reckoned among the most abused and confusing terms in the historical vocabulary.[2] These terms were unknown in the Middle Ages. Lawyers in the seventeenth century first devised them to denote the combination of laws and customs governing the kind of land tenure known as the fief. Among enlightened lib-

---

This illustration from a French manuscript of the early sixteenth century shows the narrow streets, tall houses, and numerous ground-level shops that were characteristic of European cities in the Middle Ages. (Photo: Photographie Bulloz)

[2] Perhaps more than any other medieval institution, the feudal system invites comparisons with similar arrangements in other cultures. See especially, in this regard, Peter Duus, *Feudalism in Japan*, 1966.

erals and reformers in the eighteenth century *la féodalité* meant the unjustified privileges enjoyed by the nobles and the Church. Nineteenth-century socialists, especially Marx, used the term "feudalism" to mean an economic system based upon serfdom; they considered it a stage in economic development that followed slavery and preceded capitalism. To Marxists today the essential feature of feudalism is that it exploits peasants by binding them to the soil and forcing them to pay rent to the landlords. Many books, even some recent ones, treat feudalism as if it meant no more than decentralized and weak government, or simple chaos. In popular usage "feudal" is often indistinguishable from "backward."

Most non-Marxist scholars now use "feudalism" in reference to systems of political and social, *not* economic, institutions. Large estates and serfdom were not central to the feudal system and are better referred to as the manorial system. Still, "feudalism" remains an elastic term and is used in both a narrow and a broad sense. In its restricted meaning "feudalism" refers to a set of distinct social and political institutions, defined by free contract, that established the relationship between two freemen of differing social station, a lord and his vassal of lower rank. In practice both lord and vassal came from the upper echelons of society. Feudal institutions did not include the serfs, who could not enter into a contract, and they touched only remotely and rarely the poorer freemen. In its broad sense "feudalism" refers to the society and government in which social and political institutions created by contract played a major role in defining relationships within the upper classes. Perhaps the most distinctive feature of feudal government is that the powerful men in society defined their political rights and obligations through individual contracts. In the ancient Roman Empire (as in our own society) one's rights and obligations

were defined by the public law of the state, which, with only minor exceptions, applied equally to all citizens.

Following the guidance of a great French historian, Marc Bloch,[3] many historians now divide Western feudalism into two periods. The first feudal age, which lasted from the disappearance of Roman government in the West until about 1050 or 1100, witnessed among the free classes of Europe the spontaneous development of feudal practices out of the early medieval and post-Carolingian chaos. In the second feudal age, which spans the period from about 1050 to 1300, princes began self-consciously to use and manipulate these institutions in order to buttress their own authority.

The Feudal Milieu

To understand the growth of feudalism we must first recall the chaotic conditions prevailing in the Early Middle Ages, especially in the ninth and tenth centuries. In a milieu where governmental authority counted for little, the individual freeman had to seek his security through his own efforts. He might appeal to his family, which has always been the first and most natural bastion of defense for the harassed individual. In Celtic areas of Europe (Ireland, Scotland, Wales, Brittany) traditionally powerful clans could extend such protection; therefore, a true feudalism never developed in those lands. Similarly among the South Slavs, the persistence of a social organization based on the clan (*zadruga* in Serbian) made superfluous the creation of authentically feudal relationships. Northern Italy was also an exceptional area in the history of feudalism. Perhaps because of the early importance of towns, the quest for security primarily favored the devel-

---

[3] As proposed in his *Feudal Society*, L. A. Manyon (tr.), 1963, one of the most important works in medieval history to be published in this century.

opment of communal associations, linking social equals, rather than lords and vassals, in
what might be considered artificial families or
clans. The power of the urban communes
in northern Italy stunted, although it did not
entirely suppress, the extension of feudal ties
even in the countryside.

The true homeland of Western feudalism was
the region between the Loire and the Rhine
rivers. The institutions that developed there
were subsequently exported to England in the
Norman Conquest, to southern Italy, and even
to Palestine, and they greatly influenced government and society in southern France, Spain,
and Germany beyond the Rhine. In this region the family seems to have been too scattered
or too weak to guarantee security for its members. The freeman in search of protection had
little recourse but to appeal to a neighbor
stronger than himself. If the neighbor accepted,
the two men entered by implied contract into
a close, quasi-familial relationship. Like the
bonds between father and son, the feudal relationship between the strong "lord" and the weak
freeman was initially far more ethical and emotional than juridical. It remained so until the
thirteenth century, when lawyers systematically
began to clarify and define its juridical implications and, by so doing, diluted its earlier ethical
and emotional force.

Vassalage

The honorable personal bond between the lord
and his man is called vassalage, a term that derives from a Celtic word meaning "boy" or
"servant." Vassalage was created by an act of
homage (from the French *homme*, "man," a
common synonym for "vassal"), the prospective vassal placing his hands within those of
his lord (sometimes too a kiss was exchanged)
and perhaps swearing an oath of fidelity. The
immixio manuum ("joining of hands") was the
central act in the ceremony of homage.

Vassalage imposed obligations on both the
vassal and his lord. The vassal owed his lord
primarily loyalty or, in its feudal term, fealty,
which meant that he had to render aid and
counsel, or material and moral help, to his lord.
He had to perform military service in the lord's
army and usually had to bring additional men in
numbers appropriate to his wealth. As the duty
of service became more precisely defined in
terms of nature and duration, military service
became more a matter of law than of the heart.
The vassal might be expected to serve, for example, forty days a year in a local war and still
less time if the lord intended to fight in foreign
lands. The vassal could not refuse this service,
but if asked by the lord for more time than
custom allowed, he could demand compensation or simply return home, on the argument
that the lord's need was not real. The lord
could also demand financial aid, and there were
four occasions or, in traditional terminology,
"incidents," which required that the vassals provide money without question: the ransoming
of the lord, the knighting of the lord's eldest
son, the marriage of the lord's eldest daughter,
and the lord's own departure on crusade. At
other times the vassal still had to consider requests for financial aid but could grumble and,
if the lord was weak enough, refuse.

The obligation of counsel required the vassal to give good advice, to keep the lord's secrets, and to help him reach true judgments in
legal cases which came before his court. If he
lived at a distance, the vassal might be required
to attend the lord's court at regular intervals,
for example, on Easter, Michaelmas, and Christmas. The ordinary work of the court was the
adjudication of disputes among the vassals and
the hearing of complaints brought by the lord
against his men. Feudal custom held that a
vassal could be judged only by his own peers,
that is, his fellow vassals. By the thirteenth century many great feudal courts were claiming

the right to hear appeals from the courts of the individual vassals. The acceptance of such appeals was one of the principal ways by which royal governments were able to strengthen their authority in the second feudal age.

The vassal's duties toward his lord were further complicated in the second feudal age by the development of multiple vassalage—acts of homage by the same man to several lords. In case of conflict among his different lords, whom should he serve? To escape this dilemma feudal custom required that the vassal select one of his lords as his liege, that is, the one whom he would serve against all others. The growth of multiple vassalage and liege homage was itself a sign of the waning emotional content of the feudal relationship.

The lord in turn owed his vassal protection and maintenance, or military and material support. He had to come to his vassal's aid when requested, repel invaders from his possessions, and even help him if he was sued in another's court. Failure to extend such help allowed the vassal to "defy" his lord, that is, to remove his faith from him and cease to serve him. In the formative period of feudalism the lord's obligation of material support was often carried out at his own table, but as vassals became more numerous and more distantly located and as great princes came to be included among them, sheer logistics prevented the lord from feeding all his men. Since a lord often had no cash revenues for making monetary compensations, he would distribute land as a form of payment for the vassal's allegiance. This concession of land was the fief. The granting of a fief superimposed upon the personal relationship of vassalage a second relationship, specifically concerning property, between the lord and his man. The close union of personal and property ties was, in fact, the most characteristic feature of the Western feudal relationship.

The Fief

The lord granted the fief in a special ceremony called the investiture (it usually followed immediately after the act of homage), in which he extended to his vassal a clod of earth or sprig of leaves, symbol of the land he was receiving. In a strict juridical sense the fief was a conditional, temporary, and nonhereditary grant of land or other income-producing property, such as an office, toll, or rent. At the vassal's death, disability, or refusal to serve, the fief at once returned, or escheated, to the lord who granted it. The juridical origins of the fief seem to go back to forms of ecclesiastical land tenure which grew up in the Early Middle Ages, the *precarium* (or *beneficium*). Churches were canonically forbidden to sell or give away their property, but they could grant its "use" while retaining ownership over it. In Carolingian times the emperors took to ordering churches and monasteries to make such concessions to favored laymen; this grant was called the "*precarium* by order of the king." The true fief, however, involving only laymen and linked with vassalage, does not appear until after the Carolingian Age.

Although technically not inheritable, the fief became gradually assimilated to the allodium (property held in absolute ownership), which was unconditional, permanent, and hereditary. From the start lords had found it convenient to grant a fief to the adult son of a deceased vassal, since he could at once serve in his father's stead. The son had only to make a special payment (the "relief") to the lord in order to acquire the fief. Feudal custom also soon recognized the right of a minor son to inherit, but the lord retained the privilege—the right of wardship—of serving as his guardian or of appointing someone to fulfill that function. Feudal practice was less inclined to admit daughters to the inheritance of a fief since they could not perform military service. Nevertheless, in some areas of Europe (Spain, southern France) women did acquire a right of inheritance. Their lord, however, could select their husbands for them, inasmuch as their spouses had to assume the obligations of service. Initially, vassals were forbidden to sell the fief, grant it to a church, or otherwise transfer it in whole or in part. By the thirteenth century, however, fiefs were commonly sold or granted —but only with the lord's permission, and that almost always had to be purchased.

The fief seems to have been the dominant form of land tenure in northern France and western Germany from the late ninth and tenth centuries. The Norman Conquest carried it to England in the eleventh. In the same period it became common in southern France, but it never entirely supplanted the allodium. It was still later in arriving in Spain, and in Italy its importance always remained restricted. The diffusion of the fief, even if slow and incomplete, had important social effects nonetheless. Because vassals could not dispose of their lands without the lord's consent, property relationships (and society, indirectly) were stabilized. Moreover, the economic pressure superimposed upon the moral force of vassalage gave the princes of the age an effective means of retaining the loyalty of their dependents: the disloyal vassal not only violated the ethics of his times, but also risked losing the lands that supported him.

Private Justice

In granting a fief, the lord gave his vassal all possible sources of revenue the land could produce, including, usually, the right to hold court and to profit from its fines and confiscations. This contributed to another characteristic of feudal society, private justice (the wide exercise of governmental powers by persons other than the king, that is, the exercise of public powers by private individuals as a right associated with their tenure of land). Lords and vassals, in other words, at every level of the feudal pyramid, could tax, judge, and punish their dependents.

By the second feudal age lawyers were arguing that the king, as the font of all justice, had the right of hearing appeals from the courts of his chief vassals (as well as those "rear vassals" who stood lower on the feudal ladder) and could also accept cases in the first instance which his vassals had traditionally heard. The exertion of these royal prerogatives brought about the gradual but unmistakable decline of private justice.

Stages of Feudal Development

Although there were significant local variations in the character and chronology of medieval feudal institutions, it remains possible to speak of certain broad stages of feudal development. In the ninth and tenth centuries Carolingian administration on the local level disintegrated. The power of the count waned, and the *vicarii* disappeared. Authority in the countryside largely passed into the hands of petty lords, most especially the castellans, or holders of castles. The eleventh and twelfth centuries saw a remarkable upsurge in the construction of castles in Europe. To cite one example, in the Diocese of Florence in Italy only 2 castles are mentioned in the sources before 900, 11 before 1000, 52 before 1050, 130 before 1100, and 205 before 1200. The proliferation of these fortresses reflects both the violence of European life and the growing effort to find protection from it.

The castellans initially had no official status in the shadowy structure of the post-Carolingian state, but they dominated the communities which lived in or near their fortresses. The castellan was the judge, tax collector, and military leader, and he usually controlled the local church as well. Within the confines of these small societies the institutions of feudalism developed spontaneously. The castles with their lands constituted fairly stable units.

From about 1050, counts, dukes, and some few kings were attempting to integrate these castles into fairly centralized principalities, insisting that the petty nobles assume toward them the obligations of vassals and fief holders. The use of these feudal concepts and institutions to serve the interests of princely authority initiates the second feudal age—the age of the feudal principality.

NORMAN AND ANGEVIN ENGLAND

The history of any one of several principalities—the Duchy of Normandy, the County of Flanders, the Kingdom of Naples and Sicily, among others—could be used to illustrate the political reorganization characteristic of the second feudal age. But England offers the best example of feudal concepts in the service of princes. The growth of feudalism in England was in turn intimately connected with the Norman Conquest of 1066, the central event of English medieval history.

The Norman Conquest

Duke William of Normandy (1027–1087), the architect of the Conquest, is the epitome of the ambitious, energetic, and resourceful prince of the Central Middle Ages. A bastard who had to fight twelve years to make good his claim over his own Norman duchy, William early set his ambitions on the English crown. His claims were respectable, but not compelling. He was the first cousin of the last Saxon king, the childless Edward the Confessor, who allegedly had promised to make him heir to the throne. However, before his death Edward in fact selected the Saxon Harold Godwin to succeed him, and his choice was supported by the Witan, the English royal council.

Edward died in 1066. William immediately recruited an army of vassals and adventurers to support his claim to the throne and gained a papal blessing for his enterprise, but unfavorable winds kept his fleet bottled up in the Norman ports for six weeks. Meantime Harold Hardrada, king of Norway, who also disputed Harold Godwin's claim, invaded England with a Viking army but was shattered by the Saxons at Stamford Bridge near York on September 28, 1066. The same day the channel winds shifted and William landed in England. Harold Godwin foolishly rushed south to confront him. Although his army was not, as was once thought, technically inferior to the Norman army, it was tired and badly in need of rest and reinforcements after the victory over the Vikings. At the Battle of Hastings on October 14, fatigue seems eventually to have tipped the scales of an otherwise even struggle. The Normans carried the day, leaving Harold Godwin dead upon the field. Duke William of Normandy had won his claim to be king of England.

After years of study the exact importance of the Norman Conquest in English history is still disputed. Today, however, most historians seem to believe that while the Norman Conquest did not radically alter the course of English development, it did add a new speed and decisiveness to changes already in evidence. For example, the Conquest oriented England away from Scandinavia and toward the Continent and

The Bayeux Tapestry, *reputedly woven by the wife of William the Conqueror, is a strip of linen 231 feet long and 20 inches wide depicting the Norman conquest of England in 1066. In the portion shown above, William arrives at Pevensey; below, King Harold fights in the Battle of Hastings. The tapestry was completed toward the end of the eleventh century.* (Photo: La Ville de Bayeux, Giraudon)

established a French-speaking aristocracy. Norman and Continental influences, however, were growing well before 1066; Edward had been raised in Normandy, and Normans were familiar figures in the English court and Church. Nor did William radically change the political and social institutions of Anglo-Saxon England; rather, he built upon them.

The basic unit of local administration remained the shire under the supervision of the sheriff, who had primary responsibility for looking after the king's interests. The sheriff administered the royal estates, collected the taxes (notably the Danegeld), summoned and led contingents to the national militia (the fyrd), and presided over the shire court. William left all these institutions of local government intact.

The real impact of the Conquest was felt at the upper levels of Anglo-Saxon society. The Saxon earls, as the great nobles were called, and most of the lesser nobles, or thanes, lost their estates, which William redistributed among his followers from the Continent—his barons (a title of uncertain origin, now used to connote the immediate vassals of the king). Although the fiefs that William allotted were large, they were not compact blocks of land; rather, they were strewn hither and yon across the countryside—fit to support service but not rebellion.

William did, however, redefine the relations between the king and the great men of the realm on the basis of essentially feudal concepts. The Anglo-Saxons had a form of lordship under which protection was extended to a man of lesser station in return for loyalty and service. Lords might further support their retainers with grants of land, but they gave the properties in full title. They did not make tenure conditional upon service—the essential feature of the Continental fief. William now insisted that all English land be considered a fief held directly or indirectly from the king. The barons had to serve the king, and the knights the barons, or risk losing their estates.

In 1086 William conducted a comprehensive survey of the lands of England, the report of which was the *Domesday Book*, probably so called because its judgments in their finality resembled those to be made on the Last Day. This survey, unique for its age among the European kingdoms, served two main purposes: it gave the king a clear record of his own holdings and those of his barons, and it enabled him to know how much service the land could support. In the Salisbury oath of 1086 every vassal had to swear loyalty to the king as the liege lord of all. Feudal concepts thus brought a greater precision to the obligations of English freemen toward their king and began to place a new ethical and material force behind royal prerogatives.

In order to maintain close contact with his barons and vassals William also took from the Continent the institution of the great council, or Curia Regis. Essentially, it was an assembly of bishops, abbots, barons—in fact, anyone whom the king summoned. The great council fulfilled the feudal functions of giving the king advice and serving as his principal court in reaching judgments. It was a much larger assembly than the Saxon Witan. However, as the great council could not be kept permanently in session, a small council, consisting of those persons in permanent attendance at the court whom the king wished to invite, carried on the functions of the great council between its sessions. The development of the great and small councils had major importance for English constitutional history. The great council was the direct ancestor of Parliament, while the small council was the source of the administrative bureaus of the royal government.

Angevin Kingship

William was succeeded by his second son, William Rufus, one of England's worst kings. He terrorized his subjects and antagonized the Church. At his death in 1100, probably from assassination, his younger brother, Henry I, became king. Henry began a series of administrative reforms, but a dispute over the succession at his death and a protracted civil war undermined his accomplishment. By 1154, however, a unified and pacified England passed under the rule of Henry II of Anjou, grandson of Henry I and the first of the "Angevin" kings of England.

Through combined inheritances and his marriage to Eleanor of Aquitaine in 1152, Henry II ruled over a sprawling assemblage of territories, including, besides England, nearly the entire west of France from the English Channel to the Pyrenees Mountains (see Map 8.4). A man of abounding energy who carried to completion many of the reforms of Henry I, he ranks among the most gifted statesmen of the twelfth century and among the greatest kings of England.

It was in the sphere of English government and law that Henry left a permanent mark. He made royal justice the common justice of the kingdom through the use of itinerant officials, or "justices in eyre" (*in itinere*, i.e., "on journey"), who were endowed with all the authority of the king himself. The itinerant justice traveled regularly to the courts of the shires, investigating and punishing crimes. Upon his arrival the justice would impound twelve "good men" and inquire of them under oath what crimes they had heard about since his last visit and whom they suspected of guilt. (This sworn inquest is the direct ancestor of the modern jury of presentment, or grand jury.) Those indicted by the twelve "good men" were still tried by the ancient ordeals of fire and water, which were retained until the Church condemned these procedures at the Fourth Lateran Council in 1215. Thereafter, the small, or petty, jury was used, as it is today, to judge guilt or innocence.

The itinerant justice did not forcibly interfere in civil disputes, but he did offer for sale the services of the royal court in settling them. Barons receiving fiefs from the king had also been given the right to hold a court and judge the disputes of their own knights and dependents. Normally, therefore, litigants in a civil dispute appeared before a baronial court. But as a result of Henry's reforms a litigant could purchase one of many royal writs, which ordered the sheriff to bring the case under the scrutiny of the royal court presided over by the justice in eyre. The great superiority of royal justice in civil matters was that it relied, not on ordeals or duels, but on sworn inquests or juries. These juries in civil cases were composed of "good men" from the neighborhood who were likely to know the facts at issue and were able to judge the truth or falsity of claims. Henry made no effort to suppress baronial courts, but the better justice offered by the royal court left them with a progressively shrinking role in the juridical life of England.

In time the justices built up a considerable body of decisions, which then served as precedents in similar cases. The result was the gradual legal unification of the realm, the development, in other words, of a "Common" law of England—common in that it applied to the entire kingdom and was thus distinct from the local customs by which cases were formerly decided. It differed from Roman law in that it represented not the will of the king or legislator but the principles, formed by custom, which were followed in deciding cases. This marks the beginnings of the tradition of common law, under which most of the English-speaking world continues to live.

The justices performed one other service in the interests of royal authority. They investigated the behavior of the sheriffs and saw to it that the king's business was handled capably and honestly at the level of the shire.

Central administration and bureaucracy also grew stronger under Henry's rule. The great officers who aided him were the justiciar, who governed the realm in his absence, the chancellor (secretary), and the chamberlain (treasurer). The Exchequer, or treasury, enjoyed a remarkable development in Henry's reign and

SCOTLAND
DENMARK
York
STAMFORD BRIDGE 1066
Lübeck
POMERANIA
Bremen
WALES
ENGLAND
FRISIA
SAXONY
Brandenburg
POLAND
MARCH OF LUSATIA
Goslar
London
Canterbury
Winchester
Clarendon
HASTINGS 1066
Bruges
Ghent
LOWER
Cologne
THURINGIA
FLANDERS
Aix-la-Chapelle
BOUVINES 1214
LORRAINE
FRANCONIA
Prague
BOHEMIA
Mainz
Worms
MORAVIA
Bayeux
Rouen
NORMANDY
Trier
UPPER
Verdun
LORRAINE
Reims
CHAMPAGNE
Paris
Troyes
Toul
Rennes
BRITTANY
MAINE
Orléans
Augsburg
SWABIA
Freiburg
Passau
BAVARIA
Salzburg
AUSTRIA
Nantes
ANJOU
TOURAINE
POITOU
Poitiers
Dijon
BURGUNDY
Autun
Cluny
Besançon
HUNGARY
KINGDOM OF BURGUNDY-ARLES
Clermont
Saintes
AQUITAINE
PERIGORD
AUVERGNE
LOMBARDY
LEGNANO 1176
Milan
Pavia
Roncaglia
Venice
REPUBLIC OF VENICE
Bordeaux
Canossa
Bologna
TOULOUSE
Toulouse
LANGUEDOC
GASCONY
Avignon
PROVENCE
Arles
Marseilles
Florence
Pisa
TUSCANY
PATRIMONY OF ST. PETER
NAVARRE
ARAGON
Barcelona
Sutri
Rome
Naples
Salerno
KINGDOM OF TWO SICILIES
SPAIN
French Royal Domain
987
987-1180
1180-1328
Boundary of English Holdings in France 1180
English Holdings in France 1328
Holy Roman Empire ca. 1200
Battle Site
0
100
200 miles

MAP 8.4: MEDIEVAL ENGLAND, FRANCE, AND GERMANY

assured the king substantial revenues in money. It received its name (which means "checkerboard") for the reason that calculations were performed by moving counters across a table divided into squares, much as one calculates with an abacus.

The Exchequeur combined the functions of an accounting office and a court. The accounting office, lower Exchequeur, received twice a year from the sheriffs an accounting of the moneys they had received—whether from the royal estates in their shires; fees or fines; the Danegeld; or scutage, which was the payment knights had to make when they did not serve personally in the royal army. The upper Exchequeur was a court which heard disputes about the king's fiscal prerogatives.

Thomas à Becket

The judicial reforms of Henry II led him into a bitter conflict with the English Church, which maintained its own canonical courts. In Henry's opinion the penalties these courts meted out to the guilty were too mild to deter them from future crime, and in 1164 he claimed the right to retry before his royal courts clerics accused of crime. The archbishop of Canterbury,

The Romanesque mural from the Church of Sts. Giovanni e Paolo in Spoleto portrays the murder of Thomas à Becket. The archbishop of Canterbury was murdered in 1170 after six years of opposition to Henry II's judicial policies. (Photo: André Held)

Thomas à Becket, rejected this claim. He argued that both the Bible and canon law forbade what we now call "double jeopardy," that is, a second trial and punishment for the same crime.

Thomas had been a warm personal friend of Henry's and had served him ably and faithfully as his chancellor, the chief official of his realm. Royal friendship and favor had brought him his election as archbishop of Canterbury in 1162. In the course of the six-year struggle between these former friends, Thomas first submitted, then broke with Henry and fled to France, and then was reconciled once more in 1170. A few months later he suspended those bishops who had supported the king. Henry, then in France, demanded in fateful rhetoric whether no man would free him of this pestilential priest. Four of the king's knights took the words to heart, journeyed to England, found Thomas in his cathedral, and cut him down before the high altar on December 29, 1170. His death accomplished what his life could not. Henry revoked the objectionable reforms and performed an arduous personal penance for his unwise words.

Although Henry II was unable to dominate the Church, the English monarchy at his death in 1189 was the strongest in Europe. It remained for the thirteenth century to discover how the great power of the king might be managed and controlled.

CAPETIAN FRANCE

In France the pattern of feudal development was much different from that of England. Central government all but disappeared in the turmoil following the age of Charlemagne. What governmental functions could still be performed amid the chaos were carried out by counts, castellans, and other lords of small territorial units. These factors alone would have made the rebuilding of an effective national monarchy in France considerably more difficult than in England, but, in addition, France was a much larger country, and its regions preserved considerable cultural diversity.

Nonetheless, the second feudal age did witness considerable changes in France. There are two notable developments. We can discern the emergence of several compact and effectively governed principalities, especially in the north—the Duchy of Normandy, the counties of Flanders and Champagne, the royal lands of the Île de France, and others. Second, the French kings sought with some success to establish a lord-vassal relation with the great dukes and counts who governed these principalities. The kings did not envision, and could not have achieved, the unification of the entire realm under their own direct authority. The goal of monarchical policy was a kind of federation of principalities bound together by a common fealty to the king on the part of distant dukes and counts.

The Capetians

In 987 the great nobles of France elected as their king Hugh Capet, whose descendants held the throne until 1792. Hugh was elected primarily because his small possessions in the Île de France, which included Paris and the surrounding region, made him no threat to the independence of the nobles. He and his successors for the next century made no dramatic efforts to enlarge their royal authority, but they carefully nursed what advantages they had; the central location of their lands; the title of king, which commanded a vague prestige; and a close association with the Church, which gave them an avenue of influence extending beyond their own territory. They also pursued a remarkably prudent policy of consolidating control over their own lands, and they had the good luck to produce sons. For two hundred years the kings crowned their sons during their own lifetimes and thus built the tradition that the crown was theirs, not by election, but by hereditary right.

The Capetian policy first bore fruit under Louis VI, the Fat (1108–1137). His aim was to be master of his own possessions, and he successfully reduced to obedience the petty nobles and castellans who had been disturbing his lands and harassing travelers seeking to cross them. By the end of his reign he had established effective control over the lands between the cities of Paris and Orléans. This gave him a compact block of territory in the geographic heart of France. Louis VI promoted the colonization of forests and wastelands by establishing free villages, and he courted the support of the town communes. The economic growth encouraged by the king added to his own fiscal resources. He staffed his administration with new men from the middle ranges of society at the expense of the older, entrenched, and unreliable nobility. One such man of humble origins was Abbot Suger of the monastery of Saint-Denis near Paris; Suger was in fact the chief architect of these successful policies.

Louis VI bequeathed to his successors a strong base of power in the Île de France, but his weaker son, Louis VII, could do little with it. At Suger's insistence Louis VII married Eleanor of Aquitaine, heiress to the extensive lands of the Duchy of Aquitaine. This marriage promised to more than double the lands under direct royal control. But manifest incompatibility of character and Eleanor's failure to produce a male heir set the spouses feuding, and the marriage was annulled in 1152. Eleanor, or at least her possessions, proved irresistible to Henry II of England, who married her two months later, although he was her junior by some ten years. The loss of her vast inheritance to the English monarchy was a major blow to the Capetian fortunes.

Louis VII's son by a later marriage, Philip II

Augustus, set out to reclaim from the English the provinces of Aquitaine and Normandy, and to break the near encirclement by Angevin lands of his royal demesne. To achieve this goal he skillfully exploited the quarrels of Henry II with Queen Eleanor and with his sons, Richard the Lion-Hearted and John. John, who succeeded Richard as king of England in 1199, paved the way to his own humiliation by marrying the fiancée of a noble of southern France, a flagrant violation of feudal custom. The offended noble appealed for justice to their common lord, Philip, who eagerly summoned John before the French court to answer for his crime. When John failed to appear, Philip declared his fiefs forfeit.

John then showed himself as maladroit in war as he was in love. While he dallied in England, French troops invaded Normandy and after an eight-month siege took the fortress of Château Gaillard, which Richard the Lion-Hearted had erected to defend the province. Normandy thus became part of the French royal domain (see Map 8.4). Finally, John bestirred himself to action. He organized a coalition of Philip's enemies, including Emperor Otto IV of Germany and the Count of Flanders who, though Philip's vassal, viewed with considerable apprehension the growth of royal authority. Philip beat back the invading army at Bouvines in 1214, a victory that confirmed England's loss of Normandy and brought new prestige to the Capetian throne. It was convincing proof of the power the king now could wield.

Under Philip royal influence began to penetrate to the south of France. In 1208 Pope Innocent III declared a crusade against the Albigensian heretics of the south (see Chapter 9), who enjoyed the protection of many powerful nobles. Philip's vassals flocked to the call, overwhelmed the counts of Toulouse and other prominent nobles, and seized much of their lands. The defeat of the southern nobility left a vacuum of power, which the king's authority soon filled.

Administration

In addition to increasing his lands Philip strengthened the administration of his royal demesne (he still made no effort to interfere directly in the governments of the fiefs of the kingdom). On the local level the representative of the king—the French counterpart of the English sheriff—was the *prévôt*. About 1190, apparently in imitation of the English itinerant justices, Philip began to appoint a new official, the *bailli*, to supervise the work of the *prévôt*. (When the king acquired territory in southern France, the same officer was called the *sénéchal*.) The *bailli* supervised the collection of rents and taxes, the administration of justice, and all the king's interests within a certain prescribed circuit or area, but he never assumed the full range of functions and powers that the English justice in eyre had acquired. The central administration was also developing specialized bureaus, although less advanced than the English, and the *Chambre de Comptes*, a special financial office, equivalent to the English Exchequeur, gradually assumed responsibility for the royal finances.

Louis VI and Philip Augustus made the French monarchy the unquestioned master in the Île de France, greatly enlarged the royal demesne, and insisted with considerable success that the great dukes and counts of the realm serve the king loyally. In France, as in England and widely in Europe, feudal practices did not necessarily mean weak government; on the contrary, the able and energetic princes of the age utilized these concepts and institutions to redefine the relationship between ruler and ruled in the interest of achieving a stronger central authority. The feudal system, as it was constructed in these principalities, was thus a major step toward a more ordered political life and toward the sovereign state of the early modern period.

THE GERMAN EMPIRE

In the tenth and eleventh centuries the German lands east of the Rhine show a pattern of political development very different from that of France or England. Whereas in France after the collapse of the Carolingian Empire, power became fragmented among many petty lords and castellans, in Germany it came to be concentrated in certain relatively large territorial blocks. Saxony, Franconia, Swabia, and Bavaria, known as "Stem" duchies (from the German *Stämme*, meaning a distinct people, tribe, or ethnic group), were originally districts of the Carolingian Empire that became independent political entities under powerful dukes. Because these duchies were close to the hostile eastern frontier, their inhabitants learned to appreciate the advantages of a unified leadership.

Moreover, in Germany the old idea of a Christian empire, which we have seen both in Byzantium and in the West under Charlemagne, retained considerable appeal. Perhaps because they were so close to the frontiers of Christendom, the German dukes considered themselves to be in a special way the champions of the Christian faith, and they mounted a missionary effort among the unconverted peoples. Their leader should appropriately be an emperor who, like Charlemagne, would aid the Church against its foreign enemies while promoting its interests at home.

Otto I, the Great

The last direct descendant of Charlemagne in Germany, a feeble ruler known as Louis the Child, died in 911. Recognizing the need for a common leader, the German dukes in 919 elected as king one of their number, Henry of Saxony. His descendants held the German monarchy until 1024. The most powerful of this line of Saxon kings, and the true restorer of the German Empire, was Otto I, the Great (936–973). Otto was primarily a warrior, and conquest was a principal foundation of his power. He routed the pagan Magyars at Lechfeld near Augsburg in 955 and ended their menace to Christian Europe; he organized military provinces, or marches, along the eastern frontier and actively promoted the work of German missionaries and settlers beyond the Elbe River; and in 951 he marched into Italy.

Historians are not certain what exactly drew Otto to the south. Perhaps he feared the formation of a large kingdom, including Provence, Burgundy, and Lombardy, which would eventually threaten Germany. Perhaps like Charlemagne he hoped to rescue the papacy from the clutches of the tumultuous Roman nobility, to which it had once again fallen victim. It does appear at any rate that Otto conceived of himself not just as a German king but as the leader of all Western Christians. He could not allow Italy, especially Rome, to remain in chaos or permit another prince to achieve a strong position there. And, indeed, during a second campaign in Italy in 962 Pope John XII crowned Otto Roman emperor. The title gave him no new powers, but it did provide him high prestige, inasmuch as he could claim to be the special protector of the Church and the most exalted ruler in Christendom.

The coronation of 962 not only marked the restoration of a "Roman" empire in the West (in fact it was German) but also confirmed the close relations between Germany and Italy which lasted through the Middle Ages. Although the German emperors claimed to be the successors of the Caesars and of Charlemagne, and thus the titular leaders of all Western Christendom, their effective power never extended beyond Germany and Italy and the small provinces contiguous to them—Provence, Burgundy, and Bohemia. Government of his far-flung territories presented Otto with problems even more formidable than those which confronted the English and French kings. He distributed the Stem duchies among his relatives, in the poorly founded hope that they would be loyal to him, and placed great reliance upon the Church both in Germany and Italy, using its lands and officials as adjuncts to his own fisc (crown lands) and administration. He therefore insisted upon the right to nominate or approve the nominations of the great prelates of his empire—bishops, abbots, and popes. Control of Church offices and Church lands gave the emperor enclaves of power in the Stem duchies and in Italy which no potential rival could match.

When Otto died in 973, his state was the strongest in Europe, but it was troubled by several difficulties. Foremost among them was the growing discontent of the Church with the imperial domination of ecclesiastical life. (This will be examined in the following section.) Reformers sought to liberate the Church from the emperor's tutelage, and they succeeded in undermining a principal foundation of imperial authority. But the reform did not end the efforts of the German kings to build a strong empire which would unite Germany and Italy and allow them to exercise a moral leadership over the whole of Western Europe.

Frederick I, Barbarossa

The emperor who came closest to building a lasting foundation for the German Empire was Frederick I (1152–1190) of the House of Hohenstaufen. He was called Barbarossa, meaning "red beard." Large, handsome, gallant, courageous, Frederick, like Charlemagne before him, gained a permanent place in the memories and myths of his people. He much resembles in his policies, if not quite in his achievements, the other great statesmen of the twelfth century—Henry II of England and Philip II of France. Frederick showed a broad eclecticism in his political philosophy. He claimed to be the special protector of the Church and therefore a holy figure. During his reign the German Empire was first called the "Holy Roman Empire," the title by which it was to be known until its demise in 1806. But Frederick also used the new institutions and concepts of political feudalism and effectively exploited ideas concerning the emperor's powers which the revived study of Roman law was providing.

Frederick pursued three principal goals. He hoped to consolidate a strong imperial domain consisting of Swabia, which he inherited; Burgundy, which he acquired by marriage; and Lombardy, which he hoped to subdue. These three contiguous territories would serve him much as the Île de France served the French king, giving him a central base of power from which he could dominate those more distant areas which he could not rule directly. In Germany he sought to force the great princes in the north and east to become his vassals. In Italy he claimed, as successor of the Caesars, to enjoy the sovereignty which Roman law attributed to the emperors.

Frederick's Italian ambitions disturbed the popes and the town communes, which from about 1100 had become the chief powers in the northern half of the peninsula. Both feared that a strong central government could be established only at the cost of their own independence. With active papal support the northern Italian towns, led by Milan, formed a coalition known as the Lombard League and defeated the imperial forces at Legnano in 1176. The Battle of Legnano not only marked the failure of Frederick's efforts to establish full sovereignty over the Lombard cities; it was also the first time in European history that an army of townsmen had bested the forces of the established army under noble leadership. At the Peace of Constance in 1183 Frederick conceded to the towns almost full authority within their walls; the towns in turn recognized that their powers came from him, and they conceded to him sovereignty in the countryside. Frederick did not gain all that he had wished in

Italy, but his position remained a strong one.

In Germany he was able to achieve a more resounding victory, this time over the powerful duke of Saxony, Henry the Lion, who had refused to aid him in his Italian war. Making effective use of feudal custom, Frederick summoned him in 1180 to face trial as a disloyal vassal. The court condemned Henry and confiscated his Saxon fief. With Henry humiliated and deprived of his lands Frederick seemed to be the unchallenged master in Germany (see Map 8.4).

Frederick now wanted to advance the empire's prestige in Europe and sought out a position of leadership in the Third Crusade, as it is traditionally numbered. But the aged emperor drowned while trying to ford a small stream in Asia Minor, bringing to a pathetic end a crowded and brilliant career.

His successors proved unable to build upon, or even maintain, his accomplishments. Frederick's inability to establish an enduring government over his vast territories is hardly surprising, in view of the obstacles which confronted him. Geography and culture, distance and the Alps worked against the union of Germany and Italy as a single state. In fact, the various regions of the empire were at such markedly different levels of social development that not until the nineteenth century did either Germany or Italy become unified states.

III. THE REFORM OF THE WESTERN CHURCH

Along with lay governments, the Church, too, experienced fundamental transformations in the eleventh and twelfth centuries; it then acquired characteristics it was to retain in large measure to the present day. The reform of the Church was the direct result of revolt against the traditional system of lay domination over ecclesiastical offices and lands.

MORAL CRISIS

After the disintegration of the Frankish Empire a kind of moral chaos invaded the lives of the clergy. Since the fourth century the Church had demanded that its clergy remain celibate, but this injunction seems to have been almost completely ignored in the post-Carolingian period. Also rampant in the Church was the sin of simony—the buying or selling of offices or sacraments. Many bishops and even some popes purchased their high positions, and parish priests frequently sold their sacramental services (baptisms, masses, absolutions of sins, marriages) to the people.

The constitution of the Western Church seems to have contributed to this moral breakdown. On the highest level the tradition of lay domination made the king or emperor effective head of the Church in all its temporal affairs. At the local level, ecclesiastical offices and lands were largely under lay control. Landlords were considered to own churches built upon their property. They therefore could name the priests who served in them and profit from donations made to them, freely sell the offices they controlled, or distribute Church lands to their relatives and friends. The results were disastrous. The Church was flooded with unworthy men who were little concerned with their spiritual duties, and the pillaging of Church lands and revenues left many clerics without adequate livings. For these, simony was often an essential means of support.

EARLY ATTEMPTS AT REFORM

According to canon law, the bishops bore the chief responsibility for the moral deportment of the clergy. A few reforming bishops in the tenth and eleventh centuries tried to suppress clerical marriage and simony of their priests, but they could make little headway. The powers of a single bishop were perforce limited to his own diocese, and to his own lifetime, since he could not name his successor.

Monastic discipline was the focus of a more effective attempt at reform, the center of which was the monastery of Cluny in Burgundy, founded in 910. Cluniac monasticism was marked by two constitutional novelties. The monastery was placed directly under the pope (neither lay lords nor bishops could interfere in its affairs). While formerly monasteries had been autonomous communities, electing their own abbots and supervising their own affairs, the administration was now centralized under the abbot of Cluny. He retained authority over the many daughter houses which his monks had founded or reformed and could visit them at will, freely correcting any abuses. The congregation of Cluny grew with extraordinary rapidity in the eleventh and twelfth centuries until it included no fewer than 1,184 houses, which were spread from the British Isles to Palestine.

The restoration of the German Empire in 962 opened another avenue of ecclesiastical reform. Otto I and his successors repeatedly condemned clerical marriage, simony, and the unauthorized usurpation of Church lands, but in the interests of their own authority they could not abandon their traditional control over ecclesiastical offices and lands. Their efforts did not satisfy a growing group of radical reformers who believed that complete freedom of the Church from lay domination was the only means to effective reform. To win and defend this liberty they looked for leadership to the long-degraded office of pope.

PAPAL REFORM

The first of the reforming popes, selected, ironically, by the Holy Roman Emperor, was Leo IX (1049–1054). He traveled widely and presided at numerous councils, where he promulgated decrees ordering reforms, summoned

Gregory VII believed that the pope had a weighty obligation to defend the liberty of the Church against all lay encroachments. In this nearly contemporary drawing, he receives an abbot under papal protection. (Photo: The Granger Collection)

council reformed papal elections and defined the principles by which popes to this day have been elected.

Tradition required that the pope, like all bishops, be elected by the clergy and people of his diocese. In practice, however, the emperor named him, or in his absence the powerful noble families and factions of Rome did. However, the election procedures set up by the council of 1059 conferred this prerogative upon the cardinals, the chief clergymen associated with the Church at Rome, thereby assuring that the College of Cardinals, and the reformers who controlled it, could maintain continuity of papal policy. (Even today all cardinals, no matter where they live in the world, hold a titular appointment to a church within the archdiocese of Rome.) Both the emperor and the Roman nobility were simultaneously deprived of one of their strongest powers.

suspect bishops, and deposed many of them. He was the first pope to make wide and regular use of papal legates, who, like Charlemagne's *missi dominici*, traveled through Europe, inspecting, reprimanding, and reforming. For the first time lands distant from Rome were subject to the close supervision of the papacy.

Under Pope Nicholas II the movement toward ecclesiastical liberty took several forward strides. By allying himself with the Normans of southern Italy, Nicholas freed the papacy from military dependence on the German Empire. He was the first pope who expressly, if vainly, condemned the practice of "lay investiture," that is, receiving churches and Church offices from laymen. In 1059 a Roman

Gregory VII

The climax of papal reform came with the pontificate of Pope Gregory VII (1073–1085), who brought to his office a high regard for its powers and responsibilities and a burning desire for reform. With regard to Church matters Gregory asserted that the pope wielded absolute authority—that he could at will overrule any local bishop in the exercise of his ordinary or usual jurisdiction. His ideas on the relations of Church and state, however, are less than clear. According to some historians, he believed that all power on earth, including the imperial power, came from the papacy. According to others, Gregory held merely that the normal function of kings—the repression of crime—was far lower than the sacred authority of popes. This much at least is beyond dispute: Gregory believed that all Christian princes must answer to the pope in spiritually significant matters and that the pope himself had a weighty responsibility to guide them.

The Investiture Controversy

The major collision between the papacy and the Holy Roman Empire that occurred during the pontificate of Gregory VII is traditionally called the Investiture Controversy. The name suggests that the principal issue was the practice of great laymen, most notably the emperor, of "investing" bishops with ring and staff, the symbols of their spiritual office. More fundamentally, the struggle revolved around the claims of laymen to dispose of ecclesiastical offices and revenues by their own authority and in their own interests.

At a Roman council in 1075 Gregory, convinced that Emperor Henry IV had no sincere interest in reform, condemned lay investiture and excommunicated some of Henry's advisers. Henry reacted with unexpected fury; he summoned a meeting of imperial bishops and declared Gregory not the true pope but a false monk. Not one to pause in what he thought to be the work of God, Gregory in turn excommunicated Henry, deposed him, and freed his subjects from allegiance to him. These acts struck at the fundamental theory of the Christian empire, according to which the emperor was supreme head of the Christian people, responsible only to God.

Gregory's forceful appeal to spiritual power gained remarkable success in Germany. Henry's enemies leagued against him and demanded that the emperor be judged before an assembly of lords and prelates to be held at Augsburg in February 1077. They invited Gregory to preside, and he readily accepted. Henry resolved to fight spiritual weapons with spiritual weapons. He slipped across the Alps and intercepted Gregory, then on his way to Germany, at the Apennine castle of Canossa near Modena. He came in the sackcloth of a penitent, radiating contrition, pleading for absolution. Gregory, who doubted the sincerity of the emperor's repentance, refused for three days to receive him, while Henry waited in the snow. Finally,

in the face of such persistence Gregory the suspicious pope had to give way to Gregory the priest, who, like all priests, was obligated to absolve a sinner professing sorrow.

The incident of Canossa is one of the most dramatic events of medieval history. Through the centuries since, the picture of the supreme lay magistrate of Christendom begging forgiveness from the pope has symbolized a victory of spiritual over material power, or a triumph of Church over state. The reality was more complex. Henry was the immediate victor. He had divided his opponents and stripped his German enemies of their excuse for rebelling. They named a rival emperor anyway, Rudolf of Swabia, but he was killed in battle in what seemed a divine judgment in Henry's favor. Gregory appears to have become unsure of himself after Canossa. He finally excommunicated Henry a second time in 1080 but was forced to flee Rome at the approach of an imperial army. He died at Salerno in 1085 in apparent bitterness, avowing that his love of justice had brought him only death in exile.

After years of confused struggle Pope Calixtus II and Emperor Henry V settled the Investiture Controversy through the Concordat of Worms in 1122. The terms of agreement were that the emperor would no longer invest prelates with the symbols of their spiritual office, and the pope would allow the elections of imperial bishops and abbots to be held in the presence of the emperor or his representative. This clearly permitted the emperor to influence the outcome of elections. In addition the emperor retained the right of investing prelates with their temporalities, that is, their imperial fiefs. The essence of the agreement was that the great bishops and abbots of the realm would have to be acceptable to both parties—worthy and religious men to please the Church and loyal and capable servants to please the emperor. The agreement fell short of both papal and imperial demands, but it shows the emergence of a new and important principle in Western political life: a recognition that major appointments in the Church ought to be made through consultation and compromise.

The Consolidation of Reform

In the twelfth century the popes continued to pursue Gregorian ideals—reform, liberty, and centralization—and to consolidate past advances. In their struggle to be free of lay authority the reformers had insisted that certain persons, such as clerics, widows, orphans, crusaders, and other wards of the Church, should be judged only in ecclesiastical courts, and that matters such as cases touching on sacrilege, heresy, marriage, testaments, contracts, and the like, should also, because of their religious nature, be under ecclesiastical jurisdiction, no matter who the parties might be. In the twelfth century a complex system of ecclesiastical courts developed according to this premise, paralleling and at times rivaling the courts of the kings. Judicial decisions from these courts could be appealed to Rome.

Legal scholars simultaneously sought to compile and clarify the canons of the Church—the authoritative statements from the Bible, Church councils, Church fathers, and popes which constituted the law of the Church. The most successful of many such compilations was the Concordance of Discordant Canons, or the *Decretum*, put together by the Italian jurist Gratian about 1142. With systematic compilations came trained canon lawyers to comment upon, interpret, and apply the law. These men helped make the law of the medieval Church one of the West's great juridical monuments.

Centralization gained in other ways. The popes came to exert a progressively tighter control over the canonization of saints, hitherto a local matter, and they gained a stronger voice in the election of bishops, until finally papal approval was accepted as essential to a valid choice. In papal tithes imposed upon the clergy and in the administration of the census (yearly payments made by many churches to Rome), the outlines of a centralized financial administration appear, though it remained rudimentary in the twelfth century.

THE REFORM AND MEDIEVAL SOCIETY

The reform of the Church in the eleventh and twelfth centuries left an indelible mark on both religious and secular life in the West. The successful establishment of sacerdotal celibacy set the clergy apart from the laity to a degree unknown in the ancient or Eastern Church. (The ideals of the reform have continued to influence the life of Catholic priests until the present.)

The movement for ecclesiastical reform touched nearly all aspects of contemporary life. The reform clergy gave powerful support to the efforts of princes to suppress private warfare and to establish an internal peace of which the Church was a chief beneficiary. They also helped revive intellectual life in the West. The Church actively set about building an educational system for its clergy. The bishop's school, and then the university, were the principal fruit of the reform. The dispute between Church and state also greatly stimulated fruitful speculations on the nature of Christian society and an intensive investigation of the ancient sources which defined its character.

Finally, the Gregorian reform was based on the assumption that the good man facing an evil world need not timidly flee it; rather, he can and should seek to correct its abuses and bring it closer to what God intended it to be. The reform thus helps mark the emergence of a new faith in human power and in the possible improvement of this present world, cultural attitudes which Western man has not since abandoned.

IV. THE CULTURAL REVIVAL

The reorganization of European life in the eleventh and twelfth centuries affected institutions of learning and even the direction and methodology of Western thought. Its impact was profound in the fields of vernacular literature and art also. The Western peoples entered upon a period of high creativity, which marked all forms of cultural expression, and many of the cultural attitudes developed in this period have affected Western culture until the present.

THE RISE OF UNIVERSITIES

During the Central Middle Ages, a new institution came to assume a role in the intellectual life of Europe, which it has not since relinquished. This was the university; it ranks as one of the most influential creations of the medieval world.

Up to about 1050, monastic schools had dominated intellectual development in the West (see Map 8.5). But the monastic devotion to prayer, asceticism, and mystical meditation was not especially favorable to original thought, while the isolation of monasteries restricted the experiences of the monastic scholar and made difficult the exchange of ideas which intellectual progress requires.

From about 1050 to 1200 the cathedral, or bishop's, school assumed the intellectual leadership in Europe. Traditionally, bishops had been obliged to provide for the education of their clergy, but the disorders of the Early Middle Ages and the decline of urban life had prevented their schools from assuming a prominent role in cultural life. From the late eleventh century the growth of cities, the Gregorian emphasis upon a trained clergy, the shock of the Investiture Controversy, and the stimulus of a more intimate contact with non-Christian areas all served to revitalize the long-moribund cathedral schools.

The cathedral schools were at first very fluid in their structure. The bishop's secretary, the chancellor, or a special officer of the cathedral clergy known as a *scholasticus*, was usually in charge of the school and had the responsibility of inviting learned men, or "masters," to lecture to the eager students. Both masters and students roamed from town to town, seeking the best teachers, the brightest (or best-paying) students, or the most liberal atmosphere for their work. The twelfth century was the age of the wandering scholars, or *clerici vagantes*, who have left us charming traces of their spirit or at least that of their more frivolous members, in the form of Goliardic verses, largely concerned with such unclerical subjects as wine, women, song, and their attendant joys.[4] We also know of student life through model letters composed by master rhetoricians for students without the time or eloquence to write their own letters. Such models always include letters directed to parents and almost always mention that if the affectionate and dutiful son is to continue his studies, he will need more money. Another side of student life is made manifest by disputes with the permanent residents of the towns where the schools were found. Townsmen frequently registered protests with the bishops or with the king against the students, whom they resented because of their boisterous ways and because their clerical status gave them immunity from the local police and courts. Riots involving town and gown were commonplace events, another medieval tradition which has continued to the present. To impose some order on this flux, and to protect young students from incompetent or unorthodox teachers, the twelfth-century cathedral schools gradually insisted that masters possess a cer-

---

[4] The exact etymology of the word "Goliardic" remains unknown. It possibly derives from Goliath the Philistine, who was honored as a kind of antisaint by the boisterous students.

MAP 8.5: GREAT MONASTIC CENTERS OF LEARNING

tification of their learning, a "license to teach." The chancellor or *scholasticus* awarded this *licentia docendi,* the ancestor of all modern academic degrees.

The throngs of masters and students, many of them strangers to the city where they lectured and studied, eventually grouped themselves into guilds to protect their common interests. It was out of these spontaneously formed guilds of masters and students that the medieval university grew (*universitas* was a widely used Latin word for guild). The guild formed by the masters in Paris, for example, received a royal charter about 1200 and a papal bull, *Parens Scientiarum,* in 1231. These documents confirmed the guild's autonomy and powers to license teachers. The University of Paris may thus claim to be the oldest of the north European universities. From about 1200 we may also date the beginnings of the age of the university in European intellectual life.

The university in Italy sprang from slightly different origins. Even in the Early Middle Ages professional schools for the training of notaries, lawyers, and doctors survived in some Italian cities. The Italian schools, too, seem to have enjoyed rapid growth from the late eleventh century, and growth in turn led to the formation of guilds. Here, however, the

The university as a community of scholars, teachers, and learners was a medieval innovation. Its structure was such that students exercised a degree of control that they rarely possess today. Since there were no salaries, professors relied upon tuition fees for their daily bread, and students could starve out unpopular teachers merely by refusing to attend their classes. However, in other aspects student life then was much the same as it is today. These scenes from a fifteenth-century manuscript show students gambling, opposing each other in disputations (class debates), and engaging in other activities of dormitory life. (Photo: University Library of Freiburg-im-Breisgau)

students rather than the professors constituted the dominant "university." At the oldest of these schools, the University of Bologna, the students regulated discipline, established the fees to be paid to the professors, and set the hours and even the content of the lectures.

Like all guilds, the university sought to protect and advance its "art" of thought and teaching and to preserve that art over generations through the appropriate training of the young. The ancient world, although it possessed several famous schools, had never developed a university system, in the sense of numerous institutions of higher learning, specifically organized for the pursuit and preservation of learning. The rise of the universities also marks the appearance in Western society of a class of men professionally committed to the life of thought. These institutions, and the men associated with them, have ever since played a role of unsurpassed importance in the intellectual growth of the West.

SCHOLASTICISM

In its broadest sense Scholasticism refers to the teaching characteristic of the medieval schools, that is, all the subjects taught in the four great faculties: the arts (traditionally numbered as seven), canonical and Roman law, medicine, and theology. But in a narrower and perhaps more usual sense the term refers to theology, the medieval "queen of the sciences," in which the character and originality of scholastic reasoning appear most clearly.

Theology had similarly dominated the monastic thought of the Early Middle Ages, but the monks had largely limited their interests to biblical interpretation, or exegesis. They sought in the sacred Scriptures four traditional levels of meaning (literal, moral, allegorical, and mystical) and wrote voluminous commentaries without constructing a rigorously logical system of theology.

The novelty of Scholasticism was, specifically, its application of dialectic to Christian theology. Dialectic is the art of analyzing the logical relationships among propositions in a dialogue or discourse. The monastic theologian, through exegesis, wished to discover what was true; the scholastic, on the other hand, sought to learn how propositions of faith joined one another within a larger, consistent, and logically forceful theological system.

The first thinker to explore, although still not in rigorous fashion, the theological applications of dialectic was St. Anselm of Canterbury (1033–1109). Anselm defined his own intellectual interests as *fides quaerens intellectum* ("faith seeking to understand"—in actuality faith seeking to find logical consistency among its beliefs). In a work known as the *Proslogium* he tried to show that there is a necessary, logical connection between the traditional Judeo-Christian dogma that God is a perfect being and the dogma that he really exists. God, argued Anselm, is traditionally understood to be a being than which nothing greater can be conceived, but that being must exist outside as well as within the mind. If he did not, then a being greater than he could be conceived who really did exist; this in turn would violate our initial definition. According to this logical sequence God must exist or our concept of him would be absurd and unthinkable.

This ontological argument for God's existence has challenged philosophers for centuries. Its great historical interest is this: it marks the revival of logical inquiry, the eagerness to know the "whys" of things, to find order and consistency among statements accepted as true. The scholastic interest in dialectical relationships much resembles classical Greek thought with the important exception, of course, that the scholastics initially sought order among propositions presented by faith. (Later, they would take further propositions from the ancient pagan philosophers and even, to a limited degree, from their own observations.) From the time of Anselm scholastic thought assumed that the human intellect was powerful enough to probe the logical and metaphysical patterns within which even God had to operate.

Peter Abelard (1079–1142), a second father of Scholasticism, brought a new rigor and popularity to dialectical theology. Abelard came to Paris in the early years of its intellectual growth, and his brilliant teaching helped give that city its reputation as Europe's leading center of philosophical and theological studies.

His major contribution to the growth of Scholasticism was his book *Sic et Non* ("Yes and No"), the first version of which probably appeared in 1122. Using what became the classical method of scholastic argumentation, the posing of formal questions and the citation of authorities on both sides, Abelard assembled 150 theological questions. For each question he marshaled authorities from the Bible, Church councils, and Church fathers. In every case there was conflict. He made no effort to reconcile the discrepancies but left the authorities standing in embarrassing juxtaposition. His method was an ingenious retort to those who maintained that dialectic could make no contribution to Christian theology and that it was enough to hold fast to the ancient writings. *Sic et Non* implied that one must either enlist dialectic to reconcile the conflicts or concede that the faith was a tissue of contradictions.

In the early phases of the medieval intellectual revival dialectic had to contend for supremacy with humanistic studies, which emphasized familiarity with the classical authors and the ability to appreciate and write good Latin. Chartres, a small cathedral town near Paris, was the center of this twelfth-century humanism. But by the end of the century dialectic, as cultivated at Paris, predominated partly because it seemed to offer to the inquisitive men of the twelfth century a certain avenue to truth and a sound means for organizing the truths they had inherited. Another factor was that after the middle of the twelfth century, translators working chiefly in Spain and Sicily introduced European scholars to hitherto unknown works of Aristotle, as well as to the great commentary which the Muslim Averroës had written on them. Christian thinkers now had at their disposal the full Aristotelian corpus, and it confronted them with a thoroughly naturalistic and rationalistic philosophical system. Aristotle's philosophy was built on reason alone, and his assumptions drove Western scholars to examine his works and their own faith through dialectic. The difficult task of reconciling Aristotelian reason and nature with Christian revelation and divine grace remained the central philosophical problem of the thirteenth century.

VERNACULAR LITERATURE

Scholasticism reflected the cultural interests of only a small group of intellectuals in medieval society. What the broader masses of the people valued must be sought in vernacular literature. Here, too, the themes treated and characters described largely reflect the life of the nobility, not that of the common people. But there is much reason to believe that this literature, or some oral version of it, was appreciated well beyond aristocratic circles. Townsmen and even peasants seem to have delighted in hearing of the doings of the great.

Of the vernacular literatures of Europe only Anglo-Saxon possesses a substantial number of surviving writings which antedate the year 1000. For most of the major languages of Europe an abundant tradition of literary work dates only from the eleventh and twelfth centuries. In forming the literary tastes of Europe, the Romance tongues (the vernacular languages descended from Latin) achieved a particular importance, especially the two great dialects of France, the langue d'oïl spoken north of the Loire River and the langue d'oc, or Provençal, used in the south. Castilian was slightly later in producing an important literature, and Italian, perhaps because of its similarity to Latin, did not emerge as a major literary language until the late thirteenth century.

There were three principal genres of vernacular literature: the heroic epic, troubadour lyric poetry, and the courtly romance. Heroic epics, or chansons de geste, have survived in great abundance. The oldest and probably the best of them is the *Song of Roland*, which was composed in the langue d'oïl probably in the last quarter of the eleventh century. The basis of the poem is the ambush of the rear guard of Charlemagne's army under the command of Roland by the Basques at Roncesvalles in 778, but poetic imagination (or perhaps, older legend) transformed this minor Frankish setback into a major event in the war against Islam.

With fine psychological discernment the poem examines the character of Roland. The qualities that make him a hero—his dauntless courage and uncompromising pride—are at war with the qualities required of a good vassal—obedience, loyalty, cooperation, and common sense. Roland is in serious danger but refuses for reasons of personal dignity to sound his horn in time for Charlemagne to return and save him and his men. By the time his pride relents and he does blow the horn, their deaths are assured. The sensitive examination of the conflict between Roland's thoughtless if heroic individualism and the demands of the new feudal order gives this poem its stature as the first masterpiece of French letters.

Very different from the heroic epic is troubadour lyric poetry, initially written in the langue d'oc of the south. The novelty of this complex poetry is its discovery and celebration of women and of love. The heroic epic was written for the thoroughly masculine society of the battle camp. The troubadours sang at courts, in which women exerted a powerful influence. In a mobile age, when knights and nobles would be away for long periods on crusades and wars, their mothers, wives, and daughters administered their households and estates and achieved considerable social prominence. They became the arbiters of what constituted "courtly manners"—proper behavior—in their households, and they surely influenced the literature which was heard within their walls.

The troubadour usually addressed a lady of superior social station, almost always someone else's wife, whom he had little chance of winning. Although she was not a likely means of sensual gratification, love for her did offer a hope for inward consolation; it could, if requited, elevate the poet's spirits to unspeakable joy and transform his world to eternal spring. Courtly love (at least as the troubadours present it) was not a dalliance but quite literally a way of salvation, a means of rescuing the lover from despondency and introducing him into an earthly paradise. This discovery and intensive exploration of the emotion of love represents one of the most influential creations of the medieval mind.

The courtly romance, which entered its great age after 1150, combines traits of both heroic epic and troubadour lyric poetry. It is narrative in form like the epic; but, like Provençal poetry, it allots a major role to women and love. Chrétien de Troyes, whose works probably date from shortly before 1182, is the author of the oldest surviving romances about King Arthur of Britain and his coterie of knights. Many of these tales are concerned with an analysis of the tensions which love, the rebel-

The Romanesque cathedral at Poitiers in western France is made almost entirely of stone. The roofing of churches in stone was one of the most significant architectural advances of the Central Middle Ages. (Photo: Dr. Martin Hürlimann—Zurich)

The tympanum (i.e., the recessed façade of the pediment) of the cathedral at Autun displays the mélange of mysticism and vitality that characterizes Romanesque works of stone sculpture, particularly those designed for the churches. (Photo: Jean Roubier)

lious emotion, creates in society. Western letters have since endlessly explored these themes.

ROMANESQUE ART

The conventional term used to describe the architectural and artistic style of this period is "Romanesque." It means "of Roman origins" and is, like many terms applied to the Middle Ages, misleading. Artists in the Central Middle Ages did imitate classical models, but not exclusively; they also drew on nearly every other artistic tradition to which they had access—barbarian, Byzantine, and Arab.

The proliferation of castles across the face of Europe stimulated the techniques of construction. These fortresses were built on a progressively larger scale, in contrast with the castles of the Carolingian Age, and by the thirteenth century, builders were able to work entirely in stone. Crusaders returning from the East brought with them new concepts of fortress design and perhaps also a desire to render castle life more gracious. The crafting of tapestries, furniture, and glass benefited from the new importance of cities, the strength of markets, and the growing number of artisans. Although life about 1200 was still remarkably

Durham Cathedral. (Photo: F. H. Crossley, Courtauld Institute of Art)

crude, even for the rich, it was clearly becoming less so.

Art, however, remained in most of its forms the servant of the Church. The religious reform in the eleventh century brought with it a liturgical revival. The monks of the Cluniac monasteries were especially devoted to (and occasionally criticized for) sumptuous religious services. Liturgical needs stimulated the art of metalwork (which produced chalices and other sacred vessels), glass making, and the weaving of fine fabrics for the priests' vestments. Music too advanced. Gregorian chant (named for Pope Gregory the Great, but in fact representing the traditional plain-song of the Church of Rome) had become established as the common music of the Western Church in the Carolingian epoch. The eleventh and twelfth centuries witnessed, not certainly the origins, but a great development in polyphonic music (part-singing). The coordination of the vocal parts in choral music also required effective systems of musical notation. A monk named Guido d'Arezzo is credited with giving names to the notes, some of which are still used (re, mi, fa, sol, la). The secular songs and melodies of the troubadours were another major source of enrichment for the Western musical tradition.

The most impressive artistic monuments left to us from the Romanesque period are the churches themselves. In engineering the great achievement of the Central Middle Ages was the roofing of churches in stone. From about the year 1000, small, stone-roofed churches began to appear, especially in southern Europe. At first the builders utilized the simple barrel, or tunnel, vault, but this design did not allow for windows because the roof would collapse if holes were put into the supporting sides of the tunnel. Engineers then developed and mastered the use of the groin vault, which is formed by the intersection of two barrel vaults. The area of intersection is called the bay, and the roof over the bay is supported at four points, not by the entire length of the lateral walls. Bays could be grouped next to bays, an entire church could be roofed with stone, windows could be easily cut, and the monotony of tunnel vaulting avoided. (See the photo on p. 265 for a characteristic example of groin vaulting.)

Romanesque churches were decorated on the exterior with stone sculpture. Monumental sculpture had been a dead technique in the West since the end of the Roman Empire. Romanesque statues, which exist by the thousands, show a marked quality of antirealism, a refusal to allow visual accuracy to dominate portrayals. In part this was dictated by the odd-shaped crevices, corners, columns, and capitals which the sculptor frequently had to decorate, but the artist was also striving to present a world as seen by faith. Christ, for example, had to be shown larger than others, in keeping with his dignity. Demons and monsters, many drawn from the popular imagination, abound in Romanesque sculpture. While similar to Byzantine portrayals in its antirealism, Romanesque style, unlike the Byzantine, overflows with movement, tension, excitement, and the spirit of mystical exhilaration. Romanesque statuary marvelously documents the exuberant spirit of this age of reform and crusades, when men seemed convinced that God was actively at work among them, setting right the world.

Romanesque art makes use of many prior and foreign traditions, but it still manifests its own proper spirit. It is therefore much more than a juxtaposition of borrowed forms. Rather, it is the first style and school which can be called an authentic product of the European West.

The eleventh and twelfth centuries were vigorously creative at every level of European life. By 1200 Europe was very different from the old, or "first," Europe of Charlemagne. Its economy was more diversified and productive, its society more complex, its government more effective, its religion more sensitive, and its thought and art more original and daring. But the very innovations of the age posed severe problems for European society. How could the new forms of economic endeavor be reconciled with the older hostility and suspicion toward a life of buying and selling? How could the rising power of monarchs be reconciled with the self-consciousness and self-interest of the nobility, reformed Church, and privileged towns? How could the new confidence in human reason and in nature, reinforced by familiarity with Aristotle, be synthesized with the older notions that nature was corrupt, men weak, and the afterlife the only hope? From about 1200 the West was trying to consolidate its recent advances and bring them into harmony with its older heritage. This effort at consolidation, reconciliation, and synthesis is the theme of Western history in the thirteenth century.

RECOMMENDED READING

Sources

Anselm of Canterbury. *Basic Writings: Proslogium, Monologium, Gaunilon's On Behalf of the Fool, Cur Deus Homo.* S. W. Deane (tr.). 1962.

De Troyes, Chrétien. *Arthurian Romances.* W. W. Comfort (tr.). 1958.

Douglas, David C. (ed.). *English Historical Documents.* 1955. The richest available collection of translated sources bearing on English history.

Fitzneale, Richard. *The Course of the Exchequer.* Charles Johnson (tr.). 1950.

Herlihy, David (ed.). *The History of Feudalism.* 1971.

John of Salisbury. *The Statesman's Book.* John Dickinson (tr.). 1963.

The Song of Roland. Dorothy L. Sayers (tr.). 1957.

Studies

*Barraclough, Geoffrey. *The Origins of Modern Germany.* 1963. Learned examination of medieval German history.

Chenu, M.-D. *Nature, Man and Society in the Twelfth Century.* Jerome Taylor and Lester K. Little (trs.). 1968. Seminal essays on cultural and intellectual change, by a French Dominican.

Chrimes, Stanley B. *An Introduction to the Administrative History of Medieval England.* 1966. Clear and authoritative.

*Douglas, David C. *William the Conqueror: The Norman Impact upon England.* 1966. Outstanding among many biographies.

*Erickson, Carolly. *The Medieval Vision: Essays in History and Perception.* 1976. Broad, impressionistic reflections on the character of medieval culture.

*Fawtier, Robert. *The Capetian Kings of France: Monarchy and Nation, 987–1328.* Lionel Butler and R. J. Adams (trs.). 1962.

*Ganshof, François L. *Feudalism.* P. Grierson (tr.). 1964. Standard guide to feudal institutions.

*Haskins, Charles H. *The Renaissance of the Twelfth Century.* 1927. A pioneering study.

*———. *The Rise of Universities.* 1957.

*Heer, Friedrich. *The Medieval World: Europe, 1100–1350.* 1964. Thoughtful appraisal by an Austrian scholar.

*Pirenne, Henri. *Medieval Cities.* Frank D. Halsey (tr.). 1939. Old but worth reading.

*Southern, Richard W. *The Making of the Middle Ages.* 1955. Classic essay.

Strayer, Joseph R. *On the Medieval Origins of the Modern State.* 1970.
———. *Medieval Statecraft and the Perspectives of History.* 1971. Studies by a prominent American historian.

*Tellenbach, Gerd. *Church, State and Christian Society at the Time of the Investiture Contest.* 1970.

---

* Available in paperback.

NINE

THE SUMMER
OF THE MIDDLE AGES

The thirteenth century (or, more precisely, the period between about 1200 and the Black Death of 1348 and 1349) has been traditionally considered the summer of the Middle Ages. It can claim many impressive achievements: a largely prosperous economy, which supported more people than Europe possessed at any other time during the Middle Ages; reasonably effective systems of government in the feudal monarchies; parliamentary institutions; Gothic cathedrals; the great works of scholastic philosophy and theology; and the Divine Comedy *of Dante Alighieri, one of the great masterpieces of Western literature. Moreover, these products of the medieval genius seem to share a certain spirit: a sense of logic and order and a serene confidence, not only in divine grace and faith but also in human reason and effort. Thirteenth-century men believed that God had created a harmonious world and that they could describe its ordered structure in their philosophy, imitate it in their art, and use this knowledge to guide their earthly lives.*

Today, as research probes ever deeper, we know that these favorable impressions are not entirely accurate. Thirteenth-century society was less placid than the smiles of Gothic angels persuade their admirers to believe. The population may have grown too large to be supported by available resources, and this may have been an important factor in provoking plagues and famines from the middle fourteenth century. The prosperity of the rich often rested on the rampant misery of the poor; the aspirations toward a united and peaceful Europe did not dispel the specter of war; and scholastic theology did not quench the flames of intellectual and religious revolt. In sum, the effort to achieve order and synthesis was itself a manifestation of acute tensions and conflicts. One must beware of what a recent historian has called the "golden legend" of the Middle Ages.

Medieval society in the thirteenth century could not achieve permanent solutions to the many problems it confronted. But this ultimate failure should not prevent us from recognizing its accomplishments. It strove to build both an ordered society and ordered systems of thought, in which all conflicts, social or intellectual, would be reconciled. .The effort was admirable and the achievements magnificent; we may still regard the thirteenth century as the summer of the Middle Ages.

1. ECONOMIC EXPANSION

European population continued to grow in the thirteenth century, and settlers extended cultivation further into new lands, although at a slower pace after 1250. The more dramatic economic changes occurred in the cities.[1] Large-scale production, extensive trade, complex commercial and banking institutions, and

[1] We must of course recognize that the size of towns everywhere in Europe remained small in comparison with the rural population. The largest medieval towns probably never had more than 120,000 inhabitants. In England in the fourteenth century the percentage of the population which lived in cities seems to have numbered only about 10 percent. In certain regions of Italy, that percentage was as high as 25 percent, but this was exceptional.

the amassing of great fortunes became the commonplace features of urban economic and social life. These urban centers pioneered many of the methods, and show much of the spirit, of modern business enterprises.

URBAN INDUSTRY

Medieval towns developed a new system of producing goods. Usually called the "putting-out system," it remained characteristic of the Western economy until the Industrial Revolution. Most work was performed in the home, little use was made of power, and there were no factories. Increased efficiency was achieved through finely dividing the process of production and through developing highly specialized skills. A merchant or manufacturer, who fulfilled the function of providing capital, acquired the raw material, put it out in sequence to specialized artisans, and then sold the finished products.

The making of woolen cloth, the largest industry of the medieval town, well illustrates the complex character of thirteenth-century manufacturing. The raw wool, often coming from England, Spain, or North Africa, was first prepared by sorters, beaters, and washers. Then the cleaned and graded wool was carded, or combed. The next task, the spinning, was usually done by women who worked in their own homes with a distaff, a small stick to hold the wool, and a spindle, a weight to spin and twist the strands into thread. (The distaff has since remained the symbol of the female sex.) The spinning wheel, apparently first invented in Italy in the late thirteenth century, added a new speed and quality to thread-making.

Weavers, almost always men, wove the thread into huge broadcloths that were thirty yards in length and might contain two to three thousand warp (lengthwise) threads. The cloth was then fulled, that is, washed and worked with special earths which caused the wool to

mat. This was arduous work and was often done at a water-driven fulling mill. The giant cloth was then tentered, or stretched on a frame, so that it would dry properly and shrink evenly. Next, the dry cloth was rubbed with teasels to raise the nap, and the nap was then carefully cut. Several times repeated, this last operation gave the cloth a smooth, almost silky finish, but it was extremely delicate work; one slip of the scissors could ruin the cloth and the large investment it represented.

At various stages in this process the wool could be dyed—whether as unspun wool, thread, or woven cloth. Medieval people loved bright colors, and dyers used a great variety of animal, vegetable, and mineral dyes and special earths, such as alum, to fix the colors.

The medieval woolen industry thus came to employ a large and remarkably diversified labor force, which worked materials brought from all corners of the known world. Capital and labor were sharply divided; a few great entrepreneurs controlled huge masses of capital. In Florence in about 1300, the number of wool shops ranged between 200 and 300; the number of big broadcloths produced were between 80,000 and 100,000, with a value surpassing 1.2 million gold florins; the number of persons who earned their living from the industry was upwards of 30,000.

The Guilds

To defend and promote their interests in a world still ruled by warriors and priests, the merchants and artisans took to forming associations of self-help known as guilds. The first guilds were organized by merchants, and appear about 1000.[2] By the twelfth century both

2 Merchant guilds appear at the small town of Montreuil-sur-Mer probably before 980, at Tiel from about 950 to 1024, at Valenciennes between 1051 and 1070, at Cologne in 1070, and at Saint-Omer between 1072 and 1083. Leather workers had a guild at Rouen between 1100 and 1135, and fishermen at Worms between 1106 and 1107.

artisans and merchants in special trades—for example, dealers in wool, spices, or silk—had organized their own independent guilds. A large industrial town such as Florence had more than fifty professional guilds.

The guild members exercised wide powers over their own affairs. They usually met together once a year in their church or hall to approve changes in the statutes and to elect permanent officials. These consuls, as the officials were often called, enforced the statutes, adjudicated disputes among the members, administered the properties of the guild and supervised its expenditures, maintained the quality of the product by regulating both the materials and processes, protected the members from unfair competition, and restricted the number of working hours, the number of employees, and the type of advertising. The personal security and welfare of members were also principal concerns. The guilds aided those who lost goods through fire or flood; they supported the widows and educated the orphaned children of their deceased members. Banquets, public processions, and religious ceremonies enriched the social life of the membership. Many guilds assumed a further responsibility for the beauty and welfare of their town. They were among the principal donors to hospitals and charities, and they usually built and maintained their own church, or at least a chapel in the city cathedral.

One of the chief contributions of the guilds was the apprenticeship system; the guilds were in fact the most important institutions of lay education functioning in the Middle Ages. They stipulated what the apprentice had to be taught and what proof of skill he had to present to be admitted into the brotherhood, how long he had to work and learn in the shop of the master, and what the master had to give him by way of lodging, food, and salary. (The apprentice really earned his education by helping the master produce his goods, and the salary

he received was always small.) The young man might be required to produce a "masterpiece" to show his skill, or at least treat the brothers to a lavish banquet. If, after finishing his training, he was too inexperienced or poor to open his own shop, he could work as a paid laborer, or journeyman, in the shop of an established master. By carefully saving his wages, the apprentice might eventually become a master in his own right and a full-fledged member of the guild, but most medieval artisans continued to work as salaried laborers for their entire lives. The medieval guild has thus been called with some justice, not a union of workers, but a union of bosses.

In protecting commercial skills under difficult conditions, offering a measure of insurance and social security to their members, and promoting education, the guilds played a crucial role in forming an environment favorable to commerce and manufacture. They were the incubators of modern economic enterprise.

BUSINESS INSTITUTIONS

The growth of trade and manufacturing stimulated the development of sophisticated commercial and banking institutions. Christian ethics traditionally condemned the taking of usury (which then meant any profit on a loan, however tiny); therefore, the medieval business community developed alternative instruments of credit, which served the purpose of interest-bearing loans while deftly escaping the taint of usury. One alternative to the loan was the annuity, pension, or perpetual rent. In return for a sum of money a man would agree to pay the investor a yearly rent, sometimes forever, sometimes for the length of the investor's life. The sale of rents and annuities was a favorite means of financing expensive capital improvements on property, such as the construction of houses or buildings.

More important for properly commercial

purposes was the bill of exchange, in essence a loan, but requiring repayment at a specified time in another place and currency. Thus a Florentine might borrow 100 pounds at Florence and agree to repay three months later in local money at a Champagne fair. He then bought goods at Florence, sold them in Champagne, and repaid the money. The rate of exchange between the currencies almost always concealed a substantial profit for the investor, but technically he earned it for changing money, not for making the loan.

Partnerships and business associations were another important means of recruiting capital. At Venice, Genoa, and Pisa overseas ventures were most often financed through special temporary partnerships, usually called a *commenda*. In its simplest form an investor, who remained at home, gave a sum of money to a merchant traveling abroad in return for a share of the eventual profits (usually three-quarters); the investor bore the entire loss if the ship sank or the venture failed. A merchant would usually accept many of these investments simultaneously or might himself invest in one voyage while sailing on another. The partnership lasted only for the length of the specified voyage.

THE COMPANIES

In the inland Italian towns a more permanent kind of partnership developed known as the *compagnia* (literally, "bread together," a sharing of bread). These earliest companies seem to have been partnerships among brothers. The sons of a deceased merchant, for example, might decide to leave their inheritance undivided and to trade together as a single company. By the thirteenth century two changes were transforming the character of these fraternal companies. They now quite commonly included as partners persons who were not blood relatives but could contribute capital and services, and they also accepted deposits from nonpartners in return for fixed yearly payments of interest which were called "gifts," lest they be considered usurious. The capital supplied by the partners was called the *corpo*, or "body" of the company. Money accepted in deposit from nonpartners was considered *sopra corpo* ("above the body") and could reach substantial amounts.

These companies performed a wide variety of functions and became colossal in size. They traded in any product which promised a profit, wrote bills of exchange, and fulfilled other banking services. From the late twelfth century they served the Roman Curia as papal bankers and were largely responsible for building and maintaining the financial system of the medieval papacy. They were also drawn into the risky business of extending loans to prelates and princes.

Before their failure in 1342 the Bardi Company of Florence had loaned King Edward III of England almost 900,000 florins and the Peruzzi Company had provided 600,000. These were gigantic amounts: in 1348, Pope Clement VI purchased Avignon for only 80,000 florins.[3] Clearly, the capital of these Florentine banks was the price of kingdoms.

MEDIEVAL VIEWS OF ECONOMIC LIFE

The thinkers of the thirteenth century were coming to new and more favorable, if not exactly enthusiastic, views concerning wealth. The Church fathers had taught that difference in wealth in human society was a necessary evil arising out of sin. Sin had aroused the concupiscence of men and threatened to make social life a "war of all against all." Private property, defended by the power of the state, restrained concupiscence and promoted peace. On the other hand, Thomas Aquinas, the great

---

[3] These figures are taken from Yves Renouard, *Les hommes d'affaires italiens du moyen âge*, 1949, p. 124.

A detail from a fourteenth-century manuscript copy of Dante's Divine Comedy *illustrates the section of hell reserved for usurers. Dante regarded usury as one of man's many earthly sins which condemn him in the eyes of God.* (Photo: British Museum)

thirteenth-century theologian, drew his principal argument for private property from natural law. Private property, he argued, provided incentive, assured good care of belongings, and promoted peace and order. He thus gave property and wealth more dignity than the thought of an earlier age had accorded them.

Even commercial wealth was losing some of its ancient taint. As late as ca. 1150, Gratian in the *Decretum* had quoted with approval the aphorism that "rarely or never can a merchant be saved." By the thirteenth century, however, preachers in commercial cities were eloquently comparing merchants to Christ. After all, they, like Christ, lived by peaceful enterprise and not by violence. Moreover, Christ, like a good and worthy merchant, had repurchased or "redeemed" the human race from the devil's ownership.

Nevertheless, the social thought of the thirteenth century was far from espousing laissez-faire liberalism in the marketplace. The rich man could not use his wealth as his personal inclinations might dictate. Property could be private in possession, but it had to be utilized to promote the common good. The individual, in other words, was morally obligated to use his wealth to benefit the entire community, not just himself.

II. THE STATES OF EUROPE

Through its practices and institutions the thirteenth-century European economy acquired a more stable structure. Governments, too, were moving toward a new level of constitutional stability. The thirteenth century was an age of great laws, which helped define and fix governmental and legal procedures. They thus served to implant in the West a strong tradition of constitutionalism, a lasting belief that people should be governed by fixed procedures. The thirteenth century made one other lasting contribution to Western political development: the representative assembly. European princes extended to the great estates, or classes, of society —namely, the clergy, nobility, eventually even the townsmen—the opportunity to hear and approve the major decisions of government. To make this participation possible, parliaments or assemblies of estates, came to assume a recognized if still humble place among the institutions of government.

ENGLAND

At the death of Henry II in 1189 the English monarchy wielded exceptional authority, but neither in practice nor in theory was it clearly established within what limits, if any, royal powers should operate, or how, if at all, the great men of the realm might participate in government.

Henry's son and successor was Richard I, the Lion-Hearted. Although Richard had all the virtues of a model knight—boldness, military skill, stately bearing, even a flair for composing troubadour lyrics—he had none of the attributes of a good king. He loved battles and shunned conferences. In 1191 and 1192 he was off fighting in the Holy Land on the Third Crusade, where he won some significant victories and gained some concessions for the Christians from the Muslim chief Saladin.

Chivalry, which gave him his reputation, also took his life. He died in 1199 from a neglected wound received while besieging a castle in a minor war in southern France. Richard's presence in England was restricted to two visits, lasting less than ten months, but the English government continued to function efficiently even in the absence of its chief; this is testimony to its fundamental strength.

Richard was succeeded by his younger brother, John, who rightly or wrongly is considered a wicked king (significantly, no other English monarch has borne the name). While the towns and the common people supported him, he gratuitously antagonized his powerful subjects by his insolence and capricious cruelty. His reign is largely a record of humiliations suffered at the hands of the pope, Philip II of France, and his own barons.

In 1206 John brazenly tried to make a worthless favorite archbishop of Canterbury. The clergy of Canterbury appealed to Pope Innocent III, who selected for the office the learned, pious, and popular Stephen Langton. To force John to acquiesce Innocent laid England under interdict in 1208. The interdict was a command to the English Church to go on strike. Priests were not to baptize babies, marry the promised, or bury the dead in public ceremony. (In case of need, private conferral of the sacraments was still allowed.) Parish bells were silenced, and the rhythm of life must have changed across England. But the Church's strike did not sway John at all. Only when he wanted papal support in his war against the French over the loss of Normandy did he finally submit in 1213. After the defeat at Bouvines John had to reap the bitter harvest that his long years of misrule at home and failures abroad had sown.

Magna Carta
To meet the extraordinary expenses of war the English kings had traditionally requested, and

almost always received, special aids or contributions from their barons. But after Bouvines, when John's policies had clearly been proved disastrous, the enraged barons refused further help. Encouraged by the Church, they took to arms. At Runnymede in June 1215 they forced John to grant the "Great Charter" of liberties, which had probably been inspired, if not largely composed, by Archbishop Langton. The Magna Carta resembled oaths which English kings since Henry I had taken upon their coronation; it obligated the king to respect certain rights of his subjects. But no previous royal charter of liberties equaled it in length, explicitness, and influence.

The Magna Carta disappoints most modern readers. Unlike the American Declaration of Independence it offers no grand generalizations about human dignity and rights. Its sixty-three clauses, arranged without apparent order, are largely concerned with technical problems of feudal law—rights of inheritance, feudal relief, wardship, and the like. But it did establish, more clearly than any previous document, that the king ought not to disturb the estates of the realm—Church, barons, and all free subjects—in the peaceful exercise of their customary liberties. It thus guaranteed to the clergy the freedom to elect bishops and to make appeals to Rome, protected the barons against arbitrary exactions of traditional feudal dues, and confirmed for the men of London and other towns "all their liberties and free customs." It called for one standard of weights and measures in the kingdom, which facilitated trade and, therefore, undoubtedly pleased the townsmen. To all freemen it promised access to justice and judgment by known procedures. "No free man shall be taken or imprisoned or dispossessed," the charter reads, "except by the legal judgment of his peers or by the law of the land." Finally, the king could impose new taxes only with the common consent of the realm. On the other hand, it offered almost nothing to the unfree classes, the serfs or villeins who constituted perhaps 80 percent of the population.

The Magna Carta marked a major step toward constitutionalism, that is, toward government by recognized procedures which could be changed only with the consent of the realm. Of course, the barons and the bishops never anticipated that subjects other than themselves might be called upon to give consent, but this limitation in no way compromises the importance of the principle established. Finally, future generations of Englishmen were to interpret the provisions of the Magna Carta in a much broader sense than its authors had intended, making it truly part of the "Bible of the English constitution." The document is of importance not only for what it said, but for what it allowed future generations to believe about the traditional relationship in England between authority and liberty.

Provisions of Oxford

Under John's son Henry III (1216–1272) two issues—appointments to royal offices and the imposition of taxes—again raised the storms of baronial revolt. In selecting the high officials of state and Church, Henry favored over his own English subjects Frenchmen from Poitou and Provence (the homeland of his queen) and Italians put forward by the popes. The popes also involved him in ill-considered foreign adventures: to establish his younger son, Edmund, as king of Sicily and to secure the election of his brother Richard as German emperor. The barons once more protested against the heavy charges placed upon them to support these costly failures.

At a meeting at Oxford in 1258 the barons forced Henry to accept the Provisions of Oxford, which required him to govern England under the tight control of several baronial committees. Almost at once the king and barons fell to arguing over the implementation of the provisions, and both sides agreed to accept the arbitration of the saintly king of France, Louis IX. In 1264 Louis decided in Henry's favor and exonerated him from his promise to respect the provisions; the pope concurred. But the disgruntled barons under the capable leadership of Simon de Montfort took up arms. With the support of the king's own son Edward, Simon defeated and captured Henry at Lewes and for a little more than a year was the effective ruler of England. However, the barons were too unruly to maintain a united opposition against the King. Edward changed sides, defeated the baronial army at Evesham in 1265, and Simon himself was killed in the fray. The issue was thus decided: the king, not the barons, would be the chief power in England.

Legal Reforms

The powers and procedures of the royal government received a still clearer definition under Edward I (1272–1307). Pious without being weak, committed to crusading but also concerned with the welfare of his realm, Edward ranks as one of the greatest and most influential of medieval English kings. In 1284 he seized Wales and later gave it as an appanage (a province intended to provide "bread," or support) to his eldest son. (Since 1301 the heir presumptive to the English throne has borne the title Prince of Wales). Edward left his strongest mark on English law and institutions, and is often referred to, somewhat extravagantly, as the English Justinian.

Edward produced no systematic codification of English law, which remained based principally on custom and court decisions of the past, but he did seek to correct and enlarge the common law in certain critical areas and to give the system a new pliancy. He issued the first Statutes of the Realm, initiating a series in which all the public laws of England have since been entered. Edward's statutes required the barons to show by what warrant (quo

warranto), or royal license, they exercised jurisdiction in their courts, and this marked an important step in the decline of baronial justice. His laws also limited the growth of mortmain, that is, land held by the Church. The statutes were especially important in determining the land law of England, regulating inheritance and defining the rights of lords, vassals, and the king when land changed hands through inheritance or purchase. Edward laid the foundations upon which the English (and eventually American) law of real estate rested for centuries. In enacting these statutes and in governing the kingdom Edward also placed a new emphasis on securing the consent of his subjects through Parliament.

Parliamentary Origins

Since the time of William the Conqueror the plenary meetings of the great council, or Curia Regis, had included the great barons, bishops, abbots, royal household officials—anyone whom the king wished to invite. During the reign of Henry III these plenary sessions of the royal court grew more frequent and clearly more important, and came to be called parliaments. (The word means only "conversation" and, derivatively, an assembly where conversation occurs.) It also became customary, but by no means mandatory, to invite knights from the shires to these sessions. In 1264 Simon de Montfort summoned a parliament that included two knights elected from every shire and two townsmen or burgesses from every town. Edward followed him in this precedent.

Historians cannot assign an exact date for the division of Parliament into separate houses of Lords and Commons. The knights and burgesses seem to have met informally together since the time of Edward I, and these meetings gained official recognition at least from the reign of Edward III. Two unique features of the English Parliament helped enhance the influence of Commons. First, the lower aristocracy (that is, those knights who were not the tenants in chief or immediate vassals of the king) sat with the burgesses and learned to act together in their mutual interests. (On the Continent the lower aristocracy and the townsmen sat as separate groups and rarely developed or supported common causes.) Second, representatives of the upper clergy gradually gave up active participation in the English Parliament, preferring to meet at their own convocations, and this weakened the influence of the House of Lords, which lost the function of representing the Church, and benefited the House of Commons.

Parliamentary Functions

We now think of Parliament as a limitation on royal power, but it was not this at all in its earliest development. Parliament, as the assembly of the king's vassals, had the obligation merely of giving the king advice. In addition, the king found Parliament a valuable adjunct to his own administration, for it promulgated and enlisted support for his decisions, strengthened royal justice, and facilitated the collection of taxes. It was therefore in the king's interest to make the assembly broadly representative of the free classes. In summoning the Parliament of 1295 Edward cited a dictum taken from the Justinian Code: "What touches all, by all should be approved."

Parliament's role in the collection of taxes led to the development of a true system of representation. The Magna Carta, feudal custom, and prudence had required that the king seek the consent of his subjects for new taxes. He could not ask all freeholders of the realm individually. He might seek the consent of the separate shires and the towns, but this was slow and awkward. Edward ingeniously simplified the procedure of consent. Through special writs, he ordered the shires and the towns to elect representatives and to grant them *plena potestas* ("full power") to grant him money.

These representatives, gathered in Parliament, thus had authority to consent to taxes and to bind their electors back home. Paradoxically, the unique powers of the English king laid the basis for the eventual, unique powers of Parliament.

As the supreme feudal council, Parliament was also England's highest court (an honor the House of Lords retains today). The members attending its sessions would carry petitions or appeals from decisions made in lower courts; whereas a sheriff or shire court might have been subject to intimidation, Parliament would not be. By welcoming petitions, the king thus made his justice better known and respected throughout the realm. Some historians see in the role of Parliament as high court the ultimate source of its sovereignty.[4] As with our own Supreme Court the decisions of Parliament determined the future policies of all English courts. The decisions were thus nearly the equivalent of legislation, and from them there was no appeal.

At Edward's death in 1307 the English constitution had acquired certain distinctive features. The constitution was not contained in a single written document but was defined by both custom and statute law. The king was the chief of the state, but it was recognized that the important men of the kingdom should have some participation in the decision-making processes, especially regarding taxes. Parliament gave this policy its practical implementation. In spite of later changes these principles still underlie the English constitution. This extraordinary continuity over centuries is testimony to the sound construction which the medieval English kings, lords, and commoners gave to their government and their realm.

---

[4] The idea was first strongly argued in C. H. McIlwain, *The High Court of Parliament: A Historical Essay on the Boundaries Between Legislation and Adjudication in England*, 1962.

In this fourteenth-century manuscript illumination, St. Louis hears the pleas of his humble and defenseless subjects, chiefly women and a monk. Note the hanged felons in the left panel. The picture illustrates the abiding reputation for justice that St. Louis earned for the French monarchy. (Photo: New York Public Library/Picture Collection)

FRANCE

In France as in England the thirteenth century was primarily an age of constitutional consolidation. The successor of Philip Augustus, Louis VIII, ruled for only three years (1223–1226), but his reign was notable for several reasons. He was the first Capetian king not to be crowned in his father's lifetime; the Capetians had finally established that their claim to the monarchy was based on inheritance and not upon election. He campaigned personally against the Albigensian heretics in southern France, and his victories prepared the way for the eventual unification of Toulouse and Languedoc with the royal domain (these were the last major additions to the royal lands until the

late fifteenth century). He adopted the policy of supporting younger sons and younger brothers by granting them territories, the so-called appanages. This policy, continued by his successors, ultimately created powerful and troublesome princely lines in France.

St. Louis

At Louis's death in 1226 the throne passed to Louis IX, St. Louis, one of the great figures of the thirteenth century. Louis was recognized as a saint even during his lifetime because of his austere piety, a disposition he perhaps learned from his mother, Blanche of Castile. He attended at least two masses a day, was sternly abstemious in food and drink, often washed the feet of the poor and the wounds of lepers, and was scrupulously faithful to his wife Margaret of Provence, who, like her husband, bore an aura of sanctity.[5] However, his per-

---

[5] One of Margaret's crosses was the intense jealousy of her mother-in-law. In the early years of his marriage, Louis supposedly had to meet with his wife secretly on the palace staircase to escape his mother's watchful eye. This did not, however, prevent the royal couple from having eleven children.

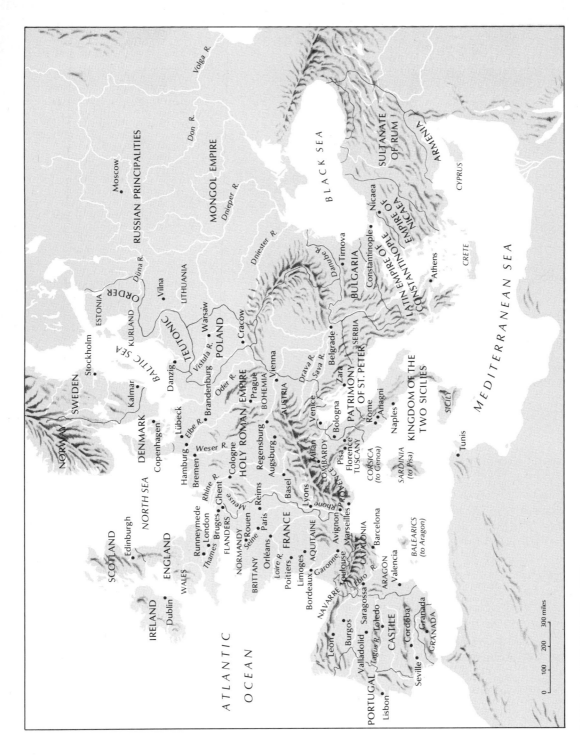

MAP 9.1: EUROPE CA. 1250

sonal asceticism did not preclude an ambitious conception of royal authority. He added new pomp to court ceremonies and freely acted against the pope's wishes whenever the interests of the monarchy or his people seemed to require it. Three great ideals informed his policies as king: more justice within his kingdom, peace with its neighbors, and war against the Muslims, who still held Jerusalem.

Legal Reforms

Louis made no attempt to extend the royal domain at the expense of the nobles of the realm or to deprive them of their traditional powers and jurisdictions, but he did expect them to be good vassals. He forbade wars among them, arbitrated their disputes, and insisted that his ordinances be respected; he was the first king to legislate for the whole of France. Although Louis did not suppress the courts of the great nobles, he and his judges listened to appeals from their decisions, so that royal justice would be available to all his subjects. The king liked to sit in the open under a great oak at Vincennes near Paris to receive personally the petitions of the humble. The prestige which the piety and fairness of his decisions lent to royal justice was his great contribution to its growth.

During Louis's reign jurists began to clarify and codify the laws and customs of France. The most important of these compilations was the Establishments of St. Louis, drawn up before 1273 and once wrongly attributed to the king himself. It contained, besides royal ordinances, the civil and feudal customs of several northern provinces and seems to have been intended for the guidance of judges and lawyers. It was not an authoritative code, but it and other compilations helped bring a new clarity and system to French law.

Louis strengthened the royal administration in other ways. He established the *enquêteurs*, or special wandering inspectors, who investi-

gated the performance of the local officials of the royal domain, namely, the *baillis* and the *sénéchaux*. In his reign the Parlement of Paris became fully independent of the royal court. (The Parlement of Paris was never, like the English Parliament, a representative assembly, but was always a tribunal or court of law.) Louis confirmed its status as the highest court in France, a position it retained until 1789.

Peace and War

Louis sought peace with his Christian neighbors. French monarchs had traditionally claimed some land south of the Pyrenees Mountains, which had formed the Spanish March under Charlemagne (see Map 6.3), and the Spanish kings of Aragon in turn claimed large areas of Languedoc in southern France (see Map 8.4). Rather than settling this dispute through war, Louis negotiated the Treaty of Corbeil (1258) with the Aragonese king, with each side renouncing its claims. This settlement defined the French-Spanish border for the next two hundred years.

Peace with England was harder to attain. The English still held Aquitaine and Gascony and were not reconciled to the loss under King John of their extensive fiefs north of the Loire River. Louis repulsed an English invasion at Saintes in 1242 but then actively sought peace with his English foe. At the Treaty of Paris in 1259 Louis relinquished several territories which his troops had occupied along the borders of Gascony, and in return King Henry III of England abandoned his claims to the lands which John had lost and agreed to perform liege homage to Louis for his fief of Gascony. The Treaty of Paris was unpopular in France; many believed that in ceding the Gascon borderlands Louis had given away more than the military situation warranted. Louis replied that these liberal terms might enable Henry's sons and his own to live thereafter in peace, as was proper for vassals and lords.

Louis, who believed that a principal duty of a Christian king was to lead a crusade, led two, one in 1248 against Egypt and the other in 1270 against Tunis. Both expeditions proved to be fiascos, but they were significant in at least one way: these were the last major Western crusades.

Philip IV

Louis's successors were able to preserve the strength, but not the serenity, of his reign. His grandson Philip IV, the Fair (1285–1314), is perhaps the most enigmatic of the medieval French kings; neither contemporaries nor later historians have agreed on his abilities. To some, Philip has seemed capable and cunning; to others, phlegmatic and uninterested, content to leave the business of government almost entirely to his ministers. If Philip lacked the personal ability to rule, he at least had the capacity to select strong ministers as his principal advisers. They were usually laymen trained in Roman law and possessing a high opinion of royal authority. They considered the king to be not merely a feudal monarch who ruled in agreement with the magnates of his realm but rather an "emperor in his own land" whose authority was free from all restrictions (the root sense of *legibus solutus*, "absolute") and subject to no higher power on earth. According to some historians, Philip's reign registers the triumph of a new "lay spirit," which overthrew the ecclesiastical and clerical domination of the earlier Middle Ages.[6]

The greatest obstacle to the advance of Philip's power was Edward I of England, master of the extensive fief of Gascony. Philip's resolve to drive England from the Continent resulted in intermittent wars from 1294 to 1302.

[6] The most extensive statement of this important thesis is Georges de Lagarde, *La naissance de l'esprit laique au déclin du moyen âge*, 3rd ed., 1956–1963.

To punish the English economically Philip tried to block the importation of English wool into Flanders. The Flemish towns revolted. Philip marched against them but was overwhelmed at Courtrai in 1302 by the towns' militias. This defeat deprived Philip of all hope of expelling the English from the Continent and confirmed the English possession of Gascony.

These costly wars had placed a heavy burden on the royal finances. To replenish the treasury Philip confiscated all the property of the Jews and drove them from his realm; he also imprisoned foreign merchants to extort money from them and arrested the members of the Knights Templars within France and brought them to trial, hoping to obtain their extensive possessions.

The Templars were originally a military-religious order, founded to aid pilgrims and to support crusades in the Holy Land. Through donations the order had grown enormously wealthy over the years, so that by the fourteenth century it had enough riches and influence to function as an international bank. To Philip, suppression of the order and confiscation of its properties offered a means to fill a depleted royal treasury. He brought the Templars to trial on false charges witnessed to by his hand-picked cronies and pressured a reluctant pope to suppress the order. But instead of transferring the order's French possessions to the royal treasury, the pope gave the properties to another religious order, the Knights Hospitalers. The royal treasury received only compensation for the costs of the trial.

Finally, Philip insisted on his right to demand from the Church "free gifts" which were truly taxes. The issue led to a protracted dispute with Pope Boniface VIII (see pp. 292–293). In seeking to dominate these international powers—the Templars and the Church itself—Philip showed his determination to become truly sovereign in his own lands.

Philip's Heritage

In trying to achieve an absolute monarchy, Philip upset the delicate feudal equilibrium of the France of St. Louis. He left at his death a deeply disturbed France. The Flemish towns remained defiant, and the strained relation of the monarchy with its principal vassal, the king of England, threatened to produce a major war. Under Philip's successors, with the outbreak of the Hundred Years' War, France entered one of the darkest periods of its history.

THE IBERIAN KINGDOMS

The Christian *Reconquista* had achieved all but final victory by 1236 with only Granada still in Muslim hands. The principal challenge now was the consolidation of the earlier conquests under Christian rule and the achievement of a stable constitutional order.

The three major Christian kingdoms that emerged from the Christian offensive were Portugal, Castile (including León), and Aragon (including Catalonia and Valencia), but they were not really united within their own territories. The Christian kings had purchased the support of both old and new subjects through generous concessions during the course of the *Reconquista*. Large communities of Jews and Muslims gained the right to live under their own laws and elect their own officials, and favored towns were granted special royal charters, known as *fueros*, that permitted them to maintain their own forum, or court. Barcelona and Valencia in Aragon and Burgos, Toledo, Valladolid, and Seville in Castile were virtually self-governing republics in the thirteenth century. Among other groups, the military aristocracy was highly privileged. The magnates, or *ricos hombres*, particularly in Castile, the largest of the Iberian kingdoms, held much of their lands not as fiefs but as allodia (properties in full title), and this reinforced their independent spirit. The clergy of course formed still another powerful and privileged group. Moreover, the Iberian kings had to reckon with three wealthy religious orders of knights, the Calatrava, Santiago, and Alcántara, which had been founded about 1200 to aid in the struggle against the infidel and which were now able to wield independent financial and military power.

To hold all these elements together under a common government was a formidable task, but the kings retained real advantages. The tradition of war against the infidel gave to kings a special prestige. And their rivals were too diverse and too eager to fight one another to be able to present a united challenge.

Sooner than other Western monarchs, the Iberian kings recognized the practical value of securing the consent of their powerful subjects to major governmental decisions, particularly regarding taxes. By the end of the twelfth century they made frequent use of representative assemblies, called Cortes. Although they never achieved the constitutional position of the English Parliament because there were too many of them, the Cortes were the most powerful representative assemblies in Europe during the thirteenth century.

In order to impose a stronger, essentially feudal sovereignty over their subjects, the Iberian kings set about systematizing the laws and customs of their realms, thus clarifying both their own prerogatives and their subjects' obligations. For example, King Diniz of Portugal reorganized royal finances and administration, suppressed the Templars, and won from the papacy concessions which gave him wide powers over the Portuguese Church. Alfonso X of Castile issued an encyclopedia of legal institutions, meant to instruct lawyers and guide judges. This code, known as the *Siete Partidas* ("Seven Divisions") was thoroughly imbued with the spirit of Roman law and presented the king as the source of all justice. Alfonso was in no position to achieve a true absolutism in his government, but the code did serve to educate the people to the high dignity of kingship. Even more than in England and France, feudal government in the Iberian kingdoms rested on a delicate compromise between royal authority and private privilege, and this apparently fragile system worked tolerably well.

With the achievement of fairly stable governments the Iberian kingdoms were free to play a larger role in the affairs of Europe. Aragon in particular, with an opening on the Mediterranean Sea, made its powers felt. In 1229 James I captured the Balearic Islands. His son Peter III made himself king of Sicily, after a revolt known as the Sicilian Vespers (1282) drove from the island a French dynasty of rulers. Sardinia was taken from the Pisans in 1326. A seemingly invincible company of Catalan mercenaries besieged Constantinople (1302–1307), then captured Athens and subjugated it to Catalan domination until 1388. The expansion of the Iberian kingdoms was to be a major theme in European history for the next several hundred years.

THE HOLY ROMAN EMPIRE

While the English, French, and Iberian kingdoms were moving toward greater unity under more centralized governments, the German and Italian territories of the Holy Roman Empire were disintegrating into a large number of small and virtually autonomous principalities. Geography and culture obstructed the effective union of the lands north and south of the Alps. Moreover, the western kings for the most part enjoyed the support of both Church and towns in their efforts to achieve ordered government; the German emperors, on the other hand, counted both Church and towns among their committed enemies, at least in Italy. This powerful opposition made a supremely difficult task impossible.

Frederick Barbarossa had negotiated an uneasy peace with the pope and the Italian towns in the last years of his reign, but the struggle was renewed soon after his death in 1190. Barbarossa's son Henry VI had married Constance, heiress to the Norman Kingdom of the Two Sicilies. Their son Frederick II thus had a legal claim to southern Italy as Constance's heir, and a moral claim to the German throne. The prospect of Italian unification under German auspices disturbed both the papacy and the free cities of Lombardy. The towns feared the direct domination of the emperor, while the papacy believed that its liberty would not survive were it to be encircled by German lands. In his brief reign of seven years Henry VI had little chance to effect the "union of the Kingdom with the Empire," as contemporaries called this fateful policy. It was a dream that was to elude his son too.

Frederick II Hohenstaufen

Frederick II (1194–1250) is one of the most fascinating personalities of the Middle Ages. A contemporary called him *stupor mundi* ("wonder of the world"). Later historians have hailed him as the first modern ruler, the prototype of the Renaissance despot, the cold and calculating statesman, a Machiavellian before Machiavelli. Frederick spoke six languages, loved learning, patronized poets and translators, founded a university at Naples, and, after a fashion, conducted scientific experiments. It had been said, for example, that a baby who hears no voices will grow up speaking Hebrew, which supposedly was man's first and most natural language. He therefore had an infant raised in total silence, to see if this were true. He wrote a scholarly tract on hunting with falcons. He also corrected Aristotle by writing on the margins of his works in several places, "It isn't so."

Several princes had contended for the German throne upon Henry VI's death. Pope

Innocent III, disappointed in them all, supported Frederick's candidacy. Innocent's successor, Honorius III, crowned Frederick emperor in 1219 on the double promise that he would renounce his mother's inheritance of southern Italy and lead a crusade to Palestine. Frederick procrastinated on both agreements, creating lasting difficulties with the Church.

Emperor Frederick influenced German development in several fundamental ways. He established on the empire's Eastern frontier a military-religious order, the Teutonic Knights, who eventually created the Prussian state; recognized Bohemia as a hereditary kingdom and Lübeck as a free imperial city; and issued the earliest charter of liberties to the Swiss cantons. His most important policy, however, was to confer upon the German ecclesiastical princes

Emperor Frederick II, in the ship showing the imperial eagles, watches his soldiers assaulting prelates on their way to a council summoned by Pope Gregory IX in 1241. This contemporary illustration of the emperor's sacrilegious behavior, taken from a manuscript, is a good example of the war of propaganda by which both the pope and emperor sought to win public sympathy. (Photo: The Granger Collection)

and the lay nobles virtual sovereignty within their own territories. The emperor retained only the right to set the foreign policy of the empire, make war and peace, and adjudicate disputes between princes or subjects of different principalities. All other powers of government passed to the princes; no later emperor could regain what Frederick gave away.

In Italy Frederick pursued a much different

policy. For the government of the Kingdom of the Two Sicilies he relied upon a trained lay bureaucracy. He rigorously centralized his administration, suppressed local privileges, imposed a universal tax in money upon his subjects, recruited his army from all classes and from Muslims as well as Christians, and issued a constitution which, in the spirit of Roman law, interpreted all jurisdiction as stemming from the emperor.

While building what some historians consider to have been the first modern state, Frederick had to face the increasingly bitter opposition of the popes and the free cities of northern Italy. Pope Gregory IX excommunicated him in 1227 because of his failure to lead an Eastern crusade. Frederick then departed on the crusade but preferred to negotiate than fight and made a treaty with the Muslims which guaranteed unarmed Christian pilgrims access to Jerusalem. The more militant among the Western Christians believed that this treaty was dishonorable. He returned to Italy in 1229 and came to terms with Pope Gregory a year later.

The Lombard towns remained fearful of his designs and finally leagued against him. He defeated them at Cortenuova in 1237, but his success once more awakened in Gregory fears of encirclement, and Frederick was again excommunicated. Both sides struggled to win the public sympathy of Europe, but the tide of history began to turn against Frederick. To break the power of the Lombard towns he unsuccessfully besieged Parma in 1248. In 1250 death cut short his efforts to unify Italy under imperial auspices.

There are some historical figures whose careers seem to summarize a given epoch and to predict the one to come. Frederick is such a figure. In Germany he reinforced a political fragmentation that had become ever more pronounced since the eleventh century. In southern Italy he completed the constitutional reorganization which the Norman kings, his forebears, had begun. He does resemble the later Renaissance tyrant and the modern statesman, but he was also perhaps the last emperor to take seriously the grand vision of the Christian empire. The chronicler who called him the wonder of the world wrote with perspicacity.

III. THE CHURCH

Since the time of the Gregorian reform of the eleventh century, the papacy had sought to build in Europe a unified Christian commonwealth, one based on faith and on obedience to Peter, in which European princes and peoples might work out their salvation in fraternal peace. In the thirteenth century, the Church came close to achieving this grand design, but it still had to face powerful challenges to both Christian unity and its own leadership.

THE GROWTH OF HERESY

From the fifth until nearly the eleventh century no major heresies had troubled the Western Church, a sure indication of intellectual and spiritual torpor. From about the year 1000, however, chroniclers begin to note with growing frequency the appearance of heretics and sporadic attempts to suppress them.

The spread of heresy in the eleventh and twelfth centuries was partially a reaction to abuses within the established Church. Angered by the wealth and moral laxity of the clergy, heretics rejected the claimed privileges of the official priesthood. Heresy had social roots also. The continuing increase of population brought many social dislocations in its wake. The young were too numerous for the positions and jobs left to them by the aged. Young men, frustrated in their hopes for a career, and unmarriageable young women filled society. The movement into new territories, the growth of towns, the appearance of new trades and industries all created strong psychological tensions, which often found an outlet in heretical movements. Within the towns, for example, heresy offered a form of social protest to the urban poor. It held potential for rich townsmen, too, inasmuch as traditional Christianity had been highly suspicious of wealth, particularly when earned in the marketplace, and gave the rich merchant little assurance of reaching heaven. Nobles envied the property and power of the Church; to them, heresy offered a justification for seizing the wealth of a corrupt Church for themselves. Heresy had a particular appeal to women. Many heretics made a special effort to recruit women, conducting schools for them and teaching them how to read the Scriptures at a time when the established Church largely neglected their education.

This was also an age of spiritual tension. Many laymen wanted a more mystical and emotional reward from religion, but were denied such satisfaction because they were given no opportunity to study the Bible, to hear it read in the vernacular, or to be moved by sermons. These were the exclusive activities of monks. A principal effort of both the new heresies and the new movements within the Church was to break this monastic monopoly of the religious experience.

THE WALDENSIANS AND ALBIGENSIANS

The first heretics appeared about the year 1000 and seem to have been reformers who denounced the Church for its failings but offered no solutions for its problems. Then about 1170 a rich merchant of Lyons, Peter Waldo, adopted a life of absolute poverty and gave himself to preaching. He soon attracted followers, who came to be known as "the poor men of Lyons," or Waldensians. The Waldensians attacked the moral laxness of the clergy and extended their denunciations to the sacraments they administered. This group was

declared heretical by the Lateran Council of 1215, but the Church never succeeded in suppressing the movement. The Waldensian Church still exists, although its theology was later much transformed by Protestant influences.

Far more powerful in their own day, though not destined to survive the Middle Ages, were the Cathari, or Albigensians, named for the town of Albi in Languedoc. The Albigensians' religious attitudes were greatly influenced by Manicheanism, an ancient belief that continued to survive among various small sects in Asia Minor and the Balkans. The Albigensians, like the Manicheans, believed that two principles, or deities, a god of light and a god of darkness, were fighting for supremacy in the universe. The good man must help the god of light vanquish the evil god of darkness, who had created and ruled the material world. The true Albigensian led a life of rigorous asceticism: he refrained from sexual intercourse, even within marriage, because it served only to propagate matter and thereby extend the dominion of darkness; and because of the taint of the reproductive process, he refused to eat all animal flesh (fish was not forbidden, thanks to the Albigensians' ignorance of the mating habits of aquatic animals). Because a sect which preached abstinence within marriage would, of course, soon bring about its own extinction, the Albigensians reached a practical compromise: those who abided by these stringent regulations were the *Perfecti* (they formed the priesthood); those who did not live by this stern code were the believers. A believer at the point of death could hope to be initiated into the ranks of the perfect through a kind of sacrament known as the *consolamentum*, which could be received only once.

The Albigensians, like the Waldensians, denied all value to the sacraments and priesthood of the established Church. They, of course, denied that Christ had ever appeared in human form and saw no coming redemption of the

world. The Albigensians more truly constituted a non-Christian religion than a Christian
heresy. Their appeal came principally from
their use of a vernacular Testament and their
willingness to preach in the vernacular to laymen and from their moral fervor. Eventually
they developed a strong organization with
councils and a hierarchy of *Perfecti* headed by
a pope.

THE SUPPRESSION OF HERESY

The Church initially responded to the heretics
by attempting to reconvert them. One of the
first and greatest leaders supporting the policy
of reconversion was a priest from Castile
named Dominic. About 1205 he began to
preach among the Albigensians of Languedoc.
Dominic insisted that his followers, whose mission was to preach, live in poverty and support
themselves by begging; they thus constituted a
mendicant, or begging, order. This new Order
of Preachers grew with amazing rapidity, and
was approved by the bishop of Toulouse (1215)
and shortly afterward by the pope. To prepare its members for their work the Dominican
Order stressed education, and thus eventually
became the intellectual arm of the medieval
Church. It counted among its members Albertus Magnus, Thomas Aquinas, and many other
important religious thinkers of the thirteenth
century.

Reconversion through preaching, persuasion,
and example remained, however, a slow and
uncertain process. Moreover, canon law failed
to provide an effective remedy against the powerful, organized heresies of the twelfth century.
The law did give the bishop the right to try a
suspected heretic before his own court, but a
heretic protected by important men in the community was virtually immune to prosecution,
inasmuch as the bishop often feared offending
the lay powers of his diocese. The lack of any
effective legal way of dealing with heretics led

to frequent riots against them—the medieval
equivalent of the lynch law.

By the early thirteenth century the Church
began to suppress heresy systematically by
force. Pope Innocent III, of whom more will
be said later, favored peaceful solutions to
heresy until his legate Peter of Castelnau, who
had excommunicated the count of Toulouse
for tolerating heresy, was murdered by one of
the count's retainers. Innocent concluded that
as long as the nobility of Languedoc abetted
heresy, nothing short of force would be effective against it. He therefore proclaimed a
crusade against the Albigensians and the nobles
who supported them. Knights from the north
of France responded with zeal, but more out of
greed for plunder than concern for orthodoxy.
They defeated the nobles of Languedoc, but the
problem of suppressing heresy remained.

In 1231 Pope Gregory IX instituted a special
papal court to investigate and punish heresy.
This was the famous papal Inquisition, which
was to play a large and unhappy role in European history for the next several centuries.
Through the Inquisition the popes sought to
impose ordered and effective procedures upon
the hunt for heretics. Like the English justices
in eyre, the inquisitors were itinerant justices
who visited the towns within their circuit at
regular intervals. Strangers to the locale, they
were not subject to pressures from the important men of the region. While the Inquisition
was doubtlessly an improvement over riots, the
procedures it adopted, which were a conscious
break with prior traditions of canonical and
medieval justice, were unfortunate. It accepted
secret denunciations and, to protect the accusers, would not reveal their names to those denounced; at times it used evidence that was
not even revealed to the accused; it denied the
right of counsel and tortured obdurate heretics.
The suspected heretic was, in fact, considered
guilty before even being summoned to court.
He could confess and repent, with the likely

consequence of a heavy penance and usually the confiscation of his property. But he had little chance to prove his innocence.[7] As an ecclesiastical court the Inquisition was forbidden to shed blood, but here too its procedures were novel: it delivered relapsed or unrepentant heretics to the secular authority with full knowledge that they would be put to death.

The weaknesses of this system soon became apparent. Secret procedures protected incompetent and even demented judges. Inquisitors such as Bernard Gui in southern France or Conrad of Marsburg would today probably be considered psychotics; they shocked and disgusted even their contemporaries with their savage zeal. In addition, the Inquisition could function only where it had the close cooperation of the secular authority. It was never established in areas (for example, England) where strong kings considered themselves fully competent to control heresy. (Kings characteristically equated religious and civil rebellion and considered heresy to be identical with treason; even Frederick II, in spite of his bitter dispute with the papacy, imposed the death penalty upon heretics.) Dependence on the secular arm meant that the Inquisition ultimately became an instrument of royal as much as ecclesiastical policy. Philip IV of France, for example, utilized the Inquisition for the suppression of the Templars.

The number of heretics who were executed is not known exactly, but they were probably not more than several hundred. Fines, confiscations of property, and imprisonment were the usual punishments for all but the most obstinate heretics. There is no denying the unfortunate effect of the Inquisition upon the medi-

eval papacy and Church, chiefly the association of the papacy with persecution and bloodshed to the inevitable erosion of its own prestige. And moral prestige has been, in all ages, the true basis of papal authority.

THE FRANCISCANS

Crusades and the Inquisition could not alone preserve the unity of the medieval Church. A spiritual regeneration was needed; the Church had to reach laymen, especially those living in towns, and provide them with a spiritual message they could comprehend. The Dominicans were the first religious order to undertake this task as their primary mission. A major role was also played by a contemporary of St. Dominic, St. Francis of Assisi.

Francis (1182?–1226) is probably the greatest saint of the Middle Ages and possibly the most sensitive poet of religious emotion. He succeeded in developing a style of piety which was both faithful to orthodoxy and abounding in new mystical insights. Since most of Francis's life is screened by legend, it is nearly impossible to reconstruct the exact course of his spiritual development. He seems to have devoted his young manhood to a self-conscious search for happiness, or, in the troubadour terminology he favored, for perfect joy. He first tried the rowdy amusements of the city. But dissatisfaction lingered; a biographer, Thomas of Celano, relates that after a severe illness Francis wandered on a May morning out to the blossoming fields but did not feel his accustomed joy. He then became a knight, but contentment still eluded him. Finally he turned to the religious life, instructed to do so, according to legend, by Christ himself, and adopted a life of poverty. Still, he believed that the test of true living, and indeed of true religion, ought to be joy: if all creatures, including men, recognized God's good providence over them, they would respond with joy. Joy would in

---

[7] The one defense the accused had was to show malice and prejudice by identifying in court his otherwise anonymous accusers. This meant, however, that his defense depended too often upon a good guess.

turn assure universal harmony in the world and bring a kind of golden age.

Disciples began to gather almost at once around the "little poor man" of Assisi. In 1208 Francis obtained papal approval for the formation of a new religious order. This Order of Friars Minor (Lesser Brothers) grew with extraordinary rapidity; within ten years it reached some five thousand members and spread from Germany to Palestine; before the end of the century it was the largest order in the Church. Although the problems of administering a huge order did not command Francis's deepest interests, he did write a brief rule for the Friars and shortly before his death gave them some further recommendations in a document known as his Testament, in which he stressed the importance of poverty and simplicity.

He visited Palestine twice to preach to the infidels. In 1224 he is said to have received the stigmata, the marks of Christ's five wounds, thus becoming the first Christian saint to exhibit these signs of superior sanctity.

The success of the Friars Minor was an authentic triumph for the Church. Like the Dominicans, they carried their message primarily to laymen in the growing towns, to the social classes where the heretics had hitherto won their greatest successes. Giving themselves to poverty and preaching, the Friars Minor came to include not only a second order of nuns but a third order of laymen. Francis and his followers thus opened orthodox religion to delight in the natural world, to mystical and emotional experiences, and to joy, which all men, they believed, including the ascetic and the pious, should be seeking.

This fresco from the basilica of St. Francis at Assisi, traditionally attributed to the Florentine painter Giotto, shows the saint preaching to the birds. He congratulates them on their bright plumage and bids them sing in praise of God. The implication is that if men too recognize God's good providence over them, they will respond with gratitude and joy. (Photo: Olinari–Scala)

PAPAL GOVERNMENT

In this period of profound social change and religious crisis the papacy faced serious obstacles in achieving its ideal of a unified, peaceful, and obedient European community. The pope of the thirteenth century whose reign best illustrates the aspirations and the problems of the medieval Church is Innocent III (1198–1216).

Innocent was somewhat ambiguous in defining his own powers.[8] He once stated that God had given him "not only the universal Church, but the whole world to govern," yet he also declared to Philip II of France that he had no wish to "lessen or disturb the jurisdiction and power of the king." Although he seems to have been willing enough to leave the princes undisturbed in the routine exercise of government, he did insist that they obey him in matters concerning the rights of the Church, the peace and common interests of Christendom, and their own personal morality. He sought with vigor and with remarkable, if always partial, success to achieve three major goals: the unity of Christendom, the hegemony of the papacy over Europe, and the clarification of Christian discipline and belief.

Within Europe heresy was the greatest threat to Christian unity, and though he ordered the crusade against the Albigensians, Innocent, in general, favored the new mendicant orders to counter the appeal of the heretics. Beyond Europe he sought reunion with the Eastern Church. At first condemning the Fourth Crusade, which was directed against fellow Christians, Innocent came to consider the fall of Constantinople to the crusaders a providential act, meant to achieve unification of Western and Eastern Churches. From 1204 to 1261 an imposed union did hold the members of the

---

[8] For a good presentation of the ambiguities of Innocent's statements, see James M. Powell, *Innocent III— Vicar of Christ or Lord of the World?*, 1963.

Eastern Church, or at least some of them, in obedience to Rome, but the violence of the Western Europeans during the crusade sowed among the conquered a lasting hatred which frustrated later efforts at permanent union.

The pope also sought to exert his leadership over the princes of Europe in all spiritually significant affairs. Some of his efforts to bend kings to his will have already been mentioned: his struggle with King John to install Stephen Langton as archbishop of Canterbury and his support of Frederick II as candidate for emperor. He also excommunicated Philip II of France for refusing to live with his queen. Innocent had occasion to reprimand the kings of Aragon, Portugal, Poland, and Norway. Indeed, no prior pope had scrutinized princely behavior with so keen an eye. Nevertheless, his interventions had uneven results, especially with regard to his dearest goal, the establishment of permanent peace among the European princes.

THE FOURTH LATERAN COUNCIL

Trained in canon law, Innocent wanted to bring a new system to Christian belief and government. In 1215 he summoned some fifteen hundred prelates to attend the Fourth Lateran Council. The Lateran Council identified the sacraments as exactly seven and reaffirmed that they are essential to salvation, imposed an obligation of yearly confession and communion on the faithful, and defined the dogma of transsubstantiation, according to which the priest in uttering the words of consecration at mass annihilates the substance of bread and wine and substitutes for them the substance of Christ. Transubstantiation unambiguously affirmed the mass as miracle, and thus conferred a unique dignity and power on the Catholic priesthood. The council also pronounced on a wide variety of disciplinary matters—the qualifications for the priesthood, the nature of priestly education, the

character of monastic life, the veneration of relics, and other devotional exercises. Only the councils of Nicaea, Trent, and perhaps Vatican II have had a greater influence on Catholic life.

THE PAPACY IN THE THIRTEENTH CENTURY

Innocent's successors pursued his goals of ecclesiastical unity, though with only moderate success. Further attempts were made to heal the schism with the Eastern Church. At the Council of Lyons in 1274 representatives of the Eastern patriarch formally submitted to papal authority, but the union soon proved illusory. Innocent's successors also continued the work of codifying Church law. In 1234 Gregory IX published an authoritative collection of decretals (papal letters) to which additions were made in 1298 and 1314. Together with the *Decretum* of Gratian, these collections formed the Body of Canon Law, which in turn made up the finished constitution of the medieval Church.

Papal administration, and especially papal finances, continued to expand during the thirteenth century. Often desperate for funds to carry on their ambitious policies, the popes extracted substantial payments for appointments to office, imposed tithes (a tenth of income) upon the clergy, and sold exemptions and dispensations from the regulations of canon law. By the late thirteenth century the popes were clearly exploiting their spiritual powers for financial profit, and this was to prove a disastrous precedent.

Boniface VIII
By the late thirteenth century the papacy was facing a rising challenge from the princes of Europe, who sought to dominate the churches within their own territories. Both Philip IV of France and Edward I of England had been taxing the clergy through the fiction of asking, and always receiving, gifts, or subventions. In

1296 Pope Boniface VIII forbade all clergy to make grants without papal permission. Such a restriction would have given the pope a powerful if not controlling voice in royal finances, which no king could tolerate. The English simply ignored the order, but Philip retaliated by forbidding all exports of coin from his realm to Rome. Boniface, surprised by the forceful reaction, dropped his demands a year later.

In 1301 Philip arrested for treason a French bishop who happened also to be a papal legate, thus striking directly at the sovereignty of the pope and the immunities of his representatives. Boniface reprimanded Philip for his behavior, but the king responded by circulating defamatory accusations against the pope. Naturally Boniface felt that both his personal character and the papal authority were being threatened. He therefore issued a bull (all solemn papal letters were called bulls because they were closed with a seal, or *bulla*), known from its first two words as *Unam Sanctam*, declaring that Philip must submit to his authority or risk the loss of his immortal soul. In no mood to accept a rebuff, Philip sent one of his principal advisers to Italy, who with the aid of a Roman faction opposed to Boniface broke into the papal palace at Anagni and arrested the pope. The citizens of Anagni rescued Boniface shortly afterward, but he died in Rome only a few months later. The vulnerability of the papacy had been clearly demonstrated.

The succeeding popes capitulated to the French king and even revoked *Unam Sanctam*. Philip's victory was complete when a Frenchman was elected pope in 1305. Clement V never reached Rome, settling in the French-speaking, though imperial, city of Avignon in 1309. For the next sixty-eight years the popes lived within the shadow of the French monarchy.

The medieval papacy hoped to serve as the vocal conscience of Europe. It was aided in this ambition by magnificent theological and legal systems and by a huge administrative apparatus. But the growth of papal power weakened the bishop's ability to maintain the moral discipline of his clergy and people, the result being an increasing measure of local chaos which permitted abuses to grow unchecked. Even the new intellectual rigor of Christian belief carried with it a certain risk for the spiritual life; cold intellectualism or a suffocating legalism might well threaten and dilute authentic piety. The Church has lived for hundreds of years with the achievements and unresolved problems bequeathed to it by the thirteenth century.

IV. THE SUMMER OF MEDIEVAL CULTURE

Whereas the twelfth century was the period of discovery and creation in the cultural growth of the medieval world, the thirteenth century was an age of intellectual synthesis. As the statesmen of Europe tried to unite law and custom in ordered constitutional systems, the cultural leaders tried to bring earlier intellectual traditions into harmony.

THE MEDIEVAL SYNTHESIS

An appreciation of thirteenth-century culture requires an understanding of the ideas and values the period was seeking to combine. The scholastics were trying to reconcile the fundamental assumptions of Aristotelian philosophy with the fundamental attitudes of Christianity, the former asserting that human reason could probe the metaphysical structure of the universe unaided, the latter insisting on the necessity of divine revelation and grace.

In their attempt to reconcile these views medieval intellectuals aimed at nothing less than uniting two historical and cultural experiences, for medieval civilization was itself the product of two quite different epochs. The violence and desperation of the late Roman and early medieval periods had implanted in the medieval mind a deep conviction that man's natural powers were inadequate to control his destiny, that he needed help through grace. The experiences of society after 1000 had, on the other hand, bred a new confidence in human capabilities. Aristotelian philosophy lent intellectual force to what experience seemed to be teaching: that man could attain, through his own efforts, some measure of truth and fulfillment in this present world.

In seeking to reconcile faith and reason, medieval man was trying to extract the common denominator of truth from the vastly different experiences through which he had passed. He wanted to construct an open intellectual system which would give a place to all truth and all values, wherever they were found, however they had been learned. The general nature of this effort at synthesis can be seen in three of the major achievements of the period: the Scholasticism of Thomas Aquinas, the Gothic cathedral, and the *Comedy* of Dante Alighieri.

Thomas Aquinas

The most gifted representative of scholastic philosophy, and the greatest Christian theologian since Augustine, was St. Thomas Aquinas (1225?–1274), whose career well illustrates the character of thirteenth-century intellectual life. At seventeen Thomas entered the new Dominican Order, perhaps attracted by its commitment to scholarship; he studied at Monte Cassino and Naples, and later, as a Dominican, at Cologne and Paris. His most influential teacher was another Dominican, Albertus Magnus, a German who wrote extensively not only on theological matters but on questions of natural science, especially biology. Thomas was no intellectual recluse; he lectured at Paris and traveled widely across Europe, particularly in the business of his order and the Church.

In his short and active life Thomas produced a prodigious amount of writing: commentaries on biblical books and Aristotelian works, short essays on philosophical problems, a lengthy compendium of Christian apologetics, the *Summa contra Gentiles*, which was probably intended for Dominican missionaries working to convert heretics and infidels. However, his most important work was one he did not live to finish. Divided into three divisions on God, Man, and Christ, the *Summa Theologica* was meant to provide a comprehensive introduction to Christian theology and to present a systematic view of the universe which would do justice to all truth, natural and revealed, pagan and Christian.

Thomas brought to his task an extraordinary subtle and perceptive intellect, and his system (not unlike the feudal constitution) rests upon several fundamental, delicate compromises. In regard to faith and reason he taught that both are roads to a single truth. Reason is based ultimately on sense experience. It is a powerful instrument, but insufficient to teach men all that God wishes them to know. Nature is good, and man can achieve some partial, temporary happiness in this life. But nature alone cannot carry man to ultimate fulfillment. Grace is still needed to bring nature to perfection and man to eternal salvation.

In respect to the fundamental structure of the universe, Thomas sought the common ground between two interpretations of reality, inherited from the ancient philosophers and called in the medieval schools realism and nominalism. The realists maintained that universal terms—the common nouns which can be predicated on many individual objects, such as man or stone— refer to "real" entities which exist independently of the mind. Somewhere, in other words, there exists a "manness" or "stoneness" in which individual men or stones somehow participate. These general natures form a hierarchy or chain of being leading up to God.

MAP 9.2: MEDIEVAL UNIVERSITIES

Their critics, the nominalists, said that the universal term or common noun is merely a *nomen* ("name"), a "breath of air," with no existence outside the mind. In the nominalist view, the universe has no knowable structure. It must be viewed as an aggregate of unique and autonomous beings. The philosopher can discern similarities among objects and place them into species and genera, but he cannot be certain that his classifications have a basis in reality.

Thomas, who was technically a moderate realist, argued that both views are correct. Each object in the universe is autonomous and unique but it is also representative of general species or classes. To possess this double dimension of meaning, each object must also be metaphysically a composite of two principles, one of which explains its unity with other objects and the other its individuality.[9] In broadest terms, the principle of unity is "act," meaning the act of being, as it is ultimately in their being that objects resemble one another. The principle of individuation is "potency," which limits act and renders an object unique. Motion or change in the universe is essentially a transition from potency to act. Only God is unlimited, unindividuated Being—"pure act" in Thomas's definition. Only God cannot change, but He ultimately supports all change. In his proofs of God's existence, Thomas argued that instability, imperfection, and change, which we see all around us, point to the existence of an "unmoved mover," a principle of absolute perfection, stability, and power.

The *Summa* shows certain characteristic weaknesses of Scholasticm. Thomas affirmed that natural truth is ultimately grounded in observation, but in fact he observed very little. His critical distinction between act and potency, which he borrowed from Aristotle, was founded not on observation or experimentation. (He admitted these principles were in fact supersensory.) Many later thinkers found his system too speculative, too elaborate. Nonetheless, the *Summa* remains an unquestioned masterpiece of Western theology. It offers comment on an enormous range of theological, philosophical, and ethical problems, and it consistently attracts with its openness, perception, and wisdom.

John Duns Scotus

Thomas's system fell under critical scrutiny already in the generation following his death. Among his early critics the most influential was a Scottish Franciscan, John Duns Scotus (1265?–1308). Drawing inspiration from St. Augustine, Duns Scotus affirmed that faith was logically prior to reason; that is, unless faith had first suggested to reason that spiritual beings—God and angels—could exist, reason would never have arrived at a concept of them. Once the mind accepted the idea of God from faith, it could then prove the necessity for God's existence. To Duns Scotus the proof of God's existence was not based, as with Aquinas, on the perception of change in the universe, for he did not trust the accuracy of sense observation; rather, it derived from an exclusively intellectual analysis of the concept of God as a necessary being. In effect, he was restating in revised form the "ontological proof" for God's existence, first formulated by Anselm of Canterbury (see pp. 260–261). Later, in the seventeenth century, René Descartes, regarded as the founder of modern philosophy, would present still another version of the same argument. It has continued to tease philosophers until the present.

Because of the complexity of his thought, Scotus is traditionally called the "subtle doctor." His followers, who continued the tradition of sometimes unintelligible speculations, were "dunces" to their derisive critics. Scotus marks the transition between the synthetic or constructive period of medieval philosophy and a new period of analysis and criticism, which begins in the fourteenth century.

The Gothic Cathedral

Artists as well as theologians were attempting to present a systematic view of the universe

---

[9] This two-dimensional view of reality is also reflected in Gothic art, in which the statues are at once individuals and yet manifestations of a higher order, and in Dante's *Comedy*, where the figures he encounters on his journey through the other world are both individual personalities and representatives of common human types.

reflective of all truth. The artistic counterpart to the scholastic *Summas* was the Gothic cathedral.

The word "Gothic" was coined in the sixteenth century as an expression of contempt for these supposedly barbarous medieval buildings. In fact, the Goths had disappeared some five hundred years before any Gothic churches were built. As used today, "Gothic" refers to the style of architecture and art which initially developed in the royal lands in France, including Paris and its surroundings, from about 1150. The abbey church of Saint-Denis near Paris, built by the Abbot Suger in 1144, is usually taken as the first authentic example of the Gothic style. The early Gothic churches were almost all urban cathedrals and were characteristically dedicated to the Virgin Mary. In the thirteenth century the Gothic style spread widely through Europe and found special application in the large churches built by the Franciscan and Dominican orders. The growth of cities also led to its expression in secular architecture: town halls, guildhalls, towers, gates, and private houses.

Technically, three engineering devices helped stamp the Gothic style: the broken rather than rounded arch; ribbed vaulting, which concentrated support around the lines of thrust and gave the buildings a visibly delineated skeleton; and the flying buttress, an external support which allowed the walls to be made higher and lighter. The flying buttress also freed sections of the walls from the function of supporting the roof and therefore permitted the use of large areas for windows. Romanesque architects had pioneered all three devices, but the Gothic engineers combined them and used them with unprecedented vigor and boldness.

Innovations were also made in the statues that adorned the buildings. Romanesque sculpture often conveyed great emotion and power but did not reflect the visible world. Sculptors now wanted their works to emulate reality, or

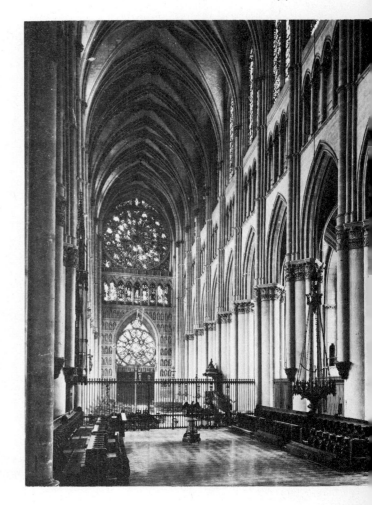

This interior view of the nave of Reims Cathedral shows the ribbed vaulting that was characteristic of Gothic churches. (Photo: ND–Giraudon)

at least its handsomest parts (decorative foliage, for example, was carved with such accuracy that the botanical models can be identified). Their statues were real and usually cheerful people, subtly exerting their own personalities without destroying the harmony of the whole.

The Gothic Spirit

These magnificent churches with their hundreds of statues took decades to construct and decorate, and many were never completed. The builders intended that the churches provide a comprehensive view of the universe and instruction in its sacred history. One principal element of the Gothic aesthetic is a strong sense of order. The naked ribs and buttresses and the intricate vaulting constitute a spectacular geometry that instills in the viewer a vivid impression of intelligence and logical relationships. The churches, reflecting the structure of the universe, taught that God, the master builder, created and still governs the natural world with similar logic.

The most distinctive aspect of the Gothic style is its use of light in a manner unique in the history of architecture. Once within the church, the visitor has entered a realm defined and infused by a warm, colored glow. In Christian worship light is one of the most ancient, common, and versatile symbols. It suggests to the worshiper mystical illumination, spiritual beauty, grace, and divinity itself.

The impressions rendered by the architecture and the stained glass were further developed by the performance of the sacred liturgy. Here music was also enlisted to convey the sense of an intricate and sublime harmony in God's care of the world. Paris in the thirteenth century witnessed a marked development of polyphonic music; the choir masters seem to have sought a musical style which would parallel the complexity and the harmony of the surrounding cathedral. Through architecture,

In contrast to Romanesque sculpture which overflows with great displays of emotion, Gothic sculpture evokes a sense of calm and orderly reality, as can be seen in the jamb figures on the central portal of Chartres Cathedral. (Photo: Marburg—Art Reference Bureau)

sculpture, and music, the believer was encouraged to feel the presence of God, to discern a universe permeated with his wisdom, sanctity, and loving concern.

Dante

Literary output in most vernacular languages grew continuously more abundant during the

In the Gothic style of church building, the roof was supported partly by columns within the building and partly by external flying buttresses which can be seen here at Notre Dame Cathedral in Paris. (Photo: ND—Giraudon)

thirteenth century, except in English, which was retarded in its development by the continued dominance of a French-speaking aristocracy. Of several masterpieces the one that best summarizes the culture of the age is the *Comedy* of Dante Alighieri.

Dante was born in Florence in 1265. Little is known of his education, but he seems to have acquired a broad learning. The *Comedy* is one of the most erudite, and hence most difficult, poems of world literature.

Two experiences in Dante's life profoundly influenced his attitudes and are reflected in his works. In 1274, when he was (as he himself affirms) only nine years old, he fell deeply in love with a young girl named Beatrice. Much mystery surrounds her, but she seems to have been Beatrice Portinari, who later married into a prominent family and died in 1290. Dante could have seen her only rarely; we do not know if she ever returned his love. Still, in his youthful adoration of Beatrice he seems to have attained that sense of harmony and joy which the troubadours considered to be the great reward of lovers. In 1302 an experience of a much different sort shattered his life. For political reasons he was exiled from Florence. He spent the remaining years of his life wandering from city to city, a disillusioned, even bitter man. He died in 1321 and was buried at Ravenna.

The Comedy

Dante composed his masterpiece from 1313 to 1321. He called it a *commedia* in conformity with the classical notion that a happy ending made any story, no matter how serious, a comedy; the adjective "divine" was added to its title only after his death. The poem is divided into three parts, which describe the poet's journey through hell, purgatory, and heaven.

The poem opens with Dante "in the middle of the way of this our life." An aging man, he has grown confused and disillusioned; he is lost in a "dark forest" of doubt, harassed by wild animals, symbols of his own untamed passions. The theme of the poem is essentially Dante's rediscovery of a former sense of harmony and joy. Leading him back to his lost peace are two guides. The first, Vergil, who represents human reason, conducts Dante through hell and then up the seven-storied mountain of purgatory to the earthly paradise, the vanished Eden, at its summit. In hell Dante encounters men who have chosen as their supreme goal in life something other than the love of God—riches, pleasures, fame, or power. Vergil shows Dante that the good life cannot be built upon such selfish choices. Reason, in other words, can enable man to avoid the pitfalls of egoistic, material existence. Reason can accomplish even more than that; for, as embodied by Vergil, it guides Dante through purgatory and shows him how to acquire the natural virtues which are the foundations of the earthly paradise—a full and peaceful earthly existence. In the dignity and power given to Vergil, Dante shares the high regard for human reason characteristic of the thirteenth century. However, reason can take man only so far. To enter heaven Dante needs a new guide—Beatrice herself, representative of supernatural revelation and grace. She takes the poet through the heavenly spheres into the presence of God, "in Whom is our peace." The peace and joy of the heavenly court set the dominant mood at the poem's conclusion, in contrast to the confusion and violence of the dark forest with which it had opened.

Like many literary masterpieces the *Comedy* has several dimensions of meaning. On a personal level it summarizes the experiences of Dante's own life; it affirms that the youthful idealism and joy he had once so easily found were not proved false by age and bitter exile. The poem further reflects the great cultural issues that challenged his contemporaries—the relations between reason and faith, nature and grace, human power and the divine will. Dante, like Aquinas, was trying to combine two opposed views of man and his abilities to shape his own destiny. One, rooted in the very optimism of the twelfth and thirteenth centuries and in the more distant classical heritage, affirmed that man was the master of himself and the world. The other, grounded in the Judeo-Christian tradition, saw him, fundamentally, as a lost child in a vale of tears. Both views had helped support human life and were therefore worth preserving. Dante's majestic panorama summarizes not only medieval man's vision of the universe but also his estimation of what it meant to live a truly wise, truly happy, and truly human life.

 *In the thirteenth century, medieval civilization attained a new stability, and medieval institutions functioned with considerable success. Large-scale manufacture, long-range commercial exchanges, and sophisticated business practices gave the economy a distinctly capitalistic aura. In political life feudal governments consolidated and clarified their constitutional procedures, and parliaments and representative assemblies came to play a recognized role in the processes of government. Confronted with heresies that threatened its unity and dominance, the Church responded in part with crusades and the Inquisition, ultimately to its own detriment. At the same time orthodox religion enjoyed an authentic spiritual renewal, of which Francis of Assisi was the chief inspiration. The papacy energetically sought to lead the Western princes as their guide and conscience, but secular entanglements and fiscal problems threatened and gradually diluted its moral authority.*

In cultural life this was a period not so much of new creations as of reordering and synthesis. The masterpieces of the age aimed at bringing together all parts of the medieval heritage into an ordered whole which would offer men a comprehensive understanding of the universe and a wise formula for living.

Medieval society in the thirteenth century seemed close to resolving its principal problems, whether economic, political, or cultural. In fact, however, the relative prosperity and peace, the institutional stability and intellectual synthesis were not to survive much beyond the year 1300. In the fourteenth century a new era of turmoil dawned for the medieval world. The closing Middle Ages was a period of spectacular disasters, but also of profound changes. These changes greatly altered the character of the civilizations in both Eastern and Western Europe.

RECOMMENDED READING

Sources

Alighieri, Dante. *The Divine Comedy.* Louis Biancolli (tr.). 1966.

Aquinas, Thomas. *Basic Writings.* Anton C. Pegis (ed.). 1945.

*Brown, Raphael (ed. and tr.). *The Little Flowers of St. Francis.* 1971. Legends collected in the early fourteenth century exemplifying the style of Franciscan piety.

De Joinville, Jean. *The Life of St. Louis.* René Hague (tr.). 1955.

Studies

Bisson, Thomas. *Assemblies and Representation in Languedoc in the Thirteenth Century.* 1964. A study of the origins of representation in southern France.

Boase, T. S. R. *Boniface VIII.* 1933.

*Copleston, Frederick. *Aquinas.* 1955.

Gilson, Etienne. *Dante and Philosophy.* David Moore (tr.).

Kantorowicz, Ernest H. *Frederick II.* E. O. Lorimer (tr.). 1957.

Mundy, John H. *Europe in the High Middle Ages.* 1973. A recent general survey.

*Panofsky, Erwin. *Gothic Architecture and Scholasticism.* 1966. Examines the parallels between two great cultural monuments of the thirteenth century.

Powicke, F. M. *The Thirteenth Century, 1216–1307.* 1953. Basic political survey of English events.

Vacandard, E. *The Inquisition.* 1924.

*Von Simson, Otto. *The Gothic Cathedral: Origins of Gothic Architecture and the Medieval Concept of Order.* 1962. Interprets Gothic style primarily in terms of its use of light.

* Available in paperback.

TEN

THE CRUSADES
AND EASTERN EUROPE

The peoples of Western Europe had remained fairly isolated from the East during the Early Middle Ages, a factor that added considerably to their economic and cultural backwardness. This isolation began to break down after the year 1000. Western pilgrims and crusaders in large numbers visited the Christian holy places in the East and for some two centuries maintained in the Latin Kingdom of Jerusalem a colony in Palestine. Western merchants established contact with the principal ports of the eastern Mediterranean and Black seas. A vigorous trade developed across the waters of the Mediterranean, and Westerners once more came to enjoy the spices and other products of the East. In the thirteenth century, some missionaries and merchants penetrated into Central Asia, and a few traveled as far as China. This greatly enlarged the geographic horizons of Europeans and made them aware that rich and brilliant civilizations existed beyond their borders. Westerners entered into intense military competition, close trade relations, and fruitful cultural exchanges with their Eastern neighbors. An appreciation of Western history therefore requires a knowledge of these Eastern peoples and the results of the increasing contact with them.

The East after the year 1000 was itself in a state of flux. The three states which dominated the region in the Early Middle Ages—the Byzantine Empire, the Arab Caliphate, and Kievan Rus—were all in manifest decline. Turkish peoples—first the Seljuks and then the Ottomans—built states which, in large part, claimed the territorial heritage of both Byzantium and the caliphate. By the fifteenth century the Ottoman Empire had come to dominate the land bridge between Europe and Asia and presented the West with a formidable military challenge. This powerful and aggressive empire gave Europeans strong incentive for searching out new trade routes around Ottoman territories to the more distant East.

The spiritual and cultural heritage of both Byzantium and Kievan Rus largely passed to a new Russian state which had its capital at Moscow and was the direct ancestor of the modern Russian Empire and the Soviet Union. Like Byzantium before it, Moscovite Russia assumed the function of guarding the eastern frontiers of Christian Europe.

The contacts, the rivalries, the economic and cultural exchanges begun or restored in the second half of the Middle Ages have continued to play a major role in the history of the peoples in both these areas of the world.

1. THE CRUSADES

In the eleventh century the Western peoples launched a series of armed expeditions to the East in an effort to free the Holy Land from Islamic rule. These expeditions are traditionally known as the crusades. Not long ago it was fashionable to consider the crusades a central event in medieval history that stimulated trade, encouraged the growth of towns, and contributed to the establishment of a stable political order in the West. More recently, many historians have alleged that the campaigns in the East were costly failures, that they worsened relations not only with the Muslims but with Eastern Christians, and that the crusading enthusiasm in Europe all too frequently found an outlet in riots and pogroms directed against those most accessible infidels, the Jews.[1]

Whatever their net effect, the crusades manifest more dramatically than any other event the spirit of Western society in the eleventh and twelfth centuries—its energy, brash self-confidence, compelling faith, and frequent bigotry. At the same time that they helped acquaint the Western peoples with ideas and techniques of civilizations more sophisticated than their own, the crusades were an initial phase in the expansion of the West—the massive exportation of European men and skills beyond the confines of their narrow continent, a movement which has since influenced civilizations in every part of the world.

ORIGINS

The origins of the crusades must be sought in a double set of circumstances: the social and religious movements in the West and the political situations in the East. In the Christian West a favorite form of religious exercise was the pilgrimage, a personal visit to a place made holy through the lives of Christ or his saints or sanctified by the presence of a sacred relic. Common in the West since the fourth century, pilgrimages gained in popularity during the eleventh century as Europe experienced religious revival and reform. Bands of pilgrims, sometimes numbering in the thousands, set forth to visit the places sacred to their religion, and of these Palestine was the most holy.

---

[1] One of the leading modern historians of the crusading movement, Sir Steven Runciman, concludes his three-volume study with the following strong condemnation: "The Holy War itself was nothing more than a long act of intolerance in the name of God, which is the sin against the Holy Ghost." *A History of the Crusades,* vol. 3, 1954, p. 480.

Inevitably, this pilgrim traffic was jeopardized by the Seljuk Turks, Muslim nomads who in the eleventh century had overrun most of the Middle East. It does not appear that the Seljuks consciously sought to prevent the pilgrims from reaching Palestine, but they did impose numerous taxes and tolls upon them, and many Christians became incensed at the domination of the holy places of Palestine by a strong, aggressive Islamic power.

Perhaps still more disturbing was the prospect that the Christian empire of Byzantium would also be overrun. The Seljuks had crushed a Byzantine army at the Battle of Manzikert in 1071, and the road to Constantinople seemed wide open. The fall of Byzantium would remove the traditional barrier to Islamic advance to the West and would be a major disaster to the Christian world. In 1095 a delegation from the emperor of Byzantium requested the help of Pope Urban II, who resolved to appeal to the Western knights and princes to go to the aid of their fellow Christians in the East. Social and religious conditions in Europe helped assure that Urban's summons would evoke a powerful response.

THE MOTIVES OF THE CRUSADERS

The crusades were viewed by those who participated in them primarily as acts of religious devotion. Even before Urban made his appeal, the idea had gained currency in the West that God would reward those who fought in a good cause; that is, that wars could be holy. The crusaders also shared the conviction manifest in the movement for Church reform that the good man ought not simply to endure the evils of the world but should attempt to correct them. This active, confident spirit is in obvious contrast to the resignation to evil and the withdrawal from the world recommended by most Christian writers of the Early Middle Ages.

Social and economic motivations also contributed to these holy enterprises. The age of mass pilgrimages and crusades, from about 1050 to 1250, corresponds with the period in medieval history in which the European population was growing most rapidly. The crusades may be considered one further example of the expanding Western frontier, similar in motivation and character to the Spanish *Reconquista* or the German push to the east. Of course, the crusades differed in at least one significant way from these other ventures. They were almost exclusively military expeditions of Europe's warrior classes; peasants did not settle in Palestine in significant numbers, as they did in the lands of Eastern Europe or in the Iberian Peninsula.

The knights of Europe were particularly sensitive to the pressures created by an expanding population, especially with regard to younger sons, many of whom could not hope to receive from their parents lands sufficient for their support. "This land which you inhabit," Pope Urban is reported to have told the knights of France in 1095, "is too narrow for your large population; nor does it abound in wealth; and it provides hardly enough food for those who farm it. This is the reason that you murder and consume one another." Moreover, the knights were educated for war, and in war they placed their chief hope for wealth, honor, and social advance. The growth of the feudal principalities, the efforts of the Church to restrict fighting, and the slow pacification of European society which these policies were bringing threatened to leave the knights poor, unhonored, and unemployed. "You should shudder, brethren," Urban is also reported to have told the knights, "you should shudder at perpetrating violence against Christians; it is less wicked to turn your sword against Muslims. . . . The possessions of the enemy will also fall to you, since you will claim their treasures as plunder." War against the infidel thus offered constructive employment for Europe's surplus and troublesome population of knights. In the following century St. Bernard of Clairvaux, whose preaching inspired thousands to join the Second Crusade, frankly affirmed that all but a few crusaders were "criminals and sinners, ravishers and the sacrilegious, murderers, perjurers, and adulterers." To have them crusading in the East therefore conferred a double benefit. As Bernard remarked, "Their departure makes their own people happy, and their arrival cheers those whom they are hastening to help. They aid both groups, not only by protecting the one but also by not oppressing the other." The crusades, in sum, were in considerable degree a violent means of draining the violence from medieval life.

THE FIRST CRUSADE

In 1095, before a council assembled at Clermont in southern France, Pope Urban II urged the knights to go to the East to aid their endangered Christian brothers and to free the Holy Land from its allegedly blasphemous masters.[2] His sermon was intended for the upper classes, but its plea had sensational results at all levels of Western society. In northern France and the Rhineland influential preachers were soon rousing the people and organizing movements which historians now call the Popular Crusade. Bands

---

[2] The exact circumstances of Urban's famous sermon remain obscure. He probably was replying to a plea for help from Emperor Alexius of Byzantium; a Greek embassy, bearing such a plea, reached him at Piacenza earlier in 1095. The chroniclers give us four versions of the sermon, but it is almost impossible to determine which, if any, have preserved Urban's own words. At any rate, certainly Alexius wanted from the West mercenary soldiers, not princes bent on establishing their own principalities in the East. The sources dealing with the summoning of the First Crusade have been conveniently gathered and translated by Peter Charanis, "Byzantium and the West," in Kenneth M. Setton and Henry R. Winkler (eds.), *Great Problems in European Civilization*, 1966, pp. 93–110.

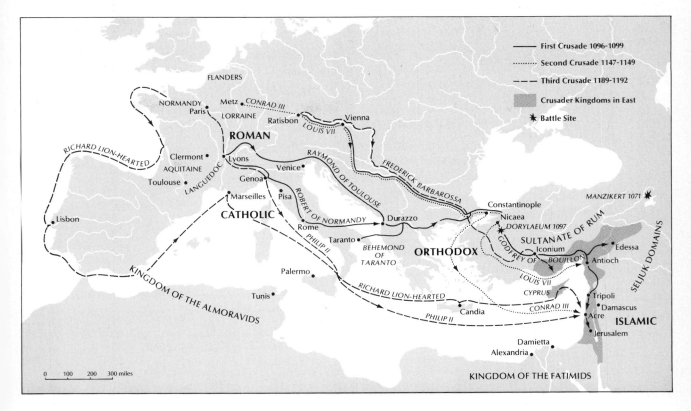

MAP 10.1: THE CRUSADES

of peasants and the poor set out for the East, miserably equipped and lacking competent leaders. They marched down the Rhine valley, through Hungary and Bulgaria, to Constantinople. Emperor Alexius of Byzantium, who could only have been shocked at the sight of this hapless army, gave them transport across the Bosporus. The Turks at once cut them to pieces.

Far better organized was the official First Crusade, which was led by nobles: Robert of Normandy, son of William the Conqueror, headed a northern French army; Godfrey of Bouillon, his brother Baldwin, and Robert of Flanders commanded an army of Lotharingians and Flemings; Raymond of Toulouse led the men of Languedoc; and Bohemond of Taranto and his brother Tancred marshaled the Normans of southern Italy. These four armies

moved by various overland and sea routes to Constantinople (see Map 10.1), arriving there in 1096 and 1097.

Although the leaders of the First Crusade had intended to conquer lands in the East in their own name, Emperor Alexius demanded from them an oath of fealty in exchange for his provisioning the armies as they marched to Palestine. Grudgingly, they agreed, promising to regard the emperor as the overlord of the lands they might reconquer from the Turks. Subsequently, both the emperor and the Western leaders accused each other of violating the terms of the oath. The failure of the crusaders and the Byzantines to find a firm basis for cooperating ultimately weakened, although it did not defeat, the enterprise.

In 1097 the crusaders entered the Seljuk Sultanate of Rum, achieving their first major

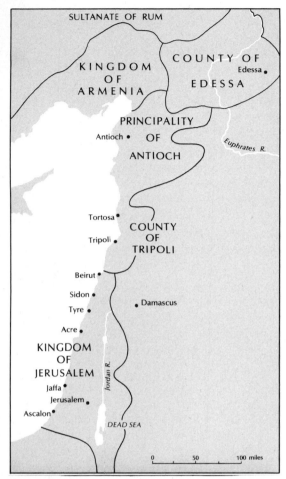

**MAP 10.2: CRUSADER KINGDOMS
12TH CENTURY**

joint victory at Dorylaeum. Baldwin, the brother of Godfrey of Bouillon, then separated his troops from the main body and conquered Edessa, where he established the first crusader state in the East.

The decisive victory of the First Crusade came in the battle for the port city of Antioch. After that, the road to Jerusalem was open before the crusaders. On July 15, 1099, they stormed the Holy City and pitilessly slaughtered the entire infidel population.

Besides a high level of organizational skill and their own considerable daring, the Westerners had a critical advantage in the tumultuous political situation in the East. The Seljuk Turks, newly risen to power, had had little opportunity to consolidate their rule and were contending with the Fatimids, the ruling dynasty of Egypt, over the possession of Palestine. In addition, the ancient schisms among the the Islamic religious sects continued to divide and weaken the community. The inability of Muslims to present a united front against the crusaders was probably the decisive factor in the final success of the First Crusade.

THE KINGDOM OF JERUSALEM

The crusaders now had the problem of organizing a government for their conquered territories. They chose as ruler Godfrey of Bouillon, but death cut short his reign in 1100, and his younger brother Baldwin, the conqueror of Edessa, succeeded him.

Baldwin set out to strengthen his realm through the application of feudal concepts and institutions. He retained a direct dominion over Jerusalem and its surroundings, including a stretch of coast extending from Gaza to Beirut. To the north three fiefs, the County of Tripoli, the Principality of Antioch, and the County of Edessa, were made subject to his suzerainty (see Map 10.2). Although King Baldwin and his successors were able to exert a respectable measure of authority over all these lands, profound weaknesses undermined the security of their hold. For one thing, the kings were never able to push their frontiers to an easily defensible, strategic border, such as the Lebanese Mountains. Furthermore, the administration remained critically dependent upon a constant influx of men and money from the European homeland. Many knights and pilgrims came, but relatively few stayed as permanent settlers. The Westerners constituted a foreign aristocracy, small in number and set

super me transierunt.

In die mandauit dominus miseri

cordiam suam: z nocte canticum eius.

Apud me oracio deo uite mee: di

cam deo susceptor meus es.

over a people of largely different faith, culture, and sympathies. The wonder is not that the crusader states ultimately succumbed, but that some of their outposts could have survived on the mainland of Asia Minor for nearly two centuries.

THE LATER CRUSADES

Although historians have traditionally assigned numbers to the later crusades, these expeditions were merely momentary swells in the steady current of Western men and treasures to and from the Middle East. The recapture of the city of Edessa by the Muslims in 1144 gave rise to the Second Crusade (1147–1149). Two

This manuscript rendering of two perfect knights jousting is thought to be a portrayal of Richard the Lion-Hearted and Saladin. (Photo: British Museum)

armies, led by King Louis VII of France and Emperor Conrad III of Germany, set out to capture Damascus to give the Kingdom of Jerusalem a more defensible frontier. However, they were soon forced to retreat ignominiously before superior Muslim forces.

The capture of Jerusalem by the Muslim chief Saladin evoked the Third Crusade (1189–1192), which was the climax of the crusading movement and its greatest disappointment. Emperor Frederick Barbarossa and kings Philip

II of France and Richard I, the Lion-Hearted, of England all marched to the East. (Frederick drowned while crossing through Asia Minor and most of his forces turned back.) Although the crusaders captured Acre, the Third Crusade ended in a stalemate. The Kingdom of Jerusalem remained limited to a narrow strip of the coast from Acre to Jaffa, but unarmed Christian pilgrims were given the right to visit Jerusalem. These were paltry fruits from so grand an effort.

In the thirteenth century the crusades clearly lost their appeal to Western knights. The population expansion in Europe, which had helped lend strength to the earlier crusades, was already leveling off. Moreover, many Europeans were shocked when the popes tried to direct crusades against the Albigensian heretics in southern France and against political enemies such as Frederick II of Hohenstaufen. With dwindling support from the West, the Christians in 1291 lost Acre, their last outpost on the Asiatic mainland. Repeatedly during the Late Middle Ages the popes attempted to organize crusades; many knights and princes vowed to participate; some traveled to the East, but none gained a major victory.

RESULTS OF THE CRUSADES

In terms of their principal professed goal the crusaders gained a partial success but not a permanent one: they held Jerusalem for nearly a century and maintained outposts on the Palestinian coast for nearly two centuries. Meanwhile, Christian pilgrims in large numbers were able to visit the holy places in Palestine in moderate safety. Even after the loss of Acre the Westerners continued to hold Eastern possessions acquired during the early crusades. When the Ottoman Turks, successors to the Seljuks, finally seized these last remnants of the crusaders' conquests, the Western peoples had already found new routes to the Far East and

were in the midst of the "Atlantic revolution," which gave them a new position in the world that the Turks did not challenge. The crusades enhanced the security of the West by slowing the Turkish advance across the Mediterranean Sea and into Europe.

Militarily, the crusades exerted a powerful influence upon the arts of war. After their initial invasions the crusaders waged a largely defensive war, and they became particularly skilled in the art of constructing castles. The numerous remains of crusader castles still found in nearly all the Eastern lands reflect this fact in such features as the overhanging tower parapets from which oil or missiles could be rained down on attackers and the angular castle entranceways that prevented the enemy from shooting directly at the gates. Islamic castles also show a similar evolution toward a more advanced military design.

The foes continually copied each other, and the Ottoman Turks in particular adopted many Western technical skills. By the fifteenth century the Ottomans, originally landlocked nomads, began to build a fleet and challenge Western maritime supremacy in the eastern Mediterranean Sea. They also learned from Western technicians the new arts of firearms, specifically cannons, without which they probably could not have conquered their vast empire.

The crusades naturally presented enormous, unprecedented problems of financing and logistical support, and therefore exerted a major stimulus upon the growth of financial and governmental institutions in the West. In the early crusades each knight or soldier had largely looked to his own support. He brought money with him (often acquired by selling or mortgaging his estates) and purchased supplies from the natives of the lands through which he marched. He replenished his funds through booty or gifts from his lord and eventually through estates granted him in Palestine. But

The Krak-des-Chevaliers in Syria is a castle formerly used by crusaders as a bastion of defense.
This aerial view reveals the extended parapets and
angular entranceways, both innovative features
of fortification developed during the crusades.
(Photo: Aerofilms Limited)

as the crusader wars became largely defensive
in character, the opportunity for booty declined and the armies could no longer live off
the land; support had to come primarily from
Europe, thus requiring permanent institutional
arrangements by which a constant flow of
money (and men) could be directed from
Europe into Palestine.

Traditional sources of revenue were inadequate, so both the popes and the princes began
to impose direct taxes upon their lands and subjects. In 1188, for example, the pope authorized, and the princes collected, the so-called
Saladin tithe, a direct tax of 10 percent imposed
on all clerical and lay revenues and destined to
finance the Third Crusade. (Previously, Euro-

pean governments had made little use of direct
taxes because they were difficult to assess and
collect.) The imposition of the Saladin tithe
and subsequent direct taxes required that institutional methods be devised for assessment,
collecting the moneys, and transferring the
funds to where they were needed. The crusades, in other words, helped the governments
of the West come of age in a fiscal sense.

One other financial recourse adopted by the papacy had great importance for the future. The popes allowed those Europeans who were too old or too weak to participate in the crusades to gain the spiritual benefits of crusading through monetary contributions, in return for which they were promised an indulgence, that is, a remission of punishment due for their sins. This practice was subsequently to draw the criticism of reformers, and it was the immediate cause of Martin Luther's split with the Roman Church in 1517.

MILITARY-RELIGIOUS ORDERS

Soon after the First Crusade a new kind of institution appeared that was founded to offer armed escorts and safe lodgings to pilgrims to Palestine but eventually assumed a major role in the task of supplying the newly acquired Eastern lands. This was the military-religious order, which combined the dedication, discipline, and organizational experience of monasticism with the military purposes of the crusade. The first of three great orders to emerge from the crusades was the Knights of the Temple, or Templars, founded sometime before 1120 by a group of French knights. The knights took the three monastic vows of poverty, chastity, and obedience and, like monks, lived together in their own convents, or communities. The Templars assumed a principal role in the maintenance of safe routes between Europe and the crusader states and in the defense of the Kingdom of Jerusalem. The order also transported and guarded moneys in support of the Eastern war, and thus became the most important banking institution of the age until its suppression by the pope in 1312.

The Knights of the Hospital of St. John of Jerusalem, or the Hospitalers, founded about 1130, enjoyed an even longer history. Never as numerous or as wealthy as the Templars, they still made a major contribution to the defense of the Kingdom of Jerusalem. With the fall of Acre the knights moved their headquarters to Cyprus, then to Rhodes, and finally to Malta. As the Knights of Malta, they ruled the island until 1798. This "sovereign order" of the Knights of Malta survives today as an exclusively philanthropic confraternity and is a principal arm of papal charities throughout the world.

About 1190, German pilgrims organized the Teutonic Knights for the defense of the roads to Palestine. These knights later transferred their headquarters first to Venice, then to Transylvania (in modern Rumania), and finally, in 1229, to Prussia, where they became the armed vanguard of the German eastward expansion and conquered for themselves an extensive domain along the shores of the Baltic Sea. In 1525 the last grand master, Albert of Hohenzollern, adopted Lutheranism and secularized the order and its territories. The German state of Brandenburg-Prussia eventually absorbed the lands, and perhaps something of the militant spirit, of these crusading knights. At all events, the long history of these orders illustrates how organizational and military skills first acquired in the crusading movement continued to affect European life over the subsequent centuries.

ECONOMY

Historians still cannot draw up an exact balance sheet that registers accurately the economic gains and losses of these holy expeditions. Certainly the crusades were costly in blood and treasure. To support its armies Europe exported large quantities of precious metals; the spoils of war and commercial profits undoubtedly brought some moneys back, but probably not enough to recoup the losses. Nevertheless, the crusades seem to have had a powerful and beneficial impact on the European economy, principally by forcing into circulation moneys and treasures which had hitherto been hoarded in the West. Although there are no exact figures, both the volume of money and the speed of its circulation in Europe seem to have increased dramatically during this period. The new abundance of money stimulated commercial exchange and business investments and helped revive the Western economy, though in this respect the crusades were less significant than such factors as population growth and the settlement of new lands within Europe.

The crusades also enlivened trade with the East. After the First Crusade most of the large Western armies went to Palestine by water, creating a lucrative business for the maritime cities of the Mediterranean Sea, especially in Italy. The Italians poured much of their profits from transporting and provisioning crusaders into commercial enterprises and established merchant colonies in many Eastern ports. Moreover, the crusades greatly strengthened the market for Eastern condiments in Europe. Knights and other pilgrims who had become familiar with sugar, spices, and similar products in the East continued to want them upon returning home, and they introduced them to their neighbors.

The Western demand for spices promoted commerce not only on the Mediterranean Sea but between the Middle East and East Asia. Furthermore, it had an impact that went beyond the narrowly commercial. In the Late Middle Ages political disruptions in Central Asia and the high taxes imposed by the Turks and Egyptians hampered trade with the East, but the call for Eastern products continued to be strong within Europe. This situation assured rich rewards to the navigators and nations who discovered surer, cheaper ways to import spices and other Eastern commodities, and thus provided a direct incentive for the geographic explorations and discoveries which introduce the modern epoch.

In familiarizing Europeans with many new products, the crusades helped raise the standard of living in the West, and this in turn intensified the pace of economic activity. From the eleventh century on, Europeans seem to have worked harder, partially perhaps to gain for themselves some of the products and the amenities of life they had observed in the East. Discoveries overseas in the sixteenth and seventeenth centuries seem to have influenced Europe in a similar fashion. New commodities altered the popular appreciation of what was essential for a good life and prompted Europeans to work more energetically to satisfy their newly raised expectations.

RELIGION AND LEARNING

As acts of piety the crusades inevitably affected the organization and practice of religion, although it is all but impossible to distinguish their impact from that of many other forces at work in the West. Their initial success added to the prestige of the popes who sponsored them, just as their subsequent failures undermined faith in papal leadership. Ecclesiastical finances and even canon law were influenced, as the Church sought to extend economic support and legal protection to both the crusaders and the families they left behind.

It is difficult to assess exactly the importance of the crusades to the intellectual life of Europe. In one area of knowledge, geography, they did make important contributions. Starting from the crusader principalities in the East, first missionaries, then merchants penetrated deep into Central Asia, and by the early thirteenth century reached China. Their reports, especially the memoirs of the Venetian Marco Polo at the close of the thirteenth century, gave Europe abundant information about East Asia, and helped inspire Western navigators to seek new ways to penetrate beyond Islamic lands.

In other fields of knowledge the crusades seem to have brought little enlightenment. Most crusaders were rough warriors who had little interest in the subtleties of Islamic learning. However, the failure of these warriors to absorb new ideas from foreign cultures does not fully measure the cultural debt which the medieval West owes to Islam. Particularly through contacts in Spain and Sicily, Westerners learned new skills (the making of paper, perhaps the use of the compass) and new ideas which influenced the development of courtly love and scientific, philosophical, and religious thought in Europe. But it may also be true that the crusades in fomenting hatred against the infidel made Europeans less receptive to foreign ideas.

In the intellectual field as in all others, then, the crusades did not radically alter the course of medieval history, either in Christian or Islamic societies, but they did powerfully reinforce existing tendencies and accelerate the pace of change on almost every level of life. Through the crusades Europeans learned about the geography of distant lands, became highly motivated to establish permanent, profitable contact with them, and acquired some experience in the conquest and administration of overseas territories. Appropriately, the crusades may be regarded as the initial chapter in the expansion of Europe, which was to be renewed and carried forward even more vigorously in the early modern period.

II. BYZANTIUM AND THE ASCENDANCY OF THE OTTOMAN EMPIRE

After the disaster at Manzikert in 1071, the Byzantine Empire was able to survive until the middle fifteenth century, but it constituted a shrinking enclave around Constantinople and could no longer exercise a strong regional leadership. Nor could it halt the expansion of the Ottoman Turks, who by the early sixteenth century became the unquestioned masters of southeast Europe and the Middle East.

THE PASSING OF EAST ROME

The beginning of the thirteenth century saw the launching of the Fourth Crusade and, unexpectedly, the subsequent fragmenting of the Byzantine Empire. The expedition was first planned as a campaign against Egypt, but the Venetian Doge Enrico Dandolo bargained the short-funded crusaders into capturing, in return for passage east, the Christian city of Zara in Dalmatia, which was opposing Venice in the Adriatic Sea. Then Alexius IV, a pretender to the Byzantine throne, hired the crusaders to seize Constantinople in return for money, military help in the Egyptian campaign, and the reunion of the Eastern and Western Churches. The crusaders restored Alexius, but he could not honor his promises. By way of compensation, the crusaders stormed and looted Constantinople in 1204. They then divided the Byzantine Empire among themselves.

A Flemish nobleman assumed the office of emperor, although he ruled directly only a small parcel of territory surrounding Constantinople. The Venetians gained three-eighths of all Byzantine possessions; this acquisition marks the foundation of the Venetian colonial empire, portions of which were retained until the seventeenth century. Byzantine refugees from Constantinople set up an empire in exile, with its capital at Nicaea in Asia Minor. In 1261 the emperor of Nicaea, Michael III Paleologus, recaptured Constantinople, but neither he nor his successors could restore the shattered unity of the old Byzantine Empire.

The decline of the Byzantine Empire allowed the hitherto subject Balkan peoples to build their own independent kingdoms and to aspire to a position of dominance in the area. First the Bulgarians in the thirteenth century, and then the Serbs in the fourteenth, created large Balkan empires. At the height of their powers these empires seemed destined to absorb the remnants of the Byzantine Empire, but by the fourteenth century it was the Ottoman Turks who presented the greatest menace to Byzantium.

THE FALL OF CONSTANTINOPLE

Turkish communities and peoples had been assuming a large military and political role in the Middle East since the late tenth century. The Seljuk Turks, who had nearly overwhelmed the Byzantine Empire with their victory at Manzikert in 1071, established the Sultanate of Rum, which dominated western Asia Minor for the next century and a half. This sultanate survived the attacks of the Western crusaders but was defeated by the far more formidable invasion of an Asiatic people, the Mongols, in the thirteenth century. The Ottoman Turks followed the Mongol invasions and settled in the area of the Sultanate of Rum. They established themselves at Gallipoli on the European side of the Straits in 1354, and within a few years their possessions entirely surrounded Byzantine territory.

The Byzantine emperors tried desperately but unsuccessfully to gain military help from the West. In 1439 Emperor John VII accepted reunion with Rome, largely on Roman terms, in return for aid, but he had no power to impose his policy of reuniting the churches upon his people; in fact many Eastern Christians preferred Turkish rule to submission to the hated Westerners.

The Ottomans were unable to mount a major campaign against Constantinople until 1453, in the reign of the Sultan Mohammed II, the Conqueror, when they attacked the city by land and water. Constantinople fell after a heroic resistance; Emperor Constantine XIII, whose imperial lineage stretched back more than fourteen hundred years to Augustus Caesar, died in this final agony of the Byzantine Empire.

The fall of Constantinople changed very little in military or economic terms. The Byzantine Empire had not been an effective barrier to Ottoman expansion for years, and Constanti-

Mohammed II, the Conqueror, here represented in a contemporary painting attributed to the Venetian artist Gentile Bellini, took Constantinople in 1453 and was one of the principal founders of the Ottoman Empire. (Photo: The Granger Collection)

nople had dwindled commercially as well as politically. The shift to Turkish dominion did not, as was once believed, substantially affect the flow of trade between the East and West. Nor was the exodus of Byzantine scholars and manuscripts into Italy that stimulated a revival of the Greek language in the West provoked by the Turkish conquest of the city. Scholars from the East, recognizing the decline and seemingly inevitable fall of the Byzantine Empire, had been emigrating to Italy since the late fourteenth century; the revival of Greek letters was well under way in the West by 1453.

The impact of the fall was largely psychological; although hardly unexpected, it shocked the Christian world. The pope sought to launch a new crusade and received from the Western princes the usual promises but no armies. Venice waged a protracted and inconclusive war against the Turks (1463–1479). Perhaps most important, the collapse of the Byzantine Empire gave further incentive to the search for new ways to East Asia, for new contacts with the lands beyond the Islamic territories of the eastern Mediterranean.

Finally, the fall did have great symbolic importance for contemporaries and perhaps even more for later historians. In selecting Byzantium as his capital in 324 Constantine had simultaneously founded a Christian Roman empire which could be considered the first authentically medieval state. For more than a thousand years this Christian Roman empire played a major political and cultural role in the history of both Eastern and Western peoples. To many historians the years of its existence mark the span of the Middle Ages, and its passing symbolizes the end of an era.

EXPANSION OF THE OTTOMAN EMPIRE

The Ottomans took their name from Osman, or Othman (1299–1326), who founded a dynasty of sultans that survived for six centuries.[3] Under Mohammed II, who from the start of his reign committed his government to a policy of conquest, the Ottomans entered upon a century of expansion. After the fall of Constantinople, which became his capital under the name of Istanbul, Mohammed subjugated Morea, Serbia, Bosnia, and parts of Herzegovina. He drove the Genoese from their Black Sea colonies, forced the Khan of the Crimea to become his vassal, and fought a lengthy naval war with the Venetians. At his death the Ottomans were

a power on land and sea, and the Black Sea had become a Turkish lake.

Early in the following century Turkish domination was extended over the heart of the Arab lands through the conquest of Syria, Egypt, and the western coast of the Arabian Peninsula. (The Arabs did not again enjoy autonomy until the twentieth century.) With the conquest of the sacred cities of Mecca and Medina the sultan assumed the title of caliph, "successor of the Prophet," claiming to be Islam's supreme religious head as well as its mightiest sword.

The Ottoman Empire was brought to its height of power by Suleiman II, the Magnificent (1520–1566), who extended the empire in both the West and the East. In 1521 he took the citadel of Belgrade, which had hitherto blocked Turkish advance up the Balkan Peninsula toward Hungary, and the next year forced the Knights of St. John, after a six-month siege, to surrender the island of Rhodes, a loss that was a crippling blow to Western naval strength in the eastern Mediterranean.

Suleiman achieved his greatest victory by annihilating the kingdom of Hungary in 1526. Then he launched his most ambitious campaign, directed against Austria, the Christian state which now assumed chief responsibility for defending the Western frontiers. However, this effort, the high-water mark of Ottoman expansion into Europe, failed, and the frustrated Suleiman returned home in 1529, turning his attention toward the East. His armies overran Mesopotamia and completed the conquest of southern Arabia. The Ottoman Empire, which now included southeastern Europe, the Middle East, Egypt, and Arabia (see Map 10.3), then entered a period of stability.

Suleiman brought his empire fully into the diplomatic as well as the military struggles of Europe, taking shrewd advantage of the rivalries that existed there. He hated Charles V, who as Holy Roman Emperor similarly pretended to rule the world, and in 1525 he joined

---

[3] For a more detailed treatment of the remarkable state and civilization of the Ottomans see Norman Itzkowitz, *Ottoman Empire and Islamic Tradition*, 1972.

In this woodcut by Peter Coeck van Aelst (1553), the sultan Suleiman is shown riding through the ruins of the hippodrome (stadium) of the Byzantine capital, Constantinople. (Photo: The Granger Collection)

Francis I of France in an alliance directed against Charles, later negotiating a commercial treaty that further cemented cooperation between France and the Ottoman Empire. Through his alliance with France, Suleiman confronted Charles V with the possibility of a war on two fronts and prevented the formation of a common Christian crusade against himself, which the popes were ceaselessly advocating. Indirectly, by weakening Charles, Suleiman contributed to the success of the Reformation, since the Holy Roman Emperor, threatened from both East and West, was unable to take effective action against Martin Luther and the German Protestant princes.

Ottoman Institutions

The Ottomans had expanded a small, landlocked community in western Asia Minor into a great empire. Several advantages account for this achievement, one of them being their geographic position. Set on the frontier between the Islamic and Christian worlds, the Ottomans could claim to be the chief warriors

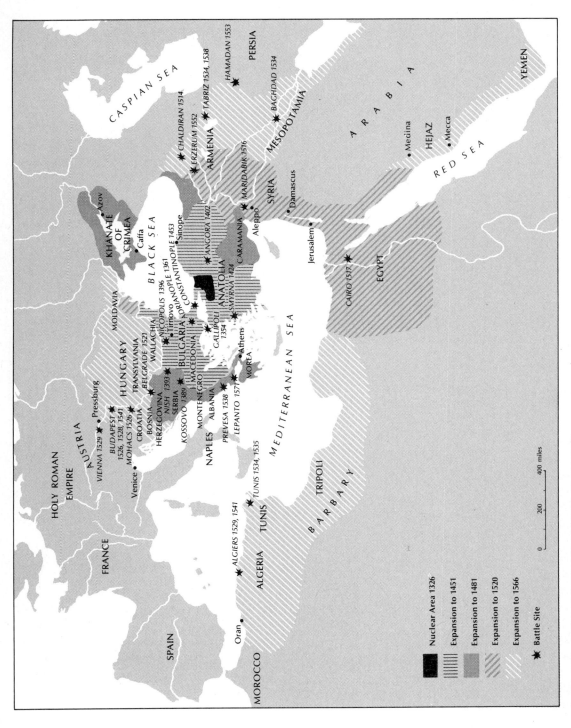

MAP 10.3: THE OTTOMAN EMPIRE 1300–1566

Nuclear Area 1326
Expansion to 1451
Expansion to 1481
Expansion to 1520
Expansion to 1566
★ Battle Site

CASPIAN SEA
PERSIA
HAMADAN 1553
TABRIZ 1534, 1538
YEMEN
CHALDIRAN 1514
ERZERUM 1552
BAGHDAD 1534
ARMENIA
MESOPOTAMIA
ARABIA
HEJAZ
Medina
Mecca
RED SEA
MARIDABIK 1516
SYRIA
Damascus
KHANATE OF CRIMEA
Azov
Caffa
BLACK SEA
ANCORA 1402
Sinope
Aleppo
Jerusalem
EGYPT
CAIRO 1517
CARAMANIA
ADRIANOPLE 1453
CONSTANTINOPLE 1453
ANATOLIA
SMYRNA 1424
MOLDAVIA
NICOPOLIS 1396
Tirnovo
BULGARIA 1393
GALLIPOLI 1354
WALLACHIA
BELGRADE 1521
HUNGARY
TRANSYLVANIA
CROATIA
MOHACS 1526
BUDAPEST 1526, 1528, 1541
VIENNA 1529
Pressburg
AUSTRIA
HOLY ROMAN EMPIRE
FRANCE
BOSNIA
HERZEGOVINA
SERBIA
NISH 1393
KOSSOVO 1389
MONTENEGRO
ALBANIA
MACEDONIA
Athens
MOREA
PREVESA 1538
LEPANTO 1571
Venice
NAPLES
MEDITERRANEAN SEA
TUNIS 1534, 1535
ALGIERS 1529, 1541
ALGERIA
TUNIS
TRIPOLI
BARBARY
Oran
SPAIN
MOROCCO

0   200   400 miles

for the faith, and the prestige thereby accruing to them won recruits and moral support from the more interior Islamic communities. Moreover, the Ottomans soon became a power in the political struggles of both Europe and the Middle East and were able to take advantage of favorable opportunities in both regions, even enlisting allies in one area to wage war in the other.

The intense rivalries sundering the Christian faiths also facilitated Ottoman expansion. Some Balkan Christians accepted papal supremacy, others adhered to the Eastern Orthodox traditions, and still others were regarded as heretics by both the Roman Catholics and the Orthodox. Often a Christian sect preferred the rule of the tolerant Ottomans to that of a rival Christian sect. In preserving peace among these dissident Christians, the Ottomans could serve as impartial referees, as Christians obviously could not.

Perhaps the greatest advantage of the Ottomans in their remarkable ascendancy was the character of their own cultural institutions. From their nomadic origins and their long experience as frontier fighters they had preserved a strong military tradition. Their devout adherence to Islam, which advocated holy wars against unbelievers, reinforced their aggressive tendencies; but the Ottomans also showed a remarkable ability to organize conquered territories and gain the support, and in some measure even the loyalty, of the subjugated peoples.

The Ottomans allowed the subject communities to live by their own laws under their own officials, requiring them only to pay taxes and supply men for the Ottoman army and administration. The Ottoman conquests did not greatly disturb the society, economy, or culture of these communities, which were also able to play a role of considerable importance in the social and economic life of the Ottoman Empire. Trade, for example, which remained vigorous in the Black Sea and the eastern Mediterranean Sea, was still largely in the hands of Greeks, Armenians, and Jews. The Ottomans themselves remained aloof from commercial undertakings and confined their careers to government service and the army.

In the course of their enormous expansion the Ottoman sultans faced the formidable problem of developing military and administrative institutions strong enough to hold together their vast empire. Like all medieval rulers the sultan originally governed with the aid of a council of chosen advisers, which was called the divan. From the time of Mohammed the Conqueror, however, the sultan came to be considered too august to participate personally in its deliberations. The function of presiding over the meetings of the divan fell to the grand vizier, who became the chief administrative official of the Ottoman state. The administration was divided into three major categories: civil, ecclesiastical, and military. The divan retained supreme responsibility over both the civil and military branches; it supervised the collection of taxes and tribute, conscription of soldiers, and conduct of foreign affairs, and made recommendations to the sultan concerning peace, war, or other major decisions of state; it also functioned as a court in disputes which were not religious in character.

Religious affairs were administered by a class of judges specially trained in Islamic law, who constituted a special corps called the *ulema*. At their head the sheikh-ul-Islam served as the supreme judge after the sultan himself in all matters of sacred law.

The army had two principal divisions: unpaid holders of fiefs granted by the sultan in exchange for military service; and paid soldiers, technically considered slaves, who remained permanently in the sultan's service. The holder of a fief was required to provide the military with armed men, the number being set in strict proportion to the revenue deriving from his estates. Among the paid soldiers the most important corps was that of the Janissaries. Slave armies had been common in Islamic states, but the Ottomans did not adopt the practice until the fifteenth century. According to the accounts of the earliest chronicles, Sultan Murad learned from a theologian in about 1430 that the Koran assigned him one-fifth of the booty captured by his army, including prisoners. Murad decided to convert his prisoners to Islam, teach them Turkish, and enlist them in a special, highly trained military contingent, the Janissaries ("new troops"). Most medieval monarchs relied upon mercenaries or poorly trained and poorly equipped feudal levies, comprised of vassals with little enthusiasm for fighting, and feudal levies continued to make up the larger part of the Turkish army. But the Janissaries soon became an elite corps of professional fighters, dedicated to the sultan and to Islam, and were in large part responsible for the Ottoman victories.

On the local level the government of the empire was content to leave many administrative responsibilities to the self-governing communities of Christians and Jews and to the holders of fiefs, who collected taxes and mustered soldiers from those settled on their lands. Apart from the fiefs the unit of local administration was the canton, or *kaza*, which was administered by a judge, or *qaid*. The cantons were grouped into departments and provinces, usually under the authority of a pasha, who was both a civil and a military official, since he bore the responsibility of leading the feudal levies of his provinces in time of war.

Sometime in the fifteenth century a new system of recruitment for the civil administration and the military was introduced—the *devshirme*, or levy of boys. In its developed form, special commissioners every five years selected young boys from among the Christian population to be given special instruction in Turkish and converted to Islam. After their training they were examined and either assigned to the corps of Janissaries or chosen for the palace administration. In the latter case they were given still more intensive training, and the most talented of them could aspire to the highest administrative offices of the empire. Even the grand vizier was usually a slave. Remarkably, in each generation the most powerful administrators were new men having no family ties with the Turkish aristocracy and no reason to ally with them against the sultan's interests. This practice of requisitioning slaves in the sultan's service is sometimes called the fundamental institution of the empire, for the sultan's power was critically dependent upon its proper functioning.

The Sultan

The sultan united in his own person supreme civil, military, and religious authority. The concept of his office was influenced by Byzantine views of imperial authority, which seem to have contributed primarily to the pomp of court ceremony and the aura of sanctity surrounding the person of the sultan, and still more by Islamic traditions concerning governmental power, particularly the notion that he was the successor of Muhammad, the legitimate ruler of all true believers. In a strict sense the sultan could not be an absolute ruler, for he was, like every member of the Islamic community, subject to the sacred law. But he was also the supreme judge of that law, and there was no way apart from revolution that his decisions could be challenged.

The early sultans devised a striking solution to a problem common to most medieval states: the peaceful transference of power from a ruler to his successor. From the fifteenth to the seventeenth century the Ottomans followed what has come to be called the law of fratricide. The sultans cohabited with numerous slave girls of the harem, who were selected much as were the male household slaves, and characteristically fathered numerous progeny. The reigning sultan selected one of the boys to be his successor. At the sultan's death, the designated heir had the right and obligation to put his brothers and half-brothers to death. (They were strangled with a silken bowstring in order to avoid the shedding of their imperial blood.) The religious judges allowed such massacres, because an orderly and peaceful succession was essential to the welfare of the empire.

The Limits of Ottoman Power

In the sixteenth century Suleiman the Magnificent had brought the Ottoman Empire to unprecedented heights of power, but already certain factors were imposing limits upon its expansion. One was geography. The Ottomans had operated effectively in areas close to their homeland in Asia Minor, but the efficiency of their army and administration inevitably diminished with distance. The unsuccessful campaign against Austria proved that the region was already beyond their reach, and the Ottomans encountered similar walls to further advance in the Iranian Plateau and the waters of the central Mediterranean. With the opening of trade routes around Africa and across the Atlantic the Ottomans were no longer at the center of the civilized world and no longer the masters of movements East and West. Although they left the commerce of their empire largely in the hands of the subject communities, they were well aware of its importance, and Suleiman therefore sent a force to destroy the Portuguese ships and trading stations in the Indian Ocean. Its failure was an ominous sign for the empire. Economically, the geographic discoveries of the period caused dislocations in the empire—the shift in trade routes, the increase in the stock of precious metal in Europe, and consequent inflation—and brought few benefits.

Within the empire there was also a deterioration in the quality of leadership. For reasons hard to explain, the sultans after Suleiman show little of the energy and ability which had marked out the earlier rulers of the House of Osman. Technical advance was continuing in the West, and it was critical for the empire to keep abreast of these changes. The great sultans had welcomed Western technicians and made use of their skills, especially in armament, but their successors after Suleiman seem distinctly less interested in learning from the West. Declining efficiency appears broadly evident in Ottoman government. The chanceries and secretariats kept precise and informative records in the fifteenth century, but they no longer do so in the late sixteenth century and seem to have been beset by mounting disorder.[4] At the death of Suleiman in 1566, it is still much too early to speak of Ottoman decadence, but the fortunes of the Ottoman Empire were already past their apogee.

III. THE BIRTH OF MODERN RUSSIA

A great Russian historian, V. O. Kliuchevsky, once defined the principal theme in the history of the Russian people to be colonization, the long, arduous, and ultimately successful struggle to settle and subdue the huge Eurasian plain

---

[4] During the period of expansion the basis of organizing conquered provinces was a document called the *defter,* a survey of the population and its possessions. The oldest surviving *defter* dates from 1431 to 1432 and deals with Albania, but the practice is undoubtedly somewhat older. These are remarkable documents, combining the qualities of a census and a property survey, and are comparable to the best records we possess from the same age in Western Europe. They illustrate the high administrative efficiency of the Ottoman government—an efficiency which noticeably deteriorates after the late sixteenth century.

Genghis Khan (1162–1227), here depicted as the illuminator of a sixteenth-century Persian manuscript imagined him to be, built an empire extending from China to central Europe. He is the most successful conqueror in history. (Photo: The Granger Collection)

which was their home.[5] The history of that struggle records defeats as well as victories. From the ninth to the twelfth centuries, the

[5] *A History of Russia*, 1911, vol. 1, p. 2, "Thus we see that the principal fundamental factor in Russian history has been migration or colonisation, and that all other factors have been more or less inseparably connected therewith." This theory bears interesting similarities with Frederick Jackson Turner's "frontier thesis" in regard to American history.

center of Rus civilization had been Kiev, on the fringes of the southern steppe. Although the Rus of Kiev maintained close contact across the steppes to the Black Sea and the Mediterranean world beyond, they could not permanently defeat the invading steppe nomads. From the twelfth century, Pechenegs and Cumans, followed by the still more terrible Mongols, mounted ever more destructive raids against the Rus settlements and cut off their contact with the Black Sea. Eventually the insecurity of the steppe forced the Rus to seek out safer homes in the forested regions to the north and west. In these areas, the Rus formed new institutions and built a new civilization, the direct ancestor of the modern Russian state.

THE MONGOLS

The resurgence of the steppe nomads was a principal factor in the decline of Kievan Rus, especially with the appearance of the Mongols on Europe's borders in the early thirteenth century. The Mongol chief Genghis Khan was then amassing the largest empire the world has ever known. In 1223 a Mongol army penetrated into Eastern Europe in what seems to have been a reconnoitering expedition. The Mongols defeated the allied princes of Rus in a battle on the Kalka River (a tributary of the Don) but almost at once returned home, only to reappear a few years later in still greater force. From 1237 to 1241 a Mongol army under a nephew of Genghis's named Batu conducted raids throughout Eastern Europe and established at Sarai on the lower Volga River the capital of a division of the Mongol Empire, which came to be called the Golden Horde. The khans, or rulers, of the Golden Horde maintained suzerainty over the lands of what is now the Ukraine and Byelorussia until the middle fourteenth century and over eastern Russia until the middle fifteenth. The princes subject to the Golden Horde had to pay tribute to the khans and secure from them a charter, called *yarlik*, which confirmed them in their office, but otherwise they were not interfered with in their rule. In spite of the duration of the Mongols' power over the East Slavs, the influence they exerted upon their languages and cultures remained relatively slight.

The nomad incursions and the formation of the Golden Horde were particularly destructive in the exposed southern steppes. A chronicler laments that Kiev, once proudly known as the "mother of Rus cities," had only two hundred houses left standing in the thirteenth century. Under nomad pressure the Rus population sought out more protected lands. In the twelfth and thirteenth centuries three new areas of East Slavic settlement came into prominence. Colonists moved west into the provinces of Galicia and Volynia along the upper Dniester River and became the forebears of the modern Ukrainians and the Byelorussians, or White Russians. After a short period of submission to the Mongols, these colonies fell under the political domination first of the grand dukes of Lithuania and then of the Polish kings, developed their own literary languages and cultural traditions, and were not politically reunited with their fellow East Slavs until the seventeenth and eighteenth centuries. (The province of Galicia, with a large Ukrainian population, remained under Polish or Austrian rule until 1944.) Other colonists moved north into the vast and empty lands ruled by the city of Novgorod, the region of Russia where Mongol rule had the shortest duration. But the poor soil of the area could not support a dense population. More important was the third new center of settlement: the Russian "Mesopotamia," the lands between the upper Volga and Oka rivers, with dense forests that offered both relative security from the nomads and a productive soil. Those who moved north to Novgorod and the Russian Mesopotamia were the ancestors of the modern Great Rus-

sians, still the largest of all the East Slavic peoples, and they formed the nucleus of a new Russian state; hence, their institutions and culture have a special interest.

Historians conventionally call the period between the twelfth and fifteenth centuries the age of feudal, or appanage, Russia—the time when Russia was divided into many princely patrimonies; for nearly all the small towns within the Russian Mesopotamia had their own princes, their own citadels, or kremlins, and their own territories. All the princes were subject to the Khan of the Golden Horde, but Mongol government remained limited to the extracting of tribute and the granting of *yarliks*. Russia lacked a central government.

In this feudal period Russian economy, society, and culture acquired distinctive characteristics. With the exception of Novgorod the towns of the north could not, like Kiev, develop an active commerce with distant areas, nor did they have close contact with Constantinople or other centers of learning. The Russian towns in the main were not commercial or industrial centers but fortresses to which the surrounding population could repair in times of danger. The economy was overwhelmingly agricultural, and the energy of the people was primarily directed to clearing the great forests. In social terms, most peasants remained freemen, and their freedom was protected by the proximity of an expanding frontier. Culturally, the Russians developed remarkable skill in constructing churches and citadels almost entirely from wood. As one historian maintains, the appropriate symbols of Russian culture in this age are the ax and the icon.[6] Art continued to serve primarily the Church. Working within the conventions of icon painting established by Byzantine masters, Russian artists were still

---

[6] Cf. the essay on Russian culture by James H. Billington, *The Icon and the Axe: An Interpretive History of Russian Culture*, 1966.

able to achieve a remarkable delicacy and serenity, which stand in sharp contrast to the harsh conditions of Russian life. Russia's supreme religious painter was Andrei Rublev (1370?–1430?), who deserves to be recognized as one of the world's great artistic geniuses, even though little survives of his work.

THE RISE OF MOSCOW

In spite of political divisions the Russians' religion and their common submission to the Mongols preserved a sense of identity and unity among them, but for long it remained uncertain which of the many petty princes would take the leadership in building a politically united nation. The town that perhaps seemed least likely to achieve this hegemony was the new settlement of Moscow, which is mentioned in a chronicle for the first time in 1147. Its early obscurity proved an advantage because the small town was passed up by raiding nomads in search of richer plunder. This city on the Moskva River had other advantages too. It was in the center of the Russian Mesopotamia, close to the hub of the tributary rivers feeding the Volga River to the north and the Oka River to the south. The princes of Moscow could pursue a "river policy" in their expansion, following the courses of streams in all directions and depending upon this network of water routes to bind their state together. The region between the Volga and the Oka rivers also formed the geographic heart of European Russia and allowed the prince who ruled it to exploit opportunities in almost any part of Russia.

Moscow gained preeminence primarily through the talents of its early princes. Like other rulers in the north they abandoned the

Page from the Slavonic Gospels. (Photo: British Museum)

disastrous rota system of inheritance characteristic of the Kievan period and after some initial hesitation adopted a policy of primogeniture. A prince's acquisitions were thus kept intact rather than being divided among many heirs, and each prince built upon the accomplishments of his predecessor. The princes set about "gathering the Russian land," as historians traditionally describe the process of reunification, through the simultaneous pursuit of two distinct goals: they acquired new territories at every opportunity, through wars, marriages, and purchases; and they sought to make of Moscow, together with the Church, the symbol and the embodiment of Russian national unity, the representative of all Russians in the face of the Mongols and Western Christians. The prestige which thus accrued to Moscow helped persuade the princes of other cities to submit to its hegemony.

Ivan I (1328–1341) was the first Muscovite prince to raise this obscure little town to a place of prominence. Chiefly through purchases from other princes but occasionally through conquest, he extended his possessions along the entire course of the Moskva River and gained enclaves of territory to the north beyond the Volga River (see Map 10.4). Ivan assiduously courted the favor of the still powerful Mongol Khan of the Golden Horde; he repeatedly visited the khan in his capital on the lower Volga River. In 1328 in recognition of his loyalty and gifts the khan gave him a special *yarlik* which made him the chief representative of Mongol authority in Russia with the right to collect the Mongol tribute from all the Russian lands. Thereafter Ivan and his successors permanently bore the title *velikii kniaz* ("great prince," or as traditionally if inaccurately rendered into English, "grand duke"). In collecting tribute for the Mongols, Ivan also increased his own treasury, thereby earning the nickname by which he is best known to history—*Kalita* ("moneybags").

Ivan no less assiduously sought to win the favor of the Russian Church and developed a strong friendship with the holder of its primal see, Peter, successor to the Metropolitan of Kiev. Like his predecessor, who had abandoned that decaying city, Peter at first had no fixed see but peregrinated among the new centers of Russian settlement. He visited Moscow frequently and by chance died there in 1326. His tomb became a national shrine, and his successors chose Moscow as their permanent see, thus making it the capital of the Russian Church before it was the capital of the Russian people.

By the late fourteenth century the power of the Mongols was declining, largely because of dissensions within the Golden Horde; the princes of Moscow shifted from their traditional role as chief servant of the khan to that of leader in the growing national opposition to Mongol rule. Though far from breaking the power of the Mongols, Prince Dmitri scored the first Russian defeat of a Mongol army in 1380, at Kulikovo on the Don River. In addition to this victory, which earned him the proud title *Donskoi* ("of the Don"), Dmitri also repulsed a Lithuanian invasion. He thus made Moscow the special defender of Orthodoxy against both the infidel Tatars and Western Christians, whom the Russians regarded as heretics, and gave it a prestige no other Russian city possessed.

The sovereign who completed the gathering of the Russian land and laid the constitutional foundations for modern Russia was Ivan III,

Andrei Rublev, considered to have been Russia's greatest religious artist of the Middle Ages, painted the icon shown here, Old Testament Trinity *(ca. 1410–1420). Although influenced by the works of earlier Byzantine artists, Rublev evoked an even greater sense of tranquillity in his own creations.* (Photo: Tretyakov Gallery)

the Great (1462–1505). His most important acquisition was Novgorod, a commercial city which had strong ties with the West and had gained control of a huge if still thinly populated area to the north. Through its vigorous trade with the Hanseatic League, a mercantile league of German cities, Novgorod had enjoyed considerable prosperity in the fourteenth and fifteenth centuries, but the consolidation of strong states along its borders—Lithuania and Poland as well as Muscovite Russia—threatened its independence. The merchant oligarchy which ruled the town wished to accept the suzerainty of the Catholic Lithuanians, while the populace, which was staunchly Orthodox in religion, looked rather to the prince of Moscow. Ivan could not allow a territory so large and so close to his own to fall under the control of a powerful foreign prince. In 1471 he demanded and received the submission of the city; when the city rebelled again in 1478, Ivan not only subdued it but incorporated Novgorod and its territories into the Muscovite state. Ivan also gathered in the principalities of Yaroslavl, Perm, Rostov, and Tver. He dispelled the shadow of Mongol sovereignty over Russia by confronting an invading army at the Oka River in 1480, although no battle was fought because the river separated the two foes and neither dared cross its waters. The enemy withdrew, quietly ending more than two centuries of Mongol rule in Russia.

Under Ivan's successor Basil III, the principalities of Pskov, Riazan, and Smolensk were added; Moscow, which in 1462 had ruled some fifteen thousand square miles of territory, by the middle of the sixteenth century ruled forty thousand square miles, and the borders of the principality of Moscow included nearly all the areas settled by the Great Russians. The princes of Moscow now confronted beyond their frontiers, not another Russian prince, but foreign sovereigns. The reign of Ivan III thus

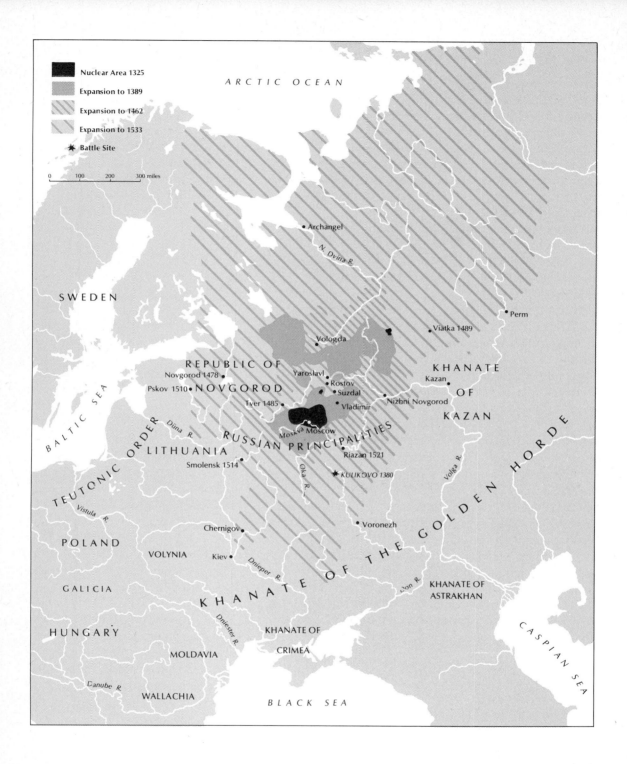

Legend
- ■ Nuclear Area 1325
- Expansion to 1389
- Expansion to 1462
- Expansion to 1533
- ★ Battle Site

0   100   200   300 miles

ARCTIC OCEAN

• Archangel

N. Dvina R.

SWEDEN

• Perm

• Viatka 1489

Vologda •

REPUBLIC OF

Novgorod 1478 •

Pskov 1510 •   NOVGOROD

Yaroslavl

• Rostov

• Suzdal

KHANATE

Kazan •

OF

KAZAN

Tver 1485 •

• Vladimir

• Nizhni Novgorod

BALTIC SEA

TEUTONIC ORDER

Düna R.

LITHUANIA

Moskva Moscow

RUSSIAN PRINCIPALITIES

Smolensk 1514 •

Riazan 1521 •

Oka R.

★ *KULIKOVO 1380*

Volga R.

KHANATE OF THE GOLDEN HORDE

Vistula R.

POLAND

Chernigov •

• Voronezh

VOLYNIA

Kiev •

Dnieper R.

Don R.

KHANATE OF
ASTRAKHAN

GALICIA

HUNGARY

Dniester R.

KHANATE OF

CASPIAN SEA

MOLDAVIA

CRIMEA

Danube R.

WALLACHIA

BLACK SEA

MAP 10.4: RUSSIA 1325–1533

begins a new epoch in the history of diplomatic and cultural relations with non-Russian peoples.

INSTITUTIONAL AND SOCIAL CHANGE

Ivan III refashioned Russian institutions to suit the newly achieved national unity. The ruler of all the Russians could no longer be considered a mere appanage prince, so Ivan adopted the title *tsar*, the Slavic equivalent of the Latin term *Caesar* and the Greek *kaîsar*, the traditional title of the Roman and the Byzantine emperors. Ivan also sought to depict himself as the successor of the Byzantine emperors. He adopted the Greek title *autokrator* ("autocrat") and introduced at his court the elaborate pomp and etiquette which had been characteristic of Byzantine practice. The Byzantine double-headed eagle became the seal and symbol of the new Russian Empire. Ivan added material as well as ideological splendor to his capital. Under the influence of his wife, Sophia Paleologus, who was the niece of the last Byzantine emperor and had been educated in Italy, he invited Italian artists to Moscow who helped to rebuild the Kremlin, the ancient citadel of the city. The Italians exerted considerable influence on Russian artistic style, especially Aristotele Fioravanti, who designed some of the Kremlin's most graceful churches and palaces.

Ivan was the first prince since the Kievan period to legislate for the whole of Russia. In 1497 he promulgated a new code of laws known as the *Sudebnik*, which was the first national legal code since the *Russkaia Pravda*, compiled by the Kievan Prince Iaroslav the Wise in the eleventh century. The new strength and splendor of the tsar inspired several monastic scholars to elaborate the theory of Moscow as the third Rome. The first Rome had allegedly fallen into heresy, and the second, Constantinople, was taken by the infidel.

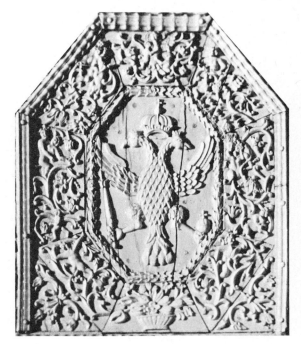

The throne of Ivan the Terrible (the grandson of Ivan III) resembles a straight high-backed chair. The ivory plates that face the wooden framework are covered with relief carvings featuring mythological, historical, heraldic, and everyday scenes. The detail shown here is of the double-headed eagle, a Byzantine emblem which was adopted by the tsar as the seal and symbol of the Russian Empire. (Photo: APN)

Moscow alone, the capital of the one Orthodox ruler, preserved the light of true religion.

In administering their state the princes of Moscow had traditionally relied upon the boyars, the hereditary nobles who were obligated to serve the prince in both the army and the civil administration. Many of the boyars held vast estates in full title, and their economic independence sometimes made them unreliable as servants. Without directly attacking the boyars, Tsar Ivan created a new class of serving gentry who were entirely dependent on the tsar's favor for their social position. He inaugurated a land grant called a *pomest'e*, which like the Western fief was made on condition of faithful service. The *pomeshchik*, as the holder of the grant was called, retained the property only so long as he fulfilled his obligations and, initially at least, the concession was not heritable. This new class acted as a counterpoise to the power of the boyars and as a principal support of the tsar's authority. Here is another example of a feudal institution contributing toward the establishment of a stronger, more centralized government.

Although Ivan's reforms were not truly completed until the reign of his grandson, the notorious Ivan IV, the Terrible, who brutally extirpated the old nobility of boyars and imposed on all landowners the status of the tsar's servants, Ivan III may be considered the founder of the modern Russian state. He created the class of serving gentry; he finished the task of gathering the Russian land and unifying its people; he brought a united Russia to face the outside world; and he declared himself to be tsar, autocrat of Russia. Ivan III bequeathed to his successors one of the most characteristic institutions of modern Russia: its centralized, autocratic government.

In the Central and Late Middle Ages the isolation of the West from the East was partially overcome through the crusades and commercial expansion. The period further witnessed the formation in the East of two new states destined to replace both the Byzantine Empire and the Islamic Caliphate as the region's principal powers. Through a combination of military skill, religious fervor, remarkably effective institutions, and the weakness of their foes, the Ottoman Turks reassembled the territories of both Byzantium and the caliphate and established in the Middle East a vast empire, which stretched from Persia to the Danube River, and from North Africa to the Russian steppes. To the north the Russians had overcome by 1500 the political fragmentation of their own "feudal" age and had regained political unity. Although the tsars in the sixteenth century were not nearly so powerful as the Ottoman sultans, they were laying the foundations for the future strength of their empire.

In Western Europe over these same centuries, changes of comparable magnitude were occurring. The West was spared the nomadic invasions which always threatened and frequently struck the Eastern peoples, but it too sustained in the fourteenth and fifteenth centuries a series of disastrous blows—famines, plagues, economic depression, and wars. These catastrophes were the cause of profound dislocations in the society of the medieval West. The following two chapters examine the nature of this crisis, which transformed the medieval world and helped create the civilization of modern Western Europe.

RECOMMENDED READING

Sources

The Chronicle of Novgorod. Robert Mitchell and Nevill Forbes (trs.). 1914. Portrays social and political life of the principal commercial town of medieval Russia.

*DeVillehardouin, Geoffrey, and Jean DeJoinville. *Chronicles of the Crusades.* Margaret R. Shaw (tr.). 1963.

Howes, Robert Craig (ed. and tr.). *The Testaments of the Grand Princes of Moscow.* 1967.

Tyre, William of. *A History of Deeds Done Beyond the Sea.* Emily A. Babcock and A. C. Krey (trs.). 1943. One of the most important crusader chronicles.

Studies

Atiya, Azia S. *Crusade, Commerce and Culture.* 1962. An evaluation of the results of the crusades in European history.

Eversley, George, and Valentine Chirol. *The Turkish Empire: Its Growth and Decay.* 1969.

Fennell, J. L. *Ivan the Great of Moscow.* 1963. A political biography.

Kliuchevsky, V. O. *A History of Russia.* C. J. Hogarth (tr.). 1911. Classic study, by Russia's greatest historian.

Lewis, Bernard. *Istanbul and the Civilization of the Ottoman Empire.* 1963. By a prominent student of Islamic cultures.

Merriman, Roger B. *Suleiman the Magnificent: 1520–1566.* 1966.

Mylonas, George E. *The Balkan States: An Introduction to Their History.* 1947. Clearly written introductory survey.

Setton, Kenneth M. *Europe and the Levant in the Middle Ages and the Renaissance.* 1974. Collected essays by a distinguished expert on Byzantium and the West.

—————— (ed.). *A History of the Crusades.* 1955 ff. Three volumes to date (1977); when completed, this work will constitute the most comprehensive history of the crusades.

Vernadsky, George. *The Mongols and Russia.* 1953.

——————. *Russia at the Dawn of the Modern Age.* 1959. Volumes in the author's *History of Russia.*

Wittek, Paul. *The Rise of the Ottoman Empire.* 1971.

---

* Available in paperback.

ELEVEN

THE WEST IN TRANSITION: ECONOMY AND INSTITUTIONS

Shadows covered wide areas of European life in the fourteenth and fifteenth centuries. The vigorous expansion into bordering areas which had marked European history since the eleventh century came to an end. The Christian West fought to halt the expansion of the Muslim Turks but did not completely succeed. Plague, famine, and recurrent wars decimated populations and snuffed out their former prosperity. The papacy and feudal government struggled against mounting institutional chaos. Powerful mystical and heretical movements and new critical currents in Scholasticism rocked the established religious and philosophical equilibrium of the thirteenth century.

But for all these signs of crisis the fourteenth and fifteenth centuries were not merely an age of breakdown. The partial failure both of the medieval economy and government and of the established systems of thought and value facilitated change and impelled men to repair their institutions and renew their culture. As Chapter 12 will show, there were vigorous developments in philosophy, religious thought, vernacular and Latin literature, and the fine arts. By the late fifteenth century the outlines of a new equilibrium were emerging. In 1500 Europeans doubtlessly remained fewer in numbers than they had been in 1300. But they also had developed a more productive economy and a more powerful technology than they had possessed two hundred years before. These achievements also equipped Europeans for their great expansion throughout the world in the early modern epoch.

A traditional interpretation of the fourteenth and fifteenth centuries has made them years of renewal, rebirth: the Renaissance. In another interpretation, now equally traditional and reputable, the fourteenth and fifteenth centuries were the "autumn of the Middle Ages," and the somber theme of their history is the decline and death of a formerly great civilization. Today, with our own vastly enlarged fund of information, it is permissible and indeed necessary to consider the age both an autumn and a renaissance. The study of any past epoch requires an effort to balance the work of death and renewal. In few periods of history do death and renewal confront each other so dramatically as in the years between 1300 and 1500.

1. ECONOMIC DEPRESSION AND RECOVERY

The plagues and famines which struck European society in the fourteenth and fifteenth centuries profoundly affected economic life. Initially, they disrupted the established patterns of producing and exchanging goods and led directly to what some scholars now call "the economic depression of the Renaissance." But the effects of this disruption were not entirely negative; in reorganizing the economy under greatly changed demographic conditions, Europeans were also able to make certain significant advances in the efficiency of economic production. To understand this paradox we must first examine how these disasters affected the population of Europe.

DEMOGRAPHIC CATASTROPHE

Scholars have uncovered some censuses and other statistical records which for the first time give an insight into the size and structure of the European population. Nearly all of these records were drawn up for purposes of taxation and they therefore usually survey only limited geographical areas—a city or a province—and are rarely complete. But although they give us no reliable figures for total population, they still enable us to discern with considerable confidence how it was changing.

Almost every region of Europe from which we possess such records shows an appalling decline of population between approximately 1300 and 1450. For example, the population of Provence in southern France seems to have been between 350,000 and 400,000 at about 1310; a century later it had shrunk to something between one-third and one-half its earlier size, and only after 1470 did it again begin to increase. The population of the city and countryside of Pistoia, near Florence, fell from about 43,000 in the middle of the thirteenth century to 14,000 by the early fifteenth. The neighboring city and countryside of San Gimignano had approximately 13,000 residents in 1332 and only 3,100 in 1428; the region still has not regained its maximum medieval size.

For the larger kingdoms of Europe the figures are less reliable, but they cannot be too far from the mark. England had a population of about 3.7 million in 1347 and 2.2 million by 1377.[1] By 1550 it was no larger a nation than it had been in the thirteenth century. France by 1328 may have reached 15 million; it too

was not again to attain its peak medieval size for several hundred years. In Germany, of some 170,000 inhabited localities named in sources antedating 1300, about 40,000 disappeared during the fourteenth and fifteenth centuries. Since many of the surviving towns were simultaneously shrinking in size, the population loss could only have been greater.

Certain favored regions of Europe, however—the fertile lands surrounding Paris or the Po valley—continually attracted settlers and maintained fairly stable populations, but they owed their good fortune more to immigration than to high birth rates or immunity from disease. It can safely be estimated that all of Europe in 1450 had no more than one-half, and probably only one-third, of the population it had had in the thirteenth century.

Pestilence

The great plague of the fourteenth century provides the most evident, although perhaps not the most satisfactory, explanation for these huge human losses. In 1347 a merchant ship sailing from Tana in the Crimea to Messina in Sicily seems to have carried infected rats. A plague broke out at Messina and from there it spread throughout Europe (see Map 11.1).

This Black Death was not so much an epidemic as a pandemic, striking an entire continent. It may not have been the first pandemic in European history (sparse sources mention a general plague from 747 to 750), but it was the first in perhaps six hundred years, and it struck repeatedly during the century. A city was lucky if more than ten years went by without an onslaught; in some part of Europe, in

---

[1] The estimate is based on the pioneering researches of J. C. Russell, *British Medieval Population*, 1948, but there is no national census for England in the period immediately preceding the Black Death and the figure of 3.7 million had to be extrapolated on the basis of presumed mortality rates. Recently, M. M. Postan, in the *Cambridge Economic History*, I, 562, stated that

the preplague population may have been nearer 7 million and that "to most historians abreast of most recent researches the higher estimates may well appear to be more consistent with the economic and social conditions of rural England at the end of the thirteenth century. . . ."

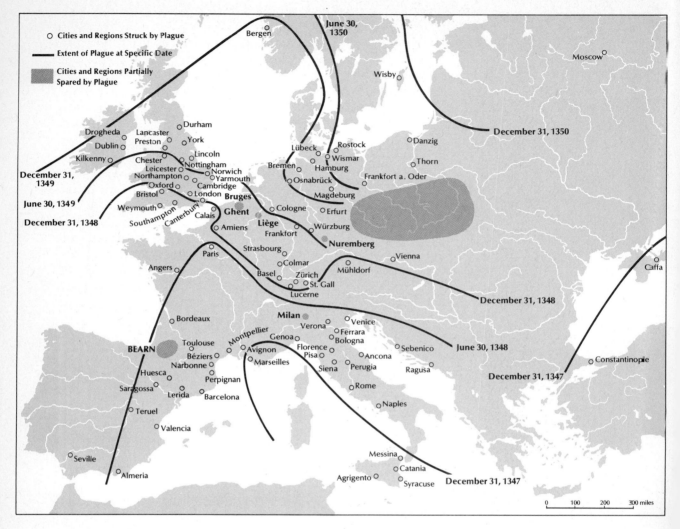

MAP 11.1: THE BLACK DEATH

[Adapted from Carpentier, E., "Autour de la peste noire; famines et épidémies dans l'histoire du XIVe siècle," in *Annales: Economies, Sociétés, Civilisations*, XVII (1962). Used by permission.]

almost every year, the plague was raging. Barcelona and its province of Catalonia, for example, lived through this record of misery in the fourteenth century: famine, 1333; plague, 1347 and 1351; famine, 1358 and 1359; plague, 1362, 1363, 1371, and 1397.

Some of the horror of the plague can be glimpsed in this account by an anonymous cleric who visited the French city of Avignon in 1348:

To put the matter shortly, one-half, or more than a half, of the people at Avignon are already dead. Within the walls of the city there are now more than 7,000 houses shut up; in these no one is living, and all who have inhabited them are departed; the suburbs hardly contain any people at all. . . .
The like account I can give of all the cities and towns of Provence. Already the sickness has crossed the Rhone, and ravaged many cities and villages as far as Toulouse, and it ever in-

creases in violence as it proceeds. On account of this great mortality there is such a fear of death that people do not dare even to speak with anyone whose relative has died, because it is frequently remarked that in a family where one dies nearly all the relations follow him, and this is commonly believed among the people.[2]

Most historians identify the Black Death as the bubonic plague, but they find it difficult to explain how this disease could have spread so rapidly and killed so many, since bubonic plague is more truly a disease of rats and small mammals than of men. If bubonic plague is to spread to a human, a flea must bite an infected rat, pick up the infection, and carry it to a human host through a bite. The infection causes the lymphatic glands to swell but recovery is not uncommon. Only if the infection travels through the bloodstream to the lungs, causing pneumonia, can the disease be spread directly from person to person. The real killer in the fourteenth century seems to have been a pneumonic plague, which infects the lungs directly; it probably was spread through coughing and was almost always fatal.

In spite of the virulence of pneumonic plague it is hard to believe that medical factors alone can explain the awesome mortalities. After all, Europeans had maintained close contact with the East, where the plague had been endemic, since the eleventh century, but not until 1347 and 1348 did it make serious inroads in Europe. In addition, pneumonic plague itself is a disease of the winter months, but the plagues of the fourteenth century characteristically raged during the summer and dissipated with the cooler weather of autumn. Some scholars consider that the weather of the age—it seems to have been unusually cool and humid—somehow favored the disease. Others argue that

acute, widespread malnutrition had severely debilitated the population and lowered resistance to all kinds of infections.

Hunger
A second cause of the dramatic fall of population was hunger. Famines frequently scourged the land; and even if they were less lethal than the plague in their initial onslaught, they were likely to persist for several years. In 1315, 1316, and 1317 a severe famine raged in the north of Europe; in 1339 and 1340 another struck the south. The starving people ate not only their reserves of grain but most of the seed set aside for planting. Only a remarkably good harvest could compensate for the loss of grain by providing both immediate sustenance and seed for future planting in satisfactory quantities.

Why was hunger so rampant in the early fourteenth century? Some historians now locate the root of trouble in the sheer number of people the lands had to support by 1300. The medieval population, they say, had been growing rapidly since about 1000, and by 1300 Europe was becoming the victim of its own success. Parts of the Continent were crowded, even glutted, with people. The county of Beaumont-le-Roger in Normandy, for example, had a population in the early fourteenth century not much below the number it was supporting in the early twentieth century. Thousands, millions even, had to be fed without the aid of chemical fertilizers, power tools, and fast transport. Masses of people had come to depend for their livelihood upon unrewarding soils. Even in good years they were surviving on the slim and uncertain margins of existence; a slightly reduced harvest during any one year took on the dimensions of a major famine. Through hunger, malnutrition, and plague the hand of death was correcting the ledgers of life, balancing the numbers of people and the resources which supported them.

---

[2] *Breve Chronicon clerici anonymi,* quoted in Francis Aidan Gasquet, *The Black Death of 1348 and 1349,* 1908, p. 46.

What effects did the fall in population have on the economy of Europe? Initially, the losses disrupted production. According to the chroniclers, survivors of the plague frequently gave up toiling in the fields or working in shops; presumably, they saw no point in working for the future when the future was so uncertain. But, in the long run, the results were not altogether negative. In agriculture, for example, the contraction of the population enabled the survivors to concentrate their efforts on the better soils. Moreover, in both agriculture and industry the shortage of laborers was a challenge to landlords and entrepreneurs to save costs either by adopting productive routines less demanding of manpower or by increased investment in labor-saving devices. Thus the decline in population eventually taught Europeans to work more efficiently through more rational productive routines and greater capital investment.

Agriculture

Perhaps the best indication of the forces working upon the European economy comes from the history of prices. The evidence is scattered and rarely precise, but it is good enough to reveal roughly similar patterns in price movements all over Europe. Most agricultural products—cereals, wine, beer, oil, and meat—shot up immediately after the Black Death and stayed high until the last decades of the fourteenth century. High food prices in a period of contracting population seem certain evidence that production was falling even more rapidly than the number of consumers.

The beginnings of an agricultural recovery become evident in the early fifteenth century. With a diminished number of Europeans to be fed, the demand for cereals, the cultivation of which dominated agriculture in the earlier centuries, lessened perceptibly and their prices declined; with fewer available workers, the cost of labor pushed steadily upward. Landlords had to compete with one another to attract

scarce tenants to their lands and did so by offering lower rents and favorable terms of tenancy. The upward movement of wages and the downward price of cereals led to a concentration on those commodities which would command a better price in the market or were less expensive to produce. Better wages in both town and countryside enabled the population to consume a more varied and more expensive diet. While the price of wheat fell, wine, beer, oil, butter, cheese, meat, fruit, and other relatively expensive foods remained high, reflecting a strong market demand.

One branch of agriculture which enjoyed a remarkable period of growth in the fifteenth century was sheep raising. Labor costs were low, since a few shepherds could guard thousands of sheep, and the price for wool, skins, mutton, and cheese remained high. In England many landlords fenced large fields, converting them from plowland into sheep pastures and expelling the peasants or small herders who had formerly lived on them; this process, called enclosure, continued into the sixteenth century and played an important role in the economic and social history of Tudor England.

By the middle of the fifteenth century, agricultural prices tended to stabilize, and this suggests a more dependable production. Farms enjoyed the advantages of greater size, better location on more profitable soil, and greater capital investments in tools and animals. Agriculture was now considerably diversified, benefiting the soil, lowering the risk of famine through the failure of a single staple crop, and providing more nourishment for the people. Europeans were consuming a healthier diet by the middle of the fifteenth century than had their ancestors two hundred years before.

Industry and Trade

The movement of prices created serious problems for the entrepreneurs within the cities. As the labor force contracted, wages in most towns surged upward and commonly reached levels two, three, and even four times higher than they had been before 1348. Although the prices of manufactured commodities also increased, they did not rise as much as wages, and this worked to reduce profit margins. To offset these unfavorable tendencies, the entrepreneurs sought government intervention. In various enactments from 1349 to 1351, England, France, Aragon, Castile, and other governments tried to fix prices and wages at levels favorable to employers. The English Parliament in the Statute of Laborers, a policy typical of the age, forbade employers to pay more than the customary wages and required laborers to accept jobs at those wages. These early experiments in a controlled economy failed. The price and wage ceilings set by law seem to have had little perceptible influence on actual prices.

A related problem troubled the business climate. Competition grew as population fell and markets contracted. Entrepreneurs tried to protect themselves by creating restricted markets and establishing monopolies. Guilds limited their membership, and some admitted only the sons of established masters. Cities too imposed heavy restrictions on the importation of foreign manufactures.

Probably the best example of the monopoly spirit is the association of north German trading cities, the Hanseatic League. The league was a defensive association formed in the fourteenth century to promote German interests and exclude foreigners from the Baltic trade. The cities initially sought this mutual protection because the emperor was too weak to defend their interests. At its height the Hanseatic League included about seventy or eighty cities under the leadership of Bremen, Cologne, Hamburg, and especially Lübeck. Maintaining its own treasury and fleet, the league supervised commercial exchange, policed the waters of the Baltic Sea, and negotiated with foreign princes. By the late fifteenth century, however, the

The German towns of the Hanseatic League dominated the trade of northern Europe in the fourteenth and fifteenth centuries. The picture shows a bustling port of the period. (Photo: Culver Pictures, Inc.)

league had begun to decline. It failed to meet the growing threat of the Dutch, who were then vigorously competing for leadership in northern commerce. The Hanseatic League was never formally abolished; it continued to meet at lengthening intervals until 1669.

THE FORCES OF RECOVERY

Attempts to raise the efficiency of workers proved to be far more effective than wage and trade regulation in laying the basis for recovery. Employers were able to counteract high wages by adopting more rational production procedures and substituting capital for labor, that is, providing the worker with better tools. Although largely inspired by hard times and labor shortages, most of the technical advances of the fourteenth and fifteenth centuries enabled the worker to practice his trade more efficiently and eventually helped make Europe a richer community.

Metallurgy

Mining and metallurgy benefited from a series of inventions after 1460 that lowered the cost of metals and extended their use in European life. Better techniques of digging, shoring, ventilating, and draining allowed mine shafts to be sunk several hundred feet into the earth, permitting the large-scale exploitation of the deep, rich mineral deposits of Central Europe. Some historians estimate (on slim evidence, to be sure) that the output from the mines of Central Europe—Hungary, the Tyrol, Bohemia, and Saxony—grew as much as five times between 1460 and 1530. During this period miners in Saxony discovered a method of extracting pure silver from the lead alloy in which it was often found (the invention was of major importance for the later, massive development of silver mines in America). Larger furnaces came into use, and huge bellows and triphammers, driven by water power, aided the smelting and working of metals. Simultaneously, the masters of the trade were acquiring a new precision in the difficult art of casting.

By the late fifteenth century, European mines were providing an abundance of silver bullion for coinage. Money became more plentiful, and this stimulated the economy. Beginnings were also laid for the exploitation of the rich coal deposits of the European north. Expanding iron production meant more and stronger pumps, gears and machine parts, tools, and ironwares; such products found wide application in construction work and shipbuilding. Moreover, skill in metalworking contributed to two other inventions: firearms and movable metal type.

Firearms

Men were constantly trying to improve the arts of war in the bellicose Middle Ages; and one weapon, or family of weapons, they sought was a device which would hurl projectiles with great force and accuracy. We do not know how Europeans first learned that certain mixtures of carbon, sulfur, and saltpeter burn with explosive force and could be used to hurl boulders at an enemy, but we do know that cannons were used in the fourteenth century during the Hundred Years' War. Their effect seems to have been chiefly psychological: the thunderous roar merely by frightening the enemy's horses probably did more damage than the inevitably misdirected shots. Still, a breakthrough had been made, and cannons gained in military importance. Their development depended primarily on stronger, more precise casting and on proper granulation of the powder to ensure that the charge would burn at the right speed so that its full force pushed the projectile. With firearms fewer soldiers could fight more effectively; capital, in the

Leonardo da Vinci's concept of a cannon foundry had its ancestry in the Chinese and Byzantine applications of rapid chemical combustion to the weapons of war. The Chinese had used fireworks for centuries; the Byzantines had concocted a "Greek fire" which they sprayed on enemy ships with devastating effect. (Photo: Royal Collection, Windsor Castle)

A page from Johannes Gutenberg's Bible marks one of the most significant technical and cultural advances of the fifteenth century: printing with movable type, a process that made possible a wider dissemination of literature and thought. (Photo: E. Harold Hugo)

form of an efficient though expensive tool, was again being substituted for labor.

Printing

The extension of literacy among laymen and the greater reliance of governments and businesses upon records created a demand for a cheap method of reproducing the written word. One important advance was the replacement of expensive parchment by paper, which had originated in the East. But even so, the scribe and copier worked slowly and, like all workmen, were commanding an increased salary. As a solution, printing was first tried by stamping paper or parchment with woodcuts, which were inked blocks with letters or designs carved on them. But the "block books" produced in this fashion represented only a small advance over handwriting, for a separate woodcut had to be carved for each page.

By the middle of the fifteenth century several masters were on the verge of perfecting the technique of printing with movable metal type. The first man to prove the practicability of the new art was Johannes Gutenberg of Mainz, a former jeweler and stonecutter. Gutenberg devised an alloy of lead, tin, and antimony which would melt at a low temperature, cast well in the die, and be durable in the press; this alloy is still the basis of the printer's art. His Bible, printed in 1455, is the first major work reproduced through printing.

In spite of Gutenberg's efforts to keep the technique a secret it spread rapidly. Before 1500 some 250 European cities had acquired presses. German masters held an early leadership, but Italians soon challenged their preeminence. The Venetian printer Aldus Manutius published works, notably editions of the Greek and Latin classics, which are minor masterpieces of scholarship and grace. Manutius and his fellow Italian masters rejected the elaborate Gothic typeface used in the north and developed their own, modeled on the clear script they found in their oldest manuscripts. They wrongly believed that it was the style of writing used in ancient Rome; they were in fact imitating the Carolingian minuscule.

The immediate effect of the printing press was to multiply the output and cut the price of books, which meant that the pleasures of reading were no longer the monopoly of the rich and the clergy but were available to a much broader range of the population. Printing also helped to standardize texts, contributing fundamentally to the advance of scholarship, science, and technology.

Printing also could spread new ideas with unprecedented speed and impact, a fact that was appreciated only slowly. The Protestant reformers of the sixteenth century were really the first to take advantage of the potential of printing for propaganda, and Catholics soon followed.

Navigation

Men as well as ideas began to travel more easily in the fourteenth and fifteenth centuries Before about 1325 there was still no regular sea traffic between northern and southern Europe by way of the Atlantic, but it grew rapidly thereafter. In navigation the substitution of capital for labor primarily meant the introduction of larger ships, which could carry more cargo with relatively smaller crews. The large ships were safer at sea; they could sail in periods of uncertain weather, when smaller vessels had to stay in port. They could also remain at sea longer and did not have to sail close to the coastline in order to replenish their supplies. Their voyages between ports could be more direct and therefore speedier.

The larger vessels required more sophisticated means of steering and navigation. Before 1300, ships were turned by trailing an oar over the side. The control provided by this method was poor, especially for sailing ships, which needed an efficient means of steering to take advantage of shifting winds. Sometime during the fourteenth century the stern rudder was developed, enabling the captain to tack effectively against the wind and control his ship more closely entering or leaving ports. Voyages thus were rendered quicker and safer, and the costs of maritime transport declined.

Ocean navigation also required a reliable means for estimating course and position, and here notable progress had been made, especially in the late thirteenth century. Scholars at the court of King Alfonso X of Castile compiled the Alfonsine Tables, which showed with unprecedented accuracy the position and movements of the heavenly bodies. Using such tables along with an astrolabe, captains could shoot the sun or stars and calculate their latitude, or position on a north-south coordinate.[3]

The compass, the origin of which is unclear, was commonly used on Mediterranean ships by at least the thirteenth century. By 1300, and undoubtedly for some decades before, Mediterranean navigators sailed with the aid of maps remarkable for their accuracy. Navigators were further aided by portolani, or port descriptions, which gave an account of harbors and coastlines and pinpointed hazards. All these technical developments gave European mariners a mastery of the Atlantic coastal waters and helped prepare the way for the voyages of discovery in the fifteenth century.

---

[3] Ships could not tell their longitude, or position on an east-west coordinate, until they could carry accurate clocks, which could in turn tell the time of a basic reference meridian (such as that of Greenwich, England) and be compared with the ship's time. Galileo's discovery of the laws of the pendulum made possible the first really accurate mechanical clocks, but they could not function aboard a swaying ship. Not until the eighteenth century were the first accurate "chronometers," or shipboard clocks, developed. Until then navigators such as Columbus who sailed across the Atlantic had no precise idea how far they were traveling.

Business Institutions

The bad times of the fourteenth century also stimulated the development of more efficient business procedures. The mercantile houses in the late fourteenth and fifteenth centuries were considerably smaller in size than those of the thirteenth century, but were more flexible in their structure. The Medici bank of Florence, which functioned from 1397 until 1498, offers a particularly clear example of fifteenth-century business organization. It was not a single monolithic structure; rather, it was founded upon separate partnerships, by which its various branches were established at Florence, Venice, Rome, Avignon, Bruges, and London. Central control and unified management were ensured, since the senior partners— members of the Medici family—were the same in all the contracts; but the branches had autonomy and, most important, the collapse of one did not threaten them all. One scholar has compared this system of interlocked partnerships to a modern holding company.

Banking operations also grew more sophisticated. By the late fourteenth century, "book transfers" had become commonplace; that is, one depositor could pay a debt to another without actually using coin by ordering the bank to transfer credit from his own account to his creditor's. At first the depositor had to give this order orally, but by 1400 such an order was commonly written, making it one of the immediate ancestors of the modern check.

Accounting methods also improved. The most notable development was the adoption of double-entry bookkeeping, which makes arithmetical errors immediately evident and gives a clear picture of the financial position of a commercial enterprise. Although known in the ancient world, double-entry bookkeeping was not widely practiced in the West until the fourteenth century. In this as in other business practices the lands of southern Europe, especially Italy, were precociously advanced, but their accounting techniques eventually spread to the rest of Europe.

Another financial innovation was the development of a system of maritime insurance, without which investors would have been highly reluctant to risk their money on expensive vessels. There are references to the practice of insuring ships in the major Italian ports as early as 1318. In these first insurance contracts the broker bought the ship and cargo at the port of embarkation and agreed to sell them back at a higher price once the ship reached its destination. If the ship sank en route, it was legally the broker's and he assumed the loss. In the course of the fourteenth century the leading companies of Florence, actively interested in providing insurance to shippers, abandoned the clumsy device of conditional sales and wrote explicit and open insurance contracts. By 1400 maritime insurance had become a regular item of the shipping business. It was to play a major role in the opening of the Atlantic.

Insurance for land transport developed a half-century later and never was intensively practiced. The first examples of life insurance contracts come from fifteenth-century Italy and were limited to particular periods (the duration of a voyage) or particular persons (a wife during pregnancy). But without actuarial tables life insurance of this sort was far more a gamble than a business.

The Economy in the Late Fifteenth Century

In the last half of the fifteenth century Europe had fairly well recovered from the economic blows of a hundred years before, and the revived economy differed greatly from what it had formerly been. Increased diversification, capitalization, and rationalization aided production and enterprise in both countryside and city. Europe in 1500 was certainly a much

smaller community than it had been in 1300. Possibly, too, the gross product of its economy may not have equaled the output of the best years of the thirteenth century. But the population ultimately had fallen more drastically than production. After a century of difficult readjustment Europe emerged more productive and richer than it had been at any earlier time in its history.

II. POPULAR UNREST

The demographic collapse and economic troubles of the fourteenth century deeply disturbed the social peace of Europe. European society

This illustration from a printed Italian handbook, which gives instructions to merchants and is dated ca. 1496, shows the interior of a bank or counting house. (Photo: New York Public Library/Picture Collection)

had been remarkably stable and mostly peaceful from the early Middle Ages until approximately 1300, and the chronicles have preserved few notices of social uprisings or class warfare. The fourteenth and fifteenth centuries, however, witness numerous revolts of peasants and artisans against what they believed to be oppression by the propertied classes.

RURAL REVOLTS

One of the most spectacular of the fourteenth-century rural uprisings was the English Peasants' War of 1381. Both the policies of the royal government and the practices of the great landlords angered the peasants. As mentioned earlier, the royal government through the Statute of Laborers (1351) sought to freeze wages and keep the workers bound to their jobs. Although this policy had little practical success, the mere effort to implement it aggravated social tensions, especially in the countryside, where it would have imposed a kind of neoserfdom upon the peasants. In addition the government made several efforts to collect from the rural villages a poll tax (a flat charge on each member of the population). Moreover, the great landlords, faced with falling rents, sought to revive many half-forgotten feudal dues, which had been allowed to lapse when rents were high in the thirteenth century.

Under leaders of uncertain background—Wat Tyler, Jack Straw, and a priest named John Ball—peasant bands, enraged by the latest poll tax, marched on London in 1381. They called for the final abolition of serfdom, labor services, tithes, and other feudal dues and demanded an end to the poll taxes. The workers of London, St. Albans, York, and other cities, who had similar grievances against the royal government, rose in support of the peasants. After the mobs burned the houses of prominent lawyers and royal officials, King Richard II, then fifteen, with considerable bravery personally met with the peasants and was able to placate them by promising to accept their demands. But as the peasants dispersed, the great landlords reorganized their forces and violently suppressed the last vestiges of unrest in the countryside; the young king also reneged on his promises.

The peasant uprising in England was only one of many rural disturbances that occurred between 1350 and 1450, including revolts in

the Île de France, Languedoc, Catalonia, Sweden, and another in England (1450). Numerous rural disturbances occurred in Germany in the fifteenth century, and a major peasant revolt there in 1524 played an important role in the history of the early Reformation.

URBAN REVOLTS

The causes of social unrest within the cities were very similar to those in the countryside. Governments controlled by the propertied classes tried to prevent wages from rising and workers from moving and also sought to impose a heavier share of the tax burden upon the poorer segments of society. In the fourteenth and early fifteenth centuries Strasbourg, Metz, Ghent, Liège, and Paris all were the scenes of riots. One of the most interesting, if not perhaps the most typical, of the specifically urban revolts was the Ciompi uprising at Florence in 1378.

Florence was one of the wool-manufacturing centers of Europe; the industry employed probably one-third of the working population of the city, which shortly before the Black Death included probably 120,000 people. The wool industry, like most industries, entered into bad times immediately after the plague. To protect themselves, employers cut production, thereby spreading unemployment. Since many of the employers were also members of the ruling oligarchy, they had laws passed limiting wages and manipulating taxation and other monetary policies to the benefit of the rich. The poorest workers were denied their own guild and had no collective voice which might have influenced the government. In all disputes they were subject to the bosses' judges and the bosses' law.

The poorest workers—principally the wool carders, known as the Ciompi—rose in revolt. They demanded, and for a short time got, several reforms. The employers would produce at least enough cloths to assure work; they would refrain from certain monetary manipulations considered deleterious to the interests of the workers; they would allow the workers their own guild; and they would give them representation in communal government. This was hardly a dictatorship of the proletariat, but it was nevertheless intolerable to the ruling oligarchy. Because the Ciompi did not have the leaders to maintain a steady influence on governmental policy, the great families regained full authority in the city by 1382 and quickly abrogated the democratic concessions. Although the Ciompi revolt was short-lived and ultimately unsuccessful, the incident marks one of the first manifestations of urban class tensions which would frequently disturb capitalistic society in future centuries.

THE SEEDS OF DISCONTENT

Each of the social disturbances of the fourteenth and fifteenth centuries was shaped by circumstances that were local and unique. Nevertheless, there were similarities in these social movements: for example, the fact that misery does not seem to have been the principal cause of the unrest. Indeed, the evidence suggests that the conditions of the working classes in both countryside and city were improving after the Black Death. The prosperity of the thirteenth century, which was chiefly a prosperity of landlords and employers, had been founded in part upon the poor negotiating position, and even the exploitation, of the workers. The depopulation of the fourteenth century radically altered this situation. The workers, now much reduced in number, were better able to bargain for lower rents, higher wages, and a fairer distribution of social benefits.

With the possible exception of the Ciompi the people who revolted were rarely the desperately poor. In England, for example, the centers of the peasant uprising of 1381 were in the lower Thames valley—a region which seems to have been more fertile, more prosperous, and less oppressed than other parts of the kingdom. (Serfdom, for example, was relatively less widespread and onerous here than in other English areas.) Also, the immediate provocation for the revolt was the imposition of a poll tax, and obviously poll taxes, or any taxes or charges, do not alarm the truly destitute, whereas they do alarm men recently arrived at some favorable position and anxious to hold onto their gains.

The principal goad to revolt in both town and country seems to have been the effort of the propertied classes to retain their old advantages and deny the workers their new ones. In the first decades after the Black Death governments failed in their efforts to increase taxes and to peg rents, wages, and prices at levels favorable to landlords and employers; meanwhile they spread hostility among the workers, who felt their improving social and economic status threatened.

The impulse to revolt also drew strength from the psychological tensions characteristic of this age of devastating plagues, famines, and wars. The nervous temper of the times predisposed men to take compulsive action against real or imagined enemies. When needed, ready justification for revolt could be found in Christian belief, for the common teaching of the Christian fathers was that neither private property nor social inequality had been intended by God. In a high-strung world many of these uprisings involved an emotional effort to attain the millennium, to reach that age of justice and equality which Christian belief saw in the past, expected in the future, and put off for the present.

The revolts of the fourteenth and fifteenth centuries brought no radical changes in governments or policies, but underlying social movements were coming to elevate the status of the workers. If the rich wanted tillers for their lands and workers for their shops, they had to offer favorable terms.

By about 1450, after a century of instability, a new equilibrium was emerging in European society, even if slowly and never completely. The humblest classes improved their lot and were fairly secure in their gains. Serfdom all but disappeared in the West; wages remained high and bread cheap. Life of course was still very hard for most workers, but it was better than it had been two centuries before. Perhaps reflective of better social conditions for the masses, the population once more began to grow, equipping Europe for its great expansion within its borders and beyond the oceans in the sixteenth century.

III. THE GOVERNMENTS OF EUROPE

War was a frequent occurrence throughout the Middle Ages but was never so widespread and so protracted as in the conflicts of the fourteenth and fifteenth centuries. The Hundred Years' War between England and France is the most famous of these struggles, but there was fighting in every corner of Europe. The in-bred violence of the age manifests a partial breakdown in the governmental systems, their failure to maintain stability at home and peace with foreign powers.

CRISIS AND THE FEUDAL EQUILIBRIUM

The governmental systems of Europe were founded upon multiple partnerships in the exercise of power under the feudal constitutions. The king enjoyed supreme dignity and even a recognized sacred character, but he was far from being an absolute ruler. In return for loyalty and service he conceded a large share of the responsibility for government to a wide range of privileged persons and institutions: the great secular and ecclesiastical princes, the nobles, religious congregations, powerful military orders such as the Templars, free cities, or communes, and even favored guilds such as the universities.

The growth of the feudal constitution in the eleventh and twelfth centuries had been a major step toward a more ordered political life, but it rested upon a delicate equilibrium. To keep an internal peace, which because of the confused borders of most feudal states often meant international peace, all members of the feudal partnership had to remain punctiliously faithful to their obligations. This governmental system worked well until the beginning of the fourteenth century, but it could not sustain the multiple blows suffered during the period of social crisis. Governments had to be slowly rebuilt, still along feudal lines, still based on shared authority. Many of the new governments that came to dominate the European political scene in the late fifteenth century, although still not absolutistic, conceded far more power for the senior partner in the feudal relationship, the king or prince.

Dynastic Instability

The forces which upset the equilibrium of feudal governments were many. One of the most evident, itself rooted in the demographic instability of the age, was the failure of dynasties to perpetuate themselves. The Hundred Years' War, or at least the excuse for it, arose from the inability of the Capetian kings of France, for the first time since the tenth century, to produce a male heir in direct line. The English War of the Roses resulted from the uncertain succession to the crown of England and the claims which the two rival houses of Lancaster and York exerted for it. In Portugal, Castile, France, England, Naples, Hungary,

Poland, and the Scandinavian countries the reigning monarchs of 1450 were not the direct, male, legitimate descendants of those reigning in 1300. Most of the founders of new lines had to fight for their position.

Fiscal Pressures

The same powerful economic forces that were creating new patterns of agriculture and trade were also reshaping the fiscal policies and financial machinery of feudal governments. War was growing more expensive, as well as more frequent. Better-trained armies were needed to fight for longer periods of time and with more complex weaponry. Above all, the increasing use of firearms was adding to the costs of war. To replace the traditional, undisciplined, unpaid, and poorly equipped feudal armies, governments came more and more to rely on mercenaries, who were better trained and better armed than the vassals who fought in fulfillment of their feudal obligations. Many mercenaries were organized into associations known as companies of adventure, whose leaders were both good commanders and businessmen. They took their enterprise where the market was most favorable, sold their services to the highest bidder, and turned substantial profits. To hire mercenaries, and win battles, was increasingly a question of money, which then became, as it has since remained, the *nervi belli* ("the sinews of war").

While war went up in price, the traditional revenues upon which governments depended sank. Until the fourteenth century the king or prince was expected to meet the expenses of government from ordinary revenues, chiefly rents from his properties; but his rents, like everyone's, were falling in the Late Middle Ages. Governments of all types—monarchies, the papacy, cities—desperately sought to develop new sources of revenue. For example, the papacy, because it could not rely on the meager receipts from its lands, built a huge financial apparatus that sold ecclesiastical appointments, favors, and dispensations from normal canonical requirements; imposed tithes on ecclesiastical revenues; and sold indulgences. In France the monarchy established a monopoly over the sale of salt (the *gabelle*). In England the king at various times imposed direct taxes on hearths, individuals (the poll tax), and plow teams, plus a host of smaller levies. The Italian cities taxed a whole range of items from windows to prostitutes. Under acute fiscal pressures governments rigorously scrutinized the necessities, pleasures, and sins of society to find sources of revenue.

Surviving fiscal records indicate that in spite of the disturbed times many governments did succeed in greatly increasing their incomes through these taxes. For example, the English monarchy never collected or spent more than £30,000 per year before 1336; thereafter, the budget rarely sank below £100,000 and at times reached £250,000 in the late fourteenth century.

This new reliance on extraordinary taxes had important political consequences. The most lucrative of them were not limited to the ruler's own demesne but extended over all his realm. They were, in other words, national, or at least territorial, taxes. Moreover, the ruler had no established right to their collection but had to seek the consent of his subjects. He therefore frequently summoned territorial or national assemblies of estates, such as Parliament in England or the Estates General in France, to grant the new taxes. But the assemblies in turn often balked at these requests or offered to grant them only in return for political concessions. Even within the Church many reformers maintained that a general council should have ultimate control over papal finances. The extraordinary expansion of governmental revenues thus raised profound constitutional questions in both ecclesiastical and secular governments.

Factional Conflicts

The aristocracy that had developed nearly everywhere in Europe also entered a period of instability in the Late Middle Ages. Birth afforded the principal access to this class, and membership in it conveyed certain legal and social privileges—exemption from most taxes, immunity from certain juridical procedures, such as torture, and so forth. The nobles looked upon themselves as the chief counselors of the king and his principal partners in the conduct of government.

By the fourteenth century, however, the nobles had long since lost whatever economic homogeneity they may once have possessed. Their wealth was chiefly in land, and they, like all landlords, faced the problem of declining rents. Frequently they lacked the funds needed for the new systems of agriculture. They were further plagued by the continuing problem of finding income and careers for their younger sons. In short, the nobles possessed no immunity from the acute economic dislocations of the times, and their class included men who lived on the brink of poverty as well as holders of enormous estates.

To maintain their position some of the nobles joined the companies of adventure to fight as mercenaries. Others hoped to buttress their sinking fortunes through marriage or by winning offices, lands, pensions, or other favors which governments could provide. Amid these social uncertainties the nobles tended to coalesce into factions, which disputed with one another over the control of government and the distribution of its favors. From England to Italy factional warfare, far more than class warfare, constantly disturbed the peace. A divided and grasping nobility added to the tensions of the age and to its taste for violence.

Characteristically, a faction was led by a great noble house and included numerous persons of varying social station—great nobles in alliance with the leading house, poor knights, retainers, servants, sometimes even artisans and peasants. At times the factions encompassed scores of families and hundreds of men and could almost be considered little states within a state, with their own small armies, loyalties, and symbols of allegiance in the colors or distinctive costumes (livery) worn by their members.

ENGLAND, FRANCE, AND THE HUNDRED YEARS' WAR

All the factors that upset the equilibrium of feudal governments—dynastic instability, fiscal pressures, and factional rivalries—helped to provoke the greatest struggle of the epoch, the Hundred Years' War.

The proclaimed issue of the Hundred Years' War was a dispute over the French royal succession. After more than three hundred years of extraordinary good luck the last three Capetian kings (the brothers Louis X, Philip V, and Charles IV) failed to produce male heirs. With Charles's death in 1328, the nearest surviving male relative was his nephew King Edward III of England, son of his sister Isabella. But the Parlement of Paris—the supreme court of France—declared that women could not transmit a claim to the crown. In place of Edward the French Estates chose Philip of Valois, a first cousin of the preceding kings. Edward did not initially dispute this decision, and as holder of the French fiefs of Aquitaine and Ponthieu he did homage to Philip.

More important than the dynastic issue was

A castle under siege during the Hundred Years' War. (Photo: British Museum)

the clash of French and English interests in the county of Flanders, whose cloth-making industry relied on England for wool. In 1302 the Flemings had rebelled against their count, a vassal of the French king, and had remained virtually independent until 1328, when Philip defeated their forces at Cassel and restored the count. At Philip's insistence the count ordered the arrest of all English merchants in Flanders; Edward then retaliated by cutting off the export of wool, which spread unemployment in the Flemish towns. The Flemings revolted once more and drove out the count. To give legal sanction to their revolt they persuaded Edward to assert his claim to the French crown, which would have given him suzerainty over Flanders as well.

The most serious of all points of friction, however, was the exact status of Aquitaine and Ponthieu. Edward had willingly performed ordinary homage for them, but Philip then insisted on liege homage, which would have obligated Edward to support Philip against all enemies. Edward did not believe that, as a king, he could undertake the obligations of liege homage to any man, and refused. Philip began harassing the frontiers of Aquitaine and declared Edward's fiefs forfeit in 1337. The attack upon Aquitaine undoubtedly pushed Edward into supporting the Flemish revolt and was the principal provocation for the Hundred Years' War.

Philip, in his eagerness for glory, had clearly embarked upon a dangerous adventure in his harassment of Aquitaine, and Edward, in supporting the Flemings, reacted perhaps too strongly to the provocation. Both men evidently took their feudal obligation of mutual respect and love very lightly. The coming of this war between the French king and his principal vassal was thus rooted in a breakdown of the feudal constitution of medieval France in both its institutions and its spirit.

The Tides of Battle

The French seemed to have a decisive superiority over the English at the outset of the war. The population of France was perhaps fifteen million; England had between four and seven million. But for most of its course the war was not really a national confrontation. French subjects (Flemings, Gascons, later Burgundians) fought alongside the English against other French subjects. The confused struggle may be fairly divided into three periods: an initial phase of English victories from 1338 to 1360; a phase of French resurgence, then stalemate, from 1367 to 1415; and a wild denouement with tides rapidly shifting from 1415 to 1453.

The series of English victories that opened the war were never fully exploited by the English, nor ever quite undone by the French. An English naval victory at Sluys in 1340 assured English communications across the Channel and determined France as the scene of the fighting. Six years later Edward landed in France on what was more a marauding expedition than a campaign of conquest. Philip pursued the English and finally overtook them at Crécy. The French knights attacked before their forces could be entirely marshaled and organized; the disciplined English, making effective use of the longbow, cut the confused French army to pieces. The scenario was repeated in 1356 at Poitiers. John II, who had succeeded Philip, attacked an English army under Edward's son, the gallant Black Prince, and incurred a defeat even more crushing. English victories, the Black Death, and mutual exhaustion prepared the way for the Peace of Brétigny in 1360. The English were given Calais and an enlarged Aquitaine, and Edward in turn renounced his claims to the French crown.

But the French could not allow so large a part of their kingdom to remain in English

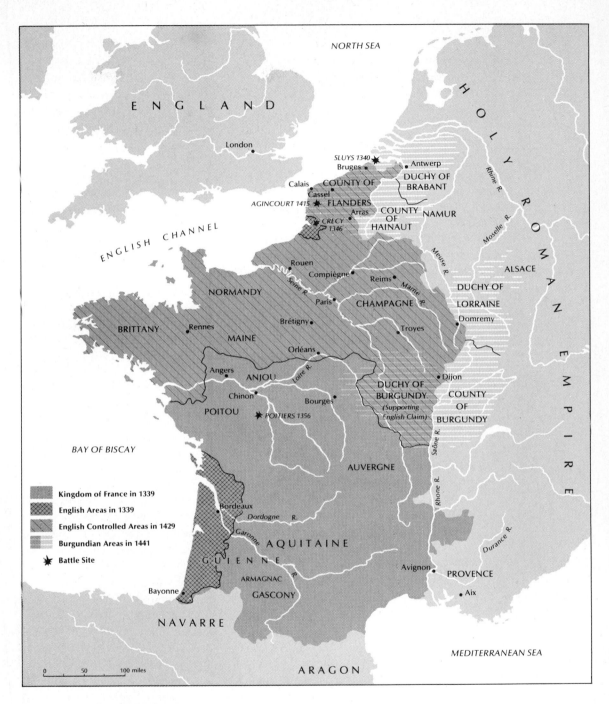

MAP 11.2: THE HUNDRED YEARS' WAR

NORTH SEA

E N G L A N D

London

SLUYS 1340 ★
Bruges • • Antwerp
Calais • DUCHY OF
Cassel COUNTY OF BRABANT
AGINCOURT 1415 ★ FLANDERS
Arras • COUNTY NAMUR
CRECY OF
1346 HAINAUT

ENGLISH CHANNEL

Rouen •
Compiègne •
Reims •
NORMANDY
Seine R. Paris • CHAMPAGNE

BRITTANY
Rennes • Brétigny •
MAINE
Orléans •
Angers •
ANJOU Loire R.
Chinon •
POITOU
Bourges •
★ POITIERS 1356

BAY OF BISCAY

DUCHY OF
BURGUNDY
(Supporting
English Claim)

ALSACE

DUCHY OF
LORRAINE
Domremy •

Troyes •

DIjon •

COUNTY
OF
BURGUNDY

AUVERGNE

H O L Y   R O M A N   E M P I R E

Rhine R.
Moselle R.
Meuse R.
Marne R.
Saône R.
Rhône R.

Bordeaux •
Dordogne R.
Garonne R.
A Q U I T A I N E

G U I E N N E

Bayonne •
ARMAGNAC
GASCONY

N A V A R R E

Avignon •
Aix •

PROVENCE

Durance R.

MEDITERRANEAN SEA

A R A G O N

Kingdom of France in 1339
English Areas in 1339
English Controlled Areas in 1429
Burgundian Areas in 1441
★ Battle Site

0   50   100 miles

hands. Seven years later, under John's successor, Charles V, they opened the second phase of the war. The French armies succeeded largely by avoiding full-scale battles and wearing down the English forces bit by bit. By 1380 they had pushed the English nearly into the sea, confining them to Calais and a narrow strip of the Atlantic coast from Bordeaux to Bayonne. Fighting was sporadic from 1380 until 1415, both sides content with a stalemate.

The last period of the war from 1415 to 1453 was one of high drama and rapidly shifting fortunes. Henry V of England invaded France and wrought disaster on the French army at Agincourt in 1415. His success was confirmed by the Treaty of Troyes in 1420, an almost total French capitulation. King Charles VI of France declared his son the Dauphin (the future Charles VII) illegitimate, named Henry his successor, appointed him regent of France, and gave him direct rule over all French lands as far south as the Loire River (see Map 11.2). Charles also gave Henry his daughter Catherine in marriage.

The Dauphin of course could not accept this forced abdication, and from his capital at Bourges he led an expedition across the Loire River. Henry drove his forces back and then embarked on a systematic reduction of towns and fortresses north of the river that were loyal to the Dauphin. Then in 1428 the English laid siege to Orléans; its fall would have given them a commanding position in the Loire valley and would have rendered the plight of the Dauphin nearly desperate.

Joan of Arc

The intervention of a young peasant girl, Joan of Arc, saved the Capetian dynasty. Convinced that heavenly voices were ordering her to rescue France, Joan persuaded several royal officials, and finally the Dauphin himself, of the authenticity of her mission and was given an army. In 1429 she marched to Orléans and

forced the English to raise the siege. She then escorted the Dauphin to Reims, the historic coronation city of France. His own coronation there confirmed his legitimacy and enlisted the support of French royalist sentiment in his cause. The tide had turned.

Joan passed from history as quickly and as dramatically as she had arrived. The Burgundians, allies of the English, captured her in 1430 and sold her to the English, who put her on trial for witchcraft and heresy. She was burned at the stake at Rouen in 1431.

Joan was a manifestation of an increasingly powerful sentiment among the people. They had grown impatient with continuing destruction and had come to identify their own security with the expulsion of the English and with a strong Capetian monarchy. This growing loyalty to the king finally saved France from its century of struggle. A series of French successes followed the execution of Joan, and by 1453 only Calais was left in English hands. No formal treaty ended the war, but both sides accepted the outcome: England was no longer a Continental power.

The Effects of the Hundred Years' War

Like all the disasters of that era, the Hundred Years' War accelerated change. With regard to warfare, it stimulated the development of firearms and the technologies needed for them and helped establish that the infantry, armed with longbow, pike, or gun, was superior in battle to mounted knights.

The war also had a significant effect on governmental institutions in England and France. The expense of fighting forced the kings on each side to look for new sources of revenue through taxation. In England the king willingly conceded to Parliament a larger role in return for grants of new taxes. The tradition became firmly established that Parliament had the right to grant or refuse new taxes, to agree to legislation, to channel appeals to the king, and to offer advice on important decisions such as those regarding peace and war. The House of Commons gained the right to introduce all tax legislation, since the Commons could speak, as the Lords could not, as representatives of the shires and boroughs. Parliament also named a committee to audit the tax records, to be sure that its will was respected. Equally important, Commons could also impeach high royal officials, an important early step in establishing the principle that the king's ministers were responsible to Parliament as well as to their royal master. By the end of the Hundred Years' War, Parliament had been considerably strengthened at the expense of royal power.

The need for new taxes produced a somewhat different outcome in France, actually enhancing the power of the French monarchs while weakening the Estates General, the national representative assembly. In 1343 Philip IV established a monopoly over the sale of salt, determining in many French provinces how much each family had to consume and how much they had to pay for it. The tax on salt, called the *gabelle*, was destined to form a major support of French finance for the entire duration of the monarchy, until 1789. In gaining support for this and other proposed taxes Philip and his successors sought the agreement of both the regional, or provincial, assemblies of estates and the national Estates General. The kings' reliance on the provincial estates hindered the emergence of a centralized assembly that could speak for the entire kingdom. By the reign of Charles VII, during the last stages of the war, the monarchy obtained the right to impose national taxes (notably the *taille*, a direct tax from which nobles and clerics were exempt) without the consent of the Estates General. By then, too, the royal government was served by a standing, professional army (the "companies of ordinance")—the first in any European country since the fall of the Roman Empire.

This representation of St. Joan of Arc, done after her death, shows her in battle dress, with the figures of the three saints who instructed her (her "voices") emblazoned upon her banner. (Photo: Archives Nationales/Giraudon)

Both England and France experienced internal dissension during the course of the war. After the death of Edward III in 1377, England faced over a century of turmoil, with the nobles striving to maintain their endangered economic fortunes through factional conflicts—that is, by preying on one another. In time these conflicts led to a struggle between two factions, the Lancastrians and the Yorkists, over the throne itself, with the English nobles quickly aligning themselves on one side or the other. The civil war that followed is known to historians as the

War of the Roses (the Lancastrian emblem was a red rose, that of the Yorkists a white one). It lasted some thirty-five years, ending in 1485, when at Bosworth Field Henry Tudor defeated the Yorkists and acceded to the throne as Henry VII. By this time prosperity had relieved the pressures on the English nobles, and the people in general, weary of war, welcomed the strong and orderly regime which Henry proposed to establish.

In France too the power of the monarchy was threatened by strife between rival factions of nobles, the Armagnacs and the Burgundians. The Armagnacs favored a vigorous prosecution of the war with England, whereas the Burgundians favored accommodation. The territorial ambitions of the Burgundians also posed a threat to the French monarchy. King John the Good of France had granted the huge Duchy of Burgundy to his younger son, Philip the Bold, in 1363. Philip and his successors greatly enlarged their possessions in eastern France, the Rhone and Rhine valleys, and the Low Countries (see Map 11.2). The dukes seem to have taken as their goal the establishment of a Burgundian "middle kingdom" between France and the Holy Roman Empire; such a state would have permanently affected the political geography of Europe and undermined the position of the French monarch. However, this threat ended in 1477 with the death of the last duke, because his daughter and heir, Mary of Burgundy, was unable to hold her scattered inheritance together, and a large part of it came under French control.

With the loss of nearly all its Continental possessions in the course of the war, England emerged from the war geographically more consolidated. It was also homogeneous in its language (English had replaced French as the language of the law courts and administration) and conscious of its cultural distinctiveness and national identity. Freed from its Continental entanglements, England was ready for its expansion beyond the seas and for a great growth in national pride and self-consciousness.

France never achieved quite the territorial consolidation of England, but with the expulsion of the English from the Continent and the sudden distintegration of the Duchy of Burgundy the French king was without a major rival among his feudal princes. The monarchy emerged from the war with a permanent army, a remunerative tax system, and no clear constitutional restrictions on its exercise of power. Most significantly, the war gave the French king greater prestige and confirmed him as the chief protector and patron of the people.

In both France and England, government at the end of the Middle Ages must still be considered decentralized and "feudal," if we mean by that term that certain privileged persons and institutions (nobles, the Church, towns, and the like) continued to hold and to exercise some forms of private jurisdiction. They retained, for example, their own courts. But the king had unmistakably emerged as the dominant partner in the feudal relationship. Moreover, he was prepared to press his advantages still further in the sixteenth century.

THE HOLY ROMAN EMPIRE

With the death of Emperor Frederick II of Hohenstaufen (1250), the Holy Roman Empire ceased to function as a major power in European affairs. The empire continued to link Germany and Italy, but real authority fell to the princes in Germany and the city republics in Italy. In 1273, after a tumultuous period known as the Interregnum, during which several rivals contended for the title, the princes chose as emperor Rudolf of Hapsburg, the first of that famous family to hold the office. Instead of rebuilding the imperial authority, Rudolf rather sought to advance the interests of his own dynasty and its ancestral possessions. His successors also characteristically sought to use the office of emperor for their own narrow dynastic advantage.

A significant event of the fourteenth century was the issuance in 1356 of the Golden Bull, which defined the constitution of the empire as it would largely remain until 1806. Although issued by the pope, the bull reflected the interests of the great German princes. The right of naming the emperor was given to seven electors—the archbishops of Mainz, Trier, and Cologne, the count palatine of the Rhine, the duke of Saxony, the margrave of Brandenburg, and the king of Bohemia. It assigned no role to the popes in naming or crowning the emperor and thus was a victory for imperial autonomy.

A development of major interest in the empire was the emergence of the Swiss Confederation of cantons (districts), which won virtual autonomy in the Late Middle Ages. In the early thirteenth century Emperor Frederick II of Hohenstaufen had recognized the autonomy of two cantons, Uri and Schwyz, and had given them the responsibility of guarding the Saint Gotthard Pass through the Alps, the shortest route from Germany to Italy. The lands of the cantons were technically part of the ancient duchy of Swabia, and in the late thirteenth century the Hapsburg princes, seeking to consolidate their possessions in the duchy, attempted to subjugate the Swiss lands as well. To resist the Hapsburg menace the cantons of Uri, Schwyz, and Unterwalden joined in a Perpetual Compact in 1291. They formed the nucleus of what was eventually to become the twenty-two cantons of present-day Switzerland.

The Swiss had to fight for their autonomy, and they acquired the reputation of being among the best fighters in Europe. Both history and legend, such as the colorful stories of William Tell, celebrate their successes. The confederated governments of the Swiss cantons represent a notable exception to the tendency, evident elsewhere in Europe, for central governments to grow stronger in the fourteenth and fifteenth centuries.

THE STATES OF ITALY

The free city, or commune, was the dominant power in Italian political life at the beginning of the fourteenth century, at least in the center and north of the peninsula. The Holy Roman Empire exerted a loose sovereignty over much of the peninsula north of Rome and the papacy governed the area around Rome, but almost all the principal cities, and many small ones too, had gained the status of self-governing city-states.

However, the new economic and social conditions of the fourteenth century were unfavorable to the survival of the smaller communes. The economic contractions of the times made it increasingly difficult for industries and merchant houses in the smaller cities to compete with their rivals in the larger ones. Moreover, with the rising costs of war the small communes found it equally hard to defend their independence. Finally, in both large and small towns Italian society was deeply disturbed by factional strife which often made political order impossible.

In response to such pressures two principal tendencies become evident in Italian political development. Much stronger governments, amounting at times to true despotisms, tended to replace the weak governments of the free commune. And regional states, dominated politically and economically by a single metropolis, replaced the numerous, free, and highly competitive communes.

Perhaps the most effective Italian despot was the ruler of Milan, Gian Galeazzo Visconti (1378–1402), who energetically set about enlarging the Visconti inheritance of twenty-one cities in the Po valley. Through shrewd negotiations and opportune attacks he secured the submission of Verona, Vicenza, and Padua, which gave him an outlet to the Adriatic Sea. He then seized Bologna, purchased Pisa, and through a variety of ways was accepted as suzerain in Siena, Perugia, Spoleto, Nocera, and Assisi. In the course of this advance deep into central Italy Gian Galeazzo worked with some success to keep his chief enemies, the Florentines and the Venetians, divided, and he seemed destined to forge an Italian kingdom and restore Italian unity.

To establish a legal basis for his power Gian Galeazzo secured from the emperor an appointment as imperial vicar in 1380, and then as hereditary duke in 1395. This made him, in fact, the only duke in all Italy and seemed a step toward the assumption of a royal title. He revised the statutes of Milan, but his chief administrative achievement, and the true foundation of most of his successes, was his ability to wring enormous tax revenues from his subjects. Gian Galeazzo was also a generous patron of Humanism and the new learning, and with his conquests, wealth, and brilliance he seemed to be awaiting only the submission of the truculent Florentines before adopting the title of king. But he died unexpectedly in 1402, leaving two minor sons, who were incapable of defending their inheritance.

Even those states that escaped the despotism of a Gian Galeazzo moved toward stronger governments and the formation of territorial or regional states. In Venice the government was placed under the domination of a small and closed oligarchy. A kind of corporative despot, known as the Council of Ten, looked over and after the Venetian state. Its mandate was the preservation of oligarchic rule in Venice and the suppression of opposition to the government.

Whereas Venice had previously devoted its principal energies to maritime commerce and overseas possessions, it could not now ignore the growth on the mainland of territorial states,

which might deprive it of its agricultural imports or jeopardize its inland trade routes. From the early fifteenth century onward Venice too initiated a policy of territorial expansion on the mainland. By 1405 Padua, Verona, and Vicenza had become Venetian dependencies.

Florence, while retaining the outer trappings of republican government, also came under stronger rule. In 1434 a successful banker named Cosimo de' Medici established a form of boss rule over the city. In his tax policies he favored the lower and middle classes of the city, and also cultivated the support of the middle classes by appointments to office and other forms of political patronage. Further, he took peace in Italy as his supreme goal. In guiding the relations between Florence and other cities and states he earned from his fellow citizens the title *pater patriae* ("father of his country"), and most historians would concur in this judgment.

Cosimo's achievements were a preparation for the rule of his more famous grandson, Lorenzo the Magnificent (1478–1492). Under Lorenzo's direction Florence set the style for Italy, and eventually for Europe, in the splendor of its festivals, the elegance of its social life, the beauty of its buildings, and the lavish support it extended to scholars and artists. With good reason, Lorenzo's lifetime is viewed by many as the golden age of Renaissance Florence.

The Papal States and the Kingdom of Naples

The popes, who were now located in Avignon in southern France, sought to consolidate their rule over their possessions in central Italy, but they faced formidable obstacles. The rugged territory with its many castles and fortified towns enabled communes, petty lords, and plain brigands to defy the papal authority easily. Continuing disorders largely discouraged the popes from returning to Rome, and the attempts to pacify the tumultuous region were causing a major drain on papal finances.

Even after its return to Rome in 1378 the papacy had difficulty maintaining authority. Not until the pontificate of Martin V (1417–1431) was a stable administration established, and Martin's successors still faced frequent revolts for the entire course of the fifteenth century.

The political situation was equally confused in the Kingdom of Naples and Sicily. With papal support Charles of Anjou, younger brother of St. Louis of France, had established a dynasty of Angevin rulers over the area. But in 1282 the people of Sicily revolted against the Angevins and appealed for help to the king of Aragon. For the next 150 years the Aragonese and the Angevins battled for dominion over Sicily and Naples. Then in 1435 the king of Aragon, Alfonso V, the Magnanimous, reunited Sicily and southern Italy and made the kingdom the center of an Aragonese empire in the Mediterranean. Alfonso sought to suppress the factions of lawless nobles and to reform taxes and strengthen administration. His efforts were not completely successful, for southern Italy and Sicily were rugged, poor lands and difficult to subdue; but he was at least able to overcome the chaos that had prevailed earlier. Alfonso was an enthusiastic patron of literature and the arts, and his court at Naples was one of the most brilliant of the early Renaissance.

Foreign Relations

Italy, by about 1450, was no longer a land of numerous, tiny free communes. Rather, it was divided among five territorial states: the Duchy of Milan, the republics of Venice and Florence, the Papal States, and the Kingdom of Naples (see Map 11.3). To govern the relations among these states the Italians conceived new methods of diplomacy. Led by Venice, the states began to maintain permanent embassies at important foreign courts.

Moreover, largely through the political sense of Cosimo de' Medici, the Italian states were able to pioneer a new way of preserving stability. The Peace of Lodi in 1454 ended a war between Milan, Florence, and Venice, and Cosimo sought to make the peace a lasting one through balancing alliance systems. Milan, Naples, and Florence held one side of the balance, and Venice and the Papal States the other. Each state felt sufficiently secure in its alliances to have no need to appeal to non-Italian powers for support. During the next forty years the balance was occasionally rocked, but never overturned, and it gave Italy an unaccustomed period of peace and freedom from foreign intervention. This system represents one of the earliest appearances in European history of the concept of the balance of power as a workable means of maintaining both security and peace.

IV. THE PAPACY

The papacy also experienced profound transformations in the fourteenth and fifteenth centuries. It continued to envision as its chief objective a peaceful Christendom united in faith and in filial obedience to Rome. But in fact the international Christian community was beset by powerful forces that worked to undermine its cohesiveness and to weaken papal authority and influence. Although the culmination of these disruptive forces came in the Reformation in the sixteenth century, their roots lie deep within the history of the previous two centuries.

THE AVIGNON EXILE

The humiliation of Pope Boniface VIII by the agents of Philip IV of France at Anagni in 1303 opened the doors to French influence at the Curia. In 1305 the College of Cardinals elected a Frenchman pope, Clement V, who

MAP 11.3: ITALY 1454

Map labels (clockwise/by region):

Legend:
1 MARCH OF MONTFERRAT
2 MARCH OF MANTUA
3 DUCHY OF MODENA
4 REPUBLIC OF LUCCA
5 COUNTY OF ASTI

THE FIVE GREAT POWERS
Republic of Florence
Duchy of Milan
Kingdom of Naples
Papal States
Venetian Republic

DUCHY OF SAVOY
Aosta
Turin
Saluzzo
Genoa
GENOA
Milan
Pavia
Lodi
Cremona
Piacenza
Po R.
Adda R.
Bergamo
Brescia
Trent
Adige R.
Vincenza
Verona
Padua
Treviso
Venice
Chioggia
ISTRIA
Parma
Reggio
Modena
EMILIA
Bologna
Ferrara
DUCHY OF FERRARA
Ravenna
ROMAGNA
Rimini
San Marino
Urbino
Ancona
MARCHES
Lucca
Pistoia
Pisa
Florence
Arno R.
Livorno
TUSCANY
Siena
SIENA
Arezzo
Assisi
Perugia
Spoleto
Orvieto
Viterbo
Rome
Tiber R.
Pontecorvo
ELBA
(to Florence)
CORSICA
(to Genoa)
SARDINIA
(to Aragon)
TYRRHENIAN SEA
ADRIATIC SEA
DALMATIA
Barletta
Trani
Bari
Benevento
Naples
Nocera
Salerno
Brindisi
Taranto
PUGLIA
Otranto
Cosenza
CALABRIA
Palermo
Messina
Reggio
SICILY
Syracuse

0   50   100 miles

The papal palace at Avignon was the site of what has been termed the papacy's "Babylonian captivity," or the Avignon exile. Rome was without the papacy from 1308 to 1377. (Photo: Photo Boudot-LaMotte)

because of the political disorders in the Papal States settled at Avignon. Though technically a part of the Holy Roman Empire, Avignon was in language and culture a French city. The popes who followed Clement expressed an intention to return to Rome but remained at Avignon, claiming that the continuing turmoil of central Italy would not permit the papal government to function effectively. These popes were, in fact, skilled administrators, and the period witnessed an enormous expansion of the papal bureaucracy, especially its fiscal machinery.

FISCAL CRISIS

Like many secular governments the papacy at Avignon faced an acute fiscal crisis. But unlike the major powers of Europe it had no adequate territorial base to supply it with funds, because the tumultuous Papal States usually drained off more money than they supplied. The powers of appointment, dispensation, tithing, and indulgences were the only resources the papacy possessed, and it was thus drawn into the unfortunate but perhaps unavoidable practice of exploiting them for financial purposes. For instance, the popes insisted that candidates appointed to high ecclesiastical offices pay a special tax, which usually amounted to a third or a half of the first year's revenues. The popes also claimed the income from vacant offices and even sold future appointments to office when the incumbents were still alive. Dispensation released a petitioner from the normal requirements of canon law. A monastery or religious house, for example, might purchase from the pope an exemption from the visitation and inspection of the local bishop. Tithes were a payment to the papacy of one-tenth of the revenues of ecclesiastical benefices or offices throughout Christendom. Indulgences, remissions of the temporal punishment attendant to a sin, were also distributed in return for monetary contributions to the papacy.[4]

These fiscal practices brought the popes greatly enlarged revenues, but they also had many deplorable results. Prelates who paid huge sums to Avignon tended to pass on the costs to the lower clergy. Parish priests, hardly able to live within the incomes left to them, were the more readily tempted to disordered moral lives. The flow of money to Avignon angered rulers; well before the close of the Middle Ages there were demands for a halt to such payments and even for the confiscation of Church property. Dispensations gravely injured the authority of the bishops, since the exempt persons or houses all but escaped their

supervision. The bishops were frequently too weak, and the pope too distant, to deal effectively with abuses on the local level. The fiscal system of the papacy thus helped sow chaos in many parts of the Western Church.

THE GREAT SCHISM

The end of the seventy-year Avignon exile led to a controversy that almost split the Western Church. Pope Gregory XI returned reluctantly to Rome in 1378 and died there a short time later. The Roman people, fearing that Gregory's successor would once more remove the court to Avignon and thereby deprive Rome of desperately needed revenues, agitated for the election of an Italian pope. Responding to this pressure, the College of Cardinals found a compromise candidate who satisfied both French and Italian interests—a Neapolitan of French-Angevin extraction. The new pope, Urban VI, soon antagonized the French cardinals by seeking to limit their privileges and by threatening to pack the College with his own appointments. Seven months after choosing Urban, a majority of the cardinals declared that his election had taken place under duress and was therefore invalid; they then named a new pope, who returned to Avignon. Thus began the Great Schism of the West, the period when two, and later three, popes contended over the rule of the Church. The schism was to last for almost forty years.

Christendom was now confronted with the deplorable spectacle of two pretenders to the throne of Peter, one in Rome and one in Avignon. Princes and peoples quickly took sides (see Map 11.4). The troubles of the papacy were at once doubled. Each pope had his own court and needed still more funds, both to meet ordinary expenses and to pay for policies which he hoped would defeat his rival. And since each pope excommunicated the other and those who supported him, everyone in

---

[4] Both the tithe and the indulgence originated as means of supporting the crusades, but income from them was frequently, and even usually, applied by the pope to his domestic needs.

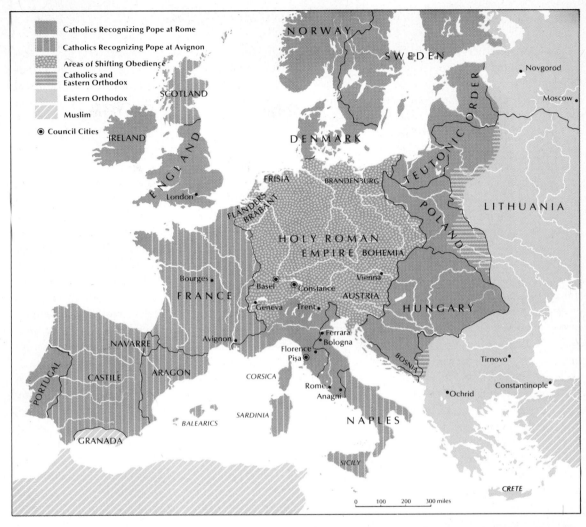

MAP 11.4: THE GREAT SCHISM 1378–1417

Christendom was at least technically excommunicated.

THE CONCILIAR MOVEMENT

Theologians and jurists had speculated earlier on who should rule the Church if the pope were to become heretical or incompetent; some concluded that it should be the College of Cardinals or a general council of Church officials. Since the College of Cardinals had split into two factions, each backing one of the rival popes, many prominent thinkers supported the theory that a general council should rule the Church. These conciliarists, as they were called, went even further. They urged that the Church be given a new constitution to confirm the supremacy of a general council. Such a step would have reduced the pope's role to that of a limited monarch. The critical need for correcting numerous abuses, particularly regarding the fiscal support and morality of the clergy, lent further strength to the idea that a general council should rule and reform the Church.

The first test of the conciliarists' position was at the Council of Pisa (1409), which was convened by cardinals of both Rome and Avignon. The council did assert its own supremacy within the Church by deposing the two popes and electing another. But this act merely compounded the confusion, for it left Christendom with three rivals claiming to be the lawful pope.

A few years later another council finally resolved the situation. Some four hundred ecclesiastics assembled at the Council of Constance (1414–1418), the greatest international gathering of the Middle Ages. The council was organized in a fashion novel for the times. The delegates elected to sit and vote by nations to offset the power of the Italians, who constituted nearly half the attendance. The council also gave recognition to the new importance of national and territorial churches, as each national church voted as a unit.

The assembled delegates immediately deposed both the new pope and the pope at Avignon after the latter refused to resign; the Roman pope submitted to the demand of the council and resigned. In his stead the council elected a Roman cardinal, who took the name Martin V. Thus the Great Schism was ended, and the Western Church was once again united under a single pope.

As the meetings continued, the views of the conciliarists prevailed. The delegates formally declared that a general council was supreme within the Church. To ensure a degree of continuity in Church government the delegates further directed that new councils be summoned periodically.

In spite of this assertion of supremacy, the council made little headway in reforming the Church "in head and members," to use the language of contemporaries. Those attending the council, chiefly great prelates, were in large part the beneficiaries of the fiscal system. They were reluctant to touch their own privileges and advantages. The real victims of the fiscal abuses, the lower clergy, were poorly represented. The council could not agree on a general program of reform. This failure illustrates a fatal flaw in the vision of conciliar rule over the Church. The council was too large, too cumbersome, and too divided to maintain an effective ecclesiastical government. The restored papacy quickly reclaimed its position as supreme head of the Western Church.

The practical weaknesses of the conciliar movement were amply revealed at the Council of Basel (1431–1443). Because disputes broke out almost at once with the pope, the council deposed him and elected another to replace him, Felix V. The conciliar movement, designed to heal the schism, now seemed responsible for renewing it. Recognizing the futility of its actions, the council at the death of Felix tried to rescue a semblance of its dignity by "electing" the Roman pope Nicholas V in 1449 and disbanding. This ended the effort to reform the Church through giving supreme authority over it to councils.

The popes retained a suspicion of councils, but in fact they had much more serious rivals to their authority in the powerful lay princes, who were exerting an ever tighter control over their territorial churches. Both England and France issued decrees that limited the exercise of papal powers within their kingdoms. The policy was soon imitated in Spain and in the stronger principalities of the Holy Roman Empire. Although these decrees did not establish national or territorial churches, they do document the deteriorating papal control over the international Christian community.

THE POPES AS PATRONS OF THE ARTS

The papacy in the fifteenth and early sixteenth centuries experienced one of the most troubled and most glorious periods of its history. The popes ruled over a disturbed Christendom, soon to experience one of its greatest crises in the Reformation. Yet never before had the papacy exerted such an influence over artistic and cultural expression in the West. The visitor to Rome today is captivated by the magnificent art which the popes of this age encouraged and supported.

According to his epitaph, Nicholas V (1447–1455) restored the golden age to Rome. A splendid, learned court had become essential to a great prince, and Nicholas intended to make the papal court second to none. The manuscripts that he assiduously collected became the nucleus of the Vatican Library. Pius II (1458–1464) is the only pope to have left us a personal memoir of his reign—his *Commentaries*, which offers a marvelous picture of the psychology of the times.

The Sistine Chapel in the Vatican is the great monument of Sixtus IV (1471–1484). He commissioned the best artists of the day—Botticelli, Perugino, Pinturicchio, and others—to paint the twelve frescoes of the lower walls.

During the reign of Sixtus's nephew Julius II (1503–1513) Michelangelo painted the glorious ceiling of the chapel (see Plate 24), which has remained a true museum of Renaissance artistic genius.

Julius also commissioned the new St. Peter's Church, with the Florentine Bramante (later succeeded by Michelangelo) as architect. Moreover, Julius achieved one of the papacy's main political goals: his military successes and reformed administration had consolidated his authority over the Papal States and ensured stability in central Italy. At this moment of unrivaled splendor and apparent success, the papacy stood on the brink of disaster.

The Reformation, which began during the reign of Julius's successor, makes it hard to judge these magnificent pontiffs fairly. Certainly they do not bear the major responsibility for the Protestant revolt, but they clearly did fail to grasp the depth and danger of the ills afflicting Christendom. The values of the day obscured and limited their vision. They flourished as princes and faltered as popes.

In the fourteenth and fifteenth centuries a series of spectacular catastrophes disrupted European life on almost every level. In the wake of plague, famine, and war, all rooted perhaps in overpopulation, the numbers of Europe's peoples fell drastically, and a severe economic depression gripped the Continent. The European nations were forced to reorganize their economies in accordance with the new scarcity of labor and the new structure of the market. By about 1450 they achieved considerable economic recovery, based upon a greater diversification in production and a marked substitution of capital for labor. In the late fifteenth century Europe was a smaller but richer community than it had been two hundred years before.

Society and government experienced a comparable crisis, as social unrest, factional strife, and war nearly everywhere disturbed the peace of Europe. But here too a new stability was achieved by about 1450, based on better conditions of life for the humbler classes and on the stronger authority claimed by many princes. The papacy also changed; it developed a huge bureaucratic and fiscal apparatus and successfully withstood the challenge of the conciliar movement. However, it failed to lead the Church to the reform many Europeans were demanding.

In European culture as well as institutions a profound crisis occurred in the fourteenth and fifteenth centuries. Yet even in this aspect of the "autumn" of the Middle Ages there was a renaissance, in the sense that out of a crisis of traditional values there emerged new creative efforts to enrich the culture of the West.

RECOMMENDED READING

Sources

Council of Constance. Louise R. Loomis (tr.). 1961.

*Froissart, Jean. *The Chronicles of England, France, Spain and Other Places Adjoining.* 1961. Covers the first half of the Hundred Years' War.

*Pernoud, Regine (ed.). *Joan of Arc: By Herself and Her Witnesses.* 1969.

Pius II, Pope. *Commentaries of Pius Second.* Florence A. Gragg (tr.). 1970. Personal, often acerbic reminiscences; unique document in papal history.

*Vespasiano da Bisticci. *Renaissance Princes, Popes and Prelates.* 1963. Biographies of prominent Italians of the fifteenth century, written by a contemporary.

Studies

*Ady, Cecil M. *Lorenzo dei Medici and Renaissance Italy.* 1952. Readable introduction to the rule and culture of the Medici.

Becker, Marvin B. *Florence in Transition.* 1967 ff. Stimulating and controversial.

*Bridbury, A. R. *Economic Growth in England in the Later Middle Ages.* 1962. Rejects thesis of a "Renaissance depression."

Brucker, Gene A. *Florentine Politics and Society.* 1962–1976. Social and political history of Florence from 1343 to 1420.

De Roover, Raymond. *The Rise and Decline of the Medici Bank.* 1963. Classic study in business history.

Hilton, Rodney. *Bondsmen Made Free.* 1973. A study of peasant violence in the Late Middle Ages.

*Mattingly, Garrett. *Renaissance Diplomacy.* 1964.

*Perroy, Édouard. *The Hundred Years' War.* 1965. Excellent survey by a French scholar.

*Schevill, Ferdinand. *Medieval and Renaissance Florence.* 1963. Readable general history.

_____

* Available in paperback.

TWELVE

THE WEST
IN TRANSITION:
THE RENAISSANCE

The Swiss historian Jacob Burckhardt published a book in 1860, which has influenced, as few books have, the understanding that most educated men and women in Europe and America have of their own past. In The Civilization of the Renaissance in Italy *he argued that the fourteenth and fifteenth centuries witnessed a true revolution in values in that country. Men allegedly shook off the religious illusions and institutional restrictions of medieval society and rediscovered both the visible world and their own true selves. The essential novelty of Renaissance culture was the accent it placed on the individual and the delight it took in the beauties and satisfactions of life. The humanistic heritage of Greece and Rome, which stressed similar values, appealed to the men of this age, and the revived interest in that heritage constituted the classical Renaissance. Moreover, according to Burckhardt, the Italy of this period deserves to be considered the birthplace of the modern world.*

Modern historians can easily criticize Burckhardt's sweeping assertions. It is difficult to believe that anyone could attain the full release from his society and its traditions that Burckhardt claimed for the men of the fourteenth and fifteenth centuries. He certainly slighted the achievements of the earlier Middle Ages and exaggerated the originality of the period he called the Renaissance. Also, he confined his vision to Italy, and historians have had difficulty applying his formulas to other regions of Europe. Nevertheless, his fundamental insight still commands the respect and agreement of many scholars.

Historians today still discuss the problems raised by Burckhardt, but they are also learning to view those problems from new perspectives. They are penetrating ever more deeply into archives and attempting to apply stronger analytical methods to the data they are gathering. They are exploring aspects of society and social experience inaccessible to

Burckhardt and other earlier historians. How long did men live and how did they grow, marry, raise their children, and meet with death? In the light of these experiences, how did they view the world, and what did they value in life? How and to what extent did their attitudes in fact change? These are the questions for which many scholars today are seeking answers, and which we too shall examine in this chapter.

1. SOCIETY AND CULTURE IN ITALY

In the fourteenth and fifteenth centuries Italy produced an extraordinary number of gifted thinkers and artists, whose collective work constituted the core of the cultural Renaissance and profoundly influenced all areas of European thought and artistic expression. To understand the character of the Renaissance requires, there- fore, a consideration of the society which, in Burckhardt's estimation, shaped the culture of the modern world.

CITIES

One basic social characteristic clearly distinguished Italy from most European areas: the number and size of its cities, particularly in the northern regions of Tuscany and the Lombard plain. In 1377, for example, only 10 percent of the people in England lived in urban centers with a population greater than 3,200—a percentage fairly typical for most of northern Europe—whereas in Tuscany about 26 percent lived in urban centers. The cities were large. Venice, for instance, counted probably 120,000 inhabitants in 1338; 84,000 in about 1422; 102,000 in 1509; and 169,000 in 1563—a figure it was not to reach again until the twentieth century.

This remarkable urban concentration affected Italian culture. The large nonagrarian population depended for its support on a vigorous commerce and active urban industries. All levels of society participated in commerce, including the great landlords, nobles, and knights —classes which in northern Europe tended to remain on their rural estates. Moreover, success in urban occupations required a level of training higher than that needed in agriculture; therefore, many Italian cities supported public schools to assure themselves of an educated citizenry. Frequently even girls were given an elementary education, since literacy was a nearly essential skill for the wives of shopkeepers and merchants. Finally, many towns were politically independent and offered their affluent citizens the opportunity to participate in governmental decisions. To many great families such participation was essential to the protection of their interests, and required a mastery of the arts of communicating with their fellow citizens. In sum, Italian urban society in the fourteenth and fifteenth centuries was remarkably well educated and committed to active participation in the affairs of business and of government.

FAMILIES

The cities were populous, but the households within them tended to be small and unstable. Average household size roughly followed the general population trends of decline and growth

in the fourteenth and fifteenth centuries, but remained small over most of this period.[1] At Florence in 1427, the average household contained only 3.8 persons; at Bologna in 1395, 3.5 persons; at Verona in 1425, 3.7 persons. Restricted household size reflected the numerous deaths in a time of plagues, but marital customs also contributed. In particular, urban males tended to be much older than their brides when they married. At Florence in 1427, most men postponed marriage until they were thirty, and some did not marry at all. Economic factors—lengthy apprenticeships required of males in the urban trades, extended absences from home on commercial ventures, the need to accumulate capital before starting a family—delayed and sometimes precluded marriage for urban men. Florentine women, on the other hand, were on the average less than eighteen years old when they married for the first time; the "modal" (most common) age of first marriage for these urban girls in 1427 was fifteen years.

Several important social and cultural results followed from this distinctive marriage pattern. Because of high mortalities, the pool of prospective grooms (men of approximately thirty years of age) was distinctly smaller than the pool of brides (girls in their middle and late teens). Girls (or rather, their fathers and families) faced acute competition in the search for scarce husbands; brides, in consequence, usually entered marriage under unfavorable terms. In particular they or their families normally had to pay substantial dowries. Families with many daughters to marry faced financial ruin. This was one reason why girls were married so young; their fathers or families were eager to settle their uncertain futures as soon as possible. Those girls who could not be married before the age of twenty had no honorable alternative

---

[1] The data on Florentine families are taken largely from a study by D. Herlihy and C. Klapisch, *Les Toscans et leurs familles* (1978).

but to enter convents. In the words of a contemporary saint, Bernardine of Siena, these unwilling nuns were "the scum and vomit of the world."

Given the wide age difference separating the spouses, the urban marriage was likely to be of short duration, ending usually with the death of the husband. Often, too, the young widow did not remarry. Florentine husbands typically tried to discourage their spouses from remarrying after their own deaths; their widows, once remarried, might neglect the offspring of their earlier unions. Accordingly, the wills of Florentine husbands characteristically gave to their widows special concessions, which would be lost in the event of remarriage: use of the family dwelling, the right to serve as guardians over their children, sometimes a pension or annuity. Moreover, at her husband's death the substantial dowry, paid by her family at her marriage, was returned to the widow to be used as she saw fit. For the first time in her life, she was freed from male tutelage, whether of father, brothers, or husband. Many widowed women obviously relished this new-found freedom. At Florence in 1427, more than one-half of the female population, age forty or over, were widowed. The city teemed with mature women, many of them widows, many attracted to the city from the countryside, some of them wealthy and able to influence urban culture.

Even while her husband lived, the Florentine woman soon attained a special position within the household. Her husband was likely to be fully occupied by affairs of business or politics. The wife assumed primary responsibility for running the household and for bringing up the children. She was also usually destined for longer contact with her children. The average baby in Florence in 1427 was born to a mother of twenty-six; the father was forty. To many Florentines of the fourteenth and fifteenth centuries, the father was a distant figure, routinely praised but rarely intimately known; the mother dominated the formative years of the children. A friar named Giovanni Dominici, writing in the first decade of the fifteenth century, complained that Florentine mothers were spoiling their children, both girls and boys. They dressed them in elegant clothes and taught them music and dancing, presumably elevating their aesthetic tastes. They did not countenance violent or brutal games or sports. The result, Dominici implies, was an effeminization of Florentine culture. Women served primarily as intermediaries between the urban generations, shaping to their own preferences the values and attitudes which the young received. Elegance and refinement are essential attributes of Renaissance culture; elegant and refined tastes seem to have been assiduously nurtured within the bosom of the urban family.

The short duration of the urban marriage, the reluctance of many widows to remarry, and the commitment of many girls to the convent limited the exposure of urban women to the risk of pregnancy, to use the language of modern demography. In the countryside, men characteristically married in their middle twenties and took as brides girls nearer in age to themselves. The duration of rural marriages was longer, and couples had more children. The urban family was less prolific and usually smaller than its rural counterpart. The city thus ran a demographic deficit in relation to the countryside. This too had an important social repercussion. The city was forced to replenish its numbers by encouraging large-scale immigration from the countryside and small towns. This promoted both physical and social mobility, as the city characteristically attracted and rewarded skilled and energetic immigrants. Many of the leaders of the cultural Renaissance —Boccaccio, Leonardo Bruni, Coluccio Salutati, Poggio Bracciolini, Leonardo da Vinci, and others—were of rural or small-town origins and came to the city to meet its constant need for men. The Renaissance city seems to have been eminently successful in identifying the talented and in utilizing well its human capital.

The unstable character of the urban household and of human relations within it prompted much reflection on the family. Earlier, social thinkers had viewed the family abstractly, in relation to man's ultimate destiny; they affirmed that it was a natural society, but did not examine how it functioned in the real world. In contrast, concern for the welfare, even the survival, of families animates writers of the fifteenth century in Italy. Foremost among them was the Florentine scholar, artist, and architect Leon Battista Alberti, who in the 1430s wrote a tract entitled *Four Books on the Family*. In it he explained how children should be reared, wives chosen, domestic affairs managed, and friends cultivated—all to assure the survival of threatened lineages. Closely related to this examination of domestic policies are numerous tracts devoted to the training of children, many of which advocated a reform of education in the humanistic spirit (see p. 374). These tracts show a new awareness of the special psychology of children. Simultaneously, the artists of the period were presenting young people, even the infant Christ, not as miniature adults, but authentically as children, looking and acting as children do. The playful baby angels known as putti appear in even the most solemn religious paintings. The very fragility of the Italian urban family seems to have inspired a deeper appreciation of the values of family life, and the contribution which every member, even the youngest, makes to domestic contentment.

Finally, the weakness of the urban family forced its members to cultivate ties with outsiders in order to seek supplementary material and moral support. Living in constant contact with the outside world, the inhabitants of the Italian cities grew more sensitive to the canons of good behavior and the art of making friends. The age produced an abundance of essays on good manners, the most famous of which was the *Book of the Courtier*, written in 1516 by Baldassare Castiglione. Castiglione intended to describe proper deportment at court, but his work affected the image of the gentleman and the lady for a much broader range of society and was destined to influence standards of behavior all over Europe.

LEADERSHIP OF THE YOUNG

A principal reason for the instability of the urban family was the high levels of mortality which prevailed everywhere in Europe in the fourteenth and fifteenth centuries. On the basis of family memoirs left to us by Florentine merchants, which record births and deaths in the household, life expectancy from birth for these relatively affluent persons was forty years in about 1300, dropping to only eighteen years in the generation struck by the Black Death, and rising to thirty years in the fifteenth century as the plagues declined in virulence. (Today in the United States a newborn may be expected to survive for some seventy years.) To be sure, the high death rates attributable to plague were strongly "age specific," that is, they varied considerably across the various levels of age. The principal victims were the very young. In many periods, probably between one-half and one-third of the babies born never reached fifteen. Society swarmed with little children, but the death of children was a common occurrence in almost every family.

According to the most recent studies, the plague (as distinct from other causes of death) took greater tolls among young adults than among the aged. In effect, a person who survived one or more major epidemics had a good chance of living through the next onslaught. This phenomenon allowed some few favored persons to reach extreme old age, in the face of the horrendous mortalities. But it also meant that young adults continued to face high risks of dying. Friars, for example, who entered the Dominican convent of Sta. Maria Novella at Florence in the last half of the fourteenth century survived an average of only twenty years after profession, when most would have been in their late teens. Although there are exceptions, the normal adult career was of short duration.

For this reason, on every level and in every activity of life, the leaders of the fourteenth and fifteenth centuries were often very young, and subject to rapid replacement. The young were not frustrated by the lengthy survival of numerous elders, who clung on to the available jobs and blocked their own careers. There was no basis for the kind of generational tensions and conflicts which have disturbed modern societies. The leaders of the age show psychological qualities which may in part at least be attributed to their youth: impatience and imagination; a tendency to take quick recourse to violence; a love of extravagant gesture and display; and a rather small endowment of prudence, restraint, and self-control. High mortality and a rapid turnover of leaders further contributed to making this an age of opportunity, especially within the cities. Early death assured room at the top for the energetic and the gifted, especially in the business and artistic fields, where birth mattered little and skill counted for much.

The power given to the young, the rapid replacement of leaders, the opportunities extended to the gifted, and the thin ranks of an older generation that might counsel restraint worked also to intensify the pace of cultural change. To be sure, notoriously poor communications hampered the spread of ideas. The quickest a man or a letter could travel on land was between twenty and thirty miles per day; to get to Bruges by sea from Genoa took thirty days, from Venice forty days. The expense and scarcity of manuscripts before the age of printing further narrowed and muffled the intellectual dialogue. On the other hand, new generations pressed upon the old at a much more rapid rate than in our own society, and characteristically they brought with them new policies, preferences, and ideas, or at least a willingness to experiment—in sum, ferment. The gifted man was given his main chance early in his life and passed early from the scene. In Italy as in all Europe the stage of the fourteenth and fifteenth centuries with its constantly changing characters often appears crowded, but the drama enacted upon it moves at a rapid, exciting pace.

LEARNING AND LITERATURE

Although university and scholastic learning retained considerable vitality in the fourteenth and fifteenth centuries, Scholasticism did not adequately serve the literate lay population. The curriculum remained largely designed for the training of teachers and theologians, whereas men committed to an active life in business and politics wanted practical training in the arts of persuasive communications: good speaking and good writing. Moreover, many laymen believed that scholastics failed to meet their religious needs. Coldly analytic in its treatment of religious questions, Scholasticism seemed indifferent to the personal, emotional, and mystical aspects of religion. As Petrarch was to note, education should train men in the art of leading a wise, pious, and happy life. The central concern of the cultural Renaissance was to develop a system of education which would do exactly that.

Humanism

One minor branch of the medieval educational curriculum, rhetoric, or the art of good speaking and writing, was concerned specifically with the skill of communicating well. Initially, the art consisted of little more than memorizing Latin formulas by rote for use in letters or legal documents. With time its practitioners began to search through the Latin classics for further

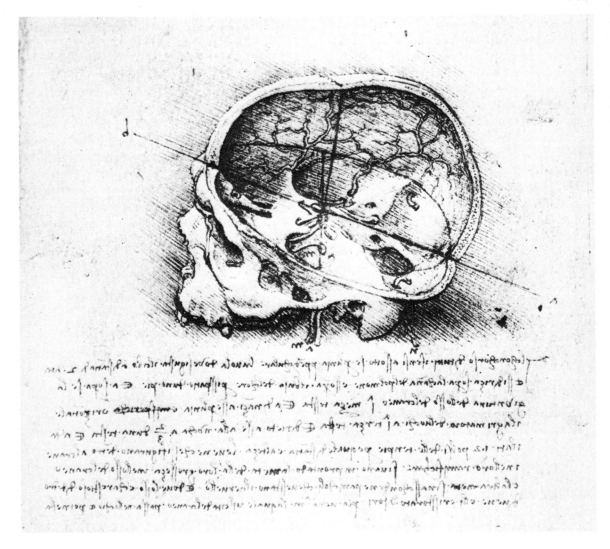

models of good writing. This return to the classical authors was facilitated by the close relationship between the Italian language and Latin, by the availability of manuscripts, and by the visual evidence preserved in countless monuments of the classical achievement. By the late thirteenth century in a number of Italian cities, notably Padua, Bologna, and Florence, writers were calling for new directions in education, urging that the classics be studied inten-

Although the humanists disparaged the narrow professional training of the medieval schools (including medicine), they advocated that all aspects of man were worthy of study: nihil humanum a me alienum, "nothing human is foreign to me." In this cross section of the human skull, done in 1489, Leonardo da Vinci states in his notes that he sought to illustrate the "confluence of the senses" at the intersection of the diagonal lines. The drawing shows his deep anatomical and psychological interests. (Photo: Royal Collection, Windsor Castle)

sively and that learning be made morally relevant in the sense of helping men to better lives.

These men were the founders of the intellectual movement known as Humanism. Basically, Humanism means classical scholarship—the ability to read, understand, and appreciate the writings of the ancient world. In classical antiquity, and again in the Renaissance, educators called the curriculum most suitable for the training of free and responsible persons the *studia humanitatis* ("the studies of mankind" or "the humanities").[2] The curriculum was designed to develop in the student primarily those qualities of intellect and will which truly distinguished men from animals. The ideal product of a humanist education was the man, trained in the classics, who possessed both *sapientia* and *eloquentia*—the wisdom needed to know the right path to follow in any situation and the eloquence needed to persuade his fellows to take it.

Renaissance Humanism was marked by three principal characteristics. First, it rejected the emphasis which the medieval schools placed on professional training, whether in theology, law, or medicine, and advocated a liberal education, based on a knowledge of moral philosophy and a command of eloquence. The truly educated person was not identified by technical mastery of a body of learning, but by the capacity to make the right moral judgments in difficult human situations. Second, Humanism stressed the supreme importance of the Latin language (later, Greek also) and the classical authors. These were the models of eloquence and the storehouses of wisdom which offered men the best possible guides to life, apart from religion itself. Third, Humanism affirmed the possibility of human improvement through education and study. Ideally, man should develop

to the fullest all his specifically human faculties—physical, moral, spiritual, aesthetic. There was nothing in this hope for human perfection antagonistic to traditional Christianity and ecclesiastical authority. The modern use of the word "Humanism" to denote a secular philosophy which denies an afterlife has no basis in the history of the Renaissance. Most Renaissance humanists read the Church fathers as avidly as the pagan authors and believed that the highest virtues included piety. Humanism was far more an effort to enrich traditional religious attitudes than a revolt against them.

Petrarch

The man who clarified these humanistic ideals and disseminated them with unprecedented success in Italy and to some extent in Europe was the Tuscan Francesco Petrarch (1304–1374), a writer by profession and one of the most attractive personalities of his age. Petrarch possessed an immense enthusiasm—and generated it in others—for the ancient authors, for educational reform, and for scholarship. He personally sought to save from neglect the ancient authors preserved in monastic libraries and launched an eager search for their manuscripts, a pursuit that was to become an integral part of the humanist movement. Petrarch had a dismal opinion of his own times and held up in contrast the ideal world of ancient Rome, when there supposedly flourished both authentic learning and virtue. For this reason he thought that the Latin classics should be the heart of the educational curriculum.

Petrarch wrote prolifically and with consistent grace and flair in both Latin and Italian. His best Latin works are his five hundred letters, all clearly composed with an eye to a readership beyond the persons addressed. He was the first to discern personality in the great writers of the past, and he directed some of the letters to them—Cicero, Seneca, Vergil, and especially St. Augustine, his favorite literary companion. He also composed an autobio-

---

[2] "Humanism" was not actually coined until the nineteenth century. In fifteenth- and sixteenth-century Italy, *humanista* signified a professor of humane studies (the *studia humanitatis*) or a classical scholar.

graphical "letter to posterity" to future generations—to us. Even today, his warmth and wit win him friends.

Petrarch pretended to disparage his Italian works, but today they are the foundation of his literary reputation. Especially admirable are his 366 sonnets, most of which express his love for a young married woman named Laura, who died in the plague of 1348. In the sonnets written both before and after her death, love represents for Petrarch not so much passion as a way to inner peace; Laura offers him not so much satisfaction as solace.

In his writings, particularly in his imaginative exchanges with St. Augustine, Petrarch examines at length an ethical dilemma characteristic of his age: how should religious people act who aspire to a life of quiet contemplation but feel themselves responsible for the welfare of family, friends, community, Church, and the world in tumultuous times? He does not resolve this dilemma, but probably no one before him explored its dimensions with equal sensitivity.

Petrarch richly deserves his esteemed place in the history of European thought. More than any writer before him, he set a new standard of excellence for Western letters by imitating the simplicity and elegance of classical literary style. He also defined a new aim in education—the art of living happily and well, as distinct from the narrow professional goals of the older Scholasticism. Finally, he helped develop a new vision of human fulfillment. To Petrarch, the ideal man was the one who spent his life in the study of letters, enjoyed them, cherished them, and found God in them.

Boccaccio

A near-contemporary of Petrarch, and second only to him in his influence on fourteenth-century Italian learning, was Giovanni Boccaccio (1313–1375). As a young author, Boccaccio celebrated in poetry the charms of his lady Fiammetta, who, unlike Beatrice and even Laura, did not conduct the poet to idealized

rapture and ultimate peace, but instead delighted him with both her beauty and her wit and sometimes baffled him with her shifting moods. She was the woman, not of mystic love, but of daily experience.

Boccaccio's great work, the short stories known as *The Decameron*, was written probably between 1348 and 1351. It recounts how a group of young Florentines—seven women and three men—fled during the Black Death of 1348 to a secluded villa, where for ten days each told a story. The first prose masterpiece in Italian, and a model thereafter for clear and lively narration, *The Decameron* is often considered a work of literary realism, principally for its frank and frequent treatment of sex. In fact, however, it hardly ever offers a realistic portrait of fourteenth-century life and society, for the narrators are consciously seeking to flee and forget the grim, real world; their servants are even forbidden to repeat unpleasant news within their charming villa. *The Decameron* was composed as an antidote to melancholy—one of the first major works in Western letters intended to divert and amuse rather than edify.

With age this one-time spinner of ribald stories became attracted to the religious life; he took orders in the Church and turned his efforts to the cure of souls. Like Petrarch, he disparaged his vernacular writings and even reprimanded a friend for allowing his wife to read the indecent *Decameron*. He died regretting the work which has earned him immortality.

The Civic Humanists

In the generation after Petrarch and Boccaccio, Florentine scholars were preeminent in the humanist movement, and under the leadership of Coluccio Salutati gave to the revived study of antiquity the character of a true movement. Through the recovery of ancient manuscripts and the formation of libraries Coluccio and his group—Leonardo Bruni, Poggio Bracciolini, and others—made accessible to scholars

Nastagio's tale, from The Decameron, *tells of a rejected suitor who encounters in the woods outside of Ravenna a phantom knight. Every Friday, the knight hunts down and kills the ghost of the lady who, in refusing his love, had caused his death. The suitor invites his own lady and her family to a Friday banquet in the woods, where they too witness the horrifying hunt. The living lady recognizes the cruelty of her ways and accepts the suitor. The depiction of this popular story given here is a detail from panels by the great fifteenth-century Florentine painter, Sandro Botticelli.* (Photo: Museo del Prado)

virtually the entire surviving corpus of classical Latin authors.

These Florentines further sought to reestablish in Italy a command of the Greek language, which, according to Bruni, "no Italian had understood in seven hundred years." In 1396 they invited the Byzantine scholar Manuel Chrysoloras to lecture at the University of Florence. In the following decades—troubled years for the Byzantine Empire—other Eastern scholars joined the exodus to the West, and they and Western visitors returning from the East brought with them hundreds of Greek manuscripts. By the middle of the fifteenth century Western scholars had both the philological skill and the manuscripts to establish direct contact with the most original minds of the classical world and were making numerous Latin and Italian translations of Greek works. Histories, tragedies, lyric poetry, the dialogues of Plato, many mathematical treatises, the most important works of the Greek fathers of the Church—in sum, a large part of the Greek cultural inheritance—fully entered Western culture for the first time.

Coluccio and his contemporary Florentine scholars are now often called civic humanists, since they stressed that participation in public affairs is essential for full human development. They linked their praise of the active life with a defense of the republican liberty of

Florence, then threatened by the despot Gian Galeazzo of Milan. The humanists argued that human advance depends on a kind of community dialogue, which allows men to learn from one another. To participate in such a dialogue the educated citizen needs wisdom founded upon sound moral philosophy and also eloquence, without which his knowledge will remain socially barren. The best education imparts both qualities, which are themselves best exemplified by the ancient classics. Moreover, if human progress depends on dialogue, the best political institutions are those which invite the participation of the citizens in the councils of government. The republican form of government was therefore claimed superior to the despotism represented by Gian Galeazzo. In one integrated argument the civic humanists thus defended the capital importance of training in the classics, the superiority of the active life, and the value of Florentine republican institutions.

Humanism in the Fifteenth Century

As the humanist movement gained in prestige, it spread from Florence to the other principal cities of Italy. At Rome and Naples one of the most able humanist scholars was Lorenzo Valla (1407–1457). Valla conclusively proved that the document known as the Donation of Constantine—one of the documents upon which the papacy based its claim to supremacy in the West—was a forgery concocted in the eighth century. According to the Donation, when Emperor Constantine left Rome in the fourth century to found Constantinople, he gave the pope Italy and the entire Western empire. Drawing on his superb historical knowledge of Latin, Valla pointed out the anachronisms in the document; many of the Latin expressions used were typical of the eighth century, not the fourth. Valla was thus one of the first scholars to develop the tools of historical criticism in interpreting ancient records.

Two fifteenth-century scholars from the north of Italy, Guarino da Verona and Vittorino da Feltre, were chiefly responsible for incorporating the diffuse educational ideas of the humanists into a practical curriculum. Guarino launched a reform of the traditional methods of education and Vittorino brought the new methods to their fullest development in the various schools he founded, especially his *Casa Giocosa* ("Happy House") at Mantua. The pupils included boys and girls, both rich and poor (the latter on scholarships). All the students learned Latin and Greek, mathematics, music, and philosophy; in addition, because Vittorino believed that education should aid physical, moral, and social development, they were also taught social graces such as dancing and courteous manners and received instruction in physical exercises like riding and fencing. Vittorino's Happy House attracted pupils from all over Italy, and his methods were widely imitated even beyond the Italian borders.

By the late fifteenth century, and still more in the sixteenth, Humanism, in the sense of classical literary scholarship, showed a declining vitality in Italy. Like most reform movements Italian Humanism declined principally because its cause had been won. By about 1450, with only a few exceptions, the monastic libraries had yielded their treasures of ancient manuscripts, and in the latter half of the century printing made the texts readily available among the educated public. Humanists were no longer needed to find the ancient authors, copy them, or propagandize for their wider dissemination. Education too had come to recognize, at least partially, the value of training in the classics. By the late fifteenth century the leaders of Italian intellectual life were no longer the humanists but philosophers, who were now able to use a command of the classical heritage to enrich and develop their own philosophical systems.

The Florentine Neoplatonists

One major theme of the cultural Renaissance, perhaps generated by the misery and melancholy of life, was an effort to depict ideal worlds in thought, literature, and art. A good example of what some scholars call the Renaissance religion of beauty is provided by a group of philosophers active at Florence in the last decades of the fifteenth century. The most gifted among them was probably Marsilio Ficino, whose career is a tribute to the cultural patronage of the Medici. Cosimo de' Medici befriended him as a child and gave him the use of a villa and library near Florence. In this lovely setting a group of scholars and statesmen met frequently to discuss philosophical questions. Drawn to the idealism of Plato (and usually called the Platonic Academy), Ficino and his fellows were particularly concerned with the place of the human soul within the Platonic cosmos and with the soul's dignity and immortality, which they passionately affirmed. To spread these ideas among a larger audience Ficino translated into Latin all of Plato's dialogues and the writings of the chief figures of the Neoplatonic tradition. He also made an ambitious effort to reconcile and assimilate Platonic philosophy and the Christian religion.

Another brilliant member of the Platonic Academy was the young Prince Giovanni Pico della Mirandola, who thought he could reconcile all philosophies. In 1486 Pico proposed to dispute publicly at Rome on some nine hundred theses which would show the essential unity of the philosophic experience. But Pope Innocent VIII, believing that the theses contained several heretical propositions, forbade the disputation. By the time of his death at thirty-one Pico had not made much progress toward the "philosophical peace," or reconciliation of philosophical systems, which he sought.

Both Ficino and Pico founded their philosophies upon two essential assumptions: all being is arranged in a hierarchy of excellence with God at the summit. Moreover, each being in the universe, with the exception only of God, is impelled through a "natural appetite" to seek the perfection of its kind; it is impelled, in other words, to achieve—or at least to contemplate—the beautiful. As Pico expressed it, however, man is unique in that he is placed in the middle of the universe linked with both the spiritual world above and the material one below. His free will enables him to seek perfection in either direction; he is free to become all things. A clear ethic emerges from this scheme: the good life should be an effort to achieve personal perfection, and the highest human value is the contemplation of the beautiful.

These philosophers believed that Plato had been divinely illumined and therefore that Platonic philosophy and Christian belief were two wholly reconcilable faces of a single truth. Neoplatonic philosophy has a particular importance for the influence it exerted on many of the great artists of the Florentine Renaissance, including Botticelli and Michelangelo.

The Heritage of Humanism

Fifteenth-century Italian Humanism left a deep imprint on European scholarship and education. The humanists greatly strengthened the command of Latin. They also restored a mastery of the Greek language in the West and elevated a large part of the Greek cultural inheritance to a position of influence in Western civilization. Moreover, they began the systematic investigation of other languages associated with great cultural traditions, most notably Hebrew, and in so doing laid the basis of modern textual and (more remotely) historical criticism. They developed new ways of investigating the character of the ancient world—through archaeology, numismatics (the study of coins), and epigraphy (the study of inscriptions on buildings, statues, and the like), as well as through the study of literary texts. Humanistic influence on the study of history was particularly profound. The medieval chroniclers had looked into the past for evidence of God's saving providence, whereas the humanists were primarily concerned with utilizing the past to illustrate human behavior and provide moral examples. Though their approach was not without its faults—such as an aversion to mundane detail and statistical data, and a sometimes bombastic and obscure rhetorical style—they certainly deepened the historical consciousness of the West and greatly strengthened the historian's technical skill. Humanistic influences on vernacular languages helped bring standardization of spelling and grammar; and the classical ideas of simplicity, restraint, and elegance of style exerted a continuing influence on Western letters.

No less important was the role of the humanists as educational reformers. The curriculum devised by them spread throughout Europe in the sixteenth century; in fact, until the early twentieth century it everywhere defined the standards by which the lay leaders of Western society were trained. Protestants, Catholics, men of all nationalities were steeped in the same classics and consequently thought and communicated in similar fashion. In spite of bitter religious divisions and heated national antagonisms, the common humanistic education helped preserve the fundamental cultural unity of the West.

Whatever the achievements of the movement in the fourteenth and fifteenth centuries, it cannot be concluded that Humanism represented a revolt against the intellectual and religious heritage of the Middle Ages. It would be more accurate to say that the humanists, rather than destroying the heritage of the past, opened it to a new and larger audience. In the thirteenth century learning had remained largely a monopoly of monks and scholastics, and its character reflected their professional and vocational needs. In the fourteenth and fifteenth centuries the humanists introduced a narrow but still important segment of lay society to the accumulated intellectual treasury of the European past, both classical and scholastic, ancient and medieval. Simultaneously, they reinterpreted that heritage and enlarged the function of education and scholarship to serve men in their present life by teaching them, as Petrarch recommended, the art of living wisely and well.

II. THE CULTURE OF THE NORTH

Most areas of Europe beyond the Alps did not have the many large cities and the high percentage of urban dwellers that supported the humanistic movement in Italy. Moreover, unlike those of Italy, the physical monuments and languages of northern Europe did not offer ready reminders of the classical heritage. Humanism and the true classical Renaissance, with a literate, trained laity, did not come to the north until the last decade of the fifteenth century. The court, rather than the city, and the knight, rather than the merchant, dominated northern culture for most of the later fourteenth and fifteenth centuries.

CHIVALRY

In 1919 a Dutch historian, Johan Huizinga, wrote *The Waning of the Middle Ages*, a stimulating study of the character of north European culture in the fourteenth and fifteenth centuries. That culture, Huizinga argued, should be viewed, not as a renaissance, but as the decline of medieval civilization. Paying chief attention to the court of the dukes of Burgundy, who were among the wealthiest and most powerful princes of the north, Huizinga examined courtly life and manners, and described the courtiers' views on love, war, and religion. He found tension and frequent violence in this society, with little of the balance and serenity that had marked medieval society in the thirteenth century. Instead, its members seemed to show a defective sense of reality, an acute inconsistency in their values and actions, and great emotional instability. Many critics now consider that Huizinga probably exaggerated the negative qualities in northern culture, but that his analysis still contains much that is accurate.

The defective sense of reality that Huizinga noted is manifest in the extravagant cultivation of the notion of chivalry. Militarily, the knight was in fact becoming less important than the foot soldier armed with longbow, pike, or firearms. But the noble classes of the north continued to pretend that knightly virtues governed all questions of state and society; they discounted such lowly considerations as money, arms, number of forces, supplies, and the total resources of countries in deciding the outcome of wars. For example, before the Battle of Agincourt, one French knight told King Charles that he should not use contingents from the Parisian townsfolk because that would give his army an unfair numerical advantage; the battle should be decided strictly on the basis of chivalrous valor.

This was the age of the perfect knight and the *beau geste* and grand feats of arms. King John of Bohemia insisted that his soldiers lead him to the front rank of battle, so that he could better strike the enemy; but he needed his soldiers to guide him, for John was blind. The feats of renowned knights won the rapt admiration of chroniclers but affected the outcome of battle hardly at all. The age was marked too by the foundation of new orders of chivalry—notably the Knights of the Garter and the Burgundian Knights of the Golden Fleece.[3] The basic supposition was that these orders would reform the world by the intensive cultivation of knightly virtues.

Princes rivaled one another in the sheer glitter of their arms and the splendor of their tournaments. They waged wars of dazzlement, seeking to confound rivals and confirm friends with spectacular displays of gold, silks, and tapestries. Court ceremony achieved unprecedented excesses.

Extravagance touched the chivalric arts of love as well. A special order was founded for the defense of women, and knights frequently took lunatic oaths to honor their ladies, such as keeping one eye closed for extended periods. Obviously people rarely made love or war in this artificial way. But men still drew satisfaction in speculating—in dreaming—how love and war would be if this sad world were only a perfect place.

THE CULT OF DECAY

Huizinga called the extravagant life style of the northern courts the "cult of the sublime," or the impossibly beautiful. But he also noted that both knights and commoners showed a morbid fascination with death and its ravages. Reminders of the ultimate victory of death and explicit treatment of decay are frequently encountered in both literature and art. One popular artistic motif was the danse macabre, or dance of death, depicting people from all walks of life—rich and poor, cleric and layman, good and bad—joined in their final, intimate dance. Another melancholy theme favored by all European artists was the Pietà—the Virgin weeping over her dead son.

This morbid interest in death and decay in an age of pestilence was not the fruit of lofty religious sentiment. The unbalanced concern with the fleetingness of material beauty shows, if anything, an excessive attachment to it, a

---

[3] Jason, leader of the Argonauts, was the first patron of the order, but the question was soon raised whether a pagan hero could appropriately be taken as a model by Christian knights. It was further pointed out that Jason had treated his wife Medea in a most unchivalrous fashion (he left her for another woman). Jason was therefore replaced as patron by the Old Testament hero Gideon.

kind of inverse materialism. Even more than that, it reveals a growing religious dissatisfaction. In the thirteenth century Francis of Assisi addressed death as a sister; in the fourteenth and fifteenth centuries men clearly regarded it as a ravaging, indomitable fiend. Clearly the Church was failing to provide consolation to many of its members, and a religion that fails to console is a religion in crisis.

Still another manifestation of the unsettled religious spirit of the age was a fascination with the devil, demonology, and witchcraft. The most enlightened scholars of the day argued at length about whether witches could ride through the air on sticks, and about their relations with the devil. (One of the more notable

The danse macabre was a common artistic theme in northern Europe, reflecting a gloomy fascination with death. This woodcut of "Skeleton Dance" is from the Nuremberg World Chronicle of 1493. (Photo: Philip Evola)

witch trials of Western history occurred at Arras in 1460. Scores of people were accused of participating in a witches' sabbath, giving homage to the devil, and even having sexual intercourse with him.) Fear of the devil and perhaps also a widespread cultivation of the occult arts in the lower levels of society are salient departures from the serene, confident religion of the thirteenth century.

Finally, men showed an inordinate desire to reduce religious images to their most concrete form. The passion to have immediate, physical contact with the objects of religious devotion gave added popularity to pilgrimages and still more to the obsession with relics of the saints, which, more often fabricated than authentic, became a major commodity in international trade, and princes accumulated collections numbering in the tens of thousands.

Huizinga saw these manifestations of northern culture as the disintegration of the cultural synthesis of the Middle Ages. Without a disciplined and unified view of the world, attitudes toward war, love, and religion lost balance, and disordered behavior followed. This culture was not young and vigorous but old and dying. However, Huizinga's root concept of decadence must be used with a certain caution. Certainly this was a psychologically disturbed world, which had lost the self-confidence of the thirteenth century; but these allegedly decadent men were not the victims of a torpid spirit. They were dissatisfied perhaps, but they were also passionately anxious to find solutions to the psychological tensions that unsettled them. It is well to recall that passion when trying to understand the appeal and the power behind other cultural movements—lay piety, northern Humanism, and efforts for religious reform.

CONTEMPORARY VIEWS OF NORTHERN SOCIETY

Huizinga wrote about chivalric society from the perspective of the twentieth century. One of the best contemporary historians of that society was Jean Froissart (1333?–1400?) of Flanders, who traveled widely across England and the Continent, noting carefully the exploits of valiant men. His chronicles give the richest account of the first half of the Hundred Years' War, and he has no equal among medieval chroniclers for colorful, dramatic narration. Nonetheless, Froissart has been criticized for his preoccupation with chivalric society; his narrative treats peasants and townsmen with contempt, or simply ignores them. Yet concerns limited to chivalry suited the purposes for which he wrote. He wished to record the wars of his day, lest, as he put it, "the deeds of present champions should fade into oblivion."

The works of contemporary English writers help to round out the picture of northern society in the fourteenth century. One of them, a poet of uncertain identity, probably William Langland, presents the viewpoint of the humbler classes. His *Vision of Piers Plowman*, which was probably written about 1360, is one of the most remarkable works of the age. The poem gives a loosely connected account of eleven visions, each of which is crowded with allegorical figures, and it is filled with spirited comment about the various classes of people, the impact of plague and war upon society, and the failings of the Church.

Geoffrey Chaucer wrote about the middle classes. His *Canterbury Tales*, perhaps the greatest work of imaginative literature produced anywhere in Europe in the late fourteenth century, recounts the pilgrimage of some thirty persons to the tomb of St. Thomas à Becket at Canterbury. For entertainment on the road each pilgrim agrees to tell two stories. Chaucer's portraits sum up the moral and social ills of the day, especially those affecting the Church. His robust monk, for example, ignores the Benedictine rule; his friar is more interested in donations than in the cure of souls; and his pardoner knowingly hawks fraudulent relics. But Chaucer's picture is balanced; he praises the student of Oxford, who would gladly learn and gladly teach, and the rural parson, who cares for his flock while others search out benefices, to the neglect of the faithful. Apart from the grace of his poetry Chaucer was gifted with an ability to delineate character and spin a lively narrative. *The Canterbury Tales* is a masterly portrayal of human personalities and human behavior which can delight readers in any age.

III. RELIGIOUS THOUGHT AND PIETY

The Scholasticism of the thirteenth century, as represented by Thomas Aquinas, was based on the bold postulate that it was within the power of human reason to construct a universal philosophy that would do justice to all truths and would reconcile all apparent conflicts among them. The simultaneous growth in ecclesiastical law had also tended to define Christian obligations and the Christian life in terms of precise rules of behavior rather than interior spirit. This style of thinking changed during the next two centuries. Many scholastics were drawn toward analysis (breaking apart) rather than synthesis (putting together) as they attempted a rigorous investigation of philosophical and theological statements. Many of them no longer shared Aquinas's confidence in human reason. Fundamentally, they hoped to repair the Thomistic synthesis or to replace it by new systems which, though less comprehensive, would at least rest on sound foundations. Piety changed too, as more and more Christian leaders sought ways of deepening interior, mystical experience.

The "Modern Way"

The followers of St. Thomas or of Duns Scotus remained active in the late medieval schools, but the most original of the philosophers were nominalists, that is, those who denied the existence, or at least the knowability, of universal natures —manness, dogness, and the like. The greatest

of these late medieval nominalists was the English Franciscan William of Ockham (1300?–1349?). The fundamental principle of his logical analysis later came to be called Ockham's razor. It may be stated in several ways, but essentially it affirms that between alternative explanations for the same phenomenon, the simpler is always to be preferred.

On the basis of this "principle of economy" Ockham attacked the traditional problem of ideal forms, such as manness or dogness. He rejected Aquinas's argument that all beings, apart from God, were metaphysically composite of a principle of unity (act) and a principle of individuation (potency). The simplest way to explain the existence of an individual object is to affirm that it exists. The mind can detect resemblances among objects and form general concepts concerning them; these concepts can be further manipulated in logically valid ways. But they offer no certain assurance that ideal forms—principles of unity in which individual objects participate—exist in the real world.

The area of reality in which the mind can effectively function is thus severely limited. The universe, as far as human reason can detect, is an aggregate of autonomous individual beings, not a hierarchy of ideal forms, natures, or ideas. The proper approach in dealing with this universe is through direct experience, not through speculations about ideal or abstract natures, the very existence of which is doubtful. Any theology based upon observation and reason would obviously be greatly restricted. It would still be possible, thought Ockham, to prove the existence of necessary principles in the universe, but man could not know whether the necessary principle, or God, is one or many.

Ockham and many of his contemporaries were profoundly impressed by the power and freedom of God and by man's absolute dependence on him. They lacked Aquinas's high assessment of human powers and his confident belief in the ordered and autonomous structure of the natural world. Living within a disturbed,

pessimistic age, the nominalists reflect a crisis in confidence, in natural reason and in themselves, which is a major theme of late medieval cultural history.

Nominalism enjoyed great popularity in the universities, and Ockhamite philosophy in particular came to be known as the *via moderna* ("modern way"). Although nominalists and humanists were frequently at odds, they shared certain common attitudes: both were dissatisfied with some aspects of the medieval intellectual tradition; both were impatient with the speculative abstractions of medieval thought; and both advocated approaches to reality that would concentrate upon the concrete and the present and consider them with a stricter awareness of method.

Social Thought

The belief of the nominalists that reality was to be found, not in abstract forms, but in concrete objects had important implications for social thought. Among the social thinkers clearly influenced by nominalism the most remarkable is Marsilius of Padua. In 1324 he wrote *Defender of Peace*, a pamphlet attacking papal authority and supporting lay sovereignty within the Church. In conformity with nominalist principles Marsilius affirmed that the reality of the Christian community, like the reality of the universe, consists in the aggregate of all its parts. The sovereignty of the Church thus rests in its membership—or, as Marsilius phrased it rather vaguely, in its "stronger and healthier part." This part in turn constituted the "human legislator," which represents the collective, sovereign will of the community. The human legislator delegates the functions of government to six great bureaus: the princely office, the

Detail from the Campin Altarpiece. (Photo: The Metropolitan Museum of Art, The Cloisters Collection, Purchase)

treasury, the military establishment, artisans, cultivators, and finally the clergy.

Marsilius is often considered an architect of the modern concept of sovereignty, and even of totalitarianism. He maintained that only those regulations supported by force are true law. Therefore, the enactments of the Church do not constitute binding legislation, because they are not supported by any coercive power. Only the human legislator can promulgate authentic law, and there is no limit on what it may do. The Church has no right to power or property and is entirely subject to the sovereign will of the state. Sovereignty is in turn indivisible, absolute, and unlimited.

Defender of Peace is noteworthy not only for its radical ideas but also for the evidence it gives of deep dissatisfactions within medieval society. Marsilius and others manifested a hostile impatience with the papal and clerical domination of Western political life. They demanded that the guidance of the Church and the Christian community rest exclusively with laymen. *Defender of Peace*, in this respect at least, was a prophecy of things to come.

STYLES OF PIETY

Religion remained a central concern of fourteenth- and fifteenth-century men and women, but new forms of piety, or religious practice, began to appear that were designed to meet the needs of laymen. Mysticism, an interior sense of the presence and love of God, had found its usual expression within the confines of the monastic orders, but by the thirteenth century this monopoly was beginning to break down. The principal mission of the Franciscans and the Dominicans became preaching to laymen, to whom these two mendicant orders hoped to introduce some of the satisfactions of mystical religion. And laymen, wishing to remain in the outside world, could join special branches of the Franciscans or Dominicans known as third orders.

Confraternities, which were religious guilds largely for laymen, grew up in the cities and, through common religious services and the support of charitable activities, tried to deepen the spiritual life of their members. Humanism preserved strong overtones of a movement for lay piety. An abundance of devotional and mystical literature was written for laymen to teach them how to feel repentance, not just how to define it. Translations of the Scriptures into many vernacular languages appeared, although the high cost of manuscripts before the age of printing severely limited their circulation.

This growth of lay piety was in essence an effort to open the monastic experience to the lay world, to put at the disposal of all what had hitherto been restricted to a spiritual elite. Frightened by the disasters of the age, men hungered for emotional reassurance, for evidence of God's love and redeeming grace within them. Moreover, the spread of education among the laity, at least in the cities, made men discontented with empty forms of religious ritual.

The Rhenish Mystics

The most active center of the new lay piety was the Rhine valley. The first of several leading figures in the region was the Dominican Meister Eckhart. A great preacher and a devoted student of Aquinas, Eckhart sought to bring his largely lay listeners into a mystical confrontation with God. The believer, he maintained, should cultivate within his soul the "divine spark." To achieve this he must banish all thoughts from his mind and seek to attain a state of pure passivity. If he succeeds, God will come and dwell within him. Eckhart stressed the futility of dogma and, implicitly, traditional acts of piety. God is too great to be contained in dogmatic categories and too sovereign to be moved by conventional piety.

The Rhenish mystics all stressed the theme that formal knowledge of God and his attributes means little if it is cultivated without love and emotional receptivity. Perhaps the most

influential of all of them was Gerhard Groote of Holland. Groote wrote sparingly, exerting his extraordinary influence upon his followers largely through his personality. After his death in 1384 his disciples formed a religious congregation known as the Brethren of the Common Life. Taking education as their principal ministry, they founded schools in Germany and the Low Countries that imparted a style of lay piety known as the *devotio moderna* ("modern devotion"). Erasmus of Rotterdam and Martin Luther were among their pupils.

The richest statement of the *devotio moderna* appeared about 1425 in *The Imitation of Christ,* a small devotional manual attributed to Thomas à Kempis, a member of the Brethren of the Common Life. *The Imitation of Christ* says almost nothing about fasting, pilgrimages, and other acts of private penitence characteristic of traditional piety. Instead, it emphasizes interior experience as an essential part of the religious life; it is also untraditional in its ethical and social consciousness. The fruit of interior conversion is not extreme acts of personal expiation, but high ethical behavior: "First, keep yourself in peace, and then you shall be able to bring peace to others."

The new lay piety was by no means a revolutionary break with the medieval Church, but it implicitly discounted the importance of many traditional institutions and practices. In this personal approach to God there was no special value in the monastic vocation. As Erasmus would later sharply argue, what was good in monasticism should be practiced by every Christian. Stressing simplicity and humility, the new lay piety was reacting against the pomp and splendor that had come to surround popes and prelates and to mark religious ceremonies. Likewise, the punctilious rules concerning fasts, abstinences, and devotional exercises; the cult of the saints and their relics; and the traffic in indulgences and pardons all seemed peripheral to true religious needs. Without the proper state of soul these traditional acts of piety were meaningless; with the proper state every act was worship.

A generation ago many Protestant scholars considered that the new lay piety was a preparation for the Reformation, while Catholic historians vigorously affirmed that it was authentically Catholic. Today, in our ecumenical age, the desire to enlist Thomas à Kempis among one's spiritual forebears seems pointless. The new lay piety was a preparation for both sixteenth-century reformations, Protestant and Catholic. It aimed at producing a more penetrating religious sentiment. The formal religion of the Middle Ages, for all its grandeur and logical intricacies, no longer fully satisfied the religious spirit and was leaving hollows in the human heart.

Although the *devotio moderna* was a religious movement, it was in many ways similar to Humanism. Both Thomas à Kempis and Petrarch expressed their distaste for the subtle abstractions and intellectual arrogance of the scholastics. Both stressed that the man who is wise and good will cultivate humility and maintain toward the profound questions of religion a "learned ignorance." Both affirmed that it is more important to educate the will to love than the intellect to the mastery of abstruse theology. Finally, both addressed their message primarily to laymen, in order to aid them to a higher moral life. The humanists of course drew their chief inspiration from the works of pagan and Christian antiquity, whereas the advocates of the new lay piety looked almost exclusively to Scripture. But the resemblances were so close that in the late fifteenth and sixteenth centuries, men like Erasmus and Thomas More could combine elements from both in the movement known as Christian Humanism.

Heresies

Efforts to repair the traditions of medieval Christianity also led to outright heretical attacks upon the religious establishment, which of course were strengthened by antagonism toward the papacy, reaction against corruption in the Church, and the social and psychological tensions characteristic of this disturbed epoch. Fundamentally, however, the growing appeal of heresies reflected the difficulties the Church was experiencing in adapting its organization and teachings to the demands of a changing world.

The most prominent of the heretics of the time was the English Dominican John Wycliffe, who was clearly influenced by the national spirit generated by the Hundred Years' War and the apparent subservience of the Avignon papacy to France. In 1365 he denounced the payment of Peter's pence, the annual tax given by the English people to the papacy. Later he publicly excoriated the papal Curia, monks, and friars for their vices.

Wycliffe argued that the Scriptures alone declared the will of God and that neither the pope, the cardinals, nor scholastic theologians could tell the Christian what he should believe. (In 1382 he began to translate the Bible into English, but died two years later without finishing.) He also attacked the dogma of transubstantiation, which asserts that the priest at mass works a miracle when he changes the substance of bread and wine into the substance of Christ. Besides attacking the special powers, position, and privileges of the priesthood in such dogmas as transubstantiation, Wycliffe assaulted with equal vehemence the authority of the pope and the hierarchy to exercise jurisdiction and to hold property. He claimed that the true Church was that of the predestined, that is, those in the state of sanctifying grace. Only the elect could rule the elect; therefore, popes and bishops who had no grace could be justly divested of their properties and had no right to rule. The chief responsibility for ecclesiastical reform rested with the prince, and the pope could exercise only so much authority as the prince allowed.

Wycliffe's adherents, mostly from among the

lower classes, were called Lollards, a name apparently derived from "lollar" (idler). Although this group may have survived in England until the age of the Tudor Reformation, Wycliffe's religious system seems to have had no direct influence on subsequent ecclesiastical history. Still, his ideas show many similarities with later Protestantism. His insistence on a purified Church, a priesthood not sacramentally distinct from the laity, a vernacular Bible, a religion more culturally responsive to the people, and lay direction of religious affairs marks out the major issues which, within a little more than a century, would divide the Western Christian community.

In distant Bohemia a Czech priest named John Huss (1369–1415) mounted an equally dangerous attack upon the dominance of the established Church. Historians dispute how much Huss was influenced by Wycliffe's ideas. Certainly he knew the works of the English heretic, but he was more conservative in his own theology—what can be understood of it. For Huss's ideas are less than clear, and it is hard even to define how he departed from orthodoxy. He seems to have held that the Church included only the predestined and he questioned, without explicitly denying, transubstantiation.

Huss was burned at the stake at Constance in 1415, more for rejecting the authority of the general council which condemned him than for his doctrinal errors. After his death Huss's followers in Bohemia defied the efforts of the emperor and Church to persuade them to submit; however, the Hussites soon divided into several rival sects—in a manner which anticipates the experience of later Protestantism—and civil war raged in Bohemia from 1421 to 1436 with no clear-cut outcome. The Hussite movement represents one of the earliest successful revolts against the medieval religious establishment. It was also the first withdrawal of an entire territory from unity with Rome.

IV. THE FINE ARTS

The social and cultural changes profoundly affected the arts, making the fourteenth and fifteenth centuries one of the most brilliant periods in Western history. Works of art have survived from this age in an unprecedented abundance, a sign that the arts were assuming broader functions in Western society. Princes and townsmen became art patrons, and the artist himself acquired a new prestige.

PATRONS AND VALUES

In the Early Middle Ages architecture, sculpture, painting, and music were primarily liturgical in character, in the sense that their chief function was to enrich Christian worship. There had, of course, always been some lay patronage of the arts—the troubadours, for example, had composed and sung songs for lay patrons—but secular music remained technically behind the music of the Church, and it is difficult today even to reconstruct its sounds.

The Church continued to promote and inspire artistic production in the fourteenth and fifteenth centuries, and many of the greatest creations of the period retained a liturgical character. But the more novel development of the age was the greatly enlarged role which laymen came to play as patrons—notably the princes of Europe and the rich townsmen in Italy and Flanders. In older histories of the Renaissance the growth of lay patronage was often equated with a secularization of art, but such a view is only partially correct. To a large degree lay patrons favored religious themes in the art they commissioned, even though much of it was no longer liturgical in function. Yet the rise of lay patronage did strongly affect the character of art. In works prepared for liturgical purposes the artist could not draw too much attention to his own work, for the Church objected to art or music which overly intruded upon the consciousness of the worshiping Christian.

Moreover, the painter and the sculptor had to accommodate the architecture of the church they were decorating. The lay patronage of religious art—and the use of that art for the decoration of homes as well as churches—in part freed the artist to form his work as he saw fit, knowing that he had the principal attention of the viewer and that the work did not have to be subservient to architecture.

Moreover, the changing religious values that have been mentioned affected artistic styles. Both the humanists and the promoters of the new lay piety insisted that religious values be made more concrete and more immediate to the believing Christian; in terms of art this meant that the viewer should become involved visually and emotionally with the sacred scenes he contemplated. The growth of naturalism in art reflected not a waning interest in religious images, but an effort to view them more intimately.

The interest of fourteenth- and fifteenth-century society in elegant living naturally extended to nonliturgical art, providing artists an abundance of opportunities. Both townsmen and nobles wished to live in attractive surroundings. Architects therefore turned their attention to the construction of beautiful homes, villas, palaces, and châteaus; adding to the beauty of these residences were tapestries, paintings, statuary, finely made furniture, and windows of tinted glass. This pursuit of elegance also gave music a new importance. In the books on good manners characteristic of the age the perfect courtier or gentleman was instructed to develop an ear for music and an ability to sing gracefully and play an instrument. No gathering within the higher levels of society could take place without the participation of singers and musicians.

Art and music also fulfilled other functions. The growing awareness of and concern with the family led patrons to commission portraits of their loved ones. In an often melancholy age art and music offered the same sweetness, delight, and spiritual refreshment which Boccaccio meant to convey in his *Decameron*. In Italy the philosophers of the Platonic Academy maintained that the contemplation of ideal beauty was the highest human activity, and it was primarily in art that the ideal beauty could be found. In the north as well, art and music were essential parts of what Huizinga called the cult of the sublime, the effort to conjure up through the mind and senses images of ideal worlds.

Finally, the social position of the artist himself was changing. In the Early Middle Ages many artists appear to have been either amateurs (in the sense of drawing their support from another career such as the monastic or clerical) or poorly paid artisans. The growing market for works of art, however, widened the ranks of professional artists and gave them greater economic rewards and prestige. The growing professionalism of the artist is perhaps most apparent in music. For example, the great churches of Europe relied more and more on professional organists and singers to staff their choirs, governments employed professional trumpeters to add splendor to their proceedings, and professional musicians entertained at the elegant fêtes of the wealthy. The high technical competence required of singers and musicians in much of the music of the Late Middle Ages probably would not have been within the reach of amateurs. The artist too was often accorded special social status; painters such as Leonardo and Michelangelo were actively cultivated by princes.

TECHNIQUES AND MODELS

The artist was also acquiring a larger array of technical skills. In music the age witnessed accelerated progress in musical notation. More diversified instrumentation became possible as

Rogier van der Weyden, a master of Flemish painting, rendered The Descent from the Cross *about 1435. By placing his figures within a restricted architectural framework he rivets the viewer's attention to the foreground. He is concerned more with the emotional rather than historical significance of the event.* (Photo: Museo del Prado)

new instruments were invented and existing ones improved. Thus in strings there were the lute, viol, and harp; in wind instruments, the flute, recorder, oboe, and trumpet; and in keyboard instruments, the organ, virginal, and clavichord.

Technical advances in painting helped artists to achieve greater depth and realism. The fourteenth-century Florentine Giotto used light and shadow, initiating a technique known as chiaroscuro to create an illusion of depth. Less than a century after Giotto, another Florentine, Masaccio, achieved a complete mastery of the scientific laws of perspective, as evidenced in his *Holy Trinity with the Virgin and St. John,* which seems almost three-dimensional (see Plate 19). The Italians heightened the naturalism of their paintings still further through the scientific study of human anatomy.

The major technical achievement in the north was the development of oil painting in the fifteenth century. Oils provided the artist with richer colors and permitted him to paint more slowly and carefully and to make changes on the painted canvas. To create an illusion of reality, the Flemish masters concentrated on precise detail rather than on perspective and chiaroscuro. Because of their painstaking exactitude the Flemish artists were the leading portrait painters of the age.

The artist was also using new models, and here the most important innovation was the heightened appreciation, especially in Italy, of the artistic heritage of the classical world. Earlier medieval artists had frequently borrowed the motifs of classical art, but they had made no effort to reflect its values—idealized beauty, admiration of the human form, simplicity, restraint, elegance, and balance. An appreciation of classical style and the values it conveyed is the achievement of Italian art, particularly in sculpture, in the fifteenth century. One of the greatest sculptors of the age, the Florentine Donatello, demonstrates those values in his *Annunciation;* though the theme is religious, the treatment is classical (see Plate 17).

In architecture the Italian masters borrowed a variety of forms from the classical style— domes, columns, colonnades, pilasters, and cornices. In the early and middle 1400s the churches and palaces merely combined classical motifs with traditional medieval techniques. A pure classical style did not really triumph until the sixteenth century, when Andrea Palladio fully captured the stateliness and grace of the ancient temples in his villas, palaces, and churches in the lower Po valley.

THE GREAT MASTERS

The two major centers of Western art in the fifteenth century were Italy and the Low Countries, then under the rule of the dukes of Burgundy. In Italy the last decades of the fifteenth century and the opening decades of the six-

teenth are traditionally called the High Renaissance. But most historians of art believe that the term "Renaissance," in the sense of conscious imitation of classical models, is inappropriate in the north of Europe in the fifteenth century, where the chief sources of inspiration remained medieval. All scholars, however, recognize the high level of creativity achieved in the north, especially by the artists and musicians of the Low Countries.

The North

The great period of painting in Flanders began with Jan van Eyck (1385?–1440), whose meticulous concern with detail achieved an intense realism that was to characterize Flemish art. In *The Virgin and Child in the Church,* Van Eyck's precision in depicting the jewels of the Virgin's crown and the fabric of her robe heightens the realism; the Virgin's vivid presence seems almost to envelop the viewer (see Plate 18). In an unstable age, when religious confusion was prevalent in the north, Van Eyck and the other Flemish masters seemed anxious to reassure the viewer of the reality and truth of the scenes they were presenting. Van Eyck's chief rival as the finest representative of Flemish art was Rogier van der Weyden, whose *Descent from the Cross* is a masterpiece of dramatic composition and emotional intensity, related by many critics to the spirit of the *devotio moderna*, then flourishing in the Low Countries.

The Low Countries enjoyed an equal prominence in music in the late fifteenth century. The choirmasters in the cathedral towns such as Cambrai, Bruges, and Antwerp, with the aid of professional singers, carried four-part choral polyphony to a new level of development. With the perfection of the a cappella (unaccompanied) vocal harmony, instrumental music was freed from its traditional subservience to voice. The masters gave their attention almost equally to secular and sacred music.

Leonardo da Vinci's mural The Last Supper *exemplifies an ideal of Renaissance painting with its superb compositional balance and its evocation of what Leonardo called "the intention of man's soul." Leonardo developed perspective by painting the figures first rather than the architectural setting. This enabled him to use architecture symbolically; for example, the large opening in the back wall acts as a halo around the head of Christ.* (Photo: Sta. Maria delle Grazie, Milan)

Among many gifted musicians may be cited Guillaume Dufay of Cambrai, author of several impressive masses as well as secular songs; and Josquin Des Prés, perhaps the most versatile of the northern composers, author of masses, motets, and chansons in almost every current style. These masters, musicians, and composers traveled widely in Europe and many of them spent some time in Italy; they therefore learned from, and deeply influenced, the local and regional musical traditions.

Italy

The art of the High Renaissance in Italy is best represented in the work of three men, each of whom stands among the major artistic geniuses of the Western past: Leonardo da Vinci (1452–1519), Raphael Santi (1483–1520), and Michelangelo Buonarroti (1475–1564).

Leonardo is celebrated for his mechanical designs as well as for his art, but his exact contribution to technology and science remains difficult to assess. He failed to complete most of the projects he contemplated, and he purposely worked in a secretive fashion (he wrote his notes in mirror writing). Although he stands somewhat apart from the mainstream of technical and scientific advance, his inventive imagination produced ingenious speculative designs for an airplane, a tank, and a submarine.

In art Leonardo's accomplishment is unmistakable. Only fifteen paintings survive, but they include some of the greatest masterpieces of Western art. He had two remarkable gifts, an ability to handle groups of people and an extraordinary skill in portraying human psychology, both exemplified by his *Last Supper*, which depicts the psychological reactions of the apostles as they hear Christ say that someone at the table will betray him. The *Mona Lisa*, a portrait of a Florentine matron in her twenties, is a fascinating psychological examination of the lady's personality.

If Leonardo was a master of design, Raphael would have to be called a master of grace. Better than any other artist he reveals the Renaissance admiration for harmony, serenity, pure beauty, and pure form. He was an extremely versatile painter from the point of view of style, readily absorbing the techniques of his masters both in Umbria (his native province) and Florence (where he served his apprenticeship)—the bright colors favored by the Umbrians, the subtle shading of color and the strength of design of Leonardo, and the vitality and power of Michelangelo. Raphael may not be as original a genius as Leonardo or Michelangelo, but he is unsurpassed in the quality of his craftsmanship and the charm of its results.

Michelangelo is probably the best example of the universal genius of the Renaissance, a man of towering accomplishments in architecture, sculpture, and painting. As an artist Michelangelo preferred sculpture to painting, but his work in both mediums is rich with subtle, dramatic vitality. He liked to portray his subjects at the moment of psychological transition. For example, his statue of David catches the young man at the instant he resolves to hurl the stone at Goliath. The statue of Moses shows the old prophet awakening to anger at the idolatry of the Israelites. Adam, painted on the Sistine ceiling, is represented just as his inert body responds to God's life-giving touch (see Plate 24).

Imbued with the neoplatonic longing to view things not as they are but as they ought to be, Michelangelo did not depict a natural world. His works seem almost a protest against the limitations of matter, from which many of his subjects struggle to be free. There is little that is placid or serene in his art, and this predilection for contorted, struggling, even misshapen figures exercised a profound influence on his successors. His work is traditionally, and justly, considered to mark the bridge between the harmonious art of the Renaissance and the distorted, dynamic style of the Mannerist school.

v. SCIENCE AND THE RENAISSANCE

In the fourteenth and fifteenth centuries numerous changes—social and economic as well as intellectual—prepared the way for the scientific revolution of the early modern epoch. Although the natural philosophers of the period made no dramatic advances in scientific theory, they succeeded in assimilating a large part of ancient science and began the slow process of questioning and revising, which ultimately led to the achievements of Copernicus, Galileo, and Newton.

THE RECEPTION OF ANCIENT SCIENCE

A critical first step toward the scientific revolution was the mastery of the natural science of the ancient world. Ancient science offered philosophers a full and coherent system or model of the natural world (sometimes called a paradigm) against which they could compare their own observations and speculations. In the twelfth and thirteenth centuries the complete corpus of the scientific works of Aristotle, together with the commentary by the Muslim philosopher Averroës, became known in the West and immediately inspired close study and extensive discussion. Albertus Magnus, for example, the teacher of Thomas Aquinas, wrote at length on biological questions; he both reflected and promoted a new interest in the life sciences in Western schools.

In the fourteenth century, nominalists at Paris and Oxford took the first, hesitant steps toward a criticism of Aristotle's world system. At the University of Paris, for example, Jean Buridan proposed an important revision in the Aristotelian theory of motion, or physical dynamics. If, as Aristotle had said, all objects are at rest in their natural state, what keeps an arrow flying after it leaves the bow? Aristotle had reasoned rather lamely that the arrow disturbs the air through which it passes and that it is this disturbance which keeps pushing the arrow forward.

But this explanation did not satisfy the nominalists. Buridan suggested that the movement of the bow lends the arrow a special quality of motion, an "impetus," which stays with it permanently unless removed by the resistance of the air. Although it was inaccurate, Buridan's explanation anticipated Galileo's theory of inertia, according to which an object at rest tends to remain at rest, and an object in motion continues to move along a straight line until it is acted upon by an external force. Buridan and other fourteenth-century nominalists also theorized about the acceleration of falling objects and made some attempt to describe this phenomenon in mathematical terms. Their ideas became the point of departure for other of Galileo's investigations of mechanics. Moreover, their use of mathematics foreshadowed the importance to be given to measurement in scientific work.

The humanists also helped to prepare the way for scientific advance. The growth of textual and literary criticism—a major humanist achievement—taught men to look with greater care and precision at works inherited from the past. Inevitably too, they acquired a sharper critical sense concerning the content as well as the language of the ancient texts. The revival of the classics placed at the disposal of Europeans a larger fund of ancient ideas, and this increased the awareness that ancient authors did not always speak in unison. Could the ancients therefore always be correct? Furthermore, the idealism of Plato and the number mysticism of Pythagoras maintained that behind the disparate data of experience there existed ideal forms or harmonies, which the philosopher should seek to perceive and describe. Once this assumption gained credence, it was natural to assume that the cosmic harmonies might be described in mathematical terms.

The Middle Ages also nourished traditions of astrology and alchemy; men sought not only to understand natural processes but also to turn that knowledge into power. Natural science and the scientists themselves would for a long time maintain close connections with these intellectual forms of magical practice.

Finally, technological and economic changes contributed to the birth of exact science. The improvement of ships stimulated, for navigational purposes, more accurate observation of the heavenly bodies. Changes in warfare raised interest in the ballistics of cannon balls, in the design of war machines and fortifications, and in military engineering generally. Artists were able to depict with high levels of accuracy the human anatomy, maps, or astronomical charts. Printing assured that ideas could be disseminated cheaply, accurately, and quickly across wide geographical areas. Craftsmen working in metal and glass were growing more skilled in the course of the Late Middle Ages. Eyeglasses became ever more popular in Europe in the thirteenth century, and glass workers ground lenses more accurately and experimented with their uses. Although the telescope was a seventeenth-century invention, the technical basis for it was laid in the Late Middle Ages.

The scientific revolution was, in sum, supported by a whole range of developments in European cultural life, many of which occurred in the fourteenth and fifteenth centuries. It remained for the fathers of modern science to draw upon these various traditions in the sixteenth and seventeenth centuries, and to form out of them and their own observations new systems or models of the natural world.

The culture of the West was changing profoundly in the fourteenth and fifteenth centuries, as it responded to new social needs. In Italy a literate lay aristocracy had come to dominate society. Traditional cultural interests and values seemed too abstract, too removed from the lives of these men, who daily faced concrete problems and wanted moral guidance. To meet this need Italian humanists developed a system of education which emphasized rhetoric and moral philosophy and looked to the works of classical antiquity for the best models of wisdom and persuasive language.

In the north of Europe the ideals of chivalry continued to dominate the culture of the lay aristocracy until late in the fifteenth century; but those ideals had become exaggerated, and they began to distort reality. The overripe chivalry of the north has helped give the Late Middle Ages its reputation for decadence.

Nominalist philosophers in the universities were effecting a critical reappraisal of the principles of thirteenth-century Scholasticism in the interest of defining precisely the borders between reason and faith. Also evident is a new style of piety which stressed the need to cultivate an interior sense of the presence and love of God.

The humanists, nominalist philosophers, and advocates of the new piety were not revolting against the accumulated cultural heritage of the Middle Ages. Rather, they wished to enrich it and make it accessible to a broader spectrum of the population. Learning, literature, art, and religion, they believed, should help men lead lives which would at once be more cultured, more contented, more pious, and more human.

The fine arts flourished during these years of change. In both Italy and the north artists adopted new techniques and gave brilliant expression to a much fuller range of values. The scientific achievements of the age were more modest, but they foreshadowed the revolutionary changes in science that were to take place in the sixteenth and seventeenth centuries.

RECOMMENDED READING

Sources

*Boccaccio, Giovanni. *The Decameron.* G. H. Mc-William (tr.). 1972.

*Cassirer, Ernst, P. P. Kristeller, and J. H. Randell, Jr. (eds.). *The Renaissance Philosophy of Man.* 1953. Selections from Petrarch, Valla, Ficino, Pico, and others.

Eckhart. *Meister Eckhart, a Modern Translation.* Raymond Bernard Blakney (tr.).

Froissart, Jean. *Chronicles of England, France, Spain and the Adjoining Countries.* Thomas Johnes (tr.). 1901.

Kempis, Thomas à. *The Imitation of Christ.* William Benham (tr.). 1909. Great classic of late medieval piety.

Langland, William. *The Vision of Piers Plowman.* Henry W. Wells (tr.). 1959.

*Marsilius of Padua. *Defender of Peace.* Alan Gerwith (tr.). 1956.

Studies

*Baron, Hans. *The Crisis of the Early Italian Renaissance: Civic Humanism and Republican Liberty in the Age of Classicism and Tyranny.* 1966. Fundamental analysis of Florentine "civic humanism."

*Berenson, Bernard. *The Italian Painters of the Renaissance.* 1968. Classical essays in the history of art.

*Burckhardt, Jacob. *The Civilization of the Renaissance in Italy.* 1958. One of the great works in European history.

Cartellieri, Otto. *The Court of Burgundy.* 1929.

Clark, J. M. *The Great German Mystics: Eckhart, Tauler and Suso.* 1949.

Crombie, Alistair C. *Medieval and Early Modern Science.* 1961.

*Herlihy, David. *The Family in Renaissance Italy.* 1974.

*Huizinga, Johan. *The Waning of the Middle Ages.* 1953.

*Kristeller, Paul Otto. *Renaissance Thought: The Classic, Scholastic and Humanistic Strains.* 1961. One of many works by a leading student of Renaissance thought.

Leff, Gordon. *William of Ockham.* 1975. Recent, authoritative examination of a difficult philosopher.

Martines, Lauro. *The Social World of the Florentine Humanists.* 1963. The humanists examined in the light of their social origins.

---

* Available in paperback.

THIRTEEN

OVERSEAS EXPANSION
AND NEW POLITICS

Between the last quarter of the fifteenth century and the middle of the sixteenth century, a renewed sense of confidence spread through Europe, accompanying a revival of prosperity, authority, and stability. The vigor that returned to economic life was particularly remarkable; this was a period of rising prices, population growth, and a rapid expansion of trade. Overseas the results of this surge of enterprise were even more spectacular: the discovery of new lands and riches, and the founding of colonies which grew into massive empires that endured into the nineteenth and twentieth centuries.

The question of why it was Western civilization that eventually spread around the globe has long fascinated historians. In the fifteenth century Europeans were less advanced in technology than Asians, and their leading rulers had none of the wealth of Indian moguls or Chinese emperors. Some scholars have suggested that Oriental societies, being much larger, were more self-sufficient and that therefore neither explorers nor international traders achieved the status they gained in the West.

Another reason the Europeans seem to have been able to launch the expansion was the restoration of stability in political life. A new assurance permeated the government of the rulers of three leading kingdoms: England, France, and Spain. Often called "new monarchs" by historians, they merited the title because of their potent reassertion of royal preeminence in their domains. Their aims were still largely personal and dynastic—they were concerned more with the fortunes of their own families than with the destinies of the people they ruled—but to this end they raised their power at home, particularly against the nobility, to new levels. By the 1550s the new monarchs had emerged from the uncertainties of the Late Middle Ages as the main political force in their realms.

The Germans, Italians, and Eastern Europeans, by contrast, began to fall behind their Western neighbors in this crucial respect. They lacked strong, unifying central governments, and thus local nobles or small political units fragmented political authority. The result was the eventual decline of these countries. From the mid-sixteenth century until the mid-nineteenth century, they slipped to lesser roles in international affairs, victims of the chief political lesson of this period: only a capable central authority could marshall the resources of a territory and win prominence on the international scene.

I. EXPLORATION AND ITS IMPACT

Few great changes in the history of the world have owed so much to the exploits of a handful of daring men as did the overseas expansion of Europe. The origins of the movement can be traced back to the crusades, the Europeans' first outward steps after centuries of defensiveness and shrinkage. Travelers such as Marco Polo and traders in the Levant had also contributed to this interest in far-off places. But the enlargement of the Ottoman Empire during the fifteenth century threatened to cut overland contacts with Asia. It was therefore necessary to find an alternative: a sea route such as the one being opened up by the explorers who were inching their way around Africa toward the Indian Ocean.

THE OVERSEAS EXPANSION

The most spectacular evidence that a long period of contraction in the West had come to an end was the territorial and economic expansion that began in the fifteenth century. The explorers, colonists, and merchants of this period transformed an inward-looking Europe into the booming and vigorous founder of empires that stretched from East Asia to the Americas.

The Portuguese

The pioneers in this transformation were the Portuguese, occupants of an inhospitable land, whose seafarers had always held an important place in the country's economic life. The need for better agricultural opportunities had long turned their eyes toward the Atlantic islands and the territories held by the Muslims (Moors) to the south. But this ambition had to be organized into a sustained effort if it was to achieve results, and in the early fifteenth century, Prince Henry the Navigator, a younger son of the king, undertook that task.

A talented leader, Henry participated in the capture of the North African port of Ceuta from the Arabs in 1415, a crusading expedition that only whetted his appetite for more victories over the infidels. At Ceuta he probably received information about legendary Christians (the fabled kingdom of Prester John) and mines of gold somewhere in the interior. A mixture of motives—profit, religion, and curiosity—spurred him on, and in 1419 he founded a center for sailors, mapmakers, astronomers (because their contributions to celestial navigation were vital), shipbuilders, and instrument makers at Sagres, at the southwestern tip of Portugal. Here men interested in discovery—mainly Ital-

ians—gathered, hoping to find a way around Africa in order to reach India. The early adventurers did not succeed, but during their gradual advance down the West African coast, they opened a rich new trade in ivory, gold, and slaves.

Then, in 1487, one Portuguese captain, Bartholomeu Dias, returned to Lisbon after an incredible voyage. He had been blown out to sea by a northerly gale and spent thirteen days without sight of land. As soon as possible he had headed east, but when he made his landfall it proved to be on the east coast of Africa, beyond the Cape of Good Hope, which thus far no one had been able to pass.

The way to India now seemed open, but before the Portuguese could send out their first expedition the news arrived that a sailor employed by the Spaniards, one Christopher Columbus, had apparently reached India by sailing west. To avoid conflicting claims, Portugal and Spain signed the Treaty of Tordesillas in 1494, which gave Portugal possession of all the lands to the east of an imaginary line about 300 miles west of the Azores, and Spain a monopoly of everything to the west. Portugal thus kept the only practical route to India (as well as the rights to Brazil, which one of her sailors may already have discovered). Three years later Vasco da Gama took the first Portuguese fleet across the Indian Ocean.

At first, he found it very hard to trade, because the Arabs, who had controlled these waters for centuries, tried to keep out all rivals. Within the next fourteen years, however, the Portuguese merchants had established themselves. The key to their success was naval power, for their ship designers had learned to combine their old square sails, which provided speed, with the Arabs' lateen sails, which increased maneuverability. The Portuguese were also the first to give their fleets effective fire power, realizing that cannon, not soldiers, won battles at sea. In addition, they deployed their ships in squadrons rather than individually, a tactic that further increased their superiority. The result was rapid and overwhelming success. A series of victories at sea reduced Arab naval strength, and bombardments brought recalcitrant cities to submission. Guided by the military skill and superb strategic sense of a brilliant commander, Affonso de Albuquerque, the Portuguese established tradings posts in the East that by 1513 extended to the rich Spice Islands, the Moluccas (see Map 13.1).

The empire Portugal created remained entirely dependent on sea power; she rarely tried to colonize overseas areas. Instead she set up a chain of trading bases, consisting of warehouses combined with forts that could be supplied and defended by sea, from West Africa to China. Generally the Portuguese restricted contacts with Africans and Asians to maintaining friendly relations and missionary and trading rights; they made no attempt to conquer. By the mid-fifteenth century, they were beginning to profit from their explorations—between 1442 and 1446 almost 1,000 slaves were brought home from Africa—and in the sixteenth century their wealth multiplied as they became major importers of luxuries from the East such as spices, which were in great demand as medicines, preservatives, and tasty delicacies. By dominating commerce with the rich Oriental civilizations, Portugal's merchants controlled Europe's most valuable trade.

The Portuguese achievement displayed all the ingredients of the West's rise to worldwide power: driving ambition, technical superiority in guns and ships, tactical skills, commercial expertise supported by military force, and careful planning and organization in the home country. Their expansion was sustained by the political and economic revival that was spreading through Western Europe at this time and by the added spur of competition. For Spain soon determined to emulate her neighbor, and when later the Dutch, English, and French took the lead in empire building, they sought to outdo their predecessors and each other. This competition gave the Europeans the crucial stimulus that other peoples had lacked, and it projected them into a dominance over the rest of the globe that would last for more than 450 years.[1]

The Spaniards

Inspired by the same centuries-old crusading ambitions as the Portuguese, the Spaniards rode the second wave of expansion to wealth and glory overseas. Because she was a much larger nation and because she happened to direct her attention toward a more sparsely populated continent than did Portugal, Spain founded her empire on conquest and colonization, not trade. But she got her start from a stroke of luck.

Christopher Columbus, an experienced Genoese sailor who had some contact with the leading Italian geographers of his day, seems to have believed (it is difficult to know for certain, for he was always a secretive man) that Asia lay only 3,500 miles beyond the Canary Islands. He arrived at this figure as the result of two mistakes: he relied on the ancient Ptolemaic estimate that the circumference of the world was 18,000 miles—6,000 miles too short—and on Marco Polo's estimate that Asia extended 1,500 miles farther east than in fact it does.

Convinced that sailing across the Atlantic to the East was perfectly feasible, Columbus took his proposal in 1484 to the Portuguese government, which refused to underwrite the venture. With a mystic belief in his own destiny, he persisted, gained the financial backing and blessing of Ferdinand V and Isabella I of Spain, and

---

[1] Current discussions of the differences that led Europe, rather than another civilization, to expand throughout the world are excellently surveyed in Joseph R. Levenson (ed.), *European Expansion and the Counter-Example of Asia, 1300–1600* (1967). See also Robert O. Collins, *Europeans in Africa* (1971), Ch. 1.

set sail in 1492. He was an excellent navigator (one of his discoveries on the voyage was the difference between true and magnetic north), and he kept his men going despite their horror of being so long at sea without sight of land. After thirty-three days he reached the Bahamas, and though disappointed that he found no Chinese or Japanese as he investigated Cuba and the west coast of Hispaniola (today's Haiti), he was certain that he had reached Asia, notwithstanding the lack of resemblance between the few natives he encountered and those whom travelers such as Marco Polo had described.

Columbus crossed the Atlantic Ocean three more times, but he made no further discoveries of significance. By the end of his life, in 1506, it was becoming apparent that he had found islands close by a new continent, not Asia. The Treaty of Tordesillas reserved the exploration of these lands for the Spaniards, who soon began to perceive them as an asset, not an obstacle.

Other Spanish voyages of discovery followed those of Columbus. In 1513 Vasco de Balboa saw the Pacific Ocean from Central America, and this rekindled the notion that an easy westward passage might be found to East Asia. But the last remaining hopes were finally dashed in 1522, when the one surviving ship from a fleet of five that had set out under Ferdinand Magellan three years before returned to Spain after the ordeal of having sailed around the world (see Map 13.1).

Magellan's ninety-eight-day crossing of the Pacific stands as a supreme accomplishment of seamanship in the age of discovery. But the perilous voyage persuaded the Spaniards that Portugal clearly had the best route to the East, and in 1529 they finally renounced all claims to trade with the Spice Islands for a payment of 350,000 ducats. The world had been divided, and Spain could concentrate on the Americas, those unexpected continents that were to become possessions of unbelievable richness.

Volunteers were amply available. When the

This facsimile of a wood engraving depicts the discovery of Santo Domingo by Christopher Columbus. It is based on a sketch attributed to the explorer himself. (Photo: New York Public Library/Picture Collection)

Muslim kingdom in southern Spain was conquered by the Castilians in 1492, a group of men with a long tradition of military service found themselves at loose ends. These were the younger sons of noble families, who were kept from inheriting land because Spanish law allowed only the eldest son to inherit. Naturally the prospect of unlimited land and military adventure across the Atlantic appealed to them, and thus the conquistador, the conqueror,

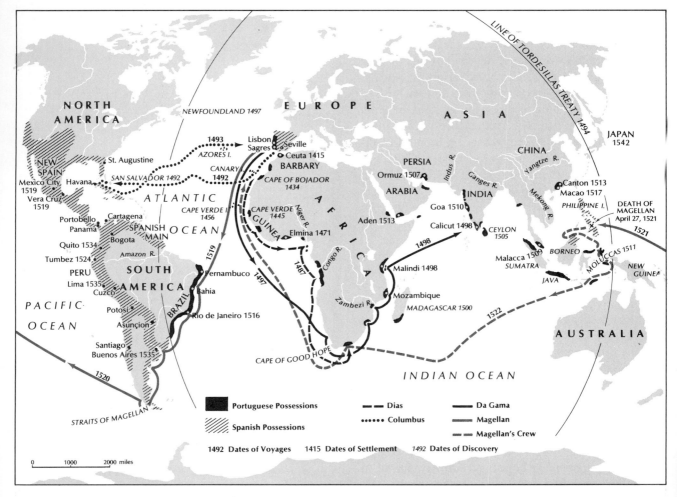

MAP 13.1: EXPLORATION AND CONQUEST IN THE 15TH AND 16TH CENTURIES

Map labels:

NORTH AMERICA · EUROPE · A S I A

NEWFOUNDLAND 1497 · Lisbon · Seville · JAPAN 1542
1493 · AZORES I. · Sagres · Ceuta 1415 · CHINA · Yangtze R.
NEW SPAIN · CANARY 1492 · BARBARY · PERSIA · Canton 1513 · Macao 1517
Mexico City 1519 · Havana · SAN SALVADOR 1492 · CAPE OF BOJADOR 1434 · Ormuz 1507 · Indus R. · Ganges R. · PHILIPPINE I. · DEATH OF MAGELLAN April 27, 1521 · 1521
Vera Cruz 1519 · ATLANTIC · ARABIA · INDIA · Mekong R.
St. Augustine · CAPE VERDE I. 1456 · CAPE VERDE 1445 · AFRICA · Goa 1510
Portobello · Cartagena · OCEAN · GUINEA · Niger R. · Aden 1513 · Calicut 1498 · CEYLON 1505 · BORNEO · MOLUCCAS 1511
Panama · SPANISH MAIN · Elmina 1471 · Malacca 1509 · SUMATRA · NEW GUINEA
Quito 1534 · Bogota · Amazon R. · 1498 · JAVA
Tumbez 1524 · PERU · SOUTH AMERICA · Congo R. · Malindi 1498
Lima 1535 · 1519 · BRAZIL · Pernambuco · 1487 · Mozambique
Cuzco · Bahia · 1497 · Zambezi R. · MADAGASCAR 1500 · AUSTRALIA
PACIFIC OCEAN · Potosí · Rio de Janeiro 1516
Asunción · 1522
Santiago · Buenos Aires 1535 · CAPE OF GOOD HOPE · INDIAN OCEAN
1520 · STRAITS OF MAGELLAN

LINE OF TORDESILLAS TREATY 1494

Legend:
- Portuguese Possessions
- Spanish Possessions
- Dias
- Columbus
- Da Gama
- Magellan
- Magellan's Crew

1492 Dates of Voyages   1415 Dates of Settlement   1492 Dates of Discovery

0   1000   2000 miles

---

was born. There were not many of them—less than 1,000 at most—but they overran much of America in search of wealth and glory.

The first and most dramatic of these leaders was Hernando Cortés, who in 1519 landed on the Mexican coast and set out to overcome the splendid Aztec civilization in the high plateau of central Mexico. His army consisted of only 600 men, but in two years, with a few reinforcements, he had won a complete victory. Guns alone made no important difference be-

cause Cortés had only thirteen muskets and some unwieldy cannon. More effective were his horses, his clever manipulation of Aztec superstitions, and the unshakable determination of his men. The Mexican Mayas also surrendered to Cortés, while the Incas of Peru fell to Francisco Pizarro. Other conquistadors repeated these successes throughout Central and South America. By 1550 the conquest was over, and the military men, never very good at governing the territories they had won, gave way to administrators who began to pull the huge empire into organized shape.

The Spanish government established in the New World the same pattern of political administration that it was setting up in its European territories (see section II). Representatives of the throne, viceroys, were sent to administer the empire and to impose centralized control. Each was advised by a local *audiencia*, a kind of miniature council that also acted as a court of law, but the ultimate authority remained in Spain.

To the rest of the world, the overwhelming attraction of Spanish America was its mineral wealth, especially its silver. In 1545 a major vein of silver was discovered at Potosí, in Bolivia, and from those mines—worked by Indian forced labor—came the treasure that made fortunes for the colonists, sustained wars that Spain was fighting against her neighbors, and ultimately enriched all of Western Europe (see accompanying table). For the balance of the sixteenth century, however, despite the efforts of other countries, Portugal and Spain remained the only conspicuous promoters and the major beneficiaries of Europe's expansion.

IMPORTS OF TREASURE TO SPAIN FROM THE NEW WORLD, 1511–1600

DECADE	TOTAL VALUE*
1511–1520	2,626,000
1521–1530	1,407,000
1531–1540	6,706,000
1541–1550	12,555,000
1551–1560	21,437,000
1561–1570	30,418,000
1571–1580	34,990,000
1581–1590	63,849,000
1591–1600	83,536,000

* In Ducats

Adapted from J. H. Elliott, *Imperial Spain, 1469–1716* (New York, 1964), p. 175.

ECONOMIC GROWTH

Most of the silver from the New World went beyond Spain to Italian and German merchants who financed the wars of the Spanish kings and also controlled the American trade. Although other sources of supply, mainly silver mines in Austria, were appearing at this time, the New World was primarily responsible for the end of the crippling shortage of precious metals, and hence of coins, that had plagued Europe for centuries. By the middle of the seventeenth century, the Continent's holdings in gold were to increase by one-fifth, and, more important, its stock of silver was to triple.

In 1556 a Spanish professor named Azpilcueta suggested that this flow explained a phenomenon that was beginning to cause wide concern —a tremendous rise in prices. The inflation was sharpest in Spain, where money lost three-quarters of its 1500 value by 1600; the depreciation elsewhere was serious but less marked —in England for example it was about two-thirds. Recent historians, however, have shown that the upward movement of prices began before substantial amounts of silver were shipped and that the rate slowed at the very time that imports from South America rose sharply. Although it is still acknowledged that the supply of precious metals directly influenced price levels and contributed to Europe's economic revival, an exclusive correlation can no longer be accepted.[2] Other factors must be taken into consideration to explain the startling changes of the late fifteenth century.

At the simplest level what happened was a gradual revival of confidence. After a century and a half of hard times, economic conditions were improving. Much of the credit for this must be given to the restoration of political sta-

[2] There is a good introduction to the problem of explaining the rise in prices in J. H. Elliott, *Imperial Spain, 1469–1716* (1964), pp. 172–191.

bility. Merchants were more inclined to risk long-distance trading under strong governments. Rulers could make treaties with foreign powers for commercial advantage and guarantee that such agreements would be upheld. The growth of population in the sixteenth century was the most dramatic result of the new sense of confidence, and the surge in the number of people was a prime contributor to the inflation because it increased the demand for goods. In general the businessman, encouraged by the discovery of new sources of silver, enlarged markets, and the improved profits generated by rising prices, was now able to widen the scope of his investments.

Records are far too poor to permit a measurement of the increase in population, but it is likely that by the early seventeenth century, Europe's population was perhaps 50 percent larger than it had been in the late fifteenth. And cities grew much faster than did the population as a whole: London for example had approximately 50,000 inhabitants in the early sixteenth century but over 200,000 a hundred years later (see Map 13.2). Significantly, wide areas of marginal farmland were reoccupied, having been abandoned in the fourteenth and fifteenth centuries because a shrinking population had provided no market for their produce. Now there were more mouths to feed, and the extra acres again became profitable.

The population rise was followed by a staggering jump in food prices. By the early 1600s wheat cost approximately five times more than in the late 1400s, an increase that far outpaced the movement of prices in general. It is not surprising, therefore, that this period witnessed the first wave of enclosures in England: major landowners put up fences around common tilling or grazing ground, traditionally open to all the animals of the locality, in order to reserve it for their own crops or their sheep, whose wool was also in increasing demand. By 1600 about an eighth of England's arable land had been enclosed.

As markets began to grow in response to population pressures, the volume of trade also shot upward; commercial profits thus kept pace with those of agriculture. Customs receipts rose steadily, as did the yield of tolls from ships entering the Baltic Sea, one of Europe's leading trade centers. In many areas, too, shipbuilding boomed. This was the heyday of the English cloth trade and the great Spanish sheep farms, of the central German linen industry and the northern Italian silk industry. Printing became a widespread occupation, and gunmaking and glassmaking also expanded rapidly. The latter had a major effect on European society, because the increasing use of windows allowed builders to divide houses into small rooms, thus giving many people a little privacy for the first time.

Leading financiers who invested in the growing volume of trade of course accumulated large fortunes. For centuries the Italians had been in the vanguard of economic advance but in the sixteenth century firms of other nations were achieving international prominence. The most successful of the new enterprises was run by a family descended from a fourteenth-century weaver, Johannes Fugger of Augsburg. The sixteenth-century Fuggers financed the Spanish King Charles I's campaign for the throne of the Holy Roman Empire and his later wars when he became the Emperor Charles V. Great bankers were thus often closely allied with monarchs, and like all merchants, they gained from the mounting power of central governments. Rulers encouraged commerce in the hope of larger revenues from customs duties and taxes, and they gave leading entrepreneurs valuable privileges. Such alliances were eventually the undoing of some houses, which were ruined by royal bankruptcies, but until the late sixteenth century, Italian and German bankers controlled Europe's finances.

The continued importance of Italy, and of the Mediterranean in general, indicates that the overseas expansion did not change Europe over-

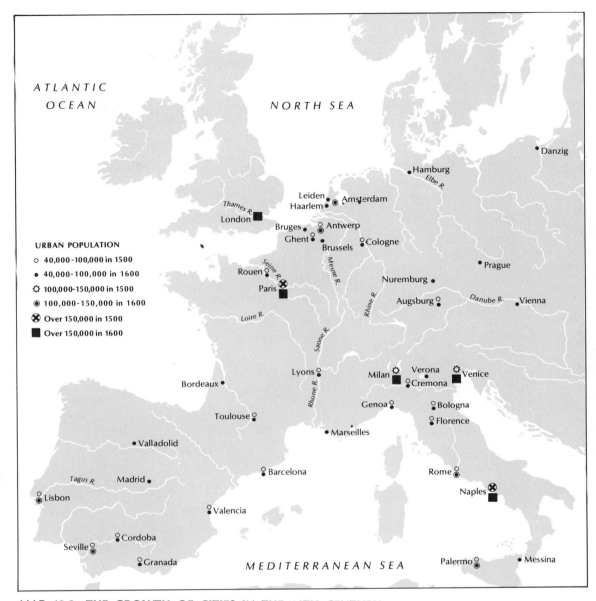

MAP 13.2: THE GROWTH OF CITIES IN THE 16TH CENTURY

URBAN POPULATION
○ 40,000–100,000 in 1500
● 40,000–100,000 in 1600
✿ 100,000–150,000 in 1500
◉ 100,000–150,000 in 1600
⊗ Over 150,000 in 1500
■ Over 150,000 in 1600

night. In fact, Italy's overland spice trade across Asia continued as it had for centuries, even though the Portuguese found it much cheaper to bring the goods west by sea. But rather than try to squeeze Italy out of the trade, Portugal simply charged the same prices and thus made a larger profit. Not until Dutch and English fleets began to enter the Mediterranean around 1600, and at the same time gained control of eastern spice shipments, did the balance shift away from the Italians. In the meantime, the boom benefited all areas of Europe.

Indeed, every level of trading activity offered opportunities for advancement. The guild sys-

tem expanded in the sixteenth century to incorporate many new trades, while the whole structure of mercantile enterprise developed in new ways. The idea took hold that a business firm was an impersonal entity, larger than the man who owned it and vested with an identity, legal status, permanence, and even profits that were not the same as those of its members. Here was yet another indication of the creativity and energy at work in economic affairs.

SOCIAL CHANGE

Not everyone shared in the new prosperity. Naturally landowners and food producers benefited most from the inflation and could amass considerable wealth. The tenant could also do well, because rents did not keep pace with food prices. But wages lagged miserably. By the early seventeenth century, a laborer's annual income had about half the purchasing power it had had at the end of the fifteenth, a decline that made its most drastic impact on Eastern Europe, where serfdom reappeared. In the West, large numbers of peasants had to leave the land, which could no longer support all of them; others were forced off by enclosures and similar "improvements." These displaced people turned to begging and wandering across country, often ending up in towns, where crime became a serious problem. Peasant uprisings directed at tax collectors, nobles, or food suppliers were almost annual affairs in one region of France or another after the mid-sixteenth century, and in England the unending stream of vagrants gave rise to a belief that the country was overpopulated. The extreme poverty was universally deplored, particularly as it promoted disorders; local nobles, not as strong as they had once been, could no longer restrain potential troublemakers, and the two centuries from

Antwerp on market day, ca. 1600. (Photo: Koninklijke Museum voor Schone Kunsten, Brussels)

the mid-sixteenth to the mid-eighteenth were the great days of the highwayman. Nobody could understand, much less control, the forces that were transforming society.

The newly strong governments of the period tried to relieve the distress, but their efforts were not always consistent. They regarded the beggars sometimes as shirkers who should be punished and at other times as unfortunates who needed to be helped. Not until the end of the sixteenth century did the more compassionate view begin to prevail.

Vagrancy was only one of the signs that Europeans were witnessing the beginnings of modern urbanization, with all of its dislocations. Major differences also developed between life in the country and life in the town. The rural worker may have led a strenuous existence, but he escaped the worst hazards of the urban dweller. Whole sections of most large cities were controlled by the sixteenth-century equivalent of the underworld, which offered sanctuary to criminals and danger to most citizens. Plagues were much more serious in towns—the upper classes soon learned to flee to the country at the first sign of disease—and famines more devastating because of the far poorer sanitation in urban areas and their remoteness from food supplies.

On the other hand the opening of economic opportunities offered many people a chance to improve their status dramatically. At courts, in royal administrations, in law, in the burgeoning cities, and overseas in growing empires, men won fortunes and titles and founded new aristocratic dynasties. The means of advancement varied: the English monarchy sold to the newly rich the lands it confiscated from monasteries after the religious struggle that split the kingdom from the Church of Rome (see section II); France put government offices on the market to raise revenue and build the bureaucracy; the New World gave minor Spanish nobles the chance to acquire vast estates; and everywhere the long boom in commerce encouraged social mobility. By the 1620s, when the upward movement began to subside, a new aristocracy had been born that was destined to dominate Europe for centuries.

It seems a paradox that the disruptive economic and social changes of the sixteenth century should have happened at a time when the "new monarchs" of England, France, and Spain were asserting their control and imposing order in their realms. The two processes were not unrelated—strong central governments gave vital support to economic growth, overseas expansion, and attempts to relieve social distress, while prosperity provided rulers with the tax revenues that were essential to their power—but they clearly had somewhat contrary effects. In the long run, however, it was the restoration of political stability that permitted the solution of the problems that arose during the sixteenth century. The creation of well-organized states, structured around powerful central governments, was even more decisive than the economic boom in shaping the future of Western Europe.

II. THE "NEW MONARCHIES"

During the last quarter of the fifteenth century, England, France, and Spain were governed by remarkable rulers, whose accomplishments have led historians to call them "new monarchs": Henry VII, Louis XI, and Ferdinand and Isabella.[3] Their reigns are generally regarded as marking the end of more than a century of fragmentation and the beginning of a revival of royal power that would ultimately create the bureaucracies characteristic of the modern state. Moreover the successors to their thrones not only inaugurated more active and aggressive policies in international affairs but also—and

[3] An excellent introduction to the scholarship on the "new monarchs" is Arthur J. Slavin (ed.), *The "New Monarchies" and Representative Assemblies: Medieval Constitutionalism or Modern Absolutism?* (1964), which also covers some subjects not treated in this

this was of momentous significance—gradually gained ground over traditional competitors for power such as the Church.

TUDOR ENGLAND

The English monarchs had relied for centuries on local cooperation to run their kingdom. Unlike other European countries, England contained only fifty or sixty families out of a population of perhaps 2.5 million who were legally nobles. But many other families, though not technically members of the nobility, had large estates and were dominant figures at the parish, county, and even national level. They were known as gentry, and it was from their ranks that the crown appointed the local officers who administered the realm—notably the justices of the peace (usually referred to as J.P.s). These voluntary, unpaid officials served as the principal public servants in the more than forty counties of the land.

For reasons of status as well as out of a feeling of responsibility, the gentry had always sought such appointments. From the crown's point of view, the great advantage of the system was its efficiency: enforcement was in the hands of those who could enforce, for as a "great man" in his neighborhood, the justice of the peace rarely had trouble exerting his authority. By the Late Middle Ages, the king had had at his disposal an administrative structure without rival in Europe. This cooperative approach to the task of governing had created a strong sense of duty among the members of the ruling class, and the king had come to consult them more frequently over the years.

In the sixteenth century an institution that had developed from this relationship, Parliament, began to take on a general importance as the chief representative of the country's wishes:

chapter—for example the rise of representative assemblies in the Low Countries and the establishment of a strong central government in Sweden during the sixteenth century.

THE
IMAGE
OF
MAN
IN RENAISSANCE ART

It has been said of the Renaissance that there are as many ways of defining it as there are branches of historic study and that the one point of agreement among experts is that the new era began when people realized they were no longer living in the Middle Ages. The Renaissance, in other words, was the first period in history to be aware of its own existence. Not only did it coin a name for itself—Renaissance means "rebirth"—but also for its predecessor, the "thousand years of darkness," which it thought followed upon the fall of ancient civilization. Both names have stuck, although today we no longer regard the Middle Ages as dark and are less sure what the Renaissance was a rebirth of.

To those who first thought in these terms—a tiny minority even among the educated in fourteenth-century Italy—"rebirth" meant the revival of the classics, the language and literature of ancient Greece and Rome; in the course of the next hundred years, however, the concept came to embrace the entire range of cultural life, including the visual arts. From this the Italian humanists distilled a new philosophy of man designed to reconcile what seemed to them two equal sources of authority: Christian revelation and the wisdom of the ancients. Its basis is still the biblical account of man's creation by the Lord "in our image and likeness," but the emphasis is now on man's freedom of will rather than his dependence on God. Thus Gianozzo Manetti, in his treatise "On the Dignity and Excellence of Man," proclaims him not only the most beautiful and perfect of all creatures but a second creator: "After that first, new and rude creation of the world [by God], everything seems to have been discovered, constructed and completed by us ... all homes, all towns, all cities, finally all buildings in the world which certainly are so many and of such a nature that they ought rather to be regarded as the works of angels than of men. ... Ours are the paintings, ours the sculptures, ours the arts, ours the sciences. ..." Is it any wonder, Manetti asks, that "the first inventors of the various arts were worshiped as gods by the early peoples"?[1] In Pico della Mirandola's oration on the same theme, the Lord speaks to the newly created Adam as follows: "The nature of all other beings is limited ... within the bounds of laws prescribed by Us. You, constrained by no limits, in accordance with your own free will ... shall ordain for yourself the limits of your nature. ... We made you neither of heaven nor of earth, neither mortal nor immortal, so that with freedom of choice ... you may fashion yourself in whatever shape you prefer. You shall have the power to degenerate into the lower forms of life, which are brutish. You shall have the power ... to be reborn into the higher forms, which are divine."[2] The humanists, then, saw man as endowed by God with gifts that make him the master of his own fate.

If Pico's exalted vision of man's potential seems to anticipate Michelangelo (see Plate 24), Manetti's celebration of man as the active and self-confident shaper of his world, with special pride in his achievements in the visual arts, suggests the new poise of Donatello (see Plate 17) and the clarity and order of Masaccio (see Plate 19). Scientific perspective, the means by which Masaccio achieved these qualities, was far more than a technical accomplishment; it permitted the painter, for the first time in the history of art, to define, exactly and measurably, man's relation to his spatial setting within the picture and at the same time to treat the fictitious painted space as an extension of the real space of our sense experience. This new structuring of space also demanded a more precise knowledge of the structure of the human body. The skeleton in Masaccio's mural, unlike those in earlier art, is anatomically correct, and in the figure of Christ we sense the same interest in the body as an organic entity. Compared to older, less consistent methods of creating pictorial space, such as that used by Jan van Eyck (see Plate 18), scientific perspective is something of a paradox: subjective and impersonal at the same time. Its system, based on a central vanishing point that corresponds to the eye of a single beholder, expresses the individualism of the new era. It was this individualism that made portraiture, neglected since the fall of the Roman Empire, once more a major concern of painters and sculptors (see the kneeling donors in Plate 19 as well as Plates 20 and 28–30). On the other hand, the effectiveness of scientific perspective depends on mathematical rules that leave little scope for personal interpretation. Perspective boasts of setting a standard of objective truth and thus allies the artist with the scientist. To Leonardo da Vinci, who was both, "seeing" was equivalent to "knowing." The ultimate result of this alliance was to be the invention of photography in the early nineteenth century, which to the painters of the time seemed at first a threat, then a liberation that permitted them to abandon the Renaissance goal of truth to nature.

"Truth to nature," however, could be interpreted in radically different ways even by Renaissance artists. Comparing the paintings by Bellini and Botticelli (Plates 22 and 23), we realize how little the two pictures have in common, although both were painted in the 1480s. Bellini's view of nature, despite its abundance of detail, is as firmly structured as the architecture in Masaccio's "Trinity," and man's place in it is defined with equal precision. What we see here is the familiar nature of everyday experience transfigured by the saint's ecstasy. Botticelli's picture, in contrast, looks as flat and patterned as a playing card. It bears out Leonardo's remark that Botticelli "paints very dull landscapes." What concerns Botticelli is man's relation not to nature but to an ideal of formal perfection embodied in the art of antiquity and reflecting man's desire, in Pico's words, "to be reborn into the higher forms, which are divine." His goal is nature perfected rather than nature observed; and since, according to Pico's God, such perfectibility is vouchsafed only to man, the rest of the natural world holds little interest for him. This unconcern with objective truth is still more evident in Parmigianino (see Plate 26) and in Bronzino (see Plate 28). The problem of reconciling ideal and real nature haunted artists and critics for centuries to come.

The conflict of ideal and reality in art, like the humanists's new view of man, originated in Italy. But whereas humanism found a ready response north of the Alps and profoundly influenced the religious Reformation, Italian Renaissance art did not become a model for the rest of Europe until the sixteenth century, and even then its authority was far from absolute. Jan van Eyck, Masaccio's contemporary, was an equally great innovator in his way, yet he perceived the visible world in terms of light and color rather than of its underlying structure (compare Plates 18 and 19). He founded a tradition so powerful that Altdorfer (see Plate 31), painting a century later, still owes more to Jan van Eyck than to any Italian source, despite the classical subject of the picture. Other Northerners, such as the remarkable Dutch painter Hieronymus Bosch (see Plate 21), mirror the conflict between the medieval and Renaissance concepts of man in their pessimistic visions of a sinful humanity remote from any hope of redemption. When, soon after 1500, Northern artists began to visit Italy in order to study classical antiquity and the "classic" masters of their own day, the new image of man they came to know tended to remain an alien element in their own work, like quotations in an unfamiliar language. Pieter Bruegel, the greatest Northern painter of the second half of the century, acknowledges the humanist vision in an oddly backhanded way; his "Land of Cockaigne" (Plate 32) is a sermon on the dignity of man, but in reverse, by showing the fate of those who fail to heed it. It was not until 1600 that the heritage of Italian Renaissance art was fully shared by the rest of Europe.

---

[1] Charles Trinkaus, *In Our Image and Likeness: Humanity and Divinity in Italian Humanist Thought* (1970), vol. 1, p. 247.
[2] *The Renaissance Philosophy of Man*, edited by Ernst Cassirer et al. (1948), p. 225.

Among the founding fathers of Renaissance art, it was Donatello who first formed the new image of man demanded by the new era. His *Annunciation* in Plate 17 shows more strikingly than any of his other works why the Renaissance proclaimed itself the rebirth of antiquity, for nowhere else does he approach the classic Greek ideal of human beauty as closely as he does here. The two figures are carved in high relief rather than in the round, but they move with such complete ease and freedom that they seem in no way constrained by their architectural setting; and their response to each other—the reverential greeting of the angel, the Virgin's gentle gesture of surprise—is equally well-balanced and natural. For the first time in a thousand years, body and spirit seem to be in complete harmony. The contrast with the Romanesque *Annunciation* in Plate 12, done three centuries earlier, could hardly be more striking.

How Donatello achieved this is little short of miraculous. Although he was an ardent admirer of ancient sculpture, he knew it only from late and inferior examples. Yet he perceived in them, with the clairvoyance of genius, the underlying ideal of classical perfection and recreated it in his own work. The framework, too, bespeaks the rebirth of antiquity: its forms derive from the ornamental vocabulary of ancient Greece and Rome, although Donatello's way of combining them is uniquely his own.

Plate 17. Donatello, THE ANNUNCIATION
ca. 1430—1435, limestone,
height of niche 7'2"
Santa Croce, Florence

The revolutionary change that took place in northern European painting about 1420 becomes strikingly evident if we compare Jan van Eyck's panel in Plate 18 with the *April* miniature in Plate 16. Suddenly the bright fairytale world of the International Gothic style has given way to an art that brings us face to face with visible reality in all its richness and depth, as if the picture surface had been turned into a window. The difference between the two is technical as well as artistic: the miniature is painted in tempera (pigments mixed with diluted egg yolk) and the panel is an early instance of the use of oils. Tempera is thin, opaque, and quick-drying; oil viscous and slow-drying. Unlike tempera, oil permits the smooth blending of tones on the picture surface, and its body may vary from translucent colored glazes to thick layers of creamy, saturated paint. Jan van Eyck knew how to exploit the greater flexibility of the new medium to full effect. Yet the panel contains a contradiction: the lovely Virgin is far too big for the architecture. Only if we recognize this mistake and its hidden purpose can we understand the subtlety of Jan van Eyck's art. Realism to him did not limit the symbolic meaning of his pictures, but rather it actually enhanced it. In this panel, the church building stands for the Church and so does the

Plate 18. Jan van Eyck
THE VIRGIN AND CHILD IN THE CHURCH
ca. 1425—1430, oil on wood, height 12"
Staatliche Museen Preussischer
Kulturbesitz, Gemäldegalerie, Berlin (West)

Virgin; therefore, the interior is just tall enough to hold her. For final proof we need only look at the altar in the background, attended not by priests but by angels.

In Masaccio's mural in Plate 19, the surface is also treated as a window. Here, however, everything is lifesize, and the painted space seems a direct continuation of the actual space surrounding the beholder. This has been achieved by means of scientific perspective, one of the great discoveries of the Italian Early Renaissance, which is a system of projecting three-dimensional shapes onto a flat surface, analogous to the way the camera lens projects them onto a piece of film. Masaccio's entire composition embodies his faith in rational order and clarity. The figures are as massive as Giotto's and as fully articulated and self-sufficient as Donatello's; the architecture resembles the classically inspired framework of Donatello's *Annunciation* rather than the Gothic interior of Jan van Eyck's panel. Like the latter, Masaccio's mural was done for a private patron; he and his wife are kneeling in prayer just outside the sacred precinct. The step on which they kneel coincides with the beholder's eye level. It is also the dividing line between time and eternity: above it, salvation; below it, a skeleton to remind us of the brevity of man's life on earth.

Plate 19. Masaccio
THE HOLY TRINITY WITH
THE VIRGIN AND ST. JOHN
ca. 1425, wall painting,
height 21'10"
Santa Maria Novella, Florence

The exploration of visible reality in fifteenth-century painting has its counterpart in the daring sea voyages beyond the limits of the known world that culminated in the discovery of America. The Portuguese led the way in these ventures. It was they who explored the west coast of Africa and opened the sea route to India; they who first circumnavigated the globe. What was the impulse behind their journeys? A quest for riches and power, surely, but also a quest for knowledge, and, equally important, a sense of religious duty, as attested by Nuño Gonçalves' panel in Plate 20. Here St. Vincent displays to the reverently kneeling king a Gospel text concerning the Apostles' mission among the infidels, and in so doing appoints him their spiritual heir. The older man with hands folded in prayer is the king's uncle, Prince Henry the Navigator, the earliest royal sponsor of voyages of discovery. Gonçalves must have learned his art in close contact with the great Flemish realists, such as Jan van Eyck. Although a less subtle painter than Van Eyck, he was a portraitist of exceptional power who has left us an unforgettable record of the rulers of Portugal.

Plate 20. Nuño Gonçalves
SAINT VINCENT COMMANDING KING
AFFONSO V OF PORTUGAL TO SPREAD
THE CHRISTIAN FAITH IN AFRICA
1471—1481, oil on panel,
height 6'9½"
National Museum of Ancient Art, Lisbon

The Dutchman Hieronymus Bosch was a pioneer of another sort, venturing farther into the unexplored regions of man's imagination than any artist before him. His vision of Hell in Plate 21 is a nightmare world of burning cities and icy rivers where sinners are punished by being surfeited with the vices they had enjoyed on earth. Thus, in the center of our panel, a huge stomach houses a devilish inn; below it, musical instruments are engines of torture (secular music was "the food of love" and hence a sinful pleasure); and in the lower right-hand corner, a sow embraces a man who is vainly trying to escape. The interpretation of Bosch's pictures has proved extremely difficult, but enough is known about them to assure us that he intended every detail to have a precise didactic meaning, however strange his imagery may seem today. He was haunted—indeed mesmerized—by the power of evil to corrupt mankind; its counterweight, the promise of redemption, is barely hinted at in his work. This state of mind reflects the conflict between the other-worldly goals of traditional Christianity and an ever greater openness to the attractions of life on earth, a crisis of conscience that was to erupt soon in the Reformation.

Plate 21. Hieronymus Bosch
HELL WING *(from the triptych,*
THE GARDEN OF EARTHLY DELIGHTS)
ca. 1500, oil on wood panel, height 7'2½"
Prado Museum, Madrid

Plate 22. Giovanni Bellini
SAINT FRANCIS IN ECSTASY
ca. 1485, oil on wood panel, height 48½″
The Frick Collection, New York

The work of the great Flemish realists was known and admired in fifteenth-century Italy. Although it had little immediate effect in Florence, birthplace of the Early Renaissance, it left a lasting imprint on Venice. Before long, the use of oils and an emphasis on light and color became hallmarks of Venetian Renaissance painting. Venetian masters, such as Giovanni Bellini, also raised landscape to a new level of importance. In Plate 22, St. Francis is so small compared to the setting that he seems almost incidental, yet his mystic rapture before the beauty of nature sets our own response to the glorious view that is spread out before us. He has left his wooden clogs behind and stands barefoot, thus indicating that the ground is hallowed by the presence of the Lord. The soft, glowing colors, the warm late-afternoon sunlight, the tender regard for every detail, recall the art of Jan van Eyck. Unlike the Northerners, however, Giovanni Bellini knows how to define the beholder's relationship to the space within the picture; the rock formations of the foreground are clear and firm, like architecture rendered by the rules of scientific perspective.

In Florence, meanwhile, the revival of antiquity kindled a new interest in the pagan deities, who now began to appear once more in their original form. The Venus in Botticelli's famous painting in Plate 23 is modeled on a classical statue of the goddess. Could such a subject be justified in a Christian civilization? How did artist and patron escape the charge of being neo-pagans? Part of the answer to these questions is provided by the Neo-Platonic philosophers of the time. They believed that the life of the universe, including that of man, was linked to God by a spiritual circuit continuously ascending and descending so that all revelation, whether from the Bible, Plato, or classical myths, was one. Thus they could invoke the celestial Venus interchangeably with the Virgin Mary as a source of divine love. Once we understand this quasi-religious meaning of Botticelli's picture, we may find it less strange that the figures look so ethereal. They are embodiments of poetic and philosophical ideas rather than creatures of flesh and blood—exquisitely beautiful but accessible only to a select and highly educated circle of initiates.

Plate 23. Sandro Botticelli
THE BIRTH OF VENUS
ca. 1480, oil on canvas, height 69"
Uffizi Gallery, Florence

Plate 24.
Michelangelo, THE CREATION OF ADAM *(detail of the Sistine Ceiling), 1508—1512, wall painting*
Sistine Chapel, Vatican

The early sixteenth century—the High Renaissance—has been called the age of genius, for it was the time that formed the concept of artistic genius. Until then, even the greatest of artists were mere makers; now they were creators, set apart from ordinary men by divine inspiration. No less exalted term would fit men such as Leonardo da Vinci, who was both artist and scientist yet full of mystery like a magician, or Michelangelo, who was driven by a truly superhuman ambition. Their works immediately became classics, equal in authority to the most renowned

works of the ancients, and their spell persists even today. This is certainly true of Michelangelo's masterpiece, the Sistine Ceiling, which had so vast an impact that it changed the course of Western art for several centuries to come. In this huge expanse of vaulted surface with its hundreds of figures, Michelangelo proclaimed a new ideal image of man: heroic, nude, and beautiful as the gods of Greece but, unlike them, troubled by inner conflicts and unfulfilled yearnings. Thus Adam, in Plate 24, reaches out for contact with the Divine (characteristically, Michelangelo does not

Plate 25.
Titian, BACCHANAL, ca. 1518, oil on canvas, height 69"
Prado Museum, Madrid

show the physical making of Adam's body); at the same time, however, his glance meets that of Eve, who nestles yet unborn in the shelter of the Lord's left arm. No other artist ever achieved so dramatic a juxtaposition of Man and God.

Some of the figures in Titian's *Bacchanal* in Plate 25 have the muscular build, the animation, the complex poses of Michelangelo's (the influence of the Sistine Ceiling had reached Venice within a few years after its completion), but they form part of a very different world: a richly sensuous, untroubled pagan paradise, inspired by

classical poetry. Titian clearly owes a good deal to Giovanni Bellini as well (compare Plate 22), although his brushwork is broader and more fluid, his colors deeper, and the play of sunlight and shadow more dramatic. These figures, unlike those in Botticelli's *Birth of Venus,* are full-blooded human beings who bring antiquity back to life with all the vigor and immediacy we could demand. If Titian lacks the heroic vision of Michelangelo, his works have a vitality whose direct appeal has hardly been dimmed by the passage of time.

In its twin centers, Florence and Rome, the High Renaissance lasted barely two decades, ending with the death of Leonardo in 1519 and that of Raphael in 1520. Michelangelo, it is true, lived until 1564, but his later work no longer had the radiant energy and assurance of the Sistine Ceiling. The next generation of artists reacted to the classic style of their great predecessors in strange and unexpected ways. Some, such as Parmigianino, pursued an ideal of unearthly grace; the long-limbed, languid figures in the *Madonna with the Long Neck* in Plate 26 have a formal perfection that defies any comparison with actual human beings. Characteristically, the meaning of the picture is so intricate that it went unrecognized until very recently. The crystal vessel displayed by the angel on the far left symbolizes the Virgin's purity; its surface, however, reflects a cross (now barely visible), and the Infant Christ, who has seen it, is frightened by this prophecy of his future suffering, while Mary, not yet aware of it, smiles at him tenderly.

The forms in Rosso's *Descent from the Cross* in Plate 27 are as

jagged and angular as Parmigianino's are smooth and sinuous. The
entire composition seems filled with
unbearable anguish whether we look
at the latticework of figures engaged
in lowering the body of Christ to
the ground or at the frozen grief of
those at the foot of the cross. The
colors, too, appear to be deliberately
off-key, designed to reinforce the
harsh expressiveness of the artist's
style. How are we to understand this
deliberate rejection of balance and
rationality? By High Renaissance
standards, the frantic Rosso and the
elegant Parmigianino are equally
anticlassical. The new trend they
represent, known as Mannerism, has
been explained as a symptom of the
spiritual crisis brought about by the
Reformation. It can be viewed
equally, however, as a response to
the perfection of High Renaissance
art, which had assumed an authority
greater even than nature and thus
had established style as an ultimate
value, an end in itself. Be that as it
may, Mannerism was to dominate
much of Italian as well as Northern
art from the 1520s to the end of the
century.

Plate 27. Rosso Fiorentino
THE DESCENT FROM THE CROSS
1521, oil on wood panel, height 11′
Pinacoteca Comunale, Volterra

Plate 28.
Agnolo Bronzino
ELEANORA OF TOLEDO AND HER SON GIOVANNI DE' MEDICI
ca. 1550, oil on canvas, height 38"
Uffizi Gallery, Florence

The elegant phase of Mannerism appealed particularly to aristocratic patrons and produced splendid portraits like that of Eleanora, the wife of Cosimo I de'Medici, by Cosimo's court painter Bronzino. The sitter in Plate 28 appears as the member of an exalted social caste rather than as an individual personality. Congealed into immobility behind the barrier of her lavishly ornate costume, Eleanora seems more akin to Parmigianino's Madonna (compare Plate 26) than to ordinary flesh and blood. Her masklike features betray no hint of inner life; she permits us to admire her, but under no circumstances would she deign to acknowledge our presence.

The ideal type underlying portraits of this kind reflects a development that was to reach its climax a hundred years later: the absolute monarchy, with all strands of state power gathered in the hands of the sovereign. El Greco's portrait in Plate 29 is based on an altogether different scale of values. The last and greatest of Mannerists, El Greco was born on the Greek island of

Crete. As a youth, he acquired the rich heritage of Venetian painting (he worked under Titian for a while), went to Rome, and finally settled in the Spanish town of Toledo. Spain had long been the home of the Counter-Reformation, and El Greco's mature work was decisively shaped by the spiritual climate of that movement. Unlike Bronzino, whose portrait of Eleanora conveys a sense of awed distance between artist and sitter, El Greco was on intimate terms with Paravicino, a scholar and poet who has left us several sonnets in praise of El Greco's genius. The contrast between the two pictures could hardly be more striking: Bronzino's forms are rigidly immobile, while El Greco's every brush stroke communicates a quivering movement; Eleanora's coldness is matched by Paravicino's emotional ardor. His frail, expressive hands and the pallid face, with its sensitive mouth and burning eyes, project an ideal image of the saints of the Counter-Reformation—mystics and intellectuals at the same time.

Plate 29.
El Greco
FRAY FELIX HORTENSIO PARAVICINO
ca. 1605, oil on canvas, height 44½"
Museum of Fine Arts, Boston

Plate 30. Hans Holbein the Younger, HENRY VIII
1540, oil on wood panel, height 32½"
National Gallery of Ancient Art, Rome

When the young German painter Albrecht Dürer visited Venice in 1495, two experiences made an indelible impresson on him: the high esteem accorded to Italian artists, and the clarity and rationality of Italian art. In his own work, Dürer spread the gospel of the Italian Renaissance with an almost religious zeal. However, the flowering of the Northern Renaissance which he had helped to bring about was as brief as the High Renaissance in Italy. By the mid-1520s, Germany and her neighbors were in the grip of the Reformation crisis; and since Protestantism opposed religious imagery, artists found themselves deprived of their principal task. The career of Holbein, Germany's greatest artist after Dürer, is characteristic of the times. When the city of Basel went Protestant he was saved by his gift for portraiture: he emigrated to England and became court painter to Henry VIII. His picture of the king in Plate 30 has the immobile pose, the air of unapproachability, and the emphasis on costume and jewelry familiar to us from Bronzino's court portraits (compare Plate 28). Its rigid frontality and physical bulk create an overpowering sensation of the king's ruthless, commanding presence. Here, we realize, stands not only the temporal sovereign, but also the creator and head of the Church of England.

Other northern artists tried their hand at subjects from classical antiquity, although more often than not they drew them from literary rather than from visual sources. Nothing could be less classical than Altdorfer's picture in Plate 31 of the battle in which Alexander defeated Darius, with its ant-like mass of sixteenth-century soldiers spread over an Alpine valley. In fact, the only classical element is the inscribed tablet in the sky, which enables us to identify the subject. The painting might well show some contemporary battle except for the spectacular sky, where we see the sun triumphantly breaking through the clouds and defeating the moon. This celestial drama, obviously correlated with the human contest below, raises the scene to the cosmic level.

Plate 31. Albrecht Altdorfer, THE BATTLE OF ISSUS
1529, oil on wood panel, height 62"
Alte Pinakothek, Munich

Plate 32.
Pieter Bruegel the Elder, THE LAND OF COCKAIGNE
1567, oil on wood panel, height 20½"
Alte Pinakothek, Munich

Although the Netherlands suffered more than any other country in the struggle between Protestants and Catholics, it was Dutch painters who led the field in developing new secular themes to replace the traditional religious subjects. The greatest of them, Pieter Bruegel, explored landscape, peasant life, and moral allegory. *The Land of Cockaigne* in Plate 32 is a fool's paradise, based on a folk tale, where tables are always laden with tasty dishes, houses have roofs made of pies, and pigs and chickens run about roasted to a turn. To reach it, one must eat his way through a mountain of gruel (see the upper right-hand corner). The lesson Bruegel teaches here is a philosophical comment on human nature; the men under the tree are not sinners in the grip of evil like those in Bosch's Hell (compare Plate 21), they are simply not wise enough to know what is best for them. By becoming slaves to their stomachs, they relinquish all ambition for the sake of a kind of animal happiness—the knight has dropped his lance, the farmer his flail, the scholar his books. "Beware of the fool's paradise," the artist seems to say; "it is more dangerous than hell because people *like* going there." And the impressive composition, in the shape of a great wheel turned on its side, shows that he must have thought the subject serious and important.

it was increasingly considered to be the only body that could give a ruler's actions a wider sanction than he could draw from his prerogatives alone. Although for a long time to come it would remain firmly subordinated to the crown, England's kings already realized that they could not take such measures as raising extraordinary taxes without Parliament's consent.

Another of the monarch's assets was England's common law, the uniform country-wide system of justice based on precedent and tradition. Like Parliament, the common law would eventually be regarded by opponents of royal power as an independent source of authority with which the crown could not interfere. But under the conditions facing the "new monarch" in the 1480s, it proved an effective tool in his work of restoring the authority of the throne after two centuries of weakness.

Henry VII

Henry VII (1485–1509), who founded the Tudor dynasty, came to the throne as a usurper in the aftermath of more than thirty years of civil conflict, the Wars of the Roses. England's nobles had been fighting one another for decades, and the situation hardly looked promising for a reassertion of royal power. Yet Henry both extended the authority of the crown and restored order with extraordinary speed.

His first concern as he set about establishing a stable rule was finances. The crown's income was about £52,000 a year, but Henry's immediate expenses were considerably higher.[4] He knew that unless he could balance his budget, his position would remain insecure. Yet extra taxes were the surest way to alienating subjects who expected a king to "live of his own," that is, from the income his lands provided, customs payments, and the traditional contributions made to him at special times such as the marriage of his daughter. It is a testimony to the care with which he nurtured his revenues that by the end of his reign he had paid off all his debts and accumulated between one and two million pounds as a reserve.

Part of his success was due to his beginning his reign with more property than any of his predecessors, a consequence of forfeitures and inheritances during the civil wars. But Henry also sharply increased the profits of justice—fees and fines—which had the added advantage of cowing unruly subjects. Moreover he radically improved his financial administration by taking the tasks of collection and supervision out of the cumbersome office of the Exchequer and placing them in his own more efficient household. By careful management of this kind, he was able to "live of his own."

Where domestic order was concerned, the main impetus behind the revival of royal authority was clearly the energy of the king and his chief servants. Henry increased the powers of the justices of the peace, thus striking severely at the independence attained by leading nobles during the previous two centuries. Under his leadership, too, the council became a far more active and influential body. The ministers not only exercised executive powers but also resumed hearing legal appeals, primarily because the government was determined to exert all its force to quell disorder. Plaintiffs could be sure that at such a hearing, where there was no jury and where deliberations would not be influenced by the power of a local lord, decisions would be quick and fair, and the popularity and business of the councillors' court grew rapidly.[5]

The dual objective of government stability and fiscal responsibility guided Henry's foreign policy. He never became involved in costly adventures, and he allowed no challenge to the Tudor dynasty's claim to the crown. In 1492 for example, after Henry half-heartedly invaded

---

[4] To give a sense of scale, a man who made £100 a year was considered very rich.

[5] The room where the royal council met had stars painted on its ceiling; the council sitting as a court eventually came to be known by the name of the room, the Star Chamber.

France as a protest against the French annexation of Brittany, Charles VIII signed a treaty promising to pay him £160,000 and guaranteeing not to support any claimants to the English throne. A succession of agreements with other rulers from Denmark to Florence bolstered the position of England's merchants, whose international trade was essential to the crown's customs revenues. Henry encouraged the manufacture and export of the country's great staple product, cloth, and protected shipping with a navigation act. Turning to more distant possibilities, he granted an Italian sailor, John Cabot, a patent to search for a westward route to China. The result of this undertaking was the discovery of enormous fishing banks off Newfoundland whose exploitation was to be the basis of the growing prosperity of many English ports in the sixteenth century.

Henry VIII and His Successors

The first Tudor was a conservative, building up his authority and finances through traditional methods and institutions that had long been at the disposal of England's kings but that the founder of the new dynasty applied with exceptional determination and vigor. The young man who followed him on the throne, Henry VIII (1509–1547), was an expansive, dazzling figure, a strong contrast to his cold and careful father (see Plate 30). Early in his reign he removed a longstanding threat from England's north by inflicting a shattering defeat on an invading Scots army at Flodden in 1513, and the following year he brought a sporadic war with France to a favorable conclusion. With his prestige thus enhanced, he spent the next fifteen years taking only a minor part in European affairs while he consolidated royal power at home with the capable assistance of his chief minister, Cardinal Thomas Wolsey.

Wolsey was not an innovator but a tireless and effective administrator who continued the consolidation of royal power begun under Henry VII. To meet the rising demand for royal justice, he expanded the jurisdiction and activities of the Star Chamber and guided another offshoot of the king's council to independent status: the Court of Requests, or Court of Poor Men's Causes.

Wolsey fell from power in 1529, ruined by the king's wish to obtain a divorce from his wife, who had failed to produce a surviving male heir. Henry had married his brother's widow, Catherine of Aragon, under a special papal dispensation from the biblical law that normally prohibited a union between such close relatives. Obsessed with continuing his dynasty, for which a male heir seemed essential—and infatuated with a young lady at court, Anne Boleyn—Henry had urged Wolsey to ask the pope to declare the previous dispensation invalid. Under ordinary circumstances there would have been no trouble, but at this moment the pope was in the power of Charles V, king of Spain and emperor of the Holy Roman Empire, who not only had a high sense of rectitude but also was Catherine's nephew. When all Wolsey's efforts ended in failure, Henry dismissed him.

For three years thereafter the king tried in vain to get his divorce. He called Parliament and gave it free rein to express bitter anticlerical sentiments; he sought opinions in European universities in favor of the divorce; he attacked his own clergy for having bowed to Wolsey's authority; he even extracted a vague recognition from the clergy of his position as "supreme lord" of the Church. Finally he placed his confidence in Thomas Cromwell, a former servant of Wolsey, who suggested a radical but simple solution: that Henry break with the pope, declare himself supreme head of the Church, and divorce Catherine on his own authority. The king agreed, thus unleashing a revolution that dramatically increased the powers of the royal government.

The instrument chosen to accomplish the

break with Rome was Parliament, the only body capable of giving the move legal sanction and an aura of national approval. Henry called the assembly in 1529 and did not dissolve it until 1536. During its sessions it acted on more matters of greater importance than a Parliament had ever considered before. It forbade litigants from making ecclesiastical appeals to Rome, thus allowing Henry to obtain his divorce and remarry, and finally declared him supreme head of the Church in England in 1534. Royal power gained enormously from these acts, but so too did the stature of Parliament, thanks to its unprecedented responsibilities and length of meeting.

Previously, election to Parliament had been considered a chore by the townsmen and landed gentry in the House of Commons, who found the expense of unpaid attendance and its encroachments on their time more irksome than did the nobles in the House of Lords (so named during Henry VIII's reign). But this attitude began to change in the 1530s as members of the Commons, returning to successive sessions, came to know one another and in time developed a remarkable esprit de corps as jealous guardians of Parliament's traditions and privileges.

Following his successful suggestion for solving Henry's conflict with Rome, Thomas Cromwell rose rapidly in his monarch's service. He was a tireless bureaucrat; he reorganized the administration of the country into six carefully distinguished departments with specific functions and gave himself the chief executive position, the secretaryship. A Privy Council, consisting of the king's principal advisers, was also established to coordinate and direct the administration.

Unquestionably the principal beneficiary of the events of the 1530s was the crown. Royal income rose markedly when Henry became head of the English Church and took over the ecclesiastical fees that previously had gone to the pope. He gained an even larger windfall when he dissolved all English monasteries and confiscated their immensely valuable lands, which were sold over the next few decades. Fortunes were made by speculators, and new families rose to prominence as major landowners.

For all the stimulus he gave to parliamentary power, Henry now had a much larger, wealthier, and more sophisticated administration at his disposal, and he left no doubt where ultimate authority lay. He did not establish a standing army, as some of the Continental kings did, but he had no need for one. He was fully capable of awing ambitious nobles or crushing an uprising.

Royal power was put to the test very soon. Where doctrine and the structure of the Church were concerned, Henry was a conservative; he allowed few changes in dogma or liturgy. As the Lutheran reform movement on the Continent created a serious split in Christendom, Henry tried to restrain the spread of Reformation ideas and persecuted heresy, but he could not avoid compromises. Perhaps realizing the shape of things to come, he had his son, Edward, tutored by a committed reformer. Moreover in the 1540s a leading Continental reformer, Martin Bucer, spent a few years in Cambridge, deeply influencing a number of future leaders of the English Church.

During the reign of Edward VI (1547–1553), who died while still a minor, the nobility attempted to resume some of their old powers in government, and the Reformation advanced rapidly in England. But Edward's half-sister Mary I tried to reestablish Roman Catholicism when she became queen in 1553, forcing many Englishmen into exile and others into two major revolts during her five-year reign. Royal power, however, was strong enough to survive these strains. The revival of the nobles was short-lived, and Mary's death, in 1558, brought an end to the reversal of religions. She was succeeded by Henry VIII's last surviving child,

Elizabeth, a woman of determination who demonstrated that the growth of the monarchy's authority had been but briefly interrupted under Edward and Mary.

VALOIS FRANCE

The rulers of France in the fifteenth century, unlike their English counterparts, lacked a well-formed organization for local government. Aristocrats dominated many sections, particularly those farthest from Paris, and great nobles had become virtually independent rulers. They had their own administrations and often their own courts and taxation, leaving the crown little say in their affairs. The size of the kingdom also placed restraints on royal power; it took more than a week to travel from Paris to the remoter parts of the domain—almost double the time for the equivalent English journey. Delays of this size inevitably hampered central authority.

The monarchy had tried to resolve the problem of ruling distant provinces by granting close relatives appanages, large blocs of territory that came into royal hands. Theoretically the kinsman would devote full attention to these lands and execute the monarch's wishes more effectively than he himself could from Paris. In practice, however, an ambitious family member often became just as difficult to handle as any powerful noble. After 1469 the crown kept control over such acquisitions—an indication that it was becoming capable of exercising authority even in areas far from the capital.

The administrative center of the government in Paris was the royal council and its chief departments: the Chancery, which had charge of all formal documents, and the Treasury. The greatest court of law in the land was the Parlement of Paris, whose members were appointed by the crown and which had remained a judicial body, unlike the English Parliament. As the central administration grew in the fifteenth

and early sixteenth centuries, various provinces received their own parlements from the crown, a recognition of the continuing strength of local autonomies. The countervailing force was the dominant system of Roman law, which enabled the monarch to govern by issuing ordinances and edicts. They had to be registered by the parlements in order to take effect, but usually this was a formality.

Representative assemblies, the estates, also reduced the power of the throne. A number of provinces had local estates, and matters such as the raising of taxes had to be arranged through them. But the national representative body, the Estates General, to which clergy, nobles, and townsmen sent delegates, never attained the prestige of the English Parliament and was never able to bind the country together or function as an essential organ of government.

Moreover French kings had a degree of independence that English monarchs never achieved in a critically important area: finances. For centuries they had supplemented their ordinary sources of income, from lands and customs duties, with extraordinary levies in the form of a sales tax (*aide*), a hearth tax (*taille*), and a salt tax (*gabelle*). Consequently the average Frenchman who was subject to taxation (all nobles and many towns were exempt) usually bore a heavier burden than his English counterpart. In earlier days the consent of the localities had been required before such demands could be made, but after 1451 the taxes could be raised on the king's authority alone, although he still had to negotiate the exact rate with provincial estates and be careful not to go beyond what would seem reasonable to his subjects.

But the most decisive contrast with England lay in France's standing army. The upkeep of the troops accounted for more than half the royal expenditures in Louis XI's reign, mainly because their numbers grew with increases in revenues. In the 1480s a force probably larger than 15,000 men, chiefly professional mercenaries and military-minded nobles, was held in permanent readiness every campaigning season from spring to fall. With the invention of the arquebus, a primitive handgun, and the need for large concentrations of pikemen to protect the gunners, the size of armies had to be increased; moreover, the development of cannon demanded the expensive skills and logistics of heavy artillery. These innovations added to the advantages of the central government because it alone could afford the cost of the new technology. At the same time, much larger resources were needed to support the army in the field. Troops were billeted in various provinces, and often the local estates had to contribute to their maintenance. As a result all Frenchmen eventually had the indirect burden of heavier taxation, and many regions of France had direct contact with royal soldiers. Although frequently short of pay, the troops were firmly under royal control and hence a vital device—rarely used but always a threat—in the strengthening of royal authority.

Louis XI and Charles VIII

When Louis XI (1461–1483) began his reign, he faced a situation as unpromising as that of Henry VII at his succession, for the country had just emerged from the Hundred Years' War, and royal powers were much reduced. English troops, present in France for most of the war years, had finally departed in the 1450s; but a new and equally dangerous menace had arisen in the east: the conglomeration of territories assembled by the dukes of Burgundy.

By the 1460s the dukes, though vassals of the French crown in their southern holdings, were among the most powerful lords in Western Europe. They ruled a loosely organized dominion that stretched from the seventeen separate provinces of the Low Countries to the Swiss Confederation, and their Burgundian capital, Dijon, had become a major cultural and political center. In 1474 Louis XI put together

a coalition against Duke Charles the Bold, who had been at war with him for some seven years, and in 1477 Charles was killed in battle with the French king's Swiss allies. Louis then reannexed the duchy of Burgundy itself; but Mary, the duke's daughter, retained the Low Countries, which would later form part of the imperial inheritance of her grandson, the Holy Roman Emperor Charles V.

The Burgundian lands added considerably to Louis's sphere of authority. His masterful maneuvering in the tortuous diplomacy of his day soon won him other territories; he was appropriately nicknamed "the Spider," because the prizes he caught in his web were more often the result of waiting or shrewd negotiation than of victories on the battlefield. Such was the case at the beginning of his reign when, by a typical combination of force and fraud, he pried two provinces on his southern border away from Spain. Simple luck enlarged his realm as well: in 1481 he inherited the enormous Angevin lands—the provinces of Anjou, Maine, and Provence. The result was that by the end of his reign, though government procedures had not noticeably changed, royal power had penetrated into massive areas where previously it had been unknown; only one major region, Brittany, remained completely beyond the crown's influence (see Map 13.3).

Louis XI's son and successor, Charles VIII (1483–1498), was equally dedicated to increasing the territories under the Valois dynasty's command. For a start he married the heiress of the duke of Brittany, thereby securing the last independent region of France, though it was not officially incorporated into the royal domain for another half-century.

In 1494, seeking further gains, Charles invaded Italy at the request of the duke of Milan, who was afraid of being attacked by Florence and Naples. After some initial successes the French settled into a prolonged struggle with the Hapsburgs for control of the rich Italian

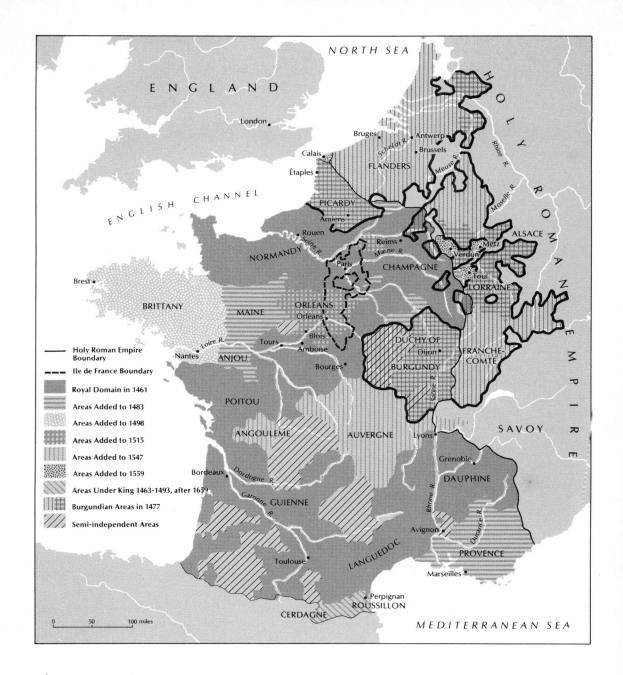

MAP 13.3: FRANCE IN THE 15TH AND 16TH CENTURIES

This map shows in detail the successive stages whereby the monarchy extended its control throughout France.

peninsula. The conflicts lasted for sixty-five years, ending in defeat for the French. Although the Italian wars failed to satisfy the territorial ambitions of Charles and his successors, they provided an outlet for the restless French nobility and gave the monarchy an opportunity to consolidate royal power at home.

The Growth of Government Power

After Charles VIII's reign France's financial and administrative machinery grew in both size and effectiveness, largely because of the demands of the Italian wars. There was rarely enough money to support the adventure; the kings therefore relied heavily on loans from Italian bankers, who sometimes helped shape France's financial policies. At the same time the crown made a determined and notably successful effort to increase traditional royal revenues.

But expenses were also rising. France was a rich country of 15 million people with the most fertile land in Europe; yet the financial needs of the monarch always outstripped his subjects' ability to pay. Nobles, many towns, royal officeholders, and the clergy were exempt from the *taille* and the *gabelle*. Thus the bulk of the taxes had to be raised from the very classes that had the least to give. Other means were therefore needed to supplement the royal income.

One solution was found in the sale of offices. The kings sold positions in the administration, the parlements, and every branch of the bureaucracy to purchasers eager to obtain both the tax exemption and the considerable status (sometimes a title of nobility) that the offices brought them. From modest and uncertain beginnings under Louis XII (1498–1515), the system widened steadily; by the end of the sixteenth century, it would provide the crown with one-twelfth of its revenues.

Many other rulers were adopting this device, and everywhere it had similar effects: it stimulated social mobility, creating dynasties of noble officeholders and a new administrative class; it caused a dramatic expansion of bureaucracies; and it encouraged corruption. The system spread most rapidly and the effects were most noticeable in France, where the reign of Francis I (1515–1547) witnessed a major increase in the government's power as its servants multiplied. Francis tried hard to continue the widening of royal control by expeditions into Italy, but in fact he contributed more to the development of the crown's authority by his actions at home.

One of the earliest and perhaps most remarkable of Francis's accomplishments was the power he gained over his formidable rival, the Church. Early in his reign he was highly successful in his Italian campaigns, and he used his position to persuade the pope in 1516 to give France's king the right to appoint all her bishops and abbots. According to this concordat, the first year's income after a new bishop took office still went to the Vatican, but in effect Francis now controlled the French Church. Its enormous patronage was at his disposal, and he could use it at will to reward servants or raise money. Since his wishes had not been blocked by the pope, he did not need to break with Rome in order to obtain the authority over the clergy that Henry VIII was soon to achieve in England.

In the 1520s he also began a major reorganization of the government. Francis formally legalized the sale of offices, and gradually the purchasers replaced local nobles as the administrators of the various sections of France. He also formed an inner council, more manageable than the unwieldy royal council, to act as the chief executive body of the realm. As part of this streamlining, in 1523 all tax-gathering and accounting responsibilities were centralized in one agency. Against the parlements, meanwhile, the king invoked the *lit de justice*, a prerogative which allowed him to appear before an assembly that was delaying the registration of any of his edicts or ordinances and declare them registered and therefore law. The Estates General was no problem because none met between 1484 and 1560.

With the monarchy's authority extended throughout his country, Francis's interests began to move outside of Europe. Jacques Cartier's voyages to North America in the 1530s and a French challenge to the Portuguese monopoly of West African trade were the first stirrings of a maritime effort that was cut short only by civil wars in the late sixteenth century.

By the end of Francis's reign, royal power was thus stronger than ever before; but signs of disunity had begun to appear that would intensify in the years to come. The Reformation was under way in the Holy Roman Empire, and it soon produced religious divisions and social unrest in France. As the reign of Francis's son Henry II (1547–1559) came to a close, the Italian wars ended in a French defeat, badly damaging the prestige of the monarchy. The civil wars that followed came perilously close to destroying all that the monarchy had accomplished during the previous hundred years.

UNITED SPAIN

The Iberian Peninsula in the mid-fifteenth century was divided into three very different kingdoms. Portugal, with some 1.5 million inhabitants, was in the midst of an expansion around the coast of Africa that was soon to bring her great wealth from the East. Castile, in the center, with a population of more than 8 million, was the largest and richest of the kingdoms. Sheep farming was the basis of her prosperity, and her countryside was dominated by powerful nobles. Castile was the last kingdom still fighting the Moors, and in the ceaseless crusade against the infidels the nobles played a leading part. They had built up both a great chivalric tradition and considerable political strength as a result of their exploits, and their status was enhanced by the religious fervor that the long struggle had inspired. The third kingdom, Aragon, approximately the same size as Portugal, consisted of three areas: Catalonia, the heart of the kingdom and a great commercial region centered on the city of Barcelona; Aragon itself, which was little more than a barren hinterland to Catalonia; and Valencia, a farming and fishing region south of Catalonia along the Mediterranean coast.

In October 1469, Isabella, future queen of Castile, married Ferdinand, future king of Sicily and heir to the throne of Aragon. Realizing that the marriage would strengthen the crown, the Castilian nobles opposed the union, precipitating a ten-year civil war. But the joined monarchy emerged victorious, more powerful, and in control of a new political entity: the Kingdom of Spain.

Ferdinand and Isabella

When Ferdinand and Isabella jointly assumed the thrones of Castile in 1474 and Aragon five years later, they made no attempt to create a monolithic state. Aragon remained a federation of territories, administered by viceroys, who were appointed by the king but who allowed local customs to remain virtually intact. The traditions of governing by consent and preserving the subject's rights were particularly strong in this kingdom, where each province had its own representative assembly, known as the Cortes. Ferdinand left the system untouched, but he did make the viceroys a permanent feature of the government and created a special council for Aragonese affairs, through which he controlled the kingdom. In Castile, however, the two monarchs were determined to assert their superiority over all possible rivals to their authority. Their immediate aims were to restore the order in the countryside that had been destroyed by civil war, much as it had been in England and France, and to reduce the power of the nobility.

The first objective was accomplished with the help of the Cortes of Castile, an assembly dominated by urban representatives who shared the wish for order because peace benefited trade. The Cortes established special tribunals to pursue and try criminals, and by the 1490s it had succeeded in ending the widespread lawlessness in the kingdom.

To reinforce their authority, Ferdinand and Isabella sharply reduced the number of great nobles in the royal council and overhauled the entire administration, particularly the financial agencies, applying the principle that ability rather than social status should determine appointments. As the bureaucracy spread, the hidalgo, a lesser aristocrat, who was heavily dependent on royal favor, became increasingly important in government. Unlike the great nobles, whose enormous wealth was little affected by the reforms that reduced their role, the hidalgos were hurt because they lost their tax exemptions. The new livelihood they found was in the service of the crown, and they became essential figures in the centralization of power in Castile as well as the overseas territories.

The monarchs achieved final control over the nobles in the 1480s and 1490s, when they took over the rich and powerful military orders into which the aristocracy was organized. The great nobles could not be crushed completely; nor did the king and queen wish to destroy them. But like the kings of England and France, Ferdinand and Isabella wanted to reduce their autonomy to a level that did not seem to threaten central authority—a process that was accomplished by 1500.

The rulers also succeeded in weakening the Spanish bishops and abbots, who were as strong and wealthy as leading nobles. After Ferdinand and Isabella destroyed the power of the Moors in Castile, the pope granted the monarchy the right to make all major ecclesiastical appointments in the newly won territory, and this right was extended to the New World shortly thereafter. In the following reign the monarchy would gain complete control over Church appointments, making Spain more independent of Rome than any other Catholic state.

Mastery over the towns and the Cortes of Castile did not pose much of a problem. Where local rule was concerned, an old official, the *corregidor*, was given new powers and a position of responsibility within the administrative hierarchy. Usually a hidalgo, he became the chief executive and judicial officer in his region, rather like the justice of the peace in England, and he also supervised town affairs. The Cortes did not seriously restrict the crown because Spanish taxes, like French, could be raised without consent. The Castilian assembly met frequently and even provided additional funds for foreign wars, but it never challenged royal supremacy during this reign.

The king and queen supervised the system of justice directly, hearing cases personally once a week. All law was considered to come from the throne, and they had full power to overrule the decisions of local courts, often run by nobles. Centralized judicial machinery began to appear, and in a few decades Castilian law was organized into a uniform code—always a landmark in the stabilization of a state.

Considering the anarchy at the start of their reign and the absence of central institutions, Ferdinand and Isabella performed greater wonders in establishing royal power than did any of the other new monarchs. A good index of the effectiveness of their growing bureaucracy is the increase in their revenues. As soon as the main administrative reforms were completed, in the 1490s, the yield of the sales tax (the *alcabala*), which was the mainstay of royal income, began to rise dramatically. Total annual revenue is estimated to have soared from 80,000 ducats in 1474 to 2.3 million by 1504, the year Isabella died.[6] Religious affairs, too, helped in the consolidation of the crown's authority. After the civil wars in Castile had come to an end, Ferdinand had turned his energies to driving the Moors from the peninsula. The reasons for his aggressive policy were clear: first, it complemented the crown's drive for power at home; second, war was a traditional

---

[6] There were approximately four Spanish ducats to the English pound, which means that Ferdinand and Isabella had an income nearly five times that of Henry VII or half that of Louis XII.

INQVISITION

At the dread auto-da-fé a public judgment of guilt was passed on those whom the Spanish Inquisition had tried. Then followed the punishment, which was carried out by the civil authorities—usually burning the heretics, as shown in this engraving. (Photo: Giraudon) interest for an ambitious ruler, and it helped keep restless nobles occupied; and finally, the element of crusade in the struggle against non-Christians stimulated the country's religious fervor, which in turn promoted enthusiasm for its rulers.

The tide of religious zeal swept on after the last Arab stronghold, Granada, capitulated in 1492. Less than three months later, all Jews were expelled from Spain. Some 150,000 of the most enterprising people in Aragon and Castile, including many leading doctors, government officials, and others who had made a vital contribution to economic and cultural life, departed overnight. It was only natural that the rulers' determination to remove anything that stood in their way should have focused on a group that did not share the popular religious passion sustaining their authority. The campaign against the Jews thus went hand in hand with growing royal power.

The same drive to consolidate their strength had prompted Ferdinand and Isabella to obtain permission from the pope in 1478 to establish their own Inquisition. Since 1483 this indigenous body had been run by a royal council and given a mandate to root out Marranos and Moriscos—Jews and Moors who under coercion had pretended to accept Christianity but in fact retained their original beliefs. After the fall of Granada, the Spanish Church attempted to convert the Moors, and in 1502 all Arabs who were not officially Christian were expelled from the country. Nonetheless suspected Moriscos and Marranos kept the Inquisition busy. The persecution welded the country into a religious unity that paralleled and supported the political centralization achieved by the monarchy. Religious policy was thus as much an instrument of political power as it was of ideological conformity.

Foreign Affairs

The fall of Granda extended Spain's dominion southward, but there were also lands to be captured to the north and east. It was in this undertaking that Ferdinand took the lead, because men controlled diplomacy and warfare, and he emphasized these activities during the twelve years he ruled on his own after Isabella's death. His first success had come in 1493, when Charles VIII rewarded Spain's support of the French expedition into Italy by returning to her the two provinces on the French border that Louis XI had taken thirty years before. Two years later, however, fearful that France's Italian invasion was threatening his Kingdom of Sicily, Ferdinand decided to enter the war in Italy.

His achievements in the next two decades were due to a combination of military and diplomatic skills unusual even among the highly capable rulers of the age. A reorganization of Spain's standing army made it the most effective force in Europe, and it rapidly achieved a commanding presence in Italy: by 1504 it had conquered Naples, and Spain had become a major power in the peninsula. Ferdinand also built the strongest diplomatic service of his time, setting up five permanent embassies—at Rome, Venice, London, Brussels, and the Hapsburg court. The ambassadors' reports and activities made him the best-informed and most effective maneuverer in the international politics of the day.

Thus by the time of his death, in 1516, the united Spain that he and Isabella created had gained enormously in territory and status both at home and abroad. The successor to the throne inherited a monarchy fully as dynamic and as triumphant over its rivals as those of England and France.

Charles V, Holy Roman Emperor

To bolster their dynasty the joint rulers had married their five children to members of the leading families of Europe. Their daughter Joanna became the wife of the Hapsburg Archduke Philip of Austria, and her son Charles became heir to both the royal throne of Spain and the Hapsburg dukedom.

A Jew kneeling before Queen Isabella during the Inquisition. (Photo: Museo Provincial, Zaragoza/Photo MAS)

Early in his reign as king of Spain, however, Charles (1516–1556) had to withstand a major onslaught on the crown's position. Educated in Flanders, he spoke no Castilian, and when he arrived in Spain late in 1517, he soon aroused the resentment of the local nobility, particularly when members of the large Flemish entourage he brought with him were given positions in the government. The young king stayed for two and a half years, during which time he was elected emperor of the Holy Roman Empire (1519). This enhanced his prestige, but it also intensified his subjects' fears that he would become an absentee ruler with little interest in their affairs. The Cortes, in particular, showed open hostility when Charles requested additional tax funds so that he could leave the country with Spanish troops for imperial purposes. As soon as he left, in 1520, revolts began to break out in Spain's towns, and the risings of these communes racked the country for two years. The troubles Charles now endured were one of the first of many major clashes during the next 150 years between the traditional dynastic aims of the leading European monarchs and the jealous sense of distinctiveness felt by their subjects.[7]

Fortunately for the crown, the communes lacked positive aims; their resentments and hopes were deep but vague. They wanted to reverse the growth of royal power and to restore their traditional autonomy—a grievance that central governments were bound to encounter as they extended their authority. To this end communes asked for the removal of Flemish royal officials and a reduction in taxation, and at first they had the strong sympathy of the Spanish nobles, who particularly disliked the foreign ruler. But the movement soon took on social overtones: the communes launched attacks on the privileged orders of society, especially the nobility, and this lost the revolt its only chance for success. For now the nobles turned against the communes and defeated them in battle even before Charles returned to Spain.

The king took warning from the uprisings and made sure that his administration was now kept entirely in Spanish hands. Henceforth the energies of his subjects were channeled into imperial missions overseas, where the conquest of Mexico was under way, and against the Ottoman Turks in the Mediterranean. Once again foreign excursions bought a monarch peace at home.

The one notable extension of royal power during Charles's reign was the large empire Spaniards were establishing in Central and South America. Closer to home, however, there was little that gave him or his Spanish subjects cause for pleasure. As Holy Roman Emperor and king of Spain, Charles ruled almost all of Continental Europe west of Poland and the Balkans, with the major exception of France, and he was almost ceaselessly at war defending his territories (see Map 13.4). To the Spaniards most of the wars helped imperial ambitions and were thus irrelevant. As far as they were concerned, aside from the widening acquisitions in the New World, Charles did little to further the expansion started by Ferdinand and Isabella.

The recurrent crises and wars outside of Spain kept Charles away from his kingdom for more than two-thirds of his forty-year reign. But in his absence a highly talented administrator, Francisco de los Cobos, shaped and clarified the government's position. He established the complete supremacy of the crown by greatly enlarging the bureaucracy and elaborating the system of councils that Ferdinand and Isabella had begun. In the 1520s this structure, which was to survive for centuries, received its final form.

There were two types of council. One was responsible for each of the departments of the

[7] Although this feeling cannot be called nationalism, it was certainly an ancestor of that powerful modern force. Incidentally, the word "communes" as used here refers to the towns and cities of Spain that had distinct legal privileges and some degree of self-government; they were the center of the revolt. Their inhabitants are called, in Spanish, "comuneros."

MAP 13.4: THE EMPIRE OF CHARLES V

This map indicates both the vastness of Charles's empire and the extent of the fighting in which he became involved. Almost every battle his troops fought—against Spanish communes, German Protestants, the Turks, and the French—is included so as to show the full measure of the emperor's never-ending ordeal.

government—finance, war, the Inquisition, and so on. The other supervised each of the territories ruled by the crown: Aragon, Castile, Italy, the Indies, and later in the century the Low Countries. At the head of this system was the Council of State, the principal advisory group, consisting of leading officials from the subsidiary councils. All the subsidiary councils reported to the king or to his deputy when he was away, but since each controlled its own bureaucracy, they were perfectly capable of running the empire in the monarch's absence.

What emerged was a vast federation, with Castile standing at its heart but with the parts, though directed from the center, allowed considerable autonomy. A viceroy in every major area (there were nine altogether from Naples to Peru) ran the administration under the supervision of the *audiencia*—the territorial council—and while on the whole these officials were left to do as they wished, they had to report to Castile in minute detail at regular intervals and refer major decisions to the central government.

Although corruption was widespread and delays in communications (it took at least eight months to send a message from Castile to Peru) made the system unwieldy, the centralization gave the monarch the power he wanted. The enormous bureaucracy was carefully staffed, primarily by hidalgos and townsmen, while great nobles were given only vice-royalties or high army posts. Flexibility was allowed at the local level, but through the hierarchy of loyal servants the crown could exercise unhampered control. As a result, Spain's administrative machine was one of the most remarkably detailed structures ever devised for ruling so vast an empire.

The Financial Toll of War

The only serious strain on Charles's monarchy was financial, the result of the constant wars the Hapsburgs had to support. A large portion of the money for the fighting came from Italy and the Low Countries, but Spain had to pay a growing share of the costs. As the sixteenth century progressed, the Spaniards increasingly resented the siphoning away of their funds into foreign wars. It was the tragedy of their century of glory that so much of the fantastic

wealth they discovered in Latin America was exported to support hostilities from which they drew almost no benefit.

The burden was by no means equally distributed. The stronger Cortes of Aragon was able to prevent substantial increases in taxation, which meant that Castile had to assume the brunt of the payments. To some extent this was balanced by a monopoly of trade with the New World that was granted to the inhabitants of Castile, but eventually the basic inequality among different Spanish regions led to civil war in the next century.

Charles's finances were saved from disaster only by the influx of treasure—mainly silver—from Latin America. Approximately 40 percent of the bullion went into the royal coffers, while the rest was taken by merchants in the Castilian city of Seville, mainly Genoese, who were given the sole right to ship goods to and from America. Starting with an annual inflow of some 20,000 ducats at the beginning of the century, Charles was receiving approximately 800,000 ducats' worth of treasure each year by the end of his reign. Unfortunately it was always mortgaged in advance to the Italian and German bankers whose loans sustained his armies.

The country and the monarchy faced increasing difficulties as the wars continued for more than a century and a half. Seville's monopoly prevented the rest of the nation from gaining a share of the new wealth, and foreigners—notably representatives of Italian and German financiers—came to dominate her economy and her commerce. Spain was squeezed dry by the king's financial demands; yet he only just kept his head above water. In 1557, the first year of the reign of Charles's successor, Philip II, the monarchy had to declare itself bankrupt, a self-defeating evasion of its mammoth debts that it had to repeat seven times in the next 125 years. There has never been a better example of the way that ceaseless war can sap the strength of even the most formidable nation.

III. THE SPLINTERED STATES

The rulers of England, France, and Spain in the mid-sixteenth century came to thrones strengthened domestically and internationally. Their predecessors had centralized their governments, largely subdued the rivals to royal power, engaged in a huge expansion overseas, and brought a fair measure of prosperity and safety from lawlessness to their subjects. Above all they had begun to free the individual from subjection to his local lord. But in the European domains east of these three kingdoms, such developments took place fitfully and only within small territorial units such as city-states. Here the centrifugal forces retained the control they had enjoyed for centuries.

THE HOLY ROMAN EMPIRE: AUTONOMOUS PRINCES

The Holy Roman Empire is a classic example of weak institutions preventing the emergence of a strong central government. Members of the leading family of Central Europe, the Hapsburgs, had been elected to the imperial throne since the thirteenth century, but they lacked the authority and machinery to halt the fragmentation of the lands they nominally ruled. In addition to some 2,000 imperial knights, some of whom owned no more than four or five acres, there were 50 ecclesiastical and 30 secular princes, more than 100 counts, some 70 prelates, and 66 cities, all virtually independent politically though officially subordinate to the emperor.

The princes, who reigned over most of the area of the Holy Roman Empire, rarely had any trouble resisting the emperor's claims; their main concern was to increase their own power at the expense of their subjects, another prince,

or the cities. The cities themselves also refused to remain subordinate to a central government. Fifty of them contained more than 2,000 inhabitants in 1500—a sizable number for this time—and twenty had over 10,000. Their wealth was substantial, because many were situated along a densely traveled trade artery, the Rhine River, and many were also political powers. But their fierce independence meant that the emperor could rarely tap their manpower or wealth.

The only central institution apart from the imperial office itself, the Diet, consisted of three assemblies: representatives of the cities, the princes, and the electors (the seven princes who elected each new emperor). Given this make-up, the Diet in effect became the instrument of the princes; with its legislation they secured their position against both the cities and the lesser nobility within their own domains.

By the end of the fifteenth century, most of the princes had achieved considerable control over their own territories. Only in the southwest of the empire were they significantly restricted by representative assemblies led by the lesser nobility. The princes were thus enjoying a success that paralleled the accomplishments of the monarchs of England, France, and Spain except that the units were much smaller. Although the Hapsburgs tried to develop strong central authority, they exercised significant control only over their personal dominions, which in 1500 comprised Austria, the Low Countries, and so-called imperial Burgundy, or Franche-Comté. To the rulers of other states of the empire, they were feudal overlords in theory but powerless in practice.

Nevertheless the need for effective central institutions met with some response in the late fifteenth century, particularly in the west and southwest of the empire. In 1495 for example a tribunal was established to settle disputes between local powers. Controlled and financed by the princes, the chief beneficiaries of its work, it made considerable headway toward ending the lawlessness that had marked the fifteenth century, an achievement similar to the restoration of order in France, Spain, and England at the same time. The tribunal's use of Roman law had a wide influence on legislation and justice throughout the empire, but again only to the advantage of the princes, who interpreted its endorsement of a leader's authority as referring only to themselves.

Further attempts at administrative reform had little effect, because ecclesiastical and secular princes reacted by tightening their hold on the multitude of territories that constituted the empire. The religious dissensions of the Reformation worsened the rivalries, dividing the empire and making Charles V no more than the leader of one side in the conflict, incapable of asserting his authority over his opponents. Charles's many commitments elsewhere diverted him repeatedly, but even when he won decisive military victories over the princes, he could not break the long tradition of local independence.

EASTERN EUROPE: RESURGENT NOBLES

In the late fifteenth century, the dominant force in Eastern and Central Europe was the Kingdom of Hungary, under the leadership of Matthias Corvinus (1458–1490). He was exactly in the mold of the other new monarchs of the day: he restrained the great nobles, expanded and centralized his administration, dramatically increased the yield of taxation, and established a standing army. The king's power thus grew spectacularly both at home and abroad. He gained Bohemia and some German and Austrian lands, and he made Vienna his capital in 1485.

Immediately after his death, however, royal authority collapsed. To gain Hapsburg recognition of his right to the throne, his successor gave up the conquests of Austrian and German territories and arranged dynastic marriages with the Hapsburgs. This retreat provided the nobles of Hungary with an issue over which to reassert their position. First they forced the

king to dissolve the standing army by refusing him essential financial support. Then, following a major peasant revolt against increasing repression by landowners, they imposed serfdom on all peasants in 1514 at a meeting of the Hungarian Diet, the governing body, which was controlled by the aristocracy. In the course of the next thirty years, the country was overrun by the Ottoman Empire, whose system of rule—reliance on local powers who would give allegiance to Constantinople—strengthened the nobility further at the expense of both the monarchy and the peasantry. By the middle of the sixteenth century, a revival of central authority had become impossible.

In Poland royal power began to decline in the 1490s, when the king turned to the lesser nobles to help him against the greater nobility. He issued a statute in 1496 that strengthened the lower aristocrats against those below them, the townsmen and the peasants. The latter virtually became serfs, for they were forbidden to buy land and were deprived of freedom of movement. In 1505 the national Diet, consisting only of nobles, was made the supreme body of the land, without whose consent no laws could be passed. Shortly thereafter the Diet officially established serfdom.

Royal and noble patronage produced a great cultural efflorescence in Poland in these decades, most famously represented by the astronomer Nicolaus Copernicus. Yet the monarchy was losing influence steadily, as was revealed by the failure of its attempts to found a standing army. At the end of Sigismund II's reign, his kingdom was the largest in Europe; but his death, in 1572, ended the Jagellon dynasty, which had ruled the country for centuries. The Diet immediately made sure that succession to the crown, which technically had always been elective and in the hands of the nobles, would henceforth depend entirely on their approval. Thus the aristocracy confirmed both its own dominance and the ineffectiveness of royal authority.

The Hungarian and Polish patterns were repeated throughout Eastern Europe. By the early sixteenth century, serfdom had been officially imposed in all the territories east of the Elbe River. In the West at the same time, labor shortages caused by the plagues of the fourteenth and fifteenth centuries had brought a permanent end to this kind of subjection. Peasants who were needed to work the land became scarce, and since estates were relatively small, desperate landowners, competing with one another for labor, had to offer the remaining serfs freedom in exchange for services. In the East much of the territory was newly settled and divided into very large holdings. Here the lords could achieve economies of scale and make do with fewer laborers per acre; consequently, they did not feel the need to make concessions. Moreover, these great landowners also held the keys to political power, and hence they could combine influence in the government with economic pressure to ensure the repression of the lowest levels of society.

The political and social processes at work in Eastern and Central Europe thus contrasted strongly with developments in England, France, and Spain in this period. Nevertheless, although the trend was toward fragmentation in the East, one class, the aristocracy, did share the vigor and organizational ability that in the West was apparent primarily in the policies of kings. To that extent, therefore, the sense of renewed vitality in Europe during these years was also apparent beyond the borders of the new monarchies. The critical difference lay in the leaders of the revival. When kings were in command, their states gained strength and status; when the nobles dominated, countries lost ground in the fierce competition of international affairs.

ITALY: INDEPENDENT CITY-STATES

The cultural and economic leader of Europe, Italy, had developed a unique political struc-

ture. In the fifteenth century five major states had managed to consolidate themselves among the numerous warring principalities and towns of the peninsula: the Kingdom of Naples; the Papal States, centered on Rome; the duchy of Milan; and two republics based on cities, Florence and Venice. The Treaty of Lodi in 1454 established a balance among them that was preserved without serious disruption for the next forty years.

This long period of peace was finally broken in 1494, when Milan asked Charles VIII of France to help protect it against Florence and Naples. Thus began the Italian wars, which soon revealed that these relatively small territories were totally incapable of resisting the force that a new political organization, the national monarchy, could bring to bear.

Venice and particularly Florence had long been regarded by Europeans as model republics —reincarnations of classical city-states and centers of freedom governed with the consent of their citizens. In truth Venice was controlled by a small merchant oligarchy and Florence by the Medici family, but the image was still widely accepted. Moreover the Italians were regarded as masters not only of politics but also of culture and manners.

It was a considerable shock to Europe therefore when the Italian states crumbled before the onslaught of French forces and then of the Spaniards and the Hapsburgs. Charles VIII drove the Medicis out of Florence in 1494 and established a new republic, but in 1512 Ferdinand of Aragon engineered their return, and eventually the Hapsburgs set up the Medici family as hereditary dukes. Ferdinand had annexed Naples in 1504, and Emperor Charles V ultimately took over Milan. The fighting finally ended in 1559 with the Hapsburgs in control; they would dominate the Italian peninsula for the next century. Only Venice and the Papal States remained independent, the former somewhat battered by a series of defeats and the latter the one gainer from the Italian wars. Julius II (1503–1513), known as the Warrior Pope, carved out a new papal territory in central and eastern Italy by force of arms.

The critical lesson of this disastrous sequence of events was that the small political unit could not survive in an age when governments were consolidating their authority in large kingdoms. No matter how brilliant and sophisticated, a compact urban state could not withstand such superior force. Italy's cultural and economic prominence took a long time to fade, but by the mid-sixteenth century, her political independence had disappeared, not to return for 300 years.

iv. THE NEW STATECRAFT

At the same time as European political life grew more elaborate and complex, innovations appeared in the relations among states and the perspectives of political observers. The newly powerful central governments were confronted by an international situation radically different from that of only a century before. Rulers had achieved levels of military and economic strength and a freedom of action that required equivalent transformations in the techniques of diplomacy. Theorists and historians who witnessed these changes began to see politics in a different light. Two Italians in particular, Niccolò Machiavelli and Francesco Guicciardini, opened the way to a totally new understanding of the phenomenon of political leadership.

Hans Holbein's The Ambassadors *shows the worldliness that was expected of diplomats (many of whom were also soldiers) in the sixteenth century. The two men are surrounded by symbols of the skills, knowledge, and refinement their job required—geography, mathematics, literature, and music. But despite this emphasis on material concerns, Holbein reminds us (in the optically distorted skull across the bottom of the painting) that death and spiritual needs cannot be forgotten.* (Photo: National Gallery, London)

INTERNATIONAL RELATIONS

The Italian states of the fifteenth century, in their intensive machinations and competition, developed various new ways of pursuing foreign policy. During the Italian wars these techniques spread throughout Europe and caused a revolution in diplomacy. Any state hoping to play a prominent role in international affairs worked under a serious disadvantage if it did not adopt the new methods.

The essential innovation was the resident ambassador. Previously rulers had dispatched ambassadors only for specific missions, such as arranging an alliance, declaring war, or delivering a message, but from the sixteenth century on, important states maintained their representatives in every major capital city or court continuously. The permanent ambassador could not only keep his home government informed

of the latest local and international developments but could also move without delay to protect his sovereign's interests.

As states established embassies, procedures and organization became more sophisticated: a primitive system of immunities evolved, formal protocol developed, and embassy officials were assigned different levels of responsibility and importance. Considerable advances were still to come, but by the mid-sixteenth century the outlines of the new diplomacy were already visible —yet another reflection of the growing powers and ambitions of central governments.

The great dividing line between established arrangements and the new diplomacy was the Italian wars, the first Europe-wide crisis of modern times. Rulers as distant as the English King Henry VIII and the Ottoman Sultan Suleiman II were drawn into the conflict between the Hapsburgs and the Valois, and gradually all states recognized that it was in the interests of everyone to accept a system in which no one power dominated the rest. In later years this interdependence, this prevention of excessive aggression, was to be known as the balance of power, yet by the mid-sixteenth century the glimmerings of the idea were already affecting alliances and peace treaties. The lesson again came from the Italians, who on a smaller scale had tried to create a balance among the leading states of the peninsula with the Treaty of Lodi.

For Charles V, ever on the defensive and an instinctive peacemaker, such orderliness had much to recommend it. But Francis I considered the Hapsburgs far too powerful, and he pursued his ambitions in Italy with all the means at his disposal, undeterred by repeated defeats. In 1535 he shocked Europe by concluding a treaty with the Muslim Suleiman, the Hapsburgs' most formidable enemy. And the sultan even paid the papacy a pension to help it pursue its own opposition to Charles V. Thus common political interests brought religious opponents together.

In military affairs the new monarchs took similar initiatives. A recent historian has called the period of Charles V's reign "more decisive for the evolution of the art of war" than any thereafter until the late eighteenth century. During this time the crossbow was finally superseded, armies combined artillery with infantry and cavalry, the division emerged as the basic military unit, city wall bastion fortification was devised, and the siege became the essential tactic of warfare. Logistics were now as important as any other military art, and strategists laid out careful systems of supply and command. An amazing feature of this military revolution was that it advanced uniformly throughout Europe. No ruler could afford to be left behind in the deadly race.

CONTEMPORARY APPRAISALS: MACHIAVELLI AND GUICCIARDINI

Political commentators soon began to seek theoretical explanations for the new authority and aggressiveness of rulers and the collapse of the Italian city-states. Turning from arguments based on divine will or contractual law, they looked to pragmatism, opportunism, and effective government as an end in itself.

The earliest full expression of these views came from the Italians, the pioneers of the methods and attitudes that were revolutionizing politics. When all military efforts proved futile in face of the superior forces of France and Spain, they naturally wanted to find out why. The most disturbing answer was given by an experienced diplomat, Niccolò Machiavelli, who was thrown out of his job when the Medicis took control of Florence in 1512. With a bitter pen he immediately set about analyzing exactly how power operated.

The result, *The Prince*, is one of the few radically original books in history. To move from his predecessors to Machiavelli is to enter a world that even the immediate Italian background does not foreshadow; Roman jurists talking of kings as the source of law and writers asserting that a monarch was not subordinate to the pope were still thinking in legalistic or moral terms. Machiavelli swept away all these conventions. If he came out of any tradition, it was the Renaissance fascination with style and method that had produced manuals on cooking, dancing, fencing, and manners. But he wrote on a subject never previously approached: power.

Machiavelli showed not why power does or should exist, but how it works. In the form of advice to a prince and without reference to divine, legal, or natural justification, the book explains what a ruler needs to do to win and maintain complete control over his subjects. Machiavelli did not deny the force of religion or law; what concerned him was how they ought to be *used* in the tactics of governing—religion for molding unity and contentment, and devotion to law for building the ruler's reputation as a fair-minded man. *The Prince* outlines the particular methods of a conqueror, legitimate heir, or usurper as well as the proper ways to deal with insurrection and the many other problems that a ruler is likely to encounter. Fear and respect are the bases of his authority, and he must exercise care at all times not to relax his control over either potential troublemakers or the image he conveys to his people.

Very few contemporaries of Machiavelli dared accept his view of politics. To men of the sixteenth century and long thereafter, "Machiavellianism" was synonymous with evil and cunning. Secular and pragmatic considerations might be gaining prominence, but Europe was not yet ready to abandon its reverence for law, divine providence, and natural morality.

The change in the perspective on power became noticeable in historical writings too.

Machiavelli's other masterpiece, the *Discourses*, developed a cyclical theory of every government moving inexorably from tyranny to democracy and back again. His conclusion, drawn particularly from a study of Roman history, is that healthy government can be preserved only by the active participation of all citizens in the life of the state. He attributed the Italians' defeat to the fact that his countrymen had relied on mercenary troops and abandoned their civic responsibilities. The vigor of the Roman republic had depended on its citizen army.

Another Italian, Franceso Guicciardini, writing in the 1530s, saw the root of the problem as the lack of unity in Italy. His great work, a *History of Italy*, rose above the particularism of previous narratives, which had dealt with events in only one city-state or region. Guicciardini's comparative analysis of the Italian states led him to conclude that government should be left in the hands of an intelligent ruler. There are no basic principles at work in history; experience, flexibility, and the ability to meet a situation on its own terms make a good ruler.

Guicciardini was the first major historian to rely heavily on original documents rather than secondhand accounts. If the conclusions he reached from his study of the sources seem dauntingly cynical—he attributed even less to underlying historical forces than did Machiavelli—the reasons for his pessimism are not far to seek. The actions of kings and princes in the early sixteenth century hardly gave much room for optimism, and shrewd observers like Machiavelli and Guicciardini must have found it difficult to avoid pessimism about public events. They were exposing the atmosphere of the times, capturing in print the obsession with power and pragmatism that drove Europe's newly powerful rulers as they extended their authority both at home and abroad.

Beginning in the late fifteenth century, the kings of England, France, and Spain consolidated their realms into strong polities with power centralized under their own command. These new monarchs, as historians have called them, extended their authority at home by undermining their traditional domestic rivals, the nobility and the Church, and pursued aggressive dynastic ambitions abroad. The Holy Roman Empire, Eastern Europe, and Italy did not experience this development. Instead local powers—cities, nobles, and princes—remained autonomous, preventing their countries from marshaling their resources and organizing themselves like the new monarchies. Ironically, though the Italian city-states were too small to retain their independence, their politicians were teaching the rest of Europe new methods of conducting international relations; and their political analysts and historians, perceiving the trends in statecraft before anyone else, broke new ground in their analysis of how power works and why states rise and fall.

Parallel to the political developments were remarkable economic advances and an expansion to other continents that reflected the vigor of a newly confident age. Europe's population was increasing, its prices were rising, and its trade was multiplying—all unmistakable signs of a healthy society. Yet the social consequences were not always benevolent, for the revival had paradoxical results. Social mobility did increase, but so did poverty. Strong central governments restored order, but they also provoked resentment. And rapid change by its very nature caused considerable bewilderment, producing signs of disquiet in the culture of the age. Of all the causes of tension, however, none equaled in impact the most shattering disruption of the sixteenth century, an upheaval that brought an end to more than a thousand years of Western Christian unity—the Reformation.

RECOMMENDED READING

Sources

*Guicciardini, Francesco. *The History of Italy and Other Selected Writings.* Cecil Grayson (tr.). 1964.

*Machiavelli, Niccolò. *The Prince and the Discourses.* Luigi Ricci (tr.). 1950.

Studies

Blum, Jerome. "The Rise of Serfdom in Eastern Europe." *American Historical Review,* Vol. 62, No. 4 (July 1957), 807–836. A discussion of why serfdom disappeared in Western Europe at the very

time that it was becoming firmly established in the East.

Boxer, Charles R. *The Portuguese Seaborne Empire.* 1970. An excellent overview of the rise and structure of the Portuguese empire.

*Brandi, Karl. *The Emperor Charles V.* C. V. Wedgwood (tr.). 1968. This is a long and detailed biography, but the narrative is well written and flows easily. Moreover, in the course of the book just about every political problem that arose in Europe during Charles's lifetime is discussed.

Cipolla, Carlo M. *Guns, Sails, and Empires: Technological Innovation and the Early Phases of European Expansion 1400–1700.* 1965. This is a lively study of the reasons the expansion succeeded, with particular emphasis on weaponry.

*Elliott, J. H. *Imperial Spain, 1469–1716.* 1964. The best introduction to Spanish history in this period, covering mainly political and economic developments.

*Elton, Geoffrey R. *The Tudor Revolution in Government.* 1959. An important study of how government worked, and how its operations were expanded, during the reign of Henry VIII.

*Gilmore, Myron P. *The World of Humanism, 1453–1517.* 1952. A thorough introduction to the entire period, with a full, though somewhat out-of-date, bibliography. For more recent work, see the bibliography in Rice, below.

*Hale, J. R. *Machiavelli and Renaissance Italy.* 1963. The clearest and most straightforward short account of Machiavelli and his times.

*Jensen, DeLamar (ed.). *The Expansion of Europe: Motives, Methods, and Meanings.* 1967. A collection of writings on the expansion, reflecting the different views historians have held about the overseas movements.

*Mattingly, Garrett. *Renaissance Diplomacy.* 1971. An elegant account of the changes that began in international relations during the fifteenth century.

*Morison, Samuel Eliot. *Admiral of the Ocean Sea: A Life of Christopher Columbus.* 1942. An exciting story, well told, that brings to life Europe's most remarkable explorer.

*Parry, John H. *The Age of Reconnaissance.* 1963.
The most complete history of Europe's expansion through 1620.

Parry, John H. *The Spanish Seaborne Empire.* 1966. Published in the same series as Boxer's book on the Portuguese empire, this is a good review of the establishment of the Spanish empire.

Potter, G. R. (ed.). *The New Cambridge Modern History.* Vol. I: *The Renaissance, 1493–1520.* 1964. The most thorough and detailed history of the period.

Raab, Felix. *The English Face of Machiavelli: A Changing Interpretation 1500–1700.* 1964. A well-written study of the people who read Machiavelli, what they thought of him, and how his reputation changed over two hundred years.

*Rice, Eugene F., Jr. *The Foundations of Early Modern Europe, 1460–1559.* 1970. The best of the recent short surveys of the period, with three pages of suggested readings that list the main books that have been published since Gilmore's bibliography.

Rich, E. E., and C. H. Wilson (eds.). *The Cambridge Economic History of Europe.* Vol. IV: *The Economy of Expanding Europe in the Sixteenth and Seventeenth Centuries.* 1967. A comprehensive survey of recent works in the field.

Wolfe, Martin. *The Fiscal System of Renaissance France.* 1972. An account of the way a central government raised money and exercised power during this period.

* Available in paperback.

FOURTEEN

REFORMATIONS
IN RELIGION

To the sixteenth-century European, the most momentous revolution of the time was not the growth of royal power, the rise of prices, or the discovery of new lands overseas but the movement that destroyed the West's religious unity: the Reformation. Two sides began to form, to be called Catholic and Protestant, each resolutely convinced of its own righteousness and the other's error, and their confrontation inspired wars for more than a century.

The new ideas of the religious thinkers Martin Luther, Ulrich Zwingli, John Calvin, and their successors stimulated a radical rethinking of traditional views of God, man, and society. At issue in the Reformation was the balance between the role of the Church and the piety of the individual in the answer to the fundamental question of Christian history: How can sinful humans gain salvation? The traditional answer was that the Church was the essential intermediary through which man could be saved. This laid the stress on community, on outward participation in rituals, and particularly on the seven sacraments, the principal channels of grace. But there was another answer that had been advocated by distinguished Church fathers such as St. Augustine: that man could be saved by his faith in God and love of him. This view emphasized the inward and personal and focused on God as the source of grace.

The two traditions were not incompatible; for centuries they had coexisted without difficulty, and elements of each would be retained by both Protestants and Catholics after the Reformation. Indeed, one of the problems theologians faced around 1500 was the absence of precise definition in many areas of doctrine. It was often difficult to tell where orthodoxy ended and heresy began. This indeterminacy might have been an asset had it reflected a commitment to flexibility and comprehensiveness by the leaders of the Church. In fact, however, as the papacy and the Church had grown in power and im-

portance during the High Middle Ages, official attitudes had shifted decisively toward the outward, sacramental, institutional view and away from the inward and personal approach. The main purpose of the Reformation was to reverse this trend. What was not clear at the outset was whether the change would be accomplished by reform from within or by a revolution and schism in the Church.

I. DISSENT AND PIETY

Dissatisfaction with the Church was evident at all levels of society in the early sixteenth century. For more than 200 years the prestige of the papacy had been steadily eroding, and increasing numbers of deeply pious people were finding the Church's growing emphasis on ritual and standardized practices unhelpful in their personal quest for salvation. What they sought was spiritual renewal and a return to the basic values of early Christianity. Their religious grievances were the root of the ferment; once the Reformation had begun, however, political, economic, and social issues influenced its course.

SOURCES OF MALAISE

The spiritual authority of the papacy had been declining for more than two centuries. During the seventy years of the Babylonian captivity, when the pontiffs had lived in Avignon, they had no longer seemed to be symbols of the universal Church but rather captives of the French monarchs. Far more demoralizing, the Great Schism that followed had threatened to undermine the unity of Western Christendom, as two and then three pretenders each claimed to be the true pope. The Council of Constance had closed this breach by 1418 but had also encouraged the conciliar movement. This attempt to subordinate papal power to the authority of Church councils ultimately failed, but it was yet another direct challenge to the pope's supremacy. Only the refusal of secular rulers to protect the reform movements that arose around 1400—in particular, the efforts of John Wycliffe and John Huss and their followers—prevented a major split like the Reformation 100 years before it actually occurred.

The papacy had also lost spiritual influence because of its secularization. Increasingly popes were conducting themselves like Italian princes. With skillful diplomacy and even military action, they had consolidated their control over the papal lands in the peninsula. They had surrounded themselves with an elaborate court and become patrons of the arts, taking over for a time the cultural leadership of Europe. But this concern with political power and grandeur had eclipsed religious duties to the point where popes used their spiritual powers to raise funds for their secular activities. The fiscal measures developed at Avignon, which furnished the papacy with income from appointments to Church offices and from dispensations and indulgences, had enlarged revenues but led to widespread abuses. High ecclesiastical offices could be bought and sold, and men (usually sons of nobles) were attracted to them by the opportunities they provided for wealth and power, not by a religious vocation.

Abuses were widespread at lower levels in the Church as well. Some prelates held several offices at a time and could not give adequate attention to any of them. The ignorance and moral laxity of the parish and monastic clergy also aroused antagonism. The lower clerical orders, particularly the ordinary parish priests, were little better off than the peasants among whom they lived, and many of them used indulgences as a fund-raising device—granting the remission of some of the temporal punishment for sin to anyone who made a donation to the Church. Many laymen found this practice a shocking attempt to sell divine grace.

These abuses provoked two major responses: anticlericalism and a call for reform within the Church. Both reactions were symptomatic of a broader quest for genuine piety that was running throughout European society by the early 1500s.

The deepest source of discontent with the Church was its failure to meet spiritual needs. The institution had grown more formal, its doctrines supported by an elaborate system of canon law and theology and its services filled with pomp and ceremony. Increasing importance was being attached to the sacraments, the role of the priest, and the doctrine that salvation could be achieved only if faith was accompanied by good works—fasting, abstinence, and similar acts of denial or expiation.

Lay people sought a more personal piety than the official devotions provided. Observation of Church rituals meant little, they felt, unless the believer could cultivate an interior sense of the love and presence of God. They looked for nourishment, therefore, to those, like the mystics, who emphasized religious individualism. Rejecting the theological subtleties of Scholasticism, they sought divine guidance in the Bible and the writings of the early Church fathers, especially St. Augustine. Lay religious fraternities dedicated to private devotions and charitable works proliferated in the cities, especially in Germany and Italy. The most widespread of them in Germany, the Brotherhood of the Eleven Thousand Virgins, consisted of laymen who gathered together, usually in a church, to sing hymns. In the mid-fifteenth century, 80 such groups had been established in Cologne, a city of some 35,000 people, and more than 100 in Hamburg, which had slightly more than 10,000 inhabitants. Churchmen, unhappy about a development over which they had no control, had tried to suppress such activities but to no avail. Itinerant preachers still roamed Central Europe in considerable numbers, urging direct communication between believers and God free from ritual and complex doctrine. To the vast crowds they drew, they seemed to echo the words of St. Augustine: "God and the soul I want to recognize, nothing else."

The most spectacular outburst of popular piety around 1500 was the ascendancy over the city of Florence of Girolamo Savonarola, a zealous Dominican who wanted to banish the irreligion and materialism he saw everywhere about him. The climax of his influence came in 1496, when he arranged a tremendous bonfire, in which the Florentines burned cosmetics, light literature, dice, and other such frivolities. But Savonarola's attempts at internal reform eventually brought him into conflict with the papacy. At that point the Church intervened, and eventually he was executed for heresy.

The widespread search for a more intense devotional life was a sign of spiritual vitality. Had the hierarchy responded by adapting religious teachings and practices to meet this need, the Church might have been spared the upheavals of the Reformation. Instead churchmen gave little encouragement to ecclesiastical reform and the evangelization of the laity. They reacted with vigor only when they detected a clear threat to their authority—when

for example they condemned the teachings of John Wycliffe and John Huss as heretical. Only in Spain was there a deliberate attempt to eradicate abuses and encourage religious fervor, and there the leadership in the effort came not from Rome but from the head of the Spanish Church, Cardinal Francisco Ximenes de Cisneros. When the papacy finally did attempt to revitalize the Church in the mid-sixteenth century, the revolt of the reformers was an accomplished fact.

PIETY AND PROTEST IN LITERATURE AND ART

Popular piety received unexpected assistance from technology. The invention of the printing press made reading material available to a much broader segment of the population and new ideas traveled with unprecedented speed. Perhaps a third of the professional and upper classes—townsmen, the educated, and the nobility—could read, but books reached a much wider audience. Throughout Europe, peddlers began to carry printed materials in their packs, selling them in country towns in all regions. Here they could be bought by a local person for reading out loud at a gathering of villagers. These evening readings to a group of people who would never have had access to written literature in the days of manuscripts became an important means of spreading new ideas.

Some publishers took advantage of this new market by printing almanacs filled with homely advice about the weather and nature that were written specifically for simple rural folk. And translated Bibles made Scripture available to ordinary people in a language that, for the first time, they could understand. For the Reformers, therefore, books were a powerful weapon, but they were used by both sides in the religious conflict and revealed the general interest in spiritual matters. Devotional tracts, lives of the saints, and the Bible itself

This sixteenth-century painting depicts the torture and execution of Savonarola and his chief followers in the main square of Florence in 1498. (Photo: Museo di San Marco, Florence/Alinari)

were the most popular titles—often running to editions of around 1,000 copies.

Printing may thus have lessened the layman's dependence on the clergy; whereas traditionally the priest had read and interpreted the Scriptures for his congregation, now many could consult their own copy. By 1522 eighteen translations of the Bible had been published. Some 14,000 copies had been printed in German alone, enough to make it easy to buy in most German-speaking regions.

Many books were profusely illustrated, and thus accessible to the illiterate as well. Perhaps the most famous was the German Sebastian Brant's *Ship of Fools* (1494), a long satire in verse describing life as a voyage. The poem

THE SPREAD OF PRINTING THROUGH 1500
Number of Towns in which a Printing Press Was Established for the First Time, by Period and Country

PERIOD	GERMAN-SPEAKING AREAS	ITALIAN-SPEAKING AREAS	FRENCH-SPEAKING AREAS	SPAIN	ENGLAND	NETHER-LANDS	OTHER	TOTAL
Before 1471:	8	4	1	1	–	–	–	14
1471–1480:	22	36	9	6	3	12	5	93
1481–1490:	17	13	21	12	–	5	4	72
1491–1500:	9	5	11	6	–	2	8	41
Total by 1500:	56	58	42	25	3	19	17	220

Adapted from Lucien Febvre and Henri-Jean Martin, *The Coming of the Book: The Impact of Printing 1450–1800*, translated by David Gerard, London, NLB, 1976, pp. 178–179 and 184–185.

(*Note:* Printing did not spread to other towns in England because the government, to ensure control over printers, ordered that they work only in London.)

dissects each passenger—the beggar, the friar, and so on—lampooning his lack of true faith or morality.

The most gifted satirist of the age, however, was François Rabelais, an incisive critic of the clergy and morality of his day. He was a monk (as well as a doctor), but he was deeply unhappy that traditional religious practices had diverged so far from the ideals of Jesus. Rabelais is most famous for his earthy bawdiness, but again and again he returned to clerical targets. His *Gargantua* and *Pantagruel* (1533 and 1535) contain numerous sardonic passages:

"Don't [monks] pray to God for us?" "They do nothing of the kind," said Gargantua. "All they do is keep the whole neighborhood awake by jangling their bells. . . . They mumble over a lot of legends and psalms, which they don't in the least understand; and they say a great many paternosters . . . without thinking or caring about what they are saying. And all that I call a mockery of God, not prayer."

Scurrilous broadsides no less stinging in tone became very popular during the Reformation. These were single sheets, often containing vicious attacks on religious opponents and usually illustrated by cartoons that used obscene imagery so that the point would be unmistakable. These propaganda pieces were the product of partisan hostility, but their broader significance should not be ignored (see illustration, p. 445). Even the most lowly of hack writers could share with a serious author like Rabelais a common sense of outrage at indifference in high places and a dismay with the spiritual malaise of their time.

This concern with spiritual and religious themes, so evident in European literature, also permeated the work of Northern artists in the late fifteenth and early sixteenth centuries. The gruesome vision of Hieronymus Bosch, for example, depicts the fears and dangers his contemporaries felt threatening them. He put on canvas the demons, the temptations, the terrible punishments for sin that men considered as real as their tangible surroundings (see Plate 21). Bosch's younger contemporary Mathias Grünewald conveyed the same mixture of ter-

Grünewald's Temptation of St. Anthony *bears witness to the terrifying impact of the supernatural on the thought of Northern artists.* (Photo: Lauros-Giraudon)

ror and devotion. Like Bosch, he painted a frightening *Temptation of St. Anthony* showing the travails of the saint who steadfastly resisted horrible attacks by the devil. These artists explored the darker side of faith, taking their inspiration from the fear of damnation and the hope for salvation—the first seen in the devils, the second in the redeeming Christ.

The supreme innovation of the finest Northern artist of this period, Albrecht Dürer, was not in painting but in the art of the woodcut. Developed in the mid-fourteenth century, the technique of cutting a picture into wood so that it could be inked and reproduced grew in importance with the invention of printing. Until touched by the genius of Dürer, however, it remained a stiff and primitive art form. His hand transformed it into a subtle, versatile means of expression, a superb vehicle for the religious themes he portrayed.

The depth of piety conveyed by these artists reflected the temper of Europe (see, for example, the religious meaning put even into a secular painting like Holbein's *The Ambassadors*, reproduced on p. 427). In art and literature as in lay organizations and the continuing popularity of itinerant preachers, men showed their concern over individual spiritual values and their dissatisfaction with a Church that was not meeting their needs. But no segment of society expressed the strivings and yearnings of the age more eloquently than the Northern humanists.

II. THE NORTHERN HUMANISTS

The salient features of the humanist movement in Italy—its theory of education, its emphasis on eloquence, its reverence for the ancients, and its endorsement of active participation in affairs of state—began to win wide acceptance north of the Alps in the late 1400s. But the Northerners added a significant religious dimension to the movement by devoting considerable attention to early Christian literature—the Bible and the writings of the Church fathers. The greatest of the Northern humanists, Erasmus, urged a return to the "philosophy of Christ," but he eventually found that the simple piety he advocated was leading in a new and, in his eyes, unacceptable direction: toward a split in the Church.

CHRISTIAN HUMANISM

The first major center of Northern Humanism was the University of Heidelberg, but by the end of the fifteenth century the influence of the movement was almost universal. As it grew, there was a quickening of activity in the world of letters and thought that paralleled the new energy in economic life, politics, and overseas enterprise. The ease of communication created by the printing press helped accelerate the exchange of ideas, for by 1500 there was at least one press in every city of any size along the Rhine River from Basel to Leiden.

The driving force behind Northern Humanism came to be a determination to probe early Christianity for the light it could throw on the origins of current religious belief. But this scholarly pursuit soon produced a conflict that arrayed humanist intellectuals against more traditional scholars.

At issue was the danger inherent in the study of Jewish writings. The protagonists were a bitter ex-Jew, Johannes Pfefferkorn, who considered Hebrew works pernicious and wanted them condemned, and Johann Reuchlin, a humanist and brilliant Herbraist, who advocated research that would illuminate the parent faith of Christianity. The controversy inspired scores of polemical pamphlets. The most famous, the *Letters of Obscure Men* (1515 and 1517), a stinging defense of Reuchlin that ridiculed his opponents, was the creation of a group of aggressive young humanists; one of them, Ulrich von Hutten, was to be among Luther's most ardent supporters. Thus Northern Humanism's broad examination of religious issues helped create the atmosphere in which Luther's much more serious criticisms could flourish.

This new direction was especially noticeable in the work of the leading French humanist of the period, Jacques Lefèvre d'Étaples, who was one of the most important biblical scholars of his day. In his commentary on St. Paul (1512), he applied the humanist principle of seeking the straightforward, clear meaning of the text and in this way built a powerful case for a return to the simple godliness of early Christianity and for the primacy of biblical authority. The revival of interest in the apostle St. Paul was a major step on the road to Reformation, and it is notable that a number of Lefèvre's comments on Paul anticipated Luther's pronouncements.

Christian Humanism, as modern scholars call the phase of the movement represented by men like Reuchlin and Lefèvre, retained an interest in classical authors and continued to utilize the methods of the Italian humanists—analysis of ancient texts, language, and style. But its purpose was different: to answer questions about the message of Jesus and the apostles so as to offer contemporaries a guide to true piety and morality. This was a deeply religious undertaking, and it dominated the writings of the most famous Christian humanists, one English and one Dutch.

THOMAS MORE AND ERASMUS

Sir Thomas More (1478–1535), a lawyer and statesman, was the central figure of English Humanism. His reputation as a writer rests primarily on a brief work, *Utopia*, published in Latin in 1516, which describes an ideal society on an imaginary island. In it More condemned war, poverty, religious intolerance, and other evils of his day and defined the general principles of morality that should underlie human society.

The first book of *Utopia* asks whether a man of learning should withdraw from the world to avoid temptation, or actively participate in affairs of state so as to guide his fellow men. The Italian civic humanists had established commitment to public responsibilities as an essential part of the humanist movement. More reopened the question from the standpoint of religious as well as ethical values and answered with a warning against evading public duties, even though rulers rarely heed the advice they are given.

The second and more famous book of *Utopia* describes the ideal commonwealth itself. In political and social organization, it is a carefully regulated, almost monastic community that has succeeded in abolishing private property—together with greed and pride—and has achieved true morality. The Utopians are non-Christian, and More implies that a society based on Christian principles can attain even greater good. Asceticism is his answer to the fall of man: weak human nature can be led to virtuousness only if severely curbed.

True to his prescriptions, More, though a layman, subjected himself to the strict discipline of a Carthusian monastery in his twenties, after which he entered public life as a member of Parliament in 1504. He rose high in government service, succeeding—against his will—to the lord chancellorship on Wolsey's fall in 1529. He gave his life for remaining loyal to the pope and refusing to recognize Henry VIII as head of the English Church. His last words revealed his unflinching adherence to the Christian principles he pursued throughout his life: "I die the King's good servant, but God's first."

The supreme representative of Christian Humanism was the Dutchman Desiderius Erasmus (1466?–1536). Erasmus early acquired a taste for ancient writers, and he determined to devote himself to classical studies.

For the greater part of his life, he wandered through Europe, writing, visiting friends, occasionally working for important patrons. He always retained his independence, however, for unlike More, his answer to the question of whether a scholar should enter public life was that he should avoid the compromises he would have to make in the service of a ruler.

Erasmus became so famous for his learning and his literary skills that he dominated the world of letters in Europe. Constantly consulted by scholars and admirers, he wrote magnificently composed letters that reflected every aspect of the culture of his times. The English humanists, particularly More, were among his closest friends, and it was during his first visit to England, in 1499, that his interests were turned away from purely literary matters toward the theological writings that became the main focus of his scholarship.

Erasmus' most famous book was *The Praise of Folly* (1509), inspired by the already popular *Ship of Fools*, but a subtler work with a deeper moral commitment. Some of it is gay, light-hearted banter that pokes fun at the author himself, his friends, and the follies of everyday life, suggesting that a little folly is essential to human existence. But in other passages Erasmus launched sharply satirical attacks against monks, the pope, meaningless ceremonies, and the many lapses from what he perceived to be the true Christian spirit.

At the heart of Erasmus' work was the message that he called the "philosophy of Christ." He believed that the life of Jesus himself and especially the teachings in the Sermon on the Mount should be the model for Christian piety and morality. For ceremonies and rigid discipline he had only censure: too often they served as substitutes for genuine spiritual concerns. People lit thousands of candles for Mary but cared little about the humility she is supposed to inspire, for they forgot that what counts is the spirit of religious devotion, not

the form. By simply following the precepts of Jesus, a Christian could lead a life guided by sincere faith. Because of his insistence on ethical behavior, Erasmus could admire a truly moral man even if he was a pagan. "I could almost say 'Pray for me, St. Socrates!'" he once wrote.

Erasmus believed that the Church had lost sight of its original mission. In the course of fifteen centuries, traditions and practices had developed that obscured the intentions of its founder, and the only way purity could be restored was by studying the Scriptures and the writings of the early Church fathers. Here the tools of the humanists became vitally important, because they enabled scholars to understand the meaning and intention of an ancient manuscript. Practicing what he preached, Erasmus spent ten years preparing a new edition of the Greek text of the New Testament so as to correct errors in the Latin Vulgate, which was the standard version, and revised it repeatedly for another twenty years.

But the calm, scholarly, and tolerant moderation Erasmus prized was soon left behind by events. The rising fanaticism of the reformers and their opponents destroyed the effort he had led to cure the ills of the Church from within. Despite its surface plausibility, the famous saying, "Erasmus laid the egg that Luther hatched," misses the fundamental difference between the two men: Erasmus, a classic nonrevolutionary, wanted a revival of purer faith, but within the traditional structure of the Church.

The final irony of Erasmus' career was that he inspired reformers in both camps and yet in the end was rejected by both. He was condemned by Catholics as heretical and by leaders of the Reformation as half-hearted. In an age of confrontation, it was impossible to keep a middle course, and Erasmus found himself swept aside by forces that he himself had helped build but that Luther unleashed.

III. THE LUTHERAN REFORMATION

That the first religious conflict should have erupted in the Holy Roman Empire is not surprising. Here popular piety had been noticeably strong, as evidenced by the waves of Rhineland mysticism and the lay religious movements. In addition the chief local authorities in many areas were ecclesiastical princes, usually aristocratic bishops such as the ruler of the important city of Cologne on the Rhine. As a result no strong intermediaries like the rulers of England, France, and Spain stood between the papacy and the people, and the popes regarded the empire as their surest source of revenue. This situation may help explain why a determined reformer, Martin Luther, won such swift and widespread support; but the reasons he made his stand must be sought in the personal development of a highly sensitive, energetic, and troubled man.

MARTIN LUTHER

Martin Luther (1483–1546) was born into a simple workingman's family in Saxony in central Germany. The household was dominated by the father, whose powerful presence some modern commentators have seen reflected in his son's vision of an omnipotent God. The boy received a good education and decided to become a lawyer, a profession that would have given him many opportunities for advancement. But in his early twenties, shortly after starting his legal studies, he had an experience that changed his life. Crossing a field during a thunderstorm, he was thrown to the ground by a bolt of lightning, and in his terror he cried to St. Anne, the mother of Mary, that he would enter a monastery.

Although the decision may well have been that sudden, it is clear that there was more to Luther's complete change of direction than this one incident, however traumatic. He was obviously a man obsessed with his own sinfulness, and he joined an Augustinian monastery in the hope that a penitential life would help him overcome his sense of guilt. Once in the order he pursued every possible opportunity to earn worthiness in the sight of God. He overlooked no possible discipline or act of contrition or self-denial, and for added merit he endured austerities such as self-flagellation that went far beyond normal requirements. To no avail: at his first mass after his ordination, in 1507, he was so terrified at the prospect of a sinner like himself transforming the wafer and wine into the body and blood of Christ that he almost failed to complete the ritual.

Fortunately for Luther his superiors took more notice of his intellectual gifts than of his self-doubts and in 1508 assigned him to the faculty of a new university in Wittenberg, the capital of Saxony. It was from his scholarship, which was superb, and especially from his study of the Bible, that he was able at last to draw comfort and spiritual peace.

A second episode that probably took place when he was in his mid-thirties marked another crucial turning point in Luther's life. Until "the experience in the tower," as it is usually called, he could see no way that he, a despicable mortal, could receive anything but the fiercest punishments from a God of absolute justice. Now, however, he suddenly understood that he had only to rely on God's mercy, a quality as great as his justice. He later described the experience in these words:

I greatly longed to understand Paul's Epistle to the Romans and nothing stood in the way but that one expression, "the justice of God," because I took it to mean that justice whereby God is just and deals justly in punishing the unjust. My situation was that, although an impeccable monk, I stood before God as a sinner troubled in conscience, and I had no confidence that my merit would assuage him. . . . Night and day I pondered until I saw the connection between the justice of God and the statement [Romans 1:17] that "The just shall live by his faith." Then I grasped that the justice of God is that righteousness by which through grace and sheer mercy God justifies us through faith. Thereupon I felt myself to be reborn and to have gone through open doors into paradise.[1]

The many advances in Luther's thinking thereafter came ultimately from this insight: that justification—expiation of sin and attainment of righteousness through a gift of grace—is achieved by faith alone.

The Indulgence Controversy

In 1517 an event occurred that was ultimately to lead Luther to an irrevocable break with the Church. In the spring a Dominican monk, Johann Tetzel, began to sell indulgences a few miles from Wittenberg as part of a huge fundraising effort to pay for the new Church of St. Peter in Rome. Originally an indulgence had been granted to a person who was unable to go on a crusade and who gave sufficient money to permit a poor crusader to reach the Holy Land. The indulgence itself released a sinner from a certain period of punishment in purgatory before going to heaven, and was justified doctrinally as a sort of credit that could be drawn from the treasury of merit built up by Jesus and the saints. But the doctrine had not been defined exactly, and clerics had been taking advantage of this vagueness to sell indulgences indiscriminately. Tetzel, an expert salesman, was offering complete releases from purgatory without bothering to mention the repentance demanded of everyone as the condition for forgiveness of sin.

The people of Wittenberg were soon flocking to Tetzel to buy this easy guarantee of salvation. For Luther, a man groping toward an evangelical solution of his own doubts, it was unforgivable that people should be deprived of their hard-earned money for spurious, worthless promises. On October 31, 1517, he nailed to the door of the university church in Wittenberg ninety-five theses, or statements, on indulgences that he offered to debate with experts in Christian doctrine.

This was no revolutionary document. It merely described what Luther believed to be correct teachings on indulgences: that the pope could remit only the penalties that he himself or canon law imposed, that therefore the promise of a general release was damnable, and that every true believer shared in the benefits of the Church whether or not he obtained letters of pardon. Within a few weeks the story was all over the empire that a monk had challenged the sale of indulgences. The proceeds of Tetzel's mission began to drop off, and the Dominicans, rallying to the defense of their brother, launched an attack against this presumptuous Augustinian.[2]

The controversy soon drew attention from Rome. At first Pope Leo X regarded the affair as merely a monks' quarrel. But in time Luther's responses to the Dominicans' attacks began to deviate radically from Church doctrine, and by 1520 he had gone so far as to challenge the authority of the papacy itself in three pamphlets outlining his fundamental position.

In *An Address to the Christian Nobility of the German Nation*, Luther made a frankly patriotic appeal to his countrymen to reject the foreign pope's authority. The Church, he said, consisted of all Christians, including laymen; hence the nobles were as much its governors as the clergy, and they had the responsibility to remedy its defects. Indeed, Emperor Charles V had an obligation to call a council to

---

[1] Quoted in Roland Bainton, *Here I Stand: A Life of Martin Luther* (1955), pp. 49–50.

[2] The Dominicans, long-time rivals of the Augustinians, were the traditional upholders of orthodoxy and prominent in the Inquisition. Luther liked to refer to them by using an old joke that split their Latin name into *Domini canes,* "dogs of the Lord."

end the abuses. *The Babylonian Captivity*, the most radical of the three works, attacked the system of the seven sacraments, the basis of the Church's power.[3] In *The Liberty of the Christian Man*, a less polemical work, Luther explained his doctrine of faith and justification, stressing that he did not reject good works but that only the faith of the individual believer could bring salvation from an all-powerful, just, and merciful God.

There could no longer be any doubt that Luther was embracing heresy, and in 1520 Leo X issued a bull excommunicating him. Luther publicly tossed the document into a bonfire, defending his action by calling the pope an Antichrist. In 1521 Charles V, theoretically the papacy's secular arm, responded by summoning the celebrated monk to offer his defense against the papal decree at a Diet of the Empire at Worms, a city on the Rhine. The journey across Germany was a triumphant procession for Luther, who had evoked widespread sympathy. Appearing before the magnificent assembly dressed in his monk's robe, he offered a striking contrast to the display of imperial and princely grandeur. First in German and then in Latin, he made the famous declaration that closed the last door behind him: "I cannot and will not recant anything, since it is unsafe and wrong to go against my conscience. Here I stand. I cannot do otherwise. God help me. Amen." On the following day the emperor gave his reply: "A single friar who goes counter to all Christianity for a thousand years must be wrong."

Charles added legality to the papal bull by issuing an imperial edict calling for Luther's

---

[3] The seven sacraments are baptism, confirmation, matrimony, the eucharist, ordination, penance, and extreme unction. Apart from some special exceptions, these ceremonies are considered by Catholics to require the attendance of a priest, because his presence (and hence the mediation of the Church) is believed to be essential to the proper administration of the sacrament.

In this broadside (see p. 438), a single sheet printed in thousands of copies and sold cheaply at fairs and stalls throughout Germany, Johann Tetzel is ridiculed for his greed. The poem describes him as a breaker of the faith who became a thief and was stopped only by the blessed Dr. Luther. The fifth and sixth lines of the second column quote the claim attributed to Tetzel: "As soon as the coin clinks in the box, the soul flies straight to heaven." (Photo: The Granger Collection)

arrest and the burning of his works. At this point, however, the independent power of the German princes and their resentment of foreign ecclesiastical interference came to the reformer's aid. Elector Frederick III of Saxony, who had never met Luther and who was never to break with the Catholic Church, nonetheless determined to protect the rebel who lived in his territory. He had him taken to the Wartburg castle, one of his strongholds, and here Luther remained for almost a year, safe from his enemies.

Lutheran Doctrine and Practice

While at the Wartburg Luther, together with his friend Philipp Melanchthon, developed the elements of Lutheranism and shaped them into the independent set of beliefs which formed the background for most of the subsequent variations of Protestant Christianity.

It is important to realize, however, that some of these positions had roots in the nominalist theology taught at Luther's old monastery. Two of the teachings in particular left a lasting impression on Luther and later reformers. First, in opposition to Aquinas and the thirteenth-century attempts to unite reason and faith, the nominalists stressed the primacy of faith, the inadequacy of reason, and the unknowableness of God. Second, as a natural corollary to his mystery, they emphasized the overwhelming power and majesty of God. Both of these beliefs were to reappear frequently in the reformers' writings. Their importance was hardly surprising, for Nominalism was by far the most influential philosophical and theological movement of the fourteenth and fifteenth centuries.

This influence is apparent in the two fundamental assertions that lay at the heart of Luther's teachings. First, faith alone—not good works, nor the receiving of the sacraments—justifies man, that is, makes him righteous in the eyes of God and wins him redemption. Man himself is a helpless and unworthy sinner who can do nothing to cooperate in his own salvation; God bestows faith on those he chooses to save. Second, the Bible is the sole source of religious authority. It alone carries the word of God, and Christians must reject all other supposed channels of divine inspiration: tradition, commentaries, or the pronouncements of popes and councils.

These two doctrines had important implications. According to Luther all men are equally capable of understanding God's word as expressed in the Bible and can gain salvation without the help of intermediaries; they do not need a priest endowed with special powers or an interceding church. Luther thus saw God's chosen faithful as a "priesthood of all believers," a concept totally foreign to Catholics, who insisted on the distinction between clergy and laity. The distinction disappeared in Luther's doctrines, because all the faithful now shared the responsibilities formerly reserved for the priests.

True to his reliance on biblical authority, Luther denied the efficacy of five of the Catholics' sacraments. Only baptism and the eucharist are mentioned in Scripture, therefore they alone can be the means by which God distributes grace. Moreover the ceremony of the eucharist was now called communion (literally "sharing") to emphasize that all worshipers, including the officiating clergyman, were equal. Confession was abolished, which reduced the priest's importance yet again, and the last sign of his distinctiveness was removed by allowing him the right to marry.

The new teachings on the sacraments transformed the mass, the ceremony that surrounds the eucharist, or Lord's Supper. According to Catholic dogma, when the priest raises the host during the mass and recites the words *Hoc est corpus meum* ("This is my body"), the sacrifice of Jesus on the cross is reenacted. The wafer and the wine retain their outward appearance, their "accidents," but their substance is transformed into the body and blood of Christ—in other words, transubstantiation takes place.

Luther asserted that the wafer and wine retain their substance as well as their accidents and undergo *con*substantiation at the moment the priest says "This is my body." The real presence of Christ and the natural substance *coexist* within the wafer and wine. Nothing suddenly happens, no miraculous moment occurs; the believer is simply made aware of the real presence of God, who is everywhere at all times. Again, it is the faith of the individual, not the ceremony itself, that counts.

Luther reduced the mystery of the Lord's Supper further by allowing the congregation to partake of the wine, which was reserved for the priest in the Catholic ceremony—a change that also undermined the position of the priest. The liturgy in general was simplified—by abolishing processions, incense, votive candles, and the like—to make it more approachable for ordinary people, and services were conducted in the vernacular.

Given the priest's reduced stature, it was vital to make God's word more readily accessible to all worshipers. To this end Luther began the gigantic task of translating the Bible. He was to complete the work in 1534, creating a text that is a milestone in the history of the German language. By then, however, his work of forming the new faith was done, for his doctrines had been put together systematically in the Augsburg Confession of 1530. Although he was to live until 1546, henceforth the progress of the revolution he had launched would rely on outside forces: its popular appeal and the actions of political leaders.

It is usually said that Lutheranism spread from above, advancing only when princes and rulers helped it along. Although this view has some basis, it does not adequately explain the growth of the movement. The response to Luther's stand was immediate and widespread. Even before the Diet of Worms, heretical preachers were drawing audiences in many parts of the Holy Roman Empire, and in 1521 there were waves of image smashing, reports of priests marrying, and efforts to reform and simplify the sacraments.

Soon men were conducting services according to Luther's teachings throughout the empire and in Sweden, Denmark, Poland, Prussia, and Hungary. Broadsides and pamphlets fresh from the printing presses spread the news of the reformer's message with breathtaking speed, stimulating an immediate response from thousands who saw the opportunity to renew their faith.

As long as his own doctrines were adhered to, Luther was naturally delighted to see his teachings spread. But from the start people were drawing inferences that he could not tolerate. Early in 1522 for example three men from the nearby town of Zwickau appeared in Wittenberg claiming to be prophets who enjoyed direct communication with God. Their ideas were both radical and, in Luther's eyes, damnable. When he returned from the Wartburg, therefore, he preached eight sermons to expose their errors—a futile effort, because the reform movement was now too dispersed to control. Capitalizing on mass discontent, radical preachers incited disturbances in the name of faith, and it was only a matter of time before social as well as religious protest exploded.

DISORDERS IN THE NAME OF RELIGION

The first trouble came in the summer of 1522, when fighting broke out between a number of princes of the empire and a group of imperial knights. The knights occupied a precarious position in the social hierarchy. Usually their holdings consisted of little more than a single castle, but they owed official allegiance to no one but the emperor himself, and inevitably they came to resent the growing power of cities and territorial rulers.

Posing as the true representatives of the imperial system—that is, as loyal supporters of the emperor's authority in contrast to the cities and princes, who wanted to be independent—

and pointing to Lutheranism as further justification, the knights launched an attack on one of the leading ecclesiastical rulers, the archbishop of Trier. The onslaught was crushed within a year, but it was now easy for the Lutherans' opponents to suggest that the new religious teachings undermined law and order.

The banner of the new faith rose over popular revolts as well. A peasant uprising began in Swabia in 1524 and quickly engulfed the southern and central parts of the empire. Citing Luther's inspiration, the peasants published a list of twelve demands the next year. However, ten of their grievances concerned social, not religious, injustices: they wanted an end to serfdom, tithes, and the restrictions and burdens imposed by their overlords, including prohibitions on hunting and fishing, excessive rents and services, and unlawful punishments. In religious matters they demanded the right to choose their own pastors and insisted that only Scripture could determine the justice of their cause.

Luther sympathized with the last two claims, and at first he considered the peasants' demands reasonable. But when it became apparent that they were spreading anarchy through the empire—burning, looting, and murdering as they went—he wrote a vicious pamphlet, *Against the Rapacious and Murdering Peasants*, calling on the nobility to cut them down without mercy so as to restore peace. A few months later the rebels were defeated in battle, and thereafter Luther threw his support unreservedly on the side of the princes and the established political and social order.

This is not to say that there was never again popular support for Lutheranism; the advance of the movement, particularly in northern Germany and Scandinavia, still depended on its appeal to the ordinary believer. Nonetheless, after the mid-1520s popular enthusiasm alone would not have sufficed; Lutheranism could not have stood up to the Catholic opposition had it not been defended by powerful princes in the empire and the kings of Denmark and Sweden.

One of the reasons the new set of beliefs could attract a number of princes was its conservatism. As long as a person accepted the doctrines of justification by faith alone and Scripture as the sole authority, he could be accepted as a Lutheran. Consequently the new congregations could retain much from the old religion: most of the liturgy, the sacred music, and, particularly important, a territorial church that, though less hierarchic, was still organized so as to provide order and authority.

Some rulers were swept up by the emotions that moved their subjects, but others were moved by more material interests. Since ecclesiastical property was abolished when reform was introduced, princes could confiscate the rich and extensive holdings of monasteries and churches in their domains. Furthermore, they now had added reason for flaunting their independence from Emperor Charles V, an unwavering upholder of orthodoxy. It was risky to adopt this policy, for Charles could strip a prince of his title. On the other side, a prince loyal to Catholicism could blackmail the pope into offering him almost as many riches as he could win by confiscation. Nevertheless, the appeal of the new faith eventually tipped the balance for enough princes to create a formidable party capable of resisting Charles' power. Gathered together at the imperial Diet of Speyer in 1529, they signed a declaration "protesting" the Diet's decree that no further religious innovations were to be introduced in the empire, and thereafter they were known as Protestants. The following year, at another imperial Diet, the Lutheran princes announced their support of the Augsburg Confession, a statement of the doctrines of the reformed faith drawn up by Melanchthon and approved by Luther; it is still the official creed of the Lutheran Church. Charles V now realized that military force would be needed to crush the heresy, and in the face of this threat, the Lutherans formed a defensive league in 1531 at the small Saxon town of Schmalkalden. Throughout the 1530s this alliance grew in strength, consolidated Protestant gains, brought new princes into the cause, and in general amassed sufficient strength to deter Charles from immediate action.

The reform party became so solidly established that it negotiated with the pope—on equal terms—about the possibility of reconciliation, but the talks collapsed, and the chances for a reunification of Christendom evaporated. Yet not until 1546, the year of Luther's death, was battle finally joined. Then, in a brief war, Charles won a crushing victory. But matters had advanced too far for the entire movement to collapse merely because of a single defeat on the battlefield. The new faith had gained acceptance among a large part of the German people, particularly in the north and the east, farthest away from the center of imperial power. Some of the great cities of the south, such as Nuremberg, which had been centers of Humanism, had also come over to the Lutheran side. By the 1550s Lutheranism had captured perhaps half the population of the Empire.

The Catholic princes also played a part in assuring the survival of the new faith. Fearful of Charles V's new power, they refused to cooperate in his attempt to establish his authority throughout the empire, and he had to rely on Spanish troops, who further alienated him from his subjects. The Protestants rallied, and in 1555 the imperial Diet at Augsburg drew up a compromise settlement that exposed the decline of the emperor's power. Henceforth each ruler was allowed to determine the religion of his territory, Lutheran or Catholic, without outside interference. Religious uniformity was at an end, and the future of Lutheranism was secure.

The influence that this first Protestant Church was to exert on all of European life was immense. The equality of believers in the eyes of God was to inspire revolutionary changes in thought and society: the appearance of antimonarchical constitutional theories, the acceptance of economic life as worthy, and the undermining of the hierarchic view of the universe. But the most immediate effect of the new faith was on religious life itself: before the century was out, the dissent led by Luther had given birth to a multitude of sects and a ferment of ideas without precedent in the history of Europe.

IV. THE GROWTH OF PROTESTANTISM

Hardly had Luther made his stand in 1517 when heresy in many different forms suddenly appeared. It was as if no more was needed than one opening shot before a volley of discontent broke out—a testimony to the deep and widespread striving for individual piety of the times. The Peasants' War, in particular, gave scores of fiery preachers the opportunity to gain a wide hearing, and their teachings were much more radical than Luther's. As new ideas proliferated, it seemed that the fragmentation of the reform movement might lead to chaotic disunity. But the work of John Calvin gave the Reformation the organization that its further advance required.

ZWINGLI

Less than two years after Luther posted his ninety-five theses, another reformer defied the Church in the Swiss city of Zurich: Ulrich Zwingli (1484–1531). A priest, a learned humanist, and a disciple of Erasmus, Zwingli began to develop a system of doctrine between 1519 and 1522 that was quite similar to Luther's. Like the Saxon reformer, he based his ideas entirely on Scripture, excluding all non-biblical authorities. He rejected the role of the Church as mediator between the believer and God, the celibacy of the clergy, and the belief in purgatory after death. However, Zwingli was less concerned than Luther to demonstrate man's inadequacy. Instead he sought chiefly to simplify religious belief and practice, freeing them from complexity and ceremony. To this end he asserted that none of the sacraments were channels of grace; they were merely signs of grace already given. Baptism does not regenerate the recipient, and communion is no more than a memorial and thanksgiving for the grace bestowed by God, who is present only in spirit—not in actuality, as Luther believed.

Despite his obvious debt to Luther, Zwingli's divergences were significant. When he met Luther in 1529, hoping to iron out differences in order to present a united front, their inability to agree on a doctrine of communion kept them apart. Zwingli had founded a new form of Protestantism, more thoroughly dependent on the individual believer and more devoid of mystery and ritual than anything Luther could accept.

Taking a line of argument closer to Sir Thomas More's than Luther's, Zwingli held that man is innately good but needs constant correction to lead a godly life. Since he recognized no distinction between secular and religious authority, he established a tribunal of clergymen and magistrates to enforce discipline among the faithful. It supervised all moral questions, from compulsory church attendance to the public behavior of amorous couples. The court could excommunicate flagrant transgressors, and it maintained constant surveillance—through a network of informers—to keep the faithful on paths of godliness.

Because Zwingli considered it vital for discipline that the faithful should receive a continuing education, he also founded a theological school and authorized a new transla-tion of the Bible. He revealed a similar intent when he established the practice of lengthy sermons at each service. Worship was stripped bare, as were the churches, and preaching began to assume tremendous importance as a means of instructing the believer and strengthening his faith. Zwingli also revived the ancient Christian practice of public confession—yet another reinforcement of discipline.

Zwingli's ideas spread rapidly in the Swiss Confederation, helped by the virtual autonomy each canton enjoyed. By 1529 six cantons had accepted Zwinglianism. As a result two camps formed in the country, and a war broke out in 1531 in which Zwingli himself was killed. Thereafter Switzerland remained split between Catholics and reformers. Zwinglianism as such never grew into a major religion, but it had a considerable effect on subsequent Protestantism, particularly Calvinism.

THE RADICALS

Both Luther and Zwingli wanted to retain a territorial church, and therefore insisted that infant baptism was the moment of entry into the church, even though this had no biblical sanction. Some radical reformers, however, extending Luther's logic, believed that as in biblical times baptism should be administered only to mature adults who could make a conscious choice for Christ, not to infants who were incapable of understanding that they were receiving grace. Soon they were contemptuously called Anabaptists ("rebaptizers") by their enemies. The term is often used to describe all radicals, though in fact it applied only to one conspicuous group.

Diversity was inevitable among these extremists, who refused to recognize church organization, rejected priests, and gave individual belief free rein, sometimes to the point of recognizing only personal communication with God and disregarding Scripture. Many groups of like-minded radicals formed sects—

voluntary associations of adult believers (rarely more than a hundred or so)—in an effort to achieve complete separation from the world and avoid compromising their ideals. They wanted to set an example for others by adhering fervently to the truth as they saw it, regardless of the consequences.

Some sects established little utopian communities, holding everything in common, including property and wives. Others, direct descendants of the mystics, disdained all worldly things and lived only for the supreme ecstasy of a trance in which they made direct contact with God himself. Many, believing in the imminent coming of the Messiah, prepared themselves for the Day of Judgment and warned their fellow men of the approaching Armageddon.

Such divergence in the name of a personal search for God was intolerable to Luther, Zwingli, and later to Calvin, each of whom believed that his doctrines were the only means of salvation. Once the major branches of Protestantism were firmly entrenched, they became as deeply committed as the Catholic Church to the status quo and to their hierarchies and traditions. The established reformers thus regarded the radicals' refusal to conform as an unmistakable sign of damnation; Heinrich Bullinger, Zwingli's successor, put it bluntly when he wrote that individual interpretation of the Bible allowed each man to carve his own path to hell. Indeed, Lutherans, Zwinglians, and Calvinists alike saw it as their duty to persecute these people who refused salvation.

The assault began in the mid-1520s and soon spread through most of Europe. The imperial Diet in 1529 called for the death penalty against all Anabaptists, and most members of a group of more than thirty Anabaptist leaders who met to discuss their ideas in 1533 eventually met a violent death. Finally, in the Rhine city of Münster, a particularly fiery sect known as the Melchiorites provoked a reaction that signaled doom even for the more moderate dissenters.

The Melchiorites had managed to gain considerable influence over both the ordinary workers of Münster and the craft guilds. Early in 1534 they gained political control of the city and began to establish their "heavenly Jerusalem" on earth. They burned all books except the Bible, abolished private property, introduced polygamy, and in an atmosphere of abandon and chaos dug in to await the coming of the Messiah.

Here was a sufficient threat to society to force Protestants and Catholics into an alliance, and they captured the city and brutally massacred the Melchiorites. Thereafter the radicals were savagely persecuted throughout the empire. To survive, many fled first to Poland, then to the Low Countries and England, and eventually to the New World.

JOHN CALVIN AND HIS CHURCH

The one systematizing force among the varied Protestant movements in the 1530s was the creation of a second-generation reformer, John Calvin (1509–1564). Born in Noyon, a small town in northern France, he studied both law and the humanities at the University of Paris. In his early twenties he apparently had a blinding spiritual experience that he later called his "sudden conversion," an event about which he would say almost nothing else. Yet from that moment on all his energy was devoted to religious activity.

In November 1533 Calvin was indicted for heresy, and after more than a year in hiding, he took refuge in the Swiss city of Basel. There in 1536 he published a little treatise, *Institutes of the Christian Religion*, outlining the principles of a new system of belief. He would revise and expand the *Institutes* for the remainder of his life, and it was to become the basis of the most vigorous branch of Protestantism in the sixteenth century.

This contemporary caricature of John Calvin mocks the subhuman character of the stern religious leader. (Photo: Gripsholm Castle, Sweden)

Later in 1536 Calvin settled in Geneva, where, except for a brief period, he was to remain until his death. The citizens of this prosperous market center had just overthrown their prince, a bishop. In achieving their independence they had allied with other Swiss cities—notably Bern, a recent convert to Zwinglianism. Rebels who had just freed themselves with the help of heretics from an ecclesiastical overlord would obviously be receptive to new religious teachings.

Outwardly Calvinism seemed to have much in common with Lutheranism. Both emphasized man's sinfulness, lack of free will, and helplessness; both rejected good works as a means of salvation; both accepted only two sacraments, baptism and communion; both regarded all positions in life as equally worthy in the sight of God; both strongly upheld established political and social authority; and both leaned heavily on St. Paul and St. Augustine

in their views of faith, man's weakness, and God's omnipotence. But the emphases in Calvinism were very different.

Luther's belief in justification by faith alone assumed that God can predestine a man to be saved but rejected the idea that damnation can also be preordained. Calvin's faith was much sterner, however, for it recognized no such distinction: if a man is damned, he should praise God's justice because his sins certainly merit such a judgment; if a man is saved, he should praise God's mercy because his salvation is not a result of his own good deeds. Either way the outcome is predestined, and nothing can be done to affect his fate. It is up to God alone to justify a person; he then perseveres in his mercy despite the person's sins; and finally he decides whether to receive the sinner into the small band of saints, or elect, whom he wishes to save. Calvin's was a grim but powerful answer to the age-old Christian question: How can sinful human beings gain salvation?

Calvin believed that the life a man leads on earth is no indication of his fate. He did suggest that someone who has been justified by God is likely to be upright and moral, but such behavior is not necessarily a sign of salvation. However, because man has to try to please God at all times, he should make every effort to lead the kind of life that will be worthy of one of the elect.

Calvin therefore developed a strict moral code for the true believer that banned frivolous activities like dancing in favor of constant self-examination, austerity, and sober study of the Bible. To help the faithful observe such regulation, he reestablished public confessions, as Zwingli had, and required daily preaching. He made services starkly simple: stripped of ornaments, they concentrated on uplifting sermons and the celebration of communion. His doctrine of communion occupied a middle ground between Luther's and Zwingli's. He rejected Zwingli's interpretation, saying instead that Christ's body and blood were actually and not just symbolically present. But unlike Luther, he held that they were present only in spirit and were consumed only spiritually, by faith.

In order to supervise the morals of the faithful more closely, Calvin gave his church a strict hierarchical structure. It was controlled by deacons and lay elders, who could function even in the hostile territories where many Calvinists found themselves. A body of lay elders called the consistory served as the chief ecclesiastical authority. They enforced discipline and had the power of excommunication, though they always worked together with the secular magistrates, who imposed the actual punishments for failures in religious duties.

Calvin's genius produced a cohesiveness and organization achieved by no other Protestant church. The *Institutes* spelled out every point of faith and practice in detail—an enormous advantage for his followers at a time when new religious doctrines were still fluid. A believer's duties and obligations were absolutely clear, as was his position in the very carefully organized hierarchy of the church. In France for example there was a cell in each town, a local synod (or council) in each area, a provincial synod in each province, and a national synod at the top of the pyramid. Tight discipline controlled the entire system, with the result that Calvinists felt themselves to be setting an example that all the world would eventually have to follow. They were part of a very privileged group, not necessarily the elect but at least possessors of the true faith. Like the children of Israel, they had a mission to live out God's word on earth, and their sense of destiny was to be one of Calvinism's greatest strengths.

Preachers from Geneva traveled through Europe to win adherents and organize the faithful wherever they could. In 1559 the city opened a university for the purpose of training them, because Calvin regarded education

as an essential means of instilling faith. Moreover, soon after the elector of the Palatinate converted to Calvinism in 1556, he turned the great university in his lands, Heidelberg, into a similar training center. From Geneva flowed a stream of pamphlets and books, which strengthened the faith of all believers and made sure that none who wished to learn would lack the opportunity.

By 1564, when Calvin died, his church was well established: more than a million adherents

The disillusionment resulting from religious conflict is reflected in this French engraving of 1600, which shows the disputes among the Pope, Calvin, and Luther, depicted as three old men pulling each other's hair, oblivious to the crucifixion and martyrdom of St. Sebastian behind them. (Photo: Giraudon)

CALVIN · LE PAPE · LUTHER

in France, where they were called Huguenots; the Palatinate converted; Scotland won; and considerable groups of followers in England, the Low Countries, and Hungary. Despite its severity Calvin's coherent and comprehensive body of doctrine proved to have wide and powerful appeal in an age of piety that yearned for clear answers.

V. THE CATHOLIC REVIVAL

Those with Protestant sympathies usually refer to the Catholic revival that started in the 1530s as the Counter Reformation, implying that action came only as a result of criticisms by Luther and others. Catholic historians call it the Catholic Reformation, implying that the movement began within the Church and was not merely a reaction to Protestantism. There is justification for both views. Certainly the papacy was aware of its loss of control over millions of Christians, but a great deal of the effort to put the Catholic Church's house in order came from men of deep faith who were determined to purify their institution for its own sake. This internal purification can quite properly be called the Catholic Reformation.

CRISIS AND REFORM IN THE CHURCH

There could be no doubt that a revival within the Catholic Church was badly needed. The first half of the sixteenth century was the lowest point in its history, and by the 1560s few observers could have expected it ever to recover. Much of Europe had been lost and even in areas still loyal the papacy was able to exercise little control. The French Church for example had a well-established tradition of autonomy, typified by the concordat of 1516, which had given Francis I and his successors the right to make ecclesiastical appointments. In Spain, too, the monarchy retained its independence and even had its own Inquisition. In the Holy Roman Empire, those states that had rejected Protestantism gave the pope no more than token allegiance.

Moreover there was still no comprehensive definition of Catholic doctrine on justification, salvation, and the sacraments. Worse yet, the Church's leadership was far from effective. Although one pope, Leo X, had attempted to correct notorious abuses such as simony in the early sixteenth century, the Vatican simply did not have the spiritual authority to make reform a vital force in the Catholic Church.

The situation changed with the pope elected in 1534: Paul III, a man not renowned for saintliness himself, but a genius at making the right decisions for the Church. By the end of his reign, in 1549, the Catholic revival was well under way.

The heart of Paul's strategy was his determination to assert papal responsibility throughout the church. Realizing that uncertainties in Catholic doctrine could be resolved only by a reexamination of traditional theology, he decided within a few months of taking office to call a church council for that purpose, despite the danger of rekindling the conciliar movement. It took ten years to overcome resistance to the idea, but in the meantime Paul relentlessly attacked abuses throughout the church, disregarding both vested interests and tradition. He aimed his campaign at all levels of the hierarchy, undeterred by powerful bishops and cardinals long used to a lax and corrupt regime. And he also founded a Roman Inquisition to destroy heresy throughout society.

Paul realized that in the long run the revival of Catholicism would depend on whether his successors maintained the effort. Within a few years therefore he made a series of appointments to the College of Cardinals, which elected the popes, that transformed it into possibly the most illustrious group that has ever held that honor at one time. Many were famous for their piety, others for their learning.

They came from all over Europe, united by their devotion to the church and their resolve to see it once again command the admiration and reverence it deserved. The result of this far-sighted policy was to be a succession of popes through the early seventeenth century who would fully restore the atmosphere of spirituality and morality that had long been missing from the papacy.

THE COUNCIL OF TRENT

The ecumenical, or general, council that Pope Paul finally succeeded in opening met at Trent, a northern Italian city, in 1545, and met irregularly until the delegates managed to complete their work in 1563. The council's history was one of stormy battles between various national factions. The non-Italians pressed for decentralization; the Italians, closely tied to the papacy, advocated a consolidation of power. Because the Italians were a large majority of the delegates, time after time the authority of the pope's office was confirmed and reinforced. The threat of a revival of conciliarism thus never materialized.

In keeping with Paul's instructions, the Council of Trent gave most of its time to the basic issue of doctrine, devoting little attention to the problem of reform. Almost all its decisions drew on the interpretations put forward by Thomas Aquinas, who now became the central theologian of the Catholic Church. Significantly the one major subject left unsettled was a definition of the extent of papal authority on matters of faith and morals.[4]

Trent's most important decrees affirmed the truth of precisely those teachings the Protestants had rejected. Catholicism from then on would be committed primarily to the outward, sacramental heritage of Christianity. In this view the Bible is not the exclusive authority—tradition also holds a place in establishing the true faith. Man's will is free; good works as well as faith are means of salvation; all seven sacraments are channels of grace; and Christ's sacrifice is reenacted in every mass. The Council of Trent endorsed the special position of the priest and insisted that God be worshiped with appropriately elaborate ceremonies and rites.

These were the principal decisions at Trent, but hundreds of minor matters also had to be settled. Thus for the first time the priest's presence was declared to be essential at the sacrament of marriage, a further reinforcement of his importance. The Vulgate, the Latin translation of the Bible prepared chiefly by St. Jerome, was decreed to be a holy text, which rebutted humanists and other scholars who had declared the Greek and Hebrew versions superior. And in direct contrast to the Protestants, gorgeous ritual was heavily stressed, which encouraged artists to beautify church buildings and ceremonies.

What the council was doing was adjusting the church to the world—an aim shared by Vatican II in the 1960s. Many ordinary people, troubled by the stern self-denial and predestination taught by most Protestant churches and sects, were delighted to embrace the traditional faith, now infused with new vigor, for the council had not hesitated to deal with morality and discipline as thoroughly as with belief. In fact, it had given its approval to the Inquisition and the "Index of Forbidden Books," which informed all Catholics of works with heretical content that they were not allowed to read.[5]

---

[4] Not until 1870, at the council known as Vatican I, was this matter settled by the assertion of the dogma of papal infallibility.

[5] The Index became a major weapon, used particularly effectively against borderline cases such as Erasmus. Later distinguished entries in the list included Michel de Montaigne, René Descartes, and Edward Gibbon. In the twentieth century, though, considerable relaxation has been allowed.

The Aftermath of Trent

The new atmosphere of spiritual dedication swept through the Catholic Church, inspiring thinkers and artists throughout Europe to lend their talents to the cause. In many ways Baroque art was to be the genre of the Counter Reformation: painters, architects, and musicians caught up by the new moral fervor in Catholicism expressed their faith in brilliant and dramatic portrayals of religious subjects and in churches that were designed to dazzle the observer in a way that most Protestants could not allow.

This outpouring was of course far more than a reflection of the decisions of a few hundred prelates assembled in a council. It was also one of many indicators of the new vigor of Catholicism. Spain experienced a great flowering of mysticism. In France the new generation of church leaders who appeared in the late sixteenth century were distinguished for their piety, learning, and observance of their duties. In Italy a similar group of talented theologians and religious writers gathered around the revitalized papal court. The inheritors of the traditional scholastic philosophy multiplied, and in the late sixteenth and early seventeenth centuries they were to become influential throughout Europe, particularly in the Holy Roman Empire, Italy, and Spain.

The most conspicuous examples of this new energy, however, were the popes themselves. Paul III's successors used their personal authority and pontifical resources not to adorn their palaces but to continue the enormous cleansing operation within the church and to lead the counterattack against Protestantism. If a king or prince refused to help, they would try to persuade one of his leading subjects to organize the struggle (for example, the Guise family in France or the dukes of Bavaria in the empire). Their diplomats and agents were everywhere, ceaselessly urging the faithful to stamp out Protestantism wherever it was found. And the pontiffs insisted on strict morality in order to set the best possible example: one pope even ordered clothes painted on the nudes in Michelangelo's *Day of Judgment* in the Sistine Chapel.

With the leaders of the church thus bent on reform, the restoration of the faith and the reconquest of lost souls could proceed with maximum effect. And they had at their disposal an order established by Ignatius Loyola in 1540 specifically for these purposes: the Society of Jesus.

IGNATIUS LOYOLA: THE MAKING OF A REFORMER

The third of the great religious innovators of the sixteenth century, after Luther and Calvin, was Ignatius Loyola (1491–1556), but unlike his predecessors he sought to reform the Catholic Church from within.

Loyola was the son of a Basque nobleman, raised in the chivalric and fiercely religious atmosphere of Spain, and he was often at the court of Ferdinand of Aragon. In his teens he entered the army, but when he was thirty a serious wound ended his career. While convalescing he was deeply impressed by a number of popular lives of the saints he read, and soon his religious interests began to take shape in chivalric and military terms. He visualized Mary as his lady, the inspiration of a Christian quest in which the forces of God and the devil fought in mighty battle. This was a faith seen from the perspective of the knight, and though the direct parallel lessened as his thought developed, it left an unmistakable stamp on all his future work.

In 1522 Loyola gave up his knightly garb and swore to become a pilgrim. He retired to a monastery for ten months to absolve himself of the guilt of a sinful life and to prepare spiritually for a journey to the Holy Land. At the monastery he had a momentous experience that, like Luther's and Calvin's, dominated the rest of his life. According to tradition it was a vision lasting eight days, during which he first saw in detail the outline of a book, the *Spiritual Exercises*, and a new religious order, the Society of Jesus.

The first version of the *Spiritual Exercises* certainly dated from this time, but like Calvin's *Institutes*, it was to be revised thoroughly many times. The book deals not with doctrines or theology but with the discipline and training necessary for a God-fearing life. The believer must undertake four weeks of contemplation and self-examination, culminating in a feeling of union with God in which he surrenders his mind and his will to Christ. If successful, he is then ready to submit completely to the call of God and the church and to pursue the commands he receives without question.

The manual was the heart of the organization of the Society of Jesus, and it gave those who followed its precepts a dedication and determination that made them seem like the Church's answer to the Calvinists. But while the end might be similar to Luther's and Calvin's—the personal attainment of grace—the method, the emphasis on individual effort and concentration, could not have been more different. For the *Spiritual Exercises* prepared a man's inward condition for grace through a tremendous act of will, and its severity relied on the belief that the will is free and that good works are efficacious.

During the sixteen years after he left the monastery Ignatius led a life of poverty and study. He traveled to Jerusalem and back barefoot in 1523–1524, and two years later he found his way to the University of Alcalá, where he attracted his first disciples, three fellow students. Suspected by the Inquisition, the little band walked to Paris, where they were joined by six more disciples. Ignatius now decided to return to the Holy Land, but the companions found themselves unable to travel beyond Venice because of war. Instead they preached in the streets, visited the poor and

the sick, urged all who would listen to rededicate themselves to piety and faith, and in 1537 achieved ordination as priests. Their activities were beginning to take definite shape, and so they decided to seek the pope's blessing for their work. They saw Paul III in 1538, and two years later, despite opposition and suspicion at the Vatican, the pope gave his approval to a plan Ignatius had drawn up for a new religious order that would owe allegiance only to the papacy.

The Jesuits

The Society, or Company, of Jesus had four principal functions: preaching, hearing confessions, teaching, and founding and maintaining missions. The first two were the Jesuits' means of strengthening the beliefs of individual Catholics or converting heretics. The third became one of their most effective weapons. Loyola, much influenced by the Christian humanists he had encountered, was convinced of the tremendous power of education. The Jesuits therefore set about organizing the best schools in Europe, an endeavor in which they succeeded so well that some Protestants sent their children to the Society's schools despite the certainty that the pupils would become committed Catholics. The instructors followed humanist principles and taught the latest ideas, including for a while the most recent advances in science. The Jesuits' final activity, missionary work, brought them their most spectacular successes among both non-Christians and Protestants.

A number of qualities combined to make the Jesuits extraordinarily effective in winning converts and turning Catholics into militant activists. First, they had a remarkable knowledge of Scripture and traditional teachings and were usually more than a match for any serious opponent. In addition they were carefully selected and received a superb training that fashioned them into brilliant preachers and excellent educators. Their discipline, de-

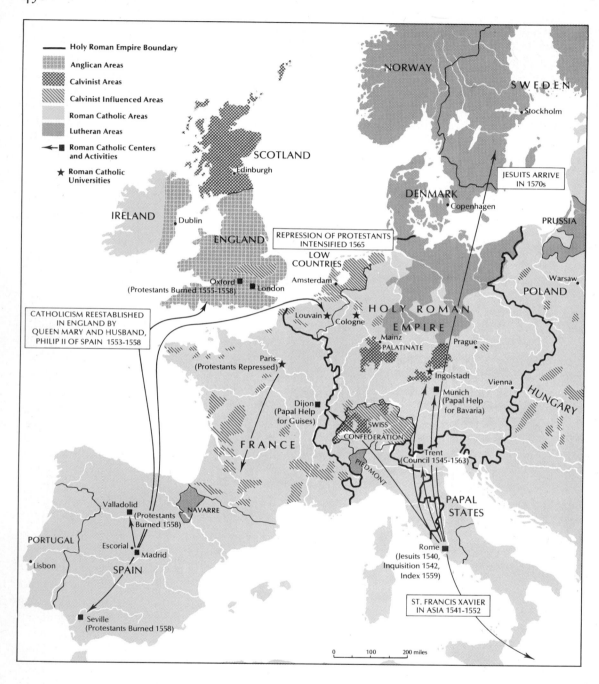

Legend:

Holy Roman Empire Boundary

Anglican Areas

Calvinist Areas

Calvinist Influenced Areas

Roman Catholic Areas

Lutheran Areas

Roman Catholic Centers and Activities

★ Roman Catholic Universities

JESUITS ARRIVE IN 1570s

REPRESSION OF PROTESTANTS INTENSIFIED 1565

CATHOLICISM REESTABLISHED IN ENGLAND BY QUEEN MARY AND HUSBAND, PHILIP II OF SPAIN 1553-1558

NORWAY

SWEDEN

Stockholm

DENMARK

Copenhagen

PRUSSIA

SCOTLAND

Edinburgh

IRELAND

Dublin

ENGLAND

LOW COUNTRIES

Amsterdam

Warsaw

POLAND

Oxford • London

(Protestants Burned 1555-1558)

Louvain ★ ★ Cologne

HOLY ROMAN

EMPIRE

Mainz

PALATINATE

Prague

Paris (Protestants Repressed) ★

Ingolstadt ★

Vienna

HUNGARY

Dijon (Papal Help for Guises)

Munich (Papal Help for Bavaria)

FRANCE

SWISS CONFEDERATION

Trent (Council 1545-1563)

Valladolid

(Protestants Burned 1558)

NAVARRE

PIEDMONT

PAPAL STATES

PORTUGAL

Escorial • ■ Madrid

Lisbon

SPAIN

Rome (Jesuits 1540, Inquisition 1542, Index 1559)

Seville (Protestants Burned 1558)

ST. FRANCIS XAVIER IN ASIA 1541-1552

0   100   200 miles

MAP 14.1: RELIGIOUS TENSIONS 1560

termination, and their awareness of the contemporary world allowed them to make clever use of their fearsome reputation, whose darker side—they were accused of the most sinister conspiracies—had little foundation in fact. But of their successes there could be no doubt; they had no equal in the forcefulness with which they advanced the aims of the Council of Trent and the papacy.

It is not inappropriate to regard the Jesuits as the striking arm of the Counter Reformation; indeed, their organization was to some extent modeled on the medieval military orders. A Jesuit at a royal court was often the chief inspiration for a ruler's militant support of the faith, and in many areas the Society was the main conqueror of heresy. Yet it must be noted that in this age of cruel persecution, the Jesuits always opposed execution for heresy; they far preferred to win a convert than to kill a man. Their presence was soon felt all over the world—as early as the 1540s, one of Loyola's first disciples, Francis Xavier, was conducting a mission to Japan. Despite many enmities (some of them richly deserved), their unswerving devotion to Catholicism was a major reason for the revival of the Roman Church.

One of the saddest spectacles in history is the diversion of the wish for a purer, simpler religion, freed from abuses and material concerns, into fanaticism and bloodletting in the late sixteenth century. What had started as a desire to improve religious practice and belief within existing institutions soon became, in Luther's hands, a determination to start anew. Inevitably the ideas of those who broke with Rome became increasingly radical, and when they received the organization provided by Calvin, they had extraordinary success in winning new adherents.

Within the Catholic Church, meanwhile, a reform movement begun by Pope Paul III in the 1530s raised that institution's moral stature and gave it the organization and aggressive force to meet its opponents on equal terms. Spearheaded by the Jesuits, Catholic reformers made many gains and ensured that Protestantism would not engulf the Continent.

But it was not enough for either side to remedy religious deficiencies and abuses. Each had to launch a fanatical and unrelenting attack on the enemy religion. In this atmosphere of hatred and violence, voices of moderation such as Erasmus' were ignored, and pleas for toleration went unheard. For there was a rare ferocity to the conflicts that now racked European civilization.

As the religious upheavals multiplied, the sources of hostility broadened, and revolutionary thought and action erupted on many other planes of society. Subjects challenged their governments; writers and artists expressed deep discontents. Lacerated by vicious warfare, Europe entered one of its most tormented centuries.

RECOMMENDED READING

Sources

* Calvin, John. *On God and Political Duty.* J. T. McNeill (ed.). 1950.
    * ————. *On the Christian Faith.* J. T. McNeill (ed.). 1957.
* Erasmus, Desiderius. *Essential Works of Erasmus.* W. T. H. Jackson (ed.). 1965.
* Loyola, Ignatius. *The Spiritual Exercises of St. Ignatius.* R. W. Gleason (ed.). 1964.
* Luther, Martin. *Martin Luther: Selections from his Writings.* John Dillenberger (ed.). 1961.

Studies

* Bainton, Roland H. *Here I Stand: A Life of Martin Luther.* 1955. The standard biography in English, with many quotations from Luther's writings.
* Cohn, Norman. *The Pursuit of the Millennium: Revolutionary Messianism in Medieval and Reformation Europe and its Bearing on Modern Totalitarian Movements.* 1961. A study of radical and extreme religious movements which indicates the kind of popular piety that existed in Europe during the medieval and Reformation periods.
* Davis, Natalie Zemon. *Society and Culture in Early Modern France.* 1975. A collection of essays about popular beliefs and attitudes, particularly on religious matters, during the sixteenth century.
* Dickens, A. G. *The Counter Reformation.* 1969. A clear and thorough introduction to the subject, handsomely illustrated.
* Elton, Geoffrey (ed.). *The New Cambridge Modern History.* Vol. II: *The Reformation, 1520–1559.* 1965. The most detailed and thorough survey of European history during this period.
* Fülop-Miller, René. *Jesuits: A History of the Society of Jesus.* 1963. The only account in English of the full history of the order.

Hexter, J. H. *More's Utopia: The Biography of an Idea.* 1965. A fascinating study of the way the book developed in More's mind, and the problems he was trying to solve.
* Huizinga, Johan. *Erasmus and the Age of Reformation.* 1957. A warm and sympathetic biography, beautifully written.
Koenigsberger, H. G., and G. L. Mosse. *Europe in the Sixteenth Century.* 1968. The best overall introduction to the period—compact, well written, and equipped with useful bibliographical notes.
* McNeill, J. T. *The History and Character of Calvinism.* 1967. A clear short history of the movement that Calvin founded.
* Strauss, Gerald. *Nuremberg in the Sixteenth Century.* 1966. A study of a German city, showing how its people lived and how they responded to Luther.
* Tawney, R. H. *Religion and the Rise of Capitalism.* 1947. A lively and powerfully argued study of the links between Protestantism and economic behavior.
* Weber, Max. *The Protestant Ethic and the Spirit of Capitalism.* Talcott Parsons (tr.). 1958. Originally published in 1904 and 1905, this study of the way in which the Reformation helped create the modern world has become a classic and has influenced much of the historical thinking about the Reformation.
Wendel, François. *Calvin: The Origins and Development of his Religious Thought.* Philip Mairet (tr.). 1963. The best overall introduction to the reformer's work.
Williams, George H. *The Radical Reformation.* 1962. A comprehensive history of the many sects and radical ideas that sprung up during the Reformation.

---

* Available in paperback.

FIFTEEN

A CENTURY OF
WAR AND REVOLT

In the wake of the rapid and bewildering changes of the early sixteenth century—the dislocations caused by the activities of the new monarchs, the rises in population and prices, the overseas discoveries, and the Reformation—Europe entered a period of fierce upheaval. It was difficult to come to terms with such radical alterations in so many elements of society: the increasing interference in local affairs by bureaucrats from distant capitals, the sudden soaring of food costs, or the questioning of hallowed authorities like the pope. Many people, often led by nobles who saw their power dwindling, revolted against their monarchs. The poor launched hopeless rebellions against their social superiors. And the two religious camps struggled relentlessly to destroy each other. From Scotland to Russia, the events of the century following the Reformation, from about 1560 to 1660, were dominated by warfare.

The pivot of the conflict was the Hapsburg family, which ruled most of southern and central Europe. Until the 1590s its chief representative was Philip II, King of Spain, whose ambitions and world-wide commitments lay at the center of forty years of international disputes. Then, after a short respite, the Thirty Years' War began and involved large areas of Europe in the bloodiest fighting the Continent had ever seen. Domestic tensions, peasant revolts, and civil wars added to the perpetual upheaval. The constant military activity had widespread effects on politics, economy, society, and thought. No country was untouched, because phenomena as diverse as population increase and political theory or taxation and the proliferation of bureaucracies were transformed by the impact of the wars. The fighting was in fact a crucial element in the long and painful process whereby Europeans came to terms with the revolutions that had begun about 1500. Almost imperceptibly, fundamental economic, political, social, and religious changes took root,

and troubled Europeans managed to come to terms with their altered circumstances. At last, in the mid-seventeenth century, the long struggle seemed to ease as conflict shifted to different issues. But by the time the long adjustment finally ended, countless lives had been sacrificed and endless suffering had been caused.

I. WARFARE

Western Europe was the scene of almost constant fighting during the late sixteenth century and the succeeding era of the Thirty Years' War. Warfare was so widespread between 1600 and 1650 that no country was immune to the effects of the mounting brutality. The effects of war were to be felt in all areas of political and social development, intensifying the sense of disorder and upheaval that had arisen during the first half of the six-

teenth century and causing basic shifts of power in political and economic structures.

THE MILITARY REVOLUTION

Dramatic changes took place in the way battles were fought and armies were organized between the early 1500s and the middle of the seventeenth century. At the beginning of the period gunpowder first came into general use. The result was not only the creation of a new

(top) *A view of the siege of Magdeburg during the Thirty Years' War. Cannon are pouring fire into the city. Star-shaped bastions are visible in the lower right and at the far left.* (Photo: New York Public Library Picture Collection) (left) *A typical system of trenches approaching a bastion.* (Photo: The Granger Collection)

type of industry, cannon and gun manufacture, but also a transformation of tactics. Individual castles could no longer be defended against explosives; even towns had to build heavy and elaborate fortifications if they were to resist the new fire power. Sieges became complicated, expensive operations, whose purpose was to bring explosives right up to a town wall so that it could be blown up. This required an intricate system of trenches, because walls were built in star shapes so as to multiply angles of fire and make any approach dangerous. Although both attack and defense thus became increasingly costly, sieges remained essential to the strategy of warfare until the eighteenth century.

In open battles, the effects of gunpowder were equally expensive. The new tactics that appeared around 1500, perfected by the Spaniards, relied on massed ranks of infantry, organized in huge squares, and made the traditional cavalry charge obsolete. Around the edge of the square were soldiers carrying pikes. They fended off horses or opposing infantry while the men with guns—in the center of the square—tried to mow the enemy down. The squares with the best discipline usually won, and for over a century after the reign of Ferdinand of Aragon, the Spaniards had the best army in Europe. Each square had about 3,000 troops, and to maintain sufficient squares at full strength required an army numbering approximately 40,000. The cost of keeping that many men clothed, fed, and housed, let alone equipped and paid, was enormous. But worse was to come: new tactics emerged in the early seventeenth century that required even more soldiers.

Since nobody could outdo the Spaniards at their own methods, a different approach was developed by their rivals. The first advance was made by Maurice of Nassau, who led the Dutch revolt against Spain from the 1580s. He relied not on sheer weight and power, but on flexibility and mobility. Then one of the geniuses of the history of warfare, Gustavus Adolphus, king of Sweden, found a way to achieve mobility without losing power. His main invention was the salvo—instead of having his musketeers fire one row at a time, like the Spaniards, he had them all fire at once. What he lost in continuity of shot he gained in a fearsome blast that, if properly timed, could shatter enemy ranks. Huge, slow-moving squares were simply no match for smaller, faster units that riddled them with well-coordinated salvos. To add to his fire power, Gustavus had his engineers devise a light, movable cannon that could be brought into action wherever it was most needed on a battlefield.

These changes brought about a further increase in the size of armies because the more units, the better they could be placed on the battlefield. Although the Spanish army hardly grew between 1590 and 1600, remaining at 40,000 to 60,000 men, the Swedes had 175,000 men by 1632; and at the end of the century, Louis XIV considered a force of 400,000 essential to maintain his dominant position in Europe.[1]

This growth had far-reaching consequences. Rulers knew the risks of relying on mercenary troops, who might change sides for a raise in pay, and Gustavus introduced conscription in the late 1620s so that his army, consisting largely of his own subjects, would be easier to control. Because it also made sense not to disband such huge forces each autumn, when the campaigning season ended, the armies were kept permanently ready.

The need to maintain so many soldiers the year round caused a rapid expansion of supporting administrative personnel. Taxation mushroomed. All levels of society felt the impact but especially the lower classes, who paid the bulk of the taxes and provided most of the recruits. To encourage enlistment rulers made military service as attractive as possible—not a difficult task at a time when regular meals, clothing, housing, and wages were not always easy to come by. Social distinctions were reduced; an able young man could rise high in the officer corps, though the top ranks were still reserved for nobles. Even the lower echelons were given important responsibilities because the new system of small, flexible units required that junior officers, who were sometimes in command of only fifty men, be given considerable initiative. The decline of the cavalry, which had always been an aristocratic preserve, similarly reduced social differentiations.

Life in the army also changed. Maneuverability demanded tighter discipline, which was achieved by the introduction of drilling and combat training. The order of command was clarified, and many ranks familiar today—major, colonel, and the various levels of general—appeared in the seventeenth century.

[1] An excellent analysis of the military revolution and its implications can be found in Michael Roberts' "Gustav Adolf and the Art of War" and "The Military Revolution, 1560–1660," in his *Essays in Swedish History* (1967), pp. 58–81 and 195–225.

Gustavus Adolphus, the Swedish monarch whose domestic and military policies gained his country a position of considerable power in the early seventeenth century, is here shown landing in Germany with his men and immediately thanking God for his success thus far. (Photo: National-museum, Stockholm)

The distinctions were reinforced by uniforms, which became standard equipment. These developments created a sense of corporate spirit among military officers, an international phenomenon that was to occupy an important place in European society for three centuries.

As Gustavus himself put it, war nourishes itself. With ever-larger armies, stimulated by national ambitions and governments in search of wider powers, it was inevitable that the devastations of warfare would proliferate. Gustavus himself enunciated the strategy of devastation—an opponent can be brought to his knees, he said, only if his strength is totally destroyed. This is a brutal concept, and it spilled over into the writings of Hugo Grotius, a great Dutch jurist who tried to lay down order and rules for international affairs. Though Grotius hoped to control war, he said that the law permits combatants to kill prisoners of war, to treat noncombatants (including women and children) as belligerents, and to ravage an enemy's territory. Such conclusions clearly reflected the appalling slaughter of the era that has come to be known as the age of religious warfare.

THE WARS OF RELIGION

Although many other issues were involved in the wars that plagued Europe from the 1560s to the 1640s, religion was the burning motivation, the one that inspired fanatical devotion and the most vicious hatred. A deep conviction that heresy was dangerous to man and hateful·to God made Protestants and Catholics treat one another callously and cruelly. Even the dead were not spared; corpses were sometimes mutilated to emphasize how dreadful their sins had been in their lifetimes. This was the bitter emotion that blended in with political and other ambitions to give Europe a century of almost ceaseless war.

Spain's Catholic Crusade

During the second half of the sixteenth century, the conflict was ignited by the leader of the Catholics, Philip II of Spain (1556–1598), the most powerful monarch in Europe. He ruled the Iberian peninsula, much of Italy, the Netherlands, and a huge overseas empire, but his main obsessions were the two enemies of his church, the Muslims and the Protestants.

Against the Muslims in the Mediterranean, Philip's successful campaigns seemed to justify the financial strains they caused. In particular, his naval victory at Lepanto, off the coast of Greece, in 1571 made him a Christian hero at the same time as it rid the western Mediterranean of Muslim interference. But elsewhere he found little but frustration. He tried to prevent a Protestant, Henry IV, from succeeding to the French crown, and after he failed he continued to back the losing side in France's civil wars even though Henry converted to Catholicism.

Philip's policy toward England was similarly ineffective. After the Protestant Queen Elizabeth I came to the throne in 1558, he remained uneasily cordial toward her for about ten years. But relations deteriorated as England's sailors and explorers tried to take some of the wealth of Philip's New World possessions for themselves. The last straw came in 1585 when Elizabeth began to help the Protestant Dutch in their rebellion against Spain.

Philip decided to end all these troubles with one mighty blow: in 1588 he sent a mammoth fleet—the Armada—to the Low Countries to pick up a Spanish army, invade England, and crush his Protestant enemies. By this time, however, English seamen were among the best in the world; and their ships, which had greater maneuverability and fire power than the Spaniards', made up in tactical superiority what they lacked in size. After several skirmishes with the Armada, they set fire to a few vessels with loaded cannon aboard and sent them drifting toward the Spanish ships, anchored off Calais. The Spaniards panicked, and some of the fleet was lost. The next day the remaining ships retreated up the North Sea. The only way home was around Scotland and Ireland, and wind, storms, and the pursuing English ensured that no more than a few stragglers reached Spain safely. This shattering reversal was comparable in scale and unexpectedness only to Xerxes' disaster at Salamis more than 2,000 years earlier.

The defeat spelled the doom of Philip's foreign policies. Though he improved the defense of the Spanish Empire, English raids multiplied in a tremendous wave of privateering in the 1590s, and his possessions were under almost constant attack thereafter. Enemies to the bitter end, both Elizabeth and Philip died before peace came in 1604.

The Dutch Revolt

Philip's most serious reversal was the revolt of the provinces he had inherited from his father in the Netherlands. Here his single-mindedness provoked a determined reaction that grew into a successful struggle for independence, the first major effort in Western Europe to resist the new authority of a monarchy.

The original focus of opposition was Philip's reorganization of the ecclesiastical structure so as to gain control over the country's Catholic church, a change which deprived the aristocracy of important patronage. The billeting of troops meanwhile aroused the resentment of ordinary citizens. Using this situation, the nobles, led by William of Orange, threatened mass disorder, but Philip kept up the pressure: he put the Inquisition to work against heretics, and summoned the Jesuits to combat religious unorthodoxy. These moves had a disastrous effect because they further undermined local autonomy and threatened the Protestants of the country.

Philip's interference in religion provoked violence in 1566: Protestant mobs swept through cities, sacking Catholic churches as they went. He therefore tightened the pressure, appointing as governor the ruthless duke of Alva, whose Spanish troops were used to suppress heresy and treason. Protestants were hanged in public, small rebel bands were mercilessly decimated, and two nobles who had been guilty of nothing worse than demanding that Philip change his policy were executed.

The reaction of one observer, the great painter Pieter Brueghel, was a searing indictment of the persecution. When he painted the famous biblical subject, the Massacre of the Innocents, he set the scene in a village in the Netherlands during the harshest season, winter. His own countrymen were the victims, and the murderers were Spanish soldiers, watched over by the sinister figure of the duke of Alva, dressed entirely in black.

Organized revolt broke out in 1572, when a small group of Dutch seamen flying the flag of William of Orange seized the fishing village of Brill, on the North Sea. The success of these "sea beggars," as the Spaniards called them, stimulated uprisings in towns throughout the Low Countries. The banner of William of Orange became the symbol of resistance, and under his leadership full-scale rebellion gathered momentum.

After the sea beggars' capture of Brill, the Spaniards advanced into the province of Holland, but they were stopped in 1574 by the opening of the dikes when they were only twenty-five miles from Amsterdam.[2] Following two more years of fighting, Philip's troops

---

[2] Most areas of the provinces of Holland and Zeeland lay below sea level and were protected by dikes. Defenders could flood them at very short notice by opening sluices in the sea walls. The forewarned population would take to boats, and the enemy soldiers, caught unawares, would have to beat a hasty retreat.

This detail from Brueghel's Massacre of the Innocents *shows the brutality of Spanish soldiers toward the local population. The figure in black at the center of the detachment of cavalry has been identified as the duke of Alva.* (Photo: Kunsthistorisches Museum, Vienna)

mutinied and rioted in Antwerp. In reaction sixteen·out of seventeen provinces united behind William to drive out the Spaniards. The next year, however, the ten southern provinces again gave their allegiance to Philip because he had restored political power to the nobility.

In 1579 the remaining seven formed the United Provinces (Map 15.1). Despite the assassination of William in 1584, they managed to hang on, for various reasons: they could always open up the dikes; Philip was often diverted by other wars, and in any case never placed total confidence in his commanders; and the Calvinists, though still a minority, became the heart of the resistance with their determination to establish freedom for their religion as well as their country. William was succeeded by Maurice of Nassau, his son, a brilliant military commander who won a series of victories in the 1590s. The Spaniards could make no progress and agreed to a twelve-year truce in 1609, but final recognition of the independence of the United Provinces did not come until the Peace of Westphalia, in 1648, after twenty-seven more years of fighting. The new state, bound together by religious, economic, and military ties, demonstrated the occasional positive effects of warfare in this period: it could unite a people and give them the means to achieve dignity and full autonomy.

Civil War in France

The warfare that religion inspired had no such redeeming effects in France. By the 1550s Calvinism was widespread among the peasants and poorer middle classes in the southern and southwestern section of the country, and its leaders had virtually created a small, semi-independent state within France. To meet this threat, a great noble family, the Guises, assumed the leadership of a Catholic party, and in response the Bourbons, another noble family, championed the Calvinists. The ensuing war split France apart.

It was ominous that in 1559, the year that Henry II, France's last strong king for a generation, died, the Protestant Huguenots organized their first national synod, an indication of impressive strength. During the next thirty years, a period when factional disputes among the nobles and religious passions overwhelmed the country, the throne was occupied by Henry's three ineffectual sons. The power behind the crown was Henry's widow, Catherine de Médicis (see the accompanying genealogical table), who tried desperately to preserve royal authority. But she was often helpless because the religious conflict intensified the factional struggle for power between the Catholic Guises and the Protestant Bourbons, both of whom were closely related to the monarchy and hoped eventually to inherit the throne.

The fighting started in 1562, and lasted for thirty-six years, interrupted only by short-lived peace agreements. Catherine first turned to the Catholics for help but later switched to the Calvinists. When they became too powerful at court, she changed sides again, and she probably gave tacit approval to a massacre in

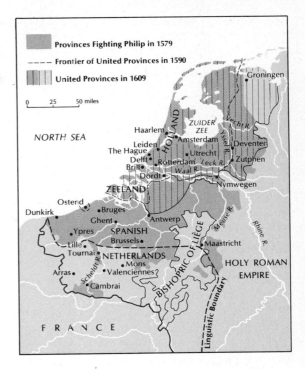

MAP 15.1: THE NETHERLANDS 1579–1609

The seventeen provinces making up the Netherlands, or the Low Countries, were detached from the Holy Roman Empire when Charles V abdicated in 1556. As the map indicates, their subsequent division into two states was determined not by the linguistic difference between French-speaking people of the south and Dutch-speaking people of the north, but rather by geography. The great river systems at the mouth of the Rhine eventually proved to be the barrier beyond which the Spaniards could not penetrate.

Paris on St. Bartholomew's Day, August 24, 1572, which destroyed the Calvinist leadership. Henry of Navarre, a Bourbon, was the only major figure who escaped. When Catherine switched again and made peace with the Calvinists in 1576, the Guises, in desperation, formed the Catholic League, which for several years virtually ran the government. In 1584 the league made an alliance with Philip II to

THE KINGS OF FRANCE IN THE SIXTEENTH CENTURY

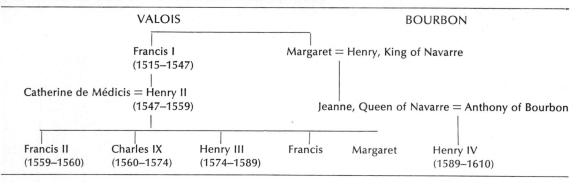

VALOIS   BOURBON

Francis I   Margaret = Henry, King of Navarre
(1515–1547)

Catherine de Médicis = Henry II
(1547–1559)

Jeanne, Queen of Navarre = Anthony of Bourbon

| Francis II | Charles IX | Henry III | Francis | Margaret | Henry IV |
| (1559–1560) | (1560–1574) | (1574–1589) | | | (1589–1610) |

destroy heresy in France and deny the Bourbon Henry's legal right to inherit the throne.

The defeat of the Armada proved to be the turning point in France's civil war. The duke of Guise lost his principal support, Spain; and Henry III, who had been a pawn of the league, ordered Guise's assassination and threw in his lot with the Bourbons. Within a few months he in turn was assassinated, and Henry of Navarre inherited the throne.

Henry IV (1589–1610) had few advantages as he began the reassertion of royal authority. The Calvinists and Catholics had formed almost independent governments, controlling large sections of France. The Catholic League was in command of the east, including the capital, Paris; the Calvinists dominated the south and southwest, remote from the central government. In addition the royal administration was in a sorry state, for power had returned to the crown's oldest rivals, the great nobles, who were now unchallenged in their domains.

Yet largely because of the assassination of the duke of Guise, Henry IV survived and recovered. The duke had been a forceful leader, a serious contender for the throne. He was succeeded by his brother, who had agreed to support a Spanish candidate for the crown. The prospect of a foreign ruler, the loss of a charismatic leader, and war weariness destroyed much of the support for the Catholic League, which finally collapsed as a result of revolts in eastern France against the Guises in the 1590s. The uprisings, founded on a demand for peace, increased in frequency and intensity after Henry IV renounced Protestantism in 1593 to win acceptance by his Catholic subjects. The following year Henry had himself officially crowned, and all of France declared its allegiance to the monarchy so as to join in the effort of repelling the Spanish invader.

When Spain finally withdrew and signed a peace in 1598, the fighting came to an end. To complete the reconciliation, Henry issued (also in 1598) the Edict of Nantes, which granted toleration to the Huguenots. Although it did not create complete religious liberty, it made Calvinism legal, protected the rights of the minority, and opened public office to Protestants.

But the effects of decades of strife could not be brushed aside. A basic change in political thought, for example, was an inevitable response to the civil wars, because a number of

From a portrayal of the Massacre of St. Bartholomew's Day by a Huguenot survivor. (Photo: Andre Held)

theorists felt obliged to reassess the relationship between a king and his subjects.

The Huguenots were the first to justify resistance to a monarch. Seizing on a vague passage in Calvin's writings about the sanctity of conscience and ignoring his endorsement of obedience to authority, they asserted that when a king goes against God's wishes and disturbs the faith, he breaks his contract with his people, thus making revolt permissible. Catholics took up a similar argument when they were fighting the king. The Jesuits developed the idea of a contract between ruler and ruled and found excellent biblical support for the overthrow of a tyrant (for example pharaoh) who turned against true religion.

These extreme positions soon lost appeal when order was restored, however, and a group whose views had previously gone unheeded gained the ascendancy: the politiques. Although most were Catholics their main premise was that peace, security, and national unity were far more important than the claims of rival churches. Representing the forces of nationalism and central authority, the politiques were the heralds of a more stable future.

Their most famous representative, Jean Bodin, made his case by examining the basic structure of the state, and his analysis influenced political theorists for centuries. His principal work is *The Six Books of the Republic* (1576), in which he tried to define the nature and the limits of authority. By aiming for a balance between power and restraint, Bodin was seeking a principle for restoring stability in an age of shattering upheaval. But in the process he also exposed the paradox that has been the primary focus of political theory ever since: control versus freedom, the need for authority and yet the equal need for individual rights. Bodin never really tried to resolve the problem, but in emphasizing this equilibrium as the essential difficulty of political thought, he not only mirrored the uncertainties of his age but also influenced everyone who grappled with the issue thereafter.

THE THIRTY YEARS' WAR

In the Holy Roman Empire fierce religious antagonisms were particularly dangerous because the empire lacked a central authority and unifying institutions. Small-scale fighting broke out repeatedly after the 1550s, always inspired by religion. And though in most of Western Europe the first two decades of the seventeenth century were a time of relative peace, which seemed to signal a decline of confessional conflict, in the empire the stage was being set for the bloodiest of all the wars fired by religion.

Known as the Thirty Years' War, this ferocious series of encounters began in the Kingdom of Bohemia in 1618 and continued until 1648. The principal battleground, the empire, was ravaged by the fighting, and eventually every major ruler of Europe became involved in the struggle. Political ambitions soon began to replace religious motives as the prime concern of the combatants, but the devastation continued to spread until international relations seemed to be sinking into total chaos. The chief victims were of course the Germans, who, like the Italians in the sixteenth century, found themselves at the mercy of well-organized states that used another country as the arena for settling their quarrels.

The immediate problem was typical of the situation in the empire. In 1609 Emperor Rudolf II promised toleration for Protestants in Bohemia, one of his own domains. When his cousin Ferdinand, a pious Catholic, suc-

This map reveals both the extent and the fluctuations of fighting in Europe from the outbreak of the Thirty Years' War to the end of the Civil War in England. The principal battles are listed so as to give a more precise indication of the timing and location of major encounters. A look at the route followed by Spain's troops as they marched to the Netherlands, always staying close to friendly Catholic territories, will pinpoint the vital importance of the Valtellina, a vulnerable pass through the Alps that they had to cross.

MAP 15.2: AREAS OF FIGHTING 1618–1660

NORWAY

SWEDEN

RIGA 1621

SCOTLAND

NORTH SEA

DUNBAR 1650

DENMARK

Copenhagen

BALTIC SEA

PRUSSIA

IRELAND

DROGHEDA 1649

Dublin

ENGLAND

STRALSUND 1628

LÜBECK 1627

STETTIN 1630

Vistula R.

WARSAW 1656

POLAND

WORCESTER 1651

NASEBY 1645

Amsterdam

UNITED PROVINCES

MAGDEBURG 1631

EDGEHILL 1642

SCHEVENINGEN 1654

London

Thames R.

STADTLOHN 1623

LÜTTER 1626

DESSAU 1626

BREITENFELD 1631

Weser R.

Elbe R.

BREDA 1625, 1637

DUNKIRK 1658

Brussels

LUTZEN 1632

SAXONY

Oder R.

ENGLISH CHANNEL

LENS 1648

SPANISH NETHERLANDS

Rhine R.

HOLY ROMAN EMPIRE

WHITE MOUNTAIN 1620

PRAGUE 1648

HOCHST 1622

CORBIE 1636

PERONNE 1654

ROCROI 1643

Scheldt R.

LOWER PALATINATE

WIMPFEN 1622

PILSEN 1622

NUREMBERG 1622

Seine R.

PHILIPPSBURG 1635

Paris

ST. ANTOINE 1652

WIESLOCH 1622

NORDLINGEN 1634

Meuse R.

AUGSBURG 1635

BAVARIA

Vienna

UPPER AUSTRIA 1626

AUSTRIA

PRESSBURG 1619

BREISACH 1638

MUNICH 1632

Loire R.

FRANCE

HUNGARY

LA ROCHELLE 1628

SWISS CONFEDERATION

VALTELLINA 1622-1637

Danube R.

SAVOY

CASAL 1629

THE MILANESE

Milan

Venice

ADRIATIC SEA

PINEROLO 1630

CHERASCO 1631

MANTUA 1630

PIEDMONT

Genoa

PAPAL STATES

PERPIGNAN 1642

CORSICA

Rome

KINGDOM OF NAPLES

SPAIN

Conflict Areas 1618-1630

Conflict Areas 1630-1648

Conflict Areas 1648-1669

Barcelona

Occupied by Spain in 1621

Route of Spanish Soldiers

SARDINIA

Boundaries in 1618   ✳ Battle Site

BALEARICS

0   100   200 miles

MEDITERRANEAN   SEA

ceeded to the Bohemian throne in 1617, he refused to honor Rudolf's promise, and the Bohemians rebelled. Since the crown was technically elective, they declared Ferdinand deposed, replacing him with the leading Calvinist of the empire, Frederick II of the Palatinate. Frederick accepted the crown, an act of defiance whose only possible outcome was war between the two religious camps.

For more than a decade, little went wrong for the Hapsburgs. Ferdinand became emperor (1619–1637), and the powerful Catholic Maximilian of Bavaria put his army at the emperor's disposal. Within a year the imperial troops won a shattering victory over the Bohemians at the Battle of the White Mountain. Leading rebels were executed or exiled, and Ferdinand II confiscated all of Frederick's lands. Half were given to Maximilian as a reward for his army, and the remainder were offered to the Spaniards, who occupied them as a valuable base for their struggle with the Dutch. It seemed as though the Catholic and imperial cause had triumphed. But in 1621 the truce between the Spaniards and the Dutch expired, hostilities reopened in the Netherlands, and religious warfare resumed in Germany (see Map 15.2).

Until 1630, however, the Protestants could do little in the face of the armies of the Hapsburgs and Bavaria. In 1622 the Spaniards occupied the Valtellina, a Swiss valley that was the best route for their troops traveling to the Netherlands. And in the empire all attempts by Protestants to help Frederick were beaten back. By 1630 Hapsburg power, bolstered by the creation of a new army, had reached its height.

The man who put together the new imperial army was Albrecht von Wallenstein, a minor Bohemian nobleman and a remarkable opportunist who had become one of the richest men in the empire. In 1624 Wallenstein, realizing that the emperor's great weakness was that he lacked his own army, offered to raise a force if he could billet it and raise its supplies among the population in whatever area it happened to be stationed. Ferdinand agreed, and by 1627 his army had begun to conquer the northern region of the empire, the last major center of Protestant strength. To emphasize his supremacy, Ferdinand issued the Edict of Restitution in 1629, ordering the restoration to Catholics of all the territories they had lost to Protestants—mainly in the northern empire—since 1552.

But these successes were more apparent than real because it was only the extreme disorganization of the empire that permitted a mercenary captain like Wallenstein to achieve such immense power. Once the princes realized their danger, they united against the Hapsburgs; and the forced contributions exacted by Wallenstein's army strengthened their determination to curb this growing menace to their independence. At an electoral diet in 1630, they made Ferdinand dismiss his general by threatening to keep his son from the imperial succession. The emperor's submission proved fatal to his cause, for Sweden and France were now preparing to unleash new aggressions against the Hapsburgs, and Wallenstein was the one man who might have been able to beat back the onslaught.

The year 1630 marked the beginning of a change in fortune. In the spring France, disturbed at Hapsburg power—both Austrian and Spanish—on her eastern border, attacked the duke of Savoy, a Hapsburg ally, and occupied his lands. Then early in 1631 Gustavus Adolphus of Protestant Sweden, fearing that Swedish territories around the Baltic Sea might be threatened, and alarmed at Ferdinand's treatment of Protestants, signed alliances with France and the elector of Saxony. In July he crossed the Baltic, and at the head of a Swedish-Saxon army destroyed the imperial force at Breitenfeld in one of the few decisive battles of the war.

Ferdinand hastily recalled Wallenstein,

whose troops finally met the Swedes in battle at Lützen in 1632. Although Gustavus' soldiers won the day, he himself was killed, and his death saved the Hapsburg dynasty from total destruction. Nothing, however, could restore Ferdinand's former position. The emperor was forced to turn against Wallenstein once more; a few months later he had him assassinated. The removal of the great general marked the end of an era, for he was the last man in more than three centuries capable of establishing unified authority throughout what is now Germany.

Encouraged by Gustavus' success, the empire's princes began to raise new armies, and by 1635 Ferdinand had to make peace with them at the Treaty of Prague. In return for their promise of assistance in driving out the Swedes, Ferdinand agreed to suspend the Edict of Restitution and to grant amnesty to all but Frederick of the Palatinate and a few Bohemian rebels. Ferdinand was renouncing most of his ambitions, and it seemed that peace might return to the battle-scarred land.

But the French could not let matters rest. In 1635 they finally declared war on Ferdinand and occupied the Valtellina. For the next thirteen years, the French and Swedes rained unmitigated disaster on Germany. Peace negotiations began in 1641, but not until 1648 did the combatants agree to lay down arms and sign the treaties of Westphalia. Even thereafter the war between France and Spain, pursued mainly in the Spanish Netherlands, continued for another eleven years; and hostilities around the Baltic among Sweden, Denmark, Poland, and Russia, which had started in 1611, did not end until 1661.

The wars killed off more than a third of Germany's population. They caused serious economic dislocations, because a number of princes—already in serious financial straits—sharply debased their coinage. Their action worsened the continent-wide depression that had begun around 1620 and had brought the great sixteenth-century boom to an end, causing the first drop in prices since 1500. Few contemporaries perceived the connection between war and economic troubles, but nobody could ignore the interminable drain on men and resources or the widespread effects of the conflict on the life of the time.

THE PEACE OF WESTPHALIA

By the 1630s it was already becoming apparent that the fighting was getting out of hand, and that it would not be easy to bring the conflicts to an end. There had never been such widespread or devastating warfare; in the view of many diplomats, the settlement had to be far more decisive and of far greater scope than any negotiated before. And they were right. When at last the treaties were signed, after seven years of negotiation in the German province of Westphalia, a landmark in international relations was passed—remarkable not only because an anarchic situation was brought under control, but because a new system for dealing with wars was created.

The most important innovation was the gathering at the peace conference of all the participants in the Thirty Years' War, rather than the usual practice of bringing only two or three belligerents together. The presence of ambassadors from Bavaria, Brandenburg, Denmark, France, the Holy Roman Empire, Saxony, Spain, Sweden, Switzerland, and the United Provinces made possible, for the first time in European history, a series of all-embracing treaties that dealt with nearly every major international issue at one stroke. Although the Franco-Spanish and the Baltic wars continued for more than ten years, the Peace of Westphalia in 1648 became the first comprehensive rearrangement of the map of Europe in modern history (Map 15.3).

The principal beneficiaries were France and Sweden, the chief aggressors during the last decade of the war. France made important

MAP 15.3: TERRITORIAL CHANGE 1648–1661

Legend:

- French Gains, 1648 and 1659
- Swedish Gains 1617 to 1661
- Brandenburg at 1618
- Brandenburg Gains 1648 and 1661
- Austrian Hapsburg Areas
- Spanish Hapsburg Areas
- Holy Roman Empire Boundary in 1618
- Areas Lost by Holy Roman Empire in 1648

Inset (upper left): **French Gains in the Southwest** — FRANCE; Bordeaux; ALBERT 1607; Bayonne; Montauban; ARMAGNAC 1607; K. OF NAVARRE 1620; Toulouse; BIGORRE 1607; FOIX 1607; 1659; Perpignan; ROUSSILLON; CERDAGNE; SPAIN

Labels on main map: TRONDHJEM; HERJEDALEN; KARELIA; NORWAY; SWEDEN; INGRIA; Stockholm; BALTIC SEA; LIVONIA; DENMARK; Copenhagen; Riga; Königsberg; PRUSSIA; NORTH SEA; WESTERN POMERANIA; EASTERN POMERANIA; Stettin; UNITED PROVINCES; Emden; BREMEN; Bremen; VER; BRANDENBURG; POLAND; Amsterdam; Osnabrück; Münster; WESTPHALIA; CLEVES; MARK; SPANISH NETHERLANDS; SAXONY 1648; HOLY ROMAN EMPIRE; Paris; LOWER PALATINATE; UPPER PALATINATE; Prague; BOHEMIA; LORRAINE; ALSACE; 1648; BAVARIA; Vienna; AUSTRIA; HUNGARY; FRANCHE-COMTÉ; SWISS CONFEDERATION; FRANCE; SAVOY; THE MILANESE; Venice; SPAIN

This map shows the territorial changes that took place after the Thirty Years' War. The treaties of Westphalia (1648) and the Pyrenees (1659) arranged the principal transfers, but the settlements in the Baltic were not confirmed until the treaties of Copenhagen, Oliva (both 1660), and Kardis (1661). The arrows indicate the direction of conquests and the date at which they were accomplished.

gains on her northeastern frontier, notably the provinces of Alsace and Lorraine; and Sweden obtained extensive territories in the Holy Roman Empire, among them Eastern Pomerania, Bremen, and Verden. The main loser was the House of Hapsburg, since both the United Provinces and the Swiss Confederation were recognized as independent states and the German princes, who agreed not to join an alliance against the emperor, were otherwise given almost complete independence.

However, the princes' autonomy was not officially established until 1657, when they elected as emperor Leopold I, the head of the House of Hapsburg, in return for two promises. First, Leopold would give no help to his cousins, the rulers of Spain; and second, the empire would be a *Fürstenstaat*, a prince's state, in which each ruler would be completely free from imperial interference. This freedom permitted the rise of Brandenburg-Prussia and the growth of absolutism within the major principalities. In addition the Hapsburgs' capitulation prepared the way for their reorientation toward the east along the Danube River —the beginnings of the Austro-Hungarian Empire.

For more than a century the settlement reached at Westphalia was regarded as the basis for all international negotiations. The Treaty of the Pyrenees in 1659, ending the war between France and Spain, and the treaties of Copenhagen and Oliva in 1660 and Kardis in 1661, ending the Baltic struggles, were considered only to have rounded out the agreements made at Westphalia. Even major new accords, such as the one that ended yet another series of wars in 1713, were viewed primarily as adjustments of the decisions of 1648.

In practice of course multinational conferences were no more effective than brief, limited negotiations as means of reducing international tensions. Wars continued to break out with monotonous frequency, and armies grew in size and skill. But diplomats did believe that the total situation was under better control and that the anarchy of the Thirty Years' War had been replaced by something more stable and more clearly defined.

Confidence was reinforced as it became clear after 1648 that armies were trying to improve discipline and avoid the excesses of the previous thirty years. The treatment of civilians became more orderly, and on the battlefield the casualty rate went from as high as one death per three soldiers in the 1630s down to one death in seven at worst, or one in twenty at best, during the early 1700s. As religious passions declined, combat became less vicious, and the aims of warfare changed significantly.

The most obvious difference after the Peace of Westphalia was that France replaced Spain as the Continent's dominant power, and that northern countries—especially England and the Netherlands—took over economic leadership from the Mediterranean, where it had been centered for 2,000 years. But behind this outward shift a more fundamental transformation was taking place. What had become apparent in the later stages of the Thirty Years' War was that Europe's states were interested in fighting only for economic, territorial, or political advantages. Dynastic aims were still important—and were to remain so for centuries —but supranational goals like religious advancement could no longer determine foreign policies.

The Thirty Years' War was the last major conflict in which two religious camps organized their forces as blocs. After 1648 such connections gave way to more purely national interests. Despite the universal wish for peace, Pope Innocent X, furious at the Catholics' compromises, denounced the treaties of Westphalia, but his voice went unheard. The declining influence of ideology meant that men would henceforth pursue the glory of their nation or ruler—not the advantage of their faith. This shift marked the final stage of a process that had long been under way: the emergence of the state as the basic unit and object of loyalty in Western civilization.

If the new aims of foreign policies, such as economic advantage, could not yet arouse the same passions as religion, they nevertheless revealed that commitment to one's country, and an interest in the way it was run, was becoming important throughout Europe. Indeed, at the very time that tensions were lessening in international affairs, they reached a new height in the internal affairs of a number of countries. Just as the mid-seventeenth century witnessed the most intense phase and also the settlement of the difficulties among states, so too did it mark the climax and the resolution of an era of upheaval and revolt within states.

II. REVOLTS

The warfare of the century from the 1560s to the 1660s affected the relations between rulers and their subjects no less than relations between countries. The additional taxes and bureaucrats required by the military created burdens that provoked the resistance to governments that was a major feature of the century. Some of these domestic conflicts had international dimensions—the Dutch revolt, the French civil wars, and the upheavals in Bohemia and Germany all blended in, as we have seen, with much wider wars—but they were equally important in shaping the internal administration of Europe's states. By the time the conflicts died away, after a particularly acute outburst in the mid-seventeenth century, they had helped create the national political structures that endured until the age of the French Revolution.

ENGLAND

The one attempt at a radical transformation of politics and society—a revolution—occurred in England. Compared to her neighbors, England seemed relatively calm during the second half of the sixteenth century and the early years of the seventeenth. But tensions were rising that were to produce the most far-reaching upheaval of the age.

Elizabeth I

The tranquillity of the period from the 1560s to the 1630s had several causes. With only occasional fighting to support, and that largely at sea, England was far less affected by war than the Continental states. Furthermore the people were already united by such common bonds as a national reformation and the institution of Parliament, so the crown did not experience the severe challenges that plagued royal authority in contemporary Spain and France. And the monarch also happened to be extraordinarily clever at the task of calming discontent.

Elizabeth I (1558–1603) has been an appealing figure to every generation because she combined shrewd hard-headedness and a sense of the possible with a charming appearance of frailty. Her qualities are easily appreciated: her dedication to the task of government; her astute choice of advisers—with the one exception of the handsome young earl of Essex, for whom she developed a disastrous infatuation near the end of her life; her careful and usually successful handling of political problems; and her ability to feel the mood of her people, to catch their spirit, to inspire their unquestioning enthusiasm.

Her concern for loyalty made Elizabeth reluctant to break openly with those who opposed her, but this also led to an indecisiveness that had unfortunate consequences, notably where the succession was concerned. Her refusal to marry caused serious uncertainties, and it was only because of the astute planning of Elizabeth's chief minister, Robert Cecil, that a crisis was avoided when she died in 1603 without naming a successor. Thanks to Cecil's diplomacy, the king of Scotland, James Stuart, succeeded without incident.

The advisers Elizabeth appointed to the Privy Council, the chief government body, were essential to her success. They distilled the flow of administrative business and worked closely with the queen, but they also represented different views. Some advocated caution, inaction, and discretion in international affairs, whereas others favored an aggressive foreign policy. Elizabeth had great skill in balancing the contrasting viewpoints and her clever maneuvering assured her of her ministers' loyalty at all times.

Even more important than her approval of a policy was the patronage that accompanied her pleasure. Because the government's powers and hence its need for officials had grown rapidly since the 1530s, dozens of new posts were being created for the crown to bestow. Whoever was the queen's favorite therefore had the best chance of nominating a successful candidate for a vacancy in the bureaucracy. But as a result of the patronage system, a swarm of parasites descended on London, hopeful of advancement. Many Englishmen viewed this development with distaste, and after Elizabeth's death it became the cause of serious cleavage between crown and subjects.

Economic and Social Change

Another force with dangerous implications for the future was the result of rapidly shifting patterns in English society. With new methods of warfare, nobles no longer had a vital military role to play. Moreover they were losing their preeminence in government; nearly all the chief ministers were new men in national life, and the House of Commons was becoming at least the equal of the House of Lords in Parliament. The nobles were also not benefiting as much from England's rising prosperity as were other sections of society. Thus they were losing their hold over the power, wealth, and government of the country.

The gentry, the new group that joined them at the head of society, ranged from people considered great men in a parish or other small locality to courtiers considered great men throughout the land. There were never more than sixty nobles during Elizabeth's reign, but the gentry may have numbered close to 20,000 by the time she died.

The majority of the gentry were doing well economically, primarily from the purchase of land that the crown had confiscated when the monasteries were dissolved, in the 1530s. They also benefited from spiraling food prices and rising rents. Many profited too from crown offices; a number became involved in industrial activity; and hundreds invested in new overseas trading and colonial ventures. The gentry's participation in commerce made them unique among the landed classes of Europe, whose members were traditionally contemptuous of business affairs, and it testified to the enterprise and vigor of these Englishmen. Long important in local administration, they wanted power at the center of government, and they flocked to the House of Commons, for they regarded Parliament as the instrument of their drive for power. Their ambitions were to pose a serious threat to the monarchy, especially when linked with the effects of rapid economic change.

In the 1550s, stimulated by the general boom in trade and by the help of leading courtiers who recognized the importance of opening new markets, England's merchants began to transform her economic situation. During the next half-century, they started commerce with Russia, the Baltic and Mediterranean lands, the Levant, and East Asia. Although cloth remained the dominant export until the middle of the seventeenth century, it was joined by a growing trade in the reexport of overseas goods, such as Newfoundland fish, which were distributed throughout Europe.

Early attempts at colonization were not successful, with the exception of those in Ireland;

but vital experience was gained, and the financial rewards were sometimes significant. Within England, moreover, there was significant industrial development. The mining and manufacture of a whole variety of commodities, from alum to wire, grew at a rapid pace, and shipbuilding became a major industry. The production of coal alone increased fourteenfold between 1540 and 1680, creating many new fortunes and an expertise in industrial and commercial techniques that took England far ahead of her neighbors.

The most revealing evidence of England's new position was the founding of nearly fifty companies devoted to overseas exploration, commerce, or colonization between 1600 and 1630. The more successful ones laid the foundations for the British Empire. In India, the Caribbean islands, Bermuda, Virginia, Maryland, New England, and Canada, colonies were started that within a century were to become the most populous offshoots of any European nation.

The economic vigor and growth that ensued, apparent also in industrial and agricultural advances, gave the classes that benefited the most—the gentry and the merchants—a cohesion and a sense of purpose that made it dangerous to oppose them when they felt their rights infringed. They increasingly regarded themselves as the leaders of the nation, second only to the nobility, whose importance was diminishing. They wanted respect for their wishes, and they bitterly resented the economic interference and political high-handedness of Elizabeth's successors.

What made the situation particularly dangerous was that many of the gentry were sympathetic to the Puritans. These religious reformers believed that the Protestant Anglican Church established by Elizabeth was still too close to Roman Catholicism, and they wanted further changes. Elizabeth had refused, and although she had tried to avoid a confrontation, in the last years of her reign she had had to silence the most outspoken of her critics. As a result, the Puritans had become a disgruntled minority, ready to add their demands to those of the gentry (some of whom were themselves Puritans). By the 1630s, when the government tried to repress such religious dissent more vigorously, there were many Englishmen who felt that the monarchy was leading the country astray and was ignoring the wishes of its subjects. Leading parliamentarians in particular soon came to believe that only revolution could restore justice to England.

Parliament and the Law

The place where the gentry made their views known to the government was Parliament, the nation's supreme legislative body. Three-quarters of the lower chamber, the House of Commons, consisted of members of the gentry. These men were better educated than before; at the end of the sixteenth century, more than half of them had attended a university, and slightly less than half had legal training. Through the House of Commons, they were beginning to make a bid for their share of government, and since the Commons had to approve all taxation, these members had no compunction about using the power of the purse to promote their ambitions.

The monarchy was still the dominant force in the country when Elizabeth died in 1603, but Parliament's challenge to that supremacy was gathering momentum. Although the queen had been known for her care with money, in the last twenty years of her reign, her resources had been overtaxed by the war with Spain and an economic depression. Consequently she bequeathed to her successor, James I, a huge debt—£400,000, the equal of a year's royal revenue—and the struggle to pay it off gave the Commons the leverage to expand their powers even further.

Trouble began to mount in 1604, at the first meeting of Parliament in the reign of James I (1603–1625). Puritans who still hoped to

change the Anglican Church by legislation and gentry who wanted to extend the powers of the House of Commons led the opposition to the king. They began to dominate proceedings, and through 1629 (after which there was no session for eleven years) they engaged in a running battle with the monarchy. They blocked the union of England with Scotland that James sought. They drew up an "Apology" explaining his mistakes and his ignorance,

The decisions and policies of English monarchs had often been challenged by Parliament, but these challenges were strongest and most successful during the reigns of James I and Charles I in sessions of the House of Commons such as the one shown here in 1624. (Photo: Historical Pictures Service, Chicago)

as a Scotsman, of English traditions. And they wrung repeated concessions from him until in

1624 they gained the unprecedented right to discuss foreign policy.

The parliamentarians used the law as justification for their resistance to royal power. The basic legal system of the country was the common law—justice administered on the basis of precedents and parliamentary statutes, decided with the assistance of juries. This system stood in contrast to Roman law, prevalent on the Continent, where royal edicts could make law, and decisions were reached by judges without juries. Such practices existed in England only in a few royal courts of law, such as the Star Chamber. Proceedings here were popular, because they were quicker, and powerful men could not influence the decisions of the judges who were usually prominent men themselves.

Common lawyers, whose leaders were also prominent in the House of Commons, resented the growth of this rival system, and they attacked royal courts in Parliament. Both James and his successor were accused of putting pressure on the judges to gain their ends—particularly after they won a series of famous cases involving a subject's right to criticize the monarch. Thus the crown could be portrayed as disregarding not only the desires of the people but the law itself. Technically the king had extensive rights, but when he exercised them without regard to Parliament's wishes, his actions began to take on the appearance of tyranny.

Rising Antagonisms

The confrontation in Parliament grew worse during the 1620s. In 1621 the House of Commons forced the king's lord chancellor, Francis Bacon, out of office for accepting bribes, and in reaction to their attacks, James had some of the members sent to prison. Under his son Charles I (1625–1649), the hostilities intensified. At the Parliament of 1628–1629, the crown faced an open challenge, whose climax was the Petition of Right, an appeal that has

become a landmark in constitutional history. The petition demanded an end to imprisonment without cause shown, to taxation without the consent of Parliament, to martial law in peacetime, and to the billeting of troops among civilians. Charles agreed, in the hope of gaining much-needed subsidies, but then broke his word.

The issue was now clearly whether Parliament, as the representative of the nation, would hold an essential position in the government alongside the king. To stop further confrontation Charles ordered Parliament dissolved, but in a move of great daring, two members denied the king even this hallowed right by holding the speaker of the House in his chair while they passed a final angry resolution.

Resentful subjects were clearly on the brink of open defiance of their sovereign. Puritans, common lawyers, and disenchanted country gentry had captured the House of Commons, and Charles could avoid further trouble only by refusing to call another session of Parliament. This he managed to do for eleven years, all the while increasing the repression of Puritanism and resorting to unpopular extraordinary measures to raise revenues.

But the smooth sailing could not last long. The leaders of the Puritan and parliamentary opposition met regularly after 1630, and they finally had the opportunity in 1639 to extract from the king the concessions they sought when the Calvinist Scots took up arms rather than accept the Anglican prayer book. Religious persecution had once again sparked military combat: the Scots invaded England, and Charles had to raise an army. To obtain the necessary funds, he turned to Parliament, which demanded that he first redress its grievances. When he resisted, civil war followed.

The English Civil War

The Parliament that met in 1640 was dominated by John Pym, a Puritan and a prominent critic of the monarch for nearly twenty years, who opened the session with a two-hour speech outlining the long-standing grievances against both church and government. Charles refused to change his policies and the Commons refused to grant a subsidy, and so the king angrily dissolved the session. But there was no way to pay for an army without taxes. By the summer of 1640, the Scots occupied most of northern England, and Charles had no alternative but to summon a new Parliament. This one sat for thirteen years, earning the appropriate name of the Long Parliament.

Pym was in complete control of Parliament for the first year. The House of Commons passed legislation abolishing the royal courts, such as Star Chamber, and establishing the writ of habeas corpus (which prevented imprisonment without cause shown) as mandatory; it declared taxation without parliamentary consent illegal; and it ruled that Parliament had to meet at least once every three years, with the additional proviso that the current assembly could not be dissolved without its consent. Meanwhile, the Puritans were preparing to reform the church. Oliver Cromwell, one of the leading members of the House, demanded abolition of the Anglican Book of Common Prayer and strongly attacked the institution of episcopacy. The climactic vote came the next year, when the Commons passed their Grand Remonstrance, outlining for the king all the legislation they had put through and asking that bishops be deprived of their votes in the House of Lords.

This was the prelude to a more revolutionary assault on the structure of the church, but significantly the Grand Remonstrance passed by only 11 votes. A moderate party was detaching itself from Pym, and the beginning of a royalist party was appearing. The nation's chief grievances had been redressed, and there was no longer a uniform desire for change. Still Charles misjudged the situation and tried to arrest five leaders of the opposition, including Pym, ostensibly for plotting treason with the Scots. But Parliament refused to order their arrest, and the citizens of London, now openly hostile to Charles, sheltered the five.

In June 1642 the king received the Commons' final demands: complete parliamentary control over the church, the appointment of ministers and judges, and the army. This would have meant the abdication of all effective royal authority, and Charles refused. Gradually England began to split in two. By the late summer both sides had assembled armies, and the Civil War was under way.

The fascination of this great revolution that sought to transform English government and society has been endless. Much attention has been given to religion and politics, to the motives of Puritans and parliamentarians; it is now clear that simple differentiations cannot be made. Half the parliamentarians joined the king; the Puritans were split; and many members of the gentry, not noticeably committed to either of these opposition groups, fought against Charles.

What made so many people overcome their habitual loyalty to the monarchy? One interesting distinction is that the royalists in Parliament were considerably younger than their opponents; this suggests that it was long experience with the Stuarts and nostalgia for Elizabethan times that created dedicated revolutionaries. Another clear division was regional. The south and east of England were primarily antiroyalist while the north and west were mostly royalist. What this implied was that the more cosmopolitan areas, which were closer to the Continent and also the principal centers of Puritanism, were primarily on Parliament's side. Frequently the decision was very much a personal matter: a great man would take his locality to one side because his old rival, the great man a few miles away, had chosen the other. Those who opposed the Church of England were unequivocally antiroyalist, but they were a minority in the country and hardly even a majority in the House of Commons. Like all revolutions, this one was animated by a small group of radicals (in this case Puritans) who alone kept the momentum going.

The Stuarts' long alienation of their subjects can account for the situation in 1640, when Charles could find no support anywhere, but by the end of 1641 many felt that the necessary remedies had been obtained. Thus apart from Puritanism—or to put it more generally, apart from opposition to the Church of England—

This contemporary Dutch engraving of the execution of Charles I shows the scaffold in front of the Banqueting House in Whitehall—a building that still can be seen in London. On the far right of the scaffold, the executioner displays the severed head for the crowd. (Photo: The Granger Collection)

the historian can point to no basic cause but only to the influence of local circumstances to explain how two sides came into being in the summer of 1642.

The Course of Conflict

The first round of fighting was indecisive—a year of small successes on both sides. Then in 1643 the antiroyalists, supported by the Scottish army, gained the first military advantage. The alliance with the Scots was Pym's last accomplishment, because shortly thereafter he died, and the first major split in the antiroyalist ranks occurred.

Increasingly during the last months of Pym's life, a group known as the Independents urged that the Anglican Church be replaced by the congregational system, in which

each local congregation, free of all central authority, would decide its own form of worship. The most important representative of the Independents in Parliament was Oliver Cromwell (1599–1658). Opposed to them were the Presbyterians, who wanted to establish a strictly organized Calvinist system, much like the one that had been created in Scotland, in which local congregations were subject to centralized authority, although laymen did participate in church government. Since both the Scots, whose alliance was vital in the war, and a majority of the members of the Commons were Presbyterians,[3] Cromwell agreed to give way, but only for the moment. In addition to the religious issue, there was also a quarrel over the goals of the war because the antiroyalists were unsure whether they ought to attempt to defeat Charles completely. This dispute crossed religious lines, though on the whole the Independents were more determined to force him into total submission, and in the end they had their way.

Meanwhile the fighting continued. Hoping to create a more potent fighting force, Cromwell persuaded the House of Commons early in 1645 to create a completely reorganized army, the New Model Army, to bring the war to an end. Whipped to fervor by sermons, prayers, and the singing of psalms, the New Model Army became a formidable force. At the Battle of Naseby in June, it won a major victory over the royalists and a year later Charles surrendered.

The next two years were chaotic. The Presbyterians and Independents quarreled over what to do with the king, and finally the Civil War resumed. This time the Presbyterians and Scots backed Charles against the Independ-

ents. But even with this alliance the royalist forces were no match for the New Model Army; Cromwell soon defeated his opponents and captured the king.

At the same time, in 1647, the Independents abolished the House of Lords and removed all Presbyterians from the House of Commons, leaving behind a "rump" of less than 100 men, about a fifth of the original membership of the Long Parliament. The Rump Parliament tried to negotiate with Charles but discovered that he continued to plot a return to power. With Cromwell's approval the Commons decided that their monarch, untrustworthy and a troublemaker, would have to die. A trial without legality was held, and though many of the participants refused to sign the death warrant, the "holy, anointed" king was executed by his subjects in January 1649, to the horror of all Europe and most of England.

England Under Cromwell: The Interregnum

Oliver Cromwell, the hero of the New Model Army, was now master of England. The republic established after Charles' execution was officially ruled by the Rump Parliament, but a Council of State led by Cromwell controlled policy, with the backing of the army. Military activity was far from over because first an Irish rebellion had to be crushed—and it was, brutally—and then the Scots revolted in support of Charles II, the executed monarch's son. This last threat was not suppressed until late in 1651.

At home Cromwell had to contend with a ferment of political and social ideas. One group, known as the Levellers, demanded the vote for nearly all adult males and parliamentary elections every other year. The men of property among the Puritans, notably Cromwell himself, were disturbed by the political egalitarianism implied by these proposals and insisted that only men with an "interest" in

---

[3] This was a majority of a depleted House, however, because a few dozen royalists had departed from the Commons during 1641, especially after the Grand Remonstrance, and they never returned.

England—that is, land—should be qualified to vote.[4]

Even more radical were the Diggers, a communistic sect that sought to implement the spirit of primitive Christianity by abolishing personal property; the Society of Friends, which stressed personal inspiration as the source of faith and all action; and the Fifth Monarchists, a messianic group who believed that the "saints"—themselves—should rule because the Day of Judgment was at hand. Men of great ability contributed to the fantastic flood of pamphlets and suggestions that poured forth in these years—the poet John Milton, Cromwell's secretary, was one of the most prominent pamphleteers—and their ideas inspired many future revolutionaries. But at the time they merely put Cromwell on the defensive, forcing him to maintain control at all costs.

Cromwell himself—as an Independent among the Puritans, a staunch parliamentarian, and a country gentleman—fought for two overriding causes: religious freedom (except for Anglicanism and Catholicism) and constitutional government. But neither came within his grasp, and he grew increasingly unhappy at the Rump's refusal to enact reforms. When the assembly tried to perpetuate itself, he dissolved it in 1653 (the final end of the Long Parliament).

During the remaining five years of his life, Cromwell tried desperately to lay down a new constitutional structure for his government. He always hoped that Parliament itself would establish the perfect political system for England. In fact, though, the three Parliaments

he called during these five years seemed to have no inclination to undertake such reforms. Cromwell refused on principle to influence proceedings—except to dismiss the assembly when he felt a selfish faction was seeking its own ends—but in so acting he ignored the realities of politics and left his ideals unfulfilled.

Cromwell was driven by noble aspirations, but he adhered to them so intensely that he could make few compromises. Finally, when he felt he had no other recourse since nobody else was as high-minded as he was, he created a blatant military dictatorship, because the alternatives seemed worse. From 1653 on he was called lord protector and ruled through eleven major generals, each responsible for a different district of England and supported by a tax on royalist estates. To quell dissent he banned newspapers, and to prevent disorder he took such measures as enlisting innkeepers as government spies.

Cromwell always remained a reluctant revolutionary; he hated power and sought only limited ends. Some revolutionaries, like Lenin, have a good idea of where they would like to be carried by events; others, like Cromwell, move painfully, hesitantly, and uncertainly to the extremes they finally reach. It was because he sought England's benefit so urgently and because he considered the nation too precious to abandon to irreligion or tyranny that he remained determinedly in command to the end of his life.

Those final years, however, were filled with plots led by Levellers, royalists, and other dissidents of every shade of belief. The court that gathered around the young Stuart heir, Charles II, who had been in exile on the Continent since 1648, was a breeding ground of conspiracy. Only a superb counterespionage system, organized by the head of Cromwell's postal services (who simply read the mails), enabled him to quench all the plots.

Gradually more traditional forms reap-

---

[4] It should be recalled that voting rights were still tightly restricted; parliamentary elections by no means assured every Englishman a voice in government. In a town only the freemen (a small group, rarely more than about 20 percent of the population) and in the country only owners of land worth at least 40 shillings in rent a year (considerably less than 10 percent) were entitled to vote.

peared. The Parliament of 1656 offered Cromwell the crown, and though he refused, he took the title of "His Highness" and ensured that the succession would go to his son. Cromwell was monarch in all but name; only he assured stability. After he died his quiet, retiring son Richard proved no match for the scheming generals of the army. To bring an end to the chaos, General George Monck, the commander of a well-disciplined force in Scotland, marched south, assumed control, invited Charles II home from exile, and thus in May of 1660 brought the interregnum to an end.

The Results of the Revolution

Cromwell's chief success had been in foreign policy: he had strengthened the navy, captured Jamaica, gained Dunkirk, and in general reasserted England's importance in international affairs. But at home only the actions taken during the first months of the Long Parliament, in 1640 and 1641—the abolition of leading royal courts, the prohibition of taxation without parliamentary consent, and the establishment of the writ of habeas corpus—persisted beyond the interregnum. Otherwise everything was much the same as before: bishops and lords were reinstated; the repression of religious dissent was resumed; Parliament was called and dissolved by the monarch; and though many old feudal rights were annulled, the king got a set annual income in their place. Inertia and tradition reasserted themselves in the end.

The obvious long-term political and social changes were so minor that one might well question whether this had indeed been a revolution. By comparison with the French and Russian revolutions, its legacy was slim at best. And yet in one fundamental way it had altered the structure of government and society. Henceforth the gentry could no longer be denied a decisive voice in politics. In essence this had been their revolution, and they had succeeded. When in the 1680s a king again tried to impose his wishes on the country without reference to Parliament, there was no need for another major upheaval. A quiet, bloodless coup reaffirmed the new role of the gentry and Parliament.

Thus a new settlement was reached after a long period of growing unease and open conflict. The English could now enjoy untroubled a system of rule that with only gradual modification was to remain in force for some two centuries.

FRANCE

Before 1789, the civil wars of the sixteenth century were the closest France came to a revolutionary situation, but the tensions did not disappear when Henry IV brought the fighting to an end. Although the monarchy managed to extend its powers over the next fifty years, resistance continued until a final violent confrontation between the central government and its opponents in the 1640s and 1650s ended in victory for the crown. That confrontation, known as the Fronde, did not develop into a radical attempt to reorganize society, but it did parallel the contemporary English revolution in that its outcome settled the political and social structure of the country for over a century.

Henry IV

Henry IV began the process of strengthening royal power as soon as the civil wars were over. During the remaining years of his reign, from 1598 to 1610, opposition was muted, and he was able to establish his authority in a variety of ways. He mollified the traditional landed aristocracy, known as the nobility of the sword, by giving its leaders places on the chief executive body, the Council of Affairs, and then, when he felt strong enough, by shunting them off to their country estates with large financial settlements that were little better than bribes.

The principal bureaucrats, known as the nobility of the robe, required more careful treatment. They were a formidable group, in control of the country's administration, and led by great officeholding dynasties that were highly suspicious of newcomers. Henry did not try to undermine their position, but he made sure to turn their interests to his benefit. Since all crown offices had to be bought, he used the system both to raise revenues and to confirm the bureaucrats in their loyalty to the king. His tactics involved not only an acceleration in the sales of offices, but also the invention of a new device, an annual fee known as the *paulette*. Regular payments of the *paulette* ensured that an officeholder's job would remain in his family when he died. This not only increased royal profits (by the end of Henry's reign, receipts from the sales accounted for one-twelfth of crown revenues), but also reduced the flow of newcomers and thus strengthened the commitment of existing officeholders to the status quo, that is, to the crown.

By 1610 Henry had succeeded in imposing his will throughout France to a degree that would have been unimaginable in 1598. His treasury was solvent, neither great nobles nor Huguenots gave him trouble, and he was secure enough to plan an invasion of the Holy Roman Empire to extend his power even further. He was assassinated as he was about to leave Paris to join his army, but he had already brought about a quite extraordinary revival of royal authority.

Economic Affairs

In economic affairs the religious wars had taken a toll that was not so quickly remedied. In the 1550s a most fruitful alliance in trading ventures had developed between merchants and nobles. Significant advances had been made overseas, where the French had begun to encroach on the Portuguese monopoly of slaves, gold, and ivory in West Africa. Great ports such as Bordeaux and Marseilles and trade centers such as Lyons had enjoyed unprecedented prosperity. France possessed more fertile agricultural land than any other country of Europe, and her manufactured goods, notably clothes, had been sought throughout the Continent.

The civil war had changed this rosy situation. Trade had suffered heavily, particularly in the once-bustling coastal areas along the Channel. The overseas effort had come to a halt, and the French had soon been replaced by the Dutch and the English as the principal challengers to the Spanish and Portuguese empires. Taxes had mounted, and a large part of the burden had fallen on the merchants in the form of heavy customs dues. Naturally men had abandoned commerce as soon as they could afford to enter the nobility and gain a tax exemption by buying a royal office. The result was that capital had been diverted from trade to unproductive expenditures, and by the end of the century the nobility had developed a lofty contempt for commerce. French trade did not recover its vitality for more than a hundred years. Agriculture had suffered less, but uprisings of peasants, the main victims of the tax system, occurred almost annually in some part of France from the 1590s until the 1670s.

Although the restoration of stability ended the worst economic disruptions, Henry could do little about the fundamental problems that faced the merchants and the peasants. Nevertheless, once the process of centralization started, the assumption developed that the government was also responsible for the health of economic affairs. This view was justified by a theory known as mercantilism that became an essential ingredient of absolutism.

Mercantilism was more a set of attitudes than a systematic economic theory. Its basic premise—an erroneous one—was that the world contained a fixed amount of wealth and that each nation could enrich itself only at the expense of others. To some thinkers this meant hoarding as much bullion (gold and silver) as possible; to others it required a favorable balance of trade—more exports than imports. All mercantilists, however, agreed that state regulation was necessary for the welfare of a country. A strong, centralized government was the only power that could encourage native industries, control production, set quality standards, allocate resources, establish tariffs, and take other measures to promote prosperity and improve trade. Thus mercantilism was as much a political as an economic viewpoint and fitted in perfectly with Henry's restoration of royal power.

The Regency and Richelieu

Unrest reappeared, however, when Henry's death left the throne to his nine-year-old son, Louis XIII (1610–1643). The widowed queen, Marie de Médicis, serving as regent, dismissed her husband's ministers, and changed his aggressive foreign policy into friendship with the Hapsburgs. The Calvinists feared for their safety, and their stronghold, the southwest, came close to open revolt. The nobles too began to reassert themselves, infuriated because Marie, an Italian, took advice from her fellow countrymen and not from the aristocrats of the kingdom. Led by the prince of Condé, a cousin of Henry IV's, they demanded an investigation of the Council of Regency and particularly of its financial dealings. In the face of these mounting troubles, Marie summoned the Estates General in 1614.

This was the last meeting of the Estates General for 175 years, until the eve of the French Revolution, and its failings demonstrated that the monarchy was the only institution around which the nation could be united. The session revealed only the impotence of those who wished to oppose the throne, and Marie put the issue beyond doubt by declaring her son to be of age and the regency dissolved. There was now nothing left

to investigate, for the Estates General could only offer advice to a king; it had no legislative powers. The remaining aristocratic dissidents were silenced by large bribes, which consumed the entire treasure left by Henry IV, and the Calvinists were partially appeased by guarantees that their status would not be changed.

For a decade after the crisis, the court lacked the energetic direction that was needed to continue the consolidation of power begun by Henry IV. But in 1624 one of Marie's favorites, Armand du Plessis de Richelieu, a churchman who rose to the cardinalate through her favor, took control of the government. For the next eighteen years, there was once more an ambitious and determined head of the central administration.

Many forces pressed on the monarchy as it concentrated its power, and it was Richelieu's great achievement that he kept them in balance. The strongest group was the bureaucracy, whose ranks had been swollen by the sale of office. Richelieu was a classic example of the great ministers of the seventeenth century in that he always paid close attention to the wishes of the bureaucrats and could then face the monarchy as the head of a vast army of indispensable royal servants. He achieved a similar balance with the nobles, whom he integrated into the regime by giving them posts as diplomats, soldiers, officials, and administrators of local regions. With prominent positions in government, the nobility was as eager as the monarch for domestic security.

But the Huguenots still stirred uneasily. Since the death of Henry IV, they had feared new repressions and had engaged in sporadic fighting with the monarchy. The conflict reached a new intensity in the mid-1620s, and the royal army embarked on a systematic destruction of their military power in their stronghold, the southwest, capturing their chief bastion, the port of La Rochelle, in 1628. Richelieu then imposed strict terms. All the guarantees established by the Edict of Nantes were abolished, and though the Huguenots were allowed freedom of worship, they no longer were permitted local independence, which might threaten the unity of the state.

Richelieu also hoped to reduce administrative expenses, but when money was needed for aggression abroad, the good intentions disappeared. The sale of office was allowed to break all bounds: by 1633 it accounted for approximately one-half of the royal revenue. Ten years later more than three-quarters of the crown's direct taxation was needed to pay the salaries of the officeholders. It was a vicious circle, and the only solution was to increase the ordinary taxes, which fell most heavily on the lower classes.

As the burden of taxation mounted, Richelieu had to improve the government's control over the realm to obtain the revenue he needed. He increased the power of the *intendants*, the government's chief agents in the localities, and established them as the principal representatives of the monarchy in each province of France—a counterpoise to the traditionally dominant nobility. The *intendants* recruited for the army, arranged billeting, supervised the raising of taxes, and enforced the king's decrees. They soon came to be hated figures because the rising taxes were creating constant unrest.

In almost every year of the seventeenth century but with greatest intensity from the 1620s to the 1670s, there was a peasant uprising in some area of France, and the main grievance was taxation. But there were other issues too, notably a dislike for the growth of the central government. The peasants were frequently led by local notables who resented the widening powers of the monarchy because the increase in taxes and the rise of the *intendants* threatened their own jurisdictions.

Thus, when Richelieu decided to ignore domestic problems and concentrate on foreign ambitions, he took a major gamble, which almost failed in 1636: troops sent to quell a peasant uprising left a serious gap in France's eastern defenses, allowing Spanish troops to invade to within 100 miles of Paris. But disaster was avoided, the French went on to increasing military success, and when Richelieu died in 1642, it appeared that the twin ambitions of absolutism at home and preeminence abroad were close to realization.

Yet it was clear that the costs of France's foreign policy during the early seventeenth century intensified her domestic problems. Those who resented the growing power of the central government were only waiting for the right moment to reassert themselves. Yet the centralization was so successful that when the moment came, in the Fronde, there was no major effort to reshape the social order or to reorganize the state into a new political system. The Fronde was certainly a strident clash between opposing forces, but it took place within the traditional political and social forms. The principal expressions of discontent came from the upper levels of society: the nobles, townsmen, and members of Parlements. Only occasionally were these groups joined by peasants, who had bitter grievances against taxation and royal officials, and only for a brief while in the city of Bordeaux was there a foretaste of the sweeping revolution that was eventually to overtake France in 1789.

The Fronde

The death of Louis XIII, in 1643, followed by a regency because Louis XIV was only five years old, provided the opportunity for those who wanted to hold back the rise of absolutism. The immediate issues strikingly resembled those of Louis XIII's own minority, under the regency of Marie de Médicis. Louis XIII's widow, Anne of Austria, took over the government and placed all the power in the hands of the Italian-born Cardinal Giulio

Mazarin, a protégé of Richelieu's who symbolized the influence of foreigners and the Catholic Church that both nobles and parlementaires disliked. Moreover, Mazarin used his position to amass a huge fortune. He was therefore a perfect target for the expression of a deep-seated resentment: anger at the encroachment of central government on local authority.

Early in 1648 Mazarin sought to gain a respite from the monarch's perennial financial trouble by withholding payment of the salaries of some royal officials for four years. In response the members of various administrative and legal institutions in Paris, including the Parlement, drew up a charter of demands. They wanted the office of *intendant* abolished, no new offices created, power of approval over the raising of taxes, and enactment of a habeas corpus law. The last two demands reflected what the English Parliament was seeking at this very time, but the first two were long-standing French grievances, intensified by the officers' fear for their class identity and authority in the face of royal power, and by general opposition to newly created officials and taxes.

Mazarin reacted by arresting the Paris Parlement's leaders, thus sparking a popular rebellion in the city that forced him and the royal family to flee from the capital—an experience the young Louis XIV never forgot. In the spring of 1649, Mazarin promised to redress the parlementaires' grievances, and he was allowed to return to Paris. But the trouble was far from over; during that summer uprisings spread throughout France, particularly among peasants and in the old Huguenot stronghold, the southwest.

The most turbulent developments took place in the city of Bordeaux, where the parlementaires lost control and minor artisans and lawyers, furious at the taxes imposed by the crown and eager to revenge themselves on the less-burdened upper orders of society, took over the municipal government. Peasants and street mobs roamed the city, directing their hostility as much at the rich and powerful as at the representatives of the king.

From Mazarin's point of view, however, a more direct threat was posed by two generals who had turned against the government: Henri de Turenne and Louis II of Bourbon, prince of Condé, who had won a series of brilliant military victories in the 1640s and paved the way for France's gains at Westphalia in 1648. Condé was particularly dangerous because he was the head of the greatest noble family in France, and many aristocrats followed his lead. Their aims had not changed much since the days of the Guises eighty years before: they wanted Mazarin removed, their local powers restored, and a more influential position at court. Some nobles made brief alliances with the regional parlementaires, but each group wanted power for itself, and thus they soon drew apart.

Capitalizing on the disillusionment that soon resulted from the perpetual unrest, Mazarin began to reassert the position of the monarchy. Turenne was simply bought over; military force and the threat to use it subdued Paris and most of the rural rebels; Condé, losing support, fled to Spain; and the vulnerable regency was brought to an end by the declaration that Louis was of age in 1652. When Bordeaux finally fell to royal troops the next year, the Fronde was virtually over. Although peasants continued their occasional regional uprisings for many years to come, no other element in French society seriously challenged the crown as the basis for order in the realm.

Mazarin's remaining years in power, until his death in 1661, were relatively free of trouble. In foreign affairs he brought the war with Spain to a triumphant conclusion at the Treaty of the Pyrenees in 1659. At home the nobles had now been weakened as never before; the royal administration, centered on the *intendants*, faced no significant resistance; and the parlements subsided into quiescence, their demands all rejected when Louis was declared of age. This outcome was very different from the situation across the Channel in 1661, but just as surely as England, France had found a stable solution for long-standing conflicts.

SPAIN

For Spain the upheavals of the mid-seventeenth century were little short of disastrous. Until they erupted, she was the most powerful state in Europe; when they were over, she had lost her preeminence and was on her way to becoming a second-class power. Yet the seeds of her difficulties—primarily administrative and financial—were already visible in the sixteenth century.

Stresses in the Reign of Philip II
Philip's chief problem was the lack of unity in his diverse domains. From his father he inherited the Low Countries, Naples, Sardinia, Sicily, and Spain and her New World territories. In 1580 Portugal and her possessions also came under his control.

To hold this sprawling empire together, Philip developed an elaborate bureaucracy. But he was an obsessively suspicious man, and he therefore determined to maintain close control over the administrative structure by keeping in touch with every decision. As a result proceedings were agonizingly slow and inefficient in both important and trivial matters. The effect on military affairs was crippling; commanders in the field were often paralyzed, waiting for orders from home before taking action. Moreover the bureaucracy was run by Castilian nobles, who were resented as outsiders in other regions of the empire.

The standing army also caused the king problems. Although the military gave the throne potent support, it was the regime's single largest expense. The cost was readily undertaken since the logistic and administrative needs of the army stimulated the growth of bureaucracy and government authority. But the populace was less appreciative of these outlays, particularly when, to meet some of the expense and to emphasize the might of the crown, soldiers were lodged in the homes of ordinary citizens without recompense. This aroused bitter resentment, especially in the Low Countries, where the Spanish troops were regarded as foreigners.

Within the Iberian peninsula, however, Philip was able to overcome the resentment by using religious belief to arouse his subjects' loyalty. Spaniards regarded their country as the bastion of Catholicism, and Philip's devoutness reflected their mood perfectly. He eradicated any sign of heresy, and his enmity toward unorthodoxy affected even the great flowering of Spanish mysticism, led by St. Theresa of Avila. Neither the king nor the ecclesiastical hierarchy could feel comfortable about the mystics because such extremes of personal faith seemed to weaken the position of the Catholic Church. Nonetheless Philip's emphasis on the nation's faith powerfully stimulated Spain's political cohesion, which was promoted rather than hindered by the military activity in behalf of the Church.

Economic Problems
In other areas, notably the economy, there was little Philip could do to relieve the strains of constant warfare. Spain was a rich country in Philip's reign, but the most profitable activities were monopolized by limited groups, often foreigners. Because royal policy valued administrative convenience above social benefit, the city of Seville was arbitrarily given control over commerce with the New World so as to simplify supervision of this enormous

source of income. Other lucrative pursuits, such as wool and wine production, were dominated by a small coterie of insiders who made large profits but needed little manpower. And the pasturage rights throughout Castile that the crown granted sheep breeders removed vast areas of land from use by growers of foodstuffs. The only important economic activity whose income spread beyond a restricted circle was the prosperous Mediterranean trade. This commerce, centered in Barcelona, brought wealth to much of Aragon.

The profits made by non-Spaniards were the most obvious example of the limited domestic benefit of Spain's vast wealth. Most of the American treasure was sent abroad to repay German and Italian bankers whose loans kept Philip's troops in the field. Apart from Seville the cities that gained most from the new wealth were Genoa and Antwerp. And the Genoese mercantile community, with long experience in international finance, dominated Seville's economic life and played a crucial role in financing Philip's campaigns. Antwerp, always important as the meeting place for traders from the Mediterranean and the North, now gained prominence as the focus of Spanish activity in the Low Countries.

Thus even though the influx of silver into Spain continued to rise (it quadrupled between the 1550s and 1590s), the money was not profitably invested within the country. Drastically overextended in foreign commitments, the king declared himself bankrupt three times during his reign. His misguided policies, especially his continuing military involvements, were causing a slow economic deterioration.

Spain's futile struggles with the Dutch and later with the French proved to be the final blows in a succession of multiplying difficulties—economic, political, and military. For a while it seemed that the problems might be overcome because the second half of Philip III's reign (1598–1621), following the truce signed with the Dutch in 1609, was a time of peace. But in fact Philip's government was incompetent and corrupt, capable neither of dealing with the serious consequences of generations of excessive war spending nor of broadening the country's limited list of exports beyond wool and wine. Moreover, when the flow of treasure from the New World began to dwindle after 1600, the crown was deprived of a major source of income that it was unable to replace (see accompanying table). The decline was caused partly by a growing use of precious metals in the New World colonies but more importantly by a demographic disaster that overtook the Indians who worked as laborers and miners. Disease, overwork, and a drastic fall in the birth rate

IMPORTS OF TREASURE TO SPAIN FROM THE NEW WORLD, 1601–1660

DECADE	TOTAL VALUE*
1601–1610	66,970,000
1611–1620	65,568,000
1621–1630	62,358,000
1631–1640	40,110,000
1641–1650	30,641,000
1651–1660	12,785,000

* In ducats

Adapted from J. H. Elliott, *Imperial Spain 1469–1716*, New York, 1964, p. 175.

reduced their numbers with incredible speed. In Mexico and northern Guatemala alone, there had been approximately 25 million natives when the Spaniards first arrived in 1519. By the 1650s there were only 1.5 million.

In the meantime tax returns at home were shrinking, and at best they never covered expenses. The most significant factor in this decrease was a drop in the population of Castile and Aragon from 10 million in 1600 to 6 million in 1700. No other country in Europe suffered a demographic reversal of this proportion during the seventeenth century. The decline began when a terrible bout of plague carried off half a million people in five years around 1600, a loss that Spain never recovered. In addition, though the wine and wool industries continued to prosper, their spectacular growth had come to a halt by the early seventeenth century, and no other important industries took their place. Worse still, Spain had to rely increasingly on the importation of expensive foodstuffs to feed her people.

It was under these conditions that Spain resumed large-scale fighting under Philip IV (1621–1665), first reopening hostilities against the Dutch in 1621 and then starting an escalating involvement in the Thirty Years' War. With her dwindling resources the burdens now became too much to bear. Through the 1620s a brilliant general, Ambrogio di Spinola, maintained the Spaniards' tradition of military victory, but his death, in 1630, removed their last able commander. The effort to continue the government's commitment to war during the subsequent decades in defiance of totally inadequate financial means was finally to bring the greatest state in Europe to its knees.

Revolt and Secession
The final crisis was brought about by the policies of Philip IV's chief minister, the Count of Olivares. His aim was to unite the kingdom, to "Castilianize" Spain. He wanted all the territories to bear equally the burden of maintaining their country's dominant position in the world. Laws would be uniform, expenses would be apportioned equitably among the provinces, and each province would receive its fair share of the nation's gains. Although Castile would no longer dominate, she would also not have to provide the bulk of the taxes and army.

Olivares' program was called the Union of Arms, and though it seemed eminently reasonable, its implementation caused a series of revolts in the 1640s that split Spain apart. The reason was quite simple. For more than a century, Castile had controlled the other provinces, which had felt increasingly that local independence was being undermined by a centralized regime. The Union of Arms was regarded as the last straw because it added new substance to this long-standing grievance. Moreover Olivares undertook his plan at a time when Spain's military and economic fortunes were noticeably in decline. France had declared war on the Hapsburgs in 1635, and thereafter Spain's position had deteriorated. The funds to support an army were becoming harder to raise, and in desperation Olivares pressed more vigorously for the Union of Arms. But all he accomplished was to provoke crippling revolts against the Castilians in Catalonia, Portugal, Naples, and Sicily.

The precipitant was France's invasion of Catalonia in 1639. Thinking that the Catalans would not refuse to share some of the effort of repelling the invaders from their own territory, Olivares ordered the troops fighting the French to be billeted in Catalonia. But instead of strengthening the government, the order provided the people with the issue that finally goaded them into open defiance in 1640.

Olivares tried to meet the revolt by asking the Portuguese to help subdue the Catalans, but this attempt to bind together the components of the Spanish Empire only aroused further defiance. By the next year both Catalonia and Portugal declared themselves independent republics and placed themselves under French protection. Plots began to appear against Olivares, and Philip dismissed the one minister who had understood Spain's problems but who, in trying to solve them, had made them worse.

The Catalonian rebellion continued for another eleven years, and it was thwarted in the end only because the peasants and town mobs transformed the resistance to the central government into an attack on the privileged and wealthy classes in the province. At this point the Catalan nobility abandoned the cause and joined the government side. About the same time the Fronde forced the withdrawal of French troops. Thus when the last major holdout, Barcelona, fell to a royal army in 1652, the Catalan nobles returned with their rights and privileges guaranteed, and the revolt was over.

The Portuguese, on the other hand, though not officially granted independence from Spain until 1668, were fully capable of defending their autonomy and even invaded Castile in the 1640s. Their revolt against the central government never became tinged with the social unrest that undermined the Catalans' unity. Portugal's nobles maintained their authority throughout the struggle and dominated the government thereafter.

The revolts in Sicily and Naples, aimed at the Castilians who ruled and taxed both provinces, took place in 1647. In Naples the unrest soon developed into a tremendous mob uprising, led by a local fisherman. The poor turned against all the representatives of government and wealth they could find, and chaos ensued until their leader was killed. The violence in Sicily by contrast was more exclusively the result of soaring taxes and was directed almost entirely against government representatives. Severe countermeasures were taken in both Naples and Sicily, and within a few months the government regained control.

Spain had experienced a period of great cultural brilliance during Philip IV's reign, but even this died away as grim times descended on the country. Overextension in foreign war, financial and economic shortcomings at home, and the excessive reliance on Castile all had helped sap the nation's strength. The revolts during the 1640s were the result of decades of growing resentment at the monarch's inability to solve these basic, pressing problems; but the domestic unrest finally brought Spain's international ambitions and thus the worst of her difficulties to an end. Like England and France, she found a new way of life in the 1660s. She was to be a stable, second-level state, heavily agricultural, and run by her nobility.

THE UNITED PROVINCES

Although the United Provinces remained locked in a struggle for survival against Spain until 1648, and in various ways became a unique state, the Dutch did not escape the domestic tensions of the seventeenth century. Despite the remarkable fluidity of their society, they too went through a period of confrontation in the mid-seventeenth century that determined the structure of their government for over a century.

The Structure of the United Provinces

The United Provinces became a unique state for a number of reasons. Other republics existed in Europe, but they were controlled by small oligarchies; the Dutch, who had a long tradition of a strong representative assembly, the estates, founded a country in which many citizens participated in their own government through elected delegates. Although powerful merchants and a few aristocrats close to the House of Orange did create a small elite,

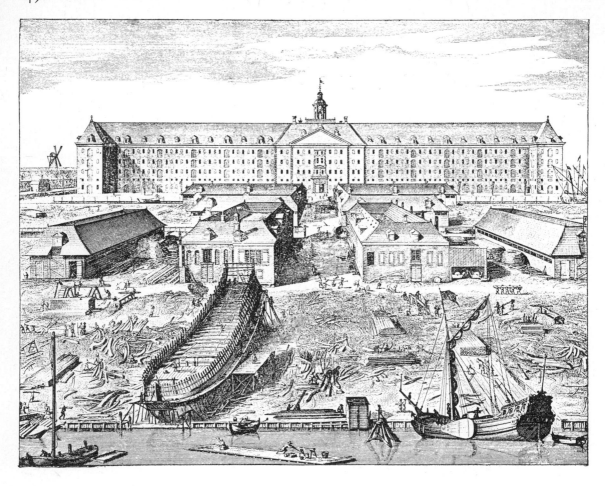

The Dutch became the best shipbuilders in Europe in the seventeenth century; the efficiency of their ships, which could be manned by fewer sailors than those of other countries, was a major reason for their successes in trade and commerce. (Photo: The Granger Collection)

the ordinary citizenry, participating in politics and united by a common cause, reduced the social differentiation prevalent elsewhere in Europe. The resultant openness and homogeneity colored the two most remarkable features of the United Provinces: economic mastery and cultural brilliance.

The most striking accomplishment of the Dutch was their rise to supremacy in the world of commerce. Amsterdam displaced Antwerp (and Genoa) as the Continent's financial capital and gained control of the trade of the world's richest markets. And in 1609 the Bank of Amsterdam was established, the first semiofficial financial institution of its kind in modern history; it made a vital contribution to the country's economy by offering the lowest interest rates in Europe. This encouraged native industries, such as shipbuilding, as well as overseas ventures, such as the East India Company, which needed substantial investments. In addition, the Dutch rapidly emerged as the cheapest shippers in international trade. As a result, by the middle of the seventeenth century they had become the chief carriers of European trade.

The openness of Dutch society permitted the freest exchange of ideas of the time. An official church, the Reformed Church, was established, but no religious groups were forbidden as long as they worshiped in private. The new state therefore gave refuge to dissenters of all kinds, whether extreme Protestant radicals or Catholics who wore their faith lightly, and the city of Amsterdam became the center of a brilliant Jewish community. This freedom attracted some of the greatest minds in Europe, and fostered remarkable artistic creativity. Patrons were easy to find among the wealthy merchants, and Dutch painting in the seventeenth century is one of the glories of Western culture. Yet it was not the result of the taste or sensibility of a few patrons and geniuses but an outpouring from many directions; and it was not the climax of a long tradition but a sudden outburst whose greatest expressions appeared in the first generation. The energy that produced the wealth and creativity reflected the pride of a tiny nation that was winning its independence.

Domestic Tensions

From the earliest days of the revolt against Spain, there had been a basic split within the United Provinces. The two provinces of Holland and Zeeland dominated the Estates General because they supplied a majority of its taxes. Their representatives formed a mercantile party, which advocated peace abroad so that their trade could flourish unhampered, government by the Estates General so that they could make their power felt, and religious toleration. In opposition to the mercantile interest was a party centered on the House of Orange, which sought to boost that family's leadership of the Dutch. This party stood for war to strengthen a popular national leader, centralized power for the House of Orange, and (after William died) strict religious orthodoxy.

The differences between the two factions came to a head in 1618, when Maurice of Nassau used the religious issue as a pretext for executing his chief opponent, Jan van Oldenbarneveldt, the principal representative of the province of Holland. Oldenbarneveldt opposed the resumption of war with Spain when the truce of 1609 expired in 1621, and his removal left Maurice in full control of the country. The mercantile party had been defeated, and war could resume in 1621.

For more than twenty years, the House of Orange remained in command, unassailable because it led the army in time of war. Not until 1648, when the family was headed by a new leader, could its opponents reassert themselves and sign the treaty of Westphalia that officially recognized the independence of the United Provinces. It then seemed that the mercantile party had gained the upper hand. But the outcome remained in the balance (there was even the threat of a siege of Amsterdam by troops loyal to the House of Orange) until William II suddenly died in 1650, leaving as his successor a posthumously born son, William III.

With serious opposition removed, the mercantile interest could now assume full power, and Jan De Witt, the representative of the province of Holland, took over the running of the government in 1653. De Witt's aims were to leave as much authority as possible in the hands of the provinces, particularly Holland; to weaken the executive in this way and prevent a revival of the fortunes of the House of Orange; to pursue trading advantage; and to maintain peace so that the economic supremacy of the Dutch would not be endangered. For more than a decade, he guided the country in its golden age. But in 1672 French armies overran the southern provinces, and De Witt, with his mercantile inclinations, lacked the military instinct to fight a dangerous enemy. The Dutch at once turned to the family that had led them to independence; a mob murdered De Witt; and the House of Orange, under William III, resumed the centralization that henceforth was to characterize the political structure of the United Provinces. The country had not experienced a mid-century upheaval as severe as those of its neighbors, but it had nevertheless been forced to endure unrest and violence before the form of its government was securely established.

SWEDEN

The Swedes, too, reached basic decisions in the mid-seventeenth century about political relations and administration of the state. Violence was avoided, but tensions had to be resolved nonetheless.

The Achievement of Gustavus Adolphus

In the early 1600s Sweden, a Lutheran country of a million people which had gained its independence from Denmark less than a century earlier, was one of the backwaters of Europe. A feudal nobility dominated the countryside and sought to control the government, a barter economy made money almost unknown, and both trade and towns were virtually nonexistent. Moreover the Swedes found themselves in a running battle with the Danes, whose well-organized, well-armed, and prosperous monarchy dominated the Baltic Sea. Sweden, by contrast, lacked a capital, central institutions, and government machinery. The task of ruling was thus entirely dependent on the king and a few courtiers; officials were appointed only to deal with specific problems as they arose.

Gustavus Adolphus (1611–1632) trans-formed this situation. At the start of his reign, he faced a war that was to involve all the states in the area—his own, Denmark, Poland, and Russia—in a struggle to control the lands around the Baltic. Without his nobles' help, however, Gustavus could not raise an army. He therefore arranged an alliance with the nobles and gave them dominant positions in a newly organized bureaucracy. By winning their support he not only staffed an administrative machine but organized an army, thus equipping himself both to govern and to fight.

During the two decades of his reign, Gustavus engaged in a remarkable series of conquests abroad. By 1629 he controlled the coastline of the eastern Baltic, making Sweden the most powerful state in the area. He then entered the Thirty Years' War, advancing victoriously through the Holy Roman Empire until his death, in 1632, during the showdown battle with Wallenstein. Although without their general the Swedes could do little more than hang on to the gains they had made, they remained for a century a force to be reckoned with in international affairs.

The system of government that Gustavus and his chief adviser, Axel Oxenstierna, established in 1611 was to be the envy of other countries until the twentieth century. At the heart of the system were five administrative departments,[5] each led by a nobleman, with the most important—the Chancellery—run by Oxenstierna, who supervised diplomacy and internal affairs. Gradually an administrative center emerged in Stockholm where, under Oxenstierna's capable leadership, the bureaucracy proved that it could run the nation, supply the army, and implement policy even during the last twelve years of Gustavus' reign, when the king himself was almost always

---

[5] They were the Chancellery, the Ministry of Justice, the Treasury, the Department of War, and the Department of the Navy.

abroad. During his absence Oxenstierna took charge, though executive power was officially vested in the Rad, an assembly of nobles.

Another major institution, the Riksdag, consisted of representatives of four estates: the nobility, the clergy, the townsmen, and (unique in Europe) the peasants. Although officially it was the highest legislative authority in the land, real power was retained by the nobles and the crown. For centuries the Riksdag functioned as no more than a sounding board that gave the appearance of popular approval to royal and aristocratic rule, which by the 1630s was already operating with an efficiency unparalleled on the Continent.

A major cause of Sweden's amazing rise was the development of the domestic economy. Early in Gustavus' reign new discoveries made possible the mining of huge deposits of copper, an important metal for cannon and coin manufacture. With the only other major source of copper being Japan, a Continental monopoly was assured. The crown maximized its profits by taking over the mining itself. To avoid dependence on one commodity, the government also encouraged iron mining. Foreign experts were brought in, and the discovery of a new smelting process made Swedish iron highly prized. At the same time, the country's traditional tar and timber exports were stepped up, and a fleet was built. By 1700 Stockholm had become an important trading and financial center, growing in the course of the century from fewer than 5,000 to more than 50,000 inhabitants—a phenomenal rise and further evidence of the general northward shift of European economic activity.

The Role of the Nobles
The one source of tension amidst this remarkable progress was the position of the aristocracy. They had been Gustavus' partners and after he died they tightened their control over the government and society.

Between 1611 and 1652 nobles more than doubled the proportion of land they owned in Sweden, and increased sixfold their holdings in Finland, which Sweden ruled. Much of this growth was at the expense of the crown, which granted away or sold its lands to help its war efforts abroad. Both peasants and townsmen viewed the developments with alarm. Peasants always fared much worse under nobles than as direct tenants of the king because the great landowners sought the maximum possible return from their possessions. And the towns felt that their place in national affairs was being completely destroyed by an excessively powerful aristocracy. Both groups were frightened when the Danish nobles took advantage of the death of their country's strong king, in 1648, to gain control of government.[6] Two years later the showdown came in Sweden.

The ruler of Sweden was Gustavus' daughter Christina, an able but erratic young queen who usually allowed Oxenstierna to run the government. In the late 1640s she was becoming increasingly hopeful that she could abdicate her throne, become a Catholic, and leave Sweden—an ambition she fulfilled in 1654. She wanted her cousin Charles recognized as her successor, but the aristocracy threatened to create a nobles' republic if she abdicated. The queen therefore summoned the Riksdag, Sweden's representative assembly, in 1650, and taking advantage of the grievances of townsmen and peasants, she encouraged the three lower estates to mount a campaign against the aristocracy. Believing that they might now gain a new importance in national affairs, the townsmen and peasants demanded the return of nobles' lands to the crown, freedom of

---

[6] In 1660 the Danish king engineered a countercoup that firmly established absolutism in that country. Denmark was thus yet another state whose political structure was settled for a long time to come during this period.

speech, and real power in the Riksdag so that the lower estates could outvote the nobles. Under this pressure the nobility gave way and recognized the future Charles X Gustavus as successor to the throne—a good choice, because Charles was an able soldier who consolidated Gustavus Adolphus' gains and confirmed Sweden's mastery of northern Europe.

But the confrontation of 1650 proved to be short-lived. Once Christina had won the argument over her successor, she removed her support from the Riksdag and rejected the demands of the lower estates. Only gradually did power shift away from the great nobles toward a broader elite of lesser nobles and bureaucrats.

EASTERN EUROPE

The major powers of eastern Europe, the Ottoman Empire, Poland, and Russia, were as affected by warfare as their western neighbors. And in Poland and Russia there were also upheavals in the mid-seventeenth century that helped determine these states' future political development.

The Ottoman Empire

In the Ottoman Empire central control was highly effective by the early 1500s. The first signs of a decline of strength at the center began to appear after the death of Suleiman, in 1566. Harem intrigues, corruption at court, and the loosening of military discipline became increasingly serious from the late sixteenth century onward. Yet the Ottomans remained·an object of fear and hostility throughout the West—their constant wars with the Hapsburgs devastated Hungary, where most of the fighting took place, and in the eastern Mediterranean they remained a formidable force, though the English and Dutch were coming to play a dominant role in the area after 1600.

The Turkish rulers had unparalleled powers. A crack army of more than 25,000 men stood ready to serve the sultan at all times, and within his domains his supremacy was unquestioned. He was both spiritual and temporal head of his empire, completely free to appoint all officers, issue laws, and raise taxes. But these powers, geared to military conquest and extending over enormous territories, never became a focus of cohesion among the disparate races of the Balkans and the Middle East who were ruled from Constantinople, because the sultan left authority in the hands of local nobles and princes as long as his ultimate sovereignty was recognized. Whenever questions of loyalty arose (as they did sporadically in the Balkans), they revealed that the authority of the central government rested on its military might. That was more than enough to prevent any serious challenges to the power of the Ottomans until they began to lose ground to the Hapsburgs in the eighteenth century.

Poland

The largest kingdom in Europe, Poland, was as disorganized as the Holy Roman Empire. The king could exercise control over his personal lands but elsewhere the country was entirely in the hands of powerful nobles, who from 1572 onward confirmed their independence by ensuring that the monarchy would be strictly elective. The Diet, an assembly of nobles, was required to meet at least once every two years, and without the approval of this body no policy could be enforced.

In Poland as elsewhere, religion was a major issue during the second half of the sixteenth century. Sigismund III (1587–1632), with the help of some members of the aristocracy and the Jesuits, crushed Protestantism. But not all the nobles favored Roman Catholicism; some belonged to the Greek Orthodox Church. Attempts were made to unite the Roman Catholics with the Greek Orthodox, and one group, known as the Uniate Church, agreed to acknowledge papal supremacy while retaining traditional Greek rites. When the Jesuits tried to increase their influence, however, the adherents of the Orthodox and Uniate churches formed a coalition for common defense that split the country into two religious camps.

Although Poland was constantly at war, Sigismund and his successors were never able to use the military situation to overcome the fragmentation of political authority and create a strong central government. Instead, the religious divisions and the power of local nobles became increasingly serious problems until, in the mid-seventeenth century, the Poles, like so many Europeans, faced a major internal clash.

The crisis arose in the Ukraine, the borderland in the southeast of Poland that had long been occupied by the soldier-farmers known as Cossacks. Like their Russian counterparts, these Cossacks were allowed considerable independence because of their importance in protecting the countryside against turbulent neighbors to the south and east. Firm adherents of the Greek Orthodox Church, they became increasingly annoyed at the government for encouraging Catholicism. Finally in 1648 they rebelled, took control of the eastern Ukraine, and in 1654 offered their allegiance to the Greek Orthodox tsar of Russia.

The Polish monarchy was much too weak to combat the revolt, and the nobility had little wish to undertake a long assault on this frontier region. Thus the Ukraine was lost—yet another casualty of the upheavals of the age—though internally Poland continued much as before, a country dominated by a small yet powerful aristocracy. Once again, the storms that swept political life had been succeeded by a sense of settlement.

Russia

The power of the central authority in Russia was already apparent in the reign of Ivan IV (1547–1584)—called the Terrible—who used his considerable military strength both at home and in conquests that extended Muscovite rule along the length of the Volga River to the southeast.

Ivan's autocracy was hampered by fewer limitations than any other ruler in Europe. Russia was still feudal; her peasants were serfs, and her great lords, known as boyars, controlled local areas but had little say in national affairs. Jealous of their regional powers, Ivan launched a vicious campaign against the boyars and enormously increased the areas of Russia under his direct control. He enlarged his bureaucracy to meet the new administrative tasks created by his conquests, but the authority of the central government was now a divisive rather than a unifying force, discredited and hated because it had grown by military might.

The reaction came after Ivan's death, when the country entered a thirty-year period that would later be called the Time of Troubles. Ivan's son Feodor, the last of the Rurik dynasty, which had ruled since the ninth century, lacked his father's vigor and could not prevent the boyars from reasserting their power. From 1591 onward he virtually handed over control of the government to his brother-in-law, Boris Godunov, whom the boyars regarded as an upstart. When Feodor died in 1598 Boris became tsar and major revolts soon broke out.

For fifteen years the country was in chaos as peasants, townsmen, and petty nobles joined in various coalitions against the government and the boyars. The final confrontation took place when the leading boyars supported a Polish claimant to the throne, and a popular army, led by townsmen and lesser nobles who had been excluded from political prominence by the higher nobility, drove the Polish claimant from Moscow. In his place a national assembly, consisting of nobles and townsmen, elected as tsar a grandnephew of Ivan the Terrible, Mikhail Feodorovich (1613–1645), founder of the Romanov dynasty.

The central government emerged from these disruptions with its powers essentially unimpaired. The boyars had been unable to weaken the tsar's ability to take firm military measures against his opponents, and under Mikhail they returned to docile inaction. They now depended on the throne for their control over local areas, and many had to serve the tsar in order to retain their estates. During the half-century after the Time of Troubles, the monarchy organized its administration systematically, codified Russia's laws, and continued the extension of its authority by the use or threat of armed force.

But the potential for domestic upheaval was not entirely removed, and indeed it was during this half-century that the groundwork for new turmoil was laid as the boyars gradually closed the last loopholes in the system of serfdom. Previously an escaped serf who remained uncaptured for a certain number of years was automatically liberated, but in 1646 the boyars persuaded Tsar Alexis (1645–1676) to abolish the limit. Now a serf remained in his status for life—a hopeless fugitive even if he did escape his master.

The result was constant agrarian unrest, met by harsh repression, which inspired even more violent uprisings. The disturbances were fed by increasing financial demands on both serfs and townsmen from the central government and local lords, and in 1648 the boiling point was reached. A major riot broke out in Moscow, the tsar was forced to hand over to the rebels a number of his financial administrators, and by the end of the year almost every large city in Russia had experienced virulent disorders, quelled only by the intervention of royal troops. This year of upheaval, as fierce in Russia as in England and France, marked the beginning of a period of more than two decades when the lower classes made a major effort, for the last time in centuries, to restrain the growing power of the central government and the landowners.

The popular discontent intensified in the 1650s and 1660s, and finally in 1668 the major revolt that had long been brewing exploded in the southern provinces of Russia, led by a Cossack, Stenka Razin, who terrorized the area and launched a fleet that caused chaos on the Caspian Sea. In 1670 Razin led two expeditions up the Volga River, capturing a succession of towns and handing them over to mob rule. His very approach incited peasants to violence, for his troops included thousands of escaped serfs who hoped to bring liberty to all their oppressed brethren. There was open advocacy of what amounted to class war: the poor against the rich, the weak against the powerful. Eventually royal troops shattered the poorly equipped army; and though marauding bands continued to harass the inhabitants of central Russia for years, the major threat was ended in 1671, when Razin was executed in Moscow.

Compounding Russia's troubles was serious dissension within the national Greek Orthodox Church. The dispute arose over the decision of the patriarch of Moscow, the head of the Russian Church, to correct the traditional liturgical books of the faith, which contained errors introduced by copyists over the centuries. A group calling itself the Old Believers, refusing to change usages hallowed by custom, objected to the revision and broke away from the established church. The schism was accompanied by violence, which forced the patriarch and his followers to become entirely dependent on the secular power to maintain their authority. This reliance on the state undermined the clergy's spiritual leadership and helped the monarchy on its way to assuming complete control over all facets of Russian society.

Having overcome two potential threats to his authority—peasant unrest in areas far from Moscow and the rivalry within the church—Alexis began to feel strong enough in his last years to pay less attention to the boyars. It was clear that a determined ruler could once again make the tsar the dominant figure in Russian society, and in the late seventeenth century it was Peter the Great who was to be that ruler.

Throughout Europe in the mid-seventeenth century long-standing tensions which had just passed through an especially virulent phase were resolved, and a period of relative stability began that was to last for over a century. In international affairs a vicious circle of brutality was broken as a degree of restraint was imposed on the anarchy of warfare. Within Europe's states, the resistance to central governments, usually the result of regional loyalties, traditional aristocratic independence, or resentment at soaring taxes, was effectively brought to an end. Whatever the outcomes—and they ranged from England's parliamentary system to France's absolutism—each country's political situation now settled into accepted forms, just as warmaking and diplomacy did after Westphalia.

Because the disturbances had been so widespread, historians have called the mid-seventeenth century an age of "general crisis." It is a rather vague term, but it does convey the flavor of a period when upheaval was common, reached crisis proportions, and then subsided into relaxation. To the extent that the crisis was general, however, one would expect it to be reflected not merely in politics but in thought, art, and society. And indeed, the mid-seventeenth century was the time when, for example, the ideas of the scientific revolution became, after much doubt, an essential part of European civilization. One must not push the connections too far, because simple parallels distort the complexities of the period; nevertheless, the progression from turbulence to calm in politics was not without its analogies in the cultural and social developments of the sixteenth and seventeenth centuries.

RECOMMENDED READING

Sources

Studies

* Franklin, Julian H. (tr. and ed.). *Constitutionalism and Resistance in the Sixteenth Century: Three Treatises by Hotman, Beza, & Mornay.* 1969. Three of the most radical tracts of the period, each justifying rebellion.

* Aston, Trevor (ed.). *Crisis in Europe 1560–1660: Essays from Past and Present.* 1965. This is a collection of those essays in which the "general crisis" interpretation was initially put forward and discussed.

Doolin, P. R. *The Fronde*. 1935. Still the best account in English of the French upheaval.

Elliott, John H. *The Revolt of the Catalans*. 1963. The standard history of the growing troubles of the Spanish monarchy in the seventeenth century.

* Forster, Robert, and Jack P. Greene (eds.). *Preconditions of Revolution in Early Modern Europe*. 1972. An excellent series of essays on resistance to central governments, and its causes, in a number of European countries.

Hellie, Richard. *Enserfment and Military Change in Muscovy*. 1971. This study shows the links between military affairs and social change in Russia during the early modern period.

Howell, Roger. *Cromwell*. 1977. The clearest and most reliable short biography of the revolutionary leader.

Koenigsberger, H. G. *Estates and Revolutions: Essays in Early Modern European History*. A most useful set of articles, primarily on political history; of particular interest is a fascinating comparison of the revolutionary parties in France and the Netherlands.

* Mattingly, Garrett. *The Armada*. 1959. This beautifully written book, which was a best seller when it first appeared, is a gripping account of a major international crisis.

* Neale, J. E. *Queen Elizabeth I: A Biography*. 1934. A lucid and affectionate account of the reign by its most distinguished twentieth-century historian.

* Pagès, Georges. *The Thirty Years' War: 1618–1648*. 1971. The most straightforward history of a highly complex period.

Parker, Geoffrey. *The Army of Flanders and the Spanish Road, 1567–1659: The Logistics of Spanish Victory and Defeat in the Low Countries' Wars*. 1972. A study of the way Spain kept the route to the Netherlands open and the methods of warfare in this period.

* ————. *The Dutch Revolt*. 1977. This brief book gives a good introduction to the revolt of the Netherlands and the nature of Dutch society in the seventeenth century.

* Rabb, Theodore K. *The Struggle for Stability in Early Modern Europe*. 1975. An assessment of the "crisis" interpretation, including extensive bibliographic references.

Roberts, Michael. *Gustavus Adolphus and the Rise of Sweden*. 1973. This is the best biography of the Swedish king, emphasizing especially his military and administrative achievements.

* Salmon, J. H. M. *The French Wars of Religion: How Important Were Religious Factors?* 1967. A collection of interpretations of the causes and nature of the civil wars.

* Shaw, Howard. *The Levellers*. 1968. This brief introduction to the ideas and activities of the most famous radical group in the English revolution is accompanied by extracts from their writings.

Stone, Lawrence. *The Causes of the English Revolution, 1529–1642*. 1972. A short but comprehensive assessment of the reasons for the outbreak of the seventeenth century's most far-reaching revolution.

Tapié, V. L. *France in the Age of Louis XIII and Richelieu*. D. McN. Lockie (tr. and ed.). 1974. The standard history of the twenty-year period when the basic development of French absolutism took place.

* Walzer, Michael. *The Revolution of the Saints: A Study in the Origins of Radical Politics*. A provocative interpretation of the revolutionary impulse in English Puritanism.

* Available in paperback.

SIXTEEN

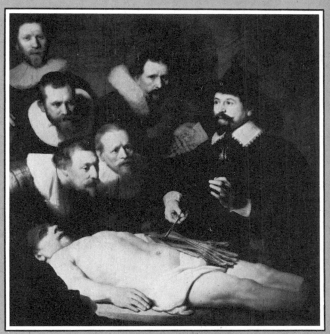

CULTURE AND SOCIETY IN THE AGE OF THE SCIENTIFIC REVOLUTION

The sense of upheaval and then crisis followed by a settling down that dominated European politics and international relations from the mid-sixteenth to the mid-seventeenth century is also visible in other areas of life. Indeed it is remarkable how well cultural and social patterns reflect the progression from uncertainty to stable resolution. Here, too, the doubts of more than a century, from the days of the Reformation, the discovery of new worlds, and the beginnings of the scientific revolution, were gradually overcome.

Not only the clearest but also the most important development along these lines was the scientific revolution. Starting with tentative and disturbing questions about the theories of ancient authorities, whose views had been accepted for centuries, scientists eventually created a completely new way of looking at nature and a new way of thinking and arguing about physical problems. Their successes were remarkable, and they became very influential, because the certainty and orderliness of their results appealed to a Europe that was seeking relief from uncertainty.

The central event in the confrontation between the old and the new was the trial and condemnation by the Roman Inquisition of one of the greatest of the seventeenth-century scientists, Galileo. But in the next generation the ideas he represented triumphed, as part of a renewed sense of settlement that descended on European society. Stability was visible throughout intellectual life: in literature as well as in art, in painting as well as in poetry. Where the Mannerist painters and the writers of the late sixteenth century emphasized doubts, upheaval, and insecurity, their successors in the Baroque period gave themselves up to enormous, grandiose ambitions, but the artists after the mid-seventeenth century increasingly stressed calm, restraint, and order. It was the exact equivalent to the resolution of tension one could see elsewhere in society.

Although for ordinary men and women these high intellectual movements had little meaning, their lives were changed in a similar direction as central governments gained considerable control over them, severely reducing the restlessness and rebelliousness that had been prevalent since the early sixteenth century. Even the inhabitants of country villages found that they were no longer as isolated and self-contained as they had once been. One of the most obvious symptoms of their unease, the tremendous outburst of witchcraft during this period, was curbed from above. And when religion no longer caused disruptions throughout Europe, the common people lost a major occasion for self-expression and violence. In general, with the powers of repression growing and their traditional local independence—and their wages—declining, ordinary people took an unavoidable part in the universal quieting down that characterized Western society in the late seventeenth century.

I. THE SCIENTIFIC REVOLUTION

To contemporaries the wars and crises of the sixteenth and seventeenth centuries seemed to dominate their lives. To us it is clear that European civilization was affected no less deeply in this period by the quiet revolution in ideas about nature that was accomplished by a handful of scholars and experimenters. We call such people scientists, but at the time they were known as natural philosophers. They were specialists in an area of philosophy then considered less important than theology; but by the time their revolution was complete, their ideas had become central to Western thought.

ORIGINS OF THE SCIENTIFIC REVOLUTION

The study of nature by Europeans took its point of departure from the ancient Greeks whose interests shaped subsequent work until the sixteenth century—Aristotle in physics, Ptolemy in astronomy, and Galen in medicine. The most dramatic advances during the scientific revolution came in the fields the Greeks had pioneered, and were to some extent caused by increasing evidence that their theories did not cover all the facts. For instance, Aristotle's belief that all objects in their natural state are at rest created a number of problems, such as explaining why an arrow kept on flying after leaving a bow; while grappling with this question, some fourteenth-century scientists came up with a new explanation, the belief that a moving body possessed impetus, which kept the motion going until it died out. Similarly, observations revealed that Ptolemy's picture of the heavens, in which all motion was circular around a central earth, could not account for the peculiar motion of some planets, which at times seemed to be moving backward. Moreover Galen's theories, often based on mistaken

anatomical information, were shown by dissections to be inadequate.

Still, it is not likely philosophers would have abandoned their cherished theories—they far preferred making adjustments than beginning anew—if it had not been for various other influences at work in the fifteenth and sixteenth centuries. First was the humanists' rediscovery of the work of a number of ancient scientists, which showed that classical writers themselves had not all agreed with the theories of Aristotle or Ptolemy. One particularly important rediscovery was Archimedes, whose studies of dynamics were an important inspiration for new ideas in physics. A second influence was an increasing interest in what we now dismiss as "magic," but which at the time was regarded as a serious intellectual enterprise. There were various sides to magical inquiry. Alchemy was the belief that by mixing substances and using secret formulae the nature of matter could be understood. A related interest was the theory of atomism, the idea that all matter was made up of tiny particles, whose composition could be changed—again a theory newly recovered from ancient writers. One of the most famous sixteenth-century alchemists, Paracelsus, was also a proponent of new medical theories, notably the belief that diseases were separate entities with lives of their own. Another magical favorite was astrology, which claimed that natural phenomena became understandable and predictable if planetary movements were properly interpreted. A similar easy key to the mysteries of nature was promised by Hermeticism, a school of thought that asserted that all of knowledge had once been given to man, that it was contained in some obscure writings, and that with the right approach and intelligence, a complete insight into the structure of the universe could be achieved.

What linked all this magic was the conviction that the world could be understood and that the answers to traditional questions consisted of simple, comprehensive keys to nature. The theories of Neoplatonism, which became very influential during the Renaissance, supported this conviction, as did some of the mystical beliefs that attracted attention in the fifteenth and sixteenth centuries. One of the latter, derived from a system of Jewish thought known as cabala, suggested that the key to the universe might consist of magical arrangements of numbers. For all its irrational elements, it was precisely this longing for new, simple solutions to ancient problems that made natural philosophers capable, for the first time, of discarding the honored theories they had inherited from antiquity, trying different ones, paying greater attention to mathematics, and eventually creating an intellectual revolution.

Two other influences deserve mention. The first was Europe's long fascination with technological invention. The architects, navigators, engineers, and weapons experts of the Renaissance were important pioneers of the belief in measurement and careful observation. For example, at the Arsenal in Venice, where huge cannon were moved and devices invented for handling great weights, Galileo got ideas and made experiments that helped his study of dynamics. A related interest was followed by the anatomists at the nearby university of Padua who created a school famous for its work in dissections and its direct investigations of nature; many of the leading figures of the scientific revolution received their training in methods of experiment and observation at Padua. It was not too surprising, therefore, that the period of the scientific revolution was marked by the invention of important new instruments which often made the discoveries possible: the telescope, the thermometer, the barometer, the vacuum pump, and the microscope. These instruments encouraged the development of a scientific approach that was

entirely new in the seventeenth century—it did not go back to the ancients, to the practitioners of magic, or to the engineers. It was pioneered by Francis Bacon and consisted of the belief that in order to make Nature reveal her secrets, she had to be made to do things she did not do normally: in Bacon's phrase, one had to "twist the lion's tail." What this meant was that one did not simply observe phenomena that occurred normally in nature—for instance, the apparent bending of a stick when placed in a glass of water—but created conditions that were *not* normal. With the telescope one could perceive secrets hidden to the naked eye; with the vacuum pump one could begin to understand the properties of air.

The influences that combined to create the scientific revolution varied greatly. Yet there is no doubt that the heart of the change lay in purely intellectual breakthroughs. A small group of brilliant men, grappling with ancient problems of physics, astronomy, and anatomy —motion, heavenly phenomena, and the structure of the body—came up with persuasive discoveries that changed Western thought forever.

THE FIRST BREAKTHROUGHS

The earliest advances were in astronomy and anatomy. By coincidence, both were contained in books published in 1543, which was also the year when the first printed edition of Archimedes appeared. *The Structure of the Human Body*, by Andreas Vesalius, a member of the Padua faculty, pointed out errors in the work of Galen, the chief medical authority for over a thousand years. Although Vesalius himself did not always follow strictly the findings of dissections—like Galen, he showed the liver as having five lobes, which is true of some animals but not of humans, though in a corner of the picture he also showed a small

An engraving of Copernicus' conception of the universe shows the sun rather than the earth at the center, the spheres to which planets were attached, and the moons of Jupiter discovered by Galileo. (Photo: British Museum)

two-lobed liver, perhaps to indicate that he knew what the human one really looked like—he opened a new era of careful observation and experimentation in studies of the body.

On the Revolutions of the Heavenly Bodies, by Nicolaus Copernicus, a Polish cleric who had studied at Padua, had far greater consequences. A first-rate mathematician, he felt that the calculations of planetary movements under Ptolemy's system had grown too complex. In Ptolemaic astronomy, the planets and the sun, attached to transparent, crystalline spheres, revolved around the earth. All motion was circular, and observed irregularities were accounted for by epicycles—movement around small spheres which were attached to the larger spheres and which themselves re-

Kepler, surrounded by the instruments of the astrologer and the astronomer, discussing his work with his patron, the emperor Rudolf II. (Photo: New York Public Library, Picture Collection)

volved. Much influenced by Neoplatonic and related ideas, Copernicus believed that a simpler picture would reflect more accurately the true structure of the universe. In good Neoplatonic fashion, he argued that the sun, as the most splendid of celestial bodies, ought rightfully to be at the center of an orderly and harmonious universe.

Copernicus' system was in fact no simpler than Ptolemy's—the spheres and epicycles were just as complex—and he had no way of proving that his theory was correct. But he was such a fine mathematician that his successors had to use his calculations even if they rejected his assumptions. He thus became part of intellectual discussion, drawn upon when Pope Gregory XIII decided to reform the calendar in 1582. The Julian calendar, in use since Roman times, counted century years as leap years, thus adding extra days which caused Easter—whose date is determined by the position of the sun—to drift further and further away from its normal occurrence in

March. The reform produced the Gregorian calendar, which we still use—ten days were simply dropped, and since then three out of every four century years have not been leap years (1900 had no February 29, but 2000 will have one). The need for calendar reform had been one of the motives for Copernicus' studies, which proved useful even though his theories remained controversial.

What developed during the half-century following the publication of his *Revolutions* was a growing sense of uncertainty. The greatest astronomer of the period, Tycho Brahe, made the most remarkable observations of the heavens before the telescope, plotting the paths of the moon and planets every night for decades. But the only theory he could come up with was an uneasy compromise between the Ptolemaic and Copernican systems. It was a disciple of his, the German Johannes Kepler, who made the first major advance on the work of Copernicus and who helped resolve the uncertainties that had arisen in the field of astronomy.

Kepler
Like Copernicus, Kepler believed that only the language of mathematics could describe the movements of the heavens. He was an open advocate of the latest magical ideas of his day —a famous astrologer, he also speculated about such subjects as the mystical meaning of geometric shapes—and he was convinced instinctively that Copernicus was right. He threw himself into the task of confirming the sun-centered (heliocentric) theory, and as a result of his study of Brahe's observations, he discovered three laws of planetary motion (published in 1609 and 1619) that opened a new era in astronomy.

The first law states that the orbits of the planets are ellipses, with the sun invariably at one focus of the ellipse. This was an enor-

KEPLER'S SECOND LAW

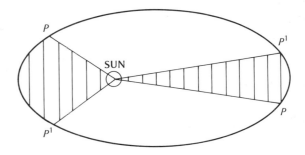

P *and* P¹ *are any two points on the orbit between which the planet passes in equal time. The area described by Sun–P–P¹–Sun is always equal.*

mous break with the past, for the assumption that circular motion is the most perfect and natural motion had been an essential part of the study of nature since Aristotle. Even Galileo was unable to reject this assumption, but Kepler followed wherever his data and his mathematics took him. The second law states that if a hypothetical line is drawn from the sun to the planet, equal areas will be swept by that line in equal times. What this means is that the planet moves faster—that is, it has to cover more of the orbit in a given period— when it is closer to the sun than when it is farther away (see figure).

The third law enters an entirely different area, describing not the motion of an individual planet, as do the first two, but a relationship among the movements of all planets. It states that the square of the ratio of the *time* it takes any two planets to complete their orbits equals the cube of the ratio of these planets' average *distance* from the sun. Formulated as an equation, $(T_1/T_2)^2 = (D_1/D_2)^3$, where T_1 and T_2 are the two planets' orbiting times and D_1 and D_2 are their average distances from the sun. This third law was Kepler's most elegant and subtle discovery, a worthy monument to his mathematical skills. However, it had little direct impact on the study of astronomy until Sir Isaac Newton used it late in the century as the foundation for his construction of a new system of the heavens.

Kepler's last major achievement was the publication in 1627 of the *Rudolfine Tables*, named after his patron, Emperor Rudolf II. The tables combined Brahe's observations of planetary positions with Kepler's theories of planetary motion and made it possible to predict celestial movements far more accurately, to the great benefit of navigators as well as astronomers. They demonstrated that Copernicus' and Kepler's discoveries had a practical value, and it became increasingly difficult to ignore or doubt the new findings. Adherents of Ptolemaic cosmology continued to hold firm for decades, but among serious observers of the heavens they were a rapidly dwindling group after the 1620s. A theory that at the beginning of Kepler's career had been uncertain at best had been transformed by the end of his life into a plausible explanation of planetary motion.

Galileo

A contemporary of Kepler's, the Italian Galileo Galilei, took the breakthrough a stage further when he became the first to perceive the connection between planetary motion and motion on earth, and his studies revealed the importance to astronomy not only of observation and mathematics but also of physics. Moreover he was the first to bring the new understanding of the universe to the attention of a wider public. Galileo's concern with technique, argument, and evidence marks him as one of the first scientists recognizable as such to modern eyes.

The study of motion inspired Galileo's most fundamental scientific contributions. When he

began his investigations, the Aristotelian view that a body is naturally at rest and needs to be pushed constantly to keep moving dominated the study of dynamics. Kepler for example believed that some steady force emanating from the sun maintains the planets' motion. Galileo broke with this tradition, developing instead a new type of physical explanation that was perfected by Newton half a century later.

Unlike Kepler, who was concerned with the strictly limited phenomena of planetary movements, Galileo wanted to uncover the principles of all motion. His observations were prolific. At the Arsenal in Venice, he watched the techniques workmen used to lift huge weights; adapting a Dutch lensmaker's invention, he built himself a primitive telescope to study the heavens; and he devised seemingly mundane experiments, employing anything from pendulums to little balls rolling down inclined planes, to test his theories. Moving from observations to abstraction, Galileo arrived at a wholly new way of understanding motion: the principle of inertia.

This breakthrough could not have been made on the basis of observation alone. For the discovery of inertia depended on mathematical imagination, the ability to conceive of a situation that cannot be demonstrated to the senses because it cannot be created experimentally: the motion of a perfectly smooth ball across a perfectly smooth plane, free of any outside forces, such as friction. Galileo's conclusion was that "Any velocity once imparted to a moving body will be rigidly maintained as long as external causes of acceleration and retardation are removed. . . . If the velocity is uniform, it will not be diminished or slackened, much less destroyed."

This insight completely undermined the Aristotelian view. Physics would never be the same again, because Galileo demonstrated that only mathematical language could describe the underlying principles of nature.

The most immediate impact of Galileo's work was on astronomy. He first became famous when in 1609 he published his discoveries that Jupiter has satellites and the moon has mountains. Both these revelations were further blows to traditional beliefs, which held that the earth is changing and imperfect while the heavens are immutable and unblemished. Now, however, it seemed that other planets have moons, just like the earth, and that these moons might have the same rough surfaces as the earth.

This was startling enough, but Galileo also sought a complete change in the methods of discovery, believing, unlike his predecessors, that the principles he had uncovered in terrestrial physics could also be used to explain phenomena in the heavens. His purposes became apparent when he calculated the height of the mountains on the moon by using the geometric techniques of surveyors, when he described the moon's secondary light—seen while it is a crescent—as a reflection of sunlight from the earth, and when he explained the movement of sunspots by referring to the principles of motion that he had found on earth. In all cases Galileo was treating his own planet simply as one part of a uniform universe. Every physical law, he was saying, is equally applicable on earth and in the heavens, including the laws of motion. As early as 1597 Galileo had told Kepler that some of his discoveries in physics could be explained only if the earth was moving, and during the next thirty years he became the most famous advocate of Copernicanism in Europe.

Galileo conveyed his arguments with devastating logic. Citing Aristotle's principle that the simplest explanation is the best explanation, Galileo asked how anyone could conceivably accept all the complexities and effort needed to keep the entire universe revolving around the earth when all the motions could be explained by the rotation of only one planet, the earth.

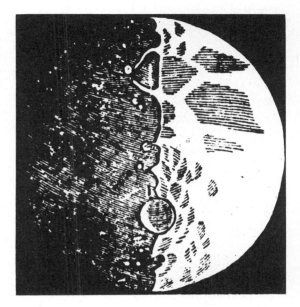

This sketch of the moon's surface appeared in Galileo's Starry Messenger (1610). *It shows what he had observed through the telescope and was interpreted as proof that the moon had a rugged surface because the lighted areas within the dark section had to be mountains. These caught the light of the setting sun longer than surrounding lower terrain and revealed, for example, a large cavity in the lower center of the sketch.* (Photo: New York Public Library Picture Collection)

When academic and religious critics pointed out that the moon looks smooth, that we would feel the earth moving, or that the Bible says Joshua made the sun stand still, he reacted with scorn to their inability to understand that his observations and proofs carried more weight than their traditional beliefs. And in response to religious objections, he asserted that "in discussions of physical problems we ought to begin not from the authority of scriptural passages, but from sense experience and necessary demonstrations."

For all the brilliance of his arguments, Galileo was now on dangerous ground. Although traditionally the Catholic Church had not concerned itself with the theories used in investigations of nature, in the early seventeenth century the situation was changing. Now deep in the struggle with Protestantism, the church was responding to the increased challenge to its authority by seeking to control any potentially questionable views held by its followers. Moreover Galileo had antagonized Jesuit and Dominican astronomers. These two orders were the chief upholders of orthodoxy in the church in this period, and it was they who referred Galileo's views to the Inquisition and then guided the attack on Copernicanism and its most brilliant proponent.

In 1616 the Inquisition forbade Galileo to teach the heretical doctrine that the earth moved; but when one of his friends was elected pope in 1623 he thought he would be safe in writing a great work on astronomy. The result was Galileo's masterpiece, the *Dialogue on the Two Great World Systems*, published in 1632 (with the approval, probably accidental, of the Inquisition). A marvelously witty, elegant book, the *Dialogue* is one of the few monuments in the history of science that the layman can find constant pleasure in reading. And so it was intended. Galileo wrote it in Italian, not the Latin that had always been used for scholarly works, because he wanted it to reach the widest possible audience.

In April 1633 he was brought before the Inquisition for having defied the order not to teach Copernicanism. In a trial that has caused controversy ever since, the aged astronomer, under threat of torture, abjured the "errors and heresies" of believing that the earth moved. Legend has it that as he left the hall, he murmured, *"Eppur si muove!"* ("And yet it does move!") and he certainly was not docile for the remainder of his life even though he was under perpetual house arrest and progressively lost his eyesight. He had his principal

work on physics, the *Two New Sciences*, published in tolerant Holland in 1638, while many of his letters ridiculed his opponents.

Galileo's condemnation discouraged further scientific activity by his countrymen. Italy had been the leader of the new discipline, but now her supremacy rapidly passed northward, to the English, Dutch, and French. Yet this only showed that the rise of science, once begun, could not be halted for long. By the late 1630s no self-respecting astronomer could deny that Galileo's findings and his *Dialogue*, added to Kepler's laws and the *Rudolfine Tables*, had established the correctness of the Copernican theory beyond reasonable doubt.

In a progression of events remarkably similar to the movement from upheaval to resolution that was taking place in politics at this very time (see Chapter 15), scientists had started out by causing tremendous bewilderment and doubt, but had ended up by creating a new kind of certainty that had far-reaching influence. And this was true not only in physics and astronomy, but also in anatomy. For with Vesalius there had begun a period in the study of the human body when many questions were raised but few answers were found. Finally, though, in 1628, another genius of the scientific revolution, the English doctor William Harvey, provided a new and more certain understanding of anatomy when he identified the function of the heart and proved that the blood circulated.

SCIENTIFIC METHOD: A NEW EPISTEMOLOGY

Both Copernicus and Galileo stressed that their discoveries rested on a way of thinking that had an independent value, and they refused to allow traditional considerations, such as the promptings of common sense or the assumptions of theology, to interfere with their conclusions. What the scientists were moving toward was a new epistemology, a new theory of how to obtain and verify knowledge, based on experience, reason, and doubt, rejecting all unsubstantiated authority. Their methods required a revolutionary definition of what could be accepted as a true description of physical reality.

The process the scientists followed after they formulated a hypothesis consisted, in their view, of three parts: first, observations; second, a generalization induced from the observations; and third, tests of the generalization by experiments whose outcome had to conform with the conclusions deducible from the generalization. A generalization remained valid only as long as it was not contradicted by experiments specifically designed to test it. The scientist used no data except the results of strict observation, and his reasoning was confined to the perception of the laws, principles, or patterns that emerged from the observations. Since measurement was the key to the data, the observations had a numerical, not a subjective, value, and the language of science naturally came to be mathematics.

Perhaps the most famous example of the method was the series of experiments Galileo conducted with inclined planes. His original hypothesis was that all objects fall at the same speed and that the difference we see between the time it takes for a stone and a feather to fall is the result only of friction and air resistance (a hypothesis recently confirmed by astronauts on the moon). He first showed that acceleration is a function of time, a proposition which he proved geometrically and then demonstrated by rolling a ball down a plane, noting the time required to make the descent: "We [then] rolled the ball only one-quarter the length of the [plane]; and having measured the time of its descent, we found it precisely one-half of the former [descent]." He

repeated such experiments a hundred times, and always the ratio of the distances was a square of the ratio of the times. From this basic regularity he proceeded to a proof, similarly resting on both geometry and experiment, that regardless of the angle of a descent, a body always reaches the bottom in the same interval of time if the vertical height of its descent remains the same.

This was a classic application of the new scientific method. Mathematics, in this case geometry, allowed Galileo to measure and describe natural phenomena. Carefully controlled experiments then verified conclusions that might seem contrary to common sense. And the progression—hypothesis, observation, generalization, and tests, conducted in the language of mathematics—provided him with a logical structure that could be defeated only on its own terms. Nothing was accepted as given. It was a self-contained mode of demonstration whose conclusions could be rejected solely if disproved by identical procedures.

Scientists in fact rarely move through all the steps toward a conclusion in the exact way this idealized scheme suggests. The French scientist Blaise Pascal, for instance, described an experiment at the foot of a deep vat filled with water that would have been impossible to perform at the time. However, he understood the relevant physical theory so well that he knew what would have happened. In other words, experiments as well as hypotheses can occur in the mind; the essence of scientific method still remains a special way of looking at and understanding nature.

THE WIDER INFLUENCE OF SCIENTIFIC THOUGHT

The principles of scientific inquiry received attention throughout the intellectual community only gradually; it took time for the power of the scientist's method to be recognized. For decades, as Galileo found out, even investigators of nature continued to use what he would have considered irrelevant criteria, such as the teachings of the Bible, in judging scientific work. If acceptance of the new method was to spread, then the literate public would have to be educated in the techniques being employed. This growing understanding was eventually achieved by midcentury as much through the efforts of ardent propagandizers as through the writings of the great innovators themselves.

Francis Bacon

Although not an important scientist himself, Francis Bacon was the greatest of these propagandists, and he inspired an entire generation with his vision of what the discipline could accomplish for mankind. His description of an ideal society in the *New Atlantis*, published in 1627, the year after his death, was the most famous of a series of seventeenth-century descendants of Sir Thomas More's *Utopia*, all af which placed the constant and fruitful advance of science at the center of their schemes. *New Atlantis* is a vision of science as the savior of the human race. It predicts a time when those doing research at the highest levels will be regarded as the most important people in the state and will work on a vast government-supported project to gather all known facts about the physical universe and its properties. By a process of gradual induction, this information will lead to universal laws that in turn will enable man to improve his lot on earth.

Bacon's view of research as a collective enterprise whose aim is the discovery of practical benefits for all made a powerful impact on a number of later scientists, particularly the founders of the English Royal Society. Many cited him as the chief inspiration for their work. Moreover Bacon advocated a total overhaul of the traditional educational curriculum: an end to the study of venerated philosophers and more attention to practical concerns. By the mid-seventeenth century, his ideas had entered the mainstream of European thought, an acceptance that testified to the broadening interest in science and its protagonists.

René Descartes

The French philosopher René Descartes made the first concentrated attempt to apply the new methods of science to theories of knowledge, and in so doing he laid the foundations for modern philosophy. The impulse behind his work was his realization that for all the importance of observation and experiment, man can be deceived by his senses. In order to find some solid truth, therefore, he decided to apply the principle of doubt—the refusal to accept any authority without strict verification—to all knowledge. He began his investigations with the assumption that he could know unquestionably only one thing: he was doubting. This allowed him to proceed to the observation, "I think, therefore I am," because the very act of doubting proved he was thinking, and thinking in turn demonstrated his existence.

The cardinal point of his philosophy was contained in the statement that whatever is clearly and distinctly thought must be true. This was a conclusion drawn from the proof of his own existence, and it enabled him to construct a proof of God's existence. We cannot fail to realize that we are imperfect, he argued, and we must therefore have an idea of perfection against which we may be measured. If we have a clear idea of what perfection is, then it must exist; hence there must be a God.

The proof may not seem entirely convincing to modern readers, particularly since one suspects that a major reason for its prominence

The portrait of René Descartes by the Dutch painter Frans Hals shows the austere thinker who fitted well into the sober atmosphere of Amsterdam. Descartes spent a number of years in the United Provinces, where the exchange of ideas was much freer than in his native France. (Photo: Hubert Joesse/EPI, Inc.)

was the desire to show that the principle of doubt did not contradict religious belief. Nevertheless the argument is a good illustration of Descartes' assertion that the activity of the mind is the vital element in the search for truth. The title he gave his great work, *Discourse on the Method of Rightly Conducting the Reason and Seeking Truth in the Sciences* (1637), is thus entirely appropriate.[1] Thought is a pure and unmistakable guide, and only by reliance on its operations can man hope to advance his understanding of the world.

Descartes developed this view into a fundamental proposition about the nature of the world and of knowledge—a proposition that philosophers have been wrestling with ever since. He stated that there is an essential dichotomy between thought and extension (tangible objects) or, put another way, between spirit and matter. Various writers, including Bacon and Galileo, had insisted that science, the study of nature, is an undertaking separate from and unaffected by faith or theology, the study of God. But Descartes turned this distinction into a far-reaching principle, dividing not only science from faith but even the reality of the world from our perception of that reality. There is a difference, in other words, between a chair and our understanding of that chair in our minds.

So insistent was he that matter and spirit remain distinct that he undertook a careful examination of human anatomy to discover the seat of the soul. He had to find a part of the body that had no physical function whatsoever, because only there could the soul, a thing of spirit, reside. His candidate was the tiny

pineal gland, which did absolutely nothing, according to the medicine of the day; modern investigations still have not disclosed the function of the hormone it secretes.

The emphasis Descartes placed on the operations of the mind gave a new direction to epistemological discussions. A hypothesis gained credibility not so much from external proofs as from the logical tightness of the arguments used to support it. The decisive test was how lucid and irrefutable a statement appeared to be to the thinking mind. Descartes thus applied what he considered to be the methods of science to all knowledge. Not only the phenomena of nature but all truth had to be investigated according to the strict principles of the scientist.

Descartes' own contributions to the research of his day were theoretical rather than experimental. In physics he was the first to perceive the distinction between mass and weight, and in mathematics he was the first to apply algebraic notations and methods to geometry, thus founding analytic geometry. When he turned to astronomy, however, he formulated a theory of planetary motion based on enormous whirling vortexes, rather like the cones of tornadoes, that has come to be regarded as one of the curiosities of the scientific revolution.

The failings of specific theories, however, do not detract from Descartes' position as a prime mover of the revolution in Western thought during the seventeenth century. His emphasis on the principle of doubt irrevocably undermined such traditional assumptions as the belief in the hierarchical organization of the universe. Possibly he put too much trust in the powers of the mind, but it is undeniable that he laid down the strict procedures that philosophy—and in fact any speculation about man or his world—had to follow. And the European intellectual community accepted

---

[1] Like Galileo's *Dialogue*, Descartes' *Discourse* was written in a vernacular language. It thus had a much more popular audience than a Latin book would have received, though after a few years it was translated into Latin so that scholars from all European countries could read it.

this approach with enthusiasm. The admiration he inspired indicated how completely the methods he advocated had captured his contemporaries' imagination.

Thomas Hobbes

A notable example of the borrowings inspired by the scientists were the writings of Thomas Hobbes, who used their method to make an extraordinarily original contribution to political theory.

A story has it that Hobbes once picked up a copy of Euclid's *Elements* and opened the book in the middle. The theorem on that page seemed totally without foundation, but it rested on a proof in the preceding theorem. Working his way backward, he discovered himself finally having to accept no more than the proposition that the shortest distance between two points is a straight line. He thereupon resolved to use the same approach in analyzing political behavior. The story is probably apocryphal because as a young man Hobbes was secretary to Francis Bacon, who doubtless gave him his first taste of scientific work. Nevertheless it does capture the essence of Hobbes' approach, for he did begin his masterpiece, *Leviathan* (published in 1651), with a few limited premises about human nature from which he rigorously deduced major conclusions about political forms.

Hobbes' premises, drawn from his observation of the strife-ridden Europe of his day, were stark and uncompromising. Man, he asserted, is selfish and ambitious; consequently, unless he is restrained, he fights a perpetual war with his fellows. The weak man is more cunning and the stronger more stupid. Given these unsavory characteristics, the state of nature—which precedes the existence of society—is a state of war, in which life is "nasty, brutish, and short." Hobbes' conclusion was that the only way to restrain this instinctive aggressiveness is to erect an absolute and sovereign power that will maintain peace. Everyone must submit to the sovereign because the alternative is the anarchy of the state of nature. The moment of submission is the moment of the birth of orderly society.

In a startling innovation Hobbes suggested that the transition from nature to society is accomplished by a contract that is implicitly accepted by all who wish to end the chaos. They agree among themselves to submit to the sovereign, thus the sovereign is not a party to the contract and is not limited in any way. A government is totally free to do whatever it wishes to keep the peace. However tyrannous, this solution is always better than the turmoil it has replaced.

Both contemporaries and later writers were strongly influenced by Hobbes, not only because his logic was compelling but also because he seemed so much like a scientist. From his observations of men, he had induced general propositions about human behavior, and from these he had deduced certain political lessons that were verified by European politics. Moreover he had applied a mechanistic view to man more thoroughly than ever before, reducing all that human beings do to simple appetites and aversions.

In doing so he contributed to the popularity of the mechanistic view of the universe, a theory derived in part from the materialistic implications of Descartes' philosophy. In its simplest form mechanism holds that the entire universe, including man himself, can be regarded as a complicated machine and thus subject to strict physical principles. The arm is like a lever, the elbow like a hinge, and so on. Even an emotion is no more than a simple response to a definable stimulus.

But this approach also aroused hostility. Although they were deeply affected by his ideas, most of Hobbes' successors denounced him as godless, immoral, cynical, and unfeeling. These were charges that could be leveled at all practitioners of science, but for a long time they were not raised, largely because the scientists dealt with areas that seemed to have nothing to do with human behavior.

Blaise Pascal

At midcentury only one important voice still protested against the new science. It belonged to a young Frenchman, Blaise Pascal, one of the most brilliant mathematicians and experimenters of the time. Before his death at the age of thirty-nine, in 1662, Pascal's investigations of probability in games of chance led him to the theorem that still bears his name, and his research in conic sections helped lay the foundations for integral calculus. He also explored the properties of the vacuum and invented a versatile calculating machine.

In his late twenties, however, Pascal became increasingly dissatisfied with scientific research, and he began to wonder whether his life was being properly spent. His doubts were reinforced by frequent visits to his sister, a nun at the Abbey of Port-Royal, where he came into contact with a new spiritual movement within Catholicism known as Jansenism.

The movement took its name from Cornelis Jansen, a bishop who had written a book suggesting that the Catholic Church had forgotten the teachings of its greatest father, St. Augustine. Jansen insisted that man was not free to determine his own fate, that salvation was entirely in the hands of an all-powerful God, and that unswerving faith was the only path to salvation. These doctrines sounded ominously like Protestant teachings, and during the years after Jansen's death, the Catholic Church and especially the Jesuits, who placed great emphasis on freedom of will, made various attempts to suppress his beliefs.

Jansenism was not a particularly popular movement at the time, and its adherents consisted of little more than the immediate circle of a prominent family of magistrates, the Arnaulds, one of whom was the head of Port-Royal. But Pascal was profoundly impressed by the piety, asceticism, and spirituality at Port-Royal, and in November of 1654 he had a mystical experience that made him resolve to devote the rest of his life to the salvation of his soul. He wrote a series of devastating critiques of the Jesuits, accusing them of irresponsibility and, as he phrased it, of placing cushions under sinners' elbows.

During the few remaining years of his life, Pascal put on paper a collection of reflections —some only a few words long, some many pages—that were gathered together after his death and published as the *Pensées* (or "reflections"). These writings revealed not only the beliefs of a deeply religious man but also the anxieties of a scientist who feared the growing influence of science. He did not wish to put an end to research; he merely wanted people to realize that the truths uncovered by science were limited and not as important as the truths perceived by faith. In the words of one of his more memorable phrases, "The heart has its reasons that the mind cannot know."

Pascal was warning against the replacement of the traditional understanding of man and his destiny, gained through religious faith, with the conclusions reached by the methods of the scientists. The separation between the material and the spiritual would be fatal, he believed, because it would destroy the primacy and even the importance of the spiritual. Pascal's protest was unique, but the fact that it was raised at all indicates how high the status of the scientist and his method had risen by the 1650s. A scant quarter-century earlier, such a dramatic change in fortune would have been hard to predict, but now many intellectuals, seeing an opportunity of ending

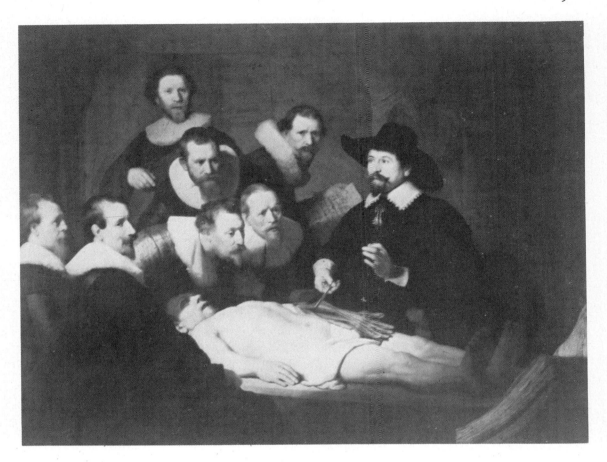

Among the many representations of the public anatomy lessons so popular in seventeenth-century Holland, the most famous is one of Rembrandt's greatest paintings, The Anatomy Lesson of Dr. Nicholaas Tulp. *(Photo: A. Dingjan)*

the uncertainties that had bedeviled their work for decades, eagerly adopted the new epistemology. Turmoil was once again giving way to assurance.

SCIENCE INSTITUTIONALIZED

There were many besides Bacon who realized that scientific work should be a common en-

deavor, pursued cooperatively by all its practitioners, and that information should be exchanged so that researchers might concentrate on different parts of a project instead of wasting time and energy following identical paths. The first major effort to apply this view was undertaken by the Lincean Academy,[2] founded under the patronage of a nobleman in Rome in 1603. Organizations of scientists had existed before, but this was the first assemblage interested in all branches of science and in

---

[2] The academy was named after Linceus, reputedly the most keen-sighted of the legendary Argonauts of ancient times.

publishing the findings of its members. After the decline of research in Italy, however, the academy gradually lost its importance.

More fruitful beginnings were made in France, where in the first decades of the seventeenth century a friar named Marin Mersenne became the center of an international network of correspondents interested in scientific work. He increased the dissemination of news by also bringing scientists together for discussions or experiments. The meetings were sporadic, but out of them developed procedures that led to a more permanent organization of scientific activity.

The first important steps toward establishing a permanent body in England were taken at Oxford during the Civil War when the revolutionaries captured the city and replaced many traditionalists at the university. A few of the newcomers formed what they called the Invisible College, a group that met to exchange information and discuss one another's work. What was important was the enterprise, not its results, for the group included only one first-class scientist: the young chemist Robert Boyle. In 1660 twelve members, including Boyle and the architect Sir Christopher Wren, formed an official organization, the Royal Society of London for Improving Natural Knowledge, with headquarters in the capital and a council to supervise its affairs. In 1662 it was granted a charter by Charles II.

The Royal Society's purposes were openly Baconian. Its aim for the first few years—until everyone realized it was impossible—was to gather all knowledge about nature, particularly whatever might be useful. For a long time the members continued to offer their services for the public good, helping in one instance to develop the science of social statistics ("political arithmetic" as it was called) for the government. Soon, however, it became clear that their principal function was to serve

as a headquarters and clearing center for research. Their secretaries maintained an enormous correspondence, encouraging foreign scholars to transmit their discoveries to the society. And in 1665 they began the regular publication of *Philosophical Transactions*, the first professional scientific journal.

As a stimulus to new discoveries, the Royal Society was without peer in seventeenth-century Europe. Imitators were soon to follow. In 1666 Louis XIV gave his blessing to the founding of the Royal Academy of Sciences, and similar organizations were established in Naples and Berlin by 1700. Membership in these societies was limited and highly prized, a symptom of the glamour that was beginning to attach itself to the new studies. By the 1660s there could be no doubt that science, secure in royal patronage, had triumphed. Its practitioners were extravagantly admired, and throughout intellectual and high social circles, there was a feverish scramble to apply its methods and its mode of thought to almost every conceivable activity.

Descartes himself had applied the techniques of science to epistemology and more broadly to philosophy in general; Bacon and Hobbes had put them at the service of social and political thought. But the borrowings were not only at these exalted levels. Formal gardens were designed to exhibit the order, harmony, and reason that science had made the most prized qualities of the time. And the arts of fortification and warfare were transformed by the adoption of principles learned from the new investigations, such as accurate measurement.

As the scientists' activities grew in popularity, amateurs known as virtuosos began to proliferate. These were usually aristocrats who spent their time playing at science. Herbariums and small observatories were added to country estates, and parties would feature an evening of star gazing. Some virtuosos took their tasks quite seriously—an early Italian enthusiast, Prince Federigo Cesi, joined in the first investigations with a microscope, a study of bees; and one English country gentleman inundated the Royal Society with meticulous observations of local sand dunes. But by and large these frivolous scientists are interesting primarily because they reveal the awe and delight aroused by a new discipline that had revolutionized man's understanding of nature.

Science was also beginning to have an impact on the general populace. Among the most eagerly anticipated occasions in seventeenth-century Holland was the public anatomy lesson. The body of a criminal would be brought to an enormous hall, packed with students and a fascinated public. A famous surgeon would dissect the cadaver, announcing and displaying each organ as he removed it.

On the whole, the influence of the scientists on laymen was not dependent on the technological improvements from their work. And by our standards much of what they did, even at the theoretical level, seems primitive at best. What this suggests is that the reverence for science and its methods developed not from a broad understanding of actual accomplishments or their potential consequences but from the fame of the spectacular discoveries which enabled a few brilliant men to provide startlingly convincing solutions to centuries-old problems in astronomy, physics, and anatomy. Thus the disturbing implications of a Hobbes, like the protests of a Pascal, could be ignored, and the new discipline could be given unblemished admiration. The entire world was coming to be viewed through the scientist's eyes —a striking victory for a recently struggling member of the intellectual community—and the qualities of regularity and harmony that he stood for began to appear in the work of playwrights and poets, artists and architects.

II. LITERATURE AND THE ARTS

Changes in culture were not as clear-cut as in politics or science, but certain parallels are evident. During the second half of the sixteenth century and into the 1610s, the tensions and uncertainties of the age were visible in the paintings of the Mannerists, and in the writings of Montaigne, Cervantes, and Shakespeare. Thereafter, two major styles dominated Europe: the Baroque, which consciously sought to arouse the emotions and achieve dramatic effects, and the Classical, which epitomized discipline, restraint, and sometimes decorum. Very gradually over the course of the seventeenth century, the emphasis moved from the values of the Baroque to those of the Classical. This shift in artistic aims bore a distinct resemblance to the sense of settlement that descended over other areas of European civilization at midcentury.

THE CULTURE OF THE LATE SIXTEENTH CENTURY

One response to the upheavals of the sixteenth century was the attempt to escape reality, to devise a distorted view of the world. It was especially noticeable in the work of the great painters of the age. Acutely sensitive to the disruptions and changes that surrounded them, they created a strange and uneasy vision of human existence.

The Mannerists

As early as the 1520s, a reaction had set in against the balance and serenity of the High Renaissance style. The artists involved in this movement, which lasted about eighty years, are generally called Mannerists. No specific characteristics united them, but they all wished to go beyond reality and to develop theatrical and disturbing qualities in their paintings. They undermined perspectives, distorted human figures, and devised unnatural colors and lighting to create startling effects. Even the great figures of the High Renaissance were affected by this orientation. Michelangelo, who lived until 1564, began to create tortured, agonized figures writhing in violent action; Titian, who died in 1576, placed a shrieking Magdalene in his last painting, a subdued Pietà.

The movement was embodied, however, in Parmigianino, an Italian, and El Greco, a Greek living in Spain. Parmigianino's *Madonna of the Long Neck* (see Plate 26), named after its most salient feature, typifies his efforts to unsettle the viewer with tricks of perspective, odd postures, and an unbalanced composition. El Greco, a man whose compelling and disturbing vision symbolized the uneasy age in which he lived, took these devices even farther. His elongated human beings, cool colors, and eerie lighting make him one of the most distinctive painters in the history of art (see Plate 29).

Michel de Montaigne

The man who expressed the most vivid concern about the upheavals and uncertainties of his age was Michel de Montaigne, the greatest humanist and philosopher of the late sixteenth century. Born into the French petty nobility, he suffered a shock at the age of thirty—the death of his closest friend—that changed the course of his life. Obsessed by death, he began one of the most moving explorations in European intellectual history.

Determined to overcome his fears, Montaigne retired to a tower in his country home in order to "essay," or test, his innermost feelings by writing short pieces of prose even about subjects he did not fully comprehend. In the process he created a new literary form, the essay, and shaped the development of the French language. But his chief influence was philosophical: he has inspired the search for self-knowledge since his time, from René Descartes and Blaise Pascal to the Existentialists of the twentieth century.

In the 1570s Montaigne's interests turned to Skepticism, which appeared in full flower in his longest essay, "An Apology for Raymond Sebond." Sebond was a Spanish theologian who tried to prove the truth of Christianity by the use of reason. Montaigne firmly rejected Sebond's belief in the power of the mind and emerged from this essay with the total uncertainty of the motto *"Que sais-je?"* ("What do I know?")

In his last years Montaigne struggled toward a more confident solution of his uncertainties, taking as his model the ancient saying, "Know thyself." By looking into his own person, each human being can find answers and values that hold true at least for himself: all truths and customs are relative, but by looking into himself, he can look into all humanity. Montaigne even came close to a morality without theology, because good and self-determination were more important to him than doctrine, and he saw everywhere religious people committing inhuman acts. Man, he argued, can know good and can achieve it by an effort of will. Trying to be an angel is wrong; being a good man is enough.

This process of self-discovery was a radical and totally secular individualism. It required a joyous acceptance of the world that finally gave Montaigne the optimistic answer to his anguish—though it was a unique, personal answer that gave comfort to few other people.

Cervantes and Shakespeare

In Spain the disillusionment that accompanied the decline of Europe's most powerful state was perfectly captured by Miguel de Cervantes (1547–1616). He was heir to a brilliant satirical and descriptive tradition that had already produced a classic literature in the sixteenth century in the writings of Erasmus and Rabelais. Cervantes saw the wide gap between the hopes and the realities of his day—in religion, in social institutions, in human behavior —and made the dichotomy the basis of the scathing social satire in his novel *Don Quixote*.

At one level Cervantes was ridiculing the excessive chivalry of the Spanish nobility in his portrayal of a knight who was ready to tilt at windmills, though he obviously admired the sincerity of his well-meaning hero and sympathized with him as a perennial loser. On another level the author brought to life the Europe of the time—the ordinary people and their hypocrisies and intolerances—with a liveliness rarely matched in literature. His view of that society, however, was far from cheery. "Justice, but not for my house," says Don Quixote as he experiences the foibles of mankind, particularly of those in authority. Cervantes avoided politics, but he was clearly directing many of his sharpest barbs at the brutality and disregard for human values that were characteristic of his fanatical times. What were Spain's repeated crusades accomplishing? Were Quixote's dreams as worthy as Sancho Panza's blunt and sensible pragmatism? These were not easy questions to answer, but they went to the heart of the dilemmas of the age. And in Spain's great enemy, England, another towering figure was grappling with similar problems.

For the English-speaking world, the most brilliant creative artist of this and all other periods was William Shakespeare, whose plays capture every conceivable mood—searing grief, airy romance, rousing nationalism, uproarious and farcical humor. Despite little education he disclosed in his imagery a familiarity with subjects ranging from astronomy to seamanship, from alchemy to warfare. It is not surprising therefore that some have doubted that one man could have produced this amazing body of work.

Shakespeare started writing in the 1590s, when he was in his late twenties, and continued until his death, in 1616. During most of this time, he was also involved with a theatrical company, and he often had to produce plays on very short notice. He thus had the best of all possible tests as he gained mastery of theatrical techniques—audience reaction.

Shakespeare rose far above his setting to timeless statements about human behavior: love, hatred, violence, sin. Of particular interest to the historian, however, is what he tells us about attitudes that belong especially to his own era. For example the conservatism of his characters is quite clear. They believe firmly in the hierarchical structure of society, and throughout the long series of historical plays, events suggest that excessive ambition does not pay. The series begins with Richard II, a legitimate monarch who is overthrown by a usurper, with catastrophic results. Repeated disasters follow as the chronicle is taken through the War of the Roses to the restoration of order by the Tudors. Again and again legality and stability are shown as fundamental virtues—a natural reaction against turbulent times. Shakespeare's expressions of nationalism are particularly intense; when in *Richard II* the king's uncle, John of Gaunt, lies dying, he pours out his love for his country in words that have moved Englishmen ever since:

This royal throne of kings, this sceptered isle,
This earth of majesty, this seat of Mars,
This other Eden, demi-paradise, . . .
This happy breed of men, this little world,
This precious stone set in the silver sea, . . .
This blessed plot, this earth, this realm, this
    England.

[*Richard II*, act 2, scene 1]

The uncertainties of the day appear in many of the plays. In *Julius Caesar* the optimistic "There is a tide in the affairs of men, which, taken at the flood, leads on to fortune" celebrates vigor and decisiveness but also warns against missing opportunities. And Hamlet offers the sober conclusion, "There's a divinity that shapes our ends, rough-hew them how we will." Shakespeare's four most famous tragedies, *Hamlet, Lear, Macbeth,* and *Othello,* end in disillusionment: the heroes are ruined by irresoluteness, pride, ambition, or jealousy. He is reflecting the Elizabethans' interest in the fatal flaws that destroy great men and in dramas of revenge, but the plays demonstrate as well his deep understanding of human nature. For all the promise of the future, one cannot forget man's weakness, the inevitability of decay, and the constant threat of disaster. The contrast appears with compelling clarity in a speech delivered by Hamlet:

> What a piece of work is man! how noble in reason! how infinite in faculties! in form and moving how express and admirable! in action how like an angel! in apprehension how like a god! the beauty of the world, the paragon of animals! And yet to me what is this quintessence of dust? Man delights not me.
> [*Hamlet*, act 2, scene 2]

Despite such pessimism, despite the deep sense of human inadequacy, the total impression Shakespeare gives is of immense vigor, of a restlessness and confidence that recall the many achievements of the sixteenth century. Prospero, the hero of his last play, *The Tempest,* has often been seen as the symbol of the new magician-cum-scientist, and references to the discoveries overseas are abundant. Yet a sense of decay is never far absent. Repeatedly men seem utterly helpless, overtaken by events they cannot control. There is a striking lack of security in the world Shakespeare's people inhabit. Nothing remains constant or dependable, and everything that seems solid and reassuring, be it the love of a daughter or the crown of England, is challenged. In this

atmosphere of ceaseless change, where all solid, safe landmarks disappear, Shakespeare forcefully conveys the tensions of his time.

THE BAROQUE AND CLASSICISM

From around 1600 onward, new concerns began to gain prominence in the arts and literature. First, in the Baroque there was an attempt to drown uncertainty in a blaze of grandeur and drama. But gradually the aims of Classicism, which emphasized formality, balance, and restraint, came to dominate European culture.

The Baroque

The word "Baroque" has been taken to indicate ornateness, grandeur, and excess as well as all the traits, including the Classical, of seventeenth-century art. Historians have applied it to music, literature, politics, and even personality traits. Its usage here will be restricted to its most precise meaning: the characteristics of a style in the visual arts that emanated from Rome in the first half of the seventeenth century. Passion, drama, mystery, and awe are the qualities of the Baroque: the viewer must be involved, aroused, uplifted. Insofar as these characteristics are reflected in other kinds of creative work, such as literature and music, it is reasonable to discuss the various examples together; but to regard all manifestations of dramatic splendor or grandiose extravagance as Baroque is to depart from the essentially visual meaning of the term.

The Baroque was closely associated with the Counter Reformation's emphasis on gorgeous display in Catholic ritual. The patronage bestowed by leading church figures and the presence of art treasures accumulated over centuries made Rome a magnet for the major painters of the period. Elsewhere the Baroque flourished primarily at the leading Catholic courts of the seventeenth century, most no-

The contrasting postures of victory and defeat are masterfully captured by Diego Velázquez in The Surrender of Breda. *The Dutch soldiers droop their heads and lances, but the victorious Spaniards hardly show triumph, and the gesture of the victorious general, Ambrosio Spinola, is one of consolation and understanding. (Photo: Prado Museum)*

tably the Hapsburg courts in Madrid, Prague, and Brussels and the ducal court of Bavaria, since the style expressed perfectly the pomp of seventeenth-century princes. Few periods have conveyed so strong a sense of grandeur, theatricality, and ornateness.

Peter Paul Rubens (1577–1640) was the principal ornament of the brilliant Hapsburg court at Brussels. His major themes typified the Baroque style: glorification of great rulers (see Plate 37) and exaltation of the ceremony and mystery of Catholicism. His secular paintings convey, by their powerful depiction of human bodies and vivid use of color, the awe-inspiring might of his subjects; his religious works similarly overwhelm the viewer with the majesty and panoply of the church and excite the believer's piety by stressing the dramatic mysteries of the faith. Toward the end of his life Rubens' paintings became more lyrical, especially on mythological subjects, but he never lost his ability to generate strong emotions.

Other artists glorified rulers of the time through idealized portraiture. The greatest court painter of the age was Diego Velázquez, some twenty-two years Rubens' junior. His portraits of members of the Spanish court depict rulers and their surroundings in the stately atmosphere appropriate to the theme (see Plate 38). Yet occasionally Velázquez hinted at the weakness of an ineffective monarch in his rendering of the face, even though the basic purpose of his work always remained the exaltation of royal power. And when he painted a celebration of a notable Hapsburg victory, *The Surrender of Breda*, he managed to suggest the sadness and emptiness as much as the glory of war.

Giovanni Lorenzo Bernini was to sculpture and architecture what Rubens was to painting,

David *by Bernini*. (Photo: Alinari–Art Reference Bureau)

and like Rubens he was closely associated with the Counter Reformation. Pope Urban VIII commissioned him in 1629 to complete both the inside and the outer setting of St. Peter's, extending and elaborating Michelangelo's original architectural plan. For the interior Bernini designed a splendid papal throne that seems to float on clouds beneath a burst of sunlight, and for the exterior he created an enormous plaza, surrounded by a double colonnade, that is the largest and most imposing square in all Europe.

The glories of Baroque Rome owe much to the work of Bernini. The elaborate fountains he sculpted can be seen throughout the city; his busts of contemporary Roman leaders set the style for portraiture in marble or stone; and his dramatic religious works reflect the desire of the Counter Reformation popes to electrify the faithful. The sensual and overpowering altarpiece dedicated to the Spanish mystic St. Theresa makes a direct appeal to the emotions of the beholder that reveals the excitement of Baroque at its best (see Plate 35). And drama is also immediately apparent in his *David*, which shows the young warrior at his supreme moment, just after he has unleashed his slingshot at Goliath. Bernini emphasized the intense exertion and concentration of this moment as an expression of human vigor, and with a touch that was characteristic of the bravado of the times he gave the figure his own face.

Similar qualities can be seen in the architecture of the age. Ornate churches and palaces were built on a massive scale that paralleled exactly the concerns of painting and sculpture. And it is significant that the three most conspicuous centers of the Counter Reformation—Rome, Munich, and Prague—were also major centers of Baroque architecture.[3]

---

[3] A good survey of Baroque architecture can be found in Nikolaus Pevsner, *An Outline of European Architecture* (1943 and later editions), Chap. 6.

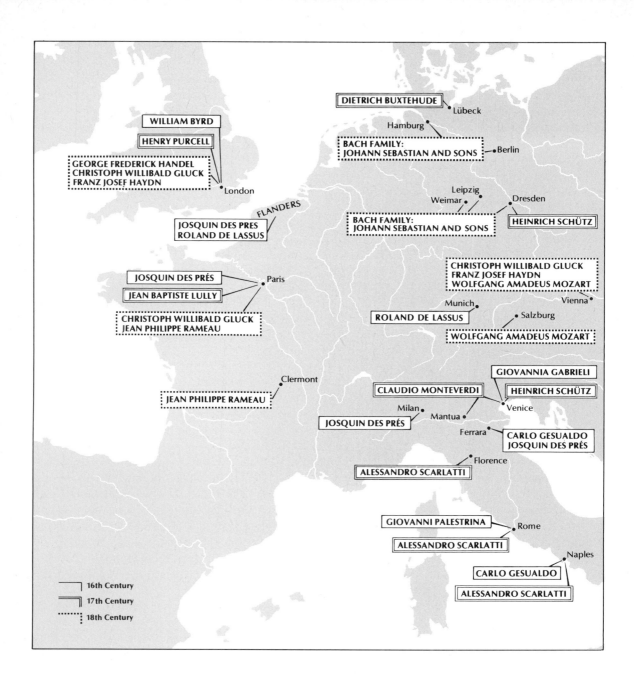

MAP 16.1: CENTERS OF MUSIC 1500–1800

The seventeenth century was significant, too, as a decisive time in the history of music. New instruments were developed, notably in the keyboard and string families, that enabled composers to create richer effects than had been possible before. Musicians also began to explore the potential of a form that first emerged in these years: the opera. Drawing on the resources of the theater, painting, architecture, music, and the dance, an operatic production could achieve a panoply of splendors beyond the reach of any one of these arts on its own. The form perfectly attuned to the courtly culture of the age, to the love of display among the princes of Europe.

The dominant figure in seventeenth-century music was the Italian Claudio Monteverdi, one of the most innovative composers of all time. He has been called with some justification the creator of both the operatic form and the orchestra. His masterpiece *Orfeo* (1607) was written for his patron, the duke of Mantua, whose court provided Monteverdi with the many skilled professionals needed to mount an opera, from scene painters to singers. The result was a tremendous success, and in the course of the next century, the opera gained in richness and complexity, attracting composers, as well as audiences, in ever increasing numbers.

There was a similar extension of the range of instrumental music. The accompaniment to *Orfeo* was still scored primarily for plucked instruments like the lute, which (except for the harp) were soon to disappear from the orchestra, but in his later works Monteverdi began to rely increasingly on strings and woodwinds. He became much freer in his use of extended melodies and readier to introduce unexpected discords, which give his works a flavor decidedly different from the music of earlier composers and reasonably familiar to modern ears.

Classicism

Classicism, the second major style of the seventeenth century, attempted to recapture the aesthetic values of ancient Greece and Rome. What this usually meant in practice was an acceptance of the strict forms embodied in the works of antiquity. Like the Baroque, Classicism aimed for grandiose effects, but it achieved them through restraint and discipline, within the bounds of a formal structure. The gradual rise of the Classical style in the seventeenth century echoed the trend toward stabilization that was taking place in other areas of intellectual life and in politics.

The epitome of disciplined expression and conscious imitation of classical antiquity is the work of Nicolas Poussin (1594–1665), a French artist who spent much of his career in Italy among the relics of Rome's glory. Poussin was no less interested than his contemporaries in momentous subjects and dramatic scenes, but the atmosphere in his canvases is always more subdued than in those of Velázquez or Rubens. The colors are muted, the figures are restrained, and the settings are serene. Peaceful landscapes, men and women in stately togas, and ruins of classical buildings are consistent features of his work, even his religious paintings (see Plate 43).

In the United Provinces different forces were at work, but they too led to a style that was much more subdued than the powerful outpourings of Rubens and Velázquez. Two aspects of Dutch society had a particular influence: Protestantism and republicanism. The Reformed Church frowned on religious art and thus reduced the demand, both ceremonial and private, for paintings of biblical scenes. Religious works therefore tended to be expressions of personal faith, not glorifications of the church. The absence of a court meant that the chief patrons were sober merchants, who were far more interested in precise, dignified portraits than in ornate displays. The result, notably in the work of the most powerful Dutch master, Rembrandt van Rijn, was an epic and compelling art whose beauty lies in its calmness and restraint.

Rembrandt explored an amazing range of themes, but his greatest paintings are his portraits. He was fascinated by human beings—their personalities, emotions, and self-revelations. Whether children or old people, simple servant girls or rich burghers, they are presented without elaboration or idealization; always the personality is allowed to speak for itself.

His most remarkable achievement in portraiture—and one of the most moving series of canvases in the history of art—is his depiction of the changes in his own face over his lifetime. The brash youth turns into the confident, successful, middle-aged man, one of the most sought-after painters in Holland. But in his late thirties the sorrows mounted: he lost his beloved wife, and commissions began to fall off. Sadness fills the eyes in these pictures. The last portraits move from despair to a final, quiet resignation as his sight slowly failed (see Plate 40). Taken together, these paintings bear comparison with Montaigne's essays as monuments to man's exploration of his own spirit—a searching appraisal that brings all who see it to a deeper understanding of human nature.

Rembrandt's large-scale, grandiose undertakings, like his smaller works, avoided startling effects. His many religious works, for example, are subdued and reverential in their approach, reflecting his own faith. The atmosphere differs sharply from the swirling passion conveyed by Rubens, who emphasized the drama of an event, whereas Rembrandt entered into the overwhelming emotions of the people present.

One could argue that Rembrandt cannot be fitted into either of the dominant styles of his time. Except for his powerful use of light, his work is far more introspective than most of the Baroque. On the other hand he did not adopt the forms of antiquity, as did Poussin and other Classical painters. Yet like the advocates of Classicism, Rembrandt in his restraint seemed to anticipate the art of the next generation. After his death, in 1669, serenity, calm, and elegance became the watchwords of European painting. An age of repose and grace was succeeding a time of upheaval as surely in the arts as in other spheres of life.

By the middle of the seventeenth century, the formalism of the Classical style was also being extended to literature, especially drama. This change was most noticeable in France, but it soon moved through Western Europe, as leading critics demanded that new plays conform to the structure laid down by the ancients. In particular they wanted the three unities observed: unity of place, which required that all scenes take place without change of location; unity of time, which demanded that the events in the play occur within a twenty-four hour period; and unity of action, which dictated simplicity and purity of plot.

The work of Pierre Corneille, the dominant figure in the French theater during the mid-century years, reflects the rise of Classicism. His early plays resemble rather complex Shakespearean drama, and even after he came in contact with the Classical tradition, his effervescent genius did not accept its rules easily. His masterpiece *Le Cid* (1636), based on the legends of a medieval Spanish hero, technically observed the three unities but only by compressing an entire tragic love affair, a military campaign, and multitudinous other events into one day. The play won immediate popular success, but the critics, urged on by Richelieu, an advocate of Classical drama, condemned Corneille for imperfect observance of the three unities. Thereafter he adhered to the Classical forms, though he was never entirely at ease with their restraints.

Passion was not absent from the strictly Classical play; the works of Jean Racine, the model Classical dramatist, portrayed some of the most intense emotion ever seen on the stage. But the exuberance of earlier drama, the enjoyment of life and of human nature, was disappearing. Only the figure of Molière was to retain these qualities, and even he respected the formalism of the Classical style. Nobody summed up the values of Classicism better than Racine in his obituary eulogy of Corneille:

> You know in what a condition the stage was when he began to write. . . . All the rules of art, and even those of decency and decorum, broken everywhere. . . . Corneille, after having for some time sought the right path and struggled against the bad taste of his day, inspired by extraordinary genius and helped by the study of the ancients, at last brought reason upon the stage.[4]

This was exactly the progression—from turbulence to calm—that was apparent throughout European culture in this period.

III. SOCIAL PATTERNS AND POPULAR CULTURE

It is difficult to draw analogies between, on the one hand, changes in the way ordinary people lived or in their customs and, on the other hand, the movement of ideas among a small, highly literate group of intellectual and artistic geniuses. There were points of contact and influence, to be sure. The magical interests of astrologers and alchemists were not far removed from the belief in hidden mysteries and spirits that influenced the inhabitants of every European village. In the late seventeenth century the first collections of folk tales were published, put together by writers who assumed that ancient wisdom was revealed in the sayings and stories of peasants. And ordinary men and women could not help but be affected by the attitudes and instructions imposed on them by their rulers. Nevertheless, one must not make the connections too close. Popular culture had roots of its own, and if we see certain trends toward restraint and order that parallel what was happening in politics and literate culture, they must not be overdrawn. Apart from anything else, the absence of social mobility and the effects of demographic trends were basic determinants of the life and outlook of the peasant and the poor; these limitations must be understood before one can even begin to consider the place of popular behavior and belief in the history of the times.

HIERARCHY AND RANK IN THE SOCIAL ORDER

Seventeenth-century men occupied well-defined places in society. According to a common view, they formed links in the great chain of being, which, ascending by degrees, united all of creation with the angels and God. Man stood in the middle of the chain between animals and angels, and within mankind there were also degrees, rising from the peasant through the well-to-do landowner or professional and the noble to the king. It was considered against the order of nature for someone to move to another level of society.

---

[4] Jean Racine, *Discours Prononcé à l'Académie Française à la Réception de M. de Corneille* (1685), in Paul Mesnard (ed.), *Oeuvres de J. Racine*, IV (1886), p. 366. Translation by Theodore K. Rabb.

MAP 16.2: CITIES OF EUROPE IN 1700

In fact, though, the people of the seventeenth century divided themselves into multiple groups and strata. Perhaps the clearest way to describe this structure is to liken society to a set of four ladders, each representing a distinct group: those on the land (about four-fifths of the population), those in the clergy, those in commerce (including artisans and shopkeepers), and those in the professions (mainly lawyers, doctors, and teachers). Within each ladder there was a sharply differentiated hierarchy, but most positions on each ladder had rough equivalents on the others. While all four were parallel, the landed ladder was clearly superior in that it rose higher and included the leaders of society, the courtiers and the great magnates.

Mobility and Privilege

The determinants of status in modern times —wealth, family background, and education —were viewed rather differently in the seventeenth century. Wealth was significant chiefly to merchants, education was important mainly among professionals, and background was vital primarily to the nobility. But in this period the significance of these three social indicators began to shift. Wealth grew increasingly respectable as ever-larger numbers of successful merchants bought their way into the nobility. Education was also becoming more highly prized; throughout Europe attendance at institutions of higher learning soared after 1550 because a smattering of knowledge was now considered to be a mark of gentility.[5] And background was being scrutinized ever more carefully (though to less effect) by oldline nobles, who were dismayed at the multiplication of "new" aristocrats.

[5] See Lawrence Stone, "The Educational Revolution in England, 1560–1640," *Past & Present*, July 1964, pp. 41–80.

The growing social importance of wealth and education indicates that mobility was possible despite the great chain of being. Thanks to the expansion of bureaucracies during the sixteenth and seventeenth centuries, it became easier for men to move to new levels, either by winning favor at court or by buying an office. High status conferred important privileges: great landowners could demand services and taxes from their tenants; city freemen, nobles, and bureaucrats were frequently exempt from taxes; and courtiers controlled portions of the vast patronage that the government disbursed. This period witnessed the rise of some of the most successful self-made men in history, particularly among the ministers who served the kings of England and France.

Somewhat different patterns were emerging in Europe's colonies. From their earliest days, the overseas settlements had reflected their countries of origin. Both the Portuguese and the Dutch for example had concentrated almost exclusively on commerce. They had small populations and were incapable of conquering large areas; instead they established a network of trading posts linked by sea that were marked by an effort to live amicably amid the native populations. The French followed a similar practice for a different reason: because the home country was rich in land and prosperous, few of its inhabitants were willing to emigrate. Spaniards and Englishmen by contrast flocked to new settlements in search of gold, land, and religious freedom. They remained overseas, occupying vast territories, subduing the natives, and creating extensive political structures that were far more elaborate than the earlier commercial outposts.

The common problem of all the colonies was their vulnerability. They were exposed to attack from the local population and from rival colonizers, and they rarely had the defensive capability to feel completely secure.

Under this pressure they often created societies imitative of but even more rigid than those of the countries they had left behind. Representatives of church and king dominated Portugal's settlements, and in her one major colony, Brazil, a few powerful landowners dominated in a way that no noble could in the homeland. Among the Dutch, as might be expected, the merchants took charge completely; and the French were subjected to strict supervision by the government—there was even an *intendant* for Canada. Spain's empire was also focused on the crown, and if its extent and remoteness permitted the emergence of a fairly independent society, great nobles and the church still stood at its head, as at home. And the English created a system in which landed gentry, such as the plantation owners of Virginia, and thriving merchants remained the leading citizens, though independent-minded New England diverted significantly from this pattern, reflecting the challenge to the traditional hierarchical view of social structure posed by Protestantism's egalitarian implications.

All the colonies, however, were distinguished from the mother countries by one institution which was vital to their economies but also degrading to its participants: slavery. The slaves posed yet another military threat to the settlers, thus reinforcing their inclination toward rigid social control.

It is important to realize that, both in Europe and in the colonies, the lower levels of society scarcely participated in the mobility caused by the growth of commerce and bureaucracy. Peasants throughout Europe were in fact entering a time of increasing difficulty at the end of the sixteenth century. Their taxes were rising rapidly, but the prices they could get for the food they grew were stabilizing. Moreover landowners were starting what has been called the "seigneurial reaction" —making additional demands on their tenants, raising rents, and taking as much as they could out of the land. The only escape was to cities or armies, both of which grew rapidly in the seventeenth century. A few lucky people improved their lot by such a move, but for the huge majority a life of poverty in cities caused even more misery and hunger than one on the land. Few were allowed to become apprentices, and day laborers were poorly paid and usually out of work. As for military careers, armies not only destroyed the well-being of the rural areas they passed through but were hardly less dangerous for their own troops. They were carriers of disease, frequently ill fed, and subject to constant hardship. For many, therefore, the only alternative to starvation was crime. In London in the seventeenth century, social events like dinners and outings took place during the daytime, because the streets were unsafe at night.

DEMOGRAPHIC PATTERNS

During the last twenty years, a number of historians have developed a new technique called family reconstitution, which uses analyses of the records of births, marriages, and deaths in parish registers to re-create the patterns of seventeenth-century life.[6] Some of the contrasts they have revealed are startling. For example in France illegitimacy appears to have accounted for only 1 percent of births in the countryside, about 4 or 5 percent in towns, and somewhat more in Paris. In England, however, illegitimacy accounted for 20 percent of births, and the rate reached 40 or 50 percent after 1700. In New England in the same period the proportion evidently rose from 10 to 50 percent. The view that sets the loose French against the proper English or re-

---

[6] An excellent introduction to the work of the historical demographers is E. A. Wrigley, *Population and History* (1969).

pressed New Englanders is thus the reverse of the truth.

Once the babies were born, no more than 25 percent reached the age of one, only 50 percent survived to be twenty, and less than 10 percent lived to be sixty. This was a society dominated by those in their twenties and thirties, able to rise because their predecessors died earlier than they do in modern times. Because only one child in two reached adulthood, a couple had to produce four children merely to replace themselves.

The likelihood that they would be able to do so was not improved by the practice of marrying relatively late or the fact that women lost the capacity to bear children in their late thirties. The average age of marriage for men was around twenty-seven and for women close to twenty-five. On the average therefore a woman would have some twelve years in which to give birth to four children if the population was to be maintained. Because of lactation the mean interval between births was almost two and a half years, which meant that the average married couple was only just raising two adults. And in fact population levels were barely being maintained for most of the seventeenth century. There had been an enormous increase before 1600, and a slight rise was sustained thereafter, but the real resumption of growth did not come until the eighteenth century.

The causes of the high mortality rate were simple but insuperable: famine, poor nutrition, disease, and war. The plague, erupting every few years from the fourteenth century on, swept away mainly the young and the old and it did not disappear until the 1720s. The upper classes, better fed and able to get away from plague centers, had a better chance for survival; but the odds were often equalized by their resort to dangerously incompetent doctors.

How and why the general population trend changed is impossible to know for certain. It is fairly clear that as early as the fifteenth century, the upper levels of society had begun limiting the size of their families in order to preserve their wealth—dowries for a daughter were expensive, and younger sons might not be able to live from family resources. Whether self-limitation was understood, let alone practiced, by other classes is difficult to say, though it is hard to offer an alternate explanation of the fact that the average gap between children sometimes rose to double the usual thirty months, particularly in troubled times. Late marriage for the upper classes was another means of controlling family size. For the lower levels of society, such postponement was a traditional economic defense: children had to work for their families until their parents' death allowed them to strike out for themselves.

Because of late marriages and low life expectancies, two married generations were rarely contemporary. Thus the extended family—more than one nuclear group of mother, father, and children living together—was extremely uncommon. Almost everyone who survived married, so there were few bachelors and spinsters, and usually each family could live on its own.

These features and consequences of demographic behavior give a sense of the basic patterns of seventeenth-century society, but we still do not know why the population grew so markedly in the sixteenth century, so little in the seventeenth, and then again so rapidly in the eighteenth. One can but suggest that repercussions were felt from the political, economic, and intellectual upheavals of the seventeenth century.

In only one area, the link between war and life expectancy, were the effects obvious. At the simplest level the Thirty Years' War alone caused the death of more than 5 million people. It also helped plunge Western Europe into a

EUROPE'S POPULATION, 1600–1700, BY REGIONS

REGION	1600*	1700	PERCENT-AGE CHANGE
Spain, Portugal, and Italy	23.6	22.7	−4
France, Switzerland, and Germany	35.0	36.2	+3
British Isles, Low Countries, and Scandinavia	12.0	16.1	+34
Total	70.6	75.0	+6

* All figures are in millions
Source: Jan de Vries, *The Economy of Europe in an Age of Crisis, 1600–1750,* Cambridge, 1976, p. 5.

debilitating economic depression, which in turn decreased the means of relieving famine. These were mighty blows at the delicate balance that maintained population growth, and disasters of such magnitude could not easily be absorbed. The few regions that managed to avoid decline were to become the leaders of Europe's economy (see accompanying table).

If the seventeenth century was almost everywhere a time of stagnation or decline in population, a period of harsh weather and recurrent famines and plagues, it was so especially for the poorest members of society. The low life expectancy, the frequent deaths of children, and the struggle to survive were constant and desperate pressures. It is small wonder that their culture embraced beliefs in dark forces and rituals of violence and protest. Nor is it surprising that as governments extended their hold over their subjects, they reduced the autonomy of ordinary villagers and limited the extremes of popular self-expression.

POPULAR CULTURE

As is natural for people living close to the land and dependent for their livelihood on the kindness of nature—good weather, health, fertility of soil—peasants in sixteenth- and seventeenth-century Europe assumed that outside forces controlled their destinies. Particular beliefs varied from place to place but there was general agreement that a mere human being could do little to assure his own well-being. The world was full of spirits and powers, and all one could do was to encourage the good, defend oneself as best one knew how against the evil, and hope that the good would win. Nothing that happened—the death of a calf, lightning striking a house, a toad jumping through a window into a home—was accidental. Everything had a purpose. Any unusual event was an omen, part of a larger plan, or the action of some unseen force.

To strengthen themselves against trouble, people used whatever help they could find. One device was to organize special processions and holidays to celebrate good times (such as harvests), to lament misfortunes, to complain about oppression, or to poke fun at scandalous behavior. These occasions, known as "rough music" in England and "charivari" in France, often used the theme of "the world turned upside down" to make their point. In the set pieces in a procession, a fool might be dressed up as a king, a woman might be shown beating

Adrianus Hubertus

her husband, or a tax collector might appear hanging from a tree. Whether ridiculing a cheating wife or lamenting the lack of bread, the community was expressing its solidarity in the face of difficulty or distasteful behavior through these rituals. It was a way of letting off steam and declaring public opinion.

This engraving reveals the popular image of witches in early modern Europe—in this case Germany. They are shown preparing for a ride, either on broomsticks or on the goats that were symbols of the devil, while the woman in the center boils up one of their evil concoctions. (Photo: Culver Pictures)

The potential for violence was always present at such gatherings, especially when religious or social differences became entangled with other resentments. The viciousness of ordinary Protestants and Catholics toward one another—it was not uncommon for one side to mutilate the dead bodies of the other—revealed a frustration and aggressiveness that was not far below the surface. When food was scarce or new impositions had been ordered by their rulers, peasants and townsmen needed little excuse to show their anger openly. In many cases women took the lead, not only because they had first-hand experience of the difficulty of feeding a family but also because troops were more reluctant to attack them. This tradition was still alive in 1789, in the early days of the French Revolution, when a band made up primarily of women marched from Paris to the royal court at Versailles to demand bread.

There was a peasant uprising in one location or another in France every year during the century up to 1675. But ordinary people also had other outlets for their problems. Recognizing their powerlessness in face of outside forces, they resorted to their version of the magic that the literate were finding so fashionable at this very time. Where the rich patronized astrologers, paying fortunes for horoscopes and advice about how to live their lives, the peasants and the poor consulted popular almanacs or sought out "cunning men" and wise women for secret spells, potions, and similar remedies for their anxieties. Even religious ceremonies were closely related to the rituals of the magical world, in which so-called "white" witches—the friendly kind—gave assistance when a ring was lost, when a new bride could not become pregnant, or when the butter would not form out of the milk.

For most Europeans, such support was all too necessary as they struggled with the unpredictability of nature. Misfortunes, they believed, could never be just plain bad luck; rather, there was intent behind everything that happened. Events were *willed*, and if they turned out badly, they must have been willed by the good witch's opposite, the evil witch. Such beliefs went back to the ancient world and for centuries had been the cause of mass scares and cruel persecutions of innocent victims—usually helpless old women, able to do nothing but mutter curses when taunted by neighbors, and easy targets if someone had to be blamed for unfortunate happenings.

In the sixteenth and seventeenth centuries, the hunt for witches intensified to levels never previously reached. This has been called the era of "the great witch craze," and for good reason. There were outbursts in every part of Europe, and tens of thousands of the accused were executed. The patterns varied—in some areas they were said to dance with the devil, in others to fly on broomsticks, in others to be possessed by evil spirits—but always the punishment was the same: burning at the stake. And the hysteria was infectious. One accusation could trigger dozens more until entire regions were swept with fear and hatred. Political and religious authorities, which often encouraged witch hunts as expressions of piety or as means of stamping out disorder, found themselves unable to stop the flow once it started. It was the perfect symptom of an age of disruption, uncertainty, and upheaval.

By the middle of the seventeenth century, however, the wave was beginning to recede. The rulers of society came to realize how dangerous to authority the witchcraft campaigns could become, especially when accusations were turned against the rich and privileged classes. Increasingly, therefore, cases were not brought to trial, and when they were, lawyers and doctors cast doubt on the validity of the testimony. Gradually, excesses were restrained and control was reestablished; by 1700 there was only a trickle of new incidents.

The decline reflected not only the more general quieting down of society but also the growing proportion of Europe's population that was living in cities. Here, less reliant on good weather or the luck of fertility, people could feel themselves more in control of their own fates. If there were unexpected fires, there were fire brigades; if a house nevertheless burned down, there might even be insurance—a new idea, just starting in the late seventeenth century. A notable shift in the world view of popular culture was under way, the inevitable result of basic changes in social organization.

CHANGE IN THE TRADITIONAL VILLAGE

A number of forces were combining to transform the atmosphere of the traditional village. Over three-quarters of Europe's population still lived in these small communities, but their structure was not what it once had been. In the east peasants were being reduced to serfdom; in the west—our principal concern—familiar relationships and institutions were changing.

The essence of the traditional village had been its isolation. Cut off from frequent contact with the world beyond its immediate region, it had been self-sufficient and closely knit. Everyone knew everyone else, and mutual help was vital. There might be distinctions among villagers—some more prosperous, others less so—but the sense of cohesiveness was powerful. It extended even to the main "outsiders" in the village, the priest and the lord. The priest was often indistinguishable from his parishioners: almost as poor and sometimes hardly more literate. He adapted to local customs and beliefs, frequently taking part in semipagan rituals so as to keep his authority with his flock. The lord could be exploitative and demanding, but he considered the village his livelihood, and he therefore kept in close touch with its affairs and did all he could to ensure its safety, orderliness, and well-being.

The first intrusion onto this scene was economic. As a result of the boom in agricultural prices during the sixteenth century, followed by the economic difficulties of the seventeenth, differences in the wealth of the villagers became more marked. The richer peasants began to set themselves apart from the poorer, and the feeling of unity began to break down. For hundreds of years, most villages had governed themselves through elected councils drawn from every part of the population. Toward the end of the seventeenth century, however, these councils started disappearing as the commitment to common interests declined.

Some of the other outside influences were more direct. In a few areas of Europe, especially in England and the Netherlands, the isolation of the villages was broken down by merchants who were experimenting with new ways of organizing labor. Traditionally, a village would raise sheep, shear them, and sell the wool at market to traders who would have it finished into cloth in towns. Now, aiming at greater efficiency, merchants were organizing production on a larger scale in a new industry that has been called the rural "putting-out" system or "cottage industry." What they were doing was buying up the raw wool in sheep-raising villages, distributing it to other villages that were now geared entirely to weaving and producing cloth, and then taking the finished material to market for sale. Entire areas came to be in the employ of merchants, dependent on them for materials and a liveli-

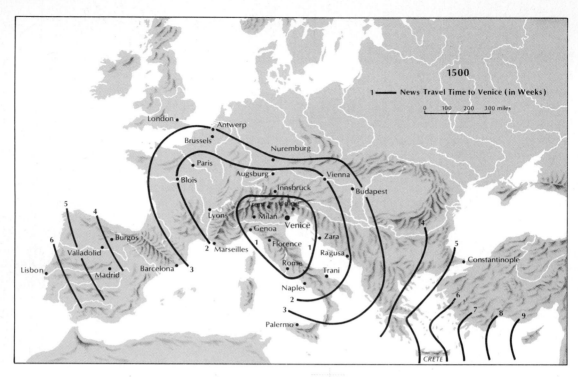

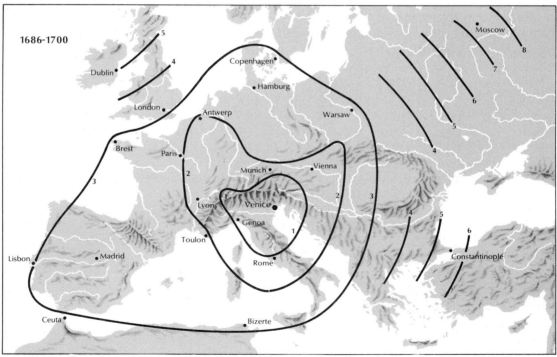

MAP 16.3: SPEED OF NEWS TRAVELING TO VENICE

hood. This created a new set of relationships, based on piecework rather than services, which again helped redirect the traditional patterns of life in the village, reducing independence and the ties of friendship and mutual help.

The isolation was also lessened as cities grew, not only because large urban centers needed ever wider regions to provide them with food and goods, but also because they attracted people who could not make ends meet in the countryside. Long-range communications became more common, especially as localities were linked into national market and trade networks, and immigrants in cities came to know fellow countrymen from distant villages (see Map 16.3).

Noneconomic forces, too, hastened the loss of autonomy. Over the course of the seventeenth century, nobles were looking more and more to central courts and capital cities, rather than to their local holdings, for position and power. Pursuing the seigneurial reaction, they treated the villages they dominated as sources of income and began to distance themselves from the inhabitants. Relations became impersonal where once they had been close and supportive. Charity, for example, was no longer thought to be the responsibility of neighbors: it was the duty of the church or the government.

The churches were taking on new roles, but these only had the effect of encouraging conformity. In Catholic countries the Counter Reformation produced better-educated priests who were trained to impose official doctrine instead of tolerating local customs. Among Protestants, ministers were similarly well-educated and denounced traditional beliefs as idolatrous or superstitious. Regardless of church, the outside world was intruding yet again. Habits did not change overnight, but in the long run the villagers were being forced to accept new values and to abandon their old beliefs.

The final blow was the growing presence of representatives of central government. In 1500 few villagers would have known what a servant of the king was, let alone have seen one. By 1700 they would all have had considerable experience with bureaucrats of one sort or another: tax collectors, recruiting officers, or army suppliers. Villagers no longer lived on their own in a small corner of the land. They were a part of the territorial state, important resources that the national government had to tap if it was to increase its power. Institutions (such as charity) had to be uniform; order had to be maintained. With their autonomy fragmenting and their customs and coherence under assault, the villages had no capacity to resist the integrating forces that were blending them into their nation states and subduing their eccentricities and traditions.

As Europeans entered the last decades of the seventeenth century, they had reason to feel that the upheavals and uncertain times they had gone through for more than 100 years were behind them. An extraordinarily successful intellectual movement, the scientific revolution, had solved many ancient problems about nature. Artists and writers had developed a new confidence. And throughout society an atmosphere of orderliness was returning

after over a century of change, disruption, and excesses like the witch craze. Religion had lost much of its power to arouse hatred and aggression; a calmer time seemed to be dawning, taking as its model the respect for reason that the scientists were encouraging.

The natural beneficiaries of these tendencies were the upper classes throughout Europe. Ordinary villagers may not have felt reconciled to the order being imposed upon them, but they proved unable to resist the forces—economic, political, and cultural—that were pressing them to conform. On the other hand, the sense of order was perfectly suited to the needs of aristocrats. They could now relax, confident that their power was secure. At dazzling princely courts, especially in France, they could enjoy the absence of turmoil and set their stamp on the culture of a new, less troubled age.

RECOMMENDED READING

Sources

* Drake, Stillman (tr. and ed.). *Discoveries and Opinions of Galileo.* 1957. The complete texts of some of Galileo's most important and readable works.
* Hall, Marie Boas (ed.). *Nature and Nature's Laws: Documents of the Scientific Revolution.* 1970. A good collection of documents by and about the pioneers of modern science.

Studies

* Butterfield, Herbert. *The Origins of Modern Science.* 1949. An elegantly written history of the scientific revolution, with a good bibliography.
* Caspar, Max. *Kepler.* C. Doris Hellman (tr.). 1959. A lucid biography of a complicated man, half-scientist, half-magician.
* Davis, Natalie Z. *Society and Culture in Early Modern France.* 1975. A fascinating set of essays on popular culture in the sixteenth and seventeenth centuries.
* Frame, Donald M. *Montaigne: A Biography.* 1965. The best biography of this influential thinker.
* Geymonat, Ludovico. *Galileo Galilei.* Stillman Drake (tr.). 1965. A straightforward and clear biography.
* Hibbard, Howard. *Bernini.* 1965. A graceful account of the life and work of the artist who was the epitome of the Baroque.

Kamen, Henry. *The Iron Century: Social Change in Europe 1550–1660.* 1971. This thorough, almost encyclopedic overview of the social history of the period also has a good bibliography.
* Kuhn, Thomas S. *The Copernican Revolution: Planetary Astronomy in the Development of Western Thought.* 1957. The most comprehensive account of the revolution in astronomy.
* ————. *The Structure of Scientific Revolutions.* 1962. A suggestive interpretation of the reasons the scientific revolution happened.
* Ladurie, Emmanuel Le Roy. *The Peasants of Languedoc.* John Day (tr.). 1966. A brilliant evocation of peasant life in France in the sixteenth and seventeenth centuries.
* Maland, David. *Culture and Society in Seventeenth-Century France.* 1970. This survey of art, drama, and literature contains a good discussion of the rise of Classicism.
* Palisca, Claude. *Baroque Music.* The best survey of this period in the history of music.
* Popkin, Richard H. *The History of Scepticism from Erasmus to Descartes.* 1964. Taking one strand in European thought as its subject, this lively study places both Montaigne and Descartes in a new perspective.
* Shearman, John. *Mannerism.* 1968. The best short introduction to a difficult artistic style.
* Tapié, V. L. *The Age of Grandeur: Baroque Art and Architecture.* A. R. Williamson (tr.). 1960. Although concentrating primarily on France and

Austria, this is the most comprehensive survey of this period in art.

* Thomas, Keith. *Religion and the Decline of Magic*. 1971. The most thorough account of popular culture yet published, this enormous book, while dealing mainly with England, treats at length such subjects as witchcraft, astrology, and ghosts in a most readable style.

White, Christopher. *Rembrandt and his World*. 1964. A brief but wide-ranging introduction to the artist's work and life.

————. *Rubens and his World*. 1968. As good on Rubens as the previous title is on Rembrandt.

---

* Available in paperback.

SEVENTEEN

THE TRIUMPH OF
ARISTOCRATS AND KINGS

Ever since the time that effective central governments had coalesced in Europe in the Late Middle Ages, nobles and rulers had engaged in a running struggle for power. After the upheavals of the mid-seventeenth century, however, it became clear that central administrations—now highly complex and commanding large bureaucracies—would dominate political life. Yet no ruler could govern without the help of the aristocracy. Of the main orders, or estates, into which society was divided—aristocrats, churchmen, townsmen, and peasants—only the aristocrats had the education, experience, and status essential for the running of a state.

The actual control they wielded over policy varied widely. In the absolutist realms they were most powerful in Austria, less so in France and Brandenburg-Prussia, and least in Russia. Moreover influence in the government was usually restricted to a small group; the class as a whole benefited only indirectly. But in England (where the ruling elite was being penetrated by members of the untitled gentry), the United Provinces, Sweden, and Poland, virtually no major decision could be executed without their approval. In effect, the aristocracy had taken possession of the administration of Europe's states and no longer had to compete with towns, representative assemblies, or the ruler himself for the fruits of power.

By the end of the seventeenth century, therefore, Europe's nobility was moving toward a new type of leadership. Historians have called this the domestication of the aristocracy, a process in which great lords who had once drawn their status primarily from the antiquity of their lineage or the extent of their lands gradually came to see service to the throne and royal favor as the best source of power.

To central administrations, eager to restore or confirm orderly government after over a century of disruptions, this alliance was more than welcome, and the rewards they bestowed—whether in patronage, privilege, or perquisites—were enormous. New power structures thus emerged in the age of Louis XIV, though the forms differed from country to country, and the fortunes of the lower classes fluctuated accordingly. Yet throughout Europe the quest for order was the underlying concern, a preoccupation that was already evident in the mid-seventeenth century and that pervaded not only political and social developments, but also thought and taste during the subsequent fifty years.

I. THE ABSOLUTE MONARCHIES

In countries that were ruled by absolutist monarchs—where all power was believed to emanate from the untrammeled person of the king—the center of society was the great court.

Here the leaders of government assembled, and around them swirled the most envied social circles of the time. At the court of Louis XIV in particular, an atmosphere of ornate splendor arose that, though primarily intended to exalt the king, inevitably glorified the aristocracy too. No other ruler could match its scale and magnificence, but many tried to imitate its style. Even at courts where nobles played a somewhat different role, this influence was inescapable.

LOUIS XIV AT VERSAILLES

In the view of Louis XIV (1643–1715), absolutism and the building of both the state and the government went hand in hand. But all three had to have a focus, preferably away from the turbulent city of Paris. To this end Louis, at a cost of half a year's royal income, transformed a small chateau his father had built at Versailles, twelve miles outside of Paris, into the largest building in Europe, surrounded by vast and elaborate formal gardens.

The splendor of the setting was designed to impress the world with the majesty of its principal occupant, and a complex ritual of daily ceremonies centered on the king gradually evolved. The name "Sun King" was another means of self-aggrandizement, symbolized by coins that showed the rays of the sun falling first on Louis and then by reflection onto his subjects, who thus owed life and warmth to their monarch. Versailles also provided an appropriate physical setting for the domestication of the nobility. Each year those who sought Louis' favor had to make an ostentatious appearance at court, and endless factions and plots swirled through the palace as courtiers jockeyed for position, competing for such privileges as handing the king his gloves in the morning. Louis regarded all men as his servants, and they were kept constantly aware of their vulnerable status.

Government and Foreign Policy

Yet this system was not merely a device to satisfy one man's whim, for Louis was a gifted state builder. In creating or reorganizing government institutions to reflect his own wishes,

he strengthened his authority at home and increased his ascendancy over his neighbors. In fact the most durable result of absolutism in seventeenth-century France was the state's winning of final control over three critical activities: the use of armed force, the formulation and execution of laws, and the collection and expenditure of revenue. These functions in turn depended on a centrally controlled bureaucracy responsive to royal orders and efficient enough to carry them out in distant provinces over the objections of local groups.

In its ideal form an absolute monarch's bureaucracy was insulated from outside pressure by the king's power to remove and transfer appointees. In the case of France, this involved creating new administrative officials—commissioners—to supersede some existing officers or magistrates who claimed their positions by virtue of property or other rights.[1] The process also required training programs, improved administrative methods, and the use of experts wherever possible. This approach was considered desirable both for the central bureaucracy in the capital and for the provincial offices.

At the head of this structure, Louis XIV was able to carry off successfully a responsibility that few monarchs had the talent to pursue: he served as his own first minister, actively and effectively overseeing administrative affairs. He thus filled two roles—as king in council and king in court. Louis the administrator coexisted with Louis the courtier, who cultivated the arts, hunted, and indulged in gargantuan banquets. In his view the two roles went together, and he held them in balance.

Among his numerous imitators, however,

---

[1] The *intendants*, who remained the chief provincial administrators, provided the model for the commissioners, because their success derived from dependence on royal approval. It should be noted that all bureaucrats were called officers, but those with judicial functions were known as magistrates.

this was not always the case. Court life was the pleasanter, easier side of absolutism. It tended to consume an inordinate share of a state's resources and to become an end in itself. The display performed certain useful functions, of course; it stimulated luxury trades, supported cultural endeavors, and thus exercised a civilizing influence on the nobility of Europe. But beyond this it tended to be frivolous and wasteful, lending an undeserved prestige to the leisure pursuits of the upper classes, such as dancing, card playing, and hunting, while sapping the energies of influential figures. Louis was one of the few who avoided sacrificing affairs of state to regal pomp.

Like court life, government policy under Louis XIV was tailored to the aim of state building. As he was to discover, there were limits to his absolutism; the resources and powers at his disposal were not endless. But until the last years of his reign, they served his many purposes extremely well. Moreover Louis had superb support at the highest levels of his administration—men whose viewpoints differed but whose skills were carefully blended by their ruler.

The king's two leading ministers were Jean Baptiste Colbert and the marquis of Louvois. Colbert was a financial wizard who had been raised to prominence by Mazarin and who regarded a mercantilist policy as the key to state building. He believed that the government should give priority to increasing France's wealth. This meant in turn that the chief danger to the country's well-being was the United Provinces, Europe's great trader state, and that royal resources should be poured into the navy, manufacturing, and shipping. By contrast Louvois, the son of a military administrator, consistently emphasized the army as the foundation of France's power. He believed that the country was threatened primarily by land—by the Holy Roman Empire on its flat, vulnerable northeast frontier—and thus that resources should be allocated to the army and to an extensive border fortification program.

Louis shifted back and forth between these considerations, but the basic tendencies of his policy can always be traced. In his early years he relied heavily on Colbert, who moved gradually toward war with the Dutch when all attempts to undermine their control of French maritime trade failed. But the war, occupying most of the 1670s, was a failure, and so the pendulum swung toward Louvois. Adopting the marquis' aims, in the early 1680s Louis asserted his right to a succession of territories on France's northeast border. No one claim seemed important enough to provoke the empire to military action; moreover its princes were distracted by a growing Turkish threat from the East. Thus France was able to annex large segments of territory, ultimately extending her frontier to Strasbourg, near the Rhine River (see Map 17.1). Finally, however, the defensive League of Augsburg was formed against Louis, and another war broke out in 1688. This one too went badly for him, and when he decided to seek peace, Louvois fell from favor. In a move that surprised all of Europe, Louis then brought back to power a former foreign minister named Simon de Pomponne, who had always stood for peace and careful diplomacy. It was characteristic of the Sun King to use his servants this way—raising and discarding them according to their position on his policy of the moment. But even this balancing process broke down in the last two decades of his reign, when France became involved in a bitter, drawn-out war that brought famine, wretched poverty, and humiliation. Louis was seeking the succession to the Spanish throne for his family, and he was determined to pursue the fighting until he achieved his aim.

The Palace of Versailles in 1668. (Photo: Louvre)

Louis XIV (seated) is shown here in full regal splendor surrounded by three of his heirs. On his right is his eldest son, on his left is his eldest grandson, and, reaching out his hand, his eldest great-grandson, held by his governess. All three of these heirs died before Louis, and thus they never became kings of France. (Photo: Wallace Collection, London)

MAP 17.1: THE WARS OF LOUIS XIV

This final and ruinous enterprise revealed both the new power of France and her limits. By launching an all-out attempt to establish his own and his country's supremacy, he showed that he felt capable of taking on the whole of Europe; but by then he no longer had the economic and military base at home or the weak opposition abroad to assure success.

The strains had begun to appear in the 1690s, when shattering famines throughout France reduced both tax revenues and manpower at home, while enemies began to unite

THE SPANISH SUCCESSION, 1700

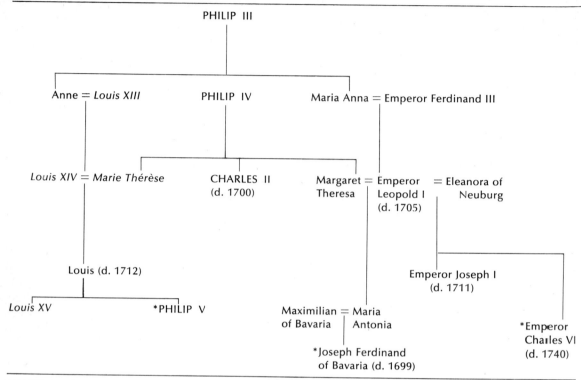

NAMES IN CAPITALS = Kings of Spain
Names in italics = Kings of France

*People designated at various times as heirs of Charles II

abroad. Louis had the most formidable army in Europe—400,000 men by the end of his reign —but both William III of the United Provinces and Leopold I of the Holy Roman Empire believed that he could be defeated by a combined assault. They worked persistently to this end, particularly after the Turkish threat to Leopold ended with the failure of the siege of Vienna, in 1683, and William gained the English throne six years later. The League of Augsburg, transformed into the Grand Alliance after William and other rulers joined it, fought a successful holding action against Louis' attempt to intervene across the Rhine, and the final showdown was precipitated when

the Hapsburg king of Spain, Charles II, died without an heir.

There were various possible claimants to the throne, and Charles himself had changed his mind a number of times, but at his death his choice was Philip, Louis XIV's grandson (see the accompanying table). Had Louis been willing to agree not to unite the thrones of France and Spain, Charles' wish might well have been respected by the rest of Europe. But Louis refused to compromise, insisting that there were no conditions to Charles' bequest. The rest of Europe disagreed and declared war on France so as to prevent Philip's unrestricted succession. Thus Louis found himself fighting virtually the entire Continent in the War of the Spanish Succession, not only at home but also overseas, in India, Canada, and the Caribbean.

Led by brilliant generals, the Englishman John Churchill, duke of Marlborough, and the Austrian Prince Eugène, the allies won a series of smashing victories. France's hardships were increased by a terrible famine in 1709. Yet the Sun King's hold over his subjects was unimpaired. Nobody rose in revolt against him; his policies were not seriously challenged; and despite military disaster he succeeded in keeping his nation's borders intact and the Spanish throne for his grandson (though he had to give up the possibility of union with France) when peace treaties were signed at Utrecht in 1713 and 1714. In sum his great task of state building, both at home and abroad, had faced and withstood the severest of all tests: defeat on the battlefield.

Domestic Affairs

The assertion of royal supremacy at home was almost complete by the time Louis came to power, but he extended the principle of centralized control to religion and social institutions. Religion was a major area of activity because two groups, the Protestant Huguenots and the Catholic Jansenists, interfered with the spiritual and confessional uniformity that the king considered essential in the absolutist state.

Of the two the Huguenots were the more obviously unintegrated. Government pressures against them mounted after 1668, when their greatest adherent, the famous Marshal Turenne, converted to Catholicism. Finally in 1685 Louis revoked the century-old Edict of Nantes, thus forcing France's 1 million Protestants either to leave the country (four-fifths did) or to convert to Catholicism. This was a political rather than a religious act, taken for the sake of unity despite the economic conse-

quences that followed the departure of a vigorous and productive minority.

Jansenism posed a more elusive problem. It had far fewer followers, though among them were some of the greatest figures in the land, such as the playwright Racine; and it was a movement within Catholicism. But the very fact that it challenged the official church hierarchy and had been condemned by Rome made it a source of unrest and disorder. What was worse, it was beginning to gain support among the magistrate class—the royal officers in the parlements, which had to register all royal edicts before they became law. The Parlement of Paris was the only governmental institution that offered Louis any real resistance during his reign. The issues over which it caused trouble were usually religious, and the link between parlementaire independence and dislike for court frivolity on the one hand, and Jansenism on the other, gave Louis more than enough reason for displeasure. He razed the Jansenists' headquarters, the Abbey of Port-Royal, and then persuaded the pope to issue a bull condemning Jansenism. He was prevented from implementing the bull—over parlementaire opposition—only by his death, in 1715.

The drive toward uniformity that lay behind these actions was reflected in all aspects of domestic policy. Louis rapidly crushed what little parlementaire protest there was; an attempt by peasants in central France to resist the government was ruthlessly suppressed; Parisian publishers came under bureaucratic supervision; and the *intendants*, the government's chief provincial officers, were given increased authority, particularly in connection with the ever-growing needs of the army.

At the outset of his rule, Louis used the government's power to improve France's economy. In this he followed a pattern familiar from earlier monarchs' reigns: an initial burst of reform measures to cure the country's economic ills, which were gradually forgotten because foreign policy demanded instant funds. In the early years, under Colbert's ministry, major efforts were made to stimulate manufacturing, agriculture, and home and foreign trade. Some industries, notably those involving luxuries like the silk production of Lyons, received considerable help and owed their rise to prosperity to royal patronage. Colbert also tried, not entirely effectively, to reduce the crippling effects of France's countless internal tolls. These were usually nobles' perquisites, and they could multiply the cost of goods shipped any distance. The government divided the country into a number of districts within each of which shipments were to be toll-free, but the system never removed the worst abuses. And finally, Louis made a concerted attempt to boost foreign trade, at first by financing new overseas trading companies and later by founding new port cities to strengthen maritime forces. Here he achieved notable success, particularly in the West Indies, which became a source of immense wealth for western France.

Louis' overall accomplishments were remarkable, and France became the envy of Europe. Yet ever since the Sun King's reign, historians have recalled the ruination caused by famine and war during his last years and have contrasted his glittering court with the misery of Frenchmen at large. Particularly after the famines of the 1690s and 1709, many contemporaries remarked on the dreadful condition of peasants in various regions. Even at Versailles there was disenchantment, expressed not only by a shrewd critic like the duke of Saint-Simon, who looked on the emptiness of court life with disdain, but also by concerned men who had not previously found fault with Louis' policies. A notable example was the great fortifications expert Sébastien le Prestre, marquis of Vauban, who had made a vital contribution to the military successes of

the reign (see Map 17.1). Late in life he called on the government to end its obsession with war because taxation was bringing the ordinary Frenchman to a state of hopeless despair.

Such warnings of course went unheeded, but in recent years historians have questioned whether France was in fact so badly off. That there was hardship cannot be denied, but its extent and lasting effect are open to question for two reasons. First, the difficulties caused none of the uprisings that were the normal reaction in the countryside either to excesses on the part of the central government or to severe food shortages. Second, France's quick recovery and unprecedented economic and demographic growth in the years following 1715 could never have taken place if the country had been as shattered as the dramatic tales of catastrophe suggest.

Nonetheless the reign of Louis XIV can be regarded as the end of an era in the life of the lower classes. In the early eighteenth century, the terrible subsistence crises, with their cycles of famine and plague, came to an end; both manufacturing and agriculture entered a period of great prosperity; and cities enjoyed spectacular new growth. It is likely that the hand of the central government seemed heavier in 1715 than a hundred years before, but the small landowner and urban worker had been struggling with taxes for decades, whether the payee was king or noble. And the Counter Reformation Church, growing in strength since the Council of Trent, provided a measure of blessing, for it began to bring into local parishes better-educated and more dedicated priests who, as part of their new commitment to service, exerted themselves to calm the outbreaks of witchcraft and irrational fear that had swept the countryside for centuries. The fortunes of Jacques Bonhomme, the symbolic French everyman, had risen noticeably by 1715.

The improvement was also apparent in the

mercantile class, which was about to enjoy a level of prosperity that outstripped even the sixteenth-century boom. Discontent at the government's interventions may have been felt by magistrates and parlementaires, who bewailed their lack of power, but these were voices in the wilderness. That there were some strains nobody could deny, but on the whole the absolutist structure had achieved its ends—a united, prosperous, and powerful France.

THE HAPSBURGS AT VIENNA AND MADRID

The pattern set at Versailles was repeated at the court of the Hapsburg Leopold I, the Holy Roman emperor (1658–1705). Heir to a reduced inheritance that gave him effective control over only Bohemia, Austria, and a small portion of Hungary, Leopold nonetheless maintained a magnificent establishment. His plans for a new palace, Schönbrunn, that was to have outshone Versailles were modified only because of a lack of funds. And his promotion of the court as the center of all political and social life turned Vienna into what it had never been before: a city of noble as well as burgher houses.

Nevertheless, Leopold himself did not display the pretensions of the Sun King. He had been a younger son and had inherited his crown only because of the death of his brother. An indecisive, retiring, deeply religious man, he had little fondness for the bravado Louis XIV enjoyed. He was a composer of no small talent, and his patronage laid the foundation for the great musical culture that was to be one of Vienna's chief glories. Whatever his inclinations, however, he found himself the holder of considerable royal authority: for more than a century, except during the Bohemian resistance of 1618 to 1621, the Hapsburg rulers had had few serious challenges to

their power. This was a tradition that Leopold felt obliged to continue, though unlike Louis XIV he relied on a small group of leading aristocrats to implement policy and run the administration.

The Thirty Years' War had revealed that the elected head of the Holy Roman Empire could no longer control the princes who nominally owed him allegiance, but within his own dominions he could maintain complete control with the cooperation of the aristocracy. The Privy Council, which in effect ran Leopold's domain, was largely filled with members of aristocratic families, and his chief advisers were always prominent nobles. But he did not switch about among representatives of various policies as Louis XIV did. Instead he carefully consulted each of his ministers and then came to decisions with agonizing slowness, even when all of them were agreed.

Unlike the other courts of Europe, Schönbrunn did not favor only native-born aristocrats. The leader of Austria's armies during the Turks' siege of Vienna in 1683 was Charles, duke of Lorraine, a prince whose duchy had long ago been taken over by the French. His predecessor as field marshal had been an Italian, and his successor was to be one of the most brilliant soldiers of the age, Prince Eugène of Savoy. None of these men were members of the Austrian nobility until Leopold gave them titles within his own dominions, but they all fitted easily into the aristocratic circles that controlled the government and the army.

Prince Eugène was a spectacular symbol of the aristocracy's continuing dominance of European politics and society. A member of one of the most distinguished families on the Continent, he had been raised in France but found himself passed over when Louis XIV awarded army commissions, perhaps because he had been intended for the church. Yet he was determined to follow a military career and therefore volunteered to serve the Aus-

MAP 17.2: THE AUSTRIAN EMPIRE 1657–1718

trians in their long struggle with the Turks. His talents soon became evident: he was field marshal of Austria's troops by the time he was thirty. For the next forty years, though foreign-born, he was a decisive influence in Hapsburg affairs, the man primarily responsible for the transformation of Vienna's policies from defensive to aggressive.

Until the siege of 1683, Leopold's innate cautiousness kept Austria simply holding the line, both against Louis XIV and against the Turks. In the 1690s, however, he tried a bolder course at Eugène's urging and in the process laid the foundations for a new Hapsburg empire along the Danube River: Austria-Hungary (see Map 17.2). He helped create the coalition that defeated Louis in the 1700s, intervened in Italy so that his landlocked do-

mains could gain an outlet to the sea, and began the long process of pushing the Turks out of the Balkans. Leopold did not live to see the advance more than started, but by the time of Eugène's death, the Austrians were within a hundred miles of the Black Sea.

However, the power of the aristocracy blocked the complete centralization of Leopold's dominions. Louis XIV supported the nobles after he had subdued their independent positions in the provinces; Leopold by contrast gave them influence in the government without first establishing genuine control over all his lands. The nobility did not cause him the troubles his predecessors had faced during the Thirty Years' War, but he had to limit his ambitions in territories outside of Austria. Moreover, as Austrians came increasingly to dominate the court, the nobles of Hungary and Bohemia reacted by clinging ever more stubbornly to local traditions and rights. Thus Leopold's was an absolutism under which the aristocracy retained far more autonomous power—and a far firmer base of local support, stimulated by nationalist sentiments—than was the case in France, despite the increased centralization achieved during his reign.

Madrid enjoyed none of the success of its fellow Hapsburg court. Its king, Charles II, was a sickly man, incapable of having children; and the War of the Spanish Succession seriously reduced the inheritance he left. Both the southern Netherlands and most of Italy passed to the Austrian Hapsburgs, and Spain's overseas possessions were already virtually independent territories, paying little notice to the homeland.

The Spanish nobility was even more successful than the Austrian in turning the trappings of absolutism to its advantage. In 1650 the crown had been able to recapture Catalonia's loyalty only by granting the province's aristocracy considerable autonomy, and this pattern recurred throughout Spain's Continental holdings. Parasitic, unproductive nobles controlled the regime almost entirely for their own personal gain. The country had lapsed into economic and cultural stagnation, subservient to a group of powerful families, and reflecting its former glory only in a fairly respectable navy.

THE HOHENZOLLERNS AT BERLIN

The one new power that emerged to prominence during the age of Louis XIV was Brandenburg-Prussia, and here again a close alliance was established between a powerful ruler and his nobles. In this case, however, thanks to effective leadership, the results were very different than in Spain.

Frederick William (1640–1688), known as the "great elector," was the ruler of scattered territories that stretched 700 miles from Cleves, on the Rhine, to a part of Prussia on the Baltic. (See Map 17.3.) Taking advantage of the uncertainties and hopes for a new order that followed the chaos of the Thirty Years' War, he made his territories the dominant principality in northern Germany and at the same time strengthened his power over his subjects. His first task was in foreign affairs, because when he took over as elector most of his possessions were devastated by war, with troops swarming over them at will. Frederick William realized that by determination and intelligent planning, even a small prince could emerge from these disasters in a good position *if* he had an army. With some military force at his disposal, he could become a useful ally for the big powers, who could then help him against his neighbors, while at home he would have the strength to crush his opponents.

By 1648 Frederick William had 8,000 troops, and he was backed by both the Dutch and the French at Westphalia as a possible restraint on Sweden in northern Europe. Without having done much to earn new territory, he did very well in the peace settlement, and he then took brilliant advantage of the Baltic wars of the 1650s to confirm his gains by switching sides at crucial moments. In the process his army grew to 22,000 men, and he began to use it to impose his will on his own territories. The fact that the army was essential to all of Frederick William's successes—giving him status in Europe and power within his territories—was to influence much of Prussia's and thus also Germany's subsequent history.

The presence of the military, and its role in establishing the elector's supremacy, was apparent throughout Brandenburg-Prussia's society. In 1653 the Diet of Brandenburg met for the last time, sealing its own fate by giving Frederick William the right to raise taxes on his own authority, though previously he had had to obtain its consent. The War Chest, the office in charge of financing the army, took over the functions of a treasury department and collected government revenue even when the state was at peace. The execution of policy in the localities was placed under the supervision of war commissars, men who were originally responsible for military recruitment, billeting, and supply in each district of Brandenburg-Prussia, but who now became the principal agents of all government departments.

Apart from the representative assemblies, Frederick William faced substantial resistance only from the cities of his realm, which had long traditions of independence. Yet once again sheer intimidation swept opposition aside. The last determined effort to dispute his authority arose in the rich city of Königsberg, which allied with the Estates General (representative assembly) of Prussia to refuse to pay taxes. But this resistance was brought to a swift conclusion in 1662, when Frederick William marched into the city with a few thousand troops. Similar pressure brought the towns of Cleves, along the Rhine, into submission after centuries of proud independence.

The nobles were major beneficiaries of this policy. It was in fact the alliance between the nobility and Frederick William that made it possible for the Diet, the cities, and the representative assemblies to be undermined. The leading families saw their best opportunities for the future in cooperation with the central government, and both within the various representative assemblies and in the localities, they worked for the establishment of absolutist powers—that is, for the removal of all restraints on the elector. The most significant indicator of their success was that by the end of the century, two tax rates had been devised, one for cities and one for the countryside, to the great advantage of the latter.

Not only did the nobles staff the upper levels of the elector's bureaucracy and army; they also won a new prosperity for themselves. Particularly in Prussia they used the reimposition of serfdom and their dominant political position to consolidate their land holdings into vast, highly profitable estates. This was a vital grain-producing area—often called the granary of Europe—and they made the most of its economic potential. To maximize their profits they eliminated the middleman by not only growing but also distributing their produce themselves. Efficiency became their hallmark, and their wealth was soon famous throughout the Holy Roman Empire. Known as Junkers, these Prussian entrepreneurs were probably the most successful group within the European aristocracy in their pursuit of both economic and political power.

Unlike Louis in France, however, Frederick William did not force his nobles to lead a life of social ostentation revolving around his person. The court at Berlin became a glittering focus of society only under his son, Frederick III (1688–1701). The great elector himself was more interested in organizing his administration, increasing tax returns, building up his army, and imposing his authority at home and abroad. He began the development of his capital, Berlin, into a major city and cultural center—he laid out the famous double avenue Unter den Linden, and he founded what was to become one of the finest libraries in the world, the Prussian State Library, in his palace —but this was never among his prime concerns. His son by contrast enjoyed the pomp of his princely status and set about encouraging the arts with enthusiasm.

Frederick III lacked only one attribute of royalty: a crown. He hungered for the distinction, and he gained it when Emperor Leopold I, who still retained the right to confer

This early eighteenth century engraving of Berlin shows a skyline marked by the many new churches with which the Electors were beautifying their capital. Yet the view also reminds us that, for all their rapid growth, eighteenth century European cities (with the exception only of the three or four largest, which were surrounded by expanding suburbs) were still very close to the agriculture of the nearby countryside. (Photo: New York Public Library Picture Collection)

titles in the empire, needed Brandenburg's troops during the War of the Spanish Succes-

sion against Louis XIV. Although none of Frederick's territories had been a kingdom previously, he was allowed to call himself "king in Prussia" (a technicality; the title soon became "king of Prussia"). At a splendid coronation in 1701, Elector Frederick III of Brandenburg was crowned King Frederick I, and thereafter the court, now regal, could feel itself to be on equal terms with the other monarchical settings of Europe.

Frederick undertook a determined campaign to improve the social and cultural atmosphere in his lands. He founded the Order of the Black Eagle to encourage aristocratic ambitions, and he made his palace a center of art and polite society to compete, he hoped, with Versailles. A major construction program in Berlin beautified the city with seven churches and a number of huge public buildings, making it an important center of Baroque architecture. Following English and French models, Frederick also created an Academy of Sciences in Berlin and persuaded the most famous German scientist and philosopher of the day, Gottfried Wilhelm von Leibniz, to become its first president. All these activities obtained generous support from state revenues, as did the universities of Brandenburg and Prussia. By the end of his reign, in 1713, Frederick could take considerable satisfaction from the transformation he had brought about. He had given his realm the prestige of a throne, the reputation derived from important artistic and intellectual activity, and the elegant manners of an aristocracy at the head of both social and political life.

PETER THE GREAT AT ST. PETERSBURG

One of the reasons the new absolutist regimes of the late seventeenth and eighteenth centuries seemed so different from their predecessors was that many of them consciously created new settings for themselves. Versailles, Schönbrunn, and Berlin were all either new or totally transformed sites for royal courts. The palaces·were far larger and grander and provided a more impressive backdrop than previous seats of government. But only one of the autocrats of the period went so far as to build an entirely new capital: Peter I of Russia, called the Great (1682–1725), who named the city St. Petersburg after his patron saint. Not surprisingly he was also the only man among his contemporaries to declare himself an emperor.

None of the monarchs of the period had Peter's terrifying energy or ruthless resolve. A man of fierce temper, he was determined to impose his will without regard for opposition, though his decisions were often made in anger and then blindly implemented. The supreme example of his callousness was the torture of his own son, a quiet, retiring boy, who was killed by the inhumane treatment he received after trying to escape from his overbearing father.

Peter left no doubt about his intention to exercise absolute control in his realm. Of all the changes brought about in his reign, the most unprecedented was the destruction of ecclesiastical independence. When the patriarch of the Russian Church died in 1700, the tsar simply did not replace him. The government took over the monasteries, using their enormous income for its own purposes, and appointed a procurator (the first one was an army officer) to supervise all religious affairs. The church was in effect made a branch of government.

In the government itself Peter virtually ignored the Duma, the traditional advisory council, and concentrated on strengthening his bureaucracy. He carried out change after change, few of which lasted any length of time, but their cumulative effect was the creation of an administrative complex many times larger than the one he had inherited. Copying Western models, especially the Swedish system, he set up carefully organized executive departments, some with specialized functions, such as finance, and others with responsibility for geographic areas, such as Siberia. The result was an elaborate but unified hierarchy of authority rising from local agents of the government through provincial officials up to the

In the eighteenth century Peter the Great of Russia outstripped the grandeur of other monarchs of the period by erecting an entirely new city for his capital. St. Petersburg (now Leningrad) was built by forced labor of the peasants under Peter's orders; they are shown here laying the foundations for the city. (Photo: Tass from Sovfoto)

staffs and governors of eleven large administrative units and finally to the leaders of the re-

gime in the capital. Peter's reign marked the beginning of the saturating bureaucratization that was to characterize Russia ever after.

In the process the tsar laid the foundations for a two-class society that persisted until the twentieth century. Previously a number of ranks had existed within both the nobility and the peasantry, and a group in the middle, known as the *odnodvortsy* (roughly, "esquires"), were sometimes considered the lowest nobles and sometimes the highest peasants. Under Peter such mingling disappeared. All peasants were reduced to a uniform level, their equality emphasized by their universal liability to a new poll tax, military conscription, and forced public work, such as the building of St. Petersburg. Below them were the serfs, whose numbers were steadily increased by harsh legislation and who spread throughout the southern and western areas of Peter's dominions where previously they had been relatively unknown. The peasants possessed a few advantages over the serfs, but their living conditions were often equally dreadful.

At the same time Peter created a homogeneous class of nobles by substituting status within the bureaucracy for status within the traditional hierarchy of titles and ranks. In 1722 he issued a table of ranks that gave everyone his place according to the bureaucratic or military office that he held. Differentiations still existed under the new system, but they were no longer unbridgeable, as they had been when antiquity of family was decisive. The result was a more tightly controlled social order and greater uniformity than in France or Brandenburg-Prussia. By definition the Russian aristocracy was the bureaucracy and the bureaucracy the aristocracy.

But this was not a relatively voluntary alliance between nobles and government, such as existed in the West; in return for his support and his total subjection of the peasantry, Peter required the aristocrats to provide manpower for his rapidly expanding bureaucracy and officers for his growing army. When he began the construction of St. Petersburg, he also demanded that the leading families build splendid mansions in his new capital. In effect the tsar was offering privilege and wealth in exchange for what was virtual conscription into public service. Thus there was hardly any sense of partnership between aristocracy and

throne—the tsar often had to use coercion to ensure that his wishes were followed.

On the other hand Peter did a good deal to build up the nobles' fortunes and their ability to control the countryside. As one recent interpreter of the tsar's policy put it, he wanted "the landowning nobility to be rich and powerful; but it must nonetheless be composed of his personal servants who were to use their wealth and power in his services."[2] It has been estimated that by 1710 he had put under the supervision of great landowners more than 40,000 peasant and serf households that had formerly been under the crown. And he was liberal in conferring new titles—some of them, such as count and baron, an imitation of German examples.

In creating an aristocratic society at his court, as in much else that he did, Peter mixed imitations of what he admired in the West with native developments. He forced the nobility to follow the ritual surrounding a Western throne; he founded an Academy of Sciences in 1725; and he encouraged the beginnings of a theater at court. Italian artists were imported, along with Dutch ship builders, German engineers, and Scandinavian colonels, not only to apply their skills, but to teach them to the Russians. St. Petersburg, unquestionably the finest example of a city built in the Classical style of eighteenth-century architecture, is mainly the work of Italians, and the Academy of Sciences long depended on foreigners for whatever stature it had. But gradually the Russians took over their own institutions—military academies produced native officers, for example—and by the end of Peter's reign the nobles had no need of foreign experts to help run the government. Within little more than half a century, the Russian Court would become the elegant, French-

---

[2] M. S. Anderson, *Peter the Great* (1969), p. 24.

speaking gathering so penetratingly described in Tolstoy's *War and Peace*. Peter the Great had laid the foundations for the aristocratic society by which his people were to be ruled for two hundred years.

The purpose of these radical internal changes was not only to consolidate the tsar's power at home but to extend it abroad. He established a huge standing army, more than 300,000 strong by the 1720s, and imported the latest military techniques from the West. One of Peter's most cherished projects, the creation of a navy, had limited success, but there could be no doubt that he transformed Russia's capacity for war and her status among European states. He extended the country's frontier to the south and west, beginning the destruction of Sweden's empire at the battle of Poltava in 1709 and following this triumph by more than a decade of advance into Estonia, Lithuania, and Poland. By the time of his death Russia was the dominant power of the Baltic region and a major influence in European affairs.

II. THE ANTI-ABSOLUTISTS

The abolutist regimes provided one model of political and social organization, but an alternative model, in most cases no less committed to uniformity and order, also flourished in the late seventeenth century: governments dominated by aristocrats or merchants. The contrast between the two was perceived by contemporary political theorists, especially opponents of absolutism, who compared France unfavorably with England. And yet the differences were often less sharp than such commentators suggested, primarily because the position of the aristocracy was similar throughout Europe. The same elite dominated both politics and society, whether in England or in France. That there were genuine differences

in social structure cannot be denied, but they were subtle and often below the surface.

THE TRIUMPH OF THE GENTRY IN ENGLAND

To outward appearances Charles II (1660–1685) was restored to a throne not radically changed from the one on which his father had sat before the interregnum. He still summoned and dissolved Parliament, he made all appointments in the bureaucracy, and he signed every law. But the crown's effective power had changed drastically. The royal courts (such as Star Chamber) had been abolished, thus lessening the king's control over judicial matters. He also could not interfere in parliamentary affairs: he could no longer arrest a member of Parliament and he could not create a new seat in the Commons. Even two ancient prerogatives, the king's right to dispense with an act of Parliament (give an exemption to a specific individual or group) and to suspend an act completely, crumbled when Charles tried to exercise them. And he could no longer raise money without parliamentary assent—instead, he was given a fixed annual income, financed by a tax on Englishmen's favorite beverage, beer.

The real control of the country's affairs had by this time passed to that large, somewhat amorphous group known as the gentry. Between 100 and 200 members of this class held hereditary titles, such as duke or earl, that made them members of the peerage who sat in the House of Lords in Parliament. About 700 other men held baronetcies, which were inheritable knighthoods (but not considered peerages); and a few hundred more were knights, which meant that they could call themselves "sir" but could not pass the honor on to their heirs. Beyond these, in a country of some 5 million people, perhaps 15,000 to

Court life under Charles II of England was similar to that of the absolute monarchs in that formal, elegant, aristocratic gatherings dominated the social scene. The occasion shown here is Charles dancing at The Hague. (Photo: The Mansell Collection)

20,000 other families were considered gentry, these being people of importance in the various localities throughout England.[3] This

proportion, approximately 2 percent, was probably not significantly different from the percentage of the population that belonged to the nobility in most Continental states.

What set the gentry apart from the nobles of other countries was their ability to determine national policy. Whereas in France, Austria, Brandenburg-Prussia, and Russia aristocrats depended on the monarch for their power and were subservient to him, the English gentry regarded themselves as an independent force. Their status was hallowed by custom, upheld by law, and maintained by their representative assembly, the House of Commons, which was both the supreme legis-

---

[3] These totals are based on the estimates made by an early statistician, Gregory King, in 1696. His calculations were performed with remarkable accuracy, and they produced the oldest figures that historians still accept today.

lative body in the land and the institution to which the executive government was ultimately responsible.

Not all the gentry took a continuing, active interest in affairs of state, and no more than a few of their number sat in the roughly 500-member House of Commons. Even the Commons did not always exercise a constant influence over the government. All that was necessary was for the ministers of the king to be prominent representatives of the gentry, whether lords or commoners, and that they be able to win the support of a majority of the members of the Commons. Policy was still set by the king and his ministers. But the Commons had to be persuaded that the policies were correct, for without parliamentary approval a minister could not long survive.

Despite occasional conflicts this structure worked relatively smoothly throughout Charles II's reign. The gentry's main fear was that his brother, James, next in line for the succession and an open Catholic, might try to restore Catholicism in England. To prevent this they even managed to force Charles to exclude James from the throne for a few years, during a confrontation known as the Exclusion Crisis. But in the end the instinctive respect for legitimacy that was characteristic of the age, combined with some shrewd maneuvering by Charles, ensured that there would be no tampering with the succession.

THE ENGLISH SUCCESSION FROM THE STUARTS TO THE HANOVERIANS

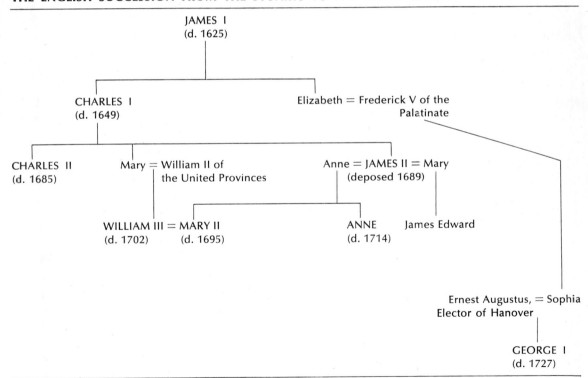

NAMES IN CAPITALS = Monarchs of England

Very quickly, however, the reign of James II turned into a disaster. Elated by his acceptance as king, James rashly attempted the very encouragement of Catholicism that Englishmen had feared. This was a direct challenge to the gentry's newly won power, and in the fall of 1688, seven of their leaders—including members of some of the oldest families in the realm—invited the Protestant ruler of the United Provinces, William III, to invade the country and take over the throne. Although William landed with an army half the size of the king's, James, uncertain of his support, decided not to risk battle and fled to exile in France.

The new king gained what little title he had to the crown through his wife, Mary (see the table on page 567), and the couple were therefore proclaimed joint monarchs by Parliament early in 1689. The Dutch ruler had taken the throne primarily to bring England into his relentless struggles against Louis XIV, and he willingly accepted a settlement that outlined the essential position of Parliament in the government of the country. The Bill of Rights was passed, settling the future succession to the throne, defining Parliament's powers, and establishing the basic civil rights of individuals; the Act of Toleration put an end to all religious persecution, though members of the official Church of England were still the only people allowed to vote, sit in Parliament, hold a government office, or attend a university; and in 1694 a statute laid down that Parliament had to meet and new elections had to be held at least once every three years.

Despite the restrictions on his authority, William exercised strong command. He guided England into a new, aggressive foreign policy, picked the ministers favorable to his aims, and never let Parliament sit when he was out of the country to pursue the war or to attend to Dutch affairs. But unlike James, William recognized his limits. He tried to have the Bill of Rights reversed and a standing army established, but he gave up these attempts when they provoked major opposition. By and large, therefore, the gentry were content to let the king rule as he saw fit. For they had shown by their intervention in 1688 that ultimately they controlled the country.

Politics and Prosperity

The political system in England now reflected the social system: a small elite controlled both the country's policy and its institutions. This group was not monolithically united, however, as was apparent when a party system began to appear in Parliament during Charles II's reign. Its most concrete early manifestation was during the Exclusion Crisis, from 1678 to 1680, when the Whig party emerged in opposition to royal prerogatives and Catholicism. The Whigs were largely responsible for the passage of the exclusion legislation. Their rivals, the Tories, stood for the independence and authority of the crown and favored a ceremonial and traditional Anglicanism.

Because the Whigs were the prime force behind the removal of James II, they controlled the government for most of William III's reign. They naturally supported him in his vendetta against Louis XIV, since France harbored both James and his followers, the romantic but ill-fated Jacobites, who tried for decades to restore James' line to the throne. The Whigs were only too happy to give England what seemed her proper place in the restraining of France's ambitions. But on the whole this was a nonpartisan issue.

Where the sustained rivalry between the Tories and the Whigs was most evident was in their competition for voters. Because the qualification for voting—owning freehold land worth 40 shillings a year in rent—had become less restrictive as a result of inflation and was not to be increased until the late 1700s, this period witnessed the largest electorate in English history before the mid-nineteenth century. It has been estimated that almost 5 percent of the population, or more than 15 percent of the adult males, could vote.[4] Although results were usually determined by the influence of powerful local magnates, as they had been for centuries, fierce politicking took place in many constituencies. And in one election— that of 1700—it brought about a notable reversal: the Tories won by opposing further war, because for the previous three years France seemed to have been contained.

Within two years, however, and despite William's death, England was again at war with Louis XIV, and soon the Whigs were back in power. Not until 1710 did a resurgence of war weariness work in the Tories' favor. Queen Anne made peace with France at Utrecht in 1713, and it was only because the Tories made the mistake of negotiating with the Jacobites after Anne died the next year without heir that the Whigs regained power when the first Hanoverian, George I, came to the throne. They then entrenched themselves, and under the leadership of Robert Walpole, they began almost a century of political control.

The system within which these maneuverings took place remained essentially unchanged until the nineteenth century, though it allowed considerable flexibility. The crown was still the dominant partner: the monarch could dismiss ministers and could influence votes in the House of Commons through the patronage at the throne's disposal. But there were strict limits to royal power. Despite party struggles the gentry as a whole retained

the upper hand. They were quiescent most of the time, but on major issues, such as war or peace, no government could survive without their support.

In this same period England was winning for herself unprecedented prosperity, and the foundations of her world power were being laid. During the reigns of the later Stuarts, the navy was built up and reorganized—largely under the direction of Samuel Pepys, the famous diarist—into the premier force on the sea, the decisive victor over France during the world-wide struggle of the early eighteenth century. In Charles II's time important new colonies were established, particularly along the North American seaboard, where the aristocracy provided the main impetus for the settlement of New Jersey and the Carolinas. The empire expanded rapidly, so that when England and Scotland joined into one kingdom in 1707, the union created a Great Britain ready for its role as a world leader.

This growth was accompanied by a rapid economic advance both at home and in world trade. A notable achievement was the establishment of the Bank of England in 1694. The bank was given permission to raise money from the public and then lend it to the government at 8 percent interest. Within twelve days its founders raised more than a million pounds, demonstrating not only the financial security and stability of England's government but also the commitment of the elite to the country's political structure.

The success of the Bank of England, the rise of the navy, and the overseas expansion were not the only symptoms of England's mounting prosperity. London was becoming the financial capital of the world, and British merchants were gaining control over maritime trade from East Asia to North America. And perhaps most significantly, the benefits of this boom helped the lower levels of society.

[4] J. H. Plumb, "The Growth of the Electorate in England from 1600 to 1715," *Past and Present*, November 1969, pp. 90–116.

There can be little doubt that with the possible exception of the Dutch, the ordinary Englishman was better off than any of his equivalents in Europe. Poverty was admittedly widespread, and London, rapidly approaching half a million in population, contained frightful slums and miserable, crime-ridden sections. Even the terrible fire of London in 1666 did little to wipe out the appalling living conditions because the city was rebuilt much as before, the only notable additions being a series of magnificent churches, including St. Paul's, designed by Christopher Wren. But the grim picture should not be overdrawn.

Compared to the sixteenth century, these years saw little starvation. The system of poor relief may have often been inhumane in forcing the unfortunate to work in horrifying workhouses, but it did provide them with the shelter and food that they had long lacked. After more than a century of crippling inflation the laborer could once again make a decent living, and the craftsman was meeting a growing demand for his work. Higher up in the social scale, more men had a say in the political process than ever before, and more could find opportunities for advancement in the rising economy of the period—in trade overseas, in the bureaucracy, or in the growing market for luxury goods. England had better roads than any other European country, lower taxes, a more impartial judicial system, and a freedom from government interference—especially since there was no standing army—that was unique for the times.

One thing is clear, however: these gains could not compare with those that the gentry had made. In fact many of the improvements, such as fairly administered justice and low taxes, were indirect results of what the upper classes had won for themselves. There is no question that the fruits of the seventeenth century's progress belonged in the first place to the aristocracy, now more surely than in previous centuries the dominant element in society.

ARISTOCRACY IN THE UNITED PROVINCES, SWEDEN, AND POLAND

In the Dutch republic the fall of Jan De Witt seemed to signal a move in the direction of absolutism rather than aristocratic control. William III, who took over the government in 1672 and led the successful resistance to Louis XIV in a six-year war, was able to concentrate government in his own hands. Soon, however, the power of the merchant oligarchy and the provincial leadership in the Estates General reasserted itself. William did not want to sign a peace treaty with Louis when it became clear that the French invasion had failed. Like his forebears in the House of Orange, he wanted to take the war into the enemy's camp and reinforce his own authority by keeping the position of commander in chief in a time of war. But the Estates General, led by the province of Holland, brought the war to a conclusion.

A decade later it was only with the approval of the Estates General that William was able to seek the English throne and thus bring the two countries into limited union—limited because the representative assemblies, the effective governing powers of the two countries, remained separate. And when William died without an heir, the Dutch provincial executive offices remained unfilled. His policies were continued by Antonius Heinsius, who now held the position of grand pensionary of Holland that Jan De Witt had once occupied. Heinsius had been a close friend of William's, but to all intents and purposes, policy was determined by the Estates General.

The representative assembly now had to

preside over the decline of a great power. In finance and trade the Dutch were gradually overtaken by the English, while in the war against Louis XIV they had to support the crippling burden of maintaining a land force, only to hand command over to England. Within half a century Frederick II of Prussia was to call the republic "a dinghy boat trailing the English man-of-war."

The aristocrats of the United Provinces differed from the usual European pattern. Instead of ancient families and bureaucratic dynasties, they boasted merchants and mayors. The prominent citizens of the leading cities were the backbone of what can be called the Dutch upper classes. Moreover social distinctions were less prominent than in any other country of Europe. The elite was comprised of hard-working financiers and traders, richer and more powerful but not essentially more privileged or leisured than those farther down the social ladder. The situation discussed in much eighteenth-century literature and political writing—the special place given to nobles, which sometimes led even to immunity from the law—was far less noticeable in the United Provinces. There was no glittering court with elegant trappings. Although here, as elsewhere, a small group controlled the country, it did so for largely economic ends and with a totally different style.

In Sweden the conditions of court life and political power more closely resembled those of Louis XIV's France, though the reigns of Charles XI and XII, the last half-century in which Sweden was still an imperial power, were marked by a continuing struggle between king and nobility. The nobles eventually established themselves as the dominant force, but not until they had gone through a long and sometimes bitter struggle with the monarch.

The chief issue was the policy of rever-

sions, whereby Charles XI forced great lords to return huge tracts of land they had received as rewards for loyalty during the precarious years of Gustavus Adolphus and Christina. The aristocrats strongly opposed the policy, but the king had the bulk of the population on his side because the crown was always a more lenient landlord for peasant tenants. By clever maneuvering Charles not only had the reversion legislation passed by the Riksdag but also had himself proclaimed virtually an absolute monarch in 1682.

The remainder of his reign was spent consolidating the power of his government at home. He stayed out of war and strengthened both his administration and his finances. The great copper mines of Sweden gave out in the 1680s, and alternatives to this lucrative source of revenue had to be built up—primarily iron and timber products, such as cannon and tar. Tolls and taxes from captured territories helped sustain the empire, but it was clear that Charles' strength depended on his avoiding the strains of war.

His successor, Charles XII, had a different set of priorities. Harking back to the glorious days of Gustavus Adolphus, he wanted to cover Sweden in military glory. His ambitions and those of Peter I of Russia embroiled the Baltic in what came to be known as the Great Northern War. At first the fighting went Sweden's way, mainly because of a brilliant victory over the Russians at Narva in 1700, which immediately established Charles as one of the ablest commanders of his day. But he then decided—the first of a series of generals to do so—that he was capable of conquering Russia. His communications and logistics broke down, and at Poltava in 1709 his invading army was shattered. The dismemberment of the Swedish Empire now began: by the time Charles was killed in battle nine years later, the Danes, Prussians, and

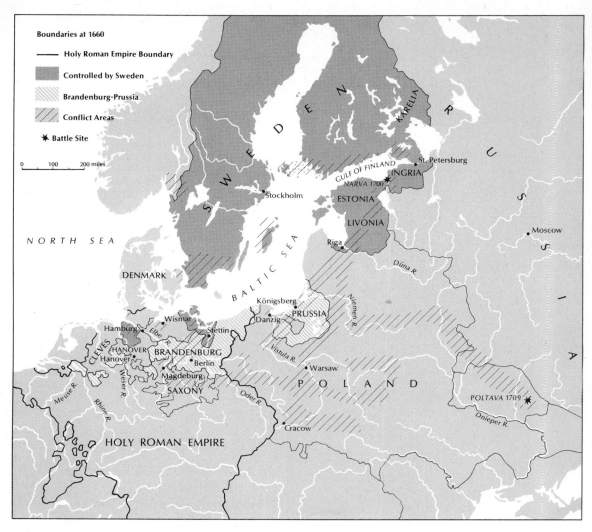

MAP 17.3: CONFLICT IN THE BALTIC AREA 1660–1721

Russians had begun to overrun Swedish possessions in Germany, Poland, and around the Gulf of Finland. (See Map 17.3.) At a series of treaties signed from 1719 to 1721, the empire was parceled out, and Sweden reverted to roughly the territory she had a century before.

Naturally the nobles took advantage of Charles XII's frequent absences to reassert their power. They ran Sweden while he was campaigning and forced his successor to accept a constitution that gave the Riksdag effective control over the country. The new structure was consciously modeled on England's political system, and the nobility came to occupy a position analogous to that of the English gentry—as the leaders of society and the controllers of politics. A splendid court arose, and Stockholm became one of the more elegant and cultured aristocratic centers in Europe.

Warsaw fared less well. In fact the strongest contrast to the French political and social model in the late seventeenth century was provided by Poland. No better object lesson can be found to demonstrate what Louis XIV was preventing in France. The sheer chaos and disunity that plagued Poland until she ceased to exist as a state in the late eighteenth century were the direct result of continued dominance by the old landed aristocracy, which blocked all attempts to centralize the government.

There were highly capable kings of Poland in this period—notably John III, who achieved Europe-wide fame by relieving Vienna from the Turkish siege in 1683. These monarchs could quite easily gather an enthusiastic army to fight (and fight well) against Poland's many foes: Germans, Swedes, Russians, and Turks. But once a battle was over, the ruler was rarely in a position to exercise anything more than nominal leadership. Each king was elected by the assembly of nobles and had to agree not to interfere with the independence of the great lords, who were growing rich from serf labor on fertile lands. The crown had neither revenue nor bureaucracy to speak of, and so the country continued to resemble nothing so much as a feudal kingdom, where power remained in the localities.

If Poland seemed a nobleman's paradise, she nonetheless produced no important cultural center like Berlin or Vienna. For that to happen some degree of central authority was necessary, a hub around which national life could revolve. Two cities in particular—London and Paris—occupied such a position, and therefore at the very beginning of the eighteenth century, they became the heart of Europe's intellectual and artistic activity.

III. THE CULTURE OF THE AGE

The quest for regularity, order, and decorum which was the most notable feature of late seventeenth-century culture contrasted strongly with the grandiose and dramatic strivings of the preceding age. The change in aesthetics offers striking evidence of the growing sense of settlement and calm in Europe after the crises of midcentury. And it was paralleled by the emergence of new kinds of cultural institutions—formal, regulated, and controlled from above unlike any that Europe had ever seen before. Not only the standards of taste but the success of individual writers, artists, and scientists reflected the preferences of a society dominated by its aristocracy.

THE ACADEMY AND THE SALON

A clear indication that the cultural atmosphere was becoming more ordered and restrained was the rise of academies and salons as mechanisms which organized intellectual life. The most carefully institutionalized setting was the official academy established under royal patronage to supervise cultural affairs. Such bodies were not entirely new—their pedigree went back to the Platonic academy, and there had been more immediate predecessors in sixteenth-century Italy—but their purpose, to set standards for artistic creations, was a departure from tradition.

France led the way in this development. The French Academy, founded by Richelieu in 1635, became the leading upholder of classical drama, while the Royal Academy of Painting and Sculpture, the Royal Academy of Architecture, and the Academy of Inscriptions and Literature, established over the next thirty-five years, performed equivalent functions in other fields. These bodies marked the beginning of a system that in France did not crumble until attacked by such nineteenth-century rebels as the Impressionists.

The cultural institutions that were founded in other countries (mostly in Italy) during this period were less prestigious but no less reflective of cultural trends. The academies were intended to preserve and promote the standards that were considered essential to good art. Just as the Royal Society was regarded as an arbiter of scientific truth, a promoter of proper method, so too in art and literature academies would set the style.

The origins of the salon were diverse and its predecessors many. Artists have frequently united in coteries when they have shared a common outlook, and rich and noble patrons have often given them encouragement. The particular form that developed in seventeenth-century France was a small, intimate gathering that usually met in the drawing room, or salon, of an aristocrat's wife.

These ambitious and often intelligent women tried to attract the most brilliant literary lights of the day. The artists for their part came in search of patronage and reputation, taking advantage of various social forces: the emergence of Paris as the cultural center of France, the clustering of the nobility in the capital as the court grew in size and importance, and the pressures of a fiercely competitive society of women with money to spare. The would-be salon entrant had to make his mark rapidly, and wit, grace, and quick repartee were essential.

The salons stimulated the intimacy and elegance that were now preferred to the heroic ideals of the midcentury. They thus became the natural center and the perfect symbol of contemporary creative expression. An atmosphere of studied gentility was strongly apparent, even to outsiders, and it was well for a writer or painter not to offend the sensibilities of those who were the chief makers and break-ers of reputations in the highly competitive world of letters and art.

The intellectual activities of most aristocrats revolved around both cultural centers, the court and the salon. At court they gathered in large, formal affairs to watch a play, a ballet, or an opera; in the salons they gathered in smaller, less formal groups, often including talented nonaristocrats, to discuss the latest gossip or cultural event. Even the enormous halls of a palace, hung with large canvases inherited from the past, contrasted with the frilly drawing rooms that served as salons, adorned with the small paintings that were the new fashion. In some ways the two were rival centers of activity, and a few prominent patronesses consciously sought to outdo a nearby prince.

Yet the contrasts should not be overdrawn. Most leading writers, musicians, and painters were equally at home in the two settings, for they needed the patronage of both; no artist could survive without nobles to commission works or pay salaries, and almost none were fortunate enough to have all their needs met by a single generous prince. Thus they turned to the multiple sources of support that the aristocracy, better educated than ever before and eager to outdo one another in patronage, were anxious to provide.

There was also a wider audience of course, because salons were urban institutions, and the city offered theaters, opera houses, and publishers. Thus it was occasionally possible for an artist to achieve popular success without gaining aristocratic approval. But this was a hazardous way of making a living, and for this reason the salon, despite its regulation of taste and expression, was a vastly preferable target for most artists. As a result the qualities of harmony and order that were so appealing to the aristocracy came to dominate the aesthetics of the age.

STYLE AND TASTE

Discussions of literature and art developed a new emphasis on lightness and grace during the late seventeenth century. The most influential literary critic of the period, Nicolas Boileau, wrote a manual of style, *Poetic Art* (1674), that exalted craftsmanship over feeling. He insisted that the perfectly shaped poem was the ultimate ideal, and he valued obedience to rule as opposed to emotion or an exuberant, disordered vision. Not surprisingly his own literary output consisted of light satires, flawlessly executed but ephemeral.

Boileau's prescriptions gained a large following in France and in other countries as well. The leading English poet of the era, for example, John Dryden, gave his energies to writing hundreds of lines of graceful verse that were often scathing but almost never profound. The sharp end of his wit could sting, as can be seen in the following lines about the duke of Buckingham, a prominent politician known for his inconsistencies and dilettantism:

A man so various, that he seem'd to be
Not one, but all mankind's epitome.
Stiff in opinions, always in the wrong;
Was everything by starts, and nothing long;
But, in the course of one revolving moon,
Was chemist, fiddler, statesman, and buffoon.
Absalom and Achitophel, ll. 545–550

Dryden was greatly admired for writing in this vein because it was a time when the elite prized sardonic aloofness.

Painters reflected these qualities only indirectly, but the change in their concerns was striking nonetheless. Gone were the vast canvases and towering themes of Rubens or Rembrandt. Instead, the leading figures of the decades around 1700 were flattering portraitists, like the Englishman Sir Peter Lely, or delicate genre painters, like the Frenchman Antoine Watteau. Their canvases were small, and their subject matter rarely departed from placid landscapes or melancholic and idealized aristocratic scenes. The art of these exquisite painters epitomizes the new interest in grace, elegance, and repose.

That is not to say that emotion was totally absent from the creative work of the age. Stark passions were expressed in the operas of Henry Purcell and the prose of John Bunyan, both writing in this period. But the characteristic of their work that distinguishes them from the previous generation of artists is precisely their discipline—their anguish pours out of a framework of monumental self-restraint. And thus we are brought back to the theme that runs through the life of the time: the emphasis on order and regularity. It is particularly apparent in the work of the greatest court writer of the epoch, the French playwright Jean Racine.

By its nature Racine's art was not for the multitude. His concern was with tragedy, and he used the Classical drama to create an intensity of emotion that had not been achieved since the days of its ancient practitioners, Euripides and Sophocles. Severely disciplined and yet overwhelming passion dominates his plays, which move to agonizing climaxes in superb, controlled language. Racine does not offer the appeal of recognizable human types; his characters are suffering men and women of unattainable nobility racked by impossible dilemmas that revolve around such perennial aristocratic preoccupations as honor and public duty. The heroine of *Phèdre* (1677) for example falls in love with her stepson and destroys him and herself as she wavers between love and honor. She wrestles with her dilemma in a series of solemn and carefully wrought but tormented speeches that give the play an almost unbearable emotional impact.

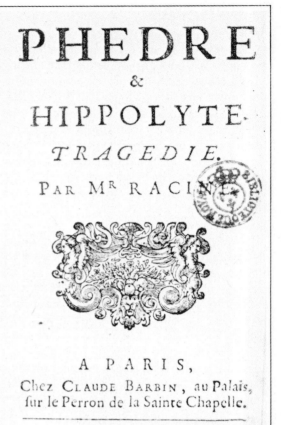

PHEDRE

&

HIPPOLYTE

TRAGEDIE.

PAR Mr RACINE.

A PARIS,

Chez CLAUDE BARBIN, au Palais,
fur le Perron de la Sainte Chapelle.

M. DC. LXXVII.

AVEC PRIVILEGE DV ROY.

Jean Racine's plays appealed strongly to the aristocratic sensibilities of his age. He was regarded as the standard by which official taste could be measured and for many years was a major figure at the court of Louis XIV. The title page of Phèdre, *one of his most enduring contributions to the French theater, is taken from the original 1677 edition. (Photo: French Cultural Services)*

There is none of the dramatic excitement—the rapid action, changes of pace, and flexible verse forms—of a Shakespearean play; it is thus all the more remarkable that *Phèdre* conveys such gripping human feelings so powerfully.

Racine's appeal to the courtiers at Versailles was enormous. He explored the discipline and aristocratic bearing that, theoretically at least, the more thoughtful among them had adopted. They saw themselves on his stage, high-minded characters determined to act as social and political models. Racine thus portrayed an idealized court setting, guided by propriety and restraint, for all the world to see.

The tastes of the middle and lower strata of

Molière's plays displayed a trenchant wit that was often aimed at the nobility. For this reason his works had a rather uneasy reception at court but were extremely popular with the Parisian middle class. Shown here is the acting company founded by Molière, La Troupe Royale, which was the prototype for the Comedie Française. (Photo: French Cultural Services)

society are much harder to define, but there were a number of distinct ways in which they entertained themselves. Urban mercantile groups usually aped their superiors, though they were clearly more at home with the bawdiness of Restoration comedy or the scintillating wit of Molière than with Racine. They were also inclined to take part in creative activity themselves. Samuel Pepys for example remarked with satisfaction that his wife's painting efforts were coming along very nicely. And music, at least for the more educated urban dweller, was as much to be played

as heard. In this respect the middle classes blended with the lower rather than the upper social levels, for singing was one of the great recreations of the ordinary man. Ballads were a major form of communication, and printers were quick to run off thousands of copies of a new song that was likely to catch on. Churches moreover gave congregations an institutionalized focus both for creating and for listening to music.

Among reading publics the nobility tended to read the classics and philosophy while the middle class read popular literature such as tales of travel, descriptions of rarities and wonders, and religious writings. The few literate members of the lower classes probably read religious works only; the rest had the Bible or a book like John Bunyan's *Pilgrim's Progress* (1667) read to them. Singing and an occasional troupe of traveling players performing the antics of standard characters like Harlequin and Columbine would have been their main recreation apart from the celebrations they themselves put on—feast day processions, "rough music," and the like (see Chapter 16).

In these interests, however, there was little reflection of the underlying concern for order so noticeable in court circles. Most people looked to music or a play for uplift or for a good time. And nowhere did they find these qualities more brilliantly represented than in the plays of the Frenchman Molière.

Molière (born Jean Baptiste Poquelin) learned his art in the same school that had taught Shakespeare half a century before: the travelling theatrical company, in which he was actor, manager, and director. After many years of touring the provinces, he came to Paris a master of his profession and founded a company, known as the Comédie Française, which soon became a national institution.

Molière followed the formal Classical style of his day, modeling his verse on that of the ancients and observing the conventions of time and place laid down so strictly by the French Academy. But his objectives could not have been more different from those of a Racine. For he never lost sight of the old tradition of farce and burlesque, which in his youth had still been the chief attraction wherever plays were performed. He used Classical style to create comedies with a serious undertone, a sustained concern with the follies of mankind. He ridiculed such types as the pretentious ladies of the salons, hypochondriacs, and the ignorant but aspiring *nouveaux riches*—these captured forever in *The Bourgeois Gentleman* (1670), whose hero was delighted to discover that all his life he had been speaking prose.

The wit was unmatched, and soon Molière was winning highly favorable attention from Louis XIV himself. But occasionally the barbs came too close. The courtiers were offended when Molière had the nobles in one of his plays speak like ordinary people. And when in *Tartuffe* he ridiculed the hypocrisy that could lie behind ostentatiously displayed religious devotion, he roused powerful enemies in the Catholic Church. The play was banned, and a number of years passed before the playwright returned to the good graces of the monarch. But when *Tartuffe* reappeared in Paris, it was an instant success.

The contrast is revealing. Molière's sparkling dialogue and superb theatrical sense ensured his acceptance at court, but the welcome had its limits, set by standards of taste that the nobility considered unbreachable. In Paris he was always idolized, and for most Frenchmen he has remained unrivaled to this day. The difference, slight though it was, gave one of the first hints of the estrangement between court and country that was to build toward the explosion of the Revolution over the next century. The aristocrats may have set the style, but they were to become increasingly insulated from the rest of society, which eventually was to find its own cultural models and heroes in the eighteenth century.

SCIENCE AND THOUGHT

The fascination inspired by the scientist and the widespread efforts to imitate scientific method in other fields were closely connected with the interest in order so characteristic of the age. The approach and the findings of science offered perfect models of regularity, harmony, and discipline, and hence they could serve both as guides and as appropriate objects of patronage and interest. The second half of the seventeenth century thus became the great age of the virtuosos, the hundreds of noblemen who dabbled in experiments and sought friendships with scientists. But it was less as participants than as eager admirers that the elite embraced science. In the eighteenth century for the first time statues were erected to honor the great discoverers. They were a new kind of hero, and they became the most widely acclaimed men of their age.

The late seventeenth and early eighteenth centuries witnessed in addition a raging controversy known as the Battle of the Books, a long dispute over the relative merits of the so-called Ancients and Moderns. In the end there could be little doubt that the advocates of the Moderns had won the dispute, largely because of the unprecedented advances in the understanding of nature during the previous century. The achievements in astronomy, physics, mathematics, and anatomy were being seen ever more frequently as a measure of human capabilities. And the qualities that the scientist seemed to represent—order, reason, and logic—corresponded with the aristocrats' aesthetic preferences in this period: balance, uniformity, and decorousness. It was only natural that the supreme scientist of the late seventeenth century, Isaac Newton, should become the idol not only of his own generation but of generations to come.

Isaac Newton

The culmination of the scientific revolution was reached in the work of Isaac Newton, who made decisive contributions in the fields of mathematics, physics, astronomy, and optics and brought to a climax the progress that had been made by Copernicus, Kepler, Galileo, Descartes, and a host of other investigators. He united physics and astronomy in a single system to explain motion throughout the universe; he helped transform mathematics by the development of calculus; and he established some of the basic laws of modern physics.

Part of the explanation of his versatility lies in the workings of the scientific community at the time. Newton was a retiring man who got into fierce arguments with such prominent

This frontispiece from the 1710 edition of Jonathan Swift's long poem, The Battle of the Books, *satirizes the controversy that broke out in the late seventeenth century over the relative superiority of Ancient and Modern writers.*

contemporaries as the English physicist Robert Hooke, who was studying gravity, and the German "universal man," Liebniz, who was working on calculus. Had it not been for his active participation in the Royal Society of London and the effort that was needed to demonstrate his views to the membership, Newton might never have pursued his researches to their conclusion. He disliked the give-and-take but felt forced in self-justification to prepare some of his most important papers for meetings of the society. There could be no better indication of how important it was that science had created its own institutions and competitiveness.

It was to refute another rival, the Cartesian approach to science, which was then much admired, that Newton wrote his masterpiece, *The Mathematical Principles of Natural Philosophy* (1687), usually referred to by the first word of its Latin title, the *Principia*. This was the last widely influential book in European history to be written in Latin, still the international language of scholarship, and useful to Newton because he was determined to have as many experts as possible see his refutation of Descartes' methods. In contrast to the Frenchman, who had placed such emphasis on the powers of the mind, on pure reason, he felt that mere hypotheses, constructions of logic and words, were not the tools of a true scientist. As he put it in a celebrated phrase, *"Hypotheses non fingo"* ("I do not posit hypotheses"), because everything he said was proved by experiment or by mathematics.

The most dramatic of his findings was the solution to the ancient problem of motion. He stated his system in three laws: first, in the absence of force, motion continues in a straight line; second, the rate of change of the motion is determined by the forces acting on it (for example friction); and third, action and reaction between two bodies are equal and opposite. To arrive at these laws, he defined the concepts of mass, inertia, and force in relation to velocity and acceleration as we know them today.

Newton extended these principles to the entire universe by demonstrating that his laws govern the motions of the moon and planets too. Using the concept of gravity, he provided the explanation of the movement of objects in space that is the foundation for current space travel. There is a balance, he said, between the earth's pull on the moon and the forward motion of the satellite, which would continue in a straight line were it not for the earth's gravity. Consequently the moon moves in an elliptical orbit in which neither gravity nor inertia gains control. The same pattern is followed by the planets around the sun. In one of his most elegant insights, Newton described the attraction mathematically in what is known as the inverse square law: gravitational force varies inversely as the square of the distance between the two bodies.[5] The result has to be an ellipse, as Kepler had already discovered.

It was largely on the basis of the uniformity and the systematic impersonal forces Newton described that the view of the universe as a vast machine gained ground. According to this theory, all motion is a result of precise, unvarying, and demonstrable forces. There is a celestial mechanics just like the mechanics that operates on earth. It was not far from this view to the belief that God is a great watchmaker who started the marvelous mechanism going but intervenes only when something goes wrong and needs repair. Newton himself for example considered the creation of the force of gravity, which is not a *necessary* property of a body, as an indication of God's intervention in the assembling of the physical universe.

These general philosophical implications were as important as the specific discoveries in making Newton one of the idols of his own and the next centuries. Aristocrats, concerned with discipline and stability, could easily in-

---

[5] In other words, the attraction increases much more rapidly than the distance closes. Stated as an equation, where G is the gravitational pull and D the distance between the two bodies, the law is $G \propto 1/D^2$.

terpret the idea that a simple structure under-lies all of nature as justification for the hierar-chical patterns of government and society that were emerging. The educated applauded Newton's achievements, and the gentry made him one of their own—he was the first scientist to receive a knighthood in England. And only a few decades after the appearance of the *Principia*, Alexander Pope summed up the public feeling in a famous couplet:

> Nature and nature's laws lay hid in night;
> God said, "Let Newton be!" and all was light.

Although he also devoted a great deal of energy to mystical and numerological investi-gations (which he kept strictly separate from his science), Newton still managed to find the time to accomplish much else of immense sci-entific value. He was the main figure in late-seventeenth-century mathematics, particularly in the study of calculus, and his work on dy-namics was a milestone in the subject. Another striking achievement, the lunar explanation of tidal action, was almost an aside in his master-piece. The differences among various tides allowed him to calculate the mass of the moon —again almost in passing. Finally, his second major work, the *Opticks* (1704), presented an analysis that influenced the study of light for more than a century.

But it was the work on motion and the heavens that won Newton his reputation. So overpowering was his stature that in these fields the steady progress of 150 years came to a halt for more than half a century after the publication of the *Principia*. There was a gen-eral impression that somehow Newton had done it all, that no important problems re-mained. In large areas of physics and astron-omy, no significant advances were made again until the late eighteenth century. There were other reasons for the slowdown—changing patterns in education, the influence of frivo-lous virtuosos, an inevitable lessening of mo-mentum—but none was so powerful as the reverence for Newton. The professional was as overawed as the aristocrat in the presence of a man who became the intellectual symbol of his own and succeeding ages.

John Locke

The second idol of the late seventeenth and eighteenth centuries, John Locke, was not himself a scientist, but a major reason for his fame was the belief that he had applied a sci-entific approach to all of knowledge.

Locke also wrote to refute Descartes, whose dualism he rejected in favor of his own theory of knowledge. He believed that at birth man's mind is a *tabula rasa*, a clean slate; contrary to Descartes, he asserted that nothing is inborn or preordained. As a human being grows, he observes and experiences the world. Once he has gathered enough data through his senses, his mind begins to work on them. Then, with the help of his reason, he perceives patterns, discovering the order and harmony that per-meate the universe. Locke was convinced that this underlying order exists and that every per-son, regardless of his individual experiences, must reach the same conclusions about its nature and structure.

This epistemology, elaborated in his *Essay Concerning Human Understanding*, published in 1690, was modeled directly on the example of the scientists. The *tabula rasa* is the coun-terpart of the principle of doubt, experience corresponds with experimentation, and reason plays the role of the process of generalization. Just as in science a single law appears again and again whatever experiments are per-formed, so in all knowledge any true principle is universal and will become apparent to every person even though individual lives are differ-ent.

Locke's thinking thus included a reverence for scientific method, a reliance on material phenomena and empiricism, and a belief in order. In all these respects, his outlook captured the interest of cultivated readers in the late seventeenth and eighteenth centuries, for he provided them with a theoretical model, built on a rejection of emotion and an elevation of reason, that allowed them to regard their mental equipment and functioning as scientific.

When Locke turned his attention to political thought, he caught the feeling of the times even more directly, because he put into systematic form the views of the English gentry and of many aristocrats throughout Europe. The *Second Treatise of Civil Government*, also published in 1690, was deeply influenced by Hobbes. From his great predecessor Locke took the notion of the state of nature as a state of war and the need for a contract among men to end the anarchy that precedes the establishment of human society. But his conclusions were decidedly different.

Employing the principles of the *Essay Concerning Human Understanding*, Locke asserted that the application of reason to the evidence of politics demonstrates the inalienability of the three rights of an individual: life, liberty, and property. Like Hobbes, he believed that there must be a sovereign power, but he argued that it has no power over these three natural rights of its subjects without their consent. Moreover this consent—for levying taxes for example—must come from a representative assembly of men of property, such as the English Parliament.

The affirmation of property as one of the three natural rights (it was changed to "the pursuit of happiness" in the more egalitarian American Declaration of Independence) is significant. Here Locke revealed himself as the spokesman of the gentry. Only people with a tangible stake in their country have any right to control its destiny, and that stake must be protected as surely as their life and liberty. The concept of liberty remained vague, but it was taken to imply the sorts of freedom, such as freedom from arbitrary arrest, that were outlined in the English Bill of Rights. All Hobbes allowed a man to do was protect his life. Locke permitted the overthrow of the sovereign power if it infringed on the subjects' rights—a course the English followed with James II and the Americans with George III.

Locke's intentions were admirable—he had a higher opinion of human nature than Hobbes, he admitted that truth was hard to find, and he tried, as Hobbes had not, to curb the potential for tyranny in sovereign power. His prime concern was to defend the individual against the state, a concern that has remained essential to liberal thought ever since. But it is important to realize that Locke's views served the elite better than the mass of society because of his emphasis on property. With Locke to reassure them, the upper classes imposed their preferences and control on eighteenth-century European civilization.

The situation of Europe's aristocracy in 1715 was a far cry from its position in 1660. Then, in the wake of a series of grave political and intellectual crises, the ancient power of the nobles, based on their local independence, had seemed radically weakened in the face of the bureaucratic state. But as the political structures of the various European countries settled into new and stable forms, it became clear that their cooperation was essential for the running of a state, and they adapted to this new role with remarkable skill. Under the absolute monarchs they became the allies and indispensable agents of government; in other countries they dominated events. In either case they came out of the transition with their power intact and even enhanced.

Thus regardless of the relative levels of order and uniformity the various regimes achieved and regardless of their degrees of absolutism, they were alike in their reliance on aristocrats. No government, however centralized, could function without the participation of the upper classes, and in most states—Peter I's Russia excepted—they took up their transformed role willingly. And the new security of aristocratic power, both political and social, showed that the age-old conflict between princes and nobles had been resolved.

Moreover the qualities of order, discipline, and stability that the elite represented and that rulers sought were making themselves felt in culture as well as in society and politics. Changes in taste and even developments in science and philosophy were seen as reinforcing the aristocratic world view. The elaborately mannered life led by this newly invigorated ruling class reflected its confidence. And its remarkable society was to last for a glittering century until its frivolities and arrogance fell before a movement that demanded a better life not merely for the few but for all.

RECOMMENDED READING

Sources

* Locke, John. *An Essay Concerning Human Understanding.* A. D. Woozley (ed.). 1964. This study of the nature of the mind appeared at the same time as Locke's *Two Treatises of Government* and presents the philosophical basis of his political ideas.

Saint-Simon, Louis. *Historical Memoirs.* Lucy Norton (ed. and tr.). 2 vols. 1967 and 1968. Lively memoirs of the court at Versailles.

Studies

Adams, Antoine. *Grandeur and Illusion: French Literature and Society 1600–1715.* Herbert Tint (tr.). 1972. A clear and comprehensive survey of French literature and its social setting during the seventeenth century, with special attention to Classicism.

Baxter, S. B. *William III and the Defense of European Liberty, 1650–1702.* 1966. A solid and straightforward account of the career of the ruler of both England and the Netherlands.

* Carsten, F. L. *The Origins of Prussia*. 1954. The standard account of the background to the reign of the great elector, Frederick William, and the best short history of his accomplishments and the rise of the Junkers.

Chandler, David. *Marlborough as Military Commander*. 1973. A fluent and energetic narrative of military affairs, centered around the colorful career of a highly intelligent general.

Cranston, Maurice. *John Locke*. 1957. The best basic introduction to the man and his ideas. (See also Dunn and MacPherson.)

Dunn, John. *The Political Thought of John Locke: An Historical Account of the Argument of the Two Treatises of Government*. 1969. An interesting interpretation, taking a very different view from MacPherson (see below).

* Goubert, Pierre. *Louis XIV and Twenty Million Frenchmen*. Anne Carter (tr.). 1970. This is not so much a history of the king's reign as a study of the nature of French society and politics during Louis' rule.

Hatton, R. N. *Charles XII of Sweden*. 1698. A thorough and well-written biography that does justice to a dramatic life.

* ———. *Europe in the Age of Louis XIV*. 1969. A beautifully illustrated and vividly interpretive history of the period that Louis dominated.

* Hazard, Paul. *The European Mind, 1680–1715*. J. L. May (tr.). 1963. This stimulating interpretation of the intellectual change that took place around 1700 has become a classic work in the history of thought.

* Koyre, Alexandre. *Newtonian Studies*. 1965. These essays have come to be accepted as the basic introduction to Newton's ideas.

Lougee, Carolyn C. *Le Paradis des Femmes: Women, Salons, and Social Stratification in Seventeenth-Century France*. 1976. An interesting study of the place of women and the importance of salons in French high society.

* MacPherson, C. B. *The Political Theory of Possessive Individualism: Hobbes to Locke*. 1962. This provocative, Marxist-inspired study of the importance of property in English political thought views Locke's ideas in largely economic terms.

Manuel, Frank. *A Portrait of Isaac Newton*. 1968. Using psychoanalytic methods, this book shows Newton and the pressures he felt in a very different light from the usual analyses that pay tribute to genius.

* Plumb, J. H. *The Growth of Political Stability in England, 1675–1725*. 1969. A brief, lucid survey of the developments in English politics that helped create Britain's modern parliamentary democracy.

Stoye, John. *The Siege of Vienna*. 1964. An exciting account of the last great threat to Christian Europe from the Turkish empire.

* Sumner, B. H. *Peter the Great and the Emergence of Russia*. 1950. This short but comprehensive book is the best introduction to Russian history in this period.

* Wolf, J. B. *Louis XIV*. 1968. The standard biography, with particularly full discussions of political affairs.

---

* Available in paperback.

EIGHTEEN

ABSOLUTISM AND EMPIRE

The Eighteenth Century—generally understood as the period between the Peace of Utrecht in 1714 and the beginning of the French Revolution in 1789—is easier to visualize as a whole than the century of extraordinary turmoil that preceded it. It was a century of consolidation and maturation: of absolutism and empire; of demographic growth; of economic prosperity based on agriculture, trade, and traditional industries; of enlightenment and cultural brilliance. These various strands were of course interwoven, but any account must take them in some sequence. The growth of Europe's population—attributable in part to good harvests and the absence of famines—is a subject that historians have recently begun to explore, and it may one day be regarded as the logical starting point of discussion. In the meantime, it is the development of the state, long the focus of historical research, that is at present best understood.

Austria, Britain, France, Prussia, and Russia, the states that would dominate Europe and most of the world until World War I, can trace their emergence to great-power status, as well as their intense rivalry with each other, back to the eighteenth century. Russia and Britain now wielded enough power to play major roles in European affairs, while Prussia's rise to great-power status offers the most spectacular example of successful state building and territorial expansion. On the Atlantic seaboard, the maritime states of France and Britain dueled for trade and colonies in a rivalry that reflected the impact of middle-class commercial interests.

It sometimes seems as if international competition was the foremost preoccupation of eighteenth-century rulers. But in fact competition among states went hand in hand with internal state building—in most cases with efforts to consolidate royal absolutism. Conflict with rival powers compelled rulers to assert their sovereignty as forcefully as possible within their own borders in order to tap the revenues and manpower they required. The issue was power, and the model of absolutism created in Louis XIV's France showed them ways to that power.

With the exception of Britain, countries in which absolutism failed to develop—such as Sweden and the Netherlands—lost influence. Poland, once Russia's mighty rival, could not raise a large standing army or overcome the self-interest of its powerful aristocracy. By the end of the century it stood helpless before the onslaught of Russia, Austria, and Prussia. Three times Poland was partitioned among them, with the final partition in 1794 ending its existence as a sovereign state altogether.

In sum, the eighteenth century saw the maturation and consolidation of the modern state internally, and the testing of each state within the state system. In this process the basic map of modern Europe emerged and the centralized character of the major European states was confirmed.

I. THE STATE SYSTEM

The international rivalry embedded in the eighteenth-century state system was not as chaotic as it sometimes appears to have been. In practice there were limitations on the aggressiveness of states, and a phenomenon that can be called balance of power did exist. It is possible to indicate the sources of the conflicts that erupted and the kinds of appetites that sought satisfaction. Diplomacy and warfare had few ironclad rules, but they did have typical procedures and bounds. In combination these helped provide a context for the development of the European states.

PATTERNS OF INTERNATIONAL RIVALRY

Two terms may be used to describe the broad sweep of international relations, provided their meaning is not exaggerated. On the one hand were the periods of hegemony, or domination by one state; on the other were periods of equilibrium, or balance of power. For reasons that probably derive from Western ethnocentrism, we tend to assume that equilibrium among the several states is natural and that disturbances by overambitious powers are unnatural.[1] Be that as it may, it is true that the great aggressors of modern times, such as Louis XIV, Napoleon, and Hitler, have been resisted and ultimately defeated after stupendous struggles. Their designs on Europe varied considerably, but to their contemporaries they seem to have appeared equally dangerous.

In fact the essential meaning of "balance of power" is this limited or negative one: the situation after a bid for hegemony had been resisted and defeated. It was a genuine goal for Europeans only in the face of some inordinate threat to their accustomed pattern of rivalry. The state system did not have a built-in equilibrium. Apart from the way states concerted to resist the few rulers who sought to dominate the entire Continent, there was little agreement about what would be tolerated. Rarely did Europe's rulers cooperate simply to maintain peace or the status quo. On the contrary they acted in their own interests against the status quo with as much force as they could.

The Peace of Utrecht restored an enormous range of options and opportunities to European states that had been curtailed while Louis XIV seemed to threaten Europe with French domination. When the threat disappeared on Louis' death, in 1715, the more limited appetites and ambitions of Europe's other sovereigns could have freer rein. No country, however, was now necessarily more secure than it had been while Louis lived; nor was the likelihood of peace with justice for all Europe any greater.

For some eighty years—between Utrecht and Napoleon Bonaparte—no state threatened to dominate Europe. In this sense a balance of power prevailed. During the first twenty or so years, there was almost no war at all because of postwar exhaustion, but this respite came only from depleted resources and special dynastic considerations, not from lessons learned or from a revulsion against war. The ideal of peace had no place in diplomacy and had nothing to do with the eighteenth-century balance of power. For despite the absence of any bid for hegemony, between Utrecht and Napoleon the century saw two international

---

[1] Thus Leopold von Ranke, the great nineteenth-century German historian, emphasized "the primacy of foreign policy" in the development of Europe. To Ranke the essence of European civilization was a common Christian culture embodied in a diversity of national states whose very competition produced a metaphysical kind of harmony. See T. von Laue, *Leopold Ranke: The Formative Years* (1950), and Ranke's famous essay, "The Great Powers," reproduced as an appendix to that book. For a classic view emphasizing the anarchy of the state system see Albert Sorel, *Europe Under the Old Regime* (tr. 1968).

The series of treaties negotiated at the peace congress at Utrecht in 1713–1714 reaffirmed the balance of power in Europe and provided that the Bourbon thrones of France and Spain would never be united. England gained various colonial and commercial spoils, including Newfoundland and Gibraltar. Spain's overseas empire went to Philip V, while the Spanish Netherlands, Milan, Sardinia, and Naples went to the Austrian Hapsburgs. (Photo: The Bettmann Archive)

conflicts (the War of the Austrian Succession and the Seven Years' War), the loss of a substantial overseas empire by France, threats of extinction against the Hapsburg Empire and Prussia, and the disappearance of the sovereign state of Poland.

There was thus no absence of aggression and bellicosity in eighteenth-century Europe. But these wars did not mobilize entire societies; the atmosphere of the period can be suggested by such incidents as the English novelist Laurence Sterne's taking his famous *Sen-*

timental Journey to France while his country was at war with her. Moreover these contests lacked the fanaticism of the religious wars while not yet calling forth the kinds of commitment that came with later wars of revolution, national unification, or ideology. They were wars in which dynastic interests and territorial ambitions interacted with disputes over trade, colonies, and prestige. Eighteenth-century wars had limited, concrete objectives. They were not total wars.

Zones of Conflict

International relations focused on four geographical regions or spheres of interest: the North, Central Europe, Eastern Europe, and the New World across the seas.

The Baltic area in the North was of strategic interest to a number of states. Russia, Sweden, Prussia, and Poland all sought direct territorial control there, which could only be achieved at some other state's expense. Maritime powers like the British and Dutch were concerned both with the trading areas that fronted on the Baltic and the rich prize of naval stores that could be found there.

Most of Central Europe constituted a fragmented power vacuum over which the great powers and their allies vied. The Bourbon-Hapsburg rivalry revolved largely around who would have the most influence there. And even lesser dominions like Saxony and Bavaria could be pardoned for dreams of grandeur that were stimulated by the absence of sizable viable states. Moreover Great Britain's dynastic tie through George I with the principality of Hanover involved her in this vortex of Central European instability, which otherwise would have been unimportant to her. Farther south the power vacuum extended into Italy, which was like a colonial area for the satisfaction of dynastic ambitions.

"Eastern Europe" is admittedly an imprecise designation. Yet in regard to the eighteenth century, it conveys a firmer concept of region than the expression "Germany." The eastern boundary of the Holy Roman Empire had lost most of its significance, but it did generally set off the classic area of Europe from the vast reaches of the continent that lay to the east. Here the most important issue was the attempt to push back the Ottomans, a task shared—in a spirit of mutual distrust—by Hapsburgs and Russians (see Map 18.1). As questions of access to the Mediterranean were raised, the maritime powers were drawn in. This is the origin of the so-called "Eastern question" that bedeviled European diplomacy for the next 200 years. However, other complicating issues, such as the ethnic diversity and latent national aspirations of the region, had not yet arisen to complicate the picture.

The fourth theater of activity was the colonized New World. Spain, Great Britain, and France, secure within their own borders, had their most important interests here, though they were not fully aware of this. By 1739 a war had begun between England and Spain that was directly attributable to a dispute in the New World: British smuggling and its repression in the Spanish Empire. Henceforth colonial tensions would severely complicate European diplomatic relations.

There were thus many possible permutations in international affairs. The abler statesmen of the times were the ones who could see past traditional commitments or superficially attractive opportunities to the veritable interests of their states. Ultimately perhaps the most important development in the state system of the eighteenth century was the rise to prominence of Britain and Russia, the two great flanking powers of Europe. Previously both had really stood on the periphery of European power politics. After Utrecht their influence would be second to none.

DIPLOMACY AND WARFARE

Diplomacy in the eighteenth century reflected an increasingly complex range of considerations. Traditional dynastic interests were still important: princes and their ministers tried to exclude challenges to the reigning family's succession, to secure client states or new territory by dynastic claims, and to arrange marriages that would bring new titles or alliances.

Dynastic considerations could promote peace in certain circumstances and war in others. When a ruler felt insecure on his throne because of possible internal challenges to his title, he might seek to improve his relations with other states in order to avoid further complications. Coincidentally this was the situation in both France and Britain after Utrecht, and it helps explain the peace that prevailed between those inexorable rivals until 1740. An episode characteristic of the diplomacy of the time involved the Polish succession—the Polish kingship having been an elective office subject to influence by the great powers. Unable to agree over the matter, the powers fought a brief limited war; France's candidate then bowed out but was compensated with the duchy of Lorraine, which would eventually pass directly under French sovereignty by virtue of the new duke's marriage to a French princess.

On the whole, though, dynastic interests gave way to policies based on a more impersonal and abstract conception of the state. Men like Frederick II of Prussia, Count Wenzel Anton von Kaunitz of Austria, and William Pitt of Britain tried to shape their diplomacy to the specific needs of their states as they conceived them. "Reasons of state" centered on security, with the only guarantee of security understood to be the power to assure it by force. The search for defensible borders and the weakening of possible challengers were obvious principles. Eighteenth-century statesmen believed that the end (security and prosperity) justified the means (the maximal use of power). Until a country was completely invulnerable, its leaders felt justified in

MAP 18.1: THE EXPANSION OF RUSSIA AND THE PARTITION OF POLAND

using the crudest and most amoral tactics in dealing with its neighbors.

Diplomats and armies shared the task of implementing "reasons of state." Emissaries were frequently put to work fabricating or embellishing claims to this province or that princely title. They were understood to be spies or at least snoopers by vocation. They offered the bribes that were a part of foreign policy and negotiated treaties sometimes knowing of their prince's intentions to violate them.

There was another, more conservative side to diplomacy: the eighteenth century marks its growth as a serious profession, parallel to the further rationalization of the state itself.

Foreign ministries or foreign offices were started and staffed with corps of experts, clerks, archives, and the like. The heads of the diplomatic machine were the ambassadors, stationed in permanent embassies abroad. This routinized management of foreign relations helped foster a sense of collective identity among the European states despite their interminable struggles. Linguistically and socially the diplomatic corps provided a veneer of sugar coating to international relations. French now reigned supreme as the common language of European diplomats; by 1774 even a treaty between Turks and Russians was drafted in that language. Socially the diplomatic corps was aristocratic and cosmopolitan. Whatever ruler they might be serving, noble ambassadors regarded themselves as members of the same fraternity.

In the wake of the exhaustion that followed the wars of Louis XIV's reign, diplomats began to play a more active role in the affairs of the Continent. Between 1715 and 1725 Europe actually saw a series of international congresses designed to settle differences in advance by means of covenants. This was only a superficial change, however, since the issues decided on were invariably minor.

Moreover the great powers dictated terms, dividing spoils and prestige at the expense of the smaller states. For example the territorial ambitions of Prussia, Austria, and Russia were reconciled at the bargaining table by their series of agreements to partition Poland's outer areas among themselves (see Map 18.1). The declaration they issued in 1772, at the time of the first partition, stated boldly that "Whatever the limitations of the respective claims may be, the acquisitions which result must be exactly equal." Rarely was such cynicism perpetrated on so grand a scale, but in its essence it was typical of the European state system. Settling disputes by negotiation could be as brutal and amoral as settling them by war.

Armies

Despite the settlement of many disputes by diplomacy, war was far from an alternative of last resort; it continued to be a commonplace instrument of statecraft. In the major Continental countries, the focus of bureaucratic innovation and monetary expenditure was the standing army, whose growth was enormous. France set the pace for this development. After 1680 the size of her forces never fell below 200,000. The growth of the Prussian army exemplifies what was happening all over Europe: between 1713 and 1786 its manpower increased from 39,000 to 200,000. But the cost, technology, and tactics of these armies served to limit the devastation and horror of eighteenth-century warfare despite the frequency of combat.

Costliness led rulers to husband their armies carefully. Princes were quick to declare war but slow to deploy their armies at full strength or commit them to battle. Observers of eighteenth-century warfare like the English writer Daniel Defoe therefore concluded that there was more money but less blood spent in war.

The techniques of building and besieging fortifications continued to preoccupy military planners. Looking back on those days from the vantage point of the French Revolution, one officer characterized eighteenth-century warfare not even as the art of defending strong places but of "surrendering them honorably after certain conventional formalities." The main body of troops—the infantry—was primarily trained for maneuvering and was taught to fire in carefully controlled line formations. A successful strategy equaled the ability to nudge an opposing army into abandoning its position in the face of superior maneuvering. Improved organization worked to counteract brutality. Better supplied by a system of magazines, more tightly disciplined by constant drilling, troops were less likely to desert or plunder than they had been during the Thirty Years' War.

Rarely was the annihilation of the opposing force the strategic objective of a battle. Some encounters were fought as if they were occurring on a parade ground, while pitched battles in open fields were usually avoided. Moreover important victories were frequently nullified when the winning army retreated toward its home bases to make winter camp. Finally, unconditional surrender was never required from an opponent. The same held true for naval battles. Commanders evinced great caution when engaging in combat and rarely followed up initial contacts by pursuing and destroying the bested squadron.

The officer corps of the military were generally the preserve of the European nobility, though they also served as channels of upward social mobility for wealthy sons of middle-class families who purchased commissions. In either case the officer ranks tended to be sinecures filled by men who lacked the professional outlook and requisite training for effective leadership. Officers were likely to be long on martial spirit and bravery but short on technical skills. The branches of service that showed the most progress were the artillery and the engineers, in which competent middle-class officers played an unusually large role.

A final element limiting the actual scale of war in the eighteenth century was the inherent weakness of coalitions of belligerents, which formed whenever a general war mushroomed. On paper these alliances looked formidable and seemed to promise vast deeds of destruction against their victims. On the battlefield, however, they were hampered by primitive communications and lack of mobility even at the peak of cooperation. Moreover the partnerships rarely lasted very long. The anarchy of the state system predictably bred distrust among supposed allies as well as enemies. Sudden abandonment of coalitions and the negotiation of separate peace treaties mark the history of almost every major war fought under this arrangement.

II. ABSOLUTISM IN CENTRAL EUROPE

The relationship between international rivalry and internal modernization is dramatically illustrated in the examples of Prussia and Austria. Already in the mid-eighteenth century these two powers were vying for domination in Central Europe and they instituted reforms to better wage this struggle. Each experienced a period of vigorous state building under their absolute rulers, the essence of which was to increase the size of armies, collect larger revenues to support them, and develop bureaucracies to administer the provinces. It did not seem to matter whether the ruler was a modern-minded atheist like Frederick II of Prussia or a pious traditionalist like Maria Theresa of Austria. In their own way each understood their vocation as ruler and the demands of the state system.

THE RISE OF PRUSSIA

The fate of Bradenburg-Prussia was entirely different from Poland's. As Chapter 17 described, Frederick William the Great Elector had begun the creation of a standing army and bureaucracy in Brandenburg and had bargained the great magnates into yielding much of their political power. These policies had raised Brandenburg from virtual obscurity to a position of second rank in the state system. Frederick I had secured the prestige of a royal throne in Prussia for the Hohenzollern family, but while patronizing new cultural activities in Berlin, he had neglected to forge ahead with the state-building process. His successor, however, more than compensated for this laxness.

Frederick William I

Under the thoroughgoing absolutism of Frederick William I (1713–1740), Prussia began her climb toward great-power status. Strikingly different from his refined father, this spartan ruler approached affairs of state as all business and little pleasure. He disdained court life and considered theaters to be temples of Satan. His standards of frugality were exorbitant: he eliminated three-quarters of the court's expenses, dismissed numerous courtiers, and cut the salaries of those who remained. Uncluttered by royal ceremonies, his days were regulated in timetable fashion as he attempted to supervise everything himself.

This painting of the Battle of Fontenoy illustrates the typical battlefield stance adopted by eighteenth-century armies. The infantry was positioned in rigid line formation when firing, which limited its effectiveness. (Photo: National Army Museum)

It could be said that Frederick William I traded the costume of the courtier for the uniform of the soldier, since his purpose was to organize the state for military power. During his reign the army grew from 38,000 to 83,000, making it the fourth largest in Europe, behind France, Russia, and Austria. While still relying on foreign mercenaries for one-third of his troops, he also instituted a form of conscription known as the canton system. Nobles, bourgeois, and skilled artisans were exempted; the children of peasants were enrolled when very young and called up as needed, serving in peacetime for three months of the year and leaving to work on the land during the harvest period. The soldiers—whether foreign mercenaries, enlistees, or conscripts—were subjected to intensive drilling, wore standardized uniforms, and were maintained by an improved supply system that at least equaled the French.

The king went even farther in the reform of the officer corps. Determined to build an effective cadre of professionals, he forbade his subjects to serve in foreign armies and compelled the sons of nobles to attend cadet schools in which martial skills and attitudes were inculcated.

In this military state Frederick William I was the number one soldier. A colorful commander in chief, he maintained a personal regiment of enormous grenadiers and always wore a uniform, which he declared that he would be buried in.[2] He did not mean that he would die in battle, however. For all his involvement with military life, he studiously refrained from committing his army to battle prematurely or needlessly. Consequently he passed this force on intact to his son, Frederick II.

The process of centralization kept pace with the growth of the army. In 1723 a government superagency was created: called the General Directory of Finance, War, and Domains, it united under one roof the administration of all functions except justice, educa-

tion, and religion. Its main task was to coordinate the collection of revenue, expenditure (mostly on the army), and local administration. The king mobilized the state's resources in one activity that even French absolutism had not affected: education. Considering it a service to both God and country to give the population some basic instruction, he made education compulsory for all children where schools existed and instructed local communities and parents to set them up where they did not. Teachers held their jobs mainly as sidelines, most coming from the clergy. Uninterested in higher intellectual pursuits, however, the king allowed the universities to decline at the same time. They did not seem to fit in with his design of building state power.

Frederick William I's dour, puritanical attitude left an impact on his reforms that helped give them what would later be considered a peculiarly Prussian flavor. Distrustful of his bureaucrats, he granted them only a minimum of discretionary power, and while insisting on absolute obedience, he held them responsible for inefficiency. This treatment was capped by the operations of a network of inspectors called fiscals, who reported directly and secretly to the king on the behavior of officials. All these policies produced a rigid, rule-book mentality among the bureaucrats that became an oppressive force in Prussia by the end of the nineteenth century.

Frederick the Great

Frederick William I's most notable triumph was perhaps the grooming of his successor. This was no mean task. Frederick II (1740–1786) seemed diametrically opposite in temperament to his father and little inclined to follow in his footsteps. The father was a Teutonic philistine, a God-fearing Protestant, and a self-conscious Hohenzollern. The prince by contrast was a sentimental, artistically inclined youth who composed music and played on the flute, wrote poetry, and fer-

---

[2] Frederick William I's militarism is the subject of numerous anecdotes but also the graver charge that he inaugurated a style that helped produce Nazism. This view was particularly common during World War II. Thus an excellent study by Robert Ergang of this dynamic ruler, published in 1941, bore the astounding title, *The Potsdam Führer: Frederick William I.*

vently admired French culture. Later he would write philosophical treatises and histories and would correspond with Voltaire. Frederick II disdained German culture, had a low estimation of his Hohenzollern relatives, and was an atheist.

But the Prussian monarchy was mobilizing all its subjects for the tasks of state building, and the young prince was not exempted. On the contrary he was compelled to work at all levels of the state apparatus so as to experience them directly, from shoveling hay on a royal farm to marching with the troops. Relentlessly the father trained his son for kingship, forcibly reshaping his personality, inculcating him with a sense of duty, and toughening him to the grinding tasks of leadership. Despite Frederick's prolonged resistance, this hard apprenticeship succeeded. In the end, as a modern psychiatrist would put it, the prince identified with the aggressor.

When he assumed the throne, in 1740, Frederick II was prepared to lead Prussia in a ruthless struggle for power and territory. While his intellectual turn of mind caused him to agonize over moral issues and the nature of his role, he never flinched from actually exercising it. He did, however, attempt to justify absolutism at home and encroachment abroad. He claimed undivided power for the ruler not because some divine qualities inhered in the dynasty but because absolute rule was the only kind that could bring results. The monarch, he stated, was the first servant of the state. In the long run, he hoped, an enlightened monarch might be in a position to lead his people into a more rational and even moral existence. Certain objectives along this road could be attained immediately; in matters like religious toleration and judicial reform, Frederick was able to implement his ideals and gained a reputation as an "enlightened absolutist."

But these were relatively peripheral matters. The paramount issue was security, and the best justification of absolutism would be its effectiveness in ensuring it. Success for Prussia depended on her improving an extremely vulnerable geographic position by acquiring more territory and stronger borders and ultimately on attaining great enough power to make her truly independent (see Map 18.2). Until such a time Frederick would not undertake social innovations domestically that might disrupt the flow of taxes, conscripts, or officers into the army or provoke the nobility against him. "The fundamental rule of governments," he wrote, "is the principle of extending their territories." This summed up what was in fact his most singular contribution to the rise of Prussia and what earned him his title of Frederick the Great.

Frederick William I had carefully avoided squandering his impressive army in engagements that would not really benefit Prussia. By coincidence the year 1740, which saw Frederick II's accession to the throne, was also the moment when a suitable objective for this army presented itself. Frederick began his reign with a sudden attack on the Hapsburg Empire. His objective was to conquer the province of Silesia. Prussia had no claim to it; it was simply a wealthy and strategically located domain contiguous to Prussia that the Hapsburgs were temporarily unable to defend effectively, for reasons that will be discussed directly. The conquest of Silesia culminated a century of Prussian state building inaugurated by the great elector back in 1648. But this same act would have equal significance for the progress of absolutism in the Hapsburg Empire.

THE HAPSBURG EMPIRE UNDER STRESS

Even after the Hapsburg dynasty lost control of Spain and its lands overseas, its personal domains remained immense. Its ambitions and its problems were correspondingly large. The Hapsburgs' empire was the antithesis of a unified state; it was rather a dynastic holding company of diverse territories gathered under one crown through marriages, bargains, and conquests: the Archduchy of Austria, the Kingdom of Bohemia (which had included Silesia), the Kingdom of Hungary, and European "colonies" like the Austrian Netherlands, Lombardy, and Tuscany (see Map 18.2). The Hapsburgs had hoped to integrate Austria, Bohemia, and Hungary into a centralized, German-speaking, Catholic superstate. But centralization was resisted by the local diets in all provinces, and forced Germanization would be opposed by the Czechs, Magyars, and Slavs. Moreover the Hapsburgs' Catholicism clashed with the strong Protestant traditions of Bohemia and Hungary.

The War of the Austrian Succession

Under the reign of Charles VI, yet another problem complicated the destinies of his multinational empire. The long history of Hapsburg intermarriage had finally issued in a failure of the male line. Charles' only heir apparent was his daughter, Maria Theresa, an unprecedented situation for the dynasty. In 1713 Charles drafted a document known as the Pragmatic Sanction, declaring that all Hapsburg dominions would pass intact to the eldest heir, male or female. He thereby hoped to prevent a succession crisis and a division of the inheritance, which would dissipate Hapsburg power. Through the labyrinthine interests of the state system, Charles sought for the next twenty-five years to secure recognition and guarantees of the Pragmatic Sanction from the European powers. By making all kinds of concessions and promises, he won this recognition on paper. But when he died, in 1740, his daughter found that such paper commitments were worthless: the succession was challenged by force from several sides. Concentrating on diplomacy alone, Charles had neglected the work of state building, leaving an empty treasury, inadequately trained

army, and ineffective bureaucracy. The Pragmatic Sanction was scarcely pragmatic.

In contrast to Austria, Prussia's treasury was full, her army primed, and her ruler self-confident. For Frederick II the moment seemed right to grab off the Hapsburg province of Silesia, with its abundant resources and geographic proximity to Prussia. Without legal claims to it, Prussia's justification was simply her own "reasons of state" combined with the Hapsburgs' faltering fortunes. Frederick struck, assuming that other problems would keep Maria Theresa occupied. This in fact was the case. France's relatively pacific policy was just ending, as a clique of military aristocrats had gained the king's support and persuaded him to resume the traditional battle against the Hapsburgs. France's entering wedge was her ally Bavaria, whose duke, Charles Albert, now put forward a tenuous claim to the disputed Hapsburg succession. Spain entered the lists against Austria also, seeing a chance to walk away with Austria's Italian colonies. Worse yet, Maria Theresa faced a rebellion led by the surviving Czech nobility in Bohemia: in 1741 four hundred of them proclaimed Charles Albert of Bavaria king of Bohemia.

The young archduchess' fate would probably have been hopeless if Hungary's Magyar nobles had followed a similar course. Their grievances, however, were not so sharp, and they listened sympathetically to Maria Theresa's moving pleas for support. In exchange for her promise of autonomy within the Hapsburg Empire, the Magyars offered her loyalty and the troops necessary to resist the invaders.

Austria's principal ally was Great Britain, but Britain was interested only in combating France on the Continent. Therefore the British pressured Maria Theresa to concede Silesia and make peace with Prussia, in order to concentrate on the Franco-Bavarian invasion. With the help of Hungarian troops and Brit-

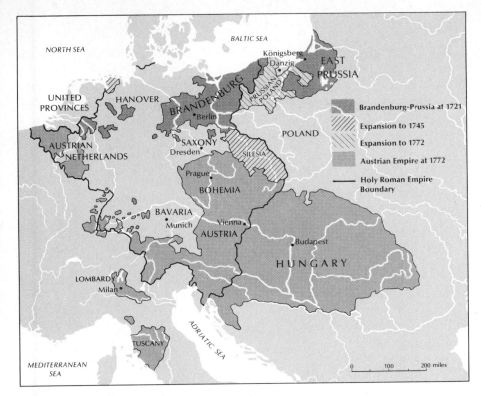

MAP 18.2: PRUSSIA 1721–1772 AND THE HAPSBURG EMPIRE

ish gold, Austria fought these opponents to a stalemate, and Frederick's conquest of Silesia proved to be the only major territorial change produced by this large-scale war. Apart from that, the Treaty of Aix-la-Chapelle in 1748 restored the status quo established by the Utrecht settlement. For England and France, who fought this war in their overseas colonies as well as in Europe, it was a stand-off. For Prussia it was a spectacular gain at Austria's expense. Austria regarded it as merely a temporary setback. The recovery of Silesia and the humiliation of Prussia became the primary objective of Austrian policy. This in turn required a major effort at state building within the Hapsburg domains.

Maria Theresa

The woman whose reign was assured not by her father's negotiations but by force of arms was a marked contrast to her archenemy, Frederick. The king of Prussia was practical and atheistic; the archduchess of Austria and Queen of Hungary was moralistic and pious. While Frederick barely tolerated a loveless marriage, the Hapsburg ruler enjoyed an unusually happy domestic life, bearing her husband numerous children and taking great personal interest in their upbringing. Her personality and her ruling style were traditional, but deceptively—under this exterior she was a shrewd innovator in the business of building and reasserting the power of her state.

Unlike Frederick, or for that matter her own son and successor, Joseph II, Maria Theresa still had a strong regard for her dynasty. She did not share the modern conception of the ruler's role as simply first servant of the state; she still believed in the divine mission of the Hapsburgs. Yet utilitarian considerations did increasingly enter into her planning, causing her to think more of her realm and less of the dynasty and the Almighty. Likewise this most pious of Catholic sovereigns—who disdained the permissive idea of religious toleration and who loathed atheists—found herself obliged to undertake stern reforms of the church. Particularly in its monastic wing, she found far too much wastefulness and self-interest; consequently she forbade the establishment of new monasteries or the taking of vows by anyone under twenty-four years of age. Moreover she abolished the clergy's exemptions from taxes, something her more easygoing French counterpart found impossible to do.

A new bureaucratic apparatus was constructed on the models of French and Prussian absolutism. At the center, in Vienna, reorganized and relatively streamlined central ministries recruited staffs of experts. For the arms and legs of this machine in the provinces, new agents were appointed, largely divorced from feudal and local interests, though in practice some concession had to be made to the enormous vested interests and regional traditions within the Hapsburg realm. The core domains (excluding Hungary and the Italian colonies) were reorganized into ten provinces, each subdivided into districts or circles that were in turn each directed by a royal official. With the help of these trusted agents, the central government could wrest new taxes from the increasingly weakened local diets. Meanwhile, by flattery and consideration, Maria Theresa lured important nobles from all corners of her domains

to Vienna to participate in its social and administrative life. It goes without saying that this was matched by military reforms, notably improvements in the training of troops and the establishment of academies to produce a more professional officer corps. By 1756 Austria was ready to face Prussia again.

III. THE MARITIME POWERS

The shift of the economic axis from the Mediterranean to the Atlantic seaboard began in the sixteenth century during the years of Spanish and Portuguese expansion. But it was left to the eighteenth century and to France and Great Britain to consolidate that shift and establish its full significance. Despite their great differences, both countries generated dynamic commercial activity, and both were beyond the state-building stage that other nations were now passing through. For the merchants and governments of France and England, colonial trade was an adjunct of state building—a question not only of profits but of power. In the process an almost global economy was created, whose mainspring was the system of plantation slavery.

THE ATLANTIC SEABOARD STATES

France After Louis XIV

Although France provided a model for absolutism, even under the Sun King centralization of power was never complete. Until the era of revolutions, the French aristocracy remained a strong group in the state that could create trouble for the monarchy.

Louis XIV's death, in 1715, released a great deal of such trouble. French absolutism was too firmly established to be swept away by an aristocratic reaction, but it could not prevent such attempts. For one thing Louis XIV's heir was still a child, and the duke of Orléans, who became regent in this interval, had no interest in the tradition of absolutism. On the contrary, to bolster his own delicate position, he supported key aristocrats in a grab for power. The regent restored the parlements to political power and replaced prominent royal bureaucrats with councils composed of France's most eminent aristocrats. The scheme quickly proved a complete failure since the councils were simply unable to govern effectively. The parlements, however, would never again surrender their power to veto royal legislation. Henceforth they became the rallying point of those who deplored the growth of centralized government and wished to restore the so-called unwritten constitution of France, which was supposed to limit the powers of the king and protect the prerogatives of various groups.

A second major problem facing France was of course her finances. The debt amassed by Louis' wartime expenditures was crushing. Since privileged groups like the nobility and clergy effectively escaped Louis' half-hearted attempts to tax them, other ways of improving the state's credit were sought. The brilliant Scottish financier John Law seemed to have the answer: a government-sponsored central bank that would issue paper notes, expand credit, and encourage investment in a new trading company for the French colonies. By tying the bank to his well-promoted East India Company, a venture promising its subscribers vast profits from the Louisiana territory, Law initiated an investment boom and a tremendous upsurge in available credit. But as was the case in England at the same time, the public's greed and credulity soon led to vast financial overextension as prices for East India Company stock rose to insanely high levels. A bust was inevitable, and when it came, in 1720, the entire scheme of bank notes and credit collapsed with it.

In different forms the same political and financial problems were to plague France through the eighteenth century until the Revolution opened up entirely new options for their solution. Meanwhile the uncertainties of regency government gave way to a long period of stability between 1720 and 1740, when Louis XV conferred almost unlimited authority on his aging tutor and adviser, Cardinal Fleury. Cautious, dedicated to the monarchy, and surrounded by talented subordinates, Cardinal Fleury made the apparatus of absolutism function quietly and with reasonable effectiveness. In these decades France turned the corner out of the low point of misfortunes that marked the end of Louis XIV's reign. Fleury's twenty-year tenure coincided with abundant harvests, slowly rising population, and commercial activity— in short with recovery.

Moreover Fleury was able to contain pressures and ambitions within the governing class. When he finally died at the age of ninety, these pressures exploded. War hawks immediately plunged France into the first of several protracted and unsuccessful wars that strained French credit to the breaking point. At home the situation likewise deteriorated. Having no one to replace Fleury as unofficial prime minister, Louis XV put his confidence in a succession of counselors, some capable and some mediocre. But he did not back any of them up when pressure from contending factions at court became uncomfortable. Lacking self-confidence and dedication to his task, the king avoided confrontations and neglected affairs of state, devoting his energy instead to the pleasures of the hunt and a succession of mistresses.

Although Louis XV clearly provided weak leadership for an extended period, France's difficulties must be seen not simply in personal but also in structural terms. The main problems—privilege, political power, and finances—posed intractable and perhaps impossible challenges to policy makers. Taxes have always been unpopular; governments that appear to levy new taxes arbitrarily seem despotic, even if the need for them is clear and the distribution equitable. One of France's soundest taxes was the *vingtième*, or twentieth, which was supposed to tap the income of all elements in French society with some measure of proportionality. The nobility and clergy, however, all but evaded the real brunt of the tax. Naturally the more aggressive royal ministers wished to remedy that situation. In the 1750s for example a plan was advanced for putting teeth into the *vingtième's* bite on the clergy's immense wealth. The plan proved to be the ruination of a capable royal official. With all its corporate might, the clergy attacked the plan; the parlements joined in the attack against the "despotism" of a crown that would arbitrarily tax its subjects. Thus not only did the privileged groups successfully block such useful reforms, but they made the monarchy's position more difficult by spreading a spirit of opposition and a fine-sounding rhetoric of liberty. In retrospect we see that the parlements were advancing their own special interests as they fought for a limitation on royal absolutism.

Another of Louis XV's ministers, René Maupeou, recognized that the parlements were an unbreachable obstacle to royal initiative, whether to do good or bad. Hence he prevailed on the king to use force as Louis XIV would have. In 1771 the parlements were dissolved and were replaced by magistrates loyal to the king. But the story could no longer end so simply as it might have a century before. Most of the articulate public now rallied to the parlements' support. The pressure of this elite "public opinion" was so great that it forced Louis XVI into restoring the parlements and dismissing Maupeou when he succeeded to the throne, wishing to begin his reign (1774–1792) with public confidence and popularity. Predictably the parlements repaid this kindness by persisting in opposing meaningful reform efforts attempted by Louis

XVI's ministers, leaving the monarchy in a hopeless impasse by the 1780s: virtually bankrupt, unpopular, and vacillating.

In the face of the structural weaknesses of the state and the special interests of the ruling classes, it is easy to forget the advances made in this most populous and wealthy European nation. Changes in population, rural economy, and the like, which will be discussed in Chapter 20, were clearly among the most important aspects of French history in the eighteenth century. So too was the commercial and maritime activity that went into the building of France's empire and the struggle to maintain it. No one knew at the time that the fate of royal ministers in the 1750s or 1770s foretold a stalemate that would help bring the Old Regime crashing down. The French peasantry at home and empire builders abroad continued to work at their callings, virtually unaffected by these storm signals.

The Growth of Stability in Great Britain

After the Peace of Utrecht, Great Britain too experienced a period of recovery. If the first half of the eighteenth century was an age of aristocratic reaction in France, it was a period of aristocratic dominance in Britain. The gentry and the wealthier freeholders, who elected the members of Parliament, represented a "political nation" of perhaps 100,000 in a population of 5 million in England and Wales in 1700. The distribution of the 558 seats in the House of Commons bore little resemblance to the relative size of the boroughs and shires. In 1793 fifty-one English and Welsh boroughs, counting less than 1,500 voters, elected 100 members of Parliament, nearly a fifth of the Commons. Many of these districts—such as Old Sarum, with an electorate of about six—were safely in the pocket of a prominent local family; little wonder that reformers would later call them "rotten." When a seat was disputed, the campaigns were seldom waged on principle but were competitions in bribery, influence, and intimidation. On a national scale loose party alignments did exist. The Whigs favored a strong Parliament and were somewhat more sensitive to commercial than to agricultural interests. The Tories usually supported the king and the policies that favored large landholders. In truth, however, the realities of politics were based on much smaller factions within these larger groups, and the principal political issue was the control of patronage and office.

But despite the oligarchic character of the social and political system, it is accurate to say that class lines remained considerably more fluid in Britain than on the Continent. The barriers separating the peerage, the gentry, and the commercial (and soon industrial) middle class were frequently pierced by marriage and by business or political associations. Some of the great Whig aristocrats in particular had substantial ties with the mercantile classes of London. Parliament, though scandalously unrepresentative of the population in the eighteenth century, at least was an institution that could be reformed and repaired. France had no similar functioning organism that could conveniently admit a larger part of the nation into participation in government.

A new dynasty, the Hanoverians, assumed the throne in 1714. Neither George I (1714–1727) nor George II (1727–1760) could speak English fluently, and while they showed some interest in their British realm, the language barrier and their concern for their Continental possessions limited royal influence and provided an opportunity for royal ministers and Parliament to grow in authority.

The dominant figure in British political history for the first half of the century was Sir Robert Walpole. He won his reputation for his skillful handling of government finances during a crisis of 1720, the collapse of the "South Sea Bubble." This panic involved shares of the South Seas Trading Company and was similar to the catastrophe that over-

took John Law's scheme in France. From 1721 to 1742 Walpole largely controlled the British government and determined its policies. He maintained his power by dispensing patronage liberally and maintaining the friendship of the king. He probably did not pronounce the words attributed to him. "Every man has his price," but the slogan would well describe political life under Walpole. The other phrase that describes his policies at home and abroad is "*Quieta non movere*," "Do not disturb the peace"—or in the vernacular, "Let sleeping dogs lie."

Although Walpole was responsible for no great new ideas or grand policies, he did contribute both to his country's economic recovery and to the growth of its political institutions. Many historians have called Walpole the first prime minister, though the office still had no official existence and the name itself was first used by his enemies as a kind of insult. He insisted that all the royal ministers follow the same policies, which of course he set himself. He insisted too that the ministers inform and consult with the House of Commons as well as the king. He himself continued to sit in its sessions in order to recruit support for his decisions. Not until the following century would the Commons have the recognized power of forcing ministers it did not approve of to resign, but Walpole took a first step toward rendering the ministers responsible before Parliament. While he was not truly the first prime minister, he certainly helped shape the office.

In Great Britain as in France, the economic expansion from about 1730 on increased the wealth and the social and political weight of the commercial and financial middle class. Walpole's policy of peace pleased the large landlords but angered the merchants and businessmen of London, who viewed the growth of French commerce and colonial settlements with apprehension. They found their champion in William Pitt, later earl of Chatham,

William Pitt is shown here addressing the House of Commons. Pitt had an abiding confidence in England's role as an imperial power, and his oratory, presence, and discerning political intelligence kept him at the forefront of British politics during the midcentury crisis. (Photo: Radio Times Hulton Picture Library)

himself the grandson of a man who had made a fortune in India. Eloquent, supremely self-confident, infused with a great vision of Britain's imperial destiny, Pitt began his career in Parliament in 1738 by bitterly criticizing the timid policies of the government and demanding that France be driven from the seas. In 1758, when the Seven Years' War was going badly for England, he was called to the ministry, with what results we shall see.

The Decline of the Dutch

The United Provinces, or Dutch Netherlands, emerged from the wars of Louis XIV in an ambiguous position. The country had survived intact, and considering her military vulnerability this was no small accomplishment. On the other hand she suffered from demographic and political ossification. The population of 2.5 million failed to rise during the eighteenth century, thus setting the Dutch apart from their rivals, the French and the British, whose numbers grew rapidly. Likewise a centralized state apparatus failed to develop even during the stress of seventeenth-century warfare. The provinces remained loosely joined in a federation that was barely able to assure the common defense of the state. So self-interested were these seven separate oligarchies that they failed to concert even to repair the ports, which were vital to shipping.

The Dutch were bound to suffer economically when French and English merchants sought to eliminate their role as the middlemen of maritime commerce. Beside this was the failure of Dutch industry to compete effectively with its rivals. Onerous indirect taxes on manufactured goods and the high wages demanded by Dutch artisans forced up the price of Dutch products excessively. Moreover manufacturers proved unable to modernize their processes and technology. High costs and antiquated organization combined especially to set back the all-important cloth industry. Leiden and Haarlem virtually disappeared from the international market.

What kept the nation from slipping completely out of Europe's economic life was her financial institutions. Shrewdly Dutch merchants gradually shifted their activity away from the competition of actual trading ventures into the safer, lucrative areas of credit and finance. With their country the first to perfect the uses of paper currency and establish a stock market and a central bank, the Dutch now became financial instead of maritime middlemen. Amsterdam's merchant-bankers loaned great amounts of money to both private enterprises and governments abroad. One estimate places the Dutch holding of the British national debt in 1776 at three-sevenths of the total. Not only did the Dutch underwrite British credit, but Dutch bankers helped funnel British money to Britain's diplomatic allies. When relations between the Dutch and British were strained in the 1770s, Dutch investment easily found new homes in North America and France. The role of the United Provinces in the colonial struggles of the eighteenth century was thus indirect but considerable.

THE EIGHTEENTH-CENTURY EMPIRES

After 1715 a new era began in the saga of European colonial development (see Map 18.3).

Three pioneers in overseas expansion had by now assumed a generally passive role, content to defend the domains already acquired. Portugal, whose dominion over Brazil was recognized at the Peace of Utrecht, henceforth retired from active contention. Likewise the Dutch could scarcely compete for new footholds and now protected their interests through cautious policies of neutrality. Although Spain continued her efforts to exclude outsiders from her vast empire, she had to rely increasingly on the power of her kindred dynasty in France for any confrontation with Britain. The stage of active competition was in fact left to these two powers.

Mercantile and Naval Competition

Great Britain, a nation that had barely been able to hold her own in maritime competition against the Dutch in the seventeenth century, now began her rise to domination of the seas. The only serious rival of this island power was France.

Their rivalry was played out in four regions. The West Indies, where France and Britain each colonized several islands profitably, constituted the fulcrum of empire, for reasons that will be discussed shortly. Directly linked to the West Indian economy was the second colonial territory: slave-providing West Africa. The third area was the North American continent, where a significant difference between the two powers developed. Britain's colonies became populous centers of settlement, whereas New France remained primarily a trading area. Finally, both nations sponsored powerful companies for trade with India and other Asian lands. These ventures were supposed to struggle for markets and influence without establishing actual colonies.

There were obvious differences and important similarities between the two royal systems. French absolutism produced a centralized structure, with its colonies being run according to uniform standards. *Intendants* and military governors ruled across the seas as they did in the French provinces. The British North American colonies by contrast were and remained somewhat independent both from each other and from the home government, where crown and Parliament both claimed colonial jurisdiction. Each colony had a royal governor but also a locally oriented legislature and strong traditions of self-government. Nonetheless the French and British faced similar problems and achieved generally similar results. Most importantly both applied mercantilist principles to the regulation of trade, and both increased naval power to protect it.

Mercantilism was a Europe-wide phenomenon, not limited to the colonial powers. It involved the regulation of economic activity so as to increase the power of the state over that of its neighbors. In this sense Prussia was as mercantilist as Britain, for both regarded the economic activities of individuals as subordinate to government policy.

A key tenet of mercantilism was the need for a favorable balance of trade and an inflow of gold and silver, with the assumption that a nation's share of bullion could increase only at its neighbor's expense. Colonies could promote a favorable balance of trade by producing valuable raw materials or crops for the mother country and providing a market for the latter's manufactured goods. Foreign states had to be excluded from these benefits as much as possible. By discriminatory tariffs, elaborate regulations, bounties, and outright prohibitions, each government sought to channel trade with its colonies in the direction of itself. Mercantilism for the colonies boiled down to an elaborate system of protectionism for this trade.

The colonies were exploited for the benefit of the mother country and not solely for the profit of those who invested or settled in them. But enormous fortunes were made by the West Indies planters as well as by merchants, manufacturers, and ship owners at home. Moreover illicit trade brought comfortable profits to more than one colonial family. For example, French planters needed North America's beef, fish, and grain and were eager to exchange their own (cheaper) sugar or molasses for it. The Hancocks of Boston among others grew dependent on this kind of smuggling to the French West Indies.

"Empire" was another way of saying "trade," but this trade depended on naval power. Rivals had to be excluded and regulations enforced. Thus there was a reciprocal relationship between the expansion of trade and the deployment of naval forces, which added to the competitive nature of colonial expansion. The merchant traders and the war vessels that supported them needed numerous stopping places for reprovisioning and refitting. This meant that ports had to be secured for them in strategic locations and denied to rivals whenever possible in Africa, India, and the Caribbean.

The Profits of Empire

Colonial commerce provided new products like sugar and new consumer demand, which in turn created an impetus for manufacturing and capital accumulation at home. This cycle increased the opportunities for the English and French middle classes. It is estimated that French commerce quadrupled during the eighteenth century, the value of its trade being somewhere in the vicinity of 200 million livres in 1716 and reaching more than 1 billion livres in 1787. By the 1770s commerce with their colonies accounted for almost one-third the total volume of both Britain's and France's foreign trade. The West Indies trade (mainly in sugar) bulked largest, and its expansion was spectacular. The value of French imports from the West Indies increased more than tenfold between 1716 and 1788, from 16 million to 185 million livres.

The West Indies seemed to be ideal colo-

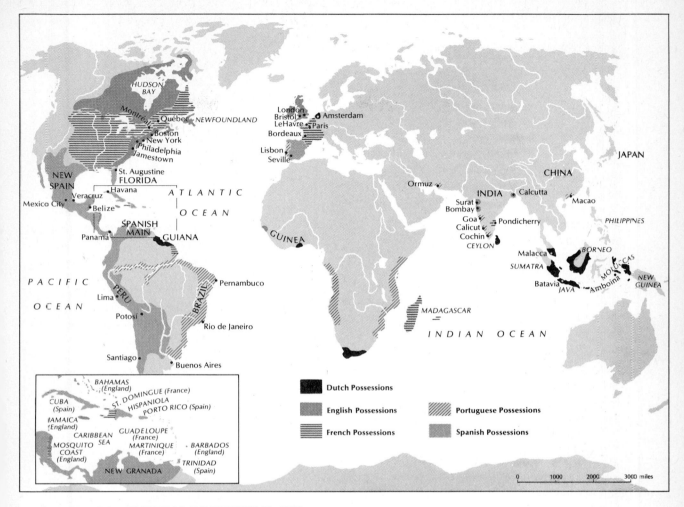

MAP 18.3: OVERSEAS POSSESSIONS 1713

nies. By virtue of their tropical climate and the isolation from European society that made slavery possible, they produced abundant crops that were difficult to raise elsewhere: tobacco, cotton, and indigo in addition to sugar, a luxury that European custom turned into a necessity. Moreover the islands could produce little else. They could not raise an adequate supply of food animals or grain to feed the vast slave population; they could not cut enough lumber for building; and they certainly could not manufacture the luxury goods demanded by the planter class. In other words the islands yielded up valuable crops and were dependent markets for most other commodities.

Numerous variations of the famous triangular trade therefore revolved around the West Indies. One pattern began with a ship departing from a British port with a cargo of manufactured products—paper, knives, pots, blankets, and the like—destined for the shopkeepers of North America. Landing at Marblehead or Philadelphia, the ship might exchange its goods for New England fish oil, fish, beef, and timber. These would then be transported to

Jamaica or Barbardos to be traded for sugar that would be turned over to British refineries many months later.

Another variation might see a frigate set out from Providence, Rhode Island (the chief slaving port in North America), with a cargo of New England rum. Landing in Africa, it would acquire slaves in exchange for the rum and then sail to the Indies to sell the slaves—for bills of exchange and for molasses, from which more rum could be distilled.

The final step in the mercantilist colonial process was the reexport of refined and distilled products made of the sugar, indigo, or tobacco provided by the overseas possessions. These were most likely to bring gold into British or French hands since finished goods could command hard cash from customers all over the Western world. For colonial commerce was superimposed on a complex and profitable pattern of European trade in which the Atlantic states carried off the lion's share. The New World's sugar, furs, fish, and tobacco were added to Baltic grain and timber; Italian and Spanish wines, fruits, olives, and silks; and Levantine and Asian spices and fabrics. To all these regions the manufacturing centers of Western Europe continued providing products like nails and pots, glassware and crockery, and shirts and stockings as well as luxuries like carriages and tapestries.

Slavery, the Foundation of Empire

Slavery was the keystone of the eighteenth-century empires. The dynamic qualities of the global trade had slavery as a starting point. Vast, backbreaking labor was necessary to transform a favorable climate and the investment of speculators into harvested crops of staples. As one British merchant put it candidly, colonial trade "increases or diminishes in proportion to the numbers of Negroes imported there, who produce the commodities with which our ships are usually loaded, and enable planters to live well and purchase great quantities of British commodities." About the same time the chamber of commerce of Nantes, France's chief slaving port, publicly argued that without slavery there would be no French colonial commerce to speak of at all.

At the height of the slave traffic, probably about 88,000 Negroes were removed from Africa annually—half in British ships, a quarter in French, and the rest in Dutch, Portuguese, Danish, and American ships. Over 600,000 slaves were imported into Jamaica in the eighteenth century, while the population of Santo Domingo comprised about half a million slaves compared with 35,000 whites of all nationalities and 28,000 mulattoes and free Negroes at the time of the French Revolution.

Traffic in slaves was competitive and risky but highly profitable for those who succeeded. The demand for slaves in the Indies, Central America, and the Southern colonies in North America kept rising, pushing prices up. In both Britain and France, slaving was originally organized monopolistically, with chartered companies holding exclusive rights in the 1660s. There was no actual colonization or conquest in Africa, but the French and to a lesser extent the British attempted to establish forts, or "factories," on African soil for the coordination and defense of these companies. Gradually the monopolies were challenged by newcomers—groups of merchants and investors who combined to launch single ships on slaving voyages. The West Indian planters, who needed more and cheaper slaves, applauded this additional source. In port cities like Bristol and Liverpool, the independent traders clustered and prospered. By the 1730s the British government was opening membership in its company almost automatically to any subject engaged in the trade. This arrangement was a midway point between the older chartered joint-stock companies and the nineteenth-century pattern of direct government attempts at colonization to promote the

THE MAGNITUDE OF THE SLAVE TRADE

The following figures represent the best current estimate of the number of persons removed from Africa and transported as slaves to the New World during the entire period of the Atlantic slave trade.

British Caribbean	1,665,000
British North America (to 1790)	275,000
United States (after 1786)	124,000
French Caribbean	1,600,000
Dutch Caribbean	500,000
Brazil	3,646,800
Spanish America	1,552,000

Source: Philip D. Curtin, *The Atlantic Slave Trade: A Census* (1969).

interests of British merchants and investors.

Europeans alone did not condemn free blacks to slavery. The actual enslavement took place in the interior at the hands of aggressive tribes whose chiefs became the middlemen of this nefarious commerce. These black traders were shrewd and hard bargainers, and prices were set in goods rather than fixed currency. The competition among Europeans for the slaves tended to drive up the prices that the natives could command in hardware, cloth, liquor, and guns. In response some traders sought to open up new areas where the natives would be more eager to come to terms. This combination of competitiveness, increasing demand, and higher prices helped spread the trade and further darken the future of Africa.

Europeans in this period scarcely penetrated the interior of the continent; they were confined by the forbidding topography and the resoluteness of the natives to coastal areas. But the Europeans' intervention disoriented African life. It spurred on civil wars among the African tribes, diverting energies into military ventures and away from agricultural development; and it drained off a vast supply of labor that was needed in Africa itself.

The chief impact of course was on the slaves themselves. Many failed to survive the process of enslavement at all, perishing either on the forced marches from the interior to the coast or on the nightmarish middle passage across the Atlantic, which was comparable to the transit in cattle cars of Nazi prisoners to extermination camps in World War II. Since the risks of slaving ventures were high and the time lag between investment and return was usually a year and a half or two years, the traders sought to maximize profits by jamming in as many captives as possible. Small ships carried as many as 500 slaves on a voyage, packed below deck in only enough space for the individual to lie at full length, pressed against neighboring bodies, and enough headroom to crawl, not stand. The food and provi-

Slave traffic was the basis for empire building in the eighteenth century, and slave ships were a cruel and common sight on international waters. This print shows a method used to quell revolts on board ship and suggests the sheer violence underlying the trade. (Photo: New York Public Library, Rare Books)

sions were likewise held to a minimum. No accurate figures are available on the mortality rate that resulted from these odious conditions. It is no wonder then that agitation against slavery tended to focus initially on the trade rather than the institution itself. After the 1780s participation in slave trafficking diminished considerably both in England and France. A dark chapter in Europe's relations with the outside world dwindled to an end, though the formal suppression of slaving did not come for several more decades.

IV. THE MIDCENTURY CONFLAGRATION

The pressures created by the competition of states, dynasties, and empires in the eighteenth century exploded in midcentury in what was to be the last large-scale war of the prerevolutionary period. For the sake of clarity, it is helpful to consider the conflagration in two parts. One, the Continental phase, known as the Seven Years' War, had at its center Austro-Prussian rivalry and the growing ambitions of Russia. The other revolved around Anglo-French competition for empire in North America, the West Indies, and India. Colonial historians have called it the Great War for Empire, and it was this sector of conflict that had produced the more striking results when the smoke cleared.

THE SEVEN YEARS' WAR

In certain respects the Seven Years' War and its colonial corollaries anticipated what would happen in the European state system on the eve of World War I. Although it lacked the elements of domestic class conflict and popular nationalism that also contributed to the crisis in Europe in 1914, the war flowed from a tangled web of interlocking alliances, im-

perial competition abroad, and one state's desire to avenge a loss of territory—Austria's loss of Silesia in this case, France's loss of Alsace-Lorraine in World War I.

At midcentury a reconsideration of alliances began within the European state system under Austria's prodding. Previously the Bourbon-Hapsburg rivalry had been the cornerstone of European diplomacy. But by the 1750s at least two other sets of fundamental antagonisms had superseded it: France's competition with Great Britain in the New World and Austria's vendetta against Prussia over Silesia. For Austria the rivalry with Bourbon France was no longer important. Its position in the Holy Roman Empire depended now on humbling Prussia. France did not yet share a concern over Prussia, but her hostility to Austria had diminished. Austria was therefore free to pursue a turnabout in alliances—a veritable diplomatic revolution—in which an anti-Prussian coalition could be forged. Russia was the key to this coalition. Aside from her personal loathing of the atheistic Frederick II, Empress Elizabeth perceived Prussia as an obstacle to Russian ambitions in Eastern Europe. Moreover Prussia's geographical vulnerability made the kingdom an inviting target.

Prussia was understandably active on the diplomatic front in the hope of compensating for that vulnerability. Upset by the initiatives of Austria's brilliant foreign minister Kaunitz, Frederick's panicky countermoves only succeeded in alienating the other powers. Frederick sought to stay out of the Anglo-French rivalry by coming to terms with both these states. Having been France's ally in the past, he sought in addition to negotiate a treaty with England. England—seeking to protect her North German client state of Hanover—willingly signed a neutrality accord with Prussia (the Convention of Westminster) in January 1756. Frederick had no intention of repudiating his friendship with France, but to the

French—who had not been informed in advance of these negotiations—the Convention of Westminster appeared as an affront if not an actual betrayal. Such accords with France's mortal enemy England seemed an unscrupulous act by an untrustworthy ally. Hence France overreacted, turned against Prussia, and thus fell into Kaunitz's design. Russia too assumed a more militant anti-Prussian position since it considered the Convention of Westminster a betrayal by *its* supposed ally England. English bribes and diplomacy could no longer keep Russia from actively joining Austria to plan Prussia's dismemberment.

Fearing encirclement, Frederick gambled on launching a preventive war through Saxony in 1756 to break apart the coalition. Although he easily conquered the duchy—the gateway to Hapsburg Bohemia—his plan backfired, for it now activated the coalition that he dreaded. Both Russia and France met their commitments to Austria, and a grand offensive design against Prussia took final shape. Poorly led, France in effect put her army at Austria's disposal for Austrian objectives.

For a time Frederick showed his genius as a general and prevailed over the coalition. His forces achieved a spectacular victory at Rossbach, Saxony, in October 1757 over a much larger combined French-Austrian army. Skillful tactics and daring surprise movements would bring other victories, but strategically the Prussian position was shaky. Frederick had to dash in all directions across his provinces to repel a variety of invading armies whose combined strength far exceeded his own. Each successive year of the war, he faced the prospect of Russian attacks on Brandenburg in the north and Austrian thrusts from the south through Silesia and Saxony. Disaster was avoided mainly because of Russia's policy of evacuating for winter quarters back east regardless of her gains, but even so the Russians occupied Berlin. On the verge of exhaustion, Prussia at best seemed to face

a stalemate with a considerable loss of territory; at worst the war could continue and bring about a total Prussian collapse. But then again all the powers were war-weary, and his enemies were extremely distrustful of each other by now.

Frederick was plucked from the jaws of despair by one of those sudden changes of reign that commonly caused dramatic reversals of policy in Europe. In January 1762 his nemesis Empress Elizabeth died and was replaced temporarily by Tsar Peter III, a fanatic admirer of Frederick. He quickly pulled Russia out of the war and returned Frederick's conquered eastern domains of Prussia and Pomerania. Kaunitz's dream collapsed. At the same time the belligerent British minister Pitt was replaced by the more pacific John Stuart, earl of Bute, clearing the way for an Anglo-French settlement that did not insist on the punishment of Prussia.

The actual terms of the Peace of Hubertusburg (1763), settling the Continental phase of the midcentury conflagration, were therefore surprisingly favorable to Prussia in view of all that had happened. Saxony was returned to its elector, but no compensation was demanded from Prussia for the devastation she had inflicted on the duchy. Silesia was recognized as Prussian by the Austrians. In short the status quo was restored. Frederick could return to Berlin, his dominion preserved. He had marshaled all the state's resources to maintain his army in the field, and this army alone had assured the survival of his state.

MOUNTING COLONIAL CONFLICTS

In the New World, rival French and British colonies had been developing along complementary lines, and both groups were prospering. The thirteen British colonies on the North American continent were experiencing a remarkable growth because of continuous immigration and natural reproduction, reaching a population of about 1.5 million by midcentury. While some pushed the frontier westward and put the soil under cultivation, others clustered around the original settlements, a few of which could by then be called cities.[3] The extension of the frontier and the growth of towns helped impart a particular vitality to the British colonial world in contrast to which New France appeared less dynamic. Since there was little enthusiasm for emigration to Louisiana or Canada, the French remained thinly spread in their substantial territories. Yet their colonies were well organized, profitable, and vigorous in their own way. Indeed French West Indian planters were able to underprice the sugar of their British competitors, and the French trading company in India was initially more effective than its British rival in expanding operations.

While French fishermen and fur traders prospered in Canada, French soldiers established a series of strongholds to support them. These included Fort Louisburg—the greatest bastion of military strength in North America —at the entrance of the Gulf of St. Lawrence and a string of forts near the Great Lakes that served as bridgeheads for French fur traders and as a security buffer for the province of Quebec (see Map 18.4). At the other end of the continent, in Louisiana, New Orleans was established to open the far end of the Mississippi River to trade. During the War of the Austrian Succession, several skirmishes were fought in the New World, but both sides were agreeable to a restitution of captured territories at the peace table, which the Treaty of Aix-la-Chapelle arranged. Obviously this was a truce, not a peace.

On the contrary imperial rivalry intensified and military preparations increased. France reinforced Louisburg, and the British established their first large military base in North America at nearby Halifax, Nova Scotia. The fishing grounds and waterways of the St. Lawrence gulf would be a major scene of contention in any future war. A second area that now loomed into prominence was the unsettled Ohio valley. Pushing south from their Great Lakes trading forts and north from their posts on the Mississippi, the French began to assume control over that wilderness. A new string of forts formed pivots for potential French domination of the whole area between the Appalachian Mountains and the Mississippi —territory claimed and coveted by British subjects in the thirteen colonies. The threat grew that the French could completely cut off the westward expansion of these colonies. Conversely the French feared that British domination in the Ohio valley would lead to encroachments on Canadian territory.

In this jockeying for position, the allegiance of the Indians was vital, and the French gradually gained the upper hand. Being traders only and not settlers, the French did not force the Indians from their native hunting grounds as the British had done repeatedly. Hence the Indians were willing to cooperate in sealing off the Ohio valley. A large land investment company called the Ohio Company of Virginia was most directly affected by this development, and in 1754 it attempted to break the French and Indian hold by sending an expedition against Fort Duquesne. Led by a young militiaman named George Washington, the expedition failed.

Thus, contrary to the British tradition of letting settled colonies pay for themselves, the home government was compelled to shoulder the burden of defense. An expedition of regulars was sent to do the job that George Washington could not. But it too met defeat in an ambush by experienced French and Indian skirmishers. Limited engagements were now giving way to a full-scale war. Each side began to reinforce its garrisons and naval squad-

---

[3] With a population of about 23,000 in 1760, for example, Philadelphia could scarcely be considered a colonial outpost. Commercially and socially (if not culturally) it was a city.

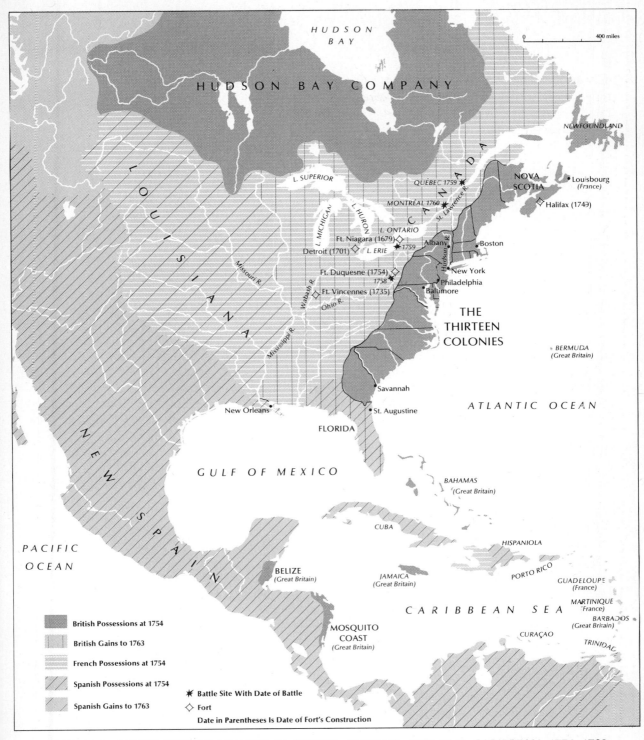

HUDSON
BAY

HUDSON BAY COMPANY

NEWFOUNDLAND

0   400 miles

L. SUPERIOR

QUÉBEC 1759

NOVA
SCOTIA

Louisbourg
(France)

MONTRÉAL 1760

Halifax (1749)

L. MICHIGAN

L. HURON

C
A
N
A
D
A

St. Lawrence R.

L. ONTARIO

Ft. Niagara (1679)

Albany

Boston

Detroit (1701)

L. ERIE

1759

New York

Missouri R.

Wabash R.

Ft. Duquesne (1754)

1758

Philadelphia

Baltimore

L
O
U
I
S
I
A
N
A

Ft. Vincennes (1735)

Ohio R.

THE
THIRTEEN
COLONIES

BERMUDA
(Great Britain)

Mississippi R.

ATLANTIC OCEAN

N
E
W

Savannah

New Orleans

St. Augustine

FLORIDA

GULF OF MEXICO

BAHAMAS
(Great Britain)

PACIFIC

OCEAN

CUBA

HISPANIOLA

S
P
A
I
N

BELIZE
(Great Britain)

JAMAICA
(Great Britain)

PORTO RICO

GUADELOUPE
(France)

MARTINIQUE
(France)

CARIBBEAN   SEA

BARBADOS
(Great Britain)

CURAÇAO

TRINIDAD

MOSQUITO
COAST
(Great Britain)

British Possessions at 1754

British Gains to 1763

French Possessions at 1754

Spanish Possessions at 1754

Spanish Gains to 1763

✳ Battle Site With Date of Battle

◇ Fort

Date in Parentheses Is Date of Fort's Construction

MAP 18.4: ANGLO-FRENCH RIVALRY IN NORTH AMERICA AND THE CARIBBEAN 1754–1763

rons. In May 1756, after some two years of unofficial hostilities, war was formally declared between Britain and France. The French and Indian War, as this arc of the Great War for Empire was called in the colonies, originated as a contest to decide the balance of power in the New World, and it remained that throughout.[4]

THE GREAT WAR FOR EMPIRE

The midcentury conflagration was to be one of Britain's high moments in history, the stuff of patriotic legends and national self-glorification. The Great War for Empire started, however, in quite another fashion. Jumping to the initiative on several fronts, the better-coordinated French struck the first blows. Calcutta, the Mediterranean island of Minorca, and several key British forts on the Great Lakes all fell, while in Europe the British expeditionary force suffered defeat and humiliation. Yet the French had certain inherent disadvantages that were to show in the long run. Spread so thinly in North America, they would be hard put to follow early success in the French and Indian War with staying power. More important, France was dependent on naval support to reinforce, supply, and move her troops; unfortunately for her, what had been a fairly even match in the 1740s turned into clear British superiority in the 1750s, with British ships of the line outnumbering French almost two to one. When William Pitt became de facto prime minister in 1758, the tide was about to turn.

Pitt brought single-mindedness, clarity of focus, and vigor to his task. Although honoring Britain's commitment to Prussia, he attached highest priority to defeating Bourbon France in the New World. His strategy for achieving this involved an immediate series of offensives and an imaginative use of the British navy. He assigned the largest segment of the British fleet to cover the French home fleet, and he waited.

The French hoped to invade the British Isles as the surest method of bringing the enemy to the peace table, and the French fleet was ordered to prepare the way. In 1759 major battles were joined between French squadrons from Brest and Toulon and the British ships assigned to cover them; the French fleet was decimated and the fate of empires decided. Henceforth the British had an almost free hand at sea. Not only were they now immune from French invasion, but they could prevent France from utilizing her superior military forces in the colonial world. Unable to transport men and supplies, she could no longer reinforce her garrisons. Unable to match the tactical assaults of British ships, she could not repel amphibious landings. In every theater of war, French colonial possessions were now falling thanks to British naval supremacy.

In the French and Indian War, for example, General James Wolfe defeated General Louis Joseph Montcalm in the battle of Quebec in September 1759. Had the French been able to reinforce Montreal, which they still held, they could have launched a counterattack against Wolfe's overextended lines. Here Pitt's strategy triumphed, since it was now precisely impossible for the French to reinforce overseas garrisons. By September 1760 this last outpost of French power in North America capitulated to the British, who had already ousted the French from the Ohio valley and the Great Lakes area. The same pattern unfolded in Africa and India. And in the West

---

[4] The classic treatment of Anglo-French rivalry in North America was written by the nineteenth-century American romantic historian Francis Parkman. See S. E. Morison (ed.), *The Parkman Reader* (1955), for a convenient selection of his writings.

THE
IMAGE
OF
MAN
IN 17TH AND 18TH CENTURY ART

The art of the time span that concerns us here—from about 1600 to the French Revolution —is designated by two awkward terms: Baroque and Rococo. They were coined at the end of the eighteenth century by advocates of the "Greek Revival" to mock the style of the previous two hundred years as bombastic, overblown, and artificial. A residue of their original negative flavor still clings to these terms today, and some scholars hesitate to use them on the ground that not all art of the seventeenth century is Baroque nor all of the eighteenth Rococo. We can sympathize with their dilemma; what does Caravaggio (Plate 33) have in common with Rubens (Plate 37), Frans Hals (Plate 39) with Poussin (Plate 43), or Tiepolo (Plate 36) with Watteau (Plate 44)? The contrasts are indeed astonishing. But earlier periods encompass a similar range of styles—compare, for example, Plates 9 and 10 or 21 and 23—yet this does not discourage us from calling them Medieval or Renaissance. The difficulty in the case of Baroque and Rococo is that, unlike Medieval and Renaissance, which refer to entire phases of Western civilization, these terms were invented specifically for art criticism and thus had a much narrower meaning from the start. In present-day use the meaning has broadened a good deal and its negative implication lessened, although we still do not speak of Baroque thought or Baroque society the way we do of Medieval thought or Renaissance society. Such terms, it seems, have a life of their own; once they have won general acceptance they are as difficult to replace as they are to do without. On the other hand, the very fact that we have no satisfactory name for the civilization of the seventeenth and eighteenth centuries tells us something about the character of this period, or at least about our perception of it: we see it, and its art, as no-longer-Renaissance and not-yet-Modern, rather than as a clear-cut entity in its own right.

It is no surprise, therefore, to encounter the same double aspect in the Baroque image of man. For the first time since recorded history began, the human form is no longer taken for granted as every artist's central concern; landscape and still life—where the presence of man is either incidental or merely implied—emerge as important subjects in painting. Man, if he (or she) happens to be an absolute sovereign claiming rule by divine right, may be glorified more than ever, but only at the risk of drowning in the allegorical apparatus (as does Marie de' Medici in Plate 37). Tiepolo (Plate 36) needs all the gods of Olympus to sing the praises of his patron, the Prince-Bishop, yet the ostensible center of all his splendid display is no more than a portrait medallion that has been pushed off to one side to make room for the soaring deities. At the other end of the scale, the image of man now includes the poor of this earth. They may be manifestations of the divine presence, as in Caravaggio (Plate 33), or they may be endowed with a dignity of suffering (as in Louis Le Nain's "Peasant Family," Plate 42) that seems to anticipate the social conscience of the nineteenth century (compare Plate 57). Whatever his station, man more often than not is shown as acted upon rather than acting, subject to forces beyond his control. The figures in Guercino's or Tiepolo's ceiling frescoes (Plates 34 and 36) are carried along by an overpowering stream of movement; Bernini's "St. Theresa" (Plate 35) is borne aloft semiconscious on a cloud as the angel of divine love prepares to pierce her heart. Even David's murdered "Marat" (Plate 46) must be understood as a secular successor of martyred Baroque saints, no less than Goya's Madrileños (Plate 48). Rembrandt, as seen by himself in old age (Plate 40), reflects a lifetime of troubled self-scrutiny. Watteau's "Gilles" (Plate 44) stands very still so that we may sense the pathos of his role as the universal butt of his fellow players' pranks. The fleeting form of Vermeer's "Girl with the Red Hat" (Plate 41) seems forever suspended in a beam of light, as does the assembled company in Velázquez's "Maids of Honor" (Plate 38). The spirited "Bathers" of Fragonard (Plate 45) share the weightlessness of the floating figures in Tiepolo's ceiling (Plate 36); they are buoyed up, and tossed back and forth, by the same irresistible currents we observe in Guercino's "Aurora" and Bernini's "St. Theresa" (Plates 34 and 35) although separated from them by more than a century.

Baroque art, then, in contrast to that of the Early and High Renaissance, no longer accepts the humanists' vision of man as the master of his own fate. Its image of man is contingent on three factors that govern man no less than they do the rest of the natural world—the flow of time, the flow of light, and the flow of motion. We sense them in Caravaggio's "Calling of St. Matthew" (Plate 33), at the very beginning of the period; light here is an active force that permits the artist to seize the most dramatic moment: Christ has just moved out of the shadows into the path of the beam illuminating his face and hand, and Matthew realizes he is being called but does not yet grasp the full meaning of the divine command. Thirty years later, in "The Jolly Toper" of Frans Hals (Plate 39), the subject is caught as he might have been by a modern camera, with the artist's dashing, open brush strokes recording a race against time. Vermeer's "Girl with the Red Hat" (Plate 41) has an equally casual pose, but we are now asked to observe not the movement of the figure but the movement of light, which settles on the surfaces in the picture like a rain of tiny droplets of color so that everything looks slightly "out of focus." Vermeer, fascinated by optical phenomena, may well have observed this effect by viewing his subject through a camera obscura, a device then in use that resembled a present-day camera but projected its images onto a translucent screen rather than a piece of light-sensitive film—one of the byproducts of the age that invented the telescope and microscope.

The use of the camera obscura by Vermeer and other painters makes us wonder how the image of man in Baroque art might be related to the scientific thought of the period. This, after all, was the first age to acknowledge that the earth was not the center of the universe but merely a planet revolving around the sun; could so shattering an insight have remained without effect on art? Was it coincidence that the great scientists of these two centuries, from Galileo to Newton, were concerned with problems of time, light, and motion (though surely not in the same way as the artists)? Having noted the parallel, we must confess that so far we are unable to establish any real links. In the Renaissance, an artist could be a humanist and a scientist as well, but now science and philosophy had become too complex, abstract, and systematic for artists to share; gravitation did not kindle their imagination any more than did calculus or Descartes's "I think, therefore I am." Still, artists and scientists (or "natural philosophers" as they were then called) could have expressed the same basic world view without necessarily being aware of each other.

Be that as it may, Baroque art had one thing in common with science: an internationalism that respected neither creeds nor national boundaries. Caravaggio had a greater impact in Catholic Spain and Protestant Holland than he did at home. Tiepolo, the Venetian, produced his largest works in Würzburg and Madrid. Poussin spent almost his entire adult life in Rome, yet his style became the acknowledged ideal of the French Royal Academy of Painting. Rubens worked in Italy for eight years and could have had as successful a career there as he did in Antwerp. Even Rembrandt, who never crossed the Alps, had admirers in Italy and in turn admired Italian art. It had taken the rest of Europe two centuries to absorb the achievements of Italian Renaissance art; the Baroque, in contrast, was an international style almost from the beginning. In this respect, too, it paved the way for the Modern era.

At the end of the sixteenth century Rome once again became the artistic capital of Europe. Now that the Catholic faith had weathered the storm of the Reformation, popes could resume the task their predecessors had set themselves a hundred years earlier: to make Rome the most beautiful city of the Christian world. The ambitious young artists they attracted soon replaced the waning tradition of Mannerism with a dynamic new style, the Baroque.

The greatest of these was Caravaggio, who coined a radically new image of man to fit the new era. In this respect, his *Calling of St. Matthew* is comparable to Michelangelo's *Creation of Adam* (Plate 24). Both are confrontations of Man and God, but the meeting now takes place in a common Roman tavern, and God has descended to man's everyday world. Matthew points questioningly at himself as two figures approach from the right. They are poor people, their bare feet and simple garments contrasting strongly with the colorful costumes of Matthew and his companions. What identifies one of the two as Christ? It is mainly his commanding gesture, borrowed from the Lord in Michelangelo's fresco and made even more emphatic by the strong beam of light that illuminates the Saviour's face and hand, thus carrying his call across to Matthew. Without this light, we would not be aware of the divine presence. Caravaggio here gives moving, direct form to an attitude no less appealing to Protestants than to Catholics—that the mysteries of faith are revealed not by intellectual speculation but spontaneously, through an inward experience open to all men.

Plate 33. Caravaggio
THE CALLING OF ST. MATTHEW
ca. 1597–1598, canvas, height 11'1"
S. Luigi dei Francesi, Rome

Plate 34. Guercino
AURORA (*ceiling*)
1621–1623, wall painting
Villa Ludovisi, Rome

Caravaggio's work, although acclaimed by artists and connoisseurs, never was widely popular in Italy. The simple people resented meeting their likes in his canvases, and the sophisticated objected to them as lacking propriety and reverence. They preferred the style exemplified in Plates 34 and 35: dynamic, illusionistic, rhetorical, spectacular in its appeal to the beholder's emotions. The *Aurora* of Guercino covers the ceiling of the main room in an aristocratic villa, but similar sweeping visions were soon to appear on the ceilings of countless churches. Through a cunning use of perspective, the walls of the room continue upward in the fresco, so that we cannot tell where the real architecture leaves off and the painted illusion begins. They leave an opening for the morning sky; Aurora, the personification of Dawn, rushes across it in her chariot drawn by dappled horses, driving the shadows of night before her. In another context, the scene might be a saint carried to heaven or a triumphant allegory of faith. If Guercino's invention strikes us as theatrical, we must keep in mind that this was the time that created the opera, a new, compound art form, and similar scenes were actually presented on the stage.

Bernini, the greatest Baroque sculptor, was also deeply involved with the world of the theater, both as a designer and a playwright. His *Ecstasy of St. Theresa* is "staged" with consummate skill. Housed in an architectural frame that has the function of a proscenium arch, the group occupies a space that is real but beyond our reach. Theresa of Avila, one of the important saints of the Counter-Reformation, had described how an angel pierced her heart with a flaming golden arrow: "The pain was so great that I screamed aloud, but at the same time I felt such infinite sweetness that I wished the pain to last forever. It was not physical but psychic pain, although it affected the body as well to some degree. It was the sweetest caressing of the soul by God." Bernini has made this visionary experience sensuously real—the angel is indistinguishable from Cupid, and the saint's ecstasy is palpably physical. Yet the two figures on their floating cloud are illuminated (from a hidden window above) in such a way that they seem almost dematerialized in their gleaming whiteness. Their visionary character is further reinforced by the stream of golden rays, which balances the heavenly wind that carries the figures heavenward, causing the turbulence of their drapery. It is hard to imagine a greater contrast than that between Bernini's group and another meeting of saint and angel, Donatello's *Annunciation* (Plate 17) carved two hundred years before, so gently human and the very opposite of theatrical. Yet it was the earlier master who ultimately made Bernini's achievement possible.

Plate 35. Gianlorenzo Bernini
THE ECSTASY OF ST. THERESA
1645–1652, marble, lifesize
Sta. Maria della Vittoria, Rome

These two paintings, however different they may be in other respects, are linked by a common purpose—the glorification of a sovereign. In the age of absolutism, great kings as well as petty rulers insisted that they embodied the power of the state by the will of God, and their desire to see themselves depicted in this superhuman role provided the artists of the period with many splendid commissions, especially in the Catholic parts of Europe. Such a task fell to Rubens when the great Flemish master, at the height of his career, was asked to produce a cycle of large pictures for the Luxembourg Palace in Paris celebrating the life of Marie de' Medici, the widow of King Henry IV and mother of Louis XIII. Plate 37 shows the artist's oil sketch for one episode, the young queen arriving on French soil after a sea voyage from Italy. Hardly an exciting subject, yet Rubens has turned it into a spectacle of drama and splendor. As Marie walks down the gangplank, Fame flies overhead sounding a triumphant blast on two trumpets, and Neptune rises from the sea with his fish-tailed crew to steady the ship and to rejoice at the queen's safe arrival, while other classical deities welcome her ashore. Everything flows together here in swirling movement: heaven and earth, history and allegory—even drawing and painting, for Rubens used oil sketches such as this one to prepare his compositions, leaving the execution of the final version mostly to his assistants. Unlike earlier artists, he liked to design his pictures in terms of light and color from the very start (most of his drawings are figure studies or portrait sketches). This unified vision was Rubens's most precious legacy to later painters.

A century and a quarter after Rubens, the Venetian painter Tiepolo faced a similar assignment in the newly completed palace of the Prince-Bishop of Würzburg in Central Germany. Here we see the last and most refined stage of illusionistic ceiling decoration represented by its greatest master, whose grace and felicity of touch had made him famous far beyond his homeland. Tiepolo's ceiling fresco in the Grand Staircase is so huge that Plate 36 shows only about a quarter of the total area. Unlike Guercino (compare Plate 34), Tiepolo no longer depends on a foreshortened architectural framework to create the necessary sense of distance between the beholder and the heavenly vision above; his illusion is achieved mainly by contrasts of light and color. Solid clusters of figures along the edges of the ceiling, larger and more strongly modeled, served to make those soaring amid the blue sky and sunlit clouds in the center seem infinitely farther away. Who they all are and how they relate to the Prince-Bishop (who is present only as a portrait medallion, not visible in our plate) is a question we are not likely to ask as we admire this celestial pageant.

Plate 37. Peter Paul Rubens
MARIE DE' MEDICI LANDING IN MARSEILLES
1622–1623, wood panel, height 25"
Alte Pinakothek, Munich

Plate 38. Diego Velázquez
THE MAIDS OF HONOR
ca. 1656, canvas, height 10′5″
Prado Museum, Madrid

Although the bulk of his work consists of portraits—mostly of the Spanish royal family and members of the court—Velázquez began his career as a painter of scenes of everyday life under the strong influence of Caravaggio. He admired the Italian master's sympathy for the common people and his handling of light, but did not share his interest in dramatic action. When, still in his twenties, Velázquez moved from his native Seville to Madrid, he was befriended by Rubens, who may have helped him to see the beauty of the numerous paintings by Titian in the king's collection (compare Plate 25). He also traveled in Italy. All these experiences are reflected in *The Maids of Honor,* painted at the height of his career. A more suitable title might be "The Painter in His Studio," for Velázquez shows himself at work on a huge canvas that juts into the picture on the left; in the center is the little Princess Margarita, who has been posing for him, among her playmates and maids of honor, which include a large dog and a dwarf. This foreground group is caught in the bright light streaming into the room from an unseen window on the right. Two other figures, a bit farther back, are less clearly seen in the shadowy, high-ceilinged gallery; in the rear a courtier, brilliantly illuminated, is framed by an open door. Evidently, something has interrupted the painting session, and most of the figures are turning to look at the beholder: an unobtrusive but commanding presence makes itself felt. What could it be? The solution, it seems, is the bright rectangle above the head of the princess, which must be a mirror rather than a painting: in it, we see two heads, those of the King and Queen.

Have they just stepped into the room, to see the scene exactly as we do? Or does the mirror reflect part of the canvas—presumably a full-length group portrait of the royal family—on which the artist has been working? Be that as it may, the painting reveals Velázquez's fascination with the action of light, which seems infinitely more varied and dramatic than the action of the figures. His rich, fluid brushwork renders the full range of its effects on shape, color, and texture, from the sparkling highlights on the princess's hair and dress to the dimly perceived canvases in the background. For Velázquez, light *creates* the visible world. No wonder that the pioneers of Impressionism two hundred years later considered him the most "modern" of seventeenth-century painters.

Frans Hals, half a generation older than Velázquez, was born in Antwerp but as a young man moved to Haarlem in the newly independent northern part of the Netherlands, where he became a portrait painter as renowned as Velázquez was in Spain. He too divided his attention between portraiture and scenes of everyday life and owed an essential debt to the influence of Caravaggio. *The Jolly Toper* is surely a portrait, but Hals seems far less concerned with the sitter's individual personality than with the effect of the picture as an "action shot"—everything is tilted, from the huge hat that frames the face like a black halo to the wine glass in the sitter's left hand, thus conveying instability and transitory movement. The brushwork itself is open and lightning-quick, each stroke so clearly separate that we are tempted to count the total number. Caravaggio's sense of the "fruitful moment" here becomes a split-second race against time.

Plate 39. Frans Hals
THE JOLLY TOPER
1627, canvas, height 32"
Rijksmuseum, Amsterdam

Plate 40. Rembrandt
SELF-PORTRAIT WITH PALETTE
1660, canvas, height 44½"
Louvre Museum, Paris

Rembrandt, the greatest genius of Dutch art, is one of a small company of artists (Leonardo da Vinci, Michelangelo, and Van Gogh are others) whose popular fame as legendary figures distorts or obscures their true achievement. He has been the subject (or better perhaps, the victim) of many fictionalized biographies that present him as a "glorious failure," deserted in mid-career by a fickle public and plunged into poverty and neglect. Actually Rembrandt's fortunes during his later years declined far less catastrophically than his romantic admirers have claimed. He retained important patrons and received some major public commissions even toward the end of his life. It is true, however, that his work from the mid-1620s to the early 1640s, with its emphasis on dramatic display, differs markedly from that of the 1650s and 1660s, which is gently lyrical and introspective. The change reflects the maturing of a powerful personality. Nowhere is this process of growth recorded more completely than in the artist's numerous self-portraits (he produced more than sixty), culminating in the self-analytical frankness and simple dignity of those he did during his final years. In the example shown in Plate 40, we see him standing at his easel, palette and brushes in hand; he gazes at the beholder (or rather, at himself) with a look, sad and tender at the same time, that seems to convey an entire lifetime's experience of thought and feeling. What makes this revelation of character possible is the magic glow of Rembrandt's light, which filters into the picture space quietly from the upper left, endowing the artist's features with their strange mute eloquence. Unlike Velázquez, Rembrandt here explores the metaphysical and expressive rather than the optical aspects of the element that

Caravaggio had introduced into Western painting as an active force.

Rembrandt was unique among the Dutch painters of his time not only for his depth of human insight but for the wide range of his subjects, which included biblical and mythological themes, landscapes, scenes of daily life, portraiture, and still lifes. Most seventeenth-century painters tended to specialize, and more so in Holland than elsewhere because of the pressure of competition. Dutch artists had to rely on private collectors rather than state or church as their chief source of support. Many of them produced "for the market," and dealing in pictures became an important trade that followed the law of supply and demand. Since the market reflects the dominant, not the most discerning, taste of the time, it could happen that some artists whom we now regard as mediocre were over-priced while others, highly esteemed today, were undervalued. The most astonishing instance of this is Vermeer, whose genius seems to us second only to Rembrandt's but who was almost forgotten until a century ago. His specialty was domestic interiors, with one or two figures, usually women, engaged in quiet everyday tasks; he also did occasional outdoors views and portraits. Some pictures, such as *The Girl with the Red Hat,* leave us in doubt: is it a portrait or a figure study? The same question arises when we look at Hals's *Jolly Toper* (Plate 39). In every other respect, however, the two canvases offer a fascinating contrast. If Vermeer is akin to any other painter of his time, it is neither Hals nor Rembrandt but Velázquez; even more than the great Spaniard, he concentrates on the optical properties of light and color. Yet the jewel-like freshness of his vision suggests that his true progenitor is Jan van Eyck (see Plate 18).

Plate 41. Jan Vermeer
THE GIRL WITH THE RED HAT
ca. 1660, canvas, height 9"
National Gallery of Art
Andrew W. Mellon Collection
Washington, D.C.

Plate 42. Louis Le Nain
PEASANT FAMILY
ca. 1640, canvas, height 44½"
Louvre Museum, Paris

That the two pictures reproduced on these pages should both have been painted by Frenchmen born within a year of each other seems almost incredible. It attests not only the extraordinary diversity of Baroque art within a single country but the intermediate position of France between North and South. Louis Le Nain, although strongly indebted to Caravaggio, is even more closely linked with the Netherlandish tradition of realism stemming from Jan van Eyck and continued by Pieter Bruegel. Poussin, in contrast, is a classicist whose sources of inspiration are Titian (compare Plate 25), the Roman High Renaissance masters, and the world of antiquity. His style was formed in Rome, where he spent almost his entire adult life, yet his patrons and his influence were largely in France. He is the father of what was to become known as the "grand manner" in painting, based on firmly held theoretical ideas about the aim of art which he expounded in his voluminous correspondence. As his starting point he took the ancient dictum that "painting is mute poetry"; like the poet, the painter must strive to elevate the mind of his audience by dealing with noble and serious themes. He will reach his goal only if he suppresses the imperfections of nature-in-the-raw and depicts instead an ideal world of nature perfected. Nor must he give too much importance to color, lest he cater to sensuous pleasure instead of appealing to man's moral impulses. Logic and order, clarity of form and composition, are to be of primary importance. In Poussin's own work such as *The Inspiration of the Epic Poet,* this prescription could yield canvases of extraordinary beauty. Others, who fol-

lowed in his footsteps and took over his formula ready-made, were less successful. There were to be a great many of them, for Poussin's doctrines became the official program of the French Royal Academy of Painting and Sculpture, founded under Louis XIV to foster a single "approved" style. It, in turn, was the model for countless similar academies in the other countries of Europe, so that "Poussinism" survived until close to the end of the nineteenth century as the ideal of conservative, state-sponsored artists.

Plate 43. Nicolas Poussin
THE INSPIRATION OF THE EPIC POET
ca. 1628, canvas, height 6'
Louvre Museum, Paris

Plate 44. Antoine Watteau
GILLES
ca. 1717, canvas, height 6'
Louvre Museum, Paris

In France, the power of the Royal Academy to enforce "Poussinism" remained unchallenged for almost half a century. During the final years of Louis XIV's long reign, however, there appeared signs of an internal revolt, led by a faction that declared its allegiance to the style of Rubens (exemplified by such pictures as our Plate 37). These "Rubenists" advocated color rather than drawing as being more true to nature and appealing to everyone, while drawing can be appreciated only by the expert few. Their argument had revolutionary implications, for it made the layman the ultimate judge of artistic values ("I don't know anything about art, but I know what I like"). The final triumph of the "Rubenists" came in 1717 with the admission to the Academy of Antoine Watteau, whose pictures violated all official canons; instead of noble and elevating themes, they depicted, in a superbly elegant and sensuous style, scenes of refined society or of comedy actors in parklike settings. Often Watteau interweaves theater and real life so that no clear distinction can be made between the two. In his *Gilles* (Plate 44) the central figure is a stock character of the French comedy stage, a kind of "straight man" who invariably becomes the victim of pranks and comic misfortunes. In his awkward white satin costume, he stands isolated from the gay throng behind him, seemingly impassive yet suffering in silent agony. If Watteau's actors lack the robust vitality of Rubens, they play their roles so well that they touch us as if they were real-life characters.

Plate 45. Jean-Honoré Fragonard
BATHERS
ca. 1765, canvas, height 25"
Louvre Museum, Paris

The victory of the "Rubenists" signaled a shift in French art and French society. After the death of Louis XIV, the power of the absolute monarchy declined and with it the art patronage of the state, so that artists came to depend increasingly on private patrons. That the latter preferred Watteau to the disciples of Poussin is hardly surprising; it was they who sponsored what later was derisively termed the Rococo, an intimate, sensuous style uninhibited by classicistic doctrines. Watteau, who died at the early age of 37, had a great many followers, although none had the emotional depth that distinguishes his art.

The last, and finest, among these is Fragonard, who painted the *Bathers* (Plate 45): his brushwork has a fluid breadth and spontaneity reminiscent of Rubens's oil sketches (compare Plate 37), and his figures move with a floating grace that also links him with Tiepolo (see Plate 36), whose work he had admired in Italy. Fragonard had the misfortune to outlive his era. After the French Revolution, he was reduced to poverty and died forgotten, in the heyday of Napoleon, when classicism, and with it the doctrines of Poussin, had once more become the order of the day.

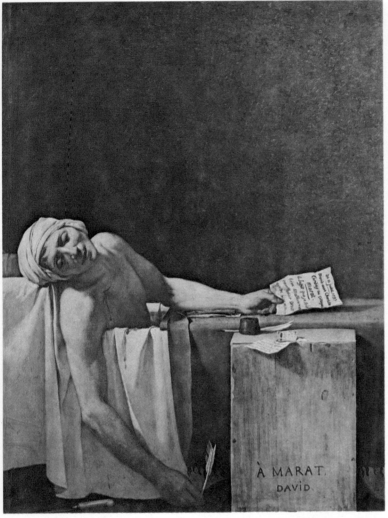

Plate 46. Jacques Louis David
THE DEATH OF MARAT
1792, canvas, height 65"
Royal Museums of Fine Arts, Brussels

The third quarter of the eighteenth century saw a gradual turning of the tide throughout European art. While Tiepolo and Fragonard were creating the last masterpieces of the Rococo, there was a growing reaction, in the name of Reason and Nature, against Baroque "artificiality." These two concepts had been proclaimed as supreme values by the thinkers of the Enlightenment; in art, they signaled a return to the doctrines of Poussin and a new admiration for the "noble simplicity and calm grandeur" of the Greeks (in the famous phrase of Johann Winckelmann, the influential German archaeologist and critic). Rome was the birthplace of this Neoclassic style, although its leading early protagonists were visitors from the north rather than Italians. It was there that Jacques Louis David, a highly gifted young French painter trained in the Rococo tradition, became a convert to the new style. After his return to Paris, David's artistic conversion became a political one as well: he passionately espoused the revolutionary ideas of the Enlightenment and, in 1789, the Revolution itself. At the height of the struggle, he painted his greatest picture, *The Death of Marat* (Plate 46). David's deep emotion has made a masterpiece from a subject that would have embarrassed any lesser artist, for Marat, one of the political leaders of the Revolution, had been murdered in his bathtub. A painful skin disease caused him to do his paperwork there, with a wooden board serving as his desk. One day a young woman named Charlotte Corday burst in with a petition and plunged a knife into him while he read it. David has composed the scene with awe-inspiring starkness as a public memorial to the martyred hero: it is Neoclassic in the clarity and simplicity of the forms and in the way the principal planes are arranged to parallel the picture surface, but the Neoclassic ideal of Nature Perfected is not in evidence. David must have realized that it could not help him achieve his purpose—to produce a historic account that was also a moving devotional image. For that he had to revert to the Caravaggio tradition of religious art, with its realism and dramatic lighting (compare Plate 33).

A few years later David became an ardent admirer of Napoleon. He was to produce several large pictures glorifying the emperor, but a favorite pupil, Antoine-Jean Gros, eclipsed him as the chief painter of the Napoleonic myth. Gros's first portrait of the great general shows him leading his troops at the battle of Arcole in northern Italy (Plate 47). It conveys Napoleon's magic as an irresistible "man of destiny" with an enthusiasm David could never match. Much as Gros respected his teacher's doctrines, his emotional nature impelled him toward the color and drama of the Baroque: hence the stormy sky, the spiral movement of the flag, the hero's disheveled, streaming hair, the violent turn of his body, the dynamic open brushwork—all of them devices of "visual rhetoric" that carry us back to Rubens (see Plate 37).

Plate 47. Antoine-Jean Gros
NAPOLEON AT ARCOLE
1796, canvas, height 29½"
Louvre Museum, Paris

Plate 48. Francisco Goya
THE THIRD OF MAY, 1808
1814–1815, canvas, height 8'9"
Prado Museum, Madrid

If Gros's *Napoleon at Arcole* may be termed Neo-Baroque, the same is true even more emphatically of Goya's *The Third of May, 1808* (Plate 48). But the great Spanish painter had never been a Neoclassicist. His early works are in a delightful late Rococo vein. During the 1780s he came to sympathize with the Enlightenment and the French Revolution. He now abandoned the Rococo for a Neo-Baroque style based on Velázquez and Rembrandt, the masters of the previous century he admired most. When Napoleon's armies occupied Spain in 1808, Goya and many of his countrymen hoped that the conquerors would bring the liberal reforms so badly needed, but the savage behavior of the French troops crushed these hopes and generated a popular resistance of equal savagery. *The Third of May, 1808,* commemorating the execution of a group of Madrid citizens, reflects this bitter experience. Its blazing color, fluid brushwork, and dramatic nocturnal light endow the picture with all the emotional intensity of religious art, yet these martyrs are dying for Liberty, not the Kingdom of Heaven and their executioners are not the agents of Satan but of political tyranny—a formation of faceless automatons impervious to their victims' despair and defiance. With the clairvoyance of genius, Goya has created an image that was to be reenacted countless times in modern history.

Indies the long duel between the two powers turned into a rout. One by one the French islands were seized, and even Martinique—known as the jewel of the French Empire—had fallen by 1761.

Not all these conquests were preserved at the peace table, however. In exchange for an end to fighting, a war-weary Britain was prepared to return certain colonies in the Treaty of Paris in 1763. France was willing to surrender Canada, and Britain chose to retain the territory—perhaps mistakenly: this removed the threat of French power, which it turned out had been a major factor in the loyalty of the British colonists to the mother country. Since British West Indian planters feared added competition from the possible inclusion of the French islands in the British system, the British government decided to accede to French demands for the return of several of these. In the long run India proved to be Britain's most important colonial territory. Her domination of the subcontinent began with the Treaty of Paris, which excluded French troops from the region, permitting only British influence to have any force.

But there would be momentous repercussions from the Peace of Paris. First, it created a new situation for the thirteen North American colonies, and Britain's triumph turned into disaster twenty years later when they successfully broke away, with French assistance. In addition, though France's ill-fated efforts in the Seven Years' War had strained her finances substantially, she was unable to resist the opportunity to strike back at Britain during the war for independence. Partly for this reason she contracted further debts that could not be absorbed by the monarchy in its existing form. Finally, it is well to remember that supporting the entire state structure were the slaves in the colonies and the peasants in most states, whose labor ultimately produced the revenues that paid for the navies and armies. Their bill would eventually come due in one form or another.

During the eighteenth century the effectiveness of Europe's states in marshaling their power and resources within the state system was increasingly apparent. French and English merchants demonstrated an extraordinary capacity to capitalize on the commercial opportunities afforded by overseas colonies, plantation economy, and slavery. But these traders were backed by their states, especially in the form of naval power. The growth of the British and French empires and with them of the global maritime economy of the eighteenth century was in one sense an aspect of the competitive state system.

In Central Europe direct territorial aggrandizement was the issue. Prussia, Austria, and Russia faced each other directly at war and at the negotiating table. Here helpless lesser states were sacrificed to the "reasons of state" of the great powers; most notable was Poland, whose disappearance from the map in three successive partitions must be accounted as one of the century's most important events.

All these interests clashed in the midcentury conflagration, a classic episode of competition in the European state system. The scale of fighting in the Seven Years' War was enormous. Yet the system was able to contain the massive aggression and survive the convulsion almost intact. Although Prussia had been driven to the brink of extinction, she actually lost little in the peace settlement; in the end Frederick II even retained Silesia. All in all, however, the Continental powers had proved to be well matched. The colonial phase of the hostilities, the great War for Empire, was more decisive, though here too a degree of balance was restored by Britain's concessions to France at the peace table. The significance of these outcomes will be best appreciated when contrasted later with the resulting upheaval of World War I.

RECOMMENDED READING

Sources

Edwards, Bryan. *The History, Civil and Commercial, of the British Colonies in the West Indies.* 2 vols. 1793. A contemporary account of Empire and slavery.

Luvvas, J. (ed.). *Frederick the Great on the Art of War.* 1966.

* Macartney, C. A. (ed.). *The Evolution of the Hapsburg & Hohenzollern Dynasties.* 1969. An excellent collection of documents.

Studies

* Anderson, M. S. *Europe in the Eighteenth Century, 1713–1789.* 1977. The best general survey of the period.

Barker, Ernest. *The Development of Public Services in Western Europe.* 1966.

* Beloff, Max. *The Age of Absolutism, 1660–1815.* 1966. An overview of state building and the state system.

* Cobban, Alfred. *A History of Modern France: Vol. I, 1715–1799.* 1966.

* Craton, Michael. *Sinews of Empire: A Short History of British Slavery.* 1974.

Dakin, Douglas. *Turgot and the Ancien Régime in France.* 1939. An insider's view of the problems and achievements of enlightened administration in France.

* Dehio, L. *The Precarious Balance: Four Centuries of the European Power Struggle.* 1965. An essay in the Germanic tradition of diplomatic history.

Dorn, Walter. *The Competition for Empire, 1740–63.* 1940. Despite its title, a good if old-fashioned general history.

* Genovese, Eugene. *The World the Slaveholders Made.* 1969. A Marxist analysis.

* Goodwin, A. (ed.). *The European Nobility in the 18th Century.* 1967.

Owen, John B. *The Eighteenth Century, 1714–1815.* 1974. A dry, detailed history of England.

Pares, Richard. *Yankees and Creoles: The Trade Between North America and the West Indies Before the American Revolution.* 1968.

* Parry, J. H. *Trade and Dominion: The European Overseas Empires in the Eighteenth Century.* 1971.

Pick, Robert. *Empress Maria Theresa: The Early Years.* 1966.

* Plumb, J. H. *England in the Eighteenth Century, 1714–1815.* 1950. Brief but informative.

* Ritter, Gerhard. *Frederick the Great.* 1968.

* Rosenburg, Hans. *Bureaucracy, Aristocracy, and Autocracy: The Prussian Experience, 1660–1815.* 1958. Difficult, highly conceptualized, important history.

Thompson, Gladys. *Catherine the Great and the Expansion of Russia.* 1962.

* Wangermann, E. *The Austrian Achievement, 1700–1800.* 1973. A concise, suggestive synthesis with an imaginatively integrated profusion of illustrations.

---

* Available in paperback.

NINETEEN

THE AGE OF
ENLIGHTENMENT

Sharp breaks in the intellectual and cultural life of Europe have been rare. Nonetheless, taken broadly rather than as literal chronological periods, the seventeenth, eighteenth, and nineteenth centuries represent three distinct phases of Western cultural development. The seventeenth century was the towering age of genius in European thought—a period of great scientific and philosophical innovation. It was also an elitist age in terms of the audience for cultural activity and the system of aristocratic patronage. If we jump ahead to the nineteenth century we encounter a decidedly middle-class intellectual and artistic milieu as well as the beginnings of mass literacy and mass culture toward the end of the century.

Obviously then the eighteenth century is transitional. In the domain of thought it was a time when the impact of science and the growth of religious skepticism matured into a naturalistic world view. Philosophy became less metaphysical and more critically concerned with practical matters, with "enlightenment." The most important eighteenth-century thinkers were not seeking to extirpate Christianity from Western civilization, but they no longer believed in it themselves and wished to counter what they took to be its spirit of complacency and to reduce its influence in temporal affairs drastically. Intellectuals developed a strong sense of their own power to enlighten their society and point it toward change. They were reformers who—contrary to Christian belief and unlike reformers within the church—believed that there was no reality beyond human society, no afterlife to divert the spirit of man from worldly concerns. In this spirit they provided an arsenal of critical ideas, particularly the notion of social utility as a standard of value, and a preoccupation with the issue of freedom.

While they were thus critics of their society, eighteenth-century intellectuals were very much at home in and proud of European culture. Theirs was an age in which publishing activity increased explosively, in which major new literary and musical genres were developed, and in which a number of cultural trends reflected the presence of an expanding middle class in a still-aristocratic age.

I. THE ENLIGHTENMENT

The eighteenth century reworked and diffused the ideas of the seventeenth. Building on seventeenth-century science, on skepticism in matters of religion, and on a heightened appreciation of Classical antiquity, intellectuals redefined the function of philosophy. They believed that human behavior and institutions could be studied rationally, like Newton's universe, and their faults corrected. They saw themselves as participants in a movement—

the Enlightenment—that was making men and women more understanding, more tolerant, and more virtuous.

THE BROADENING REVERBERATIONS OF SCIENCE

It is hard to think of two men less revolutionary in temperament than René Descartes and Sir Isaac Newton. Writing for a small, learned audience, each was conservative on matters outside the confines of science, had relatively little concern for social relations or institutions, and was a practicing Christian. Yet their legacy to succeeding generations produced what has been described as "a permanent intellectual insurrection." Their conceptual systems—along with those of John Locke and the Dutch philosopher Baruch Spinoza—were transformed and propagated in directions and in a spirit undreamed of by their authors.

While eighteenth-century scientists pondered the details of the diverging cosmologies of Descartes and Newton, nonscientists continued the process, begun in the previous century, of applying their basic methodology to all realms of human thought. Experimentation, methodical doubt, and naturalistic explanations of phenomena were fused into a "scientific" or "mathematical spirit," which at bottom meant simply confidence in reason and a skeptical attitude toward accepted dogmas. Its advocates took upon themselves the task of popularizing science, with the aim of transforming the values of Western civilization. As part of this effort men like Bernard de Fontenelle, secretary of the French Academy of Sciences from 1699 to 1741, translated the discoveries of scientists into clear and even amusing general reading. The literary talents of these enthusiasts helped make household words out of Newton and Descartes among the educated laymen of Europe.

A more calculating and ambitious propagandist of the scientific spirit was Voltaire, the Frenchman who is virtually synonymous with the Enlightenment in all its aspects. While his chief talents lay in the realm of literature and criticism, Voltaire also spent several years studying Newton's work, and in 1738 he published a widely read popularization called *Elements of the Philosophy of Newton.* However dry the study of physics, Voltaire argued, it frees the mind from dogma, and its experimental methods provide

a model for the liberation of human thought. Moreover Voltaire situated Newton's achievement in the context of the liberal England that also produced Bacon and Locke, the three of whom Voltaire adopted as his personal Trinity. In his *Philosophical Letters on the English* (1734), a celebration of English toleration and an indirect attack on what he considered French bigotry, censorship, and social snobbery, Voltaire had already noted the popularity and respect enjoyed by British literary figures and scientists. He saw this recognition of talent and distinction as a crucial component of a free society and as necessarily related to the achievements of a man like Newton.

Popularizations of scientific method stimulated public interest in science as well as public and private support for research projects. Mathematicians, cartographers, and astronomers were direct beneficiaries of the support and made notable advances in their fields. But progress was far from linear or automatic. In chemistry for example the traditions of alchemy persisted, and such phenomena as combustion long resisted objective analysis. At the end of the century, however, a major breakthrough occurred when the Englishman Joseph Priestley isolated oxygen and the Frenchman Antoine Laurent Lavoisier analyzed the components of air and water. Lavoisier also came close to explaining the process of combustion.

The more dubious side of the vogue for science could be observed in the great popularity of mesmerism. This pseudoscience of magnetic fields purported to offer its wealthy devotees relief from a variety of ailments by the use of special "electrical" baths and treatments. Although repeatedly condemned by the authoritative studies of the Academy of Sciences in Paris, mesmerism continued to attract both the educated and the credulous.

The scientific enterprise most representative of eighteenth-century attitudes was natural history, the science of the earth's development—a combination of geology, zoology, botany, and historical geography. This field of study was easy for the layman to appreciate, which made its foremost practitioner probably the most widely acclaimed scientist of the century. He was G. L. Buffon, keeper of the French Botanical Gardens—a patronage position that allowed him to produce a multivolume *Natural History of the Earth* between 1749 and 1778. Drawing on a vast knowledge of phenomena such as fossils, Buffon went beyond previous attempts to classify the data of nature, seeking to relate and generalize from them in order to provide both a theory and a description of the earth's development. A nonbeliever himself, Buffon did not explicitly attack religious versions of such events as the Creation. He simply ignored them, an omission whose significance was obvious enough to his many readers. Similarly, while he did not specifically contend that man had evolved from beasts, he implied this, writing for example, "It is possible to descend by almost insensible degrees from the most perfect creature to the most formless matter." Buffon's earth did not derive from a singular act of divine creation that would explain the origins of man. The readers of his *History* or its numerous popularizations in several languages were thus introduced to a demystified universe that had developed through evolution. Buffon's work sharpened the thrusts of science and secularism.

THE RISE OF SECULARISM

The erosion of revealed religion as a source of authority is the hallmark of the Enlightenment. The viewpoint it engendered, secularism, derived some of its impetus from seventeenth-century scientists and liberal theologians who were themselves dedicated Christians. They had hoped to accommodate religion to new philosophical standards and scientific formulations and to eliminate the superstitious imagery that could make religion seem ridiculous. They regarded the devil for example as a category of moral evil rather than a specific horned creature with a pitchfork, and they endowed the world of nature with religious significance, perceiving it as a form of revelation in which God's majesty could be discerned. Deemphasizing miracles and focusing on reverence for the Creator and on the moral teachings of the Bible would bolster religion, they hoped. And indeed their modifications retained the adherence of many educated people to Christianity during the eighteenth century. Yet in the final analysis, this kind of thinking served to diminish the force of religion and its authority in society.

A more important source of the secular outlook was the idea of toleration as propounded by the highly respected critic Pierre Bayle. Consciously applying methodical doubt to subjects that Descartes himself had excluded from such treatment, Bayle's *Critical and Historical Dictionary* (1697) put the claims of religion to the test of critical reason. Certain Christian traditions emerged as myth and fairy tale, and historical Christianity was seen as a record of fanaticism and inhumanity. Bayle's chief target was Christianity's sectarianism and attempts (like Louis XIV's revocation of the Edict of Nantes) to impose orthodoxy at any cost. Though himself a devout Calvinist, Bayle argued for complete toleration, which would allow human beings to practice any religion or none at all. A man's moral behavior rather than his creed is what should count. Ethics do not depend on Christian revelation; a Muslim, a Confucian, a Jew, even an atheist can be a moral man.

Christianity had more vehement critics than Bayle. Atheistic and blasphemous attacks were to be found in privately circulated writings rather than published books in the first half of the century. These clandestine tracts treated revealed religion as a form of hysteria that had resulted in centuries of bloodshed. Their titles tell their messages: *Critical Examination of the Apologists of the Christian Religion, Mortal Souls, The Divinity of Jesus Christ Destroyed, Faith Destroyed.* Faith was indeed destroyed here, along with such props as miracles, priests, and divine prophets.

The Enlightenment's most unstinting antireligious polemicist was Voltaire, which was the pen name of François Marie Arouet. This prolific writer was one of the century's most brilliant literary stylists, historians, and poets. Had he been satisfied with merely exploiting these talents, his fame would still have been considerable. But he was also a profoundly sincere antagonist of Christianity who was determined to bring the spirit of the clandestine literature out into the open. For tactical reasons much of his attack against *"l'infâme* ("the infamous thing"), as he called Christianity, was directed against its more vulnerable practices, such as monasticism. But his ultimate target was Christianity, which, he declared, "every sensible man, every honorable man must hold in horror."

Voltaire's masterpiece was his *Philosophical Dictionary* (1764), a best seller in its day that he was obliged to publish anonymously and that was burned by the authorities in Switzerland, France, and the Netherlands. Modeled after Bayle's dictionary, it was far blunter. In theology, he wrote, "we find man's insanity in all its plenitude." Organized religion is not simply false but pernicious, he argued. Superstition inevitably breeds fanaticism; crimes of organized religion like the St. Bartholomew's Day Massacre are not incidental but are the essence of its irrationality.

Voltaire hoped that educated Europeans would abandon Christianity in favor of deism, a naturalistic belief that accorded God recognition only as the Creator and held that the world, once created, functions according to natural laws that God cannot interfere

with. Man is now left to live in an ordered universe essentially on his own, without hope or fear of divine intervention and without the threat of damnation or the expectation of eternal salvation. Religion should be a matter of private contemplation rather than public worship and mythic creeds. Certain figures in the Enlightenment went beyond this to philosophical atheism, but on the whole Voltaire's mild and undemanding deism remained the characteristic view of eighteenth-century nonbelievers. Despite its innocuousness, however, this form of spirituality was wholly secular, and progressive churchmen who could accept many arguments of eighteenth-century science and philosophy could not accept this.

THE PHILOSOPHES

Science and secularism were the rallying points of a group of French intellectuals known as the philosophes, or philosophers. This term was employed by their traditionalist enemies to mock their pretensions, but they used it themselves with a sense of pride. For they were the avant-garde, the men who raised the Enlightenment to the status of a self-conscious movement.

The leaders of this influential coterie of writers were Voltaire (whom one meets at every turn in eighteenth-century intellectual life) and Denis Diderot (whom we will meet shortly). Its ranks included the mathematicians Jean d'Alembert and the marquis de Condorcet, the jurist baron de Montesquieu, the statesman Jacques Turgot, and the social scientists and philosophers Claude Adrien Helvétius and baron d'Holbach. Outside of France their kinship extended to a clustering of brilliant Scottish philosophers and thinkers, among them David Hume and Adam Smith; to the German playwright and critic Gotthold Ephraim Lessing and the philosopher Immanuel Kant; to such founders of the American Philosophical Society as Benjamin Franklin and Thomas Jefferson; and to the Italian economist and penal reformer the marquis of Beccaria.

The philosophes and their foreign confreres have been well described by a sympathetic historian as a close family with many distant relatives.[1] The family was troubled by a good deal of internal bickering, but its members always enjoyed a sense of common identity. What they shared above all was a critical spirit, the desire to reexamine the assumptions and institutions of society, to expose them to the tests of reason, experience, and utility. Today this sounds banal, but it was not so at a time when almost everywhere religion still dominated society. To assert the primacy of reason meant to turn away from the essence of religion: faith. It meant a decisive break with the Christian world view, which placed doctrine at the center of intellectual activity. For centuries the intellectual mentors of Western civilization had been urging man to submit to what he could know least—the divine. The philosophes hoped to change this completely. They invoked the paganism of ancient Greece and Rome, where the spirit of rational inquiry prevailed among educated men. They ridiculed the Middle Ages as the "Dark Ages," using the attitudes of that period as a contrast with their own sense of liberation and modernity. In *The Decline and Fall of the Roman Empire* (1776–1788), Edward Gibbon passed the verdict that Christianity had eclipsed a Roman civilization that had sought to live according to reason rather than myths.

The inspiration of antiquity was matched by the stimulus of modern science and philosophy. The philosophes laid claim to Newton, who made the universe intelligible without the aid of revelation, and Locke, who uncovered the workings of the human mind.

[1] Peter Gay, *The Enlightenment: An Interpretation.* (1966).

From Locke they argued that human personality is malleable—its nature is not immutably fixed, let alone corrupted by original sin. Men are therefore ultimately responsible to themselves for what they do with their lives. Inherited arrangements are no more nor less sacred than experience has proved them to be. The philosophes acclaimed the role of the enlightened intellectual in society. As the humanists had several centuries before, they placed man at the center of thought. What distinguished them from the humanists was that they placed thought in the service of change. This at any rate was their hope, and in pursuing it the philosophes launched a noisy public movement.

They appeared clamorous to their contemporaries because they had to battle entrenched authority. Intellectual freedom was absolutely essential to them, and in most places they had to fight for it against not only the church and traditionalists but also the state and its apparatus of censorship. They were often obliged to publish their works abroad and anonymously. Sometimes they were pressured into withholding manuscripts from publication altogether or into making humiliating public recantations of controversial books. Even with such cautionary measures, almost all philosophes saw some of their publications confiscated and burned; and a few were forced into exile—Voltaire himself spent several decades across the French border in Switzerland—or sent to jail: Voltaire and Diderot both spent time in the Bastille. True, the very notoriety produced by these repressions often stimulated the sale of their works, but the anxiety outweighed the advantages. Allies of the philosophes in Italy and Spain labored under even greater constraints since the Inquisition still existed in the eighteenth century to suppress heresy with surprising ruthlessness.

By the 1770s, however, the philosophes had survived their running war with the authorities. Some of them lived to see their ideas widely accepted and their works acclaimed. Thus, even if they had contributed little else to the Western experience, their struggle for freedom of expression would merit them a significant place in its history.

But they contributed far more than that. In their scholarly and polemical writings, they investigated a wide range of subjects and pioneered in several new disciplines. Some philosophes—Voltaire for example—were path-breaking historians. Moving beyond traditional historiography, which chronicled battles and rulers' biographies, they studied culture, social institutions, and government structures in an effort to understand as well as describe the past. Practically inventing social science, they dissected on a theoretical level the basis of social organization (sociology) and the human mind (psychology) and on a more practical level such matters as penology and education. These studies were in turn related to the issues of morality and the study of ethics. Their characteristic approach to ethics was utilitarian. With David Hume they tried to define value judgments about good and evil in more pragmatic terms than was common, and they concluded that social utility should become the standard for public morality. This approach to moral philosophy, however, raised the question of whether any human values were absolute and eternal. Responding to this challenge affirmatively, Kant tried to harmonize the tradition of philosophical idealism with the Enlightenment.

A major branch of Enlightenment social science was the physiocratic school. Its adherents believed that economic progress depended on freeing agriculture and trade from mercantilist restrictions and on reforming the tax structure by levying a uniform and equitable land tax. To stimulate agricultural productivity they advocated allowing the grain trade to operate according to the laws of supply and demand, which, they reasoned, would en-courage growers to expand productivity and transport their harvest to where it was most needed. In this way the chronic grain shortages that plagued France could be eliminated.

In Britain Adam Smith made a parallel attack on mercantilist restrictions in *The Wealth of Nations* (1776). Like the physiocrats, Smith believed that economic progress required that each individual be allowed to pursue his own self-interest freely rather than regimented by the state, the guild, or tradition. Smith argued that on all levels of economic activity—from the manufacturing process to the flow of international trade—a natural division of labor should be encouraged. High tariffs, guild restrictions, and the like artificially obstructed this. Both Smith and the French physiocrats were thus early proponents of the economic doctrine of "laissez faire la nature," meaning simply "let nature take its course," which would be taken up by manufacturing interests during the Industrial Revolution.

By contrast other Enlightenment figures, analyzing the origin and role of private property, concluded, on the level of theory at least, that it was a form of primitive usurpation that should be replaced by some collective principle. Men like the French philosopher and historian Gabriel Bonnet de Mably were accordingly the forerunners of a utopian socialism that would be an alternative response to the early Industrial Revolution.

All in all the Enlightenment produced not only a characteristic intellectual spirit but also a wide range of critical writings on many aspects of human society. In addition the philosophes collectively generated a single work that exemplified and fulfilled their notion of how knowledge could be useful: Diderot's *Encyclopedia*.

Diderot and the Encyclopedia

Denis Diderot never achieved the celebrity of his friend Voltaire, but his career was equally central to the concerns and achievements of the philosophes. The son of a provincial cutler, he was educated in Jesuit schools as were many other young Frenchmen but at the first opportunity headed for Paris. Continuing to educate himself while living a bohemian existence, Diderot soon developed an unshakable sense of purpose: to make himself into an independent and successful intellectual.

Within a few short years, he had published a remarkable succession of writings—novels and plays, mathematical treatises, some notable pieces of muckraking (including a devastating attack on inept medical practices), and several works dealing with religion and moral philosophy. The most original aspect of his philosophical writings is his examination of the role of passion in human personality and in any system of values derived from an understanding of human nature. In particular he affirmed the role of sexuality, arguing against artificial taboos and restrictions. As an advocate of what was sometimes called "the natural man," Diderot belies the charge leveled against the philosophes that they overemphasized reason and neglected emotion. The thread of religious criticism in these works is likewise notable. Starting from a position of mild skepticism, he soon passed to deism but ended beyond that in a position of atheism.

Diderot's unusual boldness in getting his works published brought him a considerable reputation but also some real trouble. Two of his books were condemned by the authorities as contrary to religion, the state, and morals. And in 1749 he spent 100 days in prison, being released only after making a humiliating apology.

At about that time Diderot was approached by a bookseller (roughly today's publisher) to translate a British encyclopedic reference work into French. After a number of false starts, Diderot persuaded the bookseller to sponsor instead an entirely new work that would be more comprehensive and up-to-date and would reflect the attitudes of the philosophes. The *Encyclopedia, or Classified Dictionary of the Sciences, Arts, and Occupations* would inventory all important fields of knowledge from the most theoretical to the most mundane and would constitute an arsenal of critical concepts. As the preface stated: "Our Encyclopedia is a work that could only be carried out in a philosophic century. . . . All things must be examined without sparing anyone's sensibilities. . . . The arts and sciences must regain the freedom that is so precious to them." More importantly the ultimate purpose of the encyclopedia according to the editors was "to change the general way of thinking." Or as Diderot put it in a letter to a friend, they were promoting "a revolution in the minds of men to free them from prejudice." Written in this spirit by an array of talented collaborators, the twenty-eight-volume *Encyclopedia* (1751–1772) fulfilled the fondest hopes of its editors and 4,000 initial subscribers.

In such a work religion could scarcely be ignored; nor could it be attacked frontally. Instead it was treated with artful satire or else relegated to a merely philosophical or historical plane. Demystified and subordinated, it was probed and questioned as was any other subject, much to the discomfort of learned but orthodox men.

If the *Encyclopedia* had a core, it was science. But the editors' preferences ran toward the utilitarian and technological side of science. Great attention was lavished for example on articles and plates illustrating various manufacturing processes and tools, and the roles of the mechanic, engineer, and artisan were elevated in the *Encyclopedia*'s scheme of values. The implication was that theoretical scientists could profit from closer attention to technological problems and closer collaboration with technicians. This suggested that the handicrafts and applied technology constituted a realm of knowledge comparable to pure sciences, such as physics and mathematics. At the same time it emphasized an important social perspective: the social utility of the artisan and the benefits of efficient production, as distinct from the role of the elite classes, in the advance of civilization.

Social science also figured prominently in the *Encyclopedia*. Learned articles summarized many theories about social organization and human nature, and again the emphasis was placed on the notion of social utility. On economic topics the encyclopedists tended to echo the physiocratic crusade against mercantilist restrictions on trade and agriculture. But no articles reflected the preoccupations and opinions of the popular masses on such issues as wages or social organization. While the *Encyclopedia*'s bent was not specifically middle-class, it did echo many aspirations of the bourgeoisie while threatening none of its existing prerogatives, especially in matters of property. And on political issues the *Encyclopedia* did not take a particularly controversial line on the central question of authority and sovereignty. It tended to accept absolute monarchy with equanimity, provided it was reasonably efficient and just. The major concerns of the editors were civil rights, freedom of expression, and the rule of law.

Measured from the perspective of the French Revolution—that is, with hindsight—the *Encyclopedia* thus does not seem revolutionary. Yet in the context of the times, it was. The revolution that Diderot sought was in intellectual orientation: his purpose was to spread the "critical spirit" from the precincts of the philosophes to the educated elites in general. Judging by the reaction of religious and government authorities, he was eminently successful. "Up till now," commented one French bishop, "hell has vomited its venom drop by drop." Now, he continued, it could be found assembled between the *Encyclopedia*'s covers. And the attorney general of France declared in 1758, "There is a project formed, a society organized to propagate ma-

Diderot's Encyclopedia *focused much of its attention on technology. Plates illustrating the mechanical process, such as the one shown here for casting sculpture, were provided in separate volumes.* (Photo: The Bettmann Archive)

terialism, to destroy religion, to inspire a spirit of independence, and to nourish the corruption of morals."

The *Encyclopedia* was accordingly banned, and its bookseller's license to issue the remaining volumes was revoked. Most of the contributors prudently withdrew, but Diderot was too committed. Retreating underground, he continued the herculean task until the subscribers received every promised volume, including eleven magnificent folios of illustrations. By the time these appeared, the persecutions had receded, and indeed the *Encyclopedia* was reprinted in several cheaper editions that sold out rapidly, making a fortune for their publishers. More importantly this turn of events ensured the renown of the philosophes' most impressive achievement—a work recognized both in its own time and thereafter as the landmark of an age.

II. EIGHTEENTH-CENTURY CULTURES

The Enlightenment was merely one dimension of Europe's proliferating cultural life. The economic expansion and prosperity, which will be discussed in the next chapter, were matched by a marked increase in literary output serving increasingly diverse audiences. Although the aristocracy still dominated society, people of lesser origins were prominently participating in and supporting culture. Eighteenth-century high culture was distinctly cosmopolitan, that is, spilling across national borders as well as social class lines. Its trends included an increase in travel within Europe, a dramatic expansion of publishing activity, the creation of new literary and scientific academies, and the development of new genres in fields like fiction and music. Popular culture, on the other hand, remained extremely traditional and localized.

HIGH CULTURE

As the expansive, cosmopolitan aspects of European high culture are described here, it must be remembered that the mass of Europe's population remained entirely parochial and virtually untouched by these developments. Most peasants and urban laborers continued to live within the culturally hermetic boundaries of their parish, their family, their job. But for the educated and wealthy, the numerically small but extremely influential elites,

there was a sense of belonging to an international European civilization. It was a civilization dominated by France and by the French language, which had now displaced Latin and Italian as the language of the educated. Even Frederick II of Prussia favored French over German. Whatever deleterious effects such an attitude might have—and the German dramatist Lessing considered it a disastrous prejudice—this meant that ideas and literature circulated without language barriers among Europe's elites.

Travel

Europeans' sense of their common identity was sharpened by a flood of travel literature and by their appetite for visiting foreign parts. Although transportation was slow and uncomfortable, many embarked on a "grand tour" of the Continent and Great Britain. The highlights of such a trip were visits to large cities and to the ruins of antiquity—to the glories, that is, of both the modern and the ancient world.

London, Paris, Rome, and Vienna were already large, bustling, and impressive metropolises. These and smaller cities in Germany, Italy, and the United Provinces were undertaking considerable urban improvement. With generally excellent taste, rulers and municipal authorities were continuing to embellish their cities with large plazas, public gardens, airy boulevards, theaters, and opera houses. Toward the end of the century, amenities such as street lighting and public transportation began to appear in cities, with London leading the way. From the private sector came two notable additions to the urban scene: the coffee shop and the storefront window display. Coffeehouses, where customers could chat or read, and enticing shop windows, which added to the pleasures of city walking (while also stimulating consumer demand), enhanced the rhythms of urban life for tourists and natives alike. Sophisticated

Europeans took great pleasure in their cities. When a man is tired of London, Samuel Johnson remarked, he is tired of life.

Travelers on tour invariably passed from the attractions of bustling city life to the monuments of antiquity. The philosophes called attention to pagan philosophers like Cicero; paralleling this, interest heightened in the remnants of Greek and Roman architecture and sculpture. Europeans endorsed the view of the German art historian Johann Winckelmann that Greek sculpture was the most worthy standard of aesthetic beauty. A lasting result of this fascination with antique ruins was Edward Gibbon's decision, on visiting the awesome remains of ancient Rome, to undertake *The Decline and Fall of the Roman Empire.*

The Republic of Letters

Among writers, intellectuals, and scientists, the sense of a cosmopolitan European culture devolved into the concept of a republic of letters. The phrase, introduced by sixteenth-century French humanists, was popularized by Pierre Bayle, a great progenitor of the Enlightenment, who published a critical journal that he called *News of the Republic of Letters.* The obvious import of the rubric is that the realm of culture and ideas is an intellectual homeland that cuts across all political and geographical borders. In one sense it is an exclusive republic, limited to the educated; but it is also an open society in that people may belong regardless of their social origins. For this reason European intellectuals felt that their republic of letters was a model for general social values.

Aside from the medium of the printed word, the republic of letters was organized around two institutions; the salons and the academies. Each advanced the process of social interchange, gathering together people from various countries distinguished by either status or talent. The philosophes themselves

exemplified this social mix, for their "family" was composed in almost equal measure of nobles (Montesquieu, Holbach, Condorcet) and commoners (Voltaire, Diderot, d'Alembert). Voltaire insisted that he was as good as any aristocrat but had no intention of trying to topple the aristocracy from its position; rather he sought amalgamation. As d'Alembert put it, talent on the one hand and birth and eminence on the other both deserve recognition and deference.

The salons, conducted mainly by wives of wealthy bourgeois or noble families, sought to bring together important writers with the influential aristocrats they needed for favors and funds. The marquise de Pompadour, Louis XV's mistress, was the most notable personage to run such an assembly. Since a premium was placed on style and elegance in the salons, the intellectual was required to make his ideas lucid and comprehensible to the layman, which in turn increased the likelihood that his thought would have some influence. The salons helped particularly to enlarge the audience and contacts of the philosophes and served to introduce them to a flow of foreign visitors ranging from German princes to Benjamin Franklin. Private newsletters to which interested foreigners subscribed kept them abreast of activities in the Parisian salons when they could not attend personally.

Throughout Europe freemasonry played a similar role of cultural diffusion, promoting interchange across both national and social lines and creating another cosmopolitan dimension to European intellectual life. Operating in an aura of secretiveness and symbolism, the masonic lodges fostered a curious mixture of medieval mysticism and modern rationalism. They had begun really as clubs or fraternities dedicated to humane values; thus they attracted a wide range of enlightened nobles and distinguished commoners. But toward the end of the century, they were rent by sectarian controversies, and their initial sense of universalism eroded.

Far more important for the dissemination of ideas in the eighteenth century were the learned academies. These ranged from the Lunar Society in Birmingham, a forum for the most progressive British industrialists and technologists, to state-sponsored academies in almost every capital of Southern and Central Europe, which served as conduits for advanced scientific and philosophical ideas coming from the West. In France moreover academies were established in more than thirty provincial cities—a vital development in that it promoted widespread intellectual activity and created strongholds of advanced thinking in almost every region of that large country.

These provincial academies were founded after the death of Louis XIV, as if in testimony to the liberating effect of his disappear-

A lecture at a learned gathering. (Photo: Lauros-Giraudon)

ance. They began as literary institutes, concerned with upholding traditional values like purity of style. A few remained conservative adherents to the status quo into midcentury: the motto of the Cherbourg Academy in 1755 was "Religion and Honor." But most of them gradually shifted their interests from conventional literary matters to scientific and utilitarian questions in such domains as commerce, agriculture, and local administration. They became offshoots so to speak of the *Encyclopedia*. Indeed when a Jesuit read a harangue against the *Encyclopedia* in the Lyons Academy many members threatened to resign unless he retracted his remarks. By the 1770s and 1780s, the essay contests sponsored by the provincial academies and the papers published by their members had turned to such topics as population growth, capital punishment and penology, education, poverty and welfare, the grain trade, highways, guilds, and the origins of sovereignty.

There was a parallel shift in membership. The local academies began as privileged corporations, dominated by the nobility of the region. Corresponding or associate membership was extended to commoners from the ranks of civil servants, doctors, and professionals. Gradually the distinction between regular and associate participants crumbled. More commoners were admitted to full membership, and a social fusion took place, though it remained fragile and untested until 1789. Nobles and commoners alike were eager to discuss reforms and work for the betterment of local conditions. The scientific spirit had spread to them, making them receptive to the cause of practical reform and utilitarian ideas.

Publishing and Reading

The printed word was of course the chief medium of cultural diffusion. To be sure, the eighteenth century was not an age of mass education or literacy. Rudimentary public schools in Prussia, charity schools for the poor in Britain, and parish schools run by local priests in France did not produce literacy among the majority of the lower classes. Nonetheless the proportions of those who could read were advancing slowly, and population increases caused a substantial overall gain in literacy. Both factors help explain the tremendous rise in publishing activity geared to several different reading publics.

Untapped markets for reading material were opened up by itinerant circulating libraries, which originated in England around 1740; by the end of the century, almost 1,000 had been established. Recognizing a specialized demand among women readers, publishers also began to increase the output of new kinds of fiction and "ladies' magazines." Moreover they were more receptive to women writers of fiction and poetry, especially the so-called blue-stockings of the salons, who were early literary feminists.

The most notable development in publishing during the eighteenth century was the proliferation of journals and newspapers. In England, which pioneered in this domain, the number of periodicals increased from 25 to 158 between 1700 and 1780. There were several kinds. Single-essay periodicals, whose objective was moral and aesthetic uplift and whose model was Joseph Addison and Richard Steele's *Spectator*, continued to be popular. By contrast, the miscellany contained extracts and summaries of books and covered current events and entertainment; one such, the *Gentleman's Magazine*, had the astonishing circulation of 15,000 in 1740. More sophisticated periodicals, like the *Monthly Review* and the *Journal des Savants*, specialized in critical book reviews and serious articles on science and philosophy, and they served the important function of extending the republic of letters beyond the scholar's study into the public domain. Most important for the future of reading habits in Europe was the daily newspaper, originated in England. Papers like

England broke new ground in publishing by introducing the daily newspaper. The page shown here is from a 1760 issue of "The Public Ledger," a London paper. (Photo: Radio Times Hulton Picture Library)

the *London Chronicle* were originally intended for family reading and entertainment. Gradually they assumed other functions: they took classified advertisements, they began to report news, and finally—after considerable battling—they began to cover politics and report parliamentary debates. Under France's censorship regime, newspapers did not become politically oriented until the French Revolution, at which time a politically aroused France probably surpassed England as the country of newspaper reading.

In the field of general publishing, booksellers now assumed strategic prominence. They were the intermediary between reader and author—they combined the functions of editor, printer, salesman, and (if need be) smuggler. Their judgment and marketing techniques helped create as well as fill the demand for books since they conceived, commissioned, and financed a variety of works. The system had varying results. We have seen the *Encyclopedia* originate as a bookseller's project. So too did such enduring masterpieces as Samuel Johnson's *Dictionary*, a monumental lexicon that helped purify and standardize English usage. Many respectable popularizations of scientific, historical, and philosophical treatises were likewise brought into print by publishers, who commissioned skillful stylists like Oliver Goldsmith to write them. But there was a demeaning side to this system, for booksellers also employed hack writers to turn out potboilers, romances, and other works that pandered to low tastes, paying them for quantity and speed rather than quality. These drudges led a precarious and struggling existence along with marginal theatrical people in the milieu known as Grub Street. And Grub Street had even lower depths: for the more unscrupulous booksellers and desperate writers, there was money to be made in scurrilous political pamphlets committing character assassination and of course in pornography. Sometimes the two were combined in pamphlets dwelling on the alleged perversions of kings and queens.

With the growth of publishing, the vocation of writer was taking on a variety of forms. To be sure, practically all writers aspired to hold some lucrative sinecure or to be supported by important aristocrats. But authors valued their independence as much as patronage and security; the most successful could now live off their own work without patrons. On the other hand the number of would-be writers increased enormously, and many were decidedly unsuccessful and frustrated. The explosion of the printed word therefore raised troubling questions. Would refinement and moral sensitivity be overwhelmed by vulgarity and commercialism? This is a problem gripping today's media, and it was born in the eighteenth century. On balance it seems reasonable to conclude that the new demand for books and the new economics of publishing created significant opportunity for professional writers to express

and fulfill their own talents and for literate citizens to expose themselves to a variety of ideas, new and old. The entertainment and instruction of a middle-class audience became a principal focus of writing.

POPULAR CULTURE

While the culture of aristocratic and middle-class elites has been extensively studied, the cultures of artisans, peasants, and the urban poor are only dimly known. In those sectors of society culture primarily meant recreation and was essentially public and collective. Moreover, while there was a written form of popular culture that we shall discuss, it was minor compared to the prevalent oral culture, which has left few traces in the historical record. Nonetheless it is possible to suggest some of the rich variety of cultural materials and recreations of the common people.

Popular Literature

Far removed from the markets for Voltaire and the *Gentleman's Magazine*, there existed a distinct world of popular literature—the reading matter consumed by artisans and peasants, the poor and the almost poor, those who could barely read and even those who could not read at all. From the seventeenth through the early nineteenth century but particularly in eighteenth-century France, a type of literature was specially produced for this audience. It consisted of small booklets and brochures written anonymously, printed on cheap paper, and costing only a few pennies. They were sold by colporteurs—itinerant hawkers—who knew the tastes of these customers and saw to it that they were satisfied. The booklets were often read aloud by those who could read to those who could not; but even the illiterate bought them, apparently somewhat in awe of the printed word and valuing its possession.

There were three major varieties of popular literature. The first was explicitly religious: devotional tracts, saints' lives, catechisms, manuals of penitence, and Bible stories, all written simply and vividly and generously laced with miracles. Preoccupied with fears of death and damnation, the readers sought reassurance here that a virtuous, sensible life would end in salvation. A second kind of popular literature was the almanac, which corresponded with a concern for getting along in this life as well. Almanacs and how-to-live-successfully pamphlets (forerunners of the *Reader's Digest* and Norman Vincent Peale) discussed things like cleanliness, nourishment, and the kinds of potions to take for illnesses. They also featured astrology—how to read the stars and other signs for clues about what the future might bring. The third type was entertainment literature: tales and fables, burlesques and crude satires, mixtures of fiction and history in which miraculous events frequently helped bring the story to a satisfactory conclusion.[2]

Although important information may have trickled down through these booklets, most of them were blatantly escapist. The pervasive religiosity and superstition of popular literature marks it off decisively from the growing rationalism and secularism of middle-class and avant-garde culture. Moreover it could be argued that by ignoring the real problems of famine, taxes, and material insecurity, these writings fostered submissiveness, a fatalistic acceptance of a dismal status quo. Seeing the nature of popular literature helps us understand why Voltaire had no hope of extending his ideas on religion to the masses and indeed even feared to discuss them in front of his servants.

Almanacs and pamphlets were produced for the lower classes by outsiders, printers and writers who were themselves educated. A more common and authentic form of popular culture was oral: folk tales told at the fireside on long winter nights and songs that expressed bawdiness or violence far more directly and meaningfully than the written word. Themes relating to hunger or sex or oppression were more likely to turn up in songs, often sung in local dialects that would have been incomprehensible to an educated Parisian, Londoner, or Viennese.

Groups and Recreations

If the educated had their freemasons' lodges and learned societies, the people also had organized groups. Many journeymen artisans, for example, belonged to secret societies that combined fraternal and trade-union functions. These young artisans usually toured their country, stopping periodically to work with comrades in other towns in order to improve their own skills. But the main emphasis of their associations was on camaraderie and ritual celebration. Rivalries were common between federations of such associations and occasionally degenerated into pitched battles —a far cry from the nineteenth-century ideal of labor solidarity.

Corresponding to the coffee shop and salon of the urban middle classes were the public house or "pub," the cafe in local urban neighborhoods, and the *guinguette* in the suburbs of the common people. These "dives" (as they would doubtless be called today) catered to a large, poor clientele, especially on Sunday and Monday, which working people often took as a day off. The *guinguettes* were located outside the city walls so that the wine they sold would not be subject to urban excise taxes. Wine was just beginning to be consumed by the common people in the eighteenth century. And even then it was something of a luxury except in its cheapest form, which was always adulterated or watered. In

---

[2] See Geneviève Bollème, *La Bibliothèque bleue.* (1971).

England, however, gin was the poor person's drink—cheap and plentiful until a hefty excise tax was levied following the government's realization that too many people were drinking themselves into disability and death.

More commonly drinking was not done in that morbid fashion but as part of a healthy and vibrant outdoor life. A recent study of popular pastimes in England suggests the outlines of a traditional popular culture that flourished before the Industrial Revolution. It was marked by a full calendar of holidays that provided numerous occasions for group merrymaking, eating, drinking, dressing-up, contests, and games. This was a particularly beneficial setting for boys and girls in their teens and twenties to meet each other. The highlight of a country year usually came either between spring sowing and the summer harvest or in the early autumn after the summer harvest was in, when most villages held a public feast lasting several days. In Catholic countries similar festivities were often linked with church rituals, with the most popular observances including the commemoration of saints and pilgrimages to holy places.

Popular culture involved "relaxation in noise and tumultuous merriment," preferably in public and out in the open. Football matches, for example, were a popular form of recreation in England, both for participants and observers. At times the high spirits generated on these occasions turned into good-natured riots. In August 1765 the *Northampton Mercury* reported: "We hear from West-Hadden, in this county, that on Thursday and Friday a great number of people being assembled there, in order to play a Foot-Ball Match, soon after meeting formed themselves into a tumultuous mob, and pulled up and burnt the fences designed for the inclosure of that field, and did other considerable damage."

Blood sports were another type of popular recreation in the preindustrial era. Bullbaiting, for example, involved setting loose a pack of dogs on a tied-up steer, and was often arranged by the collaboration of a butcher (who provided the steer that would subsequently be slaughtered and dispensed as meat) and a publican (who provided the yard of his inn as the arena and sold refreshments to the spectators). Cockfighting was similar in its gory results and was popular with gentlemen and commoners alike, who enjoyed wagering on the outcome. These so-called sports appear repulsive today, and by the end of the eighteenth century such cruelties to animals were being denounced by reformers and moralists. It is notable, however, that no similar attack was leveled against the gentry's organized bloodletting in the form of fox hunting.

LITERATURE, MUSIC, AND ART

Unlike the seventeenth century, sometimes classified as Baroque, the eighteenth can be given no comprehensive stylistic label. Literary styles varied, ranging from Neoclassicism in poetry to major innovation in fiction. The nature of the audience and the sources of a writer's support varied considerably. The same was true for composers. But if any trends may be singled out for attention, they are the rise of the novel and the development of the symphony.

The Novel and Poetry

For all practical purposes the novel may be said to have originated in England, where writers and booksellers were particularly aware of a growing middle-class reading public. The acknowledged pioneer of this new genre was Samuel Richardson, himself a bookseller. Epistolary in form—a series of letters telling the story—*Pamela, or Virtue Rewarded* (1740) was a melodrama of the trials and tribulations of an honest if somewhat hypo-

In this famous "Gin Lane" etching of 1750 by Hogarth, the results of excessive gin drinking by the common people are depicted as death, apathy, and decay. A cheerful and orderly companion piece called "Beer Street," however, made it clear that drinking in moderation was a perfectly acceptable habit. (Photo: Metropolitan Museum of Art, Harris Brisbane Dick Fund, 1932)

critical servant girl whose sexual virtue is repeatedly challenged but never conquered and whose wealthy employer finally agrees to marry her. *Pamela* was an instant success. Breaking away from the standard forms and heroic subjects of most previous narrative fiction, Richardson dealt with the qualities of recognizable types of people. Pamela's earnest hypocrisy, however, prompted a playwright and lawyer named Henry Fielding to pen a short satire called *Shamela*, which he followed with his own novel *Joseph Andrews*. Here comedy and adventure replaced melodrama; indeed Fielding prefaced the book with a remarkable manifesto claiming that the novel was to be a comic epic in prose. Fielding realized the full potential of this bold innovation in *Tom Jones* (1749), a colorful, robust comic panorama of English society featuring a gallery of brilliantly developed characters. Fielding was providing a literary counterpart to the world that William Hogarth was creating in his etchings—vivid exaggerations of the various social milieus, particularly the period's low life.

In general the novel was emerging as a form of fiction that told its story and treated the development of personality in a realistic social context, and in some ways it mirrored its times better than any other form of fiction. Novelists could use broad comedy, as did Laurence Sterne, or they could be totally serious, as was Johann Wolfgang von Goethe in *The Sorrows of Werther* (1774), a *Bildungsroman* (novel of development) telling the tragic story of the coming of age of a melancholy youth. In either case the writer freed himself from classic aesthetic norms and specified rules of composition. Authors could now experiment endlessly with forms and techniques and could deal with a wide range of social settings. Consequently they drew less and less on the life styles of aristocrats for their social ideals, and much of the century's fiction, in the drama as well as the novel,

focused on middle-class family life and its everyday problems of morality, love, and social relations. This reflected actual changes in middle-class values, which were increasingly emphasizing close family relations.[3]

Meanwhile a genre called the philosophical tale was being perfected by writers with more didactic objectives. The chief progenitor of the form was the great Irish satirist Jonathan Swift, notably in his well-known *Gulliver's Travels* (1726). The French philosophes naturally gravitated toward this genre of satire since it allowed them to criticize their society covertly and hence to avoid open clashes with the censors. Thus Montesquieu created a range of mythical foreign settings, exotic backgrounds, and travelers from the Levant to ridicule contemporary mores in *The Persian Letters* (1721). Likewise Voltaire achieved great success in his tale *Candide* (1759), a critique of the notion that this was the best of all possible worlds. His wholly fictional characters and incidents disguised an Enlightenment sermon against the idiocy and cruelty that he saw in European society. Voltaire and Fielding met on this ground, for both were concerned with imparting a commonsensical notion of morality and humanity.

During most of the century, the innovation that was occurring in prose fiction contrasted with the traditionalism of poetry, still the most prized form of literary expression. Here unchanged rules on what made "good literature" still prevailed. Each type of poem had its particular essence and rules; diction was supposed to be elegant and sentiments refined and elevated. The raw materials of emotion were to be muted and transformed into language and

---

[3] In his *Centuries of Childhood* (1962), Pt. 3, Philippe Ariès points out how parents were becoming much closer to their children in the eighteenth century. Instead of sending them to boarding school, they more frequently placed them in schools near home. Families also now insisted on more privacy for themselves in household architecture.

allusions that only the highly educated could appreciate. Art was viewed in this Neoclassical tradition as imitative of eternal standards of truth and beauty. It was not permissible for the poet to unburden his soul or hold forth on his own experience. The audience for poetry was the narrowest and most elitist segment of the reading public—"the wealthy few," in the phrase of William Wordsworth, who criticized eighteenth-century poets for pandering exclusively to that group.

By the end of the century, the restraints of Neoclassicism finally provoked rebellion in the ranks of English and German poets. Men like Friedrich von Schiller and Wordsworth defiantly raised the celebration of individual feeling and inner passion to the level of a creed, which eventually became known as Romanticism. Hoping to appeal to a much broader audience, these writers decisively changed the nature of poetic composition and made this literary form, like the novel, a far more flexible vehicle of expression.

Music and Art

The rise of the novel in literature was paralleled by the development of the symphony in music. But it must be noted at once that a great deal of eighteenth-century music was routine and undistinguished. For much of the century, composers were still obliged to serve under royal, ecclesiastical, or aristocratic patronage. They were bound by rigid formulas of composition and by a public taste tyrannically insistent on conventions. A pleasant melody in a predictable form was what the listener wanted from his composers. Much instrumental music was commissioned as background fare for dancing or other social occasions. Likewise Italian opera was popular and quantitatively impressive—Alessandro Scarlatti, for example, composed 115 operas. But very few of these repetitive compositions have survived the test of time; their sheer number is an obvious clue to the casual circumstances of their composition and their likely fate.

The heartland of Europe's music tradition was Austria. Here a trio of geniuses transformed the routines of eighteenth-century composition into vibrant, original, and enduring masterpieces. The early symphonies of Franz Joseph Haydn and the young prodigy Wolfgang Amadeus Mozart were conventional exercises in Rococo decorativeness. The music was light and as tuneful as its audience could wish, but it had little emotional impact. By the end of their careers, Haydn had written 104 symphonies and Mozart 41. They had stabilized the form into its familiar four movements (fast, slow, minuet, fast); they had each developed extraordinary harmonic virtuosity; but more than these accomplishments, they had infused the form with a lyricism that often crossed the border into the realm of passion. In short, the symphony had changed radically from the elegant trifles of earlier years.

The German composer Ludwig van Beethoven consummated this development and assured that the symphony, like the novel, would be adaptable and ever-malleable. In each of his nine symphonies as well as his five piano concertos, he progressively modified the standard formulas. The orchestra was much enlarged, and the movements were made far more intricate and longer. His last symphony burst the bonds of the form. Striving to make a Promethean musical statement, Beethoven introduced a large chorus singing one of Schiller's odes to conclude the composition, making it an explicit celebration in music of freedom and brotherhood. Laden with emotion and programmatic content, the music is yet recognizable as an advanced form of the eighteenth-century symphony. Thus it provides a bridge between the culture of two periods: eighteenth-century Classicism and nineteenth-century Romanticism.

The ornate interiors of eighteenth-century opera houses began filling to capacity as music grew in popularity. Italy was a focal point of the musical world, with four opera houses in Rome and three in Naples. (Photo: Librairie Larousse)

Beethoven also progressed farther than most of his predecessors in freeing himself from subordination to a powerful single patron. Haydn had pioneered in this direction by signing a lucrative contract with a London music publisher and impresario that underwrote the composition and performance of his last twelve symphonies. Beethoven relied even more on public concerts and specific commissions instead of tying himself to a particular patron.[4]

---

[4] Johann Sebastian Bach (1685–1750) is considered by many music lovers a genius on a par with Mozart and Beethoven. But in his own day, as the organist and resident composer for a number of obscure German churches, Bach was little known to the outside world. Ironically, whereas today he is admired only by "highbrows," in his time he provided what was in effect popular music for the people—organ music, hymns, and cantatas for religious worship.

Unlike fiction and music, painting did not experience notable innovations in the eighteenth century, and with the exception of Jacques Louis David (see plate 46) eighteenth-century painters were overshadowed by their predecessors as well as by their successors of the Romantic and post-Romantic schools of nineteenth-century art. Neoclassicism was a dominant style in the late eighteenth century, with its themes inspired by antiquity and its timeless conceptions of truth and beauty, similar to those of Neoclassical poetry. There were, however, at least two developments which paralleled the widening social context of the other arts. In the first place, just as composers and musicians began to perform in public concerts, so did painters begin to exhibit regularly in public, especially in the annual salons sponsored by the royal academies of art in London and in Paris. The head of London's Royal Academy, founded by George III in 1768, was Sir Joshua Reynolds. A notable portrait painter, Reynolds—solely by virtue of his talent—rose to a position of wealth and eminence, thus exemplifying the Enlightenment ideal of opportunity. Moreover, his success brought him the independence from a patron that writers, composers, and artists all aspired to.

A second development in the social history of eighteenth-century art lay in the new kinds of subject matter and themes taken up by certain artists, which paralleled what novelists and playwrights were doing. Jean Baptiste Greuze, for example, made a hit in the Parisian exhibitions of the 1770s with his sentimentalized paintings of common people in family settings caught in a dramatic situation, such as the death of a father. William Hogarth was not primarily a painter at all but an engraver working through the medium of prints and book illustrations. His art therefore had a much wider circulation than the work of any painter. And his choice of subjects ranged far and wide through the ranks of society—especially in scenes of low life among the poor and the working classes (see illustration, p. 632). Hogarth's art was not only technically brilliant, it remains a basic source for the study of English social history.

III. THE ENLIGHTENMENT AND THE STATE

On the whole the Enlightenment was not highly critical of existing forms of government, though specific policies of rulers and ministers were often criticized. In Central Europe monarchy was the starting point of most political theory or reform programs. In France the monarchy and the aristocracy were more evenly matched, and the contrasting political views of Montesquieu and Voltaire reflected this fact. With Jean Jacques Rousseau, however, we come to the century's most original political theorist—a man less concerned with actual political arrangements than with the inherent possibilities for individual and political freedom.

GERMAN ABSOLUTISM AND THE PROBLEM OF REFORM

During the late nineteenth century, German historians invented the concept of "enlightened absolutism" to describe the Prussian and Hapsburg monarchies of the eighteenth century. Apologists for German development and critics of the liberal and revolutionary traditions associated with France, they argued that the strength of an enlightened ruler was the surest basis for progress in early modern Europe. A king who ruled in the interest of his subjects, they implied, precluded violent divisions like those of the French Revolution. Heads of state came to govern in this manner only after a long evolution, for according to these historians, absolutism had evolved through three phases. First came the period of "confessional absolutism," when kings were preoccupied with religious uniformity; it was exemplified by Philip II of Spain and the notion that the prince's religion is the religion of the state. This phase was followed by a more secular and dynastic stage, "courtly absolutism," exemplified of course by Louis XIV and his famous epigram, "I am the state." In contrast to Louis' extravagant style and goals, Frederick II of Prussia marked the "enlightened" phase of absolutism, as evidenced by his dictum that the ruler is the first servant of the state.

This three-phase scheme is a distortion of history. Earlier chapters have amply demonstrated that fundamental issues differed little in these supposed stages of absolutism. Absolute monarchs strove at all times to assert their authority over the constituent elements of society and to maximize the power of their state in relation to other realms, principally by means of territorial expansion. Any notion that the Enlightenment caused the monarchs to alter this is erroneous. Still, there were visible modifications of specific practices and style in the way that absolute monarchy conducted its business. And in this the role of culture and ideas was not entirely absent.

Conceptions of "Enlightened" Rule

Some of the modifications observable in eighteenth-century absolutism may well have been prompted by prominent philosophes, with whom sovereigns like Frederick II and Catherine II of Russia (1762–1796) maintained significant contacts. Voltaire for example spent a long sojourn at Frederick's palace, while Catherine offered to buy Diderot's library to help him out of financial troubles and delay taking possession of it until his death. At various times monarchs and philosophes lavished saccharine praise on each other. How significant was this mutual admiration? For the monarchs it was probably primarily a question of public relations, of image making. Yet the

fact that they should even find it desirable to be supportive of men like Voltaire and Diderot is suggestive. They may have felt the need to justify themselves publicly and even to coopt the prestige of Europe's leading intellectuals.

Catherine the Great played this game to its limit, promising at one point in her reign to begin moving gradually toward representative government and constitutionalism—a policy that was hailed as a historic landmark by philosophe admirers who were too remote from St. Petersburg to see its falsity. In 1767 she convened the Legislative Commission, a quasi-representative body of delegates from various strata of Russian society. They were invited to present grievances, propose reforms, and debate such proposals. In the end nothing came of this except some good publicity for Catherine. She soon dissolved the commission under the pretext of having to turn her attention to a new Turkish war. Some time later she promulgated a Charter of the Nobility, which, instead of limiting the nobility's privileges, strengthened its corporate status and increased its control over the serfs in exchange for a pledge of loyalty to the throne.

No such experiment in representation was even tried in Central Europe, where other conceptions of enlightened rule and reform prevailed. German writers were particularly adept at finding theoretical justifications for the powers of an autocrat. They viewed the state as a machine and the ruler as its necessary mainspring. Progress came from sound administration, whose instrumentalities were an enlightened monarch and well-trained bureaucrats. In keeping with this notion, German universities began to train civil servants, and the rudiments of a merit system of civil service recruitment were introduced in Prussia and other states.

The orders for the bureaucracy were to come from the ruler, who was expected to dedicate himself to the welfare of his subjects in return for their obedience. The vehicle for the command-obedience chain was to be a coherent and explicit body of public law, fairly administered by the above-mentioned bureaucrats. According to its advocates, this system would produce the rule of law, the *Rechtsstaat*. A society thus based on "right" did not require a written constitution or public representation; the monarch and the bureaucrats together, following their sense of public responsibility, ensured the citizen's rights.

Many German intellectuals subscribed to this view and accordingly believed that they were living in a free and progressive society— free from arbitrary injustice, and progressive because rationality was exercised in government. Although many would sympathize with the French Revolution of 1789, they were inclined to regard the turmoil of a revolution as unnecessary for their own situation.

Joseph II and the Limits of Absolutism

The most notable sponsor of reforms from above was Joseph II, Hapsburg ruler from 1765 to 1790. Although he did not identify with the philosophes and maintained his own Catholic faith, he was actually the most "enlightened" of the major monarchs of the eighteenth century—as well as one of the most autocratic personalities. It was a difficult combination.

Joseph believed that the primary right of the people was to be governed well. But for him this entailed far more than the customary administrative and financial modernization necessary for survival in the state system. The emperor began by implementing several reforms long advocated by Enlightenment thinkers: freedom of expression, religious toleration, state control over organized religion, and legal reform. By greatly reducing royal censorship, Joseph opened the way for Vienna to become a major center of literary activity. In an edict of toleration in 1781, he emancipated Protestants and Jews, granting them the

right to worship publicly and to hold property and public office; he went so far as to ennoble some Jews. On the other hand he worked to reduce the influence of the Catholic Church by ordering the dissolution of numerous monasteries on the grounds that they were useless and corrupt. Part of their confiscated wealth was used to support the medical school at the University of Vienna. In an attempt to force the church to serve its parishioners better, he eliminated much of Rome's authority and forced the clergy to modernize rituals and services. It should come as no surprise, however, that most of his Catholic subjects preferred their traditional ways to this nationalized brand of Catholicism.

When Joseph ordered the drafting of a new criminal code, he substantiated the Enlightenment's belief in legal reform as an instrument of social progress. Certain categories of crimes, such as witchcraft, were abolished altogether. The death penalty and various brutal punishments were eliminated for most crimes; the use of torture in criminal proceedings was forbidden; motive was recognized as a factor in determining guilt. Most strikingly the code recognized no class difference in the application of criminal law. Noble offenders were subject to the same laws as were commoners and could be sentenced to the same punishments.

These significant departures from the status quo were preliminaries to the most important of Joseph's efforts at social reform: to improve the lot of the peasants. In this respect the emperor was far bolder not only than any other eighteenth-century sovereign but than most philosophes and civil servants. The question of social justice for the rural lower classes was a weak point of "enlightened absolutism" elsewhere. Catherine II not only failed to improve conditions among the serfs but allowed their status to deteriorate even further, to the point where those on royal lands, who could be bought and sold at will, were being treated almost as slaves. Frederick II had better intentions but accomplished little. He attempted to stop corporal punishment of serfs by their masters, but even this modest reform was not forced on the nobles and was carried out only on royal lands. As for the more basic issues, land ownership and labor services, nothing was done to place limits on the lords' prerogatives. While most Prussian peasants could not be sold, they could not move of their own volition or lay claim to the land they tilled, and they spent much of their time performing services directly for their lord.

Faced with a roughly comparable situation in the Hapsburg domains, Joseph attacked all aspects of the problem. He set out to eradicate the system of serfdom and transform the peasant into a free citizen in command of his person and of the land he cultivated. To begin with, Joseph abolished personal servitude and gave peasants the right to move, marry, and enter any trade they wished. He then promulgated various laws to help secure their control over the land they worked. Finally and most dramatically, he made a decisive attempt to ensure the income and limit the obligations of the peasant tenant. All land was to be surveyed and subject to a uniform tax. Twelve percent of its annual yield would go to the state, and beyond this the peasant would be obliged to pay a maximum of 18 percent of his income to the lord in lieu of his former feudal obligations. No longer would he owe the labor service to his lord that sometimes consumed more than 100 days each year.

These reforms were ordered in a purely authoritarian fashion, with no regard for public opinion and no notion of consent from any quarter. They provoked a predictably vigorous opposition from the landowning classes. But they also won scant visible support from the peasant masses, who were deeply distrustful of anything the central government did because of its religious policies. No effort was made to build support among the peasants by explaining the reforms in the hope of offsetting the nobility's reaction. As a sympathetic chronicler of Joseph's reign sadly observed, "He brought in his beneficial measures in an arbitrary manner."

The arbitrariness was not incidental to Joseph's methods. He acknowledged no other way of doing things, no limitation on his own sovereignty. His reaction to the opposition that his reforms aroused illustrates this: he moved to suppress the unexpected dissent in the firmest possible way. Not only did he restore censorship in his last years, but he elevated the police department to the status of an imperial ministry, granting it unprecedented powers. By the time he died, in 1790, he was a disillusioned man. His realm resembled less a *Rechtsstaat* than a police state.

Contrasting the century's two most notable monarchs points up the limits of "enlightened absolutism." On basic social issues like the status of the rural masses, who made up about 90 percent of the population, absolutism displayed little capacity to initiate change regardless of the ruler's intentions. Frederick II resigned himself to the impossibility of improving established practice and attempted to do little in the peasants' behalf. Joseph II tried to do a great deal in their behalf—for them, not with them—only to find that autocracy could not accomplish his objectives without provoking major upheaval.

FRENCH LIBERAL THOUGHT

Like "nature" and "reason," the word "freedom" was central to the Enlightenment. Its most important meaning to the philosophes was the freedom of the human mind to throw off centuries of what they considered ignorance and tyranny. Their foremost practical concerns were freedom of expression and of religion, which they viewed as the necessary preconditions for other kinds of liberty. If human beings were able to confront the world without bowing to the supernatural and subordinating thought to any arbitrary authority, then society's problems could be progressively dealt with. It is to the great credit of eighteenth-century intellectuals that they fought for this cause so relentlessly that freedom of thought has become a hallmark of the Western liberal tradition.

Modern standards of social and political consciousness, however, tend to set the philosophes apart from today. For in the eighteenth century, they had relatively little awareness of and concern for the potentiality of the mass of the people. Few philosophes can be considered precursors of egalitarianism. Toward the mass of impoverished peasants and laborers, the educated had two attitudes: pity and fear. Pity took the form of organized, inadequate philanthropy, sponsored by church and state and doled out condescendingly. Fear of the mob—the *canaille* ("rabble"), Voltaire called it—was axiomatic. Even in Great Britain the disfranchisement of the poor and the need for instruments of social control like the poor law were taken for granted. By today's standards, then, the perimeters of controversy in political and social thought were extremely narrow. For most writers the issue of political freedom was relevant to only a small segment of the population—the classes at the top of the social pyramid.

The Balance of Powers Versus the Royal Thesis

In France, still under the shadow of Louis XIV's stifling centralism, many people were intrigued by Britain's political institutions, as idealized in the writings of John Locke. Obvious defects like the Corporation and Test acts, which denied civil rights to dissenters and Catholics, or the corruption in the parliamentary borough system were either unknown to Frenchmen or overlooked in favor of liberties like the requirement of a writ of habeas corpus. The Continent was particularly impressed by the Glorious Revolution of 1688, and by the House of Commons, which stood up to both crown and Lords.

This inspiration is echoed in *The Spirit of Laws* (1748) by the great French jurist Montesquieu. His book was a pioneering effort in political sociology, the comparative study of governments and societies. Montesquieu was not proposing that Britain serve as a model for other countries, for he was arguing precisely that there is no absolute or universal standard of good government. The subtitle of this long and rambling discourse conveys this: *The Relation that the Laws Should Have to the Constitution of Each Government, the Customs, Climate, Religion, Commerce, etc.* Yet Montesquieu sought to display the virtues of the idealized British system, feeling that all societies could learn from it about liberty.

The sections on liberty won a wide readership in Europe and in America, where the book was influential among the drafters of the United States Constitution. Political liberty, said Montesquieu, is the absence of one dominating power in the state, whatever its kind: the king, the aristocrats, the people. The conservation of liberty depends on the separation and balance of powers, such as the executive, the legislative, and the judicial. If a single leader or group controls all functions, the country lives under despotism.

The only power in most states that can effectively check the possibility of royal despotism without itself degenerating into the despotism of the mob, he felt, is the aristocracy, the upper classes. In effect Montesquieu was arguing that "privilege was the ancestor of liberty," as one historian put it recently. This might seem paradoxical since privilege appears to be the opposite of liberty. But this was not the view of the eighteenth century, which commonly considered strong privileged groups—noblemen, corporations, chartered towns—the only effective bulwarks against encroachments of royal power. Only such intermediary bodies, independent of both the masses and the crown, could prevent tyranny. To put it another way, the price of a society free from despotism is privilege for some of its members. For Montesquieu the pivotal privileged group in France was the magistrates of the parlements (he himself was a magistrate in Bordeaux), for they were the guardians of the law. Protected by the ownership of their own offices, these men were for Montesquieu the most likely champions of French liberty.

Montesquieu thus hoped to limit the central government's power by balancing it with other power centers. Precisely the opposite argument was put forward by other thinkers: to maximize the central government's strength and thus its capacity to accomplish reforms. The separation of powers could guarantee certain kinds of freedom, but it could also perpetuate inequities and inefficiency. Executive authority could be a source of tyranny, but it could also be a stimulus to social and economic reform. Therefore Voltaire for one tended to regard an independent aristocracy not as a bulwark of freedom but on the contrary as an obstacle to change. While Montesquieu justified the power of the parlements to prevent arbitrary decrees, Voltaire argued that they were bastions of special interest that themselves exercised a heavy hand in society and repeatedly prevented necessary reforms.

Men who like Voltaire considered the monarchy as the likeliest agent for reform in France—as the best of several weak alternatives —were proponents of what was called the royal thesis. They hoped that a new power elite of enlightened administrators would cluster around the monarchy to replace the age-old power elite of nobles and priests. Voltaire did not advocate any kind of despotism, enlightened or otherwise. He merely felt that for all its dangers a strong monarchy was preferable to a strong corporate nobility.

The royal thesis seemed particularly justified when Louis XVI ascended the throne in 1774 and appointed Jacques Turgot, a contributor to the *Encyclopedia* and one of France's most progressive thinkers and talented administrators, as his finance minister. The philosophes unanimously applauded this appointment and looked forward to a truly reformist administration. The policies that Turgot initiated for tax reform and economic opportunity were relatively modest moves toward a more open society and increased initiative for private citizens. Modest though they were, however, they encroached on a number of special preserves. Turgot was therefore attacked by the entrenched interest groups, including the parlements. Within two years he was dismissed by a king who disliked agitation and controversy. The flaws in the royal thesis were numerous, but the most obvious was the disinclination of the Bourbon king himself to support it vigorously.

Rousseau

Only one major political theorist advanced well beyond the two classic eighteenth-century positions associated with Montesquieu and Voltaire. But to understand the profound originality of his thought, one must first appreciate his unique position in the republic of letters. For Jean Jacques Rousseau provided in his life and writing a critique of the Enlightenment as well as of the status quo. Obsessed with the issue of moral freedom and individual autonomy, he found society far more oppressive than most philosophes allowed.

Young Rousseau won instant fame when he submitted a prize-winning essay in a contest sponsored by a provincial academy on the topic, "Has the restoration of the arts and sciences had a purifying effect upon morals?" Unlike most respondents, Rousseau answered that it had not. He argued that the lustrous cultural and scientific achievements of recent decades were producing pretentiousness, conformity, and useless luxury. Most scientific pursuits, he wrote, "are the effect of idleness which generate idleness in their turn." The system of rewards in the arts produces "a servile and deceptive conformity . . . the dissolution of morals . . . and the corruption of taste." Against the decadence of high culture he advocated a return to "the simplicity which prevailed in earliest times"—manly physical pastimes, self-reliance, citizens instead of courtiers.

These strictures against his own society led commentators to think of Rousseau as a "primitivist," extolling the virtues of the state of nature and the "noble savage." But this was not the case. Rousseau regarded the state of nature as a state of anarchy where force ruled and men were slaves of appetite. Yet this opinion made him no less contemptuous of eighteenth-century salon society, whose artificial rituals prevented the display of genuine emotion, and valued style over substance. Worse yet, he said, the educated and refined elite nurtured a sense of superiority that undermined common sense moral standards.

For Rousseau the basis of morality was conscience, not reason. "Virtue: sublime science of simple minds," he wrote, "are not your principles graven on every heart?" This theme he returned to in his two popular works of didactic fiction, *Julie, or the New Heloise* (1761), and *Emile, or Treatise on Education* (1762). In the novel *Julie* the hero is repeatedly tempted into immoral acts by passions and appetites but triumphs over them in the end. *Emile* recounts the story of a young child raised to be a moral adult by a tutor who emphasizes experience rather than book learning and who considers education as a process of individual self-development. Both books attack the complacent secularism or deism that prevailed among intellectuals of the time, arguing for a more profound, personal religiosity. For these reasons Rousseau's fiction was highly prized by young poets, who were themselves seeking a more personal idiom of expression and who valued the force of the emotions that classical rules of composition discouraged. Thus Rousseau was both a pioneer of progressive education and a precursor of literary romanticism.

Rousseau himself was by no means a saint. On the contrary his struggle against his own passions—illustrated by the illegitimate child whom he fathered and abandoned—doubtless contributed to his preoccupation with morality and conscience. Nonetheless his life as well as his writings influenced the generation of intellectuals coming of age in the 1770s and 1780s. He was a true rebel among his contemporaries, rejecting much of the celebrity that his pen brought him. Not only did he quarrel with the repressive authorities of church and state—who repeatedly banned and burned his books—but he attacked the pretensions of his fellow philosophes, whom he considered arrogant and cynical. By the 1770s heroes of the Enlightenment like Voltaire and Diderot had won their battles and had become almost too successful to serve any longer as critics of society. They were masters of the most important academies by then, and in a sense they had themselves become the establishment. For younger writers and thinkers who were critical of the existing distribution of power and patronage, Rousseau remained an inspiration. He was a cultural hero for frustrated intellectuals and reformers, some of whom became revolutionaries in 1789.

What proved to be Rousseau's most famous work, *The Social Contract* (1762), became so only after the French Revolution, which dramatized many of the issues that it raised. The Revolution did more for the book than Rousseau did for the Revolution, which he neither prophesied nor advocated. *The Social Contract* was not meant as a blueprint for revolution but rather as an ideal standard against which the reader might measure his own society. Rousseau did not expect that this standard could be achieved in practice since existing states were too large and complex to allow the kind of participation that was the essence of his vision.

A free society in Rousseau's conception is one in which authority and sovereignty derive from the individual himself. A government that is entirely distinct from the individuals over whom it claims to exercise authority has no validity. In short Rousseau denied the almost universal idea that some men are meant to govern and others to obey. In the ideal polity, an individual has had a role in making the law to which he submits. By obeying it he is thus obeying himself as well as all his fellow citizens. For this reason he is free.

The foundation for a society of this kind lies in a primal act of sovereignty in which each citizen voluntarily subscribes to a social contract that establishes the society's ground rules. The government that is erected under such a contract is a revocable trust. To the perceptive reader *The Social Contract* suggested a community based on the voluntary participation of its members rather than the chance destiny of history or inheritance. The only legitimate "sovereign," then, is the people. This sovereign in turn creates a government that will carry on the day-to-day business of applying the laws.

Rousseau was not advocating majority rule but rather consensus as to the best interest of all citizens, even if it *appears* contrary to the welfare of some. For in fact the best interest of the community must be their best interest too since they are voluntary members of the community. This concept, which Rousseau called the general will, is paradoxical and difficult to grasp. Acceptance of the general will is an act of moral freedom, a very demanding principle. Freedom for the citizen means doing what one *ought*, not what one *wants*. It derives from conscience, which must do battle within the individual against passion, appetite, and self-interest. Thus, to use Rousseau's most striking phrase, the government must occasionally "force its citizens to be free." Freedom cannot exist in a state of nature or in any arrangement dictated by force. It is a tenuous social arrangement involving consent, participation, and subordination of individual self-interest to the commonweal.

More than any of the philosophes, Rousseau understood that the issue of freedom—one of the Enlightenment's central concerns—cannot be dealt with simply in terms of individual autonomy and well-being. The moral freedom of a man depends on the arrangements governing the collectivity of men.

Shortly after the French Revolution began in 1789, conservatives such as the Irish statesman Edmund Burke charged the philosophes with causing it. Burke thought the philosophes had subverted their society by consciously undermining all authority, particularly that of the monarchy and the church. As if substantiating Burke's claim, but in an opposite spirit, many revolutionaries made a cult of the memory of Voltaire and Rousseau. All this has confused the issue of the actual nature and impact of the Enlightenment.

The philosophes, most of whom had died by the 1770s, were far from being incipient revolutionaries. Members of Europe's cultural elite, they intended only that their society gradually reform itself. Distrustful of the uneducated masses, afraid of sedition and popular anarchy, they had everything to fear from a revolutionary upheaval. They were critics of their society but not its subverters.

Nonetheless the Enlightenment did challenge the traditional values of European society. From Voltaire's early polemics against Christianity through the sober social science of the Encyclopedia and the impassioned writings of Rousseau, new ideas and new modes of thought were diffused among important elements of Europe's educated classes. The philosophes did not offer new doctrines such as Socialism for men to implement. Rather they challenged the automatic respect for convention and authority, promoting the habit of independent-minded reflection and the conviction that change was both necessary and possible.

In and of themselves the crusades of the philosophes against religion and against glaring contemporary abuses were by no means revolutionary. But they promoted a climate in which the status quo was gradually put on the defensive and in which revolution—when provoked under other circumstances—was not unthinkable.

RECOMMENDED READING

Sources

* Crocker, L. G. (ed.). *The Age of Enlightenment.* 1969.
* Gendzier, Stephen J. (ed.). *Denis Diderot: The Encyclopedia: Selections.* 1967.
* Manuel, Frank E. (ed.). *The Enlightenment.* 1965.
Rousseau, Jean Jacques. *The Social Contract and Discourses.* 1950.
* Voltaire. *The Portable Voltaire.* 1949, 1977.

Studies

* Behrens, C. B. *The Ancien Régime.* 1967. A long essay tying together society, culture, and government. Abundantly illustrated.
Bruford, W. H. *Germany in the Eighteenth Century: The Social Background of the Literary Revival.* 1952.
* Cassirer, Ernst. *The Question of Jean-Jacques Rousseau.* 1963.
Cobban, Alfred. *In Search of Humanity.* 1960. A dry but useful discussion of the major philosophes.
* Cragg, G. R. *The Church and the Age of Reason, 1648–1789.* 1966.
* Ford, Franklin. *Robe and Sword: The Regrouping of the French Aristocracy After Louis XIV.* 1953. Should be read in conjunction with Montesquieu's ideas.
* Gay, Peter. *Voltaire's Politics: The Poet as Realist.* 1959. A lively and sympathetic portrait.

Hampson, Norman. *A Cultural History of the Enlightenment.* 1969. Possibly too interpretive to serve as an introduction, it nonetheless presents the subject most interestingly. (For a more advanced study see Peter Gay's two-volume work, *The Enlightenment: An Interpretation,* 1966 & 1969.)
Herr, Richard. *The Eighteenth-Century Revolution in Spain.* 1958. Absolutism and Enlightenment in Spain—a case study not discussed in the present text.
Kors, Alan. *D'Holbach's Coterie: An Enlightenment in Paris.* 1976.
Korshin, P. J. (ed.). *The Widening Circle: Essays on the Circulation of Literature in Eighteenth-Century Europe.* 1976.
* Krieger, Leonard. *Kings and Philosophers, 1689–1789.* 1970. A good introduction to eighteenth-century thought and government.
Malcolmson, R. W. *Popular Recreations in English Society, 1700–1850.* 1973.
* Paulson, Ronald. *Hogarth: His Life, Art, and Times* (abridged ed.). 1974.
Schackleton, R. *Montesquieu.* 1961.
Venturi, Franco. *Italy and the Enlightenment.* 1972. Essays on important Italian philosophes by a leading historian.
* Watt, Ian. *The Rise of the Novel: Studies of Defoe, Richardson, and Fielding.* 1957.
Wilson, Arthur. *Diderot.* 1972. An exhaustive, masterful biography.

---

* Available in paperback.

TWENTY

REVOLUTIONS OF THE EIGHTEENTH CENTURY

The eighteenth century forms a bridge in Western history between two fundamentally distinct epochs. Europe in 1700—the Europe of the "old regime"—largely preserved the institutions and the way of life that it had acquired over the long centuries of the past. In 1700 the economy remained based predominantly upon agriculture. People were aided in their labors by animals, wind, and water, but their technology offered them comparatively little help. In social and political life, inequality was the rule. Kings and emperors, who claimed to hold their authority directly from God, presided over realms which were composed of distinct orders or estates, each with its own obligations and privileges.

In contrast, the European society of 1800 was witnessing violent upheavals at every level. Western man had begun a radical transformation of his methods of raising food and producing goods. This Industrial Revolution, which continues in our day, achieved a stunning conquest of the material world, restructured society, changed all aspects of Western life in its early phases, and now offers similar promises and poses similar problems to all the peoples of the earth.

Concurrently with the inauguration of the Industrial Revolution, profound changes were undermining the peace of Western society. As we have seen, the leaders of the Enlightenment broke with traditional religious assumptions; they denied that morality and social order had to be based on divine revelation and supernatural grace. Human reason could replace or was equivalent to the word of God. In a larger context growing numbers of men—not only from the middle classes but from the older privileged orders as well—had come to believe that society was ill-served by traditional institutions, and they agitated powerfully to reform them. The demand for reform bore as its principal fruit the great revolutions that swept across wide areas of both Europe and North America in the late eighteenth century.

The latter 1700s thus initiate the great age of revolutions in the West. Of course all periods of the Western past have experienced change, and all have contributed to the making of our present society. But the economic changes and popular revolts begun toward the end of the century hold a pivotal position in the growth and transformation of Western civilization. Perhaps no other movements have left such visible marks on the character of our modern life —our government, our economy, and our social ideals.

I. THE INDUSTRIAL SYSTEM

Since the eighteenth century, the economy of the Western world has been in nearly continuous transformation. Humankind has achieved spectacular efficiency in raising food, producing goods, amassing wealth, multiplying itself, and changing the face of the earth. While no one can be certain, it is probable that more human beings are alive today than inhabited the earth over all the millennia before 1700. In a series of lectures given in 1880–1881, a young sociologist and economist at Oxford University named Arnold Toynbee chose (though he did not coin) the phrase "Industrial Revolution" to describe this metamorphosis.[1]

CHARACTERISTICS OF AN INDUSTRIAL ECONOMY

With a fund of information unavailable to Toynbee, it is easy to criticize the term that he more than anyone made part of the historical vocabulary. It does not for example encompass changes in agriculture or transportation, without which the Industrial Revolution properly speaking would not have occurred. The traditional dates for it in Great Britain, 1760 to 1815 or 1830, are much too confined. If great factories are the mark of an industrial society, Britain and even more the Continent would have to be considered still underdeveloped by 1830. The revolution did not end in 1830. Indeed the great advances based on the spread of the railroads, the application of chemistry to manufacturing, and the development of electrical power and the internal combustion engine did not affect the economy until the middle and late nineteenth century; moreover computers, atomic power, and automation carry the changes forward into our own future.

There are then many industrial revolutions, and they cannot be considered as marked off by precise dates. Nor was the initial transformation confined to manufacturing. But most historians would be reluctant to deny

that there was a period beginning in the late eighteenth century, initially in Great Britain, when profound changes occurred in the production of goods and food that eventually equipped a significant part of the Western world with a kind of economy unknown in all prior historical ages. This is the period of what is conventionally called the Industrial Revolution.

What essentially distinguishes an industrial, or modern, economy from the traditional economies of previous epochs? Arnold Toynbee and many later writers equated the Industrial Revolution with the application of steam power to manufacturing, which brought about the factory system. The steam engine, used to drive mills from the 1780s on, destroyed the putting-out system of domestic industry, in which artisans worked at home with their own tools on materials delivered to them by merchants or entrepreneurs. The use of steam power required that the workers congregate in great mills or factories, and they thus came to form a new social unit. But the emergence of the factory system does not seem today an adequate explanation of this economic transformation. In agriculture and transportation there were no factories; yet the progress in these economic sectors was an essential component of the Industrial Revolution, as noted before.

Perhaps the most distinctive feature of an industrial economy is its capacity for sustained growth. Its productivity is so great that it is able not only to meet its current consumption needs and replace its worn tools but also to invest in new capital equipment, which expands its means of producing. In short the wealth produced, the capital equipment, and the economy will not be the same at the end of a given period as they were at the beginning. The essential feature of an industrial economy —we might say of a modern society, in contrast to all societies we have studied so far—is that it never stays the same. Far more than in

[1] Arnold Toynbee was the uncle of Arnold J. Toynbee, the distinguished author of *A Study of History*, perhaps the most ambitious effort at developing a philosophy of history to appear in recent years. His own lectures on the Industrial Revolution were compiled and edited by friends after his death in 1883, at the age of thirty.

any other age, continuous, rapid, and all-pervasive change has been the law of Western life since the eighteenth century.

Of course the whole of European economic history before the Industrial Revolution cannot be described as stable and changeless. It would clearly be misleading to link together the Europe of Charlemagne and the Europe of the sixteenth and seventeenth centuries as if they were equally representative of a preindustrial, or traditional, economy. Preindustrial societies can experience profound changes; witness the agricultural and commercial expansion of the Central Middle Ages and the commercial boom of the sixteenth century. The economy advances, but after a spurt of growth it tends to stabilize, though on a higher plateau of productivity. The reason for this is that changes in the capacity to produce set in motion changes in levels of consumption, which absorb the new output and limit further capital investments. A society that attains some new wealth may elect to spend it on supporting a larger population or on raising the standard of living. A balance is reestablished between production and consumption, and investment is reduced. The economy has not achieved the capacity of self-sustaining growth. It is not industrial or modern.

Preconditions of Industrialization

To achieve self-sustaining growth, a society must first satisfy what many economists today call preconditions. A major obstacle to industrialization is a highly skewed distribution of wealth, which distorts the structure of demand. If a narrow aristocracy absorbs nearly all the disposable income, the economy, beyond meeting the subsistence needs of the people, will organize itself largely to serve the wealthy few. Catering to the desires of the rich, the economy will produce expensive goods, often exquisite in quality and workmanship, but always in small quantities. This structure of demand, which was widely char-

acteristic of European states in the old regime, will not easily support a change in the mode of production, which, at least initially, will tend to sacrifice quality of product to quantity of output. A powerful demand for cheap goods, mass-produced, is a prerequisite for the beginnings of industrialism.

The society which seeks to industrialize must also possess certain substantial, uncommitted resources. Poor utilization of resources is a mark of preindustrial economies. It must also contain a large and mobile population, with a high percentage of skilled and productive workers. It must further have adequate facilities for transporting raw materials to factories, products to market, and people to wherever they are needed. Efficient means of recruiting or forming capital are also essential, as continued economic growth is critically dependent upon a high rate of reinvestment. And leaders are needed who place a high premium on industrial growth, who can influence the decisions of government in its favor, and who have the freedom to introduce radical changes into established modes of production.

In broadest terms, industrialization requires a social milieu favorable to change and innovation. In the Europe of the old regime, many institutions, practices, and attitudes tended to dampen incentive, fix individuals to their station in life, and obstruct entrepreneurial freedom. The existence, widespread across Europe, of feudal or seigneurial rents and tolls—forced payments to lords for which they gave no compensation and rendered no service in return—hampered economic improvements, as increased production would largely benefit these parasitic groups. In the opinion of some economists, a set of property rights which rewards primarily those individuals who are engaged in socially beneficial activities is a precondition for industrialization. In the typical village of northern Europe, under the openfield system (see pp. 173–174), each cultivator had to follow the same routines of working the soil; he was not free to change his methods of farming without the concurrence of his neighbors. In the towns, the guilds presented a major obstacle to economic innovation. Guild regulations, which in the eighteenth century were more exactly government regulations enforced by the guilds, prescribed the techniques to be used in production and often dictated the terms and conditions under which goods could be sold, apprentices taken on, or workers hired. In sum, the guilds in the towns, like the villages in the countryside, exerted a kind of collective management over production. By restricting competition they tended to help weak members at the expense of the strong. On the other hand, the town guild, again like the rural village, blocked innovation, froze technology, and discouraged effort.

Another policy of the old regime which obstructed innovation was the licensing of monopoly companies, with exclusive rights to trade in certain regions, such as the East Indies, or to manufacture certain products. With assured markets and profits, these companies were not likely to assume the risks of new ventures, and they blocked others from doing so. Entrepreneurial effort may also have been discouraged by a cultural attitude, which still lingered in European society, that money made in trade or manufacture was somehow tainted. Particularly on the Continent, the highest aspiration of the successful businessman seems often to have been the purchase of a noble title.

The preconditions of industrialization are, in other words, political and cultural, as well as economic. From the mid-eighteenth century on, Enlightenment reformers—the physiocrats in France, Adam Smith and the liberal economists in England—launched concentrated attacks against communal management of land in the countryside, the guild control of industry in the towns, and privilege and monopoly

in all forms. In the name of economic rationalism, they denounced both the special advantages held by a favored few and special consideration extended to the poor and weak; enlightened society should countenance no privilege and no pity. Their hard but telling logic slowly affected policy. Guilds were already weak in the countryside and in towns of recent growth, like Manchester and Birmingham in England. Also, new industries, such as cotton manufacturing, largely escaped their supervision. The government of revolutionary France, in the Le Chapelier law of 1791, permanently outlawed guilds and trade associations. In the Corporation Act of 1835, the British Parliament similarly abolished the guilds, but they had long since become ineffective in their function of regulating the economy. The government policy of chartering monopolies was gradually abandoned (the English East India Company, for example, lost its exclusive trading rights in India in 1813). Legally and socially, the entrepreneur was winning unprecedented freedom.

Finally, the degree of effort made to industrialize is also decisive. Small increments in production will likely be offset by equal increases in consumption to support more babies or allow the population an improved standard of living. To sustain a high rate of reinvestment in the face of these demands, the effort must exceed a certain critical minimum.[2] Industrialization cannot be achieved slowly, by small or leisurely steps over time. It requires a strong drive—as Toynbee called it, a revolution.

THE FRONT RUNNERS: GREAT BRITAIN AND FRANCE

Of all the countries of Europe, Great Britain best satisfied the preconditions of industriali-

[2] Cf. Harvey Leibenstein, *Economic Backwardness and Economic Growth: Studies in the Theory of Economic Development.* 1967.

zation. The community was large enough to achieve significant economies of scale with relatively minor improvements in production; that is, it could reduce costs and thus save capital outlay per unit by increasing the volume of production. A contributory factor was the excellent balance of resources within the modest dimensions of the English realm. The plain to the south and east, which contained the traditional centers of English settlement, was fertile and productive. The uplands to the west and north contained rich deposits of coal and iron, and their streams had given power to mills since the Late Middle Ages.

The sea too was a major resource, for no part of the island kingdom was distant from it. At a time when water transport offered the sole economical means for moving bulky commodities, the sea brought coal close to iron, raw materials close to factories, and products close to markets. Equally important, it provided contact with distant shores. Foreign trade stimulated the economy with new or better products, such as cottons from India, that industries at home attempted to imitate.

Moreover, in the late eighteenth century, Britain witnessed a considerable expansion of canals and turnpikes. Usually short in this compact land, they were cheap to build and profitable to operate. By 1815 the country possessed some 2,600 miles of canals. In addition there were few institutional obstructions to the movement of goods. United under a strong central government since the Middle Ages, Britain was free of internal tariff barriers. Merchants everywhere counted in the same money, measured their goods by the same standards, and conducted their affairs under the protection of common law. In France, according to Voltaire's sarcastic comment, one changed laws as frequently as horses when traveling by stagecoach across it.

Other characteristics of Britain's society made her ripe for the broadcast changes of the Industrial Revolution. The population had a long tradition of skill and could adapt rather easily to the personal and collective discipline required by the factory system. In about 1700, the standard of living of the English masses was probably the highest in Europe. English society was also considerably less stratified than that on the Continent, and the propertied classes tended to be oriented toward innovation. Primogeniture was the rule among both the peers (the titled members of the House of Lords) and the country gentlemen or squires, and the need to provide for their frequently large families encouraged them to increase their estates and revenues. From their ranks came the so-called "improving landlords." Their younger sons, left without lands, had to seek careers in other walks of life, many of them in commerce and manufacturing. They frequently recruited capital for their ventures from their landed (and sometimes titled) fathers and elder brothers. Capital, therefore, like people, frequently crossed class lines in England. Another important pool of entrepreneurs was the considerable number of English religious dissenters, chiefly Calvinists and Quakers, who concentrated their energies on business enterprises because they were denied careers in government or the church.

The responsiveness of the propertied elements to investment opportunities was a remarkable feature of English society in the eighteenth century and one of the chief reasons why Britain was the home of the Industrial Revolution. These entrepreneurs and investors had a relatively greater influence on government than comparable groups on the Continent. Since the revolution of 1638, the government had been particularly sensitive to the interests of the propertied classes. They in turn had confidence in the government. The close ties between property and power facilitated the economic growth of the realm and was one important reason for the relative stability of the British regime in this age of revolutions.

Historians are not sure exactly what precipitated the takeoff of the eighteenth-century British economy or even what sectors led others in the industrializing effort. At one time scholars stressed the work of individual leaders, the improving landlords in agriculture or inventors and entrepreneurs in the cotton industry. Today it is generally recognized that agricultural changes came only slowly and that the growth of the cotton industry, however rapid, still accounted for only a small part of England's gross national product. Historians are thus inclined to lay greater emphasis on broad economic stimuli felt in several sectors simultaneously. One recently formulated theory, partially Marxist in inspiration, stresses the economic and political exploitation of overseas colonies as the critical stimulus in early industrialization. Colonies offered a huge market for inexpensive goods, especially cotton fabrics, which the new machines produced most efficiently. They provided cheap raw materials, and the large profits of the colonial trade promoted the formation of industrial capital.

Overseas trade was certainly booming in the eighteenth century, and certainly gave a powerful thrust to industrialization. Still the possession and exploitation of a colonial empire could not of itself assure early industrialization—witness Spain, Portugal, or Holland. Probably no less important was the growth of home population, which assured an enlarged domestic market and an abundance of cheap labor. Cultural changes may also have had an effect in that many men were willing to risk replacing old methods by new, and on other planes people were questioning and transforming traditional ways of thought and behavior. Then too the industrial growth itself, once initiated, seems to have exerted a reciprocal influence on trade, population, and attitudes.

The processes of this first industrialization

THE GROWTH OF ENGLAND'S FOREIGN TRADE IN THE EIGHTEENTH CENTURY

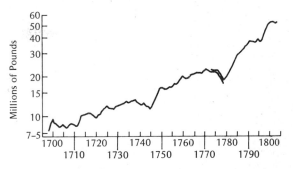

Three-year moving averages of combined imports and exports. (Adapted from Dean, Phyllis, and Cole, W. A., *British Economic Growth, 1688–1959,* Cambridge, 1964, p. 49.)

are thus highly complex and still not entirely understood. What seems certain is that a strong demand for cheap goods was growing at home and abroad in the eighteenth century, that important segments of the British community perceived this opportunity and responded to it, and that resources in England were abundant enough to support fundamental changes in traditional methods of production.

In Continental Europe France came closest to Britain in meeting the preconditions of industrialization in the eighteenth century. But the French economy labored under handicaps. France was larger, and the expense of transportation grew rapidly with distance. Waterways were not so conveniently distributed, and roads were miserable even in the age of Louis XIV's minister Colbert. Internal tariffs at provincial borders continued to restrain trade. In 1664 Colbert had created an area of free trade that embraced the older central provinces of the monarchy, but beyond it tariffs, tolls, and seigneurial dues burdened commerce. Merchants in the northeastern provinces of the Franche-Comté and Alsace for example found it easier to trade with the imperial cities of the Rhineland than with

Paris. Contrasts in legal systems and in weights and measures further complicated and slowed exchange.

After 1715 France enjoyed some seventy-five years nearly free from foreign invasions and internal uprisings; this was the calm before the terrible storms of the Revolution. The period of peace saw a remarkable proliferation of communications arteries. By 1738 the Picardy Canal linked the Somme and Oise rivers in the north. The Central Canal, built between 1783 and 1793, joined the Loire and Saône. Work was begun in 1777 on the Burgundy Canal, which enabled barges to move from the English Channel to the Mediterranean. The improvement of French roads, given major attention by Philibert Orry, a chief financial officer under Louis XV, was perhaps even more impressive. In 1738, he imposed a heavy corvée on the parishes, requiring from them contributions in labor for the construction and maintenance of roads. About a decade later the government founded the Ecole des Ponts et Chaussées ("School of Bridges and Roads"), which soon became probably the best engineering school in Europe and which still functions today. By the late eighteenth century, France had acquired a magnificent system of royal highways that many contemporaries considered unsurpassed in Europe.

Foreign trade expanded too, especially with the West Indies and the Levant, despite the military reversals in North America and India. The number of French ships engaged in foreign commerce increased about fourfold between 1716 and 1789; on the eve of the Revolution, some 1,800 vessels showed the French flag. In the same period exports of manufactured products rose by 221 percent and all other commodities by 298 percent. The great ports of Bordeaux and Marseilles enjoyed a period of prosperity unequaled since the Middle Ages.

Stable coinage aided the financing of enterprises. In 1726 the government fixed the value of the principal gold coin, the louis, and kept it stable for the remaining years of the old regime—a remarkable feat in the light of the monarchy's desperate financial needs. The collapse of John Law's investment scheme in 1720 had a regressive effect on French banking, to be sure. French investors developed a lasting suspicion of banks, paper money, and joint-stock companies. Businessmen tended to rely on resources that they or their close relatives could muster and preferred to deal in hard cash rather than commercial paper. Small size, small capital, and conservative management worked to hold back French business enterprises. But this only dampened, not suppressed, the boom of the eighteenth century.

II. ECONOMICS AND DEMOGRAPHY

The birth of the new economic system required the development of effective ways of recruiting, managing, and channeling capital into those enterprises with the greatest potential for profit. The commercial capitalism of the previous centuries was thus gradually being transformed into industrial capitalism. Changes in monetary practices affected trade and prices, and price movements had a major impact not only upon the economy but upon government as well. At a still more fundamental level, these economic changes influenced the patterns of marriages, births, and deaths in European society. In fact, they helped stimulate a population explosion, which in turn had a powerful repercussion on European life.

FINANCIAL MANAGEMENT

Critical to the takeoff of the industrialization process is a high rate of reinvestment, which in turn depends on the skillful management of money by both individuals and public institutions. Here again Great Britain was the most advanced country of Europe. From the sixteenth century on, the demands of overseas trade promoted the formation of joint-stock companies. By the seventeenth century, great concerns controlling trade with India, the South Seas, Africa, and the Levant were dominating England's overseas commerce. The financial panic in 1720 caused by the collapse of the South Sea Bubble prompted Parliament to pass the so-called Bubble Act, which required that all joint-stock ventures secure a royal charter. This limited the formation of stock companies, for a charter was difficult and expensive to obtain. Eventually, however, the joint-stock company was to become as much the child of modern capitalism as the factory.

The early industrial enterprises, chiefly partnerships, could rely on a growing banking system to meet their capital needs. In the seventeenth century the goldsmiths of London had assumed the functions of bankers. They accepted and guarded deposits, extended loans, transferred upon request credits from one account to another, and changed money. In the eighteenth century banking services became available beyond London; country banks, of which there were 300 in 1780, numbered more than 700 in 1810. The English businessman was familiar with bank notes and other forms of commercial papers, and his confidence in paper facilitated the recruitment and flow of capital.

The founding of the Bank of England in 1694 itself marked an epoch in the history of European finance. It enjoyed a phenomenal success in the eighteenth century as it has since. It assumed responsibility for managing the public debt and sold shares in the debt (equivalent to shares in the bank) to the public. It faithfully met the interest payments due to the shareholders, with the help of government revenues it was given to administer, and simultaneously placed at the disposal of the

government financial resources unavailable to any Continental state. The bank was so well run that it may have attracted investments away from the private sector of the economy. But stability in government finance also assured stability in the entire money market. Moreover the system also enlisted the tax powers of the government in the cause of industrialization. Taxes and interest payments took money from the mass of the people, who were likely to consume it, and gave it to the wealthy, who were likely to invest it. Some kind of forced savings was probably essential in preserving the high rate of reinvestment essential for industrialization.

PRICES

The eighteenth century in Britain and in France and other regions of the West as well was thus an age of increasing wealth, but the economy did not expand steadily. Rather it experienced periods of sharp fluctuation, of rapid growth and severe decline, of boom and bust. French scholars have made particularly rigorous studies of the economic cycles of the period in France as revealed primarily through the history of prices. Their analyses have provided a new and powerful if sometimes controversial tool for investigating social change in eighteenth-century France and for interpreting the French Revolution itself.[3] We are less well informed concerning price movements and business cycles in other parts of Europe and in North America, but the available information suggests that the economy in these societies was behaving comparably to France's.

For the first thirty years of the eighteenth century, prices in France and apparently in

---

[3] The French historian E. Labrousse has written the fundamental studies on price movements in eighteenth-century France; see especially his *La crise de l'économie française à la fin de l'Ancien Régime et au debut de la Révolution.* 1944.

England too remained stable. The economy similarly remained relatively stagnant, one reason being the exhaustion of the European states during the War of the Spanish Succession and the difficult decade and a half of readjustment following it. The economic eighteenth century, as some French scholars call it, began about 1730 and lasted until about 1817, the time of the peace settlements following the Napoleonic wars. Inflation in prices dominated the era. Since French money was kept stable after 1726, the strong upward movement must be attributed to other causes. The great increase in foreign trade brought a new abundance of precious metals to Europe, especially gold from Brazil. But primarily, as we shall see further, the price rise reflected the pressures of a growing population and a growing demand for food, land, goods, and employment.

The present-day reconstruction of price movements in the eighteenth century distinguishes four periods:

1. Phase A: inflation. After 1730 prices moved slowly upward. The movement accelerated between 1758 and 1770, bringing prosperity to some segments at least of French society and making these years the "splendor of Louis XV."

2. Phase B: depression. Prices leveled off about 1770 and began to move downward after 1778. The next decade was one of hard times, which aggravated the financial difficulties of the government.

3. The Revolution cycle. From 1787 to 1791 a series of bad harvests raised the prices of grain. Striking after a protracted period of hard times, these shocks helped precipitate the social and political crisis that ended France's "*ancien régime*," the Old Regime.

4. Continuation of phase A, inflation and prosperity, after 1791.

Over the long term the inflation did not affect all products, all sectors of the economy, and all segments of society equally. Prices in France between 1726 and 1789 increased by an average of about 65 percent. The cost of cereals, the basic food for the poor, rose slightly more than the average and considerably more than other agricultural products, such as wine and meat. Rents rose sharply, suggesting a shortage of available land; in relation to averages for the decade of the 1730s, rents paid in money had grown by 98 percent in the years 1786–1790. Wages on the other hand increased by a meager 22 percent in the same period, which would point to a glut of workers competing for employment.

These differentials had important social and economic effects. High rents in the countryside and low wages in the city took wealth from the poor and delivered it to the landlord and employer. This movement of money particularly benefited the entrepreneurial groups. Inflation helped drive many of the poor from the soil, to the advantage of their better-off neighbors, who were eager to expand their holdings; it was thus a principal cause of acute rural unrest. In the city it enabled the industrial entrepreneur to sell his goods for more and pay his workers less. Burdening the poor, it also worked against the economically inactive members of society—the nobles, for example, who lived from fixed rents or dues set in money. Inflation hurt the government too, for its revenues did not grow so fast as its expenditures. A large portion of French lands, owned by the aristocracy or the clergy, was tax-exempt. The government therefore relied primarily on indirect taxation that weighed on the lower classes, and they controlled less and less of the national wealth. Inflation was thus shrinking the traditional tax base of the French monarchy and paving the way for financial crisis.

These price changes were in turn influenced

by another factor, which also helped make the eighteenth century an age of revolutions—an enormous increase in the numbers of Europeans.

POPULATION

What some French historians now call the demographic eighteenth century began about 1730. Reasonable estimates put the population growth of Europe at between 60 and 80 percent over the following 100 years. Probably never before had Western Europe experienced so rapid and substantial an increase in its people, and never has it since. (In Eastern Europe, especially the lands of the Russian Empire, a comparable population explosion occurred after 1860.) The growth was particularly marked in Great Britain and France. England grew from an estimated 5 million people in 1700 to more than 9 million in 1801, the date of the first British census. Swelled by continuous immigration and a high birth rate, the population of England's North American colonies grew at probably twice the English rate —from an estimated 275,000 in 1700 to 3.93 million in 1790. The French, according to various estimates, numbered 16 to 19 million at the death of Louis XIV, in 1715, and probably 26 million or more in 1789. With an estimated 18 percent of the total population in Europe about 1750, France was by far the most populous nation in the West; the Russian Empire alone surpassed her, and only by a few million. Her proportion of Europe's inhabitants reached its peak in the age of the Revolution and Napoleon, after which it fell continuously until the present generation. The country's military and political dominance of Europe under Napoleon was in no small measure founded on this demographic preponderance.

Spain increased from perhaps 7 to 10 million and the Italian states from 9 to 13 million. Prussia was growing more rapidly, from perhaps 1.7 to 3.1 million. But all these countries remained thinly populated in comparison with France, and they were not to feel the full pressures emanating from population growth until the following century.

Much mystery surrounds the reasons for this population explosion. Historians once spoke with confidence of a "demographic transition." According to this simple and appealing theory, the population in traditional societies reproduces itself at a rate close to the biological maximum, but its growth is impeded by an equivalently high death rate. The immediate impact of industrialization is a reduction of the death rate, principally through improved measures of public health. The yawning gap between the steady birth rate, which continues high, and the dropping death rate results in substantial expansion of total numbers. Eventually, however, in the later stages of industrialization, the birth rate declines, settles to equilibrium with the death rate, and this slows to a halt the further growth of population.

The most recent research in historical demography has questioned and modified, without entirely rejecting, this classical model. The system of reproduction prevailing in traditional European society seems to have been homeostatic or self-adjusting: that is, birth rates rarely attained the biological maximum, but tended to vary in exact correspondence with death rates. This assured a stable population, which lived well within its available resources. The initial break with this homeostatic system involved births rather than deaths. In England, for example, according to rough but reliable estimates, the birth rate rose from 33.6 per thousand population in the first half of the eighteenth century to 39.7 in the latter half, a peak never since attained. Thereafter the English birth rate entered upon a path of slow, irregular but eventually substantial decline.

TABLE 20.1
THE VITAL REVOLUTION IN IRELAND

YEAR	MILLIONS OF PERSONS	YEAR	MILLIONS OF PERSONS
1712	2.8	1781	4.0
1718	2.9	1785	4.0
1725	3.0	1788	4.4
1732	3.0	1791	4.8
1754	3.2	1821	6.8
1757	3.5	1831	7.8
1772	3.6	1841	8.2
1777	3.7		

Ireland, thinly settled in the seventeenth century, experienced one of the highest rates of population growth in western Europe from c. 1700 until 1841. The increase was closely associated with the spread of potato cultivation, but it cannot be determined whether the potato removed previous limits on population size, or whether the population, growing for other reasons, turned more and more to that easily cultivated plant. The figures to 1791 are adopted from K. H. Connell, *The Population of Ireland* (Oxford, 1950), p. 25. The later figures are from official censuses.

Why did births initially increase? A likely explanation is that the booming commerce and new industries created jobs. Jobs in turn enabled young persons to depart early from the homes in which they grew up, to marry, and to begin families sooner than would otherwise have been possible. Ready employment also favored procreation; children could earn wages at early ages and were more an asset than a burden to their families. Still, this spurt in births may have occurred in advance of significant economic expansion. Did incremented births stimulate the economy, or did a stimulated economy encourage births? Historians can only affirm that the two were intimately connected.

The impact of industrialization upon deaths was slow in appearing and equally complex. In many ways, the industrial system aided people to longer lives. Established trading networks and cheap transport allowed food to be carried efficiently over great distances, and took the edge off most years of famine and dearth. Living standards, fluctuating but slowly improving, led to better care for children and the sick and better nutrition and hygiene for all. Cheap, plentiful, and washable cotton garments allowed new levels of personal cleanliness. Soon, cheap iron pipes brought clean water into households and carried sewage away, both moved by the cheap power of steam. Medical advances such as the development of the vaccination helped protect the population. On the other hand, the growth of large cities introduced millions into a biologically unfavorable environment. In many great European cities, death rates did not sink below birth rates until the second half of the nineteenth century. In most great European cities, infant mortality remained stubbornly high for well into the twentieth century.

Still, over the long term, the death rate was declining, and it fell more rapidly than the relative number of births. The theory of a demographic transition retains a certain crude validity. But it is not at all a full description of the behavior of the population in the period of industrialization. As research continues we may hope to learn more concerning this basic change in the terms of human life, one of the great turning points in Western history.

III. AGRICULTURE

The term "Industrial Revolution" misleadingly conveys that the economic changes of the time were confined to the cities, but in fact the countryside too was necessarily affected. In England in 1700, an estimated 80 percent of the population lived directly from agriculture; by about 1800 that portion had fallen to approximately 40 percent. This massive shift of labor and resources from agriculture to industry would have been inconceivable had the countryside not been able to supply a greater abundance of food with a reduced amount of labor. To be sure, change came only slowly to rural areas, especially on the Continent; the peasant cultivators clung tenaciously to traditional ways. But significant improvements were still achieved in agricultural methods, and these in turn enabled the countryside to supply the industrial towns with food, labor, capital, and markets.

THE ENCLOSURE MOVEMENT IN GREAT BRITAIN

The considerable improvement that Britain experienced in agricultural technology in the eighteenth century contributed greatly to her industrialization. In any agricultural system the central problem is the restoration of fertility to the soil, especially after repeated harvests. Since the Early Middle Ages, farmers in Europe had relied principally on resting their lands periodically under the two- and three-field system of crop rotation (see Chapter 6). This allowed bacteria in the soil to take needed nitrogen from the air. A quicker method, heavy manuring, could not be used widely because the poorly productive farms could not support sufficient animals.

The secret of improving agricultural productivity lay in suppressing the fallow periods. This required that more animals be produced to provide the necessary fertilizer. One of the first of the British landlords to seek a solution was Jethro Tull, an agriculturist and inventor. Much of his work was impeded by false assumptions prevalent in the first half of the eighteenth century—for example that plants actually devour the soil and that animal fertilizer is bad for them. But the zeal with which he conducted his experiments proved infectious. He also designed a horse-drawn hoe and a mechanical seeder, early steps in the mechanization of agriculture.

By the late eighteenth century, Norfolk, in the east of England, had achieved particular prominence for its techniques of "high farming." In the 1730s Tull's contemporary Charles "Turnip" Townshend stressed, as his nickname suggests, the value of using turnips and other field crops in a rotation system of planting instead of letting the land lie fallow. Some five decades later Thomas William Coke wrote extensively on field grasses, new fertilizers such as oil-cake and bone manure, and the principles of efficient estate management. The eighteenth-century high farmers also experimented with the selective breeding of animals. Coke improved the Suffolk breed of pigs, adding to the advances made by Robert Bakewell, a generation his senior, who had developed the Leicestershire breed of sheep and dramatically increased the weight of marketed cattle.

To make use of the new methods, the improving farmers had to be free to manage the land as they saw fit. This was all but impossible under the open-field system, which had dominated the countryside since the Middle Ages. Characteristically even the largest landlords held their property in numerous elongated strips that were open to the land of their neighbors. Owners of contiguous strips had to follow the same routines of cultivation. One could not raise grasses to graze cattle when another was raising wheat. The village as a whole determined what routines should be followed and was thus the effective manager of each holding. The village also decided such matters as how many cattle each member could graze on common meadows and how much wood he could take from the forest. The open-field system froze the technology of cultivation at the levels attained in the Middle Ages. The landlord who wished to form a compact farm and apply new methods could not function within this framework. He needed the freedom to innovate.

He could gain that freedom only by enclosing his property. But both common law and cost considerations ruled out fencing the long, narrow strips. The entire village had to be enclosed, and this required the agreement of all its members, even the poorest. Voluntary enclosures were thus nigh-on impossible to arrange. There was an alternative, however: an act of Parliament, usually passed in response to a petition, allowing the enclosure of a village even against the opposition of some of its members. The procedure was difficult and expensive. The lands of the village had to be surveyed and redistributed in compact blocks among the members in proportion to their former holdings. Frequently too roads had to be constructed to ensure access to the fields. But over the course of the eighteenth century, the high rents and returns to be earned thanks to the new methods were making enclosures very desirable investments.

The first parliamentary act authorizing the enclosure of a village was registered in 1710, but this recourse was not exercised often until after the 1750s. Then the number of acts soared: 156 passed in 1750–1760 but 906 in 1800–1810. This sweeping change all but eradicated the traditional village and the open-field system from the British countryside.

While the enclosure movement was clearly rational from an economic standpoint, it brought much human misery in its wake. The redistribution of the land deprived the poor of their precious rights in the commons and often left them with tiny, unprofitable plots. Frequently they were forced to sell their holdings to their richer neighbors and seek employment as landless laborers or urban workers.

Historians have interpreted the importance of enclosures in English economic and social history variously. They have viewed the system as a counterpart or even a precondition of industrialization in the cities. The peasant cultivator, thrown off the soil, provided the factories with cheap labor; the productive fields yielded the needed food; the prosperous gentry and its tenants purchased the manufactured products and helped provide industrial capital.

Today research is showing that enclosures did not perhaps mesh quite so neatly with industrialization. There was no massive rural depopulation in their wake; the industrial labor force seems to have recruited its members as much from artisans already established in the towns as from the dislodged rural poor.

On the other hand it would be unwise to discount the importance of this movement. It transformed the English countryside even in a physical sense, giving it the appearance it retains today: the large, verdant fields, neatly defined by hedges and walls. It resulted in the near-disappearance of the peasant cultivator, working his own land in the village of his ancestors. If enclosures did not violently push people to the towns, neither did they encourage growth in rural settlements. They were therefore a major factor in the steady shift of population from countryside to city and in the emergence of the first truly urban, truly industrial society in the modern world.

AGRICULTURE ON THE CONTINENT

Change came more slowly to the countryside in Continental regions. The centers that witnessed the most active development were the Netherlands, the Paris basin and the northeast of France, the Rhineland, and the Po valley—all areas of dense settlement where high prices for food encouraged investments in agricultural improvements. Many great landlords emulated the British in improving methods of cultivation.

Continental farmers also waged a battle for managerial freedom, though it was by no means so sweeping as the English enclosure movement. For example many French villages worked the land under a system similar to the open-field arrangement known as *vaine pâture* ("empty pasture," or fallow). This too required owners to follow the same routines of cultivation as their neighbors, with the village determining the rights of its members on common lands. From the middle of the century on, the representative assemblies of several provinces outlawed obligatory *vaine pâture* and allowed individual owners to enclose their land, and some authorized the division of communal properties. But the French monarchy did not adopt enclosures as national policy, and after 1771 even the provincial governments no longer seem to have authorized or required them. Traces of the medieval village and the medieval countryside thus lasted longer in France and other Continental regions than in England.

There is a further contrast between Great Britain and the Continent that is of considerable interest in social history. Enclosures in Britain led to the domination of rural society by great landlords and prosperous tenant farmers, who usually held the land under long leases. In France on the eve of the Revolution, probably 35 percent of the land was owned by the peasants who worked it. In this regard the French peasants were more favored than those of any other European country, Britain included.

If the soil had been worked efficiently and if the population had remained stable, the distribution of the land would clearly have been socially advantageous. But in fact small peasant proprietors rarely had the resources to adopt new techniques, and their very numbers, apparently growing rapidly, obstructed their efforts. The society of small farmers was therefore vulnerable to population pressures and was easily disturbed by violent movements in prices—two major characteristics of eighteenth-century economic history, as we have seen. Because of poor transportation one region could easily suffer a food shortage or even famine while neighboring areas were enjoying relative plenty. The pattern of land distribution in France and the character of rural society, superficially so favorable to the peasant, was thus also a source of acute unrest in the countryside.

In the regions close to the Mediterranean Sea, difficult geographical and climatic conditions—the often rugged terrain, thin soil, and a dearth of summer rain—did not readily allow the introduction of new techniques. The peasants continued to work their lands much as they had in the Late Middle Ages and for the same poor reward. The eastern regions of the Holy Roman Empire, Poland, and Russia had participated hardly at all in the commercial expansion of the early modern period; capital remained scarce and interest rates high. The political fragmentation of the empire and a paucity of transportation in Poland and Russia limited the size of the markets and the incentives to higher production. Areas close to the Baltic Sea, such as east Prussia, benefited from the growing demand for cereals in Western countries, but on the whole Eastern Europe was not to experience the full force of agricultural change until the next century.

IV. THE NEW SHAPE OF INDUSTRY

In manufacturing, the essential achievement of the Industrial Revolution was an enormous increase in the productivity of labor. This was attributable to two innovations: the development of more efficient tools and machines, and the exploitation of new sources of energy. Economists would call this process "factor substitution," whereby capital, represented by the new tools and machines, was substituted for the skills and energy of men. Initially the new tools were cheap and simple enough to be used by artisans in the home or in small workshops. But the growing complexity of machinery, in particular the application of steam, called into being a new social unit—the factory. The new system of production changed the face of the great European cities and brought in its wake acute new social and political problems.

COAL AND IRON

The most successful innovations of the Industrial Revolution were dependent upon efficient utilization of raw materials, particularly cheap metals such as iron, which could be formed into machines, and cheap fuel such as coal. Countries poorly endowed with these resources (as, for example, the Mediterranean lands of Europe) faced formidable obstacles in their industrial growth. England, on the other hand, was well supplied, and her deposits of coal were found in convenient proximity to her iron ore.

Since the Late Middle Ages, the English economy was handicapped by a shortage of wood, as the once great forests had been progressively cut down. Consequently England turned in ever greater measure to the use of coal as fuel, to heat homes, brew beer and ale, heat the vats for dyeing cloth, or fire the furnaces for making glass, pottery, or bricks. As miners began taking coal from deeper veins, they often penetrated beneath the water table and faced the critical task of pumping out the water. The need for powerful pumps stimulated experiments to harness steam in the late seventeenth century. A successful solution came with the development of the Savery and Watt engines. In the nineteenth century when steam was used to propel ships and trains, coal could be transported cheaply from mine to furnace. This allowed the price of coal to plummet.

In one process, however, coal was not satisfactory: the smelting of iron. Here the fuel had to be burned in direct contact with the iron ore, and mineral impurities in the coal combined with the iron to make an unsatisfactory product. Ironmasters traditionally used charcoal in the making of high-quality, malleable or wrought iron, but charcoal was expensive and the output of wrought iron consequently limited. In 1709 Alexander Darby succeeded in smelting ore with coke prepared from coal, but his invention had little immediate impact on the industry. Ironmasters used coke for smelting pig iron, which could be cast but not worked or machined. To refine the metal into wrought iron or steel they continued to use charcoal.

But the demand for and price of iron rose after 1760, and this stimulated the development of new techniques. In the early 1780s Henry Cort devised the puddling process, the first commercially feasible effort to purify iron using coke alone. This invention freed iron-making from dependence on forests. Ironmasters were simultaneously growing more adept at utilizing the metal. Perhaps the most skilled of them was John Wilkinson, a man with boundless faith that iron would become the basic building material of the new age. His improved techniques for boring cylinders made both better steam engines and better cannons possible. He built the first iron bridge in the world over the Severn River in 1779, experimented with iron rails, launched an iron boat, and at his death was buried in an iron coffin.

Low-cost metal, which could be precisely machined, and low-cost fuel in turn removed the chief obstacles to major and continuing improvements in the techniques of making goods.

INVENTIONS IN TEXTILE PRODUCTION

In Great Britain the industry that led all others in growth and technological improvements was the manufacture of cotton cloth. Its beginnings were modest; wool had been the traditional basis of urban industry everywhere in Europe. Spinners could not produce a sturdy thread from cotton fiber, so that weavers used it principally in combination with other threads, such as linen or wool.

In the early eighteenth century, several factors gave a powerful stimulus to both techno-

logical development and investment in cotton manufacturing. Trade with India had brought large quantities of muslin, calico, madras, and other fine cottons to England and built a healthy market. Wool could not be painted or printed, and cotton fabrics with bright designs appealed to the tastes of the age. To

In this design of a blast furnace, taken from a French copper engraving of the eighteenth century, the large water wheel powers the bellows, which in turn supply the needed jets of air to raise the temperature of the furnace. The continued importance of water power was a principal reason why many early factories were built in rustic settings. (Photo: The Granger Collection)

limit the competition that Indian cottons offered to domestically produced wool, in 1700 Parliament prohibited the importation of printed calicoes from India, Persia, and China and in 1721 even tried to prohibit the wearing of certain kinds of cotton cloth. By obstructing imports the government unwittingly provided a marvelous opportunity for the domestic entrepreneur. Fortune awaited those who could market cottons comparable in quality and price to those once imported from the East.

The industry thus had a double task: to speed its production processes and to improve the quality of the finished cloth. Spinning could be done by women in conjunction with their daily chores, but weaving was slow and difficult work, almost always done by men. In 1738 John Kay of Lancashire, by profession a clockmaker, invented a flying shuttle, propelled by hammers instead of passed by hand. It accelerated the weaving process, removed restrictions on the width of the cloth, and reduced the number of workers needed on a broadcloth loom.

Now the weavers could work more quickly and efficiently than the spinners. To speed the production of thread and restore equilibrium among the processes of manufacture, James Hargreaves devised his spinning jenny in the mid-1760s. The jenny, like the flying shuttle, required no source of power beyond the worker's muscle, and it could spin between six and eight threads simultaneously; later models could make as many as eighty. About the same time Richard Arkwright produced a spinner called the water frame that drew cotton fibers through rollers and twisted them into thread. Much dispute surrounds Arkwright's claim to this invention; it is likely that he pirated its basic design. But if his originality is questionable, he did possess qualities of imagination, daring, and drive. He was an entrepreneur, one of the first self-made men to lead the Industrial Revolution.

The water frame, as its name suggests, was too large to be driven by human exertion. Arkwright first used horses, but within a few years he built a factory driven by a water mill. In 1785 he adopted the steam engine as his source of power, and the modern factory was born. Technical advances kept apace. A weaver named Samuel Crompton combined the features of the jenny and the water frame into a spinning mule—so called because it was a hybrid—which spun a fine and strong thread, excelling in quality the best Indian product. Once more the equilibrium of the productive processes was disrupted, and the now-slower work of weaving restricted output. In 1784 Edmund Cartwright designed a power loom, though technical difficulties and the violent opposition of weavers limited its use until after the Napoleonic wars.

Other inventions accelerated other processes in cotton manufacturing during the last two decades of the century. An American, Eli Whitney, produced the cotton gin, which mechanized and enormously accelerated the separation of seed from fiber in the raw cotton. Sir Thomas Bell developed a method for printing the cotton cloth on cylindrical copper presses, and British and Continental inventors improved the chemical processes of bleaching and tinting the cloth.

Cotton production soared. Lancashire, with its great city of Manchester, and the neighboring counties became the great centers of cotton manufacture, soon serving the entire world. These were thinly settled areas before the eighteenth century, with few incorporated towns and no established guild systems to obstruct innovation. Lancashire offered the further advantages of water power, coal, and a good harbor, Liverpool. In 1743 England had imported about 1 million pounds of raw cotton; the figure was over 60 million by the turn of the century. And by the early 1820s cotton exports made up 46 percent of Britain's export trade.

HARNESSING STEAM

Arkwright's water frame, Crompton's spinning mule, and Cartwright's power loom all required energy beyond the ability of men or horses to provide. Even earlier, as we have seen, the mining industry had developed a critical need for cheap power. Since ancient times men had noticed that steam exerts strong pressure. The third-century Greek scientist Hero of Alexandria had employed a jet of steam to spin a small wheel; the account of his experiments, translated into English in 1575, helped alert scholars to a simple means by which heat could be converted into motion. However, the first experiments with engines powered by fire were based on another principle: the pressure the atmosphere exerts against a vacuum.

In the seventeenth century several scientists —among them Pascal in France and Otto von Guericke in Germany—proved that the atmosphere has weight. Guericke used atmospheric pressure to push a piston through a cylinder, overcoming the efforts of twenty men to restrain it. Sensational experiments like this one led directly to efforts to construct an "atmospheric engine." To create the vacuum some inventors tried gunpowder, but the fuel was too unstable to control. Steam was more manageable, and before the end of the century, atmospheric machines were being designed both in England and on the Continent that utilized the condensation of steam to create the needed vacuum.

The inventor of what must be considered the first commercially successful atmospheric engine was an Englishman, Thomas Savery, who described it to the public in a book published in 1702 and significantly entitled *The Miner's Friend*. Working as a pump, Savery's invention allowed the steam to come into direct contact with the water it was moving; this condensed the steam, dissipated heat, and rendered the pump woefully inefficient. However, Savery's engine at least proved that a fire pump was a practical possibility. A decade later another Englishman, Thomas Newcomen, returned to the piston and cylinder design and completely separated the engine from the pump. Although it still wasted a great deal of power, its reintroduction of the piston made it more efficient than Savery's by a third, and Newcomen engines were soon being used not only in Great Britain but in Hungary, Austria, France, and Denmark.

In the 1760s a young mechanic and instrument maker working at the University of Glasgow, James Watt, was given the task of repairing a small Newcomen engine used in scientific lectures. He recognized its two major inefficiencies: its great weight in relation to its power output and the quantities of fuel it required. Fascinated by the problem, he redesigned the machine and made the fundamental change of providing a separate chamber for the spent steam to condense in. His first engine, patented in 1769, was essentially an improved Newcomen engine, still relying on atmospheric pressure for its principal motive force.

But Watt had also recognized the advantage of using the pressure of expanding steam directly. The implementation of this idea took many years and required new levels of precision in machining cylinders and pistons, new designs for valves, and new knowledge of lubricants and the properties of steam itself. Watt's first practical model incorporating this principle, patented in 1782, was nearly three times more efficient than the Newcomen engine, its distant parent. He also devised a system of gears, called the sun and planet, for converting the reciprocating motion of the piston to the rotary motion needed to drive most machines. A still more important invention was the governor, or flywheel, which smoothed the movements of the engine.

Watt's partner, the industrialist Matthew Boulton, shared the merit of placing the inventions at the service of the economy. The site of Boulton's plant was Birmingham, which became the first great center for the manufacture of these new and powerful machines. From the 1780s on the steam engine was giving power to factories as well as pumps; some 500 were built before 1800.

Even these early machines represented a remarkable improvement over traditional sources of power, ranging as they did between 6 and 20 horsepower. The average man working hard can muster about one-tenth horsepower, or about 75 watts. This would not be enough to drive most of the major appliances in American homes today, such as washers, vacuum cleaners, dryers, even beaters and blenders. The horse itself works continuously at a power output of only one-half horsepower. James Watt himself first defined the unit of horsepower as 33,000 foot-pounds per minute, but this could be achieved only by the strongest horses and only for short periods. So poor in power output are animals—men and horses—that even before the advent of the steam engine they were far surpassed by windmills and water mills.

The largest windmills in the eighteenth century could develop probably as much as 50 horsepower, but perhaps two-thirds of this was lost in friction as the power was transmitted from the rotors to the pump or mill. The best water mills of the period seem to have produced 10 horsepower, but most of them rarely surpassed 5. Still, this would replace 10 or more horses and save the miller the expense of feeding and caring for so many animals. With such advantages the construction of water mills rapidly quickened over the course of the eighteenth century; flowing water rather than steam powered the early phases of the Industrial Revolution. But then too sometimes winds ceased and streams froze, and water and wind power could not be transmitted from where it was harnessed to where it

was needed. Steam engines could both produce more power more reliably and be placed where they were needed. To the traditional power-starved economy of Great Britain as of the world, the steam engine offered an enormous increment in its capacity to do work. More than any other invention, its appearance marks the advent of a new era.

INDUSTRY ON THE CONTINENT

Industrial growth was much slower on the Continent than in England. The numerous political divisions, tolls and tariffs, and the difficulties of transport restricted the size of markets. Continental society was more stratified than the English and did not develop effective mechanisms for recruiting the sons of nobles and gentry for business careers. It was also apparently less wealthy and could not initially generate a strong demand for industrial products. Business enterprises tended to be small, largely restricted to members of the same family, and cautious in policy. Cultural attitudes still placed high prestige on the life of the country gentleman, and this blocked the flow of men and capital from agriculture to manufactures.

Yet the Continental countries were experiencing important industrial changes, if not a revolution, in the eighteenth century. In France, cotton industries were taking root in Alsace, Normandy, and the region of Lille on the borders of the Austrian Netherlands. At Rouen, in Normandy, the largest center of cotton manufacture, production grew by 107 percent between 1732 and 1766. John Kay introduced his flying shuttle at Rouen in that period, and toward the end of the century the industry, while still comparatively backward, was adopting English-model mechanical spinners. The silk cloth industry, first promoted by Colbert, enjoyed a comparable boom, benefiting from the growing affluence of eighteenth-century fashionable society. At Lyons, the center of silk manufacture with a population of perhaps 143,000, the silk shops alone came to employ some 30,000 workers.

Coal production was also expanding. At Anzin, in northeastern France, one of the earliest centers of large-scale coal mining, output grew by 681 percent between 1744 and 1789. Iron manufacture at first lagged behind. The first foundry utilizing coke rather than charcoal went into operation only in 1769, and the industry's total output increased by only 72 percent in the half-century preceding 1789. Nonetheless, the iron as well as the coal works furnished France early if still restricted examples of the factory system; they also equipped her with an armaments industry destined to serve her well during the wars of the French Revolution.

Switzerland too was a region of early industrial growth. Her ancient mercantile traditions, abundant resources in water power, and strategic position on the passes linking northern and southern Europe gave her distinct advantages in developing cotton manufactures and other forms of light industry. French Flanders (the southern half of the Austrian Netherlands), the valley of the lower Rhine, Silesia (acquired by Prussia in 1741), and Bohemia-Moravia were other centers of modest but real industrial growth, especially in textiles. In Germany and Central Europe the wars and reforms of the French revolutionary period, while frequently disruptive, also served to eradicate many of the institutional obstacles to trade. Growth still came slowly, and no continental region could challenge the industrial supremacy of England before 1850. But well in advance of that date, these areas were laying the basis for a strong leap forward.

While changing its basic methods of raising food and producing goods, European society was also engaged in reforming its fundamental institutions and principles of government.

V. CONSTITUTIONAL CONFLICTS

The great expansion in population, the growth of the economy, and changes visible in almost every other aspect of eighteenth-century life inevitably disturbed the political equilibrium of the European states. Groups within the various societies believed, often with good reason, that these transformations were hurting their interests and that their governments were unresponsive to their legitimate needs. They therefore sought to reform the constitutional structure of the state. The latter half of the century particularly was a period of high social tension, constitutional crises, and spirited debate over the nature and function of government.

THE ESTATES

To understand the nature of the constitutional crises, we must first recall a salient characteristic of government under the old regimes. In virtually all the governments of Europe, a role of major importance was assigned to the corporations of citizens known as estates. By definition an estate was a functional group within society—clerics, who prayed; nobles, who fought and counseled; merchants, who traded; and artisans and peasants, who labored. Birth or appointment gave people admission to the various estates, and membership conferred certain distinctive rights and obligations. Through parliaments or assemblies the estates were also supposed to play a role in making government decisions.

Traditionally the clergy constituted the first estate and the nobles the second, but usually these two groups maintained a common aristocratic viewpoint. The ruler was also an estate, considered a corporation of one in his person —or rather his office; he had, in the political imagery of the day, another body that never died. This is implied in the usual acclamation of subjects at the death of their sovereign: "The king is dead. Long live the king!" Beneath these privileged orders was the estate of the people, the third estate in France or the commons in England. In most European domains this was the most amorphous and the least influential of the constituent bodies of society.

The estates were developing self-awareness and political ambition in the eighteenth century, and most remarkable, in the latter half even the third estate came to exert its latent power. In 1788 a French priest, Emmanuel Joseph Sieyès, posed the question in a pamphlet, "What is the third estate?" He replied simply that it was everything—the entire nation, the people. He noted further that in the past it had been nothing, but now its ambition was to become a force in the state. His assessment of both the past and the future was accurate. The rise to prominence and power of the people at the expense of the hitherto dominant aristocratic orders make this period, as one historian calls it, the "age of the democratic revolution."[4]

MONARCHICAL REFORMS

In the great eighteenth-century struggle over the exercise of power, the ruler was often the first to seek and effect constitutional change. The rights and immunities of the separate estates, primarily the aristocratic orders, reduced his fiscal resources and often deprived him of authority in conducting foreign affairs and pursuing internal reform. The privileges and monopolies enjoyed by provinces, towns, and guilds further restrained trade, hampered economic growth, and militated against the common welfare, of which eighteenth-century heads of state increasingly believed themselves the chief defenders.

The enlightened despots of the period made

[4] See especially R. R. Palmer, *The Age of the Democratic Revolution*. 1959–1964.

an attack on obstructive privilege a usual part of their policy, and many of them may be considered crowned constitutional reformers. Sweden offers perhaps the best example. Her estates, meeting in a four-house Diet (or Riksdag), long held the king in trammels, as he could not tax, change the laws, or make war, peace, or alliances without their agreement. The Diet itself offered no effective leadership because it was divided into hostile factions, especially among the nobles, that spent their energies in ceaseless battles for office and patronage and readily sold their support to foreign powers eager to influence Swedish policy, notably France or Russia.

In 1771 a new king trained in France and imbued with liberal ideas, Gustavus III, ascended the throne. The following year, with the aid of the army and French support, he mounted a coup d'état against the Diet. At the point of bayonets, he forced a constitution on the houses—the first comprehensive, written document of its kind adopted by a European state. It gave the king broader if still limited powers: the Diet could assemble only on royal summons and could discuss only what the king proposed, though its agreement was still necessary for new taxes and laws.

Gustavus then proceeded to remake Swedish institutions, almost without the Diet's participation. He changed the laws governing ownership and inheritance of land, opened offices to all classes, reformed the courts, tried to suppress corruption, established freedom of the press and of religion, and lifted restrictions on trade in grain. Stung by the reforms, which often touched their privileges, the nobles grew ever more disgruntled and from 1786 on openly challenged the king's authority. In 1788 they refused to support him in a war he had declared against Russia. In response, through the Act of Union and Security the next year, Gustavus once more altered the constitution, allocating to the king sole authority in foreign affairs and still further diminishing the role of the aristocracy in the Swedish state. Deprived of constitutional means of expressing their dissent, the dissatisfied nobles conspired against the king, who was shot dead at a masquerade in 1792. This dramatic incident later inspired Giuseppe Verdi's opera *The Masked Ball*, first produced in Rome in 1859. To sooth the censors, who looked askance at successful conspiracies, Verdi changed the locale to Boston, Massachusetts; he made Gustavus himself an English governor, who presumably could die on stage without undermining the public order.

If Gustavus' career offers an excellent example of fundamental reforms imposed from above, it also shows the violent opposition such policies could evoke from the aristocracy. In many European states the aristocracy was not content simply to defend its traditional privileges but agitated for a still larger share in the exercise of power.

ARISTOCRATIC RESURGENCE

Europe's aristocracies had understandable cause for discontent with the changes occurring in the eighteenth century. The growth of trade, the expansion of capital, and pervasive inflation left many nobles hard-pressed economically, and as a countermeasure many of them tried to reactivate their ancient and half-forgotten feudal prerogatives over the peasants. In the political sphere as well, monarchs were allocating a progressively smaller place to the nobles in the business of government.

Aristocracies all over Europe thus sought to advance their fortunes and consolidate what they took to be their rightful place under their countries' constitutions. Armed with the ideas of Montesquieu, they claimed that nobles had the exclusive right to serve as the chief counselors of the king as well as the obligation of leading the community in the conduct of its important affairs. By the last decades of the century, the aristocracy had in fact secured a near-monopoly over high offices in both the state and the church. In 1781 for example the rank of commissioned officer in the French army was limited almost exclusively to those who could show four generations of nobility. And on the eve of the Revolution, the 18 archbishops, 118 bishops, and 8,000 canons (high ecclesiastics) in the French Church were all of noble extraction; in contrast half this group had come from bourgeois stock in 1730. Simultaneously aristocrats demanded that the assemblies of estates, which they dominated or hoped to dominate, be granted a larger share of political power.

Perhaps the best example of a revolution led by the aristocracy in support of such claims arose in the Austrian Netherlands. The ten provinces were governed under charters granted by the Hapsburgs and other rulers that dated back to the Middle Ages. Representative assemblies, which controlled the government in all the provinces, largely determined the laws and imposed the taxes, apparently the lightest in the whole of Europe. Guilds, whose privileges similarly dated from the Middle Ages, were particularly strong in the Flemish towns and tightly regulated the economy.

In the 1780s Holy Roman Emperor Joseph II of Austria as part of a general reform of his realm sought to centralize and modernize Hapsburg administration of the southern Netherlands. He tried to abolish the special privileges enjoyed by the ten provinces, and in the interest of freeing the economy, he also sought to break the guild monopolies. Much to the alarm of the United Provinces and Britain, he tried as well to reopen the port of Antwerp, which had been closed to international trade since 1648. These changes were coupled with other liberal reforms—the abolition of torture, the introduction of religious toleration, the suppression of some few monasteries, and the important social reforms for the rural population that were discussed in Chapter 19. Finally, in 1787 he overhauled

In this engraving by a contemporary artist, Jean-Paul Laurens, Louis XVI is greeted upon his arrival at the opening session of the Estates General. The convocation of the Estates was the first in a sequence of events that would ultimately lead to the abolition of the monarchy and the king's execution. (Photo: New York Public Library, Picture Collection)

the court system, under which the estates had exercised their chief judicial and administrative prerogatives.

The patricians protested these reforms. In late 1788 the representative assemblies of two provinces refused to grant Joseph money, and the emperor retaliated by revoking their ancient charters, with the aim of bringing them under the direct and unlimited powers of the crown. The frightened aristocrats organized secret societies, called Pro Aris et Focis ("For Altars and Hearths"), the name implying an objection to Joseph's treatment of the Catholic Church. The following year, doubtless encouraged by the defiance of the Estates General in France, the provinces declared their independence. In the face of concerted opposition, Austrian rule collapsed. But the revolutionaries now found themselves divided. One party, led by a Brussels lawyer, held that independence from Austria sufficed and no further changes were required. The provinces should be ruled by their assemblies, which meant by their traditional aristocracies. But a second party, led by another lawyer, sought to limit the privileges of the provinces, guilds, and assemblies. These democrats, as they were called, now faced the aristocrats in a struggle over the constitution of the land. In 1790, with the support of the church and most of the peasants, the conservatives prevailed, and the leaders of the democratic faction were forced into exile.

The death of Joseph II the same year and the succession of his brother Leopold II further complicated the picture. Leopold was about as sympathetic to reform as a monarch could be in the eighteenth century, and he energetically sought to make a common front with the democrats against the aristocrats. The coalition was successful, and Austrian rule was restored in the provinces in December. The democrats flocked back, but the coalition between the monarch and the people never had the opportunity to reform the government freely. The increasing radicalism of the Revolution in France made Leopold progressively suspicious of the intentions of his own democratic allies. Finally, in 1792 French revolutionary armies poured into the Austrian Netherlands and ended all possibility of peacefully wrought change.

POPULAR MOVEMENTS

In their competition for power, both monarchs and aristocrats were likely to seek an ally in the politically inert but potentially powerful third estate, the people. The small Swiss city of Geneva offers an early example of popular participation in movements for reform. In England too, by the late eighteenth century, popular reform movements were assuming major importance in politics.

Geneva

Socially and juridically, the population of Geneva was divided into three groups. The patricians held the highest offices and dominated the Small Council, the executive body or board of governors of the city. The burghers, representing about a fourth of the population, elected the Great Council, which could approve but not propose legislation and which chose the chief officers from lists prepared by the Small Council. The majority of the population, called natives, had no political rights and were also excluded from certain professions.

In the 1760s the patricians and burghers entered into a protracted argument over the exercise of power in the government. The Small Council for example tried to suppress certain writings of Jean Jacques Rousseau, himself born in Geneva and an honorary citizen; the burghers protested. In addition they claimed the right to initiate legislation and present it to the Small Council. Because they

realized that this violated traditional constitutional procedure, the burghers took the step of appealing to theories of popular sovereignty—a fateful decision, for the same theories could be used against their own privileged status. They also cultivated the support of the totally disfranchised natives. In the face of violent agitation, the Small Council accepted a reform edict that enlarged the role of the Great Council in the government and extended certain minor concessions to the natives. The natives, now politically aroused, demanded that they be allowed to participate in political life. Riots broke out in 1770, and the government responded by suppressing the natives' political clubs and even threatening their leaders with death. In 1782, with the support of France, the government rescinded the reform edict. Fear of the people had brought a counterrevolution.

Great Britain

In Great Britain too a tripartite conflict arose involving the king, the aristocracy, and the people in the late eighteenth century. As elsewhere a major role in initiating a popular movement was played by a reforming monarch, George III (1760–1820). Unlike his namesake grandfather and great-grandfather, George had been born in England and knew the land, its language, and its political system well. He was also intent on advancing royal authority. He did not seek to by-pass Parliament but rather tried, much as the Whig ministers had before him, to control its members through patronage and influence. The Whigs saw the royal ambitions and the system through which it worked as a threat to their own traditional hegemony. Not only did they oppose the king and his ministers in Parliament, but they enlisted the support of reform elements originating outside of Parliament itself.

One such group, known as the Radical Dissenters, was led by such men as the clergyman Richard Price and the scientist Joseph Priestley. The appearance of daily newspapers (the *Morning Post* was founded in 1772 and the *Times* in 1785) gave them a marvelous means of spreading their views, and they leveled destructive criticism against the defects of the British political system. Characteristically they called for representation proportionate to population, stricter laws against corruption, exclusion from the Commons of royal officeholders, and freedom of the press.

The most notorious of popular agitators was a journalist by the name of John Wilkes. Ambitious, eloquent, and ruthless, Wilkes purchased a seat in Parliament with the aid of an opportune marriage. But success through traditional channels came too slowly, and he assumed the risky but promising role of a popular champion for reform. He viciously attacked in print the king's prime minister, and indirectly the king himself over the terms of the Treaty of Paris in 1763, which he considered unfavorable to Britain's imperial interests. The government arrested him for sedition and libel on a general warrant—that is, with the name of the accused omitted. During his trial crowds in London marched in his support shouting "Wilkes and liberty," and the courts quashed the indictment. The government then accused him of having authored a pornographic poem, called "An Essay on Women," and this time Wilkes fled to France. There he stayed for four years, but in 1768, still under indictment, he returned to stand once more for Parliament. At his second attempt he was elected. Three times the Commons refused to seat him, and three times he was returned. With the ardent support of radicals and to the acclaim of the London crowds, Wilkes finally won his seat.

The agitation for parliamentary reform in Great Britain was soon swept up in the larger issues raised by the outbreak of the French Revolution. The events of 1789 across the Channel naturally frightened certain social groups, but the Revolution's opponents were initially drowned out in a chorus of enthusiasm that swept the literate classes in Britain as on the Continent. It was hard after all to defend what was taken to be the traditional despotism of the French monarchy. But the increasing radicalism of the Revolution generated disenchantment and hostility.

The Wilkes affair, the agitation for parliamentary reform, and the reactions to the uprisings in France characterized the reform movements in a British context; revolutionary action did not. Wilkes and other radicals appealed not only to the London crowds but also to many underprivileged groups—traders, craftsmen, and the like—who did have the franchise and were thus able to express their political dissatisfaction by voting Wilkes and other men displeasing to the government into Parliament. This added to the effectiveness of the reform movement, but it also diluted its revolutionary thrust. Most radicals called only for the reform, not the replacement, of the British political system. They still retained some measure of respect for the nation's political traditions.

Ireland and North America

Great Britain did face revolutionary agitation in her overseas possessions, notably Ireland and North America. In Ireland a largely Protestant gentry was demanding autonomy for the country's Parliament under the British king and reform in the trade laws, which injured the Irish economy. But the religious and cultural gulf that divided the Protestant gentry from the Catholic people prevented an effective alliance between them, and the throne was usually able to purchase the loyalty of the upper classes with relatively minor concessions. In 1782 for example, in response to agitation led by the Protestant patriots Henry Flood and Henry Grattan, Britain gave the Irish Parliament the sought-for autonomy. This assured the loyalty of Irish gentry during the final phase of the American Revolution and the more difficult struggle with revolutionary France.

In her thirteen North American colonies, Britain faced a much different situation. George III and his prime minister, Lord North, attempted to force the colonies to pay the costs, past and present, of their own defense. The policy would have meant a pronounced centralization of authority within the government of the British Empire.

The prominent landlords and merchants of the Eastern seaboard took the leadership in opposing the fiscal measures and the constitutional changes they implied. Like the upper classes in many European lands, they too applied to the third constituent division of society—the people. But the resistance in North America otherwise differed profoundly from comparable movements in Europe. The American social leaders could not appeal to a body of corporate privileges that the actions of the king were allegedly violating. They therefore appealed to the traditional rights enjoyed by all British subjects, regardless of rank, and to theories of popular sovereignty as advanced particularly by John Locke; the Declaration of Independence was to give eloquent expression to these broad concepts. The same lack of a true estate system in colonial American society, the amorphous and fluid margins separating the social strata, further prevented the development of conflicts between patricians and the lower social orders, which so often occurred in Europe.

These differences partially explain the unique character of the American Revolution. Its effects on society were limited. But in the theory that supported it and in the close and continuing alliance between the upper and lower classes, it was perhaps the most democratic of the revolutions of the eighteenth century. It created the first state and government in which the exercise of power was explicitly declared to be based not on divine right or inherited privilege but on the consent of the governed. It also represented the first successful rebellion of an overseas colony against a European country. The example and effects of the American Revolution were thus of major importance in the dissolution of Europe's old regimes.

VI. THE FRENCH REVOLUTION

The pivotal event of European history in the eighteenth century—some would say in the modern epoch—was the French Revolution, which broke out in 1789. It conquered much of Europe with its arms and, slowly, all of Europe with its ideals. Those ideals essentially defined the contours of a modern, liberal society. In place of the traditional toleration of involuntary service (feudal charges on the land, vestiges of personal serfdom, slavery overseas), the Revolution preached liberty. In place of hierarchy and inherited social status, the Revolution demanded equality. In place of privileged and exclusive estates and corporations and established religions, the Revolution proclaimed fraternity. Liberty, equality, fraternity: this grand revolutionary slogan still represents a social ideal, to which most modern Europeans and Americans would subscribe.

ORIGINS

Historians have long studied and discussed the origins of this tremendous upheaval, and the explanations they have offered for it are many. The incompetence and indecisiveness of Louis XVI, and the frivolous character of his Austrian queen, Marie Antoinette, certainly affected the course of events, but could hardly have incited a national uprising. The ideas of the philosophes were surely corrosive of inherited values and institutions, and powerfully shaped revolutionary policies. But the philosophes themselves never advocated violent change, and most entertained deep suspicions of the restless, ignorant masses.

The interpretation which today most sharply divides historians holds that the revolution was rooted in class struggle. In the words of a prominent French historian, Albert Soboul, who writes from within a Marxist tradition, the uprising forms "the classical model of a bourgeois revolution." In this view, the French middle classes, gaining in wealth across the eighteenth century, resented the privileges of the nobility and the obstacles which the old regime placed in the path of capitalistic development. They fought to change social institutions in their own interest and claimed the seats of power in their own name. The Revolution, in sum, placed a bourgeois regime atop an already bourgeois economy.

This forceful theory has, however, evoked an equally vigorous rebuttal. Its critics question the coherence, some even the existence, of a capitalistic bourgeoisie in eighteenth-century France. Intense research has shown that the barrier between the second and third estates was porous and often passed, and the lines of social division frequently blurred. The gap between the nobles and the upper bourgeoisie was as nothing compared with the gulf which separated these orders, both privileged, from the common people. Perhaps most cogently, these critics point out that the revolutionary leaders were lawyers and administrators, rarely merchants or industrialists. The leaders of the new economy looked with doubt and fear upon the revolutionary course, supposedly (according to Soboul) flowing in their favor. The bourgeoisie, it is argued, did not make the Revolution. Rather, the Revolution made the bourgeoisie, in the sense that the reforms it achieved stimulated decisive growth in the capitalistic economy.

This ingenious revision of the Marxist argument still fails to answer the question: Who made the revolution? A recent explanation stresses the failure of French society to accommodate the growing numbers of its young. In an age of rapid demographic expansion, the young outnumbered their elders and were too numerous for the available places and careers which society could offer. Those who aspired to careers in the professions, as lawyers, doctors, clerics, officers, or administrators, faced exceptionally bitter competition and frequent frustration. Understandably they resented the advantage which a noble title or high connections might confer upon a rival. Numerous leaders of the epoch—Maximilien Robespierre, for example (see pp. 691–692)—were young lawyers from small towns whom the Revolution nurtured and frequently devoured. In this view, the French Revolution was at least in part a fronde of the frustrated and an upheaval of the young.

In the late eighteenth century, powerful forces, rooted in larger numbers of people, new forms of economic organization, and new values and ideas, strained French society. The monarchy sought to contain those forces within the established social and political system. Its effort to accomplish this, its abject failure, the reconstruction of a new social and political order are the great themes of French revolutionary history.

FISCAL CRISIS

Whatever the deep sources of the outbreak, this much at least is certain: the Revolution was precipitated by the impending bankruptcy of the French monarchy in 1789. The crisis struck France at a particularly difficult point—during a sharp downturn in the economy aggravated by two years of bad harvests. Unemployment and hunger stirred up the people. Why was the country facing bankruptcy in 1789? And why had reform been so drastically delayed?

In the 1730s France's economy had entered a period of expansion, and the growing resources it developed should have provided the monarchy with adequate revenues. Despite this the government faced nearly continuous fiscal straits. The chief reason for its poverty in the midst of plenty was the narrow tax base of its finances. The system of privilege largely exempted ecclesiastical and noble lands from a proportionate contribution to fiscal needs.

The last years of the reign of Louis XV witnessed both bad economic times and deepening fiscal distress. In 1771 the chancellor, René Nicolas de Maupeou, tried to force reform decrees through the Parlement of Paris, and when he met with concerted opposition, he dissolved the Parlement and exiled more than 100 aristocrats from the capital. His action almost exactly parallels Gustavus III's attack on the Swedish Diet. Maupeou abolished the sale of offices and created a new system of courts in which the judges held their positions by royal appointment, not by inheritance or purchase. While still not touching tax exemptions, Maupeou's policies seemed a first, bold step in reducing privilege in French government and society.

However, the monarchy was ill-served by the man who guided it. The aging Louis XV gave himself to his pleasures, and the extravagance of the court spread resentment against him. He died in 1774, and the court felt it advisable to carry the king once hailed as the Beloved to his final resting place at night, almost without ceremony, almost in secret. But many people in France still expected great things from the monarchy in the person of his grandson and heir, a young man who showed authentic concern for his people.

LOUIS XVI AND HIS FINANCE MINISTERS

Louis XVI was nineteen years old when he succeeded his grandfather as king of France in 1774. A man of blameless private life, he was nonetheless critically lacking in confidence in himself and was psychologically incapable of either conceiving or pursuing a firm course of action. His still younger queen, Marie Antoinette, daughter of Maria Theresa, was prone to intervening in her husband's decisions, which earned her the resentment of the court and the people.

Louis at once tried to conciliate the nobles, whose position in government had been gravely threatened by Maupeou's reforms. He restored to the parlements their former prerogatives. This was a popular gesture as it seemed to mark a move away from royal absolutism toward a limited and responsible monarchy. But it proved to be a major tactical error, for it gave a voice and a constitutional position to the nobles, the chief defenders of privilege. Louis was better served by his choice of ministers—in particular Jacques Turgot, a former *intendant* and a man of high talents steeped in the thought of the physiocrats, who assumed the office of controller general of finance.

Turgot imposed a policy of austerity to put France's house in order—no new taxes, no new loans, and no new expenses. He sought reform too; in 1774 he removed all restrictions on commerce in grain, and in 1776 he abolished the guilds. As a good physiocrat he contemplated replacing all indirect taxes that hampered trade with a single tax on land—all land —which he called the territorial subsidy and which would have represented the end of all noble privileges. Privately, he favored a system of advisory assemblies to replace the parlements, culminating in a national congress called the Great Municipality of the realm. Turgot in sum desired a constitution for France.

The king refused to support him. His economic policies aggravated the court, his philosophical ideas and support of tolerance offended the clergy, and his schemes for tax reform frightened the nobles. Above all his austerity and refusal to make certain appointments angered the queen. Louis, worn down by complaints against the minister, dismissed him in 1776. With him went the last hope for reform in France under royal leadership.

The king then turned to a Protestant banker from Geneva with a reputation for financial wizardry, Jacques Necker. A shrewd man with a strong sense of public relations, Necker abolished the last vestiges of serfdom on the royal lands, ended torture in judicial proceedings, and reorganized hospitals and prisons. He thus earned an enormous and largely unmerited popularity. His solution for the financial crisis, which was greatly aggravated when war broke out with England in 1778, was more loans, for was not France after all a rich nation? His policy of borrowing and spending helped several bankers on to fortune and raised his popularity among the financial bourgeoisie. But new loans only delayed and in delaying worsened the eventual reckoning. With bankruptcy ever closer and support decaying around him, Necker adroitly maneuvered the king into asking for his resignation. He left the government in 1781 with his reputation as a financial reformer still intact.

After a further shuffle of ministers, in 1783 Louis turned to another experienced administrator and former *intendant*, Charles Alexandre de Calonne. He first proceeded on the principle that the government's credit was based on confidence and that confidence was best assured by the court's carefree spending. Never had the fetes at Versailles been so splendid since the days of the Sun King. But fear of bankruptcy steadily mounted. Then in 1786 Calonne reversed his casual policies and proposed a single tax on all lands without exception—Turgot's territorial subsidy. Rather than submitting the reform to the Parlement of Paris, which would be certain to reject it, the king at Calonne's bidding summoned an Assembly of Notables, which met in February 1787. To Calonne's shock the 147 notables

refused to accept the decrees, and after several stormy sessions he was dismissed by the king. His successor, Loménie de Brienne, the former archbishop of Toulouse, brought the proposal for a land tax before the Parlement of Paris, which as predicted rejected it. The full dimensions of the king's mistake in restoring rights to the Parlement were now revealed. Louis dissolved it and exiled its members to the small provincial town of Troyes, but they continued to defy the government, asserting that only the Estates General could authorize new taxes.

The government now faced the mass defiance by the nobility that many historians call the prerevolution. The provincial parlements issued declarations of support for their counterparts of Paris. Riots broke out in several cities and provinces. The civil administration seemed on the verge of breakdown, and the loyalty of the army itself was uncertain. Louis was forced to retreat before the uprising of the privileged. He summoned the Estates General to convene in May 1789 and recalled Necker. The summoning of the national assembly was the critical first step in the Revolution, for it represented the failure of royal absolutism to achieve reform; it meant too entry onto the scene of the middle classes and beyond them the people.

THE ESTATES GENERAL AND THE CONSTITUENT ASSEMBLY

From February to May 1789, a period of growing scarcity of grain, the three traditional orders of France elected their representatives to the Estates General, which had last been convened in 1614. By a special royal concession, the third estate was accorded twice as many delegates as the two higher orders. The delegates also drew up lists of grievances (*cahiers de doléances*). Recent analyses of their content, pursued in France and America, have shown that the great majority were conservative in tone: they refer only to local ills and express confidence that the royal government would recognize and redress them. Only a few delegates from large cities, Paris especially, allude to the general principles of social order and of justice elaborated by the philosophes. It is impossible, in other words, to read in the *cahiers* the future course of the Revolution. Still they promoted widespread reflection on France's failings; their preparation was a stage in the raising of a revolutionary consciousness.

The popular expectation that the monarchy would provide leadership in reform proved to be ill-founded. When the representatives met on May 5, Louis proposed nothing. He even left unsettled the critical question of whether the assembly would vote by order, which would assure control by the privileged, or by head, which would give the dominant voice to the third estate, since many nobles and ecclesiastics sympathized with its cause.

In the absence of royal direction, the third estate seized the initiative and demanded that the privileged orders meet with it to constitute a national assembly. The king, who finally decided to cast his lot with the nobility and clergy, locked the third estate's delegates out of their meeting room until a session could be arranged in which he would state his will. Unable to sit in their usual hall, they retired to a tennis court, and there all but one swore that they would not bow to force. The king, in the face of this defiance, once more conceded and on June 24 allowed the three estates to form together the National Assembly, which changed its name shortly to the Constituent Assembly, empowered to give France a constitution.

Meanwhile unrest was growing daily in this year of hunger, and Louis' own ill-considered actions added to the turmoil. He gathered 20,000 soldiers around Paris and on July 11 dismissed the popular Necker. The dismissal provoked open insurrection in Paris. On July 14, in search of arms, the insurgents first attacked the military hospital of the Invalides and then the Bastille, an old fortress used as a prison. The latter was only one of several violent incidents in these troubled days, but the fall of the Bastille seemed to represent a victory of the people in the name of liberty over traditional despotism. Again the king capitulated. He removed the troops around Paris and recalled Necker. On July 17, to please the populace, he donned a cockade bearing the colors of white for the monarchy and blue and red for the city of Paris. This tricolor was to become the flag of the new France.

But these gestures hardly pacified the hungry masses. Rather, unrest reached the provincial towns, which rallied to declare their solidarity with the third estate, and then spread fully into the countryside. The sources of peasant dissatisfaction were many and long standing. Population growth and the parceling of holdings had sown widespread rural impoverishment. It has been estimated that one-tenth of the country population lived solely by begging; still larger proportions were reduced to mendicancy during years of dearth. Feudal dues and the ecclesiastical tithe weighed heavy upon those struggling to survive on the margins of subsistence. Suspicions, too, were rampant that the nobles were hoarding grain and pursuing a policy of fomenting famine in order to block reform. In July, peasants of Normandy, Franche-Comté, Alsace, the Mâconnais, and elsewhere sacked the castles and homes of the nobles and burned the documents that recorded their feudal obligations. From about July 20, this peasant insurgency blended imperceptibly into a popular panic, known as the Great Fear. Rumors flew through the countryside that "brigands" of unknown origin and loyalties—perhaps hirelings of the nobles—were marching on the villages, intent on destroying the new harvest upon which depended all hope of relieving the famine. The fear was baseless, but it prompted a mass recourse to arms in the provincial towns and villages, stirred up hatred and suspicion of the nobles, and destroyed what confidence remained in the traditional social and constitutional order. Peasant insurgency and the Great Fear showed that the royal government faced something far more ominous than bread riots in the capital; it was confronting a national and popular revolution.

Peasant unrest also frightened the delegates of the Constituent Assembly. On the night of August 4, the representatives of the nobility and clergy vied with one another in dramatically renouncing their ancient privileges, and the Assembly solemnly decreed that the feudal regime was forever abolished in France. The delegates showed a high regard for the rights of property, however, in insisting that the nobles be compensated for the feudal rents they were losing. But the peasants seem to have been satisfied with the concessions they attained. Strongly religious, traditionally suspicious of the motives of townsmen, rural France thereafter became a largely conservative presence in the further unfolding of the Revolution.

On August 26 the Assembly drew up the Declaration of the Rights of Man and of the Citizen. In phrases reminiscent of the American Declaration of Independence, the document affirmed the rights of men to practice what religion they chose, to receive quick and fair justice, to assemble, to own property, and to be represented in government. So also all citizens were obligated to assume a fair share of the tax burden.

But still the hunger continued, and social tensions remained high. On October 5 crowds of women demanding bread besieged Versailles and forced the king and the royal family to come to Paris. The Assembly followed within a few days. Versailles, Louis XIV's great palace, symbolized not only royal absolutism but the detachment of the government from the people. The government's return to Paris thus indicated the new power of the popular forces in France.

The Restructuring of France

From 1789 to 1791, the Constituent Assembly labored hard and productively on a constitution for the new France. While recognizing the rights of all French citizens, the constitution effectively transferred power from the privileged estates to the general body of the rich and the educated, in which the nobility remained as individuals without titles or privileges. In reshaping institutions, the Assembly sought to implement principles of rationality, efficiency, and humanity, much as the philosophes advocated. Especially as they touched local administration, justice, and the courts, the reforms proved remarkably durable; even today, the work of the Assembly is visible in France.

At the center, the constitution created a limited monarchy with a clear separation of powers. The king was to name and dismiss his ministers at will, but he would be required to secure their approval for his major decisions. The legislative branch would consist of a single house, the Legislative Assembly, with members elected for two years by a complex system of indirect voting. The king would exercise a suspensive veto over their enactments, but if the bill was passed by three Assemblies, it would become law even without royal approval. The franchise was to be limited to "active" citizens who paid a certain sum in taxes, and the property qualification would be even higher for those who wished to stand for public office. But some two-thirds of the adult male population attained the right to choose the electors, who in turn would choose the delegates. Although the system favored the rich, it was considerably more liberal than the political structure in for example contemporary Britain.

With regard to local government, the Con-

stituent Assembly abolished the parlements and provided a standardized provincial administration in France. The land was divided into eighty-three departments, each allowed considerable autonomy—something not characteristic of later French constitutions. Offices were no longer to be sold, and torture and unusual punishments in judicial procedures were prohibited. The Assembly called for a new codification of French law, but this desideratum was to be achieved only by Napoleon. In economic affairs the principle of laissez faire inspired the Assembly's decisions. It lifted all internal tariffs and did away with all chartered trading companies and monopolies. The law also forbade the formation of associations of workers since they too were considered hindrances to freedom of trade and contract.

In finance the Constituent Assembly decided to honor the royal debt, which it considered, as it did all forms of commitment involving property, an inviolable obligation. To find new revenue it confiscated all ecclesiastical property in November 1789, placing it "at the disposition of the nation" and simultaneously making the government responsible for the costs of religious services. On the basis of this fund of church lands (to which the property of émigré nobles and the crown would subsequently be added), the Assembly issued paper bills known as assignats, which circulated as money. The secularization of ecclesiastical holdings had one important social result. Those bourgeois and rich peasants who acquired them acquired too a vested interest in the work of the Revolution. They

MAP 20.1: FRANCE: PROVINCES AND REGIONS BEFORE 1789

(From Breunig, Charles, *The Age of Revolution and Reaction, 1789–1850*, New York: Norton, 1970, p. 18.)

were numerous and strong enough to assure that the achievements of the Constituent Assembly would never be undone.

The following July the Assembly reformed the Catholic Church in France through the Civil Constitution of the Clergy. The law reduced the number of bishops to eighty-three, reshaping diocesan boundaries to conform with those of the departments; required that both bishops and parish priests, like civil officials, be elected by those they served; and when resistance became manifest to these enactments, the Assembly demanded that all

MAP 20.2: FRANCE: REVOLUTIONARY DEPARTMENTS AFTER 1789

(From Breunig, Charles, *The Age of Revolution and Reaction, 1789–1850*, New York: Norton, 1970, p. 18.)

clerics swear to uphold the new legislation. The Civil Constitution ignored the traditional canon law and would have suppressed the autonomy of the church or for that matter the authority of the pope in France had it been able.

The Civil Constitution raised a storm of protest among both the clergy and the Catholic faithful. All but seven bishops and half the parochial priests refused to take the required oath. These were called the refractory clergy. Reforms in the French Church were a recognized need, and many of the provisions corresponded with the wishes of informed and pious Catholics. But the effort to impose reforms without consideration of traditional procedures in the church was a grave tactical error. The Revolution had hitherto found much sympathy among the lower clergy especially. But the Civil Constitution linked the cause of reform with anticlericalism and impiety. It made enemies for the Revolution when it desperately needed friends.

COUNTERREVOLUTION

The Constituent Assembly permanently changed France, but it failed to find broad social support for its reforms. The radical left denounced its deference to the monarchy, its favoring of the rich, and the restricted suffrage granted under the new constitution. The radicals organized themselves into clubs and associations of clubs to discuss, develop, and disseminate their views. One of the most powerful of the clubs was the Jacobin, so called because its members met in the former Dominican convent of St. Jacques in Paris. On the right the nobles resented the fact that the Revolution they had hoped to lead had turned against their interests. The king himself, who might have given stability to the new regime, again hesitated, now favoring and now opposing the reforms.

In June 1791 Louis and his family secretly fled from Paris. He hoped to reach the city of Metz, near the Rhine frontier, where he expected to find a garrison of troops favorable to him and where help from Austria would be close if needed. But he was recognized at the small post station of Varennes near Reims and brought back to Paris. The Assembly, which saw the critical need for royal support, pretended that the flight had been forced on him and reaffirmed his status as king. But the nearly traitorous act lent strength to the radical agitation.

The Constituent Assembly itself adopted a measure that would withdraw power from those most committed to enforcing its reforms: its own members. Still seeking popular support, it decreed that no present delegates could stand for election to the new legislature. This self-denying ordinance assured that the Legislative Assembly would be composed of men younger, less experienced, and probably more daring than their predecessors.

The new national body was elected as provided by the constitution, and it convened for the first time on October 1, 1791. Almost from the first the question of war dominated its mood and work. By an odd coincidence both the right and the left in France saw advantage in a war between France and Austria. The king and the court hoped that military defeat would discredit the new regime and restore full power to the monarchy, and many Jacobins were eager to strike down the foreign supporters of counterrevolutionaries at home and émigrés abroad. When Francis II took the throne of the Hapsburg dominions in March 1792, the other half of the stage was set. Unlike his father Leopold, who strongly rejected intervention, Francis fell under the influence of vengeful émigrés and shortsighted advisers. He determined to assist the French queen, his aunt, and he hoped to achieve territorial gains for Austria at the expense of France. With both sides geared for battle, France went to war against the Austro-Prussian coalition in April.

Each camp expected rapid victory, but both were deceived. The French offensive was quickly driven back, and soon invading armies were crossing French borders. The Legislative Assembly ordered the exile of refractory clergy and the establishment of a special corps of 20,000 national guardsmen to protect Paris. Louis vetoed both measures and held to his decision in spite of demonstrations in the capital. This was for all practical

This contemporary text and music of the Marseillaise carries a sketch of the "sons of the revolution" marching and singing. The anthem's original title was War Song for the Army of the Rhine. (Photo: The Mansell Collection)

purposes his last act as king. Meanwhile the Assembly declared the mother country to be in danger and called for volunteers from the provinces to defend the frontiers. As France mobilized for war an officer named Rouget de Lisle composed a marching song for his volunteer battalion—a song eventually known as the *Marseillaise*. Now the national anthem of France, it ranks among history's most stirring summons to patriotic war.

The *Marseillaise* accurately reflected the spirit of resistance that was developing in France. As Prussian forces began a drive toward Paris, their commander, the duke of Brunswick, recklessly demanded that Paris disarm itself and threatened to level the city if it resisted or if it harmed the royal family. This seemed the final proof that Louis was in league with the enemy. Far from intimidating the revolutionaries, the threat drove them into action. Since the Legislative Assembly had refused to act decisively in the face of royal obstructionism, the Parisians organized an insurrection. On August 10, 1792, a crowd of armed Parisians stormed the royal palace at the Tuileries, literally driving the king from the throne. The Assembly then had no choice but to declare him suspended. That night more than half its members themselves fled Paris, making it clear that the Assembly too had lost its legitimacy. Recognizing this, the representatives who remained prepared to dissolve the Assembly permanently and ordered elections for a new body, the National Convention. They left to the Convention the responsibility of declaring a republic in France and of judging her former king. More even than the storming of the Bastille in July 1789, the events of August 10, 1792, marked the passing of the old regime in France.

In the eighteenth century major transformations began in all aspects of Western life. The inhabitants of Europe and North America expanded at an extraordinary rate to unprecedented numbers, initiating a population explosion that has continued into modern times and now affects the entire world. The demographic revolution was closely related in both effect and cause to a revolution in manufacturing. The new industrial economy, if still of small size, created a new organization of production based on steam power and high engineering skill, factors that would sustain the economic growth of the following century. And the overall economic system took on a configuration that differed from the patterns of all prior periods in its capacity to transform itself ceaselessly and thus to lend a new dynamic quality to the society living from it.

These profound changes were accompanied by a crisis in social and political institutions. A tripartite struggle developed involving the ruler, the aristocracy, and the people over the proper allocation of power in the state. Several European monarchs sought to impose reform from above. The aristocracies on the other hand bitterly resented encroachments on their privileges, and some were willing to pursue the defense of their interests to the point of revolution. Both rulers and patricians appealed to the third estate, the people, often with unexpected results. The emerging claim to power of the unprivileged classes is the greatest change effected by the revolutions of the eighteenth century. No longer would the political history of the Western world focus exclusively on the elite.

The peoples of the West thus faced the task of building a new economic, social, and political order. What should its character be? How should power be managed, and how should wealth be distributed? What values should now govern human lives? These were the issues destined to occupy the Western nations as they entered the industrial and democratic age.

RECOMMENDED READING

Sources

Aspinall, Arthur, and E. Anthony Smith (eds.). *English Historical Documents, Vol. XI: 1783–1832.* 1959.

* Burke, Edmund. *Reflections on the Revolution in France.* 1969.

Higgins, E. L. (ed.). *The French Revolution as Told by Contemporaries.* 1939.

Horn, D. B., and Mary Ransome. *English Historical Documents, Vol. X: 1714–1783.* 1957.

* Kaplow, J. (ed.). *France on the Eve of the Revolution.* 1971.

* Smith, Adam. *Enquiry into the Nature and Causes of the Wealth of Nations.* 1961.

Stewart, John H. (ed.). *A Documentary Survey of the French Revolution.* 1951.

* Young, Arthur. *Travels in France During the Years 1787, 1788, 1789.* 1972.

Studies

* Ashton, T. S. *The Industrial Revolution, 1760–1830.* 1968.

* Cobban, A. *The Social Interpretation of the French Revolution.* 1968. Lively critique of the theory that the Revolution was engendered by class conflict.

* Deane, Phyllis. *The First Industrial Revolution.* 1975. Based on lectures, covering the years 1750–1850.

* De Tocqueville, Alexis. *The Old Regime and the French Revolution.* Stuart Gilbert (tr.). 1955.

Godechot, Jacques. *France and the Atlantic Revolutions of the Eighteenth Century.* 1965. Good comparative study of revolutions, by a French scholar.

* Hampson, Norman. *A Social History of the French Revolution.* 1963. Institutional rather than social; clearly organized and written.

Landes, David S. *The Unbound Prometheus. Technological Change and Industrial Development in Western Europe from 1750 to the Present.* 1969. Broad survey, effectively written, with an emphasis on technology.

* Lefebvre, Georges. *The Coming of the French Revolution.* R. R. Palmer (tr.). 1957. Short, clear, classical analysis by a prominent French historian.

* Mantoux, Paul. *The Industrial Revolution in the Eighteenth Century.* 1962. Basic introduction, with stress on inventions and factories.

Palmer, Robert R. *The Age of the Democratic Revolution. A Political History of Europe and America, 1760–1800.* 1959–1962.

Population Patterns in the Past. R. D. Lee (ed.). 1977. Collection of advanced studies.

Rudé, George F. *Paris and London in the Eighteenth Century. Studies in Popular Protest.* 1975.

* Soboul, Albert. *The French Revolution, 1787–1799.* 1975. The Revolution seen as an uprising of the bourgeoisie.

---

* Available in paperback.

TWENTY-ONE

THE TERROR
AND NAPOLEON

The end of the eighteenth century is often called the age of the dual revolution—the industrial revolution beginning in England and the social and political revolution centering in France. But where the former unfolded gradually, the latter exploded. By 1791—just two years after the fall of the Bastille—the foundations of government and society in France had been profoundly altered. The estate structure, dominated by the monarch and the nobles had been destroyed; middle-class values and leaders were in the ascendant; the peasantry had been freed from most remnants of the seigneurial system; absolutism had been replaced by constitutional monarchy, legislative representation, and local self-government; freedom of religion and expression had been inaugurated.

Yet the Revolution was far from over, and in the short view one might say that it was only just beginning. True, the gains just enumerated ultimately proved to be the most enduring and doubtless the most important. But they had been won at the price of great opposition, and the old order was far from admitting defeat. Priests, émigrés, and royalists in France were seconded by Old Regime monarchs, aristocrats, and armies elsewhere in Europe in their resistance to the Revolution. Moreover within France itself vast sections of the population were disaffected from the "patriots" of 1789 for a variety of reasons.

Challenged in 1792 by war and counterrevolution, the patriots themselves were divided. Some were alienated by the leaders of the Revolution and ultimately joined its opponents. Others were radicalized and gave their allegiance to the Jacobins. These in turn were seeking allies among the urban popular classes—the sans-culottes. Building on the momentum of August 1792, when Louis XVI had been driven from the throne, the Jacobins forged a coalition with the sans-culottes, who wanted to revolutionize the Revolution. The goals of this second revolution were more advanced than those of 1789: a democratic republic based on an ever-widening definition of social equality. Its hallmark was a posture of relentless militancy.

Each increment of revolution produced new opponents at home and abroad, but each increment of opposition stiffened the determination of the Revolution's supporters. An epochal confrontation was in the making that would engulf Europe. It began with a power struggle between revolutionary factions, a conflict of personalities as much as of political orientations; it ended in a coup that led France into a dictatorship under Napoleon Bonaparte.

I. THE SECOND REVOLUTION

The National Convention elected after the fall of the monarchy had a challenging mandate. It was supposed to consolidate the achievements of the first revolution but also establish a democratic republic, in effect moving the Revolution into a second stage. It is impossible to say how this would have proceeded had the times been calm, but of course they were not. France was immediately beset by an emergency situation—a convergence of invasion, civil war, and economic crisis. This situation demanded new initiatives which affected the course of the second revolution. To save and expand freedom, it was argued, force and terrorism were necessary. Thus the ideals of democracy and social equality were confused with problems of national defense and with the brutal dilemma of means versus ends. Although the second revolution lasted for little more than two years (1792–1794), it challenged the very foundations upon which government and society had always been organized.

THE NATIONAL CONVENTION (1792–1794)

By late 1792 revolutionary France had the makings of a new government. The Revolution had been saved from defeat by the belated success of the French army. Bolstered by units of citizen volunteers, the army halted the invading coalition at the Battle of Valmy in September, and two months later inflicted decisive defeat on the armies of the old order at Jemappes in the Austrian Netherlands, which were now occupied by the French. Meanwhile, in France a National Convention elected under universal male suffrage convened to declare the birth of a republic, to govern the country until a new democratic-republican constitution could be implemented, and to try the ex-king for treason.

Louis XVI's fate was the Convention's first major business and it proved an extremely divisive issue. While the king was found guilty of treason unanimously, there was a sharp and prolonged debate over his punishment. Some argued for clemency, while others insisted on his execution as a symbolic break with the old order as well as a fitting punishment for his betrayal. Finally, by a vote of 387 to 334, Louis was sentenced to death,

and efforts to reprieve this sentence or delay it for a popular referendum were defeated. On January 21, 1793, Louis was beheaded, put to death like an ordinary citizen. The French in general and the Convention in particular had become regicides—king-killers. This decision made compromise with the counter-revolution unlikely and total victory imperative. The Revolution would have to move forward.

France was now a republic, a country in which the influence of kings, priests, and nobles was to be eliminated, in which regionalism was supposed to give way to unity, in which social justice and reform could advance. Yet in a few months everything began to go wrong, and the Revolution faced a new and more serious crisis. By the early spring of 1793 the republic was under siege, internally divided and foundering. At least five problems faced the Convention: factionalism and conflict within its own ranks; a new invasion by a coalition of anti-French states; peasant dissatisfaction and internal civil war; economic dislocation including inflation and scarcity of bread; and growing militancy among Parisian radicals.

From the Convention's opening day two groups of deputies vied for leadership. The bitterness of their rivalry proved to be extremely divisive and threatened to paralyze the republic altogether. Yet this conflict reflected a painful reality: opinion *was* divided by what had already happened, and a consensus or stable majority was extremely difficult to find. The factional conflict originated in 1791–1792 as a quarrel within the Paris Jacobin Club and intensified after the insurrection of August 10. A group of deputies and journalists centering on Jacques Brissot had helped lead the country into war, but had then shrunk back from the vigorous measures necessary to pursue it. (This group later would be labeled the "Girondists" since several of its spokesmen were elected deputies to the Con-

Tried and sentenced by the National Convention for treason, Louis Capet (formerly Louis XVI) stoically mounted the guillotine on January 21, 1793. His execution made it clear that the Revolution had taken a sharp turn and that it would deal implacably with its enemies. (Photo: The Granger Collection)

vention from the department of Gironde.) Advocates of provincial middle-class interests, fiery orators, and ambitious politicians, they gradually fell out of step with the growing radicalization of the Parisian populace. The Girondists continued to hope that they could gain political power through the king and therefore did not cooperate in the overthrow of the monarchy.

Subsequently they blamed the violence of the September prison massacres on their Jacobin rivals. That episode—one of the bloodiest events of the French Revolution—erupted in the wake of the August 10 insurrection. As able-bodied volunteers were leaving for the war, Parisians nervously eyed the jails, which were jammed with political prisoners and common criminals. Seeing these prisoners as a potential counterrevolutionary striking force and fearing a plot to open the prisons, popular leaders like the journalist Jean Paul Marat warned of the threat. This growing sense of alarm finally exploded early in September. For three successive days groups of Parisians invaded the prisons, set up popular tribunals, and executed more than 1000 prisoners. No official dared intervene to stop the slaughter. But Brissot and his friends later blamed this spontaneous violence on their political rivals.

Brissotins or Girondists denounced the leading Parisian Jacobins—Robespierre, Marat, and Danton—as demagogues. By this time Brissot and his friends had been forced out of the Jacobin Club, and the Parisian electors sent a deputation to the Convention without a single "Brissotin," but which did include Danton, Robespierre, and Marat. This Parisian deputation became the nucleus of a group called "the Mountain," since it occupied the upper benches of the Convention's hall. The Mountain now dominated the Jacobin Club and attracted to its ranks the more democratically oriented provincial deputies. The Mountain attacked the Girondists as compromisers, as men unattuned to the new demands of the French people. The Girondists in turn denounced the Mountain as would-be tyrants who were captives of Parisian opinion to the detriment of the provinces and the propertied classes.

Between these two factions stood several hundred deputies in the center (called the Plain, in contrast to the Mountain). Committed to the Revolution, they were uncertain whom to trust and would support those men or policies that promised success in consolidating the Revolution. They disliked and feared popular agitation, but they were reluctant to turn against the popular movement, agreeing with the Mountain that the Revolution depended on it. In the debate on the king the center was split, but a majority finally embraced the Jacobins' demand for execution, whereas a few prominent Girondists had argued for clemency. Military and economic problems were eventually to propel the majority to disavow the Girondists and support the Mountain.

The Revolutionary Crisis

Within a few months the Convention faced a perilous convergence of invasion, civil war, and economic crisis which demanded new policies and imaginative responses. The military victories of 1792 were quickly forgotten when Austria and Prussia mounted a new offensive in 1793, an alliance soon strengthened by the addition of Spain, Piedmont, and England. Between March and September reversals occurred on every front, while the regular army was weakened by the emigration of officers and by poor leadership. In fact the French commander, General Dumouriez, the Revolution's first military hero the year before, sought—unsuccessfully—to bring his army back to Paris in order to topple the Convention.

The Convention's first response to the deteriorating military situation was to introduce a system of conscription. But this in turn touched off a peasant rebellion in western France. Long-simmering resentments by a traditional peasantry, who hated the small patriot middle class in the cities for monopolizing political power and who resented the Revolution's persecution of their priests, finally ignited when the republic tried to conscript them. Peasants and weavers in the Vendée region south of the Loire River began to attack the government's supporters in the region's isolated towns. Gradually this insurrection was influenced by priests and émigrés who organized the rebels into guerrilla bands and finally into what called itself the Catholic and Royalist Army. Wherever it triumphed, the Bourbons were proclaimed kings again and patriots were massacred. Several major cities were occupied briefly and for a while the rebels threatened the port city of Nantes, which could have been used for a landing of British troops if it fell from the government's control.

The bitter factionalism in the Convention had meanwhile generated conflict elsewhere in the country. Various provincial centers that sympathized with the Girondists hovered on the brink of rebellion against the Convention's leadership and against Parisian radicalism. In Normandy and Brittany forces were raised to threaten Paris, while in the south local Jacobins lost control of Marseilles, Bordeaux, and France's second largest city, Lyons. Like the Vendée rebellion, the Lyons resistance to Paris was eventually taken over by royalists who hoped to ignite the entire south of France against Paris. This was an intolerable challenge to the Convention. Labeling the anti-Jacobins in Lyons and elsewhere "federalists," the Convention sent out armed forces to suppress them. Ironically, in the United States at this time the word "federalist" referred to those who advocated a strong central government. In France it was used in the opposite sense, meaning those who sought to undermine the republic's unity. As such, the federalists were considered counterrevolutionary, for to disavow Paris meant to disavow the Revolution itself.

Parisian radicalism—against which the federalists were reacting—was in large measure provoked by severe economic troubles that were engulfing the infant republic. By February 1793 the Revolution's paper money, the assignats, had declined to 50 percent of its face value in the marketplace, and it continued steadily downward after that, to as low as one-third. This disastrous devaluation was compounded by a poor harvest. Panic over the scarcity of grain and flour swept across France, especially in the cities. Municipal leaders attempted to fix the price of bread so as to make it available to the masses, but they simply could not secure adequate supplies. Likewise the central government could not supply its armies under these conditions Human cupidity of course made matters worse; uncivic-minded Frenchmen attempted to profit from the situation by hoarding scarce commodities or by speculating in assignats.

The strongest impetus for taking vigorous measures against all these problems, military, political, and economic, came from the urban populace in Paris and other cities. But the vehemence of certain Parisian sans-culottes posed yet another threat to the Convention: the threat of excessive radicalism and anarchy. The ultraradicals, like their enemies the federalists, were unwilling to defer to the Convention. Sans-culotte spokesmen who emerged in these months communicated the view that the Convention, the Jacobin Club, and even the Paris city government were not sufficiently responsive to popular demands. They therefore demanded a purge of the Convention to rid it of its moderates, a program of revolutionary public safety, and radical economic intervention to break through the laissez-faire immobility of the government: (1) price control (called a law of the Maximum) for all necessary commodities, (2) severe laws against hoarding and speculation, and (3) forced requisitions on the peasantry, to be carried out with the assistance of an armed force or revolutionary army of the interior.

Behind these demands lay the threat of armed insurrection. Many Parisians were sympathetic to this platform, aimed at revolutionizing the Revolution. For the Jacobins the pressure from the sans-culottes was a volatile mixture: it provided aid in their struggle against the Girondists and federalists, but it posed the danger of spilling over into anarchy.

In a sense all elements of the revolutionary crisis hinged on one problem: the lack of a strong, effective government that would not simply respond to popular pressure but organize and channel it into constructive action. The first step in the creation of such a government seemed to be the purge demanded by the radicals. On May 31 the sans-culottes launched a demonstration to force home their demands, and the Plain at this point decided that the Mountain must be supported against the Girondists, who were thundering against sans-culotte "tyranny." On June 2 twenty-three Girondists were expelled by the Convention and placed under house arrest; they would subsequently be tried for treason. A turning point had come, but the future course of the Revolution was still in question.

THE JACOBIN DICTATORSHIP

The sans-culotte movement in Paris had hoisted the Mountain to power in the Convention. The question now was which side of the coalition would dominate. Popular demands swelled for terrorism against counter-revolution and for vigorous provisioning policies. The conviction was spreading among the urban masses that the sovereign people could dictate its will to the Convention by demonstrations and the threat of insurrection. At the same time federalism exploded in the provinces in response to the purge of the Girondists; Lyons and Marseilles were now in full-scale rebellion.

The high point of popular agitation came on September 5, when a massive demonstration placed demands for drastic measures before the Convention. The Convention now depended on the support of the sans-culottes; moreover certain of the measures would strengthen the government's control over the country. The demonstrators' main slogans were "Food—and to have it, force for the law" and "Let terror be placed on the order of the day." Concretely they won the passage of laws imposing general price control, forbid-

ding hoarding, creating revolutionary armies of the interior, and empowering local revolutionary committees to incarcerate citizens whose loyalty was suspect or who seemed to threaten the public safety—the so-called law of suspects.

The Revolutionary Government

Back in June the triumphant Jacobins had drafted a democratic constitution, one of the original purposes for which the National Convention had been called. It had been submitted to a referendum and overwhelmingly approved by 3 million voters; thus it provided the cornerstone for a new legitimate government. But the constitution could not be implemented in the throes of such a crisis as now faced the nation, particularly in view of her internal divisions. In October the Convention acknowledged this, formally placed the constitution aside, and proclaimed the government "revolutionary until the peace." Such luxuries of citizenship as the elections, local self-government, and guarantees of individual liberty promised in the constitution would be enjoyed only after the republic was secure from its enemies within and without.

An array of revolutionary laws and institutions now existed; it remained for a group of determined and skillful political leaders to take the reins and make them effective. Such men were to be found on the Committee of Public Safety, appointed by the Convention to supervise military, economic, and political affairs.

The committee's leading personality and tactician was Maximilien Robespierre. An austere bachelor in his mid-thirties and a provincial lawyer before the Revolution, Robespierre had been a prominent spokesman for the left in the Constituent Assembly where he had advocated the rights of women, Jews, and free Negroes, and had crusaded for the democratization of the regime. In 1792 he was an official of the Paris city government and a newspaper editor. But his principal political forum was the capital's Jacobin Club, which by 1793 he more or less dominated. Elected to the Convention from Paris, he was selfless and self-righteous in his total dedication to revolutionary causes. He sought to guide the sans-culottes and serve their interests as much as possible, but at all times he placed the survival of the Revolution above their particular grievances. Thus in his leadership he struck a delicate balance between his sense of responsibility and his sympathy for popular aspirations. The two were not always compatible. His main object was to bring the republic through the emergency by creating confidence and efficiency in the revolutionary government, and in this he succeeded. His hope of reconciling class interests in the cause of democracy was ultimately frustrated.

The legislation for creating a centralized revolutionary government was passed in December 1793, at last filling the vacuum left by the fall of the monarchy. Under a law enacted December 4—or 14 Frimaire, year II, according to the new French calendar—revolutionary committees in towns and villages were made responsible to the Committee of Public Safety, which could purge them. Local officials were redesignated national agents, their initiative was curbed, and they too were subject to removal by the Committee. Revolutionary tribunals, representatives on mission (deputies sent to the provinces as commissars), and revolutionary armies of the interior were all placed under the Committee's scrutiny and control.

Crucial links in this chain of revolutionary dictatorship were the Jacobin clubs. They too were organized into a centralized network, led by the Paris Jacobin Club. They nominated citizens for posts on revolutionary committees and exercised surveillance over them. The clubs were to be "arsenals of public opinion," to support the war effort in every way possible, and to denounce uncivic behavior among their fellow citizens.

No serious dissent was tolerated under the Jacobin reign. Freedom of expression was limited by the government's sense of the need for unity during the emergency, and the politically outspoken were purged. The first to fall were a group of ultraleftists led by Jacques René Hébert, a radical journalist and Paris official. They were accused of a plot against the republic. In reality they had questioned what they considered the Convention's leniency toward "enemies" of the people. Next came the turn of the so-called indulgents, among them Danton. They had argued—prematurely, in the government's view—for a relaxation of terrorism and centralization. They were arrested, indicted on trumped-up charges of treason, and sentenced to death by the revolutionary tribunal. This succession of purges, starting with the Girondists and ultimately ending with Robespierre himself, seemed to suggest, as one contemporary put it, that revolutions devour their own children.

The Reign of Terror

Most of those devoured by the French Revolution, however, were not its own children. They were rather an assortment of armed rebels, counterrevolutionaries, and unfortunate citizens swept into the vortex of war and internal strife. The Reign of Terror developed in response to the multifaceted crisis described on the previous pages. On the level of attitude, the Terror reflected a revolutionary mentality that saw threats and plots all around (some real, some imagined). The laws of the Terror were designed to intimidate a wide range of people perceived as enemies of the Revolution. They included the law of suspects, which led to the incarceration of 400,000 to 500,000 prisoners, and laws against the life and property of refractory priests and émigrés. They included also the price-control regulations and other legislation aimed at preventing the collapse of the Revolution from economic chaos or food shortages.

The Terror was the force behind the law— the determination and techniques to make these laws work. Its purpose was to coerce Frenchmen into abiding by the Revolution in some minimal fashion and into accepting certain sacrifices of self-interest to permit the republic and the Revolution to survive. By the same token the emphasis on organizing the Terror, on supervising it from some central point of authority, was designed to prevent anarchic violence like the prison massacres of September 1792 and the infamous *noyades* (drownings) of Nantes, in which hundreds of Vendée rebels and priests were brutally drowned in the Loire River. Wholesale slaughter was disavowed by the Committee of Public Safety, which for example prevented the indiscriminate condemnation of federalists and put a stop to violent de-Christianization. The Terror was meant to impress by the severity of examples, not by the liquidation of whole groups.

Statistical analysis of the death sentences during the Terror suggests that there was a relationship between executions and clear-and-present danger. A total of 17,000 death sentences were handed down by the various revolutionary tribunals and commissions, and an estimated 10,000 additional armed rebels were executed without trial. Over 70 percent of the sentences were passed in the two zones of intense civil war: 19 percent in the southeast (the Lyons region) and 52 percent in the west (the Vendée region). Moreover 72 percent of these were for armed rebellion. Conversely one-third of the departments had fewer than ten death sentences each and were relatively tranquil. While much of the revolutionary rhetoric and some of its legislation were aimed at the upper classes, the death sentences of the Terror hit hardest at the largest groups in the population: urban and rural common people who actively participated in the rebellions.[1]

The Paris Jacobin Club was founded by a group of progressive deputies to the Constituent Assembly of 1789. After August 1792 and the elections to the Convention, it became a forum for democratic deputies and middle-class Parisian radicals, as well as a "mother club" with which popular societies in the provinces affiliated themselves. As such, it was the closest thing the French revolutionaries had to a party apparatus. (Photo: New York Public Library, Picture Collection)

Apart from the repression of the Vendée revolt, the Terror's bloodiest episode took place in Lyons. The Convention laid siege to the city until it capitulated in October 1793. Implacable in its hostility, the Convention declared that "Lyons has made war against liberty and thus Lyons no longer exists." The entire population was disarmed, and the houses

[1] These statistics are drawn from Donald Greer, *The Incidence of the Terror.* 1935.

TURNING POINTS IN THE REVOLUTION

July 14, 1789:	Storming of the Bastille and triumph of the third estate.
August 10, 1792:	Storming of the Tuileries and end of the constitutional monarchy.
September 2–5, 1792:	Paris prison massacres.
May 31–June 2, 1793:	Sans-culotte march on the Convention and purge of the Girondists.
September 5, 1793:	Demonstration before the Convention and enactment of terroristic legislaticn and economic controls.
9 Thermidor, year II (July 27, 1794):	Fall of Robespierre.
1–2 Prairial, year III (May 20–21, 1795):	Unsuccessful insurrection by the Parisian sans-culottes for "Bread and the constitution of 1793."
18 Brumaire, year VIII (November 9, 1799):	Coup d'état by Napoleon Bonaparte and the revisionists.

of many wealthy citizens were burned. On-the-spot courts-martial were held and executions followed immediately. Some were carried out gruesomely, with the encouragement of irresponsible commissars. Almost 2,000 people were put to death, two-thirds of them from the upper classes. The fanaticism of the Parisian sans-culottes sent against Lyons reflected both their class consciousness and their revolutionary fervor during the dark days of crisis.

THE SANS-CULOTTES AND THE POPULAR REVOLUTION

After their massive revolt against the old order in 1789, the peasants were generally passive or overtly hostile to the Revolution's further progress. They contributed little as a group to the second revolution. The urban common people or sans-culottes, however, not only propelled the insurrectionary movements in the cities in 1789, but became ardent proponents of further revolutionizing in the social, political, and economic spheres. Their participation in the second revolution was essential to its success.

The role of the people in the Revolution has always been noted but until recently they have not been studied directly and in their own right. Instead their actions and concerns have been refracted through the eyes of their enemies or their spokesmen, themselves middle or upper class and far removed in their own life style from the common people. Inspired by Georges Lefebvre's classic studies of the peasants, historians have recently been writing about the French Revolution "from below"—about specific groups of common people. These studies convey their social identity, their aspirations, attitudes, and revolutionary activity as they tried to place their collective stamp on what they regarded as their Revolution.

The most dramatic impact made by the sans-culottes on the Revolution came during the famous insurrectionary *journées*, or "days" of crowd actions, demonstrations, and uprisings, that marked turning points in the Revolution's course (see list). We now know that the participants in these crowds and striking forces were not criminals and drifters, as antirevolutionary writers have claimed. They were Parisian workingmen—carpenters, cobblers, wine sellers, clerks, tailors, cafe keepers, stonemasons—mainly small-scale artisans, shopkeepers, and journeymen. The sans-culottes were not a class in the Marxist sense, for they varied in their relationship to the means of production: some, such as small workshop proprietors, owned them; others provided only their labor. But all shared the life style of Paris' popular neighborhoods and had a strong sense of community.

Popular Attitudes

The long hours of hard work that characterized the sans-culottes' existence generally yielded a modest livelihood that was painfully reduced by rises in the cost of living. Accordingly they were extremely concerned over the availability and prices of basic commodities like bread, candles, meat, and fuel. As consumers they faced the economic crisis of the revolutionary period with distress and anger. Their most basic demand was for government intervention to assure them the basic necessities of life. This incidentally is one reason that women were prominent among revolutionary activists: they were most directly concerned with putting food on their family's table. This concern was summarized by the call for "Food—and to have it, force for the law." By 1793 the Revolution's leaders were compelled to recognize this, and the right to subsistence was prominently proclaimed in the Jacobin constitution of 1793. Concretely it meant a combination of government price control, requisitioning, and a public works program to provide employment. Most of this violated the middle-class laissez-faire view of how the economy should work.

The sans-culottes, while firm believers in property rights, insisted that they must be limited by considerations of social utility. The right of an individual to a modest amount of property, like one small workshop or one store, was considered inviolate, but the sans-culottes denied that anyone had the right to "misuse" property by hoarding, speculating, or accumulating far more than he needed. Concepts of freedom and equality had a practical economic side in their opinion. As one petition put it, "What is the meaning of freedom, when one class of men can starve another? What is the meaning of equality, when the rich, by their monopolies, can exercise the right of life and death over their equals?"

Under the stress of soaring inflation and economic dislocation, the sans-culotte call for the right to subsistence and the middle-class call for laissez faire clashed dramatically. The willingness of the Mountain and the Jacobin Club to acknowledge the right to subsistence and to regulate the economy, at least during the war emergency, won them support among the people.

Bitterly antiaristocratic, the sans-culottes feared that the middle class might replace the nobility as a new kind of elite. The social attitude was reflected in everyday behavior. Extolling simplicity in dress and manners, they attacked opulence and pretension wherever they found or imagined them to be. Under their disapproving eye, high society and fancy dress generally disappeared from view. There was a revolution too in manners and morals. Vices like prostitution, pornography, and gambling were attributed to aristocrats and were denounced in the virtuous and austere society of the Revolution; drinking was the common man's vice and was tolerated.

The sans-culottes symbolized their break with the past by changing the names of their streets, cities, and public places to eliminate signs of royalism and aristocracy. The Palais Royal became the Palais d'Égalité ("Equality Palace"). Many people underwent debaptizing, exchanging their Christian names for the names of secular heroes like Gracchus, the ancient Roman reformer, or names derived from trees and plants. The Gregorian calendar was replaced with a more geometric revo-

lutionary calendar, computed from September 22, 1792, forward, in which weeks were replaced by units of ten days. Titles like "monsieur" and "madame" were dropped in favor of the simple, uniform designation of "citizen"—just as revolutionaries of a later generation would call each other "comrade."

Participatory Democracy

The Convention believed in a system of parliamentary or representative democracy, with an active political life at the grass roots but with power delegated to elected officials. And as we saw, during the emergency the Jacobins were willing to impose a virtual dictatorship in the form of the highly centralized revolutionary government. The sans-culottes, on the other hand, favored a popular scheme of participatory democracy. They believed that the local voters or in larger cities the local section assembly of citizens was the ultimate sovereign body; it could never permanently delegate its authority, even to the popularly elected Convention. In short they wanted the decision-making power actively lodged with the people rather than their deputies. To Robespierre this ideal of unrestrained direct democracy appeared unworkable and akin to anarchy.

At the beginning of the revolutionary year II (1793–1794), the forty-eight sections in Paris functioned almost as tiny autonomous republics in which the people ran their own affairs directly in the general assembly, a system an American would call town-meeting democracy. When necessary the sections co-

The Parisian citizen-soldiers were the most adamant revolutionaries of the era. Aristocrats called them sans-culottes (meaning "without knee-breeches") by way of insult, but the bitterly antiaristocratic militants proudly adopted it as their popular name. (Photo: The Mansell Collection)

operated with each other to exert collective pressure on the government. On the various *journées* the sans-culottes demonstrated their conviction that the people, if necessary in a state of armed insurrection, ought to be the ultimate arbiter of the republic. Political life in those months, especially but not exclusively in Paris, had a naive, breathless quality, generating high enthusiasm among thousands of sans-culottes, making them feel that for the first time the power of self-government was theirs.

The Convention looked on with mixed feelings. On the one hand they were uneasy allies, committed to the ideals of democracy and equality. On the other hand they were pragmatists who feared the anarchic force of this popular movement—its unpredictability, its disorder, and its inefficiency. The Mountain attempted to steer a difficult course between encouraging this civic participation and controlling it. The sans-culotte militants did a great deal for the war effort: they rooted out counterrevolutionaries, spread revolutionary usages, recruited soldiers, and formed committees for public relief. Like the Jacobin clubs in the provinces, the Parisian sans-culottes promoted the ideal of self-help.

From the sections, however, there came an endless stream of exhortations, petitions, denunciations, and veiled threats to the government. In the end the Convention decided that politically and administratively the direct democracy of the sections had to be disciplined. In the spring of 1794, it passed a series of measures restricting the meeting times, activities, and rights of the sections that removed most of their effective powers. What the government failed to realize was that once the ardor of the sans-culottes was forcibly cooled off, their support of the Convention, and their willingness to sacrifice, would also diminish. The results would leave these leaders vulnerable to reaction.

THE VICTORIES OF THE YEAR II

Even while the Mountain was curtailing the powers of the sans-culottes, however, it continued to bank on their support for the military defense of the nation. For the Revolution's more far-sighted leaders knew that France's ultimate fate rested in the hands of her armies. Drawing on the citizenry at large, the Convention forged a new armed force that overcame the coalition of hostile states arrayed against France.

Revolutionary Foreign Policy

As initially formulated in 1789, revolutionary ideology had offered no direct threat to the status quo of the European state system. It had perceived its influence as consisting only in the force of example. French power was not to be felt across the country's borders except as persuasion. Indeed the orators of the National Assembly had argued that the best foreign policy for a progressive and free society was peace, neutrality, and isolation from the diplomatic intrigues of monarchs.

But peace did not imply pacifism. When counterrevolution at home coalesced with threats from abroad, the revolutionaries were eager to resort to war against both. The hostilities that broke out in 1792 were for the most part defensive in origin as far as the French were concerned. But as in all major wars the initial objectives were rapidly forgotten, and as the conflict spilled over large parts of Europe, it disrupted the political organization and boundaries of many Continental states.

The revolutionary wars involved considerations that were perennial in international conflicts as well as certain new and explosive purposes. On the one hand the French adopted traditional objectives such as rounding off and extending their frontiers and exacting agreements from adjoining states aimed at protecting those frontiers. At the same time they pursued revolutionary principles such as the right of a people to self-determination. As early as September 1791, the National Assembly had declared that "the rights of peoples are not determined by the treaties of princes."

As we have seen in the previous chapter, there were people in many areas of Western Europe who were eager to challenge the ancient arrangements—"the treaties of princes" —that determined their political destiny. Particularly in the zone of Europe lying west of the Elbe River, several internal conflicts had already arisen before 1789, and the success of the French could not help but renew liberal and revolutionary sentiment. Patriots in Geneva, the United Provinces, and the Austrian Netherlands had already tasted repression. They were eager for another round in their various struggles and looked to France for assistance.

Refugees from these regions had fled to France and formed pressure groups that lobbied with French leaders and corresponded with rebels back home. Their fondest hopes rested on the chance that in fighting against the coalition, the French might liberate their own lands. If they were contiguous to France (as were the Austrian Netherlands, Savoy, and the Rhineland), France might then annex them to her own republic; elsewhere (in Holland, Lombardy, Ireland, and the Swiss Confederation) she might help set up independent republics by overthrowing the ruling princes or oligarchies. In the wake of war and revolutionary enthusiasm, the foreign patriots induced the Convention to declare in November 1792 that it "accords fraternity and aid to [foreign] people who wish to recover their liberty," though the French had in mind only those whose governments were actively leagued against France.

While there had been some talk of mounting a universal crusade to bring freedom to oppressed peoples, French leaders were in reality committed to a pragmatic policy. As the war spilled over into the Austrian Netherlands and Germany, they had to organize their forces and ensure a base of support abroad. This in turn required that the primary aims of war embody the spirit and stated objectives of the revolutionary society, not the age-old motive of aggrandizement through occupation and domination. Thus in December of 1792 the government proclaimed further that it would establish the freedom of those to whom it had brought or would bring armed assistance. This meant that in each land where the French prevailed, feudal practices, hereditary privileges, and repressive institutions would be abolished. A provisional government would be established to cooperate with the French forces in supervising and paying for the liberation. Full independence was a long-term promise; more immediately the occupied territory would be obliged to underwrite the expenses of French troops.

These intentions were greeted enthusiastically by progressive elements in the middle and noble classes and in some instances by artisans. But most nobles, priests, and peasants and large sections of the middle class were hostile or indifferent to them, resenting the requisitions and special taxes, though they did not necessarily wish a restoration of the old order.

By 1794 France had a permanent foothold in the Austrian Netherlands, which was shortly to be annexed to the Great Nation, as France now called herself. Apart from this, however, Robespierre proved to be relatively isolationist. Arguing that freedom had to be secured at home before it could be exported abroad, the Committee of Public Safety declined to intervene in behalf of a Polish revolutionary movement, refused to invade Holland, and designed a strategy that precluded any involvement in Italy. In short, while occupying the Austrian Netherlands and hoping to annex the left bank of the Rhine, the Convention renounced any drive for the establishment of new "sister republics."

The Revolutionary Armies

The fighting men who carried the Revolution abroad were a very different body from the corps inherited from Louis XVI. The royal army had undergone major reforms since 1789 that opened military service as a decent career to all kinds of Frenchmen. At the same time the organization of militias and national guards, with their elected officers, introduced a new concept of the citizen-soldier as against a professional army apart from civil society.

The army's chief problem came after the war began, when large numbers of royalist officers either deserted altogether or behaved disloyally. At the crucial Battle of Valmy, a remnant of the old army showed that it could fight effectively, but its numbers were too reduced by desertion and neglect to offer continued resistance. A hasty call-up of volunteers proved inadequate both in numbers and effectiveness.

The coalition launched its second major assault in 1793, and the poor performance of the French troops made it clear that drastic innovations were required. The Convention initiated far-reaching conscription and mobilization, the so-called mass levy of August 1793 (*levée en masse*). All unmarried men between the ages of eighteen and twenty-five were drafted for combat service, while older and married men were assigned convoy and guard duty or similar tasks. All social classes were affected, and in a short time almost half a million French citizens were placed under arms. With elected officers at their head, the citizen-soldiers marched off to the front under banners reading, "The French People, risen against the tyrants."

The Convention had already decided to combine these blue-uniformed recruits with their white-uniformed counterparts from the old professional army in units called demibrigades. In the future noncommissioned officers would be elected by all troops, but higher ranks would be chosen by superior officers according to merit and seniority. The expectation was that discipline would be taught to the new troops by the professionals, who in turn would absorb a spirit of patriotism from the recruits. Although the actual amalgam took several years to complete, its spirit proved immediately successful.

One reason for this success was the Convention's attitude toward military discipline in a revolutionary society. Civilian control over the military was firmly established, and discipline now applied to officers as well as men. The government insisted that generals show the will to win, confidence in the republic, and talent. A large number of young men were raised quickly through the ranks to command positions. Lazare Hoche, perhaps the most spectacular case, led an entire army at the age of twenty-five and died a military hero at twenty-seven. Other generals were less fortunate. The commander of the ill-fated Rhine army in early 1793 was branded a traitor, tried, and guillotined. The revolutionary slogan "Win or die" was a serious matter.

A dramatically new approach to military life was thus taking shape: citizen-soldiers recruited through conscription, concern for their needs and morale, generous veterans' benefits if they were wounded, quick promotions for loyal and capable men, exemplary discipline for officers who wavered in spirit or on the battlefield. The question still remained of how the new army would be used in the field, and the answer reflected the combination of revolutionary spirit and hardheaded practicality that prevailed in the republic.

The mass of soldiers in the new demibrigades did not have the necessary training to be deployed according to the traditional tactics of Old Regime armies. Conversely they were infused with a sense of patriotism that it would be well to utilize. Hence strategists perfected the new battle formation of massive columns that could move quickly without much practice in drilling. Mass and mobility characterized the armies of the French Revolution. As General Hoche put it, "No maneuvers, no art; only fire and patriotism," and the Committee of Public Safety advised its commanders, "Act offensively and in masses. Use the bayonet at every opportunity. Fight great battles and pursue the enemy until he is utterly destroyed." In this spirit the Jacobins and sans-culottes sought all-out war, and strategy was shaped to achieve it.

The Jacobins did not neglect the home front, whose contributions to the war effort were obviously crucial for victory. Economic mobilization, directed by the Convention and the Jacobin clubs, produced the necessary material support for the armies. Weapons, ammunition, clothing, and food were all produced or requisitioned in extraordinary quantities by herculean effort. Without them the military reforms would have achieved no purpose.

In late 1793 and early 1794, the armies won a series of decisive battles. They culminated in the Battle of Fleurus in June 1794, when the Austrian Netherlands was once again occupied; the annexation, officially conceded by the Hapsburgs in 1797, would last until 1814. At the Pyrenees and the Rhine, French armies were victorious, forcing their enemies one by one to come to the peace table—first Spain

and Prussia, then Piedmont, and finally Austria. An army crippled at the outset by treason and desertion, defeat, lack of training and discipline, and collapsing morale had been forged into a potent force in less than two years. Militarily the second revolution was a brilliant success.

II. FROM ROBESPIERRE TO BONAPARTE

To its most dedicated supporters, the revolutionary government had two major purposes: first, to surmount a crisis and steer the republic to victory; second, to democratize France's social fabric. Only the first objective won the widespread adherence of middle-class republicans. It is not surprising, therefore, that after the victories of the year II, the revolutionary government was overthrown and the second revolution dismantled. Jacobinism and democracy, however, had become a permanent part of the French experience, as had royalism and reaction. The political spectrum of modern Europe had been created. Within this spectrum the men of 1789 attempted to command an elusive centrist or moderate position, but they proved inadequate to the task. During the four unsteady years of the Directory regime, however, revolutionary expansion outside of France proceeded aggressively. It triumphed briefly but soon precipitated a second anti-French coalition. This challenge brought the weaknesses of the Directory regime to a head and opened the way to the ascendancy of Napoleon Bonaparte.

THE THERMIDORIAN REACTION (1794–1796)

The National Convention held a polarized nation together, consolidated the republic, and defeated the Revolution's foreign enemies. But in achieving these successes, the ruling Jacobins increasingly isolated themselves, making enemies on every side. Moderates and ultrarevolutionaries alike resented the rule that they imposed. Wealthy peasants and businessmen chafed under the economic regimentation. Moreover the pressure of events and the relentless necessity to make hard and unpopular decisions wore out the Revolution's most prominent leaders.

After the decisive victories of the year II, the Convention's unity disintegrated. As the fifth anniversary of the Bastille's fall approached, Robespierre's enemies were emboldened to rise against him. Longstanding rivalries, differences over policy, and clashes of temperament now exploded. Robespierre girded himself to denounce yet another group of unspecified intriguers, presumably to send them to the fate of Danton and Hébert. But his rivals both left and right formed a hasty coalition and struck back, denouncing Robespierre to the Convention as a tyrant and would-be dictator.

The plotting of these individuals was crucial, but Robespierre's downfall is attributable also to the fact that he was no longer needed by the Convention. Having supported him with reluctance during the emergency, the moderate deputies were now willing to abandon him. The Parisian sans-culottes might have maintained Robespierre in power despite this desertion, but as we have seen, the Jacobins had alienated them by curbing the autonomy of the sections. Many sans-culottes were therefore indifferent to the struggle of personalities that took place in the Convention that July.

On the twenty-seventh — 9 Thermidor — Robespierre was declared an outlaw by the Convention. Efforts to rally a popular force in his defense that night proved ineffective; and on the following day he and several loyal associates were seized and guillotined. French-

men perhaps did not realize it at the time, but 9 Thermidor thus became one of those crucial *journées* on which the Revolution's course was decisively altered.[2]

After Robespierre's fall the Revolution's momentum was broken, and the apparatus of the Terror was dismantled. Soon the anti-Jacobins began to attack the revolutionaries in turn. Their strident calls for retribution against the terrorists eventually produced a terrorism of their own—a "white terror" aimed against Jacobins and sans-culottes that resulted in street fighting, assassinations, and in the south of France massacres.

To survey the unfolding of the Thermidorian reaction is equivalent to viewing a film of the preceding half-decade run backward through the projector. Suspects were released, the revolutionary committees abolished, defendants before the revolutionary tribunals acquitted, and their former accusers indicted in their place. The Paris Jacobin Club was closed, while in the provinces the affiliated clubs gradually withered away under harassment and restrictive legislation. Amnesty was extended to the Girondists and to the Vendée rebels; Mountain deputies were now denounced. Paris underwent "de-sans-culottization"—the section leaders of the year II were driven out of political life and threatened with retribution. At all levels those who had borne the burden of responsibility and action in the year II suddenly found themselves attacked.

Paralleling these political reversals was a marked change in the state of public morals and social behavior. The upper classes now set

---

[2] "Thermidor" has become a generic term to denote the phase in a revolution when the pendulum swings back toward moderation or reaction. It has been argued that the drafting of the United States Constitution in 1787 was the Thermidor of the American Revolution and that Stalin's reign was the Thermidor of the Bolshevik Revolution.

the tone. For those who sought a life of pleasure and luxury, Thermidor was a reprieve from the austerity and restraint of the year II. Public virtue gave way before indulgence and license. Luxury not only reappeared but by all contemporary accounts was flaunted with scandalous vulgarity. High society, with its balls, salons, and fancy dress, was reestablished. The titles "monsieur" and "madame" replaced the republican designation "citizen." Most important, this high society of the rich showed itself bored by the spectacle of popular misery.

Unfortunately this social reaction occurred at a time of extensive mass suffering. In keeping with free-trade ideology, the Thermidorians abandoned the legislation regulating the economy. The marketplace was again permitted to operate by its "natural laws" of supply and demand, producing a skyrocketing inflation. Worse yet, France experienced a harvest in 1795 more meager than in the crisis years of 1788–1789 and 1793. But despite such ill luck, the Thermidorians declined to intervene to protect small consumers from economic ravages. They refused to try to provide a minimum supply of bread at an affordable price, a relief effort that the revolutionary government and even the Old Regime monarchs had made. In the face of near-famine, every index of social welfare now revealed disaster. Suicide and mortality rates rose markedly; police reports spoke of little else besides popular misery, discontent, and destitute people collapsing in the streets from undernourishment.

Since the government would not help, the former militants attempted to spark a political reversal to halt the reaction and force the authorities to act. Their hopes centered on the constitution of 1793, whose prompt and full implementation they now demanded. The slogan of sans-culottes in the sections during the spring of 1795 was simply "Bread and the constitution of 1793." The Thermidorians, however, were moving in precisely the opposite direction. Viewing that constitution as far too democratic, they were looking for an excuse to scrap it altogether.

The militants began demonstrating in April, and the government countered by ordering local authorities to disarm them. The only recourse left was insurrection, and it began on 1 Prairial, year III (May 20, 1795). It was a grim, mournful uprising, a rear-guard action against disaster. The sans-culottes took over the Convention briefly in cooperation with a handful of sympathetic deputies. But their hours were numbered, for the Thermidorians had retreated merely to organize their armed forces. In two days of street fighting, the sans-culottes were driven back, cut off, and defeated. Severe repression followed: 36 people were executed, some 1,200 imprisoned, and an additional 1,700 interrogated and disarmed. Probably the majority of these had not even taken part in the insurrection but were being singled out in retribution for the role of the sans-culottes during the Terror.

These *journées* were the end of the popular movement, the last time that the Parisian revolutionary crowd would be mobilized. It was now clear just how much the sans-culottes and the Jacobins had needed each other. Isolated from each other, they had both been defeated. In the process the democratic republic of the year II was lost. Whatever the possibilities had been for achieving some form of social democracy (and the issue remains ambiguous), they were now severely reduced.[3] The Thermidorian reaction seemed to

---

[3] The Convention's measures to promote social democracy included the abolition of slavery, the final abolition of seigneurial rights without compensation to the lords, and equal division of estates among heirs. Legislation for a system of free public education, a progressive income tax, a war veterans' bonus, and the distribution of the property of convicted suspects to indigent patriots was never implemented.

guarantee that the middle class would maintain control of France.

THE DIRECTORY (1796–1799)

By the end of 1795, the remaining members of the Convention assumed that the Revolution was over. The extremes had been vanquished, and the time for the "peaceable enjoyment of liberty" was at hand. They had drafted a new constitution—the constitution of the year III—and proclaimed a general amnesty, and they were prepared to turn a new page. The revolutionary government, which had replaced the fallen constitutional monarchy, had in turn been replaced by a middle-class constitutional republic. It was known as the Directory, after its five-man executive body.

The Directory's proponents, concerned above all with retaining power, openly declared that the republic would "be governed by the best citizens, who are found among the property-owning class." Accordingly the constitution abandoned the universal suffrage of 1793 and restored the propertied franchise of 1791 and the multilayered system of indirect elections. It called for a cumbersome separation of powers, designed to moderate the political process, while it guarded against the rise of a potential dictator by installing the five-man Directory. Equally important, it omitted devices to facilitate active democracy, such as referendums, and said nothing of popular rights, like the right to free education and to subsistence, all of which were specified in the 1793 constitution. The concern with eliminating the popular democracy of the year II was balanced by measures to prevent a royalist resurgence. Fearing that free elections at this point might swing the republic too far to the right, the Convention decided to coopt two-thirds of its membership into the new legislature established by the constitu-

tion. A royalist attempt to oppose this with an armed protest was crushed.

The government thus repudiated both the royalist movement and the second revolution. As regicides the directors necessarily opposed royalism; on the other hand they were determined that popular democracy and terrorism would not recur. Apart from these considerations they were inclined to forgive and forget. They attempted to command a position somewhere near the hypothetical center of the political spectrum, a stance that one historian has aptly called the mirage of the moderates.

To maintain themselves in power, the Directory politicians were obliged to remove with one hand freedoms that they had granted with the other. They repeatedly purged locally elected officials; they periodically undermined freedom of the press and of association, ostensibly guaranteed in the new constitution, by suppressing new Jacobin clubs and hostile newspapers. Above all they refused to acknowledge the legitimacy of organized opposition, whether rightist or leftist. This explains the succession of coups and purges that marked the Directory's four years. Although the repressive measures were mild compared with those of the second revolution—deportation was generally the harshest punishment meted out for dissent—their net effect was to make the regime dysfunctional. In the end a significant number of Thermidorians were obliged to abandon their own creation altogether.

The Political Spectrum

For all its dictatorial qualities, however, the Directory regime was free enough to allow most shades of the political spectrum some visibility. Obliterated previously by the Jacobin commonwealth and later by the Napoleonic dictatorship, the full range of opinions and divisions in France was clearly revealed during the years of the Directory and would persist with certain modifications down to the fall of the Third Republic, in 1940.

The most important legacy of all was probably apathy, born of exhaustion or cynicism. Most citizens, especially peasants, were weary of controversy, distrustful of politicians, and hostile to administrators and tax collectors, whatever government they served. As a result participation in the Directory regime's annual elections was extremely low.

Within this context of massive apathy, politically conscious Frenchmen were deeply divided. The ultraroyalists were uncompromising enemies of the Directory, dedicated to overthrowing it. They included émigrés, armed rebels, and refractory priests, along with their peasant followers, and many of them cooperated with the exiled Bourbons and English spies. Shading off from the ultraroyalists were the monarchists, mainly from the middle and peasant classes. They hoped to alter the republic's foundations and to drift gradually back toward royalism without necessarily overthrowing the republic by force. Their goals included allowing the émigrés to return, restoring the position of the refractory clergy, and stamping out entirely the last vestiges of Jacobinism. Since Napoleon largely acquiesced in these changes, they formed a major base of his support.

On the left of the spectrum stood the Jacobins, or democrats. They were committed not only to preserving the Revolution of 1789 and the republic but to identifying positively with the second revolution as well. They did not advocate a return to the Terror, hoping rather, like the constitutional royalists, to work legally within the new institutions of the Directory to regain power. The Jacobin policy was to promote grass-roots activism through local political clubs, petitions, peaceful demonstrations, newspapers, and electoral campaigns. The clubs attracted a small cross section of middle-class revolutionaries and sans-culotte militants, thus keeping alive the egalitarian social ideals of the year II. In addition to calling for the implementation of existing laws against counterrevolutionaries, the Jacobins advocated free public education, a veterans' bonus for soldiers, the right to subsistence, and progressive taxation.

At the far end of the spectrum emerged a tiny group of collectivists whose significance would loom much larger in the nineteenth century than it did in 1796. This was the circle of Gracchus Babeuf. They viewed the year II as simply a stage in the revolutionary process that now had to be followed by a final revolution against the middle-class republic in the name of the masses. Their objectives were a vaguely defined "real equality" and a "community of goods," a distributive type of communism. Believing that the middle-class republic was simply a new form of tyranny, they plotted its overthrow by means of a highly centralized secret conspiracy. When Filippo Buonarroti published a firsthand account of the plot in the 1820s, it became a handbook of revolution, influencing Karl Marx and ultimately Lenin.

The Directory's adherents stood somewhere in the center of this broad spectrum, shifting their ground uncertainly and unsuccessfully to find a solid position. They were hostile to the royalists, but possibly even more antagonistic to the Jacobins. Thus they sometimes collaborated with the reactionaries, as when they used the Babeuf plot as a pretext for repressing the entire left, though most democrats had deplored Babeuf's calls for insurrection and did not take his communism seriously. This propelled the Directory into a tentative alliance with the right, and the climate of public opinion became increasingly reactionary. However, when the first regular elections held in the year V (1797) produced a royalist victory, the moderates reversed themselves. Backed by General Bonaparte's army of Italy, they purged the legislature of the most notorious royalists, annulled numerous elections, suppressed about forty royalist newspapers, restored the sanctions against priests and émigrés, and allowed the Jacobins to open new clubs.

But after a few months, as the clubs began to revive a democratic spirit, the Directory grew fearful. During the elections of the year VI, democratic and conservative republicans began to campaign against each other in what almost amounted to party rivalry. The Directory again intervened, closing the clubs, manipulating the electoral assemblies, and where this failed, purging the democrats elected. It is revealing to note that almost at the same time the American republic was going through a similar process, but there the rival parties finally agreed to disagree, and organized opposition was accepted as part of the legitimate political system. In France organized opposition was not tolerated, and that crucial decision contributed to the republic's demise.

THE RISE OF BONAPARTE

While France was retreating from her Revolution internally, however, she supported and spread it more forcefully than ever abroad. For the Revolution in Europe, the Directory years marked a high point of success. Under the Directory she gradually turned to a policy of encouraging wars of liberation and the establishment of sister republics (see Map 21.1). This eventually led to the creation of progressive representative governments in the United Provinces and the Swiss Confederation, which became known respectively as the Batavian and Helvetic republics. It led also, despite the Directory's attempt to prevent it, to the spread of war and liberation to the entire Italian peninsula. This in turn came about because certain commanders in the field began to create their own diplomacy. Among them was a young brigadier general, Napoleon Bonaparte.

The Making of a Hero

Bonaparte personifies the world-historical figure—the rare person whose life decisively affects the mainstream of human events. Born in 1769 of an impoverished but well-connected family on the French-controlled island of Corsica, he scarcely seemed destined to play such a role. His youthful ambitions were limited to Corsica itself, and most of his adolescent fantasies seem to have involved leading the island to independence from France. He was sent to French military academies, where he proved a diligent student, very adept at mathematics, and an eager reader of history. Aloof from his aristocratic classmates, whose pretensions he resented, young Bonaparte was extraordinarily self-reliant and energetic. Imagination and energy would remain among his chief personality traits, but before the Revolution he lacked any notable objective. Meanwhile he became an expert in artillery.

The Revolution saw him return to Corsica, but his ambitions ran afoul of more conservative elements on the island, and eventually the heat of provincial factionalism drove him and his family off Corsica altogether. At that juncture Napoleon moved onto a far larger stage of action. His rise as a military officer was steady and rapid; it was based in part on the luck of successive opportunities but equally on his ability to make fast, bold decisions and carry them out with remarkable efficiency. On leave in Paris in 1795, he made important contacts among the leaders of the Directory and was assigned to the planning

MAP 21.1: THE REVOLUTIONARY REPUBLICS 1792–1799

bureau of the war ministry. This put him in a position to advocate a new strategy—the opening of a major front in Italy for a French strike at the Hapsburg forces from the south, pushing northward into Germany while armies on the Rhine drove in from the west. The strategy approved, he was given command of the Army of Italy in 1797.

The total number of opposing Austrians outnumbered the French, but Bonaparte moved his troops rapidly and skillfully to achieve surprise and numerical superiority in specific encounters. The end result was a major victory that brought the French the Hapsburg province of Lombardy with its capital, Milan. Bonaparte's overall plan almost miscarried since the army of the Rhine was unsuccessful in its part of the offensive. But this fact made his own victories all the more important to the Directory. Moreover Napoleon ensured his popularity with the Paris government by making his campaign self-supporting through organized levies on the Italians instead of allowing his troops the customary prerogative of looting.

On the scene in Italy, Bonaparte brought a great new sense of excitement and showmanship to the French occupation. His personal magnetism, his theatrical skill, and his ability to manipulate men and policies all won him tremendous popularity among the Italians. He encouraged them to organize their own revolutionary movement, seeing the liberation of Italy as a means of both solidifying support for his army among them and ultimately enhancing his own reputation. This distressed the Directory since its own objective was to trade off conquests in Italy for security on the Rhine frontier, but in the end the government had to accept the fruits of the young general's victories over Austria and the Treaty of Campo Formio, which he personally negotiated in October 1797. Austria recognized a new and independent state in northern Italy, the Cisalpine Republic, and made peace with France, though leaving the Rhine question to future negotiations.

Patriotic aspiration in France now focused on defeating the last member of the coalition—the hated British enemy. Bonaparte naturally yearned for the glory of accomplishing this, and he was authorized to prepare an invasion force. Previous seaborne landings directed at Ireland had failed, and Napoleon too was finally obliged to abandon the scheme because of insufficient naval capability.

In February 1798 Napoleon instead proceeded southward to launch an expedition to Egypt. The objective was to strike at Britain's colonial interests, ultimately including the approaches to India. But British naval superiority, in the form of Admiral Horatio Nelson's fleet, turned the mission into a debacle. At the Battle of the Nile, the French fleet was decimated, and the army was marooned without support in North Africa. In addition Napoleon suffered reversals in engagements with Turkish forces. Only skillful news management prevented the full dimensions of the defeat from being known in France; the expedition's exotic details—including the much-publicized element of scientific exploration—dominated the version of the events that most Frenchmen learned. Ultimately Napoleon extricated himself from this morass by slipping off through the blockade alone, to all intents and purposes abandoning his army. Since important things were happening in France, he was confident that this would be overlooked.

The Brumaire Coup

While Bonaparte was in Egypt, the Directory was faltering under the political pressures discussed earlier. Charges of tyranny and ineffectiveness accumulated against the executive. Its diplomacy had proved a failure; further expansion in Italy, which had produced several new sister republics on the peninsula, had precipitated a new coalition against France—Great Britain, Russia, Austria, Naples, and Turkey. Facing a new war in the spring of 1799, the government was denounced for tolerating corruption by war contractors and for harassing patriotic generals.

In the elections of that spring, the widespread discontent was manifested in the defeat of many government-sponsored candidates. Shortly thereafter the legislature was able to oust four of the five directors and replace them with an ill-fated consortium of Jacobins and conservatives led by Sieyès. The pretext for toppling the incumbents came from military reversals in June, when ill-supplied French forces were compelled to evacuate most of Italy and were yielding in the Helvetic Republic. Sieyès' supporters were secretly eager to alter the constitution itself. They had lost confidence in the seemingly ineffectual institutions of the Directory regime and the instability that they felt in its annual elections. They were "revisionists," hoping to redesign the republic along more oligarchic lines. The Jacobins were their main enemies, for they wished conversely to democratize the Directory gradually. The moderate or centrist position had virtually disappeared.

The military crisis briefly favored the Jacobins, who responded with a battery of emergency measures to rally the country. Simultaneously they urged legislation to guarantee freedom for newspapers, political clubs, and other forms of organized dissent. The revisionists opposed these proposals, stalled, and ultimately succeeded in having them rejected. Meanwhile the autumn brought success for the French forces in the Helvetic state and in the Batavian Republic, where they repulsed an Anglo-Russian invasion. Most of Italy was lost, but the real threat to France herself had passed. At this point the revisionists began a concerted offensive at home against the democrats, closing down their clubs and newspapers and preparing for a coup d'état against the constitution, whose main supporters were now the powerless Jacobins.

Bonaparte's return to France seemed fortuitous at this time of uncertainty. No dire military threat remained to propel the country into the arms of a general; the revisionists were primarily concerned with scrapping a relatively open-ended regime that might evolve in a democratic direction and establishing a more rigid, oligarchic republic. But they did need a general's cooperation, for generals were the only national heroes in this demoralized period, and a general would come in handy to organize whatever force might be necessary to ensure the success of the coup. Bonaparte was not the revisionists' first choice, but he proved to be the only one available. In addition his trip up from the Mediterranean was greeted with a hero's welcome; the people had only a dim knowledge of the Egyptian fiasco and saw him in his well-earned role of victor in the Italian campaign.

Contrary to the intentions of Sieyès and his coconspirators, Bonaparte proved to be the tail that wagged the dog. As the plans were prepared, he thrust himself into an increasingly prominent position, emerging as the most ambitious and boldest of those involved. It was he who addressed the legislature to denounce a mythical Jacobin plot and to demand emergency powers to set up a new provisional government. These powers were granted, and Bonaparte joined with the two remaining directors to form a new executive, charged with bringing in a new constitutional draft. Soldiers were present to prevent any resistance. The legislature was then purged, with a cooperative rump left to ratify the new arrangements. This was how the *journée* of 18 Brumaire, year VIII (November 9, 1799), unfolded.

The Brumaire coup had not been designed to create a dictatorship, let alone a military dictatorship, but that was precisely its eventual result. In the ensuing maneuvering among the revisionists, Bonaparte's ideas and personality prevailed. The general came out of the coup as the strong man in a triumvirate of consuls, and Sieyès' elaborate plans for a republican oligarchy ended in the wastebasket, he himself accepting a pension and retiring to the country.

In other respects the plotters' plans succeeded. Elections and legislative power were meant to be limited, and they were; the middle-class elite was meant to erect barriers against the advance of democracy, and it did. The social changes propounded in the revolution of the year II were permanently blocked, while those of 1789 were consummated and protected. The price was a surrender of popular sovereignty and parliamentary liberalism.

On one final point the revisionists were to be particularly deceived. With Bonaparte's cooperation they had implicitly held out the promise of obtaining a durable peace through victory. Instead, the new regime promoted expansion and continuous war of unparalleled dimensions.

III. THE NAPOLEONIC IMPERIUM

Bonaparte rapidly became a forceful and skillful dictator. Certain of his institutional and social reforms proved so durable that they survived his downfall by well over a century. At the time, however, it was his success on the battlefield against France's foes that gave him a free hand domestically. And it was again on the battlefield that his enigmatic ambitions began to grow, transforming him from a general of the Revolution to an imperial conqueror of the Continent. Bonaparte's occupation of Italy, Germany, Spain, and other lands set contradictory forces of change in motion, for nationalism, liberalism, and reaction alike were sparked by his presence.

THE NAPOLEONIC SETTLEMENT IN FRANCE

Napoleon's prime asset in his rapid takeover of France was the resignation of its citizens. Most Frenchmen were so weary politically that they were inclined to see in Napoleon what they wished to see. The Committee of Public Safety had won grudging submission only through its terroristic policies; Napoleon achieved the same result almost by default. The fact that he was highly eclectic, an effective propagandist for himself, and a man of great personal magnetism helped placate a divided France. Ultraroyalists and dedicated Jacobins were never reconciled to his regime, but most citizens fell between those extremes and were able to find something to cheer about in the general's accomplishments.

Napoleon's attitudes are not easily classified: he was not a reactionary or a Jacobin, not a conservative or a liberal, though his opinions were flavored by a touch of each persuasion. The things he was most concerned with were authority and justification of his actions through results. The men of 1789 could find in him an heir of the Revolution because of his hostility toward the Old Regime. The corporate system, the creaking institutions of absolutism, and the congealed structures of aristocratic hierarchy were all immensely distasteful to him; he considered them unjust and ineffective. Apart from these negative perspectives, Napoleon valued the Revolution's positive commitment to equality of opportunity. This was the major liberal concept of 1789 that he continued to defend. Other rights and liberties he apparently felt could be curtailed or ignored.

Ten years of upheavals had presented a grim paradox: the Revolution had proceeded in the name of freedom, and yet successive forms of repression had been mounted to defend it. Napoleon fitted comfortably into this mold; unlike the Directory, he made no pretense about it. The social gains of the Revolution would be preserved through the exercise of strong control. His field of action was far greater than that of the most powerful eighteenth-century monarch, for no entrenched aristocracy existed to resist him. Benefiting from the clearing operations of the Revolution, he could reconstruct far more than any previous ruler and thus could show more results in justification of his authority.

Tragically, however, Napoleon drifted away from his own ideal of rationalization. Increasingly absorbed in his personal power, he began to force domestic and foreign policies on France that were geared to his imperial ambitions. As a result he increasingly directed his government toward raising men and money for the military machine, abandoning the fragile revolutionary legacy in the process.

Political and Religious Settlements
Bonaparte imposed a constitution on France that placed almost unchecked power in the hands of a single man, the first consul, for ten years. It also called for his own appointment to that position. Two later constitutional revisions, which were approved in plebiscites, further increased executive authority while diminishing the legislative branch until it disappeared altogether. The first, in 1802, converted the consulship into a lifetime post; the second, in 1804, did away with the republic by proclaiming Napoleon emperor of the French with hereditary title. The task of drafting legislation was transferred from elected representatives to appointed administrators in the Council of State. This new body was charged with advising the emperor, drafting legislation under his orders, and supervising local authorities and public institutions. This marked the birth of government by experts that remained an alternative to parliamentary government throughout subsequent French history.

The system of local government established in 1800 came ironically close to restoring the centralized bureaucracy of the Old Regime, which had been unanimously condemned in 1789. Under Bonaparte local elections, which the Revolution had emphasized, were virtually eliminated. Each department was now administered by a prefect appointed by Paris. The 400-odd subprefects on the district level as well as the 40,000 mayors of France's communes were likewise chosen in Paris. With minor changes the prefect system survives in France to this day, severely limiting local autonomy and self-government.

Police-state methods finished what constitutional change began: the suppression of genuine political activity in French life. Inheriting a large police ministry from the Directory, Napoleon placed it under the control of a former terrorist, Joseph Fouché, directing him to eliminate organized opposition and dissent. Newspapers were reduced in number and drastically censored;[4] the free journalism born in 1789 was replaced by government press releases and news management—the propaganda techniques Napoleon had adopted in Italy and Egypt became standard procedure for the consulate and empire. Clubs were prohibited, certain dissidents deported, and other presumed opponents placed under surveillance by police spies. All this wrested submission from the whole range of political activists—royalist die-hards, sans-culotte militants, and liberal intellectuals. Opposition

_____

[4] Before the Brumaire coup Paris had had seventy-three newspapers; by 1811 it had only four, all hewing to the official government line.

was reduced to clandestine plotting or passive resistance in such forms as desertion from the army.

Napoleon's actions in the religious sphere were designed to promote stability at home and popularity abroad. By 1800 revolutionary policy amounted to half-hearted secularism, with Catholicism tolerated but barred from a voice in public activity. Continuing proscription of the refractory clergy made the free exercise of the religion difficult, and the orthodox Catholic world continued to stigmatize the entire Revolution as antichurch.

Napoleon judged that major concessions to Catholic sentiment were in order, provided they could be carefully controlled by the state. He proceeded to negotiate an agreement with Pope Pius VII, the Concordat of 1801, acknowledging Catholicism as the "preferred" religion of France but explicitly protecting freedom of conscience and worship for other cults. The church was now permitted to operate in full public view; indeed primary education would be more or less turned over to the clergy, and clerical salaries would be paid by the state. Bishops would again be consecrated by the pope, but they would be nominated by the consul. Most important, the concordat reserved to the state the power to regulate the place of the church within French society. One major revolutionary change was sustained: lands confiscated from the church and sold during the Revolution were to be retained by their purchasers. Another major change was abandoned: the ten-day week was dropped and the Gregorian calendar restored.

The balance of church-state relations was firmly fixed in the state's favor, for it was Napoleon's intention to use the clergy as a major prop of the new regime. With priests now responsible to the government, the pulpit and the primary school became instruments of social control, to be used, as the imperial catechism put it, "to bind the religious conscience of the people to the August person of the Emperor." Napoleon summarized his approach to religion in his statement that the clergy would be his moral prefects. Eventually devout Catholics came to fear that this highly national version of church organization would be detrimental to true Catholicism, and Pius renounced the concordat—to which Napoleon responded by removing the pontiff to France and placing him under house arrest.

The Social System

With Old Regime obstacles to civil equality removed, Napoleon believed that the Revolution was complete. It remained now to erect an orderly, hierarchical society to counteract what he regarded as the excessive individualism of revolutionary social reforms. The foundation stones of social change—the transfer of church lands, the end of the guild system, the abolition of feudalism—would be consolidated. At the same time the authority of state and family would be reasserted and the social dominance of the middle class reaffirmed.

In the absence of electoral politics, Napoleon used the state's vast appointive powers to confer status on prominent local figures, thus associating them with his regime. These regional dignitaries were chosen from among the prosperous landowners and middle class, while the common people were definitively returned to their supposedly rightful place of deferential passivity. A new source of status was added to enhance the prestige of those who served the regime well: the Order of the Legion of Honor, nine-tenths of whose members were military men. "It is with trinkets that mankind is governed," Napoleon is supposed to have said. Legion of Honor awards and local appointments under the patronage

system were precisely such trinkets, and they endured long after their creator was gone.

Napoleon helped consolidate middle-class dominance in more practical ways. A system of compulsory labor "passports" gave employers control over their workers' movements; trade unions and strikes were strictly prohibited. Leading bankers realized their long-standing ambition to have a national bank chartered that they themselves fully controlled and that enjoyed the credit power derived from official ties to the state. In education Napoleon created elite secondary schools, or lycées, designed in part to produce high civil servants and officers. They were joined to a rigidly centralized academic system that survived intact into the twentieth

Legion of Honor decorations—distributed initially at the Hôtel des Invalides in 1802—were Napoleon's way of recognizing talent, especially in the form of military service to the state. Whereas in one sense they represented the principle of equality of opportunity, they also reflected the regime's growing militarism. (Photo: The Bettmann Archive)

This etching of the Battle of Austerlitz (December 1805) dramatically captures the two faces of Napoleonic warfare: the glory and the gore. In the background an Austrian flag is being presented to the Emperor—the mark of his brilliant victory in that engagement. But in the foreground the mangled corpses of the casualties are plainly evident. As the years went on, the glory became more and more dubious, while the dead and disabled grew too numerous to contemplate. (Photo: Culver Pictures, Inc.)

century, dominating the pattern of French education and some would say retarding it. Teachers and professors were certified and assigned by Paris; an enormous bureaucracy regulated educational affairs down to the smallest detail of curriculum and maintenance.

An equally durable legal codification covered social relations and property rights. The Civil Code, renamed the Napoleonic Code in 1807, guaranteed fundamental departures from Old Regime practices, and as such it was a revolutionary document that progressives were pleased to see exported throughout Europe. Feudal aristocracy and the property relations deriving from it were obliterated.

Instead all citizens could now exercise unambiguous contractual ownership. The code established the right to choose one's occupation, to receive equal treatment under the law, and to enjoy religious freedom. At the same time it confirmed the Thermidorian and Directory retreat from the social policies of the second revolution. Property rights for example were not matched by anything resembling a right to subsistence.

Revolutionary legislation had emancipated women and children by establishing their civil liberties. Napoleon undid most of this progress by restoring the father's absolute authority in the family. A wife owes obedience to her husband, said the code, which proceeded to deprive her of property and juridical rights that had been granted during the Revolution. The rights of illegitimate children were also eliminated, and the husband's options in disposing of his estate were enlarged, though each son was still guaranteed a portion. Napoleon insisted on relatively liberal provisions for divorce—but only as far as the husband was concerned. Penal codes and criminal procedures also rolled back revolutionary libertarianism. Defendants' rights and the role of juries were both curtailed.

The Napoleonic Code, the concordat, the education system, and the patronage structure all proved extremely durable institutions. They fulfilled Napoleon's desire to create a series of "granite masses" on which French society could be permanently reconstructed. His admirers emphasize that these achievements contributed to social stability despite France's chronic lack of stable governments. One can argue that they were skillful compromises between revolutionary equality and libertarianism on the one hand and a sense of hierarchy and authority on the other. Detractors point out first that they were class-oriented, withdrawing from the mass of Frenchmen promises held out by the second revolution; and second that they created an overcentralized, rigid institutional structure that sapped French vitality in succeeding generations. Whatever their merits or defects, these institutions did take root. They did not prove ephemeral reflections of the luster of the imperial throne, as did other aspects of Napoleon's reign—notably his attempt to create a hereditary empire and a French-dominated Europe.

NAPOLEONIC HEGEMONY

Although Bonaparte was not needed to repel an imminent invasion at the time of the Brumaire coup, he was expected to provide strategy and command for a successful conclusion of the war against the second coalition. Accordingly the first consul left France at the earliest opportunity in late 1799 with an army prepared to engage Hapsburg forces in northern Italy. The outcome of this campaign would confirm or destroy the settlement he had imposed on the revisionists. A decisive victory would make him impregnable; a rout would obviously destroy his political future.

Napoleon's strategy called for a repeat of the 1797 campaign: he would strike through Italy while the army of the Rhine pushed eastward against Vienna. This time it worked. Following French victories at Marengo, in Lombardy, and Hohenlinden, in Germany, Austria sued for peace. The Treaty of Lunéville, in February 1801, essentially restored France to the position she had held after Napoleon's triumphs in 1797.

In the British Isles a war-weary government, now standing alone against Napoleon, decided to negotiate a treaty also. The Peace of Amiens, March 1801, ended hostilities and reshuffled territorial holdings outside Europe. But it was a precarious truce because it did not settle the future of French influence and expansion or commercial relations between the two nations. Napoleon soon showed that he was willing to violate the spirit of the treaty while abiding by its letter. The British and Austrians alike were dismayed by the continued expansion of French influence in Italy, the Helvetic Republic, and North America. Most important perhaps, France made it clear that she would exclude British trade rather than restore normal trading relations. Historians generally agree that the Peace of Amiens failed because neither side was strongly interested in making it last. Their century-long struggle for preeminence had yet to be decided.

A third coalition, a replay of its predecessors, formed as the treaties broke down. France's ostensible war aims were still the preservation of the regime at home and the sister republics abroad. The coalition had the ideological and diplomatic objectives of restoring the Batavian Republic and Italy to "independence," dissolving French influence elsewhere, and if possible reducing France to her original borders. But like most alliances of its sort, the third coalition was to be dismembered piecemeal.

French hopes of settling the issue directly by invading England proved unrealizable. At the Battle of Trafalgar, in October 1805, an already outnumbered and outmanned French navy was crushed by Admiral Nelson's fleet. An innovative tactician who broke rule-book procedures on the high seas as French generals had been doing on land, Nelson ensured the security of the British Isles for the remainder of the Napoleonic era.

Napoleon turned now against the Austro-Russian forces. Moving 200,000 French soldiers with unprecedented speed across the Continent, he took his enemies by surprise and won a succession of startling victories.

After occupying Vienna he proceeded against the coalition's main army in December. Feigning weakness and retreat at the moment of battle, he drew his now numerically superior opponents into an exposed position, crushed the center of their lines, and inflicted a decisive defeat. The Battle of Austerlitz was Napoleon's most brilliant tactical achievement, and the Hapsburgs were compelled to jump for the peace table. The resulting Treaty of Pressburg was extremely harsh and humiliating for Austria. Not only was a large indemnity imposed on her, but she was required to cede her Venetian provinces.

The Conquest and Reorganization of Europe

By this time Napoleon had far surpassed his role of general of the Revolution and was beginning his imperial march toward the conquest of Europe. The French sphere of influence had increased dramatically to include most of southern Germany, which was organized into the Confederation of the Rhine, a client realm of France. At the moment only Prussia stood outside this sphere. Her neutrality during the war with Austria had been effected by skillful French diplomacy and Prussian miscalculation. Only after Austria had been forced to the peace table did Prussia recognize the threat she had allowed to rise against her interests by missing her chance to combine effectively with her neighbor to the south. Belatedly she mobilized her famous but antiquated army; it was rewarded with stinging defeat by France in a number of encounters culminating in the Battle of Jena in October 1806. With Prussian military power proved a paper tiger and the conqueror ensconced in Berlin, the prestige of the ruling class disintegrated, and the masses docilely accepted the occupation that followed. Napoleon was now master of the northern German lands as well as the south. For a while it appeared that he would obliterate Prussia entirely, but in the end he restored her sovereignty after amputating part of her territory and imposing a crushing indemnity.

The subsequent reorganization of Central Europe brought Napoleon considerable gratification and prestige. He formally proclaimed the end of the moribund Holy Roman Empire in 1806—Francis II had already changed his own title to Emperor Francis I of Austria two years earlier—and proceeded to liquidate numerous small German principalities whose profusion had created such chaos. In their place he erected two new states: the Kingdom of Westphalia, on whose throne he placed his brother Jérôme; and the grand duchy of Berg, to be ruled by Joachim Murat, his brother-in-law. His ally Saxony was proclaimed a full-scale kingdom, while a new duchy of Warsaw was created out of Prussian Poland. This "restoration" of Poland had major propaganda value; it made the emperor appear a champion of Polish national aspirations in view of the fact that the rulers of Prussia, Russia, and Austria had dismembered Poland in a series of partitions ending in 1794. Moreover Napoleon could now enlist a Polish army and use Polish territory as a base of operations against the last Continental member of the coalition, Russia.

In February 1807 Napoleon confronted the colossus of the East in the Battle of Eylau; the resulting carnage was horrifying but inconclusive. When spring came Napoleon was in a desperate position. Only a dramatic victory could preserve his conquests in Central Europe and vindicate the extraordinary decisions of the past two years. Fortunately for the Emperor the Battle of Friedland in June was a French victory that demoralized Tsar Alexander I and persuaded him to negotiate. Meeting at Tilsit, the two emperors buried

their differences and proceeded to create a mighty alliance of two superstates that would dominate Europe, essentially partitioning it into Eastern and Western spheres of influence. Each would support the other's conquests and mediate in behalf of the other's interests. The Treaty of Tilsit of July 7 sanctioned Napoleon's reorganization of Europe as well as the dramatic expansion of French territory eastward. Apart from outright annexations the chief vehicle for Napoleon's rearrangements was the creation of satellite kingdoms. The old sister republics were now induced to evolve into kingdoms just as France herself had. And it happened that Napoleon had a whole family of brothers ready to assume royal crowns.

The distorted shape of Napoleonic Europe at its high point, around 1810, is best appreciated on a map (see Map 21.2). His chief satellites included the Kingdom of Holland, comprising the Batavian Republic, with brother Louis on the throne; the Kingdom of Italy, with Napoleon himself as king and stepson Eugène de Beauharnais as viceroy; the Confederation of the Rhine, including brother Jérôme's Kingdom of Westphalia; the Kingdom of Naples, covering southern Italy, with brother Joseph wearing the crown until he was transferred to Spain and passed it to brother-in-law Murat; and the duchy of Warsaw. The old Austrian Netherlands, the Rhineland, Tuscany, Piedmont, Genoa, the Illyrian provinces, and the Ionian Islands had been directly annexed to France. Switzerland persisted as the Helvetic Republic but under a new constitution dictated by France. In 1810, after yet another war with Austria, imperial policy was consummated by a marriage between the house of Bonaparte and the house of Hapsburg: Napoleon, having divorced Joséphine de Beauharnais, married Marie Louise, daughter of Francis I.

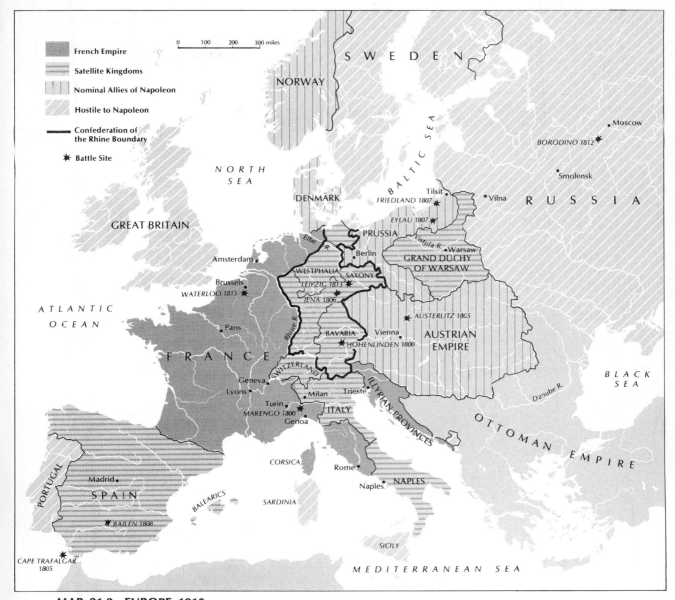

MAP 21.2: EUROPE 1810

The Continental System

Only Britain remained to be vanquished; meanwhile she stood between Napoleon and his dream of complete hegemony over Europe, not to mention the world beyond. Since Britain was invulnerable to invasion, Napoleon's objective was to destroy her influence by means of economic warfare.

Unable to blockade British ports directly, the emperor sought to close the Continent—

to blockade Britain from her markets, stop her exports, and thus ruin her trade and credit. In mercantilist fashion he reasoned that if she had nowhere to sell her manufactured goods, no gold would come into the country, which would eventually bankrupt her. At the same time overproduction would cause unemployment, and the ensuing labor unrest might turn the British people against the government and force it to make peace with France. On the other hand French advantages in Continental markets would naturally increase with the elimination of British competition.

Accordingly Napoleon mounted his so-called Continental system: he would prohibit British trade with all French allies and all commerce by neutrals carrying British products, prevent all ships coming from British ports from landing in Europe, and have any goods coming from or belonging to the British Isles impounded.

The British responded in 1807 with the Orders in Council that in effect reversed the blockade: they *required* all neutral ships to stop at British ports to procure trading licenses and pay tariffs. In other words they intervened in all trade between neutrals and most European ports. Violators became lawful prizes to seize. Napoleon's angry answer to this was the threat simply to commandeer any neutral ship that obeyed the Orders in Council by stopping at British ports.

Thus a total naval war involving neutrals grew out of the Continental system. Indeed there scarcely remained such a thing as neutral immunity since every ship was obliged to violate one system or the other and thus run afoul of naval patrols or privateers. While the British took only about 40 French ships a year after 1807 (for few were left to sail the seas), they seized almost 3,000 neutrals a year, including many American ships.

Britain was hurt by the Continental system. Her gold reserves dwindled, and internal strife did erupt in 1811, a year of widespread unemployment and rioting. France was affected adversely by the counterblockade, which cut her off from the raw materials necessary for industrial production as well as from British finished goods, extremely popular on the Continent. But the satellite states probably suffered the most, becoming economic vassals of France. In Amsterdam for example shipping volume declined from 1,350 ships entering the port in 1806 to 310 in 1809; as a result commercial revenues dropped calamitously. Out of loyalty to the people whom he ruled, King Louis Bonaparte tolerated smuggling. This so infuriated Napoleon that he ousted his brother from the throne and annexed the Kingdom of Holland to France. Smuggling was in fact the weak link in the system, creating holes in Napoleon's dike of economic sanctions that constantly needed plugging. This in turn drove Napoleon to more drastic policies.

RESISTANCE TO NAPOLEON

Having vanquished every major European power on the battlefield except Britain, Napoleon now felt that nothing stood in his way. Since Spain and Russia did not seem responsive enough to his will, the emperor chose to deal with each of them by force, assuming that his plans against Britain could then be pursued to their conclusion. On all counts he was mistaken. Napoleon's confrontations with Britain, Spain, and Russia proved in various ways that his reach had exceeded his grasp.

The Spanish Ulcer

Spain and France had a common interest in weakening British power in Europe and the colonial world. But their alliance after 1795 brought only reversals for Spain, including the loss of her Louisiana Territory and (at the Battle of Trafalgar) most of her fleet. Domestically things were no better. The royal household had been the scene of scandalous and bitter controversy for some time. A lover of Queen Maria Louisa's, Manual de Godoy, had achieved astonishing ascendancy as prime minister and proved to be a corrupt opportunist who was extremely unpopular with the people. He was despised by Crown Prince Ferdinand, who was equally hostile to Godoy's protectors, the king and queen.

Napoleon looked on the resultant turbulence with extreme irritation. At the zenith of his power, he easily drifted toward the solution of reorganizing Spain himself. As a pretext for military intervention, he put in motion a plan to invade Portugal, supposedly to partition her with Spain. Once the French army was well inside Spain, it could impose the political solution to Spain's instability that Napoleon desired.

The squabbling King Charles IV and his son were tricked, threatened, and bribed into abdicating, one after the other; a group of Spanish notables was gathered to petition Napoleon to provide a new sovereign, preferably his brother Joseph; and Joseph was duly proclaimed king of Spain. With French troops already settled around Madrid, Joseph prepared to assume his new throne, sincerely eager to rule well under a liberal constitution that was drawn up. But as he took up the crown, an unanticipated drama unfolded.

Faced with military occupation, the disappearance of their royal family, and the crowning of a Frenchman, the Spanish people rose in rebellion. It began on May 2, 1808, when an angry crowd rioted against French troops, who responded with brutal reprisals. This bloody incident, known as the Dos de Mayo and captured in Goya's famous paintings (see Plate 48), has been preserved in Spanish leg-

end. The kidnapping of Prince Ferdinand a short time later galvanized the uprising into a sustained offensive against the French and pro-French Spaniards. Local notables created juntas to organize the rebels, mainly peasants, priests, and monks, and coordinate them with regular Spanish troops.

The troops were generally ineffective against the French but did produce one telling victory: two French divisions were forced to surrender at Bailén in July, an episode that broke the aura of Napoleonic invincibility. The main brunt of professional military operations in what had now become the Peninsular War was borne by the British, whose expeditionary force first drove the French out of Portugal and eventually rolled them back across Spain under the inspired command of Arthur Wellesley, later duke of Wellington. All the while as many as 30,000 Spanish guerrilla fighters were providing another dimension to the conflict and contributing to its brutality. Their atrocities and harassment of the French kept the foreign invaders in a constant state of anxiety and led to reprisals that in turn escalated the war's bitterness.

All told the juntas, the guerrillas, and the British held a massive French army of up to 300,000 men pinned down in Spain and made it impossible for Napoleon to mobilize fully elsewhere on the Continent. He referred to the war as the "Spanish ulcer." In addition, though Napoleon had contempt for the rebel monks and peasants, other Europeans were inspired by their example that resistance to the French emperor was possible.

Meanwhile the war proved a disaster for Spanish liberals. Torn between Joseph, who would have been a liberal ruler, and the nationalist rebels, they ended by falling into an unviable position between the two. Those who supported Joseph found that he was never able to rule independently. It was Napoleon who gave the orders in Spain, relying on his generals to carry them out. Those who stood behind the rebels were able to organize a provisional government in 1812 by convening the ancient parliament, the Cortes, in the town of Cádiz. There they drafted a liberal and nationalist constitution, which pleased the British and therefore was tolerated by the local juntas. But in reality the priests, peasants, and nobles who made up the bulk of rebel sympathizers disdained the liberals and were fighting rather for the Catholic Church and the Spanish Bourbons. When in 1814 the French were finally expelled and Ferdinand VII took the throne, the liberals' joy was short-lived. Ferdinand tore up the constitution of 1812, restored the monasteries and the Inquisition, closed down the universities, revived censorship, and arrested the leading liberals. The main beneficiaries of the Spanish rebellion and the Peninsular War were thus Spanish reactionaries and the British expeditionary force.

The Russian Debacle

In 1811 Napoleon did not yet realize how his entanglement in Spain would drain French military power and encourage intellectuals and statesmen in Central Europe to contemplate nationalist uprisings against him. On the contrary never were Napoleon's schemes more grandiose than in that year. Surveying the crumbling state system of Europe, he imagined that it could be replaced with a supranational empire, ruled from Paris and Rome and based on the Napoleonic Code. He believed that the era of the balance of power was over and that nationalist strivings would not stand in his way. On both counts he was mistaken.

The key obstacle to imperial reorganization and French domination was Russia. Wishing to retain her sphere of interest in Eastern Europe and the Baltic region and increasingly discontented with the restrictions of the Con-

tinental system, Russia was a restive ally. Alexander was being pressured on the one hand to resist France by British diplomats, French émigrés, anti-Napoleonic exiles such as Baron Stein of Prussia, and nationalist reactionaries. On the other hand Russian court liberals, more concerned with domestic reforms, were eager for him to maintain peace with France; but by 1812 their influence on Alexander had waned. On his side Napoleon wanted to enforce the Continental system and reduce Russia's capacity to interfere with Europe's destiny. As he put it with characteristic bluntness, "Let Alexander defeat the Persians, but don't let him meddle in the affairs of Europe." Once again two major powers were facing each other with progressively less interest in maintaining peace.

Napoleon decided to strike, and he embarked on his most ambitious military campaign. His objective was to annihilate the Russian forces or barring that to conquer Moscow and chase the army to the point of disarray. Almost 600,000 men (many drawn from the satellite states), long supply lines, and repeated forced marches were his principal weapons. The Russian response was to retreat in collected fashion and avoid a fight until a propitious moment. Meanwhile many nobles abandoned their estates and burned their crops to the ground. At Borodino, however, the Russians turned and took a stand. In the enormous battle that ensued, they sustained 45,000 casualties but managed to withdraw in order. The French lost 35,000. At this price they were able to enter Moscow on September 14, 1812, but the Russian army was still intact and far from demoralized.

On the contrary Moscow demoralized the French. They found the city deserted, bereft of badly needed supplies. The next night it was mysteriously set ablaze, causing such extensive damage as to make it unfit for winter quarters. Realistic advisers warned the emperor that his situation was untenable, while others told him what he wished to hear—that Russian resistance was weakening. Napoleon indulged in a reverie of false optimism and indecision. Militarily it was imperative that the French begin to retreat immediately, but that would constitute a political defeat. On October 19 Napoleon finally ordered a retreat, but it was too late.

The delay forced an unrealistic pace on the army that it was in no condition to sustain. Supplies had been outrun, medical care for the thousands of wounded was nonexistent, horses were lacking. The French officers were poorly organized for the march, and the soldiers were growing insubordinate. Food shortages compelled foraging parties to sweep some distance from the main body of troops, but these men fell prey to Russian irregulars, who operated with increasing effectiveness. And there was the weather—just a normal Russian winter in which no commander would wish to find himself on a march of several hundred miles, laden with wounded and loot but without supplies, horses, and food.[5] Napoleon's poor planning, the harsh weather, and the operation of guerrilla bands made the long retreat a nightmare of suffering for the Grand Army. It is estimated that no more than 100,000 troops survived the ordeal. Worse yet, the Prussian contingent took the occasion to desert Napoleon. This opened up the possibility of mass defections from the empire and with them the formation of a new coalition.

---

[5] Whether he had planned it that way or not, the Russian commander Kutuzov drew Napoleon deep into Russia, trapped him far from his lines of supply, and then launched a counteroffensive. During World War II the Russians dealt with Germany's invasion similarly, and it has been claimed that Stalin was following Kutuzov's classic strategy. The parallel included the use of guerrilla warfare and scorched-earth tactics to harass the enemy.

German Resistance and the Last Coalition

It is testimony to Napoleon's fortitude—if also to his imperviousness to the horror around him—that he was unshaken by all this. On the lonely sleigh ride back to his main lines, he was already planning how to recoup his losses, raise new armies, and set things aright. Other statesmen were equally determined to capitalize on his defeat and destroy the empire once and for all.

Napoleon's credibility with liberal reformers in Central and Eastern Europe still stood, but it was now challenged by ringing cries for a nationalist revival in the Confederation of the Rhine that would throw off the tyrant's yoke. This type of thinking reinforced the continuing efforts of statesmen like the Prussian Stein and the Austrian Prince Klemens von Metternich to revive the struggle against Napoleon. Less spectacularly military reformers in Prussia had adopted French methods of conscription and organization, the better to oppose France. On the level of propaganda and the symbolic gesture, German publicists talked of a popular war of liberation—the ultimate tribute to the French Revolution.

Against this background of growing nationalist sentiment and military reform, the diplomats worked and waited. Finally, in March 1813, Frederick William III of Prussia signed a treaty with Russia, forming the nucleus of an offensive coalition against Napoleon. A great struggle for Germany ensued between the Russo-Prussian forces and Napoleon and his allies. Austria continued to claim neutrality and offered to mediate the dispute. At a conference in Prague, Napoleon was invited to restore all conquests made after 1802. Napoleon rejected this, and the allies sighed with relief, since the proposal was merely a stalling tactic until Austria could be persuaded to enter the war.

In August Emperor Francis I finally declared war on his son-in-law, while Napoleon learned of new defeats in Spain. Calling up underage conscripts, Napoleon was able to field one last army, but he found that his major southern German ally, Bavaria, had finally been induced to change sides. At Leipzig a major batttle raged for three days in October, at the end of which Napoleon was defeated. His last confederation allies deserted him.

With Napoleon driven back into France, the British reinforced the coalition to assure that it would not disintegrate now that Central Europe had been liberated. Final terms were offered to the emperor: he could retain his throne, but France would be reduced to her "normal frontiers." (The precise meaning of this was purposely left unclear.) Again Napoleon counted on a dramatic reversal and chose to fight. With some reluctance the allies invaded France. Napoleon led the remnants of his army skillfully but to no avail; Frenchmen had lost confidence in him, and no civilian spirit of resistance to invasion developed as it had in 1793. Paris fell in March 1814. The price for this last defeat was the demand for unconditional surrender and the emperor's abdication. Napoleon was removed to the island of Elba, between Corsica and Italy, and was granted sovereignty over it. After twenty-two years of exile, the Bourbons returned to France.

The second revolution, guided by the Jacobin dictatorship and propelled by the sans-culottes, lasted little more than two years in 1792–1794. When the crisis had been surmounted and counter-revolution vanquished, France disavowed the Jacobin leaders. The National Convention put an end to the Terror and also to the promise of social democracy. It attempted to install a moderate republican government, in essence by recreating the middle-class regime of 1791 without a king. This proved impossible. While France exported revolution to receptive states in the years of the Directory, the revolution at home foundered.

In supporting a coup whose leadership was taken over by General Bonaparte, conservatives did not foresee that his solution to the problem would be a dictatorship. But France soon succumbed to Bonaparte's one-man rule as his prestige grew thanks to his feats on the battlefield. Before long the republic disappeared, replaced by the Napoleonic Empire.

Under the empire confrontation of France with Old Regime Europe engulfed the entire Continent. France still embodied the specter of revolution, but by this time it amounted to little more than Napoleon's contempt for the inefficiency and irrationality of the old order. Even so this was a powerful challenge to the status quo. Napoleon believed that the state system was dead, that Europe must be reorganized under French hegemony, and that administrative reform and the Napoleonic Code should be spread to the new realms.

His conquests eventually overreached his ability to maintain them except by increasingly tyrannical measures, which in turn provoked a whole range of responses in Europe. Resistance coalesced, the empire came crashing down, and the Bourbons returned to France. But the clock could not really be set back from Europe's experience of revolution and Napoleonic transformation. The era of modern political and social conflicts had begun.

RECOMMENDED READING

See also titles listed for Chapter 20.

Sources

* Beik, Paul H. (ed.). *The French Revolution.* 1970.
* De Caulaincourt, Armand. *With Napoleon in Russia.* 1935.
* Herold, J. C. (ed.). *The Mind of Napoleon.* 1961.
Stewart, J. H. *A Documentary Survey of the French Revolution.* 1951.
Thompson, J. M. (ed.). *Napoleon Self-Revealed.* 1934.

Studies

The best general history of this period is a series of volumes by the great French historian Georges Lefebvre: *The French Revolution* (2 vols.) and *Napoleon* (2 vols.), all published in translation by the Columbia University Press, with full bibliographies.

Anderson, Eugene. *Nationalism and the Cultural Crisis in Prussia, 1806–1815.* 1939.
Chandler, David. *The Campaigns of Napoleon.* 1966. For military history buffs.
* Cobb, R. C. *The Police and the People: French Popular Protest.* 1970. A discussion of peasants and sans-culottes that should be compared to Soboul's.
* Connelly, Owen. *Napoleon's Satellite Kingdoms.* 1965.
Furet, F., and D. Richet. *The French Revolution.* 1970. An attempt to break with Marxist traditions in French historiography.

Gershoy, Leo. *Bertrand Barère, a Reluctant Terrorist.* 1962. Perhaps the best English-language biography of a revolutionary figure.
* Geyl, P. *Napoleon, For and Against.* 1949. Napoleon and the historians—as interpreted by a leading Dutch historian.
Godechot, Jacques. *The Napoleonic Era in Europe.* 1971. A recent textbook.
* Herold, J. C. *The Age of Napoleon.* 1963. A brilliant example of "popular" history.
* Holtman, Robert. *The Napoleonic Revolution.* 1967. More favorable to Napoleon than Herold.
Kennedy, Michael. *The Jacobin Club of Marseilles.* 1973.
* Lyons, M. *France Under the Directory.* 1975.
* Markham, Felix. *Napoleon.* 1966. Perhaps the best biography in English.
* Palmer, Robert R. *Twelve Who Ruled: The Year of the Terror in the French Revolution.* 1941. A modern classic.
* Rudé, George. *The Crowd in the French Revolution.* 1959.
———. *Robespierre: Portrait of a Revolutionary Democrat.* 1975.
Soboul, Albert. *The Parisian Sans-Culottes and the French Revolution.* 1964. An abridgment of a landmark French thesis; should be compared to Cobb's discussion.

* Available in paperback.

TWENTY-TWO

THE POLITICS
OF RESTORATION
AND REFORM

Peace brought the chance to build again. After a generation of fighting, Europe's nations in alliance had established once more that no one state should dominate the Continent. The first task, then, was to preserve the balance at last established. The wars against France, however, had been about more than territory or balance of power; they were also battles for monarchy and against revolutionary ideas. To the victors, peace and security required that revolution as well as French aggression be prevented in the future. Painfully aware that political order was as fragile as it was precious and that rulers could be not only overrun from without but also toppled from within, the allies sought to restore the social as well as the international equilibrium of prerevolutionary Europe.

To protect their hold on power, the regimes reestablished would be required to be more effective than before the Revolution—to maintain large armies and collect more taxes, to support a better-trained bureaucracy, dispense justice more evenly, and provide more services. Governments would affect the lives of their people more directly and thus depend upon popular acquiescence more heavily than in the past. For even the most reactionary rulers, therefore, restoration would always mean some compromise between refurbishment of the old and acceptance of the changes brought by revolution, war, and Napoleonic occupation.

Politics was the vehicle for reestablishing social order and for effecting the required compromises. The organization of the state could, it seemed, shape society, determine its well-being, and set the values by which it functioned. In the nineteenth century people divided with religious intensity over questions of the form of government, who should exercise its power, and what policies it should pursue. Shared by conservatives and by the liberals who fought them in the name of liberty and prosperity, this focus on politics became the hallmark of an era.

But political conflict proved hard to contain either by repression or by reform. The moderate, reforming governments that followed the revolutions of 1830 suffered no less dissension than their more conservative predecessors; and France's liberal monarchy was the first to fall in the wave of revolution that swept the Continent in 1848. In their democratic aims and then in their divisions and defeats, the revolutions of 1848 exposed the fact that recent changes in society went even deeper and were more problematical than the changes in political forms.

I. THE CONSERVATIVE ORDER

In setting the terms of peace, allied leaders sought above all to restore stability to Europe. Proper political arrangements were expected to accomplish that. Believing that international peace and domestic order were inextricably linked, they generally supported monarchical regimes that would cooperate in resisting dangerous changes at home and abroad.

The most pressing issue was the future of

The Congress of Vienna. In this watercolor, the fashionable artist J. B. Isabey presents the Congress as a kind of elegant salon in which the very clothes the statesmen wore mix the styles of the old regime and the new century. (Photo: The Granger Collection)

France. Some of the allies, including the tsar of Russia, were willing to accept a conservative republic, but most favored some sort of monarchy. The Treaty of Paris, signed in May 1814, recognized Louis XVIII, a brother of Louis XVI, as king and granted France her "natural frontiers"—those she had gained by 1792. A settlement covering all the territory affected by the Napoleonic wars would take longer. Warily watching each other, the allies agreed to call an international congress where their respective interests could be carefully weighed and balanced.

THE CONGRESS OF VIENNA

The congress met in Vienna in September 1814, an occasion for serious deliberations and elaborate pomp. The crowned heads of Austria, Prussia, Russia, and dozens of lesser states, ministers of nearly every government, advocates of special causes, expert advisers, princesses and countesses, dancers and artists, and the ambitious of every rank flocked to the Austrian capital. Their contrived gaiety made the Congress of Vienna a symbol of aristocratic restoration from the first.

The business of the congress remained the responsibility of the four great powers—Austria, Great Britain, Russia, and Prussia—an inner circle to which France was soon admitted. Prince Klemens von Metternich, who had led the Austrian Empire to this triumph, conducted the affairs of the congress with such skill that its provisions can be seen as largely his work. Tsar Alexander I came as his country's autocrat and chief diplomat, determined to use this moment of Russia's great prestige to advantage. The reserved and able Lord Castlereagh made his broad view of British interests a major factor throughout the negotiations. Prince Talleyrand, whose talents had largely shaped the markedly lenient Treaty of Paris, used all his famous shrewdness to regain for Bourbon France her traditional influence. The importance of the negotiations and the appeal of its leading personalities have made the Congress of Vienna a subject of fascination for all students of diplomacy.

The concerns of these men focused on Continental Europe, for only Great Britain among the victors had extensive holdings overseas, and British designs on South Africa, Ceylon, and Malta were modest enough to be accepted with little dispute. Europe was considered the sphere of the great powers; each closely weighed the claims of the others, and all especially watched Russia, with her mammoth armies, undefined ambitions, and quixotic tsar.

Disposing of Polish and Saxon territory proved the thorniest issue. The three partitions of Poland in the eighteenth century suggested one solution: to keep the balance of power in Eastern Europe by dividing Poland among the three Eastern monarchies. Napoleon's creation, the duchy of Warsaw, suggested another: to set up an independent but greatly reduced Poland. Because the king of Saxony had remained loyal to Napoleon too long, Prussia claimed his realm as compensation for past suffering; Russian armies, however, now held the land in question. For Austria the expansion of Russia and Prussia was an ancient nightmare no more acceptable after Napoleon than before. Her fears drove Austria closer to Great Britain, and the rift among the allies made room for France to play a major part.

In the final settlement, a triumph of diplomacy in eighteenth-century style, everyone got something (see Map 22.1). Russia received most of Poland as a separate kingdom under the tsar. Prussia got about half of Saxony and as compensation for the rest was given greatly enlarged territories in the Rhineland. Thus formidable Prussian armies would stand along the French border. The Austrian Netherlands were absorbed in a new independent Kingdom of the Netherlands, including Belgium, which created another strong buffer against France and met the British desire that no major power control the Low Countries' important river ports. In return for her loss of the southern Netherlands, Austria acquired Venezia, which with Lombardy greatly strengthened her dominance of northern Italy. The other duchies of northern Italy went to dukes with close Austrian ties (in a touch of chivalry, Marie Louise, Napoleon's now throneless Austrian wife, was given Parma to rule).

By these and similar exchanges in less pressing cases, the most extensive European settlement since the agreements at Westphalia in 1648 established the balance of power as an interlocking system.[1] Each of the victors had gained territory, and the areas that France might easily overrun were now held by states —the Kingdom of the Netherlands, Prussia in the Rhineland, and Austria in northern Italy— capable of resisting future French aggression. The final act was signed in June 1815 by the five great powers and by Sweden, Spain, and Portugal, a gracious recognition of their past importance.

The Hundred Days
The deliberations of the Congress were interrupted in March 1815 by the terrifying news

---

[1] The Kingdom of Sardinia would have liked Lombardy but got Genoa, the last of the ancient Italian republics to fall. Russia took Finland from Sweden, which in turn got Norway from Denmark.

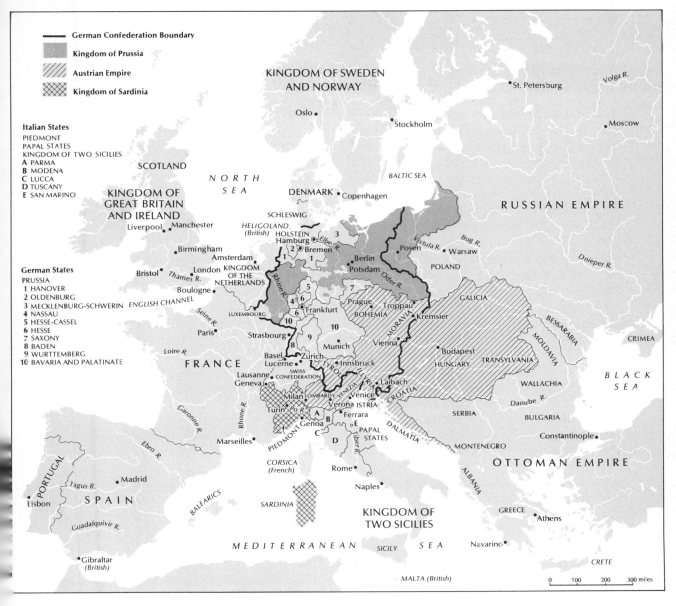

MAP 22.1: EUROPE 1815

Legend:
- German Confederation Boundary
- Kingdom of Prussia
- Austrian Empire
- Kingdom of Sardinia

Italian States
PIEDMONT
PAPAL STATES
KINGDOM OF TWO SICILIES
A PARMA
B MODENA
C LUCCA
D TUSCANY
E SAN MARINO

German States
PRUSSIA
1 HANOVER
2 OLDENBURG
3 MECKLENBURG-SCHWERIN
4 NASSAU
5 HESSE-CASSEL
6 HESSE
7 SAXONY
8 BADEN
9 WURTTEMBERG
10 BAVARIA AND PALATINATE

of Napoleon's escape. He had tried to make the best of ruling Elba and even showed something of his old flair as he designed uniforms, held receptions, and inquired into the local economy. But the island principality was far too small to contain an emperor's ambition.

Landing in the south of France, he made his way to Paris. Important parts of the French army defected, and Louis XVIII, after hoping for support that did not develop, once again climbed into his carriage and headed for the eastern border. Napoleon had become the ruler of France without firing a shot. He then tried to negotiate with the allies, but they declared him an outlaw and quickly assembled their troops. After several minor battles he was defeated for the last time at Waterloo on June 18 and surrendered to the British. They dispatched him to the more distant island of St. Helena, in the South Atlantic.

Napoleon's dashing venture lasted only a hundred days, but its effects were felt far longer. The terms of peace were altered, the possibility of a stable restoration questioned, and the meaning of Bonapartism redefined. France seemed once more a threat, and a new treaty reduced her boundaries to those of 1789 (which entailed the loss of much of the Saar to Prussia) and required her to pay the allies an indemnity. The Bourbons of course returned to the throne of France, but their claims to popularity were embarrassed by the ease with which Napoleon had regained power, and they lived with the specter of renewed revolution. During his Hundred Days Napoleon had offered a liberal government that softened the memory of his despotism (he even banned slave traffic in the French colonies), and from St. Helena he continued in his writings to broaden the appeal of Bonapartism as the best means of achieving both liberty and order. Allied diplomats, less expert in playing to popular opinion, planned instead for frequent meetings whereby together they could maintain the settlement so carefully contrived.

The Nature of the Settlement

The Congress of Vienna had not attempted simply to restore the prerevolutionary world. A Bourbon ruled again in France, but he was a king with a constitution. Despite past glories the Republic of Venice was not reestablished. Nor were the Holy Roman Empire and hundreds of its minor German principalities; instead the reorganization effected under

Napoleon was kept, with modifications, and thirty-nine German states, including Prussia and Austria, were joined in a loose and ill-defined German Confederation. The aristocrats at Vienna sought advice from teams of experts on matters of history and law, a very modern use of specialists. They laid down rules of diplomatic conduct useful to this day, and in provisions such as those establishing free navigation on international riverways, displayed their enlightened reasonableness. For a century Europe would be free of universal war, and something of that stability was due to the wisdom at Vienna, which left twice-defeated France a respected power and the interests of other states intricately connected.

The congress was less impressive, however, in the realm of ideas. Talleyrand had sought in the concept of legitimacy a general principle that would dignify the deliberations. The powers, he argued, should favor regimes that had lasted and proved acceptable to their subjects; this would obviate the need to restore every shaky and petty throne. But even so vague a principle proved inconvenient. Tsar Alexander aimed for something grander and proposed a Holy Alliance, based on an agreement that all states would conduct their affairs according to Christian teachings. Three governments refused: the sultan cared too little for Christian teachings and the pope too much, and Britain would not be committed to Continental ties. All the others signed but with public skepticism, and historians have similarly tended to dismiss the Holy Alliance as a meaningless product of Alexander's mysticism. Yet there was something modern and maybe wise in the tsar's awareness of public opinion and his desire that the conservative powers have an ethical claim with which to counter the appeal to nationality and to natural rights so freely used by their opponents.

The plan to hold frequent congresses among the great powers implied that the wartime alliance would be continued. For Castlereagh negotiation would be the means of accommodating inevitable change. But Metternich sought instead a Concert of Europe, under his leadership, to snuff out the flames of revolution wherever they occurred; and his influence dominated. The next generation of Europe's liberals, reformers, and nationalists would thus remember the Congress of Vienna not as the occasion of realistic compromise but as a brutal shuffling of territory by men indifferent to the claims of nationality or promises of constitutions, where aristocrats danced while foisting reactionary regimes on the people of Europe. For fifty years every revolution and every war in Europe would include among its goals the dismantlement of the arrangements made at Vienna.

CONSERVATIVE THOUGHT

In every period of European history, there have been leaders in politics and philosophy who could fairly be labeled conservative. But in the long battle against the French Revolution, conservatism had become what today would be called an ideology, a coherent view of human nature, social organization, political power, and the roots of change that was intended to justify social hierarchies and established institutions. Conservatives might disagree about particular policies, but conservatism had become a broad school of thought that would help shape political discourse throughout the nineteenth century.

The eloquent reasoning of Edmund Burke, whose writings appeared throughout the latter half of the eighteenth century, provided perhaps the most influential formulation of the conservative position. Society, he argued, is a partnership of the living, the dead, and those yet to be born. It depends on continuity. By granting special privileges to certain groups, it adapted to social needs in a way conducive to

order, achieving a delicate arrangement in which rank was related to social role and differences of status, having evolved through time, were acceptable to all. This "natural" order is far wiser than the "artificial" plans of radicals, however well-intentioned, who necessarily undo more than they intend and ultimately threaten society itself.

The Burkean view thus allowed for gradual change, at least in theory, but was clearly suspicious of sudden reform for immediate ends. It became more opposed to change, however, as it underwent the experience of revolution and found support in new intellectual currents. One of these was a distrust of reason, a turning away from the Enlightenment, expressed in the argument that mankind's highest achievements and deepest understanding do not result from cold calculation. This persuasion spread with the Romantic movement which deeply influenced contemporary thought. Primarily literary and artistic rather than political, Romanticism affected radicals as well as conservatives; but in its appreciation of human experience as unique, subjective, and emotional, it made an important contribution to conservatism. Romantics yearned for absolute values and ultimate meanings, and whether they found the source of these in God, historical process, or nature, they agreed that human knowledge is a puny thing compared with the great forces outside it.

Conservatives thus considered that rational plans for a just society are simply beside the point and that nations cannot be ruled by mere man-made constitutions or law. Society was seen as a great interconnecting web, an organic whole not suitable for piecemeal reform, and phrases about individual rights seemed dangerous abstractions hiding selfish interests and encouraging false hopes.

The early nineteenth-century fascination with history and the contemporary interest in

Christian philosophy gave further stimulus to conservatives, who found in history a record of how painfully civilization had evolved and how fragile it remained, and they often sought, particularly in recent events, evidence of human error and divine will to give larger meaning to their political battles. They viewed Christianity as the source of Europe's strength and Christian fear as a necessary restraint on man's selfish and prideful nature. Without it, society would dissolve into revolution and anarchy. Conservatives tended therefore to attach religion to their own politics and the church to aristocracy and monarchy. They regarded political battles as merely part of a far larger and millennial conflict.

Such views gave conservative thought both a militancy and a depth to which German contributions were perhaps the most original and lasting. For Europeans used to receiving radical ideas from France, however, two of the most striking exponents of conservatism in the restoration period were men who wrote in French, Joseph de Maistre and Louis de Bonald. Society's first task, they argued, is self-preservation. Authority alone can check the selfish wills of individuals, and authority requires undivided sovereignty, social hierarchy, and the vigilant suppression of dangerous ideas. Having experienced revolution, they were fascinated by power and demanded its vigorous use by an unfettered monarch. They declared that church and state must be closely linked, and de Maistre held the international authority of the papacy to be a social necessity. Revolution he explained as divine retribution for false ideas.

Conservatism in this form contained little that was humane or tolerant. With its praise of hangmen and censors, it spoke only to those who already shared its fears. It left little space for compromise and lambasted every concession as a dangerous weakening of the dikes restraining revolution. Like liberalism, republicanism, and socialism, nineteenth-century conservatism became an ideology that divided while calling for unity and that emphasized political power while speaking of the social good.

THE PILLARS OF THE RESTORATION

The stable international order sought at Vienna and the domestic order based on conservative principles depended ultimately on the political effectiveness of the restoration regimes. Austria, Prussia, and Russia—as the Continental guardians of the restoration—had to maintain effective, stable, and efficient regimes of their own. Only then could they shore up the similar but less secure regimes they had sponsored in Italy, Spain, and France. Yet effective administration and even stability itself often required political changes that threatened to undermine the old order. Bit by bit the great experiment of restoration broke down within a generation.

The Hapsburg Monarchy

The German, Italian, and Eastern European lands under Hapsburg rule were administered by a well-organized and centralized bureaucracy. Forged by Maria Theresa and Joseph II, it had enabled Austria to survive the Napoleonic wars without the dramatic reforms that transformed Prussia. Where any change evoked fear of revolution, the bureaucracy was a source of conservatism. Metternich and others recognized the need for more coherent and far-reaching domestic programs, but their projects—for a strong Imperial Council, for more influential diets of local landholders, and for an administration that reflected national differences—came to nothing. It was easier to guarantee order through bureaucratic restrictions, police surveillance, and energetic censorship.

Hungary, with her independent traditions

and powerful aristocracy, proved particularly troublesome to the Hapsburgs. Emperor Francis I was forced in 1825 to convene the Hungarian Diet when the counties refused to pay needed taxes, and Hungary's traditional privileges of partial autonomy were grudgingly acknowledged then and again in 1830. Finding it easier to relinquish some authority rather than make the changes that might have assured the empire's prosperity and power, Austria remained locked in a stalemate between a cautious central bureaucracy and a selfish local aristocracy. Both rested on a peasant society that had no direct voice in politics. By the 1840s Magyar had been made the official language of the Hungarian administration and schools, but this was followed in turn by demands for a more representative parliament and a campaign conducted by Lajos Kossuth in newspapers and meetings for the full panoply of liberal and national reforms.

The agitation in Hungary, stimulated by nationalist ferment in Italy, encouraged others under Hapsburg rule to claim their "natural rights." A revolt in Polish Galicia in 1846 was defeated by Austrian arms, aided by the bitter divisions between Polish peasants and their masters, and new signs of restlessness appeared in Croatia and Bohemia.

The confusion of conflicting claims was one of the monarchy's assets, for the national and religious groups opposed to Hapsburg rule were equally hostile to each other. Divided by class, religion, and language, they were not often politically effective. The growing consciousness of nationality was, therefore, a significant change. These movements, which enabled lawyers and merchants to seek popular support in their cry for governmental reform, reflected economic changes and intellectual currents sweeping Europe. Men who sought merely to strengthen noble privilege or local authority (the Magyars for example were determined to dominate the other peoples of Hungary) joined in opposition to Vienna with those who wanted better administration, parliaments, and schools.

At the center weak Ferdinand I, who had inherited his father's crown in 1835, presided over an aristocratic government that found inaction the safest compromise of internal differences. Metternich saw the need to acknowledge national sentiment within the empire and worried about Prussia's growing dominance in Germany. His chief antagonist among Ferdinand's ministers, Count Kolowrat, stressed the desperate need for fiscal reform. Their insights, like the advantages of the well-structured imperial bureaucracy, were slowly dissipated in an isolated, divided, and frightened court accustomed to relying on the effectiveness of tradition and Metternich's foreign policy.

The Russian Empire

By 1820 Tsar Alexander had abandoned an earlier enthusiasm for new ideas to become Metternich's staunchest ally. In his last years censorship became harsher, universities were more restricted, and the constitution granted the newly organized Kingdom of Poland was largely ignored. On Alexander's death, in 1825, a group of young army officers, the Decembrists, attempted a coup in the name of a constitution. Poorly planned, their isolated conspiracy was easily defeated, but they would later be remembered as part of Russia's radical tradition; Nicholas I, Alexander's younger brother who succeeded to the throne, believed that only a loyal army and his own decisiveness had prevented revolution.

Under Nicholas Russia became Europe's strongest pillar of reaction. A diligent administrator, he gave close attention to the army and extended the influence of the police into every aspect of Russian life. The bureaucracy, made more independent of the nobility, became more efficient and centralized but still could barely meet the demands of overseeing a vast land of varied peoples where communications were poor and educated men scarce. Petty corruption, the arrogance of local officials, and fear of change seriously weakened the government's capabilities.

The growth of a European market for Russian grain stimulated the economy, and many large estates became more prosperous and more specialized as they produced for export. Industry, primarily small-scale and domestic, was also growing; but the smaller lord suffered in a money economy, and the growing indebtedness of many a Russian noble became another source of social tension. Most thoughtful men, including the highest officials of the state, agreed that serfdom had become a hindrance, but the commissions ordered to study the matter could propose no solution not likely to increase unrest. Thus information was collected, and hundreds of peasant uprisings were noted with concern and suppressed with force, but the few steps taken to improve the lot of peasants remained thoroughly inadequate.

Sensing the importance of public attitudes, the government attempted to establish a kind of official philosophy based on the teachings of the Orthodox Church and utilized censors and police to enforce these precepts of autocracy. Despite fears that education bred discontent, schools were built (although literacy remained the distinction of a minority). Discussion of Russia's destiny became a compelling theme. Those who expected her to develop along familiar European lines were called Westernizers. Slavophiles, though making use of many Western (especially German) ideas, stressed rather the uniqueness of Russia. Her religion, peasant communes, and traditional culture, they argued, were the source of a unique mission in world civilization. Neither group was entirely consistent or well-defined, but within a great culture an urgent

questioning had begun about Russia's place in a changing world, giving shape to an intellectual ferment that lasted through the century.

The authority of the Russian state, however, continued to tower over these social tensions and intellectual debates. Despite loquacious exiles, bitter Poles, angry peasants, and its own immobility, the Russian government seemed enormously solid. Nicholas would watch with pride as his empire remained secure while revolution swept over most of the thrones of Europe.

The German Confederation

Germans called their battles against Napoleon the Wars of Liberation; and after that common, national experience, talk of "Germany" meant more than it had before. But the German Confederation, a tacit acknowledgment of the changes Bonaparte had wrought, was one of the Congress of Vienna's more cautious compromises. The rivalry of Austria and Prussia, distaste for reform, and the claims of German princes combined to prohibit a politically strong union. Nearly forty sovereign entities, ranging in size from the Austrian Empire and Prussia to four free cities, were made members of the loose league under the permanent presidency of Austria. Its diet, which was to meet at Frankfurt, was more a council of ambassadors than a representative assembly, and a unanimous vote was required on fundamental questions. Primarily another buffer against France, the confederation was permitted to legislate only on certain matters—restriction of the press was characteristically among them. If such advisory councils seemed unavoidable (each member of the confederation was expected to establish one), they were to be kept limited. In practice the German Confederation was important in German politics largely when Metternich wished to make it so.

He used it for example to suppress student

agitation. University fraternities, especially *Burschenschaften*, were generally nationalist and reformist, full of rhetoric about mystic brotherhood. In 1817 they celebrated the tercentenary of Luther's theses with a rally, the Wartburg Festival. Several hundred representatives gathered to drink, listen to speeches, sing songs, and cheer as a corporal's cane and a Prussian military manual were tossed into a bonfire. The symbolism was clear enough. Alarmed, governments in both Berlin and Vienna investigated and concluded that closer censorship and more careful surveillance of universities were needed. After the assassination of a reactionary writer, they called on the confederation to pass the Carlsbad Decrees of 1819, which intensified censorship, proscribed dangerous professors and students, outlawed fraternities and political clubs, and required each state to appoint commissioners to certify the ideological reliability of the universities.

Despite these alarms, there was less agitation in Germany than in most of Europe. Rather, the cultural life of these largely rural lands thrived in complacent university and market towns that seemed to eschew politics on a larger scale. The universities were strongest in philosophy and theology, and German Romanticism, when political at all, tended to become more conservative. In the last days of Beethoven and Schubert, Goethe and Hegel, German politics remained quiescent. The German states most influenced by France did adopt constitutions, but the diet Frederick William III promised for Prussia was never called, and the Council of State established in its place included only the most important military men, officials, and aristocrats. Prussian strength was not associated with representative government.

On the other hand the state continued to sponsor education and to spur economic growth. A unified tariff established in 1818 included all her territory, east and west; lowered duties (in part to discourage smuggling); and allowed free entry to raw materials. These progressive measures worked so well that within a decade many of the smaller states nearly surrounded by Prussia adopted them; and by 1833 most German governments except Austria had joined Prussia's customs union, the *Zollverein*, whose revenues, collected by Prussian inspectors, were shared and used primarily for better roads. One of the most important steps toward German unification under Prussia had been taken without nationalist intent by the government that knew how to win the benefits of liberal institutions without paying the price of liberal practice.

Germany had few modern factories, but the Zollverein proved a remarkable spur to commerce. Moreover by 1848 manufacturing and trade would be stimulated by one of the best railroad networks in Europe, built with considerable state support, especially from Prussia. These developments caused serious social dislocations. Some old trades found it difficult to compete with factory production and cheaper goods from other countries. The revolt of Silesian weavers in 1844, bloodily put down by Prussian troops, is only the most famous of many desperate and fruitless protests. Caught between rural immigrants competing for their jobs and the increased competition their products faced in the marketplace, workers looked to local governments for help; but they, too, were caught between their conservative social base and centralizing pressures from state bureaucrats eager to impose efficiency and uniformity.

Constitutional issues depended in part on accidents of dynasty. In Hanover a reactionary king set aside a four-year-old constitution in 1837, but in Prussia the reign of Frederick William IV, which began in 1840, raised prospects of significant constitutional reform. The new king, the least militaristic of Prussian

monarchs, had a liberal reputation; and though he was no friend of constitutions, in 1847 he reluctantly called for a United Landtag, to be composed of representatives of the eight provincial diets meeting in two houses. Short of revenue, in part because of its heavy investment in railroads, the government seemed in a situation like France's in 1789.

The Landtag optimistically insisted on regular sessions and some authority over the budget, but the king replied that a Prussia made by the sword would never allow petty legalisms to come between her monarchs and her people. After two months the delegates were sent home, leaving Prussia without a constitution or new taxes. Some serious ferment continued, particularly in Rhineland cities, where meetings and manifestoes demanded representative government, civil liberties, and sometimes—most frightening of all —a graduated income tax and guarantees of the right to work.

Demands for constitutional change gathered force as they combined with nationalist aims. Talk of German unification became so acceptable that both the Hohenzollern and the Hapsburg rulers paid it verbal respect. Western German reformers, and particularly those in exile, like the poet Heinrich Heine, associated their dreams of a German nation with their desire for a liberal government. Despite the difficulty of defining what territory a German nation should include or determining how it could be organized, political programs accompanied the spread of education, railroads, and economic modernization. Dismissing the Landtag settled little.

Students, burghers, and plain people were brought together in song and drink to celebrate national feeling (note the German tricolor) in Festivals like this one at Wartburg in 1848. (Photo: The Bettman Archive)

THE RESTORATION REGIMES IN SPAIN AND ITALY

The traditional governments of Germany, Russia, and the Hapsburg Empire had encountered serious domestic challenge, including open revolt. But the proposition that political authority once restored could maintain the status quo was even more doubtful elsewhere.

In Spain the Bourbon king Ferdinand VII had been restored to his throne with the expulsion of Napoleon's army. Strong enough to denounce the constitution he had promised, he was too weak to do much more. Ferdinand enjoyed some popularity because of patriotic resentment against French rule, but his government found no solution for its own inefficiency or the nation's poverty. In Spanish America the revolts led by José de San Martín and Simón Bolívar gained strength,[2] and the army that was assembled in Spain to reconquer the colonies mutinied and marched instead on Madrid in 1820.

This revolution forced the king to grant a constitution, and for three years the constitutional regime struggled to cope with Spain's enormous problems, weakened by its own dissension and its uncooperative king. But restrictions on religious orders raised powerful opposition from the church; freedom of the press produced more devastating criticism; and having a constitution was no help with the colonies. When a French army once again crossed into Spain in 1823, this time in the name of order, the Spaniards, who had fought French invasion so heroically just ten years earlier, were strangely acquiescent. With the rebellion defeated, the constitution disappeared again. Yet Ferdinand's repression nei-

[2] The history of these uprisings and of the impact of European events on Latin America is discussed in Richard Graham, *Independence in Latin America* (1972), a companion volume to *The Western Experience* in the Studies in World Civilization series.

ther ended the threat of revolution nor satisfied the more reactionary monarchists.

Restoration in Italy meant the return of the aristocracy, the reestablishment of old political boundaries, and the overwhelming dominance of Austria.[3] Yet the years of French rule had struck deep roots in Italy. The new regimes won acceptance with promises of constitutions, enlightened administration, peace, and lower taxes; but the rulers who headed them were frightened and often bitter. Unimaginative, harshly or moderately repressive, and conveniently corrupt, the governments provided the sleepy stability Metternich thought appropriate for Italians.

Such an atmosphere bred some conspiracy and rumors of far more. Across Italy secret groups, known collectively as the Carbonari, began to meet; their name, which means charcoal burners, evoked the image of Christ's poverty. Some talked of tyrannicide, some of equality and justice, and some of mild reform. They had in common the excitement of secret meetings, terrifying oaths, and ornate rituals.

The news of the revolution in Spain in 1820 was enough to prompt revolt. In Naples young army officers led the demand for a constitution, but royal concessions were followed by a more amorphous uprising in Sicily, which the Neapolitan revolutionaries then helped defeat. Their own constitutional regime died with the invasion of an Austrian army less than a year after revolution had broken out. While the Austrians were marching to

Naples, a similar revolt erupted in Piedmont. The king abdicated and the prince regent, Charles Albert, hastily granted a constitution before the new monarch arrived. When he came, the Austrian army was with him; Piedmont's constitution lasted two weeks.

The revolutions of 1821 in Italy left reactionary governments more rigid and Austrian influence more naked. They showed the inadequacies of loose, romantic conspiracies. But they contributed something as well to a radical and patriotic tradition.

THE CONCERT OF EUROPE

Like the Decembrist revolt in Russia, the uprisings in Italy and Spain were led by young army officers who were influenced by memories of Napoleonic reforms and convinced that personal advancement and efficient government required a constitution. In Italy especially their movements won some brief popular support and measured the weakness of restoration regimes that had to be sustained by outside force.

The availability of that force was Metternich's achievement. When representatives of Great Britain, Prussia, Russia, and France met at Aix-la-Chapelle in 1818 (to acknowledge payment of the French indemnity and to ratify the withdrawal of foreign troops from France), they embodied the concept of Europe the Austrian prince had envisioned at the Congress of Vienna. By their meetings at Troppau and Laibach in 1820 and 1821, however, the tenor had changed. Metternich, determined to guard against the virus of revolution anywhere in Europe, called for action against the revolt in Naples, but Great Britain disapproved of intervention in the domestic affairs of European states, and France, unwilling to antagonize opinion at home, was hesitant. Only Metternich interpreted the Con-

---

[3] Italy was divided into the Kingdom of the Two Sicilies; the Papal States; the grand duchy of Tuscany; the duchies of Lucca, Modena, and Parma; the Kingdom of Sardinia (Piedmont and Sardinia); Lombardy-Venezia, annexed to Austria; the principality of Monaco; and the republic of San Marino. All the duchies were held by friends or relatives of the Hapsburgs. The disappearance of Venice and Genoa as independent states left tiny San Marino, safe on its mountaintop, the oldest republic in the world.

gress of Laibach as a mandate for Austrian troops to march to Naples.

The breach among the powers became more apparent when they met the following year —without British representation. They approved French intervention in Spain, a royal parade to display the monarchy's revived prestige. But the subsequent hope of reestablishing European authority in Latin America brought stern warnings from Britain and the proud declaration of the Monroe Doctrine from the United States. The sphere of Metternich's concert was being delimited.

It was hardly evoked at all when the Greeks revolted against Ottoman rule in 1821. Russia was restrained from declaring war on the Ottoman Empire by Metternich's strenuous warnings. But the cries for freedom from the ancient home of democracy excited liberals throughout Europe. By 1827 the sultan seemed at last about to subdue the Greeks; but the British and French fleets intervened, and Russia declared war a few months later. Greece was granted independence in 1829 on terms arranged by the European powers, who carefully stipulated that a king should be chosen from one of the Continent's lesser ruling families. The response to revolution within the Ottoman Empire had been more like the diplomacy of imperialism that would emerge later in the century than the concert's commitment to the status quo. Diplomacy, despite Metternich's skill, proved an uncertain weapon against political change.

THE BOURBON RESTORATION IN FRANCE

The crucial test of postwar stability, however, was the domestic tranquillity of France. More than elsewhere, restoration there was a complex compromise carefully designed to build from political forms the means to maintain a balance between the old regime and the changes that followed from revolution. The charter that Louis XVIII granted by grace— not as a right—allowed the legislature more authority than Napoleon had permitted but made cabinet ministers directly responsible to the king. The old estates were now ignored, but membership in the Chamber of Peers was hereditary, and the right to vote in elections to the Chamber of Deputies was limited to men of landed wealth. Napoleon's centralized administration was kept and his taxes enthusiastically maintained.

Supporters of the new regime, shaken by how easily Napoleon had displaced it during the Hundred Days, returned to power determined to crush their enemies, and the Chamber elected after Waterloo was too reactionary even for Louis XVIII. In parts of the countryside a violent "white terror" broke out, in which some of those tainted with a revolutionary past were ousted from office or even killed. Yet Louis XVIII resisted as best he could the more extreme demands of the ultraroyalists. Land confiscated from the aristocracy and the church during the Revolution was not returned, and most of those who had benefited since 1789 were allowed to live out their lives quietly. The king and his ministers, moderate and able men, pursued a course of administrative efficiency and political restraint. From 1816 to 1820 they governed well in a relatively peaceful and prosperous country, and Paris became again Europe's most brilliant center of science and the arts.

The Catholic Church, weakened by the loss of property and still more by a scarcity of new priests in the postrevolutionary generation, revived remarkably. Missions of preachers toured the countryside calling for a return to the faith, praising the monarchy, and planting crosses of repentance. The nobles, traditionally rather skeptical, were now more pious;

and so too for the first time in more than a century were France's leading writers. To the surprise of many Catholics, however, the Concordat of 1801 remained in effect, another of Napoleon's institutional arrangements to prove a lasting one.

Despite its achievements the regime remained vulnerable and uncertain, satisfying relatively few, neither all Catholics nor anticlericals, neither ultraroyalists nor liberals. The assassination of the duke of Berry in 1820 reminded everyone of how fragile the monarchy was. The son of Louis' younger brother, the Count of Artois, he was the last Bourbon likely to produce an heir, and the royal line seemed doomed until the widowed duchess gave birth to a son eight months later. Louis XVIII feared the radicalism that appeared to be reviving throughout Europe, and he reacted to his nephew's assassination by naming more conservative ministers, increasing restrictions on the press, and dismissing some leading professors.

The air of reaction grew heavier in 1824 when the count of Artois succeeded to the throne as Charles X. A leader of the ultraroyalists, he had himself crowned at Reims in medieval splendor, a ceremony redolent with symbols of the divine right of kings and the alliance of throne and altar. The new government, led by a skillful but impolitic ultra, passed measures that gave the church fuller control of education, declared sacrilege a capital crime, and granted a cash indemnity to those who had lost land in the Revolution.

In fact the law against sacrilege was never enforced, and the indemnity, which helped end one of the most dangerous issues left from the Revolution, was a limited one. France remained freer than most European countries, but Charles' subjects worried about the intentions of a regime that disliked the very compromises on which it rested. Public criticism

grew, leading figures passed over to the parliamentary opposition, and secret societies blossomed. Disturbed by liberal gains in the elections of 1827, Charles X dutifully tried a slightly more moderate ministry, but he could not conceal his distaste for the increasingly hostile left nor offer enough concessions to win its support. By 1829 the king could stand no more. While political disputes grew more inflamed, he appointed a cabinet of ultras, but the Chamber of Deputies refused a vote of confidence. He called new elections, but instead of regaining seats the ultras lost still more.

THE REVOLUTION OF 1830

Determined not to make the mistakes of Louis XVI, Charles X reacted with firmness. In 1830 he and his ministers suddenly issued a set of secretly drafted decrees, the July Ordinances, which dissolved the new Chamber even before it met, further restricted suffrage, and muzzled the press. Having shown his fiber, the king went hunting. A shocked Paris slowly responded; crowds began to mill about, some barricades went up, and stones were thrown at the house of the king's premier. Newspapers breached the ordinances to charge that the constitution had been violated, and the government responded with troops enough to raise tempers but too few to enforce order. By the time Charles acknowledged the need to appoint more acceptable ministers, people were being killed (nearly 700 died in the three days of Paris fighting). Many troops began to mingle with the crowds, and liberal leaders started planning for a new regime. Paris was again the scene of a popular uprising, and Charles X, once again victim of what he most detested—revolution—abdicated on August 2.

For fifteen years and for the only time in her history, France had been administered by her aristocracy, who had performed with probity and seriousness. The crown had won the church's enthusiastic support, and the nation had prospered at home and enjoyed some success in foreign affairs. But the monarchy was meant above all to provide political stability, and that the restoration's most important experiment had failed to do.

The revolution, brief and largely limited to Paris, was a revolution nevertheless, and any uprising in France was a European event. Minor revolts occurred in central Italy, Spain, Portugal, and some of the German principalities, and revolution broke out in Poland. But Austria, though somewhat inhibited by France, once again extinguished revolt in Italy, and the Russian army crushed Poland's rebels. Closer to France, the Swiss cantons were forced to liberalize their constitutions. And Catholics and liberals of the southern Netherlands took the occasion to rise against Dutch rule. Once assured that France had no territorial designs on the region, Britain led in winning international guarantees for its independence and in mounting a show of force that brought Dutch acquiescence. The new state of Belgium was born.

II. THE SPREAD OF LIBERAL GOVERNMENT

Since 1815 Europe's leaders had sought to maintain the social structure and the values they believed in through carefully controlled political systems. But that control was increasingly challenged, and the battle for political change was led with growing success by liberals. The revolution that arose in France in 1830 and the revolt that created Belgium were not reversed by conservative powers, and the differences between the representative monarchies of the West and the autocratic governments of Central and Eastern Europe sharpened. The great age of liberalism began in 1830.

THE JULY MONARCHY

After Charles X's speedy abdication, the provisional government, organized largely in newspaper offices, had a faintly republican coloration. But when the Marquis de Lafayette, still a republican and a popular hero, presented Louis Philippe from the balcony of the Hôtel de Ville as the candidate for the throne, the issue had been largely settled in favor of what most men of influence preferred, a liberal monarchy. The new king headed the House of Orléans, a radical branch of the royal line (his father had voted with the Jacobins for the death of Louis XVI). His posters proclaimed him citizen-king, and the flag he chose—the Revolution's tricolor in place of the Bourbon fleurs-de-lis—signified a return to revolutionary traditions. Pressures from the people of Paris had led Louis Philippe to appear more liberal than he was, and the new government hastened to assure Europe's other monarchs that this French revolution would send no militants to sponsor or support revolution elsewhere.

Louis Philippe's regime, known as the July Monarchy, was another compromise between order and liberty. The new constitution, with stronger guarantees of political freedom, was presented as a contract the king swore to keep, not a gift he granted. Similar to the one it replaced, it lowered property requirements for voters, nearly doubling their number—though suffrage was still safely restricted to some 170,000 men of means—and the hereditary upper house was replaced by lifetime peers. More important, most of the old aristocracy resigned their offices, never to return to public life. Those who replaced them, professional people and bearers of newer (often Napoleonic) titles, differed from their predecessors more in outlook than social origin.

POLITICAL LIBERALISM

Liberalism was not a compact doctrine but rather a set of attitudes closely tied to ideas of social progress, belief in economic development, and values associated with the middle class. It varied considerably by country and changed everywhere over the course of the nineteenth century.

Liberal political values were rooted in the writings of John Locke and the philosophes; and liberals generally honored the French Revolution, despite its excesses, as a great moment in the history of freedom, while accepting those aspects of Romanticism that stressed individual creativity. A leading French liberal during the restoration, Benjamin Constant, put his case unequivocally: "The liberty of the individual is the object of all human association; on it rest public and private morality; on it are based the calculations of industry and commerce, and without it there is neither peace, dignity, nor happiness for men." By this creed freedom itself would be the source of morality, prosperity, and progress. The freedom liberals sought was primarily political and legal (their views on economic rights were frequently far more narrow), and they favored those who fought in any country for a constitution, freedom of the press and of assembly, an extension of the jury system, separation of church and state, public education, and administrative reform. Most liberals were not democrats, feeling that education and leisure were necessary for political wisdom, but nearly all believed that policies beneficial to everyone would follow from allowing ideas a free hearing and voters a free voice.

LIBERAL POLITICS IN BRITAIN

Britain's withdrawal from Metternich's Concert of Europe in the 1820s and her growing sympathy for Continental reform represented more than insular habit. She was becoming the world's leading example and advocate of liberalism; but that identification with a particular ideology only came after years of acrimony.

The end of war against Napoleon brought a depression to the British Isles as wartime markets collapsed and Europe's most developed economy stumbled before the problems of demobilization. The government's policies clearly favored the rich; it rescinded the wartime income tax and raised the tariff on grains, which increased the price of bread. These measures provoked agitation in town and country, and newspapers, political clubs, and popular meetings echoed with cries of class resentment. In 1816 a crowd demanding parliamentary reform grew violent, and the next year an alarmed government suspended habeas corpus for the first time in English history. A mass meeting for reform at St. Peter's Field, Manchester, in 1819 so terrified the local magistrates that they called out troops. In the ensuing charge hundred of demonstrators, including women and children, were wounded, and several were killed. With bitter mockery people called it the Peterloo Massacre.

Parliament decided to preserve order by passing the Six Acts of 1819, which restricted public meetings, facilitated the prosecution of radicals, and imposed a stamp tax intended to cripple the radical press. In 1820 the discovery of a clumsy plot to blow up the cabinet at dinner added to the sense of danger. When George IV followed his succession to the throne in 1820 (he had been prince regent since 1811) by instituting divorce proceedings against Queen Caroline on the ground of adul-

Massacre at St Peters or "BRITONS STRIKE HOME"!!!

This cartoon of the 1819 Peterloo Massacre captures the sense of class hatred it evoked. The hungry poor, peaceably seeking reform, are wantonly trampled by His Majesty's overfed officials. (Photo: The Mansell Collection)

tery, the public used the scandal to demonstrate its contempt. Even the Church of England was attacked as a bastion of privilege in a land where Protestant dissenters and Roman Catholics could not hold public office. Gradually agitation focused on the Corn Laws, which set tariffs on grains, of which the most important was wheat; the Combination Acts, which made it illegal for workers to organize; and Parliament itself, criticized as the unrepresentative protector of inefficient administration by a closed ruling caste.

Even an unreformed Parliament could be sensitive to public opinion, however. In 1822 George Canning replaced Castlereagh as foreign secretary and leader of the House of Commons, and he was joined by other Tories who favored temperate reforms that taken together marked a new direction. As president of the Board of Trade, William Huskisson, a member of the commercial community of London and Liverpool and an admirer of liberal economic theories, reduced some tariffs. At the Home Office Sir Robert Peel quietly ceased the prosecution of newspapers and the use of political spies. Uniformed police, instituted in London in 1829, made law and order the responsibility of civil authority, and the list of capital crimes was halved. Radicals even won the repeal of the Combination Acts; and though subsequent violence brought an amendment effectively outlawing strikes, the legality of workingmen's associations was preserved.

Such reasonable reforms were intended to make the government both more efficient and more popular, but they also reflected a widening acceptance of liberal ideas that disturbed many Tories. Increasingly their party came to depend on the unimpeachably conservative duke of Wellington, the prestigious victor over Napoleon at Waterloo, to hold their party together. Expected to resist change, he too found further concessions unavoidable. Agitation over religious freedom and other issues swelled in Ireland, and Wellington pushed through Parliament a measure he himself disliked, allowing Catholics and dissenters to vote and to hold public office. But radicals, workers, merchant reformers, and doctrinaire liberals demanded more—the reform of Parliament itself. Elections in 1830, required by the death of George IV and the accession of William IV, only raised the political temperature, and in the countryside laborers set haystacks afire by night while by day stern magistrates ordered laborers accused of seditious activity transported to Australia.

The Reform Bill of 1832

As public turmoil rose and British leaders watched with concern the course of revolution in France, a new cabinet—the most thoroughly aristocratic of the century—proposed the reform of Parliament. Initially defeated in the House of Commons, the measure passed only after a new election increased the number of reformers and after the king reluctantly threatened to create enough new peers to get the measure through the House of Lords,

where it had been defeated several times. Each setback for reform made the public mood uglier, and the king's intervention came amid demonstrations, the burning of the town hall and the bishop's palace in Bristol, and much dark talk about the French example.

The bill, far from radical, offered much less than the more outspoken radicals had wanted, but it marked a fundamental change. Suffrage was increased, especially in the counties, allowing some 800,000 men of substance to vote, well-to-do property-owners in the boroughs, property-owners and some tenants in the counties.[4] More important still, however, was the abolition of local variations, for a uniform national standard could, as many Tories complained, be easily broadened in the future. Before the Reform Bill of 1832, many boroughs that had solemnly been sending representatives to Parliament were barely villages; the most notorious, Old Sarum, was uninhabited. Perhaps a third of the members of Parliament had owed their seats to the local influence of some lord, while the bustling cities of Birmingham and Manchester had had no representatives at all. Now such "pocket boroughs" were abolished; twenty-two larger cities were assigned two representatives each and twenty-one smaller ones one apiece. Although landed interests would continue to dominate Parliament, the worst abuses had been corrected, representation was at least crudely related to population, and the voices of commerce and manufacturing were both more numerous and louder.

Restricted suffrage and social tradition (and

---

[4] This was a considerably broader electorate than in France or Belgium, though Belgium, the only country to give her elected representatives a salary, had in many respects Europe's most liberal constitution. About one Frenchman in 160 could vote in 1830, one Briton in 32 after the Reform Bill of 1832, and one Belgian in 95 by 1840 and one in 20 by 1848. Universal male suffrage permits approximately one in 5 to go to the polls.

the open ballot) still assured the dominance of the upper classes. But the political mood was different, and a series of other reform measures followed the 1832 bill. Slavery was abolished in Britain's colonies in 1833, a victory for Protestant reformers and humanitarian radicals. The Factory Act soon followed, limiting children's workweek to forty-eight hours for those six to thirteen and sixty-nine hours for those fourteen to eighteen, and a new Poor Law was passed in 1834 (see Chapter 23). The Municipal Corporations Act the next year established a uniform system for the election of town and city officials and allowed all those who paid taxes in a municipality to vote in its elections—a more direct attack on aristocratic privilege than the Reform Bill of 1832.

Grave political and social problems remained to be faced, but most Britons could now reasonably hope that these might be resolved within Parliament. When the young Victoria ascended the throne in 1837, she commenced a reign of more than six decades that would rival Queen Elizabeth I's as a period of glory and power. Like Louis Philippe, Victoria was well-informed and determined to play an active role in affairs of state. Like him too, she had some of the tastes and many of the values of a good bourgeoise. But she was subordinate (often against her wishes) to an increasingly flexible political system, whereas the new French monarchy proved as brittle as its predecessor.

LIBERAL MONARCHY IN FRANCE

In France the overriding political question of the 1830s was the July Monarchy itself, attacked from left and right. A mass held in Paris in memory of the duke of Berry became a legitimist (pro-Bourbon) demonstration, in turn prompting an anticlerical crowd to sack and loot the archbishop's palace and a nearby church. The duchess of Berry tried to spur an uprising in 1832 on behalf of her son, now the legitimist claimant to the throne; on the other hand the strike of silk workers in Lyons was considered a republican revolt and suppressed with the bitterness of class hatred by the bourgeois National Guard. Secret republican organizations with provocative names like the Society of the Rights of Man spread nonetheless, and Louis Napoleon, Bonapartist heir after the death of the emperor's son in 1832, attempted to stir a revolt in 1836 and again in 1840.

Yet all these attempts failed; and the July Monarchy, having established itself as a vehicle of monarchist stability, could even appeal to the cult of Napoleon I by bringing the emperor's body back from St. Helena and placing it with patriotic pomp in the marble crypt of the Invalides. A little self-consciously claiming its place in the revolutionary tradition of France, Orléanist rule did not usher in a period of great reforms like those in Britain in the 1830s, but the administrative system developed under the Revolution and Napoleon made such reforms less necessary. The provision for a nationwide system of public education in 1833 was a step English liberals would long envy. Gradually, as the regime benefited from the enthusiasm for railroads and visions of economic growth, its ministries became more confident and stable; the press, under some restriction, grew more tame. And many who had made their reputations under Napoleon or had been moderate republicans rallied to its support.

THE 1840s IN BRITAIN

Representative government accepts public conflict constrained in certain channels. Maintaining those constraints challenged the governments of both Britain and France in the 1840s—a challenge apparently more severe in the British Isles for most of the period but one that proved fatal to the French monarchy.

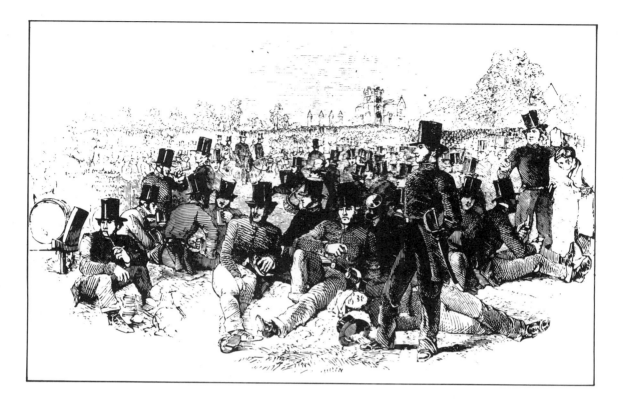

The London police, newly organized in the 1830s to deal with the increasing violence of mass demonstrations, are shown here awaiting the arrival of a Chartist procession. (Photo: The Mansell Collection)

Two great popular movements in Britain agitated for change. Chartism was a huge, amorphous movement that grew out of disappointment with the reforms of the 1830s and the frustrations of workers' organizations. Its central aim, spelled out in what was called the People's Charter, was political democracy.[5]

---

[5] The six points of the People's Charter were universal manhood suffrage, a written ballot, abolition of property qualifications for members of Parliament, payment of the members, constituencies of equal population, and annual elections. All but the last of these were adopted by 1918.

Chartists' meetings were watched with suspicion in 1839 and 1840, and their petitions to Parliament were summarily rejected. Their propaganda circulated widely, and riots on behalf of Chartist demands ended in scores of deaths. Yet by 1842 the movement was petering out. It failed despite its size to find a program that could for long mobilize the masses struggling for survival; and it failed, despite its emphasis on political rather than more threatening economic goals, to stir the consciences of those in power. Angry or desperate workers could riot here or there, but in England they were too isolated from each other and from other classes to gain even their political goals.

The other great movement, against the grain tariff, was victorious. The Anti–Corn Law League grew out of urban resentment over the high cost of bread, maintained by a tariff which benefited the landowning classes. From Manchester the movement spread throughout the country, becoming a kind of crusade, an attack on the privileges of aristocracy in the name of the "productive orders" of society, the middle and working classes united. The league propagandized with the new techniques of popular politics: parades and rallies, songs and speeches, pamphlets and cartoons. Its slogans were printed on trinkets for children, ribbons for women, drinking cups for men. Two manufacturers, Richard Cobden and John Bright, effective writers and orators, became among the best-known and most influential men in British life, spreading the gospel of liberalism across the land. To the upper classes such activity seemed in terrible taste; and conservatives argued from conviction that the nation's greatness was rooted in her landed estates. Nevertheless Sir Robert Peel's government twice passed measures lowering duties on a wide range of items, including grain. The league demanded more.

Finally, in 1845, Peel announced his support for outright repeal of the Corn Laws. The threat of famine in Ireland had decided the issue for him. Almost simultaneously the Whig leader, Lord John Russell, affirmed his conversion to the principles of free trade. Yet neither man was eager to carry the fight through the houses of Parliament. Only when Russell was unable to form a government did Peel undertake the task, and in 1846 he shepherded the measure through both the Commons and Lords. The grain tariff was reduced to almost nothing, and nearly all duties were abolished or greatly lowered.

As in 1832 the political system had bent when demands for reform gained widespread support among the middle class, but Peel's courage split his party and ended his ministry. He was jeered by angry Tories as a young backbencher, Benjamin Disraeli, rose to decry Peel's treachery to the aristocracy. Britain's adoption of free trade had not come easily, but it signified the growing weight of both public opinion and the liberal creed. In their very triumph, however, liberals broadened the sphere of political attention from questions of suffrage, efficiency, and formal justice to more difficult ones of social well-being.

THE 1840s IN FRANCE

Within government circles political conflict in the 1840s largely involved two factions, led by Adolphe Thiers and François Guizot. Both men were journalists and historians of great talent. With Thiers stood those who considered the revolution of 1830 one step in a process of evolution toward increased suffrage and constitutional reform. Those associated with Guizot, including the king himself, believed the constitution of 1830, having achieved a proper balance between liberty and order, should be preserved intact. Neither party was organized in any modern sense, and the differences between Guizot and Thiers were not very great, being at least as subtle as those between Peel and Russell, but their competition (legitimists and republicans had little voice in parliament) appeared to guarantee free and stable government. Later, it would seem a weakness that the skillful verbal duels of Guizot and Thiers failed to evoke in the nation at large the resounding echoes of English agitation over the Corn Laws.

From 1840 to 1848 the government of France was dominated by Guizot, Louis Philippe's premier during those years. A Protestant in a Catholic country, an intellectual in politics, a man who held broad principles rigidly, Guizot had in excess failings common to many liberals of the nineteenth century. He spoke of liberty, progress, and law in eloquent terms which made his cautious practices seem hypocritical. The policies he pursued were, like Louis Philippe himself, lacking in the idealism that excites or the sense of larger purpose which gives dignity to compromise. When defending himself he thought he was defending liberal government, and he cleaved to his positions to the point where rigidity itself became a principle.

The two freest and most prosperous of Europe's great nations had developed similarly since 1830. In both, liberal governments led by able men sought through reasonable compromise, the rule of law, and parliamentary government to unify their nations and to make "progress" compatible with stability. Discontent and workers' misery, though frightening, were understood in the councils of government primarily as a threat to order. In England there was a powerful aristocracy from whom reform had to be painfully wrung, but they conceded under pressure in part because they felt secure. In France the aristocracy counted for little after 1830, but more radical visions of democracy and social justice, finding little to hope for within the system, flourished outside it more strongly than across the Channel. The July Monarchy bore the insecurity of its recent and revolutionary origins; and as its core of firm supporters dwindled, it held to its narrow political forms until it, too, fell with the ease of incumbents losing an election. The differences between England and France are too often exaggerated, but they became greater after the revolutions of 1848.

LIBERAL VICTORIES IN OTHER COUNTRIES

The political victories of French and British liberalism seemed part of a general trend, not only because of the prestige and influence of those countries but because of similar developments elsewhere. In Belgium and Switzerland also liberal political institutions accompanied notable economic growth. And the strength of liberal movements in Spain and Italy further measured the weakening of that conservative dominance Metternich had sought to assure.

Belgium, Switzerland, and Spain

The Belgian monarchy established in 1830 was one of the triumphs of liberal constitutionalism. The next year the new state, which owed its existence to French restraint and British protection, took as its king Leopold I, who had lived long in England (he was an uncle of Queen Victoria) and who soon married the daughter of Louis Philippe. The constitution went farther than France's in guaranteeing civil rights and the primacy of the Chamber of Deputies, and politics continued to revolve around the coalition—rare in Europe—of Catholics and liberals, aristocrats and members of the upper-middle class who had led the revolt against the Netherlands.

Rapidly becoming the most industrialized nation on the Continent, Belgium was prosperous; and if her lower classes were more miserable and more largely illiterate than those of France, that very fact made the social isolation of her leaders politically less dangerous. Self-confident and satisfied with the new order of things, they built on the administrative traditions left from Austrian and French rule and proved themselves remarkably adept at planning railroads, reforming taxes and schools, and making timely political concessions.

Liberal institutions spread to Switzerland too as part of the international trend and were spurred by the revolutions of 1830. Beginning in 1828, some cantons adopted such measures as representative government and freedom of the press, and ten cantons formed a league in 1832 to agitate for religious freedom and for a stronger, secular central government within the Swiss confederation. These policies were resisted by seven largely Catholic cantons, dominated by their aristocracies; and the conflict, combining religious and political issues, became passionate. In 1845 the seven conservative cantons formed an alliance, the Sonderbund; two years later the leagues were at war. The Sonderbund looked for support from conservative and Catholic states, but none came—the papacy, Austria, and Piedmont had their hands full in Italy—and so the liberal sympathies of Britain and France once again proved decisive. With the Sonderbund's defeat Switzerland adopted a new constitution in 1848 influenced by the example of the United States and providing for universal male suffrage; the old union of cantons was transformed into a federal state.

In Spain the monarchy itself had turned to liberals to seek support against attacks from the right. King Ferdinand VII, who died in 1833, had carefully arranged for the succession of his three-year-old daughter, Isabella; but his brother, Don Carlos, claimed the throne.[6] Rural, regionalist, and reactionary, Carlism was a loosely organized and badly divided movement that found its support primarily in the more isolated regions of the north—Navarre, the Basque country, and parts of Catalonia and Aragon. The Carlists, who favored autocracy and the traditional claims of Spanish Catholicism, began open fighting on Isabella II's succession that ended only in 1839 with their defeat. But Don Carlos won a place in Spanish legend as a dashing and chivalric hero, the protector of old Spanish virtues, and Carlism remained a factor in every subsequent Spanish revolution.

To win liberal support the regency granted

a constitution in 1834. Cautiously modeled on the French constitution of 1814, it allowed narrow suffrage and protected the monarch's prerogatives, but it established representative institutions as a lasting feature of Spanish politics. Even so modest a step was enough to place Spain in the liberal camp, and Isabella's government relied on extensive support from Britain and France. Similar developments in Portugal under young Queen Maria II led to an alliance of the four countries in 1834, a league of constitutional regimes to offset the interventions of young princes sent from Italy and Germany to fight for Don Carlos.

Internal war led army generals to engage in politics and divided the liberals. The moderates supported the constitution of 1834 and admired Guizot's France, while the more anticlerical progressives called for a democratic constitution and the election of local officials. The progressives won a more radical constitution in 1837 and in 1840 led an uprising on behalf of General Baldomero Espartero, who displaced the queen mother as regent and established a dictatorship. Three years later General Ramón María Narváez brought a government of the moderates into power that lasted until 1854. In Spain, too, regimes needing popular support turned to parliamentary forms; in the 1840s Spain seemed to be taking its place among the liberal nations of Europe.

Italy and the Ideas of Giuseppe Mazzini

Ferment continued in Italy following the events of 1830, though order was restored throughout the peninsula and its governments remained staunchly conservative. Uprisings and demonstrations broke out in town after town, and most of them were related to the work of Giuseppe Mazzini.

A Genoese, Mazzini absorbed something of the republican and radical traditions of his native city. In exile most of his life, mainly in London, he ceaselessly conspired, corre-

---

[6] Salic law, dating from Merovingian times, prohibited the accession of women to royal thrones. Generally followed on the Continent, it meant that in 1837 Queen Victoria could not also assume rule over Hanover as her father had, and it passed to the duke of Cumberland. In Spain Ferdinand VII had abolished the Salic law by a pragmatic sanction in 1830 so that Isabella could be his heir.

In his portraits, as in much of his private life, Giuseppe Mazzini seemed more a romantic poet than a revolutionary agitator. (Photo: The Granger Collection)

crete meaning, and liberty to all. While attacking privilege he rejected socialism as materialistic, liberalism as lacking in social values, and conservatism as stiflingly paternalistic. Yet like most leaders of his generation, he put politics first; with the right kind of government, social, cultural, even moral problems would find their solution. All nations should educate men to brotherhood; every nation has its mission. Italy, having given to Europe Roman law, the Roman Catholic Church, and the Renaissance, would now create the first of this new kind of nation.

Mazzini was vague about the sources of political power and imprecise about economic organization. His unquenchable faith in the moral potential of simple people and their readiness to rise spontaneously in a great cause approached delusion. Yet he wrote tellingly about the specific grievances of peasants, artists, professional men, and intellectuals. Most of the revolts he supported ended in tragic failure, but he educated a generation to share at least a part of his dream.

Especially in northern Italy young lawyers, liberal landowners, and some members of the aristocracy began to find national implications in nearly all they did. Annual congresses of Italian scientists became quiet demonstrations; disputes over where railroad lines should be built became means of expressing discontent with Austrian rule. Literary journals and societies for agricultural improvement took up the national theme. Piedmont's efforts to win trade away from Austria by commercial treaties and projected railroads excited Italian patriots and worried the imperial government.

This ferment, more genteel than the revolution Mazzini envisioned, gained new force with the election in 1846 of Pope Pius IX. He was not the Austrian candidate, and he brought to the papacy a reputation for moderation, reformist sympathies, and deep Italian feeling. When he declared amnesty for all

sponded with acquaintances all over Europe, and published highly effective propaganda. His intent was revolutionary, and his Young Italy movement was far more democratic and radical than the Carbonari or the discontented officials who led revolts in the 1820s. Italy was his first concern, but his influence was European-wide, for he brought together patriotic visions of national independence, democracy, social reform, and progress.

The French Revolution, Mazzini argued, overemphasized negative and individual rights, leaving "humanity" a weak abstraction. He stressed instead the moral duties of man to man and the role of the nation, which gives individuals a social purpose, humanity a con-

political prisoners in the Papal States, there were jubilant demonstrations in nearly every Italian city. Talk of administrative reforms in papal territory spurred demands elsewhere for further liberal measures, including citizen militias and the abolition of censorship in Tuscany and Piedmont. When Austria tried to exercise her traditional influence, new demonstrations broke out. In fact the various Italian governments were embarrassed by their new popularity and were being pushed farther than they had meant to go when they undertook to negotiate a common Italian tariff and allowed their citizens to jeer the Austrians and talk of constitutional union.

Southern Italy had been rather removed from this agitation, but in the fall some of its towns attempted revolt, and in January 1848 well-organized revolution broke out in Palermo. By the end of the month, Neapolitan armies had been swept from Sicily except for units in a few fortresses. The Sicilian revolt, which demanded the honored Spanish constitution of 1812, led to heightened demands in Naples itself. When the Bourbon monarch granted a constitution, the dikes were broken. Early in February Piedmont and then Tuscany gained similar constitutions, all resembling France's of 1830, and the Papal States were expected to follow suit. The demand for liberal institutions, when combined with the cry for a free and independent Italy, seemed invincible.

III. THE REVOLUTIONS OF 1848

Both conservatives and liberals had assumed that political measures of the proper sort could assure domestic order. But in 1848 revolution swept across Europe from France to Hungary. Within a few weeks of each other, very different regimes gave way before rather similar demands. Social and national issues, however —issues on which political liberals did not always have a clear position—proved even more divisive than constitutional questions. One factor common to most of the uprisings was economic distress, a recession in the newly industrializing societies which followed the boom in railroad building of the 1840s and was accentuated by rising food prices after a poor harvest.

THE BEGINNINGS IN FRANCE

Economic crisis does not make a revolution; the death from starvation of more than a million Irishmen in the famine years of 1846–1849 did little more than the Chartists to shake British rule. In France, however, a faltering economy added to political pressure for a more democratic regime while Guizot held firm to the constitution he believed in and Louis Philippe to the minister he trusted.

Protest focused on a series of banquets held across the country, the most important of which was scheduled for Paris on February 22. When a frightened government banned it, some deputies announced they would attend anyway. Crowds began to gather in the streets, occasionally clashing with police, and workers who could never have afforded banquet tickets started building barricades. Revolution had begun.

The government had careful plans, though perhaps not the right generals, for dealing with insurrection; but when even the respectable citizenry of the National Guard sullenly refused to cheer their king, Louis Philippe, like Charles X before him, abdicated in favor of his grandson and left for England. Once again, however, the Paris crowds had more revolutionary aims, and on February 24 the Second Republic was declared from the Hôtel de Ville.

Political clubs and pressure groups organized quickly, and members of the provisional

This contemporary engraving of the fighting in Frankfurt on September 18, 1848 contrasts the fighting styles of troops and the people. (Photo: The Granger Collection)

government, "nominated" in the offices of two rival newspapers, were "confirmed" by cheers from the crowd outside the Hôtel de Ville. The leading figure was Alphonse de Lamartine, a handsome and eloquent poet, converted to Republicanism on the day of revolution. But the cabinet also included a scientist and several journalists; a radical republican, Alexandre Ledru-Rollin; a socialist, Louis Blanc; and even one worker, Albert Martin, always referred to with unconscious condescension by his first name only.

Despite their distrust of each other, moderates and radicals compromised with some skill. The republic adopted universal male suffrage, a degree of democracy never dared before in so large a nation; declared the citizen's right to work a principle of government; and erected a commission to hold public hearings on problems of labor. Noting that each

French revolution "owed it to the world to establish yet one more philosophic truth," the republic abolished the death penalty.

At the same time pains were taken to demonstrate the new regime's restraint. Foreign war was rejected, Lamartine's eloquence persuaded the crowd to abandon a red flag in favor of the tricolor (with a red cockade), and new taxes were levied to balance the budget. Relations with the Catholic Church were better than those of any French government in the century, and the April elections for a Constituent Assembly took place in good order, though the more radical had wanted elections postponed, with nearly 85 percent of the eligible electorate voting—striking evidence of political awareness. The result was an overwhelming majority for the moderate republicans and a serious setback for the left, which had fewer deputies than the monarchists. The Second Republic seemed solidly established.

The Spread of Revolution

As news of the events in France sped across Europe, a conservative nightmare became a reality. Nearly every capital, it developed, had citizens who found exciting promise in words like "constitution," "rights," "liberty," "free press." In Hungary the Diet cheered Kossuth's call on March 3 for representative government, and revolution broke out at the same time in the Rhineland and later in Vienna (March 12), then in Berlin (March 15), Milan (March 18), and Venice (March 22).

As spontaneous and loosely organized as the rising in Paris, these revolts followed a similar pattern. The news from France would attract excited crowds; groups of men—especially journalists, lawyers, and students—would meet in cafés to discuss rumors, newspaper accounts, and their own aspirations. Governments, as ready as local radicals to believe that revolution was at hand, would call out troops to maintain order, and with a kind of inevita-

bility, some incident would occur—a shot fired by a soldier insulted once too often or by someone in the crowd with an unfamiliar gun.

Now barricades would rise in the style that came from Paris, constructed of paving stones, a passing coach ceremoniously overturned, nearby trees, and furniture. Barricades became the peoples' voice, threatening but vague, as workers and doctors, women and children labored together through the night. When blood was shed, the crowd had its martyrs. In Paris corpses were carried around on a cart as a spur to revolutionary determination; in Berlin the king supported his fainting queen while bareheaded he paid the homage his subjects demanded to citizens his troops had killed.

When new concessions were won, the atmosphere would grow festive. New flags would fly, often a tricolor, symbolizing national union. In the almost universal dedication to politics, newspapers and pamphlets would appear in floods (100 new newspapers in Vienna, nearly 500 in Paris). Workers burst into the Tuilleries and jovially ate the lunch prepared for a king who had no time to eat it. Republicans met at the police station to read with amusement (and sometimes the shock of betrayal) police reports on their activity. Radicals would seek ever after to recapture the unanimity, the joy, the power of a day of revolution. Others, and not just conservatives, would never quite forget the fearsomeness of the mob, fanatical faces, and ugly threats.

The revolutions had in common the psychology they manifested and many of the liberal goals they demanded. Scarcity of food, depression, and the economic dislocation caused by new industry played some part in all of them; in most cities so did the fact of recent and rapid growth in the numbers of the urban poor. Peasant discontent was critical in Central Europe. Yet the revolutions of 1848 were not a single phenomenon; specific issues, the personalities who expressed them, and the forces that resolved them varied from state to state.

GERMANY AND ITALY

Frederick William IV had been replying to growing agitation in Prussia with vague assurances, a promise to reconvene the united Landtag, and a strengthening of his troops. With the incredible news of revolt in Vienna and the fall of Metternich, the king softened, relaxing censorship and calling the Landtag. Fighting broke out despite these concessions, and he gave way to demands that the hated troops leave Berlin, using the magic word "Germany" in proclamations to "my dear Berliners" and even wearing the national colors: black, gold, and red. A constituent assembly was elected in May by universal but indirect suffrage, and when it met in Berlin, where a civic guard now kept order, revolution in Prussia seemed to have triumphed.

Events in the rest of Germany confirmed that triumph. In March some 600 delegates had met in Frankfurt in a preparliamentary assembly, and no government dared oppose their call for elections by universal male suffrage to a national assembly. In May the national assembly convened at Frankfurt included 830 delegates, mostly from the smaller states of the more liberal west, more than half of them lawyers and professors. But there were businessmen, members of the liberal gentry, and even nobles suddenly awkward in such society. The great majority favored a monarchical German state with an almost democratic constitution, and the brilliant, difficult, and noisy assembly set about to write a constitution claiming for itself executive authority over a united Germany.

In the Austrian Empire, by mid-March the Hungarian Diet had established a free press and a national guard, abolished feudal obliga-

tions (with compensation to be paid the lords), and resolved to require nobles to pay taxes. Everyone noticed the parallel to 1789. The demands that Hungary be allowed to levy her own taxes and direct her own army, briefly resisted in Vienna, were soon granted, and a new cabinet, which included Kossuth, began to govern through established institutions.

A constitutional regime in Hungary alone, however, could hardly be secure; but its example encouraged students in Vienna to demand representative government for Austria and especially in the capital city. The crowds soon clashed with the troops and once fired upon became more militant. In rapid order Metternich resigned, censorship was abolished, a constitution was promised, and arms were passed out to the students. The government attempted again and again to circumscribe these concessions but quickly retreated before renewed outbursts. When students rejected the proposal that the vote be granted everyone but factory workers and servants, universal male suffrage was conceded in mid-May. At the same time Hungarian autonomy brought similar demands from Czechs in Bohemia, Croats in Croatia, and Rumanians in Transylvania (these last two domains under Hungarian rule). The old Austrian Empire had all but collapsed.

In Naples, Tuscany, and Piedmont the measures won through the March Laws in Hungary and the March Days in Berlin had been gained a few days earlier. Then the Papal States were granted a constitution, though it awkwardly preserved a veto for the pope and the College of Cardinals. With revolution in Vienna, open revolt broke out in Milan; and after five days of bitter fighting, the Austrian army retreated from the city. The Five Glorious Days of Milan added their luster to the heroic legends of March. A people aroused, it appeared, could defeat a great army. Soon

Venice too rose up to reestablish the Venetian republic.

Shortly nationalist pressure pushed Piedmont to declare war on Austria, and papal troops with papal blessing were sent to join a Neapolitan army in the common battle against Austrian rule in Italy. But a few days later Pius IX declared he could hardly fight against Catholic Austria, and Ferdinand II recalled his army from the front after his Swiss mercenaries defeated the revolutionaries in Naples. Piedmont was left alone to bear the brunt of the national war against Austria. Still, patriotic spirits remained high; and when at the end of May Piedmontese troops won a battle, the prospects for a free and independent Italy seemed good.

THE FATAL DISSENSIONS

Political freedom exposed the disagreements among those who had fought for it. In France these divisions were primarily social—between Paris and the countryside, between middle class and workers. The moderate majority of the new assembly were satisfied with what their republic had already achieved and determined that liberty should not be threatened by disorders. Workers on the other hand found conditions little improved by revolution or the new republic and agitated for a social program.

Frightened, the government dissolved the national workshops, which had been established to provide useful work for the unemployed. Only a faint echo of ideas popularized by Louis Blanc, the workshops in fact offered more relief than employment. The good bourgeois saw in them a dangerous principle, outrageous inefficiency, and wasteful expense; but they symbolized the hope of the lower classes, and unemployed men from Paris and the countryside had joined them by the tens of thousands. On news of their dissolu-

tion, barricades went up in the workingmen's quarters of Paris, and the poor fought with the ferocity of hopelessness as republican troops under General Louis Eugène Cavaignac systematically crushed the threat to order. The accidental death of the archbishop of Paris, killed while trying to mediate, seemed to prove the inevitability of civil war. After three days of fighting, June 24–26, the government troops triumphed. More than a thousand people died, and thousands more workers would be sent to prison or into exile. Paris had never seen greater bloodshed.

For the young Karl Marx and for socialists ever since, the June Days were the classic example of open class conflict, and radicals never quite recaptured their faith that democracy would lead to social justice. Given almost dictatorial powers, Cavaignac took steps to restrict the press, suppress radical societies, and discipline workers. The creation of a French republic still seemed in itself a radical step, and Cavaignac remained a convinced republican. The assembly continued to write a constitution, which, announced in November, kept universal suffrage and provided for a unicameral parliament (with no conservative upper house) and a president elected directly by popular vote. But while its official acts might have been unexceptionably republican, after June there was something a little hollow about the representativeness of the Second Republic.

In Germany and Austria revolutionary change uncovered latent conflicts among artisans, peasants, and nobles as well as between workers and members of the middle class. Furthermore revolts in these lands had not deposed their rulers, who kept control of loyal armies. Above all, nationalism, which evoked such popular enthusiasm, separated the constitution makers from each other.

Czech patriots had refused representation in the Frankfurt parliament, insisting that Slavs should not be subject to German rule. Instead a pan-Slav congress met at Prague in June. When disorder resulted, the Austrian field marshal Prince Windischgrätz, long disgusted with his emperor's weakness, bombarded Prague, crushed all resistance, and established military rule. The Frankfurt parliament congratulated him on his German victory.

It was no more sympathetic to Italian nationalism. The Austrian general Count Joseph Radetzky had retreated from Milan only as far as the great fortresses that had dominated the Lombard plain since the Middle Ages. In July, disregarding orders to negotiate, he skillfully attacked the Piedmontese and overwhelmingly defeated them. Austrian troops, once more in control of Lombardy, marched back into Milan. Radetzky too won congratulations from Frankfurt.

The German parliament also acquiesced as Prussian troops put down a Polish rising in Posen, and it called on Prussia to fight Denmark in behalf of Germans in Schleswig and Holstein, who opposed the extension of Danish authority in these duchies. In September riots broke out in Frankfurt itself, an expression of both nationalist and economic complaints; and the assembly, without revenue or a military force of its own, invited Austrian and Prussian troops to restore order.

Meanwhile many Croats had been demanding autonomy from Hungary just as Hungary had from Vienna, and General Joseph Jellachich with his emperor's encouragement built on Croat sentiment to weld an effective army that overpowered desperate Hungarian resistance and moved almost to Vienna. Before that threat the city rose again in October, but the armies of Windischgrätz and Jellachich bombarded Vienna into submission. The emperor returned, his authority reestablished in all his empire save Hungary and the Venetian Republic.

Rome too witnessed another revolutionary outburst in November; and like the June Days in Paris, the September riots in Frankfurt, and the October revolt in Vienna, this rising showed a popular fury and frustration that had not been so apparent in February and March. For hungry and desperate people, freedom added political awareness to old suspicions, and turmoil had taught the usefulness of force. The pope had proved of course not to be a nationalist; and within Rome an entrenched and reactionary administration choked each effort at reform. The appointment of Count Pellegrino Rossi, who had been French ambassador to Rome and was a friend of Guizot, to be prime minister of the Papal States would earlier have justified the wildest hopes; but now the cautious and rigid Rossi merely increased antagonisms. In November he was assassinated, Pius IX slipped away to the safety of Gaeta in the Neapolitan kingdom, and the eternal city under Mazzini's leadership assumed the ancient title of the Roman Republic.

Venice and France also remained republics, and assemblies were still busy drafting constitutions in Vienna, Berlin, and Frankfurt. There could be no doubt, however, that in general the forces of order were gaining ground at the end of the year. Nationwide elections in December selected a president for the French republic. There were four candidates: Lamartine, the most prominent figure of government from February to June, received the fewest votes; Ledru-Rollin, leader of the republican left, fared somewhat better; Cavaignac, who had held executive powers since wiping out the June uprising, made a respectable showing; and Louis Napoleon Bonaparte won 70 percent of the votes. All campaigned as republicans, but all save Napoleon symbolized disillusionment. The Louis Napoleon who once had fought with the Carbonari in Italy could claim to be the man of revolution. He was clearly also a man of order, and yet he had written more about social questions and workers' needs than any other candidate. He was supported by the Catholic Church and the monarchists, for want of anyone else. Above all he had his name.[7] In December he became the first and only president of the Second Republic.

Austria too found a strong new leader. Prince Felix von Schwarzenberg filled the place Metternich had left vacant, and in December he persuaded Ferdinand I to abdicate in favor of his eighteen-year-old son, Francis Joseph I, who had made no embarrassing commitments during the year. In Prussia the king dissolved the Landtag and promulgated a constitution of his own, very similar to Piedmont's and Belgium's. Ten months of turmoil had led back to the arrangements of February.

The Final Phase

Many of the revolutionary regimes nevertheless proved difficult to subdue. Not until May 1849 did Neapolitan armies reconquer all of Sicily, and the bombardment of Messina earned Ferdinand II the cruel nickname of King Bomba. The Roman Republic maintained better order than the regime it replaced, and for three months it fought with heroic tenacity before bowing to French troops sent by Louis Napoleon to restore the pope. In March Piedmont, pressed by radical demands and Austrian provocation, had again declared war, only to be immediately defeated. Charles Albert abdicated, and for her efforts in the Italian national cause, all the kingdom had was an enormous debt and an unpopular government, a new ruler, a constitution, and the red, white, and green flag of Italian nationalism. Ten

years later the constitution and the flag would seem quite a lot, for the time being Austria's position in the Italian peninsula was secure.

Austria invaded Hungary in January, but her forces were pushed back; and when Schwarzenberg rejected its draft constitution, the Hungarian Diet declared a republic. The Hungarians continued to battle against the armies of Austria and against Croats, Slavs, Slovaks, and Rumanians as national animosities reached new heights of fury. In June Russian intervention sealed the fate of the Hungarian republic; the conservative powers were coming to cooperate once again.

By March 1849 the Frankfurt Assembly had completed the constitution so carefully debated and elected Frederick William IV of Prussia German emperor; but after brief hesitation, he announced that the crowns he recognized came by grace of God. The Frankfurt constitution, with its universal manhood suffrage and touching list of old abuses to be abolished, its promises of civil rights and education, would never be tested. The assembly dissolved, and new revolutions broke out in the Rhineland, Saxony, and Bavaria (Baden's third revolution in a year led to a brief republic there), all of them quashed in June and July with the aid of Prussian troops.

The last of the revolutionary regimes to fall was that of the Venetian republic, defeated in August 1849 more by starvation and cholera than by Austrian artillery, though it accomplished the unprecedented feat of lobbing shells three miles from the mainland into the city.

A famous liberal historian has called 1848 "the turning-point at which modern history failed to turn,"[8] and his epigram captures the sense of destiny thwarted that still colors the liberal view of 1848. Historical analyses of

---

[7] On trial for his attempted coup in 1840, Louis Napoleon concluded his defense with these words: "I represent before you a principle, a cause, and a defeat: the principle is sovereignty of the people; the cause, that of the Empire; the defeat, Waterloo. The principle you have recognized; the cause you have served; the defeat you want to avenge."

[8] George Macaulay Trevelyan, *British History in the Nineteenth Century and After* (1937), p. 292.

that year, concerned with explaining the failure of the revolutions, generally include five broad points. First, liberal constitutions, new economic policies, and increased civil rights failed to pull strong and lasting support from the masses whose more immediate needs were neither met nor understood. Second, the revolutions of February and March were made primarily by the middle classes, strengthened by popular discontent; but when radicals sought more than representative government and legal equality, the middle classes were reminded of their concern for order and private property. Outside France the middle classes, once isolated from the masses, were too weak to retain power. Third, the leaders of the revolutions were so moved by abstract principles that, inexperienced in practical politics, they mistook arguments for power. Fourth, nationalism divided revolutionaries and prevented the cooperation that was essential for durable success. Fifth, while the military power of Austria and Russia was left intact, no major nation was ready to intervene in behalf of change. Britain was sympathetic, France

encouraging, and the United States, whose consulates were centers of republicanism, enthusiastic; but none offered the kind of help Russia gave the Austrian emperor.

From a different perspective, however, the fact of revolution so widespread and tenacious was as significant as its collapse, for 1848 also measured the failures of restoration, displayed again the power of political ideas, and uncovered the effects of a generation of social change. Many of the gains won in that year endured: the peasants of eastern Prussia and the Austrian Empire, emancipated in 1848, remained free of servile obligations; and the new constitutions were kept in Piedmont and Prussia. On all sides important lessons were learned. The monarchs triumphant in 1849 punished revolutionaries with execution, flogging, prison, and exile, but they gave increased attention to winning some popular support. Nationalists and liberals on the other hand would never again depend so optimistically on the spontaneous power of the people, and advocates of social reform became more skeptical of liberal institutions.

The period from 1815 to 1849 was an era of political experiments, each claiming to be permanent. For the most conservative regimes the problem was to achieve the administrative efficiency essential to survival while preserving as many of the privileges of inherited social rank as possible. In Western Europe the problem was in a sense reversed. The benefits of regular justice, legal equality, and broader participation in politics came to be widely (although by no means universally) acknowledged; the question was how far in this direction society could go without undermining the differences of wealth and opportunity on which, most educated people believed, civilization itself depended. The extent of suffrage aroused so much fury because it put political rights in social terms, defining by law (and therefore by conscious choice) who should participate, who constituted the political nation. Universal suffrage—few people in this period considered that the term might include both sexes—was radical because it seemed to declare men politically equal whatever their social

differences. Constitutions, by making the rules of political life formal and explicit, acknowledged such rules to be man-made and subject to change.

The battles over these issues were often narrowly political, reflecting an almost universal confidence that political systems could make the critical difference in the very nature of society. The course of that conflict established ideologies of conservatism and liberalism, and their competition proved a lasting part of European public life. With time, these positions grew more varied and complex. Conservatives often learned to live with representative government while remaining determined to defend the principles of authority and social order. Liberals, while insisting that the proper political forms and legal procedures could guarantee liberty and thus assure progress, often divided over the social responsibilities of the state. Increasingly, the focus of politics broadened. In part, political leaders, seeking wider support, deliberately took up social issues, aware that peasants and workers were a potential force or at least a threat. But society was changing too, often quite independently of political decisions and in ways for which those in power were ill-prepared. These changes, frightening and promising at the same time, are the subject of Chapter 23.

Neither the political devices of the restoration nor the timid liberalism of the 1830s achieved the stability they sought. If the revolutionary governments of 1848 fared no better, they tested still more directly the political implications of social change. In the next generation political leaders would find themselves greatly extending the authority of the state. Politics would be understood less as an autonomous sphere of activity and more in terms of its relations to the changes in social structure, economic organization, and style of life taking place in an age of industrialization.

RECOMMENDED READING

Studies

Anderson, Eugene N., and Pauline R. Anderson. *Political Institutions and Social Change in the Nineteenth Century.* 1967. Comprehensive view of constitutional and legal change.

* Artz, Frederick B. *Reaction and Revolution, 1815–1832.* 1968. First written in 1934, this remains a valuable effort to interpret the period as a whole.

* Briggs, Asa. *The Making of Modern England, 1784–1867.* 1967. A wide-ranging and readable survey of English society and politics.

Carr, Raymond. *Spain, 1808–1939.* 1966. The most balanced and comprehensive account in any language.

De Bertier de Sauvigny, Guillaume. *The Bourbon Restoration.* Lynn M. Case (tr.). 1967. An able and affectionate reappraisal of the Bourbon regime.

* Duveau, Georges. *The Making of a Revolution.* Anne Carter (tr.). 1967. Skillfully pulls together modern research on 1848 in France.

Gash, Norman. *Politics in the Age of Peel, 1830–1850.* 1953. The standard study of the changes in British politics following the reform of 1832.

Greenfield, Kent Roberts. *Economics and Liberalism in the Risorgimento: A Study of Nationalism in Lombardy*. 1966. A classic study of the connection between economic change and nationalism.

Grew, Raymond (ed.). *Crises of Political Development in Europe and the United States*. 1978. Ten essays on the patterns of political modernization in major countries.

* Hamerow, Theodore S. *Restoration, Revolution, and Reaction: Economics and Politics in Germany, 1815–1871*. 1958. A complex analysis of the relationship of social classes and the state to economic change.

* Hobsbawm, E. J. *The Age of Revolution, Europe 1789 to 1848*. 1970. A stimulating Marxist assessment.

Johnson, Douglas. *Guizot: Aspects of French History, 1787–1874*. 1963. Insightful essays focusing on the dominant figure of the July Monarchy.

Krieger, Leonard. *The German Idea of Freedom*. 1957. This profound and sometimes difficult study covers a broad period of German political thought.

* Langer, William L. *Political and Social Upheaval, 1832–1852*. 1969. Richly detailed, this study treats all of Europe in all its major aspects.

* Nicolson, Harold. *The Congress of Vienna, A Study in Allied Unity, 1812–1822*. 1946. A lively and balanced account of the process of peacemaking.

Pinkney, David H. *The French Revolution of 1830*. 1972. The study that has transformed our understanding of this revolution.

Salvemini, Gaetano. *Mazzini*. 1957. Still the best introduction to Mazzini's thought.

Seton-Watson, Hugh. *The Russian Empire, 1801–1917*. 1967. A solid, largely political survey.

* Stearns, Peter N. *1848: The Revolutionary Tide in Europe*. 1974. Brings together important recent research.

* Taylor, A. J. P. *The Hapsburg Monarchy, 1809–1918*. 1965. This concise account emphasizes the effects of nationalism on diplomacy and politics.

*Available in paperback.

TWENTY-THREE

INDUSTRIALIZATION AND
SOCIAL CHANGE

The political conflict that marked the first half of the nineteenth century was part of a larger process of social change. Social relations, long thought to be governed by rank and custom, were increasingly treated as matters of free contract between individuals, a change that freed some to seek new opportunities and left the poor unprotected. Land had always been the primary and surest source of wealth, but technology and the spread of the industrial system were changing that too, even though only a fraction of any population was directly engaged in industrial occupations. New inventions, the demand for more capital, factory organization, and more efficient transportation went hand in hand. Economic development in turn was intricately connected with population growth, urbanization, and new social groupings. The concentration of people and power in great cities altered culture, social structure, and politics.

The changes that justified optimistic visions of continuing progress also brought grave human distress. Increasingly society was perceived as consisting of antagonistic classes, and slums, poverty, and unemployment appeared to be inseparable by-products of economic growth.

Yet these changes, which affected so deeply what people believed, where they lived, what they ate, and how they related to those around them, rarely brought a sudden break in historical continuity. The institutions of government, culture, and religion continued to patch altered purposes onto old forms. While the middle class increased in size, self-confidence, and importance, the aristocracy remained socially and politically dominant in most of Europe. Western civilization once again showed its remarkable adaptability, but the strain was great. The proper relations between rich and poor, worker and employer, man and woman were called into question both by changing circumstance and by the painful dissonance between professed goals and reality.

The fact of change became the focus of intellectual as well as economic life. Liberals and socialists offered contrasting visions of the sources of change and where it must lead. And they, as much as nationalists or conservatives, argued from the study of history as to what the future must bring. In all spheres faith was placed in the rational individual, freed to calculate his own best interest, and in a proper organization of society, one that would encourage flexible adaptation to ever-changing needs. The emphasis on social organization, which showed in the concern for charity and education as well as efficient production and responsive government, underscored the need for some **social** solution to the misery of the masses.

I. PROGRESS OF INDUSTRIALIZATION

The most obvious economic change was in the way goods were produced; this transformation in the modes of production and the enormous increase in wealth that accompanied it were without precedent. They resulted, it soon became clear, from a process that fed on itself, one change stimulating another—a process in which Britain's early achievements would at least in part be repeated elsewhere. The process involved relationships governed by legal contract rather than custom, new technology, the accumulation of capital for investment, the organization of work in factories, a larger population and growing cities, more markets and wider trade. Its outcome was more production and more wealth but also more economic and social change and, for many, more misery.

THE EFFECTS OF REVOLUTION AND WAR

The preconditions of industrialization discussed in Chapter 20 had continued to develop in much of Europe during the long years of war spanning the turn of the century: the exploitation of resources had become more systematic, population was growing, transportation had generally improved, the means of recruiting capital had expanded, and the number of able political and business leaders concerned with speeding industrial growth had increased. These factors were especially evident in Great Britain, whose lead over Continental countries in goods produced, capital invested, and machinery employed had widened steadily from 1789 to 1815.

On the Continent the French Revolution and the Napoleonic era had in important respects cleared the way for future industrialization. In France, western Germany, north-ern Italy, and the Low Countries, land tenure was no longer the pressing economic and social issue; rural life was less restricted by traditional rights; and peasant proprietors, now relatively content, had become firm defenders of private property and were ready to be drawn into production for a national market. The abolition of old commercial restrictions and guilds had eliminated some obstacles to the free movement of workers and the establishment of new enterprises. Adopted on much of the Continent, French commercial law and the Napoleonic Code not only favored free contracts and an open marketplace but introduced the advantages of uniform and clear regulations. The French government had exported a common and sensible standard of weights and measures, encouraged the establishment of technical schools (the Polytechnic School in Paris long remained the world's best), and honored inventors and inventions of every sort from improved gunpowder to new techniques for raising sugar beets. Under Napoleon Europe had benefited from improved highways and bridges and a large zone of free trade; the Bank of France, as restructured in 1800, had become the European model of a bank of issue providing a reliable currency.

In the short run, however, the long warfare had slowed and disrupted economic growth. Vast resources in material and men were destroyed or consumed, and the Continental system, which had initially swung production and trade in France's favor, had collapsed with Napoleon's fall, bringing down many of the enterprises that it had artificially sustained. Both instability and renewed British competition discouraged daring investment. Great Britain, which had found compensation in American markets for her exclusion from the Continent and had avoided the shock of invasion, had suffered a severe slump in the postwar years when the anticipated

Continental demand for her goods failed to materialize and the transition to a peacetime economy had proved difficult.

PATTERNS OF INDUSTRIALIZATION

By the mid-1820s, however, British trade was reviving, and by 1830 rapid expansion was transforming the whole economy. No single industry was yet fully mechanized, but the pattern of industrialization was clearly recognizable. Cotton was the most important industry, its spinning mechanized, its weaving becoming so. Growth in one economic sector stimulated growth in others. Increased textile production for example accelerated the use of chemical dyes; greater iron production required more coal. A few factories in one place encouraged others in the same region where they could take advantage of the available work force and capital, and the concentration of production increased in turn the demand for roads, canals, and later railways. All this required more capital, and on the cycle went. In continuity, range of industries affected, national scope, and rate of increase, Great Britain's industrial growth was the greatest mankind had yet experienced; current estimates are that her gross national product was rising about 3 percent per annum.

With dazzling speed new inventions became whole industries and were integrated into the economy. The steam engine's application to rail travel is a classic case. When the patents expired on the Boulton and Watt steam engine in 1800 some 500 such engines were in use—and a number of British cotton mills had switched to steam power, although the less efficient Newcomen engines invented nearly a century before were also still being built. The first railroad was not built in England until 1825; a few years later an improved engine impressed spectators by outracing a horse, and in 1830 the first passenger line took its riders the thirty-two miles from Liverpool to Manchester in an hour and a quarter. There were 2,000 miles of such rail lines in Great Britain just over a decade later and 7,000 by 1851. Similarly the telegraph, slowly developed by a generation of scientists in many countries, rapidly progressed from an adjunct of railroading to a military necessity and a conveyor of general news. The most impressive of the early long lines was Samuel F. B. Morse's from Philadelphia to Washington, opened in 1843. Less than a decade later, Britain laid 4,000 miles of telegraph lines, and a cable to the Continent was in operation.

Yet the leap from new invention to industrialization was not necessarily direct or predictable. Often dozens of subsidiary inventions or improvements were necessary to make a new machine competitive. More often on the Continent even than in Britain, old manufacturing techniques and commercial methods persisted alongside the new. Machines themselves were usually made of wood and frequently still driven by wind, water power, or horses. But the water-driven mills, charcoal-fired smelters, and hand-powered looms that dotted the countryside would be gradually but relentlessly displaced as would hundreds of thousands of skilled artisans and rural families working in their homes who continued to produce in the old ways—a transformation that accounted for much of the human suffering occasioned by industrialization.

In 1815 many regions of the Continent, including such traditional commercial centers as Barcelona and Naples, had seemed ready to follow the British example of industrial growth, but by the 1850s the zone of industrialization had narrowed to eastern and northern France, Belgium and the Netherlands, western Germany, and northern Italy. Within this area industrial change was more uneven than in Britain. Most of Germany re-

LENGTH OF RAILWAYS (IN KILOMETERS)

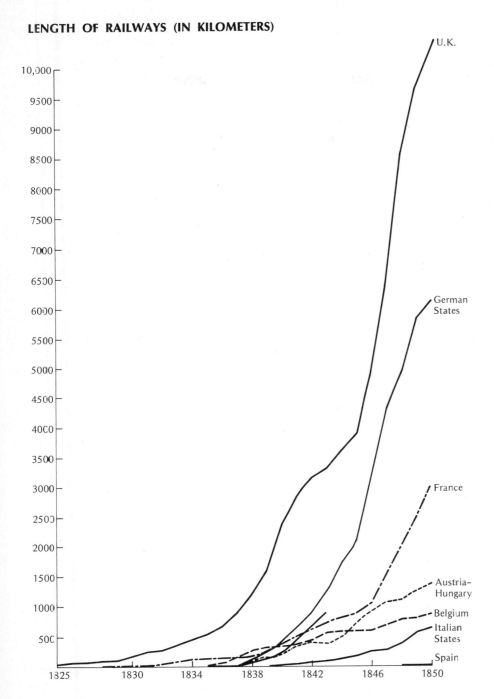

(Source: Mitchell, B. R., *European Historical Statistics, 1750–1970,* 1975, pp. 581–582.)

This train traveled from Paris to Rouen about 1860, but note that the new technology had little affected the workman's tools. (Photo: H. Roger Viollet)

mained an area of quiet villages in which peddlers and trade fairs were major avenues of commerce, though by midcentury they were crisscrossed by the Continent's largest railway network. In the 1830s and 1840s, steamboats plied all the navigable rivers of Western Europe.

Belgium, which had prospered from her former connections with Holland, continued to build on technological skills, geographical advantages, and excellent supplies of coal. Extracting twice as much coal as the rest of the Continent and the first country to complete a railway network, Belgium was the mainland's first industrialized state. The French railway system on the other hand was not finished until after the German, for it was slowed by political conflict despite early and ambitious plans. France's canals, considered good in 1815, had trebled by 1848; and her

production of iron, coal, and textiles increased severalfold in the same period. A generation earlier this would have been impressive growth, but Britain's expansion in each of these sectors was several times greater. In iron production for example the two countries were about equal in 1800, but Britain's output was six or seven times greater by 1850. She outstripped France still more in textiles and coal, producing half the world total in these as well as iron by midcentury.

Everywhere increased production led to more commerce and closer international ties as capital, techniques, workmen, and managers moved across the Channel and from Belgium and France into the rest of Europe. The Bank of France granted an emergency loan to the Bank of England in 1825, only a decade after Waterloo; and the domestic banking policies of President Andrew Jackson of the United States in response to a financial panic there in 1837 led to a wave of crises in the financial centers of Europe.

THE ROLE OF GOVERNMENT

Most observers of the new prosperity believed it followed from natural economic laws that worked their wonders more fully the freer the economy was from governmental intervention. Yet by midcentury the state was centrally involved in the process of economic growth. Railroads required franchises and the power of eminent domain before a spike was pounded. Inevitably routes, rates, and even the gauge of the track became political matters to be settled by parliaments or special commissions. In Belgium and in most of Germany, railroads were owned as well as planned by the state.

Tariffs, the dominant issue in British politics in the 1840s, became a critical question in every country. Britain's abolition of the Corn Laws in 1846 was not only an expression of

PRODUCTION IN BELGIUM, FRANCE, GERMANY, AND THE UNITED KINGDOM

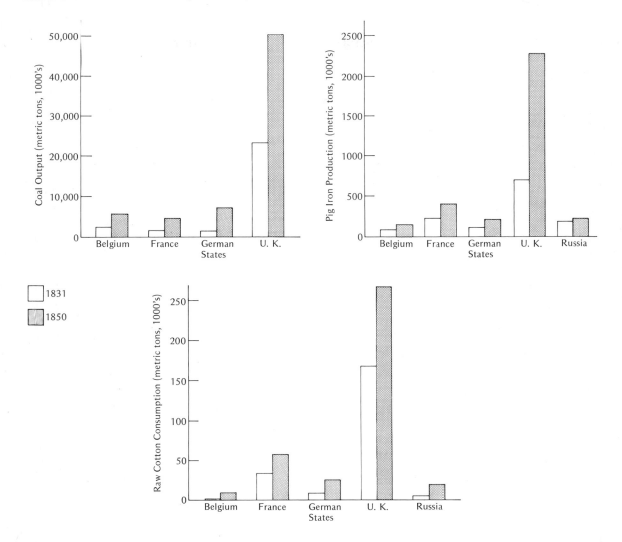

(Source: Mitchell, B. R., *European Historical Statistics, 1750–1970,* 1975.)

confidence in her position as the world's greatest producer but a decision that industrial interests had become more important to the nation's welfare than agriculture. The German Zollverein and the unification of Italy in the 1860s created larger areas of free trade; and after the Cobden-Chevalier treaty of 1860 between Britain and France, mutually reducing tariffs, a general international reduction of trade barriers allowed goods to move across borders with unparalleled freedom.

Equally important was the role of governments in banking and currency. Just before the middle of the century, Parliament granted the Bank of England a monopoly on issuing money and as a guarantee to investors required companies to register with the government and publish annual budgets. Similar steps were taken across Europe. In 1852 Louis Napoleon established the Crédit Mobilier, a joint-stock bank for starting or assisting important companies, and the Prussian government offered benefits to banks and industrialists. Before industries could effectively tap private wealth, the investor needed assurance that he risked only the money he invested, without being liable as he would be in a partnership for all a firm's debts. That assurance required new legislation establishing limited liability and encouraging the formation of corporations, and every major country passed such measures.

The growth of cities and the benefits of new technology created social demands involving government. By the 1840s most cities had a public omnibus, some sidewalks, and gas lighting in certain areas. Usually provided by private companies, such services had to be subsidized, regulated, and given legal protection by government, and as their cost and importance increased, so did the state's participation in them, usually extending to full ownership.

The role of government, the economic importance of public facilities, and the possibilities of using new techniques were exemplified by postal service, which most states had provided since the seventeenth and eighteenth centuries. With few exceptions graft-ridden and unreliable, these postal systems became intolerable in the industrial age. In Britain agitation for improvement was led by an inventor and radical who argued in terms of the new economic analysis—reduced rates would make the service pay for itself by increasing volume—and the demands of progress. He also proposed standard envelopes, payment in advance, and an adhesive stamp as means of

reducing costs and graft. Denounced as dangerous and impractical, his reforms were nevertheless passed in 1840. Within twenty years the volume of mail in Britain increased sixfold, and money orders, postal savings, and the telegraph were added to postal services. In France mail delivery was extended even to rural areas, and by the 1850s every major government was adopting the new system, including the postage stamp, which quickly became the object of a fashionable middle-class hobby.

Effective government, in short, was now expected to further industrialization—by subsidizing ports, transportation, and new inventions; by registering patents and encouraging education; by encouraging investment and enforcing contracts; by maintaining order and preventing strikes. In the 1840s the leaders of Britain, France, and Belgium busily did these things—in Great Britain the number of government employees increased about fourfold in the first half of the century—and the desire for other states to more fully follow suit was elsewhere an important part of the revolutions of 1848 and the nationalist movements of the following period.

THE RELATIVE DEVELOPMENT OF DIFFERENT NATIONS

The British celebrated their position as the masters of industrialization in 1851 with the first international industrial exhibition. Prominent people from the aristocracy, business, and government joined in the planning, and a specially designed pavilion was built in London, a sort of giant greenhouse called the Crystal Palace, that proved to be an architectual milestone. Many governments feared that Britain risked revolution by attracting huge mobs to London, but the exhibition in fact provided a significant comparison of the rela-

London's imposing Crystal Palace was designed to house the first international industrial exhibition, held there in 1851. The building was constructed of cast iron and glass, a significant innovation in architecture. (Photo: Radio Times Hulton Picture Library)

tive economic development of the participating countries.

Russia displayed primarily raw materials; Austria showed mainly luxury handicrafts. So did the Zollverein and the Italian states, but their appearance as single economic units foretold much. Although unable to fill all the space it demanded, the United States impressed viewers with collections of fossils, cheap manufactured products for domestic use, mountains of dentifrice and soap, and a series of new inventions, including Colt revolvers, a sewing machine, McCormick's reaper, and a vacuum coffin. French machines, which ranged from a much-admired device for folding envelopes to a little-noticed submarine, were generally considered the most elegant. But British machines surpassed everyone's in quantity, size, and variety. It is, explained the *Morning Chronicle*, "to our wonderful industrial discipline—our consummately arranged organization of toil, and our habit of division of labour—that we owe all the triumph."

The wealthiest nation in history by 1850,[1] Great Britain increased her lead over other countries in goods produced during the next twenty years. Important changes were taking place, however. While textiles were still important, they were no longer the leading sector of industrialization, and steel replaced the less processed forms of iron as the metal adapted to the greatest variety of crucial industrial uses.

Economic expansion in France and the German states was now comparable to Britain's a generation earlier. France's rate of growth was greater than Britain's, but it was lower than that of Germany, which was just beginning to take advantage of rich resources (especially coal), a rapidly growing population, and traditions of technical education. During the 1860s Germany passed France in the critical indexes of coal, iron, and steel production. Thus a major shift in the locus of European economic and political power was part of the extensive social change that accompanied Europe's industrialization.

II. THE STRUCTURE OF SOCIETY

Economic growth on such a scale was accompanied and indeed promoted by changes in the fabric of society. Population was rapidly rising, and cities were increasing in size and importance. Society came to be perceived as consisting of a few classes rather than as a social pyramid built on intricate personal responsibilities to those superior or inferior. Thus individuals were in theory free to take advantage of new opportunities, thereby creating greater wealth. Expansiveness and opti-

mism characterized the new industrial era, but so did child labor, tyrannical foremen, teeming slums, and unemployment. The growing prosperity and security of the middle class contrasted all the more sharply with the destitution of the urban poor.

THE GROWTH IN POPULATION

Historians nowadays increasingly stress the far-reaching effects of the growth in European population, but its causes remain uncertain. For a long time industrialization itself was thought to have brought it about, the assumption being that prosperity and opportunities for employment, particularly of children, had induced a rising birth rate. That explanation is now doubted. In fact the increase of population often occurred in rural regions, where the social effects of widespread industrialization were not likely to have been so deeply felt. There is, however, a connection between the growth of population and industry, for generally the two phenomena appeared together as they did in Great Britain, Belgium, and western Germany. The most likely factors stimulating the rise in population were a decline in disease-carrying germs, an increase in the food supply, a lowering of the age at which people married, and after 1870 some improvement in public sanitation.

Although the data are spotty at best, the most recent research suggests that the world experienced a decline in some common diseases beginning in the eighteenth century. Microbes, like locusts but less regular, have cycles of their own; and undoubtedly such remissions had occurred many times before. Now, however, better supplies of food could allow the larger numbers surviving the perilous years of infancy to reach adulthood and form families of their own.

The food supply rose because of better

---

[1] Although all estimates for this period are uncertain, it seems likely that in 1860 the per capita wealth of Frenchmen was about two-thirds and of Germans about two-fifths that of Britons.

transportation, more effective agricultural techniques, and the potato. Everywhere in Western Europe agricultural societies sprang up, experimenting with and advocating improved means of cultivation, better use of fertilizer, and by the 1840s some mechanization of farming. Primarily the work of enlightened aristocrats, these societies were aided by governments and churches in disseminating their doctrines through the countryside. The humble potato may have had particular importance, for it was easy to cultivate in a small space and yielded more calories per acre than any single crop. Not common on the Continent before 1750, it became the staple of the peasant's diet in most of Europe by 1830.[2] While infant mortality remained enormously high by modern standards, even a slight decline in death rates could make a great difference, so close to subsistence did most Europeans live.

The reasons for the trend toward earlier marriage are less clear, but apparently peasants freed from servile obligations tended to set up new households at a younger age and agricultural changes made it somewhat easier for the new husband to find a piece of land sufficient to support himself and his wife. The greater numbers of people in one generation—only a slight rise in a single decade or province—multiplied in the next generation and led to an enormous increase in the aggregate. As population grew the proportion of young and thus fertile people within it grew still faster, which increased the ratio of births to total population. The net result was that the 188 million Europeans of 1800 had become 266 million by 1850 and 295 million in 1870.

The growth in population had broad ramifications. More people consumed more food and this necessitated more intense cultivation of available soil and the use of much land previously left fallow. More people meant a larger potential work force readier to leave the countryside for industrial jobs, and that movement of population became a social change of immeasurable importance. To a lesser extent an increasing population meant an expanding market for goods other than food, an element of growth that would have stronger impact later in the century. The greater prominence of the young was in itself significant, and there is some indication that they were more restive and that the educated among them were a potential source of radical leaders.[3] There was also a distinction in birth rate by social class, which demographers call differential fertility. On the whole, the higher a man stood on the social scale, the fewer the children in his family. The distinction became more notable in the course of the century as families became more concerned with providing education and wealth for their heirs. But to contemporaries it often suggested that the lower classes, lacking foresight and moral restraint, were likely to swamp society.

Indeed one of the most influential books in the first half of the century was Thomas R. Malthus' *An Essay on the Principle of Population as It Affects the Future Improvement of Society*, first published in 1798 and reissued in

---

[2] William L. Langer makes an effective case for the potato's importance in the rise of population in "Europe's Initial Population Explosion," *American Historical Review*, 1963, pp. 1–17.

[3] In 1789 perhaps 40 percent of France's population was between twenty and forty years old and another 36 percent under twenty, the highest proportion of the young France has ever known. Mazzini limited membership in Young Italy to those under forty, and probably most of the leaders of the revolutions of 1848 would have met that standard. The relation of youth to revolution is interestingly discussed in Herbert Moller, "Youth as a Force in the Modern World," *Comparative Studies in Society and History*, April 1968.

THE WORK FORCE IN INDUSTRIAL NATIONS MID-1850S

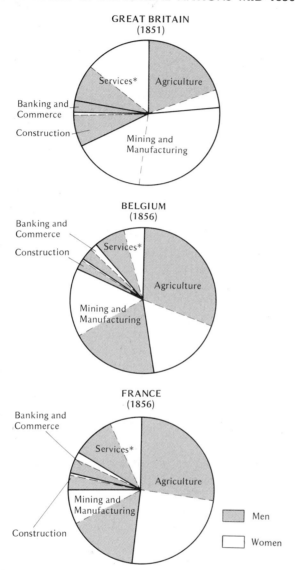

*Including transport and communication, domestic servants, and armed forces.

(Source: Bairoch, P., et al., *The Working Population and Its Structure*, Brussels, 1968.)

many subsequent revisions. Observing the Britain of his time, Malthus argued that population increases faster than the supply of food unless checked either by death (through war, famine, or pestilence) or by deliberate sexual continence. A clergyman, he advocated continence as man's best hope but remained pessimistic that mankind was capable of such restraint. Malthus was also an economist well-versed in contemporary theory, and for much of the century the demographic method and economic arguments in his controversial work deeply influenced social writing. For Malthusianism was the scientific statement of a natural law containing the harsh but convenient corollary that the misery of the poor resulted from their own improvidence. The view that economic progress rested on immutable laws and that those laws allowed little hope for the masses became a central theme of early nineteenth-century liberalism.

URBANIZATION

No demographic change was more important than the growth of cities. At the turn of the century, greater London was just reaching 1 million in population. No European city since imperial Rome had ever approached that size. Paris grew to that figure a generation later, but the third largest European city in 1800, Naples, had only 350,000 inhabitants. In all of Europe there were only twenty-two cities with populations over 100,000. By mid-century there were forty-seven. Great Britain was the leader, with six cities over the 100,000 mark; London's population had surpassed 2.5 million by 1856, Liverpool had grown from 80,000 to almost 400,000, and Manchester and Glasgow each had more than 300,000 people. By this time half of Britain's population lived in towns, making her the most urbanized nation since ancient times.

On the Continent the major capitals burgeoned. Paris reached a population of close to 1.5 million by 1850; Berlin nearly trebled, to 500,000; and a growth rate almost as great pushed Brussels to 250,000. St. Petersburg, Vienna, and Budapest all had populations between 400,000 and 500,000. Most of Europe's old cities increased by at least 50 percent in the first half of the century, and many a town became a city.

By the 1860s the English countryside was actually losing people, as were some sections of France; the tide of urbanization was overwhelming, and nearly all the subsequent increase in European population would go to swell the growth of cities, most of whose inhabitants were now immigrants as rural folk moved to nearby villages, villagers to towns, town dwellers to cities. Clearly the tide of urbanization was strongest where industry was great, but the growth of ports and national capitals demonstrated the importance of great commercial, financial, and political centers as well.

Society had neither the experience nor the means to cope with such an expansion. Urban conditions for all but the reasonably prosperous were unspeakable. Narrow alleys were littered with garbage and ordure that gave off an overpowering stench. The water supply in Paris, better than in most large cities, offered access to safe water only at fountains dotting the city (the affluent paid carriers by the bucket), and in London the private companies that provided water allowed it to flow only a few hours a day. In most cities the water supply came from dangerously polluted rivers. Sewage was an even more serious problem. A third of Manchester's houses used privies in the 1830s, and a decade later the ratio of inside toilets to population was 1 to 212. In London cesspools were a menace to health overshadowed only by still more public means of disposal.

The most dramatic inadequacy, however, was in housing of any sort. A third of Liverpool's citizens lived crowded in dark, cold cellars, and conditions in Lille were similar. In every city the poor of both sexes crowded into filthy, stuffy, unheated rooms; and over the cities, especially manufacturing and mining towns, chemical smog and coal smoke darkened the sky. It is hardly surprising that crime was rampant, that often more than a third of the births were illegitimate, and that the number of prostitutes soared (reaching perhaps 80,000 in London, where 9,000 were officially registered; 3,600 were registered in Paris).

The maintenance of public order changed its meaning. For the restoration governments the police were primarily secret agents whose job was to ferret out real or potential enemies. But the protection of lives and property in great cities, the effective handling of crowds, and the enforcement of local ordinances required something other than spies or the military. London's police force was established by Peel in 1829,[4] and Paris' Municipal Guard was created under Guizot a few years later.

For all their misery cities continued to grow; and the worst conditions were slowly alleviated by housing codes, public sewers, and reliable water supplies. These improvements were made possible in part by industrialization, which provided iron pipes, water closets, gas lighting, better heating, and sounder buildings. Urban life developed a style of its own, increasingly distinct from life in the countryside. Towns clustered around factories and railway stations, and cities teeming with the poor and indigent were also the thriving centers of communication, commerce, politics, and culture.

---

[4] The role played by Sir Robert Peel is still honored in the nickname "Bobbies."

SOCIAL CLASSES

So many kinds of change necessarily affected social grouping. In the seventeenth and eighteenth centuries, people spoke of the "orders," or "ranks," in society, implying a social pyramid rising from the lowliest peasant to the ruler and assigning each man his position in it. That position in large part defined his relations with those above and below.

By the beginning of the nineteenth century, the expression "middle" or "middling classes" had begun to appear, and by mid-century society was generally conceived in terms of broad strata, called classes. A person's social class was thought to describe the status of his occupation but also something of the values he held, his style of life, and later the political and social interests he was likely to support. Descriptive of an expanding, fluid, national society, the concept of class expressed an important change in outlook and social reality.

The Aristocracy

The class most easily identified was the aristocracy. It included all nobles and their immediate relatives, whether they held noble titles or not; members of the upper gentry, who were large landholders and lived like nobles; and in the ancient commercial cities of the Netherlands, northern Germany, and northern Italy, the established and wealthy patrician families, who dominated the cities though they might not bear titles.

The aristocracy's privileges and influence had been challenged in the eighteenth century by the French Revolution; the class was threatened in the nineteenth century by new industrial wealth, which overshadowed the fortunes of large landholders and gave greater influence to leaders from the middle class. It lost some traditional authority with every in-

In this famous engraving of London by Gustave Doré, the rhythmic sameness and cramped efficiency of new housing suggest a machine for living appropriate to the age of the railroad. (Photo: New York Public Library, Picture Collection)

crease in urbanization, every victory of constitutionalism or administrative reform. The decline of the aristocracy in the new age was so clear in fact that the continued importance of the class is easily overlooked.

In most countries aristocrats still controlled most of the wealth, were closely allied to an established church, and dominated the upper levels of administration and the military. By training and tone the most international of social classes, aristocrats remained the preeminent diplomats even under bourgeois regimes. They also stimulated some of the most influential critiques of nineteenth-century society, denouncing the middle class for selfishness and materialism, proclaiming urban life morally inferior to rural, and lamenting the loss of gentlemanly honor. The efforts of the aristocracy to defend its position, the means used, and the success achieved provide an important measure of social and political development in each country.

In much of Europe, especially the south and east, the aristocracy held on to local power and tremendous wealth, a social pattern exemplified by the Kingdom of Naples and by Russia. In both states the nobility, constituting only about 1 percent of the population, in effect ruled over most of the peasant masses. Three-fifths of the people in southern Italy lived on baronial estates. The Neapolitan aristocracy had lost many of its formal privileges under Napoleon, but with the restoration they reestablished their authority through cooperation with king and church and by providing the leading professional men. In Russia just a fraction of the nobility held one-third of the land, and most of the rest was owned by the state and administered by nobles. Russia's aristocrats, tyrants on their estates and dominant over local administration, were the chief pillar of tsarist rule.

Where the nobles made up a higher proportion of the population, the pattern was somewhat different. In Poland, Hungary, and Spain, many of the nobility were extremely poor, and they tended to alternate between desperate allegiance to an empty title and sympathy for radical change, thus becoming another and important source of instability.

In some countries, however, aristocrats sought to strengthen their influence through representative government and decentralization, thereby cooperating with political and economic reformers. The confident Magyars took this position in Hungary, and so, even more generously, did the aristocrats of northern Italy, Belgium, and Great Britain. They were thus prominent during the revolutions of 1848 in Hungary and northern Italy and in the subsequent nationalist movements in those countries. The Belgian aristocracy cooperated with liberals in 1830 and after, accepting an endless string of concessions and reforms.

Above all in England the aristocracy proved willing to exchange formal power for general influence. Of the hundred men who served as cabinet ministers in Britain between 1832 and the reform of 1867, sixty-four were sons of nobles; and perhaps four-fifths of the members of Parliament were landholders or their representatives, closely tied to the aristocracy. On the other hand younger sons and lesser aristocrats in England were more closely associated with the upper-middle class, lessening the sharpness of social division.

It was possible of course for an aristocracy to maintain its traditional hold over government even when the state became the instrument of dramatic and rapid change. This occurred in Prussia, where the most influential aristocrats were the Junkers, owners of great estates in east Prussia, some of which included sizable villages. Considered crude and ignorant by most of the aristocracies of Europe, which set great store by polished manners, elegant taste, and excellent French, the Junkers had a proud tradition of service to the state and loyalty to their king. In local government, in the bureaucracy, the army, and the court, their manners and their values— from rectitude to dueling, from arrogance to loyalty—set the tone of Prussian public life.

France is thus the European exception, for there the old aristocracy was reduced to a more minor role in national politics after 1830. Its members retained major influence in the church, army, and foreign service, but those institutions were also on the defensive. Yet even in France aristocrats maintained a strong voice in local affairs and a major influence on manners and the arts. They were everywhere, however, in danger of being isolated from important sources of political and economic power. It was small compensation to be known for elegance and leisure or a famous name. Lineage was once of such importance that tracing family lines had been a matter of state; now even pride of family was becoming a private matter.

The Peasantry

Closely related to the aristocracy in its dependence on the land and devotion to tradition, the peasant class encompassed the overwhelming majority of all Europeans. Always viewed as at the very bottom of society, peasants too were affected by the changes taking place around them. Agriculture was becoming more commercial, its production increasingly intended for a broad market rather than mere subsistence or local consumption. Profits increased with the cultivation of a single cash crop, the use of machinery, and improved fertilizers, changes primarily available to those with capital and a sizable piece of land. Large farms therefore became relatively more profitable, and landed nobles, bourgeois investors, and the richer peasants sought by every means to expand and consolidate their holdings, a trend encouraged by legislation in much of Northern Europe.

The emancipation of peasants from "feudal" obligations—during the French Revolution, by the Prussian reforms, and in 1848 in Eastern Europe—encouraged their entry into the commercial market, but it also deprived them of such traditional protections against hard times as the use of a common pasture, the right to glean what was left after the first harvest, and the practice of foraging for firewood in the forest. Similarly the decline of the putting-out system and of local industries took away critical income, especially during the winter months. Gradually and with considerable local variation, the peasant was becoming more dependent on the little piece of land to which he had some legal claim or the wages he could earn from his labor. The available land increased as more of it was cultivated, especially in the west, but it was usually of poorer quality and divided into small plots.

Improved communications increased the impact of more distant markets and brought peasants a keener sense of the opportunities and political events in the outside world. In addition, as governments became more efficient, they reached more deeply into peasant society for taxes and conscripts, enforcing regulations that often seemed alien and harsh. And the population of the now disturbed rural world was expanding, adding to economic pressure and restlessness.

Peasants are thus easily seen as passive victims of outside historical forces, but their response was also significant. The despair of reformers who were discouraged by their ignorance and illiteracy, resented their opposition to change, and were often defeated by their suspicion of outsiders, peasants tenaciously maintained old loyalties to their region, their priests, their habitual ways. Often they developed elaborate ties of family and patronage that absorbed state-appointed administrators into local social networks. Peasants were frequently shrewd judges of their short-term interests, cooperating with measures immediately beneficial to them and resisting all others with the skepticism of experience.

Their hunger for land, resentment of taxes and military service, and sense of grievance against those above them could also become a major political force. Their involvement made a crucial difference in the early days of the French Revolution and in the Spanish resistance to Napoleon, the wars of German liberation, and the strength of nationalism in Germany and Italy. Rulers were kept on edge by eruptions of peasant violence in southern England in the 1820s; Ireland in the 1830s and 1840s; Wales, Silesia, and Galicia in the 1840s; and on a smaller scale in every country from Spain to Russia. Thus the outbreaks of 1848 almost immediately brought feudal service toppling down in the Austrian Empire and eastern Prussia. At the same time rural indifference to constitutional claims and workers' demands sealed the doom of the urban revolutions.

But the peasantry was far from united. The deepest division was between those who owned land and those forced to sell their labor. Some of the former, especially in the west, grew relatively prosperous and joined the influential notables of their region. More of them lived as little dependent upon cash as possible, vulnerable to the slightest change in weather or market, supplementing their income by whatever odd jobs members of the family could manage. In most of Europe tenant-farming was more common, with endless local variations as to who paid for seed or fertilizer and how the final crop was divided. At best such arrangements provided the peasant with significant security, but they tended also to be inflexible, slow to adapt to changes in prices, markets, and technology. Rural laborers were the poorest and most insecure of all, the tinder of violence and the recruits for factory work.

A central problem for nineteenth-century European society was how to integrate the agricultural economy and the masses dependent on it into the developing commercial and industrial economy. By the 1850s the process had gone farthest in France and Great Britain but through opposite means. In Britain the peasantry was largely eliminated as the continuing enclosures of great estates reduced the rural poor to laborers, shifting from place to place and hiring out for the season or by the day. The concentration of landholding in Great Britain was one of the highest in Europe: some 500 aristocratic families controlled half the land and some 1,300 others most of the rest. In France on the other hand peasants owned approximately one-third of the land,

and their share was gradually increasing. Owners of tiny plots outnumbered the landless, and they supported themselves by favoring crops that require intense cultivation, such as grapes and sugar beets, and by maintaining small-scale craft industries.

Elsewhere the patterns lay between these two extremes, though rising populations everywhere made the landless the majority. The tradition of small landholding persisted in western Germany, northern Italy, Switzerland, the Netherlands, Belgium, and Scandinavia alongside a trend toward consolidation that reduced millions to becoming day-laborers. Emancipation in Germany usually required the peasant to pay for his freedom with part (often the best part) of the land he claimed. New historical methods which can compensate for the lack of written records have also established the importance of local variations—the quality of the soil, the favored crop, government policy, and legal custom. The fate of many a national political movement turns out on a closer look to have depended, like the resistance and uprisings often misunderstood as simply the violence of the untutored, on peasants' understanding of how in a changing world they could best preserve what little they had.

There was a clear distinction, however, between these western and central regions and eastern European domains, where Russian serfdom was the extreme. In the West the changes that increased agricultural productivity often left the life of peasants more precarious. In the East a heavy social price was paid for preserving the landholder's authority over his peasants and his claims to their labor, which ranged from a month or so a year to several days a week in Russia; and the emancipation of Russian serfs in the 1860s (see Chapter 24) proved necessary for economic expansion and minimal military and administrative efficiency. As urbanization and industrialization advanced, many writers waxed nostalgic for the bucolic purity and sturdy independence of peasant life, but the problems of the peasantry were in fact some of the gravest and most intractable of European society.

The Working Classes

Industrial laborers, however, attracted far more attention. In the 1830s and 1840s, serious French analysts wrote of the "dangerous classes" crowding into Paris. By midcentury industrial workers were the exemplars of a growing social class, though even in Britain in the 1860s they made up a small fraction of all those who lived by wages paid for physical labor; there were more domestic servants than factory hands. The conception of a working class derived less from what people did for a living or their poor pay than from their dependence on others—for employment, for defining what their job entailed, and for setting the hours and conditions of their work.

The most independent workers were the artisans. Stripped of their tight guilds and formal apprenticeships by the French Revolution, a series of laws passed in Britain up to the 1830s, and a process in Germany completed by the revolutions of 1848, artisans nevertheless continued to ply their crafts in a hierarchy of masters, journeymen, and apprentices working in small shops where conditions varied as much according to the temper of the master as the pressures of the market. Skilled workers, from carpenters and shoemakers to mechanics, moved in a less organized labor market but were distinctly better paid than the masses of the unskilled. Although vulnerable to competition from machines and new products and above all to unemployment during the frequent economic slumps, these men in general were among the beneficiaries of industrialization. Their real wages tended slowly to increase, and they could expect to earn enough to support their families in one or two bare rooms on a simple diet.

Factory workers on the whole earned too little to sustain a family, and thus the employment of women and children became as necessary to survival as it was advantageous to employers, who appreciated their greater dexterity and the lower wages they would accept. The largest factories were the cotton mills, where commonly half the laborers were women and a quarter children. In coal mines, where women and children were hired to push carts and work in the narrower shafts, they were a smaller proportion of the work force. A class was thereby formed of men, women, and children, clustered about a source of employment, dependent on cash for their subsistence, and subjected to the rigid discipline of the factory. Awakened before dawn by the factory bell, they tramped to work, where the pace of production was relentless and the dangers from machinery and irate foremen was great. Any lapse of attention during a work-day of fourteen hours or more, even stopping to help a neighbor, brought a fine and a harsh reprimand. Children were frequently beaten, as men had been before fines proved more effective, and all were spurred by the threats of piece rates and unemployment. Life was still more precarious for the millions of men without regular employment, who simply did such tasks as they could find, hauling or digging for a few pence.

Industrial workers were thus set apart by the conditions of their labor, the slums where they lived, and special restrictions such as the *livret* or passport that each French worker was required to present when applying for a job and that recorded his conduct and performance for previous employers. Understandably the powerful worried about the social volcano on which they lived, and the sensitive feared the effect of the immorality and degradation of industrial life on society.

Ignorant and exhausted workers, often strangers to each other, for the most part lacked the means necessary for effective concerted action. Their frequent outbursts of resentment and intermittent strikes usually ended in some bloodshed and sullen defeat. Sometimes the riots, demonstrations, and strikes became local revolutions, spreading across the north of England in 1811 and 1812, breaking out in Lyons in 1831 and 1834, Bristol in 1831, Lancashire in 1841, and Silesia in 1844. Significantly most of these outbursts were led by artisans, who felt most keenly the threat of change and held clearer visions of their rights and dignity. Although the authorities usually blamed the sinister plots of a few agitators for such disturbances, they nevertheless stimulated the vision of a day when laborers of many kinds, both urban and rural, might concertedly demonstrate their power. The June Days in Paris were widely understood, by all sides and perhaps exaggeratedly, as an expression of the new working class.

Trade unions were banned everywhere except in England after 1824, and even there the laws against conspiracy restricted their activity; but various local organizations had developed since the eighteenth century to take the place of the declining or outlawed guilds. By midcentury more than 1.5 million British workers may have belonged to such groups which tended, like the friendly societies, to form around a few of the more skilled workers and to meet in secret, often of necessity but also better to express a sense of brotherhood and trust. Although fond of elaborate rituals and terrifying oaths, their specific purposes were usually modest: burial costs for a member or assistance in times of illness. Equally important was the sense of community they fostered among those having in common their trade and neighborhood. In France workers' groups achieved state recognition as (carefully supervised) mutual aid

societies and were given some government subsidies under Louis Napoleon. Above all these organizations were both expressions of and efforts to create a working-class culture with values, interests, and leaders of its own. In this sense the authorities' fear that they would become hotbeds of radicalism had some basis.

There were also workers' political movements, of which Chartism was by far the largest, and cooperatives, which were intended to increase workers' control of their lives. Consumers' cooperatives were numerous by the 1830s in England, and producers' cooperatives, often established with church support in France and Italy, were the model for the French national workshops of 1848. For the most part, however, these expressions of workers' autonomy remained small in scale and local in influence.

The hundreds of strikes that occurred throughout Western Europe in the first half of the century were rarely the result of any lasting organization, but they suggested what unions might accomplish and led to heroic efforts by leaders of the working class to create them, particularly in Great Britain during the 1830s. Without funds, means of communication or common experience, these early efforts at unionizing petered out after a few years or sometimes a few months. Not even the Workingman's Association for Benefiting Politically, Socially, and Morally the Useful Classes, launched with some fanfare in 1836, managed to survive for long or bring off the general strike the more radical dreamed of. Yet these organizations, which gave the more fortunate workers some effective voice and some valuable experience of national political life, did influence Parliament in favor of factory legislation. The meetings, torchlight parades, and special newspapers and tracts all contributed to the growing sense of class. So, above all, did the repression by police and courts that usually followed. By midcentury millions of workers in Britain, somewhat fewer perhaps in France, and smaller numbers elsewhere shared heroes and rituals, believed they faced a common enemy, and accepted organization as the prime means of defending themselves in a hostile world. In Britain the national trades unions of skilled workers formed in the 1830s and 1840s (with only some 100,000 members then) would steadily increase their size and influence, reaching more than a million members a generation later.

The vast majority of the working class, however, remained essentially defenseless, possessing meager skills, dependent upon unstable employment, and living in the isolation of poverty. Ideas of *fraternité* and *egalité*, of the rights of freeborn Englishmen, and of simple patriotism, often expressed in Biblical prose, communicated a common sense of hope and outrage to millions of the men and women who attended rallies, met in dingy cafés, and read the working-class press (or listened as it was read to them)—the newspapers and pamphlets intended for workers became extensive in England after 1815, were less widespread in France in the 1830s and 1840s, and appeared everywhere in 1848. The common themes were man's natural rights, pride of work, and the claims of justice. They burst forth countless times in whole programs for change, phrases proudly tucked into petitions and posters, and anonymous gestures like the direct humor of the British coal miner who left a note to the man whose house he broke into during a strike in 1831:

> I was at yor hoose last neet, and meyd myself very comfortable. Ye hey nee family, and . . . I see ye have a great lot of rooms, and big cellars, and plenty of wine and beer in them, which I got ma share on. Noo I naw some at wor colliery that has three or fower lads and lasses, and they live in won room not half as gude as yor cellar. I don't pretend to naw very much, but I naw there shudn't be that much difference. . . .[5]

Outbursts of machine-breaking, strikes, and riot—most historians now agree—were rarely aimless but had specific targets reflecting immediate needs. Lasting gains, however, normally required some connection between the local crisis and larger, national movements. When that was not the case, and it usually was not, the workers and their families had nevertheless contributed to the creation of a subculture of which their betters knew little.

The Middle Classes

Of all the social classes, the most confident and assertive was the middle class. At the top stood the great bankers, who in London and Paris were often closely connected to the liberal aristocracy and whose political influence after 1830 was considerable. More separate from and a little contemptuous of the traditional elites stood the great industrialists and the wealthiest merchants. At the bottom were the small shopkeepers, office clerks, and schoolteachers, often distinguishable from artisans only by their pretensions. This petite bourgeoisie comprised most of the middle class numerically, but the class was epitomized by those between these groups: most merchants, managers, and upper bureaucrats and nearly all lawyers, doctors, engineers, and professors. That such disparate people could believe they shared common interests and values and therefore a similar position was the result of recent history. They opposed prescriptive privilege and saw themselves as the beneficiaries of social change which allowed the talented to gain security and influence.

---

[5] Cited in Edward P. Thompson, *The Making of the English Working Class* (1966), p. 715.

They were primarily an urban class and intimately connected with the commerce and politics of city life. In Paris they constituted nearly all of that part of the population, between one-fourth and one-fifth, prosperous enough to pay some taxes, have at least one maid, and leave an estate sufficient to cover the costs of private burial.[6] In other cities their proportion was probably somewhat smaller; among nations they were most numerous in Great Britain, a sizable fraction in France and Belgium, and a smaller minority elsewhere. Belonging to the only class which it was possible to fall out of, middle-class people established their membership by economic self-sufficiency, literacy, and respectability. Their manner, their dress, and their homes were thus symbols of their status and meant to express values of probity, hard work, fortitude, prudence, and self-reliance. No matter how favored by birth or fortune, they tended to think of themselves as self-made men.

While industrial centers were notoriously drab, the middle-class home became more ornate, packed with furnishings that boasted of elaborate craftsmanship. Women's fashions similarly featured ornamental frills, and shops translated Parisian elegance into forms available to more modest purses. Masculine garb by contrast grew plainer, a point of some pride in a practical age; and clerk and banker tended to dress alike. Those who forged great industries out of daring, foresight, and luck, those who invented or built, those who taught or tended shop or wrote for newspapers came to share a certain pride in each other's achievements as proof that personal drive and social benefit were in harmony and as a harbinger of progress yet to come.

---

[6] Perhaps the most detailed study yet made of the middle class in this period is Adeline Daumard's *La Bourgeoisie parisienne de 1815 à 1848* (1963).

More than any other, the middle class was associated with an ideology; and the triumph of the middle class in this period—so heralded then and by historians since—related as much to constitutionalism and legal equality, individual rights and economic opportunity as it did to any explicit transfer of power. The conquests of the middle class were measured not just by its rise in importance but by a more general adoption of its values. Even being in the middle, between the extremes of luxury and power and of poverty and ignorance, was seen as an advantage, a kind of inherent moderation. In the nineteenth century most of Europe's writers, scientists, doctors, lawyers, and businessmen would have felt no need to blush on finding themselves called by a London paper in 1807 "those persons . . . always counted the most valuable, because the least corrupted, members of society," or on hearing John Stuart Mill speak a generation later of "the class which is universally described as the most wise and the most virtuous part of the community, the middle rank."

SOCIAL DIFFERENTIATION

Sociologists use the term "differentiation" to describe the specialization among groups and institutions, and that too was a trend increasingly apparent in the nineteenth century. Its effects were clearest in the division of labor within a larger factory and in the tendency to separate production from the home. Thus social differentiation meant in part the increasing separation of family roles from work. It affected institutions too. Banks and markets became more specialized, and the reliance on legal contracts differentiated economic from personal or social relationships. Governments preferred to rely on their officials rather than figures traditionally prominent in the community (even when, as frequently happened, local notables were the ones appointed to office), and governmental functions themselves became more specialized. Maintaining the peace, collecting taxes, inspecting factories and schools, and administering welfare fell to separate bureaus. In addition, social tasks once performed by others such as the registering of births and deaths and the providing for education and charity, largely performed by the clergy before the French Revolution, were now increasingly absorbed by the state—another reason for the attention to politics in this period.

Just as each trade and each locality had its own history of social change, so each nation differed in the pace and manner of institutional differentiation. Britain, more than Continental states, left many public matters to local government and private groups; in France the trend toward centralization continued, and the German states tended to combine centralizing bureaucracies with considerable local autonomy. Whatever the pattern, the growth of differentiation was a major source of conflict among institutions, between levels of government, and within communities.

CHANGING CONDITIONS OF SOCIAL LIFE

Industrialization, urbanization, and greater social differentiation necessarily affected some of the most fundamental aspects of social life, including the role of the family and of women, the standard of living, and public policies for the general welfare. In each case the changes taking place at first sharpened the differences between classes, then became the subject of anguished debate, and eventually led to systematic efforts at reform.

The Family and the Role of Women

To a great many nineteenth-century observers, social change appeared to threaten the continued importance of the family, and moralists of every sort warned that the institution most central to civilization was being undermined. Recent research, however, has suggested a different view: heightened concern for the family was not only a response to real stress but an expression of increased belief in the social importance of proper child-rearing; the family proved on the whole an extraordinarily adaptable institution, and the forms of adaptation varied greatly, especially by social class. So did the place of women, and the question of women's proper role joined the long list of social issues on which nineteenth-century society sustained rigid convention yet confessed itself increasingly troubled.

For the aristocracy, family included a wide network of relatives, valuable connections to land, privilege, and power within which women played a critical but subordinate role as carriers of the dowries that joined estates, managers of large domestic staffs, and centers of the social circles in which aristocrats met. The peasant family, on the other hand, varied with local tradition, social structure, and economy. Where plots were large enough, the family unit would be likely to include grandparents or even in-laws, cousins, and nephews. Particularly in Mediterranean regions, such extended families often shared housing in the village but worked in different nearby fields. When they could, however, a young couple generally set up a household of their own. Where peasants owned land, the problem of keeping it intact while giving something to all the children was difficult, a frequent source of dispute whether law and custom required equal division of inheritance as in France, primogeniture (inheritance by the eldest son) as in England, or ultimogeniture (inheritance by the youngest son) as in parts of Germany. The elderly feared dispossession, the children that they would not get their share in time.

Yet for peasants the family remained the basic economic unit, pooling income from various sources, dividing labor in customary ways—with the women usually handling household chores and the smaller animals, the men responsible for the heavier work, and everyone working together in critical periods of planting and harvest. Often the women had more access than the men to additional sources of income—piecework from a nearby mill or domestic service for the well-to-do—and they played a central role in marketing. Men, on the other hand, were more likely to travel considerable distances, especially in difficult times, to pick up a bit of work on roads or docks or at some great landlord's harvest. As population increased, the children were more and more pushed out to seek employment in the nearest mills and towns.

For artisans too the family was often the unit of production, although the division of tasks by sex was usually more explicit, and the concentration into even small workshops had long tended to exclude women, at least from the better-paid tasks. For working-class women and children to labor long hours was thus not the change so many upper-class commentators made it seem. The strain on the family came rather from the lack of housing and the conditions of work. Not only did women and children have to supplement the father's income, but they were less and less likely to work as a family—although many employers in the early nineteenth century did prefer to hire (and fire) entire families. But they rarely worked side by side; if taught a trade, children were less likely to learn it from their parents. Hardened at an early age, adolescents in factory towns were probably more likely to leave home when their pay allowed, and urban conditions made it more difficult for the family to support the aged and the sick. Such factors did weaken family ties as did—at least in the eyes of the upper classes—the com-

mon practice for working men and women to live together without the trouble or expense of formal marriage rites. (Indeed many German towns attempted to prohibit the marriage of those without the means to support a household.) Yet among workers, too, the family survived and not only as a nuclear unit: contact was maintained with distant relatives and a mattress was provided for any coming to seek work. The fact of women's work for pay may also have slowly lessened their subordination even if it did not lead very directly to the new and superior stage of family life that Karl Marx thought it might.

In the lower-middle class, especially in France, women were as important and frequently more visible than men in operating small shops. The life of the middle-class woman, however, contrasted greatly with that of her poorer sisters, and the role allotted wife and mother became one of the most apparent and important indicators of social status. In earlier eras women had played some part in public life, in politics and business as well as high society, and they continued to be the organizers, patrons, critics, and ornaments of many of Europe's most cultivated circles. But the middle class isolated women from the harsh competition of business and politics. As the contemporary French historian Jules Michelet complained, "By a singular set of circumstances—social, economic, religious— man lives separated from woman." In Victorian England gentlemen met in their clubs or withdrew after dinner for their cigars and weighty talk. The nineteenth-century femi-

These French illustrations done in the 1840s of work in an English coal mine show the classic horrors—naked men, chained women, and straining children—that made industrialization in the English style something to be avoided. (Photo: New York Public Library, Picture Collection)

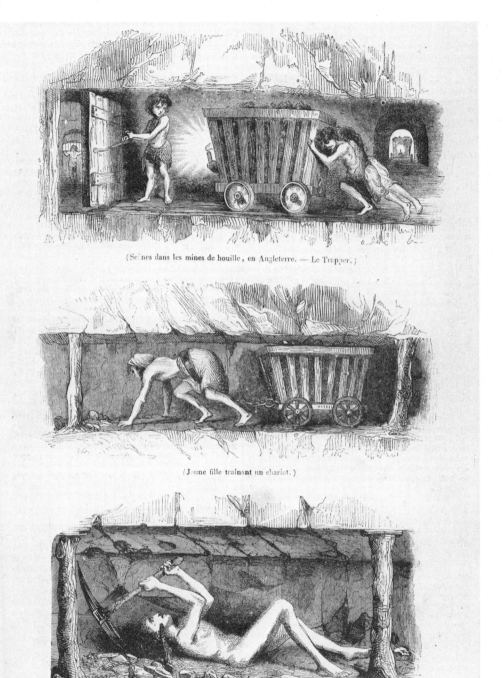

(Scènes dans les mines de houille, en Angleterre. — Le Trapper.)

(Jeune fille traînant un chariot.)

(Jeune homme employé à l'extraction du charbon.)

nine ideal was an idle and pallid creature, encased in corset or bustle, whose most vigorous expression was fainting.

There are no proven explanations of why such customs should have developed. There was of course a kind of conspicuous consumption in allowing a wife to be idle even if her husband worked hard, a certain partial imitation of aristocratic elegance; but there were signs too of an unconscious effort at maintaining a sort of counterculture. If men must be competitive, hard, and practical, women should be tender, innocent, and gracious, the weak but pure upholders of virtue and aesthetic sensibility. The middle-class woman with no estate to manage and few servants to direct was almost literally placed on a pedestal. Neither her needlework nor her piano playing were viewed as serious, but her role in maintaining the protective calm of the home and as exemplar of the moral virtues was.

Clearly these attitudes were related to the famous prudery of the age and the distrust of sexual passion. Thomas Bowdler produced in 1818 his *Family Shakespeare*, "in which . . . those words and phrases are omitted which cannot with propriety be read in a family," a strange sensitivity after 200 years; and "the anti-English pollution of the waltz . . . the most degenerating that the last or present century can see" was denounced in *The Ladies' Pocket Book of Etiquette* of 1840. The middle classes sought to maintain an orderly world through convention. At a time when prostitution and drunkenness were at new heights, this was more than repression; it was an effort to bend society to the self-discipline on which a thriving commerce, the advancement of knowledge, and personal fulfillment were thought to rest.

The special place of women emphasized the middle-class concern with the family, and the home became a private citadel largely closed to the outside world. In the family the liberal dream of combining individualism and social order came closest to achievement, for the patriarchal father, devoted mother, and carefully trained children were meant to live in disciplined harmony. Childhood itself lasted longer in the middle class, where character, manners, and education required elaborate preparation. The mother made this home; and books, newspapers, magazines, and sermons were filled with accounts of the talents that role required. Motherhood had become an honored occupation, fondly depicted in novels and the new women's magazines founded, like the Parisian *Journal des Femmes* of 1832, to make women "skilled in their duties as companions and mothers."

Before winning fame with their novels, the Brontë sisters professed envy for the working girl, who at least had her own money, but slowly respectable careers were opening to women. The governess was, along with the butler, the chief domestic, and many a bright but poor young woman used that often lonely position to gain some knowledge of the world and establish a career or enhance her prospects for marriage. In England and increasingly on the Continent, most elementary-school teachers were women, and that occupation opened significant opportunities by the 1860s Florence Nightingale offended her wealthy family by working as a nurse; but she returned from the Crimean War in 1856 a national heroine to become a major influence in public health and in the establishment of her profession, the first woman to win the British Order of Merit. On the Continent George Sand (the masculine pen name says much about the status of women) was one of the most prolific and noted writers of the age, an important figure among the artists of France, who shocked and excited her contemporaries as much by her attacks on marriage and the treatment of women as by her free personal life. In England women writers proved keen and often caustic observers of society, from Jane Austen's deft analysis of genteel life in the countryside to Elizabeth Gaskell's sympathetic picture of industrial workers and the more complex novels of George Eliot (Mary Ann Evans), who was an active participant in the major intellectual and reform movements of the period. By the 1840s, when Flora Tristan traveled across France preaching to workers of the connection between their plight and women's, the emancipation of women had become an important theme in the writings of nearly all the utopian socialists (see the next section), who found in women's role a key to the errors of middle-class society. John Stuart Mill's *Essay on the Subjugation of Women*, published in 1869, and his advocacy of suffrage for them thus stand as a milestone marking the growing strength of the women's movement.

The Standard of Living

There is more agreement among historians about the general pattern of social change in the first half of the nineteenth century than about its specific effects on the standard of living, particularly of the working class. For this period, England is the critical case; and scholars agree that between 1790 and 1840 national wealth about doubled but that the upper classes were the principal beneficiaries. Did workers gain, too? Certainly they were poor, but poverty, even of the bleakest sort, was not new (and a growing desire to correct such destitution was in itself one of the important changes of the period). The poorest peasants of Sicily who lived in caves, like those of Sweden or Ireland who lived in holes dug into the ground, may have been victims of the social system; they were hardly victims of industrialization.

What was new, then, was the terrible crowding and the workers' helpless dependence. The conditions in which workers lived made poverty more miserable, more obvious to all, and more threatening to the general welfare. In part the result of increased population, the crowding followed directly from the sudden growth of factory towns. Even if the hurriedly built housing was drier and cleaner than the peasant hovels that had served for centuries, the squeezing of whole families into a single room and the cramming of hundreds and thousands of people into areas with little light, with a single source of insalubrious water, and with no means for disposing of sewage created problems so different in scale as to be different in kind. Industrialization also added the special hazards of lead and phosphorous poisoning; and the assault of coal mining, cotton spinning, and machine grinding on the lungs made tuberculosis ubiquitous. Everywhere in Europe members of the working class were recognized generally to be thinner, shorter, and paler than other people.

Accompanying this was an often demoralizing dependence. Most new factories employed between 150 and 300 men, women, and children, which would mean many people whose well-being was largely tied to a single employer. A high proportion of these people were new to the area in which they lived, starkly dependent upon cash to pay their rent, purchase rough cotton for clothes, provide the bread that was the staple of their diet, and buy some candles and coal. For millions, employment was never steady; for millions of others unemployment was the norm. It was common for a third of the adult males of a town to be without work, especially in the winter, and pauperism was acknowledged to be the social disease of the century, a state that included some 10 percent of the population in Britain and only slightly less in France. Workers of course suffered most in the periodic depressions that baffled even the most optimistic. The depression of 1846 was nearly universal, and that of 1857 extended from North Amer-

ica to Eastern Europe. Layoffs in the Lancashire cotton industry ran so high as a result of the American Civil War that at one time more than 250,000 workers, better than half the total, lived by what they could get on relief. The recipes for the watery soup handed out by the charitable agencies of every city define the thinness of survival.[7]

At the same time there was a countertrend. In some trades and places workers were distinctly better off; in general real wages—wages measured, that is, in terms of what they could buy—may have increased somewhat. Pay rose generally in the mid-1840s and notably again in the 1850s, though these gains meant less in new factory towns, where workers could be forced to buy shoddy goods at high prices in company stores. Alcoholism was so extensive that in many a factory town paydays were staggered in order to reduce the dangerous number of drunks, and this sign of alienation may also reflect an increase in available money. Technology of course brought benefits as well. The spread of the use of soap and cotton underwear was an enormous boon to health, and brick construction and iron pipes had improved housing even for many of the relatively poor by midcentury. Luxuries such as sugar, tea, and meat were becoming available to the lower-middle class and the more prosperous artisans.

---

[7] The French chef of the Reform Club of London was much admired for his "good and nourishing" recipe: ¼ lb. leg of beef, 2 oz. of drippings, 2 onions and other vegetables, ½ lb. flour, ½ lb. barley, 3 oz. salt, ½ oz. brown sugar—and 2 gallons of water! It was by no means the cheapest soup. Cited in Cecil Woodham-Smith, *The Great Hunger* (1964), p. 173.

Gustave Doré's engraving of a London slum captures both the sullen hopelessness of the poor and the sense of the dangerous classes continuously breeding children that frightened the upper classes. (Photo: The Granger Collection)

The vigorous debate among historians over the standard of living in this period has become in large measure a test of the author's feelings about capitalism. But pessimists and optimists generally agree that whatever improvements occurred reached the masses slowly, that their effects often could not compensate for the added burdens of industrial employment, and that the chasm between the destitute and the regularly employed (who in England were called the deserving poor) became greater than ever before.

For in industrial Europe the urban poor remained a subject of baffled concern. Skilled workers and the middle classes were unquestionably more prosperous than even in the recent past, but that made the contrast with the poverty of those beneath them even more striking. A luxury restaurant in Paris (there were over 3,000 restaurants of every type there by 1830 as contrasted to only fifty or so before the Revolution) might charge twenty-five or thirty times an average worker's daily wage for a single meal; even modest ones charged twice the daily wage to a clientele that ate three or four times a day in contrast to the two meals of many workers. Despite the subtle shadings of status and wealth, the great differences of class were palpable in every aspect of daily life.

Public Life
The social questions of pauperism, public health and morals, and class divisions were debated in hundreds of speeches and pamphlets; and the parliamentary and private inquiries in Britain like the elaborate social studies in France expressed a humanitarian attempt to improve the lot of the lower class through the rational techniques that seemed to work brilliantly when applied to issues of profits and politics.

Some employers, especially in Britain and Alsace, built special housing, drab barracks that nonetheless seemed marvels of cleanliness and decency. Middle-class radicals supported the Society for the Diffusion of Useful Knowledge, founded in 1826 to carry enlightenment to the lower classes. They contributed to and gave lectures at night schools for the workingman, such as those run by the Mechanics' Institute (of which there were more than 700 in Great Britain by 1850) and by the Polytechnic Association of France (which had more than 100,000 participants on the eve of the revolution of 1848). Thousands of middle-class people personally carried the lamp of truth to the poor in the form of pious essays, moral stories, and informative descriptions of how machines worked. Bibles by the million added to this extraordinary testimony to faith in the power of the printed page and to the spread of literacy. Ambitious members of the lower-middle class were, however, more likely than workers to take advantage of these opportunities.

For the truly poverty-stricken, charities were established at an incredible rate; more than 450 relief organizations were listed in London alone in 1853, and whole encyclopedias were published in France cataloguing these undertakings. A revival of Christian zeal provided powerful impetus to such groups in Britain, and on the Continent new Catholic religious orders, most with specific social missions, were founded by the hundreds. They sponsored lectures, organized wholesome recreation, set up trade apprenticeships, provided expectant mothers with a clean sheet and a pamphlet on child care, opened savings banks that accepted even the tiniest deposit, campaigned for hygiene or temperance, gave away soup and bread, supported homes for abandoned children and fallen women, and ran nurseries, schools, and hostels. These good works were preeminently the province of women. Almost invariably they saw themselves as models of social salva-

tion, which required only that others follow their example. The Society of St. Vincent de Paul, which was organized in Paris in 1835 and soon spread to all of Catholic Europe, required thousands of educated and well-to-do men regularly to visit the poor so they might teach thrift and give hope by their example as well as their charity. Important for some lucky individuals and a significant means of informing the comfortable about the plight of the poor, the heroic efforts of these organizations were never adequate to the social challenge. Most of Europe's urban masses remained largely untouched by charity or religion.

In matters of public health, standards of housing, working conditions, and education, governments were forced to take a more active role. By modern standards the official measures were timid and hesitant, and the motives behind them were as mixed as they were in factory legislation, favored not only by humanitarians but also by landed interests happy to restrain industrialists.

It is not surprising that conditions of health remained appalling. Vaccination, enforced by progressive governments, made smallpox less threatening after the turn of the century, but beyond that any advances in medicine contributed little. The great work of immunization would come later in the century. The most important medical gain of the 1840s was probably the use of anesthesia in surgery, dentistry, and childbirth. Serious epidemics broke out in every decade. Typhus, carried by lice, was a constant threat, accounting for 1 death in 9 in Ireland between 1816 and 1819, and typhoid fever was caused by infected water in city after city. Apparently beginning along the Ganges River in 1826, cholera spread through East Asia, reaching Moscow and St. Petersburg by 1830 (100,000 died of cholera in Russia in two years). From there it spread south and west, to Egypt and North

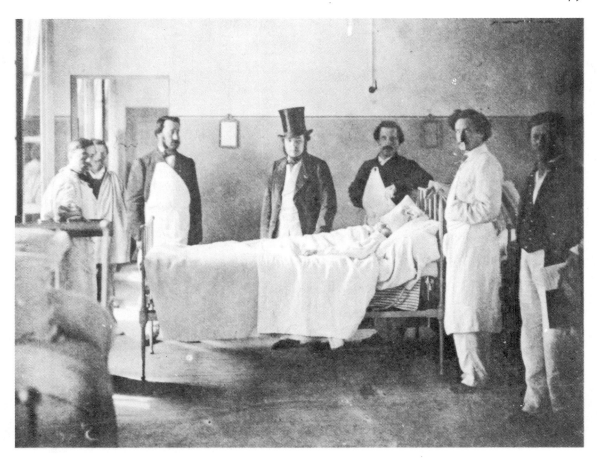

Africa, to Poland, Austria, and into Germany, to be reported in Hamburg in 1831. Despite efforts to put ports in quarantine (a move opposed by shipping interests), the disease reached northern England and later France in the same year, continuing slowly to the south, taking a ninth of Palermo's population in 1836–1837.

The reaction to the epidemic of 1831–1832 in Britain, France, and Germany, however, revealed much about social change. An official day of fasting, prayer, and humiliation in England, like the willingness of the archbishop of Paris to interpret cholera as Divine Retribu-

Photography gained wide acceptance both as a mode of portraiture and as a scientific tool in the nineteenth century. Charles Negre's photograph of "The Doctor's Visit" to the Imperial Asylum at Vincennes in 1860 combines both of these in a stark display of the hospital environment of the era. (Photo: Philadelphia Museum of Art; Collection of André Jammes)

tion, expressed criticism of an era of materialism and its belief in progress as well as the strength of traditional faith. But governments were expected to act, and, torn between two inaccurate theories of how the disease spread (contagion on contact and miasmic effluvia; the cholera bacillus was finally identified by Robert Koch in 1883), they did. Inspectors were mobilized to enforce such sanitary regulations as existed (and not infrequently were faced with riots by a populace fearful of medical body-snatchers). In Paris and Lille tenements were whitewashed by the tens of thousands, food inspected, streets and sewers cleaned on administrative order. Similar steps were taken in the German states and in Britain, where after the inadequacy of local government became apparent, a national Public Health Commission was given extraordinary powers over towns and individuals. Statistics were gathered, and over a period of years doctors and inspectors (with consciences troubled) reported on the terrible conditions they had found among lower-class neighbors whose quarters they had never visited before. There was another such epidemic in the 1840s and lesser ones thereafter, but the shock and uncertainty of what to do was never again so great. Gradually, hospitals too came under more direct state supervision as the cost and complexity of medical treatment increased. By midcentury housing and sanitary codes regulated most of urban construction throughout the West, and inspectors were empowered to enforce them. Liberalism showed its other face in England's handling of the terrible potato famine in Ireland. As the potato blight struck late in 1845, disaster for a population so dependent on a single crop was not hard to predict. For the next several years some of England's ablest officials struggled with bureaucratic earnestness to collect information, organize relief, and maintain order, yet did so in a manner so inhibited by respect for natural economic forces and the rights of property that in practice only meager relief was offered while millions starved.

The 1830s and 1840s witnessed a series of restrictions on child labor, banning employment of those under nine in textile mills in Britain and factories in Prussia, under eight in factories in France, and under ten in mines in Britain. By the end of the 1840s, similar measures had been adopted in Bavaria, Baden, Piedmont, and Russia. Generally the laws held the workday of children under twelve or thirteen to eight or nine hours and of those under sixteen or eighteen to twelve hours. In Britain and France, there were additional requirements that the very young be provided with a couple of hours of schooling each day. To be effective such regulations required teams of inspectors, provided for only in Britain, where earnest disciples of Jeremy Bentham (who is discussed in the next section) applied them diligently. This expansion of government authority had been vigorously opposed, but the appalling evidence presented to commissions of inquiry made the need apparent, and the ability to gather such evidence became one of government's most important functions.

The most bitterly controversial welfare measure of the period was Britain's Poor Law of 1834. The old system of relief required counties to supplement local wages up to a subsistence level determined by the price of bread. Expensive and inadequate to changing needs, the system was attacked by liberal economists, who charged that it discouraged workers from migrating to new jobs and cost too much. An extensive campaign led to the Poor Law of 1834, based on the quaint Benthamite notion that unemployment must be made unattractive. Those receiving relief were required to live in workhouses, where the sexes were separated and conditions kept suitably mean. Resented as a cruel act of class conflict, the new law proved unenforceable in much of the nation, though recent studies have suggested that it was less harsh in either practice or intent than its critics charged. On the Continent welfare measures kept more traditional forms while steadily shifting the responsibility for them from local and religious auspices to the state.

Public education also became a matter of national policy. Prussia had made local schooling compulsory in 1716, and a series of reforms culminated in 1807 with the creation of a bureau of education. In the following decades the government, with the cooperation of the Lutheran clergy, established an efficient system of universal education and facilities for training the needed teachers while assuring that the subject matter taught would remain rudimentary and politically safe. The network of secondary schools was also enlarged but kept quite separate, in effect excluding the lower classes. Most of the German states had similar arrangements, establishing nearly universal elementary education. In France the Napoleonic structure provided the framework for public education, in principle although not in practice providing a substitute for the extensive but more informal and largely religious schools of the old regime. The law of 1833 required an elementary school in every commune. Slowly but with remarkable continuity, the system was expanded, the quality of teachers improved, and the power of inspectors over tightfisted local authorities increased. By the revolution of 1848, three-fourths of France's school-age children were receiving some formal instruction. The conflict between the Church of England and the dissenting sects prevented the adoption of a state-controlled system of national education in Britain, a lack welcomed by those conservatives who opposed educating the masses. Nevertheless the subsidy first voted in 1833 to underwrite the construction of private schools proved an opening wedge, and it increased in amount and scope each year. From Spain to Russia elementary schools were favored by every government. Inadequate and impoverished, the public

schools of Europe offered little chance of social advancement to those forced to attend them, but few doubted that they could be a major instrument for improving society as well as a force for social peace.

III. THEORIES OF CHANGE

The overwhelming fact of political and social change demanded interpretation; and liberalism, nationalism, and socialism all sought to explain the process of development and show how it could lead to true progress, creating a civilization more knowledgeable, more prosperous, and freer than any before.

LIBERALISM

The gains of liberal politics—representative government, free speech, and laws applied equally to all citizens—accompanied the triumph of liberal economic theory and the application of liberal social policies which, though suspicious of guilds or combinations of workers, were solicitous of individual initiative and public education. Liberalism was an international movement, led primarily by men of means and education, who watched the successes of their cause throughout Western Europe and encouraged each other in the conviction that history was inevitably advancing toward the fulfillment of their common vision. That confidence rested not only on political victories but on the experience of economic growth. Liberal politics and liberal economic theory were thus closely related; yet these two aspects of liberalism have proved separable. The advocates of one were not always committed to the other, and the question of their relationship is still a matter of controversy, especially in the United States. The model of liberalism was nineteenth-century England.

Economic Liberalism

Adam Smith and the physiocrats had argued that government intervention in the marketplace merely restricted the play of economic forces that if left unfettered would increase productivity and prosperity. This belief, which had become liberal dogma, was expounded systematically by David Ricardo, whose writings represented the keystone of modern economics for generations. Ricardo was one of England's self-made men, a financier who became wealthy during the Napoleonic wars and then retired from business, thereafter contributing enthusiastically to charity, taking part in politics, and developing his economic ideas, which England's leading liberals encouraged him to publish. First issued in 1817, his *Principles of Political Economy and Taxation* presented his theory as a science in flat prose, precise but highly abstract.

The wealth of the community, Ricardo argued, comes from land, capital, and labor; and these three "classes" are compensated by rent, profit, and wages. A product's value results from the labor required to make it—the labor theory of value, which socialists would later use for very different purposes. For Ricardo this theory led to principles of property similar to Locke's and to an emphasis on labor saving as the source of profit foreshadowed by Adam Smith. Rents are determined not by individuals but by the poorest land in cultivation. The most fertile land produces more for the same labor, and that increment constitutes profit, received as rent. As population pressures bring more (and poorer) land into cultivation, rents rise because the difference between the best and worst land increases. Wages are subtracted from profit, but an "iron law of wages" (his phrase is characteristic) decrees that when labor is plentiful the worker would tend to be paid at the subsistence level. Short-term fluc-

tuations in prices are the natural regulator within the system, pushing men to activities for which demand is high. Thus Ricardan economics extended the sphere of inexorable economic laws and riveted them to Malthusian ideas about pressures of population.

Both land and labor are commodities, Ricardo said, their value quite unaffected by sentimental talk about aristocratic values or craftsmanship, and society is a congeries of competing interests. Legislation cannot raise wages or prevent the marketplace from working in its natural way; but if men acknowledge economic laws and act in their own best interest, a natural harmony and progress follow.

Ricardo called his subject political economy, and from it a powerful reform movement developed. Clearly, liberals argued, the landed interest had misused political power to benefit itself, depriving the rest of society. Throughout Europe liberal economics added important weight to demands that special privilege be eliminated and that governments be responsive to the people, who would best know their own interests. With the impressive evidence of economic growth before them, it was natural for liberals to add that politicians might well adopt something of the openness, efficiency, and energy of the men of action who were transforming business.

Utilitarianism

A second major stream of liberalism was utilitarianism, a complex and often contradictory philosophy elaborated by Jeremy Bentham. Although English, Bentham was in many respects a philosophe, ready to write a constitution for Russia or codify the laws of Latin American republics. Some of his most important writings before 1789 appeared first in French—the revolutionaries gave him French citizenship—and he combined plans of detailed reform with a theory of psychology in the

Enlightenment tradition. At first Bentham stressed reform of the legal system, and he remained all his life an opponent of the precedent-bound, technicality-loving courts of England. In contrast to most philosophes, he rejected the doctrine of natural rights as a meaningless abstraction, and unlike most liberals, he did not hesitate to advocate heavy state intervention in society.

In Bentham's thinking utility replaces natural rights as the test of proper policy, and it is measured by the standard of what provides the greatest good for the greatest number. The good is that which avoids pain and gives pleasure—a calculation that everyone makes for himself anyway and that with education he can learn to make more wisely. (Bentham called this the "felicific calculus," but his verbal pomposity was famous; his after-dinner walks were "postprandial perambulations.") The egocentrism that built great industry could also build a just and happy society. In Bentham's terms the proper estimate of pain and pleasure leads one to behave like a prudent, middle-class Christian; and the task of government is to make sure that pain and pleasure are appropriately distributed for various kinds of conduct.

Bentham's followers, sober intellectuals who called themselves philosophic radicals, became even more influential. They pressed his doctrines in every sphere, and by his death in 1832, they were among the most important reformers of Parliament, law, prisons, education, and welfare. A special group within a larger liberal movement, they shared and contributed to the tendency of liberals everywhere to take pride in pressing for humane reforms on grounds of common sense and natural harmony.

The Broader Liberalism of John Stuart Mill
Thus liberals appraised society primarily in terms of opportunities for individual growth and freedom of individual choice. Such an emphasis gave some ethical dignity to the pain of industrialization and social change. Confident and optimistic, their doctrines seemed universally valid.

Yet liberalism, to the perpetual surprise of its adherents, proved a creed of limited appeal, forever subject to attack and internal division. Enthusiasm for limited constitutional reform, so great in the 1830s, was harder to sustain in 1848. It proved difficult in practice to reconcile liberty with order and equal rights with private property, and the opportunities and freedoms proudly cited by men like Guizot seemed to others the selfishness of the well-to-do. Religious conflict in Catholic Europe, the need first to create national states in the central and eastern realms, and the problems of the dispossessed everywhere frequently made liberal practice an ineffectual ideal.

Before such problems liberals themselves divided. As maintained by some, liberalism became the narrow and at times mean justification of a social class; for others it expanded until the need for social justice and equal opportunity largely obscured the principles of competitive economics and a noninterfering state that were its original strength. In each country its temper was different, shaped by a national history liberals never wholly dominated.

Its very malleability, however, enabled liberalism to endure as a doctrine and a political force; and its transition to a broader meaning is best exemplified in John Stuart Mill, the most important liberal spokesman of the nineteenth century. Mill's father was a leading Benthamite and he raised his son in the strictist utilitarianism; but the younger Mill gradually came with searching candor to modify received doctrine. Extraordinarily learned, a philosopher, economist, and publicist, Mill's greatest influence has been through his political writings. Fearful of the intolerance and oppression of which any class or the public at large was capable, he made freedom of thought a first principle, and he advocated universal suffrage as a necessary check on the elite and proportional representation as a means of protecting minorities. Influenced by Auguste Comte (see Chapter 25) and others, he acknowledged the critical role of institutions in social organization and admitted that those institutions, even liberal ones, best suited to one stage of development might not be appropriate for another.

Mill hoped for a beneficial influence from a more open bureaucracy, from organized interest groups, and from cooperatives. Moved by the problems of the industrial poor, he tried to distinguish between production (to which liberal economics could still apply) and distribution (in which the state might intervene in behalf of justice), and he came to see that collective action by the workers could enhance freedom rather than restrict it. He sought a place for aesthetic values within the colder doctrine he inherited and in later years courageously advocated causes, such as the emancipation of women and the confiscation of excess profit, that seemed fearfully radical to most contemporaries. His liberalism, thus modified and extended, remained firm; and his essay, *On Liberty*, published in 1859, stands as one of the important works of European political theory, a careful but heartfelt, balanced but unyielding declaration that society can have no higher interest than the freedom of each of its members.

EARLY SOCIALISTS

Some men, however, envisioned a better society based on quite different principles. Among scores of socialist schemes, the ideas of Saint-Simon, Fourier, and Owen won an important place in the history of socialism by their comprehensiveness, their particular insights, and the intensity with which they were promulgated.

All three men lived through the French Revolution, had some personal experience of burgeoning capitalism, and began to develop systems for remaking the world in the early stages of industrialization, even before Napoleon's final defeat. Turning from political solutions to social problems, they developed economic and moral critiques of the contemporary world. Competition, they argued, is wasteful and cruel, inducing hard-hearted indifference to suffering, misusing wealth, and leading to frequent economic crises. Differently organized, society can instead be harmonious and orderly, providing enough for all.

As a young French officer, Claude Henri de Rouvroy, comte de Saint-Simon fought with George Washington at Yorktown. During the French Revolution he abandoned his title and built a fortune through speculation in land, which he quickly lost, and under the empire he settled down to the difficult career of a seer. For a society divided between the propertied and the propertyless, Saint-Simon proposed to substitute the direction of experts standing above the conflict: scientists, men of affairs (*industriels*), priests, and artists. These specialists, chosen for their ability, would design plans for the benefit of all, increasing productivity and therefore prosperity. The new society would recapture the integrated, organic quality of ancient Greece and the Middle Ages but with scientists and managers holding the authority once granted priests and soldiers. In a world so structured, the state would have little independent importance; for skilled men would work together, planning and directing, as in an efficient business. The artists and priests of the new order could then lead mankind to self-fulfillment and love.

Saint-Simon's theories won little hearing among the powerful of his day, but they earned a significant following especially among the bright students of the École Polytechnique. An entire cult, the New Christianity, developed among his disciples after Saint-Simon's death in 1827, only to be dissipated by internal division and public ridicule by the 1840s. Nevertheless an extraordinary number of France's leading engineers and entrepreneurs in the next generation fondly recalled the Saint-Simonian enthusiasms of their youth, and in their penchant for planning, grand economic organization, and social reform, they carried elements of his teaching into the world of affairs and respectable politics. There were important Saint-Simonian movements in every country, and later socialists would maintain his conviction that proper planning would make an economy both more just and richer.

François Marie Charles Fourier had been a traveling salesman before dedicating himself, at the same time as Saint-Simon, to a theory which he firmly believed would rank among the greatest discoveries ever made. His cantankerous and shrewd writings on contemporary society were so copious that his manuscripts have still not all been printed despite the devotion of generations of admirers. Largely self-taught, he committed to paper his fantasies of strange beasts and incredible inventions that would abound in a future age, which made him an easy target for critics.

His central concept, however, was an ideal community, the phalanstery (from "phalanx"). Once even one was created, the happiness and well-being of its members would inspire the establishment of others until all of society was converted. A phalanstery should contain some 1,600 men and women, representatives of all the types of personality identified in Fourier's elaborate psychology. He listed a dozen passions that move human be-ings and proposed to organize the phalanstery in such a way that individuals would accomplish the tasks necessary to society by doing what they wanted. Everyone would perform a variety of tasks, engaging in no one for too long; pleasure and work would flow together. Members of the phalanstery would be paid according to a formula that recognized the capital, labor, and talent each contributed. Largely self-sufficient, a phalanstery would produce some goods for export according to its particular resources, and these would be traded with similar communities.

No phalanstery was ever established exactly as Fourier planned (he even offered designs for the architecture), but communities were founded on Fourierist principles from the United States to Rumania, and if few of them survived for long, the vision did of a society in which cooperation replaces compulsion and joy transforms drudgery.

Robert Owen was one of the success stories of industrial capitalism: a self-made man, he rose from selling cloth to be the manager and part owner of a large textile mill in New Lanark, Scotland. Owen's rule transformed the town, and by the end of the Napoleonic wars, distinguished visitors were traveling from all over Europe to see the miracle he had wrought. The workday was shortened from seventeen to ten hours; new housing was constructed, eventually allowing an employee's family several rooms; inspection committees maintained cleanliness; gardens were planted and sewers installed. In nursery schools with airy, pleasant rooms, children were given exercise, encouraged to sing and dance, taught without corporal punishment from books and projects designed to be attractive, and trained in the useful arts. Most impressive of all, the subjects in this paternalistic kingdom developed a pride in their community; productivity rose and profits increased.

Owen had, he felt, disproved Ricardo's

A French engraving of Robert Owen's textile mill shows a model of order and calm in which everyone appears to have taken to heart the rules carefully posted along the wall. (Photo: The Granger Collection)

dismal laws, and he turned to projects for establishing ideal communities throughout the nation. Like Fourier's, they would be placed in a rural setting and would supply most of their own needs. Members would take meals and enjoy entertainment in common, and children would be raised communally. Educated to the age of eight, the young would then engage in productive labor until they were twenty-six; after five years in distributive or managerial jobs, adults would assume the tasks of government, cultivating the sciences and the arts in their increasing leisure. The controlled environment would assure good character among community members, and the division of tasks would provide them with varied and rich lives. Standardized production would offer more goods at lower cost (luxuries appealed to a snobbery that would disappear), and higher wages would increase the local market.

Even after losing most of his wealth with the failure of the community of New Harmony in Indiana, Owen continued to be the single most important figure in the labor movement and the workers' cooperatives that spread through England in the 1830s and 1840s. But by the time of his death, in 1858, Owen, who had converted to spiritualism, was largely ignored by the world he had sought to remake.

These early socialists imagined a society of cooperation and love, one enriched by new inventions and new means of production but based on new forms of social organization. Advocates of change, they were transitional figures seeking to combine the best of the old and new eras. Their indictment of capitalism and their insights into the nature of productivity, exchange, social planning, and education had an impact far beyond their relatively small circles of believers. A large number of Europe's best minds were touched by their theories, and the mystique of cooperation so strong in their writings remained part of the socialist and anarchist call to brotherhood and found an echo in nationalists from Mazzini on. Yet nearly everyone ultimately rejected their ideas as impractical and too radical. Bucolic isolation and artisanal production became increasingly unrealistic, and these theories were incredibly vague about problems of politics and power. The charge of radicalism, however, requires some further comment.

The criticisms of liberal society mounted by Saint-Simon, Fourier, and Owen were not so different overall from the conservative attack, and none of them was a thoroughgoing democrat. With some restrictions—Saint-Simon for example insisted on the abolition of inheritance—they even allowed private property. What most shocked contemporaries were their views on the status of women, sexual mores, and Christianity. All rejected the place allotted women in bourgeois society, and Owen not only specified that they should share in governing but believed their emancipation required a smaller role for them in the family. All wrote of sensual pleasure as good and its repression as a characteristic European error. The Saint-Simonians publicly advocated free love, and Fourier

carefully provided that neither young nor old should be deprived of the pleasures of the flesh. Owen was only slightly less outspoken in his contempt for Christian marriage. Yet all three stressed religion as the source of community feeling, brotherhood, and human ethics. Their efforts to replace what they had eliminated therefore led to imitations of Christian ritual and foggy mysticism that not only contrasted with their concern for rational planning but invited easy ridicule from a society with many reasons for rejecting their utopias.

NATIONALISM

Nationalism, a looser and more general movement whose doctrines were less specific than those of either liberalism or socialism, proved to be politically more powerful. Why this should be so, why nationalism has assumed such importance remains one of the important questions of modern history. Nationalism's deepest roots, of course, are the shared sense of a common regional and cultural identity, especially as those roots are expressed in custom, language, and religion. Such feelings, which antedate the modern period, may nevertheless have been further stimulated by the advent of increased communication and mobility. Through nationalism they were attached to the modern state, whose power and importance had increased since the state building of the seventeenth century. But it was the experience of the French Revolution and Napoleon that established nationalism as a political force capable of mobilizing popular enthusiasm, of reforming society, of creating seemingly irresistible political movements, and eventually of concentrating unprecedented power in a national state. Nationalism was also a movement of self-conscious modernization, embraced by Frenchmen eager to equal the industrial wealth of England and attracting those in other countries who aspired to achieve the prosperity and independence of Britain and France.

Nineteenth-century nationalism was thus a response to social and economic change as well as a political effort to bring middle class and masses together in order to capture established states for new programs and to build new national states where none existed. Like socialists, nationalists stressed the values of community; in most other respects they were, in the first half of the century, usually admirers of liberalism. Although they varied in content and tactics, nationalist movements not only used the latest political devices to hold out promises of freedom, economic growth, and progress but incorporated many of the major cultural trends of the period. In this, Romanticism, with its rejection of the rationalism and universalism of the Enlightenment and the French Revolution, was central. During and after the Revolution, the German intellectuals Johann Gottfried von Herder and Johann Gottlieb Fichte among others urged their countrymen to put aside the values imported from France in favor of a uniquely Germanic culture. And German Romanticism continued to be especially influential in leading Europeans everywhere to value their own traditions and dialects as the expression of national values.

The exploration of ethnic origins took many forms. A group of German scholars made philology a science, and by the 1830s and 1840s an extraordinary revival of national languages occurred across Europe. Gaelic was hailed as the mother tongue of Ireland; in Finland the first public lecture in Finnish marked a break from the dominant Swedish culture; intellectuals in Bohemia began abandoning their customary German to write in Czech. More remarkable still were the number of languages consciously contrived out of local dialects and invented vocabularies. Nor-

wegian became distinct from Danish, Serbian from other Slavic languages, and Slovak from Czech—all literary languages by the 1840s, each the work of but a handful of scholars for whom widespread illiteracy eased the task of establishing a national language.

This fascination with folk culture and a national past fostered the discovery of a special national mission. French historians wrote eloquently of France's call to carry reason and freedom across Europe, and Mazzini proclaimed the destiny of the Third Rome. The poet Adam Mickiewicz, lecturing in Paris, inspired nationalists of many countries with his descriptions of how Poland's history paralleled the life of Christ and had yet to achieve Resurrection. Francis Palacky's pioneering work stressed the role of the Czechs as leaders of the Slavs. Such visions were repeated in poetry and drama, which now blossomed in the native tongue, and justified resistance to alien rule. Cultural nationalism thus served as a weapon of middle-class self-assertion whereby men who felt cramped by social hierarchy, an unsympathetic bureaucracy, and a stagnant economy could win broader support for their own dreams of progress.

In places subject to foreign rule such as Hungary or much of Italy, movements for agricultural improvement, promoted by the liberal aristocracy, became centers of nationalism, and a national tariff, which would enlarge the area of free trade internally and protect native industry, became a nationalist battle cry. Friedrich List, a leading liberal economist, argued from the American example that only behind tariff barriers could a united Germany develop the industry and the vigorous middle class necessary for competitive strength and independence. Everywhere nationalist groups generally demanded public education, more political freedom, and efficient government. Strengthened by its promises of economic growth and its respect for native traditions, nationalism generated political movements of broad appeal, capable of mobilizing popular enthusiasm. Daniel O'Connell's inflammatory speeches won thousands to Young Ireland and its demands for the end of union with Great Britain; by the 1830s he commanded the largest movement of political protest Europe had yet seen. Politically moderate in the 1840s, nationalist movements became more militant and more radical as they benefited from social unrest—a tendency that frightened moderates during the revolutions of 1848. Those revolutions also ran afoul of conflicting national claims, especially in Central Europe. Although most nationalist movements were then defeated, nationalism was not; for its proponents learned greater respect for a strong state and military power, while governments found in nationalist policies a welcome source of popular support. In the following years nationalism would show itself to be a central force in European politics.

THE MEANING OF HISTORY

All the ideologies of change argued in terms of history, and its systematic study became the most honored of the human sciences. In England, France, and Germany, national projects were launched for publishing source documents and for training scholars to interpret them. The most popular dramas were given a historical setting, and some historians were as widely read as novelists. The Glorious Revolution of 1688, the French Revolution, and the rise of Prussia were favorite themes in their respective countries, and everywhere the search was intense for national roots in the Middle Ages and for patterns of meaning applicable to the present. Historical studies often figured prominently in contemporary political battles, their writers calling on the past to prove the need for reform or teach the dangers of revolution

while patriotically stressing the virtues of their own people.

This preoccupation with history, which affected all intellectual life, received its most powerful expression in the philosophy of Georg Wilhelm Friedrich Hegel. A Rhinelander who had felt the impact of French culture and watched Napoleon's career with fascination, thoroughly trained in philosophy and Lutheran theology, Hegel set out to establish a philosophy as comprehensive as that of Thomas Aquinas or Aristotle. He was determined to reconcile the contradictions between science and faith, Christianity and the state, the ideal and the real, the eternal and the temporal that plagued modern thought.

He sought to do so by establishing an undying purpose at the heart of history and by discovering the process of historical change. That process he described not as the simple increase of reason or wealth so often called progress, but something far more complex and subtle—the dialectic of thesis, antithesis, and synthesis. All the actions, the values, and structures of a given society constitute a thesis, an implicit statement about life. The thesis, however, is never adequate to every need, and its incompleteness generates contrary views, institutions, and practices —the antithesis. Thus every society gives birth to conflict between thesis and antithesis until finally out of their battle a new synthesis is molded. The synthesis is a new thesis that generates another round of conflict. History moves by this dialectic in a steady unfolding of the World Spirit. Its meaning is the fulfillment of human freedom and self-awareness. In the ancient East only one man was free; in Greece and Rome some were free; in the Germanic Christian kingdoms after the Reformation, all were free. Since the French Revolution men have consciously acted on history, knowing what they want and fulfilling the

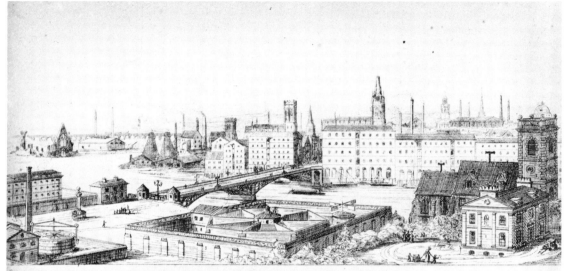

THE SAME TOWN IN 1840

1. St Michael's Tower, rebuilt in 1750. 2. New Parsonage House & Pleasure Grounds. 3. The New Jail. 4. Gas Works. 5. Lunatic Asylum. 6. Iron Works & Ruins of St Maries Abbey. 7. Mr Evans Chapel. 8. Baptist Chapel. 9. Unitarian Chapel. 10. New Church. 11. New Town Hall & Concert Room. 12. Wesleyan Centenary Chapel. 13. New Christian Society. 14. Quakers Meeting. 15. Socialist Hall of Science.

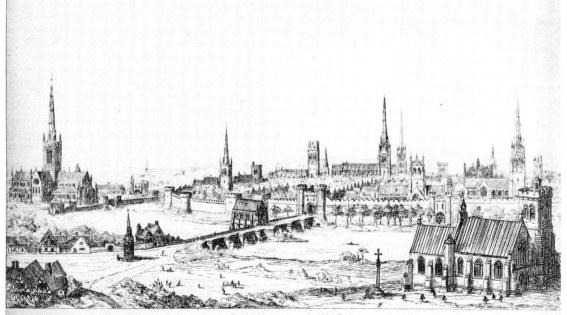

Catholic town in 1440.

1. St Michaels on the Hill. 2. Queens Cross. 3. St Thomas's Chapel. 4. St Maries Abbey. 5. All Saints. 6. St Johns. 7. St Peters. 8. St Alkmunds. 9. St Maries. 10. St Edmunds. 11. Grey Friars. 12. St Cuthberts. 13. Guild hall. 14. Trinities. 15. St Olaves. 16. St Botolphs.

A convert to Catholicism and a leading student of Gothic architecture, Augustus Pugin was one of the architects of the Houses of Parliament. These illustrations, part of a book of Contrasts *comparing Catholic and Protestant society, sum up the romantic and conservative critique of modern society. (The new prison in the foreground is Jeremy Bentham's Panopticon, designed so that a single guard can see down all the cellblocks.)* (Photo: New York Public Library, Picture Collection)

World Spirit at the same time. Thus reason, cosmic and human, work together; the meaning of history is essentially religious.

Hegel's complex and abstract philosophy was—as he would have said it had to be—both an important expression of his age and a lasting influence. He was characteristic of an era preoccupied with change in finding an eternal meaning at the core of history and his own nation as its highest articulation. After Hegel, philosophy and literary criticism tended to become increasingly historical, and historians sought more systematically for relationships among all aspects of a culture. And within a generation of his death in 1831, just after a wave of the revolutions he abhorred, some of his followers claimed to find in the Prussian state at war man's highest ethical expression, while others, led by Karl Marx, the most famous of the Hegelians, predicted the state's withering away. By then it was an intellectual habit to view society in process and to search in history for the meaning of change.

European society changed in many ways during the two generations following the Napoleonic wars. Factory organization and labor-saving machinery in 1815 showed their economic promise primarily in Britain, but by the 1850s an industrial revolution without apparent end was transforming much of Western Europe. Nearly every society experienced urbanization, expanding population, and the shift to a social structure based on modern classes.

The effort to understand these changes dominated intellectual life, and the interpretations that socialists, nationalists, and liberals made of contemporary trends and of history all promised a better future. Except for conservatives few doubted that the path of progress was marked by liberalism: freedom of speech and representative government protecting the rights of the individual, the laws of competition and self-interest working their magic. These bustling, expanding societies produced a vigorous and varied culture which expressed both the confidence and the concerns of a tumultuous era. Individualism and values associated with the middle class—rationality, probity, thrift, hard work, and a close two-generation family—were the dominant ideals.

In such an atmosphere the misery and subjugation of the lower classes seemed an intolerable contrast with the increasing wealth of society as a whole. Poverty, urban misery, and ignorance appeared no longer as natural conditions but as problems to be solved. More effective charities, better regulations, new institutions for education and welfare, or radical communities—the solutions proposed by the ideologies of change, whether piecemeal or sweeping, concentrated on improved social organization. In a civilization that expected so much of politics, this necessarily pointed to a more extensive and active role for the state.

RECOMMENDED READING

Studies

* Ashton, Thomas S. *The Industrial Revolution: 1760–1830.* 1964. A balanced "optimistic" account of the process of industrialization in Britain.

* Briggs, Asa. *Victorian Cities.* 1970. Studies of the industrial cities and their impact on British life.

The Cambridge Economic History of Europe. Vol. VI, *The Industrial Revolution and After,* 2 parts. 1965. The essay in these volumes by David S. Landes, which emphasizes the role of technology, has been revised and published separately as *Unbound Prometheus: Technological Change and Development in Western Europe from 1750 to the Present.* 1969.

Chevalier, Louis. *Laboring Classes and Dangerous Classes in Paris During the First Half of the Nineteenth Century.* 1973. This study of the Parisian poor also says much about the reactions of those better off.

* Clapham, John H. *The Economic Development of France and Germany, 1815–1914.* 1935. A sober, standard study full of useful information.

Cole, G. D. H. *A History of Socialist Thought.* 5 vols. 1953–1956. Pleasantly written compendium including each of the important movements and schools of thought.

De Ruggiero, Guido. *The History of European Liberalism.* R. G. Collingwood (tr.). 1959. A classic comparison of liberal theory in major European nations.

* Gideon, Sigfried. *Mechanization Takes Command.* 1948. Provocative analysis of the social and aesthetic implications of the machine age.

Hayes, Carleton J. H. *The Historical Evolution of Modern Nationalism.* 1931. Although now a bit dated, this remains perhaps the most useful survey.

* Heilbroner, Robert L. *The Worldly Philosophers.*
1967. A good introduction to the ideas of the economic liberals.

* Henderson, W. O. *The Industrialization of Europe: 1780–1914.* 1969. General study contrasting developments in England and on the Continent.

Himmelfarb, Gertrude. *On Liberty and Liberalism: The Case of John Stuart Mill.* 1974. Penetrating and controversial new analysis of the still controversial philosopher of liberalism.

* Lichtheim, George. *A Short History of Socialism.* 1970. Well-constructed treatment of the evolution of socialist ideas in their historical context.

* Manuel, Frank E. *The Prophets of Paris.* 1965. An excellent discussion of French utopian thinkers.

Perkin, Harold. *The Origins of Modern English Society, 1780–1880.* 1969. A serious effort to interweave all aspects of social change.

Pinkney, David H. *Napoleon III and the Rebuilding of Paris.* 1972. Careful study of the ideas and politics behind Haussmann's projects.

* Rudé, George. *The Crowd in History, 1730–1884.* 1964. Argues that there was a fundamental change in the social composition and demands of crowds after industrialization.

* Thompson, Edward P. *The Making of the English Working Class.* 1964. A remarkable work of sympathetic insight and exhaustive research.

Tilly, Charles, Louise Tilly, and Richard Tilly. *The Rebellious Century, 1830–1930.* 1975. Three studies of patterns of collective action in France, Germany, and Italy.

Walker, Mack. *German Home Towns: Community, State, and General Estate, 1648–1871.* 1971. Sensitive and original treatment of the response of small-town life to political and social change.

---

* Available in paperback.

TWENTY-FOUR

THE NATIONAL STATE
AND THE MIDDLE CLASS

In the period following the revolutions of 1848, the national state became more clearly than ever before the dominant institution of political life and the basic economic and social unit of Europe. The revolutions themselves had demonstrated the importance of public opinion, had in many cases bequeathed representative institutions for other governments to live with, and had proved the critical importance of social issues for political stability. After 1850, governments were more willing to extend the range of their activities.

Improved communications and nationwide markets also seemed to require national governments, which were in turn expected to foster industry by granting aid to railroads and banks, undertaking public works, and establishing protective tariffs. Nationalist movements promised these benefits while sustaining liberal ideas of the proper relationship between a government and its people. The national state also provided a larger field of action for the middle class who spurred its economy, manned its institutions, and sustained its cultural life. All but the most reactionary could see the benefits of having an articulate middle class that favored expansion and reform, but those in power also knew that such changes could threaten established interests.

The government most willing to experiment with new combinations of public support, innovative programs, and central control was that of Louis Napoleon in France, but the most dramatic political changes of the period were the unifications of Italy and Germany. The governments of Britain, Spain, the Austrian Empire, and Russia faced similar demands as well as an immediate need for increased military power and administrative efficiency. Throughout Europe statesmen sought modes of reform that would strengthen the state without diminishing their own power and that would convert public opinion from a threat into useful support.

The domestic political equilibrium thus achieved differed from nation to nation, but it was everywhere related to momentous shifts in international power. The Crimean War in 1853–1856 marked the breakdown of the old Concert of Europe maintained by the conservative powers after the Congress of Vienna, a change that opened the way for the wars that welded the Italian and German nations. Moreover the Conti- *nental hegemony of France in the 1850s and 1860s ended with the unification of Germany and was followed by the precarious relations manipulated by Otto von Bismarck. In a period of strong and daring statesmen, Europe's great nations found themselves charged with the direction of unprecedented accumulations of economic, military, and political power.*

I. CHANGING POLITICAL STYLES

In much of Europe the men who held power in 1850 were victors over revolution, and the waves of government repression that followed were hardly surprising. Yet Prussia, where reaction was harsh and the Junkers reasserted their influence, retained the constitution of 1850; and in the Austrian Empire, where the emperor scrapped the constitution, peasants kept their new freedom. But the most daring experiment in combining reform, popular participation, and unchallenged authority was the reign of Louis Napoleon in France. That striking venture in a new political style proved a disturbing influence as an example to others and as a factor in international relations, which became increasingly sensitive to the demands of national prestige and public opinion.

THE FRANCE OF LOUIS NAPOLEON

In 1850, with monarchists a majority in the Chamber of Deputies and Louis Napoleon the nation's president, the Second Republic was ruled by its enemies. Napoleon, often at odds with the deputies, continued the appeal to public opinion that had won him the election. When, in the third year of his four-year term, the Chamber rejected a constitutional amendment that would have permitted him a second term, he decided to mount a coup d'état.

He struck on the eve of December 2, 1851 —the anniversary of the first Napoleon's coronation as emperor in 1804 and his victory at Austerlitz in 1805. Potential opponents, including 200 deputies, were quickly taken into custody; troops occupied the streets and overran the barricades that rose. At the same time, Napoleon restored universal manhood suffrage, which the conservative Chamber had restricted with a residence requirement aimed at excluding "unstable" workers, and promised a revised constitution. Hundreds were killed, and all told between 20,000 and 30,000 were arrested with nearly 10,000 transported to Algeria. The resistance ended quickly.

Yet Louis Napoleon presented himself as the voice of the people; and three weeks after the coup his actions were ratified by more than 90 percent of the voters in a national plebiscite. The new constitution established a representative assembly, the Corps Législatif, that could debate and vote on but not initiate or amend legislation and a Senate appointed by the president, who was assured a ten-year term and almost full powers. Tired of disorder, Frenchmen were willing to settle for the façade of democracy. Exactly one year after the coup d'état, the Second Republic was transformed into the Second Empire under Emperor Napoleon III, a change even more overwhelmingly supported in another direct vote. Neither plebiscite allowed the citizen to do more than vote yes or no—accepting changes already effected or risking a rejection that might bring any number of unspecified perils in its wake.

The Second Empire found favor with most businessmen and the Catholic Church. It wooed monarchists, local notables, and peasants and played to popular opinion. The regime skillfully used the prefects who headed each *département* to strengthen its authority, and it managed to keep the press in line without official censorship. Throughout Europe people watched with surprise that a government which claimed a democratic mandate could so tightly hold the reins of power, could promise both peace and national glory, and could sponsor programs for social welfare as well as economic growth.

Varied and innovative, the Second Empire has been seen by some historians as a kind of early New Deal and by others as a precursor of Fascism, but all consider it a significant effort to cope with the political implications of a mass industrial society. Napoleon III was influenced by Saint-Simonian socialism, drawn by liberal nationalism, and obsessed by his belief in his own destiny, his Napoleonic star. Alternately decisive and weak, farsighted and misled by vague dreams of glory, he was Napoleon the Little to his opponents, Napoleon the well-meaning to his hard-headed critics, the Emperor to most Frenchmen.

The decade of the 1850s witnessed an economic boom stimulated at least in part by the policies of the regime, which sought more systematically to foster economic growth than any other government of the period. Tax incentives and laws facilitating the formation of companies with limited liability encouraged investment. The state in addition created special investment funds (of which the Crédit Mobilier was the most famous), paid entrepreneurs a respect they had rarely enjoyed in France, and launched grand public works projects.

One of these was the elaborate rebuilding of Paris, ranging from a vast new sewer and water system to the city's great boulevards and parks, most of which date from this period. A pioneering venture in city planning, these undertakings typified the imperial style. The plans were reviewed by Napoleon III himself, who favored ostentatious and regular structures, and were carried out by his extraordinarily able prefect Georges Haussmann. Slums were cleared, often with painful dislocation for their residents; boulevards, planned for their aesthetic effect and as an aid to traffic, were also expected to make uprisings more difficult; façades often received more attention than the buildings behind them. And the whole project gave rise to rumors of political spoils and speculation. Yet the result was a city healthier and more convenient, envied and imitated throughout the world. The court of Napoleon and Empress

Eugénie was brilliant, and French prestige in the arts and sciences (Louis Pasteur achieved his first fame in this period) was never higher. In the Napoleonic tradition the government awarded talent with honors and promotions. The emperor, indefatigable patron and sponsor of educational and social reform, took credit for all this—more in fact than was his due.

Foreign policy, similarly meant to be popular, was marked more by public enthusiasm than by tangible gains. The Crimean War ended with a conference in Paris in 1856, and France's intervention in Italy's war against Austria in 1859 appeared to end in victory. While maintaining good relations with Great Britain, the empire proudly showed its radical roots by supporting the national aspirations not only of Italians but of the Poles who, ever restive, rose against Russian rule in 1863.

By the 1860s however the empire's fortunes were changing. Support of Italy had antagonized French Catholics; the annexation of Nice and Savoy, France's reward for that support, had aroused British suspicions; and the French public was troubled by the cost of military glory. Eager to strengthen his domestic support, Napoleon welcomed the chance to intervene in Mexico as an inexpensive venture that would earn Catholic gratitude, but that imperial scheme ended in disaster. England, Spain, and France had sent troops there in 1861 to force payment of foreign debts; and the French remained when the others withdrew, defeating the liberal Mexican government and imposing the Archduke Maximilian of Austria as Emperor of Mexico in 1864. Unexpected Mexican resistance and opposition from the United States forced the French to abandon Maximilian, who was defeated and executed in 1867. Napoleon's vague hope to benefit from the decline of the Ottoman Empire or the expansion of Prussia fared no better when confronted with the clearer and more consistent policies of Bismarck.

The regime was also losing support at home. The church, resentful of the state's energetic intrusion into its traditional spheres of charity and public welfare, was angered by the government's close supervision of its affairs, and Catholics became more militant in their criticism of Napoleon's domestic and foreign policies. A far-reaching tariff agreement with Great Britain in 1860, followed by similar treaties with other countries, was a step toward free trade that appealed to liberal economists but upset many businessmen, particularly those dependent for survival on France's traditionally high tariffs. Laborers wanted more than public works and the government's support for mutual-aid societies. Restrictions of political freedom were increasingly resented, and ideological clashes became more intense.

Aware of these dissatisfied voices, Napoleon III sought new support by gradually making his government more responsive. In 1860 the Corps Législatif was granted permission to present resolutions and to reply to the emperor's annual address. By 1868 freedom of the press and the right of assembly had been reestablished, and the legislature was being allowed to interrogate ministers. The regime established public secondary schools for girls, encouraged the formation of workingmen's organizations, and acknowledged the right to strike. This liberalism, however, alienated some old supporters without mollifying the empire's critics. In each election the opposition, much of it republican, gained seats until it held nearly half the lower house in 1869. On the first of the year in 1870, a full-fledged parliamentary system was adopted, with ministers responsible to the bicameral assembly and a republican, Émile Ollivier, as prime minister. Eager for public favor, the new administration took a nationalist stand against Prussia in a dispute to be discussed in section II, which helped bring about the Franco-Prussian war of 1870 and the end of the Second Empire. The promise of progressive rule and social order, once enough to win middle-class support, was not enough to keep it.

NATIONALISM AND FOREIGN POLICY

Louis Napoleon was not the only ruler to recognize the political rewards of a daring foreign policy. Shortly after the Austrian Empire regained its authority with the defeat of the Hungarian revolution in 1849, Schwarzenberg sought to reassert Austria's influence over the other German states. His chance came when King Frederick William IV of Prussia, moved by the nationalist vision of leading a united Germany, called a meeting of German rulers. Many were reluctant to attend, and Schwarzenberg shrewdly reconvoked the diet of the old German confederation. This put the German states in the dangerous position of choosing between Austrian and Prussian leadership. Austria, with the clear support of Russia, then threatened Prussia with war, citing a number of issues at conflict. Before so grave a challenge, Prussia backed down, and in a conference at Olmütz in 1850, promised to abandon the scheme for a German union under her command. Hapsburg hegemony over Germany seemed assured, reestablished by a fearless minister.

The British foreign secretary also exploited the advantages of an assertive policy. Henry John Temple, Viscount Palmerston, was a flamboyant aristocrat, frequently at odds with his cabinet colleagues, who disapproved of his outspoken sympathy for liberal regimes on the Continent. Often indifferent to procedural niceties, he was shrewdly alert to public opinion. Thus Palmerston saw a national issue in the claims made by one Don Pacifico against the Greek government. An Athenian mob had burned his house because he was a Portuguese Jew, but Pacifico who was born in Gibraltar held British citizenship. Palmerston vigorously supported his demands for compensation, sending notes, threats, and finally the British fleet to Greece until an indemnity was paid.

Responsible statesmen in Great Britain were outraged, but Palmerston defended himself in one of the great speeches in the history of the House of Commons. Dramatically he recalled the pride of ancient Romans, who could say, *"Civis Romanus sum,"* "I am a Roman citizen," and know themselves secure throughout their empire. A British subject, Palmerston declared, "in whatever land he may be, shall feel confident that the watchful eye and strong arm of England will protect him against injustice and wrong." To the public at least, Palmerston was vindicated. Like Napoleon III, he recognized the appeal of nationalism.

THE CRIMEAN WAR

The restless ambitions and search for prestige that had come to characterize international relations were a direct cause of the war of France and Great Britain against Russia in 1854–1856. Nothing less would have made so serious a conflict out of the opposing claims to Jerusalem's holy places put forth by Roman Catholic and Greek Orthodox monks in 1851.

France, citing traditions ranging from the Crusades to Richelieu, supported the Latin monks and pressed the Ottoman sultan, whose empire included Jerusalem, to grant them specific privileges. For Louis Napoleon the issue provided a further chance to win Catholic support at home and to upset the balance of power established at the Congress of Vienna. Russia, rising to the defense of the Orthodox faith and anticipating the collapse of the Ottoman Empire, reacted strongly. She demanded a protectorate over Orthodox churches within the empire and in 1853 increased her pressure by occupying the Danubian principalities of Wallachia and Moldavia, lands under Ottoman suzerainty which had last been occupied by Russia in 1848 to put down revolution there. That move increased the involvement of Britain, ever inclined to see a threat to her empire in any Russian expansion. The British encouraged the sultan to resist Russia's demands.

Diplomatic activity reached fever pitch, and Britain and France sent their fleets into the Aegean Sea. Repeatedly negotiations broke down, and in October 1853 the sultan exuberantly declared war on Russia. After Russian forces destroyed an Ottoman fleet, Britain and France declared war on Russia in March 1854, a step greeted with patriotic enthusiasm in London and Paris. Austria, suspicious of a French emperor who supported nationalism in Poland and Italy and unwilling to bear the brunt of a Russian attack, remained neutral. But when Russia withdrew from the Danubian principalities in August 1854, Austria occupied them in turn, leaving the contending powers without a battlefield.

Six months after war was declared, British and French forces landed in the Crimea to continue the fighting against Russia in battles conducted with remarkable incompetence on both sides. Russia could not mobilize or effectively deploy the large armies that made her so feared, and Britain's supply system proved incapable of sustaining hostilities from such a distance. In 1855 the allies welcomed the aid of little Piedmont.

A full year after invading the Crimea, the allied forces finally took Sevastopol. That defeat, threats that Austria and Sweden might

The press did much to popularize the Crimean War. This illustration shows Florence Nightingale rushing to the front. (Photo: The Granger Collection)

enter the war, and the accession of Alexander II led Russia to sue for peace in December. The final terms were to be set at a European congress in Paris, attended by the belligerents and by Austria and Prussia.

The foreign ministers who met in Paris dealt amiably and easily with the specific issues arising from the war. Beyond establishing the status quo ante, the treaty admitted the Ottoman Empire into the European concert, guaranteed her integrity, and greatly reduced Russian influence. Russia ceded some territory at the mouth of the Danube River, surrendered her claims to any protectorate over Christians, and accepted the demilitarization of the Black Sea. Only this last point really rankled.

Napoleon III was unable, however, to launch the full assault on the treaties of 1815

he wished for; Austria and Great Britain distrusted his interest in reshaping Europe. Although the emperor wanted to include it, the question of Polish independence never got on the agenda. Italy on the other hand was discussed—the only concession Piedmont won, but even that was enough to produce patriotic outbursts in Italy and terror in Austria. The issue of the Danubian principalities with its implications of Balkan nationalism also frightened Austria. The possibility that the two provinces might be joined was too divisive to be settled then, but by 1858 they were in effect united, the basis for a Rumanian national state.

In many respects the congress had behaved liked its predecessors, but it marked an important change in the prominence of nationalism, even when formally ignored, and in the demise of that alliance of Austria, Prussia, and Russia which had preserved European peace and conservatism for so long. Russia and Austria had cooperated in opposing nationalism and revolution through the crises of 1848, but competition between them for influence in the Balkans now became one of the facts of European politics. Indeed Russia now counted for less in purely European matters and found herself turning with gratitude to signs of sympathy from Napoleon III. The fact that the congress met in Paris rather than Vienna indicated the altered prestige of the European states. The old balance of power, the old concert of conservative nations, the old diplomacy of European aristocrats, who largely ignored public sentiment—all this had been shaken.

Almost 500,000 soldiers died in the Crimean War, the highest toll of any European conflict between the Napoleonic Wars and World War I. Two-thirds of the casualties were Russian, and two-thirds of all losses resulted from sickness and bad care. Yet the outbreak of war produced a surge of enthusiasm no government could ignore. The diplomacy that led to it and the way it was conducted were shaped by concern for national prestige, and the parades of magnificently uniformed soldiers, like the heroic stories reported by an aggressive journalism for an eager public, underscored the political importance of the war. In those terms France, Piedmont, and Great Britain all gained from it; the Ottoman Empire, under Western pressure, began to adopt the modernizing institutions of the West; and Russia, sobered by defeat, launched an era of fundamental reform

unequaled since the days of Peter the Great. In Italy and Germany the way was opening for still more drastic changes.

II. TWO NEW NATIONAL STATES

Since the French Revolution the sense of common nationality had grown stronger among Germans and among Italians, supported by common experience and economic change. That nationalism, exemplified by Mazzini, was fostered by numerous organizations, defined in propaganda that ranged from clandestine pamphlets to major literature, and expressed in many a local uprising. Especially among the middle class, nationalist feeling became intense, the core of campaigns for representative government, efficient administration, a dependable system of justice, and a national economy. And the regrouping of domestic forces after 1848, which gave greater prominence to the middle class, as well as the altered international situation following the Crimean War provided new opportunities for the nationalist movements of Central Europe.

THE UNIFICATION OF ITALY

In Italy the revolutions of 1848 established that nationalism was a powerful political force. Their failure made it equally clear that separate revolts were not enough to overcome the arms of Austria, the main opponent of Italian unification. The Mazzinian program was thus cast in doubt, but so were old dreams of papal leadership in the national cause. Of the several Italian states, only Piedmont, despite having been twice defeated by the Austrians, maintained an independent foreign policy, still flew the tricolor of Italian nationalism, and kept her constitution.

Piedmont had other strengths. Her aristocracy, narrow in outlook, Catholic, and conservative, was dedicated to the service of the state; and her monarch, Victor Emmanuel II, though no liberal, ruled with a parliament and longed for a patriotic war against Austria. Although a small state, the kingdom had a tradition of military strength and bureaucratic rectitude. More recently her government had encouraged commerce and the building of railroads and had limited the privileges of the Catholic Church, setting Piedmont on the liberal course established earlier in Great Britain, France, and Belgium.

These policies acquired firmer purpose in 1852, when Count Camillo Cavour became prime minister. A member of the Piedmontese aristocracy, well-traveled in France and England, Cavour was a gentleman-farmer who believed in economic and scientific progress, representative government with limited suffrage, the rule of law, and religious tolerance. Nationalism he understood primarily as an avenue to modernization, and he found in free trade, sound finances, and railroads a power that could remake Piedmont.

Cavour pursued his liberal goals with tactical brilliance, skillfully using newspapers and parliamentary debate to mold public opinion. With some disloyalty to the cabinet of which he was a member, he suddenly formed a new parliamentary coalition of the left center and right center, a base of power from which he dominated both king and parliament from 1852 until his death in 1861. In that brief time he established himself as one of the outstanding statesmen of the century.

Piedmont's internal strength was Cavour's first concern, but he also sought to make his state the center of Italy's resurgence, the Risorgimento.[1] He welcomed exiles from other parts of the peninsula, encouraged the nationalist press, and sought every opportunity for symbolic gestures of patriotism. He was aided in this by the Italian National Society, one of whose founders was Daniele Manin, the president of the short-lived Venetian republic in 1848. The National Society propagandized for Italian unity under Piedmont's king and established secret committees in most of the cities of Italy. Its members were predominantly liberal aristocrats, local lawyers, and professors. In calling for Italian unity, they freely borrowed and effectively used the ideas of Mazzini, but this idealism was combined with hard-headed insistence on the need for international alliances and military force to defeat Austria. Economic liberalism largely replaced more generous and vaguer social theories, and talk of revolution did not lessen the commitment to a national state that would protect private property, persecute no one, and maintain social order.

Most of all Cavour depended on astute foreign policy. He had pushed for Piedmont's participation in the Crimean War and was rewarded with the discussion of the Italian question at the Congress of Paris. Using his state's enhanced international position, British sympathy, and Napoleon III's ambition, he hoped to gather the forces to defeat Austria.

This hope turned on Louis Napoleon, whose Italian connections, nationalist leanings, and restless search for prestige Cavour assiduously played upon. He was aided by liberal sympathy throughout Western Europe and even by Italian revolutionaries, whose activities helped convince many that an Italy unliberated would remain a dangerous source of European instability.

At last, in July 1858, Cavour and Napoleon III met secretly at the little spa of Plombières in eastern France to plot war against Austria. They agreed that Piedmont would acquire all of northern Italy and that the grand duchy of

---

[1] Risorgimento, now the historian's label for the whole period of Italian unification, was a term meaning "resurgence" often used by nationalists and made the title of a liberal newspaper which Cavour helped to found and edit.

Tuscany would be enlarged and become the Kingdom of Central Italy. These two large states and the Kingdom of the Two Sicilies would then form a confederation under the pope. France would receive Nice and Savoy, thus strengthening her border, and Napoleon's cousin Prince Jérôme would marry Victor Emmanuel's reluctant fifteen-year-old daughter. In his desire to tie his throne to the legitimate monarchs of Europe, Napoleon III shared the old-fashioned concerns of Louis Philippe and Napoleon I, but he also hoped to satisfy nationalism while using monarchy as a bulwark against radicalism. The arrangement contrived at Plombières would provide multiple openings for Bonapartist influence while preventing the formation of a unified Italian state that could become a threat to France. The plan, too delicately balanced to be practical, sought cautious ends through cynical daring.

After Plombières Cavour encouraged the nationalist demonstrations spreading throughout Italy but tried to prevent the kind of outbreak that might cause Napoleon to change his mind. While Cavour hunted for an excuse for war, Great Britain pressured for peace and France hesitated. But Austria, watching young Lombards and Venetians escape conscription by streaming to Piedmont as volunteers, determined to end the nationalist threat once and for all. She sent Piedmont an ultimatum so strong that Cavour needed only to reply with cautious dignity in order to have his war. On April 29, 1859, Austria invaded Piedmont, and France went to the rescue of a small state attacked by her giant neighbor.

The rapid movement of large French armies was impressive, but thereafter the war was fought with little tactical brilliance on either side. In June the Austrians were seriously defeated at Magenta, in Lombardy; but the Battle of Solferino, three weeks later, was as indecisive as it was bloody. As the Aus-

trians retreated to the fortresses controlling the Lombard plain, Napoleon lost his taste for war; and rather than face further losses, a long siege, the danger that Prussia would come to Austria's aid, and discontent at home, he unilaterally agreed to a truce. The emperors of France and Austria met at Villafranca in July to establish the terms of peace, which included ceding Lombardy but not Venezia to Piedmont and maintaining the other Italian states as before (see Map 24.1).

The Formation of the Italian Kingdom

Those states, however, had not survived the excitement of a national war. Gentle revolutions accompanied the march of Piedmontese troops throughout northern Italy. Where local patriots gathered in the streets, the dukes of Modena, Parma, and Tuscany simply fled. In these areas and in part of the Papal States, supporters of Cavour—usually members of the National Society—assumed dictatorial powers in provisional governments that adopted Piedmontese laws and currency and called for elections to representative assemblies. Thus the terms of the Villafranca truce could not be carried out. The provisional regimes cautiously went their way, carefully maintaining order, and after a few months arranged plebiscites—a device Napoleon could hardly reject —on the question of annexation to Piedmont. Italians trooped to the polls with bands playing and flags waving, peasants behind their lord and workers with their guilds. The result was as overwhelming as the plebiscites of France; and Victor Emmanuel quietly accepted the request to rule from the Alps to Rimini, on the Adriatic. The province of Savoy and the city of Nice were turned over to France.

The extension of the Piedmontese state was a triumph of moderate liberals with which more democratic nationalists were not altogether content, and sputtering revolts in Sicily

MAP 24.1: THE UNIFICATION OF ITALY 1859–1920

Within the map:

SWITZERLAND

SAVOY
(To France 1860)

AUSTRIA

TYROL
1919

Bolzano

Adda R.
Lake Como

Trent
Adige R.

Piave R.

LOMBARDY

Magenta

Milan

Peschiera

VENEZIA

Gorizia

Turin

Ticino R.

PIEDMONT

Solferino

Verona

Villafranca
Legnago

Trieste

Alessandria

Mantua

FRANCE

Verona

Venice

Fiume 1924

Po R.

PARMA

Parma

ISTRIA
1919

NICE
(To France 1860)

Genoa

Modena

Ferrara

MODENA

Bologna

ROMAGNA

Rimini

LUCCA

Lucca

SAN MARINO

Zara
1920

Pisa

Arno R.

Florence

Urbino

YUGOSLAVIA

TUSCANY

Siena

MARCHES

Ancona

Perugia

PAPAL

LISSA

ELBA

UMBRIA

STATES

CORSICA
(French)

Ajaccio

Civitavecchia

Tiber R.

Rome

A D R I A T I C   S E A

LACOSTA
1920

CAPRERA

Gaeta

Volturno R.

Bari

SARDINIA

Naples

Taranto

SASENO

ALBANIA

T Y R R H E N I A N   S E A

CORFU

GREECE

KINGDOM OF THE

TWO SICILIES

S E A

M E D I T E R R A N E A N

Palermo

Messina

SICILY

Catania

Syracuse

TUNISIA

PANTELLERIA

Annexed 1860

PELAGIE I.

MALTA (British)

Legend:

Kingdom of Sardinia at 1859

Areas Annexed in 1859

Areas Annexed in 1860

Areas Annexed in 1866

Areas Annexed in 1870

Areas Annexed from 1919 to 1924

Italian Boundary at 1924

◇ Fortress

0   50   100   150 miles

gave them a chance to lead a different sort of Risorgimento. Former Mazzinians gathered guns in Genoa and laid plans for an expedition which Cavour dared neither support nor oppose. The leader of this daring venture was Giuseppe Garibaldi. Exiled for his Mazzinian activity in the 1830s, Garibaldi had spent ten years fighting for democratic causes in South America, returning to Italy in time to take part in the wars of 1848. He had directed the heroic defense of the Roman Republic in 1849 and led the most effective corps of volunteers fighting for Piedmont in 1859. One of the most popular figures in Italy, he set sail for Sicily one night early in May 1860 with a thousand men, mainly middle-class youths from Lombardy, Venezia, and the Romagna.

No event in the nineteenth century so captured the popular imagination everywhere as that daring venture. The Expedition of the Thousand was like some ancient epic come to life in an industrial age: untrained men, wearing the red shirts Garibaldi had adopted in South America, fought with bravery and discipline, enthusiastically supported in the countryside. Garibaldi's tactics confused and defeated the Bourbon generals, despite their far larger and better-equipped forces. In two weeks the Red Shirts occupied Palermo and within two months all of Sicily except Messina. Volunteers flocked from all over Italy, and money was collected for them in the streets, at theaters, and at special meetings from New York to Stockholm.

Garibaldi proclaimed his loyalty to Victor Emmanuel, but he was equally open about his distrust of Cavour, who in turn feared the undiplomatic brashness as well as the republican and radical sentiments of the Garibaldians. When in August Garibaldi sailed across the strait and landed on the Italian mainland, declaring Rome and not just Naples to be his goal, Cavour determined to recapture control. He encouraged uprisings in the Papal States

and then sent Piedmontese troops into the region in the name of order. Carefully skirting the city of Rome, they moved south to meet Garibaldi. On September 18, between lines of suspicious men, Giuseppe Garibaldi and Victor Emmanuel rode out to shake hands. Piedmontese appointees quickly replaced the officials named by Garibaldi, who added to his legend by disdaining all proffered honors and quietly sailing with a bag of seed for his island retreat on Caprera. Plebiscites in the newly conquered provinces produced an almost unanimous vote for union, and in March 1861 the Kingdom of Italy was proclaimed before the first Italian parliament. The moderate liberalism of Cavour had triumphed.

Political and Economic Problems 1860–1876

Cavour's death shortly afterward was the first of many setbacks the new kingdom suffered, though the problems Italy now faced were in any case less susceptible to political solutions. The great differences among the regions of Italy seemed to argue for a decentralized federal system, but wartime conditions and fear of separatism prompted the government simply to extend Piedmontese administration and law. Too often, especially in the south, officials with an alien accent applying strange laws seemed almost foreign occupiers. Southern poverty and traditions of local patronage and corruption hobbled the new regime. Outbursts of brigandage in the south, occasionally supported by exiled Bourbons, the papacy, and Spanish Carlists, were an inchoate social protest which the new government met with military suppression, expending more lives than in all the wars of the Risorgimento.

Thrilled to have accomplished so much, Italian patriots could not accept the exclusion of Rome and Venice from united Italy, but both were international problems. Catholics throughout the world, convinced that papal

THE
IMAGE
OF
MAN
IN MODERN ART

The birth of the modern world is linked with two revolutions—the industrial revolution, symbolized by the invention of the steam engine, and the political revolution, which began in America and France under the banner of democracy. Both are still going on. Industrialization and democracy, as goals, are sought all over the world. Western science and political ideology (and in their wake all the other products of our civilization) are spreading to the remotest corners of the globe. Their impact has transformed every facet of our lives, at a rate so rapid and violent that many of us are said to be suffering from "future shock."

How have these twin revolutions affected the artist? His position in the modern world, when measured against the standards of the past, can only be called paradoxical. Industrialization has produced vast new wealth, but the share of our income, public or private, spent on art patronage is very much less than it was in earlier times. Yet the artist's public has grown tremendously in comparison with the past; museums, most of them founded within the past hundred years, attract millions of visitors today, and books on modern art are available in every bookshop. The artist's prestige, too, if not his financial condition, is higher than ever before. In antiquity and the Middle Ages there had been no distinction between art and craft; the Renaissance invented the concept of artistic genius but reserved it for a very few such as Leonardo da Vinci and Michelangelo, and even they were dependent on the wishes of their patrons. From the early nineteenth century on, however, artists have been acclaimed as superior to any established authority, subservient to nothing but their own impulses. They assumed, in fact, a role as exalted and as independent from the rest of society as the prophets of the Old Testament. But, like prophets, artists now had to face the prospect of being without honor in their own country. Indeed, they were expected to be. The modern artist's ideal is the bohemian, the "glorious failure" who spends his life neglected and ridiculed, only to be hailed as a genius by posterity. Actually, few of them have had careers exemplifying this pattern—Vincent van Gogh is the most famous case—yet there can be no doubt that the modern artist's lot has been more troubled than that of his predecessors in earlier periods. His freedom had to be purchased at the expense of security. Even artists who were financially successful have often felt it incumbent upon them to live as if they were not, so as to avoid becoming dependent on the public's favor which to them seemed a betrayal of their calling.

In a world without the framework of traditional constraints, the artist's latitude of action is both more frightening and more exhilarating than anybody else's. One of the modern artist's risks—and at the same time an acknowledgment of his importance—is suppression for ideological reasons. In Hitler's Germany any artist who did not work in the government-approved style was declared "degenerate" and forbidden to exhibit; a similar *lack of freedom prevails in Russia today, where the dogma of "socialist realism" is enforced, even though in the early years after the Revolution of 1917 modern artists were welcomed as kindred spirits since they, too, were revolutionary. In the West too there have been times when artists working in unfamiliar idioms were denounced by conservative politicians as "subversive." Such experiences only tend to reinforce the modern artist's distrust of the Establishment. Nor can he rely on his public, which is swayed all too often by the tides of taste and fashion. The modern artist thus seems to be forever cast in the role of the outsider, regardless of his fame or prestige.*

This basic change in the artist's condition may help to account for the fact that no coherent image of man has emerged in modern art. The shared values which enabled the artists of earlier ages to coin such an image have either disappeared or lost their reality; Jupiter (as Karl Marx once observed) could not survive against the lightning rod. Even portraiture, a continuous and vital tradition since the Early Renaissance, succumbed to the invention of photography in the mid-nineteenth century (see Plate 49). What, then, could take the place of traditional subject matter? The answer is summed up in such nineteenth-century slogans as "art for art's sake" or Walter Pater's claim that "all art aspires to the condition of music." Music, needless to say, is nonrepresentational; it arouses emotion through the harmonious and rhythmic manipulation of sound. Once it was acknowledged as the highest of the arts, painters began to think of their work as a kind of "visual music," governed by laws that could not be derived from observation of the outside world. At first they were content to give their works "musical" titles, with the subject mentioned only in second place as a sop to the public (the picture popularly known as "Whistler's Mother" was exhibited as "Arrangement in Black and Grey: The Artist's Mother" but by 1910 some painters had gone completely "nonobjective" by eliminating representation altogether, and their successors are still with us today.

Wherever we do encounter the human image in nineteenth-century art, man's condition is seen as shaped by his environment, physical or social, as in Daumier's "Third-Class Carriage" (Plate 55), Brown's "The Last of England" (Plate 56), Courbet's "Stone Breakers" (Plate 57), and Degas's "Glass of Absinthe" (Plate 58). The sympathy these pictures evoke has been consciously avoided by Seurat, whose "Bathers" (Plate 59) are so depersonalized that we perceive them only as part of their setting rather than as individuals. A "musical" title would seem entirely appropriate to such a painting. It is only in what may be broadly termed the expressionist tradition of modern art that the human image retains a central importance; but its goal is to probe extreme states of the psyche, not to define the nature of man. The beginnings of this line of development go back to the great French Romantics of the early nineteenth century: Géricault's "Madman"

(Plate 50) leads to Munch's "Scream" (Plate 61) seventy years later, and ultimately to Kienholz's "State Hospital" (Plate 64), just as Delacroix's "Chopin" (Plate 51) is prophetic of van Gogh's "Self-Portrait" (Plate 60), Rouault's "Christ" (Plate 62), and Picasso's "Weeping Woman" (Plate 63). Such images invite a twofold interpretation. They are surely signs of a general and continuing crisis due to the revolutionary changes we have been experiencing ever since the end of the eighteenth century. At the same time they afford an insight into the cause of these changes: Western man's heightened awareness of his own intellectual, moral, and emotional powers. Having so vastly expanded our range of thought, action, and feeling, we are faced with the task of redefining our own identity, to give meaning to our existence, outside the metaphysical framework that sheltered our forefathers. The modern artist senses, more sharply than the rest of us, that this is indeed a time to try men's souls.

Ingres, whose long career spans the first two-thirds of the nineteenth century, was the greatest disciple of David (see Plate 46). He is usually called a Neoclassicist and his opponents Romantics. Their quarrels recall the old debate between "Poussinists" and "Rubenists" (see Plates 43–45), with Ingres insisting that drawing is superior to color while the Romantics maintained the contrary. Actually, the views of both factions were far more doctrinaire than their pictures. In his portrait of *Louis Bertin*, Ingres's allegiance seems to be to observed reality pure and simple rather than to any theoretical convictions. There is so little "style" here that at first glance the picture looks like a superior kind of photograph. Had it been painted a decade later Ingres might well have been accused of working from a daguerreotype. In fact Ingres's realism and the development of photography sprang from the same impulse: a demand for the unvarnished scientific truth. Nothing less would do for the age of the industrial revolution. When the first practical photographic processes became available in the late 1830s, they were hailed as "the pencil of nature," and portraiture became their chief task. Thus Ingres was the last great professional in a field soon to be monopolized by the camera. His *Bertin,* however unvarnished it may seem, is a masterpiece of interpretation, endowing the sitter with a massive force of personality that is almost frightening. Individualistic, self-reliant, aggressive, Bertin seems the perfect image of the bourgeois entrepreneur, the hero of "free enterprise."

Plate 49. Dominique Ingres
LOUIS BERTIN
1832, canvas, height 46"
Louvre Museum, Paris

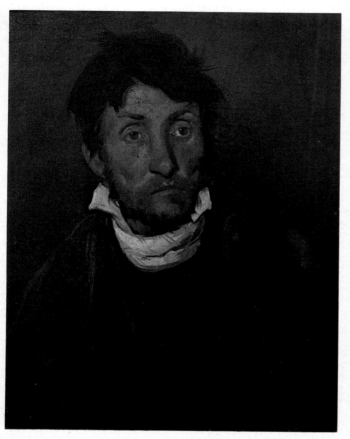

Plate 50. Théodore Géricault
THE MADMAN
1821–1824, canvas, height 24"
Museum of Fine Arts, Ghent

If Ingres's *Bertin* represents the class of men that shaped the character of post-Napoleonic Europe, the two portraits on these pages—one of a madman, the other of a great composer—seem more closely related to each other than to the forces and events of their time. Ingres shows his sitter as he wanted to be seen, squarely facing his public; Géricault's and Delacroix's subjects, in contrast, are so completely caught up in their private worlds that they remain unaware of the observer. They are indeed not portraits in the traditional sense but studies of extreme states of the human condition, and it is this that stamps them as Romantic.

Romanticism refers to an attitude of mind, rather than to a specific style, and is therefore harder to define. The word derives from the vogue for medieval tales of adventure, called "romances" because they were written in a Romance language, not in Latin. This interest in the long-neglected "dark ages," however, sprang from a revulsion against established values of any kind and had its roots in a craving for emotional experience. Almost any experience would do, real or imaginary, provided it was intense enough. The declared aim of the Romantics was to tear down the artifices barring the way to a "return to nature"—nature the unbounded, wild and ever-changing, nature the sublime and picturesque. Were man to act "naturally," giving his impulses free rein, evil would disappear. In the name of nature the Romantics worshiped liberty, power, love, violence, the Greeks, the Middle Ages, or anything that aroused their response, but actually they worshiped emotion as an end in itself. At its extreme this attitude could be expressed only through direct action, not through works of art, for the creation of a work of art demands some detachment and self-awareness. What Wordsworth, the great Romantic poet, said about poetry—that it is "emotion recollected in tranquillity"—applies also to painting. To cast his fleeting experience into permanent form, the Romantic artist needs a style. It is hardly surprising that painters such as Géricault and Delacroix preferred the vivid color, broad, open brushwork, and spontaneous emotion of Rubens, Hals, Velázquez, and Goya (see Plates 37–39, 48) to the meticulous draftsmanship and painstaking detail of Poussin, David, and Ingres (see Plate 43, 46, 49). Géricault, the older of the two, began his career as an admirer of Gros (see Plate 47), at a time when Napoleon was at the height of his glory. He died in 1824, at the age of 33. His interest in man's emotional life led him to befriend the director of the Paris insane asylum, for whom he painted a series of portraits of individual patients illustrating various types of derangement. Our picture belongs to this group. Géricault's sympathy toward the subject, his ability to see the victims of mental disease as fellow human beings rather than as accursed or bewitched outcasts, is one of the noblest fruits of the Romantic movement.

Delacroix had his first great public success in the year of Géricault's death. Until his own death almost forty years later, he remained the foremost Romantic painter of France and the acknowledged antagonist of Ingres. He rarely did portraits other than those of his personal friends and fellow victims of the "Romantic agony" such as the Polish composer Frédéric Chopin. Here we see the image of the Romantic hero at its purest: a blend of Gros's *Napoleon* and Géricault's *Madman,* he is consumed by the fire of his genius.

Plate 51. Eugène Delacroix
FRÉDÉRIC CHOPIN
1838, canvas, height 18″
Louvre Museum, Paris

Landscape had been part of the Western tradition of painting as early as Roman times (see Plate 6). In the seventeenth century it became an important subject in its own right. The Romantics, with their worship of nature, raised it to a new level of significance; landscape painting conveyed some of their most profoundly felt emotions. The *Monk at the Seashore* by the German painter Caspar David Friedrich, an early and memorable example, embodies an experience central to the Romantic imagination: that of the sublime. The tiny, lonesome figure contemplating the immensity of sea and sky becomes a moving symbol of man's insignificance when confronted with the cosmos. Turner's *Slave Ship* seeks to achieve the same effect in more dramatic fashion. First entitled *Slavers Throwing Overboard the Dead and Dying—Typhoon Coming On,* the painting is, on one level of meaning, a protest against the inhumanity of the slave trade: threatened by a storm, the captain casts his human cargo overboard. The typhoon appears to be nature's retribution for his greed and cruelty, but it is also

Plate 52. William Turner
THE SLAVE SHIP
1839, canvas, height 36"
Museum of Fine Arts, Boston

more than that, a catastrophe that engulfs everything, not merely the slaver and his victims but the sea itself with its crowds of fantastic and oddly harmless-looking fish. While we sense the force of Turner's vision, most of us today, perhaps with a twinge of guilt, tend to enjoy this explosion of color for its own sake rather than as a vehicle for the awesome emotions the artist meant to evoke. The English art critic John Ruskin, who owned *The Slave Ship,* saw in it "the true, the beautiful, and the intellectual"; to modern eyes it seems, rather, "an airy vision, painted with tinted steam" (to cite the uncharitable but acute characterization of Turner's work by John Constable, another important English landscape painter of the early nineteenth century). The very simplicity of Friedrich's *Monk at the Seashore,* painted three decades earlier, strikes us as more convincing than do the pyrotechnics of Turner.

Plate 53. Caspar David Friedrich
MONK AT THE SEASHORE
1808, canvas, height 43¼"
Schloss Charlottenburg
Berlin (West)

Plate 54. Camille Corot
SELF-PORTRAIT
ca. 1835, canvas, height 13½"
Uffizi Gallery, Florence

This self-portrait by the great French land-scapist Camille Corot is so cool and straightforward that we can hardly think of it as Romantic. It contains no hint of the emotionalism we have come to associate with the movement. Yet in at least one important respect it mirrors a characteristically Romantic attitude—it is painted out-of-doors, in brilliant sunshine. Until the early nineteenth century, painting had been confined to the studio; artists would record their impressions of nature in drawings or watercolors, but to paint out-of-doors was regarded as undesirable, technically as well as aesthetically. The equipment it demanded was far too cumbersome to be carried about, and the process itself was too slow to record the ever-changing conditions of directly observed nature. The Romantics, sensitive to transitory moods, upset this centuries-old tradition; while some of them continued to paint landscapes indoors, others insisted on working under the open sky so as to capture all the subtle gradations of light and atmosphere they experienced at a particular moment. Soon industry came to their aid by producing ready-to-use oil paints in tubes, packed in convenient boxes, as well as portable easels and stools. The pictures produced on the spot with the aid of such equipment were small in size and lacked the precise detail of earlier landscapes, but they had a freshness and immediacy never achieved before. Corot was a pioneer in this novel kind of land-scape painting; it is hardly a surprise, therefore, that he should have chosen to do his self-portrait in the same way. We see him in his working clothes, observing himself with the same directness and clarity that distinguish his views of the French and Italian countryside. The result is strangely timeless—it might have been painted yesterday rather than in the heyday of Romanticism.

Within a few decades after its beginnings in the last eighteenth century, the industrial revolution had profoundly disturbed and transformed every facet of man's existence in the Western world. It was not until the middle of the nineteenth, however, that artists began to reflect these changes in the themes they chose for their work. *The Third-Class Carriage,* by the French cartoonist and painter Honoré Daumier, is a powerful early example. It captures a peculiarly modern human condition, "the lonely crowd": these people have in common only that they are traveling together in the same railway car. They take no notice of one another— each is alone with his own thoughts. Daumier explores this state with an insight into character and a breadth of sympathy worthy of Rembrandt, whose work he revered. His feeling for the dignity of the poor also suggests Louis Le Nain (see Plate 42), whose work had recently been rediscovered by French critics. Ironically, Daumier found no public for his paintings, even though he was famous for his satirical cartoons. Only a few friends encouraged him and, a year before his death in 1879, arranged his first one-man show.

Plate 55. Honoré Daumier
THIRD-CLASS CARRIAGE
ca. 1862, canvas, height 26"
The Metropolitan Museum of Art, Bequest of Mrs. H. O. Havemeyer, 1929
The H. O. Havemeyer Collection, New York

Plate 56. Ford Madox Brown
THE LAST OF ENGLAND
1852–1853, wood panel, height 32½″
City Museum and Art Gallery
Birmingham, England

Although Daumier's *Third-Class Carriage* has a contemporary theme, its style is akin to that of the great Romantic, Delacroix (see Plate 51), whose sweeping brushwork and dramatic lighting derive from the Baroque. Other mid-nineteenth-century painters reacted against Romanticism not only in their choice of subject matter but by adopting a radically different style, as evidenced on these two pages As early as 1846, the French poet and art critic Charles Baudelaire had called for paintings that would express "the heroism of modern life." His friend, the painter Gustave Courbet, made an artistic creed of this demand. A socialist in politics who was deeply affected by the revolutionary upheavals of 1848, Courbet came to believe that the Romantic stress on emotion and imagination was merely an escape from the realities of the time. The modern artist must rely on his own direct experience alone, he must be a realist ("I cannot paint an angel because I have never seen one," he said). Courbet's realism recalls the art of Caravaggio (see Plate 33); like Caravaggio, his work was denounced for its supposed vulgarity and lack of spiritual content. The storm broke when he exhibited *The Stone Breakers* (Plate 57), the first canvas fully embodying his goals. Courbet had seen two men working on a road and had asked them to pose for him in his studio. He has painted them solidly and matter-of-factly, without any pathos or sentiment; the young man's face is averted, the old one's half-hidden by a hat. Yet Courbet cannot have picked them casually; their contrast in age is significant—one is too old for such heavy work, the other too young. Endowed with the dignity of their symbolic status, they do not turn to us for sympathy. Another of Courbet's friends, the socialist Proudhon,

Plate 57. Gustave Courbet
THE STONE BREAKERS
1849, canvas, height 22½"
Collection Oskar Reinhart, Winterthur, Switzerland

likened them to a parable from the Gospels.

Meanwhile, a concern with the "heroism of modern life" asserted itself quite independently in England as well, although the movement lacked a leader of Courbet's stature and assertiveness. Its best known product is probably *The Last of England* (Plate 56) by Ford Madox Brown, which enjoyed vast popularity in the English-speaking world during the latter half of the century. The subject— a group of emigrants watching the coast of their homeland disappear as they set out on their long overseas journey—may no longer carry the same emotional charge it once did, yet there can be no question that Brown has treated an important modern theme and that he has done so with touching seriousness. If the pathos of the scene seems a bit theatrical to us, its documentary quality gains conviction from the impersonal precision of detail, which strikes us as almost photographic; no hint of subjective "handwriting" is permitted to intervene between us and the subject.

Plate 58. Edgar Degas
THE GLASS OF ABSINTHE
1876, canvas, height 36"
Louvre Museum, Paris

For realists such as Courbet or Ford Madox Brown, subject matter was a primary consideration; style was a means to an end, the end being to present significant aspects of modern life as concretely as possible. During the last third of the nineteenth century, this relationship came to be reversed: the "how" now overshadowed the "what." A group of painters in Paris, dubbed Impressionists by a hostile critic (because their work looked so sketchy and unfinished to him), painted "slices of life" that might or might not include human beings and that no longer claimed to be significant in themselves. What gave them importance was the way they were painted, their brilliance of light and color, their freshness and originality of vision. Often the scenes the Impressionists chose were studiedly casual, like *The Glass of Absinthe* (Plate 58) by Edgar Degas. The disenchanted pair at the café table is sharply observed but, as it were, out of the corner of the artist's eye. The design, at first glance, seems as accidental as a snapshot (Degas was an enthusiastic amateur photographer), yet the longer we look, the more we realize that everything has been made to dovetail precisely, that the zigzag of empty tables between us and the luckless couple reinforces their brooding loneliness. Degas had been trained in the tradition of Ingres (see Plate 49); this may account for his strong sense of human character, which sets him apart from his fellow Impressionists. Had he been born fifty years earlier, he might well have become the greatest professional portraitist of his time.

In one respect *The Glass of Absinthe* is uncharacteristic of Impressionism: its subdued color scheme. Seurat's *Bathers* (Plate 59), in contrast, shows the brightness and intensity which led one conservative critic to complain that such

Plate 59. Georges Seurat
BATHERS
1883–1884, canvas, height 79"
The National Gallery, London

pictures hurt his eyes. The choice of subject—people enjoying their leisure on a sunny midsummer day—is equally typical of Impressionist painting. So is its shimmering surface, which results from the way the paint has been applied in separate dots or flicks of pure color. Otherwise, however, Seurat's picture hardly conforms to what we would expect of a quick "impression"; the simplified, smooth contours and the deliberate spacing of these immobile figures give the scene a timeless stability such as we have not encountered since the time of Giotto and Masaccio (see Plates 14, 19). The triumph of Im-

pressionism had indeed been short-lived. Within less than twenty years after its creation in the late 1860s, some of its chief exponents began to search for a style that would combine the virtues of Impressionism with the solidity and durability of the Old Masters. Seurat was the most consistent and methodical of these "Post-Impressionists" (as they have come to be called for lack of a more striking term). The very fact that *Bathers* is a very large canvas, carefully prepared by numerous preliminary studies, demonstrates his ambition to rival the great wall painters of the Renaissance.

Plate 60. Vincent van Gogh
SELF-PORTRAIT
1889, canvas, height 22½"
Collection Mr. and Mrs. John Hay Whitney
New York

While Seurat was reshaping Impressionism into a more severe, classical style, Vincent van Gogh pursued the opposite direction, for he believed that Impressionism did not give the artist enough freedom to express his emotions. His early interests were in literature and religion; profoundly dissatisfied with the values of industrial society and imbued with a strong sense of mission, he worked for a while as lay preacher among poor coal miners before he took up painting. Van Gogh's early work has the dark tonality of Daumier and Courbet (see Plates 55 and 57). In 1886, however, he went to Paris, where he met Seurat and other leading artists who opened his eyes to the vital importance of color. His Impressionist phase, although brief, was of key importance for van Gogh's further development; Paris had taught him to see the sensuous beauty of the visible world, yet painting continued to be a vessel for his personal emotions. In order to explore this inner reality with the new means at his command he went to Arles, in the south of France. It was there, between 1888 and 1890, that he produced his greatest pictures. The sectarian Christianity of his early years now gave way to a mystic faith in a creative force animating all forms of life—the missionary had become a prophet. We see him in that role in the *Self-Portrait* on this page, his emaciated, luminous head set off against a whirlpool of darkness. "I want to paint men and women with that something of the eternal which the halo used to symbolize," van Gogh had written, groping to define the human essence that was his aim in pictures such as this. Clearly, the methodical color dots of Seurat were inadequate for his purpose. Van Gogh's brushwork is inalienably personal, each stroke filled with so much movement that it becomes not merely a deposit of

Plate 61. Edvard Munch
THE SCREAM
1893, canvas, height 36"
National Museum, Oslo

color but an incisive graphic gesture. At the time of this *Self-Portrait* the artist had already begun to suffer fits of mental illness. Despairing of a cure, he committed suicide a year later, for he felt very deeply that art alone made his life worth living.

Van Gogh's discontent with the spiritual ills of Western civilization was widely shared toward the end of the nineteenth century. It pervades the early work of a gifted Norwegian, Edvard Munch, who came to Paris in 1889 and was influenced by van Gogh, among others. *The Scream* is an image of fear, the terrifying, unreasoned fear we feel in a nightmare. Its long wavy lines seem to carry the echo of the scream into every corner of the picture, making of earth and sky one great sounding board of fear.

Plate 62. Georges Rouault
HEAD OF CHRIST
*1905, oil on paper, mounted on canvas
height 54", Collection of the Chrysler Museum at Norfolk
Gift of Walter P. Chrysler, Jr.*

The twentieth century may be said to have begun several years late, so far as art is concerned. Between 1901 and 1906, several comprehensive exhibitions of the work of the great Post-Impressionists were held in Paris, making their achievements known to a broad public for the first time. The young painters who had grown up in the morbid mood of the 1890s were profoundly impressed, and several developed a radical new style full of violent color and bold distortions. They so shocked critical opinion that they were dubbed the Fauves (the wild beasts), a label they wore with pride. What brought them together was not a common program but a shared sense of liberation; their work was only loosely related, and the group dissolved after a few years. Nevertheless, its members exerted a lasting influence on that broad stream of modern art which we call expressionism. Among the Fauves, Georges Rouault was the only one for whom the image of man remained a central concern, the true heir of van Gogh. The savage expressiveness of his huge *Head of Christ* mirrors his anguish at the corrupt state of the world. But this expressiveness does not reside only in the "image quality" of the face; the slashing strokes of the brush speak with equal eloquence of the artist's rage and compassion. If we cover up the upper third of the picture, it ceases to be a recognizable image, yet its expressive power is hardly diminished.

Picasso's *Weeping Woman,* by comparison, strikes us as far more disciplined but at the same time more daringly distorted, as if the artist had first carved up this woman's head and hand and then reassembled the anatomical details in a new order, making them spiky and sharpedged in the process. The inner logic of the method is attested by its success: Picasso has created an image of almost unbearable intensity, reflecting his horror and despair at the time of the Spanish Civil War, which he saw as the prelude of a still greater holocaust. The First World War had produced no such emotional involvement in Picasso; he spent those years perfecting a severely formal, semi-abstract style known as Cubism. It took the agony of his own country to turn him into an expressionist. In his *Weeping Woman* he found a way to put the austere precision of Cubism to new use, forging it into a tool for the creation of images that have lost none of their shattering force during the intervening decades. It was the finest moment in an artistic career without parallel in this century.

Plate 63. Pablo Picasso
WEEPING WOMAN
1937, canvas, height 23½″
Collection Mrs. Lee Miller Penrose, London

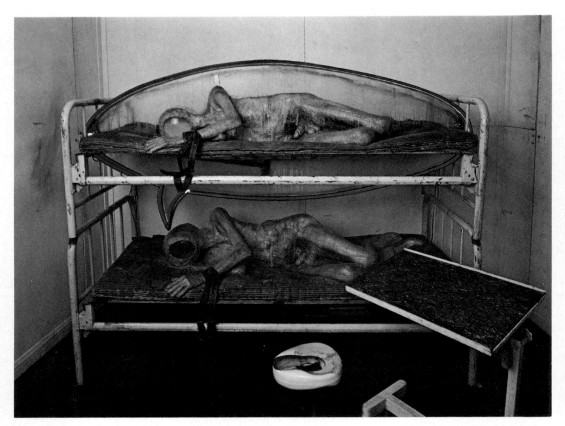

Plate 64. Edward Kienholz
THE STATE HOSPITAL
1966, mixed mediums, height 12'
Moderna Museet, Stockholm

Since the 1950s, we have been witnessing an artistic movement whose name, "Pop Art," derives from its use of popular imagery such as comic strips. To the Pop artist, our visual everyday world, shaped by the mass media and commercial culture and hitherto disdained as vulgar, is a fascinating source of raw material. The most radical results of this tendency to break down the barriers between art and reality are the so-called "environments," full-scale models of real-life situations that combine painting, sculpture, and stagecraft. Kienholz's *The State Hospital* is such an "environment": a cell in a ward for senile patients, with a naked old man strapped to the lower bunk. Neglect and mistreatment have reduced what little mental life he had almost to the vanishing point—his head is a glass bowl with live goldfish. But why the figure in the upper bunk? It duplicates the one below, but since it is enclosed within a comic-strip balloon it must be a mental image, the patient's awareness of himself. The balloon and the metaphoric goldfish bowl are alien to the horrifying realism of the scene, yet they play a vital part in it, for they make us think as well as feel. Kienholz's means may be Pop, but his aim is that of Greek tragedy.

independence required territorial sovereignty, opposed the annexation of Rome, which Napoleon III was pledged to protect; and Austrian troops, massed in Venezia, threatened the new Italian state. Within Italy the constant agitation over Rome, sometimes led by Garibaldi, weakened and divided the government.

The new nation acquired Venezia as a byproduct of the Austro-Prussian war of 1866 when both powers offered Venezia to Italy—Prussia as the reward for an alliance and Austria, at the last minute, in return for Italian neutrality. Italy honored her prior pledge to Prussia and went to war, suffering defeats on land and at sea off the Adriatic island of Lissa in the first naval engagement in Europe be-

The handshake of Victor Emmanuel and Garibaldi, which sealed the unification of Italy, as their armies met in 1860 became a favorite subject for illustrations of the Risorgimento. This one is English. (Photo: Culver Pictures)

tween ironclads. Prussia's quick victory ended the war, however, and the province of Venezia (without the Tyrol, though Garibaldi had won some of the few Italian victories there) was added to Italy. Rome, all that was left of Papal territory, was annexed when French troops withdrew during the Franco-Prussian War of 1870. Italy had gained her capital.

These were impressive achievements, even if they were less glorious than patriots had

MAP 24.2: THE UNIFICATION OF GERMANY

hoped, but they brought other difficulties to the fore. Italy passed a Law of Guarantees, assuring the full independence of the Vatican and providing an annual indemnity, but it was rejected by Pius IX, who declared himself a prisoner, refused to recognize the Italian state, and forbade Catholics to take part in national elections. Conflict with the church was a source of dangerous division, and Italy's gov-

erning class remained seriously isolated from the country at large. Because of the high property qualifications in Piedmont's constitution, now extended to all Italy, only 500,000 Italians out of a population of more than 25 million were able to vote; and this exclusion of the lower classes coupled with the abstention of Catholics made the subtleties of parliamentary conflict seem unreal.

Italy was poor, overwhelmingly agricultural, and the heir to generations of retrogressive policies; she had no coal or iron, and three-quarters of her population was illiterate. With liberal conviction the Italian government assumed the debts of the annexed states, accepted enormous military costs, and sought to balance the annual budget. Despite taxes among the highest in Europe, Italy necessarily continued to lag in schools, railways, and roads. The extension of Piedmontese law brought with it the confiscation of lands held by thousands of monasteries; but they commanded low prices because they were sold quickly, and they went to the wealthy rather than the peasants, who were supposed to benefit. Free trade within the nation and the lower Piedmontese tariffs brought many long-term benefits but instant distress to hundreds of small producers. For millions of artisans and peasants suffering the dislocations of war and social change, few tangible benefits followed from replacing reactionary dukes with a liberal national state.

Steadfastly Italy's leaders tried to foster the process of modernization. When the old Cavourians lost office to men of the left center in 1876, the change so dramatic to politicians was barely discernible to most Italians. A new generation of equally isolated middle-class leaders took charge in a country that was full of disappointments. But Italy was nonetheless free and reasonably stable, her national income rising. Her parliamentary institutions would be more severely tested later.

THE UNIFICATION OF GERMANY

The unification of Germany was completed a decade after Italy's, the work of Prussia, noted since the eighteenth century for efficient institutions that enabled her to wring impressive military strength from limited resources (see Map 24.2). Like Piedmont, Prussia began the 1850s with a new constitution at home but forced to accept Austrian terms abroad. Prussia was, however, a major European power with a long-recognized claim to economic and political leadership among the German states.

After Olmütz Austria appeared to dominate German affairs. But by 1853 all German states except those directly tied to Austria had joined the Zollverein; and Prussia's position had clearly changed by 1859, with Austria defeated in Italy and Napoleon III agreeing to a sudden truce in part at least out of fear of Prussia. Thus the Hohenzollern monarchy was the focus of nationalist opposition to Napoleon that spread through the German states. The German National Society, founded in the Rhineland in 1859 in direct imitation of the Italian National Society, propagandized vigorously for a Germany united under Prussia, citing her military power, the rapid industrialization underway in both the Rhineland and Prussia, and the liberal possibilities in Prussia's constitution.

Within Prussia the rule of William I which began in 1858 was also a turning point.[2] After a long period of reaction in which the press had been muzzled, public meetings repressed, many political leaders imprisoned, and the upper house of the legislature dominated by officials and landowners, William permitted such restrictions to be eased and turned his attention to improving the army.

The new era opened with a constitutional crisis. General Albrecht von Roon was appointed minister of war, and Helmuth von Moltke, his chief of staff, proposed a major military reorganization that would double the army's size and provide it with extensive new equipment. The plan won William's support, but the lower house of the legislature, in

---

[2] William I (1796–1888) became regent in 1858 when his brother Frederick William was adjudged insane and king on his brother's death in 1861.

which liberals had gained an unexpected majority, rejected it. Although the constitution of 1850 allowed universal male suffrage, it avoided democracy by dividing voters into three classes according to the taxes they paid, giving the two wealthier classes as many representatives as the third class, to which the overwhelming majority of the electorate belonged. In addition, the king had the right to veto any legislation and to appoint the ministers he chose. Designed to assure conservative dominance, the three-class system had the unexpected effect of magnifying the voice of new industrial wealth, and the majority of the Landtag was now prepared to challenge the monarch head on.

Liberals distrusted Prussian militarism and the Junkers who dominated the army, preferring a citizen militia; they also opposed increased expenditures. To William and his advisers, royal authority in the form of control of the army and the budget was at stake. As the conflict dragged on, they went ahead with the reorganization despite promises not to, paying for it out of general funds. Elections in 1862, however, only strengthened the opposition, which firmly insisted that the Prussian government be responsible to the legislature. William, calling on God and conscience, threatened abdication and then hesitantly named Otto von Bismarck his chief minister.

Bismarck was a Junker, better-educated than many, whose pride of caste and reactionary views were resented by liberals and whose intensity and imagination made him seem as erratic and dangerous as Napoleon III to most conservatives. For thirty years all of them would have to live with his stinging sarcasm, bruising contempt, and brilliance. Like Cavour, he saw more clearly than his king that nationalism could be used against revolution and made foreign policy the central concern as well as the justification of his program.

In the conflict with the Landtag, Bismarck gave the king firm support. He lectured the deputies on Prussia's national role and the chances too often missed in the past. If Germans looked to Prussia, it was because of her powerful army, not because of any liberal institutions; and he added, in the most famous statement he ever uttered, that "the great questions of the day will not be settled by speeches and majority decisions—that was the mistake of 1848 and 1849—but by blood and iron." He dissolved parliament and applied heavy government pressure in the subsequent elections. But despite conservative gains, the opposition increased still more. Bismarck then shifted tactics. He encouraged whatever divisions within parliament he could find, convoked it as little as possible, and ignored it whenever he could. He bribed the press with money and access to news, and he badgered and closed opposing papers. He made promotions in the civil service and judiciary dependent upon unquestionable loyalty to the government. Then, confident of the army and bureaucracy, Bismarck proceeded to spend funds and collect taxes without parliamentary authorization.

He sought to justify this defiance of Prussia's elected representatives through his foreign policy. He blocked Austria's continuing effort to reorganize the German Confederation, and his threat that perhaps the German Diet could be elected by universal suffrage stunned conservatives with its radicalism and liberals with its cynicism. While underscoring the limitations of Austria as a leader of any German national venture, he sought to win Russian friendship away from the Hapsburgs. When Russia repressed a Polish uprising in 1863 with such severity that Austria, France, and Britain joined in protest, Prussia supported the tsar. Renewed conflict over Schleswig and Holstein in the same year provided further opportunities for Prussian gains.

The Danish king outraged German nationalists by attempting to annex Schleswig and to extend his authority over Holstein. But Prussia thwarted any independent policy by the German Diet and persuaded Austria to join in war against Denmark in January 1864. Bismarck then foiled efforts at an international conference until the Danes were defeated and pressed for a plan whereby Schleswig was placed under Prussian administration and Holstein, surrounded by Prussian troops, under Austrian. The awkward arrangement, a potent source of contention between Austria and Prussia, was clearly impermanent.

Friction with Austria increased almost daily, and Bismarck prepared for war. He dangled visions of territorial gains along the Rhine before Napoleon III, won Italy's support by promising her Venezia, and gained Russia's assurance of neutrality. Both Austria and Prussia were already mobilizing when Austria convened the Holstein diet to discuss the duchy's unclear future. Bismarck denounced the move as a violation of their understandings, and Prussian troops marched into Holstein in June 1866.

Austria won the support of most of the German Confederation, but Prussia forced Hanover to surrender within two weeks. Three Prussian armies swept into Bohemia, and at the Battle of Sadowa, Austria suffered overwhelming defeat. The Austro-Prussian War lasted just seven weeks. Expert opinion had predicted a long fight, but Prussia, well-equipped and prepared, applied the lessons of the American Civil War, using railroads and telegraph to move with a speed for which Austria was unprepared.

Many Prussian conservatives had been shocked at Bismarck's belligerent treatment of Austria, but now they were eager to avenge Olmütz and to make heavy territorial demands on Austria. Yet against the wishes of his king and generals, Bismarck insisted that the Hapsburg monarchy be treated leniently; Austria surrendered no territory. But Prussia's gains elsewhere changed the face of Europe; she annexed Hanover, Nassau, Electoral Hesse, and Frankfurt, all of which had sided with Austria in the quarrel, and then established a confederation of North German states under her leadership. Austria was excluded from the new union, and the South German states agreed to a military alliance with Prussia on being told of Napoleon's hope (which Bismarck had encouraged) of some territorial compensation to balance Prussia's gains.

The North German Confederation

The constitution of the North German Confederation was in itself a triumph of Bismarckian policy. Member states, free to regulate their local affairs, were joined through a bicameral federal parliament. Its upper house, the Bundesrat, was composed of forty-three delegates sent in varying numbers from the separate states, with Prussia's seventeen more than the one-third necessary for a veto. The lower house, the Reichstag, was elected by universal manhood suffrage. Prussian dominance was assured in both. The confederation's hereditary chief executive was the king of Prussia, and he appointed the chancellor, who, responsible to no one else, shared with him full authority over foreign and military affairs. The armies of the separate states were combined under Prussian leadership.

In Prussia herself elections held during the war had strengthened the conservatives in the Landtag. The liberals still maintained a majority but chose to accept Bismarck's amazing success. After Prussia's victories, the Landtag voted a bill of indemnity, retroactively legalizing the taxes and expenditures Bismarck had imposed. Unwilling to appeal to the masses, the liberals were as soundly defeated as Austria. Encouraged that the new Reichstag would after all be elected by universal male suffrage, impressed that many conservatives were indignant at Bismarck's acceptance of any parliament for the confederation, and above all grateful to have a strong national state, most of them joined a new party, the National Liberals. Conservatives unwilling to accept the chancellor's gestures to constitutionalism countered by banding together as the Free Conservatives. Prussian politics focused on Bismarck; and Germany was set on Bismarck's course, dominated by Prussia and directed by men determined to strengthen the state and to maintain their independence of parliament.

The North German Confederation represented an enormous expansion of Prussian power and a great step toward unification. While the South German states preserved their separate status, no German nationalist could think Bismarck's federation a satisfactory or permanent solution. Instead, it seemed that the unification of Germany, like that of Italy, was to be achieved in stages, in part through diplomacy. There were other reasons, too, for stopping half-way. North Germany, Protestant and more industrial than the south, offered a sound base for the kind of Germany Bismarck envisioned, as different from the largely agricultural and Catholic south as Naples was from northern Italy. With their own rich cultural traditions and ancient dynasties (which still viewed the Hohenzollerns of Prussia as upstarts), Germany's southern states looked more to Vienna and Paris than to Berlin and remained suspicious of Prussia's militarism and cold efficiency.

Overcoming these differences was a central task of the North German Confederation, and Bismarck found the threat from France his strongest weapon. Napoleon wished to acquire Luxembourg (all parties appeared willing), and Bismarck manipulated the emperor's designs into a crisis that produced protests against cession to France of an "ancient German land" and brought France a serious diplomatic defeat. But neither such maneuvers nor the benefits of the Zollverein overcame southern resistance. A majority of the southern delegates elected to the Zollverein, led by Bavaria and Württemberg, opposed any extension of its influence, any further "Prussianization" of Germany. Something more than elections and trade were necessary if Germany was to be quickly united.

That something more was war with France. Historians once hotly disputed who was to blame for that war and whether it was "necessary." New research and changing perspectives have lessened the controversy; the war was wanted by Bismarck but first declared by France, the result of nationalism in both nations more than long-range calculation. Spain's provisional government, seeking a replacement for Queen Isabella II, forced to abdicate in 1868, settled on Leopold, prince of Hohenzollern-Sigmaringen, who under heavy French pressure finally declined. Eager to win public favor and at last score a point against Bismarck, the French government pressed on. In a famous interview at the western German spa of Ems, where William I was taking the baths, the French ambassador demanded that the Prussian king give public guarantees that the Hohenzollern candidacy would never be brought forward again. The king refused and later telegraphed a report to Bismarck of the difficult though formally correct interview. Bismarck carefully edited the Ems dispatch to make French demands seem even more imperious and the king's refusal even more abrupt, and released it to the press. Bismarck, Roon, and Moltke correctly assumed that war would follow. The French government, which could hardly afford further humiliations, responded to the patriotic fury it had helped ignite and declared war on July 19, 1870.

France hoped for support from Italy and Austria but had failed to establish any formal agreement with either, and they remained neutral. The French army, more formidable than Austria's had been, possessed modern equipment in some respects superior to the German, but the forces of the confederation were more carefully prepared and far more decisively led. By August the Germans had pushed through Alsace and encircled a French army at Metz. With heavy losses on both sides, another French army, attempting to relieve Metz, was severely defeated at Sedan in September, and there Napoleon III surrendered and was taken prisoner. Major fighting was over, but French resistance continued. Paris, quickly surrounded by German troops, held out under a long siege, and a provisional government organized from Tours continued efforts to maintain a French army in the field. For the rest of the year, German troops were subjected to a kind of guerilla harassment, and an armistice came only at the end of January, when Paris capitulated.

The brief war had profound effects. The Second Empire fell; and after bitter internal conflict, the Third Republic was established in France. Even more than defeat itself, the harsh terms of peace—France was required to pay an indemnity of 5 billion francs and to cede Alsace and Lorraine—assured the enmity between France and Germany as a central fact of international relations.

The Second Reich 1871–1879

The decision to annex Alsace-Lorraine was primarily a military one, intended to provide Germany with the strongest possible fortifications in case of future conflicts with France. But it also responded to a popular demand of German nationalists, and Bismarck still needed their support. His major concern was to complete the unification of Germany, and well before the final French surrender, he began intricate and difficult negotiations with each of the South German states. They had joined in fighting France with a mixture of enthusiasm and fear, but it took concessions, secret funds, threats, and all his skill before Bismarck got the German states, Prussia's generals, and the king to accept his terms for permanent union. When they did, William I was crowned German kaiser in the Hall of Mirrors at Versailles on January 18, 1871, his seventy-fourth birthday.

With modifications the constitution of the North German Confederation was extended to all the new nation. The upper house of parliament, the Bundesrat, received increased powers, including the right to declare war, but many domestic affairs were reserved to the twenty-five states that made up the Reich and special privileges were granted Baden, Bavaria, and Württemberg. There was no question that the great new nation created by the popular will, Bismarck's ability, and Prussian arms would be dominated by Prussia.

The Second Reich was from its inception a powerful nation.[3] Germany in 1871 was already more populous than France, and her rate of demographic growth was the fastest Europe had ever known. Less than half the population was engaged in agriculture after the first decade of unification, and Germany's industrial production increased at an astounding rate. Because she had developed later than Great Britain and more rapidly than France, her industrial equipment was more modern. The French indemnity added to the available capital, and the government aided industrial

---

[3] The old Holy Roman Empire was patriotically honored as the first Reich.

The halls of Versailles ring as Prussian soldiers hail the proclamation making King William Emperor of Germany. (Photo: The Granger Collection)

efficiency by making heavy investments in railroads, granting tax privileges, establishing tariffs, and encouraging the formation of large combines, the famous German cartels. German universities became the leading ones of Europe in the application of scientific method to every discipline.

Such rapid growth was disruptive in Germany, as elsewhere. Her nationalists stressed the traditional values of the *Volk*, the people, and nowhere were materialistic, commercial, and urban values more intensely attacked than in industrial Germany. This conflict could stimulate achievements as lasting as the work of Richard Wagner, who combined a musical revolution with Teutonic myth and individual genius with mere prejudice; but it increased the dangerous tensions among powerful conservative circles, a growing but defensive middle class, and workers increasingly aware of their distinct interests. The great achievements of the German state rested on its ability to satisfy industrialists and appeal to traditional nationalists by operating democratic institutions through autocratic means.

Bismarck, who wanted not to offend local interests and who left the army essentially autonomous, worried very much about the internal dangers to the new nation. He therefore sought to establish the supremacy of the state by moving against two apparently vulnerable groups: first the Catholic Church and then the socialist party.

Rather grandiosely named the Kulturkampf ("Battle of the Civilizations"), the conflict with the Catholic Church centered on new laws requiring state approval of church appointments, state supervision of Catholic education even in seminaries, and the abolition of religious orders. Many of these measures were part of the secularization common throughout Europe, but others were an effort at "germanization" (Poland and Alsace were heavily Catholic) intended to weaken anti-Prussian sentiment. Passed in the period from 1871 to 1875, they came at a time when the church appeared intransigently opposed to modern society, and they won the support of National Liberals, many conservative Lutherans, and much of the left.

Yet the Kulturkampf was not a great success. The severity of the laws and the harshness with which they were carried out made martyrs of many a priest and nun. A majority of bishops lost their sees, and many went into exile. Catholics rallied to their church, and many others began to fear so intrusive a state; the Catholic Center party steadily gained votes in Reichstag elections. Thus when the more flexible Leo XIII became pope, in 1878, Bismarck sought an understanding with the Vatican. Many of the laws most offensive to Catholics were allowed to lapse, and the battle of the civilizations subsided as the state turned toward the repression of other enemies.

Socialism did not offend Bismarck either in its attacks on laissez faire or in its emphasis upon the social role of the state, and he had gotten on well with the leading German socialist of the 1860s, Ferdinand Lassalle. But as socialists sought to win a mass following, founding the Social Democratic party in 1875, their attacks on autocracy, the military, and nationalism seemed more dangerous. In 1878 two attempts to assassinate the kaiser (neither by a socialist) gave Bismarck his chance, and he called for laws repressing socialism. The Reichstag refused, and the election of 1878 was fought largely on that issue, with conservatives and the Center party gaining some seats. As a result the Reichstag banned most socialist publications, prohibited socialist meetings except under police supervision, and forbade public collections for socialist causes. The Social Democrats were in effect forced underground, and another important element of society learned to hate and fear the German state. Within the Reichstag, however, socialists remained free to speak, and their party gained support with every election.

The abandonment of the Kulturkampf and the offensive against socialism were part of a larger realignment in German politics. Having preserved their strength, the conservatives and Catholics who had resisted the new Germany came to accept her, while liberals, torn between Bismarck's achievements and their old principles, grew weaker. Economic troubles, the effect of both the nation's rapid growth and a European agricultural depression, also helped forge a pro-Bismarck coalition more durable than any based on persecution. In 1879 demands for a higher tariff led the chancellor to propose and the Reichstag to grant strong protective tariffs on both manufactured and agricultural goods. The majority supporting that measure included Junker landlords, Rhineland industrialists, and the more nationalist liberals, split once again from their doctrinaire comrades. Bismarck was discovering a formula to draw together the most powerful interest groups in German society in support of a conservative state under his strong leadership.

III. A MIDDLE-CLASS CULTURE

Germany and Italy had joined the countries of western and northern Europe as nations in which the middle class enjoyed wide scope and influence. This was not just a matter of politics and economics, for the European high culture of the nineteenth century can fairly be called a culture of the middle class—one not marked by any single style; national rather than the culture of a court, salon, or village and more than ever centered in cities ("provincial" had become a pejorative term); and remarkable for quantity as well as quality, for there were more writers, artists, musicians, and scholars than ever before. For all its deliberate variety, this culture remained distinctive in its institutionalization, the forms of its expression, the themes it emphasized, and the shifting styles it favored.

CULTURAL INSTITUTIONS

Before the nineteenth century most paintings were done for a specific commission and often for a particular room; most music was composed for a special (often religious) occasion and designed to fit the talents of performers available in one palace; most books were written for a particular audience whom the author could feel he knew intimately. In the new century this had largely changed. Music moved from palaces, churches, and private salons to public concert halls; artists sold their paintings to any purchaser and, by midcentury, in stores created for that purpose; and writers found themselves engaged in commerce.

If the artist felt insecure in his dependence on an audience of unknown character and unproved cultivation, he had a larger public than ever before. That public was for the most part the same people active in politics, the professions, and business—or rather such people and their wives. They bought tickets for concerts just as they frequented restaurants with famous chefs, enjoying in both cases pleasures once part of private society and now open to all who had the inclination and money.

Theaters, institutions accustomed to commercial operations, flourished in every city, and they ranged from the new music halls to the great stages and opera houses built (usually by the state) to rank with parliament buildings as monuments of civic pride. Most major cities supported choirs, bands, and symphony orchestras, which grew larger and technically more proficient (the "Mannheim crescendo" was a new marvel of instrumental synchronization and discipline that Beethoven required of every orchestra). Conservatories and museums became national public institutions, maintaining established taste against a sea of change and considerably increasing Europe's stock of skilled artists and musicians. Some of the greatest of these institutions—the British Museum in London, the Bibliothèque Nationale in Paris, the Hermitage in St. Petersburg, the Alte Pinakothek in Munich—opened to the public in the 1840s usually in imposing new structures. The Louvre became the model museum of art, granting access to everyone and arranging its holdings by country and in chronological order. Lending libraries, charging a few pence per volume, were common even in smaller cities.

Those who sought self-improvement also flocked to public lectures on the sober implications of political economy or the wonders of science, among which photography ranked high. Daguerre announced his photographic process to the French Academy in 1839, and it persuaded the French government to purchase all rights so the new technique could be given to the world unencumbered by royalties. Important advances followed rapidly, and photography was enthusiastically applied

to the needs of science and exploration, widely used for portraits, and recognized as the newest of the arts.

But no cultural institution was more important than the press. Before 1800 the newspaper, of little importance outside of France and Britain, had been more like a newsletter, gossip column, or political pamphlet. By 1830 there were more than 2,000 European newspapers despite the censorship, special taxes, and police measures with which governments sought to restrict so awesome a social force. Where these restraints were eased, which was a central liberal demand in all countries, sales soared. By midcentury *The Times* of London

Increasing numbers of the public (note the middle-class families) flocked to the British Museum in the 1840s to view its exhibits on art and literature as well as natural history. (Photo: British Museum)

increased its 1815 circulation of 5,000 to 50,000, and two of the most popular French papers, the *Presse* and *Siècle*, both founded in 1836, had topped 70,000. In attaining such distribution, newspapers changed. The *Presse* and *Siècle* succeeded in halving their subscriptions rates (which remained substantial) by drawing their revenue primarily from advertising. Articles discussed commerce, the arts, and science as well as politics, and the papers competed for readers with serial novels by Honoré de Balzac and the elder Alexandre Dumas. The *London Illustrated News* created the picture magazine in 1842, which was copied immediately in every large country, and satirical magazines (*Punch* was founded in 1840, a few years after the *Caricature* and *Chiarivari* in Paris) made the cartoon a powerful political weapon. Honoré Daumier's biting pictures of fat bankers and complacent bourgeois raised social criticism to art.

Technology contributed to these developments. The *Times* installed a steam press in 1814, and a flood of technical improvements increased the speed and quality of typesetting and printing. Press services such as the Agence Havas and Reuters switched from carrier pigeons to the telegraph to bring bulletins to a public increasingly eager for the latest news. And paper-making machines reduced the cost and increased the volume of printing in every form.

THE CULTURAL PROFESSIONS

Newspaper work became a full-time occupation and gradually a profession—the terms "journalism" and "journalist" date from this period—and so did performing, painting, and writing. The virtuoso actor or musician could make an honored career. The violinist Niccolò Paganini, who transformed violin technique, commanded huge fees and enormous crowds wherever he played; Jenny Lind, "the Swedish Nightingale," was the rage of Europe, and Franz Liszt shaped international musical taste and standards of performance. The distinction between the amateur and professional musician became firm. Many a young man announced that he was a painter and proudly starved, in Paris if possible, out of loyalty to his career (there were 354 reg-

istered artists in Paris in 1789 but 2,159 in 1838); a few, among them England's great landscape painter J. M. W. Turner, became wealthy. The most popular writers—Balzac, Sir Walter Scott, Victor Hugo, Charles Dickens—were able to live by their pen alone, honored among the famous men of their age. Many responded to their new opportunities with appropriate industry. Scott wrote twenty-eight novels in eighteen years, and Balzac was equally prolific. Few went so far as Dumas, who employed scores of assistants to help crank out his profitable product. The artist making his way in his profession might hope for a prize or fellowship from one of the leading cultural institutions, but ultimately his fate depended on the opinion of his fellow artists and of an often untutored public not sure of its own taste.

That problem of judgment led to still another profession: the critic. The best critics won places for themselves as literary figures in their own right. But their essential role was to extend the canons of taste to a public faced with kaleidoscopic variety, just as the popular books on etiquette and gastronomy taught manners to the man of new means and prepared his bourgeois palate for *haute cuisine*.

Forms, Themes, and Styles

Although cultural life in the nineteenth century was full of uncertainties—about the role of the artist, the relationship of art to society, and the values art should express—middle-class culture remained essentially a formal one, proudly removed from the merely popular or customary. In music the forms of the symphony, concerto, quartet, and sonata, established in the eighteenth century, had been enlarged and enriched, especially by Ludwig van Beethoven, whose creative amalgam of formal structure and personal expression became the dominant model for nineteenth-century composers. His music, in whatever form, had the quality of a philosophic yet poetic essay, conceived and presented as high art to be heard in concert, studied and savored for itself and not as part of some larger entertainment or social occasion. This seriousness, intellectual and emotional, and this separation of art from any single context fit well with the changing circumstances in which music was performed by professional musicians before a paying audience. Beethoven's successors maintained that sense of music as an autonomous art and created works of such vitality that to this day most of the concert repertoire consists of music composed between 1800 and World War I.

The novel, which had also achieved its identity in the eighteenth century when it was often written in an epistolary style as if from one acquaintance to another, became the most widely enjoyed of the arts in the nineteenth century. Most often presented through an omniscient but anonymous narrator, its most common theme was the conflict between individual feeling (especially romantic love) and the roles and conventions demanded by society. Balzac attempted in his novels to encompass all the "human comedy" (the phrase contrasted with Dante's divine concerns), showing the wealthy, the ambitious, and the poor, soldiers, bankers, politicians, and writers. The novelist analyzed society and individual psychology through concrete types, and sometimes, as with Dickens, challenged the public conscience more effectively than any preacher or politician. Scott's swashbuckling stories of romance and chivalry in an earlier age probed the connection between personal character and social tension in a way that influenced writers throughout Europe. Hugo, Alexander Pushkin, and Alessandro Manzoni promulgated patriotism as they taught their readers of national brotherhood and the need to battle for liberty. Fiction presented the problems of poverty and family and city life, while deftly dissecting the frivolous aristocrat and the self-righteous middle-class merchant. A high proportion of the writer's public was women, and the issues of their lot, of love, dependence, or boredom, were more penetratingly presented in novels —Flaubert's *Madame Bovary* is the outstanding example—than anywhere else. Middle-class culture also had an intimate side, reflected in the popularity of poetry, the lithograph and watercolor, and in the demand for piano music (industrial techniques made the piano, with its iron frame, economical enough to be a common sight in middle-class parlors)—all to be enjoyed in the home and with private emotion.

The themes that run through the artistic work of the period, however, convey a tension. Romanticism's concern with the individual hero or genius—found in the paintings of Delacroix, the plays of Hugo, the poetry of Keats and Shelley—also stressed the artist's personal vision and the capture of a momentary feeling to be set like a precious stone in a carefully wrought piece of music, or poem, or painting. A logically easy step led to the cry of art for art's sake, that the merit of a work lay in its purity, independent of purpose or message. At the same time artists in the nineteenth century were fascinated by society and historical change, seeking the nature of "modernity," in the words of Charles Baudelaire, by extracting "from fashion whatever element it may contain of poetry within history." Behind this lay the desire for an integrated vision encompassing all of life, a coherent understanding that would connect culture to society, economics, and politics. There was a wish as well to integrate the arts themselves; and Baudelaire, a leading poet and critic, writing on the death of Delacroix in

1863, proclaimed it "the spiritual condition of our age that the arts aspire . . . to lend one another new powers."[4]

This reciprocity was part of the vitality of lyric opera, another of the arts to reach its height in the nineteenth century. Opera was first of all theater, combining popular appeal with aristocratic elegance, and performances were important civic events. Elaborate plots, often in historical settings, and flowery poetic texts were taken as seriously as the varied, tuneful, and complex music, the whole further enriched by ballet, colorful sets, and special effects. The two leading operatic composers were Giuseppe Verdi and his exact contemporary Richard Wagner. Verdi was an Italian national hero, whose compelling and often patriotic music, with its paeans to human virtue and its portrayal of every human emotion, remains a staple of opera houses everywhere. Wagner, however, created a kind of revolution in music by carrying the search for an artistic synthesis still further, for he wrote his own texts, often building with patriotic intent on Germanic myths, and identified his major ideas and characters with specific musical themes to create a whole in which voices, instruments, words, and visual experience were inseparable. In every form serious art intended to uplift its audience, morally and intellectually and aesthetically.

Such varied goals and ambitions, diverse audiences, and numerous professional artists led to a further characteristic of nineteenth-century culture, its frequently shifting styles. Romanticism, which emphasized the beauty of nature and the drama of human feeling, grad-

ually gave way by midcentury to a realism that dealt more matter-of-factly with everyday life; and these approaches combined and divided into scores of schools and styles, creating a highly self-conscious art in music, painting, and writing. Innovation was in itself often taken for a sign of genius, and the belief that artists must be in an avant-garde, ahead of their duller public, became a cliché. If society honored the arts, they in turn conveyed more confidence in the future or nostalgia for the preindustrial past than respect for the present. Yet in their universal criticism of the shallowness and materialism of the middle class on which they rested, the artists of the nineteenth century were spokesmen for the inner doubts that were an inherent part of middle-class culture.

Both the confidence and insecurity of this culture showed in attitudes toward religion. Most thoughtful men appear to have suffered religious shocks, felt both the loss of faith and some religious experience. On the Continent many of the middle class became bitter anticlericals, seeing in the church the barrier to progress. The Abbé Lamennais, one of the most admired of Catholic leaders, broke in the 1830s from a church that would not accept his program for associating the tenets of his faith with democracy. The Protestant David Strauss created a sensation across Europe with his *Life of Jesus*, which appeared in 1835, for it cast erudite doubt on the accuracy of the Gospel, frightening many with the apparent need to choose between historical scholarship and Christ. More typically, especially in England, stern morality and propriety were substituted for theology. Yet men worried terribly that society would lose its direction and individuals their moral purpose without religion. Protestant and Catholic missions combatted ignorance and indifference with an intensity not seen since the seventeenth century. The pious became more

---

[4] The comment on Delacroix's death is cited by Morse Peckham, *Beyond the Tragic Vision* (1962), p. 215; the reference to the artist's search for modernity is from an essay on the painter Constantin Guys in Charles Baudelaire, *The Painter of Modern Life and Other Essays*, Jonathan Mayne, tr. and ed. (1965), p. 12.

militant and turned to social action, preaching temperance, teaching reading, and establishing charities. In religion as in the arts, new organization was carrying contemporary confidence and internal conflicts more and more widely.

IV. RESHAPING THE STATE

The benefits of a strong state, sought through unification in Italy and Germany, were expected in established nations as well. For these countries too military efficiency was an ultimate test, and the defeats of Russia in 1856 and Austria in 1859 and 1866 were interpreted as proof of the need for drastic governmental change. But making the state stronger and more efficient in less developed countries required measures that often threatened the very groups in power. That dilemma tailored the pattern of reform in each country, leading to durable compromises that took different form in Russia, Austria, and Spain. In Great Britain and France, on the other hand, neither national unity nor effective institutions were at issue; but in those countries, where the middle class had achieved dominance, conflict centered rather on who else should participate in and benefit from the policies of the state—questions that brought civil war and a republic to France, further reform and modern political parties to Britain.

RUSSIA 1855–1881

Immediately after the Crimean War and only a year after assuming the throne, Tsar Alexander II issued a manifesto promising improvements in justice, education, and employment. Goals once envisaged only by liberals were adopted in defeat by the Russian autocrat. The critical reform was the abolition of serfdom. Discreetly but firmly the nobles were told to bring the institution to an end from above rather than wait for its destruction from below.

Months passed in silence while secret committees drafted proposals and most nobles dragged their feet. Intellectuals had argued against serfdom for generations, and peasants spoke through more frequent uprisings. Economic developments—a money economy, foreign trade, new industry—had further weakened the old system. Yet landowners could always argue against taking revolutionary risks just yet. Only in 1861 was serfdom abolished—by the tsar's decree.

The law of 1861 gave legal rights to more than 22 million serfs, providing in general that peasant farmers should gain title to the land they worked or its equivalent. They could either contract a long-term debt to the state, which would in turn compensate the owner, or accept one-quarter of that land free and clear. During an interim of two years, they would continue to owe all former obligations to their masters.

In practice the lord usually kept the best land for himself and through inflated land prices received additional payment for the loss of his serf labor. On the whole former serfs found themselves with less land than they needed to support their families and to make their payments; and provisions for pasture, forest, and water rights were rarely satisfactory. Thus agricultural labor, usually for the former master, remained a necessity for subsistence.

The law of 1861 also gave important responsibilities to the *mir*, or village commune, whose elected officials assigned plots, determined the crops to be planted, and paid taxes to the state for which each plot of land was assessed by the *mir*. The former serf could not leave the commune or sell his land without permission; and even after leaving, he remained liable for taxes. In this way the state made sure that the debts owed it would be met and that the new peasant society would maintain structures with which the state could deal. Indeed the commune, which came to be considered a characteristic Slavic institution, tended to resist change in favor of traditional ways; similarly few lords really became modern farmers. But this conservatism to some degree eased the adaptation to a social change immense in itself.

A few years later the government liberated all state peasants—nearly 25 million—on more favorable terms, granting on the average more land at a lower price than that available to former serfs. Still sharply segregated from more privileged members of society, with special laws and punishments, including flogging, applicable only to them, peasants remained a caste distinguishable in dress, speech, and customs.

In this 1861 photograph a Russian official is reading to peasants on a Moscow estate the "Regulations Concerning the Peasantry," the decree that abolished serfdom. (Photo: Novosti Press Agency)

Although the emancipation of the serfs, who constituted about 47 million of Russia's 74 million people, did not establish a laissez-faire economy, it provided the basis for institutions allowing some popular participation in public life. Within each district communes supported their own courts, selected their own judges, and administered the regulations on taxes and conscription. In 1864 district and provincial councils—the zemstvos, elected through a three-class system like Prussia's—were made responsible for primary schools, local roads, and measures of local welfare. Generally cautious, the zemstvos gave important political experience and a sense of political responsibility to many professional men and other members of the middle class. Cities too were granted increased autonomy and allowed to elect representative bodies.

The number of primary schools, though always inadequate, increased dramatically. In addition the government encouraged secondary and university education, relaxed censorship, and adopted a number of military reforms. The system of requiring twenty-five years of service from selected serfs was altered until by 1874 universal service, with generous exemptions and only six years of active duty, approached the concept of a citizen army.[5]

As each reform uncovered more that needed to be done, the government became more cautious. Concessions to Poland had prompted demands that culminated in the revolution of 1863. Harshly quelled by 1865, it lost Poland her separate status and strengthened conservatism in Russia. The repression

---

[5] Most soldiers were of course recruited from the peasantry. A provision reflecting the social importance of education stipulated that those who completed primary school were liable for only four years of duty, those who finished secondary school for two years, and those with university education for just six months.

extended into Russia, where the police remained independent of local controls. By 1875 the zemstvos had been forbidden to discuss general political issues, and restrictions on what could be taught or printed had been tightened.

As a consequence the movements of radical opposition flourished. The famous division of the generations, expressed in Ivan Turgenev's *Fathers and Sons,* showed in the rejection of leaders like Alexander Herzen, who from exile in London had once inspired reform but whose views belonged to the era of Mazzini and the utopian socialists. New spokesmen, called nihilists by their enemies, rejected compromise within the system and accepted the utility of violence advocated in the anarchism of Mikhail Bakunin. Populists talked of going to the people, educating the peasants to a more revolutionary view. Socialism too was spreading in the 1870s. All these doctrines were affected by pan-Slavist views, which stressed Russia's peculiar destiny and disdained the liberal parliamentarianism of the West. The intelligentsia of Russian society remained isolated and, increasingly disenchanted with a tsar liberator, moved further left. In an atmosphere of conspiracy, terrorists attempted assassination as a way to shake an oppressive regime. Usually they missed their target, but in 1881 a bomb killed Alexander II. Alexander III, his son, took the reigns of power smoothly. However inadequate, the reforms of Alexander II assured that imperial Russia could survive an assassination.

THE HAPSBURG EMPIRE 1859–1875

Following the revolutions of 1848, the Hapsburg monarchy had sought to meet its political and economic problems by creating a modern, unitary state. Under the young Francis Joseph I, the emphasis on administrative efficiency was renewed, and for the first time in its history, the entire empire was subjected to uniform laws and taxes applied by a single administration. The emperor and the aristocracy, however, were never comfortable with their earnest bureaucrats, and the innovation of centralization was not accompanied by the zeal for reform the policy required. Mounting debts and defeat in Italy were accepted as proof that it had not worked, and in 1860 Francis Joseph's October Diploma announced a new federal constitution giving considerable authority to regional diets.

Intended to reduce resentment against highhanded government, the constitution was a failure from the start. It prompted dangerous arguments among the various nationalities over what the "historic" provinces really were and won the determined opposition of liberals and bureaucrats alike. The emperor therefore reversed himself the next year in the February Patent, which established an imperial bicameral parliament. Having stirred his people to visions of local self-government and autonomous nationalities, he was now again asking for their subordination to rule from Vienna. Furthermore representatives to the lower house were to be elected by a four-class system that assured the dominance of the German-speaking middle class.

In Hungary the liberal nationalist Ferencz Deák led a campaign to reject these arrangements and reestablish instead the constitution of 1848, a far more liberal instrument. The imperial government tried the traditional tactic of recruiting support from the empire's other nationalities against the Magyars, but the response was unenthusiastic. Although not strong enough to force her will, Hungary was able to prevent the new constitution from having its intended effect. Deák then worked for a compromise, which became acceptable after the empire's defeat in the Austro-Prussian War.

In 1867 Francis Joseph was crowned king of Hungary, an autonomous state joined to Austria only in the person of the emperor and by common policies of defense and diplomacy. Thus he preserved his authority in the matters of foreign policy he cared about most by conceding to one nationality what he denied to others. Thereafter two critical issues of Hungary's domestic politics were the divergent economic interests of Austrian industry and Hungary's great landholders (a conflict that centered on the tariff) and the treatment of the non-Magyar majority of her population. On both questions the Magyar landowning aristocracy generally had its way, and after 1875 the dominant Liberal party, led by Kálmán Tisza, made Magyar the language of school and government while protecting Magyar economic interests.

In the Austrian parliament the emperor turned for support first to the German liberals, who offended him by their anticlericalism, and then to Czechs and Poles, who disturbed him with their nationalist demands. Each group won some concessions, but fundamental, lasting reforms were difficult, and government depended increasingly on a reliable, conservative bureaucracy dominated by Germans more than on parliamentary politics. Still, the Hapsburg monarch presided after 1867 over responsible ministers in both halves of his empire, assured of a determining voice in public affairs.

An awkward compromise, the Dual Monarchy gave power to wealthy landlords and merchants and rested on the dominance of Magyars (over Rumanians, Croats, and Serbs) and of Germans in cooperation with Czechs and Poles (over Slovenes, Slovaks, and Ruthenians). It lasted for fifty years as one of Europe's great powers, an empire of diversified peoples and cultures, changing even while resisting change, with more freedom in practice than in principle, sustaining at its center the graceful civilization of Vienna.

SPAIN *1854–1876*

In Spain the army, the church, big business, and regionalist interests could demand a price for their support so high as to assure the government's weakness. For nine years government under General Leopoldo O'Dónnell, the leader of the liberal coalition that displaced General Narváez in 1854, provided political stability by giving more attention to economic matters. Spain experienced on a smaller scale the waves of speculation, railroad building, economic growth, and ostentation associated with the Second Empire in France. A coalition of the political center, the government fell in 1863 before changing demands it could not meet and palace intrigue it could not stop. Its conservative replacement then sought security through repression and electoral manipulation, which ended in revolution in 1868 and the unpopular Queen Isabella II's flight to France.

The disaffection of the military in 1868 was crucial, but the revolution also won support from workers, radicals, liberals, professional groups, and businessmen. The new regime, led by General Juan Prim, sought to combine the liberal appeal of universal manhood suffrage, trial by jury, and freedom of religion and the press with the moderation implied by constitutional monarchy. It proved easier to adopt a new constitution, however, than to find a new king, as each candidate decided against entanglement in Spanish politics and the sort of international complications that precipitated the Franco-Prussian War.

The son of Victor Emmanuel II of Italy who finally agreed to accept the throne in December 1870 ruled for just two years as King Amadeus I. Associated with the Risorgimento's attacks on papal territory, the Italian royal house was anathema to Catholics, and the king was treated as an upstart and foreigner by grandees and courtiers. Finding it impossible to be either a good constitutional monarch or a strong leader, Amadeus abdicated in 1873 as republican agitation and Carlist uprisings became more serious, rather like a prime minister who had lost a vote of confidence.

The majority of the Cortes then declared Spain's first republic, which lasted a year. Republicans, divided between centralists and federalists, were further weakened by Carlist revolts and Catholic distrust. The government alienated much of its following by repressing constitutional liberties in its quest for order, and the military stepped forward to place Isabella's son, who had just come of age, on the throne as Alfonso XII.

He began his reign in 1875 under a new constitution that was closer to the one in effect from 1845 to 1869 than the more democratic one which had then replaced it. The court never again meddled in politics as Isabella had done, and the ringing freedoms proclaimed during the republic were honored at least in theory. Spain thus found stability in a government responsible to a Cortes whose majority was largely determined by manipulated elections and limited suffrage. The Conservative and Liberal parties, as they came to be called, alternated in power with little change in policy. Both provided sensible and mildly corrupt governments that offered something to most influential groups and for a generation masked the bitter divisions between regionalists and centralists, Catholics and anticlericals, the poor and men of property.

FRANCE 1870–1878

With Napoleon's capture at Sedan and the rout of French troops, the Second Empire lost its reason for existence. For the third time in France's history, a republic was announced to cheering crowds. Calling themselves the Government of National Defense, republican leaders tried valiantly to turn 1870 into

another 1792, when a republic had mobilized the nation against the monarchical armies of Europe. But German forces had already broken the back of France's army, and they surrounded Paris on September 19, less than three weeks after Sedan. The new government sent some of its members to Tours to organize resistance from there, but even the urgency of war barely covered the divisions between moderate and radical republicans, who were determined to continue the fight at all costs. Their leader, the fiery orator Léon Gambetta, daringly escaped from Paris in a balloon to accomplish remarkable feats of organization from Tours. Enthusiastic national guards and peasant boys were recruited and somehow equipped; Garibaldi arrived to help, and the French seriously harassed German troops, even recapturing Orléans, but by December the overmatched French forces were pushed back. The government retreated to Bordeaux while Paris held out against a German siege. During a winter as severe as any on record, Parisians cut the trees of their boulevards for fuel, slaughtered pets, and emptied the zoo as a starving city continued to resist. But heroism and patriotic fervor could not defeat a modern army, and at the end of January Paris capitulated. German troops marched down Haussmann's boulevards into a denuded and quiet city.

Although Gambetta wanted to continue the fighting, few others did; the armistice called for elections to establish a government that could ratify the terms of peace. In the absence of political parties or extended campaigning, the successful candidate was usually someone already well known, a local leader committed to ending the war, and thus two-thirds of those elected to the National Assembly that met in February 1871 were monarchists. Some were legitimists, who longed for a Bourbon restoration and were already calling the count de Chambord King Henry V; more were Orléanists. But there were also some republicans, mostly moderate, and a handful of Bonapartists.

Despite the moving speeches of delegates from Alsace and Lorraine, peace on German terms was accepted, and approval was quickly given for an interim government under Adolphe Thiers. The eloquent critic of Guizot, in exile during the 1850s and the empire's public opponent in the 1860s, Thiers gained at seventy-three the power he had long coveted. By naming him chief of the Executive Power, the Assembly avoided declaring whether France's permanent government would be a monarchy or a republic. It then agreed to meet next at tranquil Versailles rather than radical Paris, and adjourned.

Determined to consolidate his position, Thiers recognized Paris as the greatest threat to the sort of compromise between Orléanists and moderate republicans he represented, and one of his first acts was to disarm the city's National Guard. At the end of the German siege, many of the well-to-do had left Paris, but the poor and the radical remained, hardened by months of fighting. When troops arrived to take the city's cannons, they were met by an angry crowd; shots were fired, and by day's end two generals lay dead and most of the soldiers had joined the side of their urban brothers. Faced with insurrection, Thiers followed the advice he had given Louis Philippe in 1848: he withdrew the army to let Paris taste its revolution so he could first isolate and then crush it.

The municipal council of Paris declared a commune, once again evoking the great Revolution, and called on other cities to do the same. The Paris Commune included moderate and radical republicans, some followers of Pierre Joseph Proudhon and Jérome Adolphe Blanqui, socialists who though more militant were in the tradition of Saint-Simon and Fourier, as well as a few members of the Marxist First International. Its program, beyond democracy and federalism, was not very

specific; and it had little time to experiment with egalitarian and anticlerical measures. Its efforts to make peace with the government at Versailles were rejected, and the Assembly replied to the threat of a radical government in Paris and the Parisian "mob" by suddenly ending the moratorium on debt payment (including rents) that had been in effect during the siege and by ceasing to pay the National Guard, the only income for many. While German armies watched, troops from Versailles began their assault on Paris.

The civil war between the democrats of Paris and the Assembly at Versailles fed on the distrust and despair that accompanied the French war effort, the siege of Paris, and defeat. The city's isolation during that year of anguish, when rumors of treachery were heard at every hand, had amplified other divisions: between industrial and rural France, between urban democrats and middle-class moderates. The two sides fought out of fury for competing visions of what the nation should become now that the Second Empire had fallen. Hostages taken by the communards to win release of some of their captured leaders were killed, among them the archbishop of Paris. On both sides prisoners were shot, and the bitter and bloody fighting lasted nearly two months before troops broke into the city in May. Even then the battle continued, barricade by barricade, into the working-class quarters, where the group commanded by Louise Michel—the most famous of hundreds of militant *citoyennes* who would later tell her captors, "I belong entirely to the Social Revolution"—was among the last to fall. Solid citizens shuddered at revolutionary excess (and especially the part played by women), but on the whole the victors were more brutal. Tens of thousands of Parisians died in the streets, and summary courts-martial ordered execution, imprisonment, or deportation for tens of thousands more.

The commune raised the red specter

The Communards of Paris pulled down the statue of Napoleon I that stood atop a column in Plâce Vendôme, and none of the symbolism of that act was overlooked in this engraving. (Photo: The Granger Collection)

throughout Europe. From the first, Marxists hailed it as a proletarian rising, the dawning of a new era, though Marx was indignant with the communards' respect for property and legality and their lack of revolutionary daring. Former communards became the heroes of socialist gatherings for the next generation, and to this day the cemetery where many of them were executed remains a shrine honored by socialists and communists.[6]

Historians have been at great pains to show how little socialism, still less Marxism, there was in the Paris Commune (it respectfully left the Bank of Paris intact); yet myth has its historical importance too. This indisputably was class conflict, and the rage on both sides was

more significant than mere differences of program. After 1871 a communist revolution became a credible possibility to radical and conservative alike, and working-class movements pointed to the martyrs of the Commune as evidence of the selfish cruelty of bourgeois rule.

The Founding of the Third Republic

Thiers' government quickly reestablished effective administration, thanks to a state apparatus stronger than any political group, and the loan needed to pay the indemnity to

---

[6] A century later a Russian sputnik proudly carried not only a Soviet flag but a red flag from the Commune of 1871.

Germany was soon oversubscribed. As by-elections produced victories for moderate republicans, monarchists feared that their chance for a restoration might be slipping away. They rallied in 1873 to defeat Thiers in a close vote and united behind the Bourbon claimant, the childless count of Chambord, with the understanding that he would be succeeded by the claimant from the House of Orléans. His intransigent refusal to accept the tricolor, the flag of revolution, left the monarchists afraid to attempt a restoration yet. They borrowed time by electing Marshal Marie MacMahon as Thiers' replacement for a seven-year term. A monarchist who had fought under Napoleon III, he accepted from a sense of duty and brought to his post a dislike of politics that helped him act like the constitutional monarch for whom he was keeping the throne.

While the conservatives appointed by MacMahon risked defeats in the Assembly[7] and the monarchists grew more divided, the republicans gained in confidence. In 1875 a bill passed by one vote providing that the president of the republic should be elected by the votes of two legislative houses, and these in turn were established by laws stipulating that the Senate would be indirectly elected by local officials and the Chamber of Deputies by direct universal male suffrage.

The Third Republic was thus established without ringing phrases as the government that, in Thiers' epigram, divided Frenchmen least. A regime of compromise, for which republicans led by Gambetta had worked hard, it had earned acceptability by crushing the Commune and accepting a conservative Senate. Created by the most reluctant of

founding fathers, it endured longer than any French regime since 1789.

In the elections of 1876, the republicans captured two-thirds of the seats in the Chamber and almost half those in the Senate. Although MacMahon chose a conservative republican, Jules Simon, as premier, tension between the president and the Chamber predictably grew. The republicans accused the Catholic Church of being the political agent of legitimists and criticized the military and the Orléanist prefects. MacMahon in turn reproved Simon for not combating such charges whereupon Simon resigned, denouncing presidential interference. This was the "crisis de seize mai" (May 16, 1877), which precipitated the final step in the establishment of the republic, for MacMahon, who had previously rejected every hint that he attempt a monarchical coup, now reacted strongly He dissolved the Chamber, called new elections, and named a new ministry to manipulate their outcome. Although the republicans lost some seats, they preserved an overwhelming majority. Never again in the Third Republic did a French president use his power of dissolution; and the presidency, so strong under Thiers, declined further in authority.

When MacMahon resigned, in 1879, the two houses elected Jules Grévy, a republican who in 1848 had argued there should be no president at all. A good old man who frightened no one, Grévy exemplified the caution, the compromises, and the republican tradition on which the Third Republic rested. French public institutions preserved the remarkable continuity that characterized them after 1800 despite the changes of regime. Successive republican governments guaranteed political freedom and deferred to the middle class. Economic growth, less dramatic than in Great Britain or Germany, was also less disruptive. Like her European neighbors, France had painfully found an awkward balance, one pe-

---

[7] MacMahon's ministers, led by the able Orléanist, the duke de Broglie, were so rich in noble names that the period has come to be called the Republic of the Dukes from a study published by Daniel Halévy in 1937.

culiarly her own, between the demands for order and the need for change.

GREAT BRITAIN 1854–1880

The moderation and flexibility of Great Britain's parliamentary system, along with economic prosperity and increased population, were a source of Victorian confidence. Many claimed that special qualities in the English character—respect for tradition, the emphasis on law and Parliament, habits of toleration and deference—accounted for the combination of industrial advance and political order.[8] Yet overwhelming social change as well as the reforms of the 1830s and 1840s required the state to become more active in a wider range of activities and more responsive to the public. Ultimately dependent on elections, the government nonetheless remained the province of the upper classes, who found it difficult and sometimes repugnant to reach the masses.

Even in matters of foreign policy, however, public opinion was increasingly important. The Crimean War evoked a patriotic enthusiasm astute politicans would seek to recapture, and the ineptitude with which it was conducted forced investigations into administration and the military that increased the cry for new reforms. During the American Civil War, many liberals favored the South, as did most of the English upper classes, who viewed Southern culture with aristocratic sympathy. John Bright and many radical and working-class leaders on the other hand saw the cause of human dignity and democracy represented by the North. The revival of British radi-

calism was closely connected with the willingness of the very textile workers who suffered from the scarcity of American cotton to cheer for President Abraham Lincoln's war.

Lord John Russell built an effective coalition of liberal Tories and Whigs, and Lord Palmerston, prime minister from 1859 to his death in 1865, could at least arouse public affection—a quality that made him more popular in the nation than in Parliament. They presided over ministries of able men who soberly and sometimes imaginatively sought to lead a more efficient state to act more responsibly in behalf of social equity. Competitive examinations for entry into a restructured civil service marked an important departure achieved in 1855 after years of effort. Legal disabilities for Jews were removed, and the special taxes in behalf of the Church of England were dropped. British rule in India was thoroughly reorganized following a great mutiny in 1857 among native soldiers in the Indian army. In the same spirit the important act of 1867, which made Canada a dominion with her own representative institutions, was passed with little resistance.

The Parties of Gladstone and Disraeli

Such responsible accommodation was not sufficient, however, to meet the needs and aspirations of the lower-middle class and workers. More fundamental change followed a major political realignment that made possible the establishment of modern political parties, the extension of suffrage, and the emergence of two brilliant leaders who combined democratic appeal with masterly management of the established political system.

One of them was William Gladstone, who made his mark as chancellor of the exchequer under Palmerston. A skilled parliamentary tactician, a man of impeccable background, he was also a personal friend of some of the more doctrinaire liberal reformers and showed

---

[8] Walter Bagehot, one of the most noted political writers of the period, especially praised the Englishman's sense of deference to his social betters. Inequality and individual morality, he argued, allowed Britain to enjoy order without coercion and justice without anarchy.

open sympathy for the left-wing liberals known as radicals. Gladstone was one of the former Tories who followed Sir Robert Peel in leaving the party upon their conversion to free trade in 1846, and he was instrumental in transforming the Whigs into the Liberal party. In liberal principles he found a moral cause around which to build a strong political movement.

Gladstone became an advocate of increased suffrage as that question, in the air since 1832, became compelling. Cautiously he and Russell sponsored a complicated bill, which was defeated. The issue was then snatched from them by the rising star of the Conservatives (as the Tories were now called), Benjamin Disraeli, who led his rather startled party to support a more generous measure, passed in 1867. The right to vote was extended to all men who were borough (town) residents and paid taxes either directly or indirectly through rent. An electorate that had risen to almost a million was now doubled, and two great parties were coming systematically to compete for popular favor in terms of national issues. As the parties became better organized and disciplined, they reached far deeper into society with greater awareness of the people's concerns, and the great parliamentary clashes of Gladstone and Disraeli became a dramatic part of British public life.

Despite Disraeli's remarkable role in promoting the Reform Bill of 1867, the elections of 1868 produced a great Liberal victory, and for six years Gladstone's first and perhaps most successful ministry did much to improve British society. Great Britain, well after most European nations, at last established the basis for a national educational system by providing state aid to both church schools and locally supported secular schools. Education was compulsory only by local option and was not yet free, but a giant step had been taken. It was accompanied by important re-

forms in the two great universities, Oxford and Cambridge, which encouraged new curricula and allowed men not Anglican to compete for fellowships and teaching posts. The Liberals also reformed the army, limiting traditional privileges, improving training, and establishing shorter terms of service on the Prussian model. Even the purchase of commissions was abolished despite great resistance from the House of Lords. Ireland too received their attention. Here the Liberal government disestablished the Church of England, restricted the abuses of absentee landlords, and provided guarantees that the peasant would receive some credit for improvements he made, some protection against eviction, and some help in purchasing land for himself.

Few doubted that Great Britain would become more democratic, and many suspected that the Conservative party was doomed. Yet the elections of 1874 returned it to power, for Disraeli more than Gladstone had inherited Palmerston's appeal to nationalism. Belief in the glory and wealth of empire and willingness to expand the authority of the state in matters of public welfare was to become the strong foundation for a modern Conservative party.

Under Disraeli colonial matters received greater and more public attention, and his purchase in 1875 of a large block of shares in the Suez Canal proved the basis for subsequent British domination in Egypt. When "Empress of India" was added to Victoria's title in 1876, it sounded foreign and flamboyant to many in the upper classes but caught the imagination of citizens proud of their national power and their queen. A public health act in 1875 took the important step of establishing a national code for housing and urban sanitation. Trade unions, their legality questioned by a court decision, had been recognized in a Liberal bill of 1871, but it was the

The flotilla shown here was part of the celebration that marked the opening of the Suez Canal in 1869. The elaborate ceremonies, for which both the Empress Eugénie and Emperor Franz Joseph of Austria came to Egypt, included the first performance of Verdi's Aïda. *(Photo: Compagnie Financiere de Suez)*

Conservatives who removed restrictions that had prohibited picketing and kept strikes ineffectual.

This conception of Tory democracy was a British parallel to the policies of Bismarck and Napoleon III. Through the party system the sphere of politics was being extended and the role of the state increased beyond the intention of the upper-class men who made the system work. Its effectiveness, in addition to the wealth of industry and empire, made Britain the most powerful and most envied nation of the world.

STABILIZING INTERNATIONAL RELATIONS 1870–1881

The unification of Italy and Germany and the defeat of France had fundamentally altered the relations of the European powers, and nationalist movements within the Austrian and Ottoman empires threatened new instability.

The Balkans remained the only area of Europe not fully controlled by a single government, and the strengthened European powers were quick to perceive the opportunities and dangers that fact implied. Russia, eager to undo her defeat in the Crimean War, snatched the occasion of the Franco-Prussian War to renounce the treaty clauses banning her navy from the Black Sea and looked hopefully for chances to extend her influence. The Hapsburg monarchy, hoping to compensate for its losses in Italy and Germany and aware of the threat nationalism posed to its rule, watched

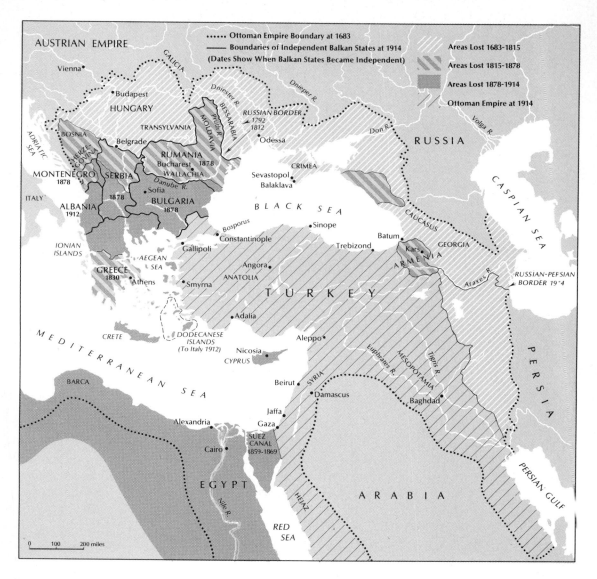

MAP 24.3: THE DECLINE OF THE OTTOMAN EMPIRE 1683–1914

the Balkans with growing concern. Great Britain's interest also increased with the political popularity of empire and the opening of the Suez Canal in 1869, which made the eastern Mediterranean appear all the more vital.

Most of the Balkan peninsula was at least nominally under Ottoman rule (see Map 24.3), but throughout the area there was a ferment of nationalism, constitutionalism, and modernizing reform. Especially strong in the autonomous countries of Serbia and Rumania, it reached into the Ottoman Empire itself, where a proclamation of 1876 established at least in theory a constitution guaranteeing parliamentary government and individual liberties. The Bulgarian uprising against Ottoman rule in 1876 was thus not an isolated event, and it won immediate support from Serbia, which had long hoped for a Balkan federation against Ottoman power and for the acquisition of Bosnia and Herzegovina. After Ottoman forces put down the revolt with shocking brutality, Russia intervened, moved by traditional ambitions and pressure from her own pan-Slav movement, which had actively encouraged Balkan nationalists.

Russia's military campaigns were poorly conducted, but her gains were sufficient within the year to force the sultan to accept the treaty of San Stefano in 1878. Russia was to acquire territory across the Caucasus Mountains (from Batum to Kars), extending her centuries-long advance southward. Both Montenegro and Serbia were to be enlarged and granted full independence, and most important, the treaty provided for a large and autonomous Bulgaria. That new state, it was universally thought, would be a Russian puppet looming over the Balkan peninsula; and the European concert, which had exercised so little voice in the unification of Italy or Germany, the fall of the Papal States, or the cession of Alsace-Lorraine, was called into action.

The combined pressure of the great powers forced Russia to agree to an international conference to establish new terms of peace in the Balkans, and at the subsequent Congress of Berlin, as at the Congress of Paris in 1856, they administered a sharp rebuff to Russia. They granted autonomy to a greatly reduced Bulgaria, and lessened the gains given Serbia and Montenegro. Austria-Hungary was authorized to occupy Bosnia and Herzegovina, which also remained under Ottoman rule, and the British occupation of Cyprus, previously agreed to between the Ottoman Empire and Britain, was confirmed.

The balance thus established in the Balkans was precarious, achieved only by extending Russian, Austrian, and British interests at the expense of a weakening Ottoman Empire, while ignoring the nationalist ambitions of many Greeks, Bulgarians, Rumanians, and Serbians.[9] This was a pattern for preserving peace in Europe that would become characteristic of imperialism.

The fact that the Congress was held in Berlin reflected Germany's prestige and her new commitment to maintaining the balance of power. Germany and her chancellor had become preeminent in Continental relations. Russia, the offended power, had nowhere to turn for allies but Berlin, for France was too radical and Great Britain a consistent foe. Bismarck thus laid the groundwork for a system of alliances to isolate France and secure Germany's position. In 1879 Austria-Hungary and Germany signed a mutual defense pact that remained the foundation of German diplomacy, promising that the two countries would fight together in case either was attacked by Russia. Then Bismarck daringly turned to isolated Russia in 1881, reviving the Three Emperors' League he had attempted a decade earlier: Austria-Hungary, Germany, and Russia swore neutrality in the event of war between any of them and a fourth power.

More important than the precise provisions were the fear of international anarchy and the new relationship these alliances implied. Bismarck used Prussia's connections with both Eastern European empires, based upon an unstable balance in the Balkans, to re-create the

---

9 The southern part of Bulgaria, Rumelia, remained under Turkish rule as a separate province. Serbia, Montenegro, and Rumania received independence but less territory than they claimed. The Rumanian provinces of Wallachia and Moldavia had been joined in 1862 and received their own prince two years later. A Hohenzollern, he became King Carol in 1881. The tsar's nephew was elected to the Bulgarian throne.

conservative alliance of the three powers. At the same time he sought the friendship of Great Britain and Italy, leaving Germany supreme and France alone upon the Continent— an arrangement to be sealed by dangerously explicit treaties as if solemn contracts could check the forces of domestic change or define the ambitions of national states.

By 1880 many of the aims of the revolutionaries defeated in 1848 had been accomplished. Italy and Germany were sovereign nations, and Hungary was autonomous. Serfdom had been abolished in Russia and religious disabilities largely removed in the United Kingdom. France and Germany enjoyed universal manhood suffrage. Representative government was firmly established in Britain, France, and Italy, and everywhere the state accepted a larger responsibility for social welfare. A dynamic middle-class culture flourished, and in a broad sense nationalism had triumphed outside Eastern Europe (few denied its potential importance there), though the policies of nationalists seemed to promote conflict, a strong army, and a vigorous state more than liberalism.

Political changes after 1850 were a response to ideas and to new economic and social conditions which radicals had been among the first to recognize, but these changes were brought about largely by the state, which radicals had failed to capture. Everywhere stronger and more specifically secular, the state increased its authority, its social role, its sovereign claims, and its expenditures. Bureaucracies expanded, their officials copying the Junkers in Germany, carrying the voice of Germanic Vienna through the Hapsburg empire, following in France the rational style of the great state schools, and carrying an upright liberalism deeper into British life. If social tension only occasionally burst into the open violence of the Paris Commune, that stability depended upon an intricate balance of forces—different in each nation—maintained by the state.

In general Europeans faced the last third of the nineteenth century with increased confidence, impressed with the evidence of economic and social progress and hopeful that institutional and moral improvement would naturally follow. They could point, and often did, to evidence that in all the ranges of human thought, they enjoyed one of history's greatest civilizations. But even as this optimism flourished, there were rumblings of discontent from intellectuals who found the fashionable faiths shallow and from groups lower in society who were only just beginning to make themselves heard. The combination of an emphasis on politics, rapid social change, and the expansion of the state could prove explosive if conflicting interests fought to see who would command the enormous power Western society had assembled.

RECOMMENDED READING

Studies

Barzun, Jacques. *Classic, Romantic, and Modern.* 1961. One of Barzun's many famous essays in defense of Romanticism.

Beales, Derek. *The Risorgimento and the Unification of Italy.* 1971. Concise, skeptical introduction to the history of Italian unification.

* Binkley, Robert C. *Realism and Nationalism: 1852–1871.* 1934. Interprets the history of this generation in terms of the victory in each country of centralizers over federalists.

* Clark, G. Kitson. *The Making of Victorian England.* 1967. Graciously knowledgeable, stimulating, and wide-ranging essay.

* Craig, Gordon. *The Politics of the Prussian Army.* 1964. Establishes that much of Prussian history can be understood in terms of the influence and needs of the army.

Hamerow, Theodore S. *The Social Foundations of German Unification, 1858–1871.* 1972. The politics and ideas of unification placed in the context of a developing economy.

* Hauser, Arnold. *Social History of Art.* Vols. III and IV. 1958. Suggestive if sometimes mechanical effort to relate artistic trends to social change.

* Howard, Michael. *The Franco-Prussian War.* 1969. Exemplary study of how war reflects (and tests) an entire society.

* Jaszi, Oscar. *The Dissolution of the Habsburg Monarchy.* 1929. A work that has shaped most subsequent studies.

Lukács, Georg. *The Historical Novel.* Hannah and Stanley Mitchell (trs.). 1962. Insightful and learned study of the nineteenth-century novel by one of Europe's leading Marxist scholars.

Mack Smith, Denis. *Garibaldi.* 1956. Ably summarizes the place recent scholarship gives Italy's popular hero.

Mosse, George L. *The Nationalization of the Masses: Political Symbolism and Mass Movements in Germany from the Napoleonic Wars Through the Third Reich.* 1975. One of the most recent and complete efforts to find the roots of Nazism in popular nationalism.

* Pflanze, Otto. *Bismarck and the Development of Germany.* 1963. A major revision of older views that has become a standard synthesis.

Stavrianos, L. S. *The Balkans, 1815–1914.* 1963. Places the international troubles of this region in the context of domestic developments.

* Taylor, A. J. P. *The Struggle for Mastery in Europe, 1848–1918.* 1971. A lively, controversial interpretation of the international relations of the period.

Thayer, William Roscoe. *The Life and Times of Cavour.* 2 vols. 1911. A solid and old-fashioned work that captures the liberal view of Cavour and the Risorgimento.

* Thompson, James M. *Louis Napoleon and the Second Empire.* 1967. A balanced assessment in the light of recent scholarship.

* Williams, Roger L. *The French Revolutions of 1870–1871.* 1969. An introduction to the recent findings and long-standing controversies about the Paris Commune.

* Woodham-Smith, Cecil. *The Reason Why.* 1971. A colorful account of the Crimean War.

---

* Available in paperback.

TWENTY-FIVE

THE AGE OF PROGRESS

The half-century from the 1860s to 1914 saw the flowering of nineteenth-century civilization. In economic organization, technology, the arts and sciences, and politics, the revolutionary changes that had occurred before 1850 had now taken root, and in some respects the result was an almost incredible success story. European power, wealth, and prestige reached new heights and spread around the world; the benefits from increased knowledge, political freedom, and unfettered capitalism in most respects exceeded the early claims made for them. The pace of change seemed to increase in every domain of human activity, and the idea of historical progress became almost an obsession.

Paradoxically, an age that described itself in such tones of optimism and confidence also subjected itself to internal criticism of extraordinary severity. Literacy spread, but intellectuals denounced the mass culture it fostered. The arts flourished, but they expressed conflicting values and attitudes that made modern civilization seem lacking in coherence. The standard of living rose, but workingmen formed militant organizations to combat their employers, and socialists considered the very success of capitalism to be evidence of its imminent collapse. Conservatives assailed the threat to civilized values posed by excessive faith in reason, rampant avarice, and purposeless tolerance of every idea and faction. Christians continued to decry materialism and the exclusion of religion from its rightful role. The late nineteenth century is often described as the triumph of the middle class and the age of liberalism, but it was characteristic of that triumph and that age that many were moved to reject it.

These conflicts placed an added strain on political life at the very time that the state was expected to wield unequaled power. Each nation developed its own pattern for meeting this challenge, and remarkably every political system survived, though few escaped the threat of revolutionary upheaval. That fact, like the continuation of international peace and the spread of European empire, seemed evidence of the health of European civilization, but the period closed in the cataclysm of World War I. From the perspective of the troubled 1930s the late nineteenth century seemed an almost idyllic period remembered nostalgically as the "belle époque" of happy stability. Yet it was also the breeding ground of twentieth-century conflict and doubt.

I. ECONOMICS AND POPULATION

Economic and demographic growth in the second half of the nineteenth century resulted from a continuation of processes already under way, but with important differences that have led historians to call this the second industrial revolution. The rapid rate of growth now came from accelerated industrial change as new technology and large-scale production fed ever-expanding markets at home and abroad. While Europe's population grew more rapidly than ever before, the value of manufacturing went up three times as fast. Prosperity spread beyond the favored groups to affect all classes, and for the first time in history, a society expected economic growth to continue year after year.

ECONOMICALLY ACTIVE POPULATION CA. 1900

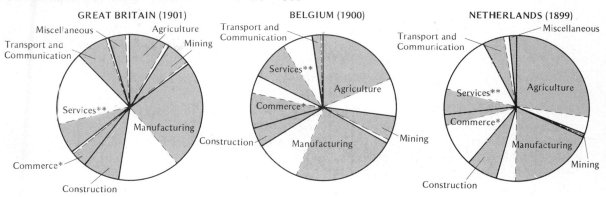

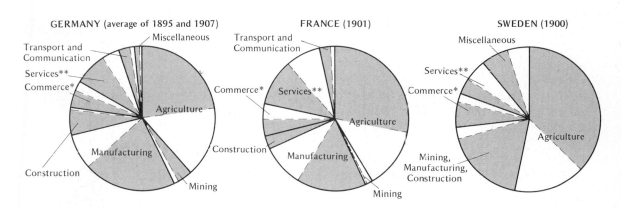

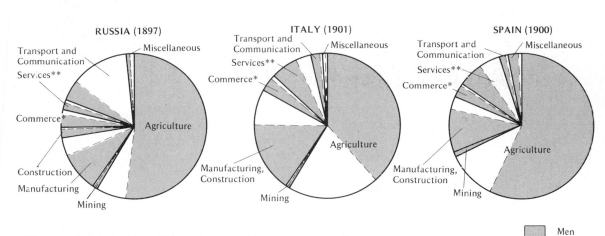

*Commerce includes banking, utilities, real estate, and insurance.
**Services includes armed forces and domestics.

Men
Women

(Source: Bairoch, P., et al., *The Working Population and Its Structure*, Brussels, 1968, p. 119.)

THE SECOND INDUSTRIAL REVOLUTION

Every nation experienced industrial progress in this period, but the expansion of the German economy following unification was spectacular. Everything seemed to foster the new nation's industrialization. Already rich in natural resources, Germany acquired more raw materials as well as factories with the annexation of Alsace-Lorraine. Her system of railroads provided excellent communications; the famous educational system produced ample numbers of the administrators and engineers the commercial sector now required. The government, which had played an active role in every facet of industrialization, continued to cooperate with business interests. Military needs stimulated basic industry, and a growing population provided an eager domestic market. Being newer than those of Britain or France, German plants employed the latest and most efficient equipment, obtaining the necessary capital through a modern banking structure. By 1900 they were far bigger than anyone else's, and firms engaged in the various

INDUSTRIAL PRODUCTION

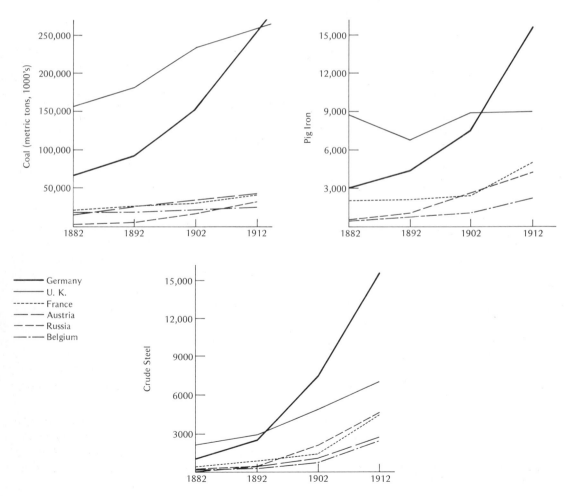

stages of production often combined in huge cartels dominating an entire field of enterprise. Germany became preeminent in new fields such as chemicals and electricity. Her salesmen appeared all over the world with catalogs in native languages and products suited to local conditions, selling with a drive and optimism British merchants resented as bad manners.

The older industrial economies of Great Britain, Belgium, and France continued to grow but more slowly; yet by 1900 France's industrial production, despite her loss of important textile and iron centers in Alsace, about equaled Great Britain's a generation earlier, when Britain led the world. French iron production more than doubled in the first twenty-five years of the Third Republic, and new processes made the nation's ore output second only to that of the United States. In value of production per capita, a figure that suggests something of a nation's standard of living, France remained ahead of Germany, though behind the British Isles.

By the turn of the century, Great Britain, whose industrial superiority had seemed a fact of nature, was clearly being surpassed in some of the critical indexes of production by the United States and Germany. Although the economy did continue to expand, its state of health became a serious issue in English public life, and economic historians remain fascinated by the question of why its growth became sluggish.

There are almost too many explanations. British plants and equipment were old and owners hesitated to undertake the cost of modernizing or replacing them. Well-established firms often made it hard for new companies to get a start. British schooling was weak in technical subjects, and education provided less opportunity for social mobility than on the Continent. Indeed social attitudes, always difficult to analyze precisely, may explain more than strictly economic fac-

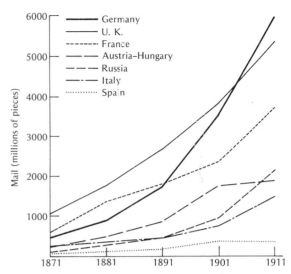

MAIL (MILLIONS OF PIECES)

The volume of mail has been used by some scholars as an indicator of modernization, reflecting increased literacy, internal communication, and commercial activity. In these terms, then, the relative position of the several nations on this chart is suggestive, and so are the points at which Germany surpasses France and then the United Kingdom or at which Italy, despite its smaller size, passes Russia.

tors. British industrialists, slow to appreciate the mere specialist and resistant to new ways, became less venturesome and perhaps a little complacent. Even so London remained the financial capital of the world—a world in which industrialization was rapidly spreading to Sweden and Italy, Russia and Japan.

Technological and Market Developments
Industrial expansion in this period was closely tied to new technology. By 1890 Europe was producing even more steel than iron, using the Bessemer converter developed in the 1860s, which permitted far higher temperatures in smelter furnaces, and subsequent discoveries made lower-grade ores profitable. British, German, and French maritime ship-

The Great Eastern, *combining steam and sail in massive square lines, looms over all other vessels in this print of 1861.* (Photo: The Granger Collection)

ping, which doubled between 1870 and 1914, depended on faster and larger steamships. New chemical processes and synthetics led to improved products ranging from dyes, textiles, and paints to fertilizers and explosives. A whole new industry developed to produce and supply electricity. The incandescent lamp created a demand for large generating stations to distribute power over a wide area, and by 1900 the manufacture of generators, cables, and motors in turn allowed increased and cheaper production in scores of other fields.

As striking as the new technology itself was the speed with which it was adapted to commercial uses. The telephone, invented in 1879, became a business necessity and an established private convenience within a few decades. The steam turbine, shown in the 1880s to be more efficient than the reciprocating engine, was widely employed for a variety of tasks, and it could soon be fueled by oil as well as coal. Home sewing machines and bicycles were created directly for the consumer market—in itself a significant reflection of the growing purchasing power of the masses. Inventions were now expected to change people's lives; the automobile in the 1890s, the airplane in the 1900s, and the radio a decade

Launching an early version of the French airplane. (Photo: J.–H. Lartigue from Rapho Guillumette)

later were all greeted with enthusiasm even before their commercial possibilities were established.

Although greater prosperity and growing populations increased the demand for food, the percentage of the population that made its living in agriculture continued to decline, down to only 8 percent in Britain, 22 percent in Belgium, and 35 percent in Germany. In France, which maintained a more balanced economy, as did the Netherlands and Sweden, 43 percent of the population lived off the land. But everywhere the wider use of machinery and chemical fertilizers increased the capital investment required for farming, and improved transportation intensified international competition. These factors encouraged much greater specialization. The most famous example is Denmark, where agriculture began to center on a highly capitalized and profitable dairy industry. But in France too wheat and sheep production declined in favor of wine grapes and sugar beets, which farmers could raise more profitably. Britain now imported almost all her grain and Germany a great deal.

The influx of agricultural produce from the Americas and Eastern Europe, especially Russia, pushed prices down at the same time that farmers desperately needed cash for the improvements required to make farming profitable, and more young men were forced to leave the countryside. European agriculture was caught in recurrent crises, and landed interests pressed their governments for help. The most common response was protective tariffs, increased by France, Germany, Austria, Russia, Italy, and Spain. Initially applied primarily to agriculture, the new tariffs were soon extended to manufactured goods as well, reversing the earlier trend toward the liberal policy of free trade.

But the trade barriers did not stop the general decline in prices. Strangely, the second industrial revolution occurred in one of the longest and most severe periods of deflation in European history. From the 1870s to 1896, prices, interest rates, and profits fell, with far-reaching effects. Handicraft industries, which had survived side by side with mechanized manufacturing throughout Europe, were forced out of business. So were numerous smaller and less efficient industrial firms. As competition sharpened, many industrialists welcomed the support governments could give through tariffs, state spending, and colonial empire. The great boom in railroad building ended, and governments had to save socially useful lines deserted by bankrupt companies. Economic demands became a central theme of politics as more and more of economic life centered on great factories owned by large corporations (and closely tied to banks and government) which employed hundreds of workers who in turn increasingly organized into industrial unions.

THE DEMOGRAPHIC TRANSFORMATION

The growing population that sustained the second industrial revolution evolved a quite different demographic profile from that of any previous period. Europe's population increased—from 295 million in 1870 to nearly 450 million by 1914—although in most of Europe birth rates had begun to decline. By the 1880s, however, mortality rates were falling still more steeply. This pattern of falling birth rates combined with a sharper decline in mortality rates has been named the demographic transition. Continuing in our own time, it has become one of the marks of modernity that has spread from Europe to the rest of the world.

Infant mortality in particular was reduced by improved sanitation, better diet, and the virtual elimination of diseases such as cholera and typhus. By the turn of the century, im-

THE TRANSFORMATION FROM SAILING VESSELS TO STEAMBOATS

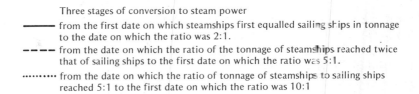

Three stages of conversion to steam power

—— from the first date on which steamships first equalled sailing ships in tonnage to the date on which the ratio was 2:1.

---- from the date on which the ratio of the tonnage of steamships reached twice that of sailing ships to the first date on which the ratio was 5:1.

········· from the date on which the ratio of tonnage of steamships to sailing ships reached 5:1 to the first date on which the ratio was 10:1

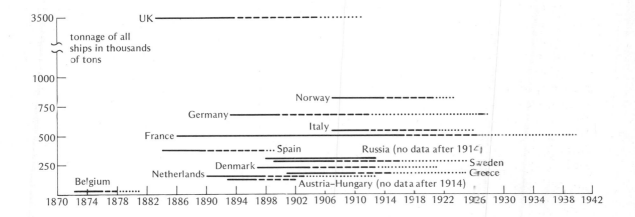

provements in medical care were lowering mortality rates still further. This left a net population growth despite a declining birth rate.[1]

Declining death rates, then, reflect the benefits of industrial prosperity, but the declining birth rates indicate a subtler change. The number of children to have was becoming more a matter of choice aided by the spread of contraception, and where bourgeois values

This chart suggests several points about the conversion to steam from sail that are indicative of the process of industrialization in general: a) most nations began the process at about the same time except for one or two early leaders, and b) nations with a smaller investment in a pre-industrial economy could convert to new technology more rapidly (Belgium and Spain, for example) so that even late-starters (such as Norway, Italy, and Greece) caught up with the others in the proportion of their ships driven by steam. Note the characteristic contrast between the United Kingdom and France. Britain, with a much larger fleet, converted to steam at a brisk pace, whereas France did so very slowly.

---

[1] "Birth rate" is used here as the more familiar term, but "fertility rate"—the ratio of the number of children born to the number of women of child-bearing age—would be more precise.

The leaders of the 1853 strike of Preston textile workers in England addressed friendly crowds but dressed differently from their men. (Photo: The Granger Collection)

took root, workers followed the upper classes in the trend toward later marriage, fewer births, and smaller families. Although the issues are complicated and the statistics un-certain, the estimates of crude birth rates in about 1910 suggest the social significance of this changing pattern: they were highest in Rumania, Bulgaria, Portugal, Hungary, Italy, and Spain, and lowest in Switzerland, Belgium, and France. Parents who were confident their children would live, who wanted them to inherit property and receive some education, chose to have fewer of them. Before 1850 population growth had been higher in West-

THE CHANGE IN NATIONAL POPULATIONS AT THE TURN OF THE CENTURY (POPULATION IN MILLIONS)

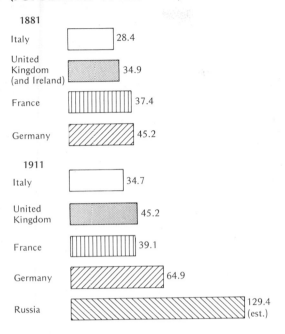

1881

Italy	28.4
United Kingdom (and Ireland)	34.9
France	37.4
Germany	45.2

1911

Italy	34.7
United Kingdom	45.2
France	39.1
Germany	64.9
Russia	129.4 (est.)

ern than in Central and Eastern Europe. That now was reversed, and the enormous increases in the populations to their east gave Frenchmen added reason to fear Germany's larger and younger population and Germans cause to worry about the Russian giant.

Another extraordinary demographic change resulted from the greatest movement of peoples in human history. Like the second industrial revolution, this wave of migration continued a century-old trend, but once again the scale of the change was unprecedented. Between 1875 and 1914 some 26 million Europeans emigrated overseas, more than half of them to the United States. The growth of population, an established pattern of internal migration to cities, larger boats and cheaper fares, unemployment in Europe and burgeoning opportunities in the New World, and visions of a better life spreading with

literacy all pushed Europe's lower classes to crowd into the steerage of ship after ship. More people left the United Kingdom in total than any other country; in proportion to population the greatest exodus was from Ireland. Before 1890 the United Kingdom, the Scandinavian countries, and Germany sent migrants in the highest proportion to their population. After 1890 the leaders were the United Kingdom, Italy, Spain, and Portugal. But every nation except France (second to the United States as the new home of European emigrants) contributed significant numbers to the movement.

Perhaps a third of those who left their native land to go overseas eventually returned home, but for every one who took a ship, countless more moved from countryside to town and town to city. Mainly the young and the poor, they were responding to new ambitions as well as perennial misery. In doing so they added to the restless change within Europe—in most cities a majority of residents had been born elsewhere—and carried European languages and cultures around the world. This economic and demographic growth reinforced the dynamism of late nineteenth-century society. New products, new businesses, new careers flourished everywhere, along with more freedom, education, and social mobility. Industrial civilization reached into the peasant hut and the urban slum.

Even the lower classes benefited from the new prosperity. Meat and white bread became an expected although not daily part of the diet for most people in the industrialized countries. Commerce offered cheap products at fixed prices, and jobs in sales and distribution brought new opportunities to rise into the lower-middle class. City crowds in London, Paris, and Berlin in 1900 were strikingly different from those of 1850 They were larger —for cities were bigger (eight European cities had a population of half a million or more in

EMIGRATION FROM EUROPE

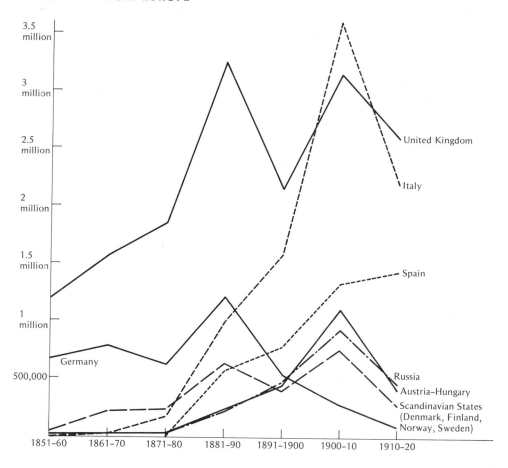

(Source: Mitchell, B. R., *European Historical Statistics, 1750–1970*, 1975, p. 135.)

1880, twenty-nine by 1910) and even workers had some free time—and they were healthier and cleaner. Their costumes told less about their trade or region; the worker could afford a dress suit, and the shopgirl could wear clothes that were not a mere uniform of her class. Fewer pickpockets and almost no beggars circulated in the streets. By 1900 nearly every city had its electric tramway, rapidly expanding the city beyond the circumferential boulevards that had replaced medieval walls, incorporating suburbs into a metropolitan area, and opening the prospect of better housing even for workers.

There was good reason then for belief in progress. Yet such rapid changes were unsettling, fatal for some occupations and hard on whole regions. In this turbulent society misery and insecurity were less tolerable and harder to excuse. Seen as the by-products of the very social system that produced so much wealth, they stimulated renewed efforts to change society itself.

II. THE CULTURE OF INDUSTRIAL SOCIETY

By any standard the fifty years before World War I was one of the great periods in the history of music, painting, and writing. Yet much of the artistic expression most admired today was disturbing to contemporaries, different from what they expected and hard to understand. Instead the public, though now more prosperous and literate, preferred commercial entertainments which offended intellectuals who found them wanting in either spontaneity or seriousness. But the expansion of knowledge, especially in the sciences, was such reassuring evidence of general progress that social theorists turned again, as the philosophes had done during the Enlightenment, to explaining it.

THEORIES OF PROGRESS: COMTE, DARWIN, AND SPENCER

The philosophy of Auguste Comte, enormously influential from midcentury on, was itself characteristic of much nineteenth-century thought. Clearly rooted in the ideas of the Enlightenment, it gave greater attention to the process of historical change. Like

Note that everywhere, both birth rates and death rates decline. The declining death rates reflect improved distribution of food and better hygiene and health care. The decline in birth rates reflects a change in social behavior. The space between them suggests the rate of population growth, very slight in the case of France, steady in England and Sweden, and sudden in Germany and Russia.

DEMOGRAPHIC TRANSITION

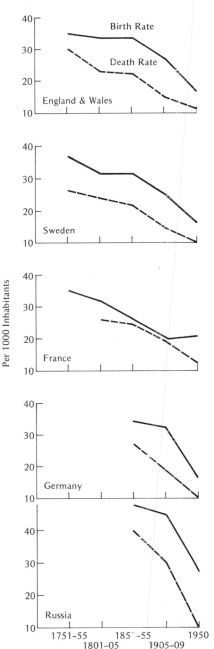

(Source: Cipolla, Carlo, *The Economic History of World Population,* Pelican, 1962.)

The new electric tram scoots above the ordinary bustle of the streets of Paris in the 1880s. (Photo: The Granger Collection)

Hegel, Comte sought to erect a comprehensive philosophical system that would encompass all of human knowledge, and like him he believed that his own era had opened the final stage of historical development. Comte was especially impressed, as were most contemporary intellectuals, by the social role of religion, the conquests of natural science, and the possibilities of human progress. For many years private secretary to Saint-Simon, Comte retained the confidence of the early socialists that society would soon be reorganized on rational principles.

He systematically elaborated his positive philosophy in ten volumes published between 1830 and 1854, and these with his other writings established positivism as an international movement even before his death, in 1857. The key to civilization, he argued, is man's understanding of the world, which has developed through three historical stages. In the first, the theological stage, mankind interpreted everything in terms of gods who lived in nature. In the second, or metaphysical, stage men learned through Christianity to think in more abstract terms. In the third, or positive, stage now dawning, human understanding was becoming scientific through objective and precise observation followed by generalization in the form of scientific laws. Every science has in fact already passed through the first two stages and into the third—astronomy first, then physics, chemistry, and biology. Now a new science, sociology (Comte coined the term), must crown the progression.

While thus honoring the role of established religion, Comte announced its demise, substituting a "religion of humanity" of his own invention. Some devoted followers accepted his complex scheme whole. But his importance rests rather in the wider agreement with his view that civilization progresses with increased knowledge discovered through scientific method and that the great contemporary need was for the scientific study of society and of man himself. This creed inspired and shaped much of the rapid development of the social sciences—economics, political science, anthropology, sociology, and psychology—achieved in the late nineteenth century.

A more concrete and more shocking theory of human progress emerged from Charles Darwin's *On the Origin of Species*, whose publication in 1859 was a milestone in the history of science.[2] With sober caution, Darwin had worked much as Comte said a scientist should. His respect for facts led him to collect evidence from every available source —his own observations from travel in the South Seas, the work of others, the lore of farmers. He first formulated his concept of natural selection in 1838, but not until Alfred R. Wallace independently developed a very similar theory could he be persuaded to publish his findings. Although Darwin's presentation was the more fully and carefully developed, the parallel theories of the two men suggest how much both owed to ideas already current. Biologists had shown the relationship

With self-conscious art, the photographer of old Charles Darwin suggests some timeless mystery. (Photo: New York Public Library, Picture Collection)

between biological form and function in impressive detail; geologists had begun to analyze the earth in terms of natural forces without recourse to sudden cataclysms or divine intervention; classical economists, especially Malthus, had stressed the importance of the cruel conflict for food, which Darwin made the essential key to natural selection.

Darwin established that the variety of species is potentially infinite—rejecting the classical and Christian idea of immutable forms in nature—and argued that there is an almost

---

[2] The full original title of Darwin's work suggests its broad and provocative implications: *On the Origin of Species by Natural Selection, or the Preservation of Favoured Races in the Struggle for Life.* The first edition sold out on the day of publication.

constant modification of species, each tested in the universal struggle for existence. He not only presented detailed evidence for evolution but described its mechanism: the fittest survived, a law of progress for all living things.

This scientific theory, expressed with caution and supported by massive evidence, almost instantly became the center of controversies that raged throughout Europe for a generation. Evolution, mutable species, survival determined by brute conflict rather than divine will—each of these challenged established assumptions in science and theology. Nor did Darwin hide his belief that the same laws apply to the development of man and beast. This seemed to many a scandalous disregard of divine providence and Christian teaching. Nowadays, except for fundamentalists, theologians and scientists generally agree that there is no necessary conflict between the concept of evolving species and Christian doctrine, but such tolerance required a distinction between the study of natural laws and religious tradition that in the nineteenth century few were willing to make. Nonetheless Darwinian ideas, often loosely understood, were enthusiastically extended to discussions of morality, politics, and society. "Social Darwinism" proved an invitingly tough-minded way to argue, in the name of human progress, for reform (a better environment makes for better people); but also for ruthless economic competition, racial differences, imperialism, and the necessity of war.

One of the grandest statements of the laws of progress was the *Synthetic Philosophy* of Herbert Spencer, published between 1860 and 1896. Spencer's ideas were closely tied to those of Comte and Darwin, and his contemporaries ranked him among the major philosophers of all time.

Spencer's central principle, which made progress "not an accident, but a necessity," was the evolution of all things from simplicity to complexity, from homogeneity to diversity. With heavy learning, he traced this process in physics and biology, sociology and psychology, economics and ethics. Such comprehensiveness was part of his appeal, and he applied his theses to physical matter, to human understanding, and to social institutions. He was admired for his claim to be hard-headed and practical; but while he refused to worry about the metaphysical abstractions of traditional philosophy, he maintained the assumptions of a narrow and rigid liberalism. He argued that the marketplace is the true test of the fittest, and that it must be uninhibited by state intervention even in behalf of welfare or public education.

When Spencer died, in 1903, much of his work was already outmoded by new developments in the several disciplines, strict laissez faire had been abandoned even by most liberals, and his sort of rationalism had come under heavy attack. His confidence that universal laws of development enshrined the values of middle-class English Protestants would soon seem quaint.

THE NATURAL SCIENCES

Discoveries in the natural sciences in this period supported the belief that a few universal principles underlie all existence. And in the nineteenth century these principles could still be understood, however imprecisely, by the educated public. The findings of science were expected to improve civilization through both their immediate application to technology and their contributions to general philosophy. Thermodynamics, the study of the relationship between heat and mechanical energy, provides an excellent example.

Building on theorems stated by Nicolas Sadi Carnot early in the century, thermodynamics became the core of nineteenth-century physics. It developed in many directions at once, treating practical problems of steam engines as well as fundamental properties of matter. By midcentury the combined work of scientists in many countries had established that formulas predicting the behavior of gases could be applied to the field of mechanics. This culminated in the mathematical formulation of the two fundamental laws of thermodynamics. One states the principle of the conservation of energy: energy can be transformed into heat or work and back again but can be neither created nor destroyed. The other declares that any closed physical system tends toward equilibrium, a state in which heat is uniformly distributed and therefore cannot produce energy.[3] In practical terms this means that heat can be made to do work only when connected through an engine to a cooler body. Philosophically it invites speculation about the universe as a giant machine in which the level of energy must inexorably decline.

The study of magnetism advanced in a similar way from the work of Michael Faraday. He had shown in the 1830s and 1840s that lines of magnetic force are analogous to gravity and that electricity can induce magnetism (and vice versa—the principle of the dynamo). In the 1860s James Clerk Maxwell's equations defined the similar behavior of light and magnetic fields. Thus gravity, magnetism, electricity, and light were all related. By the end of the century, physics had established mathematical laws of theoretical beauty and practical power extending from the universe to the atom, which was then conceived of as a miniature solar system.

The fundamental generalizations of chemistry are contained in the periodic law and periodic table published by Dmitri Mendeleev in 1869. Compounds and elements had been clearly distinguished for only half a century, and the difference between molecules and atoms came to be generally accepted only in 1860. Yet Mendeleev's table established a marvelous symmetry, so precise that the elements could all be charted by atomic weight, each eighth element having similar properties. This regularity even allowed for the prediction of unknown elements that would when discovered fill the gaps on the table.

Such achievements resulted from the efforts of hundreds of scientists, freely exchanging ideas across national boundaries, working with precise methods and the logic of mathematics. Experiments admired in the 1820s seemed crude by the 1870s, and science became the province of carefully trained professionals rather than inspired amateurs. Research demanded ever more systematic organization and larger and more expensive laboratories. The success of science stimulated a general expansion of education, and most of the disciplines that constitute the modern university achieved their separate identity, establishing professional organizations and scholarly journals, in the late nineteenth century.

Much of the theoretical scientific knowledge opened the way to very practical benefits. Thermodynamics led to the development of more efficient sources of power. The investigations of electricity led to the telegraph by midcentury and to electric lights and motors for hundreds of uses a generation later. Proof that germs were not spontaneously generated as was generally believed came from the Frenchman Louis Pasteur's studies in the 1860s of why wine spoiled; in England Joseph Lister then discovered that germs could be killed by carbolic acid; and a decade later Robert Koch in Germany showed that different diseases were caused by distinct microbes. Advances such as these moved sanitation and public medicine into the realm of systematic sciences and made vaccination an effective and broadly applicable means of reducing communicable diseases. All of society had reason to welcome the impact of science.

---

[3] The measure or amount of energy unavailable for work is called entropy, a term coined by the physicist Rudolf Clausius in 1865.

CONTRASTS IN CULTURE

The creative arts continued to flourish, benefiting from high prestige and ever larger and more sophisticated audiences. Yet the forms and styles employed grew so diverse that the arts hardly seemed to speak for a single civilization. One reason, and the one that disturbed contemporaries least, was the trend toward national styles, marked by the deliberate use of folk elements and recognizable in the special atmosphere of English or Russian novels and in the tonalities of French, German, or Russian music. Another reason was the tendency for the artist to act as social critic, thereby bringing issues of politics and values that troubled society into the realm of aesthetics. Thus the tension between the individual and society, between the artist's personal perceptions and the unstable conventions of a world undergoing rapid change, remained a central theme of nineteenth-century art. These concerns and then the reaction against them in favor of a "purer" art led to the bewildering variety of competing styles and schools. "Naturalism," "the Pre-Raphaelites," "Impressionism," "the Decadents," "Symbolism"—such self-conscious labels were frequently proclaimed with angry manifestoes against previous art and present culture.

Naturalists claimed that the artist, like a scientist, should present life in objective detail after careful research. This aim was particularly suited to the novel; and Emile Zola, with descriptions precise as acid of industrial and Parisian life, was a master of the school. Determinism, through blood inheritance or social class, was a favorite and related theme in this Darwinian age. It proved especially effective on the stage where the protagonists' destiny inexorably unfolded before the new audience slowly won over to realistic drama in the two decades before World War I.

For the realistic painters of midcentury or the Pre-Raphaelites of England (who took their name from the pious and simpler art of the early Renaissance), much of a painting's importance lay in its subject matter and message. Then a new generation of painters broke with this tradition to concentrate on capturing the effects of light and color almost as if the artist's brilliance in analyzing and recreating such effects was in itself the purpose of painting. Artists denied exhibition at the annual Paris Salon of 1867 established the Salon des Refusés, proudly contesting the validity of official taste. These are the painters we remember, for they included some of the leaders of Impressionism, whose golden age was the 1870s and 1880s, among them Auguste Renoir and Claude Monet. They and the Post-Impressionist Paul Cézanne were recognized in their own lifetime as ranking among the great artists of Western history, but painters only slightly younger, like Paul Gauguin and Vincent van Gogh, turned to still newer and more personal styles.

Thus each of the arts tended to develop on its own terms, independent of established judgments. Art nouveau, turning its back on the practical and efficient industrial world of the turn of the century, delighted in applying ornamental arabesques to everything from wrought iron to poster lettering and printed cloth. Poetry, like painting, became an increasingly private expression indifferent to conventional morality, often obscure, and constructed in terms of complex aesthetic doctrines. The fashionable fascination with death, languid despair, and perfumed aestheticism was called decadent by its critics, a label willingly accepted until it gave way to Symbolism. A movement of French poets that spread throughout Europe, symbolism interpreted the things one sees and describes as symbolic of a deeper and more spiritual reality. Art, like life itself, was to be complexly understood on several levels of meaning at once, and individual style had become a personal conquest, a private bridge between the artist's identity and

The bridge across the Firth of Forth stands as a monument to the age of iron and steel in this photograph taken shortly after the bridge's completion in 1890. (Photo: The Granger Collection)

external society. Still more radical changes in the arts occurred in the decade preceding World War I, changes that further separated the artist from the broader public but would shape the art of the twentieth century.

In contrast architecture, the most immediately social of all the arts, was the least innovative until the very end of the century. Only then were the structural and aesthetic possibilities hidden in railroad sheds, bridges, and exhibit halls developed into the skyscraper and a new architectural style. Perhaps the tension between individual and society so fruitful elsewhere was stultifying to so public and functional an art. Even when they achieved real beauty, the great buildings of the nineteenth century were eclectically dressed in the styles of other periods. Churches evoked the spiritual coherence of the High Middle Ages; banks and public buildings expressed in stone the civic virtues of Greece and Rome. Even apartment houses usually imitated some earlier epoch, as if to make new wealth feel more secure.

European popular culture changed radically in the second half of the century. Traditional festivals and games, once tied to the local region, gradually gave way to public amusements reflecting an increasingly urban life and the greater leisure and wealth of the masses. With each change to a new popular medium, from operetta to music hall to vaudeville and—

after the turn of the century—silent films, a larger part of the population shared in public entertainment. Popular culture thus tended to become more uniform within each nation and across Europe. It also became more formal (the Marquis of Queensberry rules for boxing date from 1867) and increasingly commercial, both in the music hall and on the athletic field. Leading actors and actresses became stars whose offstage lives were part of their fascination as these forms of light entertainment, along with the circus and amusement parks, boomed, their clientele swelled by families from the lower-middle and working classes. Soccer, once the sport of the English public school, became professional (most of Europe's famous clubs were formed around the turn of the century), attracting huge, noisy, Sunday crowds. While workers shared these urban entertainments, the middle classes began to crowd summer resorts and to play recently formalized games like golf and tennis. This profitable popular culture assumed and to some extent created an audience with common tastes and in doing so helped bridge the social gap between workers and the middle class, between town and city. Newspapers had similar effects as publishers learned to increase their circulation (several now approached daily sales of a million copies) through sensational articles and colorful features written in a direct and less literary style. Like the millions of popular novels (now more specialized into women's romances, adventure stories especially for children, and penny thrillers), such writing abandoned any pretense to cultivated taste, further separating formal from popular culture.

These changes were related to another of immeasurable importance: for the first time in Western history, in the major nations at least, a majority of the adult population could read and write. By the 1880s governments almost everywhere, recognizing the importance of literacy to politics and industry, had made education universal and compulsory; and school fees had been reduced or eliminated. In 1850 only in Prussia could most of the adult population read or write; by 1900 more than 90 percent of the adult population of Germany, France, and Great Britain was literate, and the proportion elsewhere was climbing rapidly. Mass schooling was usually limited to a few years of the most elementary subjects, and aside from special supplementary instructions in workers' classes, night schools, and special vocational institutes, few of the poor had any opportunity for further training. The amount and kind of education they received was one of the clearest distinctions between the middle class and those below it. Nevertheless the schooling available to everybody was steadily extended, and the barriers separating mass education from the sort of preparation that led to secondary school and university were gradually lowered.

For most contemporaries society's extraordinary commitment to education ranked with liberty, industrial prosperity, and scientific knowledge as proof of social progress. But there were some who saw in the quality of popular entertainment and mass journalism what they felt would prove to be an ominous new threat to Western culture.

III. ATTACKS ON LIBERAL CIVILIZATION

Much of liberalism's promise was being fulfilled in the last quarter of the nineteenth century. After 1870 new constitutions made governments more representative and civil rights more secure; expanding trade and production lifted the standard of living, and individuals enjoyed greater social opportunities; laws became more humane; peace, foreign and domestic, seemed more certain. Yet many intellectuals expressed contempt for middle-class society, radicals sought the end of the capitalist system, and conservatives and Christians mounted new attacks on liberal values. Moreover thinkers of many sorts strongly challenged optimistic liberal assumptions about the nature of progress and man's rationality.

MARXISM

No criticism of contemporary society has proved more influential, no nineteenth-century theory more lasting than the work of Karl Marx. Marx was born in 1818 into a middle-class Rhineland Jewish family that had prospered with the emancipation from civil disabilities brought by the revolutionary armies from France. He was an able student and received an excellent education at the leading German universities. Too radical to be permitted an academic career, he turned to journalism and became editor of a famous liberal newspaper, the *Rheinische Zeitung*. But his attacks on censorship and his views on economics led the Prussian government to demand his removal, and in 1843 Marx left for Paris. There he met other exiles and leading French radicals, men to whom he would later give the enduring label of "utopian" socialists, and he established a friendship with Friedrich Engels that would become a lifetime's collaboration.

Trained in German philosophy, abreast of contemporary economics, and in touch with the currents of radicalism, Marx began in Paris the systematic development of his own ideas. He outlined his theory in a powerful, apocalyptic tone in the *Communist Manifesto*, written jointly with Engels, which was published just before the revolutions of 1848. Little noticed at first, it proved to be one of the great pieces of propaganda of all time, a specific program and a general call to action combined with a philosophy of history. Marx devoted the rest of his life—from 1849 to 1883, which he spent in poverty-stricken exile in London—to the painstaking elaboration of his ideas in essays, letters, and the first volume of *Das Kapital*, published in 1867. Engels, who shared Marx's exile in Britain, edited the second and third volumes, which appeared in 1885 and 1894.

Marx wrote with verve on contemporary affairs—his essays on the revolutions of 1848 and Louis Napoleon's coup d'état are classics —but fundamentally he wanted, like so many thinkers of his time, to build a comprehensive philosophical system. Later in the century his followers would compare him with Darwin as the "discoverer" of the "law" of history, dialectical materialism. The dialectic came from Hegel, the struggle between thesis and antithesis leading to a synthesis as the next stage in historical evolution. Marx, however, rejected Hegel's idealism—the view that the dialectic works through ideas that constitute the spirit of the age—insisting instead that any society rests fundamentally on the organization of its economy, the mode of production.

Political systems, Marx said, grow from these material underpinnings, and in each the dominant social class expresses the needs, the values, and the interests associated with that particular mode of production. The agricultural economy of the Middle Ages required the feudal system with its particular social values and laws, upheld by the land-owning aristocracy. That system produced its antithesis in the middle class, which is based on capitalism. But capitalist and industrial society dominated by the middle class was in turn producing a new antithesis through its own contradictions and embodied in the rising proletariat. Class conflict is the mechanism of historical progress, and the triumph of the proletariat will bring a new synthesis, a classless society. History would thus lead, by its own inevitable laws, to a world similar to the one envisioned by other socialists. In the classless society, men would no longer be

forced into the inequality required for capitalist production. At present, compulsion is the primary purpose of the state, but in the new era the state would wither away, unneeded.

Revolutions, in this analysis, mark the arrival to power of a new class. They are, however, more than mere transfers of power. A new class brought changes in law, religion, and customs, which it then maintained in its own interest. The middle class, in Marxist terms, has represented a great, progressive force. But capitalism, despite all the ideologies and social institutions designed to shore it up, will fail through its own internal contradictions.

Marx's detailed analysis of capitalism took much from the classical economists (at a time when they were beginning to be outmoded). The value of a product, he insisted somewhat obscurely, comes from the value of all the labor required to produce it—to transform raw materials into manufactured goods. The capitalist makes a profit by keeping for himself part of the value added by other men's labor, by exploiting the working class. But capitalists must compete with each other, and to do so they are forced to lower prices, which in turn reduces profits. This has two effects. First, the capitalist must exploit his labor more harshly, cutting wages to the minimum required for subsistence. Second, the smaller producers will fail, which will lead to increased concentrations of capital and force more and more members of the middle class into the proletariat, composed of men with nothing but their labor to sell. Thus a shrinking capitalist class suffering from declining

Something of the power of his personality shows through this photograph of Karl Marx, the scholar (with reading glass) and bourgeois. (Photo: The Granger Collection)

profits will face a growing proletariat. Capitalism therefore lays the basis for socialism by depriving all but a few of property. The contradictions will be resolved when the whole system falls.

Many of Marx's specific predictions now seem wrong. Although some of the rich have grown richer, the poor are not poorer. Marx simply did not see much that is central to the modern economy—ever-expanding technology, the spread of ownership through public sale of stocks, and mass consumption. He did not anticipate the social effects of literacy, popular democracy, and mass communication. Marxist psychology is inadequate, with little acknowledgment of the loyalties and the irrationality so important in human personality. He sought to combine in one system Hegel's most difficult ideas, the economic theories of liberalism, the "scientific" method of positivism, and the moral vision of socialism—a combination awkward at best. Such critical terms as "class" and "state" remained ambiguous, and the concept of class struggle, applied elastically to a petty event as well as centuries of history, lost its analytic force. The goal of history, according to Marx, is the classless society; yet he sketched that desired condition only vaguely and left fundamental questions about it and about the means of obtaining it unanswered.

Despite such weaknesses, and the theory's every flaw has been widely broadcast, Marxism has deeply affected all modern thought, shaped the policies of all sorts of governments, and provided a core for some of the most powerful political movements of the last century. Such impact requires explanation, and perhaps four points can capture something of the answer.

First, Marxism not only sees society as a whole and explains historical change but demands systematic and detailed analyses of the interrelationship of social values, institutions, politics, and economic conditions. It also suggests methods for conducting such analyses, and these qualities account for its continuing importance in all the social sciences.

Second, Marxism accepts and indeed hails industrialization as inevitable and beneficial even while accepting most criticisms of industrial society. Many reformers dreamed of green gardens and simpler days; but Marx believed the machine can free man from brute labor and through greater productivity provide well-being for all. Industrialization could be made to provide solutions to the very problems it created. Thus Marxism has special appeal for societies eager to modernize.

Third, the theory is rich in moral judgments without having to defend any ethical system. Although social values are considered relative, and those of his opponents denounced as hypocritical, Marx's own rage at injustice rings out in a compelling call to generous sentiments that rejects sentimentality.

Finally, Marxism claims the prestige of science and offers the security of determinism. Knowing where destiny leads, its believers can accept the uneven flow of change, confident that any defeats are temporary. Opponents are to be recognized and fought less for what they say or do than for what they represent—for their "objective" role in the structure of capitalism. Accepting concessions does not compromise the fight, for tactics can be very flexible when the only requirement is that they assist the inevitable movement of history toward the victory of the proletariat. Marx believed that small social changes may lead to sudden qualitative ones, and Marxists thus can favor immediate reforms as well as revolution.

The variety inherent in Marx's system has been a source of bitter division as well as strength among socialists, but it has helped keep Marxism more vigorous and coherent than any other of the grand theories spawned in the nineteenth century.

The First International

Marx and Engels intended to be not merely authors of a theory but leaders of a political and social movement. When in 1864 a group of English labor leaders called a small international conference in London, Marx readily agreed to come as a representative of the German workers. The International Working Men's Association, usually called the First International, was founded at that meeting, and Marx dominated it from the start. He did his best to replace traditional radical rhetoric about truth and justice with the hard language of Marxism, and during the eight years of the First International's life, he gradually succeeded in expelling those who disagreed.

The French members were generally followers of Louis Auguste Blanqui and Pierre Joseph Proudhon, socialists for whom Marx had little use; he dismissed the Blanquists, with their fondness for violence and dreams of conspiracy, as romantic revolutionaries, and his first socialist writing had been a critique of Proudhon's plans for workers' cooperatives and his sympathy for anarchy. The International's English members did not accept Marx's emphasis on revolution or his claim that the Paris Commune was "the glorious harbinger of a new society."

The most important conflict, however, was with Mikhail Bakunin. A Russian anarchist, Bakunin had established himself as one of Europe's more flamboyant revolutionaries in 1848. Later sentenced to exile in Siberia, he escaped in 1861, eventually joining the International in 1867. Bakunin respected Marx and understood his materialist philosophy, while Marx seems to have felt some of the fascination of Bakunin's personality. But Bakunin supported nationalism and praised the revolutionary spirit of countries like Italy and Spain, whereas Marx insisted that the revolutionary cause was international and most promising in more industrial lands. The Russian's delight in conspiracies and plots seemed childish to the German expatriate; and Bakunin, who distrusted any state, found a dangerous authoritarianism in Marx and Marxism.

The 1872 meeting, at which Bakunin was expelled, was the First International's last, for Marx and Engels then let the association die. Its membership had never been large or even clearly defined. Yet it played a part in building a workers' movement by disseminating Marxism, by teaching others to view each strike or demonstration as part of a larger conflict, by stressing the international ties of workers in a period of nationalism, and by exemplifying the advantages of militant discipline. In these ways and in its intolerance of doctrinal error and its intemperate polemics, the First International helped set the tone of the growing socialist movement.

SOCIALISM AND ANARCHISM

Between 1876 and World War I, socialist parties became an important part of political life in nearly every European country. Except in Great Britain most of them were at least formally Marxist. As they began to win elections, socialists disagreed over whether to follow a more moderate policy aimed at electoral success or adhere rigidly to the teachings of Marx. The most common compromise combined moderate policies with flaming rhetoric, and the Second International, formed in 1889 with representatives from parties and unions in every country, sought to maintain doctrinal rigor and socialist unity. Thus the Marxian critique of liberalism and capitalism was spread through books, newspapers, and magazines, in parliamentary debate and every election.

Labor organizations outside of Germany were not often consistently Marxist, but their growth was another dramatic change of the period. Unions were everywhere class-conscious, frequently tempted by anarchism and suspicious of politics. Their membership soared, with millions of workers paying dues in the industrialized countries, and the strike became the common expression of social protest. Skilled artisans, threatened by new modes of production yet strengthened by their own traditions of cooperation, were often still the leaders in militant action; but the organization of labor spread especially in larger factories despite the forceful resistance of employers and of the state. In the last decades of the century European society faced the most extensive labor agitation it had ever known. Yet strikes were coming to be better organized and more orderly as well as larger, and they sometimes won important public sympathy.

Most people did not distinguish very clearly among the various radical movements and associated anarchist "propaganda of the deed" with socialists and labor organizers. Certainly anarchists were in the headlines; they assassinated the president of France in 1893, the prime minister of Spain in 1897, the empress of Austria in 1898, the king of Italy in 1900, and the president of the United States in 1901. In the 1880s and 1890s, bombs were thrown into parades, cafés, and theaters in cities all over Europe, and such incidents were followed by the arrest of radical suspects and spectacular trials.

But bomb throwers and assassins were only a tiny wing of the broad anarchist movement. Its intellectual tradition was continuous since the time of the French Revolution, and its most famous figure after Bakunin was Prince Pëter Kropotkin, an exiled Russian aristocrat. Kropotkin was a theorist whose gentleness and compassion made him a kind of spiritual leader, but his descriptions of anarcho-communism did not unify the movement. Some anarchists stressed individualism, some pacifism, and some the abolition of private property; all rejected imposed authority and sought instead a natural order in which men would cooperate as brothers. They won their largest following among the poor who felt themselves crushed by industrialization: immigrants to the United States, peasants in southern Spain, artisans, and some workers in Italy and France. Anarchism was influential in the opposition to bureaucratic centralization and to militarism, and it appealed to artists and writers who shared the anarchists' contempt for bourgeois values; but its major contribution was the heroes and martyrs it gave to the growing mystique of the radical left.

THE CHRISTIAN CRITIQUE

The attack on liberalism came not only from the left but from the pulpits of every Christian denomination. Individualism, the charges ran, is often mere selfishness; religious tolerance masks indifference to moral issues; progress is another name for materialism. Churches tended to reject the growing claims of the state, especially in education and welfare, and many Christians denounced the injustices of capitalist society as forcefully as did the socialists.

The Roman Catholic Church was particularly hostile. In 1864 Pius IX issued an encyclical, *Quanta Cura*, with a syllabus of "the principal errors of our time" attached. Taken from earlier statements by the pope, its eighty items were written in the unbending tones of theological dispute. The syllabus listed false propositions, for example, the opinion that ". . . it is no longer expedient that the Catholic religion should be held as the only religion of the State, to the exclusion of all other forms of worship." Catholics more politic than the pope were quick to point out that this denun-

ciation of formal error was not the same as advocating religious intolerance, but such subtleties were easily lost. The syllabus denounced total faith in human reason, the exclusive authority of the state, and attacks on traditional rights of the church; but its most noted proposition was the last, which declared it false to think that "The Roman Pontiff can, and ought to, reconcile himself, and come to terms with progress, liberalism and modern civilization."

The Vatican Council of 1869–1870, the first council of the church in 300 years, confirmed the impression of intransigence. It was a splendid demonstration of the Church's continued power, and prelates came from around the world to proclaim the dogma of papal infallibility. It declared that the pope, when speaking *ex cathedra* (that is, formally from the chair of Peter and on matters of faith and morals), is incapable of error. This had long been a traditional belief, and its elevation to dogma confirmed the trend toward increased centralization within the church and affirmed the solidarity of Catholics in the face of new dangers. Even as the council met, the outbreak of the Franco-Prussian War allowed the Italian government to take over Rome, and governments throughout Europe wondered if Catholics could now be reliable citizens of a secular state.

The expanding role of government, especially in matters of education and welfare, made conflicts between church and state a major theme of European life. While theories of evolution, positivism, and biblical criticism put defenders of traditional belief on the defensive, politicians worried about the influence of the churches, particularly in rural areas and among national minorities, as anonymous masses of people were increasingly called to the polls.

In the United Kingdom the Church of England had steadily been stripped of its special privileges in moves opposed at every step by the clergy, most peers, and conservatives; but religious differences continued to inflame the Irish question. Bismarck launched and then abandoned the Kulturkampf as the German government relied more and more on the Catholic Center party. In Russia the Orthodox Church became in effect a department of state, used to strengthen the dominance of Russians in the multinational empire, while the Austrian government in contrast broke its close ties (and its concordat) with the Roman Catholic Church in an effort to lessen opposition to Viennese rule. The conflict between church and state was most open and bitter, however, in Spain, Italy, and France, where it was the central political division of the 1880s and 1890s.

Generally these conflicts subsided somewhat after the turn of the century. Relatively secure states, having established the breadth of their authority, tended to become more tolerant; and anticlericalism came to seem outmoded as governments faced the rising challenge from the left. The churches too responded more flexibly, in the style of Pope Leo XIII (1878–1903), who established an understanding with Bismarck and encouraged French Catholics to accept the Third Republic.

At the same time Christianity displayed renewed vigor. There was a general revival of biblical and theological studies, marked in the Roman Catholic Church by emphasis on the theology of St. Thomas Aquinas, whose arguments for the compatibility of faith and reason brought greater clarity and confidence to Catholic positions. Christian political and social movements learned to mobilize enormous support and became more active in social work (the Salvation Army was founded in 1865).

This engagement in charity, religious missions at home and overseas, education, labor unions, and hundreds of special projects not only strengthened Christian social influence but led to outspoken denunciations of immoral and unjust conditions. In his social encyclicals, especially *Rerum Novarum* issued in 1891, Leo XIII added a powerful voice to the rising cry for reform. He restated Catholic belief in private property, the sanctity of the family, and the social role of religion but went beyond these well-known views to speak to modern industrial conditions. The Catholic Church, he wrote, not only recognizes the right of workers to their own organizations and to "reasonable and frugal comfort" but warns the state against favoring any single class and society against viewing human beings as merely a means to profit.

The churches recognized the altered circumstances that left neither public institutions nor private habit reliable supports of religion. Strongest in rural areas and with more women communicants than men, they strove to improve their position in the cities among workers and the middle class. The adjustments were neither easy nor smooth, but by 1910 Christianity was more respectable among intellectuals, more active in society, and more prominent in politics than it had been since the early nineteenth century. Whether of the political left or right, Christians found in their religion a whole arsenal of complaints against liberalism and industrial capitalism.

REVIVAL OF THE RIGHT

Until World War I European political thought remained predominantly liberal, but some of the optimism was fading. Liberals themselves made less of simple individualism and worried more about problems of community and social justice, and some writers even doubted that politics was much affected by the free exchange of ideas so dear to John Stuart Mill.

The Frenchman Georges Sorel shared the growing suspicion that public opinion owed more to prejudice than to reason. Like many intellectuals, he felt contempt for middle-class society but argued that its overthrow would not come in the way predicted by Marx. His most important book, *Reflections on Violence* (1908), postulated rather that historic changes like the rise of Christianity or the French Revolution come about when people are inspired by some great myth that stands beyond the test of reason. As a myth for his times, he proposed the general strike, a possibility then much discussed by European unions. Sorel thus contributed to the widespread syndicalist movement, which called on workers' groups, *syndicats*, to bring down bourgeois society; his larger significance was his rejection of bourgeois rationalism in favor of violence and the will. Like many contemporary writers in Italy and Germany, he found the energy for change in man's irrationality.[4]

Sorel's countryman Henri Bergson, the most eloquent and revered philosopher of his day, expounded a gentle, abstruse set of theories. In touch with contemporary movements in the arts, psychology, and religion, he too pictured much that is best in human understanding as arising not from reason but intuitively from subjective and unconscious feelings. Society therefore should encourage a spirit of energy and common endeavor, favoring the spontaneity that translates feeling into action.

The revolutionary challenge such ideas contained became clearer in the works of Friedrich Nietzsche. He too stressed the will in a philosophy that lashed contemporary civilization on every page. His disdain for ideas of equality and democracy was balanced by his hatred of nationalism and militarism; he rejected his society not only for what it was but for what it meant to be. The only hope for the future was the work of the few, of supermen who would drop the inhibitions of bourgeois society and the "slave morality" of Christianity.

Nietzsche's tone had the violence of a man trying to bring everything crashing down, but he was no mere nihilist. He wrote his passionate aphorisms as a man in terror for himself and his world. A deeply original thinker, he was a child of his times in his approach to culture and history but above all in his anger.

ANTI-SEMITISM AND THE RIGHT

Like Nietzsche's philosophy, anti-Semitism, which he detested, was part of the rising current of opposition to liberal society. Anti-Semitism in the 1890s was more than a continuation of centuries-old prejudices, and it was surprisingly universal. Venomous assertions of Jewish avarice and lack of patriotism were used to discredit the entire republic in France and opponents of imperial policy in Great Britain. Anti-Semitic parties elected sixteen deputies to the Reichstag in 1893, and the prestigious Conservative party in Germany added anti-Semitism to its program. The lord mayor of Vienna from 1895 to 1910 found anti-Semitism invaluable in winning his electoral victories, and it was an official policy of the Russian government from the terrible pogroms of 1881 on.

There is no simple explanation for a phenomenon seemingly so contrary to the major trends of the century. One reason relates to the perception of Jews as a ready symbol of liberal, capitalist society; they had received their civil rights at the hands of Napoleon and in liberal revolutions, lived primarily in urban environments, and found their opportunities for advancement in the expanding professions and businesses of the nineteenth century.

---

[4] Vilfredo Pareto and Sorel, both trained as engineers, are usually grouped together with Robert Michels as leading theorists of the new political "realism."

They were prominent leaders in many of the most venturesome enterprises, most important scientific discoveries, and most striking social theories. Nationalism, especially in Germany, had come to stress folk culture and race; by attacking Jews, conservatives could make the liberal, capitalist world itself seem alien to national traditions. Crude adaptations of Darwinism gave racial theories a pseudoscientific panache,[5] and indeed quack science generally flourished, for credulity was encouraged by the fact that much of academic science, especially physics, was no longer comprehensible to laymen. Theories of conspiracy gave concrete and simple explanations for the baffling pace of social change, offering the hope that by circumscribing specific groups—such as the Jews—society could resist change itself.

Neither irrationalism nor anti-Semitism belongs inherently to a single political persuasion, but both were used primarily by the political right in the decades preceding World War I. Rightist movements revived notably in these years, building on those social groups that felt most harmed by the changes of the century: aristocrats, rural people, and Christians. Often incongruously, they defended established constitutions—the House of Lords in Britain, the concordat with the Roman Catholic Church in France, three-class voting and government independent of the Reichstag in Germany, limited suffrage and an intrusive monarchy in Italy, the authority of the tsar in Russia. They added to this conservatism contemporary concerns about the shallowness of middle-class culture and the need for government intervention in behalf of a stable

economy. They tried, frequently with success, to make patriotism and national strength their battle cry, learning to make an effective mass appeal. Denounced by Marxists as defenders of reactionary capitalism, they declared socialism the menace of the hour and the natural consequence of liberal error.

Thus critics from the right as well as the left gained vigor from attacking the very changes that most men still labeled progress. So many simultaneous assaults created grave political crises in many states, but for most a new equilibrium followed in which government accepted more responsibility for social justice, politics became more democratic, and society grew more tolerant. Neither before nor since have Europeans generally been so free to move about as they wished and say what they liked.

IV. DOMESTIC POLITICS

Growing populations and expanding economies necessitated far-sighted policies, and every government had to meet that challenge. The Scandinavian nations became models of how to do so. When Norway voted for separation from Sweden in 1905, the decision was accepted peacefully; and the two nations lived thereafter in harmony, among the most democratic in the world.

In most countries, however, adjustment to rapid social change in the late nineteenth century was difficult, uneven, and a source of conflict. In general these conflicts centered on three different issues: first, the question of access to political life (who would be allowed to participate and to what extent); second, a question of national loyalty (were some groups—foreigners, Catholics, Jews—a threat to national life that should somehow be excluded from it); third, essentially a question of social justice (what rights to organization

---

[5] An important example is Houston Steward Chamberlain's *The Foundations of the Nineteenth Century*, published in Germany in 1899. A Germanophile Englishman and intense admirer of Wagner, Chamberlain traced all that was best in European civilization to its "Aryan" elements. The work was widely admired until the collapse of the Nazi regime.

and social welfare would workers be allowed). Each country in dealing with these issues in effect defined its social as well as its political structure. In each, international ambitions and dangers both increased domestic tensions and were ominously used to preserve domestic peace.

RUSSIA 1881–1914: LIBERAL REVOLUTION

Even in Russia political crises led to liberal concessions. To Europeans no evidence for the necessity of representative institutions was more impressive than their sudden introduction into Russia. Alexander III became tsar in 1881 on his father's assassination, an event he attributed to excessive talk about further reform following the abolition of serfdom. He used the Orthodox Church and the police to extend an official reactionary ideology through public life and gave nobles an increased role in regional zemstvos and rural administration. Local governors were authorized to use martial law, restrict or ban the religions and languages of non-Russian peoples, and persecute Jews.[6] This "Russification," meant to create a united nation, was continued with equal conviction but less energy by Tsar Nicholas II, who ascended the throne in 1894. Unrest increased, and many in the government welcomed war as a means of achieving the solidarity repression had failed to create.

War came in 1904, when Japan suddenly attacked the Russians at Port Arthur, which they had leased from China in 1898 as part of their expansion into East Asia and Manchuria.

---

[6] One of history's famous forgeries, the *Protocols of the Elders of Zion*, was published (and written) by the Russian police in 1903. The protocols purported to be the secret minutes of a Zionist congress and to reveal a Jewish conspiracy to control the world.

For years these moves had troubled the Japanese, and Russia had neither kept promises to withdraw nor acknowledged Japan's proposals for spheres of influence. The war was a disaster for Russia. Surprise attack was followed by defeats in Manchuria, the fall of Port Arthur, and the annihilation of a large Russian fleet that had sailed around the world only to be sunk in Japanese waters. In the treaty, signed at Portsmouth, New Hampshire —the United States, like Japan, wished to demonstrate her status as a world power—Russia ceded most of her recent gains, including Port Arthur and the southern half of Sakhalin Island, and recognized Japanese interest in Korea.

So dramatic a defeat increased pressure for major reforms as had the Crimean War fifty years before, but the pressure came this time from deep within society. Peasant agitation had been on the rise since a terrible famine in 1891, secret organizations had arisen to defend subject nationalities, and industrialization had begun to fill St. Petersburg and Moscow with workers organizing to improve their miserable lot. The Social Revolutionaries, a party combining the traditions of populism and terrorism, grew more active; and the Marxist Social Democrats, hitherto composed of rather disparate groups, now organized in exile and strengthened their ties within Russia.

In this atmosphere liberal members of the zemstvos held a national congress in 1904, though forbidden to by the government, and demanded civil liberties. Then in January 1905 striking workers in St. Petersburg, demanding a national constitution as well as recognition of unions, announced they would petition the tsar. They marched on the Winter Palace carrying icons and singing, "God save the tsar"; and when they had assembled, the troops opened fire, killing scores and wounding hundreds more.

"Bloody Sunday" led to agitation so widespread that in March the tsar promised to call an assembly of notables and announced immediate reforms: religious toleration, reduced restrictions on Jews and non-Russian nationals, and cancellation of part of the payments peasants owed for their land. Agitation for a constitution only grew stronger, expressed through urban strikes, peasant riots, and mutinies in both the army and navy. In August the tsar conceded more, declaring he would call a national assembly, the Imperial Duma, which was to be merely consultative and elected by limited suffrage. Many of those close to the court were shocked by so radical a step; few outside it were satisfied. The pub-

On the morning of January 9, 1905, protestors petitioning the tsar marched to the Winter Palace and were fired upon by Russian soldiers. The event, known as "Bloody Sunday," triggered a series of strikes and mutinies among the military. (Photo: Soviet Life from Sovfoto)

lic's response was a wave of strikes beginning in Moscow and spreading from city to city and trade to trade. For the last ten days of October, Russia's economic life came to a halt, the most effective general strike Europe had ever seen. It won from the tsar the October Manifesto granting a constitution.

The manifesto provided for a Duma vested with legislative authority, elected by broad suffrage, and guaranteed freedom of speech and assembly. Crowds danced in the streets. For the first time the regime's opponents were divided: moderates willing to work with this constitution became known as Octobrists; liberals who insisted on a constituent assembly and broader guarantees formed the Constitutional Democratic party, called Cadets for short; on the left socialists and revolutionaries rejected compromise, and the St. Petersburg Soviet, a committee of trade union leaders and socialists, called another general strike. It was only partially successful, however, for revolutionary fervor was dying down. Emboldened, the government arrested the leaders of the St. Petersburg Soviet in December, and when Moscow's workers rose in revolt, they were bloodily defeated.

Before the first Duma met in May 1906, Fundamental Laws announced more fully the form the constitution would be allowed to have. An upper house, half its members appointed by the tsar, would be added to the national legislature, thus making the Duma the lower house; the tsar would keep the power of veto, the right to name his ministers, and full command of the executive, the judiciary, and the armed forces. In elections boycotted by the left, the Cadets gained a large majority of the seats in the Duma, and they began the new era by demanding representative government. The Duma was dissolved after two months, but new elections, in which the left took part, produced a more radical assembly, also soon disbanded. The stalemate was broken by a new electoral law favoring the propertied classes that created a conservative majority in subsequent legislatures.

The Revolution of 1905 had nevertheless brought important changes. Russia now had parliamentary institutions and organized parties; the power of the aristocracy had been greatly reduced; and the nation was clearly set on a modern course. The prime minister from 1906 to 1911, Pëter Stolypin, reformed education and administration and strove to stimulate the economy with programs that abandoned the *mir* system in favor of full private ownership of land and created land banks and social insurance. With the aid of foreign capital, the pace of industrialization rapidly increased. Radical movements were sternly repressed, and while discontent among workers and poorer peasants remained serious, Cadets were finding it possible to work with the new system. Liberals throughout Europe rejoiced that the giant of the East had at last begun to follow the path of Western progress.

AUSTRIA-HUNGARY 1879–1914: POLITICAL STALEMATE

The Dual Monarchy did not experience the kinds of crises that set Russia on a new course and led to a more democratic equilibrium in France and Italy. Rather, social and national tensions no less grave resulted in political stalemate. Count Eduard von Taaffe was prime minister from 1879 to 1893, replacing German liberals who had sought reforms more generous than aristocracy or court could abide. His government was a coalition of German conservatives, Czechs, and Poles, but concessions to these nationalities antagonized the bureaucracy and the aristocracy, who were the pillars of the empire. The spread of education and its increased social importance made the language used in schools a divisive issue, one that exacerbated the conflicts among nationalities, eventually broke up Taaffe's coalition, and led to his downfall. Industrialization in Austria increased her economic conflicts with agrarian interests in Hungary and brought workers' agitation that Taaffe barely held in check by harshly repressing socialists while pushing through welfare measures that conservatives detested.

Subsequent governments tended to be even

less venturesome, and after 1900 they relied increasingly on decree powers and the support of the crown rather than the Austrian parliament. Universal manhood suffrage, introduced without conviction in 1907, established the Christian Socialists and the Social Democrats as the two largest parties, neither of them acceptable to the leadership of the empire. Thus they clashed to little purpose in a parliament largely ignored and with rising anger in the city of Vienna, where the Christian Socialists held sway by combining welfare programs with demagogic anti-Semitism.

Conflict with the autonomous regime of Hungary remained critical until the turn of the century. There Magyars maintained their dominance by requiring their language to be used in government and education, tightly controlling the electoral system, and maintaining administrative corruption. Their efforts to protect the interests of large landowners and to increase their independence of Vienna, however, led to contention that weakened the empire. When in 1903 they demanded greater autonomy for their own army and the adoption of Magyar as the language of command, they touched one issue about which Emperor Francis Joseph I cared too much to yield. He suspended the Hungarian constitution, ruled without parliament, and frightened the Magyars into submission by threatening to establish universal suffrage, which would leave them a political minority in their own country.

Magyars and the empire needed each other, and the new Hungarian government—led by István Tisza, son of Kálmán Tisza and a member of one of the leading Magyar families —sought to cooperate in strengthening the Dual Monarchy and lessening the open conflict of nationalities within Hungary. Magyar politics, which in the 1840s had won European admiration as a model of liberal nationalism, had turned by 1906 into the shrewd defensive strategy of a threatened aristocracy. Tisza

became one of the most influential figures in imperial politics by recognizing that mutual survival depended on avoiding dangerous changes and by using imperial foreign policy to strengthen from the outside a political system in danger at home.

SPAIN 1875-1914: THE PROBLEMS OF MODERNIZATION

As in Russia and Austria, Spain's pockets of urban industry (especially in Barcelona) existed in a larger society only partially affected by modern change. From the adoption of the constitution of 1875 until the Spanish-American War twenty-three years later, conservative and liberal parties held power alternately, tolerantly manipulating elections to assure each other's survival. Neither party, however, provided a consistent program for dealing with rising discontent at home or in the colonies. Unrest in Cuba was exacerbated by alternating policies of repression and laxity, and Cuban resistance had become guerrilla war by 1898, when the United States entered the conflict with an imperialist enthusiasm of her own. The brief war was a disaster for Spain that forced her to withdraw from Cuba and to cede Puerto Rico, Guam, and the Philippine Islands to the United States. That ferment brought to the fore a group of Spanish intellectuals known as the generation of 1898, and the question of what was wrong with the nation became the preoccupation of public life in Spain.

From 1899 to 1909 the Conservatives held power, but they grew increasingly intolerant, and they could not sustain the old political compromises. Then the liberals, already badly divided, launched a series of reforms; but these measures—restrictions on religious orders, taxation of the church's industrial properties, a progressive income tax, and toleration of strikes—hardly lessened conflict. Economic growth, particularly in the industrial centers of Bilbao and Barcelona, made old problems of rural poverty, poor communications, and regionalism more serious. Politics had become more unwieldy with the introduction of universal manhood suffrage in 1890, and while the church denounced liberals, the anarchists and socialists increased in strength. In Barcelona these conflicts burst forth in a week of violence in 1909 during which private citizens were murdered and churches were burned and looted. The revenge that followed reestablished Spain's reputation for brutality. A weak government caught between left and right and a king (Alfonso XIII had come of age in 1902) whose prestige declined with each ineffectual call for compromise could not resolve the problems tearing at Spanish society.

ITALY 1878–1914: STABILITY AND CRISIS

The Kingdom of Italy developed her own pattern of political stability. The transition was smooth to the reign of Humbert I, in 1878, and to government by the anti-Cavourian "left," which soon repealed the hated grain taxes, established the principle of compulsory education (with a modest requirement for three years of schooling not always enforced), and extended suffrage to about one adult male in eight.

The prime minister maintained his majorities through an informal system called *trasformismo*, in which he built shifting alliances on successive issues and used patronage to bargain for votes. Coming to office in 1887, Francesco Crispi, a hero of the Risorgimento, sought popularity through outspoken anticlericalism, mild reforms, and above all concern for Italy's prestige. He drew her closer to Germany and met the general agricultural depression by repressing rural revolts and establishing high tariffs that led to a harmful trade war with France. As the economic crisis

deepened and public order deteriorated, Crispi's ministry fell.

His successors, dedicated to balancing the budget, were weakened by a banking scandal that, like the collapse of the Panama Canal enterprise in France, sullied the entire parliamentary system. Returned to office in 1894, Crispi frankly relied on the army and martial law to maintain order while seeking an Italian protectorate in Ethiopia. At Aduwa in 1896, however, 25,000 Italian troops were nearly wiped out by well-prepared Ethiopian forces four times their number, the first notable defeat of a European army by African forces. Crispi fell again, and subsequent governments sought to salvage what they could, preserving Eritrea as an Italian colony and easing tensions with France.

Domestic unrest increased, and anarchist bomb throwing, socialist demonstrations, waves of strikes, and agrarian agitation culminated in riots that reached revolutionary scale in Milan in 1898. Order was restored at the cost of bloodshed, the suppression of scores of newspapers, and a ban on hundreds of socialist, republican, and Catholic organizations. A frightened Chamber of Deputies nevertheless refused to authorize continued restriction of civil liberties, and its stand was supported in the critical elections of 1900. In Italy as in France, parliament and public opinion defeated a revitalized right.

Prime minister almost continuously from 1903 to 1914, Giovanni Giolitti sought to give Italian politics a broader base. He prevented violence but not strikes, and socialists grew optimistic about parliamentarianism as the government nationalized railroads and life insurance, sponsored public health measures, and in 1911 accepted universal suffrage. Giolitti also encouraged Catholics to take part in national politics, which they had boycotted since 1870. In the decade before 1914, the Italian economy, behind that of the great industrial powers, experienced the fastest growth rate in Europe.

In an age of imperialism, Italian nationalists had yearned for an empire that would make Italy more nearly the equal of the other European powers. Their designs on Tunisia frustrated by the French in 1881, they had turned to the ill-fated venture in Ethiopia. After the clash of French and German interests in 1911 over dominance of Morocco (see Chapter 26), nationalist groups in Italy pressured the government to take Libya before someone else did. Libya was formerly part of the Ottoman empire, but Italy had carefully staked her claim through years of cautious diplomacy, and in 1912 Giolitti found the excuse for war against the sultan. Italian troops landed at the port city of Tripoli and took Rhodes and the other major Dodecanese Islands, also Ottoman possessions. The sultan ceded Libya, and the year of war produced an enthusiasm Italian governments had rarely won, a moment of unity many would want to recapture.

Giolitti's accomplishments, however, rested on his skill at obscuring political issues, influencing elections, and using silent deputies. The economic problems of the south remained grave and the discontent of more and more organized and militant workers largely unappeased. A dull and sometimes corrupt government proved an easy target for increasingly vocal critics from the left and the right. In the elections of 1913, the first under the broadened suffrage, these critics achieved notable gains.

FRANCE 1878–1914: THE TRIUMPH OF THE REPUBLICANS

By the 1880s the Third Republic had established its political style: the executive was relatively weak, the presidency reduced to a ceremonial office; most cabinets lasted only about a year in office; and the many parties had little authority over deputies tied to local interests, who were proudly independent on national issues. Stability came from the frustrating fact that shifting majorities produced new governments not very different from their predecessors—most ministers served in several cabinets—and from an able civil service.

For twenty years, from 1879 to 1899, the leading politicians were moderate republicans who found in lack of daring the best guarantee of the republic's durability and in anticlericalism their most popular plank. Strong defenders of free speech and individualism, they recognized unions but initiated few projects of public works or social welfare. In the 1880s they made elementary education in state schools compulsory and established restrictions on the Catholic Church intended to weaken its political influence, a view of progress that carried national political divisions into the villages of France.

Moderate republicans had little gift for winning popular enthusiasm, however, and political crises occurred frequently. In 1889 General Georges Boulanger gained so much popularity by his appeal to patriotism and his sympathy for workers that there was danger of a coup d'état. Then in 1892, when companies planning a canal through Panama similar to their successful Suez venture went bankrupt, investigations uncovered political graft and provoked a stormy campaign against the corruption of Jewish financiers, liberal newspapers, and republican politicians. Only as the republic's opponents seemed close to toppling the regime did its defenders pull together.

The Third Republic's great trial came with the Dreyfus case. Captain Albert Dreyfus, a Jew and a member of the General Staff, was convicted by court-martial in 1894 of providing the German military attaché with secret French documents. Although the sensational press shouted Jewish treachery, the issue be-

A French newspaper headlined Emile Zola's now-famous "J'Accuse . . . !," a denunciation of the corrupt handling of the Dreyfus Affair. The case became the cause célèbre of the nineteenth century; public speculation as to Dreyfus' guilt or innocence led to demonstrations, propaganda, street fighting, lawsuits, and political realignments. (Photo: René Dazy)

came the center of public attention only three years afterward, when evidence appeared pointing to the guilt of another officer. Generals, refusing to reopen the case, spoke darkly of honor and state secrets, and the right-wing press hailed their patriotism. The majority of Catholics, monarchists, and conservatives joined in patriotic indignation against Jews and socialists allegedly conspiring to sell out France and weaken a loyal army. The left—intellectuals, socialists, and republicans—came to view Dreyfus as the innocent victim of a plot against republican institutions. They won

the battle for public opinion, though barely, and Dreyfus was given a presidential pardon in 1899.[7] That victory set the tone of subsequent French politics, cementing traditions of republican unity on the left and greatly reducing the political influence of the church and monarchists. Years of polemics and street fights, however, left deep scars.

From 1900 until World War I, government was in the hands of republicans who called themselves radical. They set about purging the army of their opponents and launched new attacks on the church that subsided only with the passage of a law separating church and state in 1905. Yet they administered with

[7] Convicted again in 1897, Dreyfus had been court-martialed a third time in 1899 on the order of France's highest court. The verdict, guilty but "with extenuating circumstances," added new confusion and led to the presidential pardon. A few Dreyfusards continued collecting evidence and finally won acquittal in a civil trial in 1906. Dreyfus was then decorated and promoted to the rank of major.

restraint; solicitous of the "little man," of small businessmen and peasant farmers, they solidified support for the republic.

Indeed part of the Third Republic's achievement was its ability to draw radical politicians to moderate policies. A socialist even entered the cabinet in the aftermath of the Dreyfus affair (thereby earning the condemnation of the Second International for cooperating in a bourgeois state). The labor movement, more syndicalist than Marxist, doubled its membership in this period, but despite frequent strikes from the 1890s on, it never produced the more revolutionary general strike so much talked of. As prime minister from 1906 to 1909, Georges Clemenceau, once associated with the radical left, effectively combined policies of reform and conciliation. On the eve of world war, France, prosperous and stable, appeared to have surmounted her most dangerous divisions.

GERMANY 1879–1914: TENSIONS FOLLOWING UNIFICATION

German political life reflected a fragmented society in which the court, army, bureaucracy, and business were semi-independent centers of power and in which social classes were sharply demarcated. Yet Bismarck ran it until 1890 with an authority few modern figures have equaled, establishing a pattern his successors would strain to maintain.

The architect of so successful a system was understandably scornful of criticism, and a chancellor so overweening won many enemies; but Bismarck was untouchable until William II ascended the throne in 1888. Twenty-nine years old, bright but ill-prepared, William was infatuated with all things military, anxious to make himself loved, and eager to rule. He disagreed with parts of Bismarck's foreign policy and opposed the antisocialist laws, but theirs was primarily a conflict of wills. In 1890 the emperor, impatient with Bismarck's paternal arrogance, forced his resignation.

Succeeding chancellors (there were four between 1890 and 1917) served until the dissatisfaction of some powerful faction led to their replacement. In 1909 Theobald von Bethmann-Hollweg, the last peacetime chancellor of the Second Reich and the first of bourgeois origin, was chosen in part out of concern over a restive parliament, but that cautious bureaucrat was hardly the man to tame the forces of German politics.

The fundamental problems of the Second Reich were inherent in the system itself. A dynamic foreign policy whose successes could dazzle opponents at home proved impossible to sustain. Foreign policy and the political importance of the army required increases in armed strength that kept militarism at the center of politics. In 1887, when a seven-year renewal of the army bill had fallen due, Bismarck had asked for its enlargement. Resisted in parliament, he had made this an electoral issue and won a sizable victory, the last stable majority any chancellor enjoyed. Similarly in 1893, 1898, and 1911–1913, military appropriations were a source of intense conflict and propaganda; each time the army grew larger and the government's statements more nationalist.

Strident propaganda was also the mainstay of the political leagues—the Landlords', Peasants', Pan-German, Colonial, and Naval Leagues—organized in the 1890s. Well-financed by Junkers and some industrialists, they campaigned for the military, overseas empire, and high tariffs with attacks on socialists, Jews, and foreign enemies. As pressure groups they won significant victories—notably in the naval bill of 1898, which proposed to create a fleet that could compete with Britain's. Germany's conservative classes appealed to public opinion more effectively than their anti-Dreyfusard counterparts in France or the militant right in Italy.

Such movements were angrily distrusted by Europe's strongest socialist movement. Under Bismarck Germany had adopted comprehensive programs of health, old age, accident, and disability insurance that established a model of social welfare legislation unequaled elsewhere for a generation. William II was hailed as "the Labor Emperor" for supporting social security, labor arbitration, the regulation of workers' hours, and provisions for their safety. The workers, however, would not be wooed.

The Social Democrats, having been forced by harassment to rely on local organization, became powerful: they won more votes than any other party in every election from 1890 on, becoming in 1912 the largest party in the Reichstag despite the distortions of the electoral system. Socialists also dominated Germany's vigorous labor unions, which had 2.5 million members by 1912. A movement detested by the authorities, German socialism created its own subculture of newspapers and libraries and recreation centers.

In practice the Social Democrats were attentive to the concrete concerns of their constituents, but in principle and tone they remained firm revolutionaries. One of their leading theorists, Eduard Bernstein, proposed a modified doctrine in a daring book, *Evolutionary Socialism* (1897). He argued that many of Marx's predictions had proved wrong, that parts of his economic analysis were faulty, and that socialists should place less emphasis on economic determinism and revolution and seek instead to improve working conditions and strengthen democracy. Bernstein's revisionism became the focus of international debate and affected socialist movements everywhere, but it was formally rejected by the Social Democrats, who made Karl Kautsky's intransigent exposition of Marxism their official policy.

While organized factions glared and threatened, Bethmann-Hollweg presided over a bureaucracy rife with cabals and tried to hold in check a court where people spoke openly of using the army against radicals. Germany remained strong, prosperous, and apparently stable, but major political change proved impossible; even the attempt to make taxes more equitable was defeated. Thus Bethmann-Hollweg's mild program for modifying the political system came to nothing. When the Continent's most powerful nation entered into world war, the Reich was still dominated by Prussia, where voting continued by the three-class system, and ministers remained responsible to the crown and not the Reichstag.

GREAT BRITAIN 1880–1914: IMPERIALISM AND SOCIAL CHANGE

Gladstone returned to power in 1880 after a campaign that, in its effort to carry serious issues to the public, was a further step toward democracy; and in 1885 the Liberal majority led Parliament to adopt measures accepting the principle of universal manhood suffrage (it says much, however, that the requirement of an independent place of residence—which excluded domestic servants, sons living with fathers, and those without a permanent address—was enough to disqualify roughly one-third of all adult males). Gladstone's foreign policy, however, was decried as weak, and his popularity, which increased when Britain stumbled into the occupation of Egypt in 1882, was dissipated a few years later. As the Irish question became more heated, Gladstone responded with reforms that fixed fair rents and prevented the eviction of paying tenants; but Irish nationalists demanded home rule, an independent Irish parliament. When Gladstone acquiesced in 1886, his party split as badly as the Tories had a generation before over the corn laws. Joseph Chamberlain, a radical in social matters who had adopted the popular cause of imperialism, led an important group of Liberals into alliance with the Conservatives. Gladstone's perpetual compromises were beginning to seem old-fashioned in the face of these deeper divisions.

Conservative governments would hold office for sixteen of the next nineteen years, most of them under Lord Salisbury, successor to Disraeli, who had died in 1881. An able diplomat, Salisbury continued his party's emphasis on the importance of the empire and led the nation through a bitter conflict with the Dutch-speaking Boers of South Africa.

Many Boers had left Britain's Cape Colony in the 1830s, eventually establishing independent and frankly racist republics. Almost constantly at war with neighboring African peoples, they were also at odds with the expanding British interests in South Africa. In the 1850s the Boers had won recognition of the independence of their two major regimes, the Transvaal Republic (soon renamed the South African Republic) and the Orange Free State. In 1877, however, the British government had violated previous treaties by annexing the Transvaal. This produced a revolt in 1880 and Gladstone's concession of domestic autonomy in 1881. But the unstable situation had become explosive with the discovery of diamonds in the Boers' Orange Free State and gold in the South African Republic in the 1870s and 1880s (see Map 25.1). New settlers poured in, and companies amassed enormous wealth; railroads were rushed to completion and natives driven away or forced to work for meager wages.

By 1890 the Boer republics were surrounded by British colonies and swarming with Britons, whom the Boers taxed heavily but disfranchised. Cecil Rhodes, an Englishman who had gained a near-monopoly over the world's diamond production before he was thirty, used his position as prime minister of the Cape Colony to further schemes for a South African federation, and the Boers found themselves resisting raids by whites as well as blacks. When Britain refused to withdraw her troops, the Boers declared war in 1899. The British rapidly occupied the major cities, but they subdued the Boers' expert guerrilla resistance only after two more years of destroying farms and herding the homeless Boers into concentration camps. This embarrassing war, with its heavy price in blood and prestige, stirred a fierce patriotism in England that increased the Conservatives' strength.

Despite public enthusiasm for their imperial policy, the Conservatives faced growing opposition at home which they attempted to meet by sponsoring major reforms. In 1888 and 1894 they restructured local government, a major source of the aristocracy's political power, making county councils elective. They made an expanding civil service more accessible to the middle class, and an act of 1902 established a far stronger national education system that for the first time included secondary schooling.

Yet these important changes did not satisfy the working class, whose rising dissatisfaction had spilled over in strikes by London match girls in 1888 and dock workers the next year. The strikes had won public sympathy and marked the beginning of a "new unionism" of unskilled workers organized on an industry-wide basis and prepared for political activism. The formation of the Labour Representation Committee in 1900 marked the beginning of what quickly became the Labour party. Its greatest strength came from the unions, but it included the Fabian Society, a group of prominent intellectuals whose propaganda in behalf of reformist, democratic socialism gained an influence far beyond their numbers. Twenty-nine Labour members of Parliament would be elected in 1906, and within a few years the ruling Liberals would come often to depend on Labour votes in the House of Commons. British labor was further pushed to political action by a court decision, upheld by the House of Lords in 1902, which made unions liable for losses caused by strikes. Overturning the verdict that crippled unions became a central issue of the 1906 election.

In that election the Liberals won the most one-sided victory since 1833. They immediately passed measures establishing workmen's compensation, old age pensions, and urban planning. Since this legislation and the expanding arms race required new revenues, David Lloyd George, the chancellor of the Exchequer, proposed the "people's budget" in 1909. A skilled orator who delighted in the rhetoric of class conflict, he promised to place the burden of the cost of social welfare squarely on the rich.

In an unprecedented act an aroused House of Lords rejected the government's budget, forcing new elections and bringing on a constitutional crisis. Although the Liberals lost many seats, they retained office with Irish and Labour support, and King George V's threat to appoint hundreds of additional peers finally forced the upper house to accept not only the hated budget but a constitutional change forbidding the Lords to veto money bills and permitting any measure to become law when passed by the Commons in three sessions.

The peers' intemperate outburst, which cost them so much, was part of the general rise in social tension. From 1910 to 1914 strikes increased in frequency, size, and violence; a general strike became a real and much-talked-of threat. Women campaigning for the right to vote interrupted public meetings, invaded Parliament itself, smashed windows, and planted bombs. Arrested, they went on hunger strikes until baffled statesmen ordered their release. Such behavior from ladies was shocking in itself; but as the movement gained

strength, recruiting women (and some men) from every social class, its outraged attack on smug male assumptions reinforced the rising challenge to a whole social order.

Nor was the threat of violence limited to the left. In 1914 the Commons passed a bill for Irish home rule for the third time, which made it immune to a veto in the House of Lords. The Protestants of northern Ireland, with support from many Englishmen, openly threatened civil war. Squads began drilling, and the British officer corps gave frightening indications that it might mutiny rather than fight to impose home rule on Protestant loyalists.

Only the outbreak of world war generated the national unity that neither imperialism nor social reform had been able to create. If the death of Queen Victoria in 1901 had symbolized the end of an age of British expansion, the ascent of George V to the throne (1910–1936) marked the opening of new conflicts. Edward VII's brief reign (1901–1910) would soon be remembered a little sadly as the Edwardian era, a happy time of relaxed confidence that prosperity and democracy were the natural products of progress and a guarantee of peace.

V. EUROPEAN IMPERIALISM

To contemporaries the spread of empire was dramatic evidence of Europe's dynamism, and it was justified on grounds of progress—carrying higher civilization and Christianity to backward lands—as well as national interest. Imperialism became an important element in domestic European politics and an expression of the international rivalry that culminated in World War I. In 1875, after centuries of close contact with Africa, European powers lay claim to no more than a tenth of its lands. Twenty years later, seven nations had through fierce competition established dominion over almost the entire continent and had carried their rivalry to most of Asia and to the small islands of the Pacific Ocean. Won in open conquest, through protectorates, and by treaties granting special trading privileges, most of the newly acquired lands at first had few European settlers (the primary means of exploiting local wealth in the past) and most of them lay in tropical zones Europeans had heretofore found unappealing and unhealthy.

EXPLANATIONS OF IMPERIALISM

By the turn of the century, the opponents of imperialism had begun to seek explanations of the pervasive imperial fever. In 1902 J. A. Hobson, a British economist, published *Imperialism: A Study*, a critical tract that has been heavily attacked by subsequent scholars but that remains the starting point of modern analysis. Writing during the Boer War, Hobson was eager to show that imperialism offered little to restless populations or to commerce. Emigrants, he noted, preferred to go to the Americas, and Britain's trade with the European continent and the Americas was far greater and growing faster than her trade with her colonies.

The economic explanation of imperialism Hobson found in financiers, small numbers of men controlling great wealth and looking for quick profits. They used their social and political connections to induce the government to protect their investments through political dominance over undeveloped lands. Similarly their social position enabled them to exploit the missionaries, soldiers, and patriotic dreamers who glorified empire. Imperialism thus stemmed from the manipulation of public opinion in the interests of certain capitalists.

Hobson's analysis inspired the still more influential theory of Lenin. The leader of Russia's Marxist revolutionaries, Lenin provided a Marxist interpretation of a subject on which Marx had written little. In *Imperialism: The Last Stage of Capitalism* (1916), Lenin agreed that the stimulus behind empire building was basically economic and that the essence of colonialism was exploitation. But for Lenin imperialist ventures grew from the very dynamics of capitalism itself. Competition produced both monopolies and lowered profits, and surplus capital was forced to seek overseas investments. The alternative, to enlarge the domestic market by raising wages, would increase competition, thus further reducing profit. Imperialism was therefore the last "stage" of capitalism, the product of its internal contradictions. Lenin would add in 1916 that imperial rivalries, involving whole nations, led to wars that further hastened the end of capitalism. "Imperialist" became an epithet for a system considered decadent as well as immoral.

Although influenced by these views, most historians have remained uncomfortable with them. They contribute little to an understanding of the actual process of imperial conquest, in which capitalists were often reluctant participants. They do not explain why imperialists called for political control beyond treaty rights or the swift spread of European power into areas that offered small financial return; investment, like trade, remained heavier in more developed noncolonial countries. Nor do economic arguments tell us much about the role of the popular press, explorers, earnest missionaries, and ambitious soldiers in pressing hesitant politicians to imperial conquest.

Many factors help explain the sudden increase in the pace and importance of European imperialism, although all analysts today would agree that economic interests, at least in the long run, were among the most important.

A society familiar with self-made men was readier to believe that new lands offered the

chance to make one's fortune. A general increase in trade and the growing demand for rubber, oil, and rare metals spurred the search for natural resources. Stiffening competition in international commerce and rising tariffs taught businessmen to seek the backing of their governments. Technology too played a part. The steamship and telegraph made regular trade with distant places easier, and modern medicine lessened the dangers of the tropics. Coaling stations and telegraph posts acquired strategic as well as commercial importance, a fact that argued for military and political protection.

Beyond such rational calculations, however, imperialism was rooted in the values Europeans held and in their domestic society and politics. Mass-circulation newspapers gloried in imperialism, writing of adventure and wealth, Christianity and progress in the virile language of force. To the people of the late nineteenth century, exploration and conquest were high and noble adventure. Press reports made popular heroes of daring men like Henry M. Stanley, who followed the rivers of South Africa and penetrated the interior of the Congo, and Pierre de Brazza, who traveled up the Congo River, overcoming hardship and danger and dismantling a steamship so it could be carried around the rapids. Exploration seemed in itself an expression of progress, the brave adventurer the personification of individual initiative. If the explorer also gained wealth, that completed the parable.

The missionaries who risked their lives to build a chapel in the jungle and convert the heathen were as symbolically appealing as the explorer. For churches often at odds with the culture of their day and in conflict with the

state, here was a dramatic outlet and welcome reassurance of their importance in modern life. Hundreds of Social Darwinists preached the inevitable conflict of race with race and hailed the resultant spread of civilization, by which they meant of course their own. Geographical societies became prominent in every country, proudly acclaiming yet another association of new knowledge with increased power.

Where class tensions were high and domestic conflict serious, colonial expansion offered all citizens a share in national glory and gain. Rudyard Kipling's poems of imperial derring-do in exotic lands hail the simple cockney soldier; whatever his lot at home, he was a ruler abroad. Thus in politics imperialism, like nationalism, cut across social divisions. It was an important part, especially in Great Britain and Germany, of the political resurgence of the right, allowing conservative groups strong in the army, the church, and the aristocracy to ally themselves with commerical interests in a program of popular appeal. Employment as well as glory was promised as the fruit of a policy of strength. Significantly imperialism never achieved comparable political effect in France, the nation with the second largest of the European empires, though hers too was built principally by officers and clergymen. The right fumbled its effort at mass appeal in the Dreyfus affair; patriots were preoccupied with avenging the loss of Alsace and Lorraine to Germany; and French nationalism retained ideas associated with the Revolution that often conflicted with those of imperialism. But everywhere empire offered the appeal of individual daring and dramatic action in a society becoming more organized into large institutions. It gave openings to groups such as the military and the clergy often disparaged at home, and it supplemented popular theories with concrete tales of risk, gain, glory, and conquest.

A German cartoon of 1896 lampoons the Teutonic order brought to Africa by German imperialism. (Photo: The Granger Collection)

PATTERNS OF COLONIALISM

Despite the general popularity of imperialist ideas, few wholehearted imperialists held high political office even in Great Britain. The history of colonial conquest in this period was less one of long-range schemes than of individual acts and decisions that appear almost accidental when viewed singly. Frequently individual explorers, traders, or officers established their claims in a given region through treaties with native leaders and then, usually later, obtained recognition from their home government. In the process of enforcing contracts and maintaining order, they tended to exceed their original authorization and to extend their territorial claims. Governments anxious not to appear weak before their public or other powers then supported such moves; trading concessions and protectorates became colonies. This pattern of expansion required little premeditation. Applying their own laws and practices to other cultures, Europeans were shocked when natives failed to honor Western rules, and they responded with increased force.

Even Europeans attracted by non-Western cultures or devoted to helping local populations, in the name of Western religion and medicine, undermined their host societies by introducing alien ideas, institutions, and technology as well as by sheer wealth and power. There is in fact a whole other history of imperialism just now being written from the perspective of the indigenous peoples that shows how native political, economic, and religious organization was disrupted by the arrival of outsiders. To the confident men of empire, such conditions left no alternative but further European control.

Africa

In the 1870s European involvement in Africa began a rapid spread inland from a few coastal posts that would end in the partition of the entire continent by 1895 (see Map 25.1). Early signs of the domination to come were the collapse of Egyptian finances, the energetic exploration of the Congo sponsored by King Leopold II of Belgium, and the increasing conflicts between the British and the Boers.

The Suez Canal was completed in 1869, the shares in its ownership held by French investors and the khedive of Egypt, who ruled as a monarch representing the nominal suzerainty of the Ottomans. When the debt-plagued khedive sold his shares in 1875, they were purchased by the British government in one of Disraeli's most dramatic coups. Determined to protect their investments, the British and French then established joint control over Egyptian finances. In 1882, however, a nationalist revolt by the Egyptian army against both the khedive and foreign influence threatened this arrangement. The British government decided to mount a show of strength (in which the French Parlement refused to allow France a part) and the Royal Navy bombarded Alexandria to teach Egyptians that contracts must be met. In the resulting chaos the British attempted to restore order, a process that quickly led to their occupying Egypt, and the country remained under their rule until after World War II. In Tunisia a similar pattern of increased foreign investments followed by a financial crisis and intricate diplomatic maneuverings brought about French occupation in 1881. Both events accelerated the competition for African empire.

Although reluctant to accept responsibility for all their countrymen did, European governments nevertheless found themselves drawn piecemeal into scores of treaties that prescribed for societies little understood and fixed boundaries in areas whose geography was barely known. The International Association for the Exploration and Civilization of Central Africa, founded in Brussels in 1876, quickly became a private operation of Leo-

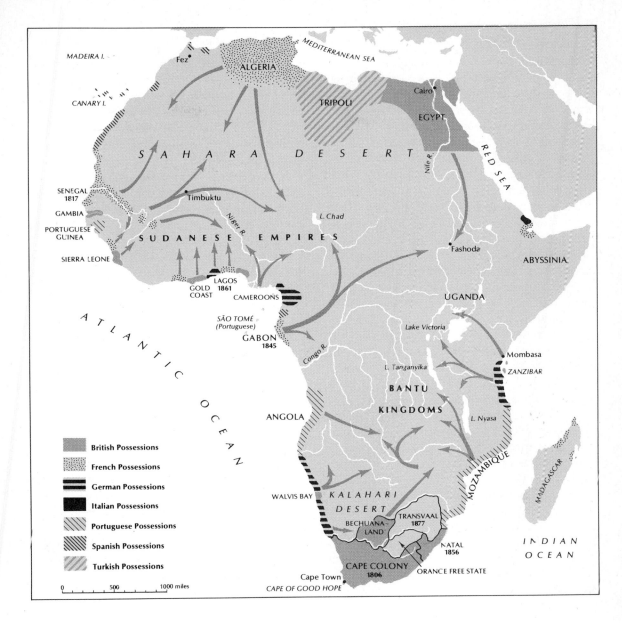

MAP 25.1: AFRICA 1885

Map legend:
- British Possessions
- French Possessions
- German Possessions
- Italian Possessions
- Portuguese Possessions
- Spanish Possessions
- Turkish Possessions

0   500   1000 miles

pold II. The association paid less attention to its lofty aims of furthering science and ending slavery than to the vast territorial claims it might make by sponsoring Stanley's explorations. From their outposts along the west coast, Frenchmen, Englishmen, Spaniards, and Portuguese hurried to push into the hinter-

lands of what are now Senegal and Nigeria.

French gains in West Africa were the most extensive of all, and in 1898 a group of soldiers who had pushed two-thirds of the way across the continent at its widest point arrived at Fashoda, on the Nile, a few days before the British, who were moving into the

Sudan. Both nations considered the encounter of their troops at Fashoda a matter of national honor, and imperialists plotted on maps how dominance over Africa was at stake. The French imagined holdings stretching from West to East across the continent, controlling the headwaters of the Nile. The British talked in terms of territory and maybe even a railway from the Cape of Good Hope to Cairo, a north-south axis through the continent. Thus the obscure outpost at Fashoda sought by no general staff brought Great Britain and France close to war for weeks. The confrontation ended when the French, divided at home over the Dreyfus affair, chose to give way.

In South Africa Cecil Rhodes typified the interconnection of local politics, private interest, and visions of empire. Confident of white and indeed Anglo-Saxon superiority, he schemed and propagandized relentlessly, stretching old claims and using trading companies and his own wealth to establish new ones. He died during the Boer War, but the British victory paved the way for the establishment of the Union of South Africa in 1910, a partial fulfillment of Rhodes' ambitions.

As the European states were drawn into the scramble, they sought through diplomacy to lessen the clear danger that clashes in Africa would lead to war in Europe. At Berlin in 1885 the powers established rules for each other. The most important was that coastal settlement by a European nation would give it claim to the hinterlands beyond. Straight lines drawn from haphazard coastal conquests cut across the little-known indigenous cultures, but they restrained the anarchy of European ambition. The powers also agreed at Berlin to prohibit slavery; and five years later they banned liquor and limited arms in the zone between the Sahara and the Cape Colony. Humanitarian considerations were not wholly forgotten, and by the turn of the century, the ruthless exploitation of the Belgian Congo was considered an international scandal. The men who bravely planted their flags and wrote out treaties for chieftains to sign did not doubt that theirs was a beneficial achievement to be measured by mission hospitals and schools, new roads and political order as well as profit. By 1912 only Liberia and Ethiopia were formally free of European domination (see Map 25.2).

Asia

In the East beyond the Ottoman Empire, Great Britain and Russia were the main contenders for influence (see Map 25.3). Persia had felt their competition since the 1830s and by the 1870s had conceded control of the Imperial Bank of Persia to British interests. Russia competed by exerting military pressure along Persia's northern frontier and in the 1890s by offering a large loan and related concessions in an effort to reduce Britain's dominance. As part of a general entente reached in 1907 (see Chapter 26), the two European powers agreed on spheres of influence: the British sphere would include the area of the Persian Gulf, in the south, and Russia's the north. Their competition, by limiting the intrusions of either power, had helped the Persian state preserve a nominal independence, but their presence increased its instability, and revolution had erupted in 1905. The technique of playing off Russian and British ambitions was less successful in Afghanistan, however, where the emir's efforts to use the Russians as a counterweight to British influence could not match Britain's determination through her presence to guarantee the security of India on Afghanistan's southeast border.

Of the lands on the Indochina peninsula, east of India and south of China, only Siam (Thailand) preserved her independence of

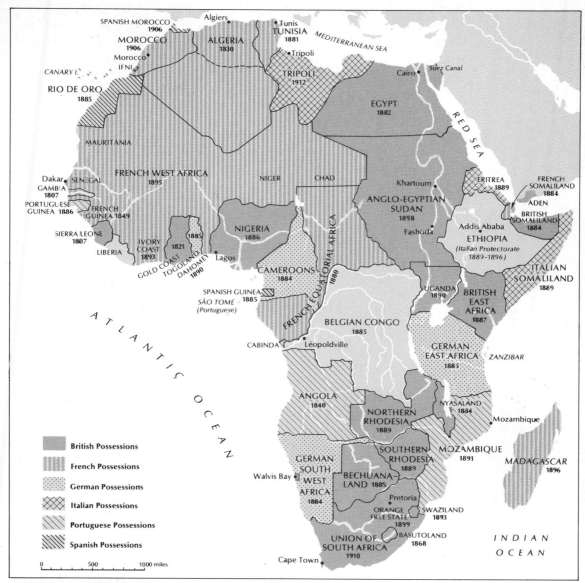

MAP 25.2: AFRICA 1914

European control, due to her own ability to modernize and to the counterbalancing pressures of three European powers present in neighboring domains. The British annexed upper Burma in 1886 and part of Malaya in 1896; the Dutch were on the island of Borneo; and French influence steadily increased in Cambodia and Cochin-China (both parts of Indochina) during the 1860s despite the indifference of the governments in Paris. When Christians were attacked or a trader murdered, the local commander pressed native rulers for further political concessions without waiting for instructions from home.

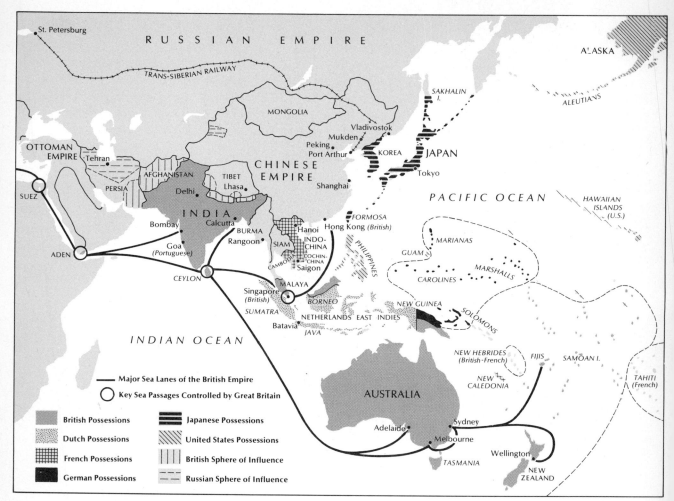

MAP 25.3: IMPERIALISM IN ASIA

Even the effort to establish for their enclave a secure frontier—a European conception that ignored social realities—usually led to war and expansion into another ancient realm. France in this way found herself at war with China in 1883; and though Parlement voted down the government of Premier Jules Ferry, France's leading imperialist, the war nevertheless resulted in a French protectorate, reorganized in 1887 as French Indochina.

The weakness of the Chinese Empire brought further European intervention in that nation. Chronically short of funds, the Chinese government sought European loans, and competing political factions tried to use European influence for their own ends. But a debt unpaid or a riot against foreigners would bring immediate pressure for further concessions, and granting them made it difficult for the Chinese to maintain their authority. British and French troops burned the emperor's summer palace in 1860 as revenge for the seizure of their envoys; by 1870 European powers had established treaty ports in which they could operate independent of Chinese rule and were claiming a share of customs duties all along the coast.

European incursions did not affect Chinese society deeply, however, until after 1895. Japan had responded to European contacts with rapid modernization during the Meiji period (1867–1912), and in 1894–1895 she tested her new strength in war against China. The Japanese won Formosa, the independence of Korea (which they annexed in 1910), and an indemnity. The war caused increased competition among the European powers for more extensive rights in China.

Its sovereignty threatened, the Chinese government responded with westernizing reforms that would lead to revolution in 1911 and the establishment of a Chinese republic. Meanwhile political turmoil and burning resentment against the foreigners erupted in attacks on Europeans and European influences. The most famous of these, the so-called Boxer Rebellion of 1900, in which scores of Western missionaries and some diplomats were murdered, prompted heavy military intervention by Russia and Germany. Thus the competition among European nations interlocked with internal stresses to spur an accelerating process of change. The only defense against European imperialism even in a great and ancient nation appeared to be a westernization that deepened European influence.

The political and economic changes transforming Europe since the eighteenth century had now been carried throughout the world, and all civilizations were forced in important ways to grow more alike. Initially the flow of culture and communication was primarily one-way: European technology, dress, etiquette, ways of doing business, wage payment, religion, and political ideas spread everywhere. Wherever they went and whether they came for gain or out of humanitarian concern, Europeans taught their Christianity and their ways of controlling power, the utility of their roads and railways and medicine, the lure of profit through international trade. Other cultures slowly developed their own ways of using European ideas of education, justice, and nationalism. In return Europeans enjoyed prestige, power, and wealth. Confident in their superiority, they were slow to borrow from non-Western cultures; but gradually, from strange foods, Eastern and African art, to Oriental religions and philosophy, European civilization came to be enriched by the cultures it had been so quick to overpower.

Within Europe progress came to be measured by prosperity, knowledge, and freedom; it reached the common man through rising standards of living, social mobility, universal education, and increased democracy. At the same time severe tensions burst forth in social and ideological conflicts that European society was hard-pressed to contain. Most nations managed to maintain political stability by making timely compromises and seeking unity in the bond of patriotism. For a generation there had been no revolutions save in backward Russia and no European war, facts often cited as proof of progress. Then suddenly in 1914 the very compromises that had kept the peace exploded into total war.

RECOMMENDED READING

Studies

* Arendt, Hannah. *The Origins of Totalitarianism.* 1958. This original analysis is also a profoundly pessimistic application of hindsight to the late nineteenth century.

* Dangerfield, George. *The Strange Death of Liberal England.* 1935. Skillfully and argumentatively written description of a society in crisis.

* Derfler, Leslie. *Socialism since Marx: A Century of the European Left.* 1973. Thoughtful discussion of the movements that stemmed from Marx.

* Eisley, Loren C. *Darwin's Century: Evolution and the Men Who Discovered It.* 1958. An attractive discussion of the history of evolutionary theory.

Fieldhouse, D. K. *Economics and Empire, 1830–1914.* 1973. Useful analysis using recent research to cast doubt on the primary importance of economic factors.

* Gallegher, John, Ronald Robinson, and Alice Denny. *Africa and the Victorians: The Climax of Imperialism.* 1961. An important revision of older views of imperialism.

* Hale, Oran J. *The Great Illusion, 1900–1914.* 1971. An able general survey in the same excellent series as the volume by Carlton Hayes.

* Hayes, Carlton J. H. *A Generation of Materialism, 1871–1900.* 1941. Though dated, still a stimulating indictment of the period.

* Hughes, H. Stuart. *Consciousness and Society: The Reorientation of European Social Thought, 1890–1930.* 1958. A graciously written and indispensable analysis of the central currents of modern thought in a time of transition.

* Joll, James. *The Anarchists.* 1965. Discusses the ideas and motives of very disparate groups.

* Kindleberger, Charles P. *Economic Growth in France and Britain: 1851–1950.* 1969. An economist's careful assessment of the evidence for the major explanations of the differences in these two economies.

Langer, William L. *The Diplomacy of Imperialism.* 2 vols. 1935. A classic work that consistently places diplomatic history in its larger context.

* Löwith, Karl. *From Hegel to Nietzsche: The Revolution in Nineteenth-Century Thought.* 1964. A sober essay on the transformations in modern thought.

* Masur, Gerhard. *Prophets of Yesterday.* 1961. Uses a broad selection of thinkers to provide a good survey of intellectual history.

* Pulzer, Peter. *The Rise of Political Anti-Semitism in Germany and Austria.* 1964. A clear and balanced survey of a difficult topic.

* Shattuck, Roger. *The Banquet Years.* 1968. A fascinating account of the artistic life in late nineteenth-century Paris.

Tannenbaum, Edward R. *1900: The Generation Before the Great War.* Interesting essays on the major facets of society.

Thayer, John A. *Italy and the Great War: Politics and Culture, 1870–1915.* 1964. Informed defense of Italian politics against its many critics.

Wagar, Warren W. *Good Tidings: The Belief in Progress from Darwin to Marcuse.* 1972. A wide-ranging account of the period's principal theme.

Weber, Eugen. *Peasants into Frenchmen: The Modernization of Rural France, 1880–1914.* 1976. Provocative treatment of the resistance of rural France to the pressures for change.

* Available in paperback.

TWENTY SIX

THE GREAT WAR

In 1914 the nations of Europe willingly took up arms. For the first time since the Napoleonic era, all the major powers engaged in battle on Continental soil, and during more than four years of unrelieved horror, the total energies of society were committed to the bloodiest conflict Europe had ever known. World War I strained the technological and organizing skills developed by the most industrialized and democratic states of the late nineteenth century. It ended with the collapse of the Russian, Austro-Hungarian, and German empires, defeated in war and torn by revolution. The new nations carved from them remade the map of Europe, and in Russia Communists established a government whose very existence altered political life throughout the West. On the winning side, the liberal Italian state never really recovered from the war, and victorious France and Great Britain emerged significantly changed.

Scholars have pondered the origins of World War I for half a century, and we can now see how a diplomatic system that seemed a triumph of flexible realism led to the disaster. Behind international relations lay domestic pressures within each country, and aggressive imperialism and nationalism were both used by conservative groups to preserve their power at home. In its causes as well as its conduct, the war was closely tied also to the economic and social changes of the preceding forty years. The machine guns, tanks, airplanes, and submarines that transformed military tactics were products of recent technology. The incredible quantities of armaments and ammunition consumed depended on modern methods of production and management. This war required the mobilization of the population to an extent possible only because of the levels of mass communication, literacy, popular participation, and efficient bureaucracy reached since the mid-nineteenth century.

The effects of the Great War were like those of a revolution. When it ended, fallen governments were replaced, buildings were rebuilt, and in the West, at least, groups previously dominant still held power; but the relations between town and country, peasant and landlord, worker and capitalist, citizen and government had been forever altered in most of Europe. The war thus had a significance beyond the immediate issue of victory and defeat. At the peace conference the desire to make sure so disastrous a conflict could never recur was strengthened by the suspicion that in 1914 a great civilization had come close to suicide.

I. THE COMING OF WORLD WAR I

Despite many dangerous moments Europe managed to avoid a war between major states for more than forty years after 1870 by accommodating world-wide interests and complex social changes, including the altered bases 'of power created by industrialization and democracy. Between nations this flexibility was managed through a traditional diplomacy conducted by gentlemen, most of them aristocrats, in secrecy and according to elaborate rules. Only later did it become clear how limited the efficacy of that diplomacy was. The experience of imperialism and the greater importance of public opinion gradually altered what could be negotiated and how negotiations were conducted, and policy came to be constrained both by military imperatives and domestic politics.

REALIGNMENTS IN THE BISMARCKIAN SYSTEM

Bismarck had established the German Empire as the arbiter of Continental peace at the Congress of Berlin in 1878, a position of strength he had sought to preserve by alliance with Austria-Hungary and the formation of the Three Emperors' Alliance. While Austria-Hungary established stronger ties with some of the Balkan States, Germany included Italy in her network of alliances intended to isolate France. Eager to increase their weight in world affairs, the Italians had identified Tunisia as a likely base for empire. But France had occupied Tunisia in 1881, and Bismarck took advantage of Italian resentment to win Italy to closer ties with Austria-Hungary and Germany, the Triple Alliance, of the following year. This treaty too was defensive, and like both earlier agreements, it had a time limit—five years. Then in 1887 Italy and the United Kingdom made a vague mutual commitment to preserve the status quo in the Mediterranean.

At its height therefore the Bismarckian system comprised the diplomatic isolation of France, good Anglo-German relations, a formal understanding with Russia, an alliance with Italy and Austria-Hungary, and additional ties extending into the Balkan and Iberian peninsulas (see Map 26.1). These accomplishments required great skill; Italy and Russia for example had more reasons for conflict with Austria-Hungary than with anyone else. Although their precise provisions were secret, the treaties were understood to imply far more than they specifically provided, and they placed Germany in a position of influence rare among sovereign states in peacetime.

Even before Bismarck fell from power, however, the system showed signs of weakness. The Three Emperors' Alliance, renewed in 1884, was allowed to lapse in 1887 because a flare-up of conflict among the Balkan States had reawakened suspicion between Austria-Hungary and Russia, a serious danger to Bismarckian diplomacy that could not be overcome. With characteristic flexibility Bismarck repaired the damage by immediately signing a separate Reinsurance Treaty with Russia, providing for the neutrality of either power if the other was at war. To preserve the Triple Alliance, which also came up for renewal in 1887, it was necessary to add recognition of Italian ambitions in the Balkans, Africa, and (in case of war with France) Corsica and Nice. Ironically, the weakest member of the Alliance could maneuver more freely than her powerful friends.

From the Germans' standpoint the keystone of the Bismarckian system was the alliance with Austria-Hungary. Beyond that their confidence rested on the assumption that enmities between France and Great Britain, Great Britain and Russia, and Italy and France would prevent any of them from aligning against the Second Reich. It was easy for Berlin to overlook one factor that might draw these powers together—common fear of Germany.

The Shifting Balance 1880–1905

The good relations all Bismarck's treaties implied required his supple skill to offset the menace of sudden attack they advertised, which of course heightened international insecurity. With his fall the system he had constructed broke down. Poorly coordinated, German diplomacy after 1890 was often inconsistent and disruptive.

Bismarck's successors did not renew the

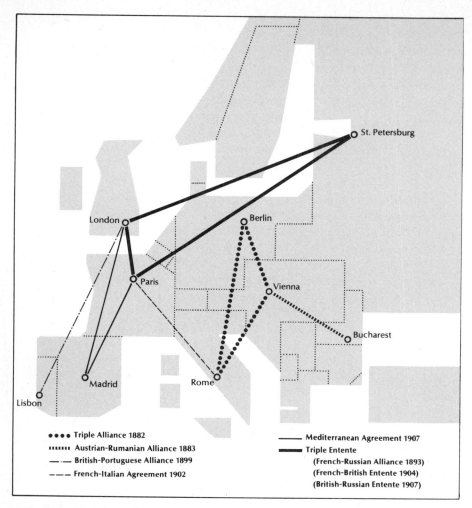

Triple Alliance 1882
Austrian-Rumanian Alliance 1883
British-Portuguese Alliance 1899
French-Italian Agreement 1902

Mediterranean Agreement 1907
Triple Entente
(French-Russian Alliance 1893)
(French-British Entente 1904)
(British-Russian Entente 1907)

MAP 26.1: THE BISMARCKIAN NETWORK OF ALLIANCES 1879–1895

understanding with Russia; a traditional dislike of Slavs reinforced by Junker objections to heavy imports of cheaper Russian grain led high German officials to prefer to keep the Triple Alliance uncluttered by a treaty with Russia.[1] The French were quick to seize the

opportunity to break out of their diplomatic isolation, and they pressed the Russian government—hesitant but already turning to France for loans and arms purchases—for an alliance. The understanding the two nations reached in 1891 became a full alliance in less than three years, a major shift in European military commitments. Russia agreed to support France if she should be attacked by Germany or by Italy with German aid, and France agreed to support Russia if she was attacked by Germany or Austria-Hungary with German aid.

[1] Renewal of the Reinsurance Treaty was one of the issues that led to the break between Bismarck and William II in 1890. The charge that it was incompatible with the Triple Alliance was at least technically incorrect, for the promise of neutrality was not to apply if Russia attacked Austria.

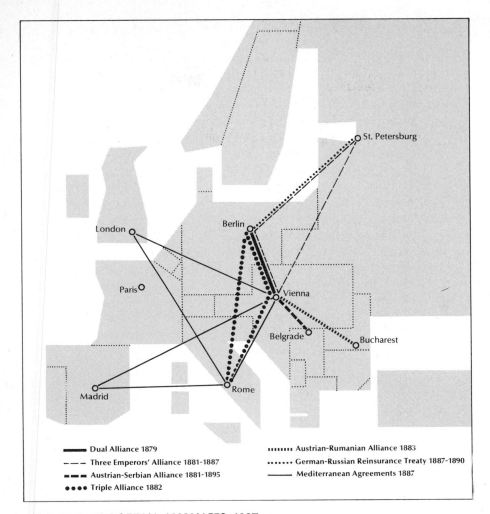

MAP 26.2: EUROPEAN ALLIANCES 1907

Dual Alliance 1879
Three Emperors' Alliance 1881-1887
Austrian-Serbian Alliance 1881-1895
Triple Alliance 1882
Austrian-Rumanian Alliance 1883
German-Russian Reinsurance Treaty 1887-1890
Mediterranean Agreements 1887

An accord between the Russian autocracy and the French republic had seemed politically impossible. But the tsar now greeted French delegates while a band played the "Marseillaise," previously prohibited as too revolutionary to be heard in Russia, and the Franco-Russian entente was to last as long as the Triple Alliance (see Map 26.2).

German diplomats in response sought to foster some understanding with the United Kingdom and to demonstrate their country's place in world affairs. Those aims conflicted.

The "new course" of *Weltpolitik* ("world politics"), backed by imperial claims and navy building, appeared more threatening with each of the verbal explosions for which the emperor became famous.

In 1896 William II sent a telegram of congratulation to S. J. P. Kruger, president of the South African Republic, after the Boers had defeated a raid on the Transvaal by a small private army organized by Englishmen who hoped to stir a revolution there. The message, deeply resented in Great Britain, was meant to show the British how much they needed German friendship; instead it encouraged distrust of Germany. During the Boxer Rebellion the Kaiser's enthusiastic talk of the "yellow peril" and instructions for his soldiers to behave like the barbaric Huns of old did nothing to enhance his reputation for stability or lessen the atmosphere of menace. Germans proclaimed the "natural" alliance between the Teutonic and Anglo-Saxon races but also took soundings about a possible Continental coalition against the United Kingdom. The navy they were building, which looked like a direct challenge to Great Britain and a threat to her links to her empire, became the central issue in all efforts at some rapprochement between the two powers. When the Germans demanded a formal alliance before they would limit their shipbuilding, the British were convinced that the German fleet was aimed at them.

During the difficult years of the Boer War, the United Kingdom had found her diplomatic independence no longer so splendid and was, as the Germans hoped, beginning to look for new international understandings. In 1902 she broke her long tradition of refusing peacetime alliances by signing a treaty with Japan. Her overall aim was of course to guard empire through alliance; her immediate purpose was to prevent France from supporting Russia's expansion into East Asia.

The colonial clashes between Great Britain and France in the last decade of the century had seemed some of the gravest threats to European peace. When the French had withdrawn from the confrontation at Fashoda in 1898, Foreign Minister Théophile Delcassé had set about turning humiliation into gain by seeking a broader understanding with Great Britain. France had learned not to demand too much, and her delegation of extraordinarily able diplomats had worked steadily for the reduction of conflicts. By the turn of the century,

she had dropped her resistance to British domination in Egypt in return for recognition of French interests in North Africa, particularly Morocco.

Similarly France had won Italian acknowledgment of her interest in Morocco by recognizing Italian ambitions in Libya, and in 1902 the two nations pledged neutrality if either was attacked by a third power. Although the Triple Alliance was renewed in the same year, Italy in fact sat on the fence between the Franco-Russian and the Austro-German alliance. The culmination of France's policy was the Anglo-French Entente Cordiale of 1904. In one sweeping effort she and Great Britain sought to eliminate all the major issues of imperial conflict between them. From Siam to Newfoundland, the Niger River to North Africa, they agreed on their spheres of influence and dominant interests.

The Entente Cordiale was nothing more than an understanding, but France was right in seeing it as a major break in the diplomatic encirclement Bismarck had created around her. Without demanding very formal guarantees, she was achieving a great deal. Edward VII's visit to Paris in 1903 and the French president's to London that year and Rome in 1905 testified to France's new place in European affairs. These understandings came in the nick of time, for they helped prevent the Russo-Japanese War of 1904–1905 from leading to conflict between France and Great Britain and effectively countered German efforts to break up the Franco-Russian alliance.

Hardening Alliances 1905–1912

Germany's diplomatic position remained strong —Britain and France were not allied; Russia's defeat at the hands of Japan and her subsequent revolution greatly reduced her influence; the chances of an Anglo-German understanding remained; and the Triple Alliance was intact. An assertive policy, German leaders reasoned, would enable them to capitalize on this situation. But the tenor of international relations was changing. Imperial ambitions, which had often threatened European relations in the preceding decades, were no longer so certain a source of antagonism as to prevent a coalition against Germany. The experience of imperialism and the politicians' increased concern for public opinion tended to transform international claims (and reactions to the Kaiser's bluster) into dangerous if vague issues of national honor. As armaments increased and treaties proliferated, each power became more obsessed with its own security. Thus within seven years three diplomatic crises—each of which at first seemed a victory for Germany—in fact brought her opponents closer together.

The first great crisis arose over Morocco. France had carefully won the acquiescence of each interested power, except Germany, in her designs on Morocco. The French planned to deal with Germany last; and the Germans, who had little direct interest there, intended to get the highest price possible for French annexation of the decaying sultanates. Wanting to test the loose understandings by which the French had improved their diplomatic position, the German chancellor Bernhard von Bülow demanded an international conference, for which there was solid basis in prior guarantees, and belligerently threatened France. Delcassé, the architect of French foreign policy, was forced from office, but the chancellor then sought more than this symbolic triumph. He reasoned that in a conference the other Triple Alliance nations would stand behind him, Russia and Great Britain would be won to the Germans' "correct" position, and a humiliated France would be left isolated once more.

The conference that met at Algeciras in 1906 did in fact produce a compromise, recognizing both international status for Morocco and the primacy of French interests, but it was a disaster for German diplomacy. Only Austria-Hungary loyally voted with her European neighbor. Italy, Russia, Great Britain, and the United States (now a participant in the Concert of Europe) supported France. The German bludgeon led to military talks between French and British officials and a far stronger sense of mutual interest.

After Algeciras Anglo-German competition for supremacy on the seas grew more serious. Both sides increased their plans for naval construction despite two great conferences at The Hague in 1899 and 1907 on disarmament and compulsory arbitration. In fact no power was willing to sacrifice any of its strength, but it was the German delegates who bluntly accepted the onus for rejecting any limitation on the sovereign right to make war. Such actions, combined with her militarism and the threats of her diplomacy, made Germany increasingly appear the major danger to peace. When an interview in the London *Daily Telegraph* quoted Kaiser William complaining that England was ungrateful for his nation's neutrality in the Boer War, the reaction was sharp and angry. British statesmen and journalists indulged in public recriminations that heightened tension while the latest efforts to settle naval questions broke down.

Also in 1907 a series of agreements showed again that imperial issues, which the Germans expected to keep their antagonists apart, were not necessarily divisive. France and Russia each reached an accord with Japan defining the areas of preeminent Japanese interest and agreeing to preserve the integrity of China. These understandings with Britain's East Asian ally opened the way for an entente between Great Britain and Russia in which the two nations resolved points of contention from the straits controlling access to the Black Sea, to Persia, Afghanistan, and Tibet. An informal coalition of France, Russia, and Britain, the Triple Entente, now balanced the Triple Alliance. Its major beneficiary was France, which had long worked for this accommodation between her two European allies. As long as they could ignore the internal politics of the places where they competed for influence, the European powers were finding it surprisingly easy to mark out and limit their interests.

Internal politics, however, could be neither ignored nor controlled in the Balkan States, and here the second crisis of the period arose. A new king and a radical nationalist government made Serbia Austria-Hungary's primary Balkan antagonist, and revolution in the Ottoman Empire in 1908—led by the Young Turks, whose movement sought to modernize the nation—foreshadowed a revival of Ottoman influence in the Balkans as well. Ever mindful of the dangers of nationalism, Austria-Hungary decided to strengthen her position there and at home by annexing Bosnia and Herzegovina, which she had occupied since the Congress of Berlin in 1878. She claimed she had Russia's agreement, but Russia, whose Slavophiles were infuriated by the annexation, demanded an international conference. Britain and France supported the call, even though they suspected the Russian foreign minister, Izvolsky, of some double dealing. Germany, angered by the precipitateness of Austria-Hungary's action, nevertheless stood by her ally. Diplomatic crises were becoming tests of alliances (and it was significant that Italy expressed resentment at not being consulted by Austria-Hungary rather than loyalty to the Triple Alliance).

The third major crisis once again involved Morocco. Both Germany and France were prepared to reach some definitive agreement, but the Germans thought to speed things up by sending the gunboat *Panther* to the Moroccan port of Agadir in 1911. They then asked for all of the French Congo in exchange for

French annexation of Morocco. Both the proposal and the method seemed excessive, and in Great Britain Lloyd George publicly decried them. The powers concerned eventually reached a compromise: France would cede parts of her Congo lands and bits of her other African territories adjacent to German colonies. But the fact of the settlement counted for less than the rising tension in Europe and the growing distrust of the Germans. After a final effort at naval agreement failed, Britain decided in 1912 to withdraw her battleships from the Mediterranean, concentrating them in the North Sea, while France sent her fleet to replace them. With this crisis and the confrontation of 1908, the loose Triple Entente was becoming at least as binding as the Triple Alliance.

Balkan Turmoil

The Balkans became the focal point for the interplay of the forces of European imperialism, nationalism, and power politics. In Serbia, Bulgaria, Rumania, and Greece, social conflicts and the strains of modernization led to governments that won support by embracing nationalism. At the same time the Balkan policies of Austria-Hungary and Russia had become enmeshed in their own bitter domestic divisions, which further reduced their diplomatic flexibility. Moreover Germany, through railway concessions in Turkey, had also developed interests in the peninsula, as had Italy, whose victory over the Ottoman sultanate in 1912 (part of her conquest of Tripoli) encouraged Greece, Bulgaria, Serbia, and Montenegro to join forces against the empire. They succeeded in driving the Ottomans from all their remaining European holdings except Constantinople. Intervention by the great powers brought peace, but the tension between Austria-Hungary and Russian-backed Serbia kept the ferment high with complex diplomatic maneuvers. Serbia had territorial designs on weakly organized areas of Albania and Montenegro, and each Balkan state had boundary disputes with the others. These conflicting claims erupted in the Second Balkan War within a few months when some Bulgarian troops launched an attack on Serbian and Greek forces. Bulgaria had gained more territory in the earlier war than the other Balkan states; and although the Bulgarian government quickly disavowed this latest move, Serbia, Greece, Rumania, and Turkey declared war and quickly defeated her. When the threats from Austria-Hungary forced Serbia to abandon some of her gains, Serbian nationalists replied by proclaiming their concern and sympathy for their fellow Slavs subject to Austrian rule in Bosnia and Herzegovina.

Thus tensions were high when on June 28, 1914, Archduke Francis Ferdinand, the heir to the Austrian and Hungarian thrones, paraded in Sarajevo, the capital of Bosnia. It was an act of some courage. One bomb just missed killing the archduke, and his car passed other conspirators who lost their courage and failed to fire. Then the car made a wrong turn; and as it backed up a young Bosnian revolutionary fired point-blank, killing both the archduke and his wife.

For the Austro-Hungarian government, convinced the Serbian government was involved in the assassination, here was a challenge that required strong action. It sent a special emissary to Berlin, where the German government, with a lack of reflection that remains remarkable, promised full support to Austria. On the other side the French president and prime minister went to Russia to declare their country's loyal backing of its ally. On July 23 the Austrians sent Serbia an ultimatum meant to be unacceptable: it gave Serbia forty-eight hours in which to apologize, ban all anti-Austrian propaganda, and agree to Austro-Hungarian participation in Serbia's investigation of the plot

This painting dramatizes the assassination of Archduke Ferdinand and his wife; the incident provided the immediate cause for World War I. (Photo: Bildarchiv der österreichischen Nationalbibliothek, Vienna)

against Francis Ferdinand—in effect to a voice in her internal government.

Serbia replied with great tact, accepting all terms except those that diminished her sovereignty and offering to submit even these to arbitration. It seemed even to Berlin that another crisis would pass. Great Britain, wanting to reduce tensions further, proposed an international conference, to which France and Russia reluctantly agreed. The Germans then declared the controversy a matter for Austrians and Serbians alone, and on July 28 Austria-Hungary declared war on Serbia.

Austria-Hungary was in fact not yet ready to fight, and Germany and Great Britain still hoped she would limit herself to occupying Belgrade and then accept a conference. But Russia, explaining that she could not allow an occupation of Serbia, on July 29 ordered a partial mobilization, making clear that it was aimed only at Austria-Hungary; the following day the Russians discovered they were not prepared for a partial call-up and announced a general mobilization instead. On July 31 Germany declared herself in a state of readiness, sent Russia an ultimatum demanding demobilization within twelve hours, and asked France what course she would take in case of a Russo-German war. France answered that she would act in her own interests and then mobilized, but she held her troops ten kilometers (about six miles) from the frontier to prevent any incidents. The Germans, who had planned next to demand the surrender of France's border fortresses as a guarantee of neutrality, were unsatisfied with this response and planned their moves for the next several days accordingly.

Germany mobilized on August 1 and declared war on Russia; and convinced this meant fighting on the Western front as well, she invaded Luxembourg and sent an ultimatum to the Belgians demanding unobstructed passage for her troops. On August 3 she declared war on France and began invading Belgium. The following day the British declared war on the Germans, and within forty-eight hours each nation had 2 million soldiers under orders. World War I had begun.

THE ORIGINS OF THE WAR

The question of what caused the Great War—or more simply who was to blame—soon became a major issue in European politics. The Allies blamed Germany so insistently that they wrote her guilt into the treaty of peace, a view that most historians have considered one-sided at the very least and that German scholars rejected with special force, which explains the furor that first greeted the recent work of the German historian Fritz Fischer, who finds strong evidence that Germany's leaders had in fact looked forward to war and nurtured almost boundless ambitions for military dominance. But the question remains without a final answer, for the causes adduced depend very much on how long-range a look one takes.

The immediate cause, the assassination, almost did not happen. The tensions that made it so significant were more deeply rooted. The Balkan States, struggling to establish their strength, played on the competition among the major nations, which in turn treated Balkan affairs as matters of their own prestige. Serbia's policy, like her nationalism and her effort to modernize, challenged Austria-Hungary, apprehensive about her declining power and thus set on teaching the Serbians a lesson while there was still time. Individual statesmen can be blamed for Austria-Hungary's untoward haste, Germany's irresponsible support of Austria-Hungary, Russia's clumsy and confused diplomacy, France's eagerness to prove to the Russians that she was a good ally, Britain's unwillingness to admit she was tied to one side, and her consequent inability to warn the Germans that an attack on France meant war with her as well.

Such an analysis may, however, make the statesmen seem to have been more autonomous and therefore more to blame than they were. The system of alliances with which each state sought security decreased the diplomats' freedom. The fact that every European power believed in the summer of 1914 that its very survival depended on its alliances meant in practice that each alliance would follow behind its least responsible member.

The fear that cemented these commitments was related to the foreign-policy goals of the major nations: Britain's conviction that empire required supremacy at sea; France's determination to revenge the defeat of 1870 and regain Alsace-Lorraine; Russia's 150 years of expansion toward the West, the Balkans, and East Asia; Italy's need to show herself a great power; Austria's dependence since Metternich on foreign policy to sustain a shaky regime; the desire of a powerful Germany fearful of encirclement for prestige abroad that might reduce conflict at home.

The arms race itself contributed to the outbreak of war. Military strength required increasing expenditures and organization, for Germany's victory over the French in 1871 had been understood in all Continental countries to prove the superiority of the Prussian system of universal conscription, large reserves, and detailed planning. Furthermore it was believed that technology gave an attacker overwhelming advantages. Thus every nation felt it needed to maintain sufficient military might, in men and matériel, to repel surprise attack. In 1889 Great Britain had adopted the principle that her navy must equal in size the two next-largest fleets combined, and in 1906 she had launched the *Dreadnought*, the first battleship armed entirely with big guns. By 1914 she had twenty-nine ships of this class afloat and thirteen under construction, and the German navy had eighteen, with nine being built. The French and German standing armies doubled between 1870 and 1914, and all able-bodied men had some military responsibilities from the age of twenty to the late fifties. Each increase in manpower and weapons was quickly matched, though in some cases only with enormous effort; France for example had but 60 percent of Germany's potential manpower and yet equaled her rival. The arms race, justified

by the fear that it was meant to allay, fed on itself. Mobilization, calling up millions of men, was considered an essential act of defense but had become by 1914 tantamount to war.

Such expenditures of money and resources, however, had to be justified to parliaments. Thus ultimately these enormous forces, like foreign policy, rested on domestic politics. In every country political parties now competing for broader popular support found nationalist programs to have effective appeal and to offer the chance of reaching across social, religious, and regional divisions. Special interests associated with the military and empire could thus join with all who feared a rising tide of socialism in dramatizing issues of national honor. This was especially the case in Germany where the very economic growth that made her powerful threatened the dominance of Prussia and of the Junker class in a still insecure new state. Throughout Europe then domestic conflict and the politics of nationalism had an important part in the statecraft that led to World War I.

Few Europeans really wanted war; yet its outbreak was hailed with joy everywhere. The strain of economic, demographic, and imperial competition prepared many to welcome with relief the open and total confrontation of armed conflict. Its excitement provided the unity and common purpose so long missed. In immediate terms world war could have been avoided; in a larger sense it was a product of the social structures it nearly annihilated.

II. THE COURSE OF THE WAR

For decades European military staffs had prepared detailed plans for the eventuality they now faced. The French intended to drive into Alsace and Lorraine in carefully coordinated and dashing maneuvers that reflected their almost mystic belief in élan. The Germans'

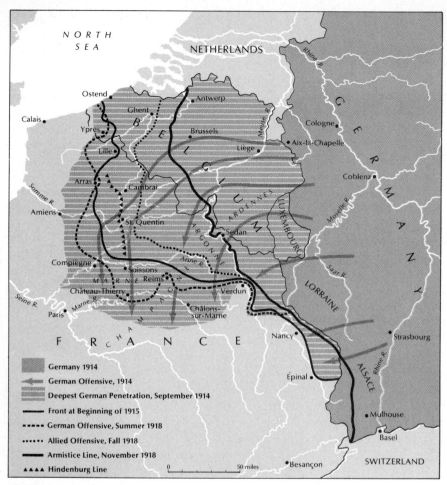

MAP 26.3: THE WESTERN FRONT

strategy rested on the Schlieffen "swinging door" plan, first adopted in 1905 to meet the awful challenge of fighting on two fronts simultaneously: using minimum forces against the Russians in the East and the expected French attack in Alsace, they would send their main armies wheeling through Belgium down on Paris and knock France out of the war before Russia could bring her massive armies into play or British aid could make a difference.

THE FIRST YEARS OF WAR

All the belligerents in 1914 assumed that modern war would be swift, with the advantage to the offense. But the first few months of hostilities established that the war being fought was not the one planned, though commanders were slow to admit it. Increased fire power gave defensive forces unexpected strength, cavalry was ineffectual, and the common soldier proved able to absorb more punishment than anyone had thought possible. After slight gains the French offensive in Alsace was stopped, with heavy losses to both sides. The Germans were more nearly successful—the French command had underestimated by half the number of troops they would engage in immediate battle—and within a month they drove to within thirty miles of Paris (see Map 26.3).

But the German fighting men were as battered as the defenders, their casualties were as high, and their lines of communication and supply were dangerously stretched. These factors, added to unanticipated Belgian resistance, infuriated and worried German commanders, and a small British force that had joined the French sooner than expected as well as Russian advances toward eastern Prussia altered the Schlieffen plan in practice. Extra German troops were sent to Alsace in hope of a breakthrough following earlier successes there, while the Russian move frightened the indecisive German chief of staff, Helmuth von Moltke (nephew of the field marshal who had led Germany to victory in 1866 and 1870), into assigning to the East troops intended to be in the West. Overwhelming though they were, the forces that cut east of Paris, instead of running beyond it, were considerably fewer than German strategy called for.

After each bloody encounter the Allies had retreated, but they were not routed; and German officers were surprised to take so few prisoners. The French commander in chief, Joseph Joffre, kept his forces together even in defeat, imperturbably confident of the ultimate success of a great French drive. In September the French launched a counteroffensive along the Marne River that saved Paris and hurled the Germans back to the natural defenses of the Aisne River. There, despite repeated Allied attacks, the Germans held. In the next few months the armies tried to outflank each other but succeeded only in extending the front northward to the sea. With changes of only a few miles, the battle lines established by the end of 1914 would remain those of the Western front for the next four years. France had not been knocked out of the war, but Germany held a tenth of her territory and nearly all of Belgium (see Map 26.4).

On the Eastern front Russian armies scored important gains in early August, taking eastern Galicia from Austria-Hungary and beginning an invasion of eastern Prussia in the North. Moltke talked in panic of a general retreat until replaced by Generals Paul von Hindenburg and Erich von Ludendorff, who soon became Germany's greatest war heroes. At Tannenberg late in August, their forces surrounded and destroyed a Russian army; and German troops pushed on almost to Warsaw before being stopped. In the South Austria-Hungary halted the Russian advance with German aid, and despite the able fighting of the Serbian army, Austrian armies took Belgrade. By the end of 1914, the Central Powers had made impressive gains at every hand, and the Ottoman Empire's entry into the war on their side extended the threat to the Allies all the way to Suez.

WAR OF ATTRITION

On the Western front especially, the great armies found themselves bogged down in a terrifying kind of siege warfare. Artillery became increasingly important, and shells were fired at rates unimaginable a few months before, devastating the pockmarked land and making any movement in it still more difficult. Dug into trenches and clinging to pillboxes, neither side could be uprooted. Military units worked out complex systems of communication by laying cables, building bridges, and maintaining roads and railways. For the first time poison gas was used, but the German troops could not follow up the momentary gains it permitted.

Again and again the Allied armies attempted to mount a great offensive, only to be stopped after gaining two or three miles and losing hundreds of thousands of men. Battles were now numbered—the Second Battle of Ypres (April–May 1915), the Second Battle of Artois (May–June), the Second Battle of Champagne (September–November), the Third Battle of Artois (September–October); and after a year's

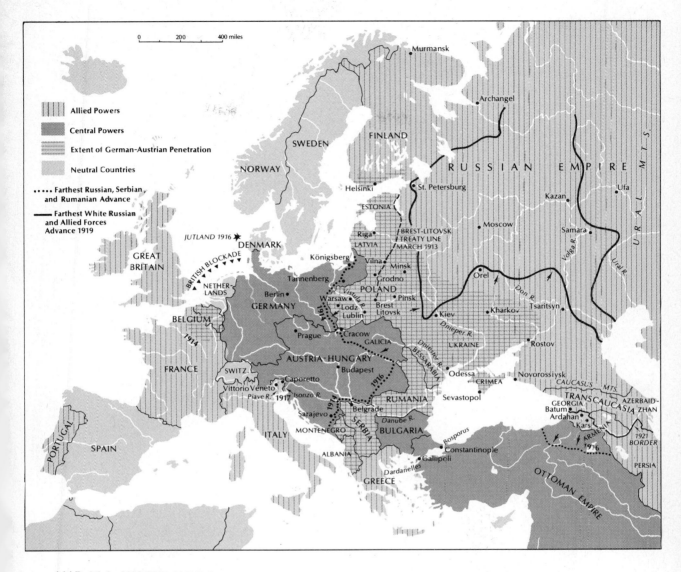

MAP 26.4: WORLD WAR I

bloodshed, the Western front remained essentially the same.

Italy's entry into the war had not broken the stalemate. She had declared her neutrality on the ground that Austria-Hungary's attack on Serbia was an offensive action and thus did

Casualties of the Battle of the Marne. (Photo: René Dazy)

not fall within the terms of the Triple Alliance, and this had kept her free to negotiate with both sides. Geography and Austria-Hungary's reluctance to give up territory the Italians sought had led them to favor the Allies. In April 1915 Italy had signed a secret agreement with Great Britain, France, and Russia, the Treaty of London, committing herself to the Allied side in return for the promise of lands along her border with Austria-Hungary (the

MAP 26.5: TERRITORIAL SETTLEMENTS 1919–1926

southern Tyrol, Istria, Trieste, and Gorizia—see Map 26.5), important Dalmatian islands, and expansion of her colonial holdings. Italy had declared war on Austria-Hungary in May and soon advanced to a line along the Isonzo River. At that line eleven battles were fought in the next two years without significant gain.

The fighting in France in 1916 brought no decisive changes either. Early in the year the Germans launched an all-out offensive against the French fortifications at Verdun. Knowing the French would be determined to hold, their aim was more to bleed the enemy than to take territory. For days shells poured down, and then the Germans attacked in overwhelming numbers. From February to July the fighting continued at full pitch. German forces captured two outlying forts, but the French managed a brief counterattack. Verdun held; and though the French losses, more than 300,000 men, weakened the subsequent Allied offensive, German casualties were only slightly less. The Allied attack in the Battle of the Somme, from July to November, brought still heavier casualties and a maximum advance of seven miles.

For two years each side had believed its offensives about to succeed only to see them halted by some unexpected flaw. The doctrine of the offensive, like general morale, was sinking in gore. If the brilliant tactics of rapid maneuver planned at war's outset could not bring victory, then attrition, systematically exhausting men and resources, seemed the only alternative.

On the Eastern front Austro-German forces launched an offensive through Galicia in May 1915, pushing forward a hundred miles, and followed it with a general offensive in July. By late September the Russians had lost Poland and Lithuania; and as the Central Powers massed on a line from Riga in the north to the easternmost part of Hungary, their new ally, Bulgaria, pressed into Serbia. The following year, however, General Alexis Brusilov, in one of the few really well conducted Russian campaigns, regained a large part of those losses. But the effort cost Russia a million men, and she lacked the organization, the supplies, and the leadership to do more. The Russian offensive brought Rumania into the war on the Allied side, but Austria-Hungary took Bucharest at the end of the year.

Naval strength did not in itself produce military success for either side during the war. The single large-scale attack by sea, the landing of Allied forces on the Gallipoli Peninsula in April 1915, was a failure. Having hoped to open the Dardanelles for shipping to Russia and to force the Ottoman Empire out of the war, the Allies were grateful to withdraw in December without serious loss.

Great Britain had nonetheless effectively maintained a blockade of Germany that was beginning to hurt. The Germans had tried to counter in 1915 by announcing a submarine blockade of Britain, but the angry reaction of neutrals led by the United States had forced them to abandon the tactic. The sinking of passenger ships—most sensationally, the *Lusitania*, killing more than a thousand civilians—gave way in 1916 to attacks on armed merchantmen and then, in the face of American warnings, to the renunciation of "unlimited" submarine warfare.

The one great naval battle of the war, at Jutland in May 1916, was indecisive. British and German fleets lost the same number of ships, though the British tonnage sunk was twice as great. Thereafter Admiral Alfred von Tirpitz's great fleet hid in its harbors and did not threaten Allied control of the sea.

THE HOME FRONT

By every measure this was war on an unprecedented scale, and adjustment to its demands strained the very fabric of society. At first the fighting produced not only enthusiasm but a

The ruins of Verdun after the seige that bled both armies stand like a broken tombstone. (Photo: Wide World Photos)

euphoric spirit of national unity. In Great Britain the Liberal government gave way within a year to a coalition; the emergency left little room for party divisions. Frenchmen hailed their "sacred union," and the leading socialist militant took a post in the cabinet. The German parliament unanimously voted war credits, and though some Germans were shocked at the invasion of Belgium, the citizenry was convinced that the nation was fighting a just and defensive war. In Russia the government seemed almost popular.

War brought immediate dislocation. As factories closed, unemployment rose despite conscription; there then followed a labor shortage as war production became crucial to survival. Everywhere agricultural output dropped, contributing to the food shortages of subsequent years. Prices rose rapidly and consumer hoarding further strained faltering systems of distribution.

In response to domestic and military crises, the powers of governments to move men, censor the press, and control the railroads, the telegraph, and shipping, and even to direct the economy were extended as never before. Unprepared for their armies' requirements of ever more ammunition and supplies, governments quickly learned to use paper money, rationing, and central planning. In this and other ways, modern warfare involved the full participation of the civilian population. The refugees from Belgium pouring into France (and the German reprisals against Belgian civilians) were only the first and clearest symptom of this pervasive change. Just as unlimited submarine warfare, poison gas, and a blockade that treated consumer goods as contraband burst the rules that had delimited warfare among civilized nations, so requirements for mobilization of the home front overrode the restraints on which liberal society had depended.

In the United Kingdom the government, which was granted unparalleled power over the lives of civilians, requisitioned supplies and forced industry to new efficiency. Its professional army shattered, Britain had, despite voluntary enlistments that raised the largest army in her history, to adopt conscription in 1916, a step that Winston Churchill considered "the greatest revolution in our system since the institution of feudalism under William the Conqueror." Rebellion in Ireland that Easter was quickly put down; yet it was a serious diversion for British troops and a disturbing reminder of how cruelly war tested every weakness in the social structure.

Germany, deprived of critical raw materials, developed the most fully controlled economy of any of the combatants. Under the brilliant direction of Walther Rathenau, German resources were allocated and her industry deployed to the needs of war. Private firms were organized into sectors of production so that the most important could be favored, inefficient firms closed, and national planning enforced. The chemical industry developed ways of making rubber substitutes, manufac-

tured fertilizers from nitrates in the air and textiles from wood pulp, and culled aluminum from local clays. Substitutes, which made "ersatz" an international word, included chestnut flour and clover meal used in the "war bread" that, like meatless days and conscription, soon made the civilian population feel the burden of all-out war.

In the first weeks of the fighting, half of France's iron ore and coal fields and more than half her heavy industry were captured or destroyed. Joffre exercised virtually dictatorial powers, and the French, too, began to develop techniques for mobilizing a whole society. Quotas and priorities were established by government and industrial committees, and supplies were allocated according to comprehensive plans. Production steadily increased. Although censorship was severe, the tradition of political dispute was in large part preserved; and if the custom of reshuffling cabinets was a source of some inefficiency, it also eased the task of recruiting men competent to undertake new administrative tasks. In France as in Great Britain civilian authority had begun to reassert itself in 1915.

These three were the states that adjusted most effectively to the revolutionary requirements of fielding huge armies while increasing industrial production and maintaining intricate networks of supply. They did it with governments that had the will and the capacity to organize their nations. Civilians were disciplined to all-out war through propaganda, compulsion, and systematic economic controls.

These were feats that the Austro-Hungarian and Russian empires could not match. Not only was their industry relatively sparse but its development was uneven, and even modern plants worked at less than capacity, hampered by lack of supplies and trained manpower. Neither government knew how or dared to squeeze from the economy the overwhelming quantities of food, ammunition, or clothes that war required. Russian armies increasingly showed the effects of fighting ill fed and ill shod, with inadequate weapons and ammunition, and without good communication. (Orders to Russian troops were broadcast uncoded, which contributed to Ludendorff's reputation as a great tactician.) Austria-Hungary could not rely in adversity on the continued loyalty of subject peoples, and soldiers were carefully dispatched to zones far from their homes so as not to be fighting against people who spoke their own tongue.

By the winter of 1916–1917, the grave strains were visible to all. Everywhere on the bloodied Continent, Europeans were thinner and more shabbily dressed, overworked, and grieved by the endless losses of husbands, sons, and homes. Poor crops and overloaded transportation systems reduced the diet further; this was the Germans' "turnip winter," when the best organized of the domestic war economies could barely keep its people healthy.

The strains of war were changing society. The queue became a kind of public rite as many of the subtler distinctions of social class disappeared. Each government awkwardly tried to restrict the consumption of alcohol and worried about rising rates of illegitimacy. Just as rationing had spread from nation to nation, becoming ever more restrictive, so did the need to employ women. British women were asked in 1915 to take any jobs they could, and by 1917 the government denied contracts to employers unwilling to hire women. The French government forbade hiring men for certain jobs that women could do; and the Krupp works, which had no women employees in 1914, counted 12,000 by 1917. In munitions industries in particular the number of women workers steadily rose to become one-third or more of the total; and women tilled the soil, served as bus conductors, fire fighters, and office

workers in addition to more direct war work. Although labor agitation remained below prewar levels, signs of growing discontent had to be taken seriously. Trade unions were treated with new respect, and officials began to talk of the benefits to be granted after the war to those making such heavy sacrifices now. Even the Kaiser spoke of ending the three-class voting system and hinted at representative government, while the House of Commons in a notable reversal declared its support in principle for women's suffrage. Meanwhile, month upon month of bloodshed in muddy, disease-filled trenches took a psychological as well as physical toll. Morale was sinking.

CHANGES IN LEADERSHIP

There were some hints in that terrible winter of the possibility of peace. In December 1916, after having gained the initiative on the Eastern front, the Central Powers indicated willingness to discuss a settlement; but the Allies' terms, stated a month later, were wholly unacceptable. Meanwhile both sides had been seeking to strengthen themselves by changes in leadership.

In the fall of 1916, Hindenburg had received overall command of German troops and with Ludendorff had taken charge of campaigns in the West. To destroy the shipping on which Britain's survival depended, the Germans returned to unlimited submarine warfare in January 1917. They were aware that this might bring the United States into the war, but they calculated that American power could not make itself felt before Britain would have to sue for peace. Britain and France also sought the formula for victory in new leadership. Joffre's intolerance of civilian leaders brought his downfall in December 1916; and General Robert Georges Nivelle, politically more tactful and personally more dashing, succeeded him as commander in chief of the French armies. He planned a massive offensive, and this one, he assured his government, would break through German defenses.

Changes in high political offices were more important. Lloyd George, who was made minister of war in June 1916, became British prime minister in December. Eloquent and energetic, once a radical orator who had terrified the upper classes, he now seemed the kind of decisive leader who could galvanize the British into a well-organized effort to win. The French turned to the fiery Clemenceau, who became premier again in November 1917 after French morale hit a dangerous low. Change had come to Russia too—through revolution. In March 1917 the tsar had abdicated, and a new provisional government had proclaimed sweeping democratic reforms while promising to continue the war. Both sides knew that Russia was now more vulnerable than ever but that her immense resources had yet to be effectively tapped.

For the Allies these changes, especially in Russia, gave the war itself new meaning. Now democracies were fighting together against authoritarian governments dominated by the aristocracy and the military. A war that involved the people more fully than any before it took on an ideological meaning. In April the United States declared war on Germany, resentful of the sinking of her ships and of German overtures to Mexico promising the return of Mexican lands taken by the United States. American entry added to the Allies' sense of democratic purpose as well as their military strength.

THE GREAT TRIALS OF *1917–1918*

In the fighting itself, however, neither new leaders nor shared ideals seemed to make much difference. On the Western front Nivelle launched his great offensive in April and May 1917 despite multiple handicaps. The Germans had strengthened their defenses along the Hindenburg line, near the French-Belgian border, and disagreements had arisen between the British and French commands. But most dangerous of all, there was grave disaffection among the French troops. Some refused to fight, and those who remained in the trenches were dispirited by two years of endless death on the same barren hills and slimy plains. Thus the offensive (the Second Battle of the Aisne and the Third Battle of Champagne) brought a toll as great as that of its predecessors and even slighter gains.

Nivelle was replaced by General Henri Philippe Pétain, the hero of Verdun, who began a concerted effort to raise the morale by recognizing many of the soldiers' grievances and by instituting regular leaves; and the government took severe measures against agitators who talked of peace. The results were encouraging, but it would be months before France dared another offensive.

The British went ahead with plans for an attack in the North, spurred by the desperate need to knock out at least some of the Germans' submarine bases, for the U-boats were sinking such enormous tonnages that the admiralty openly wondered how many months Great Britain could last. With only weak assistance from the French army, the British fared no better in the Third Battle of Ypres (July–November) than had the French in their spring offensive. The noise of battle could be heard in England, and hundreds of thousands of men fell, but there was no breakthrough. British morale too was shaken.

On the Eastern front Russian advances in July turned into almost constant retreat in the next few months. In November the Bolsheviks, a faction of the Social Democratic party, took over the government, invited all nations to join in peace without annexations or indemnities, and entered into independent negotiations with

British gas masks used in 1917 express the faceless horror of French warfare. (Photo: Gernschein Collection, Humanities Research Center, University of Texas at Austin)

the Central Powers. The most populous of the Allies had been defeated. In October German troops had joined Austro-Hungarian troops in a concentrated attack on the Italian front that issued in an overwhelming victory at the Battle of Caporetto. Italy's armies collapsed as tens of thousands died, surrendered, or deserted. But the Italians regrouped along the Piave River while Britain and France rushed in reinforcements, and the Austro-German onslaught was slowed and then stopped.

German reserves of manpower and resources were nearing exhaustion. Submarine warfare had come close to its goal of defeating Britain, but though Allied losses remained serious, they had dropped to a tolerable level with the development of the convoy in mid-1917. The convoys, enlarged by American ships, brought tons of supplies and toward the end of the year even some fresh troops.

In February 1918 the Russians stopped fighting, a gesture of peace the Central Powers did not reciprocate; they continued their breathtaking eastward march. In the Treaty of Brest Litovsk, signed in March, Russia surrendered not only Russian Poland and the Baltic provinces but the Ukraine and Transcaucasia. When she needed them most, Germany had acquired the invaluable wheat and oil of the Ukraine and a respite on one front. But the gains were so immense that merely patrolling them took great numbers of badly needed troops, and the incredibly harsh terms of the treaty stiffened the resistance of the enemy. Both Lloyd George and President Wilson, in his Fourteen Points, now stated formal war aims that expressed their confidence in victory and put revolutionary emphasis on the right to self-government.

In March also the Germans opened a great offensive on the West. With careful strategy, improved tactics, heavy artillery, and gas, they made the greatest advances seen on the Western front in four years. But the Allies held, and they sought to correct the weakness of divided command by naming General Ferdinand Foch supreme commander.

From March through June 1918 the Germans attacked British, French, and now American troops in sector after sector, scoring surprising successes; but the Allies were retaining their reserves while the Germans exhausted theirs. Enemy guns once more bombarded Paris as the Second Battle of the Marne and the Allied counteroffensive began in July. Slowly, then faster, the Germans were driven back over the familiar and devastated landscape. By the end of August, German armies had retreated to the Hindenburg line; and the Allies continued their push in battles of the Argonne and Ypres in September and October, gaining less rapidly than hoped or expected but now inexorably.

Elsewhere the Central Powers collapsed more dramatically. Meeting a large offensive begun in Palestine in September, Turkish and German troops were defeated by British and Arab forces led by T. E. Lawrence, whose exploits became part of the romantic lore in which this war was poorer than most. In October the sultan was deposed, and a new Ottoman government sued for peace. From Salonika combined Serbian, French, British, and Greek forces under French leadership drove up the Balkan Peninsula. Bulgaria surrendered at the end of the month, and the Allies moved toward Rumania.

The Austro-Hungarian Empire was disintegrating. Throughout 1918 Czech, Yugoslav, Rumanian, and Austrian Polish movements for independence had gained strength, encouraged by the Allies. On the Italian front Austria-Hungary attacked once more but withdrew after heavy losses. Defeated at the Battle of Vittorio Veneto at the end of October, her armies began simply to dissolve as the various nationalities left the battlefield for home and revolution. Czechoslovakia and the kingdom later called Yugoslavia both declared their independence, and in November Austria-Hungary would surrender unconditionally to the Italians.

Ludendorff had demanded that Germany

seek an armistice at the end of September, and in October a new government, under liberal Prince Maximilian of Baden, asked for peace on the terms of President Wilson's Fourteen Points. But Wilson now insisted on the evacuation of occupied territories and a democratic German government with which to negotiate. While German leaders hesitated, they faced the threat of revolution at home. Ludendorff resigned his command at the end of October; Kaiser William II abdicated on November 9 after a mutiny in the German fleet and revolution in Munich; and a German armistice commission met with Foch and agreed to terms on November 11. By then Allied troops were approaching the German borders in the West and had crossed the Danube in the East, taken Trieste on the Adriatic, and sailed through the Dardanelles. And revolution was sweeping Central Europe.

THE EFFECTS OF WORLD WAR I

The war itself had some of the effects of revolution. Its psychological impact is not easy to demonstrate, but there were endless examples among intellectuals of what one historian has called "minds scorched by war," and a cynical distrust of leaders and institutions seems to have spread after years of wartime promises. There was a cleavage too between those who had fought and those who stayed home, those whose lives were transformed and those who had more nearly maintained business as usual. And there was bitterness about the inequalities of sacrifice that surfaced in denunciations of war profiteers. Throughout society, there was after World War I a tendency to expect instability and change in social mores and structure. At the same time few forgot and some would yearn for the thrill of combat, the sense of common purpose, and the vision of national unity that war had brought.

Some of the psychological and social changes showed in public behavior and even in dress. Gentlemen had abandoned their top hats when forced to use public transportation, and women's clothes grew simpler and their skirts shorter. Women of the working class took to cosmetics, high-heeled shoes, and smoking and drinking in public, as did their middle-class sisters. These changes, even more than the increase in violent crime and juvenile delinquency, shocked moralists for whom they were related to casual encounters between the sexes, increased illegitimacy, and the popularity of dance halls. Such signs pointed to a more mobile and fluid society in which old customs and patterns of proper behavior had been so disrupted that they might never be recaptured. Millions of refugees represented a deep displacement, but millions more (especially peasants and women) would choose not to return to their old way of life.

Political life was directly affected and not just where revolution triumphed. In Germany ex-soldiers joined *Freikorps* ("free corps"), mercenary squads available for street fighting and marauding that preserved the camaraderie of arms. Throughout Central Europe political conflict adopted the techniques of force. Even in the West solid men of the older parties watched with apprehension the revival of the left. Clemenceau, Lloyd George, and Wilson, the spokesmen of victory, had all been vigorous reformers who understood and spoke to public opinion (even when the enthusiasm of patriotic unity came to seem a little hollow) as more traditional politicians did not. Even the most conservative governments had shown that the state could use its inflated bureaucracies and increased power to shape the economy, and no one could now deny that governments might improve the lot of the poor, a recognition that resulted in a spate of postwar legislation on housing, education, and pensions.

The relative position of the various social classes was also altered. Inflation lessened the purchasing power of aristocrats and members of the middle class who lived on investments, especially in land. Taxes (particularly in England) and the relative decline in land values also weakened the aristocracy, whose power was further lessened even where there was no open revolution by the general democratization of political life. Members of the middle class, especially those on salary or fixed income, also suffered relatively more from inflation than those on workers' wages. Middle-class life became less lavish, with fewer servants (some 400,000 English women left domestic service in the course of the war) or occasions for ostentation. A middle class confident in 1914 found itself after the war exposed and vulnerable, its savings threatened, its possibilities limited, its values challenged. Workers, particularly the skilled, were on the whole relatively well off. Although rates of pay had usually run behind inflation, the years of full employment and more jobs for women had increased family income, and trade unions used their greater influence to maintain gains of shorter hours and higher pay. Peasants, though declining in numbers, were also often better off since inflation and the demand for food had helped them to pay off their debts and own more land free and clear.

The war affected economic life in other ways. The employment of new technologies was stimulated by their wartime use, as happened with automobiles and airplanes, radio, and some chemicals. World trade had not only been disrupted but Europe's place in it permanently altered. In 1914 Europe had been the world's greatest lender of money; in 1918 its states were debtors. The physical destruction of property, aside from the billions lost in war matériel, was greatest in Belgium and France. In France alone thousands of bridges,

thousands of factories, and a million buildings were destroyed. Total European production in the 1920s would fall below the level in 1913.

All this required enormous adjustments. So did the war's simplest accomplishment: the killing of from 10 to 13 million men and perhaps half again as many civilians. Moreover, for every soldier who died, two or three were wounded; millions were maimed for life. The casualty figures tell much about the history of the first third of the twentieth century (see accompanying table).

MILITARY FATALITIES IN WORLD WAR I

Germany	2,000,000
Russia	1,700,000
France	1,500,000
Austria-Hungary	1,250,000
British Empire	1,000,000
Italy	500,000
Ottoman Empire	500,000
United States	100,000

Among the armed forces, casualties ran about 50 percent for the major combatants except France, whose losses were higher. The weakness of Russian organization shows in the fact that a smaller percentage of the population was mobilized—about 7 percent, as compared with 16 percent of the German and 19 percent of the French—and that the fatalities can only be estimated. The high percentage of mobilization in France and Germany is a measure of the desperate efforts they made. Whole classes from the elite schools of each nation were virtually wiped out. For France, with her older population and low birth rate, the war was a demographic catastrophe in which a large part of an entire generation disappeared on the Western front. And throughout Europe the one-armed, the one-legged, and the blind would live on, supported by pensions and performing menial tasks, in silent testimony to the cost of total war. With all this before them, the leaders of exhausted nations sat down to make a lasting peace.

The gigantic effort victory required had been fueled by a vision, welded in the warring, of a better world in which governments would use their increased powers to insure greater justice and fuller democracy. With Wilson as its Presbyterian voice, democracy—meaning popular participation in public life and opportunity for all—seemed a guarantee of peace. Not only would states be forever prevented from making war for selfish reasons and autocratic governments doomed, but there would be an end, Wilson suggested, to the old secret diplomacy that juggled spheres of influence and national interests without regard for public opinion. To many, such vague promises seemed radical enough, but they paled beside the revolution rolling from the East.

III. THE RUSSIAN REVOLUTION

Nothing in their experience had prepared Western statesmen for the rapid triumph of communism in Europe's largest nation. The Russian state, inadequate to the challenge of total war, was just strong enough to survive on the brink of total collapse for eight months after the February Revolution that ended the monarchy—a political change at the top of a society whose institutions were crumbling. Only the Bolsheviks found an effective means of replacing them. Winning power in the very different October Revolution, they expected to be helped by the spread of revolution along their borders and to the West. Instead they found themselves facing civil war.

THE FEBRUARY REVOLUTION

With the outbreak of war in 1914, many Russians realized that to meet this challenge government would have to be more efficient and in closer touch with Russian society. The Duma, called into brief sessions in 1915, established a committee to help coordinate the war effort, and local zemstvos made valuable contributions. But when the Cadet party demanded liberal reforms sought since 1905, the Duma's session was suspended. Resentful that the war could be used for political ends—they still did not see the connection—the tsar and his officials became more isolated from the country. Nicholas II, no more skilled a military strategist than a head of state, grandly departed to command his army, leaving Tsarina Alexandra to oppose any program for reform. Her chief confidant was Grigori Rasputin, an ignorant and corrupt mystic, whose influence symbolized the decadence of the regime.

Throughout 1916 signs of failure accumulated. Production and transportation were undependable, refugees filled the roads, inflation soared, and food shortages became critical. The resulting discontent reached into the highest circles. In November in the reconvened Duma Pavel Milyukov, the Cadets' leader, courageously delivered a bitter attack on the government; one group of nobles murdered Rasputin in December, and others talked of the need to depose the tsar. Little seemed to change. Strikes spread; and, except for the Cossacks, the soldiers called out to quell them were increasingly inclined to join the workers.

In March 1917, when strikers again filled the streets of Petrograd (St. Petersburg's new name),[2] their economic demands quickly broadened to political issues, and troops could not be relied on to oppose them. Instead, much as in 1905, the Soviet of Workers' and Soldiers' Deputies became the voice of revolution. This council of working-class leaders joined a Duma

---

[2] "St. Petersburg" was a German name, and in 1914 Nicholas had changed it to the Russian "Petrograd." The capital until 1918, the city would become Leningrad in 1924.

committee (the Duma itself was not then in session) in favoring a provisional government, and soviets organized the effective defense of Petrograd against tsarist forces that might be sent to put down the insurgents. Helpless, Nicholas II abdicated. The February Revolution, as it was dated by the Russian calendar,[3] seemed an almost easy transition in the chaos of war; and the news from Petrograd was hailed with joy and relief throughout the country.

The prime minister of the provisional government was the bland and moderate Prince

The main street of Petrograd, May 1917, as the revolutionists open fire. (Photo: Wide World Photos)

Georgi Lvov, but its central figure was Milyukov. The only socialist included was Aleksandr Kerensky, a member of the Social Revolutionary party, who led the labor representatives in the Duma and was vice chairman of the Petrograd soviet, the most important center of political power in the capital.

On many matters the new government's

---

[3] The Julian calendar, which the West had abandoned in favor of the Gregorian calendar, was still used in Russia (and today continues to be the calendar of the Orthodox Church). The revolutions that in the Gregorian system occurred on March 8–12 and November 7, 1917, each fell thirteen days earlier according to the Julian, and they continue to be called the February and October revolutions.

policy was concrete and clear: it quickly established broad civil liberties, an amnesty for political prisoners, and the end of religious persecution; it favored a constitution for Finland and independence for Russian Poland, an eight-hour day for workers, and the abolition of class privileges. Beyond these points, however, the political terrain was less known, and the provisional government left most social issues for a constituent assembly, which it promised to call soon.

The revolutionary political parties were divided. The Cadets, who dominated the provisional government, came to accept the idea of a republic, political democracy, and distribution of land with compensation to former owners. To their left the Social Revolutionaries and the Social Democratic Mensheviks, especially strong in the soviets forming across the nation, demanded more. Some of these socialists wanted **drastic** reforms but were willing to postpone them until after the war, which, like the Cadets, they still meant to win. The more radical stressed an early end to the war, though they did not yet advocate an immediate, armistice, and were contemptuous of merely political changes. The soviets were willing for the time being to allow the provisional government its chance, but they refused to be implicated in it, watching instead from the outside, ever ready to criticize. To the left of all these groups stood a small number of Bolsheviks.

THE BOLSHEVIKS

Russian Marxists had secretly formed the Social Democratic party in 1898, but its life centered mainly in the conspiratorial world of exile. At the party's second congress, held in Brussels and London in 1903, it had split into two groups, the Bolsheviks ("majority") and Mensheviks ("minority"). The points of debate between them were theoretical, organizational, and personal. Like socialists everywhere, they were divided over revisionism—the view that Marx's doctrines needed modification to fit new circumstances and to allow for the possibility of achieving socialist goals without violent revolution. The majority followed the two figures whose writings had already won them international reputations, Georgi Plekhanov and Nikolai Lenin, in cleaving to an intransigent Marxist position.

The speeches and pamphlets of these debates from the outset combined theory and economics with harsh and intolerant name-calling, but the issues had and would continue to have practical implications. Given their position and the social development of Russia, Lenin and Plekhanov had agreed that theirs should be a disciplined elite rather than a mass party, its task to instruct and lead rather than merely represent the proletariat, which by itself was always likely to settle for immediate gains far short of real social transformation. But Lenin's concept of iron discipline had left no room for Plekhanov's independent efforts to heal the breach between the two camps, and he too had been quickly consigned to the Mensheviks.

Neither group had played a central part in the Revolution of 1905, and the socialism that had spread in Russia thereafter had been mainly that of the Mensheviks and the Social Revolutionaries, who were less consistently Marxist and closer to the peasants. The Social Democrats elected to the Duma had been mostly Mensheviks. Despite the bitter loneliness and doubts of exile, Lenin had continued from Switzerland to organize his selected followers, to denounce the heresies around him, and to develop a Marxist interpretation of contemporary affairs and of the Russian situation. As he had extended Marxism to explain that imperialism was a symptom of capitalist decay, so he had increasingly expanded on the role a militant party should play in a country like Russia that was just achieving modern capitalism. To do so required recognition of the revolutionary potential in the peasants' hunger for land—a topic most Marxists had found uncongenial.

Lenin's total rejection of World War I had suggested to the Germans that his agitation might be useful behind Russian lines, and in April 1917 they arranged for him to be sent by sealed train through Germany and Scandinavia to Russia. At this time the Bolsheviks were the smallest of the socialist groups, their differences from the left wing of the Mensheviks no longer very clear. Since all the socialists welcomed the revolution but considered it bourgeois, they were uncertain of their roles.

Lenin resolved this question too with the broader view that the Russian Revolution was part of a larger revolution about to sweep all of Europe. Free of local patriotism, he asserted that socialists had no interest in a capitalist war; and he argued that with the correct tactics, they could push the revolution beyond its bourgeois phase to a "second stage." This he soon declared to be the surrender of power to the soviets as the true representatives of the revolutionary class. The Bolsheviks thus had to capture the soviets. Historians have emphasized Lenin's tactical flexibility, but in April his views seemed impossibly dogmatic even to radicals. It was the force of his personality and of his oratory that kept him leader of the Bolsheviks.

THE SUMMER CRISIS

Issues of war policy and land reform and the many disagreements among those who had overthrown the tsarist regime were not the only problems the provisional government faced in 1917. Strikes continued as workers sought some immediate benefit from revolu-

tion; nationalist movements in Latvia, Georgia, and the Ukraine threatened a disintegration of the Russian state; and the bureaucracy, like the police, had largely disappeared. The soviets meanwhile were developing a national organization that claimed authority among the troops and over railroads and telegraph lines. In May the Petrograd soviet issued its famous Order Number 1, ending traditional discipline in the army. Officers would be chosen by their men, and the military would be run by elected committees. The measure was adopted in most units, and the government, which merely watched as a good part of the army melted away, lost control over much of the rest.

Pressure for peace forced the provisional government to clarify its war aims. In May it declared that Russia had no intention of dominating other peoples; but even this vague formula was compromised by a secret addition promising that Russia would fulfill her commitments to the Allies. The split grew wider between the Cadets, convinced that honor required the country to continue the war, and the soviets, whose renewed demonstrations caused a change in the government. Milyukov resigned, four more socialists joined the cabinet, and Kerensky, as minister of war, became its leading figure, assuming the prime ministership in August. Although Social Revolutionaries and Mensheviks held a majority of the cabinet posts, the soviets still withheld their full support, demanding clear policies for ending the war and redistributing land. Kerensky, an energetic leader and effective orator, recognized that he had to seek broader backing, which meant support from outside the soviets.

The Bolsheviks too were feeling some frustration. At the first all-Russian Congress of Soviets in June they had succeeded in weakening the remaining support for Kerensky, but with just over 100 of the more than 800 delegates, they had not been able to gain full control. In July they had attempted a coup in Petrograd, but it had been decisively defeated; many Bolshevik leaders had been arrested, and Lenin had fled to Finland. The Bolshevist threat seemed over, and Kerensky tried to escape the dominance of the soviets by calling a great national congress of all other groups. He had little to offer it, however, and nothing that did not increase its grave divisions.

At the front, the July offensive, for which Kerensky had great hopes, failed after brief gains. The military situation, despite months of promising efforts at reorganization, became more desperate. In the countryside manor houses were burned and landlords murdered as the peasants rioted for land, and cities were torn by strikes and demonstrations. The social tensions of fifty years were exploding in an atmosphere of anarchy.

Convinced that a strong military hand was needed, the army's commander in chief General Lavr Kornilov decided in September to lead an attack on Petrograd; and Kerensky asked the soviets to defend the provisional government. The Bolsheviks were released from prison, and the defense of the capital was vigorously prepared. The threat passed quickly—most of Kornilov's men had refused to follow his orders—but the provisional government was more than ever dependent on the soviets. In six months in office, it had resolved few of the issues left pending in March, and Bolshevist propaganda was gaining ground with simple slogans about peace, land, and bread.

The Bolsheviks won control of the Moscow and Petrograd soviets, and Leon Trotsky was elected chairman of the latter. Trotsky had worked with Lenin in exile, but until recently he had stood somewhat aloof from both Bolsheviks and Mensheviks. Now he was firmly in Lenin's camp, and from his position in the soviet, he proceeded to organize the armed forces in Petrograd. When the Social Revolutionaries, fearful of losing their strong peasant following, supported peasant expropriation of land, the provisional government was left politically alone in a city it could not control trying to rule a nation in chaos and still at war.

THE OCTOBER REVOLUTION

To the dismay of many in his party, Lenin boldly decided to seize power. The second all-Russian Congress of Soviets was scheduled to meet on November 7, and Lenin planned to greet it with a new government. A few days before Kerensky began to take countermeasures, but he was too late.

The revolution in November (October according to the Russian calendar) was not the amorphous, general rising of March but rather a carefully planned and executed coup. Red Guards (squads of armed workers), sailors, and soldiers of the Petrograd garrison captured the Winter Palace on November 6 while comrades efficiently seized strategic points and offices throughout the city. A simultaneous movement began in Moscow, and though fighting there lasted more than a week, the outcome was hardly in doubt. On the afternoon of November 7, Lenin announced to the Congress of Soviets that the Bolsheviks held power. A young officer was sent to take command of the armies, and at each stop the noisy acclaim of the troops dissuaded their commanders from resisting. Kerensky, who had escaped the capital, tried to muster armed support, but the one group of a few hundred Cossacks who moved on Petrograd was soundly defeated. Shaky though it was, the world's first communist government had taken office.

"All power to the Soviets!" had been one of the Bolsheviks' most effective slogans, and the Congress of Soviets readily approved the one-party cabinet Lenin presented it. The rudiments of a new form of government emerged:

the Congress of Soviets, which replaced parliament; the Central Executive Committee, elected from the Congress to give advice when the larger body was not in session; and the Council of People's Commissars, the cabinet ministers. Bolshevik rule from the very first was not representative in the traditional sense, and the government did not in fact depend on any elected body. Elections for the promised constituent assembly, held at the end of November, provided the last open competition among parties in Russian history. The Bolsheviks won a quarter of the seats, other socialist parties more than 60 percent, and conservatives and liberals the rest. As the assembly met on its second day, the guards told it to adjourn, explaining that they were tired. A minority party had ruthlessly grasped the power of the state.

That ruthlessness was warranted in the Bolsheviks' thinking because of their historic role. Lenin had provided a basis for Bolshevist policy in his pamphlet "The State and Revolution," written in Finland in the summer of 1917. It kept the Marxist conception of the state as the coercive organ of the ruling class but argued that with the Bolsheviks in power, the proletariat would become the ruling class. Since backward Russia was barely ready for so advanced a revolution, only a dictatorship of the proletariat could provide the needed strength. By this reasoning Lenin accomplished three things: he justified the establishment of an authoritarian government free from the restraints of parliamentarianism; he gave theoretical sanction to dictatorship as a transition stage during which Russia's transformation would be directed by the Bolsheviks; and he preserved the Marxian vision of communism as a higher historical stage in which the state would no longer be necessary. During the dictatorship socialism would be achieved through the nationalization of land and factories. Communism would come once everyone had learned to work for the good of society and economic production could meet the needs of all.

In the interim the single party, the "vanguard of the proletariat," would have a special role. Model, teacher, and guide, it would prevent backsliding with its tight discipline; through it the masses would be heard. Lenin imagined that public criticism in party sessions would maintain efficiency and probity, combining the benefits of mass participation and dictatorship. Equality and justice remained explicit goals but sufficiently abstract to leave government unimpeded. Enthusiasm for a great cause would enable men to accept the hardships and sacrifices of the present for a glorious future.

The incongruous fusion of Marxist ideas and peasant demands that brought communism to power in the least industrial of the great nations surprised most Marxists. And ruling in such a country required an extension of socialist theory to deal with issues not foreseen in the writings of the previous fifty years. Thus Lenin, the principal architect of the first socialist state, ranks with Marx himself as a theoretician of modern communism.

THE FIRST COMMUNIST GOVERNMENT

The efficiency with which the Bolsheviks seized and wielded power went beyond theory. It rested rather on the fanatical self-confidence of able leaders hardened by years of revolutionary activity and determined now to snatch their historical moment, on the great skill and personal qualities of hundreds of officials, and above all perhaps on the decisive energy of Lenin and Trotsky.

The day after taking the Winter Palace, the new government decreed that land, livestock, and all farm equipment belonged to the state to be held "temporarily" by peasant committees—

this legitimized the rural revolution. No peasant was to work for hire, and committees of the poor would supervise the allocation of land and the distribution of agricultural produce.

In the next few months, railroads, banks, and shipping concerns were nationalized; foreign trade became a state monopoly (though there was precious little of it); and Russia's bonded debts were repudiated. Workers' committees were to share in the management of factories, and everyone was to be paid according to his work—the leading Bolsheviks assigned themselves laborers' salaries. All social titles and military ranks were abolished. "People's tribunals" replaced tsarist courts and workers' militias the police. Church and state were separated, and equality of the sexes was decreed, symbolized by the regulation that couples could obtain a divorce by mutual consent. The various nationalities of Russia were not only declared equal but granted the right of secession, and Finland severed herself from Russia in December 1917, though the Bolsheviks struggled to prevent the Ukraine and the Baltic regions from following suit. Even the alphabet was reformed and the Gregorian calendar adopted.

These revolutionary measures ratified the dissolution of traditional society. They made way too for a regime of terror. A new secret police, the Cheka, differed from the old in determination more than method. The citizens who sat on committees of the poor or the army or on the new tribunal often combined a useful revolutionary enthusiasm with personal ambition and vengeance against old enemies. Tens of thousands lost their property, their rights, and their lives for failing to perceive in a time of revolution the dangers of "mistaken" alliances, "false" ideas, or "suspicious" gestures.

Such radical policies won the Bolsheviks increased support and weakened potential opposition, but they also heightened the difficulties of operating any government at all. The old bureaucrats were gone, their replacements often ignorant and incompetent. Officials were dismissed and promoted with disrupting frequency as political suspects disappeared and talented men were transferred to meet some new crisis.

External dangers were even more pressing. Almost immediately on taking power, the Bolsheviks had asked all nations to accept peace without annexations. When rebuffed, they shocked the world by publishing secret Allied agreements. Forced to negotiate alone with the Central Powers, Russia, whose delegation was headed by Trotsky, proposed in February 1918 a policy of no peace, no war—Russia would stop fighting without a treaty. The Germans advanced to within 100 miles of Petrograd.

Desperate, the Russian government agreed to the Treaty of Brest Litovsk in March. Russia surrendered more than 1 million square miles of territory, including a third of her arable land, a third of her factories, and three-quarters of her deposits of iron and coal. She granted the independence of Finland, Georgia, and the Ukraine; left to Germany the disposition of Russian Poland, Lithuania, Latvia, and Estonia; and ceded parts of Transcaucasia to the Ottoman Empire.

The Bolsheviks had met the demand for peace, but they had done so at incredible cost. Although buoyed by confidence that revolution in Germany would nullify the Kaiser's gains, they could not be sure they would survive so serious an amputation.

Quickly the government set about legitimizing its position. In July a new constitution was promulgated. It met the problem of nationalities by declaring Russia a federation—the Russian Soviet Federated Socialist Republic (R.S.F.S.R.); Great Russia, extending through Siberia, was of course the largest member.

Political power rested with the local soviets, organized by occupation, which elected delegates to the congress of soviets of their canton, the smallest administrative unit. Each canton's congress in turn sent delegates to a congress of soviets at the next administrative level, and the process continued by steps up to the all-Russia Congress. Suffrage in the local soviet was universal for men and women but excluded members of the clergy, former high officials, and bourgeois "nontoilers." Since the public elected higher congresses only indirectly, the possibilities for control were great.

Not mentioned in the constitution was the Russian Communist party, as it was now named, which soon became the real center of political authority. Its Central Committee elected the smaller Politburo, which with the governing Council of People's Commissars shared ruling power in Soviet Russia. In Politburo and council Lenin was the dominant figure.

The Bolsheviks, however, remained surrounded by enemies. To the Allies the Treaty of Brest Litovsk appeared an act of treachery, as did Russia's repudiation of her debts. In March Allied troops in small numbers had landed in Murmansk, Archangel, and Vladivostok to prevent supplies sent to Russia earlier from being taken by the Germans, but it was clear that those detachments might also be used to support a change of regime.

In addition the government had reluctantly permitted a Czech brigade of some 30,000 men to travel the Trans-Siberian Railroad from the Eastern front to Vladivostok so they might then sail around the world to continue fighting on the Western front. As the Czechs made the long train journey, they clashed with some Hungarian prisoners of war. The fighting spread, and the Czechs, aided by Russian anti-Bolsheviks, captured one station after another along the railway.

Struck by the ease of the Czech successes, Allied leaders decided not to let their opportunity pass and ordered the Czechs to move back along the railway toward the center of Russia. At the same time a number of tsarist generals, among them Kornilov and others who had escaped from prison, were preparing to lead a small but excellent army of Cossacks. It was the beginning of a civil war that would last for two terrible years.

While Trotsky undertook to organize a Red army, opponents of the new regime formed fighting units in the Ukraine, the Caucasus territory, the Baltic region, and Siberia, aided by reinforcements and supplies from the Allies. But the civil war was not just a battle of armies, for anti-Bolsheviks of every stripe—even the Social Revolutionaries, who had now gone underground—organized in hundreds of villages and towns. Food riots, battles over land, and skirmishes between workers and bourgeois added to the violence. The first communist government in modern history was facing its gravest threat.

IV. THE PEACE

Russia's was not the only revolution in the aftermath of World War I; in the defeated states only Bulgaria's government survived. By default as well as victory, the Allies seemed free to set the terms they liked and to construct the Europe of peaceful democracies implied in so many wartime statements. Instead the diplomats assembled at the Paris Peace Conference found their task complicated by the very extent of victory and beset by more interests than they could satisfy. So grand an undertaking fed the extremes of hope and disillusionment, while far from Paris more direct means were being used to shape the postwar world.

THE REVOLUTIONARY SITUATION

From Ireland to Asia Minor, nationalist movements sought to capture power, and the peoples suddenly released from Hapsburg and Russian rule fought to define the boundaries of their new nations. In the Baltic lands, Lithuanian, Estonian, and Latvian republics marked their independence by war with Russia, but Lithuania was also at odds with the new republic of Poland. Poland in fact faced conflict on all her other borders as well—against Russians, Ukrainians, Czechs, Germans. The creation of Czechoslovakia and the new Kingdom of Yugoslavia led to renewed warfare as Czechoslovakia was attacked by Hungary, and in the Balkans the kind of hostility that had preceded World War I broke out again when Rumania attacked both Hungary and Yugoslavia.

Soviet Communists had good reason then to hope revolution would sweep from East to West, and Marxists throughout Europe looked in turn to the miraculous events in Russia as the beginning of the socialist future they had so long imagined. In March 1919 delegates from a score of countries met in Moscow to establish the Third International. Communists were active in the Baltic States, and Lenin's friend Béla Kun was to hold power as head of a Hungarian soviet in 1919 until Rumanian armies ended his brief reign. There was communist agitation in Vienna, where the provisional government of truncated Austria looked forward to union with the new German republic.

But Germany herself was the major communist goal. Marxists had long paid special attention to that highly industrialized nation with her class tensions and strong socialist movement. Defeat and a new government seemed the fulfillment of old portents. In January 1919 a communist revolt broke out in Berlin, and in the following spring another managed for a few weeks to make Bavaria a Soviet re-public. Both uprisings were quickly defeated by remnants of the German army. So Russia remained the center of the Communist world, but the chance remained that other revolutions would succeed.

THE CONFERENCE

Peace had come so suddenly that there had been little time for discussion of specific terms. But through the pressure of public opinion, the German understanding of the armistice, and American influence, President Wilson's Fourteen Points had won acceptance as a basis for defining a new European order.

In many respects similar to the programs of other statesmen, Wilson's plan dealt mainly with territorial adjustments, but it raised such changes to the level of principle, associating them with the self-determination of peoples and a democratic peace. The remaining points cautiously yet courageously set forth a vision shared by the moderate left everywhere in the West. The removal of trade barriers and free navigation of the seas had long been part of the liberal canon. International attention to the welfare of colonial populations, the reduction of armaments, and open diplomacy were more radical suggestions; but by 1918 the belief was common that had steps been taken on these issues earlier, the world's most terrible war might have been averted. Wilson's final point, and the one closest to his heart, called for a League of Nations to guarantee the safety of all. In subsequent statements the American president had enlarged on the need for "impartial justice," "peace that will be permanent," and covenants that are "sacredly observed." His language and ideals caught the imagination of the world.

At the Paris Peace Conference, it was readily agreed that the mistakes of the Congress of Vienna must not be repeated. No defeated na-

tions would take part in the early discussions—no German Talleyrand would divide the Allies. The atmosphere was one of sober business; the elegant aristocrats of 1815 had given way to commissions of expert advisers for every important issue, who were to provide the major negotiators with the detailed information they needed.

Thirty nations had joined the Allies at least formally,[4] but it was soon established that the

When Woodrow Wilson paraded through the streets, Parisians cheered the representative of a new democratic era as well as an ally in victory. (Photo: The Granger Collection)

momentous decisions would be taken by the five big powers—France, the United Kingdom, Italy, Japan, and the United States. In practice, since most questions did not directly concern Japan, primary authority resided in four

---

[4] Yugoslavia, Czechoslovakia, and Poland were treated as Allies; the new republics of Austria, Hungary, and Germany as the defeated Central Powers.

Orlando, Lloyd George, Clemenceau, and Wilson look the very epitome of their respective nations as they face the camera rather than each other in this photo, which contrasts interestingly with the picture of the Congress of Vienna in Chapter 22. (Photo: The Granger Collection)

men: Clemenceau, Lloyd George, Premier Vittorio Orlando, and Wilson.

Soon after the congress opened, in January 1919, disagreements among the principal representatives of the Big Four powers became the center around which the negotiations turned.

All were elected leaders, skilled in appealing to public opinion and sensitive to its demands. All were faced with grave domestic problems and worried by the turmoil in Central and Eastern Europe. They had to hurry.

The Treaty with Germany

To settle by May the complicated terms for peace with Germany was a remarkable achievement. Haste itself probably made the treaty more severe than it might otherwise have been. Commissions, assuming their proposals would be subject to later bargaining, tended to begin with maximum terms, but these were often simply written into the treaty itself.

The territorial provisions were not extremely harsh; Germany lost Continental lands as well as colonies, but she was preserved as a great state. The European divisions, however, were the sort to give continuing difficulty (see Map 26.5). France got Alsace-Lorraine but not the left bank of the Rhine or the establishment of an autonomous Rhineland state, which she also wanted. Instead the Allies were to occupy the Rhineland for fifteen years and the French to direct the coal-producing regions along the Saar River, but the latter were to remain under German sovereignty unless a later plebiscite determined differently. Plebiscites would also decide whether Germany surrender part of Schleswig to Denmark or of upper Silesia to Poland.

The Polish provinces of eastern Prussia, where Germans formed about 40 percent of the population, were immediately ceded to Poland. Far more controversial, however, was the creation of a Polish corridor to the sea. Within the corridor a majority of the population was Polish, but its outlet was the port of Danzig, a German city, which was restored to its ancient status as a free city. Worse, the corridor awkwardly separated eastern Prussia from the rest of Germany, and Poland would always feel insecure with an arrangement Germans never accepted.

Naturally enough the Germans were required to disarm, and though the terms were stiff, this would not have seemed unreasonable if it had proved to be a first step toward general disarmament, as the treaty implied. Germany was to have no large artillery, submarines, or military air force, and her army was to be limited to 100,000 men on long-term enlistment. The lists of matériel to be delivered to the Allies were more punitive: horses and railway carriages, quantities of coal, most of her present ships, and some new vessels to be specially built.

Most burdensome of all were the provisions for reparations. Despite fine talk of not requiring an indemnity, the Allies declared that Germany should pay for civilian damages. The claims of Belgium, a neutral attacked without warning, were easily justified; and Clemenceau could argue that the most destructive fighting had occurred in Belgium and France. But Lloyd George had campaigned on a platform of making Germany pay, and he insisted, over American objections, on including Allied military pensions as civilian costs. Pandora's box was opened. Germany was made liable for sums unspecified and without foreseeable end and forced to swear to accept "responsibility" for losses from a war "imposed . . . by the aggression of Germany and her allies." It was true that she had attacked first, and in the liberal view her militarism had been the great disruptive force in European politics for a generation. But it was false, as historians soon established, that she had deliberately planned and instigated World War I, a widespread conviction that these vague phrases echoed. The "war guilt clause" thus became a subject of controversy in every country and of bitter resentment, official and private, in every part of Germany.

Finally, in German eyes the terms of the treaty made it intolerable as a *Diktat*, a dictated settlement the country's delegates were not given a chance to argue until it was already drafted; then only minor objections were met. Although in fact the Allies had made no clear commitment regarding terms, the German military had left the civilian government to make an armistice on the basis, they said, of Wilson's Fourteen Points. The German government resigned, and parliament at first rejected the stipulation of war guilt; but when the Allies held firm, parliament angrily accepted the *Diktat.* The treaty was signed on June 28, 1919, the fifth anniversary of the assassination at Sarajevo, in the Hall of Mirrors at Versailles, where Bismarck and William I had announced the German Empire forty-eight years before—the symbolism was complete.

Treaties with the Central and Eastern States

For the Big Four the most difficult question after the treatment of Germany was the Italian boundary. All agreed that Italy, for strategic reasons, should be given the Tyrol south of the Alpine Brenner Pass, a German-speaking area formerly held by Austria; but Wilson was determined to prevent those further violations of the principle of nationality incorporated in the Treaty of London of 1915 (which promised Italy a great deal more, including much of the Slavic-speaking lands of the Dalmatian coast). By stubbornly demanding more than they expected to get, the Italians stimulated unkind references to their record in the war. Then too Wilson made a serious tactical error: in a Paris interview he in effect asked the Italian people to reject the position of their negotiators, and the Italian delegation withdrew in protest from the conference to a great outpouring of nationalist feeling at home. Eventually a compromise was reached, but from that time on Italy was another of the dissatisfied states resentfully seeking a revision of the treaties.

With the signature of the Treaty of Versailles, the Big Four dispersed to attend to their pressing domestic concerns, leaving the details of the remaining settlements (commonly named after the place where they were signed) to their foreign officers. The treaty with Austria signed at St.-Germain-en-Laye in September was closely modeled on the treaty with Germany. Provisions for reparations and demilitarization, including naval restrictions, hardly seemed appropriate for the shaky little landlocked Austrian republic. In addition to the southern Tyrol Italy was given the Istrian Peninsula and some islands but not Dalmatia, and boundaries with the other new states were settled on the basis of nationality in some cases and strategic needs in others. Treaties with Bulgaria (signed at Neuilly in November) and with Hungary (signed at the Trianon in June 1920) followed. Bohemia was given to Czechoslovakia on historical grounds, but Hungarian claims to a historical kingdom were largely ignored. Like Austria, Hungary lost almost three-quarters of the lands she had ruled in 1914. Although Bulgaria had surrendered relatively little territory, her resentment over her borders equaled that of the other defeated Central Powers.

Every state of Eastern Europe could claim injustice, usually with exaggerated statistics and with tales, too often true, of inhumane treatment. Railway lines and economic relationships, "natural" boundaries for defense, historical claims, and nationality simply did not coincide. At each point one consideration had to be sacrificed to another; and since the final dispositions were frequently influenced by favoritism, external political factors, or sheer ignorance, the inconsistencies were blatant. A major role in making these arrangements work would fall to the new League of Nations.

A number of oral agreements and the very creation of the Reparations Commission provided for by the Treaty of Versailles implied that the treaties might be modified, as logic and equity argued they should; the reparations required from Austria, for example, were divided among the defunct empire's former lands in a gesture of fairness that left some new states paying reparations to others. Many territories were to be assigned only after a plebiscite, and many others were ceded to the Allies to be dealt with later. Provisions promising minorities just treatment, an expression of the Allies' decent intent, struck sensitive states as an insulting infringement on their sovereignty. The issues for future conflict were without limit.

The final treaty was one with Turkey, not signed until August 1920 at Sèvres; much of it never went into effect. The Allies, who had encouraged Arab nationalism, were embarrassed when the Soviet regime released their secret plans for partitioning the Ottoman Empire. Now they faced indigenous movements as complex and uncontrollable as those in Eastern Europe. A Turkish revival under Mustafa Kemal assured the territorial integrity of Turkey itself despite the principle of autonomous states adopted at Sèvres. In addition Syria was to be under French influence, while a vaguely defined area—carved into Palestine, Trans-Jordan, and Iraq—was to be subject to British authority.

Aside from recognizing the presence of Britain and France, the quickly buried Treaty of Sèvres settled little, and more durable boundaries came only after the conflicts and the diplomacy of the next few years. There was confusion in particular about what the British intended by separating Palestine from Trans-Jordan. In 1917 the British foreign secretary, Arthur Balfour, had promised that a "national home" for Jews would be created in Palestine; but the Balfour Declaration, exemplifying the nationalistic propaganda and humanitarian concern of that difficult year, had also guaranteed the rights of the Arabs there. Subsequent British statements had been neither clear nor consistent. The independence of Arabia was recognized in the Sèvres agreement, but competition among native rulers left its status uncertain and the boundaries of the new state undefined. For Egypt the peace terms ratified her separation from Ottoman sovereignty and confirmed British authority—that too contested by local movements.

The Allied enthusiasm for dividing up the Ottoman Empire both abated and seemed more suspect now that neither the Russian nor the Austro-Hungarian Empire remained on the scene to demand a share. But the recognition of French and British interests in the region led to an important innovation. Colonial territories were declared "mandates" of the League of Nations and assigned to classes. The parts of the Ottoman Empire newly placed under British or French rule—Palestine, Trans-Jordan, Iraq, and Syria—were Class A mandates, states considered on the verge of self-government. Most of the reassigned African territories were Class B mandates, ones in which European rulers were to guarantee freedom of religion, prohibit trade in liquor and arms, refrain from subjecting natives to military training, and encourage commerce. Class C mandates were primarily Pacific islands, to be ruled essentially as colonies. In every case the mandate power had to submit annual reports to the League of Nations for review. Like much else in the treaties, the system of mandates can be seen as an expression of conscience and growing responsibility toward the rest of the world or as an effort to legitimize continued European dominance and wrap hypocrisy in legalism. In operation the system justified both interpretations.

Built-in Weaknesses

By 1920 it was clear that the war to make the world safe for democracy, as the Allied leaders had labeled it, had not quite accomplished that. Yet the terms of peace did concertedly promote democracy in their call for self-determination and plebiscites, provisions for the League of Nations (carefully written into each treaty at Wilson's shrewd insistence), and the development of the system of mandates. Allied victory had spurred the establishment of representative regimes throughout Central Europe, an almost requisite ticket of admission to Allied favor. Like the diplomats at Vienna a century before, the statesmen at Paris saw an integral relationship between the form of domestic government and international peace. The treaties showed the influence of democracy less happily in response to Allied public opinion that expected a peace punitive enough to justify the war.

Not since 1848 had liberal spokesmen so thoroughly dominated European politics, but the revolutions of World War I quickly went beyond nineteenth-century liberalism. The men at Paris found it hard to cope with revolution. They never managed a place for Russia at the conference nor even agreed on a consistent response to communist governments. Believers in democracy, they were baffled and frightened by the turmoil unleashed by wars for democracy. Although they supported self-determination and therefore nationalism, they were more aware than their forefathers that nationalism is not necessarily democratic. They took little account, however, of the social complexities of Eastern Europe, where land division was more explosive an issue than political forms and nationality itself no more important than the antagonism between peasant and lord. Living in a revolution they helped make and largely welcomed, the statesmen who forged the peace were not revolutionaries. If they encouraged revolutionary changes, they wanted to limit their part to legal formulas; and slogans that sounded radical in November 1918 gave way to frightened insistence on order a few months later.

Much that was accomplished at Paris reflected a cold assertion of national interest and a realistic appraisal of power. Inevitably the treaties were compromises. But it was the Allies who had asserted that their handiwork should be measured by the standards of high principle and who had injected ideology into matters of power politics. Woodrow Wilson was the most dedicated and by his lights the most consistent spokesman of this new moral and democratic politics.[5] And critics blame him for many of the weaknesses of the treaties, charging that he was intransigent or yielding in the wrong places and that he sacrificed too much to gain his dream of the League of Nations in the belief that liberal procedures would produce liberal policies.

But Wilson is more responsible for arousing hopes than betraying them. If his doctrinaire approach often meshed unfortunately with Clemenceau's skepticism and Lloyd George's easy flexibility, there were far more fundamental difficulties. Perhaps the greatest was that none of the leaders yet fully understood how much had changed. Although they created a tiny and weak Austrian republic, they could not forget the wealth and power of the Austrian Empire and therefore forbade the union of Austria, now thoroughly German, with Germany. They did not see that the deep economic, social, and psychological dislocation following the war would continue to threaten democracy and peace no matter how many representative governments were established.

CONTEMPORARY CRITICISM

Some signs of weakness in the treaty settlements appeared very early among the drafters themselves. In March 1920 the Senate of the United States rejected the documents for the final time. The most powerful nation in the world, having claimed moral leadership, would not join the League of Nations. The United States thus joined Italy in rejecting the terms of peace, and in the process she added France to the list of aggrieved states. The French had abandoned demands that Germany be further weakened in return for a joint guarantee from the United States and Great Britain against German aggression. When the United States refused to honor that agreement, France felt betrayed. Moreover France had also wanted the league to have a peacekeeping force of its own, but her allies had opposed this. Out of her dissatisfaction and alarm, she would seek to make the League of Nations not a flexible

---

[5] Yet he returned to the Paris Peace Conference after a trip home insisting that the Monroe Doctrine be written into the Covenant of the League of Nations.

instrument for modifying the war settlements but rather an agency for rigidly maintaining the status quo.

China refused to sign the treaties because of terms that gave Japan, in addition to other gains, almost a protectorate over her. Japan was offended by the conference's refusal formally to declare all races equal. For Asian, Arab, and African peoples, it was hard to believe that European diplomacy was much more principled than in the past.

The reparations clauses were soon blamed for the economic difficulties of numerous countries—those forced to pay them and those granted much less than anticipated. But the very concept had many opponents. In a brilliant and influential pamphlet, the English economist John Maynard Keynes castigated the Carthaginian peace the victors had exacted, attacking reparations in particular.[6] He argued that the Allies owed each other more money than Germany could pay and that reparations would merely slow the recovery of Europe's economy. His analysis helped undermine confidence in the terms of peace, but his prescriptions—cancellation of international war debts and recognition that the international economic system was essentially artificial—were heresies as utopian in their way as any of Woodrow Wilson's points.

Keynes was right that policies toward Russia, Germany, and the successor states were contradictory; but his criticisms, like those that for decades would ring from party platforms in every country, tended to exaggerate how much of the postwar world could be shaped by worried statesmen quarreling in Paris.

[6] John Maynard Keynes, *The Economic Consequences of the Peace* (1920); and the famous rebuttal, Etienne Mantoux, *The Carthaginian Peace: or the Economic Consequences of Mr. Keynes* (1946).

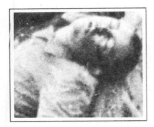

Although the European nations did not fight each other between 1871 and 1914, peace was precarious as imperialism abroad and tension at home encouraged militant posturing and an accelerating arms race. As foreign policy, economic competition, and domestic politics became more closely interrelated, any social or political conflict was likely to have international repercussions. One spark in the changing Balkans was sufficient to trigger the elaborate mechanisms of world war.

The war at first seemed to heal divisions in every nation, but the industrialization and democratization of the previous forty years had altered the nature of war. It required more in wealth, organization, manpower, and morale than any society could afford and more than the Austrian and Russian empires could provide. Defeat unleashed the divisions war had briefly masked between ideologies, classes, and neighboring nationalities; and social strain exploded into open, violent revolution in Central and Eastern Europe. Revolution in Russia, which began as an opening to democracy the West could welcome, quickly went beyond familiar concepts to bring the Bolsheviks to power. By war's end death and destruction, the changed relations of social groups, and weakened economies made even the victors appear more like the survivors of a revolution.

It fell primarily to Great Britain, France, and the United States to define international order and set the terms of peace for a torn and ravaged continent in which insecure new nations faced each other suspiciously and communism was now a reality. Led by the nonsocialist left, the great democracies approached the task bearing hopes resonant with the best in nineteenth-century optimism. Before the task was finished, disillusionment, confusion, and exhaustion measured how little freedom statesmen had to mold a new world. Like all great revolutions, World War I created a gulf between past and present that marks the beginning of a new era.

RECOMMENDED READING

Studies

Albertini, Luigi. *The Origins of the War of 1914.* 3 vols. 1952–1957. The most recent of the large-scale studies of the causes of the war.

*Bailey, Thomas A. *Woodrow Wilson and the Lost Peace.* 1963. Standard account, sympathetic to Wilson.

Carsten, F. L. *Revolution in Central Europe, 1918–1919.* 1972. An important treatment of these significant outbreaks following the war.

*Falls, Cyril B. *The Great War.* 1961. Skillful account by a noted military historian.

Fay, Sidney B. *The Origins of World War.* 2 vols. 1938. The still readable classic assessment from the interwar years.

Feldman, Gerald D. *Army, Industry and Labor in Germany, 1914–1918.* 1966. A fundamental analysis of the war's effects on institutions and power in Germany.

Ferro, Marc. *The Great War.* 1973. This stimulating, outspoken essay emphasizes economic and social factors.

*Fischer, Fritz. *Germany's Aims in the First World War.* 1967. The reassessment that became the center of controversy among German historians.

Haimson, Leopold. *The Russian Marxists and the Origins of Bolshevism.* 1955. Places the Bolsheviks in the context of Russian radicalism.

King, Jere C. *Generals and Politicians: Conflicts Between France's High Command, Parliament, and Government, 1914–1918.* 1951. Dissects the significance of the conflicts behind the lines that brought a reassertion of civilian dominance.

*Lafore, L. *The Long Fuse: An Interpretation of the Origins of World War I.* 1965. A useful, recent reinterpretation of this troublesome question.

Marwick, Arthur. *War and Social Change in the Twentieth Century: A Comparative Study of Britain, France, Germany, Russia and the United States.* 1975. Develops the case for the revolutionary effects of World Wars I and II on domestic society.

Mayer, Arno J. *Politics and Diplomacy of Peacemaking: Containment and Counterrevolution at Versailles, 1918–1919.* 1967. Argues that fear of Bolshevism shaped the peace.

*Nicolson, Harold G. *Peacemaking, 1919.* The analysis of a disappointed participant.

*Pipes, Richard. *The Formation of the Soviet Union.* 1964. A clear and comprehensive treatment.

*Tuchman, Barbara. *The Guns of August.* 1962. The strikingly written story of the war's outbreak.

*Ulam, Adam B. *Lenin and the Bolsheviks.* 1969. Combines the study of ideas and policy to explain Lenin's triumph.

Williams, John. *The Home Fronts: Britain, France, and Germany, 1914–1918.* 1972. Pulls together a variety of evidence of the war's domestic impact.

Williamson, Samuel R. *The Politics of Grand Strategy: Britain and France Prepare for War, 1904–1914.* 1969. The political background of the course that led to war.

---

* Available in paperback.

TWENTY SEVEN

DEMOCRACY
AND DEPRESSION

As war had disrupted society, so peace brought the possibility of further and more desirable change, an opportunity acknowledged in revolutions and civil wars in the lands that had known defeat and by expectations of fuller democracy and prosperity among the victors. States were more solidly identified with nationality and their citizens given more voice in government than ever before in Europe's history. Where industrialization had been slight, social and political changes encouraged its development. The institutions of parliamentarianism had spread almost everywhere, and on the whole they seemed to work. But revolution more radical than that was defeated except in Russia.

International affairs centered at first on the economic problems left by the war and on the machinery of the League of Nations. Despite complexity, distrust, and disappointments, moderation prevailed in these matters too. In institutional terms the principles represented by Woodrow Wilson came as close to realization as such peaceful dreams ever had. Great Britain and France dominated the postwar world not merely through their international power but through the influence of their political style as well.

If political organization embodied qualities associated with the middle class, European culture reflected—and stimulated—a growing malaise. New learning questioned old values and theories while the arts rejected convention. Beneath the economic recovery of Western society, forces were at work undermining the stability of intricate financial structures. As suddenly as the balance of international relations had disintegrated in 1914, the automatic regulators supposedly built into the economic system failed after the crash of 1929.

The financial crisis added immeasurably to more localized ailments of the European states. The postwar spread of democracy had not preserved political freedom in Italy or stability in much of Eastern Europe or brought about disarmament, and representative governments had left critical issues, both international and domestic, unresolved. Now they had failed to maintain prosperity. Efforts at international negotiation for economic cooperation as well as for disarmament broke down. The Great Depression, a disaster in the lives of millions, was also a disaster for the political and economic institutions of Western liberalism.

1. POSTWAR POLITICS

Nothing was clearer at the end of the war than that European political life would henceforth be different from what it had been before, for people everywhere seemed as determined as the victors themselves to effect a change. At issue was how great these changes should be and what forms they might take as the left gained strength in various nations even in the West, revolution and civil war spread across Europe east of the Rhine, and in Russia the

Bolsheviks struggled to keep power. By the early 1920s, however, a formal stability prevailed. Germany established the sort of democracy the Allies had hoped for; and between her borders and Russia's, thirteen nations, mostly new, established domestic institutions and international ties sufficient for survival. Despite political and economic uncertainties, postwar Europe broadly resembled the world envisioned at the Paris Peace Conference. Russia, the great exception, remained weak and isolated. Italy's turn to Fascism, the great surprise, might be seen merely as part of the general trend for exhausted nations to seek domestic order before all else.

THE CONSOLIDATION OF SOVIET RULE

The Bolsheviks had made peasants' demands their own, arranged a costly peace, and prevented anyone else from capturing power; but now they faced civil war and attack from experienced armies, foreign and domestic. In a land already devastated by war and defeat, in which communications were poor and the economy near collapse, the Bolsheviks adopted "War Communism," a desperate effort to gather the nation's remaining forces. They extended the nationalization of industry, requisitioned crops from the more affluent peasants, and ruthlessly used terror, police repression, and propaganda to extract from a country in chaos just enough men and supplies to fight a war. With the firm leadership of Lenin, the military talent of Trotsky, and above all the mistakes of their enemies, they were able to win.

The major threat remaining by mid-1919 was the armies gathered under former tsarist officers in Estonia, southern Russia, and the Urals. This latter army pushed toward Moscow early in the summer, but the assault from the East was stopped before troops under General Anton Denikin moved up from the basin of the River Don to take Kiev in August and reach within 300 miles of Moscow by October. At that time other "White" forces, as the "Red" Communists' internal enemies came to be called,[1] stood only thirty miles from Petrograd (see Map 26.4). Thereafter the tide turned, for the antigovernment armies could neither penetrate farther nor maintain a long siege against the Communists.

The White forces even at their peak were unable to coordinate their attacks effectively because of dissension and conflicting ambitions. Vague about the political solutions they sought, many of them behaved suspiciously like men intent on a tsarist restoration. Battlegrounds were often ill-defined, contested by units hardly more than marauding bands. And the areas under White control experienced a terror less efficient but possibly more brutal than in Red sectors. While the Communists appealed to peasants, workers, and the various nationalities, the Whites antagonized everybody, losing the popular support that was their only hope. With each defeat more of their troops melted away, and their sympathizers (including the Allies) became more cautious.

By the end of 1919 the White armies were in general retreat. The most important group, under Denikin, withdrew to the Crimea early in 1920; there a new commander, General Pëter Wrangel, stubbornly fought on before finally

---

[1] It should be noted that the term "White Russian" is used in two completely unrelated senses. For centuries before the Bolshevik revolution, and still today, it has referred to one of three major divisions of the Russian people—Great Russians, Little Russians, and White or Byelo Russians. The "White Russians" inhabit the district around Minsk in western Russia and possess a language and a literature of their own, closely related to but still distinct from those of their Great Russian neighbors. This use of the term has no connection with "Whites" used to identify the opponents of the Bolsheviks during the civil war.

heeding Allied advice and evacuating his remaining armies in November 1920.

The Communists were also successful against Poland. An Allied commission had proposed to place the Russo-Polish border along the Curzon Line, so named for the British statesman who advocated it, which assigned to Poland most areas in which ethnic Poles were clearly a majority. But cultural and historical arguments made Poland insist on a boundary that had existed in 1772, well to the east. Rejecting Russian proposals for compromise, she sent an army into the Ukraine in March 1920. Within a month it took Kiev, but Ukrainian nationalists who had fought against the Russians were unwilling to fight for the Poles. In August the Red army, by now a relatively efficient military machine, launched an assault that threatened Warsaw. An effective Polish counterattack led to terms set in 1921, establishing a frontier between Poland's demands, and the Curzon Line.

Russia's western border was now fixed. In Transcaucasia an agreement in 1921 between Russia and Turkey that ignored local independence movements assigned Armenia and Georgia, where anti-Communists had been strong, to the Soviet federation and Kars and Ardahan to Turkey. The Bolsheviks' opponents were not entirely defeated in Asian Russia until 1922, after the Japanese agreed to withdraw from eastern Siberia. Russia was then firmly in Soviet hands.

The New Economic Policy

In some ways Russia's troubles aided the new government. Like the Bolsheviks' cessions of territory, economic difficulties made them less frightening to other nations; and chaos itself made it easier to effect revolutionary changes in landholding, social structure, and political power. Now it was time to take stock.

Under War Communism regimentation and bloodshed were the means of survival, and by using them the Communist party had become an increasingly disciplined and powerful body. The militant arm of a new order, it paralleled the regular government in organization. Some saw in this a pattern for effective rule. Others argued that the loose terror had gone too far (most of the countryside was still subject to the whims of local party officials and roving bands of armed men) and that continuing crises required new policies. Cities were partially empty; a million Russians had gone into exile; tens of millions more had died; less than one-sixth as many manufactured goods had been produced in 1920 as in 1913, and the level had been far lower in some critical areas of heavy industry. Foreign trade had almost ceased. Poor harvests had left the nation faced with famine, and the continued requisitions of what food there was spurred unrest and even revolt. Black markets flourished, and bureaucratic bungling, political maneuvering, and perpetual suspicion retarded economic reconstruction in a country more lacking than ever in machinery and technicians. Thus the mutiny of sailors at the Kronstadt naval base in March 1921, though put down in a few weeks, was an ominous sign. These were just the sort of men who had made the October Revolution possible, but their demands—civil liberties, a secret ballot, and better treatment of peasants—were now rejected. Still Soviet leaders, especially Lenin, recognized the need not to depend on repression alone.

In the spring of 1921, he announced the New Economic Policy (NEP), a major turning point in the development of Communist Russia. Lenin's gift for clear and courageous analysis underlay this dramatic reversal of policy. To some Communists and many foreigners, the NEP seemed a departure from Marxism, but the failures Lenin recognized in propounding it were not failures of Marxist theory. Russia, he argued, was a special case, what today would be called a backward country; and the "citadel of capitalism"—a characteristic military metaphor—had been rushed too fast. Old habits and practices could not be uprooted overnight. Furthermore Russia lacked the cadres of technical specialists and managers a modern economy required. With noteworthy pragmatism Lenin proposed the sort of moderate course the Bolsheviks would earlier have opposed.

Under the NEP peasants were no longer subject to requisitions but rather to a tax in kind, and they could sell their surplus for profit on the open market. Retail concerns and manufacturers employing fewer than twenty workers could be run as private businesses. Even the larger industries, though they remained nationalized, could be leased to foreign entrepreneurs as a way of training Russians in efficient methods and new techniques. Fiscal reforms of the sort capitalist economists might have recommended guaranteed the stability of the currency while Russia's external trade emerged from the pattern of barter into which it had fallen.

Even with these new practices, economic recovery was slow. Millions died in the famine of 1920–1921 despite the extensive aid of the American Relief Administration, and not for another six years would production reach prewar levels. The NEP represented a surrender of the hope of creating communism all at once, but it was also a reaffirmation of Communist determination. Foreign trade, fiscal policy, large industry, wholesale commerce, and natural resources remained firmly in the hands of the state.

Creating a Communist Society

Meanwhile every social institution was recruited to help create a stable new society. The already numerous cooperatives for the sale of agricultural products and for consumer purchases were encouraged, as were trade unions. Both kinds of organization were used to strengthen allegiance to the government, teach efficiency, and instill a sense of class and national pride. Persecution of the church and organized campaigns against religion notwithstanding, by 1923 a certain relaxation permitted the Orthodox Church to function in a restricted fashion.

Russia's inadequate school system, which had nearly collapsed during the years of war and revolution, was improved and extended. Not until 1923 did enrollments pass prewar levels, but thereafter the rise was steady and impressive. The curriculum stressed official doctrines, and workers' children were favored for admission. Old practices of rote learning and ceremonial deference to teachers were to be abandoned. Higher education on the other hand developed more slowly, inhibited by the government's insistence that all subjects be taught in Marxist terms and the emigration of many of Russia's best scholars.

The problems of ruling over multiple nationalities were eased somewhat with the cession of so much territory; three-quarters of the remaining population could be called Russian. Still, non-Russian nationalities were in fact encouraged as never before. The four great Soviet republics—the Russian Soviet Federated Socialist Republic, the Ukrainian, White Russian, and (after 1922) Transcaucasian Soviet republics—were themselves divided into numerous regions for the various minorities. In theory at least each of these smaller constituent members retained considerable autonomy under a new constitution that established the Union of Soviet Socialist Republics (U.S.S.R.).

Legally the authority of the government stemmed from the hierarchy of soviets described in Chapter 26. The largest, the all-union Congress of Soviets, consisted of some 2,000 representatives. The system of indirect universal suffrage that elected them heavily favored urban voters, though rural constituencies had five times the population. At infrequent and largely ceremonial meetings, the Congress elected the 750-member Central Executive Committee, which was more nearly the equivalent of a Western parliament, though it had only advisory powers. The Committee selected both the Council of People's Commissars and the Presidium, a directorate, whose chairman was the chief of state. Precise lines of authority among competing groups were left vague, and little distinction was made between legislative and executive functions.

In practice the Communist party, which remained a restricted elite, was the most important instrument of rule. Not all officials were party members, but it dominated the upper reaches of government, and through a tightly organized hierarchy that paralleled the bureaucracy, it reached into every aspect of Soviet public life—factories, hundreds of new centers for adult education, and youth associations that soon had millions of members. These organizations stirred patriotic enthusiasm, explained the policies of the government, and prodded Russians in thousands of ways to create a modern industrial society.

At first Western artistic movements as well as technology had been welcomed and energetically adopted, but the challenge of creating a new society discouraged tolerance. In 1922 cultural activities were placed directly under the Ministry of Education. The books printed and art works exhibited were those that met the current definition of communist aesthetics: realistic in style, popular in appeal, and useful to the new order. The issues of how to translate ideology into practice, what technologies to use, and how bureaucracies should function were thrashed out within the government and the party. To be on the losing side in any of these disputes was politically and sometimes personally fatal. Experience thus led Communists to caution, and this in turn contributed to an atmosphere of apparent calm.

Even in foreign relations the Soviet Union, preoccupied with domestic problems, gave signs of accepting the world order despite the existence of the Third International. By 1924, the year of Lenin's death, every major power except the United States had recognized the new regime. And the bitter struggle for succession made it appear that even if communism remained firmly entrenched in the Soviet Union, that need not seriously disturb general European stability.

THE NEW REGIMES OF EASTERN EUROPE

From Finland to the Balkans, most of the postwar states of Eastern Europe were newly created by-products of the battle among the giants who had previously dominated these lands. Recognized as independent in the peace settlements, the new states represented the Allied commitment to self-determination, and most of them had new constitutions reflecting the latest fashions and the deepest hopes of democracy.

But in nearly every case statehood had brought war with neighboring regions; and independence, universal suffrage, and civil rights offered few solutions to the problems of conflicting nationalities and economic crisis. In most of the new states peasant revolution or military takeover threatened almost constantly, and most of the elected leaders depended on aroused national feeling for what reliable support they could muster. Peasant parties were dominant in most of these countries as they never had been in the West, and they often combined agrarian radicalism with distrust of urban values, modernizing changes, or parliaments. Social conflict in Eastern Europe was easily associated with ethnic and religious differences that increased the centrifugal pressures.

The German minorities in Poland, Czechoslovakia, Hungary, and Bulgaria were generally among the resented well-to-do. Anti-Semitism was especially virulent in Poland and Rumania,

partly an expression of rural hostility toward urban finance. Town-country antagonism also often set rural Slovaks at odds with the Czechs of industrialized western Czechoslovakia. In Yugoslavia the claims of Greek Orthodox Serbians to be the "national" people angered the Roman Catholic Croats and Slovenes. Macedonians, divided among Yugoslavia, Greece, and Bulgaria, kept up an organized agitation that added to the instability in all three countries and produced chaotic insurrection in Bulgaria from 1923 to 1925.

Rising populations, widespread illiteracy, and lack of capital plagued economic development in the new states. Only Austria and Czecho-

Trotsky sings in praise of the Red army at the 1922 meeting of the Third Internationale held in Moscow to celebrate the anniversary of the Bolshevik Revolution. (Photo: Wide World Photos)

slovakia had advanced industries of a size that could compete in European markets; elsewhere land remained the central economic issue. Independence brought the eviction of "foreign" landlords and the breakup of large estates in the Baltic countries; Bulgaria, Rumania, and Czechoslovakia also instituted significant land reforms. Everywhere, however, new policies were accompanied by resentment of any favored treatment given to certain nationalities and regions. Conservative peasants holding small plots generally proved the most resistant to agricultural modernization. In Poland and still more in Hungary (where 40 percent of the peasants were landless and the next 50 percent held less than three hectares), the great estate owners succeeded in protecting the interests of a native aristocracy.

Each state erected tariff barriers that interrupted the traditional flow of trade within the former empires. Furthermore, the successor countries began their existence burdened with a share of the debts of the Hapsburg Empire as well as complex schedules of payments due one another for lands gained or lost. Only intensive help from the League of Nations kept these claims from crippling them and enabled the financial system to function at all.

Yet gradually stable patterns emerged. The disappearance of the Russian, Austrian, and Ottoman empires had opened the way for systematic efforts at modernization. Schools were built by the thousands and functioned fairly effectively despite issues of language and nationality to which they gave rise. On the whole the traditions of the Austrian bureaucracy served its heirs well, and Turkey, which became a republic under Mustafa Kemal in 1923, borrowed Western dress and institutions as avenues to national strength. The next year the Greeks, defeated by the Turks in the last of the Balkan conflicts that followed World War I, replaced their monarchy with a republic that achieved relative stability despite the continued danger of military intervention in domestic politics.

In general the socialists and agrarian radicals prominent in the first postwar years had given way to more conservative politicians. By 1920 the defeat of Béla Kun's brief communist regime in Hungary had led to authoritarian rule under Admiral Miklós Horthy, as regent for an empty throne, who abolished the secret ballot in rural areas as part of the reassertion of Magyar dominance. But most of the governments of Eastern Europe worked more or less within their constitutions; and Czechoslovakia, under President Tomáš Masaryk and Foreign Minister Eduard Beneš, became a model of the order, freedom, and prosperity democracy was supposed to bring.

THE WEIMAR REPUBLIC OF GERMANY

Pressures for a more democratic and responsible German government grew powerful even before the armistice. Twice in 1917 Emperor William II had promised to make his cabinet subject to a majority in the Reichstag; and in October 1918, to begin this transformation from above, he appointed Prince Maximilian of Baden chancellor.

Prince Max symbolized a compromise that might have worked earlier, but he was not able to stem the uprisings sweeping through much of Germany in the name of peace, democracy, and socialism during the last weeks of war. Not only the political system but the very nation Bismarck had created threatened to break apart, and Prince Max pleaded with William to abdicate. When revolt had spread to Berlin, he announced the abdication without awaiting the Kaiser's approval. Then this liberal aristocrat who favored constitutional monarchy, this non-Prussian nobleman who opposed the dominance of Junkers and army, handed his office (quite unconstitutionally) to Friedrich Ebert, the leader of the Social Democrats. The provisional government, the first German government to include socialists, was established just in time to sign the armistice.

It talked proudly of the German "revolution," and it promulgated decrees in November promising democracy, freedom of speech, a return to the eight-hour workday, and measures to improve social security. Concerned first of all simply with survival, the provisional government avoided tackling the question of land reform lest disruption increase the real danger of starvation. Frightened of a Bolshevik revolution, it quickly reached an accommodation with the army—an army already recovering some of its confidence. Ludendorff, who had insisted that Germany had to sue for peace, later talked of holding out; and even before the terms of peace had been published, the legend began to spread of a valiant army stabbed in the back by radicals at home.

Although the German military had in fact been defeated, the nucleus of military strength remained intact. General Wilhelm Groener, who replaced Ludendorff in late October 1918 as Hindenburg's principal aide, promised to assist the new government provided it would not meddle in the army's affairs. Ebert accepted those terms, and when an uprising of left-wing Marxists called Spartacists brought most of Berlin under their control in January 1919, the army crushed the revolt and shot its leaders. The Spartacists had failed to win a large following, and Lenin's best hope for a communist revolution in Germany died with them.

Germany's new leaders remained committed democrats, and they held elections in January 1919 for a constituent assembly to meet in Weimar, a pleasant city associated with Goethe that recalled the culture of preindustrial Germany. Nearly three-quarters of the delegates elected were intent on installing a republic (Social Democrats held 40 percent of the seats), and with admirable dispatch they wrote a thoroughly democratic constitution that joined proportional representation to universal suffrage. The president, directly elected for a seven-year term, would nominate the chancellor, or prime minister, who would then have to be approved by the Reichstag. The Reichs-

rat, as the upper house was now called, would still represent the single states, but its authority was reduced. In the new Germany government would be responsible to parliament, minorities would be fairly represented, and the aristocracy would hold no political privilege. Both civil rights and private property were specifically guaranteed.

The government, however, continued to face grave threats from the left and an essentially independent army on the right. In addition Allied policies had effects quite contrary to those intended. The victors' insistence that a civilian government be established immediately allowed the generals to escape public acknowledgment of defeat and put the founders of the new republic in the position of bearing the onus of the harsh treaty terms. The decision not to occupy Germany but to maintain the blockade made military collapse less visible than Allied severity. Thus resentment combined with social and economic distress and with the unfinished business of reparations and plebiscites to feed the strength of right-wing nationalists.

In March 1920 some of these tried a revolt of their own. Wolfgang Kapp, a lesser official and outspoken nationalist, led some *Freikorps* members and others in a march on Berlin. When the army, so ready to repress revolt from the left, declared its unwillingness to fire on "fellow soldiers"—the *Freikorps* men—the government abandoned the capital. Its last-minute call for a general strike, however, produced the greatest demonstration of loyalty the Weimar regime would ever win. Workers across the nation left their jobs. In a matter of days the economy came to a halt, and the Kapp "government" gave up.

The Weimar Republic was making its way between the political extremes, but the Social Democrats lacked the strength to pursue the reforms their victory implied. The bureau-

cracy was not democratized. Nor was the army reformed, and its officer corps, though severely limited by the Treaty of Versailles, preserved its cohesion and reached another timely understanding with the politicians. The lack of reprisals following Kapp's fall contrasted strangely with the treatment of the Spartacists. Talk of nationalization produced few concrete results, and the republic could not be certain of the workers' support in future crises.

New elections showed a shift to the right and brought in ministries resting primarily on the Catholic Center and People's party, the latter dominated by industrialists who had belonged to the right wing of the former National Liberals. Although the *Freikorps* were at last outlawed, many of their members merely went into hiding; they remained prominent in the political violence that characterized the Weimar years. Scores of politicians were assassinated, including Matthias Erzberger, the Center party leader who had signed the armistice, and Walther Rathenau, a brilliant organizer of the German economy during the war and as foreign minister in 1922 a vigorous defender of German interests, shot primarily because he was a Jew. By 1924 the conservative National People's party was second in size to the Social Democrats.

The gravest problem of these years, however, was inflation. Early in 1923 French and Belgian forces occupied the Ruhr district because of Germany's failure to make coal deliveries required as reparations, and the local populace responded with passive resistance, a kind of general strike, that made the occupation fruitless. The resulting dislocation and scarcity

also drastically accelerated the already serious inflation.

The German mark, once valued at 4 to the United States dollar, was rated at 8 to 1 in 1919 and 250 to 1 in 1921, and by August 1923 the exchange was more than 2,000 to 1. New money was run off the presses at top speed, and old notes with additional zeros printed on them were rushed to the banks before they too became valueless. Prices changed within hours, always upward; by November a newspaper could sell for nearly 100 billion marks. Recovery came slowly, following the imposition of stringent new financial measures (one source of inflation had been the government's reluctance to raise taxes), a general revival of the economy, and above all a moratorium on reparations and a subsequent new schedule of payments.

At the height of the Ruhr crisis, a nationalist *Putsch* was attempted in Munich. Led by a little-known man named Adolf Hitler, the revolt was more notable for Ludendorff's participation. It was quickly defeated, though the plotters' punishment was ludicrously light: Ludendorff was acquitted and Hitler given a five-year sentence in comfortable prison quarters, where he composed *Mein Kampf* ("My Struggle") in the thirteen months of his term he actually served. It was reasonable to think in 1924 that Germany was on the road to stability. If democracy had not exactly taken root, the forms were operative; better relations with other powers now seemed possible, and the threat of internal revolution had faded.

THE FALL OF LIBERAL ITALY

At the outbreak of the Great War, the Kingdom of Italy had lived by the rules of liberal politics and economics for more than half a century; it had thus been appropriate for her

Poverty in Berlin, 1922; a family begging. (Photo: UPI)

German firms in 1923 needed a handcart to carry the weekly payroll. (Photo: Wide World Photos)

to join the Allied side. The least industrialized of the major Western powers, she had but barely met the demands of total war, and peace brought inflation and unemployment that further weakened the economy. In many places peasants simply confiscated land long promised them; and when in 1920 industrialists began to meet growing waves of strikes with lockouts, workers answered by occupying factories. Italian institutions, strong enough to survive the war, were strong enough still to prevent revolution, but an atmosphere of bitterness, fear, and violence was undermining them.

For Italy the peace treaty was as disillusion-ing as modern war. Although granted considerable territory, she got less than she had expected, and her treatment at Paris was often humiliating. Disposition of the Dalmatian port of Fiume was still being argued when in 1919 a private expedition led by Gabriele d'Annunzio dramatically captured it for Italy. The nation's most famous living poet, d'Annunzio ruled Fiume for more than a year at the head of an "army" of the unemployed, whose nationalist frenzy and vulgar slogans were a welcome contrast to the wordy frustration of diplomacy. Eventually the Italian government evicted its filibustering poet (who had declared war on Italy), but the affair showed the appeal and the effectiveness of direct action.

The Fascist movement was born amid these crises. The term *fascio,* meaning "bundle," comes from an ancient Roman symbol of authority—a bundle of sticks, individually weak but strong in unity. Echoes of imperial Rome remained part of the Fascist party mystique. The movement centered around Benito Mussolini, whose polemical skills had earlier carried him to the top of Italy's Socialist party; he was editor of the party newspaper and led its intransigent wing until expelled in 1915 for favoring Italian intervention in the war. He had then become one of Italy's noisiest nationalists. After the war Mussolini continued to agitate, using the rhetoric of the left to denounce liberalism and parliamentary indecision while using the cries of nationalism to castigate Marxists and the Allies. Inconsistencies of doctrine and tactics hid beneath activism and symbols; the party militants in their black shirts seemed a small army.

At first the Fascists had little success—they did not win a single seat in the elections of 1919—but the hesitancy and confusion of others would soon give them an advantage. The two largest political groups, the Socialists and the Popular party, were well-organized mass parties opposed to the old politics and to each other but divided internally. Left-wing Socialists split off to form a Communist party, inspired by the Bolsheviks' success which increased their reluctance to cooperate with bourgeois regimes; the Catholic Popular party demanded thoroughgoing reforms, but much of its real strength came from rural and conservative groups. The aging Giolitti, returning to the prime ministry in 1920, tried in the old ways to patch together a governing majority. In preparation for the elections of May 1921—the first held under a system of universal manhood suffrage—he brought the Fascists into a "national bloc" of candidates. The alliance, however, benefited only the Fascists, who won thirty-five seats in the new Chamber of Deputies; Giolitti's own Liberal supporters remained a

poor third behind the Socialists and the Popularists. During the campaign Fascist squads had planted bombs, beaten up opponents, and disrupted meetings, enjoying violence and intimidating moderates while denouncing Marxists as a threat to order.

When left-wing unions called a general strike in 1922, which many believed would rapidly turn into revolution, Mussolini's Black Shirts increased their threats and open violence and began taking over town councils by force. The government of Luigi Facta—a caretaker prime minister who was holding office because no one could win a majority—resigned, and the Fascists staged their March on Rome in October. Motley squads of party militants moved on the capital in a grand gesture of revolt while Mussolini cautiously waited in Milan. At the last minute Facta asked for martial law, but King Victor Emmanuel III refused—the gesture of revolt had been enough. Mussolini dashed to Rome, preserving his claims to both perfect legality and forceful conquest.

At thirty-nine Mussolini, invited by the king to form a cabinet, became prime minister of a coalition government; the violent man of order won from a desperate legislature the majority—and an overwhelming one—denied to parliamentary politicians. In the elections of 1924, Fascists won a massive victory. Intimidation and open violence contributed to this success, as did some fraud, but most Italians were willing to give the new party a chance.

In the following year, it became clearer what a Fascist regime would mean. Giacomo Matteotti, a Socialist who bravely enumerated Fascist crimes before the entire Chamber, was subsequently murdered in gangland style. As public condemnation mounted, Mussolini's government seemed about to topple, but the opponents of Fascism were no more able to unite now that they had become a parlia-

Mussolini poses triumphantly with his chiefs after the Fascist march on Rome in 1922. (Photo: Wide World Photos)

mentary minority than when they had been stronger. On the contrary, the Fascists gradually isolated first the Socialist and then the Popular party. By 1925 all opponents had been expelled from the legislature, and newspapers either printed what they were told or risked suppression. The Fascist period had begun.

To most of the world outside Italy and to many Italian moderates, it seemed merely that the country had at last found a strong and anti-socialist leader, one who could run it effectively and whose verbal excesses would undoubtedly be tempered by experience. Reasonable men found it hard to believe that a party whose program contained so many contradictions could be dangerous for long.

INTERNATIONAL ADJUSTMENTS

Gradually the remaining boundary disputes had been resolved one after another, sometimes by force, more often by complex negotiations, and occasionally with the aid of the plebiscites called for in the peace treaties. By the early

1920s, reparations rather than territory presented the most troublesome international problems. There was little agreement, for example, on how to evaluate payments in kind, which the Reparations Commission created after the war had decided Germany could offer as part of her total assigned obligation; this was the issue that had led to the French and Belgian occupation of the Ruhr in 1923. That step, however, was disastrous for all, leaving France isolated and Germany the victim of runaway inflation.

As Germany fell behind in her payments, the Allies took the position that they in turn could not pay their war debts to the United States. Some compromise was essential, and in 1924 the nations involved accepted the proposals of an international commission of financial experts, headed by the American banker Charles G. Dawes. The Dawes Plan fixed Germany's payments on a regular scale, established an orderly mode of collection, and

Germans returning to the city in 1923 after a potato raid into the countryside, where the poor could steal some precious food. (Photo: Wide World Photos)

provided for loans to her equal to 80 percent of the sum due the first year of the plan— 1 billion gold marks ($250 million; it would increase to 2.5 billion marks annually in the fifth year).[2] The plan did not, as many Europeans thought it should, admit any connection between Allied debts to the United States and German reparations to the European victors, but it did end the worst of the chaos. For the next six years, Germany, fed by loans largely from the United States, made her reparations payments on schedule. The issue seemed forever resolved with the adoption of the Young Plan in 1929, which finally set a limit to Germany's obligations (fifty-nine years), reduced annual payments, and ended foreign occupation of the Rhineland.

From 1924 to 1930 the conduct of international affairs did really reflect some of the idealism of the Paris Peace Conference. The League of Nations, formally established in 1920, successfully resolved a number of disputes. Some of its procedures were impractically elaborate, and its authority was restricted by the absence of the United States. Britain's greater concern for her empire than for the League, and France's tendency to use it for her own security. It thus dealt best with disputes in which no major power had a direct interest. Its special commissions made notable contributions, helping the disjointed economies of the new and contentious states of Eastern Europe, aiding refugees, and reporting on matters of public health and working conditions. This recognition that peace was related to social conditions was in itself an achievement, the liberal vision at its best. In the late 1920s at

least, the decisions of the Permanent Court of International Justice, organized at The Hague under the League, were treated with great seriousness; and men could imagine a world in which commonly accepted rules and even-handed justice would greatly reduce the threat of war.

The Locarno Era
Both the League of Nations and the dominant Western democracies were inclined to make general principles a subject of international relations. Efforts to outlaw war foundered on definitions of aggression, but they led to a series of treaties known as the Locarno Pact in 1925. The major agreement, entered into by Germany, Belgium, France, Great Britain, and Italy, secured Germany's western frontier; she and her neighbors promised to arbitrate their disputes; and France made a mutual-defense alliance with Poland and Czechoslovakia. A Continental war caused by German aggression now seemed impossible; France and other nations could lay aside their fears.

The Locarno era, the name given to this brief period of international optimism, was capped by the Kellogg-Briand Pact of 1928. The French had suggested that the American entry into World War I be commemorated by a friendship pact, and the Americans proposed that the accord be extended to others as well. More than a score of nations immediately signed the pact, which renounced war "as an instrument of national policy." These ill-defined declarations, accompanied by no provisions for enforcement, soon proved empty, but they expressed the hope, the belief in law, and the confidence in public opinion that marked the Locarno era.

Disarmament provided another broad path to maintaining peace, and from 1921 on some League commission was always soberly studying the problem. Naval disarmament seemed espe-

---

[2] The United States having waived her claims, the apportionment of reparations among the Allies had been decided on in 1920: 52 percent to France, 22 percent to the British Empire, 10 percent to Italy, and 8 percent to Belgium.

cially promising. Britain no longer commanded sufficient resources to maintain a fleet twice the size of any other country's, given the enormous cost of capital ships; the expense of a sizable navy in fact made every nation hope to avoid unnecessary competition. At the Washington Conference of 1921–1922, called by President Warren G. Harding, Wilson's successor, the United States, Great Britain, Japan, France, and Italy had agreed after some difficulty to fix their relative strength in capital ships at current levels,[3] not to expand their naval bases, and even to scrap some of their larger vessels. About smaller ships there had been less agreement, but the Washington Conference had produced tangible results as well as statements of good will. Never again did disarmament discussions prove so fruitful. At Geneva in 1927 and London in 1930, Italy (citing the special needs of her geography) and France (arguing that all forms of disarmament should be discussed together) refused to accept a treaty. By 1935 Japan would reject even the Washington accord.

Attempts to limit land and air arms were even less successful. League commissions could not agree on which were offensive weapons, whether a professional army was comparable to a reserve force, and whether limitations should be expressed in terms of budgets, weapons, or men. Proposals from Germany and Russia that everyone else disarm down to their level only aroused suspicion. When the conference on general disarmament that these commissions prepared was finally called in 1932, the dream of arms restrictions was more remote than ever. Hitler had come to power in Germany, and a new arms race ensued.

---

[3] This was defined as parity between the United States and Great Britain at 525,000 tons apiece in capital ships, 315,000 tons for Japan, and 175,000 tons each for France and Italy.

THE DOMINANT DEMOCRACIES

The international understandings of the Locarno era rested on the policies and influence of France and Great Britain and on the prosperity of the United States; and so, less directly, did the stability of German democracy, the maintenance of constitutional governments in Eastern Europe, and the effective isolation of the Soviet Union. The caution with which these democracies exercised their international role in turn reflected some unease within their own societies. Although much was changed after the war, few of the promised benefits had materialized. Society had not been radically reformed; indeed radicals had been as effectively defeated at the polls in Britain and France as by force in Germany and Italy. In every country the most militant Marxists felt strengthened by the presence of the Soviet Union as an international homeland for the proletariat. But that allegiance, and the founding of Communist parties that followed from it, split and weakened the left in domestic affairs.

The real social changes of this period were usually not the result of deliberate policy. Employment in services such as sales and office work increased more rapidly than in industry (and the proportion of those who were domestic servants declined). In most countries more women were gainfully employed than before the war at those jobs thought suitable for women, despite a sharp decline from the wartime peak and despite the strong tendency for women to leave work upon marriage. The number of (middle-class) youths enrolled in universities increased sharply, and the automobile, especially in Britain and France, began to alter middle-class life. Generally, the central government now spent a higher proportion of national wealth; and although most of that went to the military and to service debts and pay pensions left from war, some of it was used to lay the basis for broader measures of social security for all. Politically, both business interests and labor unions exercised a more direct influence, essentially supporting the effort to recapture economic stability. Yet, despite periods of prosperity and a genuine boom in certain industries, the 1920s did not provide the steady growth of the prewar decade. Economic uncertainty, increased by inflation and unemployment, tended, like the disillusionment over reparations or the specter of Bolshevism, to stimulate a conservatism that was essentially defensive.

France

Life in France quickly returned to prewar patterns after 1918, including the political combination of a weak executive and moderate domestic policies. Raymond Poincaré, in office since 1913, was perhaps the strongest president the Third Republic had ever had, and his term expired in 1920. Clemenceau was a likely successor, but Parlement chose a safe and colorless man instead, a French version of the "normalcy" the United States sought in Harding. The Chamber of Deputies elected in 1919 at the height of patriotic pride in victory was the most conservative since the founding of the Third Republic.

For the next decade the leading figures of French politics were Aristide Briand and Poincaré, who alternated as premier, with Briand heading the ministry of foreign affairs in 1925–1932. Briand, who after a radical youth had become a moderate, led a number of short-lived compromise cabinets, reflecting in his skillful flexibility something of both the best and the worst in the French tradition of governing. Poincaré, the strong-willed man of integrity, made the decision to occupy the Ruhr in 1923 and was called back in 1926–1929 to head a state dedicated to saving the franc, which by then had slipped to one-fifth its former value.

France had become *par excellence* the land of the lower-middle class, the artisan, and the peasant proprietor fiercely attached to his tiny plot of land. Such people were loyal to their nation and proud of their heritage—though the cornucopia of reparations they had expected never materialized, they accomplished miracles of reconstruction, carefully making their new buildings look as much as possible like those destroyed—but it took extraordinary courage to raise their taxes. Poor financing, beginning with inadequate taxes during the war, underlay the crisis of the franc, which had been one of the world's stablest currencies for a century before its postwar depreciation, and few things were as important to the French citizen as his life savings. Demographically France had been hardest hit of all nations by World War I, and that fact as well affected her postwar psychology. She epitomized the tendency common throughout the West to live as if World War I and the revolutions following had made but a temporary difference.

Competent French leaders thus presided during a period of prosperity over governments whose policies allowed domestic stagnation and encouraged rigidity in foreign affairs. Poincaré's concern for national honor and a stable currency appealed to a cautious middle class much as Briand's complicated maneuvers did to parliamentarians, but neither encouraged Frenchmen to face more difficult long-term issues of working conditions, social inequality, or mass culture.

The United Kingdom

In the United Kingdom also, the 1919 elections—the first in which women (those over thirty) were allowed to vote—produced an overwhelming victory for the leaders who had promised to extract enough from Germany to make winning the war worthwhile. Lloyd George remained prime minister, but even in its modest social legislation which included an increase in unemployment benefits his government was essentially conservative, and his conflicts with other liberal leaders added to the Liberal party's decline. Dumped by the Conservative party in 1922, Lloyd George never returned to power. For most of that decade, Britain was led by Stanley Baldwin, who had the gift of making dullness seem statesmanship. In 1924 new elections brought the Labour party (which two years before had outpolled the Liberals) briefly to power. Except for recognizing the Soviet Union, it did little to recall its leftist origins.

Throughout the period the government met problems of unemployment, Irish nationalism, and empire by extending previous policies. Although the Conservatives expanded social welfare measures, a crisis in the coal industry led to a ten-day general strike in 1926. Frightened by the bitter class conflict the work stoppage vented, Britons were quick to praise the restraint used by both sides. Nevertheless the fervent interest of the well-to-do in maintaining essential services (and breaking the strike), like the antilabor legislation that followed, did much to deepen the resentment of the British working class.

Home rule, promised Ireland before the war, had been suspended, and the Easter Rebellion of 1916 had been firmly suppressed. In 1919, however, the most militant Irish nationalists, led by the Sinn Fein (meaning "We Ourselves") party, refused to take their seats in the House of Commons and met instead at Dublin in a parliament of their own, the Dail Eireann, where they declared Ireland independent. To this defiance the London government responded slowly and ineptly, finally electing to suppress the Sinn Fein party and with it Irish independence. To support this action, the government sent reinforcements to the Royal Irish Constabulary in numbers sufficient to spread the fighting without ending it, and they soon became the most hated symbol of British repression. The Irish terrorists who resisted these British forces were by then named the Irish Republican Army. Against these civilian terrorists, the British could look only foolish or brutal; and by 1920 the two sides were fighting a bloody war.

Faced with mounting pressure at home and abroad to find a settlement, the British government in 1920 passed an Ireland act, which set up two Irish parliaments, one in the predominantly Catholic areas of the south and west, and the other in the predominantly Protestant counties of the northeast (six of the nine counties of Ulster). A Council for Ireland was to coordinate policies between the two Irish governments. This concession of home rule did not, however, appease the leaders of the Sinn Fein, who opposed both the division of the island and the continuing ties with the British crown. Almost two more years of fighting and negotiating followed. In December 1922, the Irish parliament at Dublin proclaimed, with British acquiescence, the existence of the Irish Free State, which included all Ireland except the six counties of Ulster; Northern Ireland, as the six counties were called, maintained its traditional union with Great Britain. An uneasy peace was achieved, although the political division of Ireland was destined to remain a source of aggravation, for both Irish and British governments, in the future.

Only in imperial affairs did habits of flexible compromise produce impressive success. Canadian complaints led the Imperial Conference of 1926 to a significant new definition of all dominions as "autonomous communities . . . equal in status . . . united by a common allegiance to the crown and freely associated as members of the British Commonwealth of Nations." The dominions, in other words, were recognized as completely autonomous in all domestic and foreign affairs; their ties to the British crown were entirely volitional, based on common traditions, loyalty, and friendship. Given legal sanction by the Statute of Westminster in 1931, this definition laid the foundation for a remarkable adaptation of empire to new conditions.

The Other Democracies

The second half of the 1920s was a period of notable prosperity in the Weimar Republic. But the divisions in German society, briefly obscured by defeat, had grown sharper. German workers felt that socialist governments and a republican regime had done little to benefit them. The middle class could not forgive the inflation, which had wiped out its savings. Prosperity brought moderate policies and relief from the assassinations and revolts of the earlier years, but it produced no significant group with primary loyalty to the existing regime.

The leading statesman was Gustav Stresemann, who sat in every cabinet, usually as foreign minister, from 1923 to his death, in 1929. Stresemann was closest to the businessmen of the center-right, who had few idealistic illusions and who saw the need for Germany to maintain good relations with her neighbors. If he acquiesced in army violations of the disarmament clauses of the Versailles treaty, its stringent limitations were at least partly to blame. Although Stresemann was a nationalist, a stance essential to his effectiveness, the right denounced him for his conciliatory tone toward former enemies and for bringing Germany into the League of Nations.

Throughout this period of relative calm, the political extremes were growing at the expense of the center. When President Ebert died, in 1925, a rightist coalition elected General von Hindenburg as his successor, defeating the candidate supported by both the Center and the Social Democratic parties; significantly the 2 million votes drawn to the Communist nominee would have been sufficient to defeat Hindenburg. Moreover the elections of 1930 brought Adolf Hitler's National Socialists to prominence; the Weimar Republic was far from secure.

Democracy fared rather better during the 1920s in some of the smaller Continental countries than it did in Italy and the Weimar Republic. Belgium, despite the war's destruction and conflicts over language and religion, recaptured her place among Europe's most prosperous and freest countries. The tensions between Czechs and Slovaks did not prevent Czechoslovakia from remaining a model of democratic stability and economic growth. Although the Netherlands faced nationalist unrest in her colonies, especially the East Indies, such problems hardly threatened democratic institutions at home; and the Scandinavian countries, while often at odds among themselves, continued to find in liberal institutions the means to imaginative foreign and domestic programs. There (Norway, 1907; Denmark, 1914; Sweden, 1919) and in Great Britain, women's suffrage had not destroyed the family; nor had it cleansed politics, but it seemed a natural expansion of democracy. For Europe as a whole, however, the flood tide of constitutional government that had followed the war had clearly begun to ebb.

II. THE CULTURE OF UNCERTAINTY

We are now accustomed to perceiving the arts and sciences of the twentieth century as distinct from, though closely related to, those of the previous century. When one tries to identify the major trends and the leading figures whose work expresses this broad cultural change, the decade or so just before World War I stands out as a time of significant shift.

The new directions of Western thought cannot therefore be said simply to result from the experience of total war; yet the currents most characteristic of the new era—the radical departures in psychology, physics, and philosophy as well as in art and literature—do fit with and reinforce attitudes that the war made almost commonplace: a nightmare sense of shock at what modern societies might do, skepticism toward accepted pieties, and reliance on personal feeling as a guide to conduct more than on the formal beliefs of reason or religion. The criticisms of liberal society developed in the previous generation were turned with increased animus against the bourgeois complacency and prosperity of the postwar era. Literature and the arts seemed more than ever at odds with society and traditional norms of behavior, and this tension was disseminated in popularized form in print, on the radio, and in motion pictures.

FREUDIAN PSYCHOLOGY

No figure of the half-century centered in World War I disturbed established thinking so deeply as did Sigmund Freud. A Viennese physician whose clinical studies had taken him gradually from neurology to psychiatry, he followed the method—close and detailed observation—of medical science, and his theoretical statements are as careful in their internal consistency as in their literary elegance.

Freud had done his most important work before 1914, and in many ways he was old-fashioned. For the most part, he accepted as socially necessary the norms of behavior of the nineteenth-century middle class. He was deeply influenced by ideas of evolution, and his metaphors and assumptions betray the liberal economist's conception of man.[4] His

---

[4] This point is superbly developed in Philip Rieff, *Freud, the Mind of the Moralist* (1961).

interest in the phenomenon of hysteria, his use of hypnosis, and his first ideas of the unconscious had grown from the work of French doctors with whom he had studied, but it was his genius to synthesize his particular observations into a general theory, a universal statement about the human mind, that could be tested in practical application.

In treating neurotics Freud found that they often experienced relief of their symptoms by recalling under hypnosis events they had otherwise forgotten. He deduced that it is the recollection and not the hypnosis that is crucial, later adding that though the events remembered may not actually have happened, they are the psychic reality with which the patient has been living. The center of psychic forces in the unconscious he labeled the id. Here the basic desires universal among human beings (very similar to what were called instincts) seek satisfaction, and increasingly he found the most troublesome and psychologically significant desires to be sexual. The ego tries to channel and control these desires as it is directed to do by the superego, which, rather like the conscience in more traditional conceptions, expresses a person's socially conditioned sense of what is acceptable behavior. Thus mental life is marked by perpetual tension between the id and the superego.

Most of this conflict, which is uncomfortably mediated by the ego, is unconscious. Indeed one of the mind's techniques for dealing with the id is repression from consciousness of the id's desires. Repression, however, is an enormous strain that often finds outlet in neurotic behavior. As the patient comes to face and understand what is being repressed, his neurosis is relieved.

From this conception of the human psyche, Freud developed an elaborate and subtle theory. It was a shocking one which ascribed sexual lusts to every person at every age. The

Although Freud's theories were intended to be universally valid, his consultation room in Vienna is unmistakably an expression of the European upper-middle class of the late nineteenth century. (Photo: Edmund Engelman)

idea of infant sexuality was especially offensive, but so was the notion of the Oedipus or Electra complex, the child's angry competition with the parent of the same gender whom the child has a guilt-ridden desire to kill in order to possess the parent of the opposite sex. Victorian convention could not tolerate this supposition, asserting that decent people have no such base desires. Freudian theory proclaimed such people merely the most repressed, considered religion the satisfaction of infantile and obsessive needs, and explored the greatest achievements in the arts in terms of sublimation, the diversion of the demands of the id to other and higher purposes. Psychoanalysis, the name Freud gave his body of theory and his therapeutic technique, calls on the analyst to pass no judgments but rather to help the patient discover and say things about himself that proper society holds to be quite simply unmentionable.

Freud's ideas encouraged a shift in aesthetic and intellectual perceptions. He had replaced hypnosis in treatment by free association, which allows the mind to make the connections it wishes by its own mysterious processes without the intervention of objective logic. He considered psychic reality to be as important as any other, and he discovered that dreams or slips of the tongue furnish significant signs of psychic conflict. Here was a rationale for taking dreams and fantasies as seriously as external events and for understanding both literature and life on several levels at once in terms of symbols and expressed purposes, conscious and unconscious ends. And Freud himself provided the model in essays that are persuasively organized, stylistically sensitive, and philosophically suggestive.

Implications of Freudian Theory

In the 1920s the broad implications of Freud's discoveries were beginning to gain wide public recognition. They were cited again and again as evidence of how close man remains to the primitive. If repression leads to neuroses, one extrapolation went, then greater sexual freedom and above all greater candor will produce healthier people. This remains perhaps the most widespread popular notion drawn from Freudian teaching, though it does not properly follow. Related to this is the belief that guilt is evil, a kind of Christian perversion of human nature. Freudian insights encouraged literary and personal introspection and supported the view that childhood is the most important phase of life. Although his theories stimulated new visions of a freer and happier life, Freud's dark conclusion was that "the price of progress in civilization is paid in forfeiting happiness." For civilization is based upon the repression of man's primitive and still very powerful drives, which at any moment might lead him to revolt; Freud feared the revolt he foresaw, and he died in 1939, driven into exile by Nazi anti-Semitism.

Freud and to a lesser extent his disciples developed his ideas with a wealth of examples and terminology, but psychoanalysis won more outrage than respectability during its creator's lifetime. Moreover, its followers strove with Freud to maintain the doctrine whole, treating deviations as heresies. Among these were the ideas of the Swiss C. G. Jung, who broke with Freud and developed the theory of the collective unconscious, a psychic inheritance shared by human beings everywhere and reflected especially in the symbols and rituals of religion. Jung's somewhat looser and more mystical perspectives have fascinated and influenced philosophers, theologians, and artists.

Indeed the concepts of psychoanalysis have been applied, often loosely, to works of art, periods of time, and whole civilizations. It may even be that Freudian procedures and theories have so changed behavior that they are less apposite now than when he formulated them. Only today in fact are systematic modifications of Freudian theory beginning to find acceptance.

THE HUMANITIES

Some artists in the postwar period—the Surrealists with their dreamlike canvases are an example—applied Freudian ideas directly, and in his manifesto of Surrealism (1924), the writer André Breton proclaimed the liberation of the subconscious. Quite independent of Freud, explorations of the irrational within the human mind and in society fairly exploded in prose and poetry. The novels of Proust, Kafka, and Joyce most clearly mark the change in style and content. Marcel Proust died in 1922, before he had been hailed as one of the great stylists of the French language. His long novel, *Remembrance of Things Past*, built an introverted and delicately detailed picture of upper-class Parisian life into a monumental and sensitive study of one man's quiet suffering which became a model of interior monologue, of the novel in which the subject is not action seen from the outside but feelings observed from within. Franz Kafka, who wrote in German though born in Prague, died in 1924, leaving instructions for his manuscripts to be burned. Instead, his works have come to be accepted as quintessentially modern, with their realistic and reasonable descriptions of fantasies that convey the torture of anxiety. In *The Trial* the narrator tells of his arrest, conviction, and execution on charges he can never discover, an exploration of the psychology of guilt that also seems to foreshadow the totalitarian state. James Joyce's international fame came with the publication of his novel, *Ulysses* (1922), the presentation on a mythic scale of a single day in the life of a modest Dubliner written in an exuberant, endlessly inventive game of words in which puns, clichés, parody, and poetry swirl in a dizzying stream of consciousness.

Not all of the most important writers turned away from objective, chronologically precise narrative. But even those who made use of more familiar techniques tended, like Thomas Mann in Germany, André Gide in France, and D. H. Lawrence in England, to explore topics and attitudes offensive to convention. Shock and offense seemed at times to be a form of creative expression. A movement called Dada that had originated during World War I put on displays, part theater and part art exhibition, of noisy nonsense and absurd juxtapositions to infuriate the Parisian bourgeoisie. Italian Futurists, who promised to build a new art appropriate to a technological age—"The world has been enriched by a new beauty: the beauty of speed"—balanced such positive feelings with a call to "Burn the libraries . . . demolish the venerated cities" in their manifesto of 1909. The Fauves in France and the Expressionists in Germany and Scandinavia gloried in their reputation for wildness in style, content, and conduct. Where more sober traditions prevailed, as in the carefully constructed, cerebral poetry of William Butler Yeats, pessimism and obscurity

were still the elements most readily noted. In every language serious poetry as much as serious art and music became more difficult for the layman to appreciate. Cubist and Expressionist painters, like composers using the twelve-tone scale and dissonance, deliberately eschewed the merely decorative or pleasant. The approaches that excited artists wove a frightening violence and amorality into their contemptuous disregard for tradition. Today we confidently admire works from this period as part of a continuous development, but to contemporaries the frenzied new forms were both a source and a voice of serious malaise. They also measured the widening chasm between the "serious," creative art of "high culture" and the popular culture most intellectuals disdained.

The philosopher most widely read in the 1920s was Oswald Spengler, whose *Decline of the West* appeared in 1918. Spengler treated whole civilizations as biological organisms, each with a life cycle of its own, but his book won fame less for its interesting method than for its prediction of the West's deterioration, a prediction that labeled the world war the beginning of the final act and assessed the very institutions liberals had hailed as progress to be symptoms of decay. José Ortega y Gasset's *The Revolt of the Masses*, published in 1930, was hardly more optimistic. The masses, he feared, were destined as they rose in power to destroy the highest achievements of Western civilization. Other philosophers, like contemporary artists, made much of man's irrationality, and scores of minor works that were vaguely Nietzschean, religious, or determinist rained scorn on a vapid directionless culture.

The most striking innovation in philosophy came, however, from another tradition entirely. It found its first major expression in the *Principia Mathematica* (1910), by Bertrand Russell and Alfred North Whitehead, a cornerstone of what has come to be called Analytic Philosophy. On the Continent a group known as the Vienna Circle developed a related system, Logical Positivism; and the work of Ludwig Wittgenstein, especially his *Tractatus Logico-Philosophicus* (1921), became a major influence on both schools of thought. Wittgenstein attempted in a series of numbered propositions "to set a limit to thought." He sought to define, in other words, the areas of thought in which certainty could be achieved and those in which it could not. According to Wittgenstein and others of his school, logicians and philosophers should concern themselves only with what is precise and demonstrable, and their methods, based on symbolic logic, should be analogous to mathematical reasoning. The principles and techniques of symbolic logic have come to dominate philosophy in the universities of Great Britain and the United States.

Like the earlier positivists, analytic philosophers consciously set about to learn from the methodology of the natural sciences, but what they stress is the lean language of mathematics rather than observation or experiment. The philosopher's task is to analyze every statement, stripping away connotations and values that may appeal but do not convey precise meaning. "My propositions," Wittgenstein, concludes in the *Tractatus*, "serve as elucidations in the following way: anyone who understands me eventually recognizes them as nonsensical. . . . What we cannot speak about we must consign to silence." At its most radical, such an approach rejects from consideration most of the issues theologians and moral philosophers have argued for centuries as too imprecise to merit debate. Philosophy, like the other disciplines, was turning from matters of general interest to its own specialized tasks.

THE SCIENCES

Science also had moved beyond the layman's comprehension long before the Great War.

Discoveries in the life and physical sciences were communicated and put to use with increasing rapidity, and those in one discipline were applied in sister fields, often giving birth to new hybrids such as biochemistry and biophysics. Progress in these studies represented a harmonious if accelerated continuation of the work of centuries past. But from the realm of the older natural sciences came mystifying reports of theoretical advances that upset venerable certainties.

Relativity and the Nature of Matter
One line of investigation stemmed from an experiment by two Americans, Albert A. Michelson and Edward W. Morley, in 1887. It had been assumed that the universe was filled with a motionless substance called "ether," because waves of light (or waves of any kind) could not pass through an empty space. This motionless ether presumably also provided a base from which motions of all sorts in the universe could be measured. But Michelson and Morley showed that the speed of light rays emanating from the earth was the same whether the rays traveled in the direction of the earth's movement or against it (the expected result had been that rays would travel faster in the direction of the earth's movement). The implications of this discovery had been explored in a variety of ways over the following decade and a half; then in 1905 Albert Einstein proposed an answer in his first, or special, theory of relativity (his second, or general theory of relativity, expanding the insights of the first was announced in 1915). His mathematical formulations led to striking conclusions of the highest philosophical interest: space and time are not absolute but must be measured in relation to the observer; and they also may be considered, on the most fundamental levels, as aspects of a single continuum.

As Einstein developed his theory of relativity, physicists were also achieving a new under-

Einstein's face remains one of the best known of the twentieth century, a symbol both of universal genius and of Jewish exile. (Photo: © Karsh, Ottawa/Woodfin Camp and Associates)

standing of matter. Here, a principal stimulus came from Wilhelm Roentgen's discovery of x-rays in 1895, which gave the first important insight into the world of subatomic particles.

Within two years the English physicist J. J. Thomson showed the existence of the electron, the subatomic particle carrying a negative electrical charge. The atom was clearly not the basic unit of matter. By the turn of the century Pierre and Marie Curie among others had found radium and other materials to be radioactive; that is, these materials emitted both particles and a form of electromagnetic radiation. Soon, largely through the work of Ernest Rutherford, radioactivity was identified with the breakdown of heavy and unstable atoms. The discovery that the atom was composed principally of electrically charged particles made it possible to link the structure of atoms with Dmitri Mendeleev's periodic table of elements (see Chapter 25). Elements which possessed chemically similar properties were also similar in their atomic structures. These important discoveries promised for a time to simplify and clarify the understanding of matter.

But continuing research soon revealed phenomena inexplicable in terms of Newtonian physics. In 1902 the German physicist Max Planck startled the scientific world with the announcement of the "quantum theory" of energy. Energy in the subatomic world was released or absorbed not in a continuous stream but in discrete, measurable, and apparently irreducible units, which Planck called quanta. Energy, in effect, possessed many of the properties of matter, and the theory implied that matter and energy might be interchangeable. Einstein later incorporated this insight into his theory of relativity, proposing the famous equation, $E = mc^2$. Energy, he concluded, is equivalent to mass times the square of the speed of light; at least in theory, small quantities of matter could be turned into enormous amounts of energy.

In 1919 Rutherford established that bombarding nitrogen with subatomic particles produced changes in the structure of the nitrogen atom. The ancient dream of the alchemists—the transmutation of one material into another—was now possible, although not in the ways the alchemists had envisioned. With accelerating rapidity, other atomic changes were produced in the laboratory, while the study of cosmic radiation related the structure of terrestrial matter to that found in the universe beyond.

By the mid-1920s, however, scientists contemplating the expanded knowledge of matter had to face troubling anomalies. Planck's quantum theory, though apparently verified in numerous experiments, assumed among other things that particles behave in probabilistic rather than absolutely regular patterns—a concept Einstein himself could never wholly accept. Furthermore, electromagnetic radiation, of which visible light is one form, had to be treated for some purposes as a flow of particles and for other purposes as a wave, that is, a disturbance of particles in a medium which does not cause an advance of the particles themselves. The German physicist Werner Heisenberg argued that no fixed model of the atoms of a given element was possible; only its approximate and likely structure could be described, through complex equations. In a few years matter had been found to consist mostly of empty space and not to behave with absolute regularity. Moreover, it proved impossible to measure simultaneously both the energy and the mass of a subatomic particle, because the measurement of one altered the apparent values of the other—a disturbing effect which Heisenberg appropriately named "the uncertainty principle." In the subatomic world, as in the stellar universe, the position and the purposes of the observer fundamentally affected what he observed.

Physicists who chose to philosophize about such matters now spoke in humbler and more tentative tones, describing the implications of abstract ideas more than a fixed reality. But the new theories, especially perhaps the discovery of a constant relationship between energy and mass, proved powerful tools. Physics became one of the most prestigious and highly organized (and most expensive) of human activities. Research uncovered new and special particles in bewildering number, leaving the baffled layman apprised of merely the most publicized technological results: x-ray technology, television, the electron microscope, and eventually the controlled fission of atomic energy.

The majority of physicists lived fairly comfortably with the contradictions and incompleteness of their theories. Newtonian principles, they often insisted, still obtained in most cases, as solid and predictable as ever. But the Western world had long looked to the sciences for support of its philosophy and even its theology, and it suffered a sense of loss in learning that physical laws were relative and that the very scientists who manipulated them were uncertain about what an atom looked like or what a particle was. In the twentieth century no Voltaire could build a view of society on a popularized version of the now wholly specialized disciplines. Coupled with developments in astronomy, which grappled with innumerable universes in a potentially infinite reach of space, the revolution in the understanding of matter left the world a little less certain. Some, occasionally even physicists, argued for a new mysticism or a turning to religion for the kinds of answers no longer available from science.

The Biological and Social Sciences

There was no comparable revolution in the biological and social sciences, but advances in these fields were rapidly unveiling the mysteries surrounding the human condition. Heredity had come to be better understood with the rediscovery around 1900 of the theory put forth by Gregor Mendel, the abbot of a Silesian monastery, in 1866, which distinguished between dominant and recessive characteristics and showed how they were passed on from parents to offspring. The isolation of viruses, first achieved in the 1890s, continued at a more rapid pace; and a range of important new drugs was synthesized, most notably penicillin, discovered by Sir Alexander Fleming and Sir Howard Florey in 1928. Just before the war, Sir Frederick Gowland Hopkins had identified organic substances in food that were later named vitamins A, B, C, and D. The others were discovered in the 1920s and their functions identified, findings that have made a major contribution to human health.

The other behavioral sciences were not so radically transformed during this period as psychology was by Freudian thought, but the work of the two giants of modern sociology, the Frenchman Emile Durkheim and the German Max Weber, had begun to change their own and related disciplines. Although very different sorts of scholars, they shared a concern for finding systematic and objective approaches to the study of society, and questions of methodology have remained central to the social sciences since. Durkheim, following the positivist tradition, explored the power of statistical tools, particularly in his investigation of suicides; and Weber's concept of the "ideal type" as a special form of generalization has led to the wide use of theoretical models. Both probed the social functions of apparently irrational custom and stressed the importance of religion. Weber's classic *The Protestant Ethic and the Spirit of Capitalism*, like Durkheim's concept of anomie—the disoriented condition of society when group norms have broken down—reflect the importance they also assigned to shared values as a cohesive factor in society, the very condition many feared the twentieth century had lost.

Similar themes emerged during the 1920s in

anthropology (the discipline that had benefited most from imperialism) and history, though both fields remained primarily empiricist. And the idealism of the Italian philosopher-historian Benedetto Croce also contributed to the assumption that the values of any society are relative to its time and place as well as to a broadening of the range of human behavior studied by social scientists.

The creative ferment of the 1920s seemed less troubling when it went hand in hand with technology. The public began to accept the architecture and applied design of Walter Gropius' Bauhaus school in Germany, with its emphasis on relating form to function, and the still more daring endeavors of Le Corbusier in France to envision the modern city. In motion pictures, just now winning credentials as an art form, the distortions of time and perspective through flashbacks and close-ups were less disturbing than when conveyed through words or on canvas. Even the frothiest romance or adventure story of the silent screen could express (and perhaps mold) subtle subliminal themes of social or national concern—characteristically, themes of abandonment in France, betrayal in Germany.[5] Only in this decade did Berlin ever rival Paris as an artistic center—proof of the benefits of democracy, one might argue—but intellectuals generally expressed doubts about the future of Western civilization.

That the values of Western culture were changing few denied by the late 1920s. The recognition of man's irrationality, the new scientific knowledge, and the violence that could accompany popular participation in public life were all threatening; the arts and philosophy as well as science had not only moved beyond the average man's understanding but had in large measure rejected traditional assumptions and beliefs. In essays and sermons the public was warned of a crisis of values that neither art nor science could help, a crisis apparently related to the materialism of capitalism, the dull legalism of liberal forms, and the empty gentility of the middle class.

III. THE GREAT DEPRESSION

Disturbing though they were, the attacks on familiar conceptions in the realms of the creative arts and natural phenomena did not unduly alarm the average European. His daily life was secure from war and generally from want; his world of democratic nations at peace seemed to have achieved an impressive prosperity. Then in October 1929 the American stock market crashed, inaugurating the most severe, widespread, and long-lasting of depressions in the modern history of the West. The gaps in postwar recovery were suddenly exposed, and waves of misery and instability challenged Western society and mocked liberal visions.

EUROPE'S ECONOMIC VULNERABILITY

In the mid-1920s European commerce was booming. The major nations reestablished prewar ratios between their currencies and gold, and productivity surpassed prewar levels. Some of the economic effects of war remained, however.

The dislocations of war—the destruction of plants, shifts of capital, and movements of men—had been accentuated by sudden demobilization and then by economic development itself. Not all wartime industries had been able to convert to peacetime enterprises nor all workers to regain their jobs; the prosperity of the 1920s rested heavily on new processes and on new products such as automobiles and synthetic

---

[5] Paul Monaco develops this view in *Cinema & Society: France and Germany During the Twenties* (1976).

fabrics, so that significant sectors of manufacturing declined. Italy and Great Britain, whose coal and textile industries had entered even before the war into a period of chronic depression, never fully shared in the postwar boom. Large industrial combines, closely tied to money markets, controlled concomitantly sizable shares of overall production and employment, restricting the diversification of businesses across the economic base. More people, men and women, worked in service activities such as sales and distribution that were susceptible to cutbacks.

This economic fragility was underscored by certain long-term trends. Old trade patterns had not revived. Goods traveled less freely within Europe, particularly the East, where debt-ridden and underdeveloped new countries —their industries often separated by national boundaries from traditional sources of capital —forced trade to find new routes. Germany's inflation as well as Russia's withdrawal from commerce had increased these difficulties, which had been only partly offset by industrialization in the new states and assistance from the League of Nations.

Moreover Europe did not regain its prewar percentage (about half) of world trade; its firms had lost many of their overseas markets to competitors, especially American, during the war. So it went as well with foreign investments: Britain had lost a quarter of her $18 billion, France half of her nearly $9 billion (primarily in Russia), and Germany all of her $6 billion. American investments in Europe on the other hand had multiplied seven and a half times in seven years to reach $15 billion in 1920, and they continued to rise thereafter. Furthermore a dangerous part of Europe's apparent prosperity rested on the unproductive passing of paper from the United States to Germany as loans, from Germany to the Allies as reparations, and from the Allies to the United States as payment for war debts. The United States not only dominated world trade and demanded payment of war debts but raised tariffs in 1922 and again in 1930 to levels that made it nearly impossible for Europeans to earn dollars by selling goods to her.

The turmoil in Eastern Europe and Russia had led to increased imports of grain from Canada and the United States, where more land was turned to wheat and improved technology brought larger yields. By 1925 Europe's agricultural production had recovered, but only to face a glutted market and sluggish demand due to reduced population growth and the preference for meat over grains that accompanied rising standards of living. Agricultural surpluses became a problem throughout the West that drove down prices and pushed governments to increase subsidies and tariffs. Demographic patterns added other strains. Population expansion was considerable only in Eastern and Southern Europe, but new policies in the countries of immigration, especially the United States, discriminated against nationals from just those countries where overpopulation was critical. Overseas migration slowed to a trickle while pressures of numbers built up.

The war and the disruptions of the postwar years had made people as well as economies less resilient. The demographic deficit because of casualties and a low birth rate had left the population in Western Europe somewhat older and more dependent on pensions. The trauma of war had been followed by the shocks of instability, inflation, and unreliable currencies. Those whose social status depended on savings, pensions, or salaries, especially in Germany, faced poverty in the early 1920s while those who owned real property or industry went on to greater wealth. Debtors benefited while creditors were ruined, and the sense of insecurity was never wholly lost even in the good times of 1924–1929.

FROM PANIC TO DEPRESSION

Such dislocations did not slow the economy of the United States, now the world's wealthiest nation. Speculation in stocks and real estate had been running wild and driving purchase figures unreasonably high. Then suddenly, on October 24, 1929—the notorious "Black Tuesday" of American financial history—the price of stocks on the New York Exchange began to plummet. The crash was partially precipitated by the British, who raised interest rates in order to bring back capital which had flowed to America, but it was more deeply rooted in the growing uneasiness among investors that the speculative inflation of stock prices had gone too far. Day after day tens of millions of dollars in paper assets disappeared. Such panics were not new to capitalism, and on several occasions in the previous century a collapse of the New York market had spread to Europe. But in the next few months, the financial panic settled into full-scale depression. Banks had invested heavily in stocks and real estate, and some failed, causing runs on others. Businesses cut back, consumption declined, capital became more scarce, factories closed, and unemployment rose.

The crisis in the United States was soon felt abroad. European banks and exchanges were immediately shaken; more gradually world trade declined, and the American government and businessmen began to call in their investments and loans. At first, however, it seemed that the panic might be kept from affecting the entire European economy. Then in May 1931 the Austrian bank that held two-thirds of the nation's assets nearly went under, and this precipitated a run on Austrian and German banks that spread the now familiar cycle to other sectors of the economy and to other nations.

By 1932 the world's industrial production was two-thirds of what it had been three years before. Unemployment climbed to more than 13 million in the United States, 6 million in Germany, and nearly 3 million in Great Britain. Among leading industrial nations only France, with her balanced economy, demographic stability, and relative scarcity of labor, escaped unemployment of crisis proportions.

Statesmen hoped that tested techniques of international cooperation could prevent economic disaster. One major problem disturbing financial relationships was that of war debts and German reparations. France and England maintained that they could pay their debts to the United States only if they received reparations from Germany. Although successive conferences and the Dawes and Young plans had evolved a workable system for the payment of reparations, this system too broke down amid the world economic crisis. The United States had never admitted a connection between reparations and war debts, but President Hoover's proposal in 1931 that all intergovernment debts be suspended was quickly accepted (most European states were already making only token payments, and France had defaulted). Meeting at Lausanne in 1932 the European powers in effect agreed to abandon reparations altogether. Although the moratorium originally proposed by Hoover was supposed to be temporary, any hope that the debts or reparations would ever be paid had become an illusion.

When Austria's major bank teetered on the edge of bankruptcy in May 1931, threatening all Central European finances, it had been saved by British loans. Amid the deepening Depression, this and other financial burdens forced Great Britain to abandon the gold standard, no longer guaranteeing that pounds could be converted into gold at a fixed rate. The important bloc of countries trading in sterling quickly followed suit. This was tantamount to devaluation, as the value of the pound fell

Food is distributed to unemployed demonstrators in Hyde Park, London, in 1931. (Photo: Wide World Photos)

at once below the former, officially supported exchange rate with gold. Devaluation of this principal currency in turn threatened to throw international monetary exchanges, and the trade dependent upon them, into chaos.

But international understanding might once more prevent others from rushing to devaluate. To that end the League of Nations sponsored a World Economic Conference that met in London in 1933. Begun with visions of high statesmanship, it ended in failure. Debts to the United States were removed from the agenda at American insistence, and no agreements for reducing tariffs could be reached until international exchanges rates were stabilized.

When the United States too went off the gold standard, an elaborate structure of credit and exchange that had been one of the signal achievements of liberal finance fell. France was the last major country to abandon gold. Less dependent on international trade, hit later and less suddenly by the Depression, and strongly attached to the traditions of stable finance, she resisted until 1936. A historic era in which nations, like so many bankers, supported international financial stability by honoring the laws of liberal economics had ended.[6]

National Responses

The interrelationship between politics and economics had become well understood in the nineteenth century; but whereas tariffs and taxes were acknowledged to be political issues, most governments had wished to leave large spheres of economic activity alone. During World War I, however, governments were forced to direct much of the economy, and in the following years issues of reparations, currencies, and reconstruction had drawn them more deeply into economic activity. Business increasingly turned to them for assistance, and voters who had witnessed the miracles of wartime mobilization put the responsibility on the state of leading them out of the Depression. By the early 1930s it was clear that each government had to act on its own to save its national economy.

On the whole, however, the measures taken had the effect of sinking the West deeper into the Depression. Austria and Germany in 1931 proposed a customs union, but French opposition led the World Court to forbid the step. Instead, nearly everywhere tariff barriers rose higher and import quotas were gradually extended to more and more items. The effect was a still further reduction in trade. Domestic programs varied, but the tendency was to protect interests that were politically strong, to shore up inefficient industries, and to support uncompetitive sectors of the economy—measures that slowed lasting recovery.

---

[6] Karl Polanyi has elaborated the significance of the abandonment of the gold standard in a famous essay, "The Great Transformation: The Political and Economic Origins of Our Time."

Such policies violated accepted economic precepts, but liberals were at a loss as to what else to do. Nor were socialists better prepared to solve the problems of declining commerce, insufficient capital, and unemployment, though they displayed a certain satisfaction at this new evidence of capitalism's weakness. They had a part in the governments of Germany, Austria, Sweden, Czechoslovakia, and Great Britain and were a leading force in most other countries; but their favorite nostrum, the nationalization of industry, was barely relevant. In practice socialists showed again the extent to which they had absorbed the orthodoxies of classical economics. They too usually thought governments had to reduce their budgets and ensure that exports exceeded imports. At the same time Socialist parties, closely tied to labor unions, supported whatever palliatives for unemployment could be suggested, though the dole, the most common one, strained the budgets they wanted to see balanced. As liberals and socialists tried one new measure after another, they were embarrassed by growing Communist parties, which let no one forget that while a whole system had been collapsing, Russian production had been advancing at a steady pace.

Gradually, conditions did improve. By 1937 production in Germany, Britain, and Sweden was well above the 1929 level of each, though it remained below that mark in the United States, Italy, Belgium, and France. Technological progress continued, and government intervention changed both economic and political life. But these changes were as socially divisive as the Depression itself, and the democracies that had dominated Europe faced the double threat of communism and fascism with a heavy burden of failure.

In 1919 much of Europe had been in the throes of revolution; yet the Western powers led the way to reasonable stability. New nations and a world order were created in their image, looking to democratic constitutions and the League of Nations as the means of organizing power. Despite the effects of war, social turmoil, and inflation, the new European order seemed by 1924 on its way to increased freedom and prosperity. Within a few years these achievements and the optimism that accompanied them were overshadowed by the calamity of the Depression. Liberal ideas and institutions appeared to be losing their capacity to deal with such problems as Europe was now facing, and the hopes of the 1920s quickly seemed foolish.

In retrospect the failures became clear. Britain, France, and Germany in their different ways had turned to cautious domestic policies that postponed rather than met the deepest social and economic issues. In less wealthy nations constitutions that did little to resolve conflicts of class and nationality were soon violated, while very different regimes in Russia and Italy moved with welcome dispatch. The League and the World Court showed themselves clearly most effective when the interests of no major power were at stake. Laborious negotiations for disarmament and monetary controls were often overrun by events, and the guardians of stability maintained their military forces while talking of reducing them and abandoned the gold standard while proclaiming its importance.

Individual liberty, democracy, and international law had seemed deeply rooted in Western culture when reaffirmed in the ruins of war; but those roots were not strengthened by the intellectual life of the 1920s, which turned inward to academic specialization or directly affronted the rationalism and genteel inhibitions on which bourgeois society was thought to rest. Those values, like capitalism itself, remained strong, but they would stand on the defensive throughout the next decade.

RECOMMENDED READING

Studies

*Carr, E. H. *The Twenty Years' Crisis, 1919–1939.* A balanced account that captures the sense of failure.

*Craig, Gordon A., and Felix Gilbert (eds.). *The Diplomats, 1919–1939.* 1965. Separate essays on major figures uncover the connection between international relations and domestic affairs.

*Galbraith, John K. *The Great Crash: 1929.* 1955.

A pungent, dramatic account focused on the United States.

*Gamov, George. *Thirty Years That Shook Physics.* 1966. A leading physicist, Gamov is also an able popularizer.

Gay, Peter. *Weimar Culture: The Outsider as Insider.* 1968. Sensitively explores the insecurity within German culture even in a period of great creativity.

Gerschenkron, Alexander. *Bread and Democracy in*

Germany. 1943. Emphasizes the ties between economics and politics in Germany.

*Graves, Robert, and Alan Hodge. *The Long Weekend: A Social History of Great Britain, 1918–1939*. 1963. A poet and a scholar recapture the feel of daily life among the middle classes.

*Greene, Nathaniel. *From Versailles to Vichy: The Third Republic, 1919–1940*. 1970. Balanced coverage of the interwar period.

*Hartnack, Justus. *Wittgenstein and Modern Philosophy*. Maurice Cranston (tr.). 1965. A good introduction to the topic.

*Jones, Ernest. *The Life and Work of Sigmund Freud*. Lionel Trilling and Steven Marcus (eds.). 1961. One of the best of many biographies, which studies the ideas of psychoanalysis as well as the movement that developed.

*Kahler, Erich. *The Tower and the Abyss*. 1967. Uses his learned understanding of the arts across Europe to discern the elements of decay in contemporary culture.

Lyttleton, Adrian. *The Seizure of Power: Fascism in Italy, 1919–1929*. 1973. The best study of the complicated process that brought Fascism to power.

Maier, Charles S. *Recasting Bourgeois Europe: Stabilization in France, Germany, and Italy in the Decade After World War I*. 1975. Uses the details of economic policy and political conflict to show the period as one of bourgeois defensiveness.

*Robbins, Lionel. *The Great Depression*. 1934. A distinguished British economist views the depression he has just experienced.

*Rogger, Hans, and Eugen Weber (eds.). *The European Right: A Historical Profile*. 1965. Separate chapters delineate the formation and political role in various European countries of the increasingly vigorous right.

*Rothschild, John. *East Central Europe Between the Two World Wars*. 1973. Now the best survey of the area in its critical era of independence.

*Sontag, Raymond J. *A Broken World, 1919–1939*. 1971. A senior historian's contribution to the best historical series on modern Europe.

*Stern, Fritz. *The Politics of Cultural Despair: A Study in the Use of the Germanic Ideology*. 1961. Focuses on three figures to assess the impact on politics of cultural attitudes.

*Taylor, A. J. P. *English History 1914–1945*. 1965. A wide-ranging survey by an able and provocative historian.

*Wolfers, Arnold. *Britain and France Between the Two Wars*. 1966. Traces in the relations between these two democracies the breakdown of the international system established at Versailles.

---

* Available in paperback.

TWENTY EIGHT

TOTALITARIANISM
AND WORLD WAR II

Democracy was in retreat within less than a decade after the Paris Peace Conference. By 1929 authoritarian regimes had violated or eliminated the liberal constitutions of Hungary, Spain, Albania, Portugal, Lithuania, Poland, and Yugoslavia as well as Italy. By 1936 political liberty had been suppressed in Rumania, Austria, Bulgaria, Estonia, Latvia, and Greece as well as Germany. Most of these countries were among the poorest in Europe, but their political difficulties illustrate the broader trend. Divided over issues of social reform, nationality, and religion, they suffered increased disruption with each economic crisis and foreign threat.

As the newer and poorer nations abandoned democratic forms of government, they were drawn to the political experiment unfolding in Italy, where fascism promised to mobilize all society and to combine mass politics and industrialization with stability and order. Fascist groups appeared throughout Europe, and in Germany the most radically violent of these movements took power. Fascism, which fed on all the tensions of postwar society, presented itself as the only alternative to communism and benefited from widespread fear of a radical left, which was galvanized by admiration for the Soviet Union. In Russia, however, the effort to restructure a whole society rapidly led to comparable techniques of rule. Twentieth-century ideologies, the potentialities of industrial society, and the strains of social change had generated a new political form: totalitarianism.

Even in the prosperity of the 1920s, the great democracies of the West had had difficulty finding consistent policies to meet domestic demands for social justice or the threatening problems of international relations. The stock market crash of 1929 developed into the worst depression of modern history and created an economic disaster of a magnitude that free governments did not know how to repair. The social and ideological divisions within the Western democracies were only deepened by direct challenge from Germany and Italy and the more indirect challenge from the U.S.S.R. From 1935 to 1939 the fascist states main-

tained the initiative in a series of mounting diplomatic crises. By 1939 those crises produced a war that Britain and France had desperately tried to avoid and for which Germany was psychologically and militarily far better prepared. Germany and her allies marched from conquest to conquest until they controlled the Continent by the end of 1941, when Russia and the United States were forced to fight at Britain's side.

I. THE RETREAT FROM DEMOCRACY

The transition to an authoritarian regime usually won support from at least three groups. The army, concerned about external threats and the domestic turmoil likely to accompany desired industrialization, favored a strong government. A second, more amorphous group of middle-class politicians and influential religious leaders, fearful of socialism, supported authoritarian rule to preserve established institutions.

Often they formed Catholic parties that combined rural reform with traditionalism, distrusting democratic politics and the urban masses. Liberalism, they warned, had unleashed attacks on religion and opened the door to socialism. Nationalists were a third and overlapping element, who demanded a strong state to right old defeats yet appealed to people in all social classes who felt themselves victimized by recent change. Each of these factions thus sought selective modernization, controlled change along lines that would not threaten its own influence.

The sacrifice of parliamentary government was merely the first step. Authoritarian regimes also needed some popular support and soon found themselves at odds with various established interests, often the very conservatives who had brought them to power. Thus while some regimes adopted fascist techniques, others returned in the late 1930s to a limited constitutionalism. The political turmoil that accompanied both solutions was an important part of the crises leading to World War II.

AUTHORITARIAN GOVERNMENTS

Hungary had turned to authoritarian rule relatively early, preserving the façade of constitutional institutions and relying heavily on the support of traditionally conservative groups. The Magyar aristocracy used a rigged electoral system to maintain its political dominance, protect its privileges, and stifle land reform. Ardent opponents of the Paris treaties, Hungary's leaders had drawn closer to Italy. Admiral Horthy, who had become head of state in 1920, kept that office, but monarchists and fascists put successive cabinets under severe pressure. As the Depression reached Hungary, fascist trappings increased, and successive governments became more anti-Semitic, restricting the number of Jews permitted in business or the professions. Hungary would be quick to take

what territory Hitler's policy in Eastern Europe permitted yet wary of German and Italian plans. Because the older aristocracy retained considerable influence, Hungary never became a full-fledged modern dictatorship and belatedly even dissolved some fascist parties in 1939.

In Poland domestic political divisions were complicated by the fact of powerful neighbors, and Poles disagreed on whether their national interest lay with Germany, Russia, or France. Socialists and Catholics, conservative landowners and radical peasants all had political strength, and the resulting instability had brought Marshal Józef Piłsudski to the fore. The marshal, a former Socialist, had taken power in 1926 with the aid of a military revolt. One of his followers had then been voted into the presidency while Piłsudski had served as premier; and though he had resigned after defeats at the polls in 1928, his supporters managed by persecuting the opposition to assure safer elections in the future.

From 1930 on Poland was ruled by men from the military. Constitutional changes in 1935 granted the president increased authority and gave the government a voice in the nomination of parliamentary candidates. Securely in power despite Piłsudski's death, in 1935, Poland's military men strove valiantly to strengthen a nation badly hurt by the Depression and threatened by both Russia and Germany. The noisy conflicts of fascists and socialists, however, measured the regime's failure to establish a firm popular base.

When the monarchs of Eastern Europe attempted authoritarianism, they often flirted with fascism, only to find the game so dangerous to the retention of their rule that they returned to more constitutional forms of government. In Yugoslavia Alexander I, who had ascended the throne of the new kingdom in 1921, had assumed dictatorial powers in 1929 in an effort to tame the divisive forces of Croatian, Slovenian, and Serbian nationalism. But as these conflicts continued, he tried a restricted parliamentarianism. After his death, in 1934, the regent, Prince Paul, pursued a similar course: drawn at first to Germany and Italy, he decided by 1939 that Yugoslavia's international position and internal stability would best be served by a federal and democratic system. In Bulgaria a military coup ended parliament, parties, and free speech in 1934, and the regime moved closer to Fascism as it sought both urban and rural support. But by 1936 the king was restricting the military, banning some fascist groups, and talking of constitutions.

Rumania's liberal government had begun to give way late in the 1920s before pressures from her ruling classes. Carol II, called to the throne in 1930, was an admirer of Mussolini's, and he secretly subsidized the Iron Guard, a fascist organization whose political violence and anti-Semitism imitated the worst of fascism elsewhere. In seeking popularity Carol's government became more extreme; the imposition of martial law and tight censorship was followed by an anti-Semitic campaign that stripped most Jews of land and citizenship. These policies, however, proved disruptive and brought protests from Britain and France, and by 1938 the king was leading the way in suppressing fascist activities and attempting to make a new constitution work.

THE TREND TO FASCISM

The appeal of fascism was not limited to poor nations without parliamentary traditions. In Britain Sir Oswald Moseley, once considered a likely Labour prime minister, founded the British Union of Fascists. In Belgium fascism benefited from the antagonism between Catholics and anticlericals and between Walloons and Flemings. The Flemish speakers thought of themselves as a deprived group, dominated by the French-speaking Walloons in business, church, and government. Largely rural and conservative, the Flemings came to feel considerable sympathy for fascism and especially for the Nazis, whose language was close to their own. In the Netherlands also a National Socialist movement rose to prominence in the 1930s.

There were a number of fascist movements in France, of which the *Action Française* had the longest history and broadest influence. It reached prominence in the furor of the Dreyfus case, but remained primarily an intellectual movement aimed especially at monarchists and Catholics. Under the editorship of Charles Maurras, the *Action Française* maintained a biting critique of the bourgeois republic and developed doctrines useful to fascist parties everywhere. *Action Française* failed to achieve the common touch of the most successful fascist groups, and its conflicts with the papacy helped to restrict its effectiveness. But it served as an important bridge between disaffected rightists and the uniformed young militants who filled the streets of Europe in the 1930s.

The Greek and Austrian Republics

The republican government of Greece proved particularly vulnerable to fascism. Eleutherios Venizelos, the leader of the nation's liberals, dominated the republic's brief life, which lasted little more than a decade from its founding in 1924. Yet his party had been gradually losing ground to the monarchists even before the Depression deprived Greece of vital agricultural markets and forced Venizelos to resign in 1932. Republicans attempted a coup to ward off the restoration of the monarchy, but it was defeated, and a manipulated plebescite brought King George II back to the throne in 1935. When Liberals made gains in the 1936 elections, General Joannes Metaxas proclaimed himself dictator. He then clung to power in fascist style by balancing severe censorship and the abolition of political parties with extensive social welfare, public works, and armament.

In Austria the sharp division between a Catholic German countryside and a cosmopolitan imperial Vienna without an empire to administer undermined the republic. The Socialists, out of power since 1926, had little strength beyond the city, while the Christian Socialists, whose nineteenth-century programs of welfare, nationalism, and anti-Semitism had influenced the young Hitler, moved steadily toward fascism. In the 1920s each party had established its own paramilitary organization, and their violent clashes became a regular part of Austrian politics. Within the Christian Socialist party, older Catholic politicians vied for influence with German nationalists and the party army.

Prohibited by the Western powers from economic union with Germany as well as the Anschluss—the political "consolidation" desired by Nazis and others on both sides of the frontier—Austria survived financially after 1931 through foreign loans. Chancellor Engelbert Dollfuss drew Austria closer to Italy and ruled by decree, suspending parliament, outlawing communists, and banning party uniforms (a measure aimed at the Austrian Nazis). In 1934 all parties except those in the Fatherland Front, which supported Dollfuss, were abolished. The Socialists called a general strike, and the government responded as for war. When the army bombarded Karl Marx Hof, the public housing that Viennese Socialists had been so proud of, that act symbolized the end of Austrian democracy.

A new constitution, elaborately corporative and claiming direct inspiration from papal encyclicals, was announced in 1934 but never really put into operation, and a concordat gave the Roman Catholic Church control of Austrian education. Austria's Nazis, however, remained dissatisfied, and in July a group of them assassinated the chancellor. They expected the Anschluss to follow, but a quick movement of Italian and Yugoslav troops to the frontier prevented it. For the next few years, Austria depended on Italian support, and Kurt von Schuschnigg, Dollfuss's successor, maintained a relatively mild dictatorship as he attempted to dominate the sordid squabbles for leadership within the Fatherland Front. Having destroyed the left, Austria's authoritarian government had little basis from which to resist the growing Nazi pressure.

Dictatorship and Republic in Spain

Alfonso XIII had kept Spain neutral in World War I, sparing her the direct ravages of war. But political and economic frictions were building toward a civil war that broke out in 1936.

Long before that date Spain's political system had begun to break down and her economy to suffer from the lack of capital investment and unresolved problems of land tenure. In Catalonia, the center of commercial and industrial activity, a vigorous regionalist movement flourished, drawing together various groups that opposed Madrid's policies. The army, overstaffed with ambitious officers, became increasingly active in politics; and discontented workers, divided among anarchists, socialists, and a faction soon to be called communist, staged frequent strikes that often ended in violence.

It was thus a strife-torn nation whose army in 1921 had been routed while attempting to subdue the Riffs, Berber tribes of Spanish Morocco. In the process Spain lost most of the territory she had acquired since 1909, and an embarrassed government had promised a full report, apprehensively awaited by the army. Just before it was due, in 1923, General Miguel Primo de Rivera issued a *pronunciamento* in time-honored style and forced the king to appoint him prime minister—an office he assumed as de facto dictator.

Although he began without a clear program, Primo de Rivera used the themes of modern anti-liberalism to denounce soulless materialism and petty politics. With Mussolinian techniques he built his personal prestige, assuaged the complaints of socialists and further divided the left with extensive welfare programs, and established a political party of his own. By 1926 the regime was able to claim a number of accomplishments. It had defeated the Riffs, albeit with help from France, and it had made extensive use of expert engineers and economists and adopted a corporative code, giving its domestic program a progressive flavor.

Nevertheless the dictator's simplicity and candor had begun to lose their charm; his censorship antagonized intellectuals, threats of state ownership frightened business, and the government's propensity for meddling worried both church and army. When a constituent assembly proposed not merely a corporative legislature but a kind of fascist council of ministers that the king could not dissolve, Alfonso lost his taste for imitations of Mussolini. As the Depression began to be felt in Spain, Primo de Rivera's government faltered, and in 1930 he went into exile, where he died a few months later. The king now presented himself as the protector of traditional liberties and appointed as prime minister another general, this one old and cautious enough to alarm no one. Spain's government tried both martial law and the promise of constitutionalism, but all the old problems remained. When republicans and socialists scored impressive victories in the municipal elections of 1931, Alfonso also chose exile.

The second Spanish republic represented a democratic revival. Under the republican leader, Manuel Azaña, a government of the left tried to hold its divergent supporters together with progressive labor legislation and welfare programs, but these measures were ill-adapted to Spain's economic and social structure. Granting Catalonia autonomy, one of its most successful decisions, did not end regional conflicts, and land reform based more on general principles than on specific conditions proved difficult to administer. The separation of church and state and the secularization of education infuriated half of Spain without satisfying anticlericals, many of whom continued to practice independent harassment of religious institutions and activities. Elections in 1933 installed a more conservative government with more traditional policies, but the left crew together in the popular front which triumphed in the elections of 1936.

For the five years of the republic's struggle to survive, the left had grown more radical, and antirepublicans had been preparing action of their own. A movement called the Falange had been founded by José Antonio Primo de Rivera, the dictator's son, in direct imitation of Italian Fascism; and systematic street violence was commonplace by 1936, when a group of generals announced their revolt. The Spanish Civil War, which followed, was seen from the first as part of the European battle between the fascist right and the Marxist left. The insurgent officers counted on support from Italy, Germany, and Portugal, where Antonio de Oliveira Salazar had already established his dominance over a single-party, corporative, conservative, and Catholic state.

The Common Pattern

Whether they won power or not, Europe's fascist movements had much in common. They denounced liberalism and capitalism and co-opted the socialist claim of representing a revolutionary movement. Fascists flexibly snatched every opportunity to discredit existing governments while combining a very modern mass appeal with important conservative backing.

They spoke especially to elements of the populace that felt threatened by the current of change: men of religion threatened by a secular state, businessmen threatened by government intervention, a middle class threatened by socialism, rural society threatened by urbanization, the privileged threatened by democracy, workers threatened by unemployment, everyone threatened by the Depression.

They called on the spirit of nationalism, promising a state united in common purpose without petty politics or class conflict, and they played on a kind of nostalgia for the enthusiastic patriotism of World War I. Admirers of technology and organization, fascists presented themselves as the only alternative to Marxist revolution, and they sanctioned violence as the honest tool necessary for overcoming tradition and habit.

Corporatism as a theory had a long intellectual history. In its modern version it advocated the organization of political life in terms of occupations, grouping people by trade or industry. A society so structured, the argument went, would preserve natural hierarchies while avoiding the divisiveness characteristic of parliamentary systems, which amplified differences of class and ideology; this vision of social integration gained attractiveness during the Depression. Moreover in 1931, the fortieth anniversary of Leo XIII's *Rerum Novarum,* Pope Pius XI issued another influential social encyclical, *Quadragesimo Anno* ("In the Fortieth Year"). It went further in rejecting both the injustices of capitalism and the solutions of Marxism, calling instead for a harmonious society based on religion and cooperation through corporative organization. Many anxious people found in that papal pronouncement a sympathy for fascism that seemed to justify overlooking its deeply antireligious quality. Few European societies could wholly resist the multiple appeal and simple solutions of fascism.

II. TOTALITARIANISM

Dictatorship has been recognized since ancient times as one means of maintaining political order, but the effort to create totalitarian societies has been a twentieth-century phenomenon.[1] In Italy, Germany, and Russia, a single party, mass communications, economic control, and force were combined with an official revolutionary ideology in an overwhelming drive to create a new state, highly industrialized but monolithic. With the aim of unanimity, totalitarian governments set new standards of oppression, making terror a tool of power and crushing their "enemies," whom they labeled as such not merely for public acts, but simply for belonging to certain groups, which might be defined in terms of race, occupation, region, religion, or artistic taste.

In practice none of the totalitarian regimes fully realized its goals. Italian Fascism evolved relatively slowly and never achieved the social control or demonic power of Nazi Germany, and although German and Italian totalitarianism borrowed much from the communism they abhorred, they remained significantly different in values and policy from the Bolsheviks, who sought to transform an entire economy and all its social institutions. Fascist and Nazi rule tried instead to use existing structures, working with the business community, the bureaucracy, and the army. Beneath their radical claims lay a grudging respect for the established interests that helped them to power.

---

[1] Scholars agree that Hitler's Germany and Stalin's Russia were totalitarian, but some consider the differences between those regimes more important than their similarities. Many of those who find totalitarianism a useful term also include Fascist Italy while others object that it was too inefficient and mild. A few would extend the term to Franco's Spain and to other single-party dictatorial or fascist states.

Mussolini and his Black Shirt bodyguard give the Fascist salute. (Photo: Wide World Photos)

FASCIST ITALY

A series of special laws passed by 1926 assured Mussolini's control of power in Italy. The Duce ("leader") of Fascism was declared head of state and granted the right to determine the Chamber's agenda and to govern by decree. For twenty years nearly all the laws of Italy would be issued in that way. Opposition parties were outlawed, scores of potential opponents arrested, and the civil service and judiciary purged of unreliable men.

Mussolini had a rare gift for propaganda, and Italy's newspapers were filled with unsmiling pictures of him, always in poses of command—awing visitors, captivating vast throngs, leaping hurdles on horseback, flying airplanes, harvesting grain. No story was too silly to be circulated for some effect: the Duce recited the cantos of Dante from memory; he worked all night (the light in his office was carefully left on); he inspired philosophers and instructed economists; American razor blades were inadequate to the toughness of his beard; his speed in race cars frightened experts; his stern but tender love for his subjects knew no bounds. Neither did the audacity or vulgarity of such propaganda. Disseminated day after day, it appeared to work, for Mussolini and Fascism were gradually placed beyond the range of normal criticism.

Slogans such as "the Duce is always right" or "Believe, Obey, Fight" soon covered walls from one end of Italy to the other, and mediocre party officials were humorlessly labeled supermen and saviors. The victory of an Italian athlete or the birth of a child to a prolific mother became an occasion for hailing the new order. Through the cheap theatricality of parades and balcony speeches, Mussolini's machine pumped pride and confidence into a troubled nation. Most Italians probably maintained their distrust of any government, but the good news of the propaganda was nevertheless welcomed and some of the enthusiasm real. Even in its cynicism Mussolini's sensitivity to the masses brought to Italian government a popular touch that it had lacked. The nation responded to his energy, his skillful borrowing of ideas and programs, and his arrogant confidence.

The authoritarian single party, parallel to and even competing with the state, became a hallmark of totalitarian regimes; and the Fascist party, completely subordinate to the Duce, reached into every city and town. A warning presence to other authorities and to individual citizens, the party had its own militia, secret police, and tribunals. Recruited in its early years mainly from among the unemployed and alienated, it had soon won hundreds of thousands of new members eager for the advantages of influence with the regime. There were associations for Fascist teachers, workers, and university students. In youth organizations for every age group over four years old, the next generation wore black shirts, marched, and recited official slogans. But the party never became the elite it claimed to be, and the policy of encouraging wide membership was abandoned in the 1930s in favor of fewer, more disciplined militants. Even so, the party remained more an instrument of patronage than the disciplined hierarchy described in propaganda.

Fascist doctrine, used primarily as propaganda, was neither fully practiced nor wholly consistent; but official ideology, essential to the very nature of totalitarianism, colored every aspect of life. Fascism declared itself the antithesis of the principles of 1789 yet also truly the regime of the people. While ridiculing the idea of majority rule, Fascists were extremely concerned with public sentiment and found a façade of representative institutions indispensable. The conservative principle of authority was reduced to simple obedience to the Duce. Authority was deemed purer when arbitrary than when circumscribed by rules, more effective if kept visible rather than subtle, and traditional arguments for social responsibility justified the omnipresence of the state. Crude force, the secret police, and acts of official brutality were well advertised as fulfilling the slogan: "Nothing against the state, nothing outside the state." Citizens were to replace the handshake in favor of the extended right arm of the fascist salute,[2] and regulations established the fascist names to give one's children and the form of address to use with one's friends. There was a fascist style in art and philosophy, sport and war; and the state provided academies, uniforms, medals, and pensions for those who adopted it while threatening the critical with unemployment, exile, or prison. A candid irrationalism suspicious of intellectuals and traditional culture stressed the virtues of intuitive "thinking with the blood." Revitalized by a new-found joy in war, Italians would reclaim

---

[2] The salute was a stylized form of the greeting used in ancient Rome and portrayed in the statue of Marcus Aurelius that now stands on the Capitoline Hill in Rome, where Michelangelo designed a piazza to frame it. The salute quickly became an international symbol.

"Sons of the Wolf," six to eight years old, parade past Roman ruins. They have begun their Fascist military training. (Photo: Wide World Photos)

the heritage of Imperial Rome. As the antithesis of the decadent materialism of Britain, France, and the United States, Italy would influence the world through the spread of Fascism, her millions of migrants in other lands, and her own might and empire.

Fascism promised a new society, and the government, like all totalitarian regimes, was loquacious about the new kind of person it

was creating—obedient, tough, efficient. Fascists and Mussolini himself seemed embarrassed by the stereotype of Italians as affectionate, volatile, inefficient, and artistic. Rome rather than the Renaissance, Machiavelli rather than Cavour, technology rather than opera were the traditions to be stressed.

Yet the new order in its twenty years did not remake Italy. Inconsistent policies and conflicts between party and bureaucracy added new inefficiencies, and neither government nor party overcame local customs of patronage or personal kindness. Despite the talk of discipline and sacrifice, Fascist rule produced the worst orgy of peculation Italy has ever known. The crude tyranny of Italian Fascism was not by twentieth-century standards outstandingly brutal, and the anti-Semitic policies borrowed from the Germans in the late 1930s never really took root. But freedom was crushed, the jails filled, hundreds of prominent figures exiled to dreary southern towns or desolate islands. The measure of the regime lies as much in the goals it sought as in its failure to achieve them.

Social, Religious, and Economic Policies

The government hoped to halt the rapid migration of peasants off the land into cities (a policy with clear appeal to rural employers), tried against all the best advice to increase the birth rate, and strove to make the Italian economy self-sufficient. But at the most it merely slowed the opposing trends. The regime did bring off some notable achievements, which it vigorously advertised. The Mafia was suppressed; the Pontine Marshes near Rome were drained and farmers moved into newly constructed houses there; new railroads were built and the service improved; some superhighways were started. An enormous amount of construction was sponsored by the state, usually in a monumental style, and archaeological excavations were favored as evocations of a glorious past. All these projects contributed to employment. In addition an elaborate program to enrich workers' leisure-time activities provided recreation halls, meeting rooms, and libraries in most towns as well as vacations for workers at seaside or mountain resorts. Family bonuses gave the poor an increased sense of security, and reforms of the educational system put more people in school for longer periods.

But Fascism's most publicized accomplishment was its accommodation with the Vatican. Although Mussolini and most of his early followers were thoroughly anticlerical, they soon found it worthwhile to appease Catholic interests. Crucifixes reappeared in the classrooms, chaplins were appointed to the Fascist militia, and the budget for clerical salaries and church repairs was increased. Until 1929, however, the regime had garnered only intangible benefits—the good will of many prominent Catholics and the church's failure to support antifascist movements.

Then, after lengthy and difficult negotiations, the Lateran agreements of 1929 were announced to the world. A formal treaty ended sixty years of conflict over Rome by establishing the tiny area of Vatican City within the capital as an independent state under papal sovereignty. And a concordat established religious teaching in Italian public schools, guaranteed that marriage laws would conform to Catholic doctrine, promised to restrict Protestant activities, and fixed a sum of more than $87 million as an indemnity to be paid by the state for church property confiscated during the unification of Italy.

Fascist prestige was at its height. The new agreements resolved a dispute that had seared the consciences of millions of Italians. Abroad the treaty seemed to suggest that fascism had won special favor from the papacy, and this impression was little dimmed by the sharp warning in an encyclical of 1931 against the paganism of worshiping the state or by subsequent conflicts over Catholic activities that competed with those of Fascist youth organizations. These conflicts were bitter, and relations between church and state never regained their former warmth. Still, Catholics and the Vatican were on the whole more generous in their attitude toward Mussolini's regime than they had been toward its liberal predecessors. The reduction of nineteenth-century hostilities between church and state remained one of Fascism's most important assets.

When Fascism came to power, two general principles seemed to govern its economic policy. The first was autarky, or national economic self-sufficiency, which emphasized industrialization and technological progress as the basis of military strength. The second, borrowed from socialism, favored national ownership while distrusting big business and a free market. Although this attitude was soon attenuated, the Fascist government remained more willing to intervene in the economy than its predecessors.

The government very early set the value of the lira to equal the French franc, a bid for prestige that hurt Italian exports. The accompanying import duties and credit restrictions then led to a painful deflation. In the interest of self-sufficiency and a more favorable balance of payments, the government launched its famous battle of grain in 1926. With enormous hoopla and a whole range of new incentives, Italy doubled her grain production by 1940—but only at the cost of more competitive agricultural production. Exports declined more than imports, and the official policy of autarky had a regressive effect. Output per capita declined in the fascist era.

As for big business, Fascist government proved in practice a sympathetic ally. In 1925 the leaders of Italian industry agreed to recognize only Fascist-led unions and were assured their traditional monopolistic autonomy in return. Generally the industrial giants in steel, automobiles, rubber, and chemicals found it easy to deal with (and often to manipulate) fascist bureaucracy. At the same time subsidies to weak industries, financed through the Institute for Industrial Reconstruction established in 1933, led to a significant extension of government ownership. The redistribution of land and tax reform were considered in high circles but not seriously attempted. By 1940, despite the early return to the nine-hour workday, real wages were down in both industry and agriculture, and the bureaucracy accepted a cut in salary though taxes remained high.

The Corporative State

Fascist theory and economic practice came together in the Corporative State, the most discussed aspect of fascism. By 1926 great confederations, or corporations, were established for major sectors of the economy (agriculture, commerce, industry, and so forth), each including a syndicate of employers and a syndicate of employees, a kind of official union. Both strikes and lockouts were prohibited, replaced by a grievance procedure through the corporations. The heads of syndicates were party members appointed by the government, and negotiations to establish industry-wide scales of wages were dominated by government and business. There was some basis for the Marxist charge that fascism was a device for protecting capitalists.

In 1928 the Fascist Grand Council—which included party chiefs, the heads of ministries, and leaders of parliament—became an organ of state whose duties included drawing up the list of candidates for election to the Chamber of Deputies, a list that the electorate (reduced to its wealthiest one-third) could only accept or reject as a whole. And in 1934 the number of corporations was fixed at twenty-two, each representing an entire sphere of production from extraction of raw material to manufacture and distribution.[3] For each corporation the Duce appointed a council consisting of delegates representing the syndicates and the separate phases of production (with Mussolini council president in every case), and all the

---

[3] The comprehensive intent of this organization is shown by the breadth of the twenty-two corporations, which were divided into three groups: I—grains, fruits and vegetables, wines, edible oils, beets and sugar, livestock, forestry and lumber, and textiles; II—metals, chemicals, clothing, paper and printing, construction, utilities, mining, and glass and pottery; III—insurance and banking, fine arts and liberal professions, sea and air transportation, land transportation, public entertainment, and public lodging.

councils together formed the National Council of Corporations. The importance of these institutions, however, was undercut by preparations for war and Mussolini's habit of legislating by decree. In principle this elaborate organization eliminated class conflict by unifying owners and workers behind the state; but the employers' syndicates maintained their traditional form and autonomy, and the workers' syndicates were not an extension of old unions but new organizations directed by the party. Both within the corporations and the Chamber the Fascist party was dominant, but Mussolini in turn was shrewdly alert to prevent the party from acquiring interests or policies of its own.

Resistance to Fascism

At first the new regime managed to associate some distinguished Italians with Fascism, men such as the poet Gabriele D'Annunzio, the sociologist Vilfredo Pareto, the composer Giacomo Puccini, and the playwright and novelist Luigi Pirandello. But relations with leaders in the arts and scholarly disciplines remained uneasy; many continued, as did Benedetto Croce, a quiet and safely intellectual opposition. Some, of whom the conductor Arturo Toscanini, the historian Gaetano Salvemini, and the physicist Enrico Fermi are best known to Americans, went into exile. In 1929 university rectors and deans had been required to join the party, and by 1931, when the government demanded that all professors sign a loyalty oath, only eleven refused. The government frightened most people into silence and broke up organized resistance; the remaining underground was centered in France and some secret communist groups in Italy. Internal opposition ceased to be a threat.

Within the country even the most skeptical were baffled by Mussolini's apparent successes and felt isolated and uncertain of what to believe. Indeed most Italians probably shared some pride in their nation's heightened prestige.

Outside Italy important groups in all European and many South American nations sang the praises of fascism's "bold experiment" that ended petty squabbling, ran the trains on time, kept order, and eliminated the threat of communism.

NAZI GERMANY

The Nazi regime was the most complete and terrifying achievement of totalitarianism, the beneficiary of an advanced economy and a strong administrative tradition in a society that emphasized status, regional particularism, and reciprocal distrust among Junkers, bureaucrats, professional men, and workers. Philosophies of the state were more fully developed and more widely accepted in Germany than elsewhere, as were theories that probed the weaknesses of liberalism, individualism, and rationalism. Racist ideas, current throughout Europe in the nineteenth century, won particular prominence and respectability there.

More immediately, Nazism profited from the unparalleled series of shocks German society had suffered since 1918. Defeat had brought charges of war guilt, a revolution, and a republic beloved by few. The drastic inflation of the 1920s had been followed by depression and the most extensive unemployment in Europe. German politics resounded with nationalist themes and cries of treachery, and the Weimar governments never managed to subordinate the army to civilian authority.

The Background of Nazism

Nazism itself differed from kindred movements elsewhere in its extraordinarily effective and daring leader, its simpler and more coherent ideology, and its well-organized party. As a young man, Adolf Hitler had gone to Vienna to become an artist. Rejected by the Academy, he had impressed those who knew him mainly by his bitterness and wild visions of vengeance.

World War I had been a kind of salvation for him, providing comradeship, a sense of purpose, and some status—he had been promoted to the rank of corporal. After the war he found brief employment in Munich spying on the small German Worker's party, which the army considered dangerously radical. Hitler took to addressing party rallies and began molding in the beer halls of Munich the speaking style and the personal party that in 1933 would make him Führer. His oratory combined brutal accusations with a messianic tone and repeated simple themes over and over in a spiraling frenzy, each sentence delivered with utter conviction and the menace of controlled violence.

Hitler borrowed ideas from the left and from nationalists. With none of Mussolini's experience in the world of ideological battles, he did not pretend to sophistication or subtlety. At the core of his vision were his concepts of race and universal struggle. The German people were suffering from vast conspiracies mounted by foreign powers, businessmen, Marxists, and Freemasons but above all Jews—the gutter anti-Semitism he had absorbed in Vienna was used to feed distrust of social change and provide simple explanations for any misfortune. The Jews were behind war profits, reparations, inflation, and depression; but Marxism was also Jewish, and communists were agents of the Jewish conspiracy. Internationalism and pacifism were Jewish ideas intended to destroy Germany as the bastion of Western (Aryan) civilization. Life was a desperate struggle won by the ruthless, and Germany must awake to her destiny. In Hitler's harangues Germany's defeat in World War I, the Versailles treaty, the weakness of the Weimar Republic, economic disasters, Red revolution, Jews, moral decay, and abstract art were somehow all connected in opposition to the German *Volk*, the people whose manly and primitive virtues must be welded into an irresistible force behind one leader. Admirers of an older culture, monarchists, and believers in order were invited to join the angry patriots and the unemployed in the new movement.

When in 1923 Hitler had led the party (now called the National Socialist German Workers' party) in the Munich *Putsch*, Germany was racked by many similar movements; yet the revolt had been an immediate failure. The book Hitler wrote in prison, *Mein Kampf*, became the party bible. More self-exposure than anything else, it is a turbulent and repetitious outpouring of his political views intermixed with naive but demoniac statements about how human beings are manipulated by fear, big lies, and simplistic explanations. Even in its cynicism, *Mein Kampf* touched on all the frustrations of modern German life while de-emphasizing the party's earlier, more leftist program. In prison and after his release in 1925 Hitler worked to reorganize and strengthen the party. He added the SS, an elite corps in black uniforms serving as his bodyguard and as a special police force, to the SA, the brown-shirted Storm troopers who were one of the more fearsome of the street armies. Some ideas and useful phrases were contributed to Nazi thought by Moeller van den Bruck, a literary figure respected in conservative circles, whose *The Third Reich* advocated revolution in behalf of a new, corporative and nationalist regime. The party established its own newspaper, edited by Alfred Rosenberg, which propagandized vigorously; and in 1930 Rosenberg would expand the canon of Nazi doctrine with his *The Myth of the Twentieth Century*, a wordy, turgid exposition of Hitler's racist ideas.

Nazism thus developed an ideology and the organizations to express it; yet until 1933 its crude appeal enjoyed only modest success. In 1928 the party's 60,000 members were still not enough to have much weight in German politics. It had some notable assets, however, and was establishing more. General von Ludendorff had joined Hitler in the 1923 *Putsch,* and there remained the possibility that other officers would cooperate, despite their contempt for the rabble to whom the Nazis appealed. Some circles of Bavarian conservatives and Rhineland industrialists showed interest in the movement, and in 1929 the Nazis gained national prominence by loudly promoting the petition against the Young Plan. Four million Germans declared it high treason not to renounce the "war guilt clause" of the Versailles treaty or to agree to any further reparations.

Hitler's intensity, fits of temper, and frequent bad manners offended many, but others felt the fascination of a personality that radiated power and could at times be charming. Early in the movement's history he gathered that small group of absolutely loyal men who would rule the Nazi state until its defeat: Hermann Göring, an air ace; Joseph Goebbels, journalist and party propagandist; and Heinrich Himmler. Dedicated fanatics, they worked ceaselessly to enlarge the party, orchestrate the impressive rallies inspired by Hitler's fertile sense of tactical possibilities, and spread Nazi doctrine.

The Nazis were gaining. In 1930 they became the second largest party in the Reichstag, and the following year Hitler reached an understanding with a group of Rhineland industrialists who promised to pay the party's election deficits and to provide funds for its growing armies. (Leading Nazis critical of capitalism were shunted aside.) Like Mussolini, whom he greatly admired, Hitler combined the attractions of revolution and social order, appealed to the lower classes, and reassured the respectable. To a society broken by the Depression, the party promised recovery, with higher agricultural prices for the peasants and more employment for workers (tens of thousands of whom found jobs in the SS and SA).

Nazi demonstrations, like this great rally in Nuremberg in 1938, were triumphs of mass theater. (Photo: Wide World Photos)

Hitler guaranteed as well to rebuild the army and save society from the Reds. In 1931 rightwing nationalists, some industrialists, and an important group of militarists joined the Nazis in a manifesto denouncing the "cultural Bolshevism" of the Weimar Republic and the threat of Marxism, hinting that when the Nazis seized power, they would protect only those who joined them now. They had learned to speak simultaneously like a government already in office and an underworld gang. Their propaganda and their menace increased, and they expressed their seriousness of purpose by beating up Jews and socialists.

Collapse of the Weimar Republic

The Social Democrats, who had gained in the elections of 1928, led the government that faced the Great Depression. Without great imagination, they did the best they could, but their majority in the Reichstag was shaky, and President von Hindenburg refused to authorize decree powers. In 1930 the government resigned, to be replaced by the Center party's Heinrich Brüning, a cautious, sober man with little popular appeal whom Hindenburg allowed to rule by decree for most of his years as chancellor. The elections of 1930 increased by over a hundred the number of Nazi deputies contemptuously ready to disrupt the Reichstag, and Hitler was so impressed with these successes that he became a presidential candidate when Hindenburg's term expired in 1932. Worried politicians persuaded the field marshal to run for reelection, and he won handily, but Hitler had over 13 million votes on the second ballot against the senile, eighty-four-year-old Hindenburg, now pathetically cast as the defender of the constitution. When Brüning proposed the expropriation of some East Prussian estates as part of a program of financial reform, the president dismissed him. Brüning, who proved to have been the Weimar Republic's last chance, had lost the confidence of nearly every segment of the Reichstag.

The subsequent period of palace intrigue led to Hitler. Hindenburg turned to Franz von Papen, a self-confident friend of important army officers and Junkers. Hoping to establish a conservative coalition of industrialists, Junkers, and the military, von Papen lifted Brüning's ban on the SA and SS, named four barons and a count to his cabinet, and declared martial law in Prussia, a step that was in effect a coup d'état to unseat the socialist government there.

Hindenburg then called new elections, which produced a Nazi landslide. With 230 seats they constituted some 40 percent of the Reichstag's membership and thus by far its largest party. He could find no chancellor but Hitler, who insisted on full decree powers. The field marshal refused and sent the nation to the polls again, but while the Nazis lost some seats, they remained the largest party. Hindenburg next appointed as chancellor General Kurt von Schleicher, a conventional army man who made an easy target for the abuse of Nazis, communists, and the disgruntled von Papen. Hoping to use Hitler's popularity, von Papen then led the men of Hindenburg's coterie in urging Hitler to serve as chancellor in a coalition government. The unsuccessful leader of a Munich *Putsch* ten years before took the oath of office late in January 1933.

Although he came to office legally, Hitler's arrival marked a further breakdown in the German political system. The Nazis increasingly won the votes of the right, and while the ballots cast for Marxist parties remained nearly constant, the Communist share increased. Yet no party now seemed capable of establishing a reliable majority in the Reichstag. Of the twelve men in Hitler's cabinet, only two others were Nazis, and the men around Hindenburg imagined they could use the demagogue and then discard him. Instead the Nazis established their dictatorship within two months.

Seeking to increase the party's strength, Hitler called for another election almost immediately on assuming the chancellorship. The campaign that followed was one of systematic terror, especially in Prussia, where Hermann Göring was now minister-president and the police were used as principal electoral agents. The climax came with the burning of the Reichstag, a fire that the Nazis probably set but that they loudly blamed on the communists. Hindenburg agreed to issue special laws, Ordinances for the Protection of the German

State and Nation, that ended most civil liberties, including freedom of the press and assembly. The voters gave the Nazis 44 percent of the seats, which, when combined with those of nationalist allies in other parties, assured them a bare majority.

Hitler pressed on. Communists were expelled from the Reichstag, conservatives wooed with calls to nationalism, and Center party members won over with promises to respect the privileges of the Catholic Church. In March Hitler dared to demand a special enabling act giving him as chancellor the right for four years to enact all laws and treaties independent of constitutional restraints. Of the 566 deputies left in the Reichstag, only 94 Social Democrats (out of 121) voted no. Blandishment and terror had done their work, but the tragedy went deeper: German politics offered no clear alternative to Hitler.

The Nazi regime moved quickly. It established concentration camps, first on private estates and then in larger and more permanent institutions. By July all parties except the National Socialist had been outlawed, and soon all other political organizations disappeared. In the elections of November 1933, the Nazis won more than 90 percent of the vote. They proceeded to restructure the administration of government, purge the civil service and judiciary, outlaw strikes, and clamp stricter controls on the press. In a few months Hitler had won fuller power than Mussolini had managed in years.

At this point the chancellor's most serious potential opposition was within his own party. Hitler's solution was barbarically simple. On a long weekend in June 1934, Ernst Röhm and Gregor Strasser, leaders of the Nazi left wing who took seriously the socialist aims of a Nazi revolution, were shot or stabbed. So, among hundreds of others, were General von Schleicher and his wife, some Catholic leaders, some socialists, and some taken by mistake. The Night of the Long Knives, directed primarily by the SS, meant the destruction of any serious leftist element within the party. Hitler admitted to some 74 deaths; subsequent estimates raise the figure to as many as a thousand. That summer weekend proved that any horror was possible, and the purge, like the noisy accusations of homosexuality that accompanied it, established the tone of Germany's new totalitarianism. When Hindenburg died in August, Germans voted overwhelmingly in a referendum to unite the presidency and the chancellorship in the person of Hitler, who took the occasion to assume officially the title of Führer ("Leader").

Administration and the Economy

The government undertook a systematic administrative reorganization. Called *Gleichschaltung* ("coordination"), the plan extended to all national functions and could be used against any institution or individual considered likely to inhibit the Führer's will. The federal states lost their autonomy, and the Nazi party extended its function, establishing administrative *Gaue* ("regions"). The party Gauleiter, or regional director, might or might not be the appointed governor. This duplication of state organizations was carried further in Germany than in Italy; the party even formed its own office of foreign affairs as well as a secret police, the Gestapo, which infiltrated both the bureaucracy and the army. A law of March 1933, which had expelled Jews from public service and universities, had made all government employees appointees of the Führer. New people's courts heard secret trials of cases of treason, now very broadly defined, and rewritten statutes allowed prosecution for intent as well as for overt acts. Arrest and detention without charge or trial became a regular practice.

In its economic policies the Nazi regime scored impressive successes, especially at first. Unemployment, the crying problem of German

NUMBER OF WORKERS OFFICIALLY LISTED AS UNEMPLOYED AS A PERCENTAGE OF WORKING AGE (15–64) POPULATION

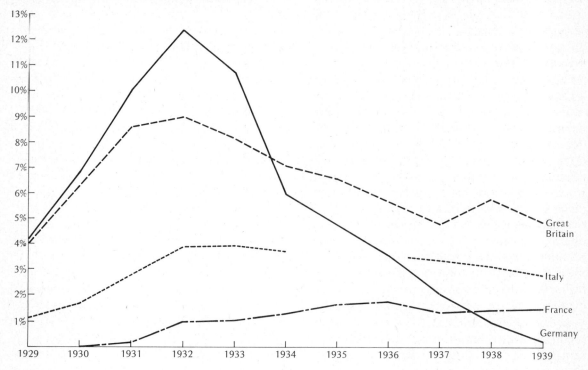

life, dropped steadily as the result of great public works projects—the construction of highways, public housing, and government offices, the reclamation of swamps and reforestation—many using special labor battalions, in which one year's service was soon made compulsory. Later the burgeoning armaments industry and a growing military establishment eliminated the problem of joblessness entirely. By spending money while more traditional governments thought it essential to balance their budgets, the Nazis reduced unemployment more effectively than any Western nation. But such programs were expensive, and they were paid for in several ways.

The government restricted internal movements of men and goods and controlled foreign trade, directing that payments be made with special marks whose value altered according to the goods and the nations involved. This currency scheme was largely the work of Hjalmar Schacht, a financial wizard who though never a Nazi contributed his skills to the new Germany. Imports were reduced, which lowered the living standard in some sectors and raised costs in many others, as part of a policy intended to make Germany as economically self-sufficient as possible. Trade thus became a weapon in international relations; Germany bought produce and raw materials from the Balkan countries, for example, at prices well above the world market but with marks redeemable only through the purchase of German manufactured products. Tantamount to barter, this system increased Germany's influence in countries dependent on her for trade.

The Nazis gained additional revenues out of property confiscated from Jews, high taxes, forced loans, and carefully staged campaigns urging patriotic Germans to contribute their personal jewelry to the state. A four-year plan launched in 1936 was directed toward economic self-sufficiency rather than domestic wealth, for by then the German state was organizing for war. Ultimately the government would cover these growing costs by printing paper currency, the effects of which would long be hidden by a war economy and the exploitation of conquered lands. By 1945 the mark would have fallen to about 1 percent of its 1933 value.

Labor policies also produced visible gains while increasing government control. Outlawing strikes reassured business without gravely damaging wage levels that unemployment would have kept from rising. The National Labor Front, which included all workers and management, froze wages and directed personnel in the interests of business and government, but it was accompanied by an extensive array of benefits. All welfare programs, including plans previously regional or private, were taken over by the state, which claimed full credit for the funds and services provided from them. A Strength Through Joy program sent German workers to summer camps or on special cruises, furnishing pleasures once available only to the well-to-do. The workers' share in an expanding economy may have declined, but workers were grateful for jobs and vacations and perhaps for the sense of their own importance all the propaganda conveyed.

The professional military had reasons of its own for gratitude to the Nazi regime: disregarding the disarmament clauses of the Treaty of Versailles (he would repudiate them formally in 1935), Hitler had set about openly and rapidly rearming Germany on becoming chancellor. While regular officers remained resentful of Nazi paramilitary organizations and disdainful of their social inferiors who now directed the state, they nevertheless appreciated the emphasis on fighting strength, and they accepted the oath of personal loyalty to Hitler required of them after he had been voted into the presidency. With the return of universal compulsory service in 1935 and the creation of an air force, Germany was soon spending several times as much on arms as Britain and France combined.

In 1938, strengthened by his diplomatic successes, Hitler asserted control more directly, removing the minister of war, the chief of staff, and more than a dozen generals. They were not merely fired but disgraced amid public tales of private vice. Baron Konstantin von Neurath, a nationalist of the old school in office as foreign minister since 1933, was replaced by Joachim von Ribbentrop, a good Nazi and no aristocrat at all. The Nazi hold on both the foreign service and the army, traditional strongholds of conservatives and aristocrats, now seemed secure.

Religious and Racial Policies

The churches presented a less tractable problem. A concordat with the Vatican in July 1933 gave the state some voice in the appointment of bishops while guaranteeing that Catholic orders and schools would be unmolested. The Protestant denominations agreed to form a new body, the Evangelical Church, under a national bishop; but when the man Hitler chose as bishop tried to "Aryanize" it, dissidents formed the separate Confessional Church. In 1935 the minister for Church Affairs was given the power to confiscate ecclesiastical property, withhold funds, and have pastors arrested. Thereafter the state fought the churches pri-

Nazi propaganda against the Jews, Catholics, and wealthy reactionaries who would subvert the Führer was disseminated by earnest young party members. (Photo: Keystone)

marily through steady harassment of individual ministers by local authorities.

Some priests and ministers cooperated with the regime, enthusiastically adopting even the pagan accretions it encouraged. But most resisted at least the more outrageous demands made of them, and individual voices spoke out against Nazism clearly and courageously. In 1937 Martin Niemoeller, the leader of the Confessional Church, was arrested for his opposition to Nazism; and Pope Pius XI condemned both the deification of the state and Nazi racial doctrine. In the following years some Catholic churches were burned, members of religious orders were frequently brought to trial on morals charges, and the claims of the Hitler Youth—the Nazi organization for adolescents—challenged religious education. The churches, although not centers of organized resistance, still permitted individuals some escape from the incessant pressures of totalitarianism.

Building a Nazi State

From the beginning the Nazis' publicity had been flamboyant, their posters striking, and their rallies well-staged; after the movement came to power, propaganda became a way of life. Torchlight parades, chorused shouts of *"Sieg Heil!"* ("Hail to victory!"), book burnings, the evocation of Norse gods, schoolyard calisthenics, the return to Gothic script: a thousand such events sought to give each citizen a feeling of participating, of being swept up—and implicated—in some great historical transformation. Joseph Goebbels at the Reich Chamber of Culture saw to it that cinema, theater, literature, art, and music all became instruments for promoting Nazism. Things primitive and brutal were praised as Aryan; one who opposed or even doubted the Führer ceased to be German.

The relentless logic and dynamism of totalitarianism showed most clearly in the government's racial policy. Nazism had always made much of its anti-Semitism, and the Nuremberg laws of 1935 not only removed Jews from the public service (anyone with one or more Jewish grandparents was considered a Jew) but declared Jews no longer citizens and prohibited marriage or sexual intercourse between Jews and Aryans. Subsequently Jews were expelled from one activity after another, required to register with the state, and give their children identifiably Jewish names. The murder of a German diplomat by a young Jewish boy in 1938 touched off a new round of terror. Many Jews were arrested, and the SS led an orgy of violence in which Jews were beaten and murdered, their synagogues burned, their homes and businesses smashed. A fine of 1 billion marks was levied on the Jews of Germany, and this was followed by still further measures to humiliate and isolate them; they were barred from the theater and concerts, forbidden to buy jewelry, forced to sell their businesses or property, denied access to certain streets, and made to wear a yellow star. Worse would come, for totalitarianism could never fulfill its vision of unanimity and total security any more than it could forgo violence. Warfare seemed its natural state.

COMMUNIST RUSSIA

Fascists insisted that only they could prevent the triumph of communism, but they learned much from the Soviet example of a revolu-

As part of its anti-Semitic policy the German government forced Jews to wear yellow stars on their clothing for immediate identification. It was the mildest of the government's discriminatory tactics. (Photo: The Bettmann Archive)

tionary movement using dictatorial powers to direct an entire society. For communists on the other hand dictatorship was incidental and supposedly temporary; and to many in Russia and in the West the Soviet Union remained the antithesis and the only consistent opponent of fascism, despite the resemblance to fascist political systems in its enforcement of ideology through a single party, its use of compulsion and terror, and its deification of the party leader. Lenin's death in January 1924 proved a turning point. For as issues of policy and leadership were slowly resolved, Joseph Stalin emerged as one of history's most effective dictators.

For more than a year, Lenin had been nearly incapacitated, but his prestige had precluded any public scramble for power, and many expected a more relaxed rule by committee to follow. In a famous letter Lenin had assessed two likely successors: Trotsky, whom he called the best man in the Politburo, though overconfident; and Stalin, whom Lenin found "too rude" though an able organizer (Stalin already held enormous power as general secretary of the party's Central Committee).

Over the next three years, Russia's leaders publicly debated the complex issues of communist theory and practical policy. Trotsky led those who clung to the traditional vision of revolution spreading across Europe, and he thus favored an uncompromising radical program at home and abroad. Stalin's stand was that the Soviet Revolution could and must survive alone through "revolution in one country." No theoretician and little informed about the world outside Russia, Stalin was not wholly at ease in these debates with more intellectual and experienced opponents. But they in turn underestimated his single-minded determination. His argument was formally adopted by the Politburo in December 1925.

Stalin used his position with skill. He was the link between the Politburo and the party organization below it, and he could count on the loyalty of party officials, many of whom he had appointed. He played effectively on personal antagonisms and on the bad feelings created by Trotsky's tactless arrogance. When the Politburo elected three new members at that December meeting, all were Stalin's associates.

Leading opponents of Stalin on the left began to cooperate with Trotsky in public agitation, but Stalin made each such move seem a threat to party solidarity and Communist rule itself. Although Grigori Zinoviev had supported Stalin, his position as head of the Comintern—the Third International—gave him independent power. He and Trotsky were expelled from the Politburo in 1926 and from the party itself in 1927. The left was broken, and Zinoviev recanted his "mistake" the following year. So did Nikolai Bukharin, perhaps the party's subtlest theoretician and a leader of the right, who believed Russia's social transformation must necessarily be slow. Trotsky, who tenaciously refused to change his mind, was exiled and then deported, continuing from abroad his criticism of Stalin's growing dictatorship.

It may seem odd that these men, all veterans of the October Revolution, did not attempt to oust Stalin; even Trotsky, who had built the Red army, never tried to use it against him. But these old Bolsheviks fervently accepted the need for party loyalty and revolutionary unity. Stalin, who favored the younger and less intellectual party members, made the most of this mystique to assure that the open debates of those years were not allowed again.

The Five-Year Plans

The First Five-Year Plan, launched in 1928, was a daring program that reflected some of the qualities that had brought Stalin to the top. It shamelessly incorporated ideas and suggestions Stalin had denounced when his opponents had put them forth just months before, but it was thoroughly his in its bold assumption that Russia could transform herself into an industrial power by mobilizing her every resource.

By 1928 Russian production had regained prewar levels in most sectors, but the recovery had come through serious concessions to free enterprise. Lenin's New Economic Policy had depended heavily on private entrepreneurs in commerce, the so-called NEP men, and on peasant owners in agriculture. The task now was to change the very nature of the economy itself by socializing it on both fronts.

As a first step the plan inaugurated the collectivization of agriculture, a measure with multiple aims: to bring socialism to the countryside; to increase production by spreading the improved techniques and the mechanization that peasants had on the whole resisted; and to give the state control over agricultural output, enabling it to feed industrial workers and to sell produce abroad so it could pay for the imported machinery industrialization required.

Although Russian peasants had many traditions of common effort, they bitterly resisted collectivization despite inducements of equipment and credit. Poor by international standards, perhaps 4 or 5 percent of them nonetheless had the means to hire labor and lend money within their villages, which gave them a hold over the entire economy. Significantly these farmer-employers would come to be called kulaks, the old, pejorative term for grasping merchants and usurers.

As agricultural prices fell—though others soared—peasants withheld their goods from the market. Famine threatened, and the government, blaming the kulaks, mounted a sweeping campaign of propaganda and police action against them. It seized their grain (informers were given a quarter of any hoard uncovered), killed hundreds of thousands of kulaks, and deported untold numbers of them to till the unbroken soil of Siberia. Meanwhile peasants destroyed crops and animals rather than let the government have them. The antagonisms of rural society were thus proving unexpectedly explosive, and Stalin had to intervene in 1930 to halt what had escalated to virtual civil war. By then more than half the peasants had joined collective farms, but the losses in animal power

Russia's First Five-Year Plan was responsible for the look of anticipation on the faces of these villagers; they are about to switch on the first electric light bulb ever to appear in Bryansk Province (1928). (Photo: Novosti Press Agency)

and able farmers had hurt production severely. Serious famine in 1932–1933 showed how badly the First Five-Year Plan had failed to reach its goals in agriculture.

The pattern of collectivization that then emerged proved to be a durable compromise. Even on collective farms peasants were permitted individual plots and privately owned tools. Larger machinery was concentrated at Machine Tractor Stations, which became the rural base for agricultural agents and party officials—modernization and political supervision went hand in hand. By 1933 output was sufficiently controlled to permit the government to concentrate on the central aim of the plan: the most massive and rapid industrialization in history.

According to the five-year forecast, industrial production was to double in less than five years and in some critical areas, such as electrical power, to increase sixfold. More than 1,500 new factories were to be put into operation, including large automobile and tractor plants; and there were projects on a still grander scale, among them a Dnieper River power station and a great coal and iron complex in a whole new city, Magnitogorsk. These goals would be met somewhat ahead of schedule, and there would be only slight exaggeration in the government's proud claim to have made Russia an industrial nation almost overnight.

All this had to be financed internally, and it was paid for primarily by the dead, displaced, and collectivized peasants. Indirect tolls were levied on the rest of the populace as well. Workers' wages were increased only slightly, and the plan postponed improvements in even such basic facilities as housing and rail service. Food and then most consumer items were rationed, with allotments varying according to one's contribution to the plan.

Most Russian laborers, unskilled or poorly trained, were unaccustomed to the pace now required; thus their rate of turnover was high, the quality of their work poor, and their output per man-hour low. The state resorted to a continuous workweek—multiple shifts kept the precious machines going—and moved special "shock brigades" of abler workers from plant to plant as a stimulus to higher production. Women and young people were urged into industrial jobs. "Socialist competition" pitted groups of workers and whole factories against each other for bonuses and prizes, and piecework payment, once a hated symbol of capitalist avarice, became increasingly common. Violators of shop rules were fined; indolence,

malingering, pilfering, and sabotage, often loosely defined, became crimes against the state. Punishment frequently included time in a corrective labor camp, so that what had initially been a mode of prison reform became another means of getting more work done.

Many of the essential managers and engineers were foreigners, but the government was eager for Russia to supply her own talent. Special courses were established in factories, and the numbers enrolled in the higher technical schools trebled. This training, like the quality of goods produced, was often inferior, but it laid a base for the future.

The plan's sober goals required a stability and discipline that led to the sacrifice of some earlier enthusiasms. In schools the formal examinations, homework, and academic degrees, once abolished, began to return; and classroom democracy gave way before the strengthened authority of the teacher. By the 1930s the virtue of marriage was being emphasized, divorce and abortion discouraged, and prolific families specially rewarded.

The five-year programs, which had taken years to devise, had to be constantly amended, requiring the development of new skills, detailed reports on every sector of the economy, and above all increased authority for the planners themselves.

The great venture mobilized every aspect of society. Associations of writers, musicians, and artists worked with party help to establish the themes and styles of propaganda useful to the plan. Mass organizations of youth and workers met for indoctrination, and kulaks and church were subject to renewed attacks. Within the party itself criticism or even skepticism about any aspect of the plan was akin to treason; hundreds of thousands of party members were expelled, and new recruits were carefully screened for absolute reliability. The state used propaganda, mass organizations, and secret police to create unanimity. "Overful-fillment" was announced in 1932, but the miracle of industrialization also marked the creation of a Russian totalitarianism holding together a society rent by rapid change. The very purpose of society seemed to lie in the statistics of production quotas met.

Growth in the Prewar Decade

The Second (1933–1937) and Third (1938–1942) Five-Year plans were continuations of the First at somewhat lower pressure. Although the emphasis on industrialization continued, the rate of capital investment was reduced, consumer goods became more available, and rationing was eliminated by 1936. Standards of quality rose, and there were new undertakings as well. Dramatic improvement in transportation, especially domestic aviation, made previously remote territories accessible and led to the serious exploitation of Arctic regions. Partly for reasons of military security, industrialization east of the Ural Mountains was stressed.

By 1939 Soviet Russia ranked third among the world's industrial producers, behind only the United States and Germany. That year she produced twenty-four times more electrical power and five times more coal and steel than in 1913. Housing and clothes were improving, though the Russian standard of living remained low compared to the West. Seven years of compulsory schooling for all remained a goal yet to be met, but the literate population had grown from less than 50 percent of those over school age in 1926 to more than 80 percent in 1939; enrollment in higher schools had trebled and the number and size of libraries and hospitals more than doubled. In these years one-seventh of the population moved to the cities, where a higher proportion lived than ever before, and over 90 percent of peasant households were on collective farms serviced by the Machine Tractor Stations.

Russia, the government proudly announced, had reached the stage of socialism, and this justified a new constitution in 1936. The changes it made were mainly formal. Direct voting by secret ballot replaced the cumbersome indirect elections, the government explained, now that the reactionary classes had ceased to exist. The body thus elected was the Soviet of the Union, one of two houses of the Supreme Soviet; the other, the Soviet of the Nationalities, represented the republics. The Supreme Soviet elected the Presidium, which legislated most of the time and whose chairman was head of state, and the Council of Ministers, the executive arm (the revolutionary term Commissars thus passed away). The constitution divided some of the larger federal republics, making eleven in all, and on paper at least left them considerable autonomy. It provided social and political guarantees that communists hailed as the most democratic in the world, and it officially noted the special position of the Communist party as "the vanguard of the working people." When new elections were held, 96 percent of the population voted, 98 percent of it for the single list the party presented in most constituencies.

Stalinism

With the new constitution many expected an easing of political controls. Amnesty had been granted some political prisoners in 1935, and the sinister secret police in operation since 1922 had been replaced by a somewhat more controlled political police, the NKVD. The campaign against religion was abating, and the white-collar classes and leaders generally were being honored—the military had officers again, and foremen were returning to factories. Opportunities for advancement in this modernizing society were great, and special awards recognized those who excelled. But tyranny remained, justified by the dangers of "capitalist encirclement."

The ubiquitous Stalin: his picture was encountered everywhere, even afloat at this Russian beach resort. (Photo: Sovfoto)

Soviet art and literature became timid; music perhaps fared better, notably in the sophisticated and dynamic works of Dmitri Shostakovich and of Sergei Prokofiev. If intellectuals were harassed less in the later 1930s than during the First Five-Year Plan, they had long since learned the necessity of caution. The Russian Academy of Science, as lavish in its support of some research as it was arbitrarily unfriendly to others, was never far from politics.

At the center of Soviet society stood Stalin, increasingly adulated. He was honored as leader and expert in every activity; works of arts were dedicated to him, factories named after him, his picture everywhere. His authority was virtually absolute, even though until 1941 he held no official position other than party secretary. Patriotism overshadowed the socialist internationalism of an earlier generation, and Soviet achievement was presented as the culmination of a long Russian development. Stalin was taking his place with Ivan the Terrible and Peter the Great among the molders of Russia.

That his power exceeded theirs showed in the great purges of the late 1930s, directed against very disparate people—engineers, Ukrainian separatists, former Mensheviks, party members —accused of being counterrevolutionaries. They were touched off by the assassination in 1934 of Sergei Kirov, who had been close to Stalin, and a member of the Politburo, an event treated as part of a large conspiracy but probably the act of young communists who admired some of Stalin's old opponents, especially Zinoviev. Zinoviev and members of the "left opposition" were tried for treason and imprisoned in 1935, tried again, and executed in 1937. Their trials were followed by others, always public: party leaders and army officers in 1937 and members of the "right opposition," Nikolai Bukharin and other old Bolsheviks, in 1939.

To the outside world the indictments seemed vague and the evidence unconvincing; yet the accused consistently confessed—and disappeared. Perhaps their admissions of guilt were merely the result of torture, but they also seemed a final act of faith by men who had always believed that anyone resisting the inevitable course of history was "objectively" a traitor.

Russia was profoundly shaken by the purges and the reign of terror, which, like the earlier campaign against the kulaks, swept the country until in 1939 Stalin once again called a halt. The dead were countless; jails and labor camps were bursting with prisoners—perhaps 10 million. More than twice that many had gone into exile. Russia's leaders, except for Stalin, were primarily from a new generation of men who had made their whole careers under communism. And the institutions and techniques of Soviet totalitarianism had grown ominously like those of Germany and Italy, even though their raison d'être was a much more fundamental transformation of society. Only in the values she professed did Russia remain closer to the humane traditions of European civilization, and it was not clear in 1939 what part the isolated and untested nation would play as Western democracy faced its greatest challenge.

III. THE DEMOCRACIES' RESPONSE

Where democracy survived the Depression, the results were unimpressive. Parties of the right center pursued sound finance and embittered the unemployed; liberals reluctantly jettisoned old principles to support higher tariffs and subsidies for business and agriculture; socialists resentfully compromised welfare projects for better-balanced budgets. Even where strong at the polls, the left was politically weakened by the fratricidal conflict between communists and socialists. If voters turned toward the militant left or the radical right, the political system became unworkable, and governments resorted to decree powers and bans on extreme parties. By the mid-1930s, when there were some promising signs of new ideas, policies, and political coalitions, international dangers brought further divisions and worse crises.

DOMESTIC UNCERTAINTY

Slow economic recovery underscored important social changes. Agriculture was becoming more productive as it became more mechanized and scientific. Better transportation, mechanical refrigeration, cheaper clothes, and more leisure were clearly raising standards of living as well as changing life styles. Throughout Europe the middle classes recouped much of the status and security threatened by inflation and depression. University enrollment, still a privilege of class, rose higher than ever before —highest in France, it rose to almost 2 percent of college-age youth in Scandinavia, Britain, Italy, and Germany (where it dropped sharply after the Nazis came to power). But small business and craft industry had suffered much more than the larger corporations, the first to benefit from the economic upturn. Economic life was clearly dominated by large-scale production and large organizations, including more

NUMBER OF MOTOR VEHICLES

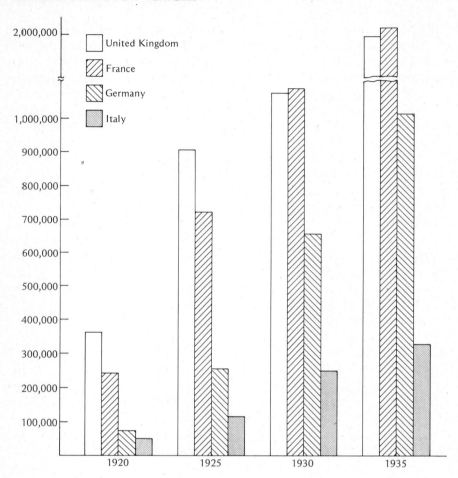

By 1935 France and the United Kingdom had one vehicle for every twenty people.

effective trade unions. Women, usually paid less than men, were now an accepted part of the industrial work force, constituting from one-quarter to one-third of such workers in the more industrialized countries; their incomes contributed to their chances for independence as well as to their families' well-being. If workers generally enjoyed a forty-hour week with more leisure time and more ways of spending it, work itself was more subject to "American" efficiency; foremen maintained relentless discipline to keep production moving at a pace set by machines.

Technology now seemed a mixed blessing even as talking motion pictures and radio did much to bridge the gap between urban and rural life and to build a popular culture common to all classes. The very form of prosperity thus stimulated discontent among intellectu-

**APPROXIMATE NUMBER OF RADIOS LICENSED FOR EVERY 100 PEOPLE
IN TWENTY SELECTED COUNTRIES (1938)**

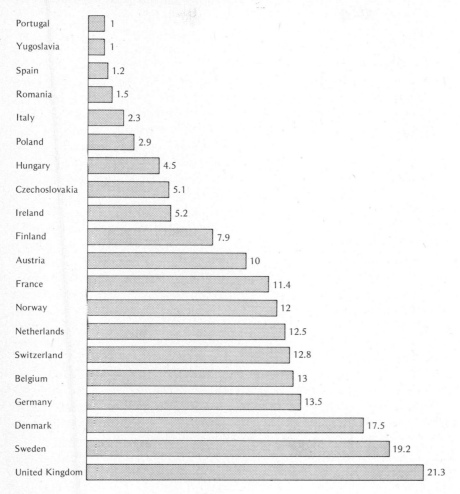

Portugal	1
Yugoslavia	1
Spain	1.2
Romania	1.5
Italy	2.3
Poland	2.9
Hungary	4.5
Czechoslovakia	5.1
Ireland	5.2
Finland	7.9
Austria	10
France	11.4
Norway	12
Netherlands	12.5
Switzerland	12.8
Belgium	13
Germany	13.5
Denmark	17.5
Sweden	19.2
United Kingdom	21.3

als disdainful of mass culture, small business-men frightened at their precarious position, and workers who disliked the conditions under which they worked and resented their limited share of national wealth. The transformation of Russian society or even the symbolic gains of better-lit factories and vacation resorts for workers glorified through propaganda in Germany and Italy, as well as the elimination of strikes there, thus contrasted with aimless dislocation in the West. Wherever freedom per-

The statistics suggest that most families in the United Kingdom had a radio, that nearly everyone could sometimes hear the radio in Finland and Austria, and that from Italy to Portugal, millions of people only heard the radio on special occasions when speakers blared in public places.

mitted, political conflict both reflected and contributed to social division.

Among the smaller democracies Switzerland, socially the most conservative, and Sweden, which combined social welfare programs and a mixed economy, fared the best. Finland and Czechoslovakia, whose economic growth and political freedom had made them models of the new postwar nations, suffered from divisions almost as grave as those that would drive Spain to civil war. At the same time, Britain and France were beset by fumbling governments that made an embarrassing contrast with the dynamic totalitarian regimes.

Great Britain

The British political system in the 1930s was able to resist the drift to extremes, but domestic moderation resulted as much from a breakdown in party structures as from political skill. The elections of 1929 had made Ramsay MacDonald prime minister again in a Labour cabinet, but neither Labour nor its Liberal allies could find acceptable remedies for the Depression. A special commission in 1931 recommended drastic economies, as financial experts in the 1930s usually did, but these required cuts in welfare and unemployment payments intolerable to most of Labour. The cabinet itself divided, and then MacDonald announced to his stunned followers the formation of a national government, including members of all three parties. MacDonald and his followers were expelled from the Labour party, his "treachery" a source of recriminations that nearly destroyed it.

Helped by ineffectual opposition, the national government won overwhelmingly in the subsequent elections; but the coalition had become a disguise for conservative rule. MacDonald nonetheless remained prime minister, weathering riots and a mutiny that greeted reduced budgets and battling the economic crisis with controls on foreign exchange and increased tariffs that split the Liberal party. When MacDonald resigned in 1935, tired and unloved, his government had overseen a slow recovery of the British economy, redefined imperial relations, and initiated some cautious steps toward

government planning. It had done so by pursuing others' policies and in the process struck a devastating blow to the proletarian movement to which MacDonald had devoted his life.

MacDonald was followed by the Conservative Stanley Baldwin, who returned for his third prime ministership armored in the complacent virtues of the middle class. His considerable political gifts masked a habit of indecision, but he easily won the elections of 1935 thanks to a divided opposition and to strong statements in favor of the League of Nations, in which he actually had little deep interest. The Parliament elected the same year would continue through 1945, the longest-lived in modern history, and the impressive talent it would prove to contain testified to the continued vitality of British political life.

But the lack of imaginative leadership in the 1930s was remarkable. As international affairs grew more ominous, the uncertainty of British policy further weakened democratic governments in Europe. One issue, however, was resolved with vigor. King Edward VIII, who acceded to the throne in 1936, was determined to marry an American divorcee; and when he abdicated, as Baldwin and the archbishop of Canterbury insisted he must, the transition to George VI went smoothly, an assertion of tradition that averted the crisis widely predicted. When Baldwin retired in 1937, his successor was his earnest Chancellor of the Exchequer, Neville Chamberlain, who was convinced that from his high office he could preserve peace in Europe.

France

The Depression hit France later and less severely than other highly industrialized countries, but when the decline came, it lasted. Politically she faced not so much a single crisis as myriad smaller problems that exhausted the old answers and undermined confidence. By the mid-1930s Frenchmen seemed more bitterly divided than at any time since the Dreyfus affair.

The left won the legislative elections of 1932 as the economic slump began to be felt, but the Socialist members refused to participate in bourgeois governments. The Radical Socialists (who were really moderate republicans) remained therefore the dominant party and sought allies toward the center and the right. Ironically the left's electoral victory thus produced unstable governments committed to reducing expenditures and protecting established interests. Outside the Chambers rightist factions, including the fascist Croix de Feu ("Cross of Fire"), grew increasingly noisy. Demonstrations led by their uniformed militants before the Chamber of Deputies building on February 6, 1934, produced more bloodshed than Paris had seen since the Commune; many believe that the Third Republic nearly died that day.

The crisis arose suddenly over the revelation of a gigantic investment swindle perpetrated by one Serge Stavisky, whose scheme, it became clear, had relied on important political connections and a strange reluctance to prosecute him. His suicide encouraged scurrilous charges that became the basis of a campaign against bourgeois government, in which proto-fascist groups used all the familiar devices, including uniforms, anti-Semitism, demonstrations, and propaganda. To meet the emergency Gaston Doumergue, a former president of the republic, was recalled from retirement to take the premiership and was given full power to govern by decree. The sober old man was supported by every party except the royalists and Marxists, and held office for nine calming months before losing his majority. But when he proposed that presidential power be permanently enlarged, many deputies were indignant. The republic still rejected strong presidents.

The left knew that in order to capture political power, it would have to heal its divisions and generate the cooperation that trade unions and others had long sought. When the Comintern, which had ruled that Communist parties must operate independently of other political organizations, declared that they could now join antifascist coalitions, the French left was able to organize a Popular Front in time for national elections in 1936. Radical Socialists, Socialists, and Communists agreed not to run against each other on the second or run-off ballot. Such rare solidarity won them a resounding victory, with the Socialists for the first time gaining more seats than the Radical Socialists and the Communists sending a sizable delegation to the Chamber. France had her first Socialist premier, Léon Blum, a learned, humane intellectual and a Jew—qualities that made conservatives distrust him all the more.

The Popular Front and the political campaign that produced its victory was in part a great rallying to the Republic and to French radical traditions, but the hopes it aroused were soon disillusioned. Even as the new government took office, it was faced with a wave of strikes by workers intent on collecting the fruits of their victory. They occupied factories, which to many Frenchmen smacked of dreaded revolution. With difficulty the government negotiated an accord, passing legislation that provided for a general 12 percent increase in wages, two-week paid vacations, a forty-hour workweek, and compulsory arbitration. Other reforms were soon added; public works were launched; the Bank of France (long the object of the left's suspicion) was restructured to give public representatives a controlling vote; and the arms industry was nationalized. The government increased pensions for veterans and subsidies for small businessmen and farmers both to stimulate the economy and to win still wider support.

But each of these measures, like the devaluation of the franc, which in 1937 could no longer be avoided, frightened the business classes. New programs proved easier to institute than to finance and the economy more accessible to regulation than stimulation. Blum's government—one of the Third Republic's most admired and most hated—had hardly begun the tax reforms needed to underwrite its plans when, after a year in office, it was defeated in the conservative Senate. The Popular Front itself soon broke up.

Subsequent governments rested on the Radical Socialists and the parties of the center, with Édouard Daladier prime minister from 1938 to 1940. French politics, while sensitive to popular sentiment and capable of innovative progress, had failed to give effective direction to a society rent by multiple factions and bitter slander. Meanwhile France's carefully constructed international position was collapsing.

THE IDEOLOGICAL STRUGGLE

The inability of the established democracies to cope with social and political strains as well as the vitality of the totalitarian nations put old and tested values on the defensive. Yet the West was also experiencing an important revival of the commitment to freedom, expressed by four major groups.

The most prominent was Marxist. The Russian Revolution had enthralled millions of Europeans with visions of economic progress in a backward nation and of social equality and high culture in a mass society. This appeal grew as capitalist economies staggered, and it reached a peak with the Russian constitution of 1936. At the same time socialists and even communists belatedly learned from fascism that all bourgeois governments were not the same. Many on the left renewed their dedication to the principles of liberty while asserting that dictatorship in Russia was a special case.

In Christian thought traditional arguments against the idolatry of the state gained new meaning. The Protestant Karl Barth and the Catholic Jacques Maritain built on firm theological orthodoxy—Barth's Pauline, Maritain's Thomist—to stress the importance of individual freedom and social justice. Similar concerns emerged in the writings of Nikolai Berdyaev, Russian Orthodox, and Martin Buber, Jewish.

Artists and writers tended in the 1930s to espouse themes of social responsibility. Poets and novelists like W. H. Auden, Thomas Mann, or André Malraux stressed the dignity of the human being, social justice, the dangers of power, and the evils of war. Much that was written was narrowly ideological, closer to political tracts than lasting art; but where they were free to do so, most European intellectuals clearly identified with the humane tradition now threatened.

Nor were liberals silent. Most vigorous in the politics and universities of Britain and France, they were heard even in Italy. In his important *History of European Liberalism*, Guido de Ruggiero probed the liberal tradition of England, France, Germany, and Italy, arguing even as he explained the decline of liberal traditions that—amended yet again—they could offer much to modern man. A decade later Benedetto Croce's historical and philosophical writings highlighted the theme of liberty as the meaning of progress, a brave perspective in 1938.

Liberal economic theory, still dominant in the academic and business worlds, was given a major restatement by John Maynard Keynes, whose *The General Theory of Employment, Interest and Money* appeared in 1936. Keynes rejected the classical view of economic man and the self-regulating economy. Few people, he argued, consistently act in their own financial interest, for no one is free of ideas, values, and tastes that shape his actions. Nor do iron economic laws inexorably dictate a pattern of booms and busts. The kind of unemployment facing Britain, which Keynes called simply intolerable, demonstrated that a free economy is not necessarily efficient and may stabilize in unproductive and unacceptable ways. At the same time he dismissed Marxism as outmoded, a vision from a time already past.

In lucid prose Keynes presented a sophisticated theory that correct governmental policies can smooth out the economic cycle. When the economy lags the government should lower the interest rates charged to borrowers, especially businesses, to encourage production, while spending money on public works and social welfare to put more money in circulation and thus stimulate consumption. As the economy expands the opposite policies should be followed to check inflation and excessive speculation. Thus he formulated the theoretical foundation for practices already partially adopted under Swedish socialism, the French Popular Front, and the American New Deal, President Franklin D. Roosevelt's program of social and economic reform inaugurated in 1933. More important, Keynes made the case for a free economy while rejecting social evils traditional thinkers had accepted. Both socialists and liberals would apply his principles when next they had the chance to direct an economy in peacetime.

Neither malaise nor conflict seemed to inhibit cultural creativity, as the new directions of the 1920s became less shocking a decade later. But two trends characteristic of the 1930s stand out. Science, social science, and the arts where not restricted by the state became more international. This was the result in part of better communication and easier mobility. But much of it was also tragically involuntary, as exiles brought the achievements of Russian ballet, Bauhaus architecture, science and scholarship from Russia, Germany, and Italy to Paris, London, and most of all the United States. And culture generally became more politicized, more ideologically divided. In Paris the Spanish painter Pablo Picasso became the dominant figure of twentieth-century art, restlessly experimenting with one new style

after another. But his most famous work, *Guernica* (see in the art folio his *Weeping Woman* of the same year), was a searing comment on war prepared for the Spanish pavilion at the Paris world's fair of 1937. Social scientists, poets, and novelists not only probed the themes of alienation and faceless mass society but actively organized to do battle in the political conflicts of the period, believing that art and social engineering could change the world. Some defended the "experiments" of Hitler and Mussolini; far more joined Marxist groups to combat the injustices of capitalist society and aid the cause of workers, minorities, or the Spanish republic. Their poetic visions tended to the apocalyptic:

> Financier, leaving your little room
> Where the money is made but not spent,
> You'll need your typist and your boy no more;
> The game is up for you and for the others. . . .[4]

But the socialist anger of W. H. Auden, the British poet who chose to live in America, was balanced by the Christian outrage of T. S. Eliot, the American poet who chose to live in Britain, "The term 'democracy' . . . does not contain enough positive content to stand alone. . . . If you will not have God (and He is a jealous God) you should pay your respects to Hitler or Stalin."[5]

INTERNATIONAL TENSIONS

In retrospect the diplomacy of the 1930s was a contest between those seeking radical changes in the international balance, led by Italy and

---

[4] W. H. Auden, "Consider This and In Our Time." In *A Little Treasury of Great Poetry*, edited by Oscar Williams, Charles Scribner's Sons, 1947, p. 689.
[5] T. S. Eliot, *The Idea of a Christian Society*, Harcourt, Brace, 1960.

Germany, and those attempting to maintain international order, led by Britain and France. To contemporaries, however, the lines did not seem so clear. The isolation of two great powers—Russia, effectively ostracized, and the United States, absorbed in her domestic affairs—made European diplomacy somewhat unreal, and the divergent policies of Britain and France often obscured their common interest. Hitler played skillfully on a certain bad conscience among the World War I victors about the Versailles treaty, and Western diplomats were ill-prepared for the strident propaganda and shifting demands of dictatorships. Foreign policy in the democracies was further weakened by reversals in domestic political platforms: the left, previously committed to disarmament and supporting the League of Nations, favored strong measures against fascist aggression, whereas the right, heretofore readier to defend national interest with a show of force, was more inclined to advocate patient compromise with fascist powers.

Even before the advent of Hitler, Wilsonian internationalism had clearly begun to fail. The complicated claims for reparations and payments of war debts had simply been abandoned rather than resolved by negotiation, and international conferences on disarmament had proved no more successful. A Far Eastern clash weakened the League of Nations still further. In 1931 Japanese troops in Manchuria occupied the major cities of the south, and China's protests led a league committee to investigate. Painfully deliberate, it recommended in 1933 that Japan be ordered to withdraw, but Japan withdrew from the league instead. The next year she renounced international limitations on her naval strength, undoing the laboriously wrought understandings of the 1920s. A four-power pact of 1933 signed by Germany, France, Italy, and Britain, reaffirming their Locarno agreements, was so obviously empty as to be wishful thinking. Later in the same year, Germany withdrew from the disarmament conference that had opened in 1932 and from the League of Nations as well.

Efforts to restrain the growing German threat through a more tightly drawn balance of power were only slightly more effective. The Eastern European nations, as frightened of Russia as of Germany, were disinclined to take unnecessary risks. The Little Entente—an alliance of Czechoslovakia, Yugoslavia, and Rumania, each also allied with France—had established a permanent council to provide fuller diplomatic and military cooperation, and Greece and Turkey were added to this French sphere by the Balkan Pact of 1934. But Hungary and Bulgaria remained outside it, authoritarian states attracted to Italy, impressed by German resurgence, and vulnerable to the economic pressures of German trade.

Austria's Nazis abandoned their attempt at a coup in 1934 when Yugoslav and Italian troops were rushed to the border to prevent the Anschluss, and for a year Italy seemed the key to the European balance of power, a position Mussolini enjoyed immensely. He encouraged the so-called Stresa Front, formed by Italy, France, and Great Britain after Germany renounced the disarmament clauses of the Versailles treaty in 1935; but the fragility of the tripower alignment showed in their separate moves thereafter. France signed a mutual assistance pact with Russia, which worried Britain, frightened Poland, and bothered so many Frenchmen that it was never given real strength. Britain reached a naval agreement with Germany, establishing that the German navy, excluding submarines, was not to exceed 35 percent of the British fleet; such dealings with Germany outraged France. And Italy was preparing all the while for an invasion of Ethiopia.

The Western powers had protested and the League of Nations condemned Germany's formal negation of the disarmament clauses, but everyone knew she had long since been rebuilding her fighting forces, and so after all had everyone else. In 1936 German troops marched into the Rhineland, demilitarized by the Versailles treaty, and this time Italy did nothing. France, unwilling to act alone as she had in 1923, consulted the British who urged acquiescence. The German troops were wildly cheered. Only the year before, France had returned the Saar to German control after a plebiscite had shown an overwhelming preference for German rule. The initiative belonged to the fascist powers.

The Ethiopian Crisis

In October 1935 Italy began an invasion of Ethiopia, seemingly an old-fashioned imperialistic venture that followed careful understandings with Britain and France. But the style of the operation, marked by enthusiastic bombings of defenseless populations and racist propaganda, signaled something new. Europeans were shocked, and the League, declaring Italy an aggressor, promptly banned the sale of essential war materials to her.

Only a few countries[6] refused to impose these sanctions, but even Germany and the United States, though not members of the League, prohibited increased shipments of restricted items. Most of Europe seemed united in this crucial test of the League's peacekeeping powers. But while the embargoes angered Italy and caused some hardship, they did not stop the war, partly because oil, the most important commodity of all, was not included on the list.

The French foreign minister, Pierre Laval, determined on a hidden course divergent from France's public position. In his successful po-

litical career, he had drifted steadily to the right, earning along the way the respectful distrust of all parties. He now sought to keep Italy a useful friend against Germany, and in secret meetings with Sir Samuel Hoare, his British counterpart, he arranged for a settlement of the Ethiopian crisis that would in effect give most of the country to Italy. When the plan was leaked to the press, public outrage swamped it and its sponsors; Hoare was dismissed, and Laval soon fell from power. The plan, however, not only delayed a decision on the crucial question of adding oil to the list of sanctions but undermined confidence in the two democracies. By May 1936 Ethiopia had capitulated, and a few months later Italians celebrated the League's formal lifting of the bans. The League of Nations could no longer be taken seriously as a force for peace.

The Spanish Civil War

Shortly after the conquest of Ethiopia, a nationalist revolt broke out in Spain led by the military. Both Italy and Germany quickly proffered their support to the insurgents, and before the end of the year, the two fascist powers signed an agreement creating the Rome-Berlin Axis, which Germany followed with the Anti-Comintern Pact between herself and Japan. The Spanish Civil War immediately deepened Europe's international and ideological division into competing camps.

Many times previously the Spanish army had claimed to represent the national will, but this civil war seemed to one side the defense of democracy against fascist aggression and a battle for social justice against reactionaries, while to the other the war was a crusade of decency and religion against the ravages of anarchists and communists. Throughout the West the public was sharply divided; and idealistic young men, most of them Marxists, went to Spain by the thousands to fight in national units like the

---

[6] They were Austria, Hungary, and Albania. Switzerland was exempt from having to impose sanctions, a recognition of her formal and permanent neutrality.

Photographs helped make the Spanish Civil War a divisive reality for all Western civilization. Robert Capa, who took this shot of a Loyalist soldier carrying a wounded comrade, became famous for his pictures of the war. (Photo: © Robert Capa/Magnum)

Lincoln or the Garibaldi Brigade (whose greatest moment was the defeat of regular Italian troops sent by Mussolini).

Spain's government had the support of republicans, socialists, communists, anarchists, labor groups, and Catalan and Basque nationalists organized in a loose coalition and calling themselves Loyalists. They were never fully controlled by the government, and local groups often went far beyond official policy in launching the radical changes the republic had prom-

ised. As the war progressed the Loyalists became increasingly dependent on Russia for supplies; by 1938 this and the Communists' greater efficiency made them prominent in a government dangerously divided.

The Nationalists were dominated by the army, which held somewhat aloof from the monarchists, fascistic Falangists, and clericals who flocked to the insurgents' standard. The accidental death of the general who had led the uprising left General Francisco Franco their leader. He had commanded the units stationed in Morocco—the revolt had in fact begun there —that were the Nationalists' best troops; and though little interested in doctrines or ideologies, he recognized the utility of a modern mass appeal in building a disciplined movement.

Most of the Spanish navy remained loyal to

the republic, and one of the insurgents' first problems was getting their armies from Morocco to the mainland, where many garrisons had risen in their favor. By July Italian and German planes were providing the needed transport. The help of the Fascist powers—Italian troops in significant numbers and military advisers, planes, tanks, and ammunition from both states—remained essential to the strength of Franco's cause. Mussolini welcomed the chance to enhance Italian prestige, and Hitler used the opportunity to test new military technology.

Only Russia gave reliable if limited aid to the Loyalists—until 1938, when Stalin decided to cut his losses. Blum's government in France favored the Loyalists but feared the domestic and international consequences of openly aiding them; Britain's Conservative government shared France's caution, but with a deeper distaste for the radicals of Madrid and a greater hope for good relations with Italy. The democracies thus chose neutrality and thought thereby to lead Germany and Italy to the same position. An international commission formed to prevent foreign intervention merely upheld the ponderous legalism that starved the republic while helping to hide the active role of the Fascist powers.

Foreign aid, trained troops, better military organization, and modern weapons made the victory of Franco's forces almost inevitable. They nearly won Madrid and the war itself in the summer of 1936, but the Loyalists held on and in a last-minute counterattack broke the Nationalists' assault. For more than two years, despite poor equipment and internal conflict, the republicans would show occasional spurts of skill and élan.

With the fall of the Spanish republic, a French gendarme leads militiamen of the International Brigade to safety across the French border. (Photo: © Robert Capa/Magnum)

Franco's troops spread slowly from their capital, Burgos, in the north, and also up from the south against the Loyalist strongholds of Madrid, Valencia, and Barcelona; but to the disgust of his Axis supporters, the general conducted a war of attrition. Not until the spring of 1939, when Russian supplies had ceased to come and Britain had signed special treaties of friendship with Italy, did the Spanish republic finally fall. Thousands of refugees wearily crossed into France while Franco filled Spain's capacious prisons with potential enemies, undid radical measures, and restored the power of the church over education. Franco then joined the Anti-Comintern Pact and took Spain out of the League of Nations.

The civil war had cost more than a million Spaniards their lives, many of them at the hands of firing squads and mobs. The bombing of Guernica by German aircraft in 1937 made men shudder before the vision of what war now meant for civilians, and the conflict between the democracies and the Axis was established as fundamental. But the democracies, fearful and divided, accepted defeat while the Axis acted.

The Anschluss and the Czech Partition

During the course of the Spanish Civil War, attention shifted to the center of Europe. In February 1938 Hitler summoned Austria's chancellor Kurt von Schuschnigg to Berchtesgaden, the Führer's fortified mountain retreat, and after a long, humiliating harangue won his promise to include Austrian Nazis in his cabinet. Feeling braver after he returned home, Schuschnigg called for a plebiscite. He hoped it would rally the people to save Austria's independence, though he could hardly hope for Socialists to forgive the suppression of their party; moreover Italy warned that she would no longer offer military backing. Hitler was furious at Schuschnigg's action, and while Austrian Nazis

rioted, Germany massed military units on the border and sent an ultimatum demanding that the plebiscite be postponed and that Schuschnigg resign.

Friendless, the Austrian chancellor had no choice; he was replaced by Artur von Seyss-Inquart, a Nazi, who invited German troops to restore order. They did so on March 13, and within a month Austria's annexation to Germany was almost unanimously approved in a plebiscite run by the Nazis. The dream of Anschluss had been fulfilled (see Map 28.1). Hitler's popularity at home rose still higher, and German influence spread more deeply into the Balkans. The lesson was clear: Germany was Europe's greatest power; alliances with the Little Entente were of small value; and when Hitler moved, Britain and France merely protested.

Two weeks after the plebiscite in Austria, Hitler demanded autonomy for the Sudetenland, an overwhelmingly German-speaking section of Czechoslovakia. The parallel with Austria was lost on no one, though the challenge to the Czech republic was far more daring, for Czechoslovakia was a prosperous industrial state protected by a respectable army, well-fortified frontiers, and mutual-aid treaties with both France and Russia. Supported by her allies, Czechoslovakia mobilized, and Hitler ordered Konrad Henlein, the Sudeten Nazi leader, to quiet down.

Internal divisions as well as geography made Czechoslovakia vulnerable. She was barely able to maintain the loyalty of the Slovaks, and she had met the threat of a pro-Nazi party—which in the elections held in 1935 had won more votes than any other—only by restricting political parties. Nor were the great powers united in their reactions to Hitler. Determined to prevent war, Chamberlain wanted to parlay directly with Germany, believing that no non-negotiable British interest was at stake in the Sudetenland, and he rejected suggestions from

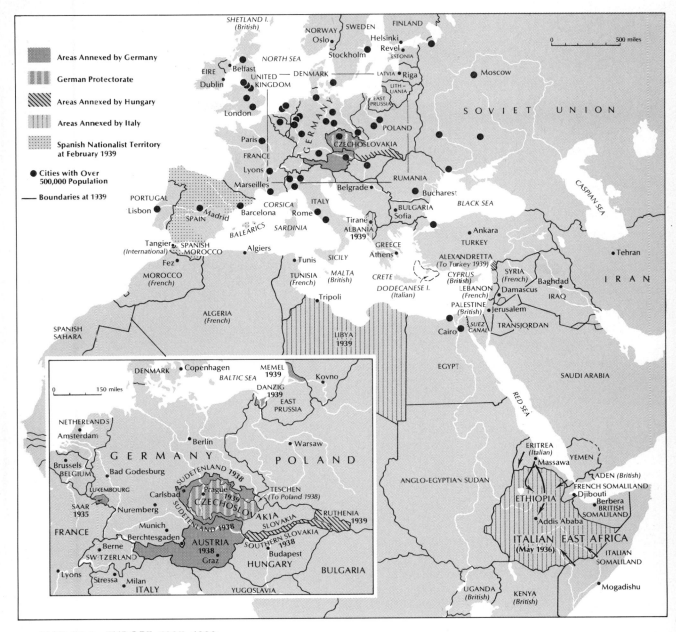

MAP 28.1: EUROPE 1935–1939

the United States and Russia for a meeting to consider means of restraining the Nazi dictator. Many Frenchmen and Englishmen, deeply alarmed at how close to war they were, wondered whether Czech sovereignty over a German population was worth such a risk.

Throughout the summer Sudeten Nazi leaders negotiated with the Czech state while demonstrations there and in Germany heated the atmosphere. In August Chamberlain, with French concurrence, sent his own emissary to mediate while German troops held maneuvers on the Czech border and Hitler pointedly toured Germany's fortifications in the west.

In September the pressure increased. Hitler's speeches became more bellicose, and war seemed imminent. Chamberlain decided, once again with French support, to visit Berchtesgaden. When he met with Hitler there on September 15, the Führer raised his demand—to annexation of the Sudetenland. After a few days Britain and France advised Czechoslovakia to submit. Desperately the Czechs sought some escape, but only Russia was ready to support resistance. On September 22 Chamberlain flew back to Germany with the good news that Czechoslovakia had agreed to Hitler's terms only to find them changed again: German troops must occupy the ceded territory immediately, leaving the Czechs no time to provide for citizens who wished to escape Nazi rule or to move factories and military supplies. A shocked Chamberlain said no, and for five days the world listened for war.

Then, persuaded by Mussolini, Hitler agreed to a meeting with Britain, France, and Italy. The brief conference took place on September 29 in Munich, where just fifteen years earlier Hitler had failed to capture the town hall. Now he dealt in nations. Hitler, von Ribbentrop, Mussolini, Chamberlain, and Daladier talked for an afternoon and evening; and Hitler was granted all he asked. Neither Russia nor Czechoslovakia was consulted. The next day Czechoslovakia submitted to the terms of the Munich Pact and to the demands added by Poland and Hungary, for the Teschen region and a piece of Slovakia respectively. At a single stroke Czechoslovakia surrendered one-third of her population, her best military defenses, and much of her economic strength.

Thus Central Europe's strongest democracy was reduced to a German dependency and a keystone of France's continental security shattered. As Daladier's plane circled the Paris airport, he watched the crowd below with dread. But it cheered him, and in Britain Chamberlain became a hero. Peace, the papers echoed, had been preserved.

THE PATH TO WAR

Europe was shaken by the Munich Pact and by the brutality and anti-Semitism goose-stepping troops carried with them into expropriated territory. Inspired by the democracies' ready capitulation, Italy began a noisy campaign to get Nice and Corsica from France.

German might, Hitler's speeches, the news of life in lands annexed or in Germany itself—all gave Jews, non-Aryans, peoples along the German borders, and whole nations reason for terror. To hold such fear in check there stood the sane temptation to believe that even the Nazis, even Hitler, could not want another world war. Then early in 1939, following the now-familiar pattern of agitation, Germany occupied all of Czechoslovakia (except for part of the Carpatho-Ukraine, taken by the Hungarians) and in the same month annexed the seaport of Memel from a terrified Lithuania. The pretext of absorbing only German peoples had now been abandoned. Chamberlain, still ready to risk personal and national honor in the hope of winning Germany to a responsible place in European councils, led those who believed that concessions could appease Hitler. But by this time most Englishmen and Frenchmen had resigned themselves to the necessity of stopping the Nazis with force.

The summer of 1939 brought more alarms. Italy invaded and annexed Albania, and the Italo-German Axis was formally tightened into the "Pact of Steel." Germany kept chancelleries quaking with demands for nonaggression agreements. Late in August the leader of the Nazi party in Danzig declared that his city must be returned to the fatherland. Everyone now knew what to expect; denunciations of the Versailles boundaries and of the persecution of Germans within the Polish corridor—cries that would once have won a sympathetic hearing—clearly meant that Poland was next. As they had all summer, Britain and France renewed their pledges to assist her.

The summer's most important contest, however, was for the allegiance of Russia, and Hitler won that too: a Russo-German nonaggression pact was suddenly announced at the height of the Polish crisis. Russia had made overtures to Britain and France for some time, suggesting that they join her in guaranteeing the territorial integrity of all the states between the Baltic and Black seas. But the Western powers had not been ready to grant the communist nation so extensive a zone of influence and had responded weakly to Russian approaches, sending lesser officials rather than their foreign ministers, who had been invited to meetings in Moscow during the summer. Despite Russian policy, which since 1935 had advocated disarmament, supported the League of Nations (Russia had entered it just as Germany had left), supplied the republican government of Spain, and offered support to Czechoslovakia, Chamberlain, like most Western statesmen, remained more willing to talk with Hitler than with Stalin.

In May 1939 Maxim Litvinov, the eloquent spokesman for this pro-Western policy, had been replaced by Stalin's tougher and less cosmopolitan friend and Russia's premier, Vyacheslav Molotov, as minister of foreign affairs. Stalin suspected the democracies would welcome a war between Germany and the Soviet Union, whereas Hitler had offered just what Russia asked: an understanding that if Germany sought any changes in her eastern border, Russia was to have a free hand in Finland, Estonia, Latvia, eastern Poland up to approximately the old Curzon Line, and the Bessarabian portion of Rumania. The Russo-German agreement was a masterpiece of cynical accommodation between the sponsors of antifascist fronts and the authors of the Anti-Comintern Pact that shocked a world still unaccustomed to totalitarian flexibility.

The last days of August resounded with formal warnings and clarifications between the Western powers and Germany, but to no avail. Hitler invaded Poland on September 1, and Britain and France mobilized and sent him an ultimatum, determined in this world conflict to make their intentions clear. On September 3, 1939, they declared war, offering battle to defend an authoritarian Poland just one year after surrendering Czechoslovakia.

IV. WORLD WAR II: 1939–1941

Appeasement had failed, not simply because it was a policy of weakness—the appeasers insisted that theirs was a serious effort to resolve differences—but because Hitler wanted war, preferably in the short bursts he was likely to win. Although Britain and France had gained some time with conciliatory policies, they had not always used it well. Memories of World War I and internal divisions made it harder to prepare for the one activity above all others to which fascism was now dedicated: the conquest of Europe. For two years the Axis would score one victory after another (see Map 28.2).

THE WESTERN FRONT

The Germans had prepared carefully for the invasion of Poland, and they attacked her with overwhelming force. Even so the speed of their victory was surprising. Poland fell in

0   300 miles

ICELAND

NORWAY

SWEDEN

FINLAND
(JUNE 1941)

Oslo

Leningrad

Helsinki

Stockholm

ESTONIA

Moscow

S O V I E T   U N I O N

N O R T H

Glasgow Edinburgh

S E A   DENMARK

Riga
LATVIA

Smolensk

Belfast

GREAT

Copenhagen

LITHUANIA

BALTIC SEA

Dublin BRITAIN INVASION OF
LOW COUNTRIES

EAST
PRUSSIA

Coventry MAY 29, JUNE 2, 1940

Berlin

Amsterdam

London NETHERLANDS

Warsaw 1

Kiev

Stalingrad

DUNKIRK EVACUATION 3
MAY 29-JUNE 2, 1940 Brussels
BELGIUM

G E R M A N Y

POLAND
SEPTEMBER 1939

ATLANTIC
OCEAN

Paris

CZECHOSLOVAKIA
(To Germany 1939)

BESSARABIA

5

MAGINOT
LINE

Nuremberg

AUSTRIA
(To Germany
1939)

Budapest

CASPIAN
SEA

3 FRANCE
JUNE 1940

Munich

Berne

HUNGARY

RUMANIA
(NOVEMBER 1940)

Vichy

SWITZ.

6

Milan

Belgrade

Bucharest

Sevastopol

PORTUGAL

Marseilles

ITALY

YUGOSLAVIA

B L A C K   S E A

Lisbon Madrid

CORSICA

Rome

BULGARIA

SPAIN
(NATIONALIST VICTORY
APRIL 1939)

Naples

Sofia

Istanbul

IRAN
(To Great Britain
and Russia
1941)

SARDINIA

ALBANIA
(To Italy 1939)

4

Ankara

SPANISH
MOROCCO

Algiers

SICILY

GREECE

TURKEY

Casablanca Oran

Tunis

Athens

SYRIA
(To Great Britain 1941)

IRAQ
(To Great Britain 1941)

MALTA
(Great Britain)

CRETE
MAY 1941

CYPRUS
(Great Britain) LEBANON

MOROCCO
(France)

TUNISIA
(France)

M E D I T E R R A N E A N   S E A

PALESTINE
(Great Britain)

ALGERIA
(France)

Tripoli

Bengazi

Tobruk

TRANSJORDAN
(Great Britain)

El Alamein

Cairo

LIBYA

EGYPT

SAUDI ARABIA

MAP 28.2: THE HEIGHT OF AXIS POWER 1942

less than a month under the impact of Europe's
first blitzkrieg, and Russia hastily marched in
to claim her share.   More nervous than ever
about the trustworthiness of her fascist partner, Russia pressed Finland for territory that
would move the Russian frontier a safer distance than the twenty miles from Leningrad
where it then lay.   The Finns, willing to negoti-

In Warsaw, German tanks, fresh from their light-ning destruction of the Polish army, pass in review before Adolf Hitler on October 5, 1939. (Photo: Wide World Photos)

ate, refused to cede all the Russians demanded, and in November the Red army marched. Finnish resistance against such odds won world-wide admiration and a brief respite during the winter but could not prevent defeat the following spring. Russia, having regained boundaries close to those the last tsars had enjoyed, could afford to wait.

The Western powers had been waiting too. Hitler suggested that with Poland gone there was no longer reason to fight, but few were tempted by his hints of peace. On the other hand, the British and French commanders were resolved not to risk their precious planes too soon or to launch the pointless assaults of World War I. Since Hitler refrained from attacking along the French border, the Allies followed

suit. This was the so-called phony war, during which arms production and mobilization speeded up, the world waited, and little happened. The strain was bad for morale. French Communists now thought the war a mistake and said so loudly, even though their party had been suppressed, but the democracies searched, as they had in the previous war, for more effective leaders. Paul Reynaud, energetic and determined, replaced Daladier as premier. Chamberlain resigned in May after a wide-ranging debate on his whole conduct of the war (Norway had just fallen), and Britain's new government included all parties under the firm hand of Winston Churchill, a Conservative who believed in empire and old-fashioned sonorous sentences, a political maverick who had been both a reformer and a defender of national interest through forty years of political life. An opponent of appeasement now given his chance by disaster, Churchill would prove one of England's greatest leaders.

The war had again become terribly real. The Allies were beginning to prepare the defense of Norway when Germany attacked, taking Denmark in a day, April 9, 1940. Norway's most strategically important points were captured in short order, giving Germany a dangerous base for assaults on British ships and cities. On May 10 and without warning, German troops flooded the Netherlands and Belgium. The Dutch, who had expected to escape war as they had since Napoleon I, surrendered in five days; the better-prepared and larger Belgian army held out for eighteen. On May 14 a skillfully executed German offensive broke through the Ardennes forest, thought to be impervious to panzer tactics, reached Sedan, and drove to the Channel, trapping the Belgian and British forces fighting there and much of the French army. The Luftwaffe controlled the air, and only Hitler's greater interest in taking Paris and their own fortitude permitted the Allies' proudest achievement in the battle for France: between May 26 and June 4, most of their 340,000 troops pinned against the sea were evacuated from the port town of Dunkirk and bravely carried across to the British Isles in a motley flotilla of naval vessels, commercial ferries, and private sailboats.

The Fall of France and the Battle of Britain
Hitler seemed invincible and the blitzkrieg some terrible new Teutonic force, a totalitarian achievement other societies could not hope to equal. In fact, however, many of the tactical ideas on which it rested were first put forward by British and French experts, including General Charles de Gaulle, an advocate of military mechanization and especially tank warfare; but German officers had the experience of defeat, which makes armies more open to new ideas, and they trained their forces well. The blitzkrieg was the result not so much of new technology as of new strategy. It combined air attacks with rapid movements of motorized columns to overcome the advantages defensive positions had previously enjoyed.

In a blitzkrieg tanks roared through and behind enemy lines, a maneuver nearly forbidden in older theories and requiring great speed and careful drill. In the flat terrain of Poland, the panzer divisions were able to encircle the enemy; in France they often assaulted troops so far in the rear that the defense was unprepared for battle. The aim was less to capture ground than to break up communications, a task furthered by the air force, which was used to disorient and terrify the retreating army. Even the machine-gunning of French roads clogged with refugees and the bombing of Rotterdam thus had their place in the campaign to demoralize.

Clearly the German tactics worked. It does not follow, however, that France's military inferiority was so great as her defeat. French commanders were able but a little too rigid and, like their nation perhaps, too inclined to think in defensive terms. They preferred larger tanks—not necessarily an unsound attitude—but they lacked the time to deploy them for maximum effect. French strategists were too slow perhaps to recognize the full importance of air power, and their air force was temporarily weakened by being in the midst of changing models. More fundamentally, Britain and France had allowed Germany years of massive arming and been reluctant to exclude from their defenses Belgium and Holland, whose neutrality made joint military planning impossible. When Germany attacked them in May, the home armies were poorly coordinated, and there was a gap along the Belgian border.

Excessive reliance on the Maginot Line, France's system of fortifications extending from the Swiss to the Belgian border, was a fatal temptation in a country of unstable governments, a tax-conscious electorate, demographic decline, and pained memories of World War I. Morale in France was not high, though the phony war and the rout of what many thought to be Europe's best army have perhaps made it seem worse than it was. Suspicions of the British, of the army, of the politicians, of the left —like the miscalculations of her officers and the inexperience of her troops—might have been rectified with time, but that above all France was not granted.

The Allied defense of France was broken after Dunkirk, and Germans renewed their attack on June 5. They took Paris in a week. Mussolini attacked France on the tenth, anxious lest he miss the war entirely; and he had in fact but barely demonstrated the inferiority of his forces before France surrendered, on June 16. The armistice was signed in the railway car used for Germany's surrender in 1918. More ironic still, the man who chose to sign for his people was the World War I hero of Verdun and marshal of France, Henri Philippe Pétain.

Pétain, who had replaced Reynaud as premier following the fall of Paris, believed France must now make her way in Hitler's Europe. He accepted terms that put the northern and eastern three-fifths of the country under Nazi occupation and allowed French prisoners of war to be kept in Germany. For a moment the nation turned to the octogenarian marshal with stunned unanimity. The headquarters of unoccupied France were established the following month at Vichy, and a reconvened parliament maneuvered by Pierre Laval named Pétain chief of state.

The new regime, a confused coalition of militant fascists and the traditional right, was never to be really independent of Germany. After adopting bits of corporatism and some fascist trappings, it settled into a lethargy of its own, ruling a truncated state as rife with intrigue, personal ambition, and shifting alliances as the Third Republic it so heartily denounced. The abler politicians of the Third Republic drifted away from Vichy, while the few convinced totalitarians preferred the more efficient atmosphere of Nazi-occupied Paris.

Great Britain stood alone. While German officers—themselves unprepared for such victories on the Continent so soon—planned an invasion, their bombers roared over England in air attacks that many believed would in themselves force Britain to sue for peace. Instead in September the projected invasion was postponed, and by the following spring the air raids were letting up. For Britain merely to survive from June 1940 to June 1941 was a kind of victory, which Churchill proudly called her "finest hour."

There had been signs that such resilience was possible. During the Norwegian campaign, which had otherwise cost Germany so little, her navy had suffered enough damage in encounters with the British to reduce its effectiveness and make it more cautious. The Dunkirk evacuation had testified to the resourcefulness of the thousands of civilians who lent the military eager assistance. And in the man-to-man air battles, British fighters, particularly their newer designs, proved at least the equal of the German.

Thus the waves of German planes flying over the island kingdom sustained losses far greater than those of the Royal Air Force, losses increased by new techniques of antiaircraft defense, including radar, an English development that was the most critical addition to military technology displayed in these years. German attacks concentrated at first on ports and shipping, then on airfields, and finally on cities, leaving great burning holes in London and destroying Coventry. But shifting targets dissipated the economic and military effects of the bombing, and the citizens of London reacted very differently from refugees on a crowded highway to terror from the skies. Britain's morale rose as, ever better organized, she fiercely carried on.

WAR IN THE EAST

The Battle of Britain was Hitler's first serious check, but Germans could be reassured by fascist victories elsewhere. They did not come easily. Italian forces, launching an offensive into Egypt from Libya in September 1940, were driven back in a successful British counterattack until the British themselves had to withdraw into Egypt because of the Axis challenge in the Balkans. When Italian forces invaded Greece from Albania in October, the Greeks pushed them back, and Hitler had to bail out Mussolini.

The Balkan States were rapidly losing their independence. Russia stretched previous agreements to annex Bessarabia in June 1940, and Germany promised to defend what remained of Rumania (after Hungary and Bulgaria each took a bit). Rumania, Hungary, and Bulgaria, all implicated in Hitler's map-making, were closely tied to the Nazi Reich. It was no great step for them to welcome German troops in March 1941 and to join Hitler in attacking Yugoslavia, which had hesitated too long, and Greece, which had fought Mussolini too well.

The attack was launched in April and swept through both countries within the month. Some Greek and British forces pulled back to Crete, only to be forced out almost immediately by history's first large glider and paratroop attack. The Allies retreated to Egypt, herself now seriously endangered by the Axis

domination of the Mediterranean. Hitler still appeared invincible in the summer of 1941.

Germany's expansion into the Balkans disturbed the Russians, but a confident Hitler suggested they interest themselves in Iran and India instead. Both sides anticipated conflict, and Stalin assumed the premiership in May as part of the preparation for war. Yet when the Germans attacked the Soviet Union on June 22, 1941, the Russians appeared genuinely surprised—at least by the timing and the size of the attack. The assault, in three broad sectors, was the largest concentration of military power that had ever been assembled.

Once more the blitzkrieg worked its magic, though everyone now understood how it operated. German armored divisions ripped through Russian lines and encircled astonishing numbers of troops. Quickly they crossed the vast lands Russia had acquired since 1939, taking Riga and Smolensk in July, reaching the Dnieper in August, claiming Kiev and the whole Ukraine in September. Then the pace slowed; but while one German force lay siege to Leningrad in the north, a second hit Sevastopol in the south and moved into the Crimea, and by December still another penetrated to the suburbs of Moscow.

There the German advance stopped temporarily, halted by an early and severe winter, by strained supply lines, and at last by sharp Russian counterattacks. Germany now held territory that had accounted for nearly two-thirds of Russia's production of coal, iron, steel, and aluminum; 40 percent of her grain and hogs. The December snows, however, raised the specter of a continuing two-front war, which Hitler had sworn to avoid. For all its losses of men and territory, the Red army was intact, and the Germans had little to live on in the wasteland the Russians systematically created as they retreated. The battle for Russia was not over as Hitler's timetable predicted it would be.

STRAINS ON THE AXIS

Baffled American servicemen survey the ruins on an airfield at Pearl Harbor; the United States had entered the war. (Photo: Navy Department/ National Archives)

By mid-December 1941 the Axis faced great threats from Russia, from within the vast lands they ruled, from the British Empire, and from the United States, the world's most powerful nation.

Despite her deep partisanship for France and Britain, the United States remained technically at peace in 1940. With the intention of keeping the country out of European conflicts, Congress had passed the second Neutrality Act in 1937. The law, which had helped withhold armaments from republican Spain, had been amended in 1939 to permit governments to buy war materials from American suppliers if the purchasers paid in cash and carried the goods on their own ships. That, everyone knew, could benefit only one side of the European conflict. In 1940 the American government sold weapons to private corporations for transfer to Great Britain and traded fifty old American destroyers for the lease of British bases in the western Atlantic, thus reducing the areas Britain needed to patrol.

A year later the United States formally accepted the role of "the arsenal of democracy," and she began extending loans, first to Britain and then the Soviet Union, to help them pay for desperately needed supplies. In August Winston Churchill and Franklin Roosevelt met at sea to draft the Atlantic Charter, which looked forward in very Wilsonian terms to a world "after the destruction of the Nazi tyranny" in which there would be collective security and self-determination for all nations so that "all the men of all the lands may live out their lives in freedom from fear and want."

Even so firm an ideological commitment, however, did not bring the United States into the war. Japanese airplanes did that. Tension between the two nations had reached a new high when Japan absorbed French Indochina in 1941. Then on December 7, confident that Russia was so occupied as to be no threat and that the United States could be rendered nearly harmless in one blow, Japan attacked the Hawaiian port of Pearl Harbor, a key U.S. naval base. The effects of the attack were devastating, and three days later Germany and Italy declared war on the United States.

American entry into the war would prove fatal to the Axis, but Hitler had fallen into the habit of underestimating his opponents.

In late 1941 he ruled virtually the entire Continent from the Atlantic to the Ukraine in the name of a new order, and he had found sympathizers and allies in every country, from Vidkun Quisling in Norway to Francisco Franco in Spain.[7] But the Nazis alienated those they conquered by their labor conscription, their racial policies, and their oppressive brutality. A high percentage of Ukrainians for example had been inclined to welcome liberation from Russian rule, but brief acquaintance with how Nazis treated "inferior" Slavs ended any enthusiasm for cooperation with the Germans and cost them an invaluable asset.

By the end of 1941, organized resistance movements in most countries were harassing the Nazi order. Mussolini perhaps the one man Hitler truly admired, had weakened the Axis with his misjudgments of his own strength. Although no contemporary could yet know it, the Axis had begun to lose the war.

---

[7] Only Sweden, Spain, Portugal, Switzerland, and Eire remained even technically neutral by grace of geography.

The democracy so optimistically extended after World War I fared badly in the following twenty years. Not only did it fail in poor and strife-torn new nations, but in the most advanced it fumbled before the social crises of the Depression and mass politics. Totalitarianism offered alternatives that fed on disenchantment with bourgeois culture and liberalism. Its fascist forms appealed to all those who had been the "losers" in the growth of the liberal, secular state, all who had been hurt or alienated by rapid change. The fear of Russian communism strengthened the view that the future lay with those who could ruthlessly mobilize masses. Ideologically and in terms of force, fascism challenged the traditional institutions and values of European culture.

Western statesmen faced the challenge only slowly. By the time they had abandoned the illusion that they could buy peace, they had lost the initative (and much of Europe), and uncertain nations faced another world war. Within two years the Axis had conquered the European Continent. Japanese airplanes then brought the United States into World War II as German submarines had done in World War I. In this most global of wars, the Allies once again stood for democracy—a democracy more socially aware and less confident than thirty years before. If Russia was as embarrassing an ally in 1941 as in 1914, the humane traditions of Western civilization clearly rested with the Europeanized societies—Russia, the Americas, and the British Empire—that set out to reconquer Europe.

RECOMMENDED READING

Studies

Branson, N., and M. Heinemann. *Britain in the 1930s*. 1971. Ably relates the interconnections of political life with the social and economic stress of the period.

*Bullock, Alan. *Hitler: A Study in Tyranny*. 1971. The best biography of Hitler and one that gives an effective picture of Nazi society.

*Carr, E. H. *The Soviet Impact on the Western World*. 1947. Although much recent scholarship adds to our understanding, this remains a valuable overall view with a participant's feeling for the importance of Soviet influence.

*Carsten, F. L. *The Rise of Fascism*. 1967. The careful synthesis of a distinguished scholar.

*Churchill, Winston. *The Second World War*. 6 vols. (also available in a one-volume condensation). 1948–1953. This powerful history is also an important document that conveys much of Churchill's greatness and prejudices.

*Fromm, Erich. *Escape from Freedom*. 1941. A psychoanalytic argument about Western man's historic reluctance to bear the burdens of freedom.

*Jackson, Gabriel. *The Spanish Republic and the Civil War, 1937–1939*. 1965. An informed, insightful treatment of a still controversial and complex period.

*Kirkpatrick, Sir Ivone. *Mussolini: Study of a Demagogue*. 1964. By a former British diplomat, this is the fullest study available in English.

Mack Smith, Denis. *Mussolini's Roman Empire*. 1976. A lucid account with much new information by the leading English scholar of modern Italy.

Nettl, J. P. *The Soviet Achievement*. 1967. Effectively tackles the difficult task of assessing both the economic development of the U.S.S.R. and its social cost.

*Nolte, Ernst. *The Three Faces of Fascism*. A learned effort to trace the intellectual history of fascism in France, Germany, and Italy.

*Schoenbaum, David. *Hitler's Social Revolution: Class and Status in Nazi Germany, 1933–1939*. 1966. An important study of the social policies, in theory and practice, of the Third Reich.

*Shirer, William L. *Rise and Fall of the Third Reich*. 1960. The somewhat tendentious and widely read account of a noted and knowledgeable journalist.

*Sontag, Raymond J. *A Broken World, 1919–1939*. 1971. A senior scholar's assessment that emphasizes international relations.

Tannenbaum, Edward R. *The Fascist Experience: Italian Society and Culture, 1922–1945*. 1972. A wide-ranging effort to recapture the meaning in practice of fascist rule.

Weinberg, Gerhard L. *The Foreign Policy of Hitler's Germany*. 1970. A major study by a leading American diplomatic historian.

*Wright, Gordon. *The Ordeal of Total War, 1939–1945*. 1968. A thoughtful and stimulating assessment of the psychological, scientific, and economic aspects of the war as well as a balanced account of its course.

* Available in paperback.

TWENTY NINE

THE SURVIVAL OF EUROPE

World War II challenged the very survival of European society, and not simply in the primitive sense that any war seems to menace civilization. The killing and destruction attacked the civilian heart of society, and the conqueror of the Continent made rapine and genocide his policy. Controlling the Continent and wide sweeps of Pacific and Asian territories, the Axis amassed a concentration of power so great that most of the remaining industrialized world had to mobilize to dislodge it. Thus the liberation of Europe began in the depths of Russia, on the sea lanes, and in North Africa, requiring enormous feats of organization and terrible sacrifice. The occupied Continental nations could contribute little more than the old-fashioned heroic work of small, secret bands.

The immediate aftermath of the war was a kind of social collapse that reduced political, economic, and social organization to a skeleton. In terms of international power, Europe appeared to have been all but conquered by the Russians and the Americans. Their conflicts, practical and ideological, were the extension of the European experience that now shaped the conditions of postwar reorganization. The Eastern European countries freed by the Soviet Union could not prevent the Russians from dominating their internal affairs; the Western states, heavily reliant on economic aid from the United States, cautiously fell back on old institutions and parliamentary forms as the basis from which to rebuild. It was doubtful whether such structures could be adequate to postwar needs.

Yet Europe accomplished a remarkable recovery. Politically an enforced moderation gave some stability to the rapidly changing world. In the West prosperity eased the accommodation to altered conditions, and the Eastern states gradually achieved an equilibrium between the relaxation of tyranny and the preservation of dictatorship, between communist alliances and national autonomy. Unprecedented increases in productivity, new techniques for directing the economies, and new policies for broadening social welfare suggested that European societies might move in directions distinctly their own. It was not clear, however, how they could achieve such autonomy.

I. THE END OF WORLD WAR II

At the beginning of 1942, Nazi power was at its height. Germany ruled most of the people and controlled most of the wealth of the Continent (see Map 29.1). Her military power that spring consisted of between 7 and 10 million men in ground forces, a superb air force, and a significant navy, including more than 150 submarines, which in the four summer months would cost the Allies nearly 400 ships. Italy added sizable forces to the Axis that were especially important in Africa. Yet Axis dominance was short-lived. Weaknesses within the fascist systems and growing Allied strength would finally turn the tide against the Axis nations.

THE THEATERS OF WAR

Germany was racing against time. If she was to consolidate her gains and make peace with Britain or defeat her, Russia must be knocked out of the war. Neither the lengthening siege

MAP 29.1: THE ALLIED VICTORY IN WORLD WAR II

of Leningrad nor the attack on Moscow had achieved that. In the summer of 1942, the Germans drove farther into southern Russia, taking Sevastopol and depriving the nation of ever more desperately needed grain. But the crucial battle of the Eastern front took place from August to October at Stalingrad (now Volgograd), a major communications center, where a breakthrough would open to Hitler the oil fields of southern Russia.

On the Continent

By September the Germans had penetrated the city, where they fought the Russians at such close quarters that sometimes the antagonists battled from within the same building. But the German offensive weakened as supplies dwindled, and Russia's heroic defense had allowed time to amass troops for a counter-attack, which broke through and encircled the German army. Hitler frantically ordered his army to stand its ground; and when it surrendered, in February 1943, less than one-third of its 300,000 men were left. The giant Russian pincers pushed on until March, costing the Germans more than half a million casualties. Stalingrad was the turning point of the European war.

The dominant Axis position in the West was deteriorating as well. By early 1943 the worst threats from U-boats had been overcome, and the air supremacy Great Britain had won over her own islands extended to the Continent by the time the Germans invaded Russia. Thousands of tons of explosives fell on Germany each month in 1942, and five times as much was dropped in 1943. The Americans favored pinpoint bombing of strategic targets; the British preferred nighttime area bombing, with a city itself as the target. The fire bombing of Hamburg in 1943 created a holocaust, but its horror would be exceeded two years later with a yet more massive raid that leveled Dresden, a city of miserable civilians and refugees and without significant industry. Indifference to the suffering of noncombatants had become a common quality of modern war.

For the Allies the major stategical dispute of the war was becoming critical: how to attack Hitler's "fortress Europe." The Russians repeatedly urged the opening of a second front

British aircraft over the ruins of Hanover. (Photo: International News)

on the Continent, and most of the American military favored an immediate invasion, whereas the British warned against the dangerously high cost of such an operation. With Roosevelt's support Churchill prevailed, and it was decided to invade Morocco and Algeria, the lightly defended western regions of North Africa then under the control of Vichy France. Success would end the Axis threat to Egypt and open southern Europe—the "soft underbelly" of the Continent, as Churchill called it—to Allied assault.

North Africa and Asia

Until 1942 the battle lines in North Africa had ebbed and flowed, as two skilled commanders—Erwin Rommel, the German "desert fox" and the British general, Bernard Montgomery—parried each other's thrusts in the deserts between Libya and Egypt. Then in October 1942 the British defeated the German *Afrikakorps* at El Alamein in Eygpt, barely seventy miles from the Nile delta. As at Stalingrad so too at El Alamein, the Nazi tide reached a high point and then began to recede. In November 1942, in the largest amphibious action yet attempted, British and American forces landed in Morocco and Algeria and attacked the *Afrikakorps* from the west. The campaign was an important test for the still green American troops; it was also a test of Allied strength and coordination, ably directed by an American commander, General Dwight D. Eisenhower. By May 1943 and after heavy losses, the Axis powers had been pushed out of Africa.

In July another mammoth amphibious assault carried Anglo-American forces into Sicily. As they advanced across the island, the Fascist Grand Council voted Mussolini out of office; and in September Allied forces landed in southern Italy. In the year since Stalingrad and the North African invasion, the course of the war had changed. Hitler still controlled most of Europe and much of the heaviest fighting lay

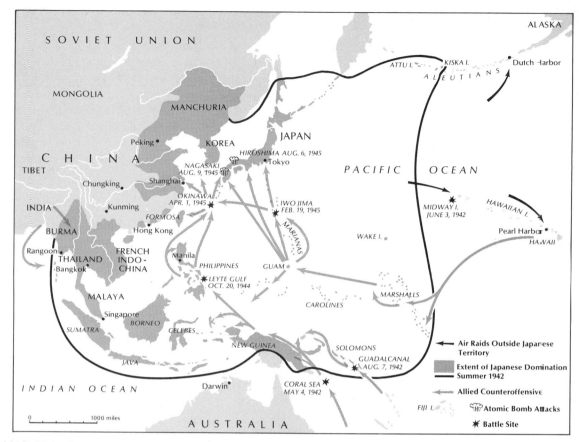

MAP 29.2: WORLD WAR II IN THE PACIFIC

ahead, but the eventual outcome no longer seemed in doubt.

Japan meanwhile had made sweeping gains in East Asia and the Pacific (see Map 29.2). Shortly after Pearl Harbor Roosevelt and Churchill had agreed to give their battle against Germany priority over the war in Asia. The decision acknowledged the bonds of Western culture, the importance of European industrial power, and the danger that Russia might not long survive without massive help. In effect the policy required the United States to postpone revenge for her defeats in the Pacific. She had lost the Philippine Islands after dramatic and costly defensive stands at Bataan and

Corregidor early in 1942. Later in May a naval engagement in the Coral Sea, just north of Australia, ended with no clear-cut victory but reduced the immediate threat of further Japanese gains. In June the Japanese landed in the Aleutian Islands, but American air power drove off their attempt to invade Midway Island. By the end of the year, U.S. forces had taken the first steps in their slow progress back through the Pacific territories.

THE DEMANDS OF TOTAL WAR

When war was declared, Germany was much the best prepared of any nation. But that advantage, critical in the early years, had largely disappeared three years later. In this total war which required the coordination of entire national economies, long-range planning, and the cooperation of every sector of society, that state in theory most devoted to militarism managed in practice less well than its enemies.

The Allies

The Soviet Union suffered the heaviest losses of any combatant whether measured in terms of people killed by war and starvation or the capacity for agricultural and industrial production that was lost. Accustomed to central planning, the Soviets quickly mobilized every resource, subjecting civilians to severe rationing and factory workers to military discipline and to increased hours of labor. Even before 1939 Stalin had adopted the policy of industrializing the more backward and safely distant regions east of the Urals, and in the months before Hitler's attack in 1941 hundreds of factories had been dismantled and moved piece by piece, and some 3500 new industrial enterprises were established there. From this base the Soviet Union was able throughout the war to produce most of the military supplies it needed, aided by the established practice of employing women (who were over half the industrial work force by war's end). The prodigies performed despite hardship and defeats testify to sustained morale. Patriotism of a rather old-fashioned and bourgeois sort became the dominant theme of Soviet public life.

Great Britain responded more slowly; not until the fall of France did the grim meaning of the war make itself felt at home. The bombing of Britain, however, seemed to stiffen civilian morale; and gradually the government developed a capacity to coordinate and command national resources with an efficiency any dictator could have admired. Although the number of workdays lost to strikes increased in the course of the war, so did production; and, as in World War I, the end of unemployment (a million workers remained without work in the first year of the war), better wages, the employment of more women, and higher taxes somewhat narrowed class differences. The United States also mobilized its full economic resources for this war, producing by the end of 1942 more war matériel than all its enemies combined. Ships, planes, arms, and munitions poured from American factories and, with food from American farms, flowed across the oceans to Britain and the Soviet Union. In this war of total economies, where organization was more important than brilliant strategy or even technological discoveries, the Allies were clearly superior.

Nazi Rule

Until 1943 German civilians experienced few real hardships and nothing comparable to the sacrifices by which the Soviets or the lowered standard of living by which the British squeezed the maximum war production from their economies. Nor was German output much greater than at the war's outset. This changed when Albert Speer was given increased powers to direct the economy, as he had been demanding. In mid-July 1943 German production was twice what it had been in 1939 despite Allied bombing, and a year later it was three times the prewar level. By then, however, advancing Allied armies were rapidly reducing the resources available to the country.

The delayed and incomplete social and economic mobilization of Nazi Germany stemmed from the very nature of the regime. The illusion, supported by breath-taking successes and official propaganda, that the war would soon be over encouraged interim measures rather than long-range planning. Disdainful of intellectuals and distrustful of established interests, the Nazis failed to achieve the effective cooperation with science and industry that marked the British and American war effort. In their incessant

Norwegians silently observe the arrival of German army reinforcements at Oslo station in 1940. (Photo: Wide World Photos)

battles for power the party, the army, and local officials often pursued conflicting or self-defeating policies. Europe's Nazi rulers had an unparalleled opportunity to bend the Continent to their purposes. Yet the much-advertised New Order remained curiously ill defined, while policies of terror and destruction reduced efficiency and undermined even its clearest goal, the exploitation of conquered territory.

Truly totalitarian control in subject lands proved beyond the German reach. Content with ruthless terror and intermittent demonstrations of their power, Nazi administrators tended in practice to leave day-to-day affairs to established institutions and local officials. Despite the fear they induced, the conquerors were never secure. Unoccupied France, governed from Vichy, was taken over in November 1942; and the French, relatively better treated than Eastern Europeans, suffered severe deprivations in the remaining years of the war, including food rations that provided about half the minimum needed for decent health. Having stockpiled critical supplies and gained access to more through conquest, Germany's most crucial need was for workers. Slave labor was the answer chosen in accordance with Nazi racial theory. The "Aryan" populations of Nordic lands and the "mixed races" of the industrial West were generally better treated and encouraged to maintain production (although a million Frenchmen, including 220,000 Jews, were taken to Germany). Slavs were rated much lower on the Nazi racial scale, and they were driven from the German borders in "population transfers" that vacated land for German settlers; eventually some 5 million were shipped like cattle to labor in Germany. By 1944 the 7 million foreign workers in Germany constituted one-fifth the work force.

But the hysteria of racial hatred dominated rational planning. Brutalized and starved workers could hardly be efficient; transporting and guarding them became an enormous, corrupting, and expensive enterprise. Hounding Jews and Gypsies or cramming Jews into ghettos was not enough; in 1942 a meeting of the regime's high officials adopted, in a phrase the century will never forget, "the final solution of the Jewish question." That solution was extermination. By 1945, nearly 6 million Jews and probably as many others—Poles, Gypsies, and Magyars especially—had died in places like Auschwitz, Buchenwald, and Dachau. These camps were also supposed to be centers of production. A Krupp arms factory, an I. G. Farben chemical plant, and a coal mine were part of the Auschwitz complex. But its chief product was corpses at a rate that reached 12,000 a day.

Such horror on such a scale challenges every concept of civilization and raises almost unbearable doubts about Western society and human nature. For contemporaries who did not know the full extent of Nazi policies, there was nevertheless plenty in public practice to stimulate opposition to Nazi rule; that opposition gradually and against great odds evolved some organization, its every act a declaration of heroic confidence that the Nazis must someday fail. Small cells of resisters formed loose networks that spread through each nation and assumed an importance far beyond their power or steadily growing numbers. Always based

German soldiers prepare to execute a Jew near Lodz, Poland. The doomed man, forced to wear the star of David, has had to dig his own grave. This was one of many photographs found in German headquarters after the Allies invaded Poland. (Photo: UPI)

on a small minority, the partisan movements achieved particular strength in Denmark and Norway, the Netherlands, France, and Yugoslavia. A number of them received material help and direction from their formal or unofficial governments in exile operating from London, which also commanded whatever fighting men had been able to escape the occupied homelands, the most notable of which was the Free French national committee, headed by General Charles de Gaulle.

Millions of Europeans came to rely on the BBC for encouragement and reliable news, for the Germans were losing the propaganda war as well. Some of the most active resistance fighters were simply individual members of neighborhood groups, but most were attached to parties with developed ideologies describing a better postwar world. The resistance movements thus revived faith in democracy and social justice even as they echoed prewar politics; in France for example moderates, Christian Democrats, Socialists, and Communists each had their organization. Generally the Christian Democrats and especially the Marxists developed the largest and most effective groups, thus laying the basis for powerful postwar parties.

The Nazis levied the harshest of reprisals for resistance. When Czechs assassinated the new "Reich protector of Bohemia and Moravia" in June 1942, the Germans retaliated by wiping out the village of Lidice, which they suspected of hiding the murderers—every man was killed, every woman and child deported; and on a single day in 1943, the Germans put 1,400 men to death in a Greek village.

Yet the underground movements continued to grow, and their maneuvers became a barometer of the course of the war. In France partisans expanded their activities from smuggling out Allied airmen and isolated dynamiting to large-scale operations closely coordinated from London. Norway's resistance helped force the Germans to keep 300,000 troops there and away from the more active fronts. In Yugoslavia the partisans, divided between two political groups, maintained an active guerrilla war; and the British decision to support the group led by Tito as the more effective all but assured his control of the country at the end of the war. After the Allied invasion of Italy, partisan groups there maintained an unnerving harassment of Fascist and Nazi forces. Even in Germany herself some members of the army and the old aristocracy began to plot against Hitler, and in July 1944 a group of conspirators planted a bomb under a table at which he was directing a conference. Although the Führer escaped serious injury, the sense of his doom had spread to the heart of Germany.

THE POLITICS OF COALITION

Almost until the end, however, Hitler remained firmly in command, and Nazi strategy was wholly committed to holding off Germany's enemies. Mussolini, a victim of his own propaganda who had consistently overestimated Italian strength and yet was reluctant to demand that Italians make the sacrifices of total war, had little influence on German plans. With his fall, the Italian Peninsula, too, came under the direct control of the German army. There was no such unanimity among the Allies. Although the nature of Nazism and its fearful power provided one simple common purpose, the Allies said less about their long-range goals than they had in World War I. And their mutual distrust complicated the conduct of the war itself.

War Aims

Stalin insisted that Russia keep the Polish territory taken in 1939; Poland could be compensated to the west at the expense of a defeated Germany. The British rightly warned that the Americans would find this unacceptable; and in fact the Anglo-American powers never forgot that Communists had encouraged revolution from Moscow to the Rhine after World War I or that Russian imperialism had sought to expand into Eastern Europe since the eighteenth century. In London the exiled leaders of the Eastern European nations agitated for their various nationalist aims while Stalin's ominous references to the need for "friendly" governments along Russia's borders made everyone shudder.

When Anglo-American successes in North Africa were not followed by invasion of the Continent, the Russians suspected that they and the Germans were being left to annihilate each other. The Americans continued to favor a direct attack on the mainland, but the British still argued in terms of tightening the blockade in the west and of encircling Germany by means of more limited assaults from the eastern Mediterranean. Churchill, it became clear, would like to have his troops so placed as to give the Western powers a voice in the disposition of Eastern Europe.

With such issues before them, Roosevelt and Churchill met at Casablanca in January 1943. There they agreed to invade Sicily (to the Russians' disgust) and to demand the unconditional surrender of Italy and Germany, an expression of moral outrage against fascism that has been heavily criticized since for strengthening the Axis powers' determination to resist. Its main purpose, however, may well have been to reassure the suspicious Allies that none would seek a self-serving, separate peace.

Sponsored Regimes

Spokesmen for the powerless governments in exile viewed what they could learn about the meeting with some misgivings, for in practice the Anglo-Americans were not above dealing with regimes that bore a fascist taint. At the time of the North African invasion, for example, Admiral Jean François Darlan, a former vice premier of Vichy and then commander of its armed forces, had happened to be in Algiers. Eisenhower's staff had quickly negotiated an agreement with him so that his forces would not resist the invasion, in return for which Darlan had been named governor-general of French Africa. De Gaulle was outraged. Since his call for continued resistance in 1940 and his organization from London of the French forces fighting with the Allies, the general had pressed his claim to represent the voice of France. His hauteur, his persistent demand for a French part in Allied policy, and his considerable success in winning support in French colonies had made his relations with Britain and the United States cool at best. Darlan's assassination in December 1942 reduced tension a bit, though the British and Americans continued

to deal with Vichy authorities in French North Africa even after the Germans occupied all of France.

The issue of what governments to foster soon extended to Italy. In July 1943, two weeks after the landing in Sicily, Italy's Fascist Grand Council met in a hasty session, voted Mussolini out of office, and had him arrested, naming Marshal Pietro Badoglio prime minister. A new coalition of monarchists and more moderate Fascists then sought an armistice. The Committees of National Liberation, composed of anti-Fascists from liberals through Communists, were now prominent throughout Italy, however, and they wanted nothing to do with the marshal, a Fascist hero who had led the campaign in Ethiopia, or with the king, who had bowed to Mussolini for twenty years.

Again the Allies were divided. Britain favored the monarchy and feared leftist influence in the Committees of Liberation; the Americans leaned toward the Committees but shared the British concern about communist influence and so joined in excluding the Russians from active participation in the Allied military government installed in Italy. Stalin accepted this, recognized the new Italian regime, and encouraged Italy's Communists to pursue a policy more flexible and accommodating than even the Socialists could swallow. But arguments about spheres of influence and the need for military control which were used against the Russians in Italy would soon be used by them elsewhere.

All this bargaining had occurred without an actual encounter among the Big Three. Finally, in December 1943, Roosevelt, Churchill, and Stalin met for the first time, at Teheran. Whereas the British had earlier served as mediators between the United States and the Soviet Union, it was the Americans who now appeared closer to a middle position. The conversations were not easy, but they provided a basis for continued cooperation. Churchill

Stalin, Roosevelt, and Churchill, meeting for the first time at Teheran, reached an understanding that laid the groundwork for Allied cooperation in pursuing the war. (Photo: UPI)

proposed an invasion of the Dardanelles, but this move was rejected and an invasion of France agreed to for the following year. There was tentative understanding that Russia would accept a boundary with Poland along the old Curzon Line, and the nature of the postwar Polish government was left open. Stalin also promised to declare war on Japan as soon as Germany surrendered. The Big Three maintained their unity largely by postponing action on difficult and divisive issues; but that at least assured the continued, vigorous prosecution of the war.

THE ROAD TO VICTORY

By late September 1943 the Allies were well entrenched in Italy and rapidly amassing still greater power. Germany could not hope to win but might prevent cataclysmic defeat by taking advantage of her shortening lines of communication and defensive strength. Meanwhile the Allied air assault subjected Germany to constant pounding, and the war in Russia was exhausting the German capacity to fight.

Military Victory

Although the Allies captured Naples in October, their campaign in Italy was bogged down in difficult terrain and faced fierce German resistance with an insufficient number of troops, for their main forces were assigned to the forthcoming invasion of France. It took the Allies five months to fight their way past a costly new beachhead at Anzio; not until May 1944 did they finally seize the old Benedictine abbey of Monte Cassino, less than seventy-five miles inland, and then only after a destructive bombardment. Rome, the first European capital to be liberated, fell in June.

Mussolini, who had been rescued from prison the previous September in a daring maneuver by German troops, had proclaimed a fascist republic in the north and was now frankly a German puppet. For Italians, with their country a battleground for foreign armies, the war also became a civil war against fascism. In December 1943 King Victor Emmanuel III announced his intention to abdicate in favor of his son (though he did not actually do so until 1946), and Badoglio gave way to a cabinet drawn from members of the Committees of National Liberation. The new government joined the Allied cause, and the slow push northward was aided by partisan risings against Nazi occupation. German resistance now converged on the so-called Gothic Line, running from Pisa to Rimini. Not until this line was pierced, in September 1944, could further drives lead to the capture of Ravenna (in December), Bologna, Verona, and Genoa (in April 1945). At that point German resistance ceased.

Russia's successes were more spectacular. In the spring of 1943, the Germans still had vitality enough to launch an offensive of their own, but it slowed within weeks. In July the Russian army began a relentless advance that continued with few setbacks for almost two years. Its armies now outnumbered the Germans, and it enjoyed a growing edge in matériel as well. Soviet forces reached the Dnieper and Kiev by November. In February 1944 they were at the Polish border; they retook the Crimea in the spring; in August Rumania surrendered; Finland and Bulgaria fell a few weeks later. When the Allied leaders met next, at Yalta in February 1945, Russian troops held part of Czechoslovakia and stood on the German frontier of Poland.

The opening of the final act of the war in Europe was the Allied invasion of France across the English Channel. The Germans knew that such an attack must come, but they believed that it would concentrate on the area around Calais, the shore closest to England. The Allies encouraged this belief through various feints and then actually landed in Normandy to the west of Caen on June 6, 1944. The operation was enormous: it called for putting 150,000 men ashore within two days, supported by 5,000 ships and 1,500 tanks. But the Anglo-Americans were now expert in amphibious assaults, they held overwhelming control of the air, and the Germans failed to coordinate their defenses.

In a complex series of costly landings, Eisenhower's Allied force poured onto the French beaches, the first of more than a million men to disembark within a few months. In July they broke through the German defense and began a series of rapid drives through France. A second amphibious attack, in southern France in mid-August, led to swift advances inland greatly aided by well-organized French resistance groups. On August 24 the Parisian underground rose against the Germans, and French forces under Charles de Gaulle quickly entered the cheering city. Brussels fell a week later, and ten days after that American troops crossed the German frontier.

Hitler's desperate replies to the Allied blows included the launching in June of a new "miracle" weapon, the relatively ineffective V-1 pilotless plane, followed in September by the far more dangerous V-2 rocket. Had the Nazis earlier recognized the potential of this new weapon and pushed its development, its effects might have been devastating. The V-2 flew faster than the speed of sound and was almost impossible to intercept; but these

Charles de Gaulle, the symbol of French resistance, greeted by Parisians on the day of the city's liberation in 1944. (Photo: © Robert Capa/ Magnum)

rockets were hard to aim, too few, and utilized too late to be decisive. More threatening was a counterstroke in December through the Ardennes on either side of Bastogne that rocked the Allied line back. The Battle of the Bulge, which cost about 70,000 men on each side before the Allies regained the initiative in January, was the last offensive the Germans would mount.

Competing Allies

As Allied troops drove farther into the Continent, the Big Three met again, this time at Yalta, for their last wartime conference; and the decisions they made that February, though widely hailed at the time, have become the most controversial of World War II. The hurried meeting dealt with four broad issues:

1. The creation of a United Nations Organization. The U.S.S.R.'s request for 16 votes to counterbalance the votes of the British Commonwealth and of U.S.-dominated Latin America was reduced to 3, and the veto she also demanded was restricted slightly.

2. Russian entry into the war against Japan. Russia agreed to declare war against Japan within ninety days after the defeat of Germany; she was to receive in compensation the territories she had surrendered to Japan in 1905 and was guaranteed a sphere of influence in Man-

churia. The agreement clearly strengthened her position in Asia.

3. The treatment of Germany. The assignment of zones of occupation to each of the Big Three presented little problem, and Russia reluctantly accepted the proposal that France also be given a zone to occupy. But the reparations and "labor services" the Russians demanded were enormous, and agreements on specific terms had to be postponed.

4. The establishment of new governments in the liberated nations. This, the most difficult issue of all, could not be postponed much longer; and yet every effort at accord merely exposed the distrust between Russia and the Western powers.

By this time the form of Italy's government had been largely set, and de Gaulle was reasserting the independence of France; but the degree of Soviet dominance in Eastern Europe was an open question. There were indications that Soviet leaders might show restraint. In most of the Eastern nations they occupied, the Russians were tolerating all the old antifascist parties and seemed to support fairly broad coalitions, but Soviet officials rejected participation by the Western powers in the affairs of the new governments and restricted Allied observers. Four months earlier, when Churchill visited Moscow, Stalin had agreed to the prime minister's bold suggestions that Russia should have overwhelming predominance in Rumania and the largest influence in Bulgaria, that the British be given a free hand in Greece, and that Russia and Britain have an equal interest in Yugoslavia and Hungary. And Stalin in fact did nothing when Churchill strongly intervened in the civil war raging in Greece, routing the leftists.

Such crude understandings, however, offered little protection against the cold self-interest Russia had shown on other occasions. As Soviet troops had approached Warsaw in August 1944, the underground there arose against the Germans. But these partisans were closely tied to the anti-communist Polish government in London, and the Russians had simply halted their advance until the Germans wiped out the Polish resistance fighters.

At Yalta no real agreement could be found about the borders of Poland or the independence of her government. The general formula adopted, with its references to democratic governments and assurances of free elections for all liberated nations, was subject to many interpretations and settled little. An adamant Stalin, a pugnacious Churchill, and a weary and ill Roosevelt turned back to the wars they still faced in Germany and against Japan.

The End of the War

As the Allies pushed into Germany from all sides, it became clear that Berlin would be the final battle. Eisenhower feared that Hitler intended to make a last desperate stand in his famed mountain redoubt at Berchtesgaden in the south German mountains (in fact German resistance was everywhere collapsing); he therefore halted the eastward advance of American and British armies at the Elbe River in preparation for the battle in the south, which was never joined. The Russians took Berlin. Hitler had characteristically ordered the German garrison to defend the capital to the death, which assured the maximum destruction of the city. Hitler himself committed suicide on April 30, 1945; his aides burned the body, and the remains have never been found. Four days later a group of German officers signed the final, unconditional surrender. The war in Europe was over.

But in Asia the world conflict continued. Despite massive bombing and repeated naval victories, progress toward Japan had been agonizingly slow the past three years. Hundreds of islands in the Pacific and thousands of miles of jungle had to be laboriously reconquered in the face of fierce resistance.

Survivors of Hiroshima, victims of a new weapon of war, one of science's most impressive achievements. (Photo: Wide World Photos)

As the American forces, commanded by Douglas MacArthur, closed in on Japan, they unleashed an air bombardment of unprecedented intensity. During the three months after Germany's surrender, the raids obliterated Japan's navy, industrial plants, and large parts of her cities—nearly 200,000 people were killed in Tokyo in just one week. But still the Japanese would not surrender.

On August 6 the new president of the United States, Harry S Truman (Roosevelt had died in April), authorized the use of a new weapon, developed after years of secret research, the atomic bomb. In one blow half of the city of Hiroshima was wiped off the face of the earth and a quarter of its 320,000 inhabitants killed. Two days later Russia declared war on Japan, and on August 9 the Americans dropped a more powerful atomic bomb on the city of Nagasaki.

Faced by total annihilation, the Japanese surrendered unconditionally on September 2. Remarkable accomplishments in science and technology, sustained by great wealth and reinforced by scores of European scientists driven to sanctuary in the United States, had permitted a great democracy to end World War II by unleashing a new order of terror upon mankind. Later, some would question the decision to use so terrible an instrument; but even in the jubilation of victory, statesmen busily reordering a shattered world had to recognize that another war could mean the end of civilization.

II. RECOVERY BETWEEN TWO GIANTS

Wartime conditions did not disappear for years. It took the better part of a decade for the millions of refugees and displaced persons to find settled lives; the rationing of food and clothes continued in many countries into the 1950s; some of the most severely bombed cities, such as London and Dresden, were still engaged in reconstruction in the 1960s. Moreover troops from the two world powers, the United States and Russia, swarmed over the Continent, symbols as well as instruments of a new era of foreign domination. The very task of European reorganization was to depend on aid, restrictions, and policies determined by outsiders.

THE CONDITIONS OF PEACE

Unlike the treaties prepared at the Paris Peace Conference after World War I, the settlements of 1945 were limited, relatively informal, and indeterminate arrangements. Although the leaders of Russia, Britain, and the United States met at Potsdam for two weeks in July 1945, they hardly hammered out broad new policies. Indeed they barely knew each other, for of the Big Three only Stalin had also been present at the Yalta Conference five months before. President Truman had been in office only three months, and in the midst of the meeting, Winston Churchill was defeated in the British elections and replaced by Clement Attlee.

The Settlement

Nevertheless the Allies did agree on basic regulations for the future of Germany: the dissolution of all Nazi institutions, the restoration of free speech and democratic politics, the abolition of all armaments production, and the control of heavy industry. For a while the Americans had leaned toward a plan devised by Secretary of the Treasury Henry Morgenthau, which would have banned industrial activity and restricted Germany to agrarian pursuits, but in the end the Potsdam conferees took no such radical measures.

The resolution of most political issues was left to unspecified future meetings. Ostensibly Allied forces were merely occupiers and were not to influence local politics except to repress Nazism. In fact the distrust between Russia and the Western powers led unintentionally to a peculiarly harsh retribution—Germany was not only occupied but effectively divided into two states. But the absence of definitive decisions at Potsdam long continued to bedevil the Allies, particularly in regard to Berlin; divided into four occupation zones and originally administered by an Interallied Control Council, the city was isolated in the midst of the eastern (Russian) sector to be the focus of contention for more than twenty years.

The one deliberate political "punishment" levied on Germany at the conference was the relocation of her eastern border to the west, at the rivers Oder and Neisse, which thus enlarged Poland. This shift produced huge new flows of refugees, which increased when Czechoslovakia, independent again, expelled all her Germans. Some 12 million displaced persons thus had to be resettled by the harassed occupying powers.

It was agreed that a Council of Foreign Ministers of the four principal Allies (France was now included) would continue to meet after Potsdam; and though the council soon became a forum for quarrels between the Russians and the others, it did draft a series of peace treaties in 1946. The nations that had fought the Axis in Europe gathered in Paris early in 1947 to sign treaties with Germany's cobelligerents: Italy, Rumania, Hungary, Bulgaria, and Finland, each of which ceded minor territories to her neighbors. Austria, however, like Germany, obtained no formal treaty and remained divided in four occupied zones, with the difference that the Austrians held their own capital, Vienna, from which to establish a unified government that could prepare the way for eventual independence.

The Potsdam conference also laid down the terms of the peace with Japan. Under the settlement the Soviet Union made some gains, and the European nations regained their colonies in Asia. But the prime beneficiaries were China and above all the United States, whose troops occupied Japan and most of the other strategic islands in the Pacific. Little account needed to be taken of Europe in these arrangements, America alone possessed the means of manufacturing the atomic bomb, and her power and wealth extended across the world.

Within Europe the first concern was to root out fascism. In the lands the Germans had occupied, notably France, this took the form of

summary executions of ordinary collaborators and emotional prosecutions of leading figures like Pierre Laval and Marshal Pétain. In Germany herself, however, the vastness of the problem made enforcement of anti-Nazi regulations against all but the highest leaders difficult. Millions of forms were filled out and hundreds of trials held. But the energy needed to sustain the drive against former Nazis soon waned, and only those prosecuted early received significant punishments.

Children in postwar Bratislava. (Photo: UPI)

An American lieutenant colonel talks to some two hundred German civilians forced to observe this scene inside Landsberg concentration camp. (Photo: Wide World Photos)

To signify that their massacres and genocide had gone beyond the limits that a civilized world could endure, even in wartime, an international tribunal tried Hitler's closest associates for war crimes. Held in Nuremberg in 1945 and 1946, the trials were also intended to inform the German people of the full horror of Nazi rule and to establish some acceptable standards of warfare. Yet to many, trials not conducted by some neutral body seemed a veneer for vengeance and without juridical basis. But the sincerity of those solemn hearings is reflected in the restrained judgments that followed—only twelve of the twenty-two prime defendants were condemned to death, and three were acquitted.

The United Nations

Although the League of Nations had failed, many looked ahead during the war to the time when effective international cooperation could once again be organized. Thus the Atlantic Charter, issued in 1941 by Great Britain and the United States in the hope of establishing collective security, led gradually to the United Nations Organization.

Its first agency, the United Nations Relief and Rehabilitation Administration (UNRRA), established late in 1943 to aid countries reconquered from the Axis, came to play a major role in the reconstruction of postwar Europe. The following year Italy, though a former enemy, was allocated $50 million, mainly in medical supplies. A related effort concentrated on economic rehabilitation. To avoid the devastating inflation that had followed World War I, the United Nations Conference at Bretton Woods, New Hampshire, in 1944 created an International Monetary Fund and an International Bank for Reconstruction and Development. The two institutions, with nearly $20 billion in assets, played a major role in maintaining the stability of currencies and international exchange after the war.

But the main aim of the United Nations was to achieve international security, based on the continued cooperation of the wartime Allies. At a meeting at Dumbarton Oaks in Washington, D.C., in 1944, representatives of the United States, Russia, and the British Commonwealth agreed to create an international organization to preserve peace throughout the world. A few months after the discussions in 1945 at Yalta, fifty-one countries approved the United Nations Charter at a special conference held in San Francisco. The charter established a General Assembly of all members to determine policy; a decision-making Security Council of eleven members to supervise "the maintenance of international peace"; and various economic, social, and legal agencies. Permanent Security Council seats were reserved for the great powers—the United States, the Soviet Union, China, Great Britain, and France—with the remainder rotating by election from among the other member states. But the Big Five were given the right to veto any council action, and Russia's opposition to much that was proposed eventually shifted some of the initiative to the General Assembly, where a two-thirds majority could overrule a veto. In this maneuvering both Russia and the United States needed the support of the so-called Third World, the nations of Asia, Africa, and Latin America that were not formally tied to one of the two major blocs. The superpowers were led from necessity to recognize the importance of these areas and to acknowledge their drives for independence.

Despite the position of Britain and France on the Security Council, therefore, and the election of Scandinavians as the UN's secretary-general (chief executive officer) until 1961, most of the organization's attention was focused on Asia and Africa after 1945, and many major decisions depended entirely on the United States or Russia. Even the UN's relief work after 1945 was primarily an American undertaking. Thus the United Nations, though structurally similar to the League of Nations, in fact represented a redistribution of international power in which Europe no longer occupied central place.

The Devastation

In contrast to World War I, a majority of fatalities in World War II were civilians, killed by bombs, conquerors, or concentration camp officials. Russia alone lost about 20 million people, and the Germans murdered more than 12 million in concentration camps, half of them Jews who had never seen combat. Elsewhere the casualties were not on this scale—perhaps 5 million Western Europeans and a similar number in all other theaters of war. For every person killed, two were either wounded or taken captive. Leaving aside some 25 million refugees (about half of them Germans) who had to be resettled after the war, it can be estimated that the total casualties of World War II— dead, wounded, or crippled by inhumane treatment—far exceeded 50 million.

The physical destruction was likewise unprecedented. In 1945 Europe's industrial capability, crippled by the obliteration of factories, communications facilities, and large segments of cities, was perhaps half of what it had been in 1939. In France alone some 2 million buildings needed reconstruction, and only one-tenth of the country's vehicles were usable. Less than half of such major cities as Frankfurt, Dresden, Brest, and Toulon were still standing. The Continent's most important ports, bridges, and rail lines had been destroyed by Allied bombs. Ironically, Germany's industry was in better shape than any on the Continent west of Russia, its fixed assets higher in 1945 than in 1939 despite Allied bombing.

Agriculture was also hard hit: France's cattle population had been reduced by half, and large areas of farmland in France, Italy, and Germany could not be cultivated. The need for food was so urgent during the first months of peace that supplies were sometimes dropped by parachute to speed distribution; in the winter of 1945–1946, starvation stalked the Continent, and in some places, such as Vienna, thousands died—many of them children—before sufficient food arrived. Disease was also an ever-present danger, although a newly developed drug, penicillin, did help limit the epidemics that erupted as a result of inadequate sanitation and medical facilities.

Some experts estimated that it would take twenty years for the Continent to regain its prewar prosperity. The very necessities of life were in desperately short supply, and Europeans had few means of producing goods themselves, and often only an illicit black market made essential supplies available to the few who could afford them. Impoverished and ravaged nations thus looked to the United States and Russia for relief.

III. RECOVERY IN A EUROPE DIVIDED

Europe, whose political and ideological divisions in the 1930s had led to world war, emerged more firmly divided than ever. To those who had been on the winning side, the postwar world often seemed like the aftermath of defeat rather than victory. By 1948 almost all the European countries (save only the traditional neutrals, Switzerland and Sweden) had become aligned with one or the other of the two superpowers, the Soviet Union or the United States (see Map 29.3). And in each European country the form of its recovery from the war bore the stamp of one of the two great blocs of economic and political power.

THE POLITICS OF CONSTRAINT

Nowhere was the direct influence of foreign domination so visible as in Eastern Europe, but in the West as well political life was constrained by the shadow of the superpowers and the conflicts of the cold war. While the European

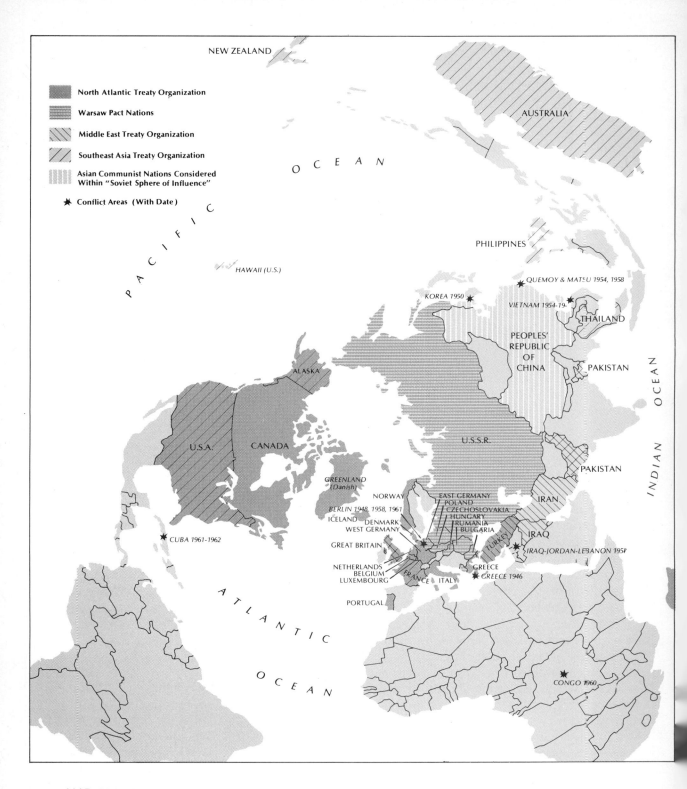

MAP 29.3: THE COLD WAR OF THE 1950s

Legend:
- North Atlantic Treaty Organization
- Warsaw Pact Nations
- Middle East Treaty Organization
- Southeast Asia Treaty Organization
- Asian Communist Nations Considered Within "Soviet Sphere of Influence"
- ★ Conflict Areas (With Date)

Labels on map:
NEW ZEALAND
AUSTRALIA
PACIFIC OCEAN
PHILIPPINES
HAWAII (U.S.)
QUEMOY & MATSU 1954, 1958
KOREA 1950
VIETNAM 1954-19-
THAILAND
PEOPLES' REPUBLIC OF CHINA
PAKISTAN
ALASKA
U.S.A.
CANADA
U.S.S.R.
PAKISTAN
INDIAN OCEAN
GREENLAND (Danish)
NORWAY
EAST GERMANY
POLAND
CZECHOSLOVAKIA
HUNGARY
RUMANIA
BULGARIA
IRAN
BERLIN 1948, 1958, 1961
ICELAND
DENMARK
WEST GERMANY
IRAQ
GREAT BRITAIN
TURKEY
IRAQ-JORDAN-LEBANON 1958
CUBA 1961-1962
NETHERLANDS
BELGIUM
LUXEMBOURG
FRANCE
ITALY
GREECE
GREECE 1946
PORTUGAL
ATLANTIC OCEAN
CONGO 1960

states relaxed their grasp of old colonial empires, their subordination to the Soviet Union and the United States made them in turn seem colonies themselves.

Eastern Europe: The Politics of Puppets

In 1945 Soviet troops held the entire area from the Adriatic to the Baltic just short of a line stretching between Trieste and Hamburg. In the Soviet Union, whose economic future would largely determine the recovery of all of Eastern Europe, industrial production was less than two-thirds of its prewar level, and the Five-Year Plan announced in 1946, which was designed to increase Russia's industrial output by more than 50 percent over her 1940 level, depended openly on her ransacking East Germany and the other occupied areas for materials. Three formerly independent states, Estonia, Latvia, and Lithuania, became Soviet republics, and Russia further extended her western border with annexations of territories once belonging to East Prussia, Poland, Hungary, and Rumania. Elsewhere the subordination of local institutions to communist orthodoxy soon became no less blatant.

The Russians restrained the forces of revolution in Eastern Europe, more explosive in 1945 than in 1918, that were fed by long-ignored issues of land distribution and industrial development. But they used these issues, skillful political maneuvers, and the crudest coercion to establish communist governments subservient to Russia. The exclusion of leading anti-communists from a ruling coalition was usually the first step in the common procedure, followed by propaganda campaigns, electoral pressures, and sudden arrests that eliminated noncommunists from positions of power. Finally a heavy-handed dictatorship set about creating a Soviet satellite with purge trials and secret police.

Rumania was first to feel the full weight of these techniques, and late in 1947 King Michael was forced into exile by the Communists. Po-

land had explicitly been promised free elections; but when these were held in 1947 a series of repressive measures against the minority National Peasant party left the dominant Independent Socialists with an overwhelming majority. The United States and Britain complained but to no avail. A few months later the leader of the National Peasant party fled to London, and his followers were purged. The Catholic Church was persecuted, the Independent Socialist party subordinated to the Workers' party (communist), and a Russian placed in command of the army. In short order Poland was firmly tied to the Soviet Union economically and politically.

A similar pattern developed elsewhere. Hungary's coalition government at first had an anti-Communist majority, but another dubious election, in 1949, gave the Communists complete control, and close links with Russia were quickly established. Following much the same course, Albania and Bulgaria became solid members of the communist bloc by 1950.

Czechoslovakia, with a notable democratic tradition, did not succumb so easily. The Communists constituted the largest postwar party but not a majority, and the president and foreign minister, Eduard Beneš and Jan Masaryk, were heirs to the liberal politics of prewar Czechoslovakia. But in 1948, when peaceful means had proved unsuccessful, the Communists threatened with Russian support to take over the country by force. Bowing to this pressure, Beneš placed the government under Communist control; a month later Masaryk died in a mysterious fall from a window; and late in the year a one-party election gave the Communists complete ascendancy, and Beneš resigned.

Yugoslavia on the other hand did not meekly follow the Russian lead, though communists dominated her government after Marshal Tito easily won the 1945 national election. Tito had had close contacts with the West throughout the war, and he resisted the Soviet Union's repeated efforts to control his foreign policy and interfere in domestic affairs. An open break came in 1948. Yugoslavia had joined with Russia and other Eastern European states the previous year to create the Cominform, an agency designed to coordinate international communist political activity, but she was now expelled from the organization and denounced by her neighbors, who also severed economic relations. While remaining communist in politics and ideology, Yugoslavia established ties with the West that gave her an independence not enjoyed by Soviet allies. Tito's insubordination seemed recklessly daring, but he demonstrated how a small state could use the tense balance between the superpowers to survive without total reliance on either of them.

In East Germany the Russians followed the same procedures as in the states of Eastern Europe. Early in 1946 they forced the major political group, the Social Democratic party, to merge with the Communist party, which put the Russians in complete control thereafter. Interpreting the economic restrictions imposed at Potsdam as severely as possible, they dismantled scores of factories, appropriated the Germans' postwar production, and forbade trade with the West—the latter two actions in violation of the Potsdam agreements. As West Germany began to revive economically in 1947, however, the Russians gradually allowed the eastern zone to increase its industrial activity, and in 1949 gave it independent status as the German Democratic Republic. The first elections, in 1950, confirmed the Communists' dominance.

Western Europe: The Politics of the Past
In circumstances that seemed unprecedented, each Western country was nevertheless drawn toward its prewar pattern of parliamentary life. The reestablishment of functioning institutions

and reconstruction of a viable economy took precedence over vaguer visions of reform. Before such needs, old ways were the natural recourse however much such conservatism belied the broader hopes of resistance movements and wartime rhetoric.

In West Germany elections held in 1946 produced a victory for the Christian Democrats over their somewhat less conservative opponents, the Social Democrats, both parties being firmly rooted in Germany's pre-Nazi political traditions. To speed the process of recovery, the Americans and British then combined their zones into a single economic unit and soon relaxed restrictions on economic activity. Early in 1949 the area occupied by the Western powers was granted its independence, the ad hoc division of Germany thereby acknowledged with the proclamation of the Federal Republic of Germany.

West Germany's federal structure, reinforced during the occupation period, allowed considerable autonomy to local states. But the truncated new state was more centralized and its political system (dominated by the two large parties) more stable than the old Weimar Republic which it otherwise strongly resembled. The chancellor for the next fourteen years was the Christian Democratic leader Konrad Adenauer, who was seventy-three years old in 1949 and who had been mayor of Cologne from 1917 to 1933. Under his firm and conservative leadership, West Germany, closely allied with the United States, rapidly prospered in an atmosphere of efficient calm.

In France the new Fourth Republic looked much like the Third. Political life was shaped by three large parties—the Communists, the Socialists, and a new Catholic party of the left, the MRP (Popular Republican Movement), which soon forced de Gaulle out of office as provisional president despite economic policies that included the nationalization of many im-

The Brandenburg gate in Berlin, a monument to Prussia's past military achievements, blocked by barbed wire in 1961 as the dividing line between East and West. (Photo: Wide World Photos)

portant industries. And whereas de Gaulle favored a strong president directly elected, the left wrote a constitution providing for a single representative chamber intended to dominate the executive—a position traditional to the left —only to have it rejected in a national referendum. The constitution narrowly adopted in 1946 then returned to the familiar bicameral system with most executive authority in the hands of a prime minister responsible to parliament (its only major innovation the granting of a larger voice to colonial representatives).

Governments were once again dependent on unstable coalitions, an instability increased by the fact that the Communists, the largest party, were the least tempted by compromise. The political balance thus shifted toward the shaky center as cabinets confronted strikers and agitation on the left and a dramatic revival of de Gaulle's popularity on the right.

In Italy more than 54 percent of the electorate voted in 1946 to replace the monarchy with a republic; and subsequent governments were dominated by the Christian Democrats, a sprawling Catholic party that combined much conservative sentiment with a more radical core inherited from the prefascist Popular party. From 1945 to 1953 the leader of the Christian Democrats and the central figure of Italian politics was Alcide De Gasperi. Prime minister during most of this time, he ostracized the Communists and took advantage of divisions among Socialists to bring Italy into close alliance with the United States. In the crucial elections of 1948, the Christian Democrats, aided by extensive American pressure, won an absolute majority, and the threat that the largest Communist party in the West might obtain power began to fade. With a program of moderate reform, including efforts to revitalize the economy of southern Italy and stimulate industry in the north, and a strong parliamentary leader manipulating a diffuse coalition of interests, Italy returned to the unheroic political traditions subverted by Fascists in the 1920s.

Among the smaller nations of Western Europe, the resumption of old ways was equally evident. Spain and Portugal, ostracized for their links with the Nazis, remained defiant dictatorships. In the democracies the traditional parties reemerged, though they were often faced by active Communist minorities and forced to promote domestic welfare through interventionist social and economic policies. Belgium for example retained her monarchy and returned to a government of shifting alliances as the old Socialist and Catholic parties jockeyed for power. Although the antagonism between the Walloons and Flemings persisted, the Belgians were nonetheless able to begin a rapid economic recovery and to provide broad-

ened welfare services. The Netherlands and the Scandinavian countries, where the Communists were generally not strong, underwent a similar growth of prosperity and social programs guided by often fragile coalition governments, most often led by Socialists.

In many respects postwar politics brought greater change in Great Britain than in Continental countries where the regimes themselves were new. Winston Churchill's defeat in the elections of 1945 was a turning away from wartime unity and sacrifice, for the Labour party won its enormous majority by promising to launch domestic reforms long postponed. Under Clement Attlee, who had led the party since 1935, it nationalized the Bank of England and a wide range of major industries and services, including the coal-mining, transportation, electrical, and—after great controversy—iron and steel industries. It also instituted extensive welfare programs and established public housing, national insurance, and free medical care for all Britons. At the same time, the government began to withdraw from the overseas empire to which men like Churchill had been so attached, granting India independence in 1947.

THE INTERNATIONAL CONTEXT

The mainlines of politics in most European states were now shaped by the intense competition between the Soviet Union and the United States. Each of these dominant powers professed a comprehensive ideology held to be universally valid and deeply rooted in the European experience. Each had well-organized allies in almost every nation. And each believed the other side fanatically determined to triumph by any means. In the postwar atmosphere of dislocation, domestic instability, and colonial revolt, the world dominance of one or the other of these superpowers seemed at stake in nearly every political conflict. The struggle between

Russian communism and American democratic capitalism reached the intensity of war without open battle—the Cold War began.

Foreign Pressures
President Truman increasingly agreed with his advisers (and with Churchill) that only the strongest measures could stop Soviet expansion, and he determined to devote the full weight of American manpower and money to containing Russian influence. When, therefore, the Western powers began to encourage the economic recovery of Germany, the Russians countered in July 1947 by closing off overland access to

In a little less than a year, 277,264 flights were completed in the Berlin airlift. (Photo: Fenno Jacobs/Black Star)

Berlin. War seemed imminent, and for nearly a year all supplies to West Berlin were ferried to the city in a remarkable airlift. By the time the crisis had been resolved, West and East Germany had become autonomous republics bearing the political trappings of the alliance to which they belonged.

In 1947 the American president also announced the Truman Doctrine, promising military and economic aid to nations threatened by Communist takeovers. Money and supplies at once poured into Greece, rent for more than a year by a recurrence of civil war in which the Communists were being helped by neighboring Yugoslavia. The American response, combined with Yugoslavia's break with Russia, enabled the Greek government to crush the opposition by 1949. Turkey, slowly moving toward the establishment of democratic institutions, received similar assistance.

A few months after the announcement of the doctrine, U.S. Secretary of State George Marshall unveiled a more far-reaching plan. To stimulate European recovery—and eliminate the economic conditions in which communism prospered—he offered massive economic aid to all nations still struggling to recover from the effects of the war. But Russia forbade the Eastern European states to participate in the American-sponsored program and established her own Council of Mutual Economic Assistance (Comecon) instead.

These antagonisms became major domestic issues as Communist parties throughout the West opposed the Marshall Plan despite its obvious benefits. In the East the last vestiges of noncommunist political activity were removed, symbolized by the exile of Poland's National Peasant party leader in 1947 and the resignation of Czechoslovakia's Eduard Beneš in 1948. In the West Communists were excluded from coalition governments in France and Italy in 1947 and from all government positions in Switzerland in 1950; West Germany banned the party itself in 1956.

Local issues were thus tinged by international implications. Every trade agreement was a litmus test of a country's intentions; strikes were denounced as communist-inspired attempts at subversion; spy scandals made sensational headlines; and travel between East and West became almost impossible. The relatively limited question of whether the city of Trieste belonged to Italy or Yugoslavia became the subject of intense great-power maneuvers. Unmistakably Europe had become a battleground in the Cold War.

And the two halves of Europe followed the lead of their powerful patrons. When the news arrived that the Soviet Union had tested her own atomic bomb in 1949, it was seen as a direct challenge to the United States, and Truman met it by announcing that American scientists were working on an even more devastating explosive, the hydrogen bomb. But the loss of the U.S. monopoly over atomic weapons made ground forces seem essential to deter further Soviet aggression without resort to the total annihilation of atomic war. Consequently in 1949 the North Atlantic Treaty Organization (NATO) was created to coordinate the military planning of the United States, Canada, and ten Western European states,[1] which in effect now received U.S. military aid. The Russians replied with the Warsaw Pact in 1955, which performed the same function for the Eastern Europeans. And when the communist North Koreans invaded South Korea in 1950, the United States at once felt duty-bound to seek the approval of the Western-controlled UN Assembly and to send troops to repel the incursion. Europe was but the most important zone of a cold war now world-wide.

The Loss of Empire

The most dramatic evidence of the decline in European power was the rapid dwindling of colonies and influence overseas. World War II had severely shaken the colonial empires, which no longer had the material means to suppress

---

[1] Great Britain, France, Belgium, the Netherlands, Luxembourg, Italy, Portugal, Denmark, Norway, and Iceland were the European members. Greece and Turkey would be added in 1952 and West Germany in 1955.

the increasingly powerful demands for independence in their overseas possessions. For a few months after the war ended, Great Britain and France enjoyed the luxury of their old rivalries in the Middle East. But in 1946 both withdrew from the new states of Lebanon and Syria, Trans-Jordan became independent, foreign troops left Iraq and Iran, and negotiations began for British forces to depart from Egypt and the Sudan.

At the same time, despite Arab hostility, Great Britain undertook concrete planning for the establishment of separate Jewish and Arab states in Palestine. Mounting terror campaigns from both sides notwithstanding, the British decided to remove all their troops in May 1948, and the United Nations, eager to give Jews a refuge following Hitler's persecutions, endorsed the creation of the state of Israel. The Arabs invaded the day the British left but were driven back despite a huge numerical superiority, and UN mediators were able to bring about a shaky truce that confirmed Israel's existence.

Colonialism weakened in Asia as well. The French recognized Vietnam as a free state in 1945; Ceylon and Burma gained their independence from Great Britain in 1948; and Indonesia won her freedom from the Dutch after a long struggle in 1949. Where only half-hearted efforts were made to grant true autonomy, however, as in Indonesia and Vietnam, Europeans found themselves fighting wars they could not win. In Vietnam, for instance, a French-educated Communist leader, Ho Chi Minh, organized a brilliant guerrilla campaign that became a serious and costly war, culminating in the capture of a major French base at Dien Bien Phu in 1954 and the expulsion of the French.

Throughout Asia the end of European domination left a heritage of ties to international capitalism, of bureaucracy and parties organized on Western models, and of nationalist and socialist ideas increasingly tempered by local traditions and such indigenous forms as passive resistance, developed to a fine political art by India's religious leader and social reformer Mohandas K. Gandhi. Local cultures often remained decisively important, however, and the prospect of Indian independence produced serious conflict only gradually reduced by dividing the subcontinent, with most Muslims giving allegiance to the newly created state of Pakistan and most Hindus loyal to India.

The resolution of all these struggles was outside European control. The creation of Israel, for example, depended primarily on UN intervention and above all on the diplomatic recognition of the new nation by the United States and the Soviet Union. Similarly the critical conflict in Iran was between the Russians, whose influence rapidly waned, and the Americans, whose economic aid rose with equal speed. Although Africa was less directly affected by the Cold War, the competition between the great powers encouraged formal independence there as well.

As the Europeans withdrew from these lands long under their hegemony, the U.S.-Soviet conflict remained. Pakistan committed herself to the West; India tried to steer a middle course; a major communist revolt broke out in Burma immediately after independence; and in Vietnam the French were encouraged by the United States while Ho Chi Minh was strongly supported by Russia and by the most formidable of the newly communist states, China, where Mao Tse-tung had seized power in 1948 after long civil conflict.

As a counterweight to these advances in Asia, the United States promoted the economic revival of a now democratic Japan and gave strong economic and military support to Taiwan (a large island off China still held by the Chinese nationalists). The American government also founded the Southeast Asia Treaty Organization (SEATO), a Pacific equivalent to NATO, in which Britain, Pakistan, Australia, New Zealand, and various Asian states joined with the United States in common defense. The creation of SEATO marked the further institutionalization of the Cold War on a world-wide scale.

In all these developments Europeans could be little more than spectators. Great Britain did attempt to use the Commonwealth of Nations, binding together all her former colonies under technical allegiance to the royal family, as a means of continuing her influence. But it was little more than a grand international club, incapable even of restraining conflicts among its members (between India and Pakistan for example) and rejected by the fiercely anti-British republic of Eire, which the British formally recognized in 1949. The main accomplishment of a similar French organization, the *Union Française*, was the survival of France's language and culture in her former colonies. Although right-wing elements within Europe resented these many losses, most Europeans were reconciled to the disappearance of world-wide possessions by a political and economic revival at home that could hardly have been foreseen during the late 1940s.

THE BASIS OF ECONOMIC REVIVAL

The greatest and most far-reaching changes in postwar Europe took place in the realm of economic affairs. Here, in contrast to domestic and international politics, renewed vitality led to innovations that eventually transformed society. Initially, however, in economic matters, too, it was rather the dependence of Europe's debt-ridden and disrupted nations on support from the superpowers that was most apparent.

Source of Strength
Europe proved to have extraordinary resources. The homeland of the Industrial Revolution, its populations possessed high levels of experience and skill. World War II, for all its destructive impact, had in many respects promoted the efficient utilization of these resources, taking up the considerable slack that a decade of depression had caused.

Full production and employment in wartime help explain one notable social phenomenon in Europe: the maintenance and in some countries the growth of the number of births. During World War I the birth rate had plummeted, and this had aggravated and perpetuated the wartime losses of human lives. Western Europe at least had a nearly opposite experience in World War II. The birth rate in France for example had declined by 45 percent in 1914–1918, but during World War II it increased 11 percent by comparison with the preceding decade; through the 1930s in fact, deaths had outnumbered births so persistently that many observers thought the country embarked on a path of "race suicide." Similarly, England's birth rate had fallen by 25 percent in the First World War and showed a relative increase of 18 percent during the Second. The figures followed an upward curve as well in almost all the neutral countries (Ireland, Spain, Sweden, Switzerland), whose economies had benefited from sales to the belligerents. In Germany herself the birth rate had dropped by 50 percent in World War I and by only 22 percent in World War II, despite the mobilization of millions of men and the death of many of them; Italy shows the same kind of pattern.

In sum, in the midst of the fighting, Western Europe witnessed the beginnings of a "baby boom," comparable to though never so large as that which occurred in the United States during the same period. Relatively high birth rates were maintained until 1963, when a slow decline ensued. Given the war losses, the increase in births undoubtedly helped stimulate and sustain economic recovery.

In 1945 Europe like the United States also

had access to a large backlog of unexploited technology, much of which derived from military research. Atomic power, the jet engine, the rocket engine, television, computers, antibiotics, and frozen and dehydrated foods are only the best known of numerous technical advances destined to have major economic impact. And the increased economic importance of advanced technology benefited a Europe richer in technology, experience, and organization than in natural resources.

Finally, even the destruction and dislocations caused by the war contributed to recovery in that rebuilt factories could utilize the best available machinery and methods. The millions of refugees, some highly skilled, formed a large and usually cheap increment to the labor force; and the need to construct thousands of factories, offices, housing units, and other buildings was a powerful stimulus to economic growth. Defeated Germany also enjoyed the negative benefit of having no large military expenditures. Thus, in the depths of distress during the early years of peace, the Europeans, who never lost their resilience, established the basis of subsequent prosperity.

The Role of Russia and the United States
The recovery of Eastern Europe depended heavily on the Soviet Union, which through strenuous efforts was able to reach and surpass its prewar industrial output by 1953, and leaders such as Politburo member Nikita Khrushchev confidently predicted that the U.S.S.R. would exceed America in industrial production by 1970.

Impressive as these achievements were, the very size of Russia's economy raised unexpected problems that have continuously slowed down the relative rate of growth. As Soviet production and wealth expanded, the costs of administration increased disproportionately, and the inefficiencies of the nation's centralized man-

agement became more pronounced. The absence of a free market deprived planners of an effective means of judging costs, profits, and performance. In several critical areas the "command economy" of the U.S.S.R. proved less successful than the West's mixed economy, combining national planning and private enterprises. Russian agriculture in particular has been a major disappointment. In 1953 the cereal harvest was only slightly larger than in 1913, when the population had been smaller by a quarter.

Nevertheless, the growth of Russian industry and its developed technology provided an important market for and stimulus to production in the countries of the communist bloc. After 1945 these states attempted to organize their economies on the Russian model. All but Poland collectivized farmlands, and all instituted five-year plans to achieve rapid industrialization. The results on the whole were not altogether satisfactory, and the governments adopted elements of a mixed economic system in greater or lesser measure—"goulash socialism," as Hungary's compromise has been called: the state retains the ownership of most means of production, but managers operate within the structure of a largely free market. The formula proved most successful in the already advanced nations of Czechoslovakia and East Germany. Even under the new conditions a prewar heritage of economic and social modernization proved an invaluable asset; and Eastern Europe, though dramatically less prosperous than the West, had the highest rate of economic growth in its history by the 1950s.

The Western European nations, looking across the Atlantic for help, found the United States slow to appreciate the depths of their plight in 1945. In 1946 the United States extended to Great Britain a long-term credit of $4.4 billion and subsequently provided a credit of $1.2 billion to France. Following these steps, several developments—aside from the escalating competition for international power with the Soviet Union—persuaded the American government to adopt the systematic policy of aid embodied in the Marshall Plan. The economies of the European countries continued to founder; currency reserves were nearing depletion, which would have halted imports, removed all limits to inflation, and dealt a final blow to hopes of steady recovery.

Announced in 1947, the Marshall Plan was funded with the massive sum of more than $5 billion when Congress approved it in 1948. The distribution of the aid reflected not the alliances of World War II but the alignments of the Cold War—in 1948, for example, Italy received more than $600 million to finance a broad program of industrial reconstruction. Over the next four years, the Marshall Plan channeled into Europe more than $15 billion under the direction of the Organization for European Economic Cooperation (OEEC), which eighteen Western states had established for this purpose. Subsequently the European Payments Union (1950–1958) was created to regulate currency exchanges. Imports from the United States, made possible by credits under the Marshall Plan, benefited America while helping the OEEC countries to rebuild their productive plants and to lay the foundations for rapid recovery.

In 1948, 1949, and 1950, the combined gross national product of the OEEC participants spurted at the unprecedented annual rate of 25 percent, and by 1952 it was approximately half again as large as it had been in 1938. In spite of a bigger population, per capita income had also increased by more than a third. Western Europe had never been wealthier, and this was only the platform for further advances. In the decade of the 1950s, Europe achieved the highest rate of growth it had ever recorded. The Marshall Plan was a spectacular success that built on the experience and renewed enthusiasm of the Western European peoples.

Government Policies

In stimulating and sustaining their nations' recovery, the policies of the OEEC governments were of major importance. Nearly everywhere in Europe the state was expanding the public sector of the economy and assuming leadership in planning for economic growth. The United Kingdom's Labour government began its program of systematic nationalization of industry, starting with the coal mines, in 1947. The French government in 1945 and 1946 took over the Bank of France and other major banks, large insurance companies, utilities, coal mines, and the Renault automotive works (made vulnerable by its owner's collaboration with the Germans). Italy, through a legacy from the Fascist regime, already controlled the biggest publicly held complex of industries anywhere in Western Europe. Two huge, state-owned aggregates—the Institute for Industrial Reconstruction, which consisted of more than 100 companies, and the National Hydro-carbon Corporation, which directed the production of gas, oil, and other energy sources—dominated the economy. West Germany alone made no effort to expand the number of publicly owned industries, but there, too, the government had an important role (as it had during the war, under Speer) in coordinating economic growth that would come to be known in the late 1950s as the German miracle.

In one sense nationalization proved a disappointment, as state ownership gave no assurance of efficient management, good labor relations, or a high return on capital. But it helped governments develop all-encompassing economic plans that would guide both public and private enterprises to function in the general interest. Through the Monnet Plan (1946–1950) and subsequent designs for balanced economic growth, France set the model of loose but effective control. Utilizing refined methods of national income accounting, economists and other "technocrats" were able to turn the flow of investments in directions favored by the government. In doing so, they successfully built on institutions and policies many of which had developed under the Vichy regime. Britain created a National Economic Development Council in 1961 and adopted a five-year plan in 1962 for similar purposes. Comparable plans overseeing the operations of a mixed economy were devised and followed in almost all European and Mediterranean countries from Sweden to the new state of Israel. In West Germany a private trade association with close government ties, the Federation of German Industries, as well as a small number of the largest banks exercised effective influence over the economy.

The policies of European governments were closely comparable in another respect: all undertook to promote the welfare of their citizens and in particular to protect workers and their families against sickness, impoverished old age, and unemployment. Great Britain provided the earliest and (Sweden excepted) probably the most complete example of what has come to be called the welfare state. Its cornerstone was the National Health Service, inaugurated in 1948, which assumed nearly the total cost of medical, dental, and hospital care for all residents of the United Kingdom. The Continental governments instituted similar programs, including such benefits as family allowances—payments for the support of minor children—which in turn may have helped sustain the birth rate.

Welfare programs had considerable economic impact. They relieved people of the need to save in anticipation of sickness and old age. At the same time, to meet welfare costs, the state developed more efficient methods for collecting taxes. The government thus accumulated large monetary reserves, which it could invest according to its economic plans, further enlarging its role in leading the nation to recovery.

From 1948 on the OEEC sought to coordinate the policies of participating governments, for the free international movement of the factors of production—capital and labor—as well as of finished products was recognized as critical to the achievement and maintenance of high domestic growth rates. But efforts to change this organization into a tariff union failed, though a small "common market" was established in 1948: Benelux, a customs union embracing Belgium, the Netherlands, and Luxembourg. At the same time, an important group of Western leaders were urging that the European states take steps to achieve political integration. Following a meeting at The Hague in 1948, chaired by Winston Churchill, to discuss the formation of a Council of Europe, their planning did get as far as the creation the next year of a Council of Ministers and a Consultative Assembly, with headquarters at Strasbourg. The new organization had very limited powers, however; and it became clear that few governments, least of all Great Britain's, were willing to surrender any sovereignty or significant decision-making power to a supranational authority.

Two leading French integrationists, the economist Jean Monnet and Foreign Minister Robert Schuman then decided to proceed by working for fuller integration in one limited sector at a time. Their efforts led to the creation of the French-German Coal and Steel Authority in 1950 as an imaginative solution to problems that had plagued relations between the two countries. In 1952, propelled by the euphoria of recovery, these two nations joined with Italy and the three Benelux states to establish the European Coal and Steel Community (ECSC), the real kernel of a common market. Each member appointed a representative to the ECSC's executive body, which was then left significantly autonomous in its task of planning and coordinating the production and distribution of the coal and steel critical to industrial growth. As the union proved its economic value and steadily increased its authority, it excited renewed visions of a close economic and political federation.

IV. THE LIMITS OF RENEWAL

By the early 1950s, recovering from the war was no longer the focus of European life, and that in itself was a striking achievement. Instead, economic growth and the consumer goods it brought were giving European society a new look of health and stability. Not surprisingly in such an atmosphere the political balance shifted toward the center and center right. Having adopted extensive welfare measures and accepted a large governmental role in economic planning (often including the nationalization of major industries), European society seemed resistant to further or more fundamental change. And this resistance was strengthened by the pressures of the Cold War which even in domestic affairs divided and isolated much of the left. In the Soviet Union, too, a somewhat comparable shift occurred. East and West, moderate governments in stable societies were tempted to assert themselves more than they had before; but the effect of such assertiveness in the years 1956–1958 was to establish once again Europe's secondary position on the world stage.

THE DOMESTIC BALANCE

A move toward the political center or simply more relaxed rule of course meant something quite different in Franco's Spain, Great Britain,

or Soviet Russia. But everywhere the business of daily life in peacetime seemed at least to take precedence. Prosperity, based on sophisticated technology and expanding trade, became again a common European goal.

Governments of Moderation

In Britain the Conservatives regained power in 1951 and held it for the next thirteen years despite Churchill's retirement in 1955. Although rationing ended and taxes were lowered, the new measures introduced by the Labour government were not undone, the Conservatives promising rather to accomplish similar ends with an administration that would be more efficient and less intrusive. In 1952 the coronation of Queen Elizabeth II seemed to mark the beginning of a new and more pleasant era.

West Germany under Adenauer vied with Britain as America's primary European ally, joining NATO in 1955 and winning diplomatic recognition even from the Soviet Union. In a notable easing of international tension a peace treaty with Austria was signed by all the former Allies in the same year and quickly led to the withdrawal of occupation forces and the full recognition of Austria's sovereignty. In Italy, although the formation of political coalitions became more complex after the fall of De Gasperi in 1953 and despite the Communists' continued importance as the nation's second largest party, the Christian Democrats dominated every government. Within that party the factions of the center and the right increased their strength, and programs of social reform and public welfare tended to be subordinated to the party's ties to business, the Catholic Church, and the United States.

The dictatorships of Spain and Portugal, bolstered by good relations with the United States, faced minimal domestic oppositions. Only in Europe's smaller democracies—the Scandinavian and Benelux countries and Austria—were Socialist parties (firmly anti-communist) likely

PERCENT OF ANNUAL INCREASE IN GNP 1950–1960 AT CONSTANT PRICES IN SELECTED COUNTRIES

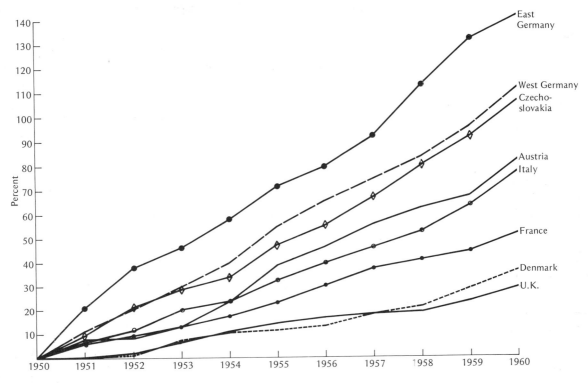

to remain in office in the 1950s. The stability bravely hoped for in the Marshall Plan was achieved with unexpected speed; the threat of chaos and despair or revolution had clearly passed.

Note that even for the United Kingdom, the growth rate averaged about 3 percent a year, about the same as in the period of industrial "take-off" in the nineteenth century.

The Soviet Union

Equally remarkable, something similar proved to be true in the Soviet Union after the passing of Stalin, whose dictatorship had grown even more intense and repressive in the years following World War II. Intellectuals and artists were required to follow more closely the official view, whether socialist realism in the arts or the fallacious genetic theories of Trofim Lysenko. Clearly the regime was anxious to counteract the effects of wartime appeals to

regional sentiment and postwar contacts with the West. But the tough intolerance, like the ugly touches of anti-Semitism, also reflected the personality of Joseph Stalin. There were signs of a new wave of purges when he died of a stroke in 1953.

After thirty years of dictatorship, such a loss was necessarily traumatic in itself; and the problem of succession, always difficult in an absolutist system, was one the Soviet Union had faced but once before. There were other issues too. Shortly before his death Stalin had hinted that the pace of industrialization might be slowed in favor of other needs, since Russia was meeting the high goals of the current Five-Year Plan, and had implied the possibility of less contentious relations with the West.

The succession went surprisingly smoothly. Party and state officials performed their duties, and at the very top a form of collective leadership emerged even while its members engaged in intense competition for power. Only in 1956–1957 did it become clear that Nikita Khrushchev was emerging victorious.

Khrushchev's triumph showed again that control of the Communist party was central to political power in Russia, but it had to do with policies as well. Some of his competitors, initially more powerful, had favored a sharper break with old policies (emphasizing the needs of consumers, for example, or the advantages of more decentralized decision making) than officialdom could accept. Khrushchev took a more conservative position. And though the infighting was ruthless and included executions as well as sudden dismissals, his preeminence was marked not by the purge of his opponents but by their assignment to minor and distant positions—steps approved by majority votes in the Presidium and Central Committee. The political forms of the Soviet Union now worked for moderation.

Khrushchev's rise within the government was most dramatically signaled by his speech at the Twentieth Party Congress in 1956. He launched a full attack on "the cult of personality" devoted to his predecessor, presenting a kind of bill of particulars of Stalin's excesses, his paranoid distrust, his interference in the conduct of war, his responsibility for the purge trials of the 1930s. Nothing like this had occurred before in the Soviet Union; myths that for a generation had been central to a great nation's enormous sacrifices were being attacked by its own leader. Khrushchev's charges circulated widely in secret and then more openly with effects the deepest of which cannot yet be measured. Suddenly streets and squares were renamed; statues and pictures disappeared. The thaw[2] following Stalin's death reached its peak, and a freer, more open society appeared in prospect.

Built-in counterpressures quickly made themselves felt. The needs of the party, the problems of administering a vast socialist state, rumblings of excitement from other peoples of the Soviet bloc who believed a real thaw might mean autonomy for them—all this led Khrushchev to clamp controls on criticism once more. But the restraints were never again so rigid or so arbitrary as under Stalin. When in 1957 the Soviet Union celebrated the fortieth anniversary of the Russian Revolution by launching the world's first space satellite, Russia's status as one of the most powerful and stable nations was dramatically confirmed.

FORAYS AT INDEPENDENCE

On the Continent prosperity and peace raised the prospect that European nations might pursue policies quite independent of American or Soviet influence. Efforts to do so, however, led to disaster; in fact no single European state could afford for long to contravene the policies of the superpower on whose protection it depended.

France and Britain

The effort, led by the United States, to strengthen European defenses clearly pointed to the rearming of Germany, a measure the French could hardly welcome and Russia was determined to prevent. As a safeguard the French proposed in 1952 the creation of a European Defense Community, in effect a common European army that would benefit

---

[2] The metaphor of the thaw, which has come to be generally applied to these changes, is derived from a novel of that title by the noted Russian fiction writer and journalist Ilya Ehrenburg.

from German strength without the risks of a separate German military force.

The proposal was accepted by most of the European members of NATO and pushed hard by the United States; but its implication of permanent Continental engagement was distasteful to the British, and growing doubts increased by resentment of extraordinary pressure from the United States led the French Parlement to reject the EDC in 1954.

There was in short a limit to which European governments could be pushed, and American intransigence in the face of Khrushchev's professed desires to improve relations (John Foster Dulles, secretary of state under President Dwight D. Eisenhower, Truman's successor, considered even Churchill a bit weak in his opposition to the communist menace) only strengthened that view. In any case, with a kind of stalemate in Europe, the more immediate confrontations of the Cold War shifted to other parts of the world, particularly those in which European dominance had recently been overcome.

Great Britain, her economy beginning to lag badly behind those of other European countries and fearful of losing her special role as America's primary ally, attempted one dramatic foreign venture. In Egypt, once a crucial part of the British Empire, Gamal Abdel Nasser's government raised growing distrust in the West, for he had made it a policy to turn to the communist bloc for help in industrializing his nation. When the Western powers, following the United States, refused aid for the construction of a high dam across the Nile at Aswan, Nasser announced the nationalization of the Suez Canal, still owned by a British-controlled company. Britain led in demanding strong measures and after international efforts at compromise broke down, conspired with Israel and France to take military action. Israel's attack on Egypt in October 1956 was followed by an Anglo-French bombardment and occupation of the canal banks. Within a week, however,

the protests of the Soviet Union and the opposition of the United States enabled the United Nations to force a cease-fire. Shortly afterward foreign troops withdrew.

Nothing had been gained by this sudden outburst of an outdated imperialist mentality, and much was lost in prestige and in good relations with Arab states and the whole Third World. Although Britain soon became the third nation to possess a hydrogen bomb, she was increasingly dependent even for her own defense on American policy.

The Satellite Nations

Until 1953 the communist governments of Eastern Europe outdid themselves in mimicry of the Soviet fatherland, including the idolization of Stalin and the ruthless use of secret police and internment camps. But Russia's open exploitation of her neighbors' resources to aid her own industrial growth was inevitably resented, and Stalin's death allowed that resentment to show.

Within three months the workers of East Berlin were in the streets proclaiming a general strike in protest against increased production quotas that they believed to be primarily for the benefit of the Soviet Union. Russian tanks rushed in to put down the revolt, but it had long-lasting effects. Walter Ulbricht became the new leader of East Germany; and while strengthening the party's dictatorship, he offered a reform program of higher wages and better living conditions. He also won from the Russians recognition of East German sovereignty and the end of occupation. Still tightly tied to the Soviet Union and limited in her autonomy, East Germany developed a voice of her own in the councils of communist countries and expanded her trade with West Germany and other states outside the Soviet orbit.

A far more serious outburst erupted in Poland following Khrushchev's speech attacking Stalin in 1956. This too began as a workers' protest, but it quickly gathered support from the growing faction of the national Communist party critical of Russian policies in Poland. Again Soviet forces intervened, to be jeered and sometimes attacked, and the Polish party elected Wladyslaw Gomulka party secretary in preference to the pro-Russian candidate. Gomulka, who remained the dominant figure in the government until 1970, was a firm communist who insisted, however, that socialist states must follow somewhat different paths from Russia's in accordance with their national traditions. He convinced Soviet leaders of his loyalty to the Russian alliance, a loyalty he subsequently proved on many occasions, and he thereby won their acquiescence to his more independent course. Russia and Poland began to deal with each other more nearly as sovereign equals. The presence of Russian troops was limited; Poland demanded and got a share of the reparations Germany paid; and she negotiated economic aid from the United States. Gomulka also mitigated the repression of the Catholic Church, and by the 1960s he conceded greater independence to Polish intellectuals and allowed increased contacts with the West.

Another revolt in 1956 ended more tragically. Rioting broke out in Hungary in October following a series of conflicts within her Communist party. From the outset the uprising was even more markedly anti-Russian than Poland's, and at first the Russians withdrew, seeming disposed in this case too to accept increased national autonomy. But then Imre Nagy, who had been arrested the year before for "right-wing deviationism," was recalled as premier. Bowing to popular pressure, he showed that he was willing to break the alliance with Russia and favor neutrality. The Russian attitude hardened, and then the Soviet army attacked in force to crush the revolution in ten days of bitter fighting.

Many in Hungary expected Western aid, for which rebel radio stations pleaded, but none came. Indeed Washington, hurling denunciations of Russian imperialism, was embarrassed by the fact that while Russian tanks were crunching across Hungary, the troops of three American allies were invading Egypt. Russia had made clear that the satellite states would not be permitted to break their alliance to her, and the West had confessed that a Russian sphere did indeed exist. A wave of refugees left the country, and Nagy himself was kidnapped by the Russians and executed in 1958. Hungary was punished with harsh repression, a heavy-handed Soviet presence, and a general worsening of working conditions, but her new premier, Janos Kadar, who had supported the more moderate phase of the rising, slowly led her on a more national course.

Czechoslovakia fared no better. The most industrialized of the states in the Russian orbit, she had not taken easily to communism. Although the regime was secure after trials and purges in the 1950s, the economy remained sluggish, and the divisions between the dominant Czechs and the Slovaks hardened.

Greater geographic isolation aided some of the other communist nations to achieve greater autonomy. Albania, the most backward country on the Continent, increasingly allied herself to mainland China in diplomatic and dogmatic opposition to Russia. Rumania, which with Bulgaria had been among the most Stalinist of the satellite regimes, found the adjustments to Soviet policy after 1953 more difficult to make. While maintaining a strict domestic dictatorship her insistence on an independent foreign policy made her the most venturesome of the Russian-dominated regimes in establishing good relations with Western powers.

Yugoslavia had never been a satellite state. After her expulsion from the Cominform in 1948, she improved her relations with her non-Communist neighbors and benefited from American aid. Reconciliations with Khrushchev in 1954 and 1957 did not reduce her independence or her trade with the West nor

diminish Tito's prestige as a leader capable of dealing with both the Soviet Union and the United States. Partly of necessity, Yugoslavia developed a Communism of her own that by the 1960s was relaxing central economic controls and encouraging local participation in decision making. No other communist nation was able to move so far from the common model.

Two New Starts in the West
The launching of Sputnik in 1957, remarkable enough in itself, had also signaled the continued advance of the superpowers. The suppression of revolt in Eastern Europe had, like the debacle at Suez, further defined the limits constraining single European states. And almost simultaneously, two events reflected distinctly

Soviet tanks occupy the streets of Budapest after the revolt had been crushed. (Photo: UPI)

different responses to this situation: the fall of the Fourth Republic in France and the founding of the European Common Market.

Under the Fourth Republic the French government had in many respects performed very well—how well would become clear only in the prosperity of the 1960s. But coalition governments also shared the best-known weaknesses of the Third Republic. With the Communist party ostracized since 1947 but still sizable, the other three large parties—the Socialists and more often the Radical Socialists and the MRP (Popular Republicans)—had to seek alliances to capture a parliamentary majority. It appeared briefly in 1954 as if the able Radical Socialist Pierre Mendès-France could continue to make the system work, as so often happened (in the nick of time) in the past. He extricated France from Vietnam, sought ways to grant Algeria independence, and tried to win his party to a program of economic planning that would bring it closer to the Socialists. But too many issues divided his own supporters, and the extremes of left and right were gaining strength at the expense of the center. The MRP was challenged by the rising Gaullist party and by conservatives; and in the elections of 1956 the Communists gained and the Socialists declined while on the right a movement of resentful small shopkeepers and farmers—people by-passed by the benefits of modernization—briefly won political importance.

One ministry after another proved unable to cope with the divisive issues before it, the most demanding of which was the growing revolt against French rule in Algeria. Beset by colonial uprisings in Africa and Asia since 1945, the French army had expended itself in repressive measures only to have "the politicians" concede autonomy or independence.[3] In the spirit of the Cold War, many officers saw themselves fighting alone against communist conspiracy around the world, and they were determined not to permit their efforts to be scuttled in Algeria, a French colony since 1830, in which a sizable French population had lived for generations. At the same time leftists and intellectuals expressed outrage at the atrocities committed by a furious army and at the kind of democracy that waged war against Algerians seeking to govern themselves.

Algerian nationalists had taken to open revolt in 1954, and for the next four years, the Algerian question brought down more French governments than any other issue. Then in 1958 a group of French army officers turned from fighting Algerians to seize political control of Algeria from which they threatened to move against the indecisive government of metropolitan France. Uncertain that any ordinary ministry could effectively resist and preferring de Gaulle to the military insurgents, a majority in the National Assembly welcomed his announcement that he would serve and invested him with extraordinary powers for six years. He led France for the next ten.

Long convinced that its weakness required a thorough reform of the Fourth Republic, de Gaulle had been shrewdly ambiguous in his pronouncements on Algeria. The army, the center, and the right all found him acceptable, and he used his strength to consolidate support and win France to a new constitution. Overwhelmingly approved by popular referendum in September 1958, it established the Fifth Republic as a presidential regime whose chief executive would be indirectly elected for a seven-year term. To no one's surprise de Gaulle was chosen president two months later. Gaullists became by far the largest party in the Parlement, where the Communists were reduced to a handful.

The president moved cautiously on the Algerian question, quietly weakening and dispersing the leaders of the military revolt. Only gradually did it become clear that de Gaulle favored Algerian self-determination, a proposal approved by three-quarters of the voters in a referendum held in January 1961. Effectively isolated, the most intransigent of the officers formed the Secret Army Organization (OAS) and for eighteen months indulged in terrorism in France and Algeria. But the French presi-

---

[3] In 1958 in North Africa alone, eight new states chose to be autonomous within the French Union: Senegal, Mali, the Ivory Coast, Mauritania, Niger, Upper Volta, Cameroun, and Gabon. Chad followed the same course in 1960. French Somaliland (Afars and Issas Territory) preferred to remain a territory; and Guinea, Togo, the (Brazzaville) Congo, and the Central African Republic chose full independence.

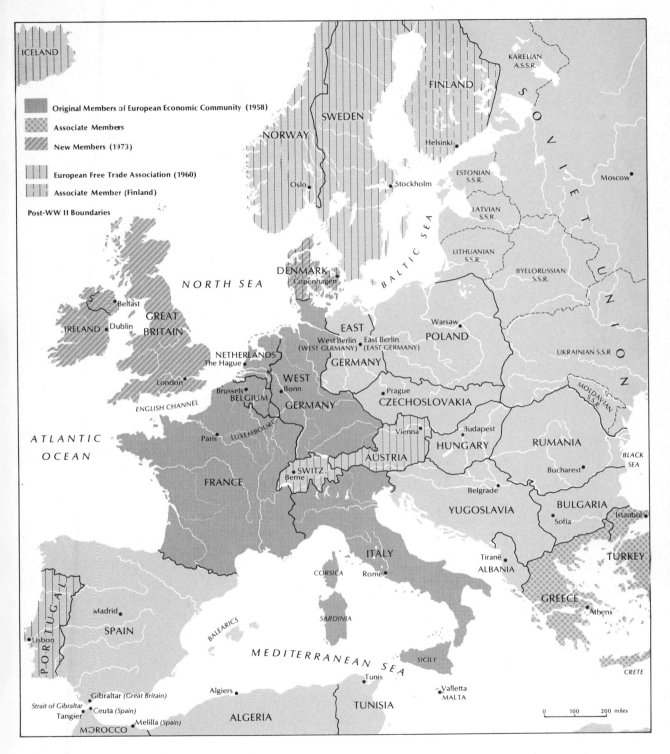

ICELAND

Original Members of European Economic Community (1958)

Associate Members

New Members (1973)

European Free Trade Association (1960)

Associate Member (Finland)

Post-WW II Boundaries

KARELIAN
A.S.S.R.

FINLAND

SWEDEN

NORWAY

Helsinki

S
O
V
I
E
T

Oslo

Stockholm

ESTONIAN
S.S.R.

Moscow

LATVIAN
S.S.R.

BALTIC SEA

LITHUANIAN
S.S.R.

DENMARK
Copenhagen

NORTH SEA

BYELORUSSIAN
S.S.R.

U

Belfast

GREAT
BRITAIN

IRELAND Dublin

EAST
West Berlin East Berlin
(WEST GERMANY) (EAST GERMANY)

Warsaw

POLAND

UKRAINIAN S.S.R

N

NETHERLANDS
The Hague

GERMANY

London

WEST

MOLDAVIAN
S.S.R.

Z

ENGLISH CHANNEL

Brussels

GERMANY

Prague

BELGIUM

Bonn

CZECHOSLOVAKIA

Paris LUXEMBOURG

Vienna

Budapest

HUNGARY

RUMANIA

BLACK
SEA

ATLANTIC
OCEAN

AUSTRIA

SWITZ.

Berne

FRANCE

Bucharest

Belgrade

BULGARIA

YUGOSLAVIA

Sofia

Istanbul

ITALY

CORSICA

Rome

Tiranë

ALBANIA

TURKEY

Madrid

SARDINIA

GREECE

Athens

SPAIN

BALEARICS

Lisbon

P
O
R
T
U
G
A
L

MEDITERRANEAN SEA

SICILY

CRETE

Tunis

Valletta
MALTA

0   100   200 miles

Gibraltar (Great Britain)

Strait of Gibraltar Ceuta (Spain)

Tangier

Algiers

Melilla (Spain)

MOROCCO

ALGERIA

TUNISIA

MAP 29.4: EUROPE SINCE WORLD WAR II

dent, having arranged peace with the Algerian rebels, declared war on the army rebels. By the end of 1962, they had disbanded, Algeria was independent, and France's strong presidential regime could turn to other questions.

The establishment of the European Economic Community, known as the Common Market, was in itself a kind of practical compromise between grand visions of a united Europe such as lay behind the formation of the Council of Europe in 1948 and the concrete achievements of the Coal and Steel Community founded four years later. The six nations belonging to the latter—Belgium, the Netherlands, Luxembourg, France, Germany, and Italy—in 1957 signed the Treaty of Rome (Britain among others declined to do so) which created the new Community to go into effect January 1, 1958. Formally it was a limited agreement, an addition to the Coal and Steel Community establishing an agency to coordinate the development of atomic energy and binding the six nations to a careful series of steps leading to the elimination of tariffs between the member states and to a common tariff toward all other nations. The France of the Fourth Republic, which long favored the creation of international European agencies with independent authority, had played a leading part along with the three smaller states in pressing for the new agreement. "Europe," the French government said at the time, "will not be made all at once, or according to a single, general plan. It will be built through concrete achievements." That larger hope was still far from realization, and it would take some time to tell whether the opening words of the new treaty would ever have more than rhetorical weight in declaring its signatories "Determined to establish the foundations of an ever closer union among the European peoples."

The European nations regained a place among the economic, social, and cultural leaders of the world even in an age in which rapid development was no longer a Western monopoly. They recovered from war with astonishing speed and on the whole adjusted to the loss of empire and international dominance realistically. Indeed the achievement was so great that visions of a still more prosperous and egalitarian united Europe no longer seemed merely utopian. But there was disillusionment, too. Neither the communists nor the democratic opponents of fascism managed in victory to create the societies they promised, and prosperity did not itself resolve old conflicts. Political leaders operating in a prewar style attempted domestic compromise and the assertion of national autonomy in international affairs, but that led to a test of power no European state save the Soviet Union could meet. The contrived stability of de Gaulle's Fifth Republic and the optimism of the founders of the European Economic Community, uncertain as the prospects were for either, at least implied the possibility of trying other approaches.

RECOMMENDED READING

Studies

Allsop, Kenneth. *The Angry Decade: A Survey of the Cultural Revolt of the 1950s.* 1969. Captures very well postwar disillusionment.

*Aron, Raymond. *The Imperial Republic: The United States and the World, 1945–1973.* 1974. A leading French thinker analyzes the period of American dominance.

Beer, Samuel H. *British Politics in the Collectivist Age.* 1965. A comprehensive treatment of the new political life of Great Britain.

*Crossman, Richard H. (ed.). *The God That Failed.* 1950. The moving testimony of former Marxists about their lost faith in the era of Stalin and the Cold War.

*Crouzet, Maurice. *The European Renaissance Since 1945.* 1971. An optimistic essay on the politics, society, and culture of postwar Europe.

*Dahrendorf, Ralf. *Society and Democracy in Germany.* 1969. A German sociologist assesses the special qualities of German society.

Dawidowicz, Lucy S. *The War Against the Jews, 1933–1945.* 1976. A full and balanced assessment of the twentieth century's greatest horror.

*Deakin, F. W. *The Brutal Friendship.* 1966. A detailed account of the Axis primarily in terms of Hitler's relations with Mussolini.

Feis, Herbert. *Churchill, Roosevelt, Stalin: The War They Waged and the Peace They Sought.* 1957. A balanced and insightful account of Allied relations.

Fejto, François. *A History of the People's Democracies: Eastern Europe Since Stalin.* 1971. A careful study of the conflicts and variety among Eastern European states under Soviet dominance.

Halle, Louis J. *The Cold War as History.* 1967. Sets the historical context of the great ideological and military division of the modern world.

*Hoffmann, Stanley, et al. *In Search of France.* 1965. A group of distinguished scholars attempt to define the unique patterns of French political and social life.

*Laquer, Walter. *Europe Since Hitler.* 1972. One of the ablest of the surveys of contemporary Europe.

Michel, Henri. *The Shadow War: The European Resistance, 1939–1945.* 1972. Combines recent scholarship in a solid study of the most attractive (and romanticized) aspect of World War II.

*Paxton, Robert. *Vichy France: Old Guard and New Order, 1940–1944.* 1972. Stresses the continuity and lasting significance for French society and institutions of this twilight period.

Postan, Michael M. *An Economic History of Western Europe, 1945–1964.* 1967. A noted economic historian analyzes the roots of European recovery.

Sherwin, M. J. *A World Destroyed: The Atomic Bomb and the Grand Alliance.* 1975. A scholarly and balanced account of this controversial and complicated subject.

*Snell, John L. *Illusion and Necessity: The Diplomacy of Global War, 1939–1945.* 1963. A clear assessment of the interrelationship of the great issues among warring powers.

*Ulam, Adam B. *The Rivals: America and Russia Since World War II.* 1972. Surveys the wide-ranging effects of the Cold War in geopolitical, ideological, and social context.

---

* Available in paperback.

THIRTY

THE PRESENT IN
HISTORICAL PERSPECTIVE

The most striking fact about Europe today is its wealth. The achievement of advanced industrial societies, this prosperity has opened new horizons for millions, altered the way most people live, and created new problems. In their efforts to create industrial wealth and to deal with the issues that accompany its creation, the countries of Europe provide a remarkable laboratory for studying the problems of developed societies and the varied ways of meeting them. Somewhat paradoxically, the social groups and political parties that propose and contest various solutions are, like the ideologies they use, not so very new; but the need for new policies and different alignments has given them new directions.

With the relaxation of tensions between the United States and the Soviet Union and the greater world-wide attention to underdeveloped and developing nations, the relationship of European countries to the rest of the world has necessarily altered too. Individually more prosperous and influential than all but a few of the nations of the world, only collectively can they equal or surpass the power and influence of the superpowers. The international ties of the European states reflect the peculiarities of this position. Within Europe itself governments maintain their sovereign interests alongside the growth of greater European unity.

Attitudes toward the present thus remain ambivalent, prospects for the future uncertain. One reason for studying the past is to better understand the present, and the tendency for Westerners to see themselves in terms of their place on some scale of historical evolution has grown stronger in the last two centuries. The French Revolution, industrialization, theories of liberalism and progress, World War I, the Russian Revolution, totalitarianism, and World War II not only have made social change a central preoccupation of modern life but have opened a continuing debate about the direction in which it leads. Predictions that society is steadily, even inevitably, marching toward greater individualism, democracy, and wealth have been countered by equally confident predictions of dehumanization, cultural and moral decline, and loss of freedom. In every case predictions rest on the assessment of social organization, technological development, and human rationality that the commentators draw from history; for the present is always understood as a period of transition to a different future.

1. PROBLEMS OF ADVANCED SOCIETIES

Europe's economic growth in the past twenty years, particularly in Western Europe, has probably been greater than at any other time in its history. Often the triumph of a mixed economy, of that combination of private enterprise and state planning practiced in most European states, this growth produces far-reaching changes and the serious problems—economic, social, and cultural—characteristic of advanced societies. Such steadily increasing

NATIONAL WEALTH: WORLD LEADERS

GROSS NATIONAL PRODUCT IN 1974 *(in billions of dollars)*			GROSS NATIONAL PRODUCT/PER CAPITA, FREE MARKET COUNTRIES IN 1975 *(in dollars)*			
United States	1267.1	(EEC 1080)	Kuwait	11,726	*Finland*	5,645
U.S.S.R.	722.2		Qatar	ca. 8,500	*Austria*	4,996
Japan	405.7		*Sweden*	8,459	New Zealand	4,414
West Germany	349.6		*Switzerland*	8,463	Japan	4,133
France	265.3		USA	7,087	*United Kingdom*	4,089
China	223.0		*Norway*	7,058	Israel	3,608
United Kingdom	175.6		*Denmark*	7,006	Saudi Arabia	3,220
Italy	143.6		Canada	6,995	*Italy*	2,704
Canada	123.3		*West Germany*	6,871	Puerto Rico	2,685
		(East Europe 105.5)	Australia	6,364	*Spain*	2,428
			France	6,360	Venezuela	2,415
			Belgium	6,352	Philippines	2,324
			Luxembourg	6,102	*Ireland*	2,176
			Netherlands	5,949	*Greece*	2,140
			Iceland	5,665		

European nations in italics.

productivity requires high rates of investment and frequent changes in production and marketing, which reduce costs while adding new products, releasing workers to the service sector of society which becomes steadily larger. Standards of consumption rise throughout society, and the cycle of growth continues. In all this, European traditions of technical skill, high levels of education, ease of communication, effective government, and social flexibility have been important advantages. Such rapid growth, however, threatens to transform society in disagreeable ways through pollution, urban crowding, and the weakening of old social ties. It also raises fundamental questions about how the benefits of prosperity should be distributed.

SOCIAL EFFECTS

The most obvious by-product of industrial growth is the pollution that contaminates air, waterways, and countryside, pouring from factories and automobiles and littering the landscape. Especially shocking in Europe where monuments and scenic places revered for centuries have become seriously threatened, the problem calls for coordinated planning and severe restrictions that governments intent upon encouraging growth have been reluctant to take. The Rhine is now one of the most polluted of international waterways, and high concentrations of mercury have been recorded in Geneva's Lac Leman. It is dangerous to bathe in or eat fish from much of the Baltic and Mediterranean seas. Escaped industrial gasses have caused illness and death in the outskirts of Milan, and the magnificent palaces of Venice are dangerously sinking, apparently because the earth beneath their pilings gives way as underground water is pumped up on the mainland for industrial use. The remaining monuments of ancient Greece and Rome and the ornate façades of Gothic churches show signs in city after city of crumbling and cracking from the vibrations and fumes of modern traffic.

There are, of course, signs that mankind and modern technology can clean up as well as pollute. Through stern regulations Great Brit-

WORLD INDUSTRIAL LEADERS

LEADING MANUFACTURING COUNTRIES, 1973
(Millions of dollars)

United States	404,376
Russia	216,563
Japan	147,824
West Germany	138,539
Great Britain	74,666
France	52,328
Italy	33,106
Canada	31,106
East Germany	25,274
Argentina	23,970

LEADING STEEL-PRODUCING COUNTRIES, 1971
(Millions of metric tons)

Russia	121
United States	109
Japan	83.6
West Germany	40.3
Great Britain	24.2
France	22.9
China	20.9
Italy	17.4
Poland	12.7
Belgium	12.4

LEADING COAL-MINING COUNTRIES, 1973
(Millions of metric tons)

Russia	744
United States	543
China	428
East Germany	247
West Germany	216
Poland	196
Great Britain	131
Czechoslovakia	109
Australia	94
India	88

LEADING IRON ORE MINING COUNTRIES, 1971
(Millions of metric tons)

Russia	203
United States	82
Australia	62
France	56
China	55
Canada	44
Brazil	43
Sweden	33
India	32
Liberia	23

LEADING PRODUCERS OF ELECTRICAL POWER, 1975 *(Millions of kilowatt hours)*

	1974	1975
United States	1,864,961	2,000,916
Russia	975,000	1,038,625
Japan	468,511	475,794
West Germany	311,676	301,802
Canada	279,072	272,624
Great Britain	276,072	272,219
France	179,880	178,514
Italy	146,376	145,551
China	112,000	97,168
Poland	91,596	
East Germany		84,505
Spain		82,385
Sweden		80,573

LEADING AUTOMOBILE MANUFACTURING COUNTRIES, 1973 *(Millions of passenger cars)*

United States	9.7
Japan	4.5
West Germany	3.6
France	3.2
Italy	1.8
Great Britain	1.7
Canada	1.2
Russia	.9
Spain	.7
Brazil	.5

WORLD INDUSTRIAL LEADERS (continued)

LEADING PRODUCERS OF NUCLEAR POWER,
1973 (Millions of kilowatt hours)

United States	112,740
Great Britain	27,997
Canada	14,256
France	13,968
West Germany	11,755
Japan	11,000
Russia	7,500
Switzerland	5,896
Spain	4,800
Italy	3,142

ain has eliminated the smog that plagued London since the sixteenth century and killed thousands of people as recently as 1952. The Thames has become a clean river for the first time in centuries. Nearly every building in Paris has been cleaned in the last decade, stripping away the somber, dark patina of soot accumulated through one hundred and fifty years of industrialization. Cities like Rome and Vienna have found that banning traffic from the narrow medieval streets of the old centers of the city can lead to a renewal that makes those sections among the most attractive, and most expensive, for shops and apartments. Everywhere ecological movements have become more influential, and several international agencies are pledged to press for enforceable European standards. But it remains too early to say whether enough can or will be done to prevent the disasters pessimists predict.

Cities present other problems as well. While the inner core of older cities may lose population (exacerbating problems of urban decay), the agglomeration grows, and in effect the larger cities continue to spread. In France one person in five and in Great Britain nearly that proportion lives within an hour's drive of the capital city. Volgograd stretches for 45 miles along the river after which it was named.

In general the new highways, extended subways, and bus lines that push the city outward rarely keep pace with the congestion of traffic at its core. As similar skyscrapers rise in the centers (to loud laments), similar residential districts sprawl across the outskirts. In the 1950s new housing tended, East and West, to look like dreary concrete barracks and often provided few of the services necessary to create a sense of community. In nearly every coun-

The results of the rush to meet the demand for new housing in these Parisian suburbs range from crowded new houses meant to evoke Norman cottages to high-rise apartments on a bleak hilltop. The remaining trees mark the forests displaced, and the smog hints at the great city beyond. (Photo: Viva/Woodfin Camp and Associates)

WORLD POPULATION, 1970

		ANNUAL GROWTH RATE IN PERCENT
World	3,860,000,000	2
Asia	2,204,000,000	2.3
Europe	472,000,000	.7
Africa	374,000,000	2.7
Latin America	308,000,000	2.8
U.S.S.R.	250,000,000	1.0
USA and Canada	233,000,000	.8
Oceania	21,000,000	2.0

EUROPEAN POPULATION

	472,000,000	.7
Northern and Western Europe	233,000,000	.4
Southern Europe	132,000,000	.9
Eastern Europe	107,000,000	.7

ESTIMATED METROPOLITAN POPULATION, 1970

London	11,540,000
Paris	8,714,000
Moscow	7,061,000
Essen	6,789,000
Leningrad	3,950,000
Madrid	2,990,000
Birmingham	2,981,000
Rome	2,920,000
Warsaw	2,664,000
Manchester	2,541,000
Athens	2,425,000
Katowice	2,424,000
Hamburg	2,407,000
Barcelona	2,333,000
West Berlin	2,240,000
Budapest	2,060,000 (city only)
Glasgow	2,008,000
Leeds	1,945,000
Stuttgart	1,935,000
Liverpool	1,823,000
Vienna	1,890,000
Cologne	1,788,000
Milan	1,750,000
Bucharest	1,700,000
Kiev	1,632,000 (city only)
Mannheim	1,578,000
Munich	1,502,000
Lisbon	1,500,000

try efforts at better planning led to the creation of whole new cities, often bleak and artificial, surrounding the metropolis; five towns of 24,000 people each were planned around Paris, twenty-four such towns now surround Moscow. The more recent trend has been toward new centers on a smaller scale, carefully planned to have shopping, recreational, and cultural centers of their own as well as some light industry so that most of the working population need not commute. Many of these, especially perhaps in Scandinavia (Tapiola, outside Helsinki, being one of the most successful), have proved very attractive, mixing large and small modern buildings, pleasant streets, and restful green spaces. Thus, despite the uneven results and the absence of wholly satisfactory solutions, Europe contains the world's most interesting experiments in urban planning. Even those who lament the impersonality and social strains that seem to accompany these developments concede that simply in the narrow terms of living space and hygiene more Europeans are comfortably housed than ever before.

The Distribution of Benefits

By any measure—real wages, per capita income, or consumer expenditures—the standard of living of the working classes has risen impressively in the past two decades. The gap between the very rich and wage earners has narrowed only slightly, however, in the West (the poorest third of the population gets a larger share of national wealth in Sweden and the Netherlands than in other Western societies, less than elsewhere in France), and in communist Europe professional people and officials

live at a much higher standard and with far greater freedom of choice than workers or peasants. The full impact of these inequalities has been softened throughout Europe by complex provisions for social security, free education, subsidized or free medical care, and a wide variety of family benefits and services; and social differences are generally more acceptable in periods of rapid economic growth when nearly everyone's lot is improving.

In the 1970s, however, unemployment has steadily risen in the West (though not to the level commonplace in the United States), ex-

This pedestrian mall in downtown Stockholm represents a widely adapted and attractive solution to urban crowding, a concept in which Scandinavian planners have been leaders. (Photo: Jerry Frank/DPI)

posing the weak position of those in declining industries and crafts and small-scale agriculture. Above all, foreign immigrants have been hardest hit. As unemployment virtually disappeared in the industrial countries in the 1960s, large numbers of people from the less developed periphery moved to the more prosperous regions—southern Italians to northern Italy, Swit-

ACTIVE WORK FORCE

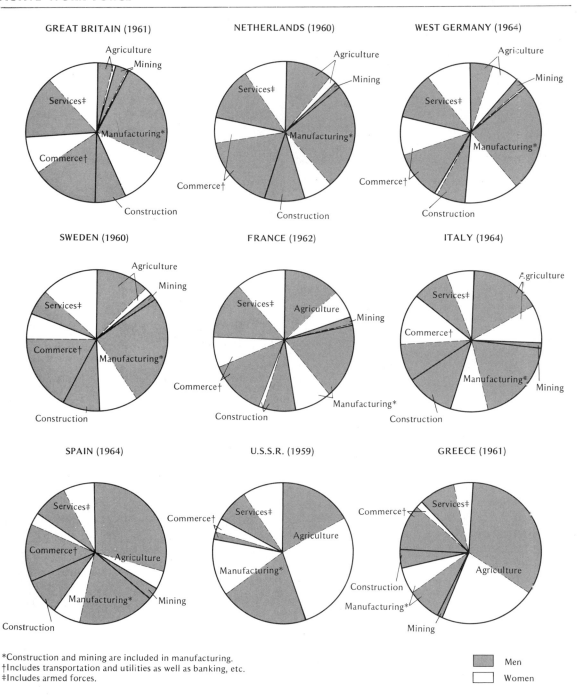

GREAT BRITAIN (1961)

NETHERLANDS (1960)

WEST GERMANY (1964)

SWEDEN (1960)

FRANCE (1962)

ITALY (1964)

SPAIN (1964)

U.S.S.R. (1959)

GREECE (1961)

*Construction and mining are included in manufacturing.
†Includes transportation and utilities as well as banking, etc.
‡Includes armed forces.

Men

Women

zerland, and Germany; Spaniards, Portuguese, and North Africans to France; Yugoslavs and Turks to Germany; Caribbean and African blacks from former colonies to England. In general they found employment as domestic servants, street sweepers, and the least skilled industrial workers—by the 1970s contributing 17 percent of the work force in Switzerland, over 6 percent in Germany (approximately 2 million people), and over 2 percent in France. Often different in physical appearance, language, and culture, these migrants were drawn together and forced by poverty to live in crowded slums that quickly became ghetto subcultures, resistant to and misunderstood by the larger society. Without the full protection of citizenship, resented by native workers competing for jobs and higher pay, despised as sources of crime and heavy welfare costs, these migrants recreated some of the gravest social problems of the early nineteenth century, now exacerbated by prejudices of race and color.

There are, of course, other groups that have not fully shared in the general prosperity. In every country whole regions labeled as backward have been made the target of special subsidies and tax incentives intended to encourage their industrialization, often with disappointing results. Neither in general do women receive equal pay or equal opportunity for advancement despite the fact that 36 percent of the work force are women in Britain, France, and Germany, with the proportion higher in Sweden and Finland, lower elsewhere. On the average, women workers earn between two-thirds (in Britain) and three-fourths (in France) as much as men. Although in Sweden, France, and Britain women have leading roles in many occupations of high prestige, nowhere are they more than a small minority in such positions except for the medical profession in the Soviet Union, which they dominate.

Access to the professions and important man-

GROWTH RATES—in Annual Percentage, 1960–1970, in Western Europe		
GDP/PER CAPITA		PRODUCTIVITY/ MAN HOUR
6.9	Greece	Spain 8.6
6.3	Spain	Sweden 7.4
5.2	Portugal	Netherlands 7.2
4.8	Italy	Greece 6.9
4.8	Finland	Portugal 6.8
4.6	France	West Germany 6.5
4.3	Belgium	France 6.2
4.2	Austria	Italy 6.0
4.1	Norway	Austria 5.9
4.0	Denmark	Belgium 5.5
4.0	Netherlands	Norway 5.3
3.6	West Germany	Finland 4.9
3.5	Sweden	Switzerland 4.9
3.4	Ireland	Denmark 4.8
2.3	Switzerland	Ireland 4.0
2.1	United Kingdom	United Kingdom 3.1

agerial positions is restricted even more by education than by sex. Traditionally in Europe secondary education has been the great dividing point, at which a small fraction of young people were admitted to schools that prided themselves on the demanding and usually classical curriculum considered essential preparation for university work; many more attended a secondary school of somewhat more vocational emphasis whose graduates did not normally attend universities, and half or more of all students beyond the ages of twelve or fourteen went directly to work. Throughout Europe the elites have shared a high formal culture, access to which was with few exceptions first a matter of social class and only second a matter of academic inclination. After World War II, the communist regimes of Eastern Europe gave preference to the children of workers and party members but only slowly enlarged the number allowed entrance into college-preparatory programs. In the West the proportion of school-age youths undertaking the more prestigious education has steadily increased. And that change has been accompanied by a move toward "comprehensive" schools, more like the American high school, which less sharply segregate the college-bound.

In each country such reforms in the late 1960s and early 1970s have been the subject of controversy, often even riots and demonstrations. Reform at the secondary level has been paralleled by major reforms of universities which, despite the creation of hundreds of new institutions, have in many places swollen in enrollments far beyond their capacity. The particular pattern in each nation reflects its own traditions of culture and class distinction, but the emerging tendency is clear. Those European nations with the highest proportion of twenty to twenty-four years old enrolled in universities (roughly 15 to 20 percent) are the Netherlands, Sweden, Denmark, France, Italy, and Norway, where traditions of democratic access if not equality are stronger. Those with the lowest proportion (less than 10 percent in Yugoslavia, Spain, and Portugal) are the least developed. And nearly all the rest of Europe, both East and West, falls in between. The present balance, however, is everywhere only a temporary and much-criticized compromise, subject to pressures for further change and expansion.

As the battles over education make clear, the citizens of Europe's advanced societies look to the state as a major instrument of social justice. In practice this has meant less the elaboration of utopian programs for social change, even in Eastern Europe, than efforts to guarantee a minimum standard of living. In the communist nations, for example, housing and transport are relatively cheap, and in the West governments extensively subsidize both (about one-third of new housing in Germany is government sponsored, one-half in Great Britain, two-thirds in Sweden and France). Social wel-

fare payments of wide-ranging variety are an important part of the family economy for nearly everyone, not just the poor. Similarly, a high proportion of private medical expenses are paid through the state in most countries, and governments have encouraged a steady increase in the number of physicians and hospital beds available. Not surprisingly, rates of infant mortality have declined and rates of longevity have improved so that among Europe's most advanced nations they are the highest in the world. The variations among countries and among regions and classes within the same country reflect, on the other hand, important and troublesome disparities. These government expenditures in addition to those for other services and for defense mean that taxes are relatively high (between 21 and 24 percent of the GNP in the wealthiest nations of Europe and 33 percent in the United Kingdom). Insofar as these taxes are levied with the same social concerns so as to fall most heavily on the rich (and in fact they often do not), that can, as liberal economists have argued, discourage investment, thereby creating yet another incentive for government planning and the nationalization of critical industries.

The important social and economic role of the state makes its citizens highly sensitive to the government's responsiveness to particular needs and concerns. If representative governments that allow free speech may be assumed to score highest in this regard, the modern state even in the freest of Western societies is often seen as distant, bureaucratic, officious, and dominated by special interests. This has led to varied but serious protests in each country and undoubtedly underlies the remarkable revival of regionalism and regionalist movements across Europe. To all such protests each state has responded according to its own institutions and customs, but much of the diverse political conflict in contemporary Europe can best be understood to reflect the often similar and interrelated problems of advanced industrial societies.

THE SEARCH FOR POLITICAL SOLUTIONS

As political systems attempt to deal with these problems, they enter unchartered territory; and there is an understandable tendency to give priority to more familiar issues, such as domestic order, national defense, and the stimulus of economic growth. Even so, European governments in the last two decades have shown notable concern that the public feel some satisfaction with the direction of social change. Even in this period of relative stability political leaders have had to live with the possibility of revolution and with the less drastic competition of communist, socialist, and capitalist governments, both free and dictatorial, existing side by side.

Toward Broader Political Participation

Formally, at least, the British and West German political systems have been models of stability, in which two dominant parties have smoothly alternated in power and pursued policies of an underlying continuity. In Britain the Conservatives were in office from 1951 to 1964 and 1970 to 1974. While placing greater emphasis in economic matters on the role of the private sector—they returned iron and steel to private hands and stopped further nationalization—they accepted the extensive welfare programs and mixed economy they inherited. The Labour governments that have held office from 1964 to 1970 and, by a thin majority, since 1974 have been severely constrained by the plight of the British economy, pressuring their trade-union constituents to accept wage limits and cutting public expenditures in an effort to balance the budget sufficiently to halt the fall of the value of the pound and to reassure such creditors as the International Monetary Fund whose loans have become essential to prevent collapse.

All these governments have shared in the efforts to improve public services, especially transportation, and to make education more democratic by encouraging comprehensive high schools and an impressive expansion of higher education. Each party, however, has been internally divided on newer issues of lowering the voting age to eighteen, joining the Common Market, special measures to protect black immigrants from discrimination, and devolution which allows Scotland and Wales to have directly elected representative assemblies of their own for dealing with local matters— all measures which eventually passed. Even as the ties of union established in 1707 are loosened, Britain's overwhelming problem remains economic. Plants have not been modernized nor productivity improved at the pace required to compete with the leading industrial nations, while runaway inflation, rising to more than 20 percent a year from 1975 to 1977, threatened to reduce further the rate of investment. Analysts have found it easier to lay the blame—on the enormous cost to Britain of World War II, unimaginative and weak managers, an inadequate educational system, the selfish conservatism of labor unions, the high costs of welfare and defense—than prescribe the solution. Membership in the European Economic Community and above all the development of the rich oil fields of the North Sea will, it is now hoped, give Britain another chance.

In economic terms the contrast with West Germany could hardly be greater, and within the Federal Republic (which in terms of industrial output stands second only to the U.S.S.R. among European nations) political issues have tended to be overshadowed by the satisfying fact of prosperity. Even the significant change in government from the Christian Democrats to

An expanding market for consumer products was an important part of the economic boom in Europe in the '60s and early '70s. These washing machines are being tested at a factory in Italy, one of the world's largest exporters of home appliances. (Photo: Tony Howarth/Woodfin Camp and Associates)

the Social Democrats has not lessened the commitment to encouraging investment, expanding trade, and preventing inflation. Often surprisingly conservative in their economic policies, the Social Democrats have nevertheless pursued democratization in other ways, lowering the voting age to eighteen, carrying through educational reforms, and expanding social services (steps that have incidentally brought greater centralization and given the bureaucracy more power). Their most venturesome measure requires all firms with more than 2000 employees to have a central board of directors half of whose members are elected representatives of labor. First Adenauer, with his close ties to the United States and to de Gaulle, and then the socialist leader Willy Brandt, with his personal warmth and optimistic gestures to the East, slowly won for Germany the central place in European affairs now enjoyed by their successors.

The Italian Republic, whose economic miracle was perhaps even more remarkable than Germany's, has never had a national government not dominated by the Christian Democrats, a party far more heterogeneous than its

German namesake. It includes some groups more traditionalist and others far more radical, and ministers holding office for brief periods and unable to control their own majority have been a characteristic weakness of the country's political life. In fact elements of Italy's Christian Democratic party were closely tied to most of the nation's major political currents, so that the process of coalition building always began within the semisecret confusion of the dominant party. While the Christian Democrats sought allies from among smaller parties in the center, the Communists, Italy's second largest party, and a smaller group of monarchists and neo-Fascists on the right maintained loud and often effective opposition.

Room for maneuver was thus limited, and until 1958 the center coalitions supported governments that postponed most major reforms and left the most important economic initiatives to the state-owned holding companies. While the economy boomed, politics often sank into immobility beneath labyrinthine deals. From 1958 on, however, there was growing talk of an "opening to the left," an understanding that would woo Socialists from their Communist allies and permit a left-center coalition. Italy's rapid modernization, the need for administrative reform, and the change in Catholic attitudes associated with Pope John XXIII, all pointed to this course.

Finally achieved in 1963, the new coalition lasted until 1972, and it accomplished some of the promised changes. But the Socialists were more divided than ever, and the Christian Democratic factions lost none of their autonomy; the process of compromise remained infinitely complex; and few ministries survived a whole year. Unprestigious governments and a sprawling, inefficient bureaucracy nevertheless maintained a tension-filled nation in reasonable peace and freedom during a period of rapid social transformation.

The slowing of economic growth, rising burdens of public debt, and rampant inflation have greatly weakened the Christian Democrats, however, in favor of a coalition of Socialists and Communists who have gained control of many of Italy's most important regional governments (which finally came into being in the 1970s as part of an effort to decentralize government and make it more responsive) and of most of her major cities. In contrast to the Christian Democrats, the Communists have a reputation for probity and efficiency; and the left has proved even on the explosive issues of divorce and abortion to be closer to the majority of Italians than the Catholic party. In an atmosphere of perpetual crisis, the Christian Democrats have been able to rule since 1975 only with the tolerant abstention of Communist deputies, arranged through prior consultation with them on all major issues. That cooperation was severely tested in 1978 with the assassination of Aldo Moro. A leading Christian Democratic advocate of an understanding with the Communists, Moro was captured by a terrorist group called the "Red Brigades," held hostage, and finally shot. But the sense of national outrage that followed seemed to strengthen the government.

The growing influence of the left in France was a somewhat more surprising outcome of the years of Gaullist supremacy, for by 1962, when his followers won a firm majority in the Chamber of Deputies, Charles de Gaulle seemed to have established the stability and even the popularity of the Fifth Republic. France had become the fourth nation in the world to have nuclear weapons, an achievement accomplished without help from any other nation, and exercised an independent position in world affairs. At home too the regime had a style all its own centered in the powerful personality of de Gaulle. Economic and social policy was firmly in the hands of able, even brilliant, technocrats;

not only was parliament docile but the bickering and factionalism of traditional political life
seemed dead as de Gaulle relied instead on plebiscites and public relations to maintain presidential government's tie to public opinion.
That France prospered in such stability was
tangibly apparent on every side. Nevertheless,
the presidential election of 1965 conducted by
direct universal suffrage according to a constitutional amendment adopted three years earlier,
required a run-off ballot between François Mit-
terand, the rising leader of the left, and de Gaulle
before the general could win a majority. The
opposition was strengthened by discontent
among workers convinced they were not receiving their share of France's prosperity, by a
broader dissatisfaction with many of the effects
of rapid economic growth, including urban
problems, inadequate housing, and the neglect
of underdeveloped regions, and by criticisms
especially from intellectuals of an often arbitrary bureaucracy and of de Gaulle's sometimes
pompous paternalism.

In May 1968 the regime was nearly toppled
by the surprisingly effective revolt of students
in the Parisian universities, a revolt that began
with specific objections to an overcrowded, excessively centralized, and outmoded educational
system but quickly became a broader attack on
the society of consumption and the technocratic policies Gaullists represented. As the
students occupied buildings and battled with
police, millions of workers went on strike.
With firmness and skill, the storm was weathered; most workers, ambivalent at best toward
the students who appeared rich and privileged
to them, were interested rather in higher wages.
And the Communists somewhat uncomfortably
kept their distance from the student radicals,
whose rising so frightened much of French society that Gaullists were able to gain impressively in the elections held that June. But the
Fifth Republic was never the same. The gov-

ernment promised and carried out extensive reforms of education, increasing options and access and giving students and parents a larger
voice at every level; it reformed much in its
own administration, and turned to broader programs of welfare and social improvement, including somewhat vague plans to give workers
a role in factory management. A few months
later, de Gaulle put forth a complex set of proposals for administrative reforms leading to
some regional decentralization. Characteristically, the proposals were both vague and far-
reaching, and the electorate was asked to approve them in a referendum, while leaving all
the details to the president. This time the
voters refused, and in April 1969 de Gaulle
resigned.

His successor, Georges Pompidou, was a
firm Gaullist whose new government was both
more open and more willing to reconsider established policies. The election of Valéry Giscard
d'Estaing as president in 1974 marked a further
evolution. A member of the government's
majority but not of the Gaullist party, he had
campaigned with a direct informality that
seemed to promise a more accessible, democratic, and relaxed administration, one that
might even lead to a new coalition of the center
reaching from reform-minded Gaullists to the
Socialists. Instead, the Socialists stayed closer
to the Communists with whom they had contracted a common electoral program in 1972
that included nationalization of many industries,
more even distribution of income, and better
housing. Significantly, in addition to these
more common Marxist goals, it also called for
more decentralized political authority and steps
to assure greater opportunities for leisure, a
more vigorous cultural life, and pleasanter
cities. French political life, despite the fact
that most voters appear closest to the center, is
now organized between a Marxist left and a
technocratic right of about equal strength.

The Chances of Revolution

For a few weeks in May 1968 it had seemed as if the students of Paris might recapture the revolutionary spirit of 1848, as their barricades of paving stones and trees, their imaginative posters and endless slogans paid homage to a revolutionary tradition. In France, Germany, Italy, Great Britain, and the United States students in 1968–1969 behaved as an independent political force, mounting attacks on university regulations and national foreign policy that became denunciations of a middle-class and capitalist society which they portrayed as hypocritical and repressive. In general these protests led to reforms of education and amended government policies in other spheres, but in the short term at least they strengthened the old order. Labor unions and parties of the left were suspicious of youthful anarchy while reformers and liberals were as appalled as conservatives by the violence and indifference to legal procedure. As revolutions, these movements thus failed in a cloud of angry rhetoric disproportionate to their strength, but in the long term they influenced a style of protest that others would take up and publicized criticisms that remain in the modern consciousness about the society of consumption, the value of work and competition, the trustworthiness of elites, and the injustices of hierarchy. These concerns are now reflected in the programs of the left in nearly every Western country, while fear of disorder and of a declining belief in traditional values has increased among conservatives.

Students were active as well in the movement that briefly transformed Czechoslovakia in 1968, where Alexander Dubček, as first secretary of the Communist party, led the adoption of a program calling for freedom of speech, assembly, and religion and the granting of greater autonomy to Slovakia. These liberal and nationalist goals, very much like those expounded in the revolutions of 1848, were seen in Moscow as an intolerable danger, and Czech resistance to Soviet pressure was overcome in August by the armed invasion of troops from the Soviet Union, East Germany, Hungary, and Poland. Within a few months all the liberal reforms save a grant of Slovakian autonomy had been reversed, the Soviet troops invited to remain, and Dubček ousted from office.

Despite the enormous concentration of power in the hands of the modern state, revolutions nevertheless remain a possibility. In Greece they have come primarily as military coups, first in 1967, when a group of army officers overthrew the unstable parliamentary system and eventually the monarchy itself and then in 1973 when they in turn gave way to civilian leaders who arrested the officers and restored democracy. Despite harsh, even brutal, repression, Greece's military rulers had found it necessary gradually to restore freedoms that further exposed their unpopularity. Having to strengthen a fragile but modernizing economy, weakened by conflict with Turkey over control of Cyprus, they had to draw closer to Western Europe where there was little disposition to treat with Greek dictators.

The restoration of political freedom in Portugal and Spain was even more remarkable. Although less dictatorial than the Salazar regime which it succeeded on his death in 1968, the government of Marcello Caetano continued along essentially the same lines. But although opposition at home was effectively stymied, that proved impossible in Portugal's African colonies. The last of Europe's colonial powers to hang on to its empire, Portugal used force and cruel repression in Portuguese Guinea, Angola, and Mozambique only to see liberation movements there grow stronger. Portugal was subject to increasing condemnation in the United Nations, among African states and other European nations while the government's political and economic strength at home was

sapped despite censorship and further restrictions on the right of assembly. Suddenly in April 1974 a group of Portuguese army officers seized control, ousting the old regime, promising full freedom and civil rights at home and self-determination for the colonies. Crowds filled the streets to dance and cheer before smiling soldiers whose rifles were decorated with flowers.

If the euphoria could not last, some sense of joyful release has been sustained as Portugal has come to grips with a series of staggering problems. A poor and backward country hoping to modernize, Portugal, with its agriculture in disarray, many of its skilled managers seeking employment in Switzerland and Brazil, faced raging inflation and declining production while peasants claimed the land they had long coveted, socialist and communist unions competed to capture a following in critical industries, and rural and business groups battled to make their interests heard. The army leaders themselves were divided ideologically (among communists, socialists, Christians, and conservatives) and over policy, both domestic and colonial. Seven governments in little over two years tried to cope with these problems; and if they are not yet resolved, important steps have been taken. Extensive nationalizations of banks and industry were followed by free elections in 1975 and 1976. A series of attempted revolts of the left and the right, usually led by military factions, have all been defeated; and since 1976 with the election of the moderate General António Ramalho Eanes as president, there has been reasonable stability. The Socialists are the largest party, though not a majority, and their minority government under Mário Soares

Angry young faces, rock throwing, and burning automobiles could be seen in many European and American cities in 1968. This demonstration took place in Prague. (Photo: P.P./Magnum)

succeeded until his first defeat in 1977 in drawing Portugal closer to the other governments of Western Europe than ever before.

The political transformation in Spain has been less dramatic, but it follows on the most rapid industrial growth in Europe. Not until the 1950s did Spanish production exceed the level of 1935, so slow was the nation's recovery from the years of civil war. By the 1960s, however, the money attracted through tourism, the encouragement of efficient large-scale agriculture at the expense of the small producer, and systematic government programs of industrialization on the familiar European model all began to have effect. The gross national product of 1960 had increased fivefold fifteen years later; and a new generation of leaders in business, the professions, and the Church kept some distance from the old pieties of the Franco regime while sporadic strikes and demonstrations (in which Basque nationalists and priests were prominent) expressed a growing discontent with the government's corruption, suppression of freedom, and social conservatism. Still the aging Franco skillfully kept his hand on power even after his retirement from the conduct of daily affairs in 1973 and the formal naming of Don Juan Carlos, the son of the Bourbon claimant to the throne, as his successor. When Franco died in 1975, the revolution many feared did not take place; and the new king proved both more flexible and adept than most anticipated. Political repression and censorship were steadily relaxed, and successive prime ministers edged toward genuinely representative government. The army remains powerful, the police highly political, and some censorship in force; but while Communists and Socialists compete for popular support, the parties of the center and the right jockey for influence, and Catalonian and Basque nationalists agitate, the Spanish nation, suddenly quite modern and more prosperous than ever before, seems nevertheless to be moving toward a democracy healthier than that expunged forty years earlier.

For the military to seize power in an unstable, developing country, as they did in Greece and Portugal, was nothing new; similar actions were common in Europe in the 1920s and 1930s and have since occurred throughout the Middle East, Asia, and Latin America. In the recent European experience, however, the trend even after a *coup d'état* has been toward mixed economies and political freedom. For radicals, social change and prosperity have strengthened the belief in revolution; and among revolutionaries, small groups tempted by terrorism, both because of the apparent vulnerability of highly organized societies and as an expression of their own alienation, have achieved notoriety throughout the West. Advocates of such tactics often see them as a form of the guerrilla warfare frequently effective in movements of national liberation, and it was in line with that example that bombs and assassination spread to metropolitan France during the Algerian crisis and were used with rising frequency by Basque nationalists in Spain in the 1970s. The Palestine Liberation Organization spread its terrorist tactics to European airports and the killing of Israeli athletes at the Munich Olympic games in 1972.

Only in Northern Ireland, however, have the techniques of terrorism escalated to the level of a kind of continuous war. There the Irish Republican Army, an underground organization repudiated by the Irish Republic, and extremist Protestant groups have killed hundreds of innocent people and pushed the British government to abandon its program for local rule that would include both Protestants and Catholics. Centuries of religious and national conflict, discrimination, and repression enable both groups to find sufficient local support to sustain them against the political and military efforts of the British government. One of the purposes of such movements, of course, is to expose established government as an instrument of oppression, and groups of young radicals in Italy and Germany (where the women in these groups far outnumber the men) use kidnapping, assassination, and bombing in large part to provoke a response that will ultimately undermine confidence in the state. As in Northern Ireland, the opposition thus produced can be as significant as the initial terrorism, whether it is neofascist armed guards, the politicization of the police, or measures like those recently introduced in West Germany to screen subversives out of the civil service.

The Varieties of Communism

Communism remained much the most powerful radical movement in Europe, one highly organized in parties and trade unions in the West and in the complex organs of the state in the East. The communist movement, however, was no longer united. Its second major division (after Yugoslavia's break with the Cominform in 1948) was the antagonism between the Soviet Union and China that became public and seemingly permanent in the 1960s, to be echoed by small groups of Maoists in Western Europe who from the extreme left criticized and harried the large Communist parties in the name of the principles represented by Chairman Mao Tse-tung. As its fatherland, the Soviet Union remained the model and dominant force of European communism; but domestic developments within Russia and across the Continent combined with the relaxation of the Cold War to introduce considerable national variety in a movement once considered monolithic.

The Soviet Union's most impressive achievement, one admired throughout the world, was her industrial growth. By the 1960s her economy was second in overall production and wealth only to that of the United States. In 1961 she sent the first man into orbit around the earth; and as the world's largest producer

Children taunt ill-at-ease British soldiers in Belfast; hatreds centuries old have been passed on to the new generation. (Photo: Jim Anderson/Woodfin Camp and Associates)

of steel, iron, and more recently oil, the U.S.S.R. was apparently gaining on the West. With this basis for confidence, Khrushchev, brash and outspoken, became an international personality and did much to humanize the image of the Soviet government. But when, in 1962, he allowed long-range Soviet missiles to be placed on the island of Cuba, which since 1959 had been ruled by a Marxist government under Fidel Castro, the result was a major international crisis that brought the world to the brink of war. In the face of a vigorous response by the American president John F. Kennedy, Khrushchev agreed to dismantle the missiles. The Soviet regime had no desire to risk its achieve-

ments and its empire in a world conflagration. Many Kremlin leaders worried as well about the restiveness in Eastern Europe and the growing rift with China. The results of Khrushchev's foreign policy weakened him at home, while his opponents in the Central Committee bided their time.

A further weakness was the perennial disappointment of Soviet agriculture. Khrushchev's

The Soviet Union gained immense prestige as the first nation to launch a space vehicle in 1957, initiating a peaceful, but frenzied, race for preeminence in space between the superpowers. By the '70s, however, the tone was more one of cooperation, reflected here in this exhibit held in Los Angeles in 1977. (Photo: Wide World Photos)

plans to apply the latest technology and to expand production across millions of acres of land in Asian Russia did not have the desired result. In addition the very success of heavy industry led to increased demand for better quality controls, more plentiful consumer products, and more adequate urban housing. All these economic issues cut to the heart of Soviet policy and were a source of conflict within the highest circles.

When Khrushchev antagonized the military in the process of solidifying his authority, they felt strong enough to speak against him in the Politburo and Central Committee. He was voted out of office in 1964 and sent into quiet retirement. The Soviet Union was developing practices that, though preserving dictatorial power and a tradition of internal battles for power, permitted orderly transitions.

Khrushchev's successors were cool and tough party technicians, Aleksei Kosygin and Leonid Brezhnev. A firm grip on power, strengthened as Brezhnev emerged as the dominant figure, provided no simple resolution of the problems that had weakened Khrushchev. The cold-blooded invasion of Czechoslovakia established the limits to freedom or autonomy to be allowed in Eastern Europe, but significantly greater diversity could not be prevented. The relatively low yield of Russian agriculture continued to produce crises in bad years and had to be met in 1972 and 1975 by huge purchases of grain from the United States which were made possible by better relations with the administration of President Richard M. Nixon. An emphasis on consumer production begun in the 1960s was later partially reversed, and for the latest technology the Soviet Union has contracted with Western firms, particularly in Italy and France, to build huge new plants in Russia.

The issue of civil rights for at least some forms of dissent has proved impossible to squelch either in world opinion or at home. When Boris Pasternak was awarded the Nobel prize for literature in 1958, he was forbidden permission to go to Stockholm to receive it. But his work, especially the novel *Doctor Zhivago*, had, like Khrushchev's denunciation of Stalin, done much to disseminate a view of the seamy and repressive aspects of Soviet life. The case of Alexander Solzhenitsyn caused still more international furor. His *Gulag Archipelago* was a haunting account of the terrors of the Soviet concentration camps, and he too was prevented from receiving the Nobel prize awarded him in 1970. Four years later he was arrested and then deported, to become an outspoken critic of the Soviet regime, thereby joining his voice to a score of Russian writers

and scientists whose criticisms, widely published outside the U.S.S.R., are increasingly known in their own country. To this criticism is added the plight of Soviet Jews subject to discrimination and attack, then intermittently permitted to emigrate. Although international conventions (and American policy since 1976) have underscored the demands for greater liberty, they have not shaken the Soviet regime nor undermined its place in world affairs. But they have given focus to questions about the use of power and the nature of the Soviet government that troubles thoughtful people everywhere.

For all the Eastern European communist states except Rumania, ties to the Soviet Union remained the keystone of foreign policy; and political orthodoxy continued to be a domestic requirement. Each country, however, increased its trade and communication with Western Europe. The Catholic Church, influential in Hungary, Czechoslovakia, and Poland, has been particularly outspoken in the latter, where recently more criticism has been allowed, significant private ownership is permitted (and more riots and demonstrations against food prices have occurred). Bulgaria sought better relations with other Balkan States, and Rumania formed economic ties with Yugoslavia and attempted to establish herself as a nonaligned state, while East Germany, the second industrial power among communist states (the seventh in Europe and the eleventh in the world), oscillated between friendlier relations and renewed tensions with West Germany, between repression and concessions at home to meet the sort of discontent expressed in bloody riots in the early 1970s.

Each country thus cautiously evolved foreign ties and domestic policies that reflected something of her history and traditional culture. Yugoslavia, the maverick among communist states, cautiously established better relations with her more orthodox neighbors while firmly maintaining her independence. Domestically, too, she stood between East and West, combining something of a market economy and decentralized factory management (in which workers were given a large voice) with state ownership, elections allowing more than one candidate for each office within a single party, and greater freedom for dissent—with occasional crackdowns on figures like Milovan Djilas, a life-long Communist whose systematic and Marxian critique of Soviet society and of party officials as a new ruling class led to years of imprisonment, or like the professors associated with the theoretical journal *Praxis*, the only officially tolerated voice of criticism, who all were suspended from their positions in 1975.

Europe as a whole thus offers an extraordinary variety of experiments in social systems ranging from the capitalism of Switzerland and West Germany to the mixed economies of Western Europe, the market communism of Yugoslavia, and other varieties of communism in Eastern Europe and the Soviet Union, with Europe's least developed nation, communist Albania, completing the spectrum as China's best ally outside Asia. This sense of variety and experiment and of new efforts to combine a directed economy with social justice and political freedom has been invigorated by the striking developments within Western European Communist parties known as Eurocommunism. Italy's Communist party, the largest in the world in a non-communist country, has been the model and major stimulus of Eurocommunism. In Antonio Gramsci, who died in a Fascist prison, the party had one of the ablest of modern Marxist theoreticians; his emphasis on the importance of local history and culture in determining the path to communism gave the party's flexibility a justification beyond mere tactical pragmatism. And through the years of opposition and close ties to the Italian Socialist party, the Communists have developed,

under the leadership of Enrico Berlinguer, a suave and attractive politician, a detailed program for the reform of Italian society, which accepts the principles of formal democracy—including civil rights, multiple parties, and free elections.

The successes of the Italian party have increased its influence at home and abroad and led the French Communist party, once among Europe's most Stalinist, to a similar stance. Both parties denounced the invasion of Czechoslovakia in 1968 and have come to insist on the independence of national parties. The Italian party even accepted NATO, and the French one not only ceased to oppose France's nuclear weapons but, determined to prove its respect for the voice of the electorate, in 1976 officially rejected the dictatorship of the proletariat as an item of party dogma. With the liberalization in Spain after the death of Franco, the Spanish Communist party, under Santiago Carrillo (whose years of exile were spent in the United States rather than the Soviet Union), has adopted similar views and moved even closer toward democratic socialism, positions outlined in Carrillo's book, *Eurocommunism and the State*, published in 1977.

This form of communism, ready to cooperate with other parties on single points and insistent on its own democratic convictions, has in essence been accepted by most Western European Communist parties (with the notable exceptions of Portugal's and Finland's).[1] Despite heavy Soviet pressure and public denunciations of these Western Communists as "bour-

---

[1] Communist parties attract nearly a third of the electorate in Italy, one-fifth in France and Finland, one-eighth in Spain, and much less elsewhere: about 5 percent in Sweden, 4 percent in Denmark, 3 percent in Belgium, 2 percent in Greece and the Netherlands, and less than 1 percent in West Germany and Great Britain.

geois ideologists," the Russians have been unable to restore the unity of European communism. On the sixtieth anniversary of the Russian Revolution in 1977, Eurocommunism thus stood as a third schism in the communist ranks; and part of its Western appeal was its claim to seek Europe's independence from both Soviet and American influence. Many voters even on the left remain skeptical, of course, of the Communists' dedication to liberal freedoms, noting that the parties themselves remain highly centralized, intolerant, suspicious of the Common Market, and in foreign affairs closely tied to Soviet and anti-American positions. But Eurocommunism has now opened the possibility that Communists might again share power in Italy and France for the first time since 1947 and that this Western form of communism might begin to exert a significant attraction in Eastern Europe (Dubček, ostracized in his own country, has published his critiques of the Czechoslovakian regime in Italian Communist journals). The sharp distinction between communists and anti-communists, which once seemed the most fundamental of political divisions, has broken down.

II. EUROPE'S PLACE IN THE WORLD

The decline of European power has been so prominent a theme of history since World War I that Europeans themselves are often not fully aware of the privileged position they still retain. Yet in terms of per capita wealth or aggregate industrial power Europe (quite aside from the question of whether the Soviet Union should be considered a European power) stands among the richest regions of the world. And the fading of the Cold War, the rise of China and Japan, the importance of the developing nations, and the movement toward greater Eu-

ropean unity all open the possibility of greater European influence in a world no longer simply divided into Soviet and American spheres of influence.

THE WEALTH OF EUROPE

There is no single, certain measure of a society's wealth. Gross national product per capita is probably the best indicator of the general standard of living, but that estimate can really only be made for nations that collect and publish rather full statistics and that engage in a free market which establishes some useful equivalence of national currencies—a requirement that omits all Communist countries. Of the regions of the world North America clearly came first at about $7000 per person in 1975; Western Europe was second at about $4200 per person. Eastern Europe would undoubtedly have placed third, followed by the Middle East (about $1300 per person), Latin America ($1000), Asia ($500), and Africa ($200?). Calculated by nations, the position of Western Europe stands out still more; Sweden, Switzerland, and Norway have higher per capita incomes than the United States (and some economists predict that France and perhaps West Germany may surpass the United States in the future). Of the six richest nations with free markets, three are thus in Western Europe; of the twenty-five richest, fifteen are Western European. Equally significant, over the past fifteen years rates of growth in Western Europe have been higher than among all other developed nations except Japan. It is not surprising that nearly half of the world's largest banks are Western European; and as a bloc, Western Europe, with its more than 300 million people, stands close to the United States and ahead of Russia, Japan, and Eastern Europe among the world's great centers of wealth.

TELEPHONES PER EACH 100 INHABITANTS, 1975

USA	69.5	Greece	22.1
Sweden	66.1	Spain	22.0
Switzerland	61.1	Czechoslovakia	17.6
Canada	57.2	East Germany	15.2
New Zealand	50.2	French Guiana	14.9
Denmark	45.4	Ireland	14.1
Iceland	41.7	Kuwait	12.3
Luxembourg	41.0	Portugal	11.3
Japan	40.5	Bahrein	10.0
Australia	39.0	Hungary	9.9
Finland	38.9	Bulgaria	8.9
United Kingdom	37.9	Poland	7.5
Netherlands	36.8	Argentina	7.8
Norway	35.0	South Africa	7.8
West Germany	31.7	United Arab Emirates	7.3
Belgium	28.5	U.S.S.R.	6.6
Austria	28.1	Namibia	6.2
France	26.2	Yugoslavia	6.1
Italy	25.9		

WESTERN EUROPE, 1970s: Proportion of Medical Expenses Paid Through State Plans

	Percent		Percent
United Kingdom	95	Spain	42
Ireland	76	Sweden	35
Finland	70	Greece	30
West Germany	69	Norway	26
Austria	67	France	24
Denmark	67	Italy	21
Luxembourg	59	Belgium	16
Switzerland	50	Netherlands	6
Portugal	42		

WESTERN EUROPE, 1970: Automobiles per Every 100 Inhabitants

Sweden	28	Netherlands	19
Luxembourg	27	Italy	19
France	25	Austria	16
United Kingdom	22	Finland	15
Switzerland	22	Ireland	13
Denmark	22	Portugal	7
West Germany	22	Spain	7
Belgium	21	Greece	3
Norway	19		

WESTERN EUROPE, 1972: Television Licenses per Every 100 Inhabitants

Sweden	32.0	France	23.0
United Kingdom	30.5	Norway	23.0
West Germany	30.0	Austria	21.0
Denmark	28.0	Italy	19.0
Netherlands	28.0	Ireland	16.0
Finland	25.0	Spain	13.0
Luxembourg	25.0	Portugal	6.0
Switzerland	24.0	Greece	3.0
Belgium	23.0		

Productivity and Trade

This extraordinary productivity rests on heavy investment and advanced technology in industry and agriculture, excellent communications, and sophisticated marketing. Although the coal fields of Britain, West Germany, and Eastern Europe, the iron ore fields of France and Sweden, and the new oil discoveries of the North Sea compensate somewhat for Europe's poorer endowment in mineral resources compared to the United States and the Soviet Union, the world's largest producers of these essential resources, Europe's industrial economy is based on the efficient transformation of raw materials. Western Europe as a whole manufactures more steel than either Russia or the United States, more automobiles than the two superpowers combined, and generates more electrical power than Russia (but about two-thirds as much as the United States). With only about 3 percent of the world's farmland, Western Europe produces 15 percent of the world's eggs, potatoes, and wheat (of which France alone is the fifth largest producer after the U.S.S.R., the United States, China, and India), and nearly one-third of the world's dairy products and sugar beets. Europe as whole, including all of the Soviet Union, produces about one-third of the world's crops (compared to 13 percent in North America).

It follows that Western Europe holds a lead-

WORLD TRADE, 1976: Approximate Value in Billions of Dollars

United States	118.0	Sweden	17.4
West Germany	90.2	Switzerland	12.9
Japan	55.8	Australia	11.9
France	52.9	Poland	10.3
Great Britain	44.1	Venezuela	10.1
Netherlands	35.0	East Germany	10.1
Italy	34.8	Denmark	8.7
Canada	34.7	Brazil	8.7
U.S.S.R.	33.3	Kuwait	8.6
Belgium-		Czechoslovakia	8.6
Luxembourg	28.8	Nigeria	8.1
Saudi Arabia	27.7	Spain	7.7
Iran	20.0	Austria	7.5

ing place in world trade (accounting for about 40 percent of the total and a comparable percentage of world shipping). The largest part of this trade flows among the Western European nations themselves, accounting for a higher proportion of their total wealth than in other developed and large nations. Trade figures nevertheless indicate something of a nation's international influence; of the world's ten biggest trader nations, eight are European; of the twenty-five largest, fifteen are in Europe. And the determination to expand trade still further is reflected in the continuing modernization of the rail and highway systems, joint ventures like the controversial supersonic Concorde airplane, and huge projects like the planned Rhine-Danube canal in Germany or the still larger French plan for a canal connecting the Rhine and the Rhone, an idea talked about in the time of Charlemagne. Among nations so dependent on trade, lowering tariffs and sharing markets are vital.

Energy and Inflation

For all their expansive prosperity, European nations must grapple with serious economic problems. The most easily understood is the need for oil. In 1973, when the oil-exporting states first banded together to raise international prices, Europe imported nearly two-thirds of its energy in the form of petroleum. And the hope of becoming self-sufficient in energy by 1985 quickly proved overly optimistic, for that depended heavily on nuclear power (in 1976 over half of the world's nuclear power plants in operation and nearly half of those under construction were in Europe) which has proved more costly than anticipated and raised questions of pollution and safety that have raised doubts as to its practicality. Continued prosperity in the advanced industrial nations will require some answer not yet clear to their rapacious demand for energy.

A second and subtler problem has been inflation, rising to an annual rate of increase in 1975–1976 (more than 20 percent in Britain and Italy, 30 percent in Portugal) that undermined planning, savings, and trade while pinching salaried employees and many workers between rising costs and lagging incomes, thus increasing agitation and discontent. Only West Germany among major capitalist nations has consistently managed to hold the rate of inflation below 5 percent. The general causes of the inflation are well known—governments spending more than their income, more money in circulation, the higher prices of imports, the tendency of businesses to maintain or increase profits by raising prices rather than increasing efficiency, the assumption on all sides that prices are bound to go up—but the solution is difficult. Government expenditures reflect social policies and political pressures not easily reversed, and organized workers are not inclined to absorb the losses that would follow from not seeking higher wages. In fact the debate as to what interests should be sacrificed can easily become an exercise in social conflict, as it has tended to do in Britain and Italy.

Equally serious, inflation has been accompanied by a decline in investment and endemic un-

employment, particularly among those socially most vulnerable—the unskilled, immigrants from the countryside and foreign countries, and the young—thus giving a structural rigidity to social problems productivity had been expected to solve and making terms like "stagflation" and "crisis" part of everyday vocabulary. Like the large loans to nations with weak economies extended by the International Monetary Fund, by more fortunate nations, private banks, and by the Common Market, political responses have concentrated more on temporary than long-term solutions.

EUROPE AND INTERNATIONAL RELATIONS

In international affairs as well as economic matters individual European nations have not since World War II had the dominant role familiar in previous centuries but have been able when acting jointly to increase greatly their influence. Europe is still the second most populous continent although its population is growing less rapidly than in any other (and more rapidly in southern Europe and eastern Russia than in the North or West, changes whose weight will be felt in the future). As the danger of armed conflict on the Continent appeared to fade, the division into those belonging to the Warsaw Pact and to NATO no longer served as the central focus, though it remained a fundamental fact of international relations in Europe; and both the role and the real strength of NATO became less certain. Restive with their lack of a voice in American policy, the European members have seen disappointment with the al-

liance matched by the American government's concern that it was expected to carry too much of the burden of mutual defense. Even after the withdrawal of France, announced in 1964 and completed two years later, and despite their inability to agree upon uniform or interchangeable weapons, the NATO countries have nevertheless maintained their military ties, including a coordinated command and regular, joint maneuvers.

Attempts at Independent European Policies
European influence has increased through a number of looser organizations such as the Organization for Economic Cooperation and Development (OECD), which groups a score of the economically advanced nations, and the Trilateral Commission, a privately based group that includes business and political leaders from Japan, the United States, and Europe. Such organizations have come to play an important part in aiding developing nations and in preventing the recession of 1975 from leading to the erection of disruptive national trade barriers.

But it is among the Western European nations themselves[2] that new ventures at international organization have gone far enough to raise the possibility of a change in the balance of world power at some point in the future. Such a possibility was envisioned, for example,

---

[2] Geographers list eighteen nations as belonging to Western Europe: Austria, Belgium, Denmark, Finland, France, Greece, Iceland, Ireland, Italy, Luxembourg, Netherlands, Norway, Portugal, Spain, Sweden, Switzerland, the United Kingdom, and West Germany. All of these save Portugal, Spain (which can expect to be admitted soon), and Finland belong to the Council of Europe, which also includes Cyprus, Malta, and Turkey.

Belgium, Denmark, Iceland, West Germany, Italy, Luxembourg, Netherlands, Norway, Portugal, Turkey, the United Kingdom, Canada, and the United States belong to NATO as do France and Greece although their armed forces no longer are under NATO command.

Traffic jams became an almost universal symptom of prosperity. This one shows vacationers returning to Rome from the resorts and beaches to the south of the city. (Photo: Wide World Photos)

with the founding of the Council of Europe in 1949. Although it has little autonomy, the Council remains a notable expression of the dream of European unity. Its Ministerial Committee, made up of the foreign ministers of the member states, meets twice a year; and its Parliamentary Assembly, housed in Strasbourg, is made up of delegates chosen by the members' parliaments. Neither body can pass binding legislation, but their discussions are not without influence. The Council's statutes require its members to uphold individual and political freedom and to honor the rule of law, requirements that have effectively excluded the Eastern European states as well as Spain and Portugal and led to the withdrawal of Greece while subject to military dictatorship. Most remarkable is the provision that permits individuals as well as nations to petition the council's Human Rights Commission against governmental abuses. When in 1977 the attorney general of Great Britain admitted Irish charges that torture had been used six years earlier against some men suspected of membership in the Irish Republican Army and promised to punish those guilty, it did seem as if some of the bright dreams the Council represents (and symbolized in its adoption of the "Ode to Joy" from Beethoven's Ninth Symphony as its anthem) might yet be realized.

But the strongest surge toward European unity has come from the Common Market, the development of which was closely tied to general changes in the international position of the major European states. The first of these had to do with the superpowers. The Soviet Union, more confident of her prestige and security, favored a relaxation of tensions in the West, despite intransigence in Berlin, as the rift with China became more public and threatening after 1960. The United States, which had consistently favored some form of closer European union, became less involved in such movements and less inclined to consider resistance to Russia its primary purpose as Western Europe appeared stronger and more stable and as American attention turned to Asia and the Middle East. The efforts at détente, marked by the invitation to the Soviet Union from the Western powers to a summit conference in 1960, led despite many setbacks to the Soviet-American agreements on space exploration in 1967 and the beginning of the Strategic Arms Limitation Talks in 1969. This reduction in tension had the effect of releasing European energies to concentrate on European affairs and gave more room for the new European role implied in 1966 when de Gaulle visited Russia, Premier Kosygin addressed the House of Commons, and Foreign Minister Gromyko went to Rome, where he even called on the pope.

Second, de Gaulle's flamboyant search for a French policy independent of the superpowers opened new paths for other European countries. Although he opposed the loss of sovereignty to any alliance or a European organization, he worked hard for the strengthening of Europe as well as of France. He rejected the British bid to enter the Common Market in 1963 partly to express his reaction to the special favors offered Britain and denied France by American defense plans but partly also to stress that Britain must declare herself first and foremost a European power. His exchanges of visits with Communist leaders, like a 1964 trade agreement with Rumania, hinted at the possibility of a single Europe. He viewed France's possession of nuclear weapons not as a deterrent on the scale of the superpowers' stockpiles but as proof that Europeans, beholden to no one, could defend themselves. At times he even competed with Tito as the best European friend of the nonaligned, developing nations of the Third World. France was second to the United States in the extent of her foreign aid.

De Gaulle's lack of enthusiasm for NATO

A French missile-firing nuclear submarine is launched at Cherbourg. More than other nations, France sought to maintain an independent, technologically advanced military force. (Photo: Wide World Photos)

was therefore part of a continuing search for independent avenues. He made it clear that in a crisis his country must side with the United States, as he himself did in the crises over Berlin and Cuba, but that very limitation encouraged other states to seek their own course within a general pro-Western framework. Thus even though de Gaulle's policies were often quixotic and highly personal, frequently at odds with those of France's closest friends, they carried a special message for Europeans.

A third major current was the increase in German strength. The political importance of

Europe's pariah had been masked by her division into two states, each dependent on one of the superpowers. And if Adenauer's close allegiance to the United States helped win his country respectability, it also postponed an independent resolution of the international questions that followed from division. The situation changed as East Germany became one of the world's most industrialized and prosperous communist nations and West Germany became a world economic power.

The building of the Berlin wall in 1961 to isolate the two sectors of the city was an immediate and crude response to the embarrassing flood of refugees who chose to escape the iron-curtain countries and a deliberate move to escalate international tension. It was also, however, a step in the process of absorbing East Berlin into the eastern republic and part of the long process that led toward the acceptance of two sovereign nations. By 1968 Russia found tension over Germany less useful than in the past.

Adenauer's concern in his later years for his close relations with de Gaulle, despite the domestic pain it cost him, similarly contributed to the subtle realignment. Willy Brandt's willingness to deal with communist nations and his patient negotiating skill carried Germany much further toward an independent accommodation. The treaty between West Germany and the Soviet Union signed in 1970, which earned Brandt a Nobel peace prize, marked a major milestone. While leaving open the possibility of a peaceful reunification of the divided country, it ratified the Oder-Neisse Line as Germany's eastern boundary, pointed to a settlement of the status of Berlin, and opened the way for extensive relations between Eastern Europe and the Continent's second most powerful nation.

The European Economic Community

While individual European states tested the opportunities for asserting themselves more independently, the European Economic Community proceeded through gradual and flexible stages, stretching over more than fifteen years, to remove obstacles to the free flow of goods, capital, and labor among its six members and, bit by bit, to coordinate its economic policies. Great Britain, reluctant to accept permanent involvement in the political affairs of the Continent or to loosen her Commonwealth ties, had in 1959 led in the creation of a counterpoise to the EEC, joining with Sweden, Norway, Denmark, Austria, Switzerland, and Portugal in the European Free Trade Association (EFTA), which remained more limited in its goals (free trade but not a common tariff among its members), looser in its structure, and far less successful than the EEC. In the decade of the 1960s, the "inner six" enjoyed nearly unprecedented growth and prosperity, while the United Kingdom remained at the bottom of the list of major European countries in the rate of economic expansion. In 1961–1963, 1967, and 1971 successive British governments sought to join the EEC, but the first two times Britain's desire for special terms with regard to the Commonwealth nations, differences over agricultural policies, and de Gaulle's opposition prevented agreement. Following the French president's resignation and concessions from both parties, Great Britain, accompanied by Ireland and Denmark, formally joined in 1972. In a surprising referendum Norwegians voted not to follow suit, but in a referendum held in 1975 to quiet opposition within Great Britain two-thirds of the voters supported the decision to enter the Common Market.

The Community's progress has often been slow and disappointing. Although the elimination of trade barriers evolved more rapidly than planned, the goals of further integration were not met on schedule, and a monetary union with a common currency though much discussed is not expected before 1980. Agricultural prices and subsidies have been the greatest difficulty, resulting in huge and costly stockpiles of produce as each nation presses for the protection of its own farmers. Expansion to nine members has made agreement more difficult to obtain, for unanimity is required on new issues despite the considerable autonomy granted the EEC's executive to carry out policies previously agreed to. The process of integration continues nevertheless. Decisions of the Community's Court of Justice lead toward regulations and legal protections that are increasingly uniform as do provisions covering the rights of migrant workers. And special programs, including significant expenditures intended to bring poorer regions, such as the northwestern part of the British Isles and southern Italy, closer to the Community's general level of prosperity, are giving it a voice in matters long considered the exclusive concern of national governments. In 1977 the heads of the nine EEC governments agreed on terms for direct elections to be held within each country in 1978 to choose representatives to the Community's parliament, where they will be seated by party rather than nationality.[3] That agreement, the session's chairman proclaimed, "marks the birth of the European citizen."

By far the world's greatest trader, the European Economic Community is an important element in world affairs and one that exercised considerable influence on the political changes in Greece, Portugal, and Spain, all of which hope to become members of the EEC. When the Community was formed, many of its members still had colonies, and the need to sustain something of the older trade patterns on which the economies of those colonies depended led to the creation of preferential trade agreements and associate status for such countries, arrangements subsequently extended under various terms to more than fifty states. The remaining EFTA states have eliminated most trade barriers between them and the Community; and agreements with Spain and Greece, while protecting them from a sudden flood of goods from the more developed nations of the Community, imply eventual membership by the 1980s when Portugal, too, is expected to belong. Many believe that the ties only slightly less close to Turkey, Algeria, Morocco, and Tunisia will lead in the same direction; and when in 1972 the EEC offered preferential tariffs to all Mediterranean nations, all but Libya responded favorably. Agreements with most of the nations of sub-Sahara Africa and with present and former colonies in the Caribbean and Pacific grant them access to the markets of the Community, often with guarantees to stabilize their income from exports while protecting their industries. In addition the Community provides sizable amounts of aid to developing countries. In relations between East and West, which may be deeply affected by the Common Market's trade with and loans to the communist countries of Eastern Europe, beginning with Yugoslavia, and in the relations between industrial and developing nations, especially in Africa, Europe may have a major part to play in the 1980s.

---

[3] France, Great Britain, Italy, and West Germany each has eighty-one representatives (the large number being necessary to assure Scotland and Wales more representatives than Denmark or Ireland); the Netherlands has twenty-five but Belgium twenty-four (having surrendered one so that the Flemings and Walloons would have equal representation); Denmark has sixteen (after the gift of a representative from Belgium), Ireland fifteen, and Luxembourg six.

III. A NEW ERA

Westerners today are almost unanimously convinced that they have entered a new historical era—an era as distinct from the past as the periods of nineteenth-century industrialization, the Enlightenment, the Renaissance, and the Middle Ages were from each other. Obviously this conviction rests on widely shared conceptions of historical change, but it is strongly supported by the evidence of Europe's place in world affairs and striking technological developments that have repercussions throughout society.

THE SENSE OF CHANGE

A concern, almost an obsession, with where we stand in historical evolution is part of the self-awareness of modern man. In every country politicians are fond of forecasting what "history will say" about their even quite minor decisions; change seems so central a trait of current life that the word "revolution" becomes a commonplace, and we speak easily of contemporary "revolutions" in everything from world politics to the roles of the sexes and food processing. At least in part this expresses a fear for the future and an effort to predict it or even control it by extending a surveyor's line from some point in the past through the present and on to the decades ahead. In part it follows from the hopes and the habits of thought of the past two centuries.

Analyses of how the world today differs from the past emphasize different aspects of society. Some begin with politics as the organization of power within and between nations. Some focus on economic distribution and the modes of production. Others concentrate on social structures and institutions. Finally, some stress changes in social values, attitudes, and ideas. Yet all these approaches tend to concur that a major historical change has occurred in the last few years.

If one dates the new era from the 1940s, the Axis domination of Europe then marks the tragic end of one epoch, Russian and American influence and European recovery the beginning of another. To put the date in the 1950s places more emphasis on the autonomy of a new, postwar Europe but points to the same evidence of more prosperous European societies but ones that no longer directly dominate the world. Or the real watershed, some would argue, lies in the 1960s, with the increasing strength of the Common Market, the growing independence of its members from the Cold War, and the end of a long period of European self-doubt and foundering extending back to the eve of World War I. Seen in any of these ways, our own era becomes the one in which a new age is clearly taking shape and in which Western technology, institutions, and ideas both Communist and capitalist have taken root around the world.

The changed role of European nations in world affairs is one obvious indication of change. In 1940 France dropped from the ranks of the world's most powerful states; Germany did so five years later; and in the 1950s even victorious Great Britain could no longer sustain a position comparable with that of the United States or the Soviet Union. Russia alone among the European states attained the position of a superpower. The economic crises of the postwar period and the loss of colonial empires confirmed a process of relative decline in Western Europe's strength. And many shared the Spenglerian gloom of Arnold Toynbee in his multivolume *Study of History* in placing this decline on a world-historical scale as the end of the European millennium.

The Locus of Power

Subsequent recovery has not restored Europe's former international dominance. The Common Market countries roughly equal the United States or Russia in population and productive capacity, but they are not one nation. Rather the European states have come to exercise their diplomatic influence in the interstices of Cold War competition. The Soviet Union has found a limit to the effectiveness of her power even in Eastern Europe, and the United States could not prohibit communism in Cuba or defeat it in Vietnam; and both superpowers, faced with economic problems at home and concerned over the rising strength of China and Japan, have had to seek good relations with European nations less dependent on them than in the past.

Political and economic relations between the communist states of Eastern Europe and the capitalist ones of the West will be a central issue. Economic expansion in both groups as well as the strength of the left in Western Europe foreshadow rapidly growing ties that will pull European governments closer together. A second long-range question regards the changing relationship of these countries to the Third World. Already the major European powers are coming to play a somewhat more independent role in the Middle East, showing a deepening interest in South America, and establishing stronger economic and political connections with the independent nations of Africa. Developing nations may have reason to prefer an association with industrial countries less overwhelming and ideologically committed than Russia or the United States.

At the same time the increasing importance of Japan, China, and eventually perhaps India and Brazil, will open new diplomatic opportunities. It is not hard to imagine on a global scale international understandings among half a dozen major powers and scores of lesser ones much like those among European nations in the eighteenth and nineteenth centuries. In such a world the wealth and the diplomatic skill of Europe will count for much.

Two favorite descriptions of the contemporary era, "the Atomic Age" and "the Space Age," express the critical role technology will play in that world. In both fields the Soviet Union and the United States achieved rough parity in the 1960s. Although European scientists contributed much to the progress these two giants have made, no other nation can match their capacity to sustain the immense organization and expend the massive funds large atomic arsenals and space flight require. On the other hand Britain and France produce nuclear weapons; and Western Europe is a leader in peaceful applications of nuclear energy and the use of satellites for communications and other purposes.

In most branches of technology, Western Europe probably surpasses Russia, and it lags behind the United States and Japan only in specific sectors, notably the application of computer technology. Its automated assembly lines, refineries, and switchyards are in fact often models for similar facilities in Eastern Europe and the United States. On the whole then Europe has essentially regained the position it held on the eve of World War II but not that of the nineteenth century. Such a rapid adaptation in a period of headlong technological advance has precipitated Europe into the postindustrial age.

POSTINDUSTRIAL SOCIETY

The somewhat misleading term "postindustrial society" was coined to indicate that the conditions and problems characteristic of the most advanced societies constitute a new historical stage. No longer is industrial production the dominant, absorbing activity in such countries; rather the white-collar occupations constitute some of the largest job categories, and service activities such as sales and distribution employ as many workers as production (a fact related to the changes in "proletarian" parties).

Postindustrial society then tends to take its lead from the professional groups. Expert managers, staff specialists, and technicians, usually highly specialized in their functions and often in their training, form a very large part of society—about the same proportion as the entire middle class in the nineteenth century. Even the very wealthy tend to exercise their influence through their connections with these groups. This in itself represents a crucial change in social structure. Furthermore, the majority of people—members of the lower-middle class, industrial workers, and most farmers—have become more similar in standard of living and even life style. Most European families now spend less than half their income on food and could easily reduce that proportion if they chose to. At the bottom of this society and often sadly separated from the rest of it are the rural poor and urban slum dwellers. Although a far smaller proportion of the population than the "deserving poor" of the nineteenth century, they are often cruelly distinguished by lack of education and by language or race.

Both the white-collar and working classes tend to be highly mobile, ready to shift jobs and location as new opportunities arise; and this is essential for the flexible adjustment to new demands on which advanced countries depend. But increased mobility and related changes affect the very fabric of society, most clearly perhaps with regard to the family. More than ever likely to be living at some distance from grandparents or cousins, the members of a family are rarely able to work together even in fields or factories, mines or small shops. Rather, increased leisure allows them to take their recreation together.

As domestic servants become scarce, household appliances become an essential benefit of the consumer society. Combined with smaller families, this means that women can approach salaried labor not merely as an interim measure to occupy their time until marriage or temporarily to supplement family income but as a lifelong occupation. The women's liberation movement, generally more prominent in the United States than in Europe, thus results

from the recognition of social opportunities as well as ideas of equality, on both counts opening the possibility of a redefinition of traditional social roles. Specialization on the other hand extends the period of training and therefore dependency; the teen-ager of today would have been considered a young adult, already working, through most of history. And society has come to recognize that increased longevity requires special provisions for the needs of the retired and the elderly.

In theory a mobile society would identify the talents of each citizen (of either sex) and provide the training to allow those talents to be used to the full. Education would thus become the critical social filter, selecting the talent and providing the training society needs. In practice this has proved difficult even in communist countries, nor have European societies settled the question of what sort of education is in fact most beneficial to the individual and to society.

An assumption underlying the concept of postindustrial societies is that everywhere they become more alike. To Europeans this change has seemed to come in the form of influences from the United States, and reactions to that challenge have reflected judgments about American society viewed as fluid, democratic, and open but also violent, crass, and culturally shallow. European economies, which in 1939 were barely familiar with installment buying, now enthusiastically employ easy purchase terms and credit cards to stimulate consumption. In the 1950s Coca-Cola was attacked as lamentable Americanization, but now supermarkets, discount stores, and packaged products are common. Television has not only become a focal point in most homes and altered the style of politics, but Eurovision allows national networks to share Europe-wide transmissions. Cities continue to expand and to grow more similar in appearance. Paid vacations, often both winter

The supermarket, once the key symbol of American affluence, was rapidly adapted to differing national tastes. This one is in France. (Photo: Viva/Woodfin Camp and Associates)

and summer, and the ubiquitous automobile carry commercial blight and common behavior to the seashores and mountains, whose isolation poets praised a few generations ago. Regional and class differences are no longer so readily and publicly identified by the clothes people wear, the places they go, or the diversions they enjoy.

As this happens, new problems arise requiring concerted social action, and matters once largely resolved by custom—such as diet, dress, popular culture, or the appearance of the countryside—become the object of deliberation. More people have more choices to make about their way of life, their occupations, their housing, and their leisure; but as such choice is extended—for example in the recent spread of legislation making divorce and abortion easier —it can also be burdensome to the individual and a challenge to traditional social values. These concerns and the tensions to which they give rise stand as another mark of modern society.

The Role of the State
Not only do postindustrial societies require that the state play a very active economic and social role but that role also seems to become

more similar from nation to nation. As always the government is a final source of social stability, but this control extends far beyond mere police power to a legal and political part in labor disputes and corporate mergers, a responsibility for general welfare and the distribution of resources, and a major part in general planning for social change as well as economic growth.

In principle the welfare state as accepted throughout Europe implies the constant reallocation of wealth from the well-to-do in favor of the poor. In practice the middle of society probably benefits as much as the less fortunate, and the accompanying tax burden is too great to fall on the rich alone. But for most Europeans the fear of going hungry, of facing illness without medical care, or of being destitute in old age has been greatly reduced. Public welfare appears almost as essential a part of state activity as the building of superhighways.

The state is also expected to assure the fiscal policies, at least some of the investments, the trade arrangements, the education system, detailed information on economic and social matters, and the means of communication that postindustrial societies require. Such tasks tend to make the government bureaucracy a model of postindustrial society itself: efficiently organized for special functions, open to people of talent and technical training who can expect promotion on merit (as well as seniority), approaching specific problems with rational objectivity. In practice, of course, no government agency is so removed from special interests and political prejudices, and this makes the bureaucracy itself a central issue of modern politics. Such tasks also lead the state into extensive long-range planning. In the French system a planning office with a large staff of experts and a consultative assembly representing affected interests both creates long-range programs and drafts legislation for parliamentary action.

Most other Western countries are beginning to adopt similarly comprehensive arrangements and have discovered how to manage the economy indirectly through tax and fiscal policies as well as through nationalized industries and direct subsidies much as they indirectly shape society through policies on housing, welfare, and education. In communist nations on the other hand, the advantages of indirect controls and more decentralized decision making are coming to be appreciated. Despite fundamental differences in the two systems, there is thus reason to see them drawing closer even in the roles assigned to the central governments. And the institutions with which governments deal —political parties, businesses, unions, education systems, hospitals—tend to manifest a similarly bureaucratic organization.

Not surprisingly the wave of changes since World War II and the picture of the future that can follow from them produce resistance and serious criticism. Just as contemporary change continues a process centuries old, so the criticisms of those changes build on a long tradition of disenchantment with claims of progress. For many the new era threatens much that was fundamental to Western civilization and that made European culture so vital. In that view society since World War II offers disturbing indications that ours is an age of crisis.

THE CRISIS OF SOCIETY

Applied to society, the metaphor of a crisis suggests some breakdown or spasm (the term was once primarily medical) which challenges survival itself and after which nothing is likely ever to be quite the same. The idea of crisis is usually accompanied by other terms loosely used—"breakdown," "revolution," "depression," "failure"; but the imprecision of "crisis" makes it useful to describe a feeling that things cannot go on as they are and appropriate to a time that seems on the eve of something drastically new. One of the favorite terms in current commentary and central to Marxist analysis, it is most often applied to the functioning of society, the state of contemporary culture, and the issue of what values people hold.

The dominant style of Western social analyses is to write as if society is a patient whose illness needs diagnosis. Such a view, common in novelists and congenial to modern psychology and sociology as well, is assumed in most contemporary assessments of our age; thus any private act, any social behavior, any publication is likely to be taken as a symptom of some larger tendency or need. Combined with an intense historical consciousness, including a fear that Western civilization may be in decline and a nostalgia for other eras, this orientation easily leads to a kind of cultural hypochondria.

Clearly there is much that does not function well. The totalitarian regimes of the 1930s and 1940s were terrifying evidence of that; worse, part of their justification was a disgust with the civilization from which they sprang—a civilization many denounced as materialistic, torn by ideological and class conflicts, lacking in universally accepted values either aesthetic or moral. If totalitarianism has subsided, it is not certain that such criticism is now less valid. Even in democracies the political process often seems far removed from the people, a sort of private game based on the manipulation of public opinion. And save for self-interest the great parties have largely lost the refreshing clarity of purpose with which they emerged from the resistance movements. The Christian Democrats, who dreamed of a Christian social vision above politics and were among the first to see the promise of European unity, have become but another coalition mediating among established influences, weak in France, stronger but hardly more creative in Germany and Italy. The socialists, once sure their hour had come, remain torn between allies on the left and in the center; no longer confident of many of their old panaceas, they are neither the incisive critics nor the innovative leaders they once showed promise of being. In Britain and Germany much of their strength lies in closely resembling their opposition.

On the Continent generally issues of civil liberties and charges of corruption still challenge the political system. In the Scandinavian countries and Britain, where such questions are less troubling, governments have hardly done better in consistently meeting the needs of a new era. Disillusionment in the communist regimes is only a little more effectively disguised, and everywhere policies that were supposed to have furthered freedom or equality can be shown merely to have left the poor and unfortunate more subordinate to the rich and powerful. Thus critics are sure of a despairing answer when they ask what Western nation is now moved by a great purpose or what government is truly free, honest, efficient, and farsighted.

Meritocracy and Bureaucracy

Indeed the state itself is an object of suspicion, not so much in the classic Marxist sense as the captive agent of the ruling class nor in the traditional liberal view as a threat to individual liberty, but simply in itself as a concentration of power dedicated to its own interests. And the criticism is applied with equal vigor to other large organizations, business corporations, political parties, and universities.

Max Weber saw bureaucracy, with its functional organization, uniform application of rules, and awards of status according to ability, as central to modern society. And its growth has been a result of efforts to make society more equitable as well as of the need to assemble great amounts of information and to act with rational efficiency. The undeniable achievements of such an approach encouraged a view of society itself as a meritocracy in which in every generation and in all fields new leaders would be selected by essentially objective criteria. Since the 1960s, however, this extension of a liberal vision has been subject to severe attack.

· Elites that confidently claim to have earned their position may be as self-interested as and sometimes more offensive than an aristocracy born to privilege. The process of selection has remained relatively restrictive after all, and even formal criteria—examinations and superiors' recommendations—are often narrow and warped by political favoritism and social prejudice. If the virtue of bureaucracy is the evenhanded application of general rules (and many deny that it accomplishes that in practice), its weakness is faceless impersonality. Citizens often find themselves helpless before regulations that defeat the purpose intended, unable to locate the source of decisions that seriously affect their lives and treated in the dehumanized terms of multiple forms to be filled and filed. Even in societies committed to justice and freedom, the individual often cannot find any authority willing to consider his whole person and his real, human needs.

The reaction against the world of meritocracy and bureaucracy, though strong, has been marked by a certain hopelessness. Political movements throughout the West have denounced the trend toward more and more social regulation; but without solutions to offer, they have appealed in the rhetoric of nostalgia primarily to groups whose importance has been waning. From Russia to the United States, politicians' promises to make government (and society) less officious have produced few clear results. Intellectuals, artists, and students have spoken out more effectively. In England the playwright John Osborne was typical of a whole group of "angry young men" who shook the complacency of the late 1950s with their attacks on the establishment. Soviet dissidents unmasked rule in the name of the proletariat as just another autocracy. The disturbances and riots in East Germany, Poland, Hungary, and Czechoslovakia underscored that complaint; and student revolts from Berkeley to Harvard to the Sorbonne, in Britain, Germany, and Italy have directly attacked all the central assumptions of meritocracy. Yet so far at least, all this outrage has produced more alienation than change.

Alienation

To Marx one of the great evils of industrial capitalism was the separation of men from the product of their labor so that they were deprived of a craftsman's pride in what they did. On the cleaner, well-lit, and partially automated assembly lines of the postindustrial era, there is evidence that a similar alienation continues. It underlies much of the agitation even among prosperous workers; and the frequent strikes, especially common in Great Britain and Italy, have to do as much with issues of the workers' privileges and dignity as with their wages. Many lament the cultural loss in the disappearance of artisanship generally. Perhaps, the argument runs, a society is poorer if it has more things but almost none individually carved or blown or tailored with great care to be treasured by fabricator and owner.

Craftsmanship is not the only victim of technological unemployment, for in many fields people find themselves threatened by new methods and by younger specialists with more recent training. Perhaps new efforts to provide additional training on the job, to make factory work more interesting (in which the Swedish have pioneered), and to give workers a voice in management (something the Germans have tried extensively, the French, Italians, and Americans have experimented with, and the British Labour party is now beginning to demand) can make a real difference. The question remains whether the modern cult of efficiency leaves room for such human and aesthetic considerations, whether the rewards of leisure and wealth can compensate for a sense of alienation from one's own labor.

More troubling still are the deeper signs of a general alienation: the attraction to crime, the escapism of commercial pornography, alcoholism, and drug abuse. The very freedom prosperity provides brings a heavy burden of self-direction. Yet in large, highly organized societies individuals today often feel powerless even though they are confronted with a more bewildering array of personal choices than most of mankind ever faced. It is significant that social control—perceived to operate through advertising, religion, and custom as well as institutions—has become a favorite subject for social research.

THE CULTURAL CRISIS

The end of World War II and the fall of the Axis brought the sudden stimulus of ideas and artistic styles long banned, as works produced in secret could be brought into the open. In all the arts but especially painting, a flood of exciting works came from the United States, whose culture had been enriched by European émigrés, free there to continue their creativity. Artists already famous in the 1930s, like the painter Pablo Picasso and the poet T. S. Eliot, could simultaneously be honored as grand old figures and savored with a freshness usually reserved for the young. There was great

continuity between the cultural outburst that followed liberation and the prewar world even though the new European works focused on the intervening experience of dictatorship and war.

Neo-realism flourished, especially in Italy, where the novels of Ignazio Silone and Alberto Moravia gave incisive, detailed accounts of the daily lives of little people buffeted by movements and events beyond their control, and where the films of Roberto Rossellini and Vittorio de Sica combined the harsh eye of the candid camera with sympathy for the minor characters who are society's victims and its strength. French films and the plays of the German Bertolt Brecht, who moved to East Berlin in 1949, pursued similar themes with more formal ideological purpose. The arts had never been more international, and works produced in one country were quickly appreciated throughout the West.

The New Wave

The *nouvelle vague* of the 1960s in literature and film was primarily a French phenomenon, but the term can fairly be extended to describe a major and continuing shift in the arts. The novels of Alain Robbe-Grillet and the films of Jean François Truffaut, Ingmar Bergman, and Federico Fellini are more like personal essays, held together by the sensitivity and imagination of a single creator that the audience is permitted to share in whatever way it can. In painting abstract expressionism, which dominated earlier, has given way to a great variety of styles often deliberately garish and disturbing—Pop Art, Op Art, and the satirically representational. And composers have shifted their explorations from the twelve-tone scale and dissonance, avant-garde interests for more than a generation, to the new sounds of *musique concrète* (using everyday noises as well as musical sounds care-

Cosmopolitan taste, leisure, luxury, and entertainment combine to make Carnaby Street in London a kind of mecca for Europeans and Americans attracted by the carnival-like assault on conventional taste associated with the Beatles. (Photo: Max Fortel/DPI)

fully arranged on spliced tapes) and of electronic music in the manner of the American John Cage and the German Karlheinz Stockhausen. Even sculpture, generally a more conservative art, is experimenting with the use of common objects, new materials of every sort, and strange forms. Sculptors work on a gigantic scale—the Englishman Henry Moore's huge reclining figures with their combination of line, solid masses, and empty spaces (influenced by African art) are perhaps the most admired.

The arts have again become radical, questing for new modes of expression, deliberately shocking and yet highly personal, sometimes almost private. But few artistic conventions remain to be burst (the inhibitions on displays of sex in motion pictures eroded rapidly in the 1960s), and to do something new becomes more difficult although, in the tradition of the avant-garde, still required. One trend is to absorb and distort technology. Thus some artists have made use of electric lights, random noise, plastics, or mechanical motion, giving them aesthetic meanings much as artists had long done with nature. Another is to break the barriers between "serious" and commercial art, for each uses the other; much that begins as formal art quickly reaches the populace in articles of mass production and slick packages of advertising. In the process commercial art and popular movies have become more sophisticated, and some popular music, led by the Beatles, has become artistically more serious and complex. This intersection of "high" and "popular" culture, lessening a division within Western civilization that has lasted for centuries, may foretell a new explosion of creativity; the more common comment is to note the decay both of folk culture and of the traditional canons of high art.

Classical and Modern

During the Enlightenment, when the comparison of ancient and modern culture became a popular theme, writers were tempted to feel that the moderns had the better of it, combining ancient wisdom with new knowledge. Contemporary commentators are less confident.

The high-bourgeois culture of the nineteenth century remains strong. Symphony orchestras are numerous and of superb quality, their concerts well attended. Paintings old and new sell for ever higher prices. The great literary works of all ages are taught in schools and universities and still read with pleasure. Yet the tendency for such interests to be made academic, a matter of special study by experts, may suggest some decline in their power to attract. The very forms of that culture—long novels and epic poems, symphonies, operas, enormous museums—have by current standards become terribly expensive in time and money. Ironically

their place appears least threatened in the Soviet Union, where the state is committed to excluding the competition offered by much of contemporary Western culture. Nowhere is ballet more honored or more old-fashioned. But one wonders whether people elsewhere will continue to receive the long preparation, maintain the patience, or preserve the values necessary to appreciate the West's traditional culture.

Paperback books, records, and reproductions of paintings have carried the arts more broadly into society, but the fear remains that they are not an integral part of it. To many the signs are disturbing: the tendency for the creative life itself to become institutionalized in universities; the frenetic search for new techniques that bespeaks some deep dissatisfaction; the danger that serious culture will be eroded by the commercial, the shocking, the fashionable aspects of mass culture. The arts have expanded to encompass almost all forms of communication and fabrication. This, like the increased interest in good design and attractive cities, may mark the hope of the new era, or it may indicate a fatal loss of focus and of that common core of values and tradition on which great cultures in the past have rested.

THE CRISIS OF VALUES

On no other issue are contemporary moralists so agreed as that the lack of universally respected values is the source of serious discontent and a symptom of fatal decay. But historical self-consciousness and the science of psychology suggest that social values change with time and place. Once value systems are seen as relative, however, it becomes difficult to insist on imposing any particular set. The symptom of social disintegration becomes one of its causes.

Existentialism

Existentialism, one of the most influential movements of this period, has offered a radical solution. Jean Paul Sartre, French philosopher and writer, has been existentialism's most important figure, but his ideas are based in turn on the prewar work of German philosophers, especially Karl Jaspers and Martin Heidegger. Once again the intellectual continuity across the war is striking.

Sartre extended relativism to its ultimate implication: life is absurd, without purpose or meaning. But from this point he slowly built: a person becomes what he is through the things he does in a lifetime; individual actions follow from decisions; and each decision to act is a moral choice. Thus Sartre constructed a radical individualism but one that keeps men morally responsible (and in the highest sense free) whatever their fate. There is in existentialism a sense of the heroic that had special meaning perhaps to those formed in the resistance movement and that was expressed with great power in the writings of Albert Camus, most encouragingly perhaps in his early novel *The Plague*.

As a statement of man's condition existentialism blends remarkably with the mainstream of modern thought; there are Christian existentialists and existentialist Marxists, and positivists, liberals, and Freudians have incorporated its insights. But its very breadth of appeal is also a weakness. The values an existentialist chooses rest after all on blind experience or some other philosophy. Like neo-realism, existentialism belonged to the early postwar period and spoke more clearly to the abnormal years of terror and rebuilding than to a time of routine and prosperity.

Older Doctrines

In the public anguish over values that has marked this period, Christian voices, individually strong, have collectively had a rather uncertain effect.

After the war the leading theologians—once again mainly men of an older generation who were already well known two decades earlier, like Jaspers, Karl Barth, and Jacques Maritain—were studied with new interest. The Protestant Paul Tillich and the Catholic Pierre Teilhard de Chardin achieved a large following with their systematic efforts to establish the relevance of Christianity to every facet of modern life and to accommodate contemporary modes of thought. Pope John XXIII was beloved as few popes have ever been by non-Catholics as well as Catholics for his gentleness, his tolerance, and his receptiveness to change. All this combined with the postwar vigor of Christian political parties and a rise in church attendance in the 1950s suggested a major revival of Christianity.

Yet by the 1960s society seemed to have been little affected. Although some theologians hailed the benefits of the greater openness about sex in literature, dress, and practice, most found it anathema. While churches became socially more aware and sometimes even radical, Marxist parties and the modern state accomplished more. Civil marriages (and divorces) increased, and religious vocations declined. When Christians evoked rigid, traditional standards of morality, they could be dismissed as reactionaries; when they embraced modern psychology or worked for social change, they were accused of opportunism. But when they charged that society was in a moral crisis, they were widely heard.

If Christians have been outspoken about the crisis of values in this generation, philosophers have on the whole been silent. In Britain and the United States, the dominance of logical positivism and analytic philosophy is all but complete, so that philosophy has become a highly specialized, quasi-mathematical discipline inclined to view the ethical questions troubling most thoughtful people as too loosely defined to merit comment. But elsewhere there are few signs of philosophical creativity. We still seem to take our intellectual problems very largely as formulated in the nineteenth century, by Kierkegaard, Marx, Nietzsche, and Freud. (Significantly the nineteenth-century schools of thought less critical of Western society or more optimistic about human nature are largely ignored.) Ours may be an era dominated by science, but philosophy today is less affected by the theories of natural science than at any time since Voltaire applied Newton to society or Hobbes sought to analyze the mechanics of politics.

There have in fact been few efforts at constructing grand philosophical systems in the nineteenth-century style, although the widespread revival of interest in Hegel, especially through the work of the German philosopher Edmund Husserl, has given a common vocabulary to much of the discourse among existentialists and Marxists eager to reconcile an emphasis on human consciousness with respect for reason, on the meaning of history with assertions of human liberty.

Some have suggested that the absence of systematic philosophies is in itself a historic change: the end of ideologies following from the end of class conflict in postindustrial society. But dissatisfaction has certainly not disappeared nor conflict either. And theories of conflict seem in the 1970s to be supplanting the emphasis on consensus so common in the 1950s. Above all, Marxism remains impressively alive. Freed somewhat by the new variety within communism, it dominates European intellectual life, spreading into much of academic history, sociology, and anthropology and stimulating a variety of literary movements and a range of new insights in literary criticism. Many of the century's most influential intellectuals, like Antonio Gramsci in Italy and Georg Lukacs in Hungary, have been theoreticians of Marxism. Part

of its appeal remains its humane concerns; yet the record of its rule as well as its historical determinism and ethical relativism makes it unreassuring as a source of social values.

But there are few alternatives. The death of liberalism has been so confidently announced for so long that one may conclude it survives; but as a systematic doctrine, rather than tolerant practice, it is in disarray, although the "new philosophers" who in France have launched an assault on Marxism suggest a revival is possible. Conservative social theories which contributed richly to Western thought now appear primarily by implication in ideas of biological determinism or theology. The most influential aspect of conservative thought was its critique of "mass" culture and technological progress, but those concerns too have largely been absorbed by the left much as the social theorists of the Frankfurt school combined a distaste for modern society which was common among German intellectuals with a heavy debt to Marxism in their influential writings on psychology, sociology, and philosophy. Herbert Marcuse, who like most of the Frankfurt group spent World War II in the United States—Hitler as well as Marx helped to make Western intellectual life more international—found himself a hero to leaders of the student revolts of 1968, although few of the new generation shared his admiration of Freud as well as Marx.

The Social Sciences

In the West the social sciences have enjoyed an enormous increase in prestige and analytic power, primarily through the application of behavioral methods of model building and of quantitative research, first in economics, then in sociology, political science, and history. But these methods all begin by seeking to be "value free." Another of the important movements in social science is structuralism, and its roots too lie in the early part of the twentieth century, in the work of the Swiss linguist Ferdinand de Saussure, who coined the term "semiology" to describe the study of the signs by which people communicate. For the French anthropologist Claude Lévi-Strauss, a leading structuralist, every aspect of supposedly primitive society—its kinship systems, customs, rituals, and myths—can be analyzed as the extension of complex, integrated structures of thought. Not consciously held, these structures nevertheless reflect the nature of the human mind. This radical subjectivism, which can lead Lévi-Strauss to an admiration of premodern societies comparable to that of many modern artists, speaks only indirectly to questions of values. In contemporary matters Lévi-Strauss, like Sartre whose historical relativism he opposes, considers himself a Marxist.

Linguistics in the social sciences and biology in the natural sciences are currently the fields of most rapid development and the ones that energetically invade and synthesize their neighboring disciplines. Abstract and mathematical, their excitement remains largely confined to specialists who inevitably disparage the few attempts to carry their new findings into discussions of social issues. Never has any previous civilization supported so much scholarship, so many centers of learning, or so many artists. But there is no test to tell whether that achievement should be a source of comfort or is itself a sign of some dangerous dispersion. Scholars barely able to keep abreast of their own disciplines speak ominously of a knowledge explosion, and professors of humanities defensively decry the dearth of interest in the things they study. Doubt about human rationality and disdain for elites have made anti-intellectualism respectable even among intellectuals, and alienation or some eternal human quest has led to a remarkable revival of interest in the occult. Computers, after all, can also be used to plot astrological charts.

THE CONSOLATION OF HISTORY

Beyond doubt there is cause for concern. The question is whether these signs mark a fatal crisis or even a fundamental transformation. Seen in historical perspective, they may not be quite so terrible nor this era so drastically different as our heightened sense of change leads us to believe. One should at least consider how many great crises Western civilization has survived and how strongly traditional values and institutions still intricately attach the present to the past.

Historical Proportion

Since every era tends narcissistically to believe its own problems the most important and therefore the gravest, the assumption needs to be carefully probed. Although Europe is a lesser force in the world than it was in the nineteenth century, it is surely not so seriously threatened as were the Greeks by Xerxes, the Romans by the barbarians, or medieval Christendom by Islam. European countries are more comparable in wealth and power to the United States than the struggling medieval principalities were to Constantinople. No twentieth-century war has been more devastating than the Black Death. It is doubtful that the ideological conflict and spiritual crisis of the present are so severe as those that followed the Reformation. Nor is it clear why centuries of peasant revolts, the alcoholism of Hogarth's London, or the highway robbery, cock fighting, prostitution, and public hangings of the nineteenth century were any less signs of alienation than the manifestations that trouble us today. If social change now is rapid, we have learned to expect and even anticipate it; the changes that followed the fifteenth century or those in the hundred years after 1760 may well have been more shocking and harder to absorb.

We should not assume that earlier ages enjoyed a comforting unanimity cruelly denied to us. At few moments in Western history has a single philosophy or set of values enjoyed undisputed hegemony. The view that other eras were informed by a single spirit is largely the product of distance which makes outlines clearer and fissures more obscure. The rights of throne and altar or the forms of transubstantiation were once questions as socially shattering as those of public and private ownership or the right to an abortion. Neither is it certain that village life was less cruel than the impersonal city or that peasants were less materialist than the modern middle class. The crises of the past that strained and altered Western civilization ultimately left it with new vitality.

The tendency to assume that the quality of social life has deteriorated may also reflect a rise in expectations. We have learned to smile at the simple optimism of nineteenth-century visions of progress, but we expect "autonomy" and "spontaneity" and "self-fulfillment" for every individual. Society is asked to reinforce in all people qualities Western thinkers traditionally believed to be beyond most of mankind. Today's intellectuals are not demonstrably more at odds with the mass of society than the elites of other times, but they resent it more. There is greater concern today, however badly practice lags, for racial equality, good education, and humane treatment of society's misfits than at any time in the past.

Contemporary anxiety over the family as a social institution is a good example of how higher expectations as well as changing behavior affect the perception of the present. That the family may be about to disappear or is at least threatened now as never before is a cliché rarely challenged. But it has been a cliché for centuries, hurled from thousands of pulpits; and serfdom, slavery, poverty, and maybe human nature have also endangered the family. But since the eighteenth century, the demands placed on it have steadily increased. Paradoxically this began at the very time that industri-

With vacations available to everyone, camping along the seashore, especially (as here) in Spain, is an inexpensive attraction to families of tourists from all over Europe. (Photo: Aurness/Woodfin Camp and Associates)

alization separated household members for nearly all their waking hours, moved millions of people to new places, and deprived the family of the traditional social support of relatives and village custom. Yet the institution survived, and the Victorians tried hard to make the family function according to the highest Christian norms while adding still other requirements. Marriage is now expected to be a matter of mutual choice and to be more a delightful partnership than a mere division of labor;

the rearing of children lasts longer and is intended to be far more intensive. Protected by the state and honored by religion, the family is supposed to provide a secure place for happiness and mutual growth, and its joys of sex and solidity are propagandized in the mass media in utopian terms that risk making reality drab at best. That contraceptives allow more couples to postpone marriage and that laws make it easier to abandon the commitment to it need not mean that the institution is crumbling. It is more likely that the family itself, its social functions, and the social roles within it are simply being yet again redefined.

The Western Tradition

The painful questioning of values in modern society is in large part a continuation of a Western tradition. Ambivalence toward the past and toward change, for example, is an ancient one, especially pronounced since the French Revolution and the Romantic era. Similarly the conflict between individual and society so explosive today was a theme of Sophocles and central to early Christianity, neatly dissected by Hobbes, restated in quite different terms by Rousseau, and was a major preoccupation throughout the nineteenth century. And today's interest in communal living and a return to nature draws on the anarchists and utopian socialists of the nineteenth century as well as a Christian practice continuous from medieval monasteries through Anabaptists to the present. The threat of the overbearing state has been a subject of endless discussion since Machiavelli.

The distrust of rationalism as a force that can inhibit creativity and the obverse, a fear of mankind's dark irrationality, twist through the novels and plays of the nineteenth century, are floodlit in the writings of Freud, and have concerned theologians since Augustine. The arguments about free will and determinism continue between Catholics and Protestants, existentialists and Marxists. When a modern Westerner approaches the most important issues of the day, he necessarily brings with him some part of a cultural heritage long concerned with similar problems. In this way the past is constantly reinvoked in the present, and current conflicts are given some shape and limit by the past.

Continuity in Modernization

The impressive pattern of social change in the last two hundred years has come to be called modernization—a typical Western conception that sees history moving in a single direction and tends to assume that the changes which have transformed the West will be repeated elsewhere until "developing" countries become more like their European models. Clearly all societies are feeling the effects of expanding technology, the trend toward secularization, the increased role of the state, and the growth of bureaucracy. But Western history also continues to demonstrate, as it always has, that the specific effects of such trends will be fundamentally affected by local conditions and customs and by deliberate choice. The West has both retained its unity and preserved its diversity through these centuries of change. National and regional differences in manners and taste alter even the most similar institutions and continue to find expression in the most modernized societies. Despite greater travel and better communication, a universal technology, comparable standards of living, and an international style in dress and architecture, London, Paris, New York, Rome, or Berlin each remains unique.

Since the establishment of the national monarchies, European governments have used sumptuary laws, mercantilist measures, and social legislation to alter the effect of economic forces. Handicrafts, for example, have often been favored by political measures and public taste although industrial competition threatened their survival; and individual farms are in most countries sustained through the social choice of subsidies as well as by rural tenacity. A sociologist has noted that the different forms and scale of organization in contemporary industries, and even the way they use technology, reflect whether those industries were founded before the industrial revolution as were the building trades, during the nineteenth century as was the textile industry, or in the twentieth century as were the smaller and more decentralized electronics firms.[4] As concern now rises for the protection of the environment, public policy once more limits private interest. But then some of Europe's most famous parks can be traced back to the common lands and hunting preserves of the Middle Ages. Technological imperatives alone do not shape society.

Secularization describes the historical development whereby religion shifts from the center to the periphery of social concern and functions once performed by the church are given over to other, secular agencies. This is primarily an institutional change and one that need not denote a decline of belief. In fact the nineteenth and twentieth centuries have probably been more "religious" than the eighteenth. As the practice of faith has ceased to be a matter of universal custom, it has become a matter of conscious, personal choice.

Even the growth of the state, in power and in social penetration, has brought with it new restrictions on the exercise of government influence. The use of representative forms and

legal codes has been one way of restraining the state, and more recently the Scandinavian device of the ombudsman paid to respond to individual complaints has come to be widely adopted. Local resistance to central control has revived from Ireland, Scotland, and Wales to Brittany and Languedoc, Catalonia, and the Basque country, from regions of Italy to the Croatian portions of Yugoslavia and the Slovak provinces of Czechoslovakia, from Sweden to the Soviet Union. The dialects and customs that the state once strived to suppress were, it was believed just a few years ago, doomed to be eliminated through force of example by radio, television, and easy travel. Instead once isolated regions have used familiarity with dominant cultures to assert their equality. Now the fashionable question is whether the national state is a machine for war-making that has lost its function.

But the most effective defense against the intrusive power of the state may be a subtle change in the boundary between the affairs considered to be properly public and those protected as private. The nuclear family and the individual dwelling have steadily widened the zone of formally sanctioned privacy. In the nineteenth century religious tolerance, security of the postal service, and the secret ballot were steps in a gradual enlargement of privacy to include one's personal convictions (steps which often required a revolution). That recognition of individualism in the twentieth century extends even to our styles of dress, sexual practices, and conscientious objection to military service.

The growth of bureaucracy, another of the themes of modernization, has strengthened institutions independent of state control as well as the state itself; and these institutions have proved a major source of continuity, carrying within them old values and attitudes to be applied to new situations. The West's courts of justice, parliaments, churches, universities, and

---

[4] A. L. Stinchcombe, "Social Structure and the Invention of Organization Forms," in Tom Burns (ed.), *Industrial Man* (1969), 153–194.

banks are powerful establishments with independent but continuous traditions that extend back often to the Middle Ages and beyond. And the tendency now is to seek ways to make all social institutions, from welfare agencies to factories, more responsive to the individual and more accessible. Many French and a few American firms now allow their employees to set their own hours, and the German system of worker representation on management councils has parallels in France, Italy, and Yugoslavia as well as in some countries within the Soviet sphere. These schemes may or may not work, but any artisan of the early nineteenth century would have understood the need to try them.

The Vatican Council that opened in 1962 under the inspiration of Pope John XXIII was perhaps the most noted of all these efforts at institutional reform. Dedicated to *aggiornamento* ("renewal"), the council sought to bring the Catholic Church up to date not only in its organization but in its social policy, expressing concern for developing nations, respect for Jews, and belief in religious liberty. The church's leadership was made more international, and the decision to say masses in the vernacular instead of Latin put the understanding of the individual believer above institutional uniformity. Yet efforts to go much further,

to give national or regional church councils autonomous authority, for example, or to abandon the celibacy of priesthood, have been firmly resisted. Even while showing impressive adaptability, Western institutions tend to slow the process of change, carefully weaving the new into the old social fabric.

Predictions of the future that take several centuries of history into account can still be wrong, but knowledge of the past should at least leave the present more comprehensible. In the light of historical experience we have little reason to feel sorry for ourselves or to feel confident of our superiority. Every age has been a time of transition, and all have given wise prophets cause to predict an apocalypse. Over the last century Western society has dealt with many of its social needs on the assumption of ever-expanding prosperity and received reassurance from its dominance in the world. Now many believe that continued economic growth and unchallenged dominance must end. If that should happen, such fundamental change would make the future in important respects more like the distant past, with the significant difference that non-Western societies are likely to be more similar to the West in ideologies, social organization, and technology than ever before, adding new perspectives and possibilities to a rich and varied tradition.

Prelates from around the world, in Rome for the Vatican Council, stand as Pope Paul VI is carried on his throne into St. Peters. The ancient and splendid ceremonies sustained their fascination to the modern world as the Church itself undertook a wide-ranging aggiornamento. (Photo: Wide World Photos)

In terms of well-being, creativity, or general decency, Europe as a whole and Western Europe in particular compares well with any society past or present. Yet the limits on the autonomy of its sovereign states seem to weigh more heavily than their world-wide influence. Where free expression is allowed, the inadequacies and inequities of Europe's societies produce criticism more resounding than the praise their prosperity and freedom can win, and the ideas of its extraordinary intellectual tradition and the continued creativity of its culture come to focus on defining the nature of the current crisis.

Western civilization seems to be entering a new era troubled by many signs of crisis; yet that description could fit most of the past two thousand years. It has since Roman times been a diverse civilization, built of Greek philosophy and Roman institutions and an Eastern religion, a mixture of many races and cultures and political systems, all borrowing from and competing against each other. Such qualities have helped make the West particularly adaptable and ready to learn from the outside world. It still is. Its long history has been filled with wars and revolutions that have bred a flexible toughness in its institutions, and its future is probably no more doubtful than futures normally are. As for the present a troubled civilization still finds nourishment and individuals still seek guidance in the Western experience.

RECOMMENDED READING

Studies

*Barraclough, Geoffrey. *An Introduction to Contemporary History*. 1967. An historian's assessment of the main currents of world history, making Europe no longer its dominant center.

Blackmer, Donald L. M., and Sidney Tarrow (eds.). *Communism in Italy and France*. 1975. American social scientists study the nature and meaning of communist strength in two Western democracies.

Boulding, Kenneth E. *The Meaning of the Twentieth Century*. An economist's stimulating look at the present and the future.

Brown, B. E. *Protest in Paris: Anatomy of a Revolt*. 1974. The student revolt subject to scholarly study.

Carré, Jean-Jacques, et al. *French Economic Growth*. 1975. Several experts analyze Europe's leading example of capitalist planning.

Ehrmann, Henry W. *Politics in France*. 1976. Social and institutional change are incorporated into this survey.

*Ellul, Jacques. *The Technological Society*. 1964. One of the most striking and influential of contemporary attacks on the effects of technology.

Grosser, Alfred. *Germany in Our Time*. 1971. A thoughtful study of the place of Germany in modern Europe.

Heidenheimer, Arnold J., Hugh Heclo, and Carolyn Teich Adams. *Comparative Public Policy: The Politics of Social Choice in Europe and America*. 1975. Studies the background and implications of the varied approaches to social policy.

Heilbronner, Robert G. *An Inquiry into the Human Prospect*. 1974. A hopeful discussion of the prospects for old Western values in a new society.

Hughes, H. Stuart. *The Sea Change: The Migration of Social Thought, 1930–1965*. A study by a leading intellectual historian of the implications for contemporary understanding of the spread of European social thought to America.

Kindleberger, Charles P. *Europe's Postwar Growth*.

1967. The comparative study of Europe's advanced economies and the policies of growth.

Mowat, R. C. *Creating the European Community.* 1973. A diplomatic historian turns to Europe's most striking international achievement.

Parker, Geoffrey. *The Logic of Unity.* 1975. The very useful analysis of the force of European unity by a geographer.

Payne, Stanley G. *Politics and Society in Twentieth-Century Spain.* 1976. A series of essays putting Spain's rapid development in historical perspective.

*Poster, Mark. *Existential Marxism in Postwar France.* 1975. The close investigation of this central theme provides a framework for understanding much of contemporary European thought.

Rostow, Walt W. *The World Economy: History and Prospect.* 1977. A leading student of economic development assays the directions of the future.

Silvanian, S. (ed.). *Eastern Europe in the 1970s.* 1972. A series of essays that highlight the prospect for important change in this region.

*Stromberg, Ronald N. *After Everything: Western Intellectual History Since 1945.* 1975. A disenchanted and provocative essay on contemporary intellectual fashions.

Willis, F. Roy. *European Integration.* 1973. Consideration of the economic, social, and political meaning of integration by a leading expert on contemporary Europe.

---

* Available in paperback.

INDEX

1/ Museum of Fine Arts, Boston, Harvard University—MFA Expedition 2/ Hirmer Verlag München 3/ Editions Skira, Geneva 4–5/ Hirmer Verlag München 6/ Scala New York/Florence 7/ European Art Color, Peter Adelburg, N.Y.C. 8/ Scala New York/Florence 9/ Editions Skira, Geneva 10/ Kunsthistorisches Museum, Vienna 11/ Leonard von Matt from Rapho Guillumette 12/ Editions Skira, Geneva 13–15/ Scala New York/Florence 16/ Giraudon 17/ Scala New York/Florence 18/ Staatliche Museen Preussischer Kulturbesitz Gemäldegalerie Berlin (West) 19/ Scala New York/Florence 20/ Alberto Augusto de Abreu Nunes 21/ Scala New York/Florence 22/ The Frick Collection, New York 23–28/ Scala New York/Florence 29/ Museum of Fine Arts, Boston, Isaac Sweetser Fund 30–31/ Scala New York/Florence 32/ Alte Pinakothek, München 33–35/ Scala New York/Florence 36/ Eberhard Zwicker, Würzberg 37/ Verlag Joachim Blauel, München 38/ Scala New York/ Florence 39/ Rijks-museum, Amsterdam 40/ Giraudon 41/ National Gallery of Art, Washington, D.C. 42/ Service de Documentation Photographie de la Réunion des Musées Nationaux 43/ Giraudon 44–45/ Service de Documentation Photographie de la Réunion des Musées Nationaux 46/ Scala New York/Florence 47/ Giraudon 48/ MAS 49/ Service de Documentation Photographie de la Réunion des Musées Nationaux 50/ Museum voor Schone Kunsten, Gent 51/ Service de Documentation Photographie de la Réunion des Musées Nationaux 52/ Boston Museum of Fine Arts 53/ Walter Steinkopf, Berlin 54/ Scala New York/ Florence 55/ The Metropolitan Museum of Art 56/ Reilly & Constantine, Birmingham, England 57/ Oskar Reinhart Collection, "Am Römerholz," Winterthur 58/ Service de Documentation Photographie de la Réunion des Musées Nationaux 59/ National Gallery, London 60/ Mr. & Mrs. John Hay Whitney 61/ O. Vaering, Oslo 62/ Chrysler Museum at Norfolk 63/ The Tate Gallery, London 64/ Moderna Museet, Stockholm

COLOR
ILLUSTRATION
SOURCES

Mortimer Chambers is Professor of History at the University of California at Los Angeles. He was a Rhodes scholar from 1949–1952 and received an M.A. from Wadham College, Oxford, in 1955 after obtaining his doctorate from Harvard University in 1954. He has taught at Harvard University (1954–1955) and the University of Chicago (1955–1958). He was Visiting Professor at the University of British Columbia in 1958 and the State University of New York at Buffalo in 1971. A specialist in Greek and Roman history, he is coauthor of *Aristotle's History of Athenian Democracy* (1962) and editor of a series of essays entitled *The Fall of Rome* (1963). He has contributed articles to the *American Historical Review* and *Classical Philology* as well as other journals.

Raymond Grew is Professor of History at the University of Michigan. He earned both his M.A. (1952) and Ph.D. (1957) from Harvard University in the field of modern European history. He was a Fulbright Fellow to Italy (1954–1955) and Guggenheim Fellow (1968–1969). In 1962 he received the Chester Highby Prize from the American Historical Association, and in 1963 the Italian government awarded him the Unita d'Italia Prize. He is an active member of the A.H.A., the Society for Italian Historical Studies, and the Society for French Historical Studies. He is the author of *A Sterner Plan for Italian Unity* (1963) and is presently the editor of *Comparative Studies in Society and History*. His articles and reviews have appeared in a number of European and American journals.

David Herlihy, Professor of History at Harvard University, is the author of several books on the economic and social history of the Middle Ages: *Pisa in the Early Renaissance, A Study of Urban Growth* (1958), *Medieval and Renaissance Pistoia, The Social History of an Italian Town* (1968), and *Medieval Culture and Society* (1968). He received his M.A. from the Catholic University of America in 1953 and his Ph.D. from Yale University in 1956. He is former president of both the American Catholic Historical Association and the Midwest Medieval Conference. He was a fellow of the Guggenheim Foundation (1962–1963), the American Council of Learned Societies (1966–1967), and the Center for Advanced Study in the Behavioral Sciences (1972–1973). His articles have appeared in *Speculum, Economic History Review*, and *Annales-Economies-Sociétes-Civilisations*.

ABOUT
THE
AUTHORS

Theodore K. Rabb is Professor of History at Princeton University. A specialist in early modern European history, he received his B.A. degree from Oxford University (1958) and his Ph.D. from Princeton University (1961). He was a Guggenheim Fellow in 1970. He has taught at Harvard University, Stanford University, Northwestern University, Johns Hopkins University, and the State University of New York at Binghamton. He is co-founder and coeditor of the *Journal of Interdisciplinary History*, a member of the National Research Council, and a fellow of the Royal Historical Society. He is the author of *The Thirty Years' War* (1964) and *Enterprise and Empire* (1967), and coeditor of *Action and Conviction in Early Modern Europe* (1969). He has contributed articles to the *American Historical Review*, *Journal of Modern History*, *Commentary*, *Past & Present*, the *Economic History Review*, and other journals.

Isser Woloch is Professor of History at Columbia University. He received both his M.A. (1961) and Ph.D. (1965) from Princeton University in the field of eighteenth- and nineteenth-century European history. He was a Fulbright Fellow (1962–1963) and an A.C.L.S. Fellow (1973–1974). He has taught at Indiana University and at the University of California at Los Angeles, where in 1967 he received a Distinguished Teaching Citation. He was also a member of the Institute for Advanced Study at Princeton (1973–1974). His works include *Jacobin Legacy: The Democratic Movement Under the Directory* and *The Peasantry in the Old Regime: Conditions and Protests*, both published in 1970, and *The French Veteran: From the Revolution to the Restoration* (forthcoming). His articles have appeared in the *Journal of Modern History*, *Journal of Interdisciplinary History*, and *Societas*.

This book was set on the Linofilm in Janson, a recutting made direct from the type cast from matrices made by Anton Janson some time between 1660 and 1687. Janson's original matrices were, at last report, in the possession of the Stempel foundry, Frankfurt am Main.

Of Janson's origin nothing is known. He may have been a relative of Justus Janson, a printer of Danish birth who practiced in Leipzig from 1614 to 1635. Some time between 1657 and 1668 Anton Janson, a punch cutter and type founder, bought from the Leipzig printer Johann Erich Hahn the type foundry that had formerly been a part of the printing house of M. Friedrich Lankisch. Janson's types were first shown in a specimen sheet issued at Leipzig about 1675. Janson's successor, and perhaps his son-in-law, Johann Karl Edling, issued a specimen sheet of Janson types in 1689. His heirs sold the matrices in Holland to Wolffgang Dietrich Erhardt of Leipzig.

A NOTE ON THE TYPE

CONTEMPORARY EUROPE

0   100   200   300   400 Miles

ICELAND

NORWEGIAN SEA

LAPLAND

NORWAY

SWEDEN

FINLAND

Trondheim

GULF OF BOTHNIA

Bergen

Oslo

Helsinki

Leningra

SHETLAND I.

Stockholm

Klaipeda

ESTONIAN S.S.R.

ORKNEY I.

Göteborg

Skagerrak

Kattegat

BALTIC SEA

Riga

LATVIAN S.S.R.

SCOTLAND

Glasgow

Edinburgh

NORTH SEA

DENMARK

Copenhagen

LITHUANIAN S.S.R.

NORTHERN IRELAND

Belfast

Kaliningrad (Königsberg)

(EAST PRUSSIA)

Minsk

BYELORU

IRELAND

UNITED KINGDOM

Dublin

Liverpool

Hull

Hamburg

Gdansk (Danzig)

Szczecin (Stettin)

Vistula R.

Warsaw

WALES

ENGLAND

Elbe R.

Berlin

Oder R.

POLAND

London

NETHERLANDS

Amsterdam

The Hague

Rhine R.

HANOVER

GERMAN DEMOCRATIC REPUBLIC

Cologne

Bonn

Dresden

Wroclaw

(SILESIA)

Lvov

ATLANTIC OCEAN

ENGLISH CHANNEL

Brussels

BELGIUM

GERMANY

Prague

MORAVIA

CZECHOSLOVAKIA

CARPATHIA

Dnieste

NORMANDY

Rouen

LUX.

Luxembourg

GERMAN FEDERAL REPUBLIC

BOHEMIA

RUTHENIA

BRITTANY

Seine R.

Paris

LORRAINE

Strasbourg

BAVARIA

SLOVAKIA

TRANSYLVAN

Loire R.

Orléans

ALSACE

BADEN

Munich

Vienna

Budapest

Tours

FRANCE

Berne

AUSTRIA

HUNGARY

RUMA

BAY OF BISCAY

Geneva

SWITZERLAND

La Coruña

Bordeaux

Lyons

Rhône R.

Milan

CROATIA-SLAVONIA

Trieste

BANAT

WALLACHIA

Bucha

GALICIA

PIEDMONT

LOMBARDY

VENEZIA

Venice

BOSNIA

Belgrade

Danub

Oporto

Bilbao

GASCONY

LANGUEDOC

PROVENCE

Genoa

Po R.

YUGOSLAVIA

BU

LEÓN

Ebro R.

NAVARRE

Marseilles

Toulon

Florence

SERBIA

Sarajevo

MONTE-NEGRO

Sofia

PORTUGAL

Duero R.

OLD CASTILE

ANDORRA

ARAGON

CATALONIA

TUSCANY

ADRIATIC SEA

ALBANIA

Saloni

Saragossa

Madrid

Barcelona

CORSICA (France)

Rome

CAMPANIA

Tiranë

Lisbon

Tagus R.

SPAIN

Valencia

Palma

APULIA

GREECE

Cordoba

NEW CASTILE

LA MANCHA

BALEARIC I. (Spain)

SARDINIA (Italy)

ITALY

Naples

A

Seville

ANDALUSIA

Málaga

CCRFU

Strait of Gibraltar

Gibraltar (England)

Palermo

Tangier (International)

Ceuta (Spain)

SICILY

Rabat

Melilla (Spain)

Oran

Algiers

Tunis

PANTELLERIA (Italy)

Valletta

MALTA

Casablanca

MOROCCO

TUNISIA

Tripoli

MEDITERRANEAN

Bengazi

ALGERIA

TRIPOLITANIA

LIBYA